Java 2
Platform

Jamie Jaworski

SAMS

Java 2 Platform Unleashed

Copyright ©1999 by Sams

International Standard Book Number: 0-672-31631-5

Library of Congress Catalog Card Number: 98-83248

Printed in the United States of America

First Printing: April 1999

01   00   99   4   3   2   1

Trademarks

Warning and Disclaimer

EXECUTIVE EDITOR
Tim Ryan

ACQUISITIONS EDITOR
Jeff Taylor

DEVELOPMENT EDITORS
Jon Steever
Tim Ryan

MANAGING EDITOR
Patrick Kanouse

PROJECT EDITOR
Rebecca Mounts

COPY EDITORS
Sara Bosin
Carol Bowers
Sean Medlock
San Dee Philips
Christina L. Smith
Kate Talbot
Rhonda Tinch-Mize

INDEXER
Christine Nelsen

TECHNICAL EDITOR
Jeff Perkins

SOFTWARE DEVELOPMENT SPECIALIST
Dan Scherf

PRODUCTION
Michael Henry
Linda Knose
Tim Osborn
Staci Somers
Mark Walchle

Contents at a Glance

Table of Contents

PART III APPLICATION PROGRAMMING 193

9 CREATING WINDOW APPLICATIONS 195

10 WRITING CONSOLE APPLICATIONS 223

Dedication

This book is dedicated to my son and favorite writer, Jason Jaworski.

Acknowledgments

I'd like to thank everyone who helped to see this book to completion. In particular, I'd like to thank Margot Maley of Waterside Productions for making the book possible, Jeff Taylor, Tim Ryan, Rebecca Mounts, and Jon Steever of Macmillan Computer Publishing for their numerous suggestions that improved the overall quality of the book, and Jeff Perkins for his excellent technical input. Finally, I'd like to thank Emily, Lisa, and Jason for their patience, love, and understanding.

About the Author

Jamie Jaworski is a professional Java programmer who develops advanced systems for the United States Department of Defense. He has used Java in several research and development projects, including a terrain analysis program and a genetic algorithm demonstration. He is also the author of *The Java Developer's Guide*, and *Mastering JavaScript*.

Tell Us What You Think!

As the reader of this book, *you* are our most important critic and commentator. We value your opinion and want to know what we're doing right, what we could do better, what areas you'd like to see us publish in, and any other words of wisdom you're willing to pass our way.

As the Executive Editor for the Web Publishing team at Macmillan Computer Publishing, I welcome your comments. You can fax, email, or write me directly to let me know what you did or didn't like about this book—as well as what we can do to make our books stronger.

Please understand that I won't have time to help you with technical problems related to the topic of this book, and that due to the high volume of mail I receive, I might not be able to reply to every message.

When you write, please be sure to include this book's title and author as well as your name and phone or fax number. I will carefully review your comments and share them with the author and editors who worked on the book.

Fax: 317-817-7070

E-mail: java@mcp.com

Mail: Tim Ryan, Executive Editor
         Java
         Macmillan Computer Publishing
         201 West 103rd Street
         Indianapolis, IN 46290 USA

Introduction

Never before has a new programming language received so much attention and become so popular so quickly. In the first year of its existence, Java took the Web by storm and became its adopted programming language. Since then, Java has become the language of choice for developing both Internet and intranet applications, and is used for both business and consumer software development. The Java phenomenon has captivated the imaginations of programmers around the world and is leading the way toward the next era of distributed application development.

Java's appeal lies in its simplicity, its familiarity, and the careful selection of features that it includes and excludes. Java was not designed by a government committee or a clique of academics. It shares its spirit with C more than any syntactical similarities. It is a programming language that was designed *by* programmers *for* programmers.

This book shows you how to program in Java, with the emphasis on version 1.2 of the Java Development Kit (JDK). It provides you with plenty of programming examples and arms you with the mindset needed to write Java code in a manner that is simple, efficient, and true to the nature of the language.

Note: In December of 1998, Sun released the final production version of Java, calling it Java 2 Platform. However, the actual version number of the JDK that you download from Sun is JDK 1.2, so we use the terms Java 2 and JDK 1.2 interchangeably throughout this book.

Who Should Read This Book

This book is for Java programmers. If you are not already a Java programmer, I suggest that you pick up an introductory Java book, such as *Sams Teach Yourself Java 1.2 in 21 Days* by Laura Lemay and Rogers Cadenhead. This book takes up where the introductory books leave off. It is an intermediate-to-advanced book that assumes you know how to use Java programming statements and that you have a basic understanding of exceptions and threads programming. If you have written programs in C or C++, you should have the background necessary to understand the material presented in this book. The syntax of Java is very similar to C and C++.

If you want to learn how to program using the JDK 1.2, this book is for you. You will learn how to program using all of the application programming interfaces (APIs) of the JDK 1.2. You'll use these APIs to develop Java applets, standalone window and console applications, beans, servlets, and distributed objects. You'll learn how to work with GUI controls, Swing components, TCP/IP sockets, remote method invocation, CORBA, multimedia, JDBC, and plenty of other new Java technologies. If you want to upgrade your Java programming skills to JDK 1.2, this book will show you how.

Conventions Used in This Book

This book uses certain conventions that make it easier for you to use.

A monospaced font is used to identify program code. Anything that you type while using Java is displayed in a **bold monospaced font**. An *italic monospaced font* is used to identify placeholders used in Java syntax descriptions.

NOTE

Notes like this are used to call your attention to information that is important to understanding and using Java.

TIP

Tips like this are used to identify ways that you can use Java more efficiently or take advantage of undocumented features in the Java Development Kit and Java-enabled browsers.

WARNING

Warnings like this are used to help you to avoid common problems encountered when using Java, and to keep you clear of potential programming difficulties.

In order for you to understand where you are going and where you have been, each chapter begins with a short description of the information that will be presented and ends with a summary of the material that has been covered.

Getting Started

To use this book, you'll need a computer and operating system that support version 1.2 of the Java Development Kit. There are a wide variety of operating systems that support the JDK 1.2, including Windows 98, Windows 95, Windows NT, and Solaris. Ports of the JDK 1.2 to Linux, Macintosh OS, OS/2, and other operating systems are in the works. This book focuses on using Java under Windows 95, but all of the book's examples are pure Java and will run with any JDK 1.2 implementation (with the exception of those examples that show how to work with Microsoft's implementation of Java).

The CD-ROM that accompanies this book contains all the source code and complete applications found in the book. The CD-ROM is a hybrid that will work on Windows 95, Windows 98, Macintosh, and UNIX platform.

The best way to use this book is to start with Chapter 1, "What's New in JDK 1.2," and proceed through each chapter in order, working through each programming example that is presented. You will learn to use the JDK 1.2 by compiling, running, analyzing, and understanding the sample programs. You can get additional hands-on practice by tinkering with the sample programs, modifying them, and augmenting their capabilities.

4

Programming with Java 2/JDK 1.2

PART

I

IN THIS PART

CHAPTER 1

What's New in JDK 1.2

The JDK 1.2 is a major upgrade of the Core and Standard Extension APIs of the Java Development Kit. It includes version 1.1 of the Java Foundations Classes (JFC), CORBA support, a more secure and flexible security model, improvements to the APIs of JDK 1.1, and performance enhancements. In this chapter you'll learn about the new capabilities added to JDK 1.2 and how these capabilities can be used to enhance your Java applets and applications. When you finish this chapter, you'll have a good understanding of what the JDK 1.2 provides and how to use this book to upgrade your Java programming skills to JDK 1.2.

The Java Foundations Classes

Probably the single most important new feature added to JDK 1.2 is version 1.1 of the Java Foundations Classes (JFC). JFC is a set of APIs for building the GUI-related components of Java applets and applications. JFC 1.1 was released separately from the JDK in February of 1998 so that they could be used with the then-current JDK 1.1. JDK 1.2 integrates JFC 1.1 as a Core API and adds the Java 2D and Drag and Drop APIs. The APIs included with JFC include the following:

- The Abstract Windowing Toolkit
- Swing
- Java 2D
- Drag and Drop
- Accessibility

These five APIs are introduced in the following subsections.

Abstract Windowing Toolkit (AWT)

If you've programmed in Java before, you know about the AWT. It provides the capability to create platform-independent, GUI-based programs and is a very important contributor to Java's popularity. Any programmer who has written programs using the arcane APIs of Microsoft Windows immediately appreciates the clarity, simplicity, and power of the AWT. Not only is the AWT a better API for developing Windows applications, it is a better API for programming window-based applications on platforms ranging from Motif to OS/2.

The AWT of JDK 1.2 has been augmented with many new classes and interfaces that add drawing, printing, and image-processing capabilities, and support the Accessibility, Drag and Drop, and Java 2D APIs. You'll learn to use the AWT in Chapter 6, "GUI Building," Chapter 7, "Working with the Canvas," and Chapter 9, "Creating Window Applications."

Swing

Of all the new capabilities provided by the JFC 1.1, one API, referred to as Swing, has far-reaching consequences for Java programmers. Swing is the code word used by the JavaSoft programming team for the next generation of the AWT. Swing extends AWT by supplying many more types of GUI components, providing 100% pure Java implementations of these components, and allowing the appearance and behavior of these components to be easily tailored.

The new components that are included with Swing include everything from tabbed panes and fancy borders to sliders and spinners. These new components, in and of themselves, make Swing an outstanding addition to the Java API. The Swing Component Gallery, located at `http://java.sun.com/products/jfc/swingdoc-current/comp_gal.html`, exhibits some of these new components. Swing also comes with a great demo program named `SwingSet`.

The Swing components are 100% pure Java. This means that they don't depend on the native windows implementation to support them. It also means that Swing components are available and consistent across all platforms. Although Swing components are implemented in terms of the underlying AWT, these components do not use AWT components. In fact, many of the traditional AWT components, such as buttons, lists, and dialog boxes, have been reimplemented as Swing components. Because of this, the AWT components behave more consistently across different platforms and are capable of providing additional features not supported by their native windowing platforms.

The most talked about feature of Swing is its support for pluggable look and feel (PL&F). If you like to customize your desktop, dabble in new color schemes, and do what it takes to make your windows fit your tastes and needs, PL&F is for you. The Swing PL&F architecture makes it easy to customize both the appearance and the behavior of any particular Swing control or any group of those controls. Swing also comes with several predefined L&Fs, including the default Metal L&F, the Motif L&F, and the Windows L&F. L&Fs for Macintosh and other platforms are also being developed.

You'll learn to program using Swing in Part IV, "Swing Programming."

Accessibility

The Accessibility API is a JFC API that has been added to JDK 1.2. It provides support for the use of assistive technologies with other JFC components. *Assistive technologies*, such as screen magnifiers and speech recognition systems, are intended for use by disabled users, but are also valuable tools for the average non-disabled user. These technologies provide non-standard ways of interacting with software applications. The

Accessibility API of JDK 1.2 allows software developers to comply with the Federal Rehabilitation Act and Americans with Disabilities Act.

The Accessibility API consists of classes and interfaces for incorporating accessibility features into applets and applications. These classes and interfaces are provided in the `javax.accessibility` package. Chapter 9 covers the use of the Accessibility API.

Java 2D

If you develop any kind of graphics-related software, you'll appreciate the new Java 2D API. This API provides comprehensive support for two-dimensional drawing, image processing, graphics rendering, color management, and printing. It consists of an imaging model that supports line art, text, images, spatial and color transformations, and image compositing. The model is device-independent, allowing displayed and printed graphics to be rendered in a consistent manner. The Java 2D API is incorporated into the `java.awt` and `java.awt.image` packages. Chapter 20, "Working with 2D and 3D Graphics," covers the Java 2D API.

Drag and Drop

One of the nicer features of most windowing environments that has been conspicuously missing from Java is support for drag and drop. *Drag and drop* is typically used to organize desktops, manage files, open documents, and execute applications. The Drag and Drop API allows the JDK 1.2 to provide platform-independent support of drag and drop. It supports drag and drop within Java applications, between Java applications, and between Java and native platform applications. The Drag and Drop API is implemented in the `java.awt.dnd` package and is supported by classes and interfaces in other JFC packages. Chapter 16, "Working with Drag and Drop," shows how to use the Drag and Drop API.

Other New Capabilities

Besides integrating JFC 1.1 as a set of Core APIs, the JDK 1.2 provides a number of other new capabilities. These capabilities are covered in the following subsections.

Java IDL

The Common Object Request Broker Architecture (CORBA) is a standard approach to developing distributed objects for use in distributed object-oriented systems. CORBA was developed by the Object Management Group (OMG), a consortium of software companies and other organizations. The capability to use Java objects within CORBA is referred to as Java IDL and has been incorporated into JDK 1.2. Java IDL provides an API and a set of tools for interfacing Java objects with CORBA objects, and for developing CORBA objects in Java. Java IDL also includes a Java Object Request Broker (ORB) and an ORB name server. Chapter 41, "Java IDL and ORBs," shows how Java and CORBA can be used together.

The Collections API

The Collections API is a set of classes and interfaces that provide an implementation-independent framework for working with collections of objects. This API consists of eleven classes and eight interfaces that have been added to the `java.util` package. These classes and interfaces provide support for generic collections, sets, bags, maps, lists, and linked lists. These classes and interfaces can be easily extended to provide support for custom object collections. The Collections API is covered in Chapter 11, "Using the Utility and Math Packages."

The Java Extensions Framework

JDK 1.2 provides the capability to extend the Core API classes. Extensions are implemented as Java Archive (JAR) files that are installed in a particular directory or downloaded from a URL. Appendix E, "The Java Extensions Framework," shows how to work with both installed and downloaded extensions.

Reference Objects

Reference objects, introduced with JDK 1.2, store references to other objects. They are similar in function to C and C++ pointers, but do not provide access to specific memory addresses. The `java.lang.ref` package provides six classes that implement reference objects. These classes also provide the capability to notify a program when a referenced object is subject to garbage collection. This capability enables reference objects to be used to implement object-caching mechanisms. Chapter 10 introduces reference objects.

Package Version Identification

Package version identification is also a new capability that was introduced with JDK 1.2. It allows applets and applications to obtain version information about a particular Java package. This version information enables large complex applications to evolve over time, with some application packages being upgraded independently of others. The new `Package` class provides methods for obtaining package version information. This version information is stored in the manifest of `.jar` files. Chapter 10, "Writing Console Applications" covers the methods of the `Package` class.

Input Method API

The Input Method API is an addition to the JDK's internationalization support that enables text-editing components to receive foreign language text input through input methods. It is designed to support large character sets, such as Chinese, Japanese, and Korean. An input method lets users enter thousands of different characters using keyboards with far fewer keys. Typically, a sequence of several characters is typed and then converted to create one or more characters. The input method framework is covered in Chapter 19, "Internationalization."

Enhancements

In addition to the new capabilities identified in previous sections, the JDK 1.2 provides significant enhancements to APIs, tools, and language features that were introduced in JDK 1.1 and 1.0. These enhancements are covered in the following subsections.

Security

The security model enforced by the JDK has evolved from JDK 1.0 through JDK 1.1 to JDK 1.2. The model enforced by JDK 1.2 is both more secure and more flexible than that of preceding JDK releases. It eliminates security flaws found in previous JDK versions. Its flexibility has been enhanced because it provides users with the capability to specify security policies simply by editing the security permissions contained in their policy text files. In addition to policy improvements, the JDK 1.2 provides enhanced support and tools for working with digital certificates. Chapter 3, "The Extended Java Security Model," and Chapter 8, "Applet Security," cover the security enhancements of JDK 1.2.

JavaBeans

The JavaBeans support provided with JDK 1.2 includes the Glasgow JavaBeans release. The Glasgow release adds the runtime containment and services protocol, support for drag and drop, and the JavaBeans activation framework. The runtime containment and services protocol provides beans with the capability to interoperate with other beans and to learn information about their execution environment. The new drag and drop support provides beans with a more complete graphical user interface capability. The JavaBeans activation framework allows beans to be selectively instantiated and used to support dynamic program requirements. Part VII, "Creating JavaBeans," covers JavaBeans programming. Chapter 29, "Glasgow Developments," covers the new features added with the Glasgow JavaBeans release.

Reflection

Reflection support was introduced in JDK 1.1. Reflection enables classes, interfaces, and objects to be examined and their public fields, constructors, and methods to be discovered and used at runtime. These capabilities are used by JavaBeans, object inspection tools, Java runtime tools such as the debugger, and other Java applications and applets. JDK 1.2 provides the capability to identify a field, method, or constructor as suppressing default Java language access controls. This permits reflection to be better used with the more flexible JDK 1.2 security model. Chapter 10 covers the use of reflection.

Audio

JDK 1.1 provided the capability for applets to play audio files that were in the Sun Audio (AU) format. JDK 1.2 provides a new sound engine that allows audio files to be played by both applets and applications. The sound engine also provides support for the Musical Instrument Digital Interface (MIDI), the Microsoft Windows audio file format (WAVE), the Rich Music Format (RMF), and the Audio Interchange File Format (AIFF). Chapter 21, "Using Audio and Video," covers these new audio capabilities.

JAR

Java Archive (JAR) files were introduced in JDK 1.1. These files provide the capability to store multiple files within a single archive file. JAR files help you organize applets, applications, beans, and class libraries and provide more efficient use of network resources. JDK 1.2 JAR enhancements include improved tools for working with JAR files and new classes for performing JAR file input and output. Chapter 8 covers the use of JAR files.

RMI and Serialization

The Remote Method Invocation (RMI) API was introduced in JDK 1.1. It provides the capability for Java objects executing on a local computer to invoke the methods of objects that execute on remote computers. Object serialization is used to pass objects as parameters and return values in the remote method invocations.

The RMI API has been significantly enhanced in JDK 1.2. The Remote Object Activation framework supports remotely activated objects and object references that persist across multiple object activations. Serialization improvements provide the capability for alternative objects to be written to and read from streams in support of serialization. RMI is covered in Part 9, "Developing Distributed Applications." Object serialization is covered in Chapter 40, "Using Object Serialization and JavaSpaces."

JDBC

JDBC provides the capability to access databases from Java. According to JavaSoft, JDBC doesn't stand for anything. However, it is sometimes associated with "Java database connectivity." JDBC was introduced in JDK 1.1. JDK 1.2 includes an improved version of the JDBC-ODBC bridge driver and support for JDBC 2.0. Part X, "Database Programming," covers all aspects of JDBC.

Native Interface

The Java Native Interface (JNI) provides the capability for Java objects to access methods written in languages other than Java. In JDK 1.2, the JNI includes new capabilities for controlling the manner in which native methods interact with the Java Virtual Machine. Chapter 53, "Native Methods," shows how to develop native methods using the Java Native Interface.

Performance

The overall performance of the JDK tools has been greatly improved. First and foremost is the inclusion of a just-in-time (JIT) compiler with the JDK. Other performance enhancements include the use of native libraries for some performance-critical Core API classes, improvements to multithreading performance, and reduction in memory usage for string constants.

Important Language Changes

In JDK 1.2, the stop(), suspend(), and resume() methods of the Thread class have been deprecated because of errors and inconsistencies that may occur as the result of their use. Instead of using the stop() method, it is recommended that threads monitor their execution and stop by returning from their run() method. A thread may determine that its execution should be stopped as the result of monitoring the state of a shared variable. In addition, it is recommended that threads suspend and resume their own execution as the result of monitoring interface events, such as the value of shared variables. The wait() and notify() methods of the Object class should be used to cause a thread to wait on changes to the value of a shared variable.

> **NOTE**
>
> In addition to changes to the Thread class, other classes, interfaces, and methods have been deprecated in JDK 1.2. A complete description of these changes is included with the JDK 1.2 documentation. A *deprecated* API element is one that is still supported for backward-compatibility but is being phased out of future JDK versions.

Tools Changes

The tools provided with JDK 1.1 have been improved in JDK 1.2, and new tools have been added. The new keytool and javasigner tools replace the javakey tool of JDK 1.1. New tools included with JDK 1.2 include the following:

- rmid—Remote activation system daemon
- keytool—Maintains a database of key pairs and digital certificates
- javasigner—Used to sign JAR files and verify the signatures of signed files
- policytool—Edits the local system security policy
- tnameserv—Implements the CORBA Common Object Services (COS) Naming Service

Appendix C, "The JDK 1.2 Toolset," summarizes the use of the tools provided with JDK 1.2.

Summary

In this chapter you learned about the new capabilities added to JDK 1.2. You learned about the JFC 1.1, the other new Core APIs added to JDK 1.2, the Servlets Standard Extension API, and improvements to the APIs of JDK 1.1. The next chapter, "The JDK 1.2 API," provides an overview of the packages that are contained in the Core and Standard Extension APIs of JDK 1.2.

The JDK 1.2 API

Chapter 1, "What's New in JDK 1.2," provided an overview of the new features incorporated into JDK 1.2. This chapter examines the JDK 1.2 API in closer detail. It provides an overview of the API packages and identifies the packages that have been added since JDK 1.1. It then describes all of the packages of JDK 1.2, highlighting important classes and interfaces. When you finish this chapter, you'll know your way around the packages of JDK 1.2 and know what packages to use for different programming needs.

API Overview

The JDK 1.2 API consists of 57 packages, all of which are in the Core API. Of the 53 Core API packages, 22 are part of the Java Foundations Classes (JFC). Figure 2.1 provides an overview of the JDK 1.2 packages.

The Core API is the minimum subset of the Java API that must be supported by the Java Platform. All classes and interfaces that are part of the JDK but are not in the Core API are in the Standard Extension API. The JFC are Core API classes and interfaces that support GUI development for applets and applications.

Figure 2.2 identifies the packages provided with JDK 1.1. By comparing Figure 2.1 with Figure 2.2, you can see that JDK 1.2 added 35 packages to the 22 packages provided with JDK 1.1. This is a substantial addition. The new JDK 1.2 packages are represented in **boldface** in Figure 2.1.

Core API

The Core API grew significantly from JDK 1.1 to 1.2. Of the 35 Core API packages that were added in JDK 1.2, 19 are in the JFC (10 Swing and 9 non-Swing), 9 are Java IDL (CORBA and CosNaming), 2 are security, 2 are utility packages (JAR and MIME support), 1 is JavaBeans, 1 is RMI, and 1 is object references (java.lang.ref). The bulk of the new JDK 1.2 packages are JFC and CORBA.

The following subsections summarize the JDK 1.2 Core API packages and identify what's new and what has been updated.

The java.applet Package

The java.applet package is one of the smallest packages in the Core API. It consists of one class and three interfaces that provide the basic functionality needed to implement applets. The Applet class provides methods to display images, play audio files, respond to events, and obtain information about an applet's execution environment. The

`AppletContext` interface defines methods that allow an applet to access the context in which it is being run. The `AppletStub` interface supports communication between an applet and its browser environment, and is used to develop custom applet viewers. The `AudioClip` interface provides methods that support the playing of audio clips. The `java.applet` package is covered in detail in Part II, "Applet Programming."

FIGURE 2.1.

The packages of JDK 1.2.

Core API Packages

JFC	
• **com.sun.java.image.codec.jpeg**	• **org.omg.CORBA**
• **com.sun.java.accessibility**	• **org.omg.CORBA.ContainedPackage**
• **com.sun.java.swing**	• **org.omg.CORBA.ContainerPackage**
• **com.sun.java.swing.border**	• **org.omg.CORBA.InterfaceDefPackage**
• **com.sun.java.swing.event**	• **org.omg.CORBA.ORBPackage**
• **com.sun.java.swing.plaf**	• **org.omg.CORBA.TypeCodePackage**
• **com.sun.java.swing.table**	• **org.omg.CORBA.portable**
• **com.sun.java.swing.text**	• **org.omg.CosNaming**
• **com.sun.java.swing.text.html**	• **org.omg.CosNaming.NamingContextPackage**
• **com.sun.java.swing.text.rtf**	
• **com.sun.java.swing.tree**	
• **com.sun.java.swing.undo**	
• java.awt	
• **java.awt.color**	
• java.awt.datatransfer	
• **java.awt.dnd**	
• java.awt.event	
• **java.awt.font**	
• **java.awt.geom**	
• **java.awt.im**	
• java.awt.image	
• **java.awt.image.renderable**	
• **java.awt.print**	

- java.applet
- java.beans
- **java.beans.beancontext**
- java.io
- java.lang
- **java.lang.ref**
- java.lang.reflect
- java.math
- java.net
- java.rmi
- **java.rmi.activation**
- java.rmi.dgc
- java.rmi.registry
- java.rmi.server
- java.security
- java.security.acl
- **java.security.cert**
- java.security.interfaces
- **java.security.spec**
- java.sql
- java.text
- java.util
- **java.util.jar**
- **java.util.mime**
- java.util.zip

2

THE JDK 1.2 API

FIGURE 2.2.

The packages of JDK 1.1.

Core API Packages
- java.applet
- java.awt
- java.awt.datatransfer
- java.awt.event
- java.awt.image
- java.beans
- java.io
- java.lang
- java.lang.reflect
- java.math
- java.net
- java.rmi
- java.rmi.dgc
- java.rmi.registry
- java.rmi.server
- java.security
- java.security.acl
- java.security.interfaces
- java.sql
- java.text
- java.util
- java.util.zip

The JFC Packages

The JFC packages provide the capability to create graphical user interfaces for applets and applications. The JFC packages subsume and extend the AWT of JDK 1.1. The number of JFC/AWT packages grew from 4 in JDK 1.1 to 23 in JDK 1.2. The 19 new packages include 10 Swing packages, written entirely in Java, that provide a pluggable look and feel for GUI controls. Other new packages support accessibility, drag and drop, 2D graphics, and imaging.

The `java.awt` Package

The java.awt package implements the core classes and interfaces of the Abstract Windowing Toolkit (AWT). It is a large package, containing 63 classes and 14 interfaces. These classes and interfaces provide the standard AWT GUI controls, as well as drawing, printing, and other capabilities. The java.awt package is covered in Chapter 6, "GUI Building," Chapter 7, "Working with the Canvas," Chapter 9, "Creating Window Applications," Part V, "Enhancing Your Applets and Applications," and Part VI, "Multimedia Programming."

The `javax.accessibility` Package

The javax.accessibility package provides seven classes and seven interfaces that support the use of assistive technologies for disabled users. It is covered in Chapter 9.

The `java.awt.color` Package

The `java.awt.color` package is part of the Java 2D API. It provides five classes that support the capability to work with different color models. The `java.awt.color` package is covered in Chapter 20, "Working with 2D and 3D Graphics."

The `java.awt.datatransfer` Package

The `java.awt.datatransfer` package provides four classes and three interfaces that support clipboard operations. It is covered in Chapter 15, "Using the Clipboard."

The `java.awt.dnd` Package

The `java.awt.dnd` package supports the new JDK 1.2 drag-and-drop capability. It contains 15 classes and four interfaces and is covered in Chapter 16, "Working with Drag and Drop."

The `java.awt.event` Package

The `java.awt.event` package provides the foundation for JDK 1.1-style event processing. It contains 21 classes and 13 interfaces, and is covered in Chapter 6.

The `java.awt.font` Package

The `java.awt.font` package is new to JDK 1.2. It provides 15 classes and two interfaces that support advanced font capabilities. The `java.awt.font` package is covered in Chapter 20.

The `java.awt.geom` Package

The `java.awt.geom` package is another new JDK 1.2 package that is part of the Java 2D API. It provides 30 classes and one interface that support standard geometrical objects and transformations. The `java.awt.geom` package is covered in Chapter 20.

The `java.awt.im` Package

The `java.awt.im` package is a new package that supports the Input Method API. It contains two classes and one interface. The Input Method API is covered in Chapter 19, "Internationalization."

The `java.awt.image` Package

The `java.awt.image` package is a Java 2D API package that supports image processing. It provides 38 classes and 8 interfaces that support common image filters. The `java.awt.image` package is covered in Chapter 20.

The `com.sun.image.codec.jpeg` Package

The `com.sun.image.codec.jpeg` package provides three classes and four interfaces that support JPEG image compression. It is covered in Chapter 20.

The `java.awt.image.renderable` Package

The `java.awt.image.renderable` package provides four classes and three interfaces that support image rendering. It is covered in Chapter 20.

The `java.awt.print` Package

The `java.awt.print` package is a Java 2D API package that supports the printing of text and graphics. It contains four classes and three interfaces. This package is covered in Chapter 18, "Printing."

The Swing Packages

The Swing packages are an important addition to the JDK 1.2. Swing is a 100 percent Java extension to the AWT that provides many new GUI components, improvements to existing components, and the capability to select from a variety of GUI look-and-feels, such as Metal, Windows, Motif, and Macintosh. Swing consists of 10 packages that are summarized in the following subsections and covered in detail in Part IV, "Swing Programming."

The `javax.swing` Package

The `javax.swing` package is the core Swing package. It contains 90 classes and 23 interfaces that provide the foundation for the Swing API. This package is introduced in Chapter 12, "Introducing Swing."

The `javax.swing.border` Package

The `javax.swing.border` package provides nine classes and one interface that implement borders and border styles. It is covered in Chapter 13, "Working with Swing Components."

The `javax.swing.event` Package

The `javax.swing.event` package provides 23 classes and 23 interfaces that implement Swing events and event listeners. It is covered in Chapter 12 and Chapter 13.

The `javax.swing.plaf` Package

The `javax.swing.plaf` package provides 42 classes and one interface that support the use of the pluggable look and feel. It is covered in Chapter 14, "Changing the Look and Feel of Your Swing Components."

The `javax.swing.table` Package

The `javax.swing.table` package provides seven classes and four interfaces that implement the Swing table component. It is covered in Chapter 13.

The `javax.swing.text` Package

The `javax.swing.text` package provides 59 classes and 21 interfaces that implement text processing components. It is covered in Chapter 12.

The `javax.swing.text.html` Package

The `javax.swing.text.html` package consists of 22 classes that provide basic HTML editing capabilities. This package is covered in Chapter 12.

The `javax.swing.text.rtf` Package

The `javax.swing.text.rtf` package consists of a single class, `RTFEditorKit`, that provides the capability to edit Rich Text Format (RTF) documents. It is covered in Chapter 12.

The `javax.swing.tree` Package

The `javax.swing.tree` package provides four classes and seven interfaces that provide the capability to work with `javax.swing.JTree` components. The `JTree` component is a GUI component that displays a set of hierarchical data as an outline. The `javax.swing.tree` package is covered in Chapter 13.

The `javax.swing.undo` Package

The `javax.swing.undo` package provides five classes and two interfaces that support the implementation of undo and redo capabilities. It is covered in Chapter 13.

The JavaBeans Packages

Two JavaBeans packages are provided with JDK 1.2. The `java.beans` package was present in JDK 1.1. The `java.beans.beancontext` package has been added to support the implementation for a bean container that provides an execution context for beans during design and runtime execution.

The `java.beans` Package

The `java.beans` package contains 15 classes and eight interfaces that provide the basic JavaBeans functionality. The `java.beans` package is covered in Part VII, "Creating JavaBeans."

The `java.beans.beancontext` Package

The `java.beans.beancontext` package provides 11 classes and eight interfaces that implement an execution context for beans. The `java.beans.beancontext` package is covered in Chapter 29, "Glasgow Developments."

The `java.io` Package

The `java.io` package provides 50 classes and 10 interfaces that implement stream-based input and output. Chapter 17, "Input/Output Streams," shows how to use `java.io` to perform a wide variety of input and output.

The Language Packages

The three `java.lang` packages implement the core classes of the Java language and runtime environment. The `java.lang.ref` package is new to JDK 1.2. This package introduces reference objects, which are objects that are used to reference other objects.

The `java.lang` Package

The `java.lang` package provides 29 classes and three interfaces that implement fundamental Java objects. Because of its importance, the `java.lang` package is included with all Java platforms, ranging from EmbeddedJava to the full-blown JDK. The `java.lang` package is covered in Chapter 10, "Writing Console Applications."

The `java.lang.ref` Package

The `java.lang.ref` package provides five classes that implement the new JDK 1.2 reference object capability. Reference objects are objects that are used to refer to other objects. They are similar to C and C++ pointers. The `java.lang.ref` package is covered in Chapter 10.

The `java.lang.reflect` Package

The `java.lang.reflect` package contains seven classes and one interface that provide the capability to implement runtime discovery of information about an object's class. The `AccessibleObject` and `ReflectPermission` classes are new to JDK 1.2. The `java.lang.reflect` package is covered in Chapter 10.

The `java.math` Package

The `java.math` package provides two classes, `BigDecimal` and `BigInteger`, that provide the capability to perform arbitrary-precision arithmetic. This package is covered in Chapter 11, "Using the Utility and Math Packages."

The `java.net` Package

The `java.net` package provides 21 classes and five interfaces for TCP/IP network programming. The `java.net` package is covered in Part VIII, "Network Programming."

The RMI Packages

The five Remote Method Invocation (RMI) packages provide the capability to use distributed objects within Java. The `java.rmi.activation` package is new to JDK 1.2. It supports persistent remote object references and automatic object activation. Part IX, "Developing Distributed Applications," covers programming with the RMI packages.

The `java.rmi` Package

The `java.rmi` package provides three classes and one interface that support basic RMI capabilities. The `MarshalledObject` class is new to JDK 1.2. It supports object persistence for remote object activation. The `Naming` class provides static methods for accessing remote objects via RMI URLs. The `RMISecurityManager` class defines the default security policy used for remote object stubs. The `Remote` interface is used to identify an object as being remotely accessible. The `java.rmi` package is covered in Chapter 38, "Building Distributed Applications with the `java.rmi` Packages," and Chapter 39, "Remote Method Invocation."

The `java.rmi.activation` Package

The `java.rmi.activation` package supports persistent object references and remote object activation. It contains seven classes and four interfaces. Chapter 39 shows how to work with these classes and interfaces.

The `java.rmi.dgc` Package

The `java.rmi.dgc` package supports distributed garbage collection. It contains two classes and one interface. The `Lease` class creates objects that are used to keep track of object references. The `VMID` class implements an ID that uniquely identifies a Java virtual machine on a particular host. The DGC interface is implemented by the server side of the distributed garbage collector. The `java.rmi.dgc` package is covered in Chapter 38.

The `java.rmi.registry` Package

The `java.rmi.registry` package supports distributed registry operations. It contains one class and two interfaces. The `LocateRegistry` class provides methods for accessing the Registry on a particular host. The `Registry` interface provides methods for associating names with remotely accessible objects. The `RegistryHandler` interface provides methods for accessing a Registry implementation. These methods have been deprecated in JDK 1.2. The `java.rmi.registry` package is covered in Chapter 38.

The `java.rmi.server` Package

The `java.rmi.server` package provides the low-level classes and interfaces that implement RMI. It contains 11 classes and nine interfaces. The SocketType class is new to JDK 1.2. The `java.rmi.registry` package is covered in Chapter 38.

The Security Packages

The five `java.security` packages support the implementation of the JDK 1.2 configurable security policy and cryptographic security mechanisms. These packages are covered in Chapter 3, "The Extended Java Security Model," and Chapter 8, "Applet Security."

The `java.security.cert` and `java.security.spec` packages are introduced in JDK 1.2. The `java.security.cert` package supports digital certificates. The `java.security.spec` package provides specifications for the keys used in common cryptographic algorithms.

The `java.security` Package

The `java.security` package provides 37 classes and eight interfaces that form the foundation for the Security API. Refer to Chapter 3 and Chapter 8.

The `java.security.acl` Package

The `java.security.acl` package provides five interfaces that form the basic elements for implementing security access controls. This package is covered in Chapter 8.

The `java.security.cert` Package

The `java.security.cert` package provides seven classes and one interface that implement digital certificates. It is covered in Chapter 8.

The `java.security.interfaces` Package

The `java.security.interfaces` package provides eight interfaces that support implementation of the NIST digital signature algorithm. It is covered in Chapter 8.

The `java.security.spec` Package

The `java.security.spec` package provides nine classes and two interfaces that provide specifications for cryptographic keys. It is covered in Chapter 8.

The `java.sql` Package

The `java.sql` package provides six classes and 18 interfaces that provide Java database connectivity. This package is covered in Part X, "Database Programming."

The `java.text` Package

The `java.text` package provides 20 classes and two interfaces that support internationalization. The `java.text` package is covered in Chapter 19.

The Utility Packages

The four `java.util` packages provide a variety of useful classes and interfaces for both applets and applications. These packages are covered in Chapter 11.

The `java.util.jar` and `java.util.mime` packages are new to JDK 1.2. The `java.util.jar` package provides classes for working with Java Archive (JAR) files. The `java.util.mime` package provides classes for working with Multipurpose Internet Mail Extensions (MIME) types.

The `java.util` Package

The `java.util` package, like `java.lang` and `java.io`, is fundamental to any Java platform. It provides 34 classes and 13 interfaces that cover a wide variety of common programming needs. Most of the new classes and interfaces support the Collections API. The `java.util` package is covered in Chapter 11.

The `java.util.jar` Package

The `java.util.jar` package provides seven classes for working with JAR files. It is covered in Chapter 11. Chapter 8 shows how to use the `jar` tool to create JAR files.

The `java.util.mime` Package

The `java.util.mime` package provides two classes for working with MIME types. The `MimeType` class provides an object representation of a MIME type. The `MimeTypeParameterList` class provides the capability to work with a MIME type's parameters. The `java.util.mime` package is covered in Chapter 11.

The `java.util.zip` Package

The `java.util.zip` package provides 14 classes and one interface for working with compressed files. It is covered in Chapter 11.

The CORBA Packages

The six new CORBA packages represent a sizable addition to the Core API and a significant capability for the Java programmer. These packages allow Java objects to make remote method invocations of CORBA objects. They also allow Java objects to be accessed as CORBA objects. The following subsections summarize these packages.

Chapter 41, "Java IDL and ORBs," shows how to use these packages to interface Java with CORBA.

The `org.omg.CORBA` Package

The `org.omg.CORBA` package consists of 57 classes and 42 interfaces that implement the foundation for supporting Java-CORBA integration.

The `org.omg.CORBA.ContainedPackage` Package

The `org.omg.CORBA.ContainedPackage` package contains a single class, `Description`, that describes the type and value of a contained object.

The `org.omg.CORBA.ContainerPackage` Package

The `org.omg.CORBA.ContainerPackage` package contains a single class, `Description`, that describes the type, value, and object of a contained in the container object.

The `org.omg.CORBA.InterfaceDefPackage` Package

The `org.omg.CORBA.InterfaceDefPackage` package contains a single class, `FullInterfacedescription`, that describes an interface definition.

The `org.omg.CORBA.ORBPackage` Package

The `org.omg.CORBA.ORBPackage` package defines the `InvalidName` exception, which is raised when an invalid name is passed to an object request broker.

The `org.omg.CORBA.TypeCodePackage` Package

The `org.omg.CORBA.TypeCodePackage` package defines the `BadKind` and `Bounds` exceptions, which are used to signal exceptions related to type usage and constraints.

The `org.omg.CORBA.portable` Package

The `org.omg.CORBA.portable` package consists of five classes and three interfaces that are used to support vendor-specific CORBA implementations.

The `org.omg.CosNaming` Package

The `org.omg.CosNaming` package consists of 20 classes and two interfaces that implement a tree-structured naming service.

The `org.omg.CosNaming.NamingContextPackage` Package

The `org.omg.CosNaming.NamingContextPackage` package consists of 13 classes that implement aspects of the naming service's name context. The name context implements nodes within the tree-structured naming scheme.

Standard Extensions

The Servlet API is a Standard Extension API, which provides the capability to perform server-side programming with Java. Java Servlets are used to replace Common Gateway Interface programs on Web servers. They can also be used to implement other, non-Web services. The Servlet API consists of the `javax.servlet` and `javax.servlet.http` packages. The `javax.servlet` package consists of three classes and six interfaces that allow Servlets to communicate with clients, process client requests, and send return responses to these requests. The `javax.servlet.http` package contains four classes and five interfaces that support the Hypertext Transfer Protocol (HTTP). Chapters 47, "Sun's Java Web Server," and Chapter 48, "Programming Other Servers," cover the Servlets API.

Other APIs

In addition to the Core and Standard Extension API packages covered in the previous sections, JavaSoft is currently developing other APIs that support other programming needs. Many of the APIs will become incorporated into future versions of the JDK as Core API or Standard Extension API packages. The new APIs covered in this book are described in the following subsections.

Java 3D

The Java 3D API provides the capability to create three-dimensional graphics applets and applications. It consists of classes and interfaces that support 3D objects and transformations. The Java 3D API is covered in Chapter 20.

The Java Media Framework

The Java Media Framework provides support for playing audio, video, and other multimedia within Java applets and applications. It supports a wide range of audio and video formats and provides animation capabilities. The Java Media Framework is covered in Chapter 21, "Using Audio and Video."

The Speech API

The Speech API adds speech recognition and synthesis capabilities to Java. The Speech API is covered in Chapter 23, "Integrating Speech and Telephony Capabilities."

The Telephony API

The Telephony API provides the capability to develop telephony applications, such as call center applications. The Telephony API is covered in Chapter 23.

JavaMail

JavaMail provides a set of classes and interfaces for developing client and server components of email systems. JavaMail is covered in Chapter 34, "Using JavaMail."

Java Naming and Directory Services

The Java Naming and Directory Interface (JNDI) allows Java applets and applications to access naming and directory services using protocols such as the Lightweight Directory Access Protocol (LDAP). The JNDI API is covered in Chapter 35, "Naming and Directory Services."

The Java Management API

The Java Management API provides a Java-based framework for managing enterprise networks and network resources. It is covered in Chapter 36, "Working with the Java Management API."

JavaSpaces

JavaSpaces supports the development of distributed applications by providing persistent distributed object capabilities. It is covered in Chapter 40, "Using Object Serialization and JavaSpaces."

JavaCommerce

The JavaCommerce API provides the capability to build electronic commerce applications in Java. It is covered in Chapter 50, "Java Commerce and JavaCard."

Summary

This chapter examined the JDK 1.2 API in close detail. It provided an overview of the API packages and identified the packages that have been added since JDK 1.1. It described all of the packages of JDK 1.2, highlighting important classes and interfaces. The next chapter will focus on Java security and the new extendible security model that is supported by JDK 1.2.

The Extended Java Security Model

CHAPTER 3

One of the most appealing features of Java in its debut as a Web programming language was the comprehensive security built into the Java runtime environment. The Java sandbox provided a mechanism for untrusted code to be downloaded from the Web and executed in a secure manner. The sandboxes of JDK 1.0 and 1.1 had some holes, but Sun encouraged the Internet community to find those holes and then quickly fixed them. The security model implemented by the Java sandbox has been strengthened and at the same time made more flexible from JDK 1.0 to JDK 1.2. In addition, JDK 1.2 provides a number of security mechanisms that can be used within the sandbox.

In this chapter you'll study the new security features of JDK 1.2 that can be used to secure Java applets and applications. You'll learn how to specify the security policy for your Java installation and how to use permissions to implement fine-grain access controls that extend the capabilities permitted to certain applets. You'll learn about the use of digital certificates and the cryptographic architecture supported by the JDK 1.2 Security API. When you finish this chapter, you'll understand how to use the security features of JDK 1.2 to enhance the security and functionality of your applets and applications.

Configurable Security Policy

One of the most powerful security features introduced in JDK 1.2 is the capability to specify a security policy for applets and applications. This feature gives software developers a great deal of flexibility in the functionality that they can incorporate into their applets and applications. At the same time, it provides users with total control over the access they allow to these programs. The configurable security policy of JDK 1.2 allows Java software developers to provide the capabilities their users want, and enables users to limit those capabilities based on their degree of trust in the source of the Java software they execute.

The Evolution of the Sandbox

To understand how the configurable security policy works and why it is useful, it is helpful to trace the evolution of Java security. JDK 1.0 introduced the *"sandbox"* approach to applet security. In this approach, all standalone Java applications are trusted by default and are allowed unrestricted access to your system resources (file system, network, and other programs). Applets that are loaded over the network are, by default, untrusted and prevented from accessing your local file system and other programs. In addition, applets are only allowed to make network connections to the host from which they are loaded.

The objective of the JDK 1.0 sandbox is to protect users from malicious applets that are downloaded from the Web. With the exception of a few security holes (which were subsequently corrected), the JDK 1.0 sandbox met this objective. However, in blocking potentially hostile applet accesses, the 1.0 sandbox also removed useful applet capabilities. Figure 3.1 summarizes the operation of the JDK 1.0 sandbox.

FIGURE 3.1.
The JDK 1.0 sandbox.

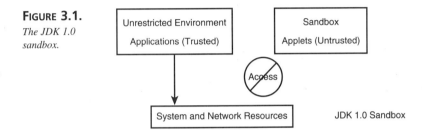

In addition to extending the sandbox for signed applets, JDK 1.0 also allows the SecurityManager class to be subclassed to implement a custom security policy for standalone Java applications, such as those that load applets. If SecurityManager is overridden, the capabilities of standalone applications can be restricted. However, the capability to implement a custom SecurityManager is provided for software developers but not users. If a user runs a standalone Java application, it is executed with unrestricted privileges unless the application polices itself.

For an example of the security provided by the JDK 1.0 sandbox, consider the applet shown in Listing 3.1. This applet reads the file specified in an applet's fileName parameter and displays the file's contents in a TextArea object. (If a security exception occurs, it is displayed in the TextArea object instead.) When you view the applet using Microsoft Internet Explorer 4.0, you receive the security exception shown in Figure 3.2. The applet in Listing 3.1 and the HTML file (used to access the applet) in Listing 3.2 can be accessed on my Web server at http://www.jaworski.com/ju/ReadFileApplet.htm. You can also set the applet up on your Web server using the files contained in the \ju\ch03 directory of this book's CD-ROM.

3

THE EXTENDED
JAVA SECURITY
MODEL

FIGURE 3.2.

A security exception is thrown when an applet tries to go outside of the sandbox.

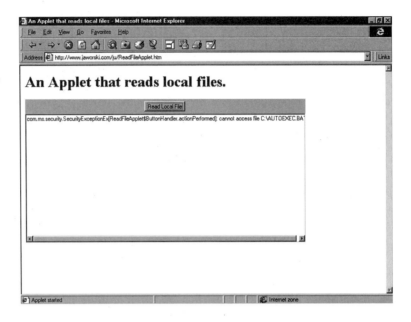

LISTING 3.1. THE ReadFileApplet.

```java
import java.applet.*;
import java.awt.*;
import java.awt.event.*;
import java.io.*;

public class ReadFileApplet extends Applet {
 TextArea text = new TextArea();
 Button goButton = new Button("Read Local File");
 Panel panel = new Panel();
 String fileName = "";
 public void init() {
  fileName = getParameter("fileName");
  setLayout(new BorderLayout());
  goButton.addActionListener(new ButtonHandler());
  panel.add(goButton);
  add("North",panel);
  add("Center",text);
 }
 class ButtonHandler implements ActionListener {
  public void actionPerformed(ActionEvent e){
   String s = e.getActionCommand();
   if("Read Local File".equals(s)){
    try {
     FileInputStream inStream = new FileInputStream(fileName);
     int inBytes = inStream.available();
     byte inBuf[] = new byte[inBytes];
```

```
        int bytesRead = inStream.read(inBuf,0,inBytes);
        text.setText(new String(inBuf));
      }catch(Exception ex){
        text.setText(ex.toString());
      }
    }
  }
 }
}
```

LISTING 3.2. THE `ReadFileApplet.htm` FILE.

```
<HTML>
<HEAD>
<TITLE>An Applet that reads local files</TITLE>
</HEAD>
<BODY>
<H1>An Applet that reads local files.</H1>
<APPLET CODE="ReadFileApplet.class" HEIGHT=300 WIDTH=600>
<PARAM NAME="fileName" VALUE="C:\AUTOEXEC.BAT">
Text displayed by browsers that are not Java-enabled.
</APPLET>
</BODY>
</HTML>
```

The JDK 1.1 sandbox is designed to maintain the security of the JDK 1.0 approach while allowing certain applets to be designated as *trusted*. Trusted applets are allowed to perform accesses that exceed the bounds of the sandbox. The Security API of JDK 1.1 provides the capability to digitally sign an applet and then verify that signature before an applet is loaded and executed. This capability enables browsers to authenticate that an applet is signed by a trusted party and that it has not been modified since the time of its signature. Given this additional level of security assurance, signed applets are considered to be as trustworthy as (or more than) standalone application programs. Figure 3.3 shows how the JDK 1.1 sandbox extends the JDK 1.0 sandbox.

FIGURE 3.3.
The JDK 1.1 security approach.

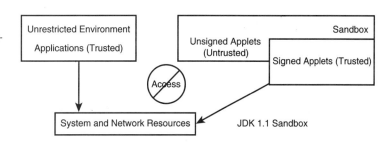

When I configure Internet Explorer 4.0 to trust `www.jaworski.com` and to allow applets from trusted hosts to access local files, I can execute the `ReadFileApplet` in Listing 3.1 and have it read, as well as display the contents of my `AUTOEXEC.BAT` file, as shown in Figure 3.4.

FIGURE 3.4.

JDK 1.1 security allows trusted applets to go outside of the sandbox.

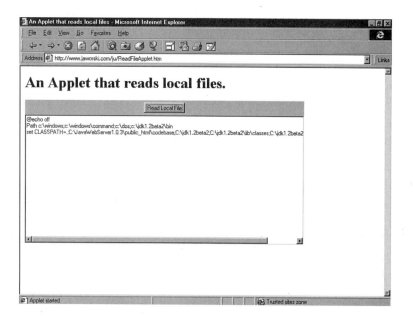

The JDK 1.1 security approach is a significant improvement on the JDK 1.0 approach because it allows applet designers to add useful capabilities like reading from and writing to the local file system, launching programs, and advanced networking. The shortcomings of the JDK 1.1 sandbox stem from its bipolar approach to security—an applet is either untrusted and confined to the sandbox, or it is trusted and given unrestricted access outside the sandbox. Applications are always trusted and given unrestricted access.

The problem with the JDK 1.1 approach is that it violates the security principle of *least privilege*. This principle states that an application should be given only those privileges that it needs to carry out its function and no more. According to least privilege, trusted applets and applications should be limited in the privileges they are allowed. For example, now that Internet Explorer 4.0 is reconfigured to run the `ReadFileApplet`, it will allow all applets from `www.jaworski.com` full access to my local file system. If Internet Explorer 4.0 implemented least privilege, I would be able to select the applets from `www.jaworski.com` that would have the privilege of accessing my local files.

JDK 1.2 introduces a security architecture for implementing least privilege. This architecture is based on the capability to specify a security policy that determines what accesses an applet or application is allowed, based on its source and on the identities of those who have signed the applet on application code.

The security policy feature of JDK 1.2 allows you to specify the following types of policies easily and without programming:

- Grant all applets from `http://www.trusted.com/` permission to read files in the `C:\tmp` directory.

- Grant all applets (from any host) permission to listen on TCP ports greater than 1023.

- Grant all applets signed by Mary and Ted (hypothetical Java programmers) that are from `http://www.trusted.com` permission to read and write to files in the `C:\tmp` directory.

- Grant all applications loaded from the `C:\trusted` directory permission to set security properties.

The next section shows how to specify the details of a particular security policy. Figure 3.5 shows how JDK 1.2 extends the JDK 1.0 and 1.1 sandboxes using a configurable security policy.

3

THE EXTENDED
JAVA SECURITY
MODEL

> **NOTE**
>
> To restrict the capabilities of a Java application, you must run it under a `SecureClassLoader`, as described in the section "Application Security" later in this chapter.

Specifying a Security Policy

Specifying a custom security policy is easy to do. All you have to do is edit the appropriate policy configuration file. JDK 1.2 provides you with a number of ways to do this:

- You can create or edit the default system policy file located at `<java.home>\lib\security\java.policy`, where `<java.home>` identifies the location of your JDK 1.2 installation. It is specified by the value of the `java.home` system property. By default, `java.home` is `C:\jdk1.2`. If you edit `java.policy`, the new policy will apply to all users of your JDK 1.2 installation.

FIGURE 3.5.

The JDK 1.2 configurable security policy.

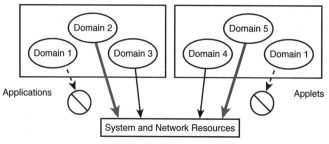

JDK 1.2 Configurable Security

- You can set the value of the `policy.java` system property to the name of an alternative security policy file.

- You can create or edit the user policy file located at *<user.home>*\.`java.policy`, where *<user.home>* identifies the current user's home directory. It is specified by the value of the `user.home` system property.

- You can set the value of the `java.security.policy` property to a different user security policy file using the `-D` command-line option. For example, suppose that you want to run the `Test` class using the `test.policy` user security policy file. You could use the `-D` option as follows:

```
java -Djava.security.policy=="test.policy" Test
```

  You can also use the `-Djava.security.manager` option to ensure that the policy is installed. The double equal sign specifies that the policy should be the only policy that is in effect. A single equal sign specifies that the policy is added to the current policy that is in effect.

- You can change the class used to implement the security policy from `java.security.PolicyFile` to another class by editing the `java.security` file located at *<java.home>*\lib\security\java.security. Change the line `policy.provider=java.security.PolicyFile` to `policy.provider=OtherClass`, where `OtherClass` is the fully qualified name of the class to be used.

When the Java byte code interpreter is run, it loads in the system policy followed by the user policy. If neither of these policies is available, the original sandbox policy is used.

You can also use the `-Djava.security.manager` option to ensure that the policy is installed. The double equal sign specifies that the policy should be the only policy that is in effect. A single equal sign specifies that the policy is added to the current policy that is in effect.

The Contents of the Security Policy File

The policy file (system or user) consists of a series of statements, referred to as *grant entries*, that identify the permissions granted to code (applet or application) based on the location from which it is loaded and any signers of the code.

> **NOTE**
>
> In JDK 1.2, all code, whether it is an applet that is loaded from a remote host or an application from the local file system, is associated with a *code source*. This code source is defined by the URL from which the code is loaded and a list of signers of the code. These signers are identified by the names associated with the signer's public keys. These names are referred to as *aliases*. The aliases and keys are stored in a user's keystore, as shown in Figure 3.6.

FIGURE 3.6.

The keystore *stores aliases, keys, certificates, and other information about entities.*

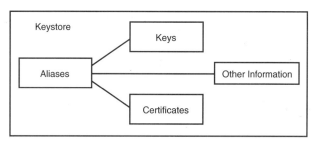

3

THE EXTENDED
JAVA SECURITY
MODEL

A keystore is a repository for the aliases, certificates, public keys, and other information about the entities (organizations and individuals) that are recognized by a user. A user's keystore resides in the .keystore file located in the user's home directory. The .keystore file is generated and maintained using JDK 1.2's keytool program. On Windows systems, the user's home directory is defined by the user.home property. If the HOMEDRIVE and HOMEPATH environment variables are defined, user.home is the concatenation of HOMEDRIVE and HOMEPATH. Otherwise, the value of user.home is the same as java.home.

> **NOTE**
>
> You'll learn more about the keytool in Chapter 8, "Applet Security."

The grant entries of the security policy identify a code source (URL and list of signers), followed by the permissions granted to that code source. The permissions (also referred to as *permission entries*) specify the actions that a code source may take with respect to a protected resource. If all this seems too abstract, hang in there. After we cover the syntax of grant entries and provide a few examples, the process of setting up a security policy will appear quite simple.

The Syntax of Grant Entries

Grant entries begin with the keyword `grant`, followed by optional `SignedBy` or `CodeBase` clauses, followed by an opening bracket ({), followed by a list of permission entries, followed by a closing bracket (}) and a semicolon. The syntax of a grant entry follows:

```
grant [SignedBy "signer_names"] [, CodeBase "URL"] {
  permission entries
};
```

The `SignedBy` clause contains a comma-separated list of the aliases of the signers of the code to which the grant entry applies. If the code has not been signed or the signers don't factor into the policy, the `SignedBy` clause may be omitted. Examples of `SignedBy` clauses follow:

```
SignedBy "Bill"
SignedBy "Bill,Ted"
SignedBy "Bill,Ted,Alice"
```

The aliases are not case sensitive. For example, "Bill" and "bill" are equivalent.

The `CodeBase` clause identifies the URL of the location from which the code is loaded. Examples follow:

```
CodeBase "http://www.trusted.com"
CodeBase "http://www.trusted.com/omega/version5/"
CodeBase "file:/local/applets/"
```

The first example specifies that the grant entry applies to all code that is loaded from `www.trusted.com`. The second example specifies that the grant entry applies to all code that is loaded from `/omega/version5/` (and all subdirectories) of `www.trusted.com`. The third example specifies that the grant entry applies to all code that is loaded from the `\local\applets` directory (and all subdirectories) of the local file system.

If the `CodeBase` clause is omitted, the grant entry applies to all code locations. Note that syntactically the `CodeBase` clause may appear before the `SignedBy` clause. If both clauses are present, they are separated by a comma.

Permission Entries

Each grant entry specifies one or more permission entries to define the permissions that are granted to the code source described by the `SignedBy` and `CodeBase` clauses. A permission entry consists of the keyword `permission`, followed by the fully qualified name of a Java permission class, followed by an optional target name, action list, and SignedBy clause. The syntax of a permission entry is as follows:

```
permission permission_class_name [ "target_name" ]
            [, "action_list"] [, SignedBy "signer_names"];
```

The permission class name identifies the permission to be granted. It is the fully qualified name of the Java class that implements the permission. Examples of permission class names follow:

```
java.io.FilePermission
java.net.SocketPermission
java.util.PropertyPermission
```

The java.io.FilePermission class is used to control the accesses that code may make of the local file system. The java.net.SocketPermission class is used to control the ways in which code may access TCP/IP sockets. The java.util.PropertyPermission class is used to control the ways in which code may access Java properties.

TIP

The implementation of permissions in terms of permission classes is covered in the section "Policy Permissions" later in this chapter. When reading it, just try to get a feel for what permissions are and how they are used to specify a security policy.

Two important characteristics of a permission are its *target* and its *action list*. The target identifies the resource or service to which access is being granted. For example, the target of java.io.FilePermission is the name of the file or directory to which access is being granted. The target of java.util.PropertyPermission is the property to which access is being granted.

The action list identifies the actions that the code source is permitted to make on the target. For example, actions related to java.io.FilePermission include read, write, delete, and execute. Actions related to java.net.SocketPermission include accept, connect, listen, and resolve. The action list is a comma-separated list of actions enclosed in quotation marks. Some permissions, such as java.RuntimePermission, are service-related and do not have actions. In these cases, the action list may be omitted.

NOTE

A complete list of the predefined permissions, targets, and actions is provided in the section "Policy Permissions" later in this chapter.

The last element of a permission entry is an optional `SignedBy` clause. Any `SignedBy` clause that is included with a permission entry indicates a signed permission entry. This means that the permission class itself must be signed by everyone in the specified signer list or must be a class that is found on the `CLASSPATH`. For example, the following permission entry requires the code for `com.jaworski.DevicePermission.class` to be signed by `jamie` or to be accessible from the `CLASSPATH`.

```
permission com.jaworski.DevicePermission "transmitter", "send, receive",
SignedBy "jamie";
```

In this example, the `com.jaworski.DevicePermission` class has `"transmitter"` as its target and `"send"` and `"receive"` as the permitted actions.

An Example Security Policy

Having covered the syntax of the security policy file, in this section I'll create an example policy and go through it on a line-by-line basis, explaining what its grant and permission entries mean and what the resultant policy permits and restricts. After that, I'll list and explain the `java.policy` file that is the default for JDK 1.2.

Listing 3.3 shows the `example.policy` file. It contains four grant entries. The first grant entry specifies the `CodeBase` as the URL `http://www.trusted.com/verified/`. This indicates that the grant entry applies to code that is loaded from that URL. Because there is no `SignedBy` clause, the grant entry applies to all code from this URL. The grant entry contains a single permission entry. This permission entry grants permission for the code to open up a client TCP socket to the host `other.trusted.com` on port 23 (the Telnet port).

The second grant entry specifies the `CodeBase` as the URL `http://jaworski.com` and the signer list as `jason` and `emily`. This indicates that the grant entry applies to all code that is loaded from `jaworski.com` that is signed by both Jason and Emily. The grant entry contains three permission entries. The first permission entry grants the code source permission to `read`, `write`, and `delete` all files and directories in the local file system. The `"-"` target indicates all files in the file system. The second permission entry grants the code source permission to read and write all Java properties. The `"*"` target indicates all properties. The third permission entry grants the code source permission to print to the local print queue.

The third grant entry has a `CodeBase` corresponding to all code that is loaded from the `\local\trusted` path of the local file system. There are no code signers. The grant entry has a single permission entry that grants the code source permission to create its own class loader.

The last grant entry does not specify a CodeBase or a signer list. This means that the grant entry applies to all code, no matter where it is loaded from or who signs it. The grant entry contains a single permission entry. This entry grants the code source permission to read the java.version property.

> **NOTE**
>
> You can use Java-style comments in a security policy configuration file.

LISTING 3.3. THE example.java POLICY FILE.

```java
// example.java

/* Grant all code that is from the /verified path of www.trusted.com
   permission to create a TCP socket and connect it to other.trusted.com
   on port 23.
*/

grant CodeBase "http://www.trusted.com/verified/" {
  permission java.net.SocketPermission "other.trusted.com:23", "connect";
};

/* Grant all code from jaworski.com that is signed by Emily and Jason the
   following permissions:
        1. Permission to read, write, delete, or execute any file
           in the local file system.
        2. Permission to read or write any property.
        3. Permission to send a print job to the local print queue.
*/

grant CodeBase "http://jaworski.com", SignedBy "jason,emily" {
  permission java.io.FilePermission "-", "read,write,delete,execute";
  permission java.util.PropertyPermission "*", "read,write";
  permission java.lang.RuntimePermission "queueJob";
};

/* Grant all code from the /local/trusted path of the local file system
   permission to create its own class loader.
*/

grant CodeBase "file:/local/trusted" {
  permission java.lang.RuntimePermission "createClassLoader";
};
```

3

THE EXTENDED
JAVA SECURITY
MODEL

continues

LISTING 3.3. CONTINUED

```
/* Grant all code from any location, signed or not, permission to read
   the java.version property.
*/

grant {
    permission java.util.PropertyPermission "java.version", "read";
};
```

Listing 3.4 shows the default `java.policy` file that comes with JDK 1.2. This file is located in the `\jdk1.2\lib\security` directory and contains a single grant entry. This grant entry does not specify a `CodeBase` or a list of signers. This means that the grant entry applies to all code. The grant entry contains 11 permission entries. The first permission entry grants permission for code to listen on TCP or UDP sockets on ports 1024 and higher. The target `"localhost:1024-"` identifies the host on which the code executes (using `localhost`) and ports 1024 and higher (using `1024-`).

Permission entries 2 through 11 are similar. They grant permission to read the properties `java.version` through `line.separator`.

LISTING 3.4. THE DEFAULT `java.policy` FILE.

```
grant {
    // allows anyone to listen on un-privileged ports
    permission java.net.SocketPermission "localhost:1024-", "listen";

    // "standard" properties that can be read by anyone

    permission java.util.PropertyPermission "java.version", "read";
    permission java.util.PropertyPermission "java.vendor", "read";
    permission java.util.PropertyPermission "java.vendor.url", "read";
    permission java.util.PropertyPermission "java.class.version", "read";
    permission java.util.PropertyPermission "os.name", "read";
    permission java.util.PropertyPermission "os.version", "read";
    permission java.util.PropertyPermission "os.arch", "read";
    permission java.util.PropertyPermission "file.separator", "read";
    permission java.util.PropertyPermission "path.separator", "read";
    permission java.util.PropertyPermission "line.separator", "read";
};
```

Policy Permissions

Security policy is implemented by the `java.security.Permission` classes and their subclasses. The permissions classes are used to specify that permission has been granted to specific system services and resources. Most subclasses of `java.security.Permission`, such as `java.net.SocketPermission` and `java.io.FilePermission`, are defined in the packages that provide the services and resources being protected. The `Permission` class hierarchy is shown in Figure 3.7. The `java.security.Permisson` class is subclassed by `java.security.BasicPermission`, `java.io.FilePermission`, and `java.net.SocketPermission`. The `java.security.BasicPermission` class provides a common subclass that implements permissions specifying targets that are named with the hierarchical naming convention used by properties and fully qualified class names. This naming convention separates naming levels using periods, as in `level1name.level2name.level3name`.

The `java.security.BasicPermission` class has seven subclasses that are identified in Figure 3.7. These seven classes, and the `java.io.FilePermission` and `java.net.SocketPermission` classes, are covered in the following subsections.

The `java.security.AllPermission` class defines a permission that implies all other permissions. This permission should be used only with extreme care.

FIGURE 3.7.
The `Permission`
class hierarchy.

```
Java Permission Hierarchy
        java.security.Permission
            java.security.BasicPermission
                java.awt.AWTPermission
                java.io.SerializablePermission
                java.lang.reflect.ReflectPermission
                java.lang.RuntimePermission
                java.net.NetPermission
                java.security.SecurityPermission
                java.util.PropertyPermission
            java.io.FilePermission
            java.net.SocketPermission
```

The `java.awt.AWTPermission` Class

The `java.awt.AWTPermission` class is used to control access to AWT resources. This class defines the following three targets:

- `accessEventQueue`—Grants permission to access the system event queue.
- `accessClipboard`—Grants permission to the system clipboard.
- `showWindowWithoutWarningBanner`—Grants an applet permission to create a window without a warning banner.

None of these targets requires an action to be specified.

The `java.net.NetPermission` Class

The `java.net.NetPermission` class is used to control access to network resources and defines the following targets:

- `requestPasswordAuthentication`—Grants permission to ask the registered authenticator for a password.
- `setDefaultAuthenticator`—Grants permission to set the authenticator to be used with networking code, such as in HTTP authentication.

Neither of these targets requires an action to be specified.

The `java.util.PropertyPermission` Class

The `java.util.PropertyPermission` class is used to control access to system properties. The target of this permission is a system property. The wildcard `"*"` is used to specify all properties. A wildcard character may also appear at the end of a hierarchical property name following the last period. For example, `"java.*"` specifies all properties beginning with `"java."`. The read and write actions may be specified with the target property.

The `java.lang.reflect.ReflectPermission` Class

The `java.lang.reflect.ReflectPermission` class is used to circumvent the access checks performed on reflected objects. It allows all members of an object to be accessed, no matter what access is specified via the public, protected, and private keywords. Only the `"suppressAccessChecks"` target is defined for this permission. No actions may be specified. Reflection is covered in Chapter 10, "Writing Console Applications."

The `java.lang.RuntimePermission` Class

The `java.lang.RuntimePermission` class is used to control access to services of the Java runtime environment. It defines the following targets:

- `createClassLoader`—Grants permission to create a class loader.
- `getClassLoader`—Grants permission to retrieve a class loader.
- `setContextClassLoader`—Grants permission to set the context class loader of a thread.
- `setSecurityManager`—Grants permission to change the current security manager.
- `createSecurityManager`—Grants permission to create a new security manager.
- `exitvm`—Grants permission to exit the runtime system.

- setFactory—Grants permission to set the socket factory, URL stream handler factory, content handler factory, and other aspects of how networking is implemented.

- setIO—Grants permission to set/reset the standard input, output, and error streams.

- modifyThread—Grants permission to alter a thread's execution.

- stopThread—Grants permission to stop a thread's execution.

- modifyThreadGroup—Grants permission to alter a thread group.

- getProtectedDomain—Grants permission to retrieve the protected domain of a class.

- readFileDescriptor—Grants permission to create an input stream using a file descriptor.

- writeFileDescriptor—Grants permission to create an output stream using a file descriptor.

- loadLibrary—Grants permission to load a dynamic link library. The name of the library is appended to "loadLibrary.".

- accessClassInPackage—Grants permission to load a class from a specified package. The name of the package is appended to "accessClassInPackage".

- defineClassInPackage—Grants permission to define a class as part of the specified package. The name of the package is appended to "defineClassInPackage".

- queuePrintJob—Grants permission to initiate a print job.

- accessDeclaredMembers—Grants permission to access the members of a class.

None of these targets requires actions to be specified.

The `java.security.SecurityPermission` Class

This class is used to grant a variety of security-related permissions. These permissions are specified as hierarchical target names:

- addIdentityCertificate—Grants permission to add certificates for Identity objects.

- removeIdentityCertificate—Grants permission to remove certificates for Identity objects.

- setIdentityPublicKey—Grants permission to set the public key of Identity objects.

- setIdentityInfo—Grants permission to set information related to Identity objects.

- setSystemScope—Grants permission to set the system's identity scope.

3

THE EXTENDED
JAVA SECURITY
MODEL

- getPolicy—Grants permission to get the installed Policy object.
- setPolicy—Grants permission to set the installed Policy object.
- clearProviderProperties—Grants permission to clear the properties of a specified security provider. The provider name is appended to "clearProviderProperties".
- putProviderProperty—Grants permission to set the property of a security provider. The property name is appended to "putProviderProperty".
- removeProviderProperty—Grants permission to remove a specified property from a security provider. The property name is appended to "removeProviderProperty".
- insertProvider—Grants permission to insert a specified security provider in the list of available providers. The provider name is appended to "insertProvider.".
- removeProvider—Grants permission to remove a specified security provider. The provider name is appended to "removeProvider.".
- getProperty—Grants permission to retrieve a specific security property. The property is appended to "get Property."
- setProperty—Grants permission to set a specific security property. The property is appended to "setProperty.".
- setSignerKeyPair—Grants permission to set the public and private key pairs for a signer.
- getPrivateKey—Grants permission to retrieve the public key of a signer.

None of these targets requires actions to be specified.

The `java.io.SerializablePermission` Class

This class is used to grant permission to use serialization. The enableSubstitution permission grants permission for objects in object input and output streams to be replaced. The enableSubclassImplementation permission allows subclasses of ObjectInputStream and ObjectOutputStream to override an object's serialization property.

The `java.io.FilePermission` Class

The java.io.FilePermission class is an important class in that it is used to grant permission for file and directory operations. The targets for this permission are file and directory names. The "-" target is used to specify all files in the file system. The target "*directory*/-" is used to specify all files in the file system that are in *directory* or its subdirectories. The target "*directory*/*" is used to specify all files in the file system that are in *directory* but not its subdirectories.

The actions that can be specified are read, write, delete, and execute. The read, write, and delete actions apply to files and directories. The execute action applies to executable files and operating system commands.

The `java.net.SocketPermission` Class

The java.net.SocketPermission class is used to grant permission to TCP/IP socket programming. The targets of this permission are of the form `"host"` or `"host:port_range"`, where host can be specified as one of the following:

- *host name*
- *IP address*
- **.domain* (All hosts in a domain or subdomain)
- *** (All hosts)

The port range can be specified using the following notation (where *n* and *m* represent port numbers):

- *n* (A single port)
- *n-* (All ports greater than or equal to *n*)
- *-n* (All ports less than or equal to *n*)
- *n-m* (All ports between *n* and *m* inclusive)

The actions that are defined for this permission are as follows:

- accept—Permits socket connections to be accepted from remote hosts.
- connect—Permits TCP, UDP, and multicast socket connections to remote hosts.
- listen—Permits listening on TCP, UDP, and multicast sockets on the local host.
- resolve—Allows DNS lookups to be performed.

TCP/IP network programming is covered in Part 8.

Extending the Sandbox

Having covered the development of a security policy in detail, let's put it all together and show how the security capabilities of an applet can be extended by adding permissions to the JDK security policy. Listing 3.5 contains the source code of the ExtendedApplet applet. This applet attempts to read the user.name system property, which is forbidden by the default JDK 1.2 security policy. The user.name property contains the current user's login name. The file extended.htm, shown in Listing 3.6, is an HTML file that is used to access ExtendedApplet.

> **NOTE**
>
> An introduction to applets and HTML is provided in Chapter 5, "JDK 1.2 Applet Writing Basics."

LISTING 3.5. THE ExtendedApplet SOURCE CODE.

```java
import java.applet.*;
import java.awt.*;
import java.util.*;
public class ExtendedApplet extends Applet {
 String text;
 int x = 30;
 int y = 120;
 public void init() {
   try {
     text=System.getProperty("user.name");
   }catch(Exception ex){
     text=ex.toString();
   }
 }
 public void paint(Graphics g) {
   g.setFont(new Font("TimesRoman",Font.BOLD,12));
   g.drawString(text,x,y);
 }
}
```

LISTING 3.6. THE extended.htm HTML FILE.

```html
<HTML>
<HEAD>
<TITLE>Extended Applet</TITLE>
</HEAD>
<BODY>
<H1>An Applet that reads the user.name property.</H1>
<APPLET CODE="ExtendedApplet.class" HEIGHT=300 WIDTH=600>
Text displayed by browsers that are not Java-enabled.
</APPLET>
</BODY>
</HTML>
```

I've compiled ExtendedApplet.java and put the ExtendedApplet.class and extended.htm files on my Web server in the http://www.jaworski.com/ju/ path. You can run ExtendedApplet by opening the URL http://www.jaworski.com/ju/extended.htm with the appletviewer:

```
appletviewer http://www.jaworski.com/ju/extended.htm
```

Run `appletviewer` from a directory other than your `ch03` directory to make sure that `ExtendedApplet.class` is loaded from my Web server and not your local file system. When you run `appletviewer`, the applet should display the exception shown in Figure 3.8.

FIGURE 3.8.
The `ExtendedApplet` *generates an* `AccessControlExc eption`.

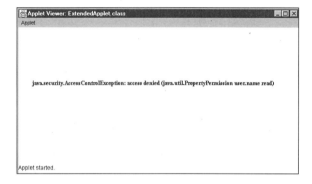

NOTE

If you use `appletviewer` to view `ExtendedApplet` from your local file system, `appletviewer` will not throw the access control exception.

Now, let's extend the capabilities of applets by adding the following permission to your `java.policy` file.

```
permission java.util.PropertyPermission "user.name", "read";
```

This file should be located in the `C:\jdk1.2\lib\security` directory. Modify the file as shown in Listing 3.7.

LISTING 3.7. THE MODIFIED `java.policy` FILE.

```
grant {
    // allows anyone to listen on un-privileged ports
    permission java.net.SocketPermission "localhost:1024-", "listen";

    // "standard" properties that can be read by anyone

    permission java.util.PropertyPermission "java.version", "read";
```

LISTING 3.7. CONTINUED

```
    permission java.util.PropertyPermission "java.vendor", "read";
    permission java.util.PropertyPermission "java.vendor.url", "read";
    permission java.util.PropertyPermission "java.class.version", "read";
    permission java.util.PropertyPermission "os.name", "read";
    permission java.util.PropertyPermission "os.version", "read";
    permission java.util.PropertyPermission "os.arch", "read";
    permission java.util.PropertyPermission "file.separator", "read";
    permission java.util.PropertyPermission "path.separator", "read";
    permission java.util.PropertyPermission "line.separator", "read";
    permission java.util.PropertyPermission "user.name", "read";
};
```

Now that you've added the permission for all code to access the user.name property, rerun appletviewer http://www.jaworski.com/ju/extended.htm. The applet should now display your login name, as shown in Figure 3.9. Note that Figure 3.9 displays my login name, not yours. I suggest that you edit java.policy one more time to remove the permission to read the user.name property.

FIGURE 3.9.

The
ExtendedApplet
*displays my login
name.*

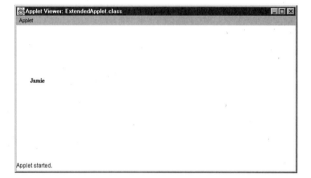

Application Security

The previous section shows how to configure your security policy to give additional privileges to applets. You can also require applications to be governed by your security policy. In order to do this, you must run the applications under a SecureClassLoader. Normally, all classes that are loaded from the CLASSPATH are treated as system classes, are trusted, and not subject to the security policy. These classes are loaded with a null system ClassLoader.

JDK 1.2 allows local classes to be loaded from a second class path that is specified by the system property java.app.class.path. If you specify the second class path when you invoke the java interpreter, you can load an application using a `SecureClassLoader` that will require the application to abide by the security policy. For example, the following command loads `MyApplication` from the `C:\untrusted` directory using a `SecureClassLoader` object:

```
java -Djava.app.class.path="/untrusted" MyApplication
```

The `SecureClassLoader` object will ensure that `MyApplication` obeys the security policy that is in effect.

Cryptographic Support

The JDK 1.1 expanded the security capabilities of JDK 1.02 to support application-level security. This new security support is provided by the Security API of the `java.security` packages and includes support for message digests, digital signatures, digital certificates, and key management. JDK 1.2 extended the capabilities provided by JDK 1.1 to include support for X.509 version 3 certificates and added new tools for working with certificates. The *Java Cryptography Extension* (*JCE*) is a separate add-on to the Security API that implements cryptographic algorithms that are subject to U.S. export controls. The JCE is available at `http://www.javasoft.com`.

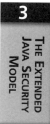

The application-level security controls provided by the Security API can be used to protect information from unauthorized modification and disclosure as it traverses the Internet. They can also be used to authenticate the contents of messages and files and the identities of applications and individuals.

In this section you'll be introduced to the cryptographic capabilities provided by the Security API. Don't worry if you are unfamiliar with the basics of cryptography—they will be summarized in the next section.

> **NOTE**
>
> This section provides an overview of the cryptographic capabilities of the Security API. Chapter 8, "Applet Security," investigates the `java.security` packages and shows how to use the security-related tools of the JDK.

Overview of Cryptography

Cryptography is the study of algorithms and protocols for securing messages during transmission and storage. However, cryptographic techniques can be applied to other applications, such as identity verification and data authentication.

One of the most fundamental applications of cryptography is to disguise a message so that it can only be read by those who know how to recover the original message content. *Encryption* is the process of disguising a message, and *decryption* is the process of recovering the original message. An encrypted message is referred to as *ciphertext*, and an unencrypted or decrypted message is referred to as *plaintext*. Figure 3.10 provides an overview of these concepts.

FIGURE 3.10.
Encryption and decryption.

> **NOTE**
>
> Cryptographic techniques are oriented toward the protection of messages. However, these techniques can be used to protect other forms of data, such as files, database records, and Java byte codes.

Although a number of approaches to encryption have been developed over the years, most current encryption algorithms are based on the use of secret keys. A *key* is a sequence of binary digits that are used to encrypt or decrypt data. In key-based cryptography, the encryption and decryption algorithms are publicly known. Data is encrypted using one key and decrypted using another. Figure 3.11 provides an overview of key-based encryption. It is important that the decryption key be kept secret, or else anyone will be able to use it to decrypt messages.

FIGURE 3.11.
Key-based encryption.

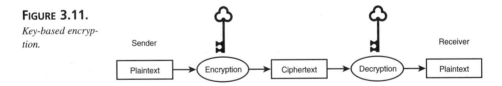

In some encryption algorithms, the encryption and decryption keys are the same, or the decryption key can be calculated from the encryption key within a useful time frame. These algorithms are known as *secret-key algorithms* or *symmetric algorithms*. Secret-key algorithms require the encryption key to be kept secret and require the sender and receiver to coordinate on the use of their secret keys. The *Data Encryption Standard* (*DES*) is an example of a secret-key algorithm.

Other encryption algorithms, known as *public-key algorithms* or *asymmetric algorithms*, are based on the use of separate encryption and decryption keys. Public-key algorithms require that it be computationally unfeasible to calculate the decryption key from the encryption key. Because of this requirement, the encryption key can be made public without affecting the security of the encryption algorithm. Figure 3.12 shows how public-key cryptography works.

FIGURE 3.12.
Public key cryptography.

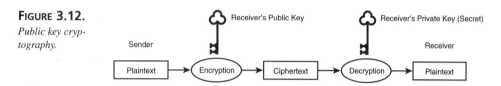

In public-key cryptosystems, each communicating entity (individual, organization, software program, and so on) is assigned a public key and a private key. Entities encrypt messages using the public key of the receiver. The receiver decrypts messages using his, her, or its private key. The public key cannot be used to determine the private key, so it does not need to be kept secret and can be openly published. Because of this feature and others, public-key encryption is very popular in open communication environments, such as the Internet. The RSA encryption algorithm is an example of a public-key algorithm.

Cryptographic techniques are not limited to preserving the secrecy of messages. They are also used to maintain message integrity and to verify the authenticity of a message. *One-way functions* are used in these applications. A one-way function is one that is easy to compute, but computationally unfeasible to reverse. A real-life example of a one-way function is a shredding machine. It is easy to put a document in a shredder and produce paper strips, but it is very difficult to reverse the process. *Message digest functions* are also one-way functions. They compute values, referred to as *message digests* or *hash values*, that are used as fingerprints for messages. Good message digest functions have the following properties:

- Given a particular message digest value, it is computationally unfeasible to compute a message that will produce that value under the message digest function.

- It is computationally unfeasible to find two messages that yield the same message digest value under the message digest function.

Figure 3.13 illustrates the use of message digest functions. Note that there is nothing secret about a message digest function—it is publicly available and uses no keys. The MD5 and MD4 algorithms are examples of message digest algorithms.

FIGURE 3.13.
Message digest functions.

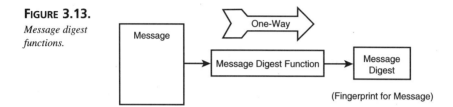

A *digital signature* is a value that is computed from a message using a secret key. It indicates that the person who holds the secret key has verified that the contents of the message are correct and authentic. Digital signatures often use public-key encryption algorithms with a slight twist—a private key is used for encryption, and a public key is used for decryption. This approach is often implemented as follows:

Signature generation:

1. A message digest is computed.
2. The message digest is encrypted using the private key of a public/private key pair, producing the message's digital signature.

Signature verification:

1. The signature is decrypted using the public key of a public/private key pair, producing a message digest value.
2. The message digest value is compared with the message digest calculated from the original message.
3. If both digest values match, the signature is authentic. Otherwise, either the signature or the message has been tampered with.

The preceding approach to signature generation/verification has the following features of real-world signatures, as well as other features that provide additional benefits:

- Unforgeability—Because the signer uses his private key and the private key is secret, only he can sign messages with that key.
- Verifiability—Since the signer's public key is openly available, anyone with access to the message and signature can verify that the message was signed by the signer and that neither the message nor signature have been altered.
- Single use—A signature is unique to a particular message. It is computationally unfeasible to use a signature with another message.
- Non-repudiation—After a signer has signed a message and the message and signature have been sent to others, the signer cannot claim that he didn't sign the message. (Unless the signer can prove that his private key was stolen.)

- Sealing—A signed message is digitally sealed; it cannot be altered without inv alidating the signature.

Figure 3.14 summarizes the mechanics of using digital signatures. An example of a digital signature algorithm is the National Institute of Standards and Technology's (NIST) Digital Signature Algorithm (DSA).

FIGURE 3.14.
Digital signatures.

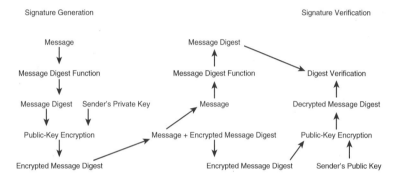

Digital certificates, based on digital signatures, are messages signed by a *certification authority* that certify the value of an entity's public key. The X.509 certificates of the International Standards Organization are a popular digital certificate format. Figure 3.15 illustrates the use of digital certificates.

3

THE EXTENDED JAVA SECURITY MODEL

FIGURE 3.15.
Digital certificates.

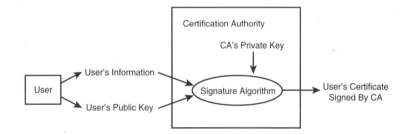

Central to the use of digital certificates is the notion of a *certification authority* (*CA*). A certification authority is an entity that is trusted to verify that other entities are who they claim to be and that they use a particular public key with a particular public-key encryption algorithm. To obtain a certificate from a CA, you usually have to submit documentation that proves your identity or that of your organization. For example, the certification process helps prevent unauthorized individuals from setting up business on the Web using the identity of Microsoft or Bank of America.

In a large networking environment, such as the Internet, multiple levels of CAs may be required. In this case a high-level CA, such as Verisign, Inc., the U.S. Post Office, or the National Security Agency, may provide certificates for second-level CAs. These second-level CAs may then provide certificates for other organizations. Individual companies may themselves act as a certification authority for their employees. A hierarchical certification structure, like that shown in Figure 3.16, is the result. Certification of an entity at the leaves and branches of this hierarchy depends on the certification of entities at higher levels within the hierarchy. These hierarchical certification relationships are referred to as *certification chains*.

FIGURE 3.16.

Certification authorities form a tree-like hierarchy.

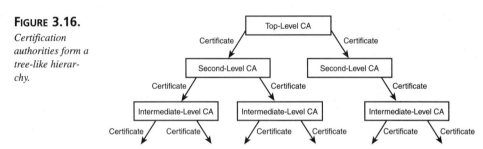

We'll study the use of digital certificates later in this chapter in the section "Using Certificates." Before we do that, we'll look at how the JDK 1.2 cryptographic architecture supports the topics discussed so far.

The JDK 1.2 Cryptographic Architecture

The Java Security API provides a flexible framework for implementing cryptographic functions and other security controls. It contains the *hooks* for message digest and digital signature computation, key generation and management, and certificate processing. It includes standard algorithms (such as MD5 and DSA) that support these security functions, but leaves out encryption algorithms (due to the restrictions of U.S. export controls). Instead of promoting a small set of cryptographic algorithms, the Java Security API implements an approach where different cryptographic packages may be provided by vendors and then be plugged in and installed within the common Security API framework.

Package Providers

The Provider class of java.security lays the foundation for using pluggable packages of cryptographic algorithms that support common functions such as message digest computation, digital signing, certificate processing, and key generation. The Provider class is a subclass of the `Properties` class of `java.util`. It encapsulates the notion of a cryptographic provider in terms of a provider name, version number, and information about the services provided by the provider.

The rationale for the `Provider` class is that it can be used to separate specific implementations of a cryptographic function (such as Company A's implementation of MD5, Company B's implementation of SHA-1, and Company C's implementation of MD5) from their provider-specific implementation. For example, several DSA packages may be available—some faster than others, some approved by the U.S. Department of Defense, and others supported by the Citizens Against Big Brother.

> **NOTE**
>
> The JDK 1.2 comes with a default provider, named "SUN", that includes an implementation of the MD5 and SHA-1 message digest algorithms, the DSA, and a DSA key generation capability.

The `Security` Class

The `Security` class provides a set of static methods that are used to manage providers. Providers are ranked in order of preference, with the most preferred provider receiving a rank of 1 and less preferred providers receiving a larger number. The methods of the `Security` class can be used to install providers, adjust their preference ranking, and retrieve information about the providers that are installed.

Cryptographic Engines

The Security API supports the notion of *cryptographic engines*. These engines are generic algorithm types—such as message digest, digital signature, and key generation—that support common cryptographic functions. The engines of the Security API include the `MessageDigest`, `Signature`, `KeyPairGenerator`, `KeyFactory AlgorithmParameters` and `AlgorithmParameterGenerator` classes.

The `MessageDigest` class, as you would expect, supports the computation of a message digest. The `Signature` class is an engine for calculating digital signatures based on provider-furnished digital signature algorithms. The `Signature` class supports both the creation of a digital signature and the verification of a digital signature.

The `KeyPairGenerator` class is an engine that provides a mechanism by which provider-furnished key generation algorithms may be accessed. Unlike `MessageDigest` and `Signature`, key generation is difficult to implement in an algorithm-independent manner.

Because of this, `KeyPairGenerator` supports both algorithm-independent and algorithm-specific key generation—the difference being in the way that the algorithms are initialized. The `KeyFactory` class is used to translate algorithm-specific keys into objects that can be handled in a generic fashion.

The `AlgorithmParameters` class is used to manage the parameters of cryptographic algorithms, and the `AlgorithmParameterGenerator` class is used to generate parameters for algorithms. Specific implementations of the engine classes are provided by cryptographic package providers.

In addition to the engine classes described in the previous paragraphs, JDK 1.2 introduces the `java.security.cert` package to support the processing of digital certificates. The `Certificate` class provides an abstract class for managing certificates. It is extended by the `X509Certificate`, which supports X.509 certificate processing. The `X509Extension` interface is provided to support the extensions of X.509 version 3. The `java.security.cert` package also provides classes for working with revoked certificates.

Using Certificates

X.509 identifies a particular format and content for digital certificates. This format has been popularized by Netscape's Secure Sockets Layer (SSL), the Java Archive (JAR) file format, and Privacy Enhanced Mail (PEM), as well as other emerging Internet security standards. X.509 certificates contain the following information:

- The version of X.509 being used with the certificate (1, 2, or 3).
- The entity's name and public key.
- A range of dates for which the certificate is valid.
- A serial number assigned by the CA.
- The name of the CA.
- A digital signature created by the CA.

The current version of X.509 is 3, although version 1 certificates are still in use. Version 3 added the capability to add custom extensions to certificates, such as email and IP addresses.

With respect to Java, the primary use for digital certificates is to support code authentication, as shown in Figure 3.17. Developers of Java code can digitally sign their code using their private keys. Users of the code verify the developers' signatures using the developer's public keys. Developers use digital certificates as a secure way to inform users of their public keys. Users manage developer certificates, identities, and public keys using the `keytool`, and establish developer-specific policies using the `policytool`.

NOTE

Chapter 8, "Applet Security," shows how to use the security-related tools of JDK 1.2.

FIGURE 3.17.

Certificates are used to support code authentication.

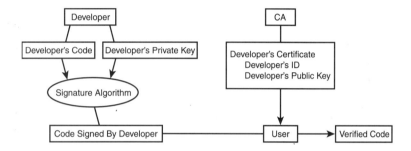

Summary

In this chapter you studied the new security features of JDK 1.2. You learned how to specify the security policy for applets and applications and how to use permissions to implement fine-grain access controls. You learned a little bit about cryptography, delved into the JDK 1.2 cryptographic architecture, and covered the use of digital certificates. In the next chapter you'll explore the different ways in which Java can be used to develop software applications.

Overview of JDK 1.2 Programming

Although Java became popular as the programming language of the Web, it has evolved beyond that to become a language for developing a wide range of software. For example, you can use Java to write applets, window and console applications, beans, servlets, and distributed objects. Don't worry if you're not familiar with these terms, because you'll learn about them in this chapter. You'll also learn how to move your legacy C and C++ code to Java. When you finish this chapter, you'll have a better understanding of which types of software you can develop with Java and how to convert your existing software to Java-based applications.

Applet Programming

Java is most closely associated with *applets*. An applet is a Java program that is executed in the context of a Web page. It's loaded and executed by any Java-capable Web browser that displays a Web page referencing the applet.

Applets are referenced in Web pages using the Hypertext Markup Language (HTML) <APPLET> tag. Chapter 5, "JDK 1.2 Applet Writing Basics," shows how to use this tag to include applets in Web pages.

Applets consist of compiled Java code that is stored on a Web server, along with the Web pages from which they are referenced. The applet code can be stored in the same directory as the Web pages or in separate directories that are used to store only applets.

Applets can be used in a variety of ways. They can be used to create fancy Web page widgets, such as animated advertisements, drop-down menus, or advanced forms. They can also be used to implement complex Web-based applications, such as database frontends, Web-based training systems, and terminal emulators, and to bring entertainment to the Web by providing custom multimedia players and, of course, a wide range of games. The major advantage of applets is that they transform passive Web pages into programs that interact with Web users.

Applets are developed by creating subclasses of the Applet class of the java.applet package. You create special methods that support applet initialization, the starting and stopping of an applet, and applet termination. You also provide GUI controls in your applets and methods for handling GUI events. The Applet class is covered in Chapter 5 in the section "The Applet Class."

The Java execution environments of Web browsers and the tools of the JDK provide a high level of security, aimed at protecting Web users from malicious applets. As you learned in Chapter 3, "The Extended Java Security Model," the security mechanisms provided by these execution environments are modeled after a sandbox—applets are permitted unrestricted access *within* the sandbox, but are blocked from making any accesses *outside* the sandbox. The extended security model, introduced with JDK 1.2, provides a more flexible approach to permitting trusted applet access outside the sandbox.

If your main interest in Java software development is applet programming, you're in luck. Part II of this book, "Applet Programming," begins with the next chapter.

Application Programming

Most of the programs that we run on a day-to-day basis are standalone programs that we execute on our PCs. With the advent of the Macintosh and Microsoft Windows, most of these programs are window-based. Java is a great language for developing these window-based programs. The JDK provides an extensive API for window program development. The Abstract Window Toolkit (AWT) of the `java.awt` packages allows window programs to be developed in a platform-independent manner. Once you develop a window program in Java, you can run it on Microsoft Windows (98, 95, NT, and CE), Macintosh, UNIX, OS/2, and other windowing environments. This is an incredible capability, considering the difficulty involved in porting non-Java window programs from one windowing environment to another.

In addition to the powerful windowing capabilities provided by the AWT, JavaSoft has introduced the Swing API with JDK 1.2. This API provides a broad range of advanced GUI controls, ranging from spinners to multilevel list boxes. It also provides the capability to easily tailor the look and feel of the overall GUI presented to the user. You'll learn how to develop Java window applications in Part III, "Application Programming." You'll learn how to use the Swing API in Part IV, "Swing Programming."

> **NOTE**
>
> The AWT, Swing, Java 2D API, Accessibility API, and Drag and Drop API are all part of the Java Foundations Classes (JFC) 1.1, which is integrated with the Core API of JDK 1.2.

In addition to being used to write attractive window programs, Java can also be used to write console programs. These programs read data entered by the user at the keyboard and write data to the user's console window. If you're an old-timer, you probably remember using console programs on MS-DOS or UNIX systems. Java console programs don't have to be simple. You can develop a range of sophisticated applications as console programs. For example, in Chapter 32, "Server Programs," you'll develop a multithreaded Web server as a console program. You'll learn the basics of how to write console programs in Chapter 10, "Writing Console Applications."

JavaBeans Programming

Since the advent of structured programming, the goal of software engineering has been the development of software components that can be reused in a variety of software applications. This goal was partially achieved by the last generation of component development tools pioneered by Microsoft's Visual Basic and Borland's Delphi. These tools supported the development of Component Object Model (COM) software components that could be reused in Microsoft Windows programs. JavaBeans picks up where these tools left off and provides the capability to develop platform-independent software components that can be reused in applets, standalone applications, and server programs.

JavaBeans are Java-based software components that are designed for maximum reuse. They are intended for use in visual software development environments. You use visual development tools to construct JavaBeans. Once a bean has been developed, you use the drag-and-drop capabilities of visual tools to add beans to your applets and applications and tailor them to your particular needs.

Beans are often visible GUI components, but they can also be invisible algorithmic components. You can use beans for developing user programs such as applets and applications. However, you can also use beans in server programs and in distributed applications. JavaSoft provides a bean bridge so that beans can even be used in legacy COM-based applications, such as Microsoft Word and Excel.

Beans are self-contained software components that easily can be tailored and added to a wide range of software applications. Since the introduction of JavaBeans, thousands of Java beans have been developed, hundreds of which are available as off-the-shelf software components. If you are interested in writing Java-based software components, be sure to read Part VII, "Creating JavaBeans."

Servlet Programming

Most of us are familiar with applets, standalone applications, and GUI-based software components because they're designed for end users. We use these types of programs on a daily basis to perform our work, interact with the world, or entertain ourselves. Another category of software that we may be less familiar with is *server* software. Server programs run behind the scenes to provide vital data and services for our user applications. Examples of server programs are Web servers, mail servers, file servers, database servers, and so on. Server programming is covered in Chapter 32, "Server Programs."

In addition to these large server programs, there is a need for small customized server programs that perform specialized tasks. For example, the Common Gateway Interface (CGI) programs are executed by Web servers to perform Web searches, process form data, and provide dynamic feedback to Web users. CGI programs are designed to be small, fast, and efficient, and are written to support specialized Web applications.

Recognizing the need for this type of server programming, JavaSoft has developed the Java Server Toolkit and the Servlet API. The Java Server Toolkit is a client-server framework for building Internet and intranet servers. It implements the functions that are common to many servers, such as listening for client connections, processing client connections in a multithreaded manner, and servicing requests made by clients over these connections.

The Servlet API is used to develop custom server-side programs for the processing of client requests. It can be used as a Java API for writing CGI programs, and is supported by all major Web server products. However, the Servlet API extends beyond CGI programming. It is envisioned that servers of all types (not just Web servers) will support the use of servlets for servicing client requests.

You'll learn about server programming in Java in Part VIII, "Network Programming," and in Part XI, "Server-Side Java."

Developing RMI Objects

Now that we live in a networked world, the natural course of software development is to create applications that are distributed over a network. The client-server computing of applets and Web servers is an example of a distributed application. However, future distributed applications will consist of many objects that are distributed over several computers.

For example, a financial application running on your personal computer may invoke methods of objects that run on another computer belonging to your company's intranet. These objects may search company databases for the information used by your financial application, process that data according to your company's business rules, and make that data available to your financial application. The results calculated by your financial application may be automatically forwarded to an information distribution object, which will make the results available to other employees within your company as well as selected vendors and customers. Figure 4.1 depicts this example distributed application.

FIGURE 4.1.

An example of a distributed application.

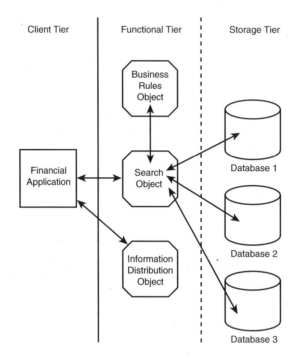

Client Tier Functional Tier Storage Tier

Business Rules Object

Financial Application

Search Object

Information Distribution Object

Database 1

Database 2

Database 3

JavaSoft provides a Java-based approach to developing distributed objects that can be used to build distributed applications. This approach is referred to as *remote method invocation (RMI)*. RMI allows Java objects executing on one host to invoke the methods of objects that execute on remote hosts—hence the name remote method invocation. The remotely invoked objects perform services and may return values that are used by the local objects.

The Remote Method Invocation (RMI) API of Java is a Java-specific approach to developing distributed systems. RMI's major advantage is that it is fully integrated with the Java object model, highly intuitive, and easy to use. In addition to the RMI API, the JDK provides a number of tools for building distributed systems.

What RMI means for you as a software developer is that you can build distributed applications with remote Java objects that are purchased off-the-shelf or custom-developed by others. You can also develop distributed objects that can be used by others. Part IX, "Developing Distributed Applications," covers the use of RMI in developing remotely accessible objects and integrating these objects into distributed applications.

Developing CORBA Objects

RMI is a 100% Java solution for developing distributed applications. If you have the flexibility to develop your distributed applications entirely (or almost entirely) in Java, RMI is the way to go. However, large enterprise applications tend to be heterogeneous, and sometimes Java alone is not enough. In these cases, a mixed-language distributed object development approach, such as that supported by the Common Object Request Broker Architecture (CORBA) is a better solution to distributed application development.

CORBA's strong point is that it supports a language-independent model. It provides a standard architecture for developing distributed object-oriented systems. This architecture specifies how a client object written in one language can invoke the methods of a remote server object developed in a different language. Figure 4.2 provides an overview of this architecture.

CORBA makes use of objects that are accessible via Object Request Brokers (ORBs).

FIGURE 4.2.
Using CORBA to build distributed applications.

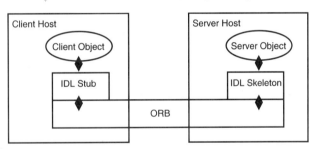

ORBs are used to connect objects to one another across a network. An object on one computer (client object) invokes the methods of an object on another computer (server object) via an ORB.

The client's interface to the ORB is a stub that is written in the Interface Definition Language (IDL). The stub is a local proxy for a remote object. The IDL provides a programming-language independent mechanism for describing the methods of an object.

The ORB's interface to the server is through an IDL skeleton. The skeleton provides the ORB with a language-independent mechanism for accessing the remote object.

Remote method invocation under CORBA takes place as follows. The client object invokes the methods of the IDL stub corresponding to a remote object. The IDL stub communicates the method invocations to the ORB. The ORB invokes the corresponding methods of the IDL skeleton. The IDL skeleton invokes the methods of the remote server object implementation. The server object returns the result of the method invocation via

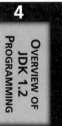

4

OVERVIEW OF JDK 1.2 PROGRAMMING

the IDL skeleton, which passes the result back to the ORB. The ORB passes the result back to the IDL stub, and the IDL stub returns the result to the client object.

JDK 1.2 provides support for interfacing Java objects with CORBA objects. This support is provided through Java IDL (an ORB), the `idltojava` compiler (used to generate stubs and skeletons), and `tnameserv`, an object naming service.

The capability to interface with CORBA objects means that Java can be used to develop industrial-strength enterprise objects for use in large, heterogeneous distributed applications. This capability opens yet another door for the Java programmer. Chapter 41, "Java IDL and ORBs," shows how to use Java IDL to interface Java objects with CORBA objects. If distributed application development is of interest to you, also check out Chapter 54, "Dirty Java," where you'll learn how Java can be used to support Microsoft's approach to distributed application development (known as the *Distributed Component Object Model* or *DCOM*).

Other Possibilities

The preceding sections covered some of the broad areas of Java software development. Within each of these areas, there are numerous specialty areas for Java software development. Part V, "Enhancing Your Applets and Applications," shows how to use the capabilities provided by the Java API to add features such as drag-and-drop and internationalization to your programs. Part VI, "Multimedia Programming," shows how to take advantage of the new multimedia features supported by JDK 1.2. Part X, "Database Programming," shows how to use JDBC to access online databases from your applets, applications, and server programs. The rest of this chapter provides suggestions on how to move your existing legacy software, written in C and C++, to Java.

Moving C/C++ Legacy Code to Java

Java is a powerful language that provides many useful features to the software developer. However, if your software organization is typical of most, you will have to trade off moving to Java with the constraints imposed by a dependency on in-place legacy code. This section summarizes the pros and cons of moving existing legacy code to Java. It identifies a spectrum of approaches for accomplishing software transition and discusses the issues involved with each approach. It also covers approaches to translating C and C++ code to Java. This section assumes that the transition of C/C++ code to Java is being performed by a moderately large software organization. Some of the software porting issues become insignificant if only a few small programs are translated into Java.

Why Move to Java?

When you're deciding whether to move existing applications to Java, you must consider the trade-off between the advantages and disadvantages of such a move. This section identifies many of the advantages of Java programs over C-based and C++-based applications. The following section considers some disadvantages of using Java and identifies roadblocks to any software-transition effort.

Platform Independence

One of the most compelling reasons to move to Java is its platform independence. Java runs on most major hardware and software platforms, including Windows 98, 95, and NT, Macintosh, and several varieties of UNIX. Java applets are supported by Java-compatible browsers, such as Netscape Navigator and Internet Explorer. By moving existing software to Java, you can make it instantly compatible with these software platforms. Your programs become more portable, and any hardware and operating-system dependencies are removed.

Although C and C++ are supported on all platforms that support Java, these languages are not supported in a platform-independent manner. C and C++ applications that are implemented on one operating system platform are usually severely intertwined with the native windowing system and OS-specific networking capabilities. Moving between OS platforms requires recompilation, at a minimum, and significant redesign in most cases.

Object Orientation

Java is a true object-oriented language. It does not merely provide the capability to implement object-oriented principles; it enforces those principles. You can develop object-oriented programs in C++, but you are not required to do so; you can use C++ to write C programs as well. Java does not allow you to slip outside the object-oriented framework. You either adhere to Java's object-oriented development approach or you do not program in Java.

Security

Java is one of the first programming languages to consider security as part of its design. The Java language, compiler, interpreter, and runtime environment were each developed with security in mind. The compiler, interpreter, API, and Java-compatible browsers all contain several levels of security measures that are designed to reduce the risk of security compromise, loss of data and program integrity, and damage to system users.

Considering the enormous security problems associated with executing potentially untrusted code in a secure manner and across multiple execution environments, Java's security measures are far ahead of even those developed to secure military systems. C and C++ do not have any intrinsic security capabilities. Can you download an arbitrary untrusted C or C++ program and execute it in a secure manner?

Reliability

Security and reliability go hand in hand. Security measures cannot be implemented with any degree of assurance without a reliable framework for program execution. Java provides multiple levels of reliability measures, beginning with the Java language itself. Many of the features of C and C++ that are detrimental to program reliability, such as pointers and automatic type conversion, are avoided in Java. The Java compiler provides several levels of additional checks to identify type mismatches and other inconsistencies. The Java runtime system duplicates many of the checks performed by the compiler, and performs additional checks to verify that the executable bytecodes form a valid Java program.

Simplicity

The Java language was designed to be a simple language to learn, building on the syntax and many of the features of C++. However, in order to promote security, reliability, and simplicity, Java has left out those elements of C and C++ that contribute to errors and program complexity. In addition, Java provides automated garbage collection, freeing you from having to manage memory deallocation in your programs. The end result of Java's focus on simplicity is that it is easy to learn how to write Java programs if you have programmed in C or C++. Java programs are also less complex than C and C++ programs, due to the fact that many of the language elements that lead to program complexity have been removed.

Language Features

The Java language provides many language features that make it preferable to C or C++ for modern software development. On the top of this list is Java's intrinsic support for multithreading, which is lacking in both C and C++. Other features are its exception-handling capabilities, which were recently introduced into C++, its strict adherence to class and object-oriented software development, and its automated garbage-collection support. In addition to these features, Java enforces a common programming style by removing the capability to slip outside of the class- and object-oriented programming paradigm to develop C-style function-oriented programs.

Standardization

Although C and C++ have been standardized by the American National Standards Institute (ANSI), many C and C++ compilers provide custom enhancements to the language, usually through additional preprocessor directives. These enhancements usually make their way into source code programs, resulting in a general lack of standardization. Java does not yet suffer from any standardization problems because its syntax and semantics are controlled by a single organization.

The Java API

The predefined classes of the Java API provide a comprehensive, platform-independent foundation for program development. These classes provide the capability to develop window and network programs that execute on a wide range of hosts. The Java API's support of remote method invocation, database connectivity, and security are unmatched by the API of any other language. In addition, no other language provides as much platform-independent power as Java's API.

Transition to Distributed Computing

Sun has taken important steps to support fully distributed computing with its support of RMI, CORBA, and JDBC. These APIs provide the capability to develop and integrate remote objects into standalone programs and applet-based Web applications.

Rapid Code Generation

Because Java is an interpreted language, it can be used to rapidly prototype applications that would require considerably more base software support in languages such as C or C++. The Java API also contributes to the capability to support rapid code generation. The classes of the Java API provide an integrated, easy-to-use repository for the development of application-specific software. Because the Java API provides high-level windows, networking, and database support, custom application prototypes can be constructed more quickly using these classes as a foundation.

Ease of Documentation and Maintenance

Java software is essentially self-documenting when doc comments and the javadoc tool are used to generate software documentation. The excellent Java API documentation is an example of the superior documentation capabilities provided by Java. Because Java software is inherently better structured and documented than C or C++ software, it is generally easier to maintain. In addition, the package orientation of Java software provides considerable modularity in software design, development, documentation, and maintenance.

Reasons Against Moving to Java

Java's many benefits make it an attractive language for developing new applications and porting existing legacy code. The previous section discussed some of the advantages of porting existing code to Java. This section identifies some of the disadvantages of any migration from C or C++ to Java.

Compatibility

Although Java is supported on many platforms, it is not supported on all of them. If your target hardware or software platform does not support Java, you are out of luck. Your alternatives are to switch to a different platform or to wait for Java to be ported to your existing software platform.

Also, your operating system or browser platform may not support the latest version of Java. For example, Netscape Communicator 4.0 supports JDK 1.1, but Microsoft Internet Explorer supports *most* of JDK 1.1 but not *all* of it. Earlier browsers support JDK 1.02. In order to develop Java software that is compatible with a wide range of users, you must ensure that your users are upgraded to an execution platform that runs the version of Java required by your software.

Compatibility may also be a problem at the design level. Suppose that your target software platform does support the latest version of Java. If your legacy code is unstructured and incompatible with a class- and object-oriented model, the effort required to migrate the software may be prohibitive.

Performance

Java is interpreted, and although its execution is efficient, it might not meet the performance demands of applications in which execution speed is of paramount importance. Examples of these types of applications include numerical "number crunching" programs, real-time control processes, language compilers, and modeling and simulation software.

Just because your application fits into one of these categories does not necessarily rule out Java. For example, the Java compiler is written in Java and performs admirably for small programs. However, its performance is greatly enhanced when it is compiled into native machine code instructions. Java-to-C translators allow programs to be developed in Java and translated into C for native machine code compilation. (See http:// www.cern.ch/WebOffice/Projects/Newspaper/tools/toba/doc/ for an example.) The translation process generally improves the performance of Java programs. Some Java development tools, such as Symantec Visual Café for Java Professional, provide the capability to create native binary code executable files (.exe) directly from Java code.

Probably the biggest boost to Java's performance is the HotSpot technology from JavaSoft. HotSpot allows Java programs to execute as fast as or faster than compiled programs. HotSpot increases execution performance by integrating a just-in-time compiler and a code optimizer with the Java interpreter.

Retraining

Although Java is simple, easy to learn, and based on C++, some training will be required to get programmers up and running with it. This is especially true if the programmers haven't been using C++ in a structured, object-oriented fashion. I never really appreciated the object-oriented programming features provided by C++ before I began programming in Java. Until I had adopted the Java program-development mindset, I was trying to apply my outdated and inefficient C++ programming techniques to Java software development. After I had made the mental transition to the Java object-oriented programming model, I became much more comfortable and efficient in writing Java programs.

Impact on Existing Operations

Moving legacy code to Java may result in adverse effects on company operations that are supported with legacy software. This is especially true when the legacy code is implemented in the poorly structured, convoluted manner that typically evolves from extensive software patches and upgrades. In the case when existing system software is tightly coupled and fragile, a transition to Java (or any other language) may break the software application to the point where a complete software redevelopment is required.

Cost, Schedule, and Level of Effort

Any software transition effort is subject to cost and schedule constraints. Moving current legacy software to Java might not be cost-effective, given the current software investment and its expected operational life. The software transition may also have a significant impact on system availability and prior scheduled activities. Transition from C or C++ to Java might also require a significant level of effort that would exceed the expected budget for the maintenance of the legacy code.

Transition Approaches and Issues

There are many ways to integrate Java into existing software applications. This section identifies some of these approaches and explores the issues involved in making the transition to a Java-based software environment.

Interfacing with Existing Legacy Code

One of the easiest ways to introduce Java to an operational environment is to use it to add functionality to existing legacy code. Java programs do not replace existing legacy

4

OVERVIEW OF JDK 1.2 PROGRAMMING

software; they merely enhance it to support new applications. This approach involves minimal impact to existing software, but introduces a potentially thorny maintenance issue because Java is added to the current list of languages that must be used to maintain the system.

Incremental Reimplementation of Legacy Code

You can reimplement legacy code in Java in increments, moving over to a Java-based software-development approach while minimizing the impact on existing legacy software. This approach assumes that the legacy software is developed in a modular fashion and can be replaced in an incremental manner. If this is the case, legacy software can be migrated to Java on a module-by-module basis, with the legacy code ultimately replaced by new Java software.

Off-Boarding Access to Legacy Objects

If in-place legacy code can be upgraded using Java software that is implemented on separate hardware platforms, Java can be used to *off-board* many of the functions performed by the legacy code. The use of off-board server software allows the investment in legacy code to be preserved, while expanding the services provided by the system as a whole.

Full-Scale Redevelopment

In some cases, it is more cost-effective to keep legacy code in place while completely redeveloping system software from scratch. This is typically the case when the system is subject to large-scale reengineering, or when it is so fragile that it breaks as the result of the simplest upgrades. If full-scale system redevelopment is necessary, this is actually an advantage to Java software development because the developed software is under no legacy-compatibility constraints and can take full advantage of Java's capabilities.

Translation Approaches and Issues

Translation of existing C and C++ code into Java can be performed in several different ways, depending upon the compatibility of the existing software with Java. This section describes some of the different approaches to software translation.

Automated Translation

Tools and utilities have been developed that allow Java source code and bytecode to be translated into C to support native machine code compilation. Future Java integrated software-development environments are planned, where either Java or C++ code may be generated based on the configuration of the development software. These development tools will allow easy movement between C++ and Java and require a common set of libraries that can be used by either Java or C++ programs. Automated translation between these two languages will be supported to some extent.

The degree to which C++ programs may be automatically translated into Java will depend on the planning and effort put into the code's design. Factors to be considered include compatible libraries, the use of single inheritance, the use of object-oriented programming capabilities, and the minimization of the use of incompatible language features.

Manual Translation

Manual translation of C and C++ to Java will probably be the most common approach to moving C and C++ legacy programs to Java. This approach requires you to use two editor windows—one for the legacy C++ code being translated, and the other for the Java program being created. Some of the translation is accomplished by cutting and pasting C++ statements into the Java window, making the corrections necessary to adjust for language differences. Other parts of the translation require that new Java classes, interfaces, variables, and methods be developed to implement C++ functions and data structures that cannot be directly translated from C++ to Java. The effectiveness of the manual translation process will be determined by the degree to which the C++ legacy code meets the compatibility considerations identified at the end of the previous section.

Source-Level Redesign

In many cases, manual translation is hampered because the C++ legacy code is written in a style that renders it impossible to migrate using cut-and-paste translation methods. In these cases, a class- and object-oriented design of the legacy code needs to be extracted from the legacy code and used as the basis for the Java source code development. A two-level approach to software translation is followed. The legacy code is reverse-engineered to an object-oriented design, and the recovered design information is used to develop a Java software design, which is in turn translated into Java source code. Code is not translated from one language to another. Instead, legacy code is translated into general design information that is used to drive the Java design and implementation.

4

OVERVIEW OF
JDK 1.2
PROGRAMMING

Summary

In this chapter you've explored the broad range of Java software development. You learned how Java is used to develop applets, console and window applications, beans, servlets, and objects for distributed systems. You also learned how to move your legacy C and C++ code to Java. In the next chapter you focus on applets and learn how they're used to bring interactive content to the Web.

Applet Programming

PART

II

JDK 1.2 Applet Writing Basics

CHAPTER 5

This chapter introduces the classes of the `java.applet` package and explains how applets are integrated within Web documents using the HTML <APPLET> tag. It describes how applets use window components and identifies the major phases in an applet's life cycle. Applet audio capabilities, JavaBeans, and Java Plug-In are also covered. When you finish this chapter, you will have a good understanding of how applets work.

Applets and the World Wide Web

Applets are Java programs that are integrated into Web pages. When a Web page containing an applet is displayed by a Web browser, the applet is loaded and executed. The applet's output is displayed within a subset of the browser's display area. Figure 5.1 illustrates this concept.

FIGURE 5.1.

How an applet is displayed by a Web browser.

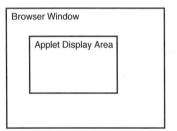

```
Browser Window

    Applet Display Area
```

The `Applet` class is a subclass of the `Panel` class, and an applet is implemented as a panel within a Web document. You'll learn more about the `Panel` class when you study window programming in Chapter 9, "Creating Window Applications." Because the `Applet` class is a subclass of the `Panel` class, it inherits all the methods of the `Panel` class and is capable of using most window GUI components. In addition, applet events are handled in the same manner as in standalone Java window programs.

The Applet Class

The `java.applet` package is one of the smallest packages in the Java API. It consists of a single class, the `Applet` class, and three interfaces: `AppletContext`, `AppletStub`, and `AudioClip`.

The `Applet` class contains a single default parameterless constructor, which is generally not used. Applets are constructed by the runtime environment when they are loaded and do not have to be explicitly constructed.

The `Applet` class contains 23 methods that are used to display images, play audio files, respond to events, and obtain information about an applet's execution environment (or *context*).

The getImage() and getAudioClip() methods are used to retrieve an Image or AudioClip object that is identified by an URL. The play() methods are used to play audio files at specified URLs. JDK 1.2 introduces the newAudioClip() method, a static method that allows AudioClip objects to be created without an applet context.

NOTE

The newAudioClip() method is the only new Applet method introduced with JDK 1.2.

The init(), start(), stop(), and destroy() methods are used to implement each of the four life cycle stages of an applet. The init() method is invoked by the runtime environment when an applet is initially loaded. It is invoked to perform any required initialization processing. The start() method is invoked by the runtime system when an applet is started, or when it's restarted as a result of a user switching between Web pages. The stop() method is invoked by the runtime system when the user switches from the Web page containing the applet to another Web page or program. The destroy() method is invoked when an applet's execution is terminated, usually as the result of the user exiting the browser. The isActive() method is used to determine whether an applet is currently active.

The getAppletContext() method is used to obtain the AppletContext object associated with an applet. The AppletContext interface defines methods by which an applet can access its execution environment. The getAppletInfo() method returns a String object that provides information about an applet. This information can include version, copyright, and authorship data, as well as applet-specific data. The getAppletInfo() method is overridden by Applet subclasses to provide this information. The getCodeBase() method returns the base URL specifying the applet's location. The getDocumentBase() returns the URL of the document in which the applet is contained. The getParameter() method is used to obtain parameter data that is passed to an applet in an HTML file. The getParameterInfo() method returns an array that describes all the parameters used by an object. It is overridden by Applet subclasses in the same manner as the getAppletInfo() method.

The resize() methods are used to resize an applet. The setStub() method is used to set the AppletStub associated with the applet. It should not be used unless you are constructing your own custom applet viewer. The showStatus() method is used to display a status message using the applet's context. The getLocale() method returns the Locale object associated with the applet. It is used to support language-independent applet programming.

The `AppletContext` interface defines methods that allow an applet to access the context in which it is being run. This is typically a Web browser, such as Netscape Navigator or Microsoft Internet Explorer, but could also be the applet viewer. The `AppletContext` interface of an applet is accessed using the `getAppletContext()` method of the `Applet` class. `AppletContext` provides seven methods that allow an applet to obtain information about and manipulate its environment. The `getApplets()` method returns an `Enumeration` object that contains all applets that are accessible in the applet's context. The `getApplet()` method returns an `Applet` object whose name matches a `String` parameter. The `getAudioClip()` method returns an `AudioClip` object that is referenced using an URL. The `getImage()` method returns an `Image` object that is identified by an URL. The two `showDocument()` methods are used to instruct a Web browser to display the Web document located at a particular URL. The `showStatus()` method is used to display a status message via the Web browser executing the applet.

The `AppletStub` interface is used to implement an applet viewer. It is not generally used by applets. It provides six methods that are used to retrieve applet information that can be used to support applet viewing.

The `AudioClip` interface defines three methods: `play()`, `stop()`, and `loop()`. The `play()` method plays an audio clip. The `stop()` method terminates the playing of an audio clip. The `loop()` method starts and plays an audio clip in a continuous loop.

A Brief HTML Primer

Web documents are written in *Hypertext Markup Language* (*HTML*). HTML uses *tags* to describe the structure of Web documents. Tags are used to identify headings, paragraphs, and lists, as well as other elements of Web pages such as links, images, forms, and applets. In order to use applets in your Web documents, you need to learn about a few basic HTML tags. Although a complete introduction to HTML is beyond the scope of this book, this section provides a quick summary of the basic HTML tags that you will need to use the examples in this book.

> **NOTE**
>
> For more information on HTML, point your Web browser to
> `http://www.jaworski.com/htmlbook/`. Here you'll find links to introductory
> tutorials on HTML, as well as links to more advanced HTML topics.

Using HTML Tags

HTML tags begin with a < and end with a >, and the name of the tag is placed between them. The tag name may be written using any combination of upper- or lowercase characters. I write tags in uppercase to set them apart from the text to which they apply. For example, the title tag is written <TITLE>, the head tag is written <HEAD>, and the body tag is written <BODY>.

HTML supports two types of tags—*separating tags* and *surrounding tags*. Separating tags are placed between the text elements to which they apply. For example, the break tag, written <BR>, is used to insert a line break within a line of text. It is placed at the point in the line where the break is desired, as shown in the following HTML:

```
This line ends at the break tag.<BR>This text is displayed on the next
line.
```

Surrounding tags consist of pairs of tags that surround the text to which they apply. The first tag in the pair is the *opening tag* and the second tag is the *closing tag*. The closing tag contains a / between the opening < and the tag's name. Examples of surrounding tags are <HTML> and </HTML>, <HEAD> and </HEAD>, and <BODY> and </BODY>. You'll learn about these tags in subsequent sections.

Some HTML tags are allowed to specify *attributes*. Attributes are used to identify properties of the tag and are included in the tag between the tag name and the closing >. When attributes are used with surrounding tags, they are included in the opening tag but not in the closing tag. For example, the <APPLET> tag uses attributes to identify the name of the class to be loaded, the dimensions of the applet display region within the browser window, and other properties of the applet. The following HTML is an example of an <APPLET> tag that uses attributes:

```
<APPLET CODE="TestApplet.class" WIDTH=300 HEIGHT=300>
[alternate text to be displayed]
</APPLET>
```

The opening <APPLET> tag has three attributes: CODE, WIDTH, and HEIGHT. The CODE attribute has the value of "TestApplet.class" and identifies the name of the applet's bytecode file. The WIDTH and HEIGHT attributes both have the value 300 and specify a 300×300 pixel applet display region within the browser window. The text [alternate text to be displayed], appearing between the opening and closing <APPLET> tags, identifies text that a browser should display if it does not support Java applets.

The <HTML>, <HEAD>, and <BODY> Tags

HTML documents are written in ASCII text, with the <HTML> and </HTML> tags marking the beginning and end. They consist of a single head and a single body. The head is used to identify information about the HTML document, such as its title, while the body contains the information displayed by the HTML document. The head and body are identified using the <HEAD>, </HEAD>, <BODY>, and </BODY> tags. The following HTML illustrates the use of these tags:

```
<HTML>
<HEAD>
The document title appears here.
</HEAD>
<BODY>
The information displayed by the HTML document appears here.
</BODY>
</HTML>
```

The <TITLE> Tag

The title of an HTML document is typically displayed at the top of the browser window, as shown in Figure 5.2. The title is placed in the head of the Web document and is surrounded by the <TITLE> and </TITLE> tags.

FIGURE 5.2.

The title of a Web document appears in the title bar at the top of the window.

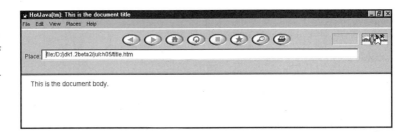

The HTML used to create the Web page in Figure 5.2 is shown in Listing 5.1.

LISTING 5.1. USING THE <TITLE> TAG.

```
<HTML>
<HEAD>
<TITLE>This is the document title</TITLE>
</HEAD>
<BODY>
This is the document body.
</BODY>
</HTML>
```

The Heading and Paragraph Tags

The heading and paragraph tags are the most common tags found within the body of a Web document. The heading tags are used to specify document headings, which in turn are used to organize Web documents into sections and subsections in the same manner in which the chapters of this book are organized into sections and subsections. HTML supports six heading levels. First-level headings are identified by the <H1> and </H1> tags, second-level headings are identified by the <H2> and </H2> tags, and so on. The HTML in Listing 5.2 shows how all six heading levels are displayed.

LISTING 5.2. USING HEADING TAGS.

```
<HTML>
<HEAD>
<TITLE>HTML Headings</TITLE>
</HEAD>
<BODY>
<H1>Heading Level 1</H1>
<H2>Heading Level 2</H2>
<H3>Heading Level 3</H3>
<H4>Heading Level 4</H4>
<H5>Heading Level 5</H5>
<H6>Heading Level 6</H6>
</BODY>
</HTML>
```

Figure 5.3 shows how this HTML file is displayed by my Web browser.

FIGURE 5.3.

HTML heading levels.

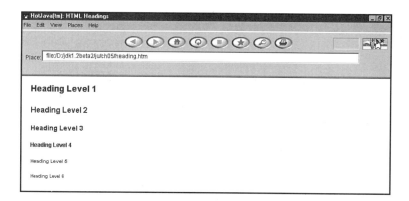

Paragraph tags are used to mark paragraphs within HTML documents. Spaces, tabs, carriage returns, and line feeds are referred to as *whitespace* characters in HTML. One or more whitespace characters are normally displayed as a single space by Web browsers. In order to mark the beginning and end of a paragraph, the HTML paragraph tags, <P> and </P>, must be used. The HTML shown in Listing 5.3 illustrates the use of paragraph tags. Figure 5.4 shows how this HTML is displayed by a Web browser.

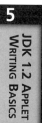

Listing 5.3. Using paragraph tags.

```
<HTML>
<HEAD>
<TITLE>HTML Paragraphs</TITLE>
</HEAD>
<BODY>
<H1>How paragraphs are marked in HTML</H1>
<P>This is paragraph 1.</P><P>This is paragraph 2.</P>
<P>This is paragraph 3.
This text also belongs to paragraph 3.
Notice that carriage returns and       multiple spaces      do
not affect the way paragraphs are formatted.</P>
</BODY>
</HTML>
```

Figure 5.4.

HTML para-graphs.

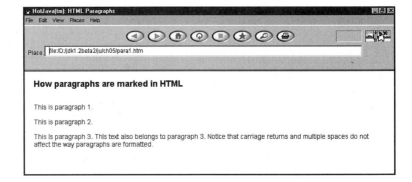

The paragraph tag may also be written as a single separating tag, <P>, although this is considered bad form. The previous example could also have been written to display identically using separating paragraph tags rather than surrounding paragraph tags.

The <APPLET> and Parameter Tags

Although there are a number of different HTML tags that you can learn, the <APPLET> and parameter tags are the primary tags of interest to Web programmers.

The <APPLET> tag is a surrounding tag. It may surround zero or more parameter tags. It may also surround *alternative text*. Alternative text is text that appears between the <APPLET> and </APPLET> tags that is not included in a parameter tag. It is displayed by browsers that are not Java-enabled as an alternative to the applet's display.

The parameter tag is used to pass named parameters to a Java applet. It is a separating tag that has two attributes: NAME and VALUE. The NAME attribute identifies the name of a parameter, and the VALUE attribute identifies its value. The following are examples of the use of parameter tags:

```
<PARAM NAME="speed" VALUE="slow">
<PARAM NAME="duration" VALUE="long">
<PARAM NAME="delay" VALUE="short">
```

An applet uses the getParameter() method of the Applet class to retrieve the value of a parameter. The parameter tag may only appear between the <APPLET> and </APPLET> tags.

The <APPLET> tag supports 11 attributes: ALIGN, ALT, ARCHIVES, CODE, CODEBASE, HEIGHT, HSPACE, NAME, OBJECT, VSPACE, and WIDTH.

- The ALIGN attribute specifies the alignment of an applet's display region with respect to the rest of the line being displayed by a browser. This line may consist of text, images, or other HTML elements. Values for this attribute are TOP, TEXTTOP, BOTTOM, ABSBOTTOM, BASELINE, MIDDLE, ABSMIDDLE, LEFT, and RIGHT. The TOP attribute value causes the top of an applet to be aligned with the top of the line being displayed by a browser. The TEXTTOP attribute causes the top of an applet to be aligned with the top of the text being displayed in the current line. The BASELINE and BOTTOM attributes cause the bottom of the applet to be aligned with the baseline of the text in the line being displayed. The ABSBOTTOM attribute causes the bottom of an applet to be aligned with the bottom of the current line being displayed. The MIDDLE attribute causes the middle of the applet to be aligned with the middle of the text displayed in the current line. The ABSMIDDLE attribute causes the middle of the applet to be aligned with the middle of the line being displayed. The LEFT and RIGHT attributes cause the applet to be aligned at the left and right margins of the browser window.

- The ALT attribute identifies text that should be displayed by a browser if it understands the <APPLET> tags, but does not support Java applets or has applet processing disabled.

- The ARCHIVES attribute identifies class archives that are preloaded to support applet execution.

- The CODE attribute is a relative URL that identifies the name of the bytecode file of the applet.

- Normally, the URL of the Web document displaying the applet is used as the base URL for locating the bytecode file referenced by the CODE attribute. The CODEBASE attribute is used to change the base URL to another location.

- The HEIGHT attribute identifies the height of the display area required by the applet.

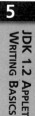

- The HSPACE attribute specifies the number of pixels to be used as the left and right margins surrounding an applet.
- The NAME attribute is used to assign a name to an applet. This name is used to support inter-applet communication.
- The OBJECT attribute identifies a file that contains a serialized representation of an applet.
- The VSPACE attribute specifies the number of pixels to be used as the top and bottom margins surrounding an applet.
- The WIDTH attribute identifies the width of the display area required by the applet.

Of the 11 applet attributes, only the CODE, HEIGHT, and WIDTH attributes are required.

The HTML file sample.htm, which is shown in Listing 5.4, shows how an applet may be specified in a Web document.

LISTING 5.4. THE sample.htm FILE.

```
<HTML>
<HEAD>
<TITLE>Using the Applet Tag</TITLE>
</HEAD>
<BODY>
<H1>An Applet that Displays Text at a Designated Location</H1>
<APPLET CODE="SampleApplet.class" HEIGHT=300 WIDTH=300>
<PARAM NAME="text" VALUE="Applets are fun!">
<PARAM NAME="x" VALUE="50">
<PARAM NAME="y" VALUE="50">
Text displayed by browsers that are not Java-enabled.
</APPLET>
</BODY>
</HTML>
```

The applet specified in the applet tag displays the text Applets are fun! at the coordinates 50,50 within the 300×300 pixel applet display area, as shown in Figure 5.5.

The source code of the SampleApplet applet is provided in Listing 5.5.

LISTING 5.5. THE SampleApplet.java SOURCE CODE FILE.

```
import java.applet.*;
import java.awt.*;
public class SampleApplet extends Applet {
 String text = "error";
 int x = 0;
 int y = 20;
```

```
public void init() {
  text = getParameter("text");
  try {
   x = Integer.parseInt(getParameter("x"));
   y = Integer.parseInt(getParameter("y"));
  }catch(NumberFormatException ex){
  }
 }
 public void paint(Graphics g) {
  g.setFont(new Font("TimesRoman",Font.BOLD+Font.ITALIC,36));
  g.drawString(text,x,y);
 }
}
```

Compile SampleApp.java using the command javac SampleApplet.java. Then open the sample.htm file using your Web browser. This should result in a display similar to that shown in Figure 5.5.

FIGURE 5.5.

The display of SampleApplet.

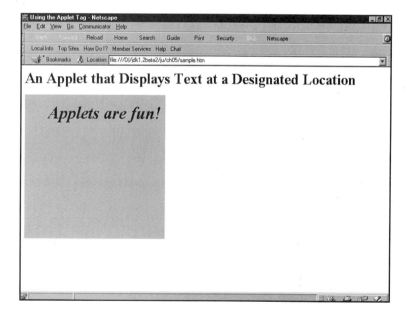

The SampleApplet class extends the Applet class. It declares three field variables: text, x, and y. The text variable is used to hold the text that is displayed in the Applet display area. The x and y variables specify the location where the text is to be displayed. The default value of the text variable is set to "error". The default value of the x variable is set to 0. The default value of the y variable is set to 20.

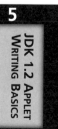

The init() method is invoked by the Java runtime system to perform any required initialization. The init() method uses the getParameter() method of the Applet class to get the value of the text, x, and y parameters. The parseInt() method of the Integer class is used to convert the String value returned by the getParameter() method to an int value.

The paint() method is invoked by the Java runtime system to update the Java display area. It is automatically passed a Graphics object as a parameter. This object is used to draw on the applet's display area. The paint() method uses the setFont() method of the Graphics class to set the current font to a 36-point bold italic TimesRoman font. The drawString() method of the Graphics class is used to display the value of the text variable at the x,y coordinate.

Other HTML Tags

The HTML tags covered in the preceding sections are the minimum needed to get you started using applets with HTML documents. There are many more HTML tags that you can use with your Web pages. The URL http://www.jaworski.com/jdg contains links to Web documents that describe these other HTML tags.

The Life Cycle of an Applet

An applet has a well-defined life cycle, as shown in Figure 5.6. Applets do not need to be explicitly constructed. They are automatically constructed by the runtime environment associated with their applet context—the Web browser or applet viewer. The init() method provides the capability to load applet parameters and perform any necessary initialization processing. The start() method serves as the execution entry point for an applet when it is initially executed and restarted as the result of a user returning to the Web page that contains the applet. The stop() method provides the capability to stop() an applet's execution when the Web page containing the applet is no longer active. The destroy() method is used at the end of an applet's life cycle to perform any termination processing.

Responding to Events

Because the Applet class is a subclass of the Panel class and therefore part of the window class hierarchy, applets handle events in the same manner as other window components. All the window event handling approaches that you will learn for window applications will also apply to Applet event handling. The init(), start(), stop(), and destroy() methods that were covered in the previous section are used to handle events that are generated by the Java runtime system. These methods are specific to applets and do not apply to other window components.

FIGURE 5.6.

The stages of an applet's life cycle.

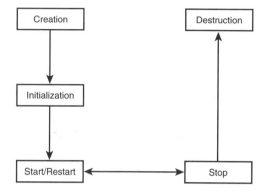

Using Window Components

Because the Applet class is a subclass of the Panel class, it can use most of the GUI components that are used by standalone window programs. This includes labels, buttons, checkboxes, radio buttons, lists, text components, canvases, and scrollbars. You will learn to use these components in the next chapter. The only major GUI components that cannot be used within an applet are menu components. Menu components are attached to Frame objects, which are associated with an application window. It is possible for an applet to create and open a separate application window in the form of a Frame object, but such an application window would only be trusted to the extent allowed by the applet security policy. This prevents the window from masquerading as other programs running on the user's system.

Adding Multimedia Features

The Applet class provides the capability to display images and play audio files. Images are displayed on the Canvas object associated with the applet's display area. Before JDK 1.2, applets only supported audio files that were in the Sun audio format (.au files). JDK 1.2 introduces a new sound engine and the capability to play audio files in both applets and applications. The new sound engine supports the following audio file formats:

- MIDI (type 0 and type 1)—The Musical Instrument Digital Interface, a digital format for musical instruments.

- RMF—The Rich Music Format, an audio file format created by Headspace, Inc. for online playback through the Beatnik plug-in.

- WAVE—The Microsoft Windows audio file format.
- AIFF—The Audio Interchange File Format, typically used with Macintosh and Silicon Graphics computers.
- AU—The Sun audio file format.

Support for the preceding formats greatly enhances the audio capabilities of Java applets and applications.

The play() method of the Applet class can be used to play an audio file that is identified by an URL. A more flexible approach is to load an object that implements the AudioClip interface and then invoke the object's play(), loop(), and stop() methods. The getAudioClip() method can be used to load an audio file by identifying its URL.

The JDK 1.2 also introduced the newAudioClip() method of the Applet class. This static method allows AudioClip objects to be created independently of an applet context, reducing the dependency of applets on the capabilities provided by differing browsers.

In addition to image display and audio playback, Java also provides the capability to include animation in applets and standalone window programs. Chapter 22, "Creating Animations," covers this topic.

An Audio Player Applet

The AudioPlayer applet, developed in this section, shows how easy it is to include multimedia features in applets. The source code for the AudioPlayer applet is shown in Listing 5.6.

> **NOTE**
>
> You need a sound board and speaker(s) to run this applet. You also need to be connected to the Internet.

LISTING 5.6. THE SOURCE CODE OF THE AudioPlayer APPLET.

```
import java.applet.*;
import java.awt.*;
import java.awt.event.*;
import java.net.*;
```

```java
public class AudioPlayer extends Applet {
 AudioClip music;
 Image background;
 public void init() {
URL codeBase = getCodeBase();
  music = getAudioClip(codeBase,"spacemusic.au");
  background = getImage(codeBase,"space.gif");
  setLayout(new BorderLayout());
  Panel buttons = new Panel();
  Button playButton = new Button("Play");
  Button stopButton = new Button("Stop");
  Button loopButton = new Button("Loop");
  playButton.addActionListener(new ButtonHandler());
  stopButton.addActionListener(new ButtonHandler());
  loopButton.addActionListener(new ButtonHandler());
  buttons.add(playButton);
  buttons.add(stopButton);
  buttons.add(loopButton);
  add("South",buttons);
 }
 public void stop() {
   music.stop();
 }
 public void paint(Graphics g) {
 g.drawImage(background,0,0,this);
 }
 class ButtonHandler implements ActionListener {
  public void actionPerformed(ActionEvent e){
   String s = e.getActionCommand();
   if("Play".equals(s)) music.play();
   else if("Stop".equals(s)) music.stop();
   else if("Loop".equals(s)) music.loop();
  }
 }
}
```

Compile AudioPlayer.java using javac AudioPlayer.java. The HTML file that is used to display the applet is shown in Listing 5.7. Note that the CODE, WIDTH, and HEIGHT attributes of the applet have been specified. You will need two additional files to run the applet: space.gif and spacemusic.au. These files are located in the ch05 directory.

LISTING 5.7. THE `audio.htm` FILE.

```
<HTML>
<HEAD>
<TITLE>Audio Player</TITLE>
</HEAD>
<BODY>
<APPLET CODE="AudioPlayer.class" WIDTH=300 HEIGHT=350>
[AudioPlayer applet]
</APPLET>
</BODY>
</HTML>
```

Open the `audio.htm` file with `appletviewer` using the following command:

`appletviewer audio.htm`

The `appletviewer` will create a window display similar to the one shown in Figure 5.7.

FIGURE 5.7.

The `audio.htm` *file, as displayed by* `appletviewer`.

You can also use your browser to load the applet over the Internet. The `audio.htm`, `AppletViewer.class`, `AppletViewer$ButtonHandler.class`, `space.gif`, and `spacemusic.au` files are located in the `\java` directory of my Web server. Use your browser to go to `http://www.jaworski.com/java/audio.htm`. It will display the window shown in Figure 5.8.

Your browser loads the `audio.htm` file and then the `AudioPlayer.class` and `AudioPlayer$ButtonHandler.class` files. The applet itself loads the background image and an audio file. To play the audio file, click on the Play button. The space music is played, using your sound board and speakers. When the music file ends, the sound ends. If you click on the Loop button, the music is played continuously. Clicking the Stop button causes the music to cease.

FIGURE 5.8.

The audio.htm
*file, as displayed
by HotJava.*

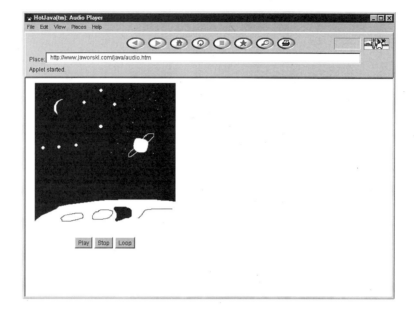

The AudioPlayer class is fairly simple. It declares two field variables, music and back-ground, which are used to hold the audio file and background image. The music variable is declared as type AudioClip, which is an interface defined in the java.applet package.

The AudioPlayer class contains three access methods: init(), stop(), and paint().

The init() method is invoked by the browser's runtime system when an applet is initially loaded. It performs any initialization required before the main part of the applet is executed. The stop() method is invoked when an applet is terminated as the result of an applet's Web page no longer being displayed by the browser. You never need to invoke init() or stop() directly. They are invoked by the runtime system.

The init() method of AudioPlayer begins by loading the audio and image files. The getCodeBase() method returns the URL of the directory where the applet file is located. The getAudioClip() method of the Applet class loads an audio file that is referenced by this URL and the spacemusic.au file name. The space.gif file is loaded in a similar manner.

After the audio and image files are loaded, the layout of the applet is set to a BorderLayout object. You'll learn about layouts in the next chapter. A Panel object is created and assigned to the buttons variable. The Play, Stop, and Loop buttons are created and added to the buttons panel. ButtonHandler objects are used to handle the events associated with these buttons. The buttons panel is then added to the bottom of the applet display area.

When the applet is no longer being displayed by the browser, the stop() method of the AudioPlayer class invokes the stop() method of the AudioClip interface to stop the music.

The paint() method draws the space.gif image assigned to the background variable on the Graphics context of the applet's display area.

The actionPerformed() method of the ButtonHandler inner class handles the three prominent events associated with the applet. These events are the clicking of the Play, Stop, and Loop buttons. When the Play button is clicked, the play() method of the AudioClip interface is invoked to play the audio clip. When the Stop button is clicked, the stop() method of the AudioClip interface is invoked to stop the music. Finally, when the Loop button is clicked, the loop() method of the AudioClip interface is invoked to cause the music to be played in a never-ending loop.

A Word About JavaBeans

As you learned in Chapter 4, "Overview of JDK 1.2 Programming," JavaBeans are software components that are designed for maximum reuse. They support the software component assembly model pioneered by Microsoft's Visual Basic and Borland's Delphi. For most people, they are the simplest way to create applets. Using a visual design tool, you just drag and drop beans into your applet. After that, all you need to do is to adjust the beans' properties to your liking and specify how the beans are to interact with each other.

However, the power of JavaBeans goes beyond rapid applet development. JavaSoft has developed the JavaBeans Bridge for ActiveX 1.0, which allows beans to interoperate with ActiveX. This means that you can use JavaBeans as ActiveX components in a number of Windows applications, including Microsoft Office, Visual Basic, and even Internet Explorer. Part VII of this book is dedicated to JavaBeans. You'll learn to develop your own beans, use them in applets, and work with bridges.

Java Plug-In

One of the biggest problems facing applet developers is maintaining backward compatibility with older browsers, such as Navigator 3.0 and Internet Explorer 3.0, that don't support JDK 1.1, let alone JDK 1.2. In order to provide applets that work with most of the installed browser base, applet developers were forced into a "least common denominator" approach. This approach generally results in applets that do not exceed the capabilities of JDK 1.02. JavaSoft developed Java Plug-In as a solution to this problem. Java Plug-In, formerly known as Activator, allows users to use various versions of Sun's Java Runtime Environment with their browser instead of the Java Virtual Machine provided by the browser vendor. This frees users of Internet Explorer from having to use Microsoft's broken JVM, and allows users of older Netscape browsers to conveniently upgrade to JDK 1.1 and JDK 1.2 runtime environments. Java Plug-In works with Navigator 3.0 or later and Internet Explorer 3.02 or later. Java Plug-In acts as an ActiveX control when used with Internet Explorer and as a browser plug-in when used with Navigator.

Summary

This chapter introduced the classes of the `java.applet` package and explained how applets are integrated within Web documents. It included a short introduction to HTML and explained how to use the HTML `<APPLET>` tag. It described how applets use window components and identified the major phases in an applet's life cycle. Applet multimedia capabilities, JavaBeans, and Activator were also introduced. Chapter 6, "GUI Building," shows how to build a graphical user interface for your applets.

GUI Building

CHAPTER 6

One of the reasons for Java's massive appeal is the Abstract Windowing Toolkit (AWT). This API allows powerful graphical user interfaces to be developed quickly and easily. If you have ever programmed in Microsoft Windows, you will greatly appreciate the simplicity and efficiency of the GUI-programming capabilities of the AWT. Also, most of its classes and interfaces can be used for both applets and applications.

In this chapter, you'll learn how to build a GUI using the classes of the AWT. You'll work with labels, buttons, text fields, checkboxes, choices, lists, and scrollbars. You'll learn how to use components and containers, and how to handle events. When you finish this chapter, you'll be able to build a basic GUI using the AWT classes.

> **NOTE**
>
> Part 4 of this book introduces Swing programming. Swing extends the AWT to provide numerous components for GUI building and to support pluggable look and feel. Many of the AWT components that you'll learn about in this chapter have Swing counterparts.

Labels

The most basic GUI component is the *label*, which is simply text that is displayed at a particular location of a GUI container. The Label class of the java.awt package provides the capability to work with labels. This class provides three Label() constructors: a default parameterless constructor for creating blank Label objects, a constructor that takes a String object that specifies the label's text, and a constructor that takes a String object (the label's text) and an alignment constant. The alignment constant may be one of the following:

- CENTER
- LEFT
- RIGHT

The alignment constants determine the justification of text within the label. The Label class provides six methods for working with the label's text and alignment, and for performing other operations. The setText() and getText() methods are used to access the label's text. You'll see an example of using labels in the section "Handling Events," later in this chapter.

Buttons

Buttons are another fundamental GUI component. Unlike labels, which are used solely to provide information to the user, buttons allow users to interact with your applets and applications. The clicking of a button triggers an event that can be handled by your GUI. You'll learn about event handling in the next section.

The Button class of java.awt provides the capability to use labeled buttons in your GUI. The Button class has two constructors: a default parameterless constructor that creates unlabeled buttons, and a constructor that takes a String object (the button's label) as a parameter. The Button class provides 10 methods for getting and setting the buttons label and handling button-related events. These methods are as follows:

- setLabel()—Sets the label displayed on the button.
- getLabel()—Returns the label displayed on the button.
- paramString()—Returns the button's state as a String object.
- addNotify()—Causes the button's peer to be created. This peer is the native windowing system's button implementation. This method is automatically invoked when a Button object is added to a container and should not be invoked directly by user code.
- addActionListener()—Adds an object that implements the ActionLister interface to the list of objects that are used to handle the button's action events.
- removeActionListener()—Removes an object from the list of objects that are used to handle the button's action events.
- processActionEvent()—Causes events to be processed by sending them to the registered ActionListener objects.
- processEvent()—Manages overall event processing for the button.
- getActionCommand()—Returns the command associated with the button's action event. This defaults to the button's label.
- setActionCommand()—Sets the command associated with the button's action event.

Most of these methods are used for handling button-related events. The following section provides an introduction to Java event handling.

Handling Events

The user communicates with window programs by performing actions such as clicking a mouse button or pressing a key on the keyboard. These actions result in the generation of events. The process of responding to an event is known as *event handling*. Window programs are said to be *event-driven* because they operate by performing actions in response to events.

The JDK 1.02 supported an approach to event handling referred to as an *inheritance model*. In this approach, events are handled by subclassing window components and overriding their action() and handleEvent() methods. These methods return true or false to indicate whether they have successfully handled an event. If a true value is returned, the event processing is complete. Otherwise, the event is sent to the object's container for further processing.

The JDK 1.02 approach to event handling was replaced by an *event delegation model* in JDK 1.1; however, the old inheritance event model was still supported. The event delegation model provides the capability to deliver events to specific objects—a capability that was lacking in JDK 1.02. The event delegation approach is less complex and more efficient. It uses special classes, called *adapter classes*, whose objects listen for the occurrence of events on behalf of objects of other classes.

> **NOTE**
>
> The JDK 1.02 event model is being phased out, and you should no longer use it. JDK 1.2 relies heavily on the JDK 1.1 event delegation model. When you study Swing in Part 4, you'll find that it relies entirely on the event delegation model, which wasn't frozen in JDK 1.1. In fact, there are new event classes that have been added in JDK 1.2—especially in Swing. However, the term "JDK 1.1 event model" is often used to refer to the event delegation model, since it was introduced with JDK 1.1.

In the event delegation model, event handling is delegated to specific event handling adapter classes. In this model, a source object generates events that are listened for by a listener object. The source object is usually a window GUI component, such as a button. The listener object is an adapter class that implements an event listener interface. The source object provides methods that allow listener objects to register themselves to listen for its events. For example, an object that handles the clicking of a button implements the ActionListener interface. This object is registered with a particular button via the button's addActionListener() method.

NOTE

Many of the adapter classes are provided in the `java.awt.event` package. These classes can be extended to support custom event handling.

The JDK 1.1 event model is a significant improvement over that of Java 1.02, which required GUI components to be subclassed in order to handle events. Although it is still possible to do so in JDK 1.1, it is no longer necessary. Events can be handled by adapter classes that are separate from the component from which the event is generated.

The following subsections describe the classes and interfaces used for JDK 1.02 event handling, followed by those used for JDK 1.1 event handling.

JDK 1.02 Event Handling

In the JDK 1.02 inheritance model, the `Event` class encapsulates all `Windows` event processing. The `Event` class defines the entire list of events handled by window programs using *class constants*. These constants are used to identify the events that are passed to event-handling methods. You can review the Java API description of the `Event` class to familiarize yourself with these constants.

The `Event` class provides three constructors for creating events, but you probably won't need to use these constructors because events are internally generated by the Java runtime system in response to user interface actions. The `Event` class also provides methods for determining whether the Ctrl, Shift, or Meta (Alt) keys were pressed during the generation of an event.

JDK 1.1 Event Handling

In the JDK 1.1 event delegation model, the `java.util.EventObject` class is the top-level class of an event hierarchy. This class provides a `source` field variable to identify the object that is the source of an event, a `getSource()` method to retrieve this object, and a `toString()` method to convert an event into a `String` representation. It provides a single constructor that takes the object that is the source of the event as an argument.

The `java.awt.AWTEvent` class extends the `java.util.EventObject` class to support AWT events. It provides several variables, constants, and methods that are used to identify events and determine whether they are consumed. The `AWTEvent` class is extended by the following classes of `java.awt.event`:

- `ActionEvent`—Generated by user interface actions, such as clicking on a button or selecting a menu item.
- `AdjustmentEvent`—Generated by scrolling actions.
- `ComponentEvent`—Generated by changes to the position, focus, or sizing of a window component, or by a keyboard input or other mouse action.
- `InputMethodEvent`—Generated by changes to the text being entered via an input method.
- `InvocationEvent`—Generated by the invocation of the `invokeLater()` and `invokeAndWait()` methods of the `java.awt.EventQueue` class.
- `ItemEvent`—Generated by a component state change, such as selecting an item from a list.
- `TextEvent`—Generated by text-related events, such as changing the value of a text field.

The `ComponentEvent` class is further extended by the following classes:

- `FocusEvent`—Generated by a change in the status of a component's input focus.
- `InputEvent`—Subclassed by `KeyEvent` and `MouseEvent` to cover events generated by keyboard actions and low-level mouse events.
- `ContainerEvent`—Generated by events associated with adding and removing components from a container.
- `PaintEvent`—Generated by the painting/repainting of a window.
- `WindowEvent`—Generated by events such as the opening, closing, and minimizing of a window.

The `AWTEvent` class and its subclasses allow window-related events to be directed to specific objects that listen for those events. These objects implement `EventListener` interfaces. The `java.util.EventListener` interface is the top-level interface of the event listener hierarchy. It is an interface in name only because it does not define any constants or methods. It is extended by the following interfaces of `java.awt.event`:

- `ActionListener`—Implemented by objects that handle `ActionEvent` events.
- `AdjustmentListener`—Implemented by objects that handle `AdjustmentEvent` events.
- `ComponentListener`—Implemented by objects that handle `ComponentEvent` events.
- `ContainerListener`—Implemented by objects that handle `ContainerEvent` events.
- `EventQueueListener`—Implemented by objects that monitor the system event queue.

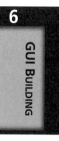

- FocusListener—Implemented by objects that handle FocusEvent events.
- InputMethodListener—Implemented by objects that handle InputMethodEvent events.
- ItemListener—Implemented by objects that handle ItemEvent events.
- KeyListener—Implemented by objects that handle KeyEvent events.
- MouseListener—Implemented by objects that handle clicking-related MouseEvent events.
- MouseMotionListener—Implemented by objects that handle movement-related MouseEvent events.
- TextListener—Implemented by objects that handle TextEvent events.
- WindowListener—Implemented by objects that handle WindowEvent events.

As a convenience, the java.awt.event package provides adapter classes that implement the event listener interfaces. These classes may be subclassed to override specific event handling methods of interest. The adapter classes of java.awt.event are as follows:

- ComponentAdapter—Implements the ComponentListener interface and handles ComponentEvent events.
- ContainerAdapter—Implements the ContainerListener interface and handles ContainerEvent events.
- FocusAdapter—Implements the FocusListener interface and handles FocusEvent events.
- KeyAdapter—Implements the KeyListener interface and handles KeyEvent events.
- MouseAdapter—Implements the MouseListener interface and handles clicking-related MouseEvent events.
- MouseMotionAdapter—Implements the MouseListener interface and handles movement-related MouseEvent events.
- WindowAdapter—Implements the WindowListener interface and handles WindowEvent events.

These adapter classes are convenience classes, in that they provide stubs for the methods of the interfaces that you don't want to implement yourself.

The java.awt.EventQueue class supports the queuing of events. It allows event listeners to monitor the queue and retrieve specific events for processing.

The java.awt.AWTEventMulticaster class provides the capability to listen for multiple events and then forward them to multiple event listeners. It provides a thread-safe mechanism by which event listeners can be added and removed from its event listening destination list.

The Buttons Applet

The Buttons applet, shown in Listing 6.1, ties together what you've learned about the Label and Button classes and AWT event handling. Listing 6.2 shows an HTML file that can be used to run the Buttons applet with the appletviewer tool.

The Buttons applet declares and constructs a Label object called "Default Label" and assigns the object to the label variable. It then creates three Button objects, labeled "One," "Two," and "Three," and assigns them to the button1, button2, and button3 variables. It then creates two Panel objects and assigns them to the panel1 and panel2 variables. Panel objects are objects that are used to contain and organize other GUI objects. You'll learn about them in the section "Components and Containers," later in this chapter.

The init() method sets the layout for the applet to an object of the BorderLayout class. Layouts are used to determine how GUI objects are displayed within a container. You'll learn about them later in this chapter in the section "Using Layouts." The Applet class is a subclass of the Panel class. This allows applets to act as containers.

The add() method of the Panel object referenced by panel1 is invoked to add the label to the panel. The addActionLister() method is used to set up objects of the ButtonHandler class to handle the events associated with the three buttons. The buttons are then added to the second panel. The first panel is then added to the top (north) part of the applet display area, and the second panel is added to the center of the applet display area.

The ButtonHandler class is an inner class of the Buttons class. It is used to handle events associated with the clicking of the applet's buttons. It implements the actionPerformed() method of the ActionListener interface. The actionPerformed() method is invoked to handle the clicking of the buttons for which the ButtonHandler objects are registered. It uses the getActionCommand() method to get the label of the button that was clicked. It then invokes the setText() method to set the label of the Label object to the button's label.

Figure 6.1 shows how the Buttons applet is displayed. When you click any of the three buttons, the label is updated to identify the button that was last clicked, as shown in Figure 6.2.

FIGURE 6.1.

The initial display of the Buttons *applet.*

FIGURE 6.2.

The label is updated to identify the button that was clicked.

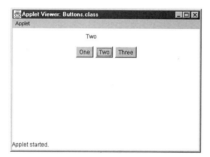

LISTING 6.1. THE Buttons APPLET.

```java
import java.applet.*;
import java.awt.*;
import java.awt.event.*;

public class Buttons extends Applet {
 Label label = new Label("Default Label");
 Button button1 = new Button("One");
 Button button2 = new Button("Two");
 Button button3 = new Button("Three");
 Panel panel1 = new Panel();
 Panel panel2 = new Panel();
 public void init() {
  setLayout(new BorderLayout());
  panel1.add(label);
  button1.addActionListener(new ButtonHandler());
  button2.addActionListener(new ButtonHandler());
  button3.addActionListener(new ButtonHandler());
  panel2.add(button1);
  panel2.add(button2);
```

continues

LISTING 6.1. CONTINUED

```
  panel2.add(button3);
  add("North",panel1);
  add("Center",panel2);
 }
 class ButtonHandler implements ActionListener {
  public void actionPerformed(ActionEvent e){
   String s = e.getActionCommand();
   label.setText(s);
  }
 }
}
```

LISTING 6.2. AN HTML FILE FOR RUNNING THE Buttons APPLET.

```
<HTML>
<HEAD>
<TITLE>Labels, Buttons, and Events</TITLE>
</HEAD>
<BODY>
<APPLET CODE="Buttons.class" WIDTH=400 HEIGHT=250>
</APPLET>
</BODY>
</HTML>
```

Components and Containers

The Component class is the superclass of the set of AWT classes that implement graphical user interface controls. These components include windows, dialog boxes, buttons, labels, text fields, and other common GUI components. The Component class provides a common set of methods that are used by all these subclasses, including methods for working with event handlers, images, fonts, and colors. More than 100 methods are implemented by this class. It is a good idea to browse the API pages of the Component class to get a feel for the kinds of methods that are available.

Although Component contains many GUI-related subclasses, its Container subclass is used to define components that can contain other components. It provides methods for adding, retrieving, displaying, counting, and removing the components that it contains. The Container class also provides methods for working with layouts. The layout classes control the layout of components within a container.

The Container class has three major subclasses: Window, Panel, and ScrollPane. Window provides a common superclass for application main windows (Frame objects) and

`Dialog` windows. You'll learn about these classes in Chapter 9, "Creating Window Applications." The `Panel` class is a generic container that can be displayed within an applet or window. It is subclassed by the `java.applet.Applet` class as the base class for all Java applets. The `ScrollPane` class is a scrollable container that can have vertical and horizontal scrollbars.

In the `Buttons` applet, we used two `Panel` objects to act as containers for the `Label` and `Button` objects that were displayed as part of the applet's GUI.

Using Layouts

The method by which the components of a `Container` object are organized is determined by an object that implements the `LayoutManager` interface. The layout of a `Container` is specified using the `setLayout()` method of the `Container` class. It passes an object that implements the `LayoutManager` interface as a parameter. For example, in the `Buttons` applet, the applet's layout was set as an object of the `BorderLayout` class.

The `LayoutManager` and `LayoutManager2` Interfaces

The `LayoutManager` interface provides a set of methods that are implemented by classes that control the layout of a container. These methods include those that add or remove components from a layout, specify the size of the container, and lay out the components of the container. The `LayoutManager2` interface extends the `LayoutManager` interface to deal with constraint-based layouts.

The `BorderLayout` Class

The `BorderLayout` class is used to lay out the GUI components contained in a `Container` object. It lays out components along the north, south, east, and west borders of the container and in the center of the container. The center component gets any space left over from the north, south, east, and west border components. It is the default layout for `Window`, `Frame`, and `Dialog` objects and provides the capability to specify the horizontal and vertical gap between the laid-out components and the container.

The `CardLayout` Class

The `CardLayout` class is used to lay out the components of a `Container` object in the form of a deck of cards in which only one card is visible at a time. The class provides methods that are used to specify the first, last, next, and previous components in the container.

The FlowLayout Class

The FlowLayout class is used to lay out the components of a Container object in a left-to-right, top-to-bottom fashion. It is the default layout used with Panel objects. It allows the alignment of the components it lays out to be specified by the LEFT, CENTER, and RIGHT constants.

The GridLayout Class

The GridLayout class is used to lay out the components of a Container object in a grid in which all components are the same size. The GridLayout constructor is used to specify the number of rows and columns of the grid.

The GridBagLayout Class

The GridBagLayout class lays out the components of a Container object in a grid-like fashion in which some components may occupy more than one row or column. The GridBagConstraints class is used to identify the positioning parameters of a component that is contained within an object laid out using a GridBagLayout. The Insets class is used to specify the margins associated with an object that is laid out using a GridBagLayout object. Refer to the API description of the GridBagLayout class for more information on how to use this layout.

The Layouts Applet

The Layouts applet, shown in Listing 6.3, provides an example of using containers and layouts. This applet is run using the HTML file provided in Listing 6.4. When you run the Layouts applet using appletviewer, it displays the opening window shown in Figure 6.3. You can click the Border, Flow, Card, Grid, and GridBag buttons in the top panel to change the layout displayed in the panel below it. Figures 6.4 through 6.7 show the other layouts that are displayed. When you select the Card layout, a bottom panel is displayed (see Figure 6.4) that contains the First, Last, Next, and Previous buttons. These buttons are used to move through the card deck of buttons displayed in the middle panel. Play with the applet to familiarize yourself with its operation before going on to the next section, which describes how the Layouts applet works.

FIGURE 6.3.

An example of a BorderLayout.

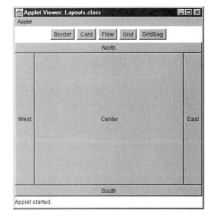

FIGURE 6.4.

An example of a CardLayout.

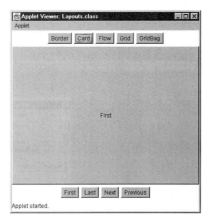

FIGURE 6.5.

An example of a FlowLayout.

FIGURE 6.6.

An example of a `GridLayout`.

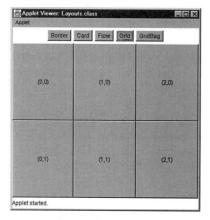

FIGURE 6.7.

An example of a `GridBagLayout`.

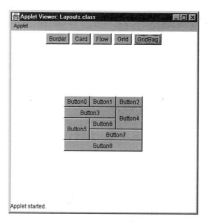

LISTING 6.3. THE Layouts APPLET.

```java
import java.applet.*;
import java.awt.*;
import java.awt.event.*;

public class Layouts extends Applet {
 Panel[] panels;
 Panel currentPanel;
 static int border=0;
 static int card=1;
 static int flow=2;
 static int grid=3;
 static int gridBag=4;
 String[] layouts = {"Border","Card","Flow","Grid","GridBag"};
 String[] cards = {"First","Last","Next","Previous"};
 Button[] layoutButtons = new Button[layouts.length];
```

```
Button[] navigateButtons = new Button[cards.length];
Panel layoutButtonPanel = new Panel();
Panel navigateButtonPanel = new Panel();
public void init(){
 setLayout(new BorderLayout());
 setupButtons();
 add("North",layoutButtonPanel);
 setupDisplayPanels();
}
void setupButtons() {
 for(int i=0;i<layouts.length;++i) {
  layoutButtons[i] = new Button(layouts[i]);
  layoutButtons[i].addActionListener(new ButtonHandler());
  layoutButtonPanel.add(layoutButtons[i]);
 }
 for(int i=0;i<cards.length;++i) {
  navigateButtons[i] = new Button(cards[i]);
  navigateButtons[i].addActionListener(new ButtonHandler());
  navigateButtonPanel.add(navigateButtons[i]);
 }
}
void setupDisplayPanels() {
 panels = new Panel[5];
 for(int i=0;i<5;++i) panels[i]=new Panel();
 panels[border].setLayout(new BorderLayout());
 panels[card].setLayout(new CardLayout());
 panels[flow].setLayout(new FlowLayout());
 panels[grid].setLayout(new GridLayout(2,3));
 GridBagLayout gridBagLayout = new GridBagLayout();
 panels[gridBag].setLayout(gridBagLayout);
 panels[border].add("North",new Button("North"));
 panels[border].add("South",new Button("South"));
 panels[border].add("East",new Button("East"));
 panels[border].add("West",new Button("West"));
 panels[border].add("Center",new Button("Center"));
 String cardButtons[] = {"First","Second","Third","Fourth","Last"};
 String flowButtons[] = {"One","Two","Three","Four","Five"};
 String gridButtons[] =
{"(0,0)","(1,0)","(2,0)","(0,1)","(1,1)","(2,1)"};
 for(int i=0;i<cardButtons.length;++i)
  panels[card].add("next card",new Button(cardButtons[i]));
 for(int i=0;i<flowButtons.length;++i)
  panels[flow].add(new Button(flowButtons[i]));
 for(int i=0;i<gridButtons.length;++i)
  panels[grid].add(new Button(gridButtons[i]));
 Button gridBagButtons[] = new Button[9];
 for(int i=0;i<9;++i) gridBagButtons[i] = new Button("Button"+i);
 int gridx[] = {0,1,2,0,2,0,1,1,0};
 int gridy[] = {0,0,0,1,1,2,2,3,4};
 int gridwidth[] = {1,1,1,2,1,1,1,2,3};
```

continues

LISTING 6.3. CONTINUED

```
int gridheight[] = {1,1,1,1,2,2,1,1,1};
GridBagConstraints gridBagConstraints[] = new GridBagConstraints[9];
for(int i=0;i<9;++i) {
 gridBagConstraints[i] = new GridBagConstraints();
 gridBagConstraints[i].fill=GridBagConstraints.BOTH;
 gridBagConstraints[i].gridx=gridx[i];
 gridBagConstraints[i].gridy=gridy[i];
 gridBagConstraints[i].gridwidth=gridwidth[i];
 gridBagConstraints[i].gridheight=gridheight[i];
 gridBagLayout.setConstraints(gridBagButtons[i],gridBagConstraints[i]);
 panels[gridBag].add(gridBagButtons[i]);
 }
 add("Center",panels[border]);
 currentPanel=panels[border];
}
void switchPanels(Panel newPanel,boolean setNavigateButtons) {
 remove(currentPanel);
 currentPanel=newPanel;
 add("Center",currentPanel);
 remove(navigateButtonPanel);
 if(setNavigateButtons) add("South",navigateButtonPanel);
 validate();
}
class ButtonHandler implements ActionListener {
 public void actionPerformed(ActionEvent ev){
  String s=ev.getActionCommand();
  if(s.equals("Border")) switchPanels(panels[border],false);
  else if(s.equals("Card")) switchPanels(panels[card],true);
  else if(s.equals("Flow")) switchPanels(panels[flow],false);
  else if(s.equals("Grid")) switchPanels(panels[grid],false);
  else if(s.equals("GridBag")) switchPanels(panels[gridBag],false);
  else if(s.equals("First")){
   CardLayout currentLayout=(CardLayout)currentPanel.getLayout();
   currentLayout.first(currentPanel);
  }else if(s.equals("Last")){
   CardLayout currentLayout=(CardLayout)currentPanel.getLayout();
   currentLayout.last(currentPanel);
  }else if(s.equals("Next")){
   CardLayout currentLayout=(CardLayout)currentPanel.getLayout();
   currentLayout.next(currentPanel);
  }else if(s.equals("Previous")){
   CardLayout currentLayout=(CardLayout)currentPanel.getLayout();
   currentLayout.previous(currentPanel);
  }
 }
}
}
```

LISTING 6.4. AN HTML FILE FOR DISPLAYING THE Layouts APPLET.

```
<HTML>
<HEAD>
<TITLE>Layouts</TITLE>
</HEAD>
<BODY>
<APPLET CODE="Layouts.class" WIDTH=400 HEIGHT=350>
</APPLET>
</BODY>
</HTML>
```

How the Layouts Applet Works

The Layouts applet begins by declaring a number of variables for use in the applet. These variables are used as follows:

- panels—An array of panels used to hold an example of each of the five layouts.
- currentPanel—Identifies the current panel being displayed.
- border—Constant used to identify a BorderLayout.
- card—Constant used to identify a CardLayout.
- flow—Constant used to identify a FlowLayout.
- grid—Constant used to identify a GridLayout.
- gridBag—Constant used to identify a GridBagLayout.
- layouts—An array of labels for the layout buttons.
- cards—An array of labels for the card navigation buttons.
- layoutButtons—The buttons displayed in the top panel.
- navigateButtons—The buttons displayed in the bottom panel when a CardLayout is selected.
- layoutButtonPanel—The panel used to display the layout buttons.
- navigateButtonPanel—The panel used to display the card navigation buttons.

The init() method sets the applet's layout to a BorderLayout. Note that this layout does not change. Only the layout of the middle panel is changed by clicking the layout buttons. The init() method invokes the setupButtons() method to initialize the layout and navigation buttons. It adds the panel used to display the layout buttons at the top (north) of the applet's display. It then invokes the setupDisplayPanels() method to set up the panels that are used to display the various layouts.

The setupButtons() method initializes the elements of the layoutButtons and navigateButtons arrays, sets up their event handlers, and adds the buttons to the layoutButtonPanel and navigateButtonPanel.

The setupDisplayPanels() method creates each of the five layout panels, lays them out, and adds buttons to them. The buttons are used for display purposes and do not handle any events. The panels are indexed by the border, flow, card, grid, and gridBag constants. The gridx, gridy, gridwidth, and gridheight arrays are used to set up the GridBagConstraints object for the GridBagLayout. These constraints determine the position and dimension of the objects being laid out. The panel with the BorderLayout is the first panel displayed, and is added to the center of the applet's display area.

The switchPanels() method is used to remove the current layout panel being displayed and to add the new panel identified by the newPanel parameter. The setNavigateButtons parameter determines whether the card navigation buttons panel is displayed at the bottom of the applet's display area. The validate() method causes the applet to be laid out and its components to be redisplayed.

The ButtonHandler class provides the event handling for the layout and card navigation buttons. This event handling is performed by the actionPerformed() method. The layout buttons are handled by invoking the switchPanels() method to display a new layout panel. The navigation buttons are handled by invoking the first(), last(), next(), and previous() methods of the CardLayout class to display other buttons in the card deck.

Using a null Layout for Absolute Positioning

In the preceding sections, you learned how to use the standard AWT layouts to organize the way GUI components are displayed within a container. But what if you want to organize your GUI in a way that is not easily supported by the standard layouts? The answer is to use a null layout and to position and size your components using absolute values. The setBounds() method of the Component class is used to specify both the position and dimensions of how a component is displayed. Because setBounds() is defined in the Component class, it can be used with all of the Component subclasses.

> **NOTE**
>
> The upper-left corner of a container is position (0,0). The x-coordinate increases as you move to the right. The y-coordinate increases as you move down.

The `Positions` Applet

The `Positions` applet, shown in Listing 6.5, illustrates the use of the `null` layout. The HTML file contained in Listing 6.6 is used to display this applet. The applet's display is shown in Figure 6.8. Note that this GUI organization is not easily supported by any of the standard layouts.

The `Positions` applet is short and simple, but it shows how the `null` layout can be used to produce custom layouts. Two labels and two buttons are declared and initialized. These buttons and labels identify the (x,y) coordinates at which they are located. The `init()` method sets the applet's layout to `null`, invokes the `setBounds()` method for each of the labels and buttons, and then adds the labels and buttons to the applet container. The `setBounds()` method used in this example takes the following four parameters:

- The horizontal position of the component.
- The vertical position of the component.
- The component's width.
- The component's height.

Other variations of the `setBounds()` method are also available. Consult the API description of the `Component` class for more information.

FIGURE 6.8.

The `Positions` *applet displays GUI components using a* `null` *layout.*

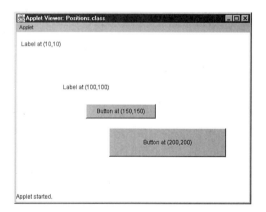

LISTING 6.5. THE `Positions` APPLET.

```
import java.applet.*;
import java.awt.*;
import java.awt.event.*;
```

continues

LISTING 6.5. CONTINUED

```
public class Positions extends Applet {
 Label label1 = new Label("Label at (10,10)");
 Label label2 = new Label("Label at (100,100)");
 Button button1 = new Button("Button at (150,150)");
 Button button2 = new Button("Button at (200,200)");
 public void init() {
  setLayout(null);
  label1.setBounds(10,10,200,30);
  label2.setBounds(100,100,200,30);
  button1.setBounds(150,150,150,30);
  button2.setBounds(200,200,250,60);
  add(label1);
  add(label2);
  add(button1);
  add(button2);
 }
}
```

LISTING 6.6. AN HTML FILE DISPLAYING THE Positions APPLET.

```
<HTML>
<HEAD>
<TITLE>Positions</TITLE>
</HEAD>
<BODY>
<APPLET CODE="Positions.class" WIDTH=500 HEIGHT=350>
</APPLET>
</BODY>
</HTML>
```

Text Components

The TextComponent class is the superclass of all text-based classes. It provides a common set of methods used by its TextField and TextArea subclasses. It does not provide any constructors and cannot be instantiated. It provides methods for getting and setting the text that is displayed in a text object, setting the text object to an editable or read-only state, handling text-editing events, and selecting text that is contained within an object.

TextField

The TextField class implements a one-line text entry field. It provides four constructors that are used to specify the width of the text field in character columns and the default text to be displayed within the field. It provides several methods for accessing the field's size and for specifying whether the characters typed by the user should be displayed. The setEchoCharacter() method is used to specify a character that is to be displayed in lieu of text typed by the user. This method is used to implement password-like fields.

TextArea

The TextArea class implements scrollable text entry objects that span multiple lines and columns. It provides five constructors that allow the number of rows and columns and the default text display to be specified. It provides several methods that return the dimensions of the text area and then insert, append, and replace the text that is contained in that text area. It also provides the capability to set the text to read-only or edit mode.

The Text Applet

The Text applet, shown in Listing 6.7, illustrates the use of the TextField and TextArea classes. Listing 6.8 provides an HTML file for displaying this applet. When you run the applet with appletviewer, it displays the GUI shown in Figure 6.9. Enter text in the text field and then click the Append button. The text is appended to the text displayed in the text area, as shown in Figure 6.10. The Clear button is used to clear the text displayed in the text area.

The Text applet begins by declaring and initializing the TextField, TextArea, and Button objects. The init() method sets the applet's layout to null and uses setBounds() to position and size the GUI components. The event handlers for the Append and Clear buttons are registered, and all of the components are added to the applet container.

The actionPerformed() method of the ButtonHandler class handles the clicking of the Append button by using the getText() method to get the text contained in the TextArea and TextField objects. It appends the text from the TextField object to the text of the TextArea object, and then invokes the setText() method to put the appended text back into the TextArea object. The Clear button is handled by using setText() to set the text of the TextArea object to a blank string.

FIGURE 6.9.

The Text *applet's initial display.*

FIGURE 6.10.

The text area is updated with the text field's contents.

LISTING 6.7. THE Text APPLET.

```
import java.applet.*;
import java.awt.*;
import java.awt.event.*;

public class Text extends Applet {
 TextField textField = new TextField();
 TextArea textArea = new TextArea();
 Button append = new Button("Append");
 Button clear = new Button("Clear");
 public void init() {
  setLayout(null);
  textField.setBounds(10,10,280,25);
  textArea.setBounds(10,50,280,150);
  append.setBounds(10,210,75,25);
  clear.setBounds(100,210,75,25);
  append.addActionListener(new ButtonHandler());
  clear.addActionListener(new ButtonHandler());
  add(textField);
  add(textArea);
  add(append);
```

```
  add(clear);
}
class ButtonHandler implements ActionListener {
 public void actionPerformed(ActionEvent ev){
  String s=ev.getActionCommand();
  if(s.equals("Append")) {
   String text = textArea.getText()+textField.getText();
   textArea.setText(text);
  }else if(s.equals("Clear")) textArea.setText("");
 }
}
}
```

LISTING 6.8. AN HTML FILE FOR DISPLAYING THE Text APPLET.

```
<HTML>
<HEAD>
<TITLE>TextFields and TextAreas</TITLE>
</HEAD>
<BODY>
<APPLET CODE="Text.class" WIDTH=300 HEIGHT=300>
</APPLET>
</BODY>
</HTML>
```

Checkboxes

The Checkbox class is used to implement labeled checkbox and radio button GUI controls. If a Checkbox object is not associated with a CheckboxGroup object, it is implemented as a traditional checkbox. If a Checkbox object is associated with a CheckboxGroup object, it is implemented as a radio button.

The Checkbox class provides five constructors that allow the checkbox label, initial state, and CheckboxGroup object to be specified. The Checkbox class provides methods for getting and setting the label and state of the checkbox and its CheckboxGroup object, if any. The state of the checkbox is boolean. The Checkbox class also provides methods for identifying event handling code.

The CheckboxGroup class is used with the Checkbox class to implement radio buttons. All Checkbox objects that are associated with a CheckboxGroup object are treated as a single set of radio buttons. Only one button in the group may be set to "on" at a given point in time. The CheckboxGroup provides a single, parameterless constructor. It also provides methods for getting and setting the Checkbox object.

The `CheckboxTest` Applet

The `CheckboxTest` applet, shown in Listing 6.9, illustrates the use of checkboxes and radio buttons. It uses the `CheckboxPanel` and `CheckboxGroupPanel` classes that are defined in Listings 6.10 and 6.11. Listing 6.12 provides an HTML file for displaying the `CheckboxTest` applet.

The initial display of the `CheckboxTest` applet is shown in Figure 6.11. A list of check-boxes is displayed on the left, and a list of radio buttons is displayed on the right. When you click on a checkbox or radio button, the event is handled by displaying the action performed in the text area at the bottom of the applet display area.

The `CheckboxTest` applet begins by declaring objects of the `CheckboxPanel`, `CheckboxGroupPanel`, and `TextArea` classes. The `init()` method sets the applets layout to a `BorderLayout` object, creates a new `CheckboxHandler` object, and declares the `sports` array for setting up the checkboxes. A new `CheckboxPanel` object is created by passing a prompt, the `sports` array, a orientation constant, and the `CheckboxHandler` object as parameters to the object's constructor. The `CheckboxPanel` object is added to the left (west) side of the applet display area. A `CheckboxGroupPanel` object is created in a similar fashion and added to the right (east) of the applet's display. Finally, the `TextArea` object is added to the bottom (south) of the applet's display.

The `itemStateChanged()` method of the `CheckboxHandler` class handles the `ItemEvent` that is generated by clicking a checkbox or radio button. It invokes the `getItemSelectable()` method to obtain a reference to the object that was selected (or deselected). It uses the `getState()` method to determine the object's selection status and the `getLabel()` method to retrieve the object's label. The selection results are then displayed to the `TextArea` object at the bottom of the screen.

Checkboxes are easy to use but tedious to construct and organize. The `CheckboxPanel` class provides a more convenient approach to creating and organizing checkboxes. Typically, checkboxes are created in groups and organized in a panel that is given a title. The `CheckboxPanel` class provides a constructor for quickly creating objects of this type. It also provides access methods for getting and setting the value of an individual check-box within the panel, based on the checkbox's label.

Two `CheckboxPanel` constructors are provided. The first constructor uses a `title` string for the panel, an array of labels to be associated with the checkboxes, an `orientation` parameter that specifies whether the panel is to be organized in a vertical or horizontal fashion, and an `ItemListener` object to handle checkbox events.

A `GridLayout` object is used to organize the `Label` and `Checkbox` objects placed within the panel. The title is added at the top of vertical panels and on the left side of horizontal panels. Then the checkboxes are created, one at a time, and they fill in the rest of the panel.

The second constructor is similar to the first constructor, except that it uses an additional `state[]` array to set the initial state of the checkboxes that are added to the panel. The state of each checkbox is set using the `setState()` method of the `Checkbox` class.

The `getState()` method takes the label of a checkbox as its parameter, and searches the checkboxes contained in the panel for one whose label matches the specified label. It then returns the state of this checkbox. If no matching checkbox is found, it returns `false`.

The `setState()` method is similar to the `getState()` method. It is used to update a checkbox with a given label.

The `CheckboxGroupPanel` class extends the `CheckboxPanel` class to work with radio buttons. The `Checkbox` panel constructors are overridden to place the checkboxes in the panel of a single group. If the second constructor is used, only one checkbox should be specified as being in the "on" state.

The `putInGroup()` method uses the `getComponents()` method inherited from the `Container` class to create an array of the components contained in the panel. It creates a `CheckboxGroup` object and then indexes through the array, putting all checkboxes into this group using the `setCheckboxGroup()` method. The first component is skipped because it is the title of the panel.

FIGURE 6.11.

The `CheckboxTest` applet.

LISTING 6.9. THE CheckboxTest APPLET.

```java
import java.applet.*;
import java.awt.*;
import java.awt.event.*;

public class CheckboxTest extends Applet {
 CheckboxPanel checkboxPanel;
 CheckboxGroupPanel checkboxGroupPanel;
 TextArea textArea = new TextArea(5,20);
 public void init() {
   setLayout(new BorderLayout());
   CheckboxHandler ch = new CheckboxHandler();
   String sports[] =
{"Baseball","Basketball","Football","Hockey","Soccer"};
   checkboxPanel = new CheckboxPanel("What team sports do you like?  ",
     sports,CheckboxPanel.VERTICAL,ch);
   add(checkboxPanel,"West");
   String ages[] = {"under 20","20 - 39","40 - 59","60 - 79","80 and
over"};
   checkboxGroupPanel = new CheckboxGroupPanel("What is your age?  ",
     ages,CheckboxPanel.VERTICAL,ch);
   add(checkboxGroupPanel,"East");
   add(textArea,"South");
 }
 class CheckboxHandler implements ItemListener {
  public void itemStateChanged(ItemEvent e){
    String status;
    Checkbox checkbox = (Checkbox) e.getItemSelectable();
    if(checkbox.getState()) status = "You checked: ";
    else status = "You unchecked: ";
    status+=checkbox.getLabel();
    textArea.setText(status);
  }
 }
}
```

LISTING 6.10. THE CheckboxPanel CLASS.

```java
import java.awt.*;
import java.awt.event.*;

public class CheckboxPanel extends Panel {
 public static int HORIZONTAL = 0;
 public static int VERTICAL = 1;
 public CheckboxPanel(String title,String labels[],int orientation,
   ItemListener ih) {
  super();
  int length = labels.length;
  if(orientation == HORIZONTAL) setLayout(new GridLayout(1,length+1));
```

```
 else setLayout(new GridLayout(length+1,1));
 add(new Label(title));
 for(int i=0;i<length;++i){
  Checkbox ch = new Checkbox(labels[i]);
  ch.addItemListener(ih);
  add(ch);
 }
}
public CheckboxPanel(String title,String labels[],boolean state[],
 int orientation,ItemListener ih) {
 super();
 int length = labels.length;
 if(orientation == HORIZONTAL) setLayout(new GridLayout(1,length+1));
 else setLayout(new GridLayout(length+1,1));
 add(new Label(title));
 for(int i=0;i<length;++i){
  Checkbox ch = new Checkbox(labels[i]);
  ch.setState(state[i]);
  ch.addItemListener(ih);
  add(ch);
 }
}
public boolean getState(String label) {
 Checkbox boxes[] = (Checkbox[])getComponents();
 for(int i=0;i<boxes.length;++i)
  if(label.equals(boxes[i].getLabel())) return boxes[i].getState();
 return false;
}
public void setState(String label,boolean state) {
 Checkbox boxes[] = (Checkbox[])getComponents();
 for(int i=0;i<boxes.length;++i)
  if(label.equals(boxes[i].getLabel())) boxes[i].setState(state);
}
}
```

LISTING 6.11. THE CheckboxGroupPanel CLASS.

```
import java.awt.*;
import java.awt.event.*;

public class CheckboxGroupPanel extends CheckboxPanel {
 public CheckboxGroupPanel(String title,String labels[],int orientation,
   ItemListener ih) {
  super(title,labels,orientation,ih);
  putInGroup();
 }
 public CheckboxGroupPanel(String title,String labels[],boolean state[],
   int orientation, ItemListener ih) {
```

continues

LISTING 6.11. CONTINUED

```
 super(title,labels,state,orientation,ih);
 putInGroup();
}
void putInGroup() {
 Component components[] = getComponents();
 int length = components.length;
 CheckboxGroup group = new CheckboxGroup();
 for(int i=1;i<length;++i){
  Checkbox checkBox = (Checkbox) components[i];
  checkBox.setCheckboxGroup(group);
 }
}
}
```

LISTING 6.12. AN HTML FILE FOR DISPLAYING THE CheckboxTest APPLET.

```
<HTML>
<HEAD>
<TITLE>Checkboxes and Checkbox Groups</TITLE>
</HEAD>
<BODY>
<APPLET CODE="CheckboxTest.class" WIDTH=400 HEIGHT=350>
</APPLET>
</BODY>
</HTML>
```

Choices and Lists

The Choice class is used to implement pull-down lists that can be placed in the main area of a window. These lists are known as *option menus* or a *pop-up menu of choices* and allow the user to select a single menu value. The Choice class provides a single, parameterless constructor. It also provides access methods that are used to add items to the list, count the number of items contained in the list, select a list item, handle events, and determine which list item is selected.

The List class implements single- and multiple-selection list GUI controls. The lists provided by the List class are more sophisticated than those provided by the Choice class. The List class lets you specify the size of the scrollable window in which the list items are displayed and select multiple items from the list. The List class has three constructors. The first one takes no parameters and constructs a generic List object. The second one allows the number of rows of the visible window to be specified. The third one allows the number of rows to be specified, as well as whether or not multiple selections are allowed.

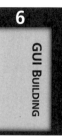

The List class provides several access methods that are used to add, delete, and replace list items, count the number of items in the list, determine which items are selected, handle events, and select items within the list.

The Chooser Applet

The Chooser applet, shown in Listing 6.13, illustrates the use of choices and lists. It uses the MyChoice and MyList classes, shown in Listings 6.14 and 6.15. Listing 6.16 provides an HTML file for running the Chooser applet.

The Chooser applet lets you decide what you want to eat for your next meal. Make sure that you have food on hand when you run the ChoiceListApp program. Its opening window is shown in Figure 6.12. The choice list, shown on the left side of the window, is used to select a meal. This selection determines which menu items are displayed in the list shown on the right side of the window. More than one item can be selected from the entree list. The text field on the bottom of the screen identifies the selections that you have made. Select Lunch from the choice list. Notice that the entree list is updated with some typical lunch items. The text field tells you that you are now ordering lunch. When you select Dinner from the choice list you get some dinner entrees, as shown in Figure 6.13. The text field is updated to list your new selections.

The Chooser applet declares several field variables. The mealChoice variable is used to refer to the MyChoice object that displays the meals identified in the meals array. Two MyList variables are declared. The mealList array holds the three MyList objects used for breakfast, lunch, and dinner. These items are stored in the mealChoices array. The currentList variable points to the current menu entree list being displayed. The text variable refers to the TextField object displayed on the bottom of the window.

The init() method sets the applet's layout to BorderLayout and invokes the setupChoice() and setupLists() methods to set up the MyChoice and MyList objects. The text field is initialized to be 40 characters wide, and then the user interface objects are placed in the appropriate places in the applet display area.

The setupChoice() method constructs the mealChoice object and sets up its event handler. The setupLists() method sets up the mealList object by indexing through the mealChoices[] array and setting up the individual MyList objects.

The ChoiceHandler inner class handles the events associated with the MyChoice object assigned to mealChoice. It does so by updating the MyList object displayed on the right side of the applet display. It uses the remove() method of the Container class to remove the currently displayed MyList object, and then adds the MyList object corresponding to the selected meal choice. The validate() method is invoked to update the applet's display.

The `ListHandler` inner class handles the events associated with the meal lists that are implemented as `MyList` objects. It invokes the `getSelectedItem()` method of the `Choice` class to determine which meal was selected, and the `getSelectedItems()` method of the `List` class to obtain an array containing the selected list items associated with the meal. It combines the meal choice and associated entrees into a string that is displayed in the `TextArea` object.

The `MyChoice` class simplifies the construction of a `Choice` object. Rather than constructing a `Choice` object and adding all of the items in the choice list, the `MyChoice` constructor takes an array of labels and adds them to the `Choice` object as it is constructed. The `addItem()` method of the `Choice` class throws the `NullPointerException`, and is handled by adding a blank item to the choice list when a `null` pointer is encountered.

The `MyList` class is similar to the `MyChoice` class in that it allows a list to be constructed using an array of list items. The `MyList` constructor also allows the number of rows displayed in the list and the multiple-selection parameter to be specified.

FIGURE 6.12.

The `Chooser`
applet's initial display.

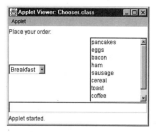

FIGURE 6.13.

The `Chooser`
applet's display is
updated based on
your selections.

LISTING 6.13. THE `Chooser` APPLET.

```
import java.applet.*;
import java.awt.*;
import java.awt.event.*;

public class Chooser extends Applet {
 MyChoice mealChoice;
 MyList currentList;
```

```
MyList mealList[];
String meals[] = {"Breakfast","Lunch","Dinner"};
String mealChoices[][] = {
 {"pancakes","eggs","bacon","ham","sausage","cereal",
  "toast","coffee","juice"},
 {"pizza","hamburger","hot dog","burrito","salad","fries",
  "chips","soda","milk"},
 {"spaghetti","carne asada","barbequed chicken","soup","salad",
  "bread","wine","beer","soda","milk"}
};
TextField text;
public void init() {
 setLayout(new BorderLayout());
 setupChoice();
 setupLists();
 text = new TextField(40);
 add("North",new Label("Place your order:"));
 add("South",text);
 add("West",mealChoice);
 currentList = mealList[0];
 add("East",currentList);
}
void setupChoice(){
 mealChoice = new MyChoice(meals);
 mealChoice.addItemListener(new ChoiceHandler());
}
void setupLists(){
 mealList = new MyList[meals.length];
 ListHandler lh = new ListHandler();
 for(int i=0;i<meals.length;++i){
  mealList[i] = new MyList(5,true,mealChoices[i]);
  mealList[i].addItemListener(lh);
 }
}
class ChoiceHandler implements ItemListener {
 public void itemStateChanged(ItemEvent e){
   for(int i=0;i<meals.length;++i)
    if(meals[i].equals(mealChoice.getSelectedItem())){
     Chooser.this.remove(currentList);
     currentList = mealList[i];
     Chooser.this.add("East",currentList);
     text.setText(meals[i]);
    }
   Chooser.this.validate();
 }
}
class ListHandler implements ItemListener {
 public void itemStateChanged(ItemEvent e){
   String order = mealChoice.getSelectedItem()+": ";
```

continues

LISTING 6.13. CONTINUED

```
    String items[] = currentList.getSelectedItems();
    for(int i=0;i<items.length;++i) order += items[i]+" ";
    text.setText(order);
  }
 }
}
```

LISTING 6.14. THE MyChoice CLASS.

```
import java.awt.*;

public class MyChoice extends Choice {
 public MyChoice(String labels[]) {
  super();
  int length = labels.length;
  for(int i=0;i<length;++i) {
   try {
    add(labels[i]);
   }catch (NullPointerException ex) {
    add("");
   }
  }
 }
}
```

LISTING 6.15. THE MyList CLASS.

```
import java.awt.*;

public class MyList extends List {
 public MyList(int rows,boolean multiple,String labels[]) {
  super(rows,multiple);
  int length = labels.length;
  for(int i=0;i<length;++i) {
   try {
    add(labels[i]);
   }catch (NullPointerException ex) {
    add("");
   }
  }
 }
}
```

LISTING 6.16. AN HTML FILE FOR RUNNING THE Chooser APPLET.

```
<HTML>
<HEAD>
<TITLE>Choices and Lists</TITLE>
</HEAD>
<BODY>
<APPLET CODE="Chooser.class" WIDTH=300 HEIGHT=200>
</APPLET>
</BODY>
</HTML>
```

Scrollbars

The Scrollbar class is used to implement vertical and horizontal scrollbars. It provides three constructors that allow the orientation of the scrollbar to be specified, as well as parameters that control the scrollbar's operation. It provides several methods that allow the scrollbar's parameters and current value to be read and set.

When you use scrollbars in your Java programs, you will most likely use them to scroll through a Graphics object that is associated with a Canvas object or the main application window. (These objects are covered in the following chapter.) You create and place scrollbars in your window in the same manner as any other window component. Their position and size within the window are determined by the layout associated with the window.

Scrollbars are created using the Scrollbar()constructor. Three forms of this constructor are provided. The default constructor takes no parameters and is not particularly useful, unless you want to create a Scrollbar object and then specify its orientation and use later in your program. The second constructor allows the orientation of a Scrollbar object to be specified. The third Scrollbar() constructor uses the five parameters that are needed to create a working scrollbar: orientation, value, visible, minimum, and maximum.

The orientation of a scrollbar is specified by the VERTICAL and HORIZONTAL constants defined by the Scrollbar class. The minimum and maximum parameters specify the minimum and maximum values associated with the scrollbar's position. These values should map to the object being scrolled. For example, if you are scrolling a 1,000-line text object, appropriate minimum and maximum values for a vertical scrollbar would be 0 and 999. Horizontal values could be determined using the maximum width of the text to be scrolled (in pixels).

The `value` parameter identifies the starting value associated with the scrollbar. The `value` parameter is usually set to the `minimum` value of the scrollbar. However, suppose you wanted to initiate the display of an object with its center displayed on the screen. You would then set the scrollbar's `value` parameter to the average of its `minimum` and `maximum` values.

The `visible` parameter is used to specify the size of the viewable area of the object being scrolled. For example, if you are scrolling a 1,000-line text object and the viewable area of the window is 25 lines long, you would set the `visible` variable to 25.

The `Scrollbar` class provides several methods for getting and setting the parameters of a `Scrollbar` object. The `getOrientation()`, `getValue()`, `getVisibleAmount()`, `getMinimum()`, and `getMaximum()` methods retrieve the parameter values discussed so far. The `getValue()` method is used to determine the position to which the user has scrolled.

The `setUnitIncrement()` and `setBlockIncrement()` methods are used to specify the size of a scrollable unit and page relative to the minimum and maximum values associated with a scrollbar. For example, when scrolling text, you can set the line increment of a vertical scrollbar to one so that only one line of text is vertically scrolled. You can set the page increment to 10 to allow 10 lines of text to be scrolled when the user clicks between the tab and arrows of a scrollbar. The `getUnitIncrement()` and `getBlockIncrement(.)` methods provide access to the current line- and page-increment values.

The `setValue()` method allows you to directly set the current position of a scrollbar. The `setValues()` method allows you to specify a scrollbar's `value`, `visible`, `minimum`, and `maximum` parameters.

Scrollbars implement the `Adjustable` interface. In order to respond to user scrollbar operations and implement scrolling of the object associated with a scrollbar, you must handle the `AdjustmentEvent` generated by user manipulation of the scrollbar. This event is handled by implementing the `AdjustmentListener` interface. The `adjustmentValueChanged()` method of `AdjustmentListener` is invoked to handle scrollbar events. It is passed an object of class `AdjustmentEvent`.

The `AdjustmentEvent` class provides methods that can be used to retrieve the scrollbar for which the event was generated, the new value of the scrollbar, and the type of scrolling action that took place.

The `Scroller` Applet

The `Scroller` applet, shown in Listing 6.17, introduces the use of the `Scrollbar` class. Listing 6.18 provides an HTML file for running the `Scroller` applet.

Figure 6.14 shows the initial display of the Scroller applet. It consists of horizontal and vertical scrollbars and a label that displays the result of using either of the two scrollbars. Play with the scrollbars and watch how the label is updated.

The Scroller applet uses the MyScrollbar class to facilitate the creation and use of the horizontal and vertical scrollbars. The horizontal scrollbar is constructed with a range of 0 to 100, an initial setting of 50, and a visible window of 10 units. The vertical scrollbar is constructed with a range of 0 to 1000, an initial setting of 500, and a visible window of 100 units. The applet is laid out using a BorderLayout, with the horizontal scrollbar on top, the vertical scrollbar at left, and the label in the center.

The MyScrollbar class extends Scrollbar and provides the capability to display the results of scrollbar operations using a TextArea object.

The MyScrollbar constructor takes a number of parameters that determine the characteristics of a scrollbar. These parameters are forwarded to the superclass constructor. A TextArea object is also passed as a parameter. The orientation parameter is set to the HORIZONTAL and VERTICAL constants of the Scrollbar class. These constants specify whether the scrollbar should be displayed horizontally or vertically. The min and max parameters specify a range of integer values that are associated with the scrollbar. The value parameter sets the initial position of the scrollbar between the min and max values. The visible parameter identifies the size of the visible portion of the scrollable area. This determines how the current scrollbar position is updated as the result of a page-up or page-down scrollbar operation. The addAdjustmentListener() method is used to set up an object of the HandleScrolling inner class as a scrollbar event handler.

The adjustmentValueChanged() method of the HandleScrolling class handles scrollbar events by using the getValue() method of the AdjustmentEvent class to obtain the current scrollbar position, and then displaying this value in the text area. Note that the HandleScrolling class implements the AdjustmentListener interface.

FIGURE 6.14.

The Scroller *applet shows how scrollbars work.*

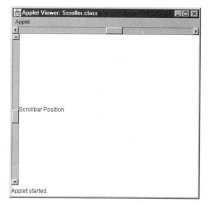

LISTING 6.17. THE Scroller APPLET.

```java
import java.applet.*;
import java.awt.*;
import java.awt.event.*;

public class Scroller extends Applet {
 Label label = new Label("Scrollbar Position");
 MyScrollbar hscroll = new MyScrollbar(Scrollbar.HORIZONTAL,
   50,10,0,100,label);
 MyScrollbar vscroll = new MyScrollbar(Scrollbar.VERTICAL,
   500,100,0,1000,label);
 public void init() {
   setLayout(new BorderLayout());
   add("Center",label);
   add("West",vscroll);
   add("North",hscroll);
 }
}
class MyScrollbar extends Scrollbar {
 Label position;
 String direction = "     Horizontal";
 public MyScrollbar(int orientation,int value,int visible,int min,int max,
   Label label) {
   super(orientation,value,visible,min,max);
   position=label;
   if(orientation==Scrollbar.VERTICAL) direction = "     Vertical";
   addAdjustmentListener(new MyScrollbar.HandleScrolling());
 }
 class HandleScrolling implements AdjustmentListener {
   public void adjustmentValueChanged(AdjustmentEvent e){
     position.setText(direction+" Position: "+e.getValue());
   }
 }
}
```

LISTING 6.18. AN HTML FILE FOR RUNNING THE Scroller APPLET.

```html
<HTML>
<HEAD>
<TITLE>Scrollbars</TITLE>
</HEAD>
<BODY>
<APPLET CODE="Scroller.class" WIDTH=400 HEIGHT=350>
</APPLET>
</BODY>
</HTML>
```

The `ScrollPane` Class

Java 1.1 introduced the `ScrollPane` class to simplify the development of scrollable applications. The `ScrollPane` class is like a combination of a panel and vertical and horizontal scrollbars. The great thing about it is that it performs all of the scrollbar event handling and screen redrawing internally. The fact that the `ScrollPane` class handles events is significant. By handling events internally, it allows scrolling-related operations to run significantly faster.

The `ScrollPane` class extends the `Container` class and therefore can contain other components. It is designed to automate scrolling for a single contained component, such as a `Canvas` object. It provides two constructors—a single parameterless constructor and a constructor that takes an `int` argument. The parameterless constructor creates a `ScrollPane` object that displays scrollbars only when they are needed. The other constructor takes one of the three constants: `SCROLLBARS_ALWAYS`, `SCROLLBARS_AS_NEEDED`, and `SCROLLBARS_NEVER`. These constants determine if and when scrollbars are displayed by the `ScrollPane` object.

The initial size of the `ScrollPane` object is 100×100 pixels. The `setSize()` method can be used to resize it. The `ScrollPane` class provides methods for accessing and updating its internal scrollbars, but in most cases this is both unnecessary and ill-advised. Other methods are provided to get and set the current scrollbar positions.

Summary

In this chapter, you learned how to build a GUI using the classes of the AWT. You worked with labels, buttons, text fields, checkboxes, choices, lists, and scrollbars. You learned how to use components and containers, and how to handle events. In the next chapter, you'll learn how to draw graphics and text on `Canvas` object.

Working with the Canvas

CHAPTER

7

In this chapter you'll learn the basics of using the `Canvas` and `Graphics` classes of the `java.awt` package. You'll also learn how to use the `Font` class to control the way text is displayed. Understanding these classes is essential to developing GUI-based applets and applications. More advanced use of canvas- and graphics-related classes is covered in Chapter 18, "Printing," and Chapter 20, "Working with 2D and 3D Graphics."

The `Canvas` and `Graphics` Classes

The `Canvas` class of `java.awt` provides a general GUI component for drawing images and text on the screen. It does not support any drawing methods of its own, but provides access to a `Graphics` object through its `paint()` method. The `paint()` method is invoked upon the creation and update of a canvas so that the `Graphics` object associated with a `Canvas` object can be updated. The `paint()` method should not be directly invoked, but it can be indirectly accessed using the `repaint()` method. The `Canvas` class is used to provide custom drawing and event handling. You can use the `Graphics` object associated with your applet's class by overriding its `paint()` method.

> **NOTE**
>
> The `Canvas` and `Graphics` objects can be used by Java applications as well as Java applets.

The `Graphics` class is where all of the low-level drawing methods are implemented. These methods can be used directly to draw objects and text, or can be combined to display more elaborate screen objects. The `Graphics` drawing methods allow a number of geometrical shapes to be drawn and filled, including lines, arcs, ovals, rectangles, rounded rectangles, and polygons. A special `draw3DRect()` method is provided for drawing rectangles that are shaded to give them a three-dimensional appearance. The `Graphics` class also provides the capability to draw bitmapped images and text on the canvas. The "Using Text and Fonts" section later in this chapter covers the drawing of text and introduces the `Font` and `FontMetrics` classes. These classes control the specific manner in which text is displayed.

Displaying Bitmapped Images

The `drawImage()` method of the `Graphics` class is used to display bitmapped images on the `Graphics` object associated with a canvas. It takes as its arguments an object of the

Image class, an object that implements the ImageObserver interface, the x- and y-coordinates where the image is to be displayed, and other parameters.

The Image class is an abstract class that provides format-independent access to graphical images. Image objects are created by invoking methods of other classes that create images. Examples of these image-creating methods are the createImage() methods of the Component and Toolkit classes and the getImage() methods of the Toolkit and Applet classes. The getImage() methods are the most handy methods for retrieving an image that is stored in a disk file or at a URL. Java currently supports GIF- and JPEG-formatted images through these methods.

The ImageObserver interface is defined in the java.awt.image package. This interface provides a set of constants and methods that support the creation and loading of images. The Component class implements the ImageObserver interface, and in most cases, the ImageObserver object used as the parameter to the drawImage() method can be supplied using the this identifier to reference the current Canvas or Frame object being painted.

The DisplayImage Applet

The DisplayImage applet shows how bitmapped images can be drawn in an applet window using the drawImage() method of the Graphics class. Its source code is shown in Listing 7.1. Listing 7.2 provides an HTML file to be used to display the applet.

LISTING 7.1. THE SOURCE CODE FOR THE DisplayImage APPLET.

```
import java.awt.*;
import java.applet.*;
import java.net.*;

public class DisplayImage extends Applet {
 int screenWidth = 400;
 int screenHeight = 400;
 Image image;
 public void init() {
  setBackground(Color.white);
  image = getImage(getDocumentBase(),"test.gif");
  resize(screenWidth,screenHeight);
 }
 public void paint(Graphics g) {
  g.drawImage(image,0,0,this);
 }
}
```

LISTING 7.2. THE DisplayImage.htm FILE USED WITH THE DisplayImage APPLET.

```
<HTML>
<HEAD>
<TITLE>Displaying an Image</TITLE>
</HEAD>
<BODY>
<APPLET CODE="DisplayImage.class" HEIGHT=500 WIDTH=500>
</APPLET>
</BODY>
</HTML>
```

Before running the DisplayImage applet, copy the test.gif image from the \ju\ch07 directory of the CD-ROM to your ju\ch07 directory. The DisplayImage program uses the test.gif file.

DisplayImage shows how a bitmapped image can be displayed using the Graphics class. When you run the applet, it will display the bitmapped image shown in Figure 7.1.

NOTE

Make sure that your TCP/IP software is operating before displaying any of the applets in this chapter. The best way to do this is to connect to the Internet.

FIGURE 7.1.

The DisplayImage applet.

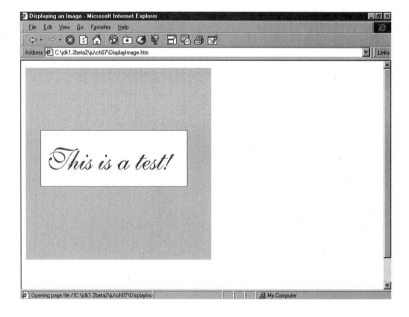

The functionality of the `DisplayImage` applet isn't all that astounding. Its purpose is to illustrate the use of the methods involved in loading and displaying image files. You can easily upgrade the applet to display arbitrary GIF or JPEG files by passing the image file name as an applet parameter.

`DisplayImage` declares three field variables. The `screenWidth` and `screenHeight` variables control the size of the applet window. The `image` variable is used to refer to the loaded image.

The `setBackground()` method of the `Component` class is used to set the applet background to white. The `getImage()` method of the `Applet` class is used to load the image in the `test.gif` file and assign it to the `image` variable. The `getDocumentBase()` method is used to obtain the URL from which the applet's HTML file is loaded. This URL is then used in the loading of `test.gif`.

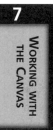

The `paint()` method draws the image referenced by the `image` variable on the default `Graphics` object of the applet window. It accomplishes this using the `drawImage()` method of the `Graphics` class. The arguments to `drawImage()` are the image to be displayed, the x- and y-coordinates where the image is to be drawn, and the object implementing the `ImageObserver` interface associated with the image. The `this` identifier is used to indicate that the applet window is the `ImageObserver`.

Drawing and Painting

Some programs, such as the Microsoft Windows Paint program, are used to construct images by *painting* on the screen. These paint programs create an image array of color pixels and update the array based on user paint commands. These commands may consist of pixel-level drawing operations or more general operations that draw geometrical objects such as circles, rectangles, and lines. Painting programs are characterized by the fact that the pixel array is the focus for the drawing that takes place.

Drawing programs, such as CorelDRAW, support drawing operations using a more object-oriented approach. When you draw a circle or line with a drawing program, you do not merely update the pixels of the canvas—you add an object to the list of objects that are displayed on the canvas. Because drawing programs operate at a higher object level, you can select, move, resize, group, and perform other operations on the objects that you've drawn.

The `Graphics` class is oriented toward providing the methods that are needed to support higher-level drawing programs rather than lower-level painting programs. However, it does support important painting operations, such as displaying bitmapped images, as you saw in the `DisplayImage` program.

When using the `Graphics` class to support graphical operations, you will generally maintain a list of the objects that you've drawn and use that list of objects to repaint the screen as required.

The `Draw` Applet

The `Draw` applet shows how the higher-level drawing operations of the `Graphics` class are used to display and maintain a list of the objects that are drawn on a canvas. The source code of the `Draw` applet is shown in Listing 7.3. Its corresponding HTML file is shown in Listing 7.4.

LISTING 7.3. THE SOURCE CODE FOR THE `Draw` APPLET.

```
import java.applet.*;
import java.awt.*;
import java.awt.event.*;
import java.lang.Math;
import java.util.Vector;

public class Draw extends Applet {
 Button lineButton = new Button("Line");
 Button ovalButton = new Button("Oval");
 Button rectButton = new Button("Rectangle");
 Button clearButton = new Button("Clear");
 MyCanvas canvas = new MyCanvas(TwoPointObject.LINE);
 int screenWidth = 400;
 int screenHeight = 400;
 public void init() {
  setBackground(Color.white);
  setLayout(new BorderLayout());
  add("Center",canvas);
  setupButtons();
  resize(screenWidth,screenHeight);
 }
 void setupButtons() {
  lineButton.addActionListener(new ButtonHandler());
  ovalButton.addActionListener(new ButtonHandler());
  rectButton.addActionListener(new ButtonHandler());
  clearButton.addActionListener(new ButtonHandler());
  Panel panel = new Panel();
  panel.add(lineButton);
  panel.add(ovalButton);
  panel.add(rectButton);
  panel.add(clearButton);
  add("North",panel);
 }
 class ButtonHandler implements ActionListener {
  public void actionPerformed(ActionEvent ev){
```

```
       String s=ev.getActionCommand();
       if(s.equals("Clear")) canvas.clear();
       else if(s.equals("Line"))
        canvas.setTool(TwoPointObject.LINE);
       else if(s.equals("Oval"))
        canvas.setTool(TwoPointObject.OVAL);
       else if(s.equals("Rectangle"))
        canvas.setTool(TwoPointObject.RECTANGLE);
      }
     }
    }
    class MyCanvas extends Canvas {
     int tool = TwoPointObject.LINE;
     Vector objects = new Vector();
     TwoPointObject current;
     boolean newObject = false;
     public MyCanvas(int toolType) {
      super();
      tool = toolType;
      addMouseListener(new MouseHandler());
      addMouseMotionListener(new MouseMotionHandler());
     }
     public void setTool(int toolType) {
      tool = toolType;
     }
     public void clear() {
      objects.removeAllElements();
      repaint();
     }
     public void paint(Graphics g) {
      int numObjects = objects.size();
      for(int i=0;i<numObjects;++i) {
       TwoPointObject obj = (TwoPointObject) objects.elementAt(i);
       obj.draw(g);
      }
      if(newObject) current.draw(g);
     }
     class MouseHandler extends MouseAdapter {
      public void mousePressed(MouseEvent e){
       current = new TwoPointObject(tool,e.getX(),e.getY());
       newObject = true;
      }
      public void mouseReleased(MouseEvent e){
       if(newObject) {
        objects.addElement(current);
        newObject = false;
       }
      }
     }
     class MouseMotionHandler extends MouseMotionAdapter {
```

continues

LISTING 7.3. CONTINUED

```java
public void mouseDragged(MouseEvent e){
  int x = e.getX();
  int y = e.getY();
  if(newObject) {
   int oldX = current.endX;
   int oldY = current.endY;
   if(tool != TwoPointObject.LINE) {
    if(x > current.startX) current.endX = x;
    if(y > current.startY) current.endY = y;
    int width = Math.max(oldX,current.endX) - current.startX + 1;
    int height = Math.max(oldY,current.endY) - current.startY + 1;
    repaint(current.startX,current.startY,width,height);
   }else{
    current.endX = x;
    current.endY = y;
    int startX = Math.min(Math.min(current.startX,current.endX),oldX);
    int startY = Math.min(Math.min(current.startY,current.endY),oldY);
    int endX = Math.max(Math.max(current.startX,current.endX),oldX);
    int endY = Math.max(Math.max(current.startY,current.endY),oldY);
    repaint(startX,startY,endX-startX+1,endY-startY+1);
   }
  }
 }
}
}
class TwoPointObject {
 public static int LINE = 0;
 public static int OVAL = 1;
 public static int RECTANGLE = 2;
 public int type, startX, startY, endX, endY;
 public TwoPointObject(int objectType,int x1,int y1,int x2,int y2) {
  type = objectType;
  startX = x1;
  startY = y1;
  endX = x2;
  endY = y2;
 }
 public TwoPointObject(int objectType,int x,int y) {
  this(objectType,x,y,x,y);
 }
 public TwoPointObject() {
  this(LINE,0,0,0,0);
 }
 public void draw(Graphics g) {
  if(type == LINE) g.drawLine(startX,startY,endX,endY);
  else{
   int w = Math.abs(endX - startX);
```

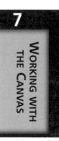

```
      int l = Math.abs(endY - startY);
      if(type == OVAL) g.drawOval(startX,startY,w,l);
      else g.drawRect(startX,startY,w,l);
    }
  }
}
```

LISTING 7.4. THE Draw.htm FILE.

```
<HTML>
<HEAD>
<TITLE>A Drawing Applet</TITLE>
</HEAD>
<BODY>
<APPLET CODE="Draw.class" HEIGHT=400 WIDTH=400>
</APPLET>
</BODY>
</HTML>
```

The Draw applet is quite a bit more sophisticated than the DisplayImage applet with respect to the capabilities that it provides. When you run Draw with your browser, you will see the opening window shown in Figure 7.2.

FIGURE 7.2.

The Draw opening window.

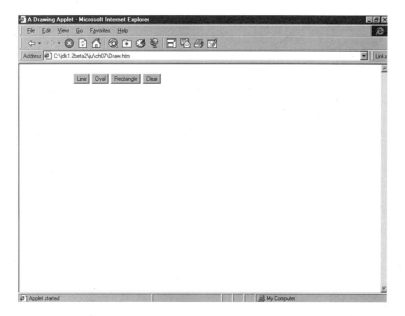

The Draw applet is initially configured for you to draw lines in its window area. You can draw a line by clicking the left mouse button and dragging the mouse. When you have finished drawing the line, release the left mouse button and the drawn line will be completed. The coordinate where you press the left mouse button is the beginning of the line, and the coordinate where you release the left mouse button is the end of the line. Go ahead and draw several lines, as shown in Figure 7.3.

FIGURE 7.3.

Drawing lines with the Draw applet.

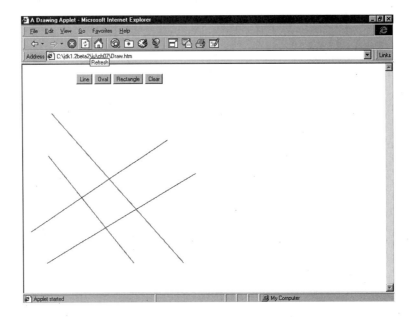

The Draw applet supports the drawing of lines, ovals, and rectangles. Click the Oval button to change the drawing tool to draw ovals. You draw an oval in the same way that you draw a line. When you click the left button of your mouse, mark the upper-left corner of the oval. Drag the mouse to where you want the lower-right corner of the oval and release the left mouse button. Try drawing a few ovals, as shown in Figure 7.4.

Now click the Rectangle button to begin drawing rectangles. Draw rectangles in the same way that you draw ovals. Go ahead and draw a rectangle, as shown in Figure 7.5.

You can experiment with the applet before going on to find out how it works. If you want to clear the drawing screen, click the Clear button.

FIGURE 7.4.

Drawing ovals with the Draw *applet.*

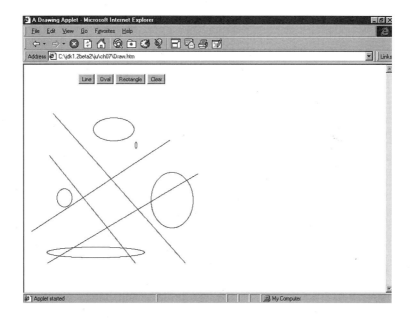

FIGURE 7.5.

Drawing rectangles with the Draw *applet.*

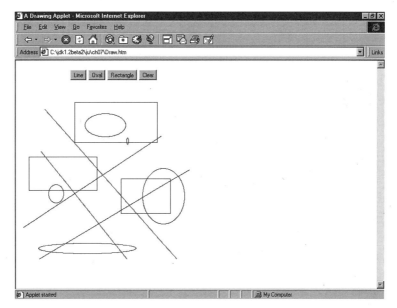

7

WORKING WITH
THE CANVAS

The Draw applet is a little (but not much) longer than the applets you've developed so far in this book. It consists of three major classes and three event handling inner classes. The Draw class is the main class used to implement the applet. The MyCanvas class is used to implement the main canvas component of the applet. The TwoPointObject class is used to implement the line, oval, and rectangle objects that are drawn on the screen. It is called TwoPointObject because it supports objects that can be characterized by a starting point (mouse down) and an ending point (mouse up).

The Draw applet declares several variables. Four button variables are declared and initialized to implement the Clear, Line, Oval, and Rectangle buttons. The canvas variable is used to refer to the MyCanvas object that implements the applet drawing. This object is constructed by passing the TwoPointObject.LINE constant as an argument. This tells the constructed object that the line tool should be initially used to support drawing. The height and width of the Draw window is set to 400×400 pixels.

The applet's init() method sets the background color to white, sets the applet's layout to a BorderLayout object, and adds the MyCanvas object to the center of the applet window. It then sets up the button event handlers and lays out the buttons via setupButtons().

The actionPerformed() method of the MenuItemHandler class handles the clicking of the buttons. The Clear button is handled by invoking the clear() method of the MyCanvas class to clear the canvas to a blank state. The Line, Oval, and Rectangle buttons are handled by invoking the setTool() method of the MyCanvas class to set the current drawing tool. It uses the LINE, OVAL, and RECTANGLE constants defined in the TwoPointObject class.

MyCanvas

The MyCanvas class extends the Canvas class to provide custom drawing capabilities. The tool variable is used to identify the current drawing tool that is in effect. The objects variable is declared as a Vector. It is used to store all of the objects drawn by the user. The current variable is used to refer to the current TwoPointObject object being drawn by the user. The newObject flag is used to track whether the user has begun drawing a new object.

The MyCanvas constructor invokes the constructor of the Canvas class using the super-class constructor call statement, and then sets the tool variable to the toolType argument passed to the constructor.

The setTool() method changes the tool used to draw an object.

The clear() method invokes the removeAllElements() method of the Vector class to remove all drawing objects stored in the Vector referenced by the objects variable.

The paint() method is used to paint and repaint the screen. It uses the size() method of the Vector class to determine how many objects are stored in the objects vector and sets the numObjects variable to this value. It then iterates through each object stored in objects and draws each one on the canvas. The elementAt() method of the Vector class is used to retrieve an object from the objects vector. The object is cast into an object of class TwoPointObject and assigned to the obj variable. The draw() method of the TwoPointObject class is invoked to draw the object on the current Graphics context.

Notice that the paint() method does not have to know how to support limited area repainting. Only full canvas painting needs to be implemented by paint(). Support of limited area repainting is provided by the local AWT implementation.

The MouseHandler and MouseMotionHandler inner classes handle the events associated with pressing, releasing, and dragging the mouse. They do this by extending the MouseAdapter and MouseMotionAdapter classes of java.awt.event. The MouseHandler class handles the pressing and releasing of the mouse button via the mousePressed() and mouseReleased() methods. The MouseMotionHandler class handles the dragging of the mouse via the mouseDragged() method.

The mousePressed() method handles the event that is generated when the user clicks the left mouse button in the canvas. The method is called by the Java runtime system with the position of the mouse click. A new TwoPointObject object is created, with the tool variable and the position of the mouse click as its arguments. The newly created object is assigned to the current variable, and the newObject flag is set to true.

The mouseReleased() method is used to handle the event that is generated when the user releases the left mouse button. This action marks the completion of the drawing of an object. The event is handled by adding the object referenced by the current variable to the objects vector. The newObject flag is then set to False. The object referenced by the current variable is updated with its ending position during the processing of the mouseDragged() event handling method. The newObject flag is checked to make sure that the mouse was not clicked outside of the current window and then released.

The mouseDragged() method performs somewhat more sophisticated event handling than the mousePressed() and mouseReleased() methods. It checks the newObject flag to make sure that an object is currently being drawn. It then sets the oldX and oldY variables to the ending position of the object being drawn. These variables will be used to determine which portion of the canvas needs to be repainted. Repainting the entire canvas is not visually appealing because it causes previously drawn objects to flicker.

If the current drawing tool is not a line, an oval or a rectangle is being drawn by the user. The x- and y-coordinates of the mouse motion are provided via the MouseEvent argument to the mouseDragged() method. These coordinates are checked to determine whether the mouse was dragged below and to the right of the object being drawn. If this is the case, the ending position of the current object is updated. If the mouse is dragged to the left or above the starting point of the object, the current position of the mouse is ignored. This is to ensure that the starting position of the oval or rectangle is indeed its upper-left corner. The new `width` and `height` of the area to be repainted are calculated as the maximum area covered by the previous ending position and the current object ending position. This is to ensure that the repaint operation will erase any previous boundaries of the object being drawn. The `max()` method of the `java.lang.Math` class is used to determine this maximum area. The `repaint()` method of the `Component` class is then used to repaint the area updated as the result of the mouse drag. This version of the `repaint()` method takes as its parameters the x- and y-coordinates of the upper-left corner of the area to be redrawn and the width and height of this area.

Line drawing is not restricted in the same manner as oval and rectangle drawing. If it were, you would not be able to draw lines that go up and to the right or down and to the left. The `else` part of the `if` statement updates the starting position of the area to be repainted as the upper-leftmost point of the line being redrawn. It then updates the ending position of the area to be repainted as the lower-rightmost point of the line. The canvas is then repainted using the starting coordinates and the updated width and height of the repainted area.

To get a better feel for the process of local screen repainting, try experimenting with the way the `repaint()` method is used to update the canvas display.

TwoPointObject

The `TwoPointObject` class is used to keep track of the objects drawn by the user. It records the type of object and its starting and ending coordinates. It also draws the objects on a `Graphics` object passed as a parameter.

`TwoPointObject` defines the `LINE`, `OVAL`, and `RECTANGLE` constants, which are also used by the `MyCanvas` class. The `type` variable is used to record the type of object being drawn. The `startX`, `startY`, `endX`, and `endY` variables identify the starting and ending coordinates of the object.

Three `TwoPointObject` constructors are declared. The first constructor takes as its parameters the type of object being drawn and its starting and ending coordinates. The second constructor leaves out the ending coordinates and sets them to be the same as the starting coordinates. The last constructor takes no parameters and creates a line at the coordinates 0,0.

The `draw()` method checks the `type` variable to determine which type of object is to be drawn. If the object is a line, it uses the `drawLine()` method of the `Graphics` class to draw a line from its starting to ending coordinates. If the object is an oval or a line, the w and l variables are assigned the width and length of the object to be drawn. The drawOval() and drawRect() methods are used to draw an oval or rectangle, respectively.

Using Text and Fonts

The Font class of java.awt provides a platform-independent method of specifying and using fonts. The Font class constructor constructs Font objects using the font's name, style (PLAIN, BOLD, ITALIC, or BOLD + ITALIC), and point size. Java's fonts are named in a platform-independent manner and then mapped to local fonts that are supported by the operating system on which it executes. The getName() method returns the logical Java font name of a particular font, and the getFamily()method returns the operating system-specific name of the font. You'll learn the name of the standard Java fonts in the next programming example in this chapter.

The FontMetrics class is used to return the specific parameters for a particular Font object. An object of this class is created using the getFontMetrics() methods supported by the Component class and other classes, such as the Graphics and Toolkit classes. The FontMetrics methods provide access to the details of the implementation of a Font object.

The bytesWidth(), charWidth(), charsWidth(), getWidths(), and stringWidth() methods are used to determine the width of a text object in pixels. These methods are essential for determining the horizontal position of text on the screen.

When text characters are displayed, they are displayed relative to a baseline. The *baseline* is the line drawn through the bottom of nondescending characters. For example, if you drew a line at the bottom of most text displayed on this line, you would get the text's baseline. Some characters, such as *g* and *y*, descend below the baseline. The number of pixels that the characters of a font descend below the baseline is known as the font's *descent*. The number of pixels that the characters of a font extend above the baseline is known as the font's *ascent*.

In addition to a font's ascent and descent, a third parameter, referred to as the font's *leading*, is used to describe the amount of vertical spacing, in pixels, used between the descent of a line of text and the ascent of the line of text below it. The overall height of a font is the sum of its leading, ascent, and descent, and is equal to the distance between baselines (in pixels) of vertically adjacent lines of text. The getLeading(), getAscent(), getDescent(), and getHeight() methods of the FontMetrics class are used to access these important font-related parameters. Figure 7.6 provides a graphical description of these parameters.

FIGURE 7.6.
Font parameters.

The getMaxAdvance(), getMaxAscent(), and getMaxDescent() methods are provided for backward-compatibility with earlier Java versions.

Using the `Toolkit` Class

The Toolkit class provides a link between the platform-independent Java implementation and its platform-specific characteristics. Among the many interesting methods implemented by this class are the getFontList(), getFontMetrics(), getScreenSize(), and getScreenResolution() methods. The getFontList()method returns a list of fonts that are accessible from Java. The getFontMetrics() method identifies the font metrics for a particular font. The getScreenSize() method identifies the screen dimension in terms of horizontal and vertical dots. The getScreenResolution() method identifies the screen resolution in dots per inch.

The getFontList() is the method of interest for this chapter. You'll use it to get a list of the fonts available to Java in the next section.

The getFontList() method is deprecated in JDK 1.2. With the advent of the Java 2D API (refer to Chapter 20), the getFontFamilyNames() method of the GraphicsEnvironment class is now preferred.

The `FontTest` Applet

The FontTest applet illustrates the use of the Font, FontMetrics, and Toolkit classes and shows how to draw text on a Graphics object. Its source code is shown in Listing 7.5. Listing 7.6 provides an HTML file for displaying the applet.

LISTING 7.5. THE SOURCE CODE OF THE FontTest APPLET.

```
import java.applet.*;
import java.awt.*;

public class FontTest extends Applet {
 Toolkit toolkit;
 Font defaultFont;
 String fontNames[];
```

```
int screenWidth = 400;
int screenHeight = 400;
public void init() {
 setupFonts();
 setSize(screenWidth,screenHeight);
}
void setupFonts() {
 toolkit = getToolkit();
 defaultFont = getFont();
 fontNames = toolkit.getFontList();
}
public void paint(Graphics g) {
 int styles[] = {Font.PLAIN,Font.BOLD,Font.ITALIC};
 String styleNames[] = {"Plain","Bold","Italic"};
 int size = 12;
 int y=10;
 for(int i=0;i<fontNames.length;++i) {
  if(fontNames[i]!="ZapfDingbats") {
   for(int j=0;j<styles.length;++j) {
    Font newFont = new Font(fontNames[i],styles[j],size);
    FontMetrics fm = g.getFontMetrics(newFont);
    g.setFont(newFont);
    String text = fontNames[i]+"-"+styleNames[j];
    int x = (screenWidth - fm.stringWidth(text))/2;
    g.drawString(text,x,y+fm.getLeading()+fm.getAscent());
    y += fm.getHeight();
   }
  }
 }
}
}
```

LISTING 7.6. THE FontTest.htm FILE.

```
<HTML>
<HEAD>
<TITLE>Using Fonts</TITLE>
</HEAD>
<BODY>
<APPLET CODE="FontTest.class" HEIGHT=400 WIDTH=400>
</APPLET>
</BODY>
</HTML>
```

The FontTest applet does not provide much functionality. Just run it and it will display a list of the fonts that are currently available to Java, with each name written in its font. Figure 7.7 shows its display. The applet's importance is not in what it does, but in how it does it. By closely examining this applet, you'll be able to quickly come up to speed on working with Java fonts.

FIGURE 7.7.

The FontTest *out-put.*

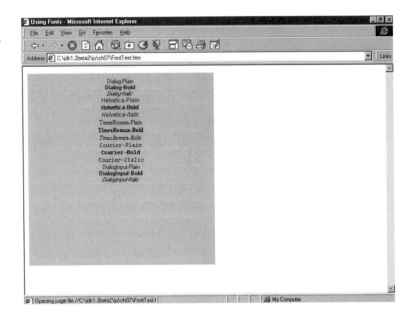

The FontTest class declares a number of field variables. The toolkit variable is used to refer to the Toolkit object associated with the applet window. The defaultFont variable identifies the default font used by the applet. The fontNames[] array is used to store the names of the fonts that are accessible to Java.

The setupFonts() method obtains the Toolkit object associated with the applet's window, using the getToolkit() method, and assigns this object to the toolkit variable. The current font used by the applet is accessed by getFont() and assigned to the defaultFont variable. The Toolkit object is then used to obtain the current list of font names via the getFontList() method of the Toolkit class. That's all for the applet's setup.

The paint() method is where the primary processing of interest takes place. The styles[] and styleNames[] arrays are used to identify the various text styles and their associated string descriptions. The y variable identifies the vertical screen position where text is displayed. The size variable identifies the point size used to display a font.

The paint() method uses two for statements. The outer statement iterates through the list of font names, and the inner statement iterates through the font styles. The ZapfDingbats font, a symbol font, is skipped. At each pass through the inner loop, a new font is created with the specified name, style, and size. The getFontMetrics() method of the `Graphics` class is used to obtain the `FontMetrics` object associated with the newly created font, and this object is assigned to the `fm` variable. The `setFont()` method of the `Graphics` class is used to set the current font to the new font.

The next line of text to be displayed is created by concatenating the font name and its style name. The horizontal position at which the text is to be displayed in order for it to be centered is calculated based upon the width of the text (in pixels) returned by the `stringWidth()` method of the `FontMetrics` class and the initial width of the applet window area. The vertical position where the text is to be displayed is its baseline, and is determined by adding the leading and ascent values of the font with the y variable. These values are obtained using the `getLeading()` and `getAscent()` methods of the current `FontMetrics` object. The y variable identifies the point of maximum descent of the previously displayed line of text. It is then updated for the current line of text by adding the height of the current font returned by the `getHeight()` method of the `FontMetrics` class.

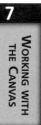

Fonts, Colors, and Text Components

The `Font` and `FontMetrics` classes are not confined to text that is drawn on `Graphics` objects. These classes can also be used with the `TextField` and `TextArea` classes. These classes automatically calculate the correct text-display locations using the native text objects supported by the local operating-system platform. In addition to changing text fonts, the `TextField` and `TextArea` classes also support the display of text using different foreground and background colors. The following applet shows how fonts and colors can be quickly incorporated into a Java applet to implement features associated with What-You-See-Is-What-You-Get (WYSIWYG) editors.

The `Edit` Applet

The `Edit` applet shows how the `Font` and `Color` classes can be used with a `TextArea` component. Its source code is shown in Listing 7.7. Its HTML file is provided in Listing 7.8.

The `Edit` applet uses the `FontDialog` and `ColorDialog` classes that are introduced in subsequent sections. In order to compile and run `Edit.java`, you will need the `FontDialog.java` and `ColorDialog.java` files. Java will automatically compile the `FontDialog.java` and `ColorDialog.java` files when `Edit.java` is compiled.

LISTING 7.7. THE SOURCE CODE OF THE Edit APPLET.

```java
import java.applet.*;
import java.awt.*;
import java.awt.event.*;

public class Edit extends Applet {
 Button clearButton = new Button("Clear");
 Button fontButton = new Button("Font");
 Button colorButton = new Button("Color");
 TextArea text;
 Frame frame;
 FontDialog fd;
 ColorDialog cd;
 Font currentFont = new Font("Courier",Font.PLAIN,12);
 Color currentColor = Color.black;
 public void init() {
  setBackground(Color.white);
  setLayout(new BorderLayout());
  text = new TextArea(25,80);
  text.setFont(currentFont);
  add("Center",text);
  setupButtons();
 }
 void setupButtons() {
  clearButton.addActionListener(new ButtonHandler());
  fontButton.addActionListener(new ButtonHandler());
  colorButton.addActionListener(new ButtonHandler());
  Panel panel = new Panel();
  panel.add(clearButton);
  panel.add(fontButton);
  panel.add(colorButton);
  add("North",panel);
 }
 class ButtonHandler implements ActionListener {
  public void actionPerformed(ActionEvent ev){
   String s=ev.getActionCommand();
   if(s=="Clear"){
    text.setText("");
   }else if(s=="Font"){
    frame = new Frame();
    frame.show();
    fd = new FontDialog(frame,currentFont,
     new FontSelectHandler());
    fd.show();
   }else if(s=="Color"){
    frame = new Frame();
    frame.show();
```

```
     cd = new ColorDialog(frame,currentColor,
      new ColorSelectHandler());
     cd.show();
   }
  }
}
class FontSelectHandler implements ActionListener {
 public void actionPerformed(ActionEvent e){
  currentFont = fd.getFont();
  fd.dispose();
  frame.dispose();
  requestFocus();
  text.setFont(currentFont);
 }
}
class ColorSelectHandler implements ActionListener {
 public void actionPerformed(ActionEvent e){
  currentColor = cd.getColor();
  cd.dispose();
  frame.dispose();
  requestFocus();
  text.setForeground(currentColor);
  text.setText(text.getText());
  text.setVisible(true);
 }
}
}
```

LISTING 7.8. THE `Edit.htm` FILE.

```
<HTML>
<HEAD>
<TITLE>Text Editing</TITLE>
</HEAD>
<BODY>
<APPLET CODE="Edit.class" HEIGHT=400 WIDTH=600>
</APPLET>
</BODY>
</HTML>
```

The `Edit` applet opening display is shown in Figure 7.8.

Type some text into the applet's text area. Click the Font button to launch the font dialog box, shown in Figure 7.9. Use this dialog box to select a 24-point Bold Italic Helvetica font. The text's display is updated, as shown in Figure 7.10.

FIGURE 7.8.

The Edit *applet opening display.*

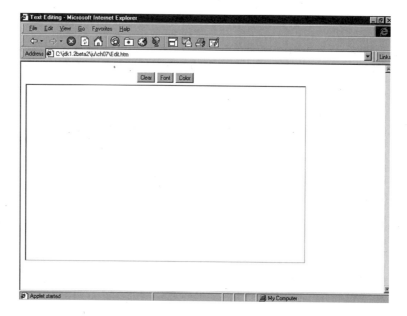

FIGURE 7.9.

The font dialog box.

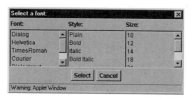

Select the Color menu item from the Format menu. The color dialog box is displayed, as shown in Figure 7.11. Use this dialog box to change the color associated with the text's display. Try using primary colors such as blue or green. Other colors might not display correctly, depending on the number of colors supported by your video card and the current color map associated with the display.

The Edit applet makes use of the FontDialog and ColorDialog classes covered in the following sections. It declares variables to implement the Clear, Font, and Color buttons, the text area, and a frame window for displaying dialog boxes. It also declares variables for referencing the font and color dialog boxes and the current font and color in use.

The init() method sets the background color and layout, creates the TextArea object, and sets the current font. It then adds the TextArea object to the center of the applet's display and invokes setupButtons().

FIGURE 7.10.
Updated text.

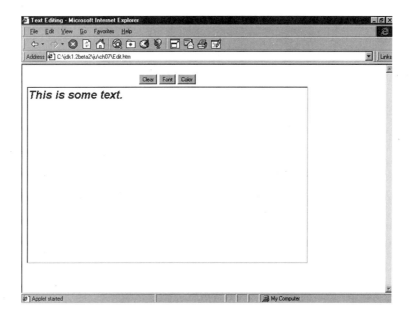

FIGURE 7.11.
*The color dialog
box.*

The `setupButtons()` method sets up each button's event handler, organizes the buttons into a `Panel` object, and adds the panel to the applet's display area.

The `ButtonHandler` class handles the clicking of the buttons. The Clear button is handled by invoking the `TextArea` object's `setText()` method to clear its text. Clicking of the Font button results in a new `FontDialog` object being created to solicit the user to change the current font. You'll learn about this class in the next section. The clicking of the Color button results in a `ColorDialog` object being created to provide the user with opportunity to change the color of the current text. The `ColorDialog` class is covered later in the chapter. Note that a `Frame` object is created to provide a window in which the `FontDialog` and `ColorDialog` boxes are displayed.

The `FontSelectHandler` class handles the event that occurs when the user closes the font dialog box. You'll create this event in the `FontDialog` class. The `actionPerformed()` method invokes the `getFont()` method of the `FontDialog` class to retrieve the font selected by the user. It then disposes of the dialog box and its frame, and sets the current font of the TextArea object to the retrieved font.

The ColorSelectHandler class handles the event that occurs when the user closes a color dialog box. You'll create this event in the ColorDialog class. The actionPerformed() method invokes the getColor() method of the ColorDialog class to retrieve the color selected by the user. It then disposes of the dialog box and its frame, and sets the current color of the TextArea object to the retrieved color. The setText() and getText() methods are used to reset the text using the new color. The setVisible() method causes the TextArea object to be redisplayed.

The FontDialog Class

The FontDialog class provides a handy encapsulation of the dialog boxes commonly used to select a font from the list of available fonts provided by the system. The source code of the FontDialog class is shown in Listing 7.9.

LISTING 7.9. THE SOURCE CODE OF THE FontDialog CLASS.

```
import java.awt.*;
import java.awt.event.*;

public class FontDialog extends Dialog {
  String fontName;
  int fontStyle;
  int fontSize;
  String fontNames[];
  String styleNames[] = {"Plain","Bold","Italic","Bold Italic"};
  String sizeNames[] = {"10","12","14","18","24","36","72"};
  int styles[] = {Font.PLAIN,Font.BOLD,Font.ITALIC,Font.BOLD+Font.ITALIC};
  int sizes[] = {10,12,14,18,24,36,72};
  MyList fontList;
  MyList styleList = new MyList(5,false,styleNames);
  MyList sizeList = new MyList(5,false,sizeNames);
  Toolkit toolkit;
  Font newFont;
  boolean fontChanged;
  ActionListener ah;
  public FontDialog(Frame parent,Font currentFont,ActionListener ah) {
    super(parent,"Select a font:",true);
    toolkit = parent.getToolkit();
    newFont = currentFont;
    setupFonts();
    setupPanels();
    setBackground(Color.lightGray);
    setForeground(Color.black);
    this.ah=ah;
```

```
 pack();
 addWindowListener(new WindowEventHandler());
}
void setupFonts() {
 fontName=newFont.getName();
 fontStyle=newFont.getStyle();
 fontSize=newFont.getSize();
 fontNames = toolkit.getFontList();
 fontList = new MyList(5,false,fontNames);
}
void setupPanels() {
 Panel mainPanel = new Panel();
 mainPanel.setLayout(new GridLayout(1,3));
 Panel fontPanel = new Panel();
 fontPanel.setLayout(new BorderLayout());
 Label fontLabel = new Label("Font:");
 fontPanel.add("North",fontLabel);
 fontPanel.add("Center",fontList);
 Panel stylePanel = new Panel();
 stylePanel.setLayout(new BorderLayout());
 Label styleLabel = new Label("Style:");
 stylePanel.add("North",styleLabel);
 stylePanel.add("Center",styleList);
 Panel sizePanel = new Panel();
 sizePanel.setLayout(new BorderLayout());
 Label sizeLabel = new Label("Size:");
 sizePanel.add("North",sizeLabel);
 sizePanel.add("Center",sizeList);
 mainPanel.add(fontPanel);
 mainPanel.add(stylePanel);
 mainPanel.add(sizePanel);
 Font plainFont = new Font("Helvetica",Font.PLAIN,12);
 Font boldFont = new Font("Helvetica",Font.BOLD,12);
 mainPanel.setFont(plainFont);
 fontLabel.setFont(boldFont);
 styleLabel.setFont(boldFont);
 sizeLabel.setFont(boldFont);
 Panel buttonPanel = new Panel();
 buttonPanel.setLayout(new FlowLayout());
 Button selectButton = new Button("Select");
 Button cancelButton = new Button("Cancel");
 ButtonHandler bh = new ButtonHandler();
 selectButton.addActionListener(bh);
 cancelButton.addActionListener(bh);
 buttonPanel.add(selectButton);
 buttonPanel.add(cancelButton);
 buttonPanel.setFont(boldFont);
 add("Center",mainPanel);
 add("South",buttonPanel);
}
```

continues

LISTING 7.9. CONTINUED

```java
public boolean isChanged() {
 return fontChanged;
}
public Font getFont() {
 return newFont;
}
void updateNewFont() {
 if(fontList.getSelectedIndex() != -1) fontName =
 ➥fontList.getSelectedItem();
 if(styleList.getSelectedIndex() != -1)
  fontStyle = styles[styleList.getSelectedIndex()];
 if(sizeList.getSelectedIndex() != -1)
  fontSize = sizes[sizeList.getSelectedIndex()];
 newFont = new Font(fontName,fontStyle,fontSize);
 fontChanged = true;
}
class ButtonHandler implements ActionListener {
 public void actionPerformed(ActionEvent e){
  String s = e.getActionCommand();
  if("Select".equals(s)) {
   updateNewFont();
   ah.actionPerformed(new ActionEvent(FontDialog.this,
    ActionEvent.ACTION_PERFORMED,"Select"));
   FontDialog.this.setVisible(false);
  }else if("Cancel".equals(s)) {
   FontDialog.this.dispose();
  }
 }
}
class WindowEventHandler extends WindowAdapter {
 public void windowClosing(WindowEvent e){
  FontDialog.this.dispose();
 }
}
}
```

The FontDialog class creates the font dialog box, shown in Figure 7.9. This type of dialog box is used in most text-processing applications. You can reuse the FontDialog class, as it is currently defined, in your Java applets. You can also subclass FontDialog and add your own custom enhancements.

The FontDialog class declares a number of variables that are used in the generation and processing of the font dialog box. The fontName, fontStyle, and fontSize variables are used to keep track of the parameters of the currently selected font. The fontNames array identifies the names of the fonts that are currently supported by the system. The styles, styleNames, sizes, and sizeNames arrays are used to maintain int and String lists of the font styles and sizes that are displayed in the dialog box. The fontList, styleList, and sizeList variables refer to the MyList objects displayed in the dialog box. The MyList class is shown in Listing 7.10. The toolkit variable refers to the Toolkit object of the window containing the font dialog box. The fontChanged variable keeps track of whether the user has selected a new font, and the newFont variable maintains the Font object that is selected by the user.

The FontDialog constructor uses the superclass constructor call statement to create a modal dialog box with the title Select a font:. The toolkit associated with the window containing the dialog box is obtained using the getToolkit() method of the Window class. The newFont variable, representing the user's font selection, is set to the default value of the currently selected font. This font is passed to the FontDialog constructor using the currentFont parameter. The FontDialog constructor invokes the setupFonts() and setupPanels() methods to perform the bulk of the dialog box setup. It then sets the background and foreground colors and stores the ActionListener object passed via the ah variable. This ActionListener object is used to handle an event generated by the FontDialog class. The constructor then packs the dialog box window and assigns an event handler to it.

The setupFonts() method assigns default values to the fontName, fontStyle, and fontSize variables based on the values of the current font stored in the newFont variable. The getFontList() method of the Toolkit class is used to set the fontNames[] array to the list of fonts currently supported by the system. These names are converted to a list using the MyList() constructor.

The setupPanels() method performs all of the grunt work, adding the lists to the dialog box and rearranging them in an appealing fashion. The mainPanel variable is used to refer to the overall panel into which the fontPanel, stylePanel, and sizePanel objects are inserted. The mainPanel is layed out as a three-column set of subpanels. These subpanels are identified by the fontPanel, stylePanel, and sizePanel variables. Each of these subpanels is layed out using a BorderLayout object. The label identifying the contents of the panel is added to the top of the panel. The center of each panel contains the three MyList objects identified by the fontList, styleList, and sizeList variables.

The Helvetica font is used for the contents of the font dialog box. The labels at the top of each column are set in a boldface style. A second panel, referred to by the buttonPanel variable, is created with two buttons: Select and Cancel. These buttons provide the user with controls needed to accept or abort a font selection. An object of the ButtonHandler class is used as the buttons' event handler. The mainPanel is added to the center of the font dialog box, and the buttonPanel is added to the bottom.

Two access methods are provided with the FontDialog class. The isChanged() method is used to query a FontDialog object to determine whether the user made a font selection. The getFont() method returns the font selected by the user.

The ButtonHandler class handles the clicking of the Select and Cancel buttons. The Cancel button results in the destruction of the FontDialog object. The object is destroyed using the dispose() method of the Window class. The Select button invokes the updateNewFont() method to create a font based on the user's current list selections and assign that font to the newFont variable. The actionPerformed() method of the ActionListener object passed to the FontDialog constructor is invoked. This enables additional event handling to be performed outside the FontDialog class. The font dialog box is then hidden but not destroyed. Note that an ActionEvent object is passed as an argument to the actionPerformed() method. The setVisible() method of the Component class is used to hide the dialog box.

The updateNewFont() method checks the MyList objects referred to by the fontList, styleList, and sizeList variables to update the fontName, fontStyle, and fontSize variables based on the user's selection. These variables are then used to construct a new Font object, which is assigned to the newFont variable. The fontChanged flag is then set to indicate that a user font selection has occurred.

LISTING 7.10. THE MyList CLASS.

```
import java.awt.*;

public class MyList extends List {
  public MyList(int rows,boolean multiple,String labels[]) {
    super(rows,multiple);
    int length = labels.length;
    for(int i=0;i<length;++i) {
     try {
      add(labels[i]);
     }catch (NullPointerException ex) {
      add("");
     }
    }
  }
}
```

The MyList class, shown in Listing 7.10, provides a constructor that simplifies the construction of List objects.

The `ColorDialog` Class

The `ColorDialog` class is very similar to, but simpler than, the `FontDialog` class. It allows the user to select a color from the list of colors defined in the `Color` class. It provides a dialog box that is similar to that of `FontDialog`, but is much simpler because only one list—the list of available colors—is supported. The source code of the `ColorDialog` class is shown in Listing 7.11.

LISTING 7.11. THE SOURCE CODE OF THE `ColorDialog` CLASS.

```
import java.awt.*;
import java.awt.event.*;

public class ColorDialog extends Dialog {
 Color colors[] =
{Color.black,Color.blue,Color.cyan,Color.darkGray,Color.gray,
Color.green,Color.lightGray,Color.magenta,Color.orange,Color.pink,
➡Color.red,
 Color.white,Color.yellow};
 String colorNames[] = {"black","blue","cyan","darkGray","gray","green",
 "lightGray","magenta","orange","pink","red",
 "white","yellow"};
 MyList colorList = new MyList(5,false,colorNames);
 Color newColor;
 boolean colorChanged;
 ActionListener ah;
 public ColorDialog(Frame parent,Color currentColor,ActionListener ah) {
  super(parent,"Select a color:",true);
  setupPanels();
  setBackground(Color.lightGray);
  setForeground(Color.black);
  this.ah=ah;
  pack();
  addWindowListener(new WindowEventHandler());
 }
 void setupPanels() {
  Panel colorPanel = new Panel();
  colorPanel.setLayout(new BorderLayout());
  Label colorLabel = new Label("Color:");
  colorPanel.add("North",colorLabel);
  colorPanel.add("Center",colorList);
  Font plainFont = new Font("Helvetica",Font.PLAIN,12);
  Font boldFont = new Font("Helvetica",Font.BOLD,12);
  colorLabel.setFont(boldFont);
  colorList.setFont(plainFont);
  Panel buttonPanel = new Panel();
  buttonPanel.setLayout(new FlowLayout());
```

continues

LISTING 7.11. CONTINUED

```
Button selectButton = new Button("Select");
Button cancelButton = new Button("Cancel");
ButtonHandler bh = new ButtonHandler();
selectButton.addActionListener(bh);
cancelButton.addActionListener(bh);
buttonPanel.add(selectButton);
buttonPanel.add(cancelButton);
buttonPanel.setFont(boldFont);
add("Center",colorPanel);
add("South",buttonPanel);
}
public boolean isChanged() {
 return colorChanged;
}
public Color getColor() {
 return newColor;
}
class ButtonHandler implements ActionListener {
 public void actionPerformed(ActionEvent e){
  String s = e.getActionCommand();
  if("Select".equals(s)) {
   if(colorList.getSelectedIndex() != -1)
    newColor = colors[colorList.getSelectedIndex()];
   colorChanged = true;
   ah.actionPerformed(new ActionEvent(ColorDialog.this,
    ActionEvent.ACTION_PERFORMED,"Select"));
   ColorDialog.this.setVisible(false);
  }else if("Cancel".equals(s)) {
   ColorDialog.this.dispose();
  }
 }
}
class WindowEventHandler extends WindowAdapter {
 public void windowClosing(WindowEvent e){
  ColorDialog.this.dispose();
 }
}
}
```

The ColorDialog class declares the colors array as an array of color constants and the
colorNames array as the names associated with these color constants. The colorList
variable refers to the MyList object that presents the colorNames array to the user. The
newColor variable identifies the color selected by the user, and the colorChanged variable indicates whether a user color selection has been made.

The `ColorDialog` constructor invokes the `Dialog` constructor to set the title of the dialog box. It then invokes the `setupPanels()` method to perform most of the setup of the dialog box's internal components. The foreground and background colors are set and then the dialog box is packed and resized.

The `setupPanels()` method creates and adds two panels to the dialog box. These panels are identified by the `colorPanel` and `buttonPanel` variables. The panel identified by the `colorPanel` variable contains the Color: label and the `MyList` object referred to by the `colorList` variable. The button panel is implemented in the same manner as in the `FontDialog` class.

The `isChanged()` and `getColor()` methods are used to determine whether the user has selected a color and, if so, to return the color selected.

The `ButtonHandler` class handles the clicking of the Select and Cancel buttons. The Select button is handled by invoking the `getSelectedIndex()` method of the `List` class to see if a color was selected and setting the `newColor` variable to the selected color. The `colorChanged` flag is updated to indicate that a color has been selected. The `actionPerformed()` method of the `ActionListener` object passed to the `ColorDialog` constructor is invoked in the same manner as in the `FontDialog` class. The `setVisible()` method causes the dialog box to be hidden.

The Cancel button is handled by simply disposing of the dialog box.

Summary

This chapter covers the details of using the `Canvas` and `Graphics` classes. It also shows you how to use the font-related classes of the `java.awt` package. The `DisplayImage` applet demonstrates Java's support of bitmapped images. The `Draw` applet illustrates the drawing methods of the `Graphics` class, and the `FontTest` applet shows you how to draw text on a `Canvas` object. The `Edit` applet shows how fonts and colors are used with text components. Chapter 8, "Applet Security," shows you how to use the applet security features of JDK 1.2.

Applet Security

CHAPTER 8

Applet security is a major concern among Web users and applet developers. From a user's perspective, an exploitable applet security flaw could result in sensitive data being modified or disclosed, or their computer being rendered inoperable. From a developer's perspective, strong applet security is necessary to make Web users comfortable with using applets. However, too high a level of security limits their applets' capabilities.

The JDK 1.2 security model meets both user and developer needs. It allows users to maintain high levels of security, by default, and also to relax these security controls to take advantage of additional applet capabilities that are provided by developers they trust.

In this chapter, you'll learn how to use the JDK 1.2 security model to develop applets that extend the bounds of the applet sandbox and use previously restricted capabilities. First, you'll learn how to package your applets as Java Archive (JAR) files and how to digitally sign these files. You'll then learn how the JDK 1.2 security model supports trusted applets and how users can configure their Java Runtime Environment (JRE) to use trusted applets. You'll also learn about digital certificates and how they are used to support applet security. You'll get hands-on experience using the JDK 1.2 security tools and cover the JDK 1.2 Security API. When you finish this chapter, you'll be thoroughly introduced to applet security.

Using JAR Files and Digital Signatures

A JAR file is a compressed archive file that is created using the Java archive tool (jar), which is similar to the PKZIP program developed by Phil Katz. It combines multiple files into a single archive file that is compressed using the ZLIB compression library. Although jar is a general-purpose file archive and compression tool, its main purpose is to combine the files used by an applet into a single compressed file for efficient loading by a Java-enabled Web browser.

> **NOTE**
>
> A description of the ZLIB compression format is available at the URL
> http://www.cdrom.com/pub/infozip/zlib/.

Using jar with applets can greatly improve browser performance. Because all of the files used by an applet are combined into a single file, a browser only needs to establish a single HTTP connection with a Web server. This reduces the communication processing overhead on both the browser and the server. File compression reduces the time required to download an applet by 50% or more. This benefits both the applet's user and publisher.

Another feature of JAR files is that they support the capability to sign archived files. This allows browsers to differentiate between untrusted applets and those applets that may be trusted to perform sensitive processing in a secure manner (because they are signed by a reputable identity). The sensitive processing that is permitted of trusted applets is determined by the local Java security policy.

Using the JAR Tool

The jar tool is easy to use. You invoke it using the following command line:

```
jar [options] [manifest] jar-file input-file(s)
```

The *jar-file* is the file that is to be used as an archive. The .jar extension should be supplied in the command line. The *input-file(s)* are written as a space-separated list of files to be placed in the archive. Filename wildcard characters may be used (for example, *.class).

The *manifest* is a file that contains information about the archived files. It need not be supplied—jar will create one automatically and store it as META-INF\MANIFEST.INF within the archive. Information about the manifest file can be found in the file docs\guide\jar\manifest.html that is included with the JDK 1.2 API documentation.

The jar *options* are used to control the input and output of the jar tool. They are described in Table 8.1.

TABLE 8.1. THE jar TOOL OPTIONS.

Option	Description
c	Creates a new (empty) archive file.
t	Displays the archive's table of contents.
x [*file(s)*]	Extracts the specified *file(s)*. If no files are specified, all files are extracted.
f	Identifies the file to be created, listed, or extracted.
v	Generates verbose output.
u	Used to update an existing JAR file.
C	Used to change directories during execution of the jar command.
0	Stores files but does not compress them.
M	Skips creation of the manifest file.
m *manifest*	Uses the supplied manifest file.

> **NOTE**
>
> The syntax of the jar tool is similar to the UNIX tar command.

> **NOTE**
>
> The @ character may be used in a jar command, followed by a file name. When this occurs, command arguments are taken from the file (one argument per line) and inserted into the command at the position of the @ character.

Examples of using the jar tool are provided in the following sections.

Creating a JAR file

If you have ever used the UNIX tar command or the DOS PKZIP program, you will find the jar tool to be familiar and easy to use. In this section, you'll learn how to create a JAR file for the Edit applet that you developed in Chapter 7, "Working with the Canvas."

We'll use the Edit applet because it uses several .class files, which makes it a good candidate for archival and compression. Start by copying the Edit.java, MyList.java, FontDialog.java, and ColorDialog.java files to your ch08 working directory and then recompile these files. The following 11 .class files are created in your ch08 directory:

```
ColorDialog.class
ColorDialog$ButtonHandler.class
ColorDialog$WindowEventHandler.class
Edit.class
Edit$ButtonHandler.class
Edit$FontSelectHandler.class
FontDialog.class
Edit$ColorSelectHandler.class
FontDialog$ButtonHandler.class
FontDialog$WindowEventHandler.class
MyList.class
```

Let's use jar to archive and compress them into a file named edit.jar:

```
jar cf edit.jar *.class
```

List your directory to verify that the JAR file was created:

```
Directory of C:\jdk1.2\ju\ch08

.               <DIR>        04-22-98 11:27a .
..              <DIR>        04-22-98 11:27a ..
COLORD~1 JAV        2,448    02-08-98  9:20a ColorDialog.java
EDIT~1   JAV        1,968    02-08-98 10:50a Edit.java
FONTDI~1 JAV        3,667    02-08-98 10:42a FontDialog.java
MYLIST~1 JAV          310    02-08-98  9:19a MyList.java
COLORD~1 CLA        2,908    04-22-98 11:34a ColorDialog.class
COLORD~2 CLA        1,324    04-22-98 11:34a
➥ColorDialog$ButtonHandler.class
COLORD~3 CLA          615    04-22-98 11:34a
➥ColorDialog$WindowEventHandler.class

EDIT~1   CLA        1,914    04-22-98 11:34a Edit.class
EDIT$B~2 CLA        1,545    04-22-98 11:34a Edit$ButtonHandler.class
EDIT$F~2 CLA        1,016    04-22-98 11:34a Edit$FontSelectHandler.class
FONTDI~1 CLA        3,880    04-22-98 11:35a FontDialog.class
EDIT$C~2 CLA        1,214    04-22-98 11:34a Edit$ColorSelectHandler.class
FONTDI~2 CLA        1,101    04-22-98 11:35a FontDialog$ButtonHandler.class
FONTDI~3 CLA          609    04-22-98 11:35a
➥FontDialog$WindowEventHandler.class
MYLIST~1 CLA          431    04-22-98 11:35a MyList.class
EDIT     JAR       11,527    04-22-98 11:36a edit.jar
        16 file(s)         36,477 bytes
         2 dir(s)     197,722,112 bytes free
```

Note that `bj.jar` is only 11,527 bytes long. Because the 11 class files are 16,557 bytes, the `jar` tool compressed them to 70% of their original size. Now that the `.class` files are archived, delete them using `del *.class`.

Listing the Contents of a JAR File

Let's use the list option of the `jar` command to see what's inside the `edit.jar` file:

```
C:\jdk1.2\ju\ch08>jar tf edit.jar
META-INF/MANIFEST.MF
ColorDialog$ButtonHandler.class
ColorDialog$WindowEventHandler.class
ColorDialog.class
Edit$ButtonHandler.class
Edit$ColorSelectHandler.class
Edit$FontSelectHandler.class
Edit.class
FontDialog$ButtonHandler.class
FontDialog$WindowEventHandler.class
FontDialog.class
MyList.class
```

The only thing that looks out of place is the META-INF/MANIFEST.MF entry. That's the file used to keep a manifest of the JAR file's contents.

Viewing a JAR File

You're probably wondering how you would include the edit.jar file in an applet. The answer is that you add the ARCHIVE="edit.jar" attribute to the applet tag. This attribute tells the browser to load the edit.jar archive file to find the Edit.class file and other related classes. Listing 8.1 shows the file Edit.htm that is used to display the Edit applet.

LISTING 8.1. THE Edit.htm FILE.

```
<HTML>
<HEAD>
<TITLE>Text Editing</TITLE>
</HEAD>
<BODY>
<APPLET CODE="Edit.class" ARCHIVE="edit.jar" HEIGHT=400 WIDTH=600>
</APPLET>
</BODY>
</HTML>
```

You can view the Edit applet using the appletviewer tool, as follows (see Figure 8.1):

```
appletviewer Edit.htm
```

FIGURE 8.1.

The Edit applet viewed by appletviewer.

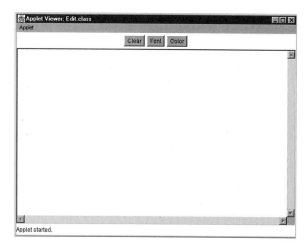

Extracting the Contents of a JAR File

The x option of the jar tool lets you extract the file's contents. You can use it to re-create the .class files that you deleted:

```
C:\jdk1.2\ju\ch08>jar xvf edit.jar
 extracted: META-INF\MANIFEST.MF
 extracted: ColorDialog$ButtonHandler.class
 extracted: ColorDialog$WindowEventHandler.class
 extracted: ColorDialog.class
 extracted: Edit$ButtonHandler.class
 extracted: Edit$ColorSelectHandler.class
 extracted: Edit$FontSelectHandler.class
 extracted: Edit.class
 extracted: FontDialog$ButtonHandler.class
 extracted: FontDialog$WindowEventHandler.class
 extracted: FontDialog.class
 extracted: MyList.class
```

You can list your directory to see exactly what came back:

```
C:\jdk1.2\ju\ch08>dir

 Volume in drive C has no label
 Volume Serial Number is 2747-15D2
 Directory of C:\jdk1.2beta3\ju\ch08

 .               <DIR>        04-22-98 11:27a .
 ..              <DIR>        04-22-98 11:27a ..
 COLORD~1 JAV       2,448     02-08-98  9:20a ColorDialog.java
 EDIT~1   JAV       1,968     02-08-98 10:50a Edit.java
 FONTDI~1 JAV       3,667     02-08-98 10:42a FontDialog.java
 MYLIST~1 JAV         310     02-08-98  9:19a MyList.java
 META-INF        <DIR>        04-22-98 12:05p META-INF
 EDIT~1   CLA       1,914     04-22-98 12:05p Edit.class
 EDIT     HTM         159     04-22-98 11:48a Edit.htm
 COLORD~1 CLA       1,324     04-22-98 12:05p
➡ColorDialog$ButtonHandler.class
 COLORD~2 CLA         615     04-22-98 12:05p
➡ColorDialog$WindowEventHandler.class

 COLORD~3 CLA       2,908     04-22-98 12:05p ColorDialog.class
 EDIT$B~1 CLA       1,545     04-22-98 12:05p Edit$ButtonHandler.class
 EDIT$C~1 CLA       1,214     04-22-98 12:05p Edit$ColorSelectHandler.class
 EDIT$F~1 CLA       1,016     04-22-98 12:05p Edit$FontSelectHandler.class
 FONTDI~1 CLA       1,101     04-22-98 12:05p FontDialog$ButtonHandler.class
 FONTDI~2 CLA         609     04-22-98 12:05p
➡FontDialog$WindowEventHandler.class
 MYLIST~1 CLA         431     04-22-98 12:05p MyList.class
```

```
EDIT     JAR       11,527  04-22-98 11:36a edit.jar
FONTDI~3 CLA        3,880  04-22-98 12:05p FontDialog.class
        17 file(s)          36,636 bytes
         3 dir(s)      194,150,400 bytes free
```

Note that the META-INF directory is created. This directory contains a single manifest file named MANIFEST.MF. The manifest file identifies each file in the JAR file, the digest algorithm used to calculate a digest of the file, and the file's digest value. Listing 8.2 provides an example manifest file.

LISTING 8.2. AN EXAMPLE MANIFEST FILE.

```
Manifest-Version: 1.0
Created-By: Manifest JDK 1.2beta3

Name: ColorDialog$ButtonHandler.class
SHA-Digest: w1HOCEWkiOt+ui0IpayJLHasnHQ=

Name: ColorDialog$WindowEventHandler.class
SHA-Digest: G2HtKJluU0aiT/7tB6YqXaBQea0=

Name: ColorDialog.class
SHA-Digest: z4qdRsSiiLgDBUAjsAmx02TQzuw=

Name: Edit$ButtonHandler.class
SHA-Digest: Huerm63Agb8edXJJsafVA623MPs=

Name: Edit$ColorSelectHandler.class
SHA-Digest: IZTp5mlHM8ar5zMHQwzDcN+tkuo=

Name: Edit$FontSelectHandler.class
SHA-Digest: Ez6+lfCLTC6UvJW+0QIZo6uBkMc=

Name: Edit.class
SHA-Digest: v2/cnmrXXlH1LsOx4kcAB4BN0jE=

Name: FontDialog$ButtonHandler.class
SHA-Digest: FrMHhW4wSQeywVXTQ7CjOnIi+yk=

Name: FontDialog$WindowEventHandler.class
SHA-Digest: Z4mmLOnJcgS2+XA1CWx1ImYkYV8=

Name: FontDialog.class
SHA-Digest: urXQWWNi9bd842Wq3lMHFZKO+tQ=

Name: MyList.class
SHA-Digest: yH75rAxTz5Lbesv/g0Tqll5QKdU=
```

Delete the .class files and the META-INF directory before going on to the next section.

Signing Applets

The next thing that we're going to do is to digitally sign the `edit.jar` file. Chapter 3, "The Extended Java Security Model," provides an introduction to digital signatures, but we'll briefly review their use here.

A *digital signature* is a value that is computed from an object, such as an applet file, using a secret key. It indicates that the person who holds the secret key has verified that the contents of the object are correct and authentic.

Digital signatures often use public-key encryption algorithms—a private key is used for encryption, and a public key is used for decryption. To sign an object, the signer first calculates a digest of the object using a message digest algorithm, such as MD5. The digest serves as a fingerprint for the object. The digest is then encrypted using the private key of a public/private key pair to produce the object's digital signature.

The signature of a signed object is verified by decrypting the signature using the signer's public key. This produces a digest value. The object's digest is then calculated and compared to the decrypted digest value. If the calculated digest value and the decrypted digest values match, the signature is verified. Refer to Figure 3.14 in Chapter 3 for an illustration of this process.

Creating a Keystore

Before we can sign an applet, we need to create a public/private key pair and make it available to the `jarsigner` tool. We'll use the `keytool` to create a keystore with the public/private key pair. A *keystore* is a database of keys and digital certificates that authenticate the values of the public keys. You'll learn to use the `keytool` to work with digital certificates later in this chapter in the section "Working with Certificates."

> **NOTE**
>
> The `keytool` and `jarsigner` tools of JDK 1.2 replace the `javakey` tool of JDK 1.1.

Keystore entries are associated with the identities of the subjects (people, organizations, software processes, and so on) to which a particular key belongs. These identities are referenced using aliases. For example, you might use the alias "John" to refer to John Doe's public key, "abc" to refer to the public key of the ABC Corporation, or "Me" to your own public and private keys. Aliases are case-insensitive. This means that "me", "Me", and "ME" are equivalent.

8

APPLET SECURITY

You generate a public/private key pair for yourself using the -genkey command of keytool. For example, the following command generates a key pair for the alias "Me" in the keystore "MyStore":

```
keytool -genkey -alias "Me" -keystore "MyStore"
```

The keytool then prompts you to enter a password for the keystore:

```
Enter keystore password:  MyPassword
```

Enter a password, and then keytool prompts you for the following additional information:

```
What is your first and last name?
  [Unknown]:  Jamie Jaworski
What is the name of your organizational unit?
  [Unknown]:  Software Development
What is the name of your organization?
  [Unknown]:  Jaworski & Associates
What is the name of your City or Locality?
  [Unknown]:  San Diego
What is the name of your State or Province?
  [Unknown]:  California
What is the two-letter country code for this unit?
  [Unknown]:  US
Is <CN=Jamie Jaworski, OU=Just Me, O=Jaworski & Associates, L=San Diego,
S=California, C=US> correct?
  [no]:  yes
```

Finally, you are prompted to enter a password for your private key:

```
Enter key password for <Me>
        (RETURN if same as keystore password):
```

I showed how I filled in this information. You would enter your own information, of course. This information is used to associate an X.500 *distinguished name* with the alias. The distinguished name is used as part of X.509 digital certificates. The following distinguished name subparts are supported:

- Common Name (CN)—A person's name, such as Jamie Jaworski.
- Organizational Unit (OU)—A part of an organization, such as software development.
- Organization (O)—Company, institution, or other organization, such as Jaworski & Associates.
- Locality name (L)—City.
- State name (S).

- Country (C)—Two-letter country code.

This information can be supplied directly with the `-dname` option.

The last password is separate from the keystore password and is used to access the private key of the public key pair. This password can be specified directly using the `-keypass` option. If the password is not specified, the keystore password is used. The `-keypasswd` command is used to change this password.

The `-keyalg` option may be used to specify the algorithm used to generate the key pair.

NOTE

If the `-keystore` option is not supplied, `keytool` generates a keystore named `.keystore` that is stored in the directory specified by the `user.home` system property.

Currently, only the National Institute of Standards and Technology (NIST) Digital Signature Standard (DSA) key pair-generation algorithm is supported.

The `-genkey` command automatically generates a self-signed X.509 digital certificate for the key pair. The `-sigalg` option may be used to specify a signature algorithm. Currently, only DSA is supported. The `-validity` option may be used to specify the number of days for which the certificate associated with the key pair is valid. If this option is not used, the certificate is valid for 90 days.

8

APPLET SECURITY

NOTE

Make sure that you create a keystore of your own before going on to the next section.

Signing a JAR File

Now that you have created a keystore with your public and private keys, you can use the `jarsigner` tool and your private key to sign a JAR file. The `jarsigner` tool is used for both signature generation and signature verification. We'll cover signature generation in this section and signature verification in the next section.

To sign a JAR file, you enter a `jarsigner` command in the following form:

```
jarsigner -keystore keystore -storepass storePassword -keypass keyPassword
JARFileName alias
```

The parameters to this command are as follows:

- *keystore*—The name of the keystore to use, such as MyStore.
- *storePassword*—The keystore password, such as MyPassword.
- *keyPassword*—The private key password, such as MyPassword.
- *JARFileName*—The name of the JAR file to be signed, such as `edit.jar`.
- *alias*—The alias of the signer, such as Me.

Additional command parameters are available for the `jarsigner` command. Use `jarsigner -help` to obtain a description of these parameters.

I used the following command to sign the `edit.jar` file:

```
jarsigner -keystore MyStore -storepass MyPassword -keypass MyPassword
edit.jar Me
```

If the `-keystore` option is not specified, the default (`.keystore`) keystore is used.

Signing a JAR file causes the file to be updated as follows:

- A signature (`.SF`) file is added to the META-INF directory. The name of this signature file is the first eight characters of the alias used to sign the file. This name may be changed using the `-sigFile` option.
- A signature block file (`.DSA`) file is added to the META-INF directory. The name of the signature block file is generated in the same way as the signature file.

The signature file identifies each file in the JAR file, the digest algorithm used in the signing process, and a digest value. The digest value is the digest computed from the file's entry in the manifest file. Listing 8.3 provides an example signature file.

LISTING 8.3. AN EXAMPLE SIGNATURE FILE.

```
Signature-Version: 1.0
SHA1-Digest-Manifest: Tskq+b1DaL4RUZxFfDGGyNkTTSY=
Created-By: SignatureFile JDK 1.2beta3

Name: ColorDialog$ButtonHandler.class
SHA1-Digest: 81+YE73yybQfZLZVz4dZxERJNio=

Name: Edit$FontSelectHandler.class
SHA1-Digest: y1/rJWyOTC+joWOnJM6ZL9fYlnI=
```

```
Name: FontDialog$ButtonHandler.class
SHA1-Digest: IzZObN+lcU8F1UN0SE8M7PR9tP8=

Name: FontDialog$WindowEventHandler.class
SHA1-Digest: O2L7SWIGmBGqVcFXz6j/dSKg2pw=

Name: MyList.class
SHA1-Digest: IMKvGp/HqIdw/6jxjUd+CtLMAmA=

Name: Edit.class
SHA1-Digest: N312zs8HBLOmLkcIA5MAs/xXC4A=

Name: FontDialog.class
SHA1-Digest: AGiOIM3EjO0RxwY/NRVkUrn8RuM=

Name: ColorDialog$WindowEventHandler.class
SHA1-Digest: yGf1SzyPh/AKEozcQK60du0Auig=

Name: ColorDialog.class
SHA1-Digest: hOJAXgIblOMG0tREBAcmH4Aqe6s=

Name: Edit$ColorSelectHandler.class
SHA1-Digest: 5iY/2gP4j64FTrrlPm1KEWEW/Q8=

Name: Edit$ButtonHandler.class
SHA1-Digest: 1jKW3bcg9iz9j36ozAtq1WdpoDQ=
```

The signature block file contains the signature of the signature file and a certificate that authenticates the public key corresponding to the private key used in the signature generation. The signature block file is a binary file.

NOTE

By default, `jarsigner` uses the SHA-1 digest and DSA signature algorithms to sign and verify JAR files. Other digest and signature algorithms may be installed and used instead of SHA-1 and DSA.

NOTE

A JAR file may have multiple signers. Each signer signs the JAR file in succession.

Verifying the Signature of a JAR File

The `jarsigner` tool is also used to verify the signature of a signed JAR file. This is accomplished using the `-verify` option. The following `jarsigner` command form is used:

```
jarsigner -verify JARFileName
```

For example, the following command verifies the signature of `edit.jar`:

```
jarsigner -verify edit.jar
```

If the signature is valid, `jarsigner` produces the following output:

```
jar verified.
```

If the signature is invalid, `jarsigner` responds with an exception identifying why the failure occurred:

```
jarsigner: java.util.zip.ZipException: invalid entry size (expected 900
but got 876 bytes)
```

The `jarsigner` signature verification process is optimized for performance. This process consists of the following:

1. Verifying that the signature block (`.DSA`) file contains a valid signature for the signature (`.SF`) file.

2. Verifying that the signature file entries are valid digests for each of the corresponding manifest (`MANIFEST.MF`) file entries.

3. Verifying that the digests in the `MANIFEST.MF` file are valid for each of the files in the JAR file.

Any error encountered in the verification process results in the generation of a security exception.

Specifying an Applet Security Policy

The signing of JAR files provides the basis for developing an applet security policy. JAR files that are received from trusted sources whose signatures can be verified may be given greater privileges than JAR files that are unsigned or from an untrusted source. Chapter 3 covers the specification of a custom security policy. In this section, we'll show how to develop an applet security policy based on digital signatures.

Listing 3.1 in Chapter 3 shows the ReadFileApplet, which generates a security exception as the result of the applet trying to read a user's AUTOEXEC.BAT file. In this section, we'll develop a trusted version of ReadFileApplet that will successfully read your AUTOEXEC.BAT file without generating a security exception.

Copy the ReadFileApplet.java and ReadFileApplet.htm files from your ch03 directory to your ch08 directory, and compile ReadFileApplet.java. This produces two class files: ReadFileApplet.class and ReadFileApplet$ButtonHandler.class. Create a ReadFileApplet.jar file using the following command:

```
jar cf ReadFileApplet.jar ReadFile*.class
```

Now edit the ReadFileApplet.htm file to include the ReadFileApplet.jar file in an ARCHIVE attribute, as shown in Listing 8.4.

LISTING 8.4. AN UPDATED ReadFileApplet.htm.

```
<HTML>
<HEAD>
<TITLE>An Applet that reads local files</TITLE>
</HEAD>
<BODY>
<H1>An Applet that reads local files.</H1>
<APPLET CODE="ReadFileApplet.class" ARCHIVE="ReadFileApplet.jar"
 HEIGHT=300 WIDTH=600>
<PARAM NAME="fileName" VALUE="C:\AUTOEXEC.BAT">
Text displayed by browsers that are not Java-enabled.
</APPLET>
</BODY>
</HTML>
```

> **NOTE**
>
> You may need to create an AUTOEXEC.BAT file for use in the example, if you don't have one already.

Now delete the ReadFileApplet.class and ReadFileApplet$ButtonHandler.class files and run the ReadFileApplet in appletviewer as follows:

```
appletviewer ReadFileApplet.htm
```

When you click the Read Local File button, appletviewer will generate a security exception, as shown in Figure 8.2.

FIGURE 8.2.

*Appletviewer gen-
erates a security
exception when
trying to run an
untrusted applet.*

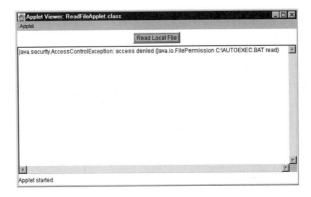

Now we'll sign the applet and create a security policy that will trust the applet to read
your AUTOEXEC.BAT file. Sign the applet using the keystore that you generated earlier in
this chapter:

```
jarsigner -keystore MyStore -storepass MyPassword -keypass MyPassword
ReadFileApplet.jar Me
```

Substitute your keystore, passwords, and alias, as necessary.

Next, create the policy file shown in Listing 8.5 and save it as my.policy in your ch08
directory. This policy specifies that the keystore "MyStore" should be used for signature
verification. It grants any code signed by "Me" permission to read the AUTOEXEC.BAT file.
Substitute your keystore and alias for "MyStore" and "Me". For more information on
security policy specification, refer to Chapter 3.

Now use appletviewer to run ReadFileApplet with the new policy:

```
appletviewer -J-Djava.policy=my.policy ReadFileApplet.htm
```

The -J option passes the -D option to the java interpreter. The -D option sets the
java.policy property to my.policy.

Now click the Read Local File button. The appletviewer displays your AUTOEXEC.BAT
file, as shown in Figure 8.3.

Figure 8.3.

The `ReadFileApplet` *is trusted to read your* `AUTOEXEC.BAT` *file.*

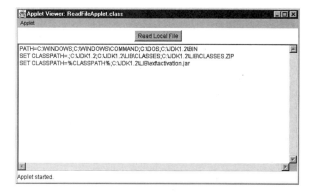

Working with Certificates

In the previous example, you worked with JAR files that you signed yourself. You'll also create JAR files that you'll distribute to your users. As a user, you'll use JAR files signed by other trusted developers. In this section, you'll learn how to export digital certificates so that they can be used by others to verify the signatures of your JAR files. You'll also learn how to import the digital certificates of others.

A digital certificate is an object (file or message) signed by a certification authority that certifies the value of an person's public key. The X.509 certificates of the International Standards Organization are a popular digital certificate format. These are the certificates supported by the `keytool`.

8

APPLET SECURITY

> **Note**
>
> Digital certificates are introduced in Chapter 3.

The `keytool` allows you to import certificates that are created and signed by others. These certificates verify the public keys of other individuals. The `keytool` also allows you to export certificates that can be imported by others. We'll cover certificate exporting in the next section, and certificate importing in the section after that.

Exporting Your Certificates

When you generate your public/private key pair, `keytool` generates a self-signed certificate for your public key. You can export this certificate using the `-export` command. This command is of the following form:

```
keytool -export -keystore keystore -alias alias -file fileName
```

You must substitute appropriate values for `keystore`, `alias`, and `fileName`.

For example, the following exports my self-signed certificate to the file `MyCert`:

```
keytool -export -keystore MyStore -alias Me -file MyCert
```

The command prompts me for a password and then tells me the status of the export:

```
Enter keystore password:  MyPassword
Certificate stored in file <MyCert>
```

I can now give this certificate to others so that they can import it into their keystores.

The `-csr` command is used to create a *certificate signing request (CSR)*. The output of this command is a file containing certificate information that is to be provided by a certification authority. The certification authority signs a certificate with its private key that attests to the validity of your public key. A certification authority is a party that is trusted by the public to verify the public keys of others. You can import the certificate received from the certification authority, and you can also distribute it to others. The format of the `-csr` command is as follows:

```
keytool -csr -keystore keystore -alias alias -file fileName
```

For example, the following creates a CSR in the file `MyCSR`:

```
keytool -export -keystore MyStore -alias Me -file MyCSR
```

The command prompts you for a keystore password.

Importing the Certificates of Others

In order to use the certificates of others, you must import them into your keystore as follows:

```
keytool -import -keystore keystore -alias alias -file fileName
```

The file specified by `fileName` contains the certificate to be imported.

The following command imports the certificate contained in the `MyCert` file into the `OtherStore` keystore, giving it the alias `Jamie`:

```
keytool -import -keystore OtherStore -alias Jamie -file MyCert
```

The command prompts you for a password:

```
Enter keystore password:  NewPassword
```

Then it generates the following type of output:

```
Owner: CN=Jamie Jaworski, OU=Software Development, O=Jaworski &
Associates, L=San Diego, S=California, C=US
Issuer: CN=Jamie Jaworski, OU=Software Development, O=Jaworski &
Associates, L=San Diego, S=California, C=US
Serial Number: 353e7a26
Valid from: Wed Apr 22 16:15:50 PDT 1998 until: Tue Jul 21 16:15:50 PDT
➡1998
Certificate Fingerprints:
        MD5:  70:BE:34:E8:D0:5A:A1:87:74:23:D4:81:0F:EC:AD:95
        SHA1: D9:61:50:41:8C:47:75:35:D8:3A:C2:72:B1:44:A1:64:18:85:63:AB
Trust this certificate? [no]:
```

Finally, `keytool` asks you whether or not to trust the certificate. You should only trust the certificates of those individuals that you trust.

Other `keytool` Commands

The `-list` command lists the contents of the keystore or of a single entry.

For example, the following lists all entries in `MyStore`:

```
keytool -list -keystore MyStore
Enter keystore password:  MyPassword

Your keystore contains 1 entry:

me, Wed Apr 22 16:15:59 PDT 1998, keyEntry,
Certificate MD5 Fingerprint:
➡70:BE:34:E8:D0:5A:A1:87:74:23:D4:81:0F:EC:AD:95
```

To list a single entry, use the `-alias` option.

The `-delete` command deletes an alias from a keystore. It is used as follows:

```
keytool -delete -keystore keystore -alias alias
```

The `-printcert` command displays a certificate that is stored in a file. The command

```
keytool -printcert -file MyCert
```

generates the following output:

```
Owner: CN=Jamie Jaworski, OU=Software Development, O=Jaworski &
       ➡Associates, L=San Diego, S=California, C=US
Issuer: CN=Jamie Jaworski, OU=Software Development, O=Jaworski &
        ➡Associates, L=San Diego, S=California, C=US
```

```
Serial Number: 353e7a26
Valid from: Wed Apr 22 16:15:50 PDT 1998 until: Tue Jul 21 16:15:50 PDT
                                                            ➥1998
Certificate Fingerprints:
      MD5:  70:BE:34:E8:D0:5A:A1:87:74:23:D4:81:0F:EC:AD:95
      SHA1: D9:61:50:41:8C:47:75:35:D8:3A:C2:72:B1:44:A1:64:18:85:63:AB
```

Finally, the -help command can be used to obtain a list of all the commands supported by keytool. The command

keytool -help

generates the following output:

```
KeyTool usage:

-csr         [-v] [-alias <alias>] [-sigalg <sigalg>]
             [-file <csr_file>] [-keypass <keypass>]
             [-keystore <keystore>] [-storepass <storepass>]

-delete      [-v] -alias <alias>
             [-keystore <keystore>] [-storepass <storepass>]

-export      [-v] [-alias <alias>] [-file <cert_file>]
             [-keystore <keystore>] [-storepass <storepass>]

-genkey      [-v] [-alias <alias>] [-keyalg <keyalg>]
             [-keysize <keysize>] [-sigalg <sigalg>]
             [-dname <dname>] [-validity <valDays>]
             [-keypass <keypass>] [-keystore <keystore>]
             [-storepass <storepass>]

-help

-import      [-v] [-noprompt] [-alias <alias>]
             [-file <cert_file>] [-keypass <keypass>]
             [-keystore <keystore>] [-storepass <storepass>]

-keyclone    [-v] [-alias <alias>] -dest <dest_alias>
             [-keypass <keypass>] [-new <new_keypass>]
             [-keystore <keystore>] [-storepass <storepass>]

-keypasswd   [-v] [-alias <alias>]
             [-keypass <old_keypass>] [-new <new_keypass>]
             [-keystore <keystore>] [-storepass <storepass>]
```

```
[-list]       [-v ¦ -rfc] [-alias <alias>]
              [-keystore <keystore>] [-storepass <storepass>]

-printcert    [-v] [-file <cert_file>]

-selfcert     [-v] [-alias <alias>] [-sigalg <sigalg>]
              [-dname <dname>] [-validity <valDays>]
              [-keypass <keypass>] [-keystore <keystore>]
              [-storepass <storepass>]

-storepasswd  [-v] [-new <new_storepass>]
              [-keystore <keystore>] [-storepass <storepass>]
```

The JDK 1.2 documentation describes all the commands and options of keytool.

The `java.security` Packages

The security tools covered in this chapter are implemented in terms of the Security API, which consists of the following five packages:

- `java.security`
- `java.security.acl`
- `java.security.cert`
- `java.security.interfaces`
- `java.security.spec`

The java.security package is the core Security API package. It provides the classes and interfaces that support encryption and the computation of message digests and digital signatures. This package also provides key generation and management support, and the classes used in security policy implementation. The java.security.acl package consists of interfaces that can be used to implement access control policies. The java. security.cert package provides support for X.509 certificates. The java.security.interfaces package defines interfaces that are used to access the National Institute of Standards and Technology (NIST) Digital Signature Algorithm. The java.security.spec package provides algorithm-independent and algorithm-dependent classes that are used for keys and other algorithm parameters. The java.security.cert and java.security.spec packages are new to JDK 1.2.

8

APPLET SECURITY

Summary

In this chapter, you learned how to develop applets that extend the bounds of the applet sandbox and use new JDK 1.2 security features. You learned how to package your applets as Java Archive (JAR) files and how to digitally sign these files. You learned how to configure your runtime environment to use trusted applets. You also learned about digital certificates and how they are used to support applet security. You were introduced to the JDK 1.2 security tools and learned about the JDK 1.2 Security API. In the next chapter, you'll learn how to write window applications in Java.

Application Programming

PART
III

IN THIS PART

Creating Window Applications

CHAPTER 9

In Part II, "Applet Programming," you learned to write applets. While applets are Java's claim to fame, they are only one aspect of Java's software development capabilities. In this chapter, you'll learn to develop full-blown window applications using Java. You'll learn about the differences between applications and applets, how to open and organize windows, and how to work with menus and dialog boxes. You'll also learn how to use the new Accessibility API of JDK 1.2. When you have finished this chapter, you will know how to write platform-independent window programs using Java.

Differences Between Applications and Applets

Applets are Java programs that execute within the context of a Web page. They interact with the user while his Web page is active and stop their execution when his Web page is no longer active. Applets are valuable because they are simple to use. A user only needs to open an applet's Web page to download and execute an applet.

Most of the programs that we are accustomed to using are standalone or networked application programs. A *standalone application* is a program that executes using the resources of a single computer. A *networked application* is an application that uses resources that are available over a network. A *distributed application* is an application that consists of objects that execute across multiple computers. You'll learn how to develop networked applications in Part VIII, "Network Programming," and distributed applications in Part IX, "Developing Distributed Applications."

Standalone applications consist of *window applications* and *console applications*. Window applications are programs that make use of a windowing system, such as those supported by Microsoft Windows, the Macintosh OS, Motif, and OS/2. Console programs are character-based programs, such as those supported by DOS and UNIX shells.

Window applications are introduced in this chapter, and console applications are covered in the following chapter. However, you'll see examples of both types of applications throughout the remainder of this book. Window applications have an advantage over applets in that they are given more security privileges by default. Among other things, they are allowed to read and write to the local file system, establish network connections to multiple hosts, and launch other programs. Applets have an advantage over applications in their ease of installation and use. The great thing about both applications and applets is that they share the same GUI controls. This means that all the GUI programming skills that you learned for applets carry over to applications.

Because window applications execute separately from a Web page, they must perform additional functions like opening and closing windows, setting up and implementing menu bars, and working with dialog boxes. These are the skills that you'll learn in this chapter.

> **NOTE**
>
> The JDK 1.2 security model allows applications to be restricted in their behavior and applets to be given greater privileges. However, the model defaults to giving applications more privileges than applets. Refer to Chapter 3, "The Extended Java Security Model."

Designing Window Programs

The design of most window programs usually involves two basic steps: laying out the program's graphical user interface, and providing the functionality that implements the interface.

The first step addresses one of the most important features of window programs—their look and feel. Window programs are preferred to console programs when their look and feel are interesting, innovative, and help the user to accomplish a particular purpose.

A program's look consists of all those characteristics that determine its appearance, such as window size, layout, background and foreground colors, menus, and GUI controls. A program's feel is determined by the availability of easy-to-use GUI controls and the contribution of these controls to the program's ultimate intended use. It is the result of the designer's selection and implementation of GUI controls that enhance a program's capability to satisfy user expectations.

The window's GUI design begins by creating an application window, using the Frame class, and determining the basic characteristics of the window, such as its size, title, background and foreground colors, and general layout. Next, a menu bar is added to the window and the program's menus and menu items are added to the menu bar. The GUI controls that are to be used in the window are determined, designed, and attached to the window's panels and frame.

At this point, you know what your program will look like and you can concentrate on what it will do. The first step in bringing your program's user interface to life is to add the event-handling software required to respond to events that are generated through user interaction. The event-handling software will not immediately implement all user actions, but it should respond to them and provide hooks for the eventual implementation of all user interface actions. The event-handling software is then fleshed out to provide all the functionality required of the application program. The program's design and implementation reaches an *Alpha stage* when all required user-interface functions have been implemented.

The next stage of program development is to refine and test the program to make it more responsive to its intended purpose. A series of *Beta versions* of the program are developed that implement user feedback and fix any identified errors or deficiencies. Finally, the program is refined to handle unusual user inputs and to process errors and exceptions.

Figure 9.1 provides an overview of the process of designing and implementing window programs.

FIGURE 9.1.

The process for window design and implementation.

Layout the program's graphical user interface.
Create a frame and specify its characteristics.
Determine the frame's layout.
Add a menu bar.
Add panels and GUI components.

Add the functionality that implements the interface.
Add event handling software.
Provide hooks for handling all user interface actions.
Flesh out event handling software.
Refine and test software functions.
Handle errors and exceptions.
Respond to user feedback.

Window Classes

The `Window` class provides an encapsulation of a generic `Window` object. It is subclassed by `Frame` and `Dialog` to provide the capabilities needed to support application main windows and dialog box support.

The `Window` class contains a single constructor that creates a window that has a frame window as its parent. The parent frame window is necessary because only objects of the `Frame` class or its subclasses contain the functionality needed to implement an independent application window.

The `Window` class implements important methods that are used by its `Frame` and `Dialog` subclasses. The `pack()` method is used to arrange the components contained in the window according to the window layout style. The `show()` method is used to display a window. Windows are hidden (invisible) by default, and are only displayed as a result of invoking their `show()` method. The `toFront()` and `toBack()`methods are used to position windows relative to their frame window. The `dispose()`method is used to release the resources associated with a window and delete the `Window` object. The `getWarningString()` method is used to retrieve the warning message associated with untrusted windows. Warning messages are associated with windows that are created by applets.

A `Window` object does not have a border or a menubar when it is created. In this state, it may be used to implement a pop-up window. The default layout for a `Window` object is `BorderLayout`.

Frame

The `Frame` class is used to provide the main window of an application. It is a subclass of `Window` that supports the capabilities to specify a window icon, cursor, menu bar, and title. Because it implements the `MenuContainer` interface, it is capable of working with `MenuBar` objects. You'll learn about menus later in this chapter in the section "Constructing Menus."

The `Frame` class defines several constants that are used to specify different types of cursors to be used within the frame. As of JDK 1.1, a separate `Cursor` class is available for working with cursors.

`Frame` provides two constructors: a default parameterless constructor that creates an untitled frame window, and a constructor that accepts a `String` argument to be used as the frame window's title. The second constructor is typically used.

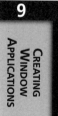

Frame extends the set of access methods that it inherits from Window by adding methods to get and set the window title, icon image, and menu bar. Methods for removing the menu bar and specifying whether the window is resizable are also provided.

Dialog

The Dialog class is a subclass of the Window class that is used to implement dialog box windows. A dialog box is a window that takes input from the user. The Dialog class allows dialog boxes to be constructed that are modal. *Modal* dialog boxes must be closed before control returns to the window that launched them. The Dialog class also provides the capability to construct *non-modal* dialog boxes that do not need to be closed before other program windows can be accessed.

The Dialog class provides four constructors. These constructors allow the Window object containing the dialog box to be specified, as well as the modal flag and the dialog box's title.

The Dialog class provides only a handful of access methods. These methods are used to get and set the dialog box's title, determine whether it is modal, and get and set its resizable properties.

FileDialog

The FileDialog class is used to construct dialog boxes that support the selection of files for input and output operations. It is a subset of the Dialog class and provides three constructors. These constructors take as arguments the Frame window that contains the dialog box, the title to be used at the top of the dialog box, and a mode parameter that can be set to the LOAD or SAVE constants defined by FileDialog.

FileDialog provides methods that are used to access the directory and filename of the user-selected file and to specify an object that implements the FileNameFilter interface.

Opening and Closing Windows

The opening and closing of windows marks the beginning and end of any window program. The Frame class enables these fundamental window operations to be accomplished. A Frame object implements an application main window, inheriting many methods from the Window, Container, and Component classes.

To open an application window, a Frame object is created and its show() method is invoked. The show() method is inherited from the Window class. To close an application window, the window closing event must be handled. The window is disposed of by using the dispose() method of the Window class, or more commonly by invoking the System.exit() method after performing any necessary program-termination processing.

The Frame class and its ancestors provide a number of methods that control the way in which a window is displayed. The setBackground() and setForeground() methods inherited from the Component class are used to specify a window's background and foreground colors. The setFont() method, also inherited from Component, is used to specify the default font to be used with a window. The Frame class itself provides a number of methods that control a window's appearance. The setTitle() method allows a window's title to be changed, the setMenuBar() method enables a menu bar to be attached to a window, and the setResizable() method toggles whether a window can or cannot be resized. The setIconImage() method allows the window's minimized icon to be changed. This method is not supported by all Java implementations, and therefore should be avoided if cross-platform compatibility is a concern.

Hello Windows!

Now that you've covered the basic classes involved in opening and closing windows, we'll create a simple window application that illustrates the use of these classes.

Traditionally, the first program that programmers write when learning a new programming language is one that displays the text "Hello World!" to the console window. The main purpose of the program is to show you how to develop a simple program that actually produces some noticeable effect. The same rationale applies to the HelloWindows program, shown in Listing 9.1. This program shows you how to open an application window and write the text "Hello Windows!" to the window.

LISTING 9.1. THE HelloWindows PROGRAM.

```
import java.awt.*;
import java.awt.event.*;

public class HelloWindows extends Frame {
 public static void main(String args[]){
  HelloWindows app = new HelloWindows();
 }
 public HelloWindows() {
  super("Hello Windows!");
  setSize(200,200);
  addWindowListener(new HelloWindows.WindowEventHandler());
  show();
 }
 public void paint(Graphics g) {
  g.drawString("Hello Windows!",50,90);
```

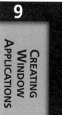

continues

LISTING 9.1. CONTINUED

```
}
class WindowEventHandler extends WindowAdapter {
  public void windowClosing(WindowEvent e){
    System.exit(0);
  }
 }
}
```

When you compile and run the program, it opens a small window in the upper-left corner of your desktop and displays the text "Hello Windows!" in the middle of the window. Figure 9.2 shows the window displayed by the HelloWindows program.

FIGURE 9.2.

The HelloWindows
program display.

Let's take a look at HelloWindows to find out what makes it work. You should notice that we import classes from the java.awt and java.awt.event packages. The Frame, Graphics, and WindowAdapter classes are the primary classes that are imported. The Frame and Graphics classes are fundamental to developing window programs. The Frame class is used to create Frame objects that implement application main windows, and the Graphics class is used to update the screen display. The WindowAdapter class is used to process user-generated window events, such as closing the window.

The HelloWindows class extends the Frame class. This is a typical approach to developing window programs. By subclassing Frame, your application class implements a main application window. You still use the same old main() method for implementing the entry point to your program. In HelloWindows, the main() method simply creates an object of class HelloWindows.

The HelloWindows constructor uses the super() constructor call statement to invoke the Frame constructor with the string "Hello Windows!". The Frame constructor creates a new application window frame with the specified text as its title. The setSize() method sets the size of the window to 200×200 pixels. The setSize() method is inherited from the Component class by way of the Container, Window, and Frame classes. The addWindowListener() method is invoked to associate window-related events with a newly created object of class WindowEventHandler. Finally, the show() method causes the window to be displayed. It is inherited from the Window class.

When the window is initially displayed or redisplayed as the result of being uncovered or brought to the foreground, the paint() method is invoked. It paints the window according to the current application state.

The paint() method used by HelloWindows overrides the paint() method inherited from the Component class. It uses the drawString() method to display the text "Hello Windows!" at the screen coordinates (50,90) within the application window.

Window coordinates are organized in the same way they are for applets, with the upper-left corner of the window being (0,0). The coordinates of the upper-right corner of the window are (*width*,0), where *width* is the horizontal width of the window in pixels. The coordinates of the lower-left corner of the window are (0,*height*), where *height* is the vertical height of the window in pixels. Finally, the coordinates of the lower-right corner of the window are (*width*,*height*).

The WindowEventHandler class subclasses the WindowAdapter class of java.awt.event to handle the event associated with the window's closing. This event occurs when the user closes the main application window using the capabilities that are provided by the native windowing system. In Microsoft Windows 95 and 98, this occurs when you click on the little "'x'" in the upper-right corner of the window.

The window-closing event is handled by invoking the exit() method of the System class to terminate the program. You might be wondering what would happen if the windowClosing() method did not handle the window closing event. Try deleting the line with the System.exit(0) method invocation, recompiling, and rerunning HelloWindows to see what happens when you try to terminate the application. Your program will no longer terminate when you attempt to close it.

Constructing Menus

Java provides a rich set of menu-related classes for creating and interacting with pull-down menus. The MenuComponent class is the superclass of all menu-related classes. It extends the Object class. The getFont()and setFont()methods are the most useful methods provided by MenuComponent. Its two direct superclasses, MenuBar and MenuItem, provide most of the methods for creating and using menus. The CheckboxMenuItem class extends the MenuItem class and supports menu items that can be checked on or off. The Menu class extends the MenuItem class and implements a collection of MenuItem objects that can be assigned to a MenuBar object. The PopupMenu class extends the Menu class to provide a menu that can be popped up inside a component to enable user menu selections. Finally, the MenuShortcut class can be used to create a keyboard shortcut to a menu item.

9

CREATING
WINDOW
APPLICATIONS

A `Frame` object can have one and only one `MenuBar` object, which is set using the `setMenuBar()` method. A *menu bar* is a collection of menus, each one represented as a separate pull-down menu. Common examples are the File, Edit, and Help pull-down menus found in many window applications. The `MenuBar` class allows a special menu to be designated as a Help menu, but this feature is not implemented in Windows 95 or NT. It is implemented by Solaris and other flavors of UNIX, however.

A `Menu` object contains one or more `MenuItem` objects, which can be a normal user-selectable `MenuItem` object, a `CheckboxMenuItem` object, or another `Menu` object. Java supports *tear-off menus*, which are menus that can be removed from a menu bar. A tear-off menu is constructed in the same manner as a regular menu—you only need to set the Boolean tear-off value in the `Menu()` constructor. Tear-off menus are not implemented within Windows 95 or NT, but they are implemented in Solaris and other UNIX derivatives.

The `MenuItem` class is the superclass of the `Menu` class. This allows a menu to be a menu item and is used to construct cascading, multilevel menus. `MenuItem` is also the superclass of the `CheckboxMenuItem` class and provides the capability to implement menu items that can be checked or unchecked. If a `MenuItem` object is constructed directly with the `MenuItem` constructor, it becomes a normal menu item that is selected from a pull-down menu.

The `MyMenu` Class

The creation and organization of menu bars, menus, and menu items into a program's menu is a straightforward but tedious process. You have to create a menu bar, create and add menus to the menu bar, add menu items to the menus, and then add the menu bar to the program's application window. This usually involves the use of a large number of constructors and access methods. To illustrate the use of the menu-related classes and to simplify the menu-creation process, you'll create two classes, `MyMenu` and `MyMenuBar`, that can be used to quickly construct menus for Java programs. These classes implement multiple levels of menus, check box menu items, and menu-disabling options. The special Help menu and tear-off menus are not implemented, however, because they are transparent to Windows 95 and NT.

NOTE

In Chapter 13, "Working with Swing Components," you'll learn about the menu classes provided by Swing. Swing's menu classes, unlike the AWT menu classes, are subclasses of the `java.awt.Component` class. The `MyMenu` and `MyMenuBar` classes can be easily tailored to support Swing.

The MyMenu class is used to construct menus using an array of objects consisting of String objects that represent menu labels, or arrays of objects that represent submenus. Menu labels can be either check box menu items or normal menu items, and can be either initially enabled or disabled (grayed out). Check box menu items can be initially checked or unchecked. The first character of the label's text string is used to indicate which type of label it is. The character conventions are as follows:

+	A check box menu item that is initially checked and enabled.
#	A check box menu item that is initially checked and disabled.
-	A check box menu item that is initially unchecked and enabled. If the label consists of just -, it indicates a separator.
=	A check box menu item that is initially unchecked and disabled.
~	A normal menu item that is initially disabled.

Any other character indicates a normal, enabled menu item. If the first character is !, it is ignored. This allows any menu item to begin with any character.

These conventions apply to menu options. Only the ~ and ! options are used with the menu's main label. Using these options greatly simplifies the process of creating a menu. The source code for the MyMenu class is shown in Listing 9.2.

LISTING 9.2. THE MyMenu CLASS.

```
package ju.ch09;

import java.awt.*;
import java.awt.event.*;

public class MyMenu extends Menu {
 public MyMenu(Object labels[],ActionListener al,ItemListener il) {
  super((String)labels[0]);
  String menuName = (String) labels[0];
  char firstMenuChar = menuName.charAt(0);
  if(firstMenuChar == '~' || firstMenuChar =='!'){
   setLabel(menuName.substring(1));
   if(firstMenuChar == '~') setEnabled(false);
  }
  for(int i=1;i<labels.length;++i) {
   if(labels[i] instanceof String){
    if("-".equals(labels[i])) addSeparator();
    else{
     String label = (String)labels[i];
     char firstChar = label.charAt(0);
     switch(firstChar){
     case '+':
```

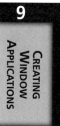

continues

LISTING 9.2. CONTINUED

```
      CheckboxMenuItem checkboxItem = new
CheckboxMenuItem(label.substring(1));
      checkboxItem.setState(true);
      add(checkboxItem);
      checkboxItem.addItemListener(il);
      break;
    case '#':
      checkboxItem = new CheckboxMenuItem(label.substring(1));
      checkboxItem.setState(true);
      checkboxItem.setEnabled(false);
      add(checkboxItem);
      checkboxItem.addItemListener(il);
      break;
    case '-':
      checkboxItem = new CheckboxMenuItem(label.substring(1));
      checkboxItem.setState(false);
      add(checkboxItem);
      checkboxItem.addItemListener(il);
      break;
    case '=':
      checkboxItem = new CheckboxMenuItem(label.substring(1));
      checkboxItem.setState(false);
      checkboxItem.setEnabled(false);
      add(checkboxItem);
      checkboxItem.addItemListener(il);
      break;
    case '~':
      MenuItem menuItem = new MenuItem(label.substring(1));
      menuItem.setEnabled(false);
      add(menuItem);
      menuItem.addActionListener(al);
      break;
    case '!':
      menuItem = new MenuItem(label.substring(1));
      add(menuItem);
      menuItem.addActionListener(al);
      break;
    default:
      menuItem = new MenuItem(label);
      add(menuItem);
      menuItem.addActionListener(al);
     }
    }
   }else{
    add(new MyMenu((Object[])labels[i],al,il));
   }
  }
 }
```

```
public MenuItem getItem(String menuItem) {
 int numItems = getItemCount();
 for(int i=0;i<numItems;++i)
  if(menuItem.equals(getItem(i).getLabel())) return getItem(i);
 return null;
 }
}
```

The MyMenu class specifies that it is in the package ju.ch09. Make sure that you place it in the ju/ch09 directory and compile it. You'll be using it in subsequent chapters.

MyMenu contains no field variables. It consists of a single constructor and the getItem()access method. The getItem() method retrieves a menu item that's contained in the menu and based on the menu item's label. It uses the getItemCount() and getItem() methods of the Menu class to retrieve the menu items contained in a menu, and the getLabel() method of the MenuItem class to match a menu item with the search string.

The MyMenu constructor constructs a menu from an array of menu labels and nested menu arrays (representing submenus). It also takes ActionListener and ItemListener objects as arguments. These objects are set up as the event handlers for the regular and check box items of the menu. For example, to construct a typical File menu, labeled File, with the New and Open menu items followed by a separator and an Exit menu item, you would use the following MyMenu constructor:

```
String fileMenuLabels[] = {"File","New","Open","-","Exit"};
// EventHandler must implement the ActionListener and ItemListener
➥interfaces.
EventHandler eh = new EventHandler();
MyMenu fileMenu = new MyMenu(fileLabelMenus,eh,eh);
```

The first object in the array must be a String object that is the main label associated with the menu. The following objects are String objects identifying the labels of the menu items contained in the menu, separators, or second-level arrays representing submenus. For example, the following creates a multilevel menu:

```
String goMenuLabels[] = {"Go","Beginning","End","Previous","Next"};
String editMenuLabels[] = {"Edit","Copy","Cut","-","Paste","-",
➥goMenuLabels};
// EventHandler must implement the ActionListener and ItemListener
➥interfaces.
EventHandler eh = new EventHandler();
MyMenu editLabel = new MyMenu(editMenuLabels,eh,eh);
```

Using the MyMenu class is much easier than constructing each of the individual menu items and adding them to a menu.

Let's step through the MyMenu constructor to see how it works. It uses the super() class constructor call statement to construct a Menu object using the first label in the labels array. This label may contain either the ~ or ! character as the first character. MyMenu() checks for these characters and readjusts the menu's label accordingly. If the first character of the menu's label is ~, MyMenu() will disable the entire menu using the setEnabled() method of the MenuItem class.

After setting up the menu's main label, MyMenu() iterates through the list of objects contained in labels. If the object is an instance of the String class and is therefore a label, MyMenu() checks the first letter of the label and processes it accordingly. If the object is not an instance of the String class, MyMenu() calls itself again, passing the object to itself as another array of objects. It then adds the resulting MyMenu object to itself using the add() method of the Menu class. This allows submenus to be processed in a recursive fashion.

MyMenu() processes the menu item labels by using a switch statement to check the first character of the label to see if it matches the +, #, -, =, ~, or ! character. If it does not match any of these characters, the label is added as a normal menu item. If the label equals -, a separator is added.

If the first character is +, an enabled and checked CheckboxMenuItem object is added to the menu. The setState() method of the CheckboxMenuItem class is used to set the state of the menu item to be checked. If the first character is #, a checked, but disabled, CheckboxMenuItem object is added. The setEnabled() method of the MenuItem class is used to disable the menu item. The cases in which the first character of the label is - or = are processed in a similar manner, except that the CheckboxMenuItem object is initially unchecked.

When the first character of the label is ~, a normal MenuItem object is added to the menu. The menu item is disabled.

The ! character is an escape character that is used to create a normal menu item beginning with any of the special characters previously mentioned. When the first character of a label is !, the actual label generated begins with the subsequent character.

The MyMenuBar Class

The MyMenuBar class uses the MyMenu class presented in the previous section to quickly create an entire menu bar. Whereas the MyMenu class uses an array of labels and submenus to create a menu, the MyMenuBar class uses an array of these arrays to create the entire menu bar. For example, the following statements will construct a menu bar with File, Edit, and Help menus, each consisting of individual menu items:

```
String menuBarLabels[] = {
 {"File","New","Open","-","~Save As","-","Exit"};
 {"Edit","Copy","Cut","-","~Paste"};
 {"Help","Index"};
};
// EventHandler must implement the ActionListener and ItemListener
➥interfaces.
EventHandler eh = new EventHandler();
MyMenuBar menuBar = new MyMenuBar(menuBarLabels,eh,eh);
```

Note that the Save As and Paste menu items are initially disabled.

The source code of the `MyMenuBar` class is shown in Listing 9.3.

LISTING 9.3. THE MyMenuBar CLASS.

```
package ju.ch09;

import java.awt.*;
import java.awt.event.*;

public class MyMenuBar extends MenuBar {
 public MyMenuBar(Object labels[][],ActionListener al,
   ItemListener il) {
  super();
  for(int i=0;i<labels.length;++i)
   add(new MyMenu(labels[i],al,il));
 }
 public MyMenu getMenu(String menuName) {
  int numMenus = getMenuCount();
  for(int i=0;i<numMenus;++i)
   if(menuName.equals(getMenu(i).getLabel())) return((MyMenu)getMenu(i));
   return null;
 }
}
```

The `MyMenuBar` constructor simply iterates through the outer array and passes the first-level elements (which are themselves `Object` arrays) to the `MyMenu` constructor. The `MyMenu` objects are then added to the `MyMenuBar` object being constructed using the `add()` method inherited from the `MenuBar` class.

The `getMenu()` method retrieves a `MyMenu` object from a `MyMenuBar` object based on the label associated with the `MyMenu` object. It uses the `getMenuCount()` and `getMenu()` methods of the `MenuBar` class to retrieve each `MyMenu` object contained in the menu bar. The `getLabel()` method of the `MenuItem` class is used to check the labels of the `MyMenu` objects against the search string.

The MenuApp Program

The MenuApp program illustrates the use of the MyMenuBar and MyMenu classes. Its source code is shown in Listing 9.4.

LISTING 9.4. THE MenuApp PROGRAM.

```java
import java.awt.*;
import java.awt.event.*;
import ju.ch09.MyMenu;
import ju.ch09.MyMenuBar;

public class MenuApp extends Frame {
 MyMenuBar menuBar;
 MenuApp.EventHandler eh = new MenuApp.EventHandler();
 public static void main(String args[]){
  MenuApp app = new MenuApp();
 }
 public MenuApp() {
  super("Menu Madness");
  setup();
  setSize(400,400);
  addWindowListener(eh);
  show();
 }
 void setup() {
  setBackground(Color.white);
  setupMenuBar();
 }
 void setupMenuBar(){
  String gotoMenu[] = {"Go To","Beginning","End","-","Line Number"};
  Object menuItems[][] = {
   {"File","New","Open","-","~Save","~Save As","-","Exit"},
   {"Edit","Copy","Cut","-","~Paste"},
   {"Search","Find","~Find Next","~Find Previous","-", gotoMenu},
   {"View","-Hex","+Line Number","+Column Number"},
   {"Help","About Menu Madness"},
  };
  menuBar = new MyMenuBar(menuItems,eh,eh);
  setMenuBar(menuBar);
 }
 class EventHandler extends WindowAdapter implements ActionListener,
   ItemListener {
  public void actionPerformed(ActionEvent e){
   String selection=e.getActionCommand();
   if("Exit".equals(selection)){
    System.exit(0);
   }else if("New".equals(selection) || "Open".equals(selection)){
    menuBar.getMenu("File").getItem("Save").setEnabled(true);
    menuBar.getMenu("File").getItem("Save As").setEnabled(true);
```

```
    }else if("Copy".equals(selection) || "Cut".equals(selection)){
     menuBar.getMenu("Edit").getItem("Paste").setEnabled(true);
    }else if("Find".equals(selection)){
     menuBar.getMenu("Search").getItem("Find Next").setEnabled(true);
     menuBar.getMenu("Search").getItem("Find Previous").setEnabled(true);
    }else if("About Menu Madness".equals(selection)){
     menuBar.getMenu("Help").setEnabled(false);
    }
   }
   public void itemStateChanged(ItemEvent e){
   }
   public void windowClosing(WindowEvent e){
    System.exit(0);
   }
  }
}
```

MenuApp shows how the MyMenuBar and MyMenu classes are used to easily create a menu bar and to support the processing of menu-related events. When the program is executed, it displays a blank opening screen and a menu bar with five pull-down menus, as shown in Figure 9.3.

FIGURE 9.3.

The MenuApp opening window.

Click on the File menu and select New, as shown in Figure 9.4. This will cause the Save and Save As menu items to become enabled. You can verify this by clicking on the File menu once again.

Click on the Edit menu and select Copy, as shown in Figure 9.5. This results in the Paste menu item becoming enabled.

Click on the Search menu and then on Go To, as shown in Figure 9.6. The Go To menu item is a second-level menu that is attached to the Search menu.

9

CREATING
WINDOW
APPLICATIONS

FIGURE 9.4.

The File menu.

FIGURE 9.5.

The Edit menu.

FIGURE 9.6.

The Search menu.

Click on the View menu and select Hex, as shown in Figure 9.7. Notice that the Hex check box becomes checked, as shown in Figure 9.8.

FIGURE 9.7.

The View menu.

FIGURE 9.8.

The View menu after checking Hex.

Click on the Help menu and select About Menu Madness, as shown in Figure 9.9. This Help menu isn't much help at all because it is programmed to disable itself, as shown in Figure 9.10.

FIGURE 9.9.

The Help menu.

9

CREATING
WINDOW
APPLICATIONS

FIGURE 9.10.

The Help menu disabled.

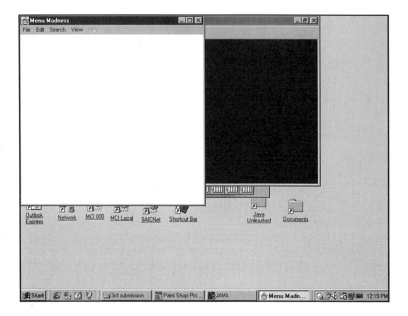

You've completed the tour of the MenuApp program. Select Exit from the File menu to terminate the program's operation.

Inside MenuApp

The MenuApp class consists of two variables, menuBar and eh. The menuBar variable is an object of class MyMenuBar that is used to hold the application's menu bar. The eh variable is assigned an object of the EventHandler class. This object is used to handle both window- and menu-related events. It is used to show how multiple event handlers can be combined into a single event handler.

The MenuApp constructor creates a 400×400 frame window with the title "Menu Madness," and invokes the setup() method to set up the background color and the menu bar. The setup() method invokes setupMenuBar() to actually perform the menu bar setup.

The setupMenuBar() method creates a gotoMenu array as the labels of a submenu that will be attached to the Search menu. The menuItems array is used to define the labels associated with the menu bar and its first-level menus. The gotoMenu array is included as an object in this array. Notice the use of the first-character conventions for disabling menu items and specifying menu items that are check boxes. The menu bar is created, assigned to the menuBar variable, and set as the menu bar for the MenuApp frame.

Creating the menu bar with the `MyMenuBar` class was a snap. However, creating the menu bar is only half of the work. You also need to write event-handling code that acts on the menu items selected by the user. The `EventHandler` inner class illustrates the use of a single event handler to handle multiple types of events. `EventHandler` extends the WindowAdapter class. This allows it to handle window events, such as the window closing event. It handles this event in the standard way, by overriding the `windowClosing()`method.

`EventHandler` also implements the `ActionListener` and `ItemListener` interfaces, and therefore the `actionPerformed()` and `itemStateChanged()` methods. The `actionPerformed()` method is used to handle the events associated with the selection of normal menu items, and the `itemStateChanged()` method is used to handle events associated with check box menu items.

The Exit menu item is handled by terminating the program's execution. The New and Open menu items cause the Save and Save As menu items to be enabled. The `getMenu()` method of `MyMenuBar` and the `getItem()` method of `MyMenu` are used to retrieve the Save and Save As `MenuItem` objects. The `setEnabled()` method of the `MenuItem` class is used to enable these menu items. Note that the Save and Save As menu items, as well as some other menu items, are not handled. Selecting these menu items does not cause any action to be performed.

The Copy and Cut menu items are processed in a similar manner as the New and Open menu items. Selecting Copy or Cut enables the Paste menu item.

The Find menu item enables the Find Next and Find Previous menu items.

The handling of the About Menu Madness menu item shows how an entire menu can be disabled.

Popup Menus

In addition to the traditional menus that are pulled down from a menu bar, Java provides support for *popup menus*, which are menus that appear when you perform a mouse action that triggers them. In Windows 95 platforms, this is the right-button click. Try right-clicking on your Windows 95 desktop. This should cause a popup menu to be displayed.

Popup menus are supported via the `PopupMenu` class, which is a subclass of the `Menu` class. This class provides two constructors—a default parameterless constructor, and a constructor that takes a `String` parameter. The `String` parameter is used as the popup menu's title. In Windows 95, the title is not displayed.

The show() method of the PopupMenu class causes a popup menu to be displayed. Its arguments are the Component object in which the menu is to be popped up and the x- and y-coordinates where the menu is to be placed (relative to the component).

Additional support for popup menus is provided in the MouseEvent and ComponentEvent classes of the java.awt.event package. The isPopupTrigger() method of MouseEvent is used to determine whether a mouse event is the native window event associated with popup menus. The getComponent() method of ComponentEvent returns the component in which a mouse event takes place.

Using Dialog Boxes

The Dialog class is used to construct a window that is displayed separately from the application menu. The window associated with a Dialog object is not allowed to contain a menu bar. It may be specified as being *modal*, meaning that it is displayed on top of the main application window until it is hidden or disposed of using the show()and dispose()methods. Most dialog boxes are used to display information to the user and get the user's response via a button click.

The MessageDialog Class

The MessageDialog class provides a custom component that implements the most common types of dialog boxes. Its source code is shown in Listing 9.5.

LISTING 9.5. THE MessageDialog CLASS.

```
package ju.ch09;

import java.awt.*;
import java.awt.event.*;

public class MessageDialog extends Dialog {
 public MessageDialog(Frame parent,String title,boolean modal,String
text[],
  String buttons[], WindowListener wh, ActionListener bh) {
  super(parent,title,modal);
  int textLines = text.length;
  int numButtons = buttons.length;
  Panel textPanel = new Panel();
  Panel buttonPanel = new Panel();
  textPanel.setLayout(new GridLayout(textLines,1));
  for(int i=0;i<textLines;++i) textPanel.add(new Label(text[i]));
  for(int i=0;i<numButtons;++i){
   Button b = new Button(buttons[i]);
   b.addActionListener(bh);
```

```
   buttonPanel.add(b);
  }
  add("North",textPanel);
  add("South",buttonPanel);
  setBackground(Color.lightGray);
  setForeground(Color.black);
  pack();
  addWindowListener(wh);
 }
}
```

The `MessageDialog` constructor uses the `parent`, `title`, `modal`, `text`, `buttons`, `wh`, and `bh` parameters. The `parent`, `title`, and `modal` parameters are passed to the `Dialog` constructor of its parent class. Two `Panel` objects are created and assigned to `textPanel` and `buttonPanel`. The `textPanel` layout is specified as a `GridLayout` object, and the `buttonPanel` layout is the default `FlowLayout` object. The `text` lines are arranged in a vertical grid in the `textPanel`. The `buttons` are laid out in a centered horizontal fashion within the `buttonPanel`. The layout for the `MessageDialog` object is `BorderLayout` by default. The `ActionListener` object passed via `bh` is set up as the event handler for each button. The `textPanel` is added to the top of the dialog box, and the `buttonPanel` is added to the bottom. The foreground and background colors are set to light gray and black. The dialog box is packed, and the `WindowListener` object passed via `wh` is set up as the event handler for the dialog box.

The `MessageApp` Program

The `MessageApp` program shows how the `MessageDialog` class can be used to implement traditional dialog box functions found in typical window programs. Its source code is shown in Listing 9.6.

LISTING 9.6. THE `MessageApp` PROGRAM.

```
import java.awt.*;
import java.awt.event.*;
import ju.ch09.MyMenu;
import ju.ch09.MyMenuBar;
import ju.ch09.MessageDialog;

public class MessageApp extends Frame {
 MyMenuBar menuBar;
 MessageDialog dialog;
 DialogHandler dh = new DialogHandler();
 public static void main(String args[]){
  MessageApp app = new MessageApp();
```

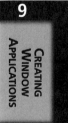

9

CREATING
WINDOW
APPLICATIONS

continues

LISTING 9.6. CONTINUED

```java
}
public MessageApp() {
 super("MessageApp");
 setup();
 setSize(400,400);
 addWindowListener(new WindowEventHandler());
 show();
}
void setup() {
 Object menuItems[][] = {
  {"File","Exit"},
  {"View","Information","Confirmation","Selection"},
 };
 MenuItemHandler mih = new MenuItemHandler();
 menuBar = new MyMenuBar(menuItems,mih,mih);
 setMenuBar(menuBar);
}
class MenuItemHandler implements ActionListener, ItemListener {
 public void actionPerformed(ActionEvent ev){
  String s=ev.getActionCommand();
  if(s=="Exit"){
  System.exit(0);
  }else if(s=="Information"){
  String text[] = {"Don't look now, but your shoelace is untied."};
  String buttons[] = {"OK"};
  dialog = new MessageDialog(MessageApp.this,"Information",false,
  text,buttons,dh,dh);
  dialog.setLocation(75,75);
  dialog.show();
  }else if(s=="Confirmation"){
  String text[] = {"Do you really want to do this?"};
  String buttons[] = {"Yes","No","Cancel"};
  dialog = new MessageDialog(MessageApp.this,"Confirmation",false,
  text,buttons,dh,dh);
  dialog.setLocation(75,75);
  dialog.show();
  }else if(s=="Selection"){
  String text[] = {"What direction do you want to go?",
   "North: cold", "South: warm", "East: humid", "West: arid"};
  String buttons[] = {"North","South","East","West"};
  dialog = new MessageDialog(MessageApp.this,"Selection",false,
  text,buttons,dh,dh);
  dialog.setLocation(75,75);
  dialog.show();
  }
 }
 public void itemStateChanged(ItemEvent e){
```

```
    }
  }
  class WindowEventHandler extends WindowAdapter {
   public void windowClosing(WindowEvent e){
    System.exit(0);
   }
  }
  class DialogHandler extends WindowAdapter implements ActionListener {
   public void windowClosing(WindowEvent e){
    MessageApp.this.show();
    dialog.dispose();
   }
   public void actionPerformed(ActionEvent e){
    MessageApp.this.show();
    dialog.dispose();
   }
  }
 }
}
```

The MessageApp opening window is shown in Figure 9.11. It supports the File and View pull-down menus.

FIGURE 9.11.

The MessageApp
opening window.

Select the Information menu item from the View pull-down menu, as shown in Figure 9.12.

A helpful Information dialog box is displayed, as shown in Figure 9.13. This type of dialog box is typically used to provide information to the user. When the dialog box is displayed, the user acknowledges the information by clicking on the OK button.

FIGURE 9.12.

Selecting Information from the View menu.

FIGURE 9.13.

The Information dialog box.

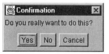

Selecting Confirmation from the View menu results in a Confirmation dialog box being displayed to the user, as shown in Figure 9.14. This type of dialog box requests confirmation from the user before attempting to perform an operation that may require the user's approval. If the user clicks the Yes button, the action is performed. If the user clicks No, the operation is not performed. If the user clicks Cancel, an entire series of actions leading up to the confirmation dialog box is aborted.

FIGURE 9.14.

The Confirmation dialog box.

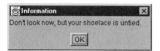

Choosing the Selection menu item from the View menu results in a multiple-choice Selection dialog box displayed to the user. The user is allowed to pick from one of several alternative paths of program execution. (See Figure 9.15.)

FIGURE 9.15.

The Selection dialog box.

The MessageApp constructor creates a 400×400 window titled "MessageApp." It uses the MyMenuBar class to construct the program's menu bar. No special processing of note is performed in the application window's construction. The dialog boxes, previously shown, are created by the program's event-handling software.

The MenuItemHandler class handles the events associated with the program's menu bar. The Exit menu item is handled by terminating the program. If the Information menu item is selected, a new MessageDialog object is created with the information shown in Figure 9.13, and the dialog box is displayed to the user using the show() method. The setLocation() method is used to move the dialog box to an offset within the main application window. The dialog box is not modal. The Confirmation and Selection menu items are handled in a similar manner. They create the dialog boxes shown in Figures 9.14 and 9.15 using the MessageDialog() constructor.

The event handling for each dialog box is performed by the methods of the DialogHandler class. These methods display the main application window and then dispose of the dialog box.

The Accessibility API

The Accessibility API provides the capability to use assistive technologies, such as screen magnifiers and speech recognition, within window applications and applets. These technologies can be used by disabled and non-disabled users to simplify their interaction with GUI components. The Accessibility API consists of the classes and interfaces of the javax.accessibility package. These classes and interfaces provide "hooks" for the incorporation of assistive technologies.

- Accessible—Defines general methods for incorporating accessibility features into an application.
- AccessibleAction—Used to define the actions that are supported by an assistive object.
- AccessibleBundle—Superclass of AccessibleState and AccessibleRole.
- AccessibleComponent—Interface implemented by visual components that support assistive technologies.
- AccessibleContext—Provides information about an assistive object.
- AccessibleHyperlink—Provides the capability to add assistive services for hyperlinks.
- AccessibleHypertext—Provides the capability to add assistive services for hypertext.

- `AccessibleResourceBundle`—Provides localized accessibility properties for a particular locale.
- `AccessibleRole`—Defines the roles for GUI components that support accessibility.
- `AccessibleSelection`—Provides methods for an assistive object to identify child objects and determine user selections.
- `AccessibleState`—Provides methods for accessing the state of GUI components that support accessibility.
- `AccessibleStateSet`—Provides methods for accessing the set of states of GUI components that support accessibility.
- `AccessibleText`—Defines methods for assistive technologies that present text to the user.
- `AccessibleValue`—An interface that is implemented by assistive objects (such as scrollbars) that yield a value within a range of values.

Unfortunately, no assistive technologies are currently available to take advantage of the hooks offered by the `javax.accessibility` package. However, it is anticipated that these technologies will be available in the near future.

Summary

In this chapter, you learned how to develop window applications using Java. You learned about the differences between applications and applets, how to open and organize windows, and how to work with menus and dialog boxes. You also learned about the Accessibility API of JDK 1.2. In the next chapter, you'll learn how to write console programs using Java.

Writing Console Applications

Before applets, the Web, Windows, and the Macintosh, most programs were text-based console applications. These programs received user keyboard entries and displayed text output to the user. Although most of the programs we use today are GUI-based, console programs still play a role in some systems and applications. For example, I still use console programs with my Linux computer, and I still run the Java compiler from a DOS shell.

In this chapter you'll learn to write console programs in Java. You'll learn to read user keyboard input, process it, and display text output to the user's console. You'll also learn about some useful classes and interfaces in the `java.lang`, `java.lang.reflect`, and `java.lang.ref` packages. When you finish this chapter, you'll be able to write your own console programs.

Differences Between Console and Window Applications

In previous chapters you learned to use Java to write applets and window applications. You learned how to open windows, display GUI components, and handle events associated with those components. You don't need to do any of these things in console programs. There are no windows or GUI components, and in simple programs, the only event that you usually need to handle is the entering of keyboard data by the user.

Console programs are not limited to user interaction. They just minimize its complexities. Advanced console programs access databases via JDBC, use TCP and UDP sockets for network communication, and interface with distributed systems using RMI, CORBA, and DCOM. The primary difference between console programs and window applications and applets is that console programs lack a graphical user interface.

Console programs have the same entry point as window applications—a `main()` method with a `String[]` argument. Like window applications, the following program template is shared by all console programs:

```
class programClass {
 public static void main(String[] args) {
   .
   .
   .
 }
}
```

Console programs start by reading the `args` array to see which parameters were passed to the program at the command line. After reading these parameters and performing any necessary initialization, the program then responds to input entered from the keyboard or received from a file, socket, remote method invocation, or other input source.

Keyboard Input and Console Output

The most basic I/O performed by a console program is reading data entered at the user's keyboard and writing data to the user's console. We'll cover keyboard input and console output in this chapter. Later chapters of this book will show how to perform I/O via files, TCP/IP socket programming, JDBC, remote method invocation, CORBA, and DCOM.

The System class of the java.lang package provides all that you need for your programs to communicate with the user via the keyboard and console. The System.in variable provides access to the standard input stream, which defaults to the keyboard. The System.out variable provides access to the standard output stream, which is the console by default. The System.err variable provides access to the standard error stream, which is also usually the user's console. These three variables refer to stream objects of the java.io package. Each of these streams can be redirected to other inputs and outputs, such as file I/O and socket I/O.

> **NOTE**
>
> Chapter 17, "Input/Output Streams," covers stream-based input and output in great detail. This chapter provides you with just enough information on stream I/O to allow you to write console programs.

The System.in variable refers to an object of the InputStream class. This class provides basic methods for reading data, but is usually used to construct more powerful input classes, such as the BufferedReader class. The BufferedReader class provides the readLine() method for reading an entire line at a time from a stream. It returns the value null if the end of a stream has been encountered.

The following lines of code illustrate the use of these classes and methods:

```
BufferedReader keyboardInput;
keyboardInput = new BufferedReader(new InputStreamReader(System.in));
String newLine;
while(((newLine = keyboardInput.readLine())!=null)) {
// Process each input line
}
```

The first line declares the `keyboardInput` variable to be of the `BufferedReader` class. The second line uses the `InputStream` object referenced by `System.in` to construct a `InputStreamReader` object. The `InputStreamReader` object is then used to construct an object of the `BufferedReader` class. This object is assigned to the `keyboardInput` variable.

The `while` statement reads a line of input at a time by invoking the `readLine()` method of the `BufferedReader` object assigned to the `keyboardInput` variable. It then assigns this input (as a `String` object) to the `newLine` variable. The `while` statement checks to see if the input is `null` to determine whether the end of the input stream was encountered. If not, it processes the new line within the body of the `while` loop. In practice, `readLine()` will not return a `null` value when reading from the keyboard. Instead, it blocks (waits) until the user enters a line of input. However, it is good practice to test for end of input just in case the user redirects a file as input in place of the keyboard.

The `System.out` and `System.err` variables refer to objects of the `PrintStream` class that are directed to the user's console. The `PrintStream` class provides the `print()` and `println()` methods for printing data to an output stream.

BlackJackApp

In this section you'll learn to write a console program that illustrates keyboard input and console output. The `BlackJackApp` program is a simplified, character-based version of the popular blackjack card game. This example, while entertaining, also illustrates the basics of console application programming. The source code for this program is shown in Listing 10.1.

LISTING 10.1. THE SOURCE CODE OF THE BlackJackApp PROGRAM.

```
// BlackJackApp.java
// Import all the Java API classes needed by this program.
import java.lang.System;
import java.lang.Integer;
import java.lang.NumberFormatException;
import java.io.InputStreamReader;
import java.io.BufferedReader;
import java.io.IOException;
import java.util.Random;
class BlackJackApp {
 public static void main (String args[]) throws IOException {
  // Create a BlackJackGame object ...
  BlackJackGame game = new BlackJackGame();
  // and play it!
  game.play();
```

```
  }
}
class BlackJackGame {
 // Variable declarations
 int bet;
 int money;
 Deck deck;
 Hand playersHand;
 Hand dealersHand;
 BufferedReader keyboardInput;
 // Method declarations
 public BlackJackGame() { // Constructor
  bet = 0;
  money = 1000;
  deck = new Deck();
  keyboardInput =
   new BufferedReader(new InputStreamReader(System.in));
 }
 void play() throws IOException {
  System.out.println("Welcome to Blackjack!");
  System.out.println("You have $"+Integer.toString(money)+".");
  do {
   placeBet();
   if(bet>0) {
    initialDeal();
    if(playersHand.blackjack()) playerWins();
    else{
     while(playersHand.under(22) && playerTakesAHit()) {
      playersHand.addCard(deck.deal());
      playersHand.show(false,false);
     }
     while(dealersHand.mustHit())
      dealersHand.addCard(deck.deal());
     dealersHand.show(true,false);
     showResults();
    }
   }
  } while (bet>0);
 }
 void placeBet() throws IOException, NumberFormatException {
  do{
   System.out.print("Enter bet: ");
   System.out.flush();
   bet = Integer.parseInt(keyboardInput.readLine());
  } while(bet<0 || bet>money);
 }
 void initialDeal() {
  System.out.println("New hand...");
  playersHand = new Hand();
  dealersHand = new Hand();
```

continues

LISTING 10.1. CONTINUED

```java
    for(int i = 0;i<2;++i) {
     playersHand.addCard(deck.deal());
     dealersHand.addCard(deck.deal());
     }
    dealersHand.show(true,true);
    playersHand.show(false,false);
   }
   void playerWins() {
    money += bet;
    System.out.println("Player wins $"+Integer.toString(bet)+".");
    System.out.println("Player has $"+Integer.toString(money)+".");
   }
   void dealerWins() {
    money -= bet;
    System.out.println("Player loses $"+Integer.toString(bet)+".");
    System.out.println("Player has $"+Integer.toString(money)+".");
   }
   void tie() {
    System.out.println("Tie.");
    System.out.println("Player has $"+Integer.toString(money)+".");
   }
   boolean playerTakesAHit() throws IOException {
    char ch = ' ';
    do{
      System.out.print("Hit or Stay: ");
      System.out.flush();
      String playersDecision = keyboardInput.readLine();
      try{
       ch = playersDecision.charAt(0);
      }catch (StringIndexOutOfBoundsException exception){
      }
      if(ch == 'H' || ch == 'h') return true;
      if(ch == 'S' || ch == 's') return false;
    } while(true);
   }
   void showResults() {
    if(playersHand.busted() && dealersHand.busted()) tie();
    else if(playersHand.busted()) dealerWins();
    else if(dealersHand.busted()) playerWins();
    else if(playersHand.bestScore() > dealersHand.bestScore()) playerWins();
    else if(playersHand.bestScore() < dealersHand.bestScore()) dealerWins();
    else tie();
   }
} // End of BlackJackGame class
class Deck {
 // Variable declarations
 int cards[];    // Array of 52 cards
 int topCard;    // 0-51 (index of card in deck)
 Random random;
```

```
// Method declarations
public Deck() { // Constructor
 cards = new int[52];
 for(int i = 0;i<52;++i) cards[i] = i;
 topCard = 0;
 random = new Random();
 shuffle();
}
public void shuffle() {
 // Repeat 52 times
 for(int i = 0;i<52;++i) {
  // Randomly exchange two cards in the deck.
  int j = randomCard();
  int k = randomCard();
  int temp = cards[j];
  cards[j] = cards[k];
  cards[k] = temp;
 }
}
int randomCard() {
 int r = random.nextInt();
 if(r<0) r = 0-r;
 return r%52;
}
Card deal() {
 if(topCard>51) {
  shuffle();
  topCard = 0;
 }
 Card card = new Card(cards[topCard]);
 ++topCard;
 return card;
}
} // End of Deck class
class Hand {
 // Variable declarations
 int numCards;
 Card cards[];
 static int MaxCards = 12;
 //Method declarations
 public Hand() { // Constructor
  numCards = 0;
  cards = new Card[MaxCards];
 }
 void addCard(Card c) {
  cards[numCards] = c;
  ++numCards;
 }
 void show(boolean isDealer,boolean hideFirstCard) {
  if(isDealer) System.out.println("Dealer:");
```

continues

10

WRITING CONSOLE
APPLICATIONS

LISTING **10.1.** CONTINUED

```
   else System.out.println("Player:");
   for(int i = 0;i<numCards;++i) {
    if(i == 0 && hideFirstCard) System.out.println("  Hidden");
     else System.out.println("  "+cards[i].value+" of "+cards[i].suit);
   }
  }
 boolean blackjack() {
  if(numCards == 2) {
   if(cards[0].iValue == 1 && cards[1].iValue == 10) return true;
   if(cards[1].iValue == 1 && cards[0].iValue == 10) return true;
  }
  return false;
 }
 boolean under(int n) {
  int points = 0;
  for(int i = 0;i<numCards;++i) points += cards[i].iValue;
  if(points<n) return true;
  else return false;
 }
 int bestScore() {
  int points = 0;
  boolean haveAce = false;
  for(int i = 0;i<numCards;++i) {
   points += cards[i].iValue;
   if(cards[i].iValue == 1) haveAce = true;
  }
  if(haveAce) {
   if(points+10 < 22) points += 10;
  }
  return points;
 }
 boolean mustHit() {
  if(bestScore()<17) return true;
  else return false;
 }
 boolean busted() {
   if(!under(22)) return true;
   else return false;
 }
} // End of Hand class
class Card {
 // Variable declarations
 int iValue;   // Numeric value corresponding to card.
 String value; // "A" "2" through "9" "T" "J" "Q" "K"
 String suit; // "S" "H" "C" "D"
 // Method declarations
 public Card(int n) { // Constructor
  int iSuit = n/13;
  iValue = n%13+1;
```

```
     switch(iSuit) {
       case 0:
        suit = "Spades";
        break;
       case 1:
        suit = "Hearts";
        break;
       case 2:
        suit = "Clubs";
        break;
       default:
        suit = "Diamonds";
     }
     if(iValue == 1) value = "Ace";
     else if(iValue == 10) value = "Ten";
     else if(iValue == 11) value = "Jack";
     else if(iValue == 12) value = "Queen";
     else if(iValue == 13) value = "King";
     else value = Integer.toString(iValue);
     if(iValue>10) iValue = 10;
    }
    int getValue() {
     return iValue;
    }
} // End of Card class
```

When you run `BlackJackApp`, it produces the following output:

```
Welcome to Blackjack!
You have $1000.
Enter bet:
```

The `BlackJackApp` program will provide you with $1,000 with which to play blackjack. You can place a bet between 0 and the amount of money you have. The program, acting as dealer, will deal two cards to you and two to itself. For example, after I entered a bet of $10, I received the following program output:

```
Welcome to Blackjack!
You have $1000.
Enter bet: 10
New hand...
Dealer:
  Hidden
  2 of Hearts
Player:
  Queen of Clubs
  3 of Spades
Hit or Stay:
```

I was dealt a queen of clubs and a three of spades. This gave me a total of 13 points. Points are calculated as follows:

Card point	*Value*
Ace	1 or 11 (whichever is better)
2 through 10	Face value of card (that is, 2 through 10)
Jack, Queen, King	10

The objective of the game is to get as close to 21 as you can without going over. Whoever gets the closest wins. If you go over 21 you lose, unless the dealer does also, in which case you tie.

When you are dealt your initial two cards, you are shown one of the dealer's cards. This helps you determine whether you should take another card, referred to as *hitting*, or *stay* with the cards that you have. You can enter h or s to inform the dealer of your decision. If you enter h, you will be dealt another card. If you enter s, the dealer will begin to play its hand.

> **NOTE**
>
> If the point total of your first two cards is 21, you have blackjack and immediately win.

The dealer must take a hit until the total points in its hand is 17 or over, at which point it must stay. When both you and the dealer have finished playing your hand, the total number of points acquired by each is used to determine the winner. Play is repeated until you enter a $0 bet.

The following program output shows a game played between myself and the BlackJackApp program:

```
Welcome to Blackjack!
You have $1000.
Enter bet: 10
New hand...
Dealer:
   Hidden
   2 of Hearts
Player:
   Queen of Clubs
   3 of Spades
Hit or Stay: h
```

```
Player:
  Queen of Clubs
  3 of Spades
  7 of Spades
Hit or Stay: s
Dealer:
  Queen of Spades
  2 of Hearts
  5 of Spades
Player wins $10.
Player has $1010.
Enter bet: 20
New hand...
Dealer:
  Hidden
  7 of Clubs
Player:
  King of Clubs
  9 of Spades
Hit or Stay: s
Dealer:
  2 of Clubs
  7 of Clubs
  9 of Clubs
Player wins $20.
Player has $1030.
Enter bet: 0
```

On the initial deal, I bet 10 bucks. I was given a queen of clubs and a three of spades, for a total of 13 points. The dealer was given a two of hearts and another (hidden) card. I elected to take a hit and was dealt a seven of spades, bringing the total in my hand up to 20 points—beginner's luck! The dealer turned over the hidden card to reveal a queen of spades. He then drew a five of spades for a total of 17 points. Because the dealer reached 17, he was forced to stay, and I had won $10. Feeling a little lightheaded, I proceeded to double my bet to $20. I was dealt a king of clubs and a nine of spades for a total of 19 points. I decided to stay with that hand. The dealer's hand was revealed to be a two of clubs and a seven of clubs. The dealer drew a nine of clubs for a total of 18 points. I had won again! At that point I elected to take the money and continue writing this book. I entered a 0 bet to end the game.

The point this is not to turn you into a blackjack gambler, but to serve as a more interesting example of console programming.

Overview of `BlackJackApp`

The `BlackJackApp.java` file is long, but don't let that daunt you. I'm going to break it down, class by class and method by method, to explain its operation.

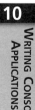

10

WRITING CONSOLE APPLICATIONS

The program begins by declaring the BlackJackApp class, the class that implements the blackjack application. The main() method consists of two Java statements. The first declares the game variable as having class type BlackJackGame and assigns it a new object of class BlackJackGame. The second statement invokes the play() method of the object referenced by game. Because BlackJackApp does not require any command-line arguments, the args array is not processed.

The BlackJackGame Class

The BlackJackGame class is rather long. It declares six variables and nine methods. The variables are data structures that represent the state of a blackjack game. The bet variable identifies the amount bet by the player. The money variable identifies how much money the player has left. The deck variable references an object of class Deck that is used to represent a deck of cards. Two Hand variables are declared, representing the player's hand and the dealer's hand. The keyboardInput variable refers to a BufferedReader object that is used to read data entered at the user's keyboard.

The BlackJackGame() constructor initializes four of the six variables of the BlackJackGame class. The player's bet is set to 0, and the player is given $1000. The playersHand and dealersHand variables are not initialized until the cards are dealt. A new Deck object is created and assigned to the deck variable. Finally, the keyboardInput variable is assigned a new object of class BufferedReader. This object is created using the BufferedReader() and InputStreamReader() constructors with the System.in variable as an argument.

The second method defined for BlackJackGame is the play() method. This method is invoked in the main() method of BlackJackApp to cause the BlackJackGame object, referenced by game, to be played.

The play() method begins by displaying the Welcome to Blackjack! text and the amount of money available to the player. The second println() method takes three arguments. First it displays You have $, then it displays the contents of the money variable, and then it displays a period (.). It converts the integer value of money to a String value before printing it. The block of statements within the do statement prompts the player to bet and then play a hand of blackjack.

If bet is greater than 0, the initialDeal() method is invoked. This method is used to deal a new hand to the player and to the dealer. It causes the playersHand and dealersHand variables to each be initialized with an object of class Hand. The blackjack() method is used to check whether the player was dealt a blackjack (21 points). If so, the player wins the bet and the playerWins() method is invoked.

If the player was not fortunate enough to have a blackjack, a `while` statement checks to see if the player has 21 points or less in his hand and whether he wants to take another card. The `playerTakesAHit()` method is invoked to prompt the player to hit or stay. The statements enclosed within the first `while` statement invoke methods for the `Hand` object referenced by the `playersHand` variable. The first method causes a card to be added to the player's hand by dealing it from the deck. The second method determines if and how the player's hand should be displayed.

The second `while` statement is used to play the dealer's hand. It invokes the `mustHit()` method with the object referenced by the `dealersHand` variable to determine whether the dealer has fewer than 17 points in his hand and, therefore, must take a hit. If the dealer must take a hit, the `addCard()` method is invoked to deal a card to the dealer.

After the dealer's hand is played, the `show()` method is invoked to display it to the console. The `showResults()` method is then invoked to show the results of the hand.

The `placeBet()` method is invoked by the `play()` method to prompt the player to enter a bet. It uses a `do` statement to repeatedly prompt the user to enter a bet between 0 and the amount of money that he has left. The statement block enclosed by the `do` statement displays the prompt, reads the line entered by the user, converts it to an integer, and then assigns it to the `bet` variable.

The `initialDeal()` method is invoked by the `play()` method to deal a new hand to the player and the dealer. It displays the `New hand...` text to the console window to inform the player that a new hand is being dealt. It then creates two new objects of class `Hand`, initializes them with the `Hand()` constructor, and assigns them to the `playersHand` and `dealersHand` variables.

After creating the two new hands, the `initialDeal()` method executes a `for` statement to sequentially deal two cards to the player and two to the dealer via the `addCard()` method. After the player and dealer have been dealt their hands, the `show()` method is invoked to display the new hands. (You'll find out what the `boolean` values are used for when you study the `show()` method.)

The next three methods, `playerWins()`, `dealerWins()`, and `tie()`, are used to update the `money` variable based on the `bet` variable and the outcome of the hand. These methods also display the results to the player by converting the values of `bet` and `money` to `String` objects.

The `playerTakesAHit()` method prompts the user to hit or stay. The `flush()` method is used to flush all output to the console in the absence of a new line character. The `readLine()` method is used to read the line entered by the user.

The showResults() method is the last method declared for the BlackJackGame class. This method uses a series of nested if statements. The first if statement checks to see if the player's hand and the dealer's hand are both busted (over 21 points). If so, the tie() method is invoked to display the results to the player.

The second if statement checks to see if the player's hand is busted. Because the else part of the first if statement was executed, it is impossible for both the player and the dealer to be busted. So if the player is busted, the dealer wins.

The third if statement is executed in the else parts of the first and second if statements. It uses the same logic as the second if statement to determine whether the dealer busts and the player wins.

The fourth if statement is only executed if neither the player nor the dealer busts. It checks the points in both of their hands to see if the player is higher than the dealer and, therefore, is the victor.

The fifth if statement is only executed if neither busts and the player is not higher than the dealer. If the dealer is higher than the player, the dealer wins. If the dealer is not higher than the player, the final else part is executed. At this point, neither has busted but neither is higher than the other, so both must have the same number of points and a tie is declared.

The Deck Class

The Deck class declares three variables and four methods. The cards variable is used to simulate a deck of cards. The topCard variable is an integer that identifies the next card to be dealt from the deck. The random variable is used to generate random numbers.

The constructor for the Deck class allocates an array of 52 integers and assigns it to cards. A for statement is used to assign 0 to cards[0], 1 to cards[1], 2 to cards[2], and so on, until 51 is assigned to cards[51]. This creates a deck of cards in which all the cards are ordered by suit and by value. The integers 0 through 51 are logically mapped to playing cards, as follows:

0 through 12 are mapped to the ace of spades through the king of spades.

13 through 25 are mapped to the ace of hearts through the king of hearts.

26 through 38 are mapped to the ace of clubs through the king of clubs.

39 through 51 are mapped to the ace of diamonds through the king of diamonds.

The topCard of the deck is set to 0. It is used as an index into the cards array. The random variable is assigned a new object of class Random. Finally, the shuffle() method is invoked to shuffle the new deck of cards.

The `shuffle()` method shuffles the deck of cards by randomly switching two cards in the deck 52 times. It does this by invoking the `randomCard()` method to generate a random integer between 0 and 51.

The `randomCard()` method returns an integer between 0 and 51, inclusive. It begins by declaring a variable r and assigning it a random integer value generated by applying the `nextInt()` method to the `random` variable. The `nextInt()` method is defined in the `java.util.Random` class. If the value assigned to r is less than 0, it is changed to a positive integer. The `randomCard()` method then returns an integer between 0 and 51 by returning the random integer modulus 52.

The `deal()` method is used to deal a card off the top of the deck. It does this by using the `topCard` variable as an index into the `cards` array. It starts at 0 and is incremented until it is greater than 51, indicating that all the cards in the deck have been dealt. In this case, the deck is reshuffled and `topCard` is set to 0 once again. This creates the effect of another deck being used because the player and dealer don't have to throw back any cards they're holding before the deck is shuffled.

The `Card` class is used to translate the integer card values to `String` values that can be displayed on the console. A card is dealt by constructing a new instance of `Card`, using the value of `cards` indexed by `topCard` as an argument. The `topCard` is then incremented to move to the next card in the deck. Note that `deal()` returns the object of class `Card` that was created using the `Card()` constructor.

The Hand Class

The `Hand` class is used to implement a hand of cards as played by both the player and the dealer. It declares three variables and eight methods.

The `numCards` variable identifies the number of cards contained in the hand. The `cards` array has the same name as the `cards` array declared in the `Deck` class, but is logically and physically distinct. Because it is declared in a separate class, it is contained in objects that are instances of the `Hand` class and not of the `Deck` class. The `MaxCards` variable is declared to be `static`. It is used to identify the number of components to be allocated within `cards`.

The constructor for the `Hand` class sets `numCards` to 0 to indicate an empty hand, and then creates a `MaxCards` size array of `Card` objects and assigns it to `cards`.

Cards are added to a hand using the `addCard()` method. This method takes an object of class `Card` as an argument and adds it to the first available position within the `cards` array. It then increments `numCards` so that it will index the next available position within `cards`.

The show() method displays either the dealer's or the player's hand. It takes two boolean arguments that specify whether the hand belongs to the dealer, and if so, whether the first card should be hidden when the hand is displayed. The isDealer parameter is used in the initial if statement to determine whether a dealer or a player heading should be displayed. A for statement is then used to iterate numCards times in order to display each card of the hand. The statement block enclosed by the for statement uses the hideFirstCard parameter to determine whether the first card should be hidden or displayed.

The blackjack() method returns a boolean value indicating whether the hand is blackjack. If the number of cards is exactly two, it uses the iValue variable of the Card objects contained in the cards array to determine whether the current hand is blackjack. The iValue variable is discussed with the Card class. It identifies the number of points associated with a card. A card with iValue = 1 is an ace. Aces can be either 1 or 11 points.

The under() method returns a boolean value indicating whether the number of points in a hand is less than the argument passed via the n parameter. It declares a points variable of type int and uses a for statement to sum the points for all cards in the hand. It then checks to see if the number of points in the hand is less than n and returns an appropriate value of true or false.

The bestScore() method returns an integer value identifying the best possible point score for the hand. It adjusts the value associated with aces to either 1 or 11, depending upon whether it causes the hand to go over 21 points.

The mustHit() method is used to play out the dealer's hand. If the bestScore of the dealer's hand is lower than 17, the dealer must take a hit. If it is 17 or higher, the dealer must stay.

The busted() method determines whether the number of points in a hand is under 22.

The Card Class

The Card class is used to translate the integer value of cards, maintained by objects of the Deck class, into objects of type String. It declares three variables and two methods.

The iValue variable is used to keep track of the number of points associated with a card. It is an abbreviation for *integer value* and is used to differentiate it from the value variable, which references a text string that is used to describe the face value of a playing card. The suit variable is used to identify the suit of a playing card.

The Card() constructor takes an integer argument (0 through 51) that is a card value from the Deck class. Card() first determines the suit of the card identified by the n parameter. It does this by dividing n by 13 and assigning the result to an integer variable named iSuit. It determines the point value of the card by calculating n modulus 13 and adding 1. It adjusts this value later in the method. Card() then uses a switch statement to assign the correct text string to the suit variable.

The getValue() method is used to return the value of iValue, the point value of the card.

The `java.lang` Packages

In the BlackJackApp program, you learned to use the System class of java.lang to perform keyboard input and console output. The java.lang package is one of the most important packages of the Core Java API. It provides a number of classes and interfaces that are fundamental to Java programming. This section covers the classes and interfaces of the java.lang, java.lang.reflect, and java.lang.ref packages. It contains several console programs that illustrate the use of these classes and interfaces.

The `Object`, `Class`, and `Package` Classes

Object and Class are two of the most important classes in the Java API. The Object class is at the top of the Java class hierarchy. All classes are subclasses of Object and therefore inherit its methods. The Class class is used to provide class descriptors for all objects created during Java program execution. The Package class is new to JDK 1.2. It is used to provide version information about a package.

Object

The Object class does not have any variables and has only one constructor. However, it provides 11 methods that are inherited by all Java classes and support general operations used by all objects. For example, the equals() and hashCode() methods are used to construct hash tables of Java objects. *Hash tables* are like arrays, but are indexed by key values and dynamically grow in size. They make use of *hash functions* to quickly access the data that they contain. The hashCode() method creates a *hashcode* for an object. Hashcodes are used to quickly determine whether two objects are different.

The clone() method creates an identical copy of an object. The object must implement the Cloneable interface. This interface is defined within the java.lang package. It contains no methods and is used only to differentiate clonable classes from nonclonable classes.

The getClass() method identifies the class of an object by returning an object of Class. You'll learn how to use this method in the next programming example. (See the "A Touch of Class" section.)

The toString() method creates a String representation of the value of an object. This method is handy for quickly displaying the contents of an object. When an object is displayed, using print() or println(), the toString() method of its class is automatically called to convert the object into a string before printing. Classes that override the toString() method can easily provide a custom display for their objects.

The finalize() method of an object is executed when an object is garbage-collected. The method performs no action, by default, and needs to be overridden by any class that requires specialized finalization processing.

The Object class provides three wait() and two notify() methods that support thread control. These methods are implemented by the Object class so that they can be made available to threads that are not created from subclasses of class Thread. The wait() methods cause a thread to wait until it is notified or until a specified amount of time has elapsed. The notify() methods are used to notify waiting threads that their wait is over.

Class

The Class class provides over 30 methods that support the runtime processing of an object's class and interface information. This class does not have a constructor. Objects of this class, referred to as *class descriptors*, are automatically created and associated with the objects to which they refer. Despite their name, class descriptors are used for interfaces as well as classes.

The getName()and toString()methods return the String containing the name of a class or interface. The toString() method differs in that it prepends the string class or interface, depending on whether the class descriptor is a class or an interface. The static forName() method loads the class specified by a String object and returns a class descriptor for that class.

The getSuperclass() method returns the class descriptor of a class's superclass. The isInterface()method identifies whether a class descriptor applies to a class or an interface. The getInterfaces() method returns an array of Class objects that specify the interfaces of a class, if any.

The newInstance()method creates an object that is a new instance of the specified class. It can be used in lieu of a class's constructor, although it is generally safer and clearer to use a constructor rather than newInstance().

The getClassLoader()method returns the class loader of a class, if one exists. Classes are not usually loaded by a class loader. However, if a class is loaded from outside the CLASSPATH, such as over a network, a class loader is used to convert the class byte stream into a class descriptor. The ClassLoader class is covered later in this chapter in the "ClassLoader" section.

The Class class contains a number of other methods that begin with get and is. These methods are as follows:

- getClasses()—Returns an array of all classes and interfaces that are members of the class.

- getComponentType()—Returns the component type of an array.

- getConstructor() and getConstructors()—Return Constructor objects for the class.

- getDeclaredClasses(), getDeclaredConstructor(), getDeclaredConstructors(), getDeclaredField(), getDeclaredFields(), getDeclaredMethod(), and getDeclaredMethods()—Return the classes, constructors, fields, and methods that are declared for a class or interface.

- getDeclaringClass()—Returns the class in which the referenced class is declared (if any).

- getField() and getFields()—Returns a specific Field object or all Field objects of a class or interface.

- getMethod() and getMethods()—Returns a specific Method object or all Method objects of a class or interface.

- getModifiers()—Returns the class or interface modifiers as a coded integer.

- getResource() and getResourceAsStream()—Locates system resources. *System resources* are objects that are used by the runtime system or local Java implementation.

- getSigners()—Returns the signers of a class. See Chapter 8, "Applet Security," for more information about class signing.

- isArray()—Returns true if the Class object represents an array.

- isAssignableFrom()—Used to determine whether an object of one class can be assigned to an object of another class.

- isInstance()—Equivalent to the isinstanceof operator.

- isPrimitive()—Returns true if the object represents a primitive type.

Package

Java software development is based upon the use and reuse of packages. Both Java 1.0 and Java 1.1 used packages. However, the Package class is new to JDK 1.2. It provides methods for obtaining package version information stored in the manifest of .jar files. The Package class provides fourteen methods that can be used to retrieve information about packages. The static getPackage() and getAllPackages() methods provide

Package objects that are known to the current class loader. The getName(),
getSpecificationTitle(), getImplementationTitle(), getSpecificationVersion(),
getImplementationVersion(), getSpecificationVendor(), and
getImplementationVendor() methods return name, title, version, and vendor information about the specification and implementation of packages. The getSealBase()
method returns the base URL of a signed package. The isSealed() method is used to
determine if a package is sealed. The isCompatibleWith() method is used to determine
whether a package is comparable with a particular version. The hashCode() and
toString() methods override those inherited from the Object class.

A Touch of Class

In order to give you a feel for how the Class methods can be used, let's create and run a
small program called ClassApp. The program's source code is shown in Listing 10.2.

LISTING 10.2. THE SOURCE CODE OF THE ClassApp PROGRAM.

```
import java.util.*;

public class ClassApp {
 public static void main(String args[]) {
  Vector v = new Vector();
  Class cl = v.getClass();
  do {
   describeClass(cl);
   cl = cl.getSuperclass();
  }while(!cl.getName().equals("java.lang.Object"));
 }
 public static void describeClass(Class classDesc){
  System.out.println("Class: "+classDesc.getName());
  System.out.println("Superclass: "+classDesc.getSuperclass().getName());
  Class interfaces[] = classDesc.getInterfaces();
  for(int i=0;i<interfaces.length;++i)
   System.out.println("has interface: "+interfaces[i].getName());
  System.out.println();
 }
}
```

The program shows how the Class methods can be used to generate runtime class and
interface information about an arbitrary object. It creates an instance of the Vector class
of the java.util package and then uses the getClass(), getSuperclass(), and
getName() methods of the Class class.

A do loop invokes the describeClass() method for the class identified by cl and then
assigns cl to the class's superclass. The loop repeats until cl becomes the class descriptor of the Object class.

The describeClass() method uses the getName() method to get the name of the class and its superclass. The describeClass() method displays this information to the console. It uses the getInterfaces() method to get all interfaces implemented by a class and the getName() method to get and display the name of each interface.

Compile and run the ClassApp program. Its output is as follows:

```
Class: java.util.Vector
Superclass: java.util.AbstractList
has interface: java.util.List
has interface: java.lang.Cloneable
has interface: java.io.Serializable

Class: java.util.AbstractList
Superclass: java.util.AbstractCollection
has interface: java.util.List

Class: java.util.AbstractCollection
Superclass: java.lang.Object
has interface: java.util.Collection
```

It steps up the class hierarchy from Vector to CGObject to display information about each class. See if you can modify the program to work with objects of other classes. You can do this by assigning the class of these objects to the cl variable in the main() method.

The ClassLoader, SecurityManager, and Runtime Classes

The ClassLoader, SecurityManager, and Runtime classes provide a fine level of control over the operation of the Java runtime system. However, most of the time you will not want or need to exercise this control because Java is set up to perform optimally for a variety of applications. The ClassLoader class allows you to define custom loaders for classes that you load outside of your CLASSPATH—for example, over a network. The SecurityManager class allows you to define a variety of security policies that govern the accesses that classes may make to threads, executable programs, your network, and your file system. The Runtime class provides you with the capability to control and monitor the Java runtime system. It also allows you to execute external programs.

ClassLoader

Classes that are loaded from outside the CLASSPATH require a class loader to convert the class byte stream into a class descriptor. ClassLoader is an abstract class that is used to define class loaders. It uses the defineClass() method to convert an array of bytes into a class descriptor. The definePackage() method is used to define a package. The loadClass() method is used to load a class from its source, usually a network. The resolveClass() method resolves all the classes referenced by a particular class by loading and defining those classes. The findSystemClass()method is used to load classes that are located within the CLASSPATH and, therefore, do not require a class loader. The findLoadedClass() method is used to access a class that has been loaded. The findLocalClass() method is used to find a class that is on the local system.

The checkPackageAccess() method is used to determine whether the invoking object's thread is permitted to access a particular package. The static currentClassLoader() method returns a reference to the ClassLoader that is currently in use. getParent() returns a class loader's parent.

The getResource(), getResourceAsStream(), getSystemResource(), and getSystemResourceAsStream() methods are used to access application- or system-specific resources. Resources are additional files or other objects that are associated with an application or the runtime system. The getPackage() and getPackages() methods are used to access packages.

The setSigners() method is used to set the signers of a loaded class.

SecurityManager

The SecurityManager class is an abstract class that works with class loaders to implement a security policy. It contains several methods that can be overridden to implement customized security policies. These methods are of the form checkX(), where X is the access being checked. You can extend SecurityManager and override these methods to implement custom security policies. As of JDK 1.2, it is preferable to configure security policy using the security policy configuration methods described in Chapter 3, "The Extended Java Security Model."

Runtime

The Runtime class provides access to the Java runtime system. It consists of a number of methods that implement system-level services.

The getRuntime() method is a static method that is used to obtain access to an object of class Runtime. The exec() methods are used to execute external programs from the Java runtime system. The exec() methods provide a number of alternatives for passing parameters to the executed program. These alternatives are similar to the standard C methods for passing command-line and environment information. The exec() methods are subject to security checking to ensure that they are executed by trusted code. The RuntimePermission class is used to implement permissions related to runtime security checking.

The `exit()` method is used to exit the Java runtime system with an error code. It is similar to the `exit` function found in standard C libraries.

The `totalMemory()`, `freeMemory()`, and `gc()` methods are used to obtain information about the runtime system and control the memory used by it. The `totalMemory()` method identifies the total memory available to the runtime system. The `freeMemory()` method identifies the amount of free (unused) memory. The `RuntimeMemoryAdvice` interface is new to JDK 1.2. It provides constants for determining the safety level associated with available memory. `RuntimeMemoryAdvice` is implemented by the `Runtime` class. The `waitForMemoryAdvice()` and `getMemoryAdvice()` methods are used to determine the current memory safety level.

The `gc()` method is used to run the garbage collector to free up memory allocated to objects that are no longer being used. In general, you should not use the `gc()` method, but rather let Java perform its own automated garbage collection.

The `getLocalizedInputStream()` and `getLocalizedOutputStream()` methods are used to convert local (usually ASCII) input and output streams to Unicode-based streams.

The `load()` and `loadLibrary()` methods are used to load dynamic link libraries. This is usually performed in conjunction with native methods, which are described in Chapter 53, "Native Methods."

The `runFinalization()` method causes the `finalize()` method of each object awaiting finalization to be invoked. The `runFinalizersOnExit()` method can toggle on or off whether finalization occurs when the runtime system exits. The `traceInstructions()` and `traceMethodCalls()` methods are used to enable or disable instruction and method tracing. You will most likely never need to use any of these methods in your programs. They are used in programs such as the debugger to trace through the execution of Java methods and instructions.

Using `Runtime`

Most of the methods provided by `Runtime` are not typically used in application programs. However, some methods are pretty useful. The program in Listing 10.3 shows how the `Runtime` methods can be used to display memory status information.

LISTING 10.3. THE SOURCE CODE OF THE RuntimeMemApp PROGRAM.

```
import java.lang.System;
import java.lang.Runtime;
import java.io.IOException;
```

continues

LISTING 10.3. CONTINUED

```
public class RuntimeMemApp {
 public static void main(String args[]) throws IOException {
  Runtime r = Runtime.getRuntime();
  System.out.println(r.totalMemory());
  System.out.println(r.freeMemory());
 }
}
```

This program uses the static getRuntime() method to get an instance of Runtime that represents the current Java runtime system. The totalMemory() method is used to display the total number of bytes of runtime system memory. The freeMemory() method is used to display the number of bytes of memory that are unallocated and currently available.

When you run the program, you should get results that are similar to the following:

```
1048568
845136
```

Listing 10.4 demonstrates how to use the Runtime exec() method to execute external programs. This example assumes that you are using Windows 95 and may not work with other Java implementations. However, it can be easily tailored to launch application programs on other operating systems.

LISTING 10.4. THE SOURCE CODE OF THE RuntimeExecApp PROGRAM.

```
import java.lang.System;
import java.lang.Runtime;
import java.io.IOException;
public class RuntimeExecApp {
 public static void main(String args[]) throws IOException {
  Runtime r = Runtime.getRuntime();
  r.exec("C:\\Windows\\Explorer.exe");
 }
}
```

This program uses getRuntime() to get the current instance of the runtime system and then uses exec() to execute the Windows Explorer. The double backslashes (\\) are Java escape codes for a single backslash (\). When you run this program, it should launch a copy of the Windows Explorer. Under Windows 95, the exec() function works with true Win32 programs. It cannot be used to execute built-in DOS commands.

The `System` Class

You are no stranger to the `System` class because you have used it in several previous programming examples. It is one of the most important and useful classes provided by `java.lang`. It provides a standard interface to common system resources and functions. It implements the standard input, output, and error streams, and supplies a set of methods that provide control over the Java runtime system. Some of these methods duplicate those provided by the `Runtime` class.

Standard Streams

The `in`, `out`, and `err` variables are, by default, assigned to the standard input, output, and error streams. The `setIn()`, `setOut()`, and `setErr()` methods can be used to reassign these variables to other streams.

Properties-Related Methods

The `System` class provides several properties-related methods. *Properties* are extensions of the `Dictionary` and `Hashtable` classes and are defined in the `java.util` package. A set of system properties is available through the `System` class that describes the general characteristics of the operating system and runtime system you are using. The `getProperties()` method gets all of the system properties and stores them in an object of class `Properties`. The `getProperty()` method gets a single property, as specified by a key. The `setProperties()` method sets the system properties to the values of a `Properties` object. The `setProperty()` method sets the value of a particular property. The `identityHashCode()` method returns the hash code associated with an object. The sample program presented in Listing 10.4 introduces you to these system properties.

Security Manager-Related Methods

The `getSecurityManager()` and `setSecurityManager()` methods provide access to the security manager that is currently in effect. The `setSecurityManager()` method can be used to implement a custom security policy. However, as of JDK 1.2, the best way to implement a custom policy is via the policy permissions covered in Chapter 3, "The Extended Java Security Model."

Runtime-Related Methods

Several of the methods defined for the `Runtime` class are made available through the `System` class. These methods include `exit()`, `gc()`, `load()`, `loadLibrary()`, `runFinalizersOnExit()`, and `runFinalization()`.

Odds and Ends

The `arraycopy()` method is used to copy data from one array to another. This function provides the opportunity for system-specific memory-copying operations to optimize memory-to-memory copies.

The `currentTimeMillis()` method returns the current time in milliseconds since January 1, 1970. If you want more capable date and time methods, check out the `Date` class in `java.util`.

The `getenv()` method is used to obtain the value of an environment variable. However, this method is identified as obsolete in the Java API documentation and can no longer be used.

Time and Properties

The short program in Listing 10.5 illustrates a few of the methods provided by the `System` class. If your heyday was in the 1960s, it will allow you to keep track of the number of milliseconds that have elapsed since the good old days. It also gets and displays the `System` properties. Take a look through these properties to get a feel for the type of information that is provided. Finally, the `exit()` method is used to terminate the program, returning a status code of 13.

LISTING 10.5. THE SOURCE CODE OF THE SystemApp PROGRAM.

```
import java.lang.System;
import java.util.Properties;
public class SystemApp {
  public static void main(String args[]) {
    long time = System.currentTimeMillis();
    System.out.print("Milliseconds elapsed since January 1, 1970: ");
    System.out.println(time);
    Properties p=System.getProperties();
    p.list(System.out);
    System.exit(13);
  }
}
```

The program generated the following output on my computer:

```
Milliseconds elapsed since January 1, 1970: 887133030120
-- listing properties --
java.specification.name=Java Platform API Specification
awt.toolkit=sun.awt.windows.WToolkit
java.version=1.2beta2
java.awt.graphicsenv=sun.awt.Win32GraphicsEnvironment
java.tmpdir=c:\windows\TEMP\
```

```
user.timezone=PST
java.specification.version=1.2beta2
user.home=C:\JDK1.2BETA2\BIN\..
java-vm.name=non-JIT
os.arch=x86
java.awt.fonts=C:\WINDOWS\Fonts
java.vendor.url=http://www.sun.com/
user.region=US
file.encoding.pkg=sun.io
java.home=C:\JDK1.2BETA2\BIN\..
java-vm.specification.vendor=Sun Microsystems Inc.
java-vm.specification.version=1.0
java.class.path=.;C:\JavaWebServer1.0.3\public_html\c...
line.separator=

os.name=Windows 95

java.vendor=Sun Microsystems Inc.
java.library.path=C:\JDK1.2BETA2\BIN;.;C:\WINDOWS;c:\wi...
java-vm.version=1.2beta2
file.encoding=8859_1
java.specification.vendor=Sun Microsystems Inc.
user.name=Jamie
user.language=en
java.vendor.url.bug=http://java.sun.com/cgi-bin/bugreport...
java.class.version=45.3
os.version=4.0
path.separator=;
java-vm.specification.name=Java Virtual Machine Specification
file.separator=\
user.dir=C:\jdk1.2beta2\ju\ch10
java-vm.vendor=Sun Microsystems Inc.
```

Wrapped Classes

Variables that are declared using the primitive Java types are not objects and cannot be created and accessed using methods. Primitive types also cannot be subclassed. To get around the limitations of primitive types, the java.lang package defines class *wrappers* for these types. These class wrappers furnish methods that provide basic capabilities such as class conversion, value testing, hash codes, and equality checks. The constructors for the wrapped classes allow objects to be created and converted from primitive values and strings. Be sure to browse the API pages for each of these classes to familiarize yourself with the methods they provide.

The Boolean Class

The Boolean class is a wrapper for the boolean primitive type. It provides the getBoolean(), toString(), valueOf(), and booleanValue() methods to support type and class conversion. The `toString()`, `equals()`, and `hashCode()` methods override those of class `Object`.

The `Character` Class

The `Character` class is a wrapper for the `char` primitive type. It provides several methods that support case, type, and class testing and conversion. Check out the API pages on these methods. We'll use some of them in the upcoming example.

The `Byte`, `Short`, `Integer`, and `Long` Classes

These classes wrap the `byte`, `short`, `int`, and `long` primitive types. They provide the `MIN_VALUE` and `MAX_VALUE` constants, as well as a number of type and class testing and conversion methods. The `parseInt()` and `parseLong()` methods are used to parse `String` objects and convert them to `Byte`, `Short`, `Integer`, and `Long` objects.

The `Double` and `Float` Classes

The `Double` and `Float` classes wrap the `double` and `float` primitive types. They provide the `MIN_VALUE`, `MAX_VALUE`, `POSITIVE_INFINITY`, and `NEGATIVE_INFINITY` constants, as well as the `NaN` (not-a-number) constant. `NaN` is used as a value that is not equal to any value, including itself. These classes provide a number of type and class testing and conversion methods, including methods that support conversion to and from integer bit representations.

The `Number` Class

The `Number` class is an abstract numeric class that is subclassed by `Byte`, `Short`, `Integer`, `Long`, `Float`, and `Double`. It provides six methods that support conversion of objects from one class to another.

All Wrapped Up

The program in Listing 10.6 shows some of the methods that can be used with the primitive types when they are wrapped as objects. Look up these methods in the API pages for each class and try to figure out how they work before moving on to their explanations.

LISTING 10.6. THE SOURCE CODE OF THE `WrappedClassApp` PROGRAM.

```
import java.lang.System;
import java.lang.Boolean;
import java.lang.Character;
import java.lang.Integer;
import java.lang.Long;
```

```
import java.lang.Float;
import java.lang.Double;
public class WrappedClassApp {
 public static void main(String args[]) {
  Boolean b1 = new Boolean("TRUE");
  Boolean b2 = new Boolean("FALSE");
  System.out.println(b1.toString()+" or "+b2.toString());
  for(int j=0;j<16;++j)
   System.out.print(Character.forDigit(j,16));
  System.out.println();
  Integer i = new Integer(Integer.parseInt("ef",16));
  Long l = new Long(Long.parseLong("abcd",16));
  long m=l.longValue()*i.longValue();
  System.out.println(Long.toString(m,8));
  System.out.println(Float.MIN_VALUE);
  System.out.println(Double.MAX_VALUE);
 }
}
```

The program examines some of the more useful methods provided by the wrapped classes. It creates two objects of class Boolean from string arguments passed to their constructors. It assigns these objects to b1 and b2 and then converts them back to String objects when it displays them. They are displayed in lowercase, as boolean values are traditionally represented.

The program then executes a for loop that prints out the character corresponding to each of the hexadecimal digits. The static forDigit() method of the Character class is used to generate the character values of digits in a number system of a different radix.

The static parseInt() and parseLong() methods are used to parse strings according to different radices. In the example, they are used to convert strings representing hexadecimal numbers into Integer and Long values. These values are then multiplied together and converted to a string that represents the resulting value in base 8. This is accomplished using an overloaded version of the toString() method.

The sample program concludes by displaying the minimum float value and the maximum double value using the predefined class constants of the Float and Double classes.

The program's output is as follows:

```
true or false
0123456789abcdef
50062143
1.4E-45
1.7976931348623157E308
```

The Math Class and Comparable Interface

The Math class provides an extensive set of mathematical methods in the form of a static class library. It also defines the mathematical constants E and PI. The supported methods include arithmetic, trigonometric, exponential, logarithmic, random number, and conversion routines. You should browse the API page of this class to get a feel for the methods it provides. The example in Listing 10.7 only touches on a few of these methods.

LISTING 10.7. THE SOURCE CODE OF THE MathApp PROGRAM.

```
import java.lang.System;
import java.lang.Math;
public class MathApp {
 public static void main(String args[]) {
  System.out.println(Math.E);
  System.out.println(Math.PI);
  System.out.println(Math.abs(-1234));
  System.out.println(Math.cos(Math.PI/4));
  System.out.println(Math.sin(Math.PI/2));
  System.out.println(Math.tan(Math.PI/4));
  System.out.println(Math.log(1));
  System.out.println(Math.exp(Math.PI));
  for(int i=0;i<3;++i)
   System.out.print(Math.random()+" ");
  System.out.println();
 }
}
```

This program prints the constants e and π, $|{-}1234|$, $\cos(\pi/4)$, $\sin(\pi/2)$, $\tan(\pi/4)$, $\ln(1)$, e^π, and then three random double numbers between 0.0 and 1.1. Its output is as follows:

```
2.718281828459045
3.141592653589793
1234
0.7071067811865476
1.0
0.9999999999999999
0.0
23.14069263277926
0.5214844573332809 0.7036104523989761 0.15555052349418896
```

The random numbers you generate will almost certainly differ from those shown here.

The Comparable interface is a new interface that was added with JDK 1.2. This interface defines the compareTo() method. Objects of classes that implement the Comparable interface can be compared to each other and sorted.

The `String` and `StringBuffer` Classes

The `String` and `StringBuffer` classes are used to support operations on strings of characters. The `String` class supports constant (unchanging) strings, whereas the `StringBuffer` class supports growable, modifiable strings. `String` objects are more compact than `StringBuffer` objects, but `StringBuffer` objects are more flexible.

String Literals

`String` literals are strings that are specified using double quotes. `"This is a string"` and `"xyz"` are examples of string literals. `String` literals are different than the literal values used with primitive types. When the `javac` compiler encounters a `String` literal, it converts it to a `String` constructor. For example, this:

```
String str = "text";
```

is equivalent to this:

```
String str = new String("text");
```

The fact that the compiler automatically supplies `String` constructors allows you to use `String` literals everywhere that you could use objects of the `String` class.

The + Operator and `StringBuffer`

If `String` objects are constant, how can they be concatenated with the + operator and be assigned to existing `String` objects? In the following example, the code will result in the string `"ab"` being assigned to the s object:

```
String s = "";
s = s + "a" + "b";
```

How can this be possible if `String`s are constant? The answer lies in the fact that the Java compiler uses `StringBuffer` objects to accomplish the string manipulations. This code would be rendered as something similar to the following by the Java compiler:

```
String s = "";
s = new StringBuffer("").append("a").append("b").toString();
```

A new object of class `StringBuffer` is created with the `""` argument. The `StringBuffer` `append()` method is used to append the strings `"a"` and `"b"` to the new object, and then the object is converted to an object of class `String` via the `toString()` method. The `toString()` method creates a new object of class `String` before it is assigned to the s variable. In this way, the s variable always refers to a constant (although new) `String` object.

10

WRITING CONSOLE
APPLICATIONS

`String` Constructors

The `String` class provides several constructors for the creation and initialization of `String` objects. These constructors allow strings to be created from other strings, string literals, arrays of characters, arrays of bytes, and `StringBuffer` objects. Browse through the API page for the `String` class to become familiar with these constructors.

`String` Access Methods

The `String` class provides a very powerful set of methods for working with `String` objects. These methods allow you to access individual characters and substrings; test and compare strings; copy, concatenate, and replace parts of strings; convert and create strings; and perform other useful string operations.

The most important `String` methods are the `length()` method, which returns an integer value identifying the length of a string; the `charAt()` method, which allows the individual characters of a string to be accessed; the `substring()` method, which allows substrings of a string to be accessed; and the `valueOf()` method, which allows primitive data types to be converted into strings.

In addition to these methods, the `Object` class provides a `toString()` method for converting other objects to `String` objects. This method is often overridden by subclasses to provide a more appropriate object-to-string conversion.

Character and Substring Methods

Several `String` methods allow you to access individual characters and substrings of a string. These include `charAt()`, `getBytes()`, `getChars()`, `indexOf()`, `lastIndexOf()`, and `substring()`. Whenever you need to perform string manipulations, be sure to check the API documentation to make sure that you don't overlook an easy-to-use, predefined `String` method.

String Comparison and Test Methods

Several `String` methods allow you to compare strings, substrings, byte arrays, and other objects with a given string. Some of these methods are `compareTo()`, `endsWith()`, `equals()`, `equalsIgnoreCase()`, `regionMatches()`, and `startsWith()`.

Copy, Concatenation, and Replace Methods

The following methods are useful for copying, concatenating, and manipulating strings: `concat()`, `copyValueOf()`, `replace()`, and `trim()`.

String Conversion and Generation

A number of string methods support `String` conversion. These are `intern()`, `toCharArray()`, `toLowerCase()`, `toString()`, `toUpperCase()`, and `valueOf()`. You'll explore the use of some of these methods in the following example.

Stringing Along

The program in Listing 10.8 provides a glimpse at the operation of some of the methods identified in the previous subsections. Because strings are frequently used in application programs, learning to use the available methods is essential to being able to use the `String` class most effectively.

LISTING 10.8. THE SOURCE CODE OF THE `StringApp` PROGRAM.

```
import java.lang.System;
import java.lang.String;
public class StringApp {
 public static void main(String args[]) {
  String s = "  Java Unleashed 1.2 ";
  System.out.println(s);
  System.out.println(s.toUpperCase());
  System.out.println(s.toLowerCase());
  System.out.println("["+s+"]");
  s=s.trim();
  System.out.println("["+s+"]");
  s=s.replace('J','X');
  s=s.replace('U','Y');
  s=s.replace('2','Z');
  System.out.println(s);
  int i1 = s.indexOf('X');
  int i2 = s.indexOf('Y');
  int i3 = s.indexOf('Z');
  char ch[] = s.toCharArray();
  ch[i1]='J';
  ch[i2]='U';
  ch[i3]='2';
  s = new String(ch);
  System.out.println(s);
 }
}
```

This program performs several manipulations of a string s, which is initially set to "Java Unleashed 1.2 ". It prints the original string and then prints upper- and lower-case versions of it, illustrating the use of the `toUpperCase()` and `toLowerCase()` methods. It prints the string enclosed between two braces to show that it contains leading and trailing spaces. It then trims away these spaces using the `trim()` method and reprints the string to show that these spaces were removed.

10

WRITING CONSOLE APPLICATIONS

The program uses the `replace()` method to replace `'J'`, `'U'`, and `'2'` with `'X'`, `'Y'`, and `'Z'`, and prints out the string to show the changes. The `replace()` method is case sensitive. It uses the `indexOf()` method to get the indices of `'X'`, `'Y'`, and `'Z'` within s. It uses the `toCharArray()` to convert the string to a `char` array. It then uses the indices to put `'J'`, `'U'`, and `'2'` back in their proper locations within the character array. The `String()` constructor is used to construct a new string from the character array. The new string is assigned to s and is printed.

The program's output is as follows:

```
Java Unleashed 1.2
JAVA UNLEASHED 1.2
java unleashed 1.2
[   Java Unleashed 1.2 ]
[Java Unleashed 1.2]
Xava Ynleashed 1.Z
Java Unleashed 1.2
```

The `StringBuffer` Class

The `StringBuffer` class is the force behind the scenes for most complex string manipulations. The compiler automatically declares and manipulates objects of this class to implement common string operations.

The `StringBuffer` class provides three constructors: an empty constructor, a constructor with a specified initial buffer length, and a constructor that creates a `StringBuffer` object from a `String` object. In general, you will find yourself constructing `StringBuffer` objects from `String` objects, and the last constructor will be the one you use most often.

The `StringBuffer` class provides several versions of the `append()` method to convert and append other objects and primitive data types to `StringBuffer` objects. It provides a similar set of `insert()` methods for inserting objects and primitive data types into `StringBuffer` objects. It also provides methods to access the character-buffering capacity of `StringBuffer` and methods for accessing the characters contained in a string. It is well worth a visit to the `StringBuffer` API pages to take a look at the methods that it has to offer.

Strung Out

The program in Listing 10.9 shows how `StringBuffer` objects can be manipulated using the `append()`, `insert()`, and `setCharAt()` methods.

LISTING 10.9. THE SOURCE CODE OF THE `StringBufferApp` PROGRAM.

```
import java.lang.System;
import java.lang.String;
import java.lang.StringBuffer;
public class StringBufferApp {
 public static void main(String args[]) {
  StringBuffer sb = new StringBuffer(" is ");
  sb.append("Hot");
  sb.append('!');
  sb.insert(0,"Java");
  sb.append('\n');
  sb.append("This is ");
  sb.append(true);
  sb.setCharAt(21,'T');
  sb.append('\n');
  sb.append("Java is #");
  sb.append(1);
  String s = sb.toString();
  System.out.println(s);
 }
}
```

The program creates a `StringBuffer` object using the string `" is "`. It appends the string `"Hot"` using the `append()` method and the character `'!'` using an overloaded version of the same method. The `insert()` method is used to insert the string `"Java"` at the beginning of the string buffer.

Three appends are used to tack on a newline character (`\n`), the string `"This is "`, and the `boolean` value `true`. The `append()` method is overloaded to support the appending of the primitive data types as well as arbitrary Java objects.

The `setCharAt()` method is used to replace the letter `'t'` at index 21 with the letter `'T'`. The `charAt()` and `setCharAt()` methods allow `StringBuffer` objects to be treated as arrays of characters.

Finally, another newline character is appended to sb, followed by the string `"Java is #"` and the `int` value 1. The `StringBuffer` object is then converted to a string and displayed to the console window.

The output of the program is as follows:

```
Java is Hot!
This is True
Java is #1
```

Threads and Processes

This section describes the classes of java.lang that support multithreading. It also covers the Process class, which is used to manipulate processes that are executed using the System.exec() methods.

Runnable

The Runnable interface provides a common approach to identifying the code to be executed as part of an active thread. It consists of a single method, run(), which is executed when a thread is activated. The Runnable interface is implemented by the Thread class and by other classes that support threaded execution.

Thread

The Thread class is used to construct and access individual threads of execution that are executed as part of a multithreaded program. It defines the priority constants that are used to control task scheduling: MIN_PRIORITY, MAX_PRIORITY, and NORM_PRIORITY. It provides seven constructors for creating instances of class Thread. The four constructors with the Runnable parameters are used to construct threads for classes that do not subclass the Thread class. The other constructors are used for the construction of Thread objects from Thread subclasses.

Thread supports many methods for accessing Thread objects. These methods provide the capabilities to work with a thread's group; obtain detailed information about a thread's activities; set and test a thread's properties; and cause a thread to wait, be interrupted, or be destroyed.

ThreadGroup

The ThreadGroup class is used to encapsulate a group of threads as a single object so that they can be accessed as a single unit. A number of access methods are provided for manipulating ThreadGroup objects. These methods keep track of the threads and thread groups contained in a thread group and perform global operations on all threads in the group. The global operations are group versions of the operations that are provided by the Thread class.

ThreadLocal

The ThreadLocal class is used to implement variables that are local to a thread. The get(), set(), and initialize() methods are used to set and retrieve the values of these variables.

Process

The `Process` class is used to encapsulate processes that are executed with the `System.exec()` methods. An instance of class `Process` is returned by the `Runtime` class `exec()` method when it executes a process that is external to the Java runtime system. This `Process` object can be destroyed using the `destroy()` method and waited on using the `waitFor()` method. The `exitValue()` method returns the system exit value of the process. The `getInputStream()`, `getOutputStream()`, and `getErrorStream()` methods are used to access the standard input, output, and error streams of the process.

ProcessApp

The simple program in Listing 10.10 actually performs some pretty complex processing. It is provided as an example of some of the powerful things that can be accomplished using the `Process` class.

LISTING **10.10.** THE SOURCE CODE OF THE ProcessApp PROGRAM.

```java
import java.lang.System;
import java.lang.Runtime;
import java.lang.Process;
import java.io.InputStreamReader;
import java.io.BufferedReader;
import java.io.IOException;
public class ProcessApp {
 public static void main(String args[]) throws IOException {
  Runtime r = Runtime.getRuntime();
  Process p = r.exec("java SystemApp");
  BufferedReader kbdInput =
   new BufferedReader(new InputStreamReader(p.getInputStream()));
  String line;
  while((line = kbdInput.readLine())!=null)
   System.out.println(line);
 }
}
```

The program uses the static `getRuntime()` method to get the current instance of the Java runtime system. It then uses the `exec()` method to execute another separate copy of the Java interpreter with the `SystemApp` program that was developed earlier in this chapter. It creates a `BufferedReader` object, `kbdInput`, that is connected to the output stream of the `SystemApp` program. It then uses `kbdInput` to read the output of the `SystemApp` program and display it on the console window.

The `exec()` methods combined with the `Process` class provide a powerful set of tools by which Java programs can be used to launch and control the execution of other programs.

The `Compiler` Class

The `Compiler` class consists of `static` methods that are used to compile Java classes in the rare event that you want to compile classes directly from a program or applet. These methods allow you to build your own customized Java development environment.

Exceptions and Errors

The `java.lang` package establishes the Java exception hierarchy and declares numerous exceptions and errors. Errors are used to indicate the occurrence of abnormal and fatal events that should not be handled within application programs.

The `Throwable` Class

The `Throwable` class is at the top of the Java error-and-exception hierarchy. It is extended by the `Error` and `Exception` classes and provides methods that are common to both classes. These methods consist of stack tracing methods, the `getMessage()` method, and the `toString()` method, which is an override of the method inherited from the `Object` class. The `getMessage()` method is used to retrieve any messages that are supplied in the creation of `Throwable` objects.

The `fillInStackTrace()` and `printStackTrace()` methods supply and print information that is used to trace the propagation of exceptions and errors throughout a program's execution.

The `Error` Class

The `Error` class is used to provide a common superclass to define abnormal and fatal events that should not occur. It provides two constructors and no other methods. Four major classes of errors extend the `Error` class: `AWTError`, `LinkageError`, `ThreadDeath`, and `VirtualMachineError`.

The `AWTError` class identifies fatal errors that occur in the Abstract Window Toolkit packages. It is a single identifier for all AWT errors and is not subclassed.

The `LinkageError` class is used to define errors that occur as the result of incompatibilities between dependent classes. These incompatibilities result when class Y depends on class X, which is changed before class Y can be recompiled. The `LinkageError` class is extensively subclassed to identify specific manifestations of this type of error.

The `ThreadDeath` error class is used to indicate that a thread has been stopped. Instances of this class can be caught and then rethrown to ensure that a thread is gracefully terminated, although this is not recommended. The `ThreadDeath` class is not subclassed.

The `VirtualMachineError` class is used to identify fatal errors occurring in the operation of the Java Virtual Machine. It has four subclasses: `InternalError`, `OutOfMemoryError`, `StackOverflowError`, and `UnknownError`.

The `Exception` Class

The `Exception` class provides a common superclass for the exceptions that can be defined for Java programs and applets.

The `Void` Class

The `Void` class is used to reference the `Class` object representing the `void` type. It is provided for completeness. It has no constructors or methods.

Reflection and the `java.lang.reflect` Package

The classes and interfaces of the `java.lang.reflect` package enable classes, interfaces, and objects to be examined, and their public fields, constructors, and methods to be discovered and used at runtime. These capabilities are used by JavaBeans, object inspection tools, Java runtime tools such as the debugger, and other Java applications and applets.

The `java.lang.reflect` package consists of the `Member` interface and seven classes: `AccessibleObject`, `Array`, `Constructor`, `Field`, `Method`, `Modifier`, and `ReflectPermission`.

The `Member` Interface

The `Member` interface is used to provide information about a `Field`, `Constructor`, or `Method`. It defines two constant variables and three methods. The `DECLARED` constant identifies the class members (fields, constructors, and methods) that are declared for a class. The `PUBLIC` constant identifies all members of a class or interface, including those that are inherited. The `getName()` method returns the name of the referenced `Member`. The `getModifiers()` method returns the modifiers of the referenced `Member` encoded as an integer. The `Modifier` class is used to decode this integer. The `getDeclaringClass()` method returns the class in which the `Member` is declared.

The `AccessibleObject` Class

The `AccessibleObject` class is introduced with JDK 1.2. It is the superclass of the `Constructor`, `Field`, and `Method` classes. It was added to the class hierarchy to provide the capability to specify whether an object suppresses reflection access control checks. The `isAccessible()` method identifies whether the object suppresses access control checks. The `setAccessible()` method is used to set the accessibility of an object or array of objects.

The `Array` Class

The `Array` class is used to obtain information about, create, and manipulate arrays. It consists of 21 `static` methods. The `getLength()` method is used to access the length of an array.

The `get()` method is used to access an indexed element of an array. The `getBoolean()`, `getByte()`, `getChar()`, `getDouble()`, `getFloat()`, `getInt()`, `getLong()`, and `getShort()` methods are used to access an indexed element of an array as a particular primitive type.

The `set()` method is used to set an indexed element of an array. The `setBoolean()`, `setByte()`, `setChar()`, `setDouble()`, `setFloat()`, `setInt()`, `setLong()`, and `setShort()` methods are used to set an indexed element of an array to a value of a particular primitive type.

The `newInstance()` method is used to create new arrays of a specified size.

The `Constructor` Class

The `Constructor` class is used to obtain information about and access the constructors of a class. It consists of nine methods.

The `getName()` method returns the name of the constructor. The `getDeclaringClass()` method identifies the class to which the constructor applies.

The `newInstance()` method is used to create a new instance of the class to which the constructor applies. The `getParameterTypes()` method provides access to the parameters used by the constructor. The `getModifiers()` method encodes the constructor's modifiers as an integer that can be decoded by the `Modifier` class. The `getExceptionTypes()` method identifies the exceptions that are thrown by the constructor.

The `equals()`, `hashCode()`, and `toString()` methods override those of the `Object` class.

The `Field` Class

The `Field` class is used to obtain information about and access the field variables of a class. It consists of 25 methods.

The `getName()` method returns the name of the variable. The `getDeclaringClass()` method identifies the class in which the variable is declared. The `getType()` method provides access to the data type of the variable. The `getModifiers()` method encodes the variable's modifiers as an integer that can be decoded by the `Modifier` class.

The `get()` method is used to access the value of the variable. The `getBoolean()`, `getByte()`, `getChar()`, `getDouble()`, `getFloat()`, `getInt()`, `getLong()`, and `getShort()` methods are used to access the value as a particular primitive type.

The `set()` method is used to set the value of the variable. The `setBoolean()`, `setByte()`, `setChar()`, `setDouble()`, `setFloat()`, `setInt()`, `setLong()`, and `setShort()` methods are used to set the value to a particular primitive type.

The `equals()`, `hashCode()`, and `toString()` methods override those of the `Object` class.

The `Method` Class

The `Method` class is used to obtain information about and access the methods of a class. It consists of 10 methods.

The `getName()` method returns the name of the method. The `getDeclaringClass()` method identifies the class in which the method is declared.

The `invoke()` method is used to invoke the method for a particular object and list of parameters. The `getParameterTypes()` method provides access to the parameters used by the method. The `getModifiers()` method encodes the method's modifiers as an integer that can be decoded by the `Modifier` class. The `getExceptionTypes()` method identifies the exceptions that are thrown by the method. The `getReturnType()` method identifies the type of object returned by the method.

The `equals()`, `hashCode()`, and `toString()` methods override those of the `Object` class.

The `Modifier` Class

The `Modifier` class is used to decode integers that represent the modifiers of classes, interfaces, field variables, constructors, and methods. It consists of 11 constants, a single parameterless constructor, and 12 `static` access methods.

The 11 constants are used to represent all possible modifiers. They are `ABSTRACT`, `FINAL`, `INTERFACE`, `NATIVE`, `PRIVATE`, `PROTECTED`, `PUBLIC`, `STATIC`, `SYNCHRONIZED`, `TRANSIENT`, and `VOLATILE`.

The `toString()` method returns a string containing the modifiers encoded in an integer. The `isAbstract()`, `isFinal()`, `isInterface()`, `isNative()`, `isPrivate()`, `isProtected()`, `isPublic()`, `isStatic()`, `isSynchronized()`, `isTransient()`, and `isVolatile()` methods return a `boolean` value indicating whether the respective modifier is encoded in an integer.

The `ReflectPermission` Class

The `ReflectPermission` class is a permission class introduced with JDK 1.2. It is used to specify whether the default language access checks should be suppressed for reflected objects. Chapter 3 covers the use of permissions in setting up a security policy.

A Reflection Example

The `java.lang.reflect` provides a number of useful methods for discovering information about the members of a class or interface. In most cases, you will use it with the `Class` class of `java.lang`. The example in Listing 10.11 shows how `Class` and the classes of `java.lang.reflect` can be used together to create a program that discovers and displays information about classes and interfaces.

LISTING 10.11. THE SOURCE CODE OF THE `ReflectApp` PROGRAM.

```
import java.lang.reflect.*;
public class ReflectApp {
 public static void main(String args[]) {
  String parm = args[0];
  Class className = void.class;
  try {
   className= Class.forName(parm);
  }catch (ClassNotFoundException ex){
   System.out.println("Not a class or interface.");
   System.exit(0);
  }
  describeClassOrInterface(className,parm);
 }
 static void describeClassOrInterface(Class className,String name){
  if(className.isInterface()){
   System.out.println("Interface: "+name);
   displayModifiers(className.getModifiers());
   displayFields(className.getDeclaredFields());
   displayMethods(className.getDeclaredMethods());
  }else{
   System.out.println("Class: "+name);
   displayModifiers(className.getModifiers());
   displayInterfaces(className.getInterfaces());
   displayFields(className.getDeclaredFields());
   displayConstructors(className.getDeclaredConstructors());
   displayMethods(className.getDeclaredMethods());
  }
 }
 static void displayModifiers(int m){
  System.out.println("Modifiers: "+Modifier.toString(m));
 }
```

```
static void displayInterfaces(Class[] interfaces){
 if(interfaces.length>0){
  System.out.println("Interfaces: ");
  for(int i=0;i<interfaces.length;++i)
   System.out.println(interfaces[i].getName());
 }
}
static void displayFields(Field[] fields){
 if(fields.length>0){
  System.out.println("Fields: ");
  for(int i=0;i<fields.length;++i)
   System.out.println(fields[i].toString());
 }
}
static void displayConstructors(Constructor[] constructors){
 if(constructors.length>0){
  System.out.println("Constructors: ");
  for(int i=0;i<constructors.length;++i)
   System.out.println(constructors[i].toString());
 }
}
static void displayMethods(Method[] methods){
 if(methods.length>0){
  System.out.println("Methods: ");
  for(int i=0;i<methods.length;++i)
   System.out.println(methods[i].toString());
 }
}
}
```

Compile the program and run it as follows. It takes the fully qualified name of a class or interface as a command-line argument. The following output shows the information that it generates when the `java.lang.reflect.AccessibleObject` class is used as an argument. It identifies the class modifiers as `public` and `synchronized` and identifies `ACCESS_PERMISSION` and `override` as field variables. It also shows that `AccessibleObject` has a single parameterless constructor and three methods.

```
java ReflectApp java.lang.reflect.AccessibleObject
Class: java.lang.reflect.AccessibleObject
Modifiers: public synchronized
Fields:
private static final java.security.Permission
➥java.lang.reflect.AccessibleObject
.ACCESS_PERMISSION
private boolean java.lang.reflect.AccessibleObject.override
Constructors:
protected java.lang.reflect.AccessibleObject()
Methods:
```

```
public static void java.lang.reflect.AccessibleObject.setAccessible
➡(java.lang.reflect.AccessibleObject[],boolean) throws
➡java.lang.SecurityException
public void java.lang.reflect.AccessibleObject.setAccessible(boolean)
➡throws java.lang.SecurityException public boolean
java.lang.reflect.AccessibleObject.isAccessible()
```

Try running ReflectApp with other classes and interfaces. It's a great way to learn about the definition of classes and interfaces.

ReflectApp takes the first command-line argument and uses the forName() method of Class to create a Class object representing the class or interface identified by the argument. This Class object is assigned to the className variable. The describeClassOrInterface() method is invoked to display information about the class or interface.

The describeClassOrInterface() method uses the isInterface() method of Class to determine whether the Class object refers to an interface or class. It uses getInterfaces() to retrieve all of the interfaces of a class and invokes displayInterfaces() to display those interfaces.

The describeClassOrInterface() method uses getModifiers(), getDeclaredFields(), getDeclaredConstructors(), and getDeclaredMethods() to retrieve the Modifier, Field, Constructor, and Method objects associated with a class or interface. It invokes displayModifiers(), displayFields(), displayConstructors(), and displayMethods() to display information about these objects. These display methods use the toString() method to convert the objects into a useful display string.

Reference Objects and the `java.lang.ref` Package

JDK 1.2 introduces *reference objects*, which are objects that store references to other objects. The java.lang.ref package provides five classes that implement reference objects. These classes also provide the capability to notify a program when a referenced object is subject to garbage collection. This capability allows reference objects to be used to implement object caching mechanisms.

The Reference class is the top-level class of the reference class hierarchy. It provides the capability to store a reference to another object. The object being referenced is referred to as the *referent*. The Reference class provides the following methods for getting and setting references to the referents:

- get() and set()—Used to retrieve and set the referent.

- `register()` and `unregister()`—Used to register and unregister the reference object with a `ReferenceQueue` object.
- `clear()`—Clears the reference to the referent.
- `isEnqueued()`—Reports on whether a reference object has been queued with a `ReferenceQueue` object.

The classes of the reference object hierarchy are used to work with referents of varying degrees of *reachability*. Reachability refers to the ease with which an object can be referenced. The following degrees of reachability are defined:

- Strongly reachable—An object can be reached without the use of reference objects.
- Weakly reachable—An object that is not strongly reachable, but can be reached via a `WeakReference` object. An object becomes eligible for finalization when all of its weak references are cleared.
- Phantomly reachable—An object that is not strongly or weakly reachable, but can be reached via a `PhantomReference` object. If an object is phantomly reachable, it has been finalized. An object becomes unreachable when all of its phantom references are cleared or unreachable.

`Reference` objects can be registered with a reference queue. When the garbage collector determines that a referent has a change in reachability, the reference object is added to the queue. A program can be notified of the queuing of a reference. The program can then remove the reference from the queue in order to access the referent. When a reference object is removed from a queue, it becomes unregistered. A reference object can only be registered with a single reference queue. The `ReferenceQueue` class implements reference queues. It provides the `remove()` method for removing an object from the queue. The `register()` and `unregister()` methods of the `Reference` class are used to register and unregister objects with a `ReferenceQueue` object.

The subclasses of `Reference` are used to implement the reachability levels. These classes are as follows:

- `WeakReference`—When the referent of a registered `WeakReference` object is no longer strongly reachable, the `WeakReference` object is cleared and added to the `ReferenceQueue` to which it is registered. The referent is then subject to finalization.
- `PhantomReference`—When the referent of a registered `PhantomReference` object is no longer strongly or weakly reachable, the `PhantomReference` object is cleared and added to the `ReferenceQueue` to which it is registered. Because `PhantomReference` objects refer to objects that have been finalized, its `get()` method always returns `null`.

The `ReferenceApp` Program

Although the reference classes are intended to be used to build caching systems, reference objects can be used in other ways. The `ReferenceApp` program (Listing 10.12) provides an example of the use of reference objects. It creates two `String` objects and assigns them to `s1` and `s2`. It then creates two `WeakReference` objects that refer to the `String` objects, and assigns the reference objects to `g1` and `g2`. It shows that `g1` and `g2` reference the original `String` objects by displaying the values returned by the `get()` method. The `WeakReference` object referenced by `g2` is assigned to `g1`. The value of the referent of `g1` is then displayed to show that it is now the second `String` object.

The output of `ReferenceApp` is as follows:

```
g1 = The value of a String object 1
g2 = The value of a String object 2
g1 = The value of a String object 2
```

LISTING 10.12. THE `ReferenceApp` PROGRAM.

```
import java.lang.ref.*;

public class ReferenceApp {
 public static void main(String args[]) {
  String s1 = "The value of a String object 1";
  String s2 = "The value of a String object 2";
  GuardedReference g1 = new WeakReference(s1);
  GuardedReference g2 = new WeakReference(s2);
  System.out.println("g1 = "+(String) g1.get());
  System.out.println("g2 = "+(String) g2.get());
  g1=g2;
  System.out.println("g1 = "+(String) g1.get());
 }
}
```

Summary

In this chapter you learned to write console programs in Java. You learned how to read user keyboard input, process the input, and display text output to the user's console. You also learned about some useful classes and interfaces in the `java.lang`, `java.lang.reflect`, and `java.lang.ref` packages. In the next chapter you'll learn how to use the classes and interfaces of the `java.util` and `java.math` packages.

Using the Utility and Math Packages

CHAPTER 11

The `java.util` family of packages and the `java.math` package provide a number of classes and interfaces that can be used to simplify the development of window and console applications, applets, or just about any Java code that you write. These utility classes include the new JDK 1.2 Collections API, as well as Java Archive (JAR), ZIP file, and MIME type support. The math classes provide support for large-number arithmetic. In this chapter you'll learn how to work with all the useful utility classes contained in the `java.util`, `java.util.mime`, `java.util.zip`, `java.util.jar`, and `java.math` packages. When you finish this chapter, you'll be able to make productive use of these classes in your own programs.

The `java.util` Package

The `java.util` package provides 34 classes and 13 interfaces that support the new Collections API, date/calendar operations, internationalization, change observation, parsing, random number generation, and basic event processing. These classes and interfaces are covered in the following subsections.

The Collections API

The most notable change to the `java.util` package in JDK 1.2 is the introduction of the classes and interfaces of the Collections API. These classes and interfaces provide an implementation-independent framework for manipulating collections of objects. We'll first review the pre-JDK 1.2 collections classes and interfaces. Then we'll cover the new classes and interfaces introduced with JDK 1.2.

Pre-JDK 1.2 Collections Classes and Interfaces

JDK 1.1 provided the `Enumeration` interface and the following six classes for working with collections of objects:

- `Vector`—An expandable array of objects.
- `Stack`—A last-in-first-out stack of objects.
- `BitSet`—A growable bit vector.
- `Dictionary`—A list of key-value pairs.
- `Hashtable`—A dictionary that implements a hash table.
- `Properties`—A hash table that provides the capability to associate a list of properties with their values.

The `Enumeration` interface and the preceding six classes proved to be very valuable in working with different types of object collections. Their success inspired the JDK 1.2

Using the Utility and Math Packages

CHAPTER 11

271

11

USING THE
UTILITY AND
MATH PACKAGES

Collections API. The following subsections cover the `Enumeration` interface and the six classes in the preceding list.

The `Enumeration` Interface

The `Enumeration` interface provides two methods for stepping through an indexed set of objects or values: `hasMoreElements()` and `nextElement()`. The `hasMoreElements()` method enables you to determine whether more elements are contained in an `Enumeration` object. The `nextElement()` method returns the `nextElement()` contained by an object.

`Enumeration`-implementing objects are said to be *consumed* by their use. This means that the `Enumeration` objects cannot be restarted to reaccess through the elements they contain. Their elements may be accessed only once.

> **NOTE**
>
> The `Enumeration` interface has been replaced by the `Iterator` interface in the JDK 1.2 Collections API. You can still use `Enumeration`, but it is being phased out.

The `Vector` Class

The `Vector` class provides the capability to implement a growable array. The array grows larger as more elements are added to it. The array may also be reduced in size after some of its elements have been deleted. This is accomplished using the `trimToSize()` method.

`Vector` operates by creating an initial storage capacity and then adding to this capacity as needed. It grows by an increment defined by the `capacityIncrement` variable. The initial storage capacity and `capacityIncrement` can be specified in `Vector`'s constructor. A second constructor is used when you want to specify only the initial storage capacity. A third, default constructor specifies neither the initial capacity nor the `capacityIncrement`. This constructor lets Java figure out the best parameters to use for `Vector` objects. Finally, a fourth constructor was added with JDK 1.2 to create a `Vector` out of a `Collection` object.

The access methods provided by the `Vector` class support array-like operations and operations related to the size of `Vector` objects. The array-like operations allow elements to be added, deleted, and inserted into vectors. They also allow tests to be performed on the contents of vectors and specific elements to be retrieved. The size-related operations allow the byte size and number of elements of the vector to be determined, and the vector size to be increased to a certain capacity or trimmed to the minimum capacity needed. Consult the `Vector` API page for a complete description of these methods.

> **NOTE**
>
> The Vector class has been retrofitted in JDK 1.2 to extend the AbstractList class and implement the List interface.

VectorApp

The VectorApp program illustrates the use of vectors and the Enumeration interface. (See Listing 11.1.)

LISTING 11.1. THE SOURCE CODE OF THE VectorApp PROGRAM.

```
import java.lang.System;
import java.util.Vector;
import java.util.Enumeration;

public class VectorApp {
 public static void main(String args[]){
  Vector v = new Vector();
  v.addElement("one");
  v.addElement("two");
  v.addElement("three");
  v.insertElementAt("zero",0);
  v.insertElementAt("oops",3);
  v.insertElementAt("four",5);
  System.out.println("Size: "+v.size());
  Enumeration enum = v.elements();
  while (enum.hasMoreElements())
   System.out.print(enum.nextElement()+" ");
  System.out.println();
  v.removeElement("oops");
  System.out.println("Size: "+v.size());
  for(int i=0;i<v.size();++i)
   System.out.print(v.elementAt(i)+" ");
  System.out.println();
 }
}
```

The program creates a Vector object using the default constructor, and uses the addElement() method to add the strings "one", "two", and "three" to the vector. It then uses the insertElementAt() method to insert the strings "zero", "oops", and "four" at locations 0, 3, and 5 within the vector. The size() method is used to retrieve the vector size for display to the console window.

The elements() method of the Vector class is used to retrieve an enumeration of the elements that were added to the vector. A while loop is then used to cycle through and

Using the Utility and Math Packages

CHAPTER 11

273

11

USING THE
UTILITY AND
MATH PACKAGES

print the elements contained in the enumeration. The `hasMoreElements()` method is used to determine whether the enumeration contains more elements. If it does, the `nextElement()` method is used to retrieve the object for printing.

The `removeElement()` of the `Vector` class is used to remove the vector element containing the string `"oops"`. The new size of the vector is displayed and the elements of the vector are redisplayed. The `for` loop indexes each element in the vector using the `elementAt()` method.

The output of the `VectorApp` program is as follows:

```
Size: 6
zero one two oops three four
Size: 5
zero one two three four
```

The `Stack` Class

The `Stack` class provides the capability to create and use storage objects called *stacks* within your Java programs. You store information by pushing it onto a stack, and remove and retrieve information by popping it off the stack. Stacks implement a last-in-first-out storage capability. The last object pushed onto a stack is the first object that can be retrieved from the stack. The `Stack` class extends the `Vector` class.

The `Stack` class provides a single default constructor, `Stack()`, that is used to create an empty stack.

Objects are placed on the stack using the `push()` method and retrieved from the stack using the `pop()` method. The `search()` method allows you to search through a stack to see if a particular object is contained on the stack. The `peek()` method returns the top element of the stack without popping it off. The `empty()` method is used to determine whether a stack is empty. The `pop()` and `peek()` methods both throw the `EmptyStackException` if the stack is empty. Use of the `empty()` method can help to avoid the generation of this exception.

StackApp

The `StackApp` program demonstrates the operation of a stack (see Listing 11.2). It creates a `Stack` object and then uses the `push()` method to push the strings `"one"`, `"two"`, and `"three"` onto the stack. Because the stack operates in last-in-first-out fashion, the top of the stack is the string `"three"`. This is verified by using the `peek()` method. The contents of the stack are then popped off and printed using a `while` loop. The `empty()` method is used to determine when the loop should terminate. The `pop()` method is used to pop objects off the top of the stack.

LISTING 11.2. THE SOURCE CODE OF THE StackApp PROGRAM.

```java
import java.lang.System;
import java.util.Stack;

public class StackApp {
 public static void main(String args[]){
  Stack s = new Stack();
  s.push("one");
  s.push("two");
  s.push("three");
  System.out.println("Top of stack: "+s.peek());
  while (!s.empty())
    System.out.println(s.pop());
 }
}
```

The output of the StackApp program is as follows:

```
Top of stack: three
three
two
one
```

The BitSet Class

The BitSet class is used to create objects that maintain a set of bits. The bits are maintained as a growable set. The capacity of the bit set is increased as needed. Bit sets are used to maintain a list of *flags* that indicate the state of each element of a set of conditions. Flags are boolean values that are used to represent the state of an object.

Two BitSet constructors are provided. One allows the initial capacity of a BitSet object to be specified. The other is a default constructor that initializes a BitSet to a default size.

The BitSet access methods provide and, or, and exclusive or logical operations on bit sets, enable specific bits to be set and cleared, and override general methods declared for the Object class.

BitSetApp

The BitSetApp program demonstrates the operation of bit sets. See Listing 11.3.

LISTING 11.3. THE SOURCE CODE OF THE BitSetApp PROGRAM.

```java
import java.lang.System;
import java.util.BitSet;

public class BitSetApp {
```

Using the Utility and Math Packages

CHAPTER 11

275

11

USING THE
UTILITY AND
MATH PACKAGES

```
public static void main(String args[]){
  int size = 8;
  BitSet b1 = new BitSet(size);
  for(int i=0;i<size;++i) b1.set(i);
  BitSet b2 = (BitSet) b1.clone();
  for(int i=0;i<size;i=i+2) b2.clear(i);
  System.out.print("b1: ");
  for(int i=0;i<size;++i) System.out.print(b1.get(i)+" ");
  System.out.print("\nb2: ");
  for(int i=0;i<size;++i) System.out.print(b2.get(i)+" ");
  System.out.println();
  System.out.println("b1: "+b1);
  System.out.println("b2: "+b2);
  b1.xor(b2);
  System.out.println("b1 xor b2 = "+b1);
  b1.and(b2);
  System.out.println("b1 and b2 = "+b1);
  b1.or(b2);
  System.out.println("b1 or b2 = "+b1);
 }
}
```

The program begins by creating a BitSet object, b1, of size 8. It executes a for statement to index through b1 and set each bit in the bit set. It then uses the clone() method to create an identical copy of b1 and assign it to b2. Another for statement is executed to clear every even-numbered bit in b2. The values of the b1 and b2 bit sets are then printed. This results in the display of two lists of boolean values. The bit sets are printed as objects, resulting in a set-oriented display. Only the bits with true boolean values are identified as members of the displayed bit sets.

The xor() method is used to compute the exclusive or of b1 and b2, updating b1 with the result. The new value of b1 is then displayed.

The and() method is used to calculate the logical and of b1 and b2, again, updating b1 with the result and displaying b1's new value.

Finally, the logical or of b1 and b2 is computed, using the or() method. The result is used to update b1, and b1's value is displayed.

The output of BitSetApp is as follows:

```
b1: true true true true true true true true
b2: false true false true false true false true
b1: {0, 1, 2, 3, 4, 5, 6, 7}
b2: {1, 3, 5, 7}
b1 xor b2 = {0, 2, 4, 6}
b1 and b2 = {}
b1 or b2 = {1, 3, 5, 7}
```

The `Dictionary`, `Hashtable`, and `Properties` Classes

The `Dictionary`, `Hashtable`, and `Properties` classes are three generations of classes that implement the capability to provide key-based data storage and retrieval. The `Dictionary` class is the abstract superclass of `Hashtable`, which is, in turn, the superclass of `Properties`.

Dictionary

`Dictionary` provides the abstract functions used to store and retrieve objects by key-value associations. The class allows any object to be used as a key or value. This provides great flexibility in the design of key-based storage and retrieval classes. `Hashtable` and `Properties` are two examples of these classes.

The `Dictionary` class can be understood using its namesake abstraction. A hard-copy dictionary maps words to their definitions. The words can be considered the keys of the dictionary, and the definitions are the values of the keys. Java dictionaries operate in the same fashion. One object is used as the key to access another object. This abstraction will become clearer as you investigate the `Hashtable` and `Properties` classes.

The `Dictionary` class defines several methods that are inherited by its subclasses. The `elements()` method is used to return an `Enumeration` object containing the values of the key-value pairs stored within the dictionary. The `keys()` method returns an enumeration of the dictionary keys. The `get()` method is used to retrieve an object from the dictionary based on its key. The `put()` method puts a `Value` object in the dictionary and indexes it using a `Key` object. The `isEmpty()` method determines whether a dictionary contains any elements, and the `size()` method identifies the dictionary's size in terms of the number of elements it contains. The `remove()` method deletes a key-value pair from the dictionary, based on the object's key.

> **NOTE**
>
> The `Dictionary` class has been rendered obsolete by the `Map` interface, as of JDK 1.2. However, its `Hashtable` and `Properties` subclasses are still in use.

Hashtable

The `Hashtable` class implements a hash table data structure. A *hash table* indexes and stores objects in a dictionary using hash codes as the objects' keys. *Hash codes* are integer values that identify objects. They are computed in such a manner that different objects are very likely to have different hash values and therefore different dictionary keys.

Using the Utility and Math Packages

CHAPTER 11

277

11

USING THE
UTILITY AND
MATH PACKAGES

The `Object` class implements the `hashCode()` method. This method allows the hash code of an arbitrary Java object to be calculated. All Java classes and objects inherit this method from `Object`. The `hashCode()` method is used to compute the hash code key for storing objects within a hash table. `Object` also implements the `equals()` method. This method is used to determine whether two objects with the same hash code are, in fact, equal.

The Java `Hashtable` class is very similar to the `Dictionary` class from which it is derived. Objects are added to a hash table as key-value pairs. The object used as the key is hashed, using its `hashCode()` method, and the hash code is used as the actual key for the value object. When an object is to be retrieved from a hash table, using a key, the key's hash code is computed and used to find the object.

The `Hashtable` class provides three constructors. The first constructor allows a hash table to be created with a specific initial capacity and load factor. The *load factor* is a `float` value between 0.0 and 1.0 that identifies the percentage of hash table usage that causes the hash table to be rehashed into a larger table. For example, suppose a hash table is created with a capacity of 100 entries and a 0.70 load factor. When the hash table is 70 percent full, a new, larger hash table will be created, and the current hash table entries will have their hash values recalculated for the larger table.

The second `Hashtable` constructor just specifies the table's initial capacity and ignores the load factor. The default hash table constructor does not specify either hash table parameter.

The access methods defined for the `Hashtable` class allow key-value pairs to be added to and removed from a hash table, to search the hash table for a particular key or object value, to create an enumeration of the table's keys and values, to determine the size of the hash table, and to recalculate the hash table as needed. Many of these methods are inherited or overridden from the `Dictionary` class.

HashApp
The `HashApp` program illustrates the operation and use of hash tables. See Listing 11.4.

LISTING 11.4. THE SOURCE CODE OF THE HashApp PROGRAM.

```
import java.lang.System;
import java.util.Hashtable;
import java.util.Enumeration;

public class HashApp {
 public static void main(String args[]){
  Hashtable h = new Hashtable();
```

continues

LISTING 11.4. CONTINUED

```
    h.put("height","6 feet");
    h.put("weight","200 pounds");
    h.put("eye color","blue");
    h.put("hair color","brown");
    System.out.println("h: "+h);
    Enumeration enum = h.keys();
    System.out.print("keys: ");
    while (enum.hasMoreElements()) System.out.print(enum.nextElement()+",
➥ ");
    System.out.print("\nelements: ");
    enum = h.elements();
    while (enum.hasMoreElements()) System.out.print(enum.nextElement()+",
➥ ");
    System.out.println();
    System.out.println("height: "+h.get("height"));
    System.out.println("weight: "+h.get("weight"));
    System.out.println("eyes: "+h.get("eye color"));
    System.out.println("hair: "+h.get("hair color"));
    h.remove("weight");
    System.out.println("h: "+h);
  }
}
```

The program begins by creating a Hashtable object using the default constructor. It then adds four key-value pairs to the hash table using the put() method. The hash table is then printed using the default print method for objects of class Hashtable.

The keys() method is used to create an enumeration of the hash table's keys. These keys are then printed one at a time by indexing through the enumeration object.

The elements() method is used to create an enumeration of the hash table's values. This enumeration is printed in the same way as the key enumeration.

The values of the hash table are again displayed by using the get() method to get the values corresponding to specific key values.

Finally, the remove() method is used to remove the key-value pair associated with the weight key, and the hash table is reprinted using the default print convention.

The program output is as follows:

```
h: {height=6 feet, weight=200 pounds, eye color=blue, hair color=brown}
keys: height, weight, eye color, hair color,
elements: 6 feet, 200 pounds, blue, brown,
height: 6 feet
weight: 200 pounds
eyes: blue
```

Using the Utility and Math Packages

CHAPTER 11

279

11

USING THE
UTILITY AND
MATH PACKAGES

```
hair: brown
h: {height=6 feet, eye color=blue, hair color=brown}
```

The Properties *Class*

The Properties class is a subclass of Hashtable that can be read from or written to a stream. It also provides the capability to specify a set of default values to be used if a specified key is not found in the table. The default values themselves are specified as an object of class Properties. This allows an object of class Properties to have a default Properties object, which in turn has its own default properties, and so on.

Properties supports two constructors: a default constructor with no parameters, and a constructor that accepts the default properties to be associated with the Properties object being constructed.

The Properties class declares several new access methods. The getProperty() method allows a property to be retrieved using a String object as a key. A second overloaded getProperty() method allows a value string to be used as the default in case the key is not contained in the Properties object.

The load() and save() methods are used to load a Properties object from an input stream and save it to an output stream. The save() method allows an optional header comment to be saved at the beginning of the saved object's position in the output stream.

The propertyNames() method provides an enumeration of all the property keys, and the list() method provides a convenient way to print a Properties object on a PrintStream object.

PropApp

The PropApp program illustrates the use of the Properties class by retrieving the System properties and displaying them to the console (see Listing 11.5). This program is similar to the SystemApp program of Chapter 10, "Writing Console Applications."

LISTING 11.5. THE SOURCE CODE OF THE PropApp PROGRAM.

```
import java.lang.System;
import java.util.Properties;

public class PropApp {
 public static void main(String args[]){
  Properties sysProp = System.getProperties();
  sysProp.list(System.out);
 }
}
```

The program uses the getProperties() method of the System class to retrieve the system properties and assign them to the sysProp variable. The system properties are then listed on the console window using the list() method.

The program's output will vary from machine to machine. Its output, when run from my computer, is as follows:

```
-- listing properties --
java.specification.name=Java Platform API Specification
awt.toolkit=sun.awt.windows.WToolkit
java.version=1.2beta2
java.awt.graphicsenv=sun.awt.Win32GraphicsEnvironment
java.tmpdir=c:\windows\TEMP\
user.timezone=PST
java.specification.version=1.2beta2
user.home=C:\JDK1.2BETA2\BIN\..
java-vm.name=non-JIT
os.arch=x86
java.awt.fonts=C:\WINDOWS\Fonts
java.vendor.url=http://www.sun.com/
user.region=US
file.encoding.pkg=sun.io
java.home=C:\JDK1.2BETA2\BIN\..
java-vm.specification.vendor=Sun Microsystems Inc.
java-vm.specification.version=1.0
java.class.path=.;C:\JavaWebServer1.0.3\public_html\c...
line.separator=

os.name=Windows 95
java.vendor=Sun Microsystems Inc.
java.library.path=C:\JDK1.2BETA2\BIN;.;C:\WINDOWS;c:\wi...
java-vm.version=1.2beta2
file.encoding=8859_1
java.specification.vendor=Sun Microsystems Inc.
user.name=jaworskij
user.language=en
java.vendor.url.bug=http://java.sun.com/cgi-bin/bugreport...
java.class.version=45.3
os.version=4.0
path.separator=;
java-vm.specification.name=Java Virtual Machine Specification
file.separator=\
user.dir=C:\jdk1.2beta2\ju\ch11
java-vm.vendor=Sun Microsystems Inc.
```

Using the Utility and Math Packages

CHAPTER 11

281

11

USING THE
UTILITY AND
MATH PACKAGES

JDK 1.2 Collections Classes and Interfaces

The Collections API of JDK 1.2 added 10 new interfaces and 13 new classes to those that you studied in the previous section. These additional classes and interfaces provide a powerful API for working with different types of object collections.

The new collections interfaces introduced with JDK 1.2 are as follows:

- Collection—Defines methods that implement the concept of a group of objects, referred to as *elements*. The Collection interface corresponds to a mathematical *bag*, which is a collection that allows duplicate objects. It defines a full spectrum of methods for adding, removing, and retrieving objects from the collection, as well as methods that operate on the collection itself.

- List—Extends the Collection interface to implement an ordered collection of objects. Because lists are ordered, List's objects can be indexed. The ListIterator interface provides methods for iterating through the elements of a list.

- Set—Extends the Collection interface to implement a finite mathematical set. Sets differ from lists in that they do not allow duplicate elements.

- SortedSet—A Set whose elements are sorted in ascending order.

- Comparator—Provides the compare() method for comparing the elements of a collection.

- Iterator—Provides methods for iterating through the elements of a collection. In JDK 1.2, the Iterator interface replaces the Enumeration interface.

- ListIterator—Extends the Iterator interface to support bidirectional iteration of lists.

- Map—Replaces the Dictionary class as a means to associate keys with values. The Map interface provides similar methods for performing operations on the map and its elements.

- SortedMap—A Map whose elements are sorted in ascending order.

- Map.Entry—An inner interface of the Map interface that defines methods for working with a single key-value pair.

Figure 11.1 shows the hierarchical relationships between the classes and interfaces of the Collections API.

FIGURE 11.1.
The Collections API class and interface hierarchy.

Collections API Hierarchy

```
           Interfaces                                    Classes

Enumeration                              java.lang.Object
Collection                                   AbstractCollection
    List                                         AbstractList
    Set                                              AbstractSequentialList
        Sorted Set                                       LinkedList
Comparator                                       ArrayList
Iterator                                         Vector
    List Iterator                                    Stack
Map                                          AbstractSet
    SortedMap                                    HashSet
Map.Entry                                        TreeSet
                                         AbstractMap
                                             HashMap
                                             TreeMap
                                             WeakHashMap
                                         Arrays
                                         BitSet
                                         Collections
                                         Dictionary
                                             Hashtable
                                                 Properties
```

The new collections classes introduced with JDK 1.2 are as follows:

- `AbstractCollection`—The `AbstractCollection` class provides a basic implementation of the `Collection` interface. It is extended by other classes that tailor `AbstractCollection` to more specific implementations.

- `AbstractList`—The `AbstractList` class extends the `AbstractCollection` class to provide a basic implementation of the `List` interface.

- `AbstractSequentialList`—The `AbstractSequentialList` class extends the `AbstractList` class to provide a list that is tailored to sequential access, as opposed to random access.

- `LinkedList`—The `LinkedList` class extends the `AbstractSequentialList` class to provide an implementation of a doubly linked list. A *linked list* is a list in which each element references the next element in the list. A *doubly linked list* is a list in which each element references both the previous and next elements in the list.

- `ArrayList`—The `ArrayList` class extends `AbstractList` to implement a resizable array.

- `AbstractSet`—The `AbstractSet` class extends the `AbstractCollection` class to provide a basic implementation of the `Set` interface.

- `HashSet`—The `HashSet` class extends `AbstractSet` to implement a set of key-value pairs. It does not allow the use of the `null` element.

Using the Utility and Math Packages

CHAPTER 11

283

11

USING THE
UTILITY AND
MATH PACKAGES

- TreeSet—The TreeSet class extends AbstractSet to implement the Set interface using a TreeMap.

- AbstractMap—The AbstractMap class provides a basic implementation of the Map interface.

- HashMap—The HashMap class extends AbstractMap to implement a hash table that supports the Map interface.

- WeakHashMap—The WeakHashMap class extends AbstractMap to implement a hash table that supports the Map interface and allows its keys to be garbage collected when no longer in ordinary use.

- TreeMap—The TreeMap class extends AbstractMap to implement a sorted binary tree that supports the Map interface.

- Arrays—The Arrays class provides static methods for searching and sorting arrays and converting them to lists.

- Collections—The Collections class provides static methods for searching, sorting, and performing other operations on objects that implement the Collection interface.

The right half of Figure 11.1 shows the Collections API class hierarchy. The following subsections show how to work with the new Collections classes and interfaces. Four examples are provided that show you how to work with lists, sets, maps, and the conversion capabilities of the Arrays class.

Working with Lists

Lists are collections whose objects are ordered. Because lists are ordered, their elements can be indexed. Lists allow duplicate elements. Most lists allow the null value to be an element.

The ListApp program of Listing 11.6 shows how to create and use lists. This program creates a LinkedList object that is referenced by the list variable. The add() method if used to add the strings "is", "is", "a", and "a" to the LinkedList object. The add() method is then used to add the null value to the list. The addLast() method is used to add "test" as the last element of the list. The addFirst() method is used to add "This" as the first element of the list. The displayList() method is then invoked to display the elements of the list.

The displayList() method displays the following results:

```
The size of the list is: 7
This
is
is
```

```
a
a
null
test
```

The displayList() method uses the size() method to determine the number of elements in the list. It invokes the listIterator() method to return an object that implements the ListIterator interface. The argument to the listIterator() method is the index of the first element of the list to return in the ListIterator object. In this case, we used 0 so that the whole list would be returned.

The hasNext() method of the ListIterator interface is used to iterate through the list, and the next() method is used to retrieve the next element of the list. Note that the list can contain the null value, and special provisions are made for printing this value.

LISTING 11.6. THE ListApp PROGRAM.

```java
import java.util.*;

public class ListApp {
 public static void main(String args[]){
    LinkedList list = new LinkedList();
    list.add("is");
    list.add("is");
    list.add("a");
    list.add("a");
    list.add(null);
    list.addLast("test");
    list.addFirst("This");
    displayList(list);
 }
 static void displayList(LinkedList list) {
  System.out.println("The size of the list is: "+list.size());
  ListIterator i = list.listIterator(0);
  while(i.hasNext()){
   Object o = i.next();
   if(o == null) System.out.println("null");
   else System.out.println(o.toString());
  }
 }
}
```

Working with Sets

Sets differ from lists in that they are unordered and cannot contain duplicates of the same element. The SetApp program, shown in Listing 11.7, illustrates the use of sets. It performs the same type of processing as ListApp, but it does so using sets instead of lists.

LISTING 11.7. THE `SetApp` PROGRAM.

```java
import java.util.*;

public class SetApp {
 public static void main(String args[]){
    HashSet set = new HashSet();
    set.add("This");
    set.add("is");
    set.add("is");
    set.add("a");
    set.add("a");
    set.add(null);
    set.add("test");
    displaySet(set);
 }
 static void displaySet(HashSet set) {
  System.out.println("The size of the set is: "+set.size());
  Iterator i = set.iterator();
  while(i.hasNext()){
   Object o = i.next();
   if(o == null) System.out.println("null");
   else System.out.println(o.toString());
  }
 }
}
```

`SetApp` begins by creating an `HashSet` object and assigning it to the `set` variable. It then adds the same elements to the set as `ListApp` did to its list. Note that because sets are not ordered, there are no `addFirst()` and `addLast()` methods. The `displaySet()` method is invoked to display the set. It displays the following results:

```
The size of the set is: 5
This
is
a
null
test
```

Note that the set did not allow duplicate elements, but did allow the `null` value as an element. The `displaySet()` method uses the `size()` method to determine the number of elements in the set. It uses the `iterator()` method to create an `Iterator` object. The `Iterator` object is used to step through and display the elements of the set.

Working with Maps

Maps differ from lists and sets in that they are ordered collections of key-value pairs. Maps are a generalization of the `Dictionary`, `Hashtable`, and `Properties` classes that you studied earlier in this chapter. The MapApp program of Listing 11.8 uses an object of the TreeMap class to create a sorted list of key-value pairs. The TreeMap class implements a sorted binary tree.

LISTING 11.8. THE MapApp PROGRAM.

```java
import java.util.*;

public class MapApp {
 public static void main(String args[]){
    TreeMap map = new TreeMap();
    map.put("one","1");
    map.put("two","2");
    map.put("three","3");
    map.put("four","4");
    map.put("five","5");
    map.put("six","6");
    displayMap(map);
 }
 static void displayMap(TreeMap map) {
  System.out.println("The size of the map is: "+map.size());
  Collection c = map.entrySet();
  Iterator i = c.iterator();
  while(i.hasNext()){
   Object o = i.next();
   if(o == null) System.out.println("null");
   else System.out.println(o.toString());
  }
 }
}
```

The MapApp program begins by creating a TreeMap object and assigning it to the map variable. It then adds six key-value pairs to the map. These key-value pairs associate the names of the numbers from 1 through 6 with their values. The displayMap() method is then invoked to display the program's results:

```
The size of the map is: 6
five=5
four=4
one=1
six=6
three=3
two=2
```

The displayMap() method uses the size() method to determine the number of elements (key-value pairs) in the map. It invokes the entrySet() method to create a Collection object containing the values of the map. The iterator() method of the Collection

Using the Utility and Math Packages

CHAPTER 11

287

11

USING THE
UTILITY AND
MATH PACKAGES

object is used to obtain an Iterator object for the collection. The Iterator object is used to step through and display the elements of the collection. You should note that the TreeMap object uses the key to sort its key-value pairs.

Sorting and Converting

The Arrays and Collections classes provide a number of static methods for searching, sorting, and converting arrays and Collection objects. The ConvertApp program of Listing 11.9 provides an example of these capabilities. This program creates an array of names, sorts the array, converts it to a list, and then displays the values of the list.

LISTING 11.9. THE ConvertApp PROGRAM.

```
import java.util.*;

public class ConvertApp {
 public static void main(String args[]){
  String strings[] = {"Jason","Emily","Lisa","Jamie","Pierre",
   "Stanley","Gloria","Ben","Ken","Lela"};
  Arrays.sort(strings);
  List list = Arrays.asList(strings);
  displayList(list);
 }
 static void displayList(List list) {
  System.out.println("The size of the list is: "+list.size());
  ListIterator i = list.listIterator(0);
  while(i.hasNext()){
   Object o = i.next();
   if(o == null) System.out.println("null");
   else System.out.println(o.toString());
  }
 }
}
```

ConvertApp begins by creating an array of first names. It then uses the static sort() method of the Arrays class to sort the array. The asList() method of Arrays is invoked to convert the array to a List object. The displayList() method is then invoked to display the list. Its output follows:

```
The size of the list is: 10
Ben
Emily
Gloria
Jamie
Jason
Ken
Lela
```

Lisa
Pierre
Stanley

The displayList() method uses the method of the List interface to determine the size of the list and step through the elements of the list.

Date and Calendar-Related Classes

Another major set of classes supported by the java.util package are classes for working with dates and calendars. The original JDK 1.0 provided the Date class to encapsulate date and time as an object. In JDK 1.1, many of the functions of the Date class were deprecated in favor of more international handling of date and time. The Calendar, GregorianCalendar, SimpleTimeZone, and TimeZone classes were added to provide more comprehensive and international support of date and time. The DateFormat class of the java.text package was also added to support international date formatting.

> **NOTE**
>
> A *deprecated* API element is one that has been replaced by an improved alternative. In most cases, the deprecated element may still be used. However, compiler warnings are generated to inform you that an improved alternative exists.

Date

The Date class encapsulates date and time information and allows date objects to be accessed in a system-independent manner.

Four of the six Date JDK 1.0 constructors have been deprecated. Only the default constructor that creates a Date object with the current system date and time, and a constructor that creates a Date object from a long value, are not deprecated in JDK 1.2.

The access methods defined by the Date class support comparisons between dates and provide access to specific date information, including the time zone offset. However, many of the JDK 1.0 methods have been deprecated in favor of methods provided by the Calendar, DateFormat, and TimeZone classes.

Calendar

The Calendar class provides support for date conversions that were previously implemented by the Date class. The support provided by Calendar is more comprehensive and

Using the Utility and Math Packages

CHAPTER 11

289

11

USING THE
UTILITY AND
MATH PACKAGES

international. The Calendar class is an abstract class that can be extended to provide conversions for specific calendar systems. The GregorianCalendar subclass supports the predominant calendar system used by many countries.

The Calendar class provides two constructors—a default parameterless constructor that constructs a calendar with the default TimeZone and Locale objects, and a constructor that allows the TimeZone and Locale objects to be specified. It supplies many constants for accessing days of the week, months of the year, hours, minutes, seconds, milliseconds, and other values.

The Calendar class provides a number of methods for performing data comparisons, arithmetic, and conversions. The getInstance() method returns a locale-specific calendar that is a GregorianCalendar object, by default.

GregorianCalendar

The GregorianCalendar class is a subclass of the Calendar class that supports calendar operations for most of the world. It supports the eras B.C. and A.D. by defining them as class constants. It provides seven constructors that allow GregorianCalendar objects to be created using a combination of different date, time, time zone, and locale values. Its methods override those provided by the Calendar class.

TimeZone

The TimeZone class is used to encapsulate the notion of a time zone. It allows you to work in the local time zone, as well as time zones that are selected by a time zone ID. The TimeZone class keeps track of daylight savings time.

The TimeZone class provides a single, parameterless constructor that creates a TimeZone object corresponding to the local time zone. The TimeZone class does not define any field variables.

The access methods of TimeZone allow you to get a list of available time zone IDs, retrieve the local time zone (from the operating system), get the local time zone offset (and adjust it for daylight savings time), and create TimeZone objects for other time zone IDs.

SimpleTimeZone

The SimpleTimeZone class extends TimeZone to provide support for GregorianCalendar objects. It creates SimpleTimeZone objects using the time zone IDs and offsets defined in the TimeZone class. It provides methods for changing the way daylight savings time is calculated.

DateApp

The DateApp program illustrates the use of the date-related classes covered in the previous sections. It shows how Date, GregorianCalendar, and TimeZone objects are created and how to use their methods to access date/time information. The DateApp program is presented in Listing 11.10.

LISTING 11.10. THE SOURCE CODE OF THE DateApp PROGRAM.

```java
import java.lang.System;
import java.util.Date;
import java.util.Calendar;
import java.util.GregorianCalendar;
import java.util.TimeZone;

public class DateApp {
 public static void main(String args[]){
  Date today = new Date();
  GregorianCalendar cal = new GregorianCalendar();
  cal.setTime(today);
  System.out.println("Today: ");
  displayDateInfo(cal);
  cal.clear();
  cal.set(2000,0,1);
  System.out.println("\nNew Years Day 2000: ");
  displayDateInfo(cal);
 }
 static void displayDateInfo(GregorianCalendar cal){
  String days[] = {"","Sun","Mon","Tue","Wed","Thu","Fri","Sat"};
  String months[] = {"January","February","March","April","May",
   "June","July","August","September","October","November",
   "December"};
  String am_pm[] = {"AM","PM"};
  System.out.println("Year: "+cal.get(Calendar.YEAR));
  System.out.println("Month: "+months[cal.get(Calendar.MONTH)]);
  System.out.println("Date: "+cal.get(Calendar.DATE));
  System.out.println("Day: "+days[cal.get(Calendar.DAY_OF_WEEK)]);
  System.out.println("Hour: "+(cal.get(Calendar.HOUR)+12)%13);
  System.out.println("Minute: "+cal.get(Calendar.MINUTE));
  System.out.println("Second: "+cal.get(Calendar.SECOND));
  System.out.println(am_pm[cal.get(Calendar.AM_PM)]);
  TimeZone tz=cal.getTimeZone();
  System.out.println("Time Zone: "+tz.getID());
 }
}
```

The program creates a Date object and a GregorianCalendar object using the default Date() and GregorianCalendar() constructors. The Date object is assigned to the today variable, and the GregorianCalendar object is assigned to the cal variable. The cal variable is updated with the current date by invoking its setTime() method with the Date object stored in today. The displayDateInfo() method is then invoked to display date and time information about the cal variable.

The clear() method of the Calendar class is invoked to reset the date of the GregorianCalendar object stored in cal. The set() method is used to set its date to New Year's 2000. There are several versions of the set() method, each of which takes a different set of parameters. The version used in DateApp takes the year, month, and date as parameters. Note that the month value ranges from 0 to 12, where the year and date values begin at 1. The displayDateInfo() method is invoked again to display information about the new calendar date.

The displayDateInfo() method creates the days, months, and am_pm arrays to define string values corresponding to the days of the week, months of the year, and a.m./p.m. It then prints a line corresponding to date and time values. These values are retrieved using the get() method of the Calendar class and the Calendar constants corresponding to date/time values. The getTimeZone() method of Calendar is invoked to retrieve the local TimeZone object. The getID() method of the TimeZone class is used to retrieve the local time zone ID string.

The output of the DateApp program follows. When you run the program, you will obviously get a different date for the first part of the program's processing. The following are the results that were displayed when I ran the program:

```
Today:
Year: 1998
Month: July
Date: 28
Day: Tue
Hour: 10
Minute: 57
Second: 6
AM
Time Zone: America/Los Angeles

New Years Day 2000:
Year: 2000
Month: January
Date: 1
Day: Sat
Hour: 12
Minute: 0
Second: 0
AM
Time Zone: America/Los Angeles
```

Internationalization Classes

The java.util package provides a number of classes that support internationalization. These classes are described in this section. Examples of their use are provided in Chapter 19, "Internationalization."

The Locale Class

The Locale class supports internationalization by describing geographic, political, or cultural regions. Locale objects are used to tailor program output to the conventions of that region. They are created using the Locale() constructors, which take language and country arguments and an optional variant argument. The variant argument is used to specify software-specific characteristics, such as operating system or browser. The Locale class defines constants for the most popular languages and countries. The access methods of Locale support the setting and retrieving of language, country, and variant-related values. Examples of using the Locale class are provided in Chapter 19.

The ResourceBundle Class

The ResourceBundle class also supports internationalization. ResourceBundle subclasses are used to store locale-specific resources that can be loaded by a program to tailor the program's appearance to the particular locale in which it is being run. Resource bundles provide the capability to isolate a program's locale-specific resources in a standard and modular manner.

The ResourceBundle class provides a single parameterless constructor. The parent field variable is used to identify the ResourceBundle class that is the parent of a particular class. This parent can be set using the setParent() method. The parent is used to find resources that are not available in a particular class.

The ResouceBundle access methods are used to retrieve the resources that are specific to a particular locale. The ResourceBundle class and its subclasses are covered in Chapter 19.

The ListResourceBundle Class

The ListResourceBundle class extends the ResourceBundle class to simplify access to locale-specific resources. It organizes resources in terms of an array of object pairs, where the first object is a String key and the second object is the key's value. The getContents() method returns the key-value array.

The `PropertyResourceBundle` Class

The `PropertyResourceBundle` class extends the `ResourceBundle` class to organize locale-specific resources using a property file. An `InputStream` object is supplied to the `PropertyResourceBundle()` constructor to enable reading of the property file.

Other `java.util` Classes and Interfaces

The `java.util` package provides a number of other classes and interfaces that provide capabilities that can be used in many of your programs. These remaining classes and interfaces are covered in the following subsections.

The `Random` Class

The `Random` class provides a template for the creation of random number generators. It differs from the `random()` method of the `java.lang.Math` class in that it allows any number of random number generators to be created as separate objects. The `Math.random()` method provides a `static` function for the generation of random `double` values. This `static` method is shared by all program code.

Objects of the `Random` class generate random numbers using a linear congruential formula. Two constructors are provided for creating `Random` objects. The default constructor initializes the seed of the random number generator using the current system time. The other constructor allows the seed to be set to an initial `long` value.

The `Random` class provides eight access methods, seven of which are used to generate random values. The `next()`, `nextInt()`, `nextLong()`, `nextFloat()`, and `nextDouble()` methods generate values for the numeric data types. The values generated by `nextFloat()` and `nextDouble()` are between 0.0 and 1.0. The `nextGaussian()` method generates a Gaussian distribution of double values with mean 0.0 and standard deviation 1.0. The `nextBytes()` method generates a random byte array.

The `setSeed()` method is used to reset the seed of the random number generator.

RandomApp

The `RandomApp` program demonstrates the use of the `Random` class (see Listing 11.11). It creates an object of class `Random` using the default constructor and assigns it to `r`. This causes the random number generator to be seeded using the current system time. Three `for` loops are used to print random `int`, `double`, and Gaussian-distributed `double` values. Each loop prints four values.

LISTING **11.11.** THE SOURCE CODE OF THE RandomApp PROGRAM.

```
import java.lang.System;
import java.util.Random;

public class RandomApp {
 public static void main(String args[]){
  Random r = new Random();
  for(int i=0;i<4;++i) System.out.print(r.nextInt()+" ");
  System.out.println();
  r = new Random(123456789);
  for(int i=0;i<4;++i) System.out.print(r.nextDouble()+" ");
  System.out.println();
  r.setSeed(234567890);
  for(int i=0;i<4;++i) System.out.print(r.nextGaussian()+" ");
  System.out.println();
 }
}
```

The following is the output generated by the program when it was run on my computer:

```
-854287801 -2056322098 1372478715 1217144804
0.664038103272266 0.45695178590520646 0.39050647939140426
0.8933411602003871
0.11378145160284903 0.4122962630933344 -1.5726230841498485
0.07568285309772235
```

It will produce different results when it is run on your computer because the first line that is printed uses the Random() constructor to generate the output data.

The StringTokenizer Class

The StringTokenizer class is used to create a parser for String objects. It parses strings according to a set of delimiter characters. It implements the Enumeration interface in order to provide access to the tokens contained within a string. The StringTokenizer class is similar to the StreamTokenizer class covered in Chapter 17, "Input/Output Streams."

StringTokenizer provides three constructors. All three have the input string as a parameter. The first constructor includes two other parameters: a set of delimiters to be used in the string parsing, and a boolean value used to specify whether the delimiter characters should be returned as tokens. The second constructor accepts the delimiter string, but not the return token's toggle. The last constructor uses the default delimiter set consisting of the space, tab, newline, and carriage-return characters.

The access methods provided by StringTokenizer include the Enumeration methods, hasMoreElements() and nextElement(), hasMoreTokens() and nextToken(), and

Using the Utility and Math Packages

CHAPTER 11

295

11

USING THE
UTILITY AND
MATH PACKAGES

countTokens(). The countTokens() method returns the number of tokens in the string being parsed.

TokenApp

The TokenApp program prompts the user to enter a line of keyboard input and then parses the line, identifying the number and value of the tokens that it found (see Listing 11.12).

LISTING 11.12. THE SOURCE CODE OF THE TokenApp PROGRAM.

```
import java.lang.System;
import java.io.*;
import java.util.StringTokenizer;

public class TokenApp {
 public static void main(String args[]) throws IOException {
  BufferedReader keyboardInput = new BufferedReader(
   new InputStreamReader(System.in));
  int numTokens;
  do {
   System.out.print("=> ");
   System.out.flush();
   StringTokenizer st = new StringTokenizer(keyboardInput.readLine());
   numTokens = st.countTokens();
   System.out.println(numTokens+" tokens");
   while (st.hasMoreTokens())
    System.out.println(" "+st.nextToken());
  } while(numTokens!=0);
 }
}
```

The program begins by creating a BufferedReader object using the System.in stream as an argument to its constructor. A do loop is used to read a line of input from the user, construct a StringTokenizer object on the input line, display the number of tokens in the line, and display each token as parsed using the standard delimiter set. The loop continues until a line with no tokens is entered.

The program's output is as follows:

```
=> this is a test
4 tokens
 this
 is
 a
 test
=> 1 2 3 4.5 6
5 tokens
 1
 2
```

```
 3
 4.5
 6
=> @ # $ % ^
5 tokens
 @
 #
 $
 %
 ^
=>
0 tokens
```

Observer and Observable

The Observer interface and Observable class are used to implement an abstract system by which observable objects can be observed by objects that implement the Observer interface. *Observable* objects are objects that subclass the abstract Observable class. These objects maintain a list of observers. When an observable object is updated, it invokes the update() method of its observers to notify the observers that it has changed state.

The update() method is the only method that is specified in the Observer interface. The update() method is used to notify an observer that an Observable object has changed. The method takes the Observable object and a second notification message Object as its parameters.

The Observable class is an abstract class that must be subclassed by Observable objects. It provides several methods for adding, deleting, and notifying observers and for manipulating change status. These methods are described in the class's API page.

The EventObject Class and the EventListener Interface

The EventObject class is the top-level class of the Java event hierarchy. *Events* represent actions that occur during the course of program execution. Most events are generated as the result of user actions, such as mouse clicks and keyboard actions. The java.awt.event package declares event classes that are subclasses of EventObject. The EventObject class contains a single constructor that identifies the object that is the source of the event. This object is accessible through the source field variable. The EventObject class also provides the getSource() method for accessing the event source.

Events are *handled* by responding to their occurrence and providing feedback to the user. Java 1.1 provided the capability to deliver events to specific objects—a capability that was lacking in Java 1.0.

It makes use of special classes, called *adapter classes*, whose objects *listen* for the occurrence of events on behalf of objects of other classes. These classes implement event listener interfaces that specify methods for identifying and responding to the occurrence of related events. The `EventListener` interface is the top-level interface that all listener interfaces must implement. It is an empty interface and does not declare any methods.

The `PropertyPermission` Class

The `PropertyPermission` class is used to create permissions to access specific system properties. You should not use this class yourself. Instead, specify property permissions in your local security policy. Chapter 3, "The Extended Java Security Model," covers the development of a JDK 1.2 security policy.

The `java.util.zip` Package

The `java.util.zip` package provides 1 interface and 14 classes to support the compression and decompression of files and streams and to support checksum calculation. These classes are described in the following sections.

Checksum

The `Checksum` interface provides four methods that support checksum calculation. The `getValue()` method returns the current value of a checksum. The `reset()` method resets a checksum to its initial value. The two `update()` methods update a checksum based on a single byte or an array of bytes.

Adler32

The `Adler32` class implements the `Checksum` interface to compute an Adler-32 checksum. The Adler-32 checksum is computed quickly, but is less reliable than the `CRC32` checksum.

CRC32

The `CRC32` class implements the `Checksum` interface to calculate a standard 32-bit cyclic redundancy code.

CheckedInputStream

The `CheckedInputStream` class extends the `FilterInputStream` class of `java.io` to include a checksum calculation for data read from the stream. The checksum is used to verify the integrity of the stream's data. The CheckedInputStream() constructor creates a CheckedInputStream object from an InputStream object and an object that implements the Checksum interface. The getChecksum() method returns the Checksum object associated with the stream. Other methods support low-level input.

CheckedOutputStream

The CheckedOutputStream class extends the FilterOutputStream class of java.io to include a checksum calculation for data written to the stream. The checksum is used to verify the integrity of the stream's data. The CheckedOutputStream() constructor creates a CheckedOutputStream object from an OutputStream object and an object that implements the Checksum interface. The getChecksum() method returns the Checksum object associated with the stream. Other methods support low-level output.

Deflater

The Deflater class supports compression using the compression approaches described in Request For Comments (RFCs) 1950, 1951, and 1952. RFCs are publicly available Internet standards that can be found at ftp://ds.internic.net/rfc/. The Deflater class supports the following compression levels and strategies, as defined by its field constants:

- BEST_COMPRESSION—Most compression
- BEST_SPEED—Fastest compression
- DEFAULT_COMPRESSION—Default trade-off between compression and speed
- DEFAULT_STRATEGY—Default compression strategy
- DEFLATED—Simple deflation
- FILTERED—Emphasizes Huffman coding over string matching
- HUFFMAN_ONLY—Uses Huffman coding and not string matching
- NO_COMPRESSION—Turns compression off

The compression level can be selected when constructing a Deflater object.

The methods of the Deflater class support data compression, the selection of a compression level and strategy, and the use of preset data dictionaries. These methods perform block-oriented compression on byte arrays.

Inflater

The Inflater class is used to decompress data that is compressed by the Deflater class. This decompression is also covered in RFCs 1950, 1951, and 1952. The Inflater() constructor provides the nowrap parameter to support GZIP- and PKZIP-compatible compression. GZIP compression is the Gnu public version of the commercial PKZIP compression algorithm developed by Phil Katz.

The methods of the Inflater class support decompression and the use of preset data dictionaries. These methods perform block-oriented decompression on byte arrays.

DeflaterOutputStream

The DeflaterOutputStream class extends the FilterOutputStream class to provide support for stream-oriented compression. Its two field variables, buf and def, identify the output buffer used to write compressed data and the type of compressor in use. The DeflaterOutputStream() constructors allow the OutputStream and Deflater objects to be specified, as well as the output buffer size.

The deflate() method writes the next block of compressed data to the output stream. The finish() method completes the compression of the output stream by writing all compressed data to the stream. Other methods support low-level data output.

InflaterInputStream

The InflaterInputStream class is the input analog of the DeflaterOutputStream class. InflaterInputStream reads and decompresses data that is written to a compressed output stream using a DeflaterOutputStream object. It extends the FilterInputStream class of java.io.

InflaterInputStream defines three field variables: buf, inf, and len. These variables identify the input buffer used for decompression, the type of decompressor to be used, and the length of the input buffer. The InflaterInputStream() constructors allow InputStream and Inflater objects to be specified, as well as the input buffer size.

The fill() method is used to fill the input buffer with compressed data. Other methods are used to read uncompressed data from the stream.

GZIPOutputStream

The GZIPOutputStream class extends DeflaterOutputStream to support GZIP compression. It adds the crc field variable to calculate a CRC-32 checksum on the compressed data. The GZIPOutputStream() constructors allow the OutputStream object and the output buffer size to be specified.

GZIPInputStream

The GZIPInputStream class is the input analog of the GZIPOutputStream class. It extends InflaterInputStream and defines two additional variables and a constant. The crc variable identifies the CRC-32 checksum of the compressed data. The eos variable identifies the end of the output stream. The GZIP_MAGIC constant identifies the *magic number* of the GZIP header. Magic numbers are used to uniquely identify files of a given format. The GZIPInputStream() constructors allow the InputStream object and the input buffer size to be specified.

ZipFile

The ZipFile class is used to read .zip compressed files. The ZipFile() constructor opens a ZIP file for reading. A File object or a String object containing a file name may be provided to the ZipFile() constructor.

The methods of the ZipFile class support the reading and examination of .zip files. They are as follows:

- entries()—Returns an Enumeration object containing the .zip file entries.
- getEntry()—Returns a ZipEntry object corresponding to the pathname passed as a string argument.
- getInputStream()—Returns an InputStream object corresponding to the ZipEntry object passed as an argument to the method. The InputStream object is used to read the contents of the ZipEntry object.
- getName()—Returns the pathname of the .zip file.
- close()—Closes the .zip file.

ZipEntry

The ZipEntry class encapsulates a .zip file entry. It represents a compressed file that is stored within the .zip file. The DEFLATED and STORED constants are used to identify whether a .zip entry is compressed or merely stored as uncompressed data within the .zip file. The ZipEntry() constructor is used to create a named .zip file entry. Several methods are provided to read the following aspects of a ZipEntry object:

- Name of the entry
- Comment string
- Size of the compressed and uncompressed data
- CRC-32 checksum of the compressed data

- Extra field data
- Compression method
- Modification time of the entry
- Whether the entry is a directory

Other methods are provided to set the comment string, CRC, extra field data, entry size, and time of modification. The toString() method is overridden to convert a ZipEntry object to a String object.

ZipOutputStream

The ZipOutputStream class extends the DeflaterOutputStream class to support the writing of file streams that are compressed in the .zip file format. The DEFLATED and STORED constants are used to identify whether data should be compressed (DEFLATED) or stored as uncompressed data (STORED). The ZipOutputStream() constructor creates a ZipOutputStream object from an OutputStream object.

In addition to low-level output methods, the ZipOutputStream class provides the following methods:

- putNextEntry()—Starts the writing of a new ZIP entry.
- closeEntry()—Closes the current entry and positions the stream for writing the next entry.
- setMethod()—Sets the compression method.
- setLevel()—Sets the compression level.
- setComment()—Sets the .zip file comment.
- finish()—Completes the writing of the zipped output stream.

ZipInputStream

The ZipInputStream class is the input analog to the ZipOutputStream class. It is used to read a compressed .zip format file. The ZipInputStream class extends the InflaterInputStream class.

The ZipInputStream() constructor creates a ZipInputStream object from an InputStream object. In addition to low-level input methods, it provides the getNextEntry() method for reading the next .zip file entry and the closeEntry() method for closing a .zip file entry.

The UnzipApp Program

The UnzipApp program, shown in Listing 11.13, illustrates the power of the
java.util.zip in working with compressed files. This short program can be used to
unzip files in the .zip format.

LISTING 11.13. THE SOURCE CODE OF THE UnzipApp PROGRAM.

```java
import java.lang.System;
import java.util.*;
import java.util.zip.*;
import java.io.*;

public class UnzipApp {
 public static void main(String args[]) throws IOException {
  if(args.length==0) System.exit(0);
  ZipFile f = new ZipFile(args[0]);
  Enumeration entries = f.entries();
  System.out.println("Decompressing "+args[0]+" ...");
  while(entries.hasMoreElements()){
   ZipEntry entry = (ZipEntry) entries.nextElement();
   System.out.println("  "+entry.getName());
   InputStream in = f.getInputStream(entry);
   FileOutputStream out = new FileOutputStream(entry.getName());
   for(int ch=in.read();ch!=-1;ch=in.read()) out.write(ch);
   out.close();
   in.close();
  }
  f.close();
 }
}
```

 To show how the program works, I've included the file rfcs.zip on the CD-
ROM included with this book. This file contains the files rfc1950.txt,
rfc1951.txt, and rfc1952.txt in compressed form. These files document the
conventions and formats used for ZLIB, DEFLATE, and GZIP.

The UnzipApp program takes a single argument—the name of the file that you want to
unzip. To unzip rfcs.zip, use:

```
java UnzipApp rfcs.zip
```

The program's output is as follows:

```
Decompressing rfcs.zip ...
  rfc1950.txt
  rfc1952.txt
  rfc1951.txt
```

Using the Utility and Math Packages
CHAPTER 11

303

11

USING THE
UTILITY AND
MATH PACKAGES

The files `rfc1950.txt`, `rfc1951.txt`, and `rfc1952.txt` are created and placed in your current working directory.

The program makes use of the `ZipFile` and `ZipEntry` classes of `java.util.zip` and the `Enumeration` interface of `java.util`. It creates a new `ZipFile` object from the filename that you pass to the program as a command-line argument. It then invokes the `entries()` method of `ZipFile` to create an `Enumeration` object of `ZipEntry` objects corresponding to the entries into the `ZipFile` object.

A `while` statement is used to loop through the `Enumeration` object and process each entry. The `hasMoreElements()` method of the `Enumeration` interface is used to determine whether all entries have been processed. The individual `ZipEntry` objects are extracted from the `Enumeration` object via the `nextElement()` method and assigned to the `entry` variable. The `getName()` method of the `ZipEntry` class is used to retrieve the filename associated with each `ZipEntry` object.

The `ZipEntry` objects are extracted to individual files by using the `getInputStream()` method of `ZipFile` to read the contents of the `ZipEntry` object and write this data to files that are created using the `FileOutputStream` class of `java.io`.

The `java.util.jar` Package

The `java.util.jar` package provides classes and methods for working with `.jar` files. The `.jar` files are archive files used to combine all of the resources used by an applet into a single file. You learned about `.jar` files in Chapter 8, "Applet Security." The `java.util.jar` package is new to JDK 1.2. It provides seven new classes that are covered in the following subsections.

The `JarFile` Class

The `JarFile` class extends the `ZipFile` class to provide support for `.jar` files. It provides the capability to add and work with the `.jar` file manifest. The `JarFile` constructors are used to create `JarFile` objects that take their input from an input stream. The `getManifest()` method returns the file's manifest. The `getJarEntry()` returns a named `.jar` file entry as an `JarEntry` object. The `createZipEntry()` method is used to create a `JarEntry` object. The `getInputStream()` method returns an input stream for reading the `.jar` file.

The `JarEntry` Class

The `JarEntry` class extends the `ZipEntry` class to provide support for `.jar` file entries. It provides a single constructor for creating a named `.jar` file entry. The `getAttributes()`

method returns an `Attributes` object that specifies the manifest attributes for the entry. The `getIdentities()` method returns an array of `Identity` objects that identifies the identities of the signers of the .jar file entry.

The Manifest Class

The `Manifest` class provides the capability to work with manifest entries and their attributes. It provides methods for reading and manipulating manifest entries, main attributes, and per-entry attributes.

The Attributes Class

The `Attributes` class implements the `Map` interface and provides a mapping between attribute names and their values. It provides methods for reading and modifying the attribute names and values.

The Attributes.Name Class

The `Attributes.Name` class is an inner class of the `Attributes` class that is used to encapsulate an attribute name. It provides a number of constants that represent commonly used manifest attributes.

The JarInputStream Class

The `JarInputStream` class is a subclass of the `ZipInputStream` class that supports the reading of .jar files. It provides methods for reading `JarEntry` and `Manifest` objects.

The JarOutputStream Class

The `JarOutputStream` class is a subclass of the `ZipOutputStream` class that supports the writing of .jar files. It provides the capability to specify a `Manifest` object in one of its constructors.

The JarApp Program

The `JarApp` program illustrates the use of the `JarFile`, `JarEntry`, `Manifest`, and `Attributes` classes. It reads a .jar file and displays the JAR entries, main attributes, and manifest entries of the .jar file.

 I've added the file `TCanv.jar` to the files contained on the CD-ROM for this chapter. You can use `JarApp` to display the contents of the `TCanv.jar` file, as follows:

Using the Utility and Math Packages

CHAPTER 11

305

11

USING THE
UTILITY AND
MATH PACKAGES

```
java JarApp TCanv.jar
Entries:
  tcanv16m.gif
  TCanvBeanInfo.class
  tcanv32c.gif
  META-INF/MANIFEST.MF
  TCanv.class
  tcanv32m.gif
  tcanv16c.gif
Main attributes:
  Manifest-Version 1.0
Manifest entries:
  tcanv16m.gif java.util.jar.Attributes@df93530
  TCanvBeanInfo.class java.util.jar.Attributes@57e4cd07
  TCanv.class java.util.jar.Attributes@c88bc2f1
  tcanv32c.gif java.util.jar.Attributes@9381af57
  tcanv16c.gif java.util.jar.Attributes@272d3530
  tcanv32m.gif java.util.jar.Attributes@8de1af57
```

JarApp begins by creating a `JarFile` object from the name of the `.jar` file passed as an argument to the program. It uses the `entries()` method to retrieve an `Enumeration` of the `JarEntry` objects contained in the `.jar` file. It invokes `getManifest()` to retrieve a `Manifest` object for the `.jar` file.

The `JarApp` program iterates through the `Enumeration` of `JarEntry` objects and uses the `getName()` method to display the names of the files that are contained in `TCanv.jar`:

```
tcanv16m.gif
TCanvBeanInfo.class
tcanv32c.gif
META-INF/MANIFEST.MF
TCanv.class
tcanv32m.gif
tcanv16c.gif
```

It invokes the `getMainAttributes()` method of the `Manifest` object to retrieve an `Attributes` object that describes the main attributes of the `.jar` file. It invokes `displayCollection()` to display the single attribute (`Manifest-Version`) and its value (`1.0`).

Next, `JarApp` invokes the `getEntries()` method of the `Manifest` object to return a `Map` object containing the manifest entries and their values. It invokes `displayCollection()` to display these values:

```
tcanv16m.gif java.util.jar.Attributes@df93530
TCanvBeanInfo.class java.util.jar.Attributes@57e4cd07
TCanv.class java.util.jar.Attributes@c88bc2f1
tcanv32c.gif java.util.jar.Attributes@9381af57
tcanv16c.gif java.util.jar.Attributes@272d3530
tcanv32m.gif java.util.jar.Attributes@8de1af57
```

The `displayCollection()` method displays a collection of key-value pairs. It invokes the `iterator()` method of the `Collection` object to obtain an `Iterator` object. It then uses the `Iterator` object to step through the collection and display each key name and its corresponding value.

LISTING 11.14. THE JarApp PROGRAM.

```java
import java.util.*;
import java.util.jar.*;
import java.io.*;

public class JarApp {
 public static void main(String args[]) throws IOException {
  // Create JarFile object
  JarFile f = new JarFile(args[0]);
  // Get JarEntry objects
  Enumeration entries = f.entries();
  // Get Manifest
  Manifest manifest = f.getManifest();
  // Display the names of the entries
  System.out.println("Entries:");
  while(entries.hasMoreElements()){
   JarEntry entry = (JarEntry) entries.nextElement();
   System.out.println("  "+entry.getName());
  }
  // Display the names of the main attributes
  System.out.println("Main attributes:");
  Attributes attributes = manifest.getMainAttributes();
  displayCollection(attributes.entrySet());
  // Display the manifest entries and their attributes
  System.out.println("Manifest entries:");
  Map manifestEntries = manifest.getEntries();
  displayCollection(manifestEntries.entrySet());
  f.close();
 }
 static void displayCollection(Collection collection) {
  if(collection.size()==0) System.out.println("  None");
  else{
   Iterator iterator = collection.iterator();
   while(iterator.hasNext()){
    Map.Entry entry = (Map.Entry) iterator.next();
    String desc = entry.getKey().toString()+" ";
    desc+=entry.getValue().toString();
    System.out.println("  "+desc);
   }
  }
 }
}
```

The `java.util.mime` Package

The `java.util.mime` package is new to JDK 1.2. It is a very small package consisting of the `MimeType` and `MimeTypeParameterList` classes. These classes are used to provide support for Multipurpose Internet Mail Extensions (MIME) types (refer to RFCs 2045 and 2046). Chapter 33, "Content and Protocol Handlers," provides an introduction to MIME types.

The `MimeType` class provides methods for constructing `MimeType` objects that represent different MIME types, for accessing the primary and subtypes of a MIME type, for working with MIME type parameters, and for comparing MIME types. It also provides methods for supporting stream-based I/O for different MIME types.

The `MimeTypeParameterList` class is used to encapsulate the parameter list of a MIME type. It provides methods for getting and setting the parameters that are in the MIME type parameter list.

The `java.math` Package

The `java.math` package includes two classes, `BigDecimal` and `BigNumber`, that can be used to perform arbitrary precision mathematical calculations. The `BigDecimal` class supports decimal arithmetic, and the `BigInteger` class supports integer arithmetic. Both of these classes extend the `Number` class.

BigDecimal

The `BigDecimal` class is implemented as an arbitrary precision integer number and a non-negative scale value that identifies the number of digits to the right of the decimal point. `BigDecimal` provides eight modes for rounding support. These modes are defined using class constants:

- `ROUND_CEILING`—Use `ROUND_UP` for positive numbers and `ROUND_DOWN` for negative numbers.
- `ROUND_DOWN`—Round toward zero.
- `ROUND_FLOOR`—Use `ROUND_DOWN` for positive numbers and `ROUND_UP` for negative numbers.
- `ROUND_HALF_DOWN`—Use `ROUND_UP` if the discarded fraction is greater than .5. Use `ROUND_DOWN` otherwise.
- `ROUND_HALF_EVEN`—Use `ROUND_HALF_UP` if the digit to the left of the discarded fraction is odd. Use `ROUND_HALF_DOWN` if the digit to the left of the discarded fraction is even.

- `ROUND_HALF_UP`—Use `ROUND_UP` if the discarded fraction is greater than or equal to .5. Otherwise, use `ROUND_DOWN`.
- `ROUND_UNNECESSARY`—An exception is thrown if rounding is required.
- `ROUND_UP`—Round away from zero.

These modes provide a great deal of flexibility in the rounding policy used by the `BigDecimal` class.

The `BigDecimal` class provides constructors that allow `BigDecimal` objects to be created from `String`, `double`, and `BigInteger` objects. The methods of `BigDecimal` support arithmetic operations, comparisons, rounding and scaling, and conversions to other types and classes.

BigInteger

The `BigInteger` class is similar to `BigDecimal`, but it is limited to integer operations. It does not have any public field values, like `BigDecimal`, because it does not deal with rounding. Its constructors allow `BigInteger` objects to be constructed from strings, byte arrays, and randomly within a specified range. Its methods support arithmetic, logical, bitwise, and comparison operations. Its methods also support modular arithmetic, greatest common divisor calculation, and prime number generation and testing.

The BigNumApp Program

The `BigNumApp` program illustrates the ease by which large number computations can be performed. It calculates the first number greater than a trillion (10 to the 12 power) that is probably prime. Listing 11.15 contains the source code of the `BigNumApp` program.

LISTING 11.15. THE SOURCE CODE OF THE BigNumApp PROGRAM.

```java
import java.lang.System;
import java.math.BigInteger;

public class BigNumApp {
 public static void main(String args[]){
  BigInteger n=new BigInteger("1000000000000");
  BigInteger one=new BigInteger("1");
  while(!n.isProbablePrime(7)) n=n.add(one);
  System.out.println(n.toString(10)+" is probably prime.");
  System.out.println("It is "+n.bitLength()+" bits in length.");
 }
}
```

The `BigNumApp` program creates a `BigInteger` equal to one trillion and assigns it to `n`. It then creates a `BigInteger` equal to 1 and assigns it to the one variable. It uses a `while` loop to test numbers greater than a trillion until it finds one that is probably prime with a certainty of 7. This certainty value means that the probability of the number being prime is $(1 - (1/2^{**}7))$, which is greater than 99%. The `bitLength()` method is to determine the length of the prime number in bits.

The program's output is as follows:

```
1000000000039 is probably prime.
It is 40 bits in length.
```

Summary

In this chapter you learned about the classes and interfaces of the `java.util` family of packages and the `java.math` package. You learned how to use the new JDK 1.2 Collections API, work with dates and calendars, work with `.zip` and `.jar` files, and perform large number arithmetic. In the next chapter you'll learn how to use the new Java Swing API to enhance the look and feel of your applets' and applications' user interfaces.

Swing Programming

PART

IV

IN THIS PART

CHAPTER 12

Introducing Swing

Swing is one of the major improvements in the JDK between versions 1.1 and 1.2. It is also one of the key APIs of the Java Foundations Classes (JFC). What makes Swing so important is the power that it provides in developing GUIs for applets and applications. The number and quality of the GUI controls provided by Swing is unrivaled by any other GUI toolkit.

Up until now, you have been developing your applet and application GUIs using the traditional GUI controls of the AWT. In this chapter, you'll be introduced to the GUI controls of Swing. You'll learn what Swing is, where it comes from, and its relationship to the AWT and the JFC as a whole. You'll cover the Swing component hierarchy and learn about the Swing packages. You'll then develop an example Swing-based GUI. When you finish this chapter, you will be thoroughly introduced to Swing. The following chapter will then expand upon your Swing programming skills.

What Is Swing?

Swing is a major component of the JFC, which is the result of a large collaborative effort between Sun, Netscape, IBM, and other companies. Swing provides a large number of useful GUI controls that originated with Netscape's Internet Foundations Classes (IFC). The Swing components go far beyond the IFC, to the point where there is no visible resemblance between Swing components and those of the IFC. Swing also provides the capability to quickly and easily change the *look and feel (L&F)* of a single component or group of components. This capability, known as *pluggable look and feel (PL&F)*, is a hallmark feature of Swing. Chapter 14, "Changing the Look and Feel of Your Swing Components," focuses on Swing's PL&F features.

> **NOTE**
>
> To make optimal use of Swing, your video card should be set to 16-bit or higher color. This setting supports 65,536 color combinations.

Swing, AWT, and the JFC

Figure 12.1 shows the relationship between Swing, the AWT, and the JFC. The JFC subsumes and extends the original AWT and consists of the following major APIs:

- AWT
- Swing

it in salable condition accompanied by
this receipt within 30 days.

If you are not satisfied with your
purchase for any reason you may return
it in salable condition accompanied by
this receipt within 30 days.

If you are not satisfied with your
purchase for any reason you may return
it in salable condition accompanied by
this receipt within 30 days.

Barnes & Noble, Inc
8871 Ladue Road
Ladue, MO 63124
314-862-6280
314-862-6280 04-12-00 S02542 R005

CUSTOMER RECEIPT COPY

Java 2 Platform Unleashe   49.99
0672316315

SUB TOTAL   49.99
SALES TAX   3.36
TOTAL   53.35
AMOUNT TENDERED
VISA   53.35
CARD #:   4313020689003541
EXP DATE: 0201
AMOUNT   53.35
AUTH CODE   045183

TOTAL PAYMENT   53.35
Thanks for shopping at Barnes & Noble!
#52093 04-12-00 05:40P KARA

Booksellers Since 1873

- Java 2D

- Drag-and-Drop

- Accessibility

Although Swing is separate from the AWT, it is implemented in terms of basic AWT classes. The AWT provides the interface between the underlying native windowing system and the Java GUI components. Swing uses this interface, but does not rely on AWT components that make use of native windowing system objects. Instead, Swing components are written in pure Java. This provides significant advantages. It allows Swing components to be independent of the native windowing system, which means they can run on any windowing system that supports the AWT. It also allows Swing components to be independent of any limitations of the native windowing systems. This independence allows Swing to control and tailor its look and feel—hence the emergence of PL&F.

FIGURE 12.1.
Swing, IFC, JFC, and AWT.

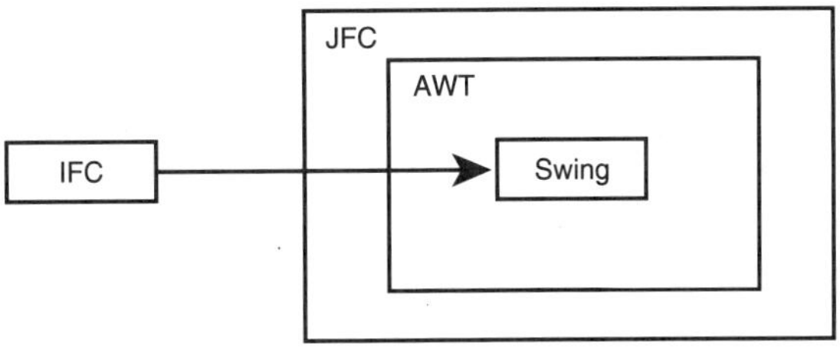

Swing also provides a pure Java implementation of many of the traditional AWT components. These components have the same functionality as the AWT components and all of the advantages of Swing. Swing is compatible with the AWT, and Swing components can be used interchangeably with AWT components. However, Swing components can only be used with the JDK 1.1 event model. They do not support the JDK 1.0 event model.

NOTE

The latest version of Swing can be found at `http://www.javasoft.com/products/jfc/index.html`. Swing is packaged as part of the JFC.

The Swing Component Hierarchy

Swing consists of 9 packages, and hundreds of classes and interfaces. However, the JComponent class of com.sun.java.swing is the top-level class of the Swing component hierarchy. As such, it is a good starting point for learning about Swing components. The JComponent class is a subclass of the java.awt.container class, and is therefore both a component and container in the AWT sense. Because JComponent is the superclass of all Swing components, all Swing components descend from java.awt.Container and java.awt.Component.

Figure 12.2 shows the Swing component hierarchy. The first thing that you should notice is that all components begin with the letter *J*, followed by the type of component supported by the class. JComponent has the following direct subclasses:

- AbstractButton—The top-level button class. It is subclassed by JButton (traditional and enhanced GUI buttons), JToggleButton (checkboxes and radio buttons), and JMenuItem (menus and menu items).

- JComboBox—A combination of a text field and drop-down list.

- JInternalFrame—A frame that supports all standard frame operations and can be used as an internal GUI component. The JDesktopIcon inner class is used to implement an iconified form of an internal frame.

- JLabel—A label that may contain text, an image, or both. It is extended by the DefaultTableCellRenderer class, which is used to display the cells of a table.

- JLayeredPane—A panel that supports several layers. It is extended by JDesktopPane, which provides the capability to manage layered frames as a desktop.

- JList—A list component that can be tailored in a variety of ways.

- JMenuBar—A menu bar that can be added to any container. It displays a pop-up menu of menu items.

- JOptionPane—A single class that supports a number of common dialog boxes.

- JPanel—The Swing analog of the AWT Panel class. It is extended by the ColorChooserPanel, which provides support for color selection.

- JPopupMenu—A pop-up menu that supports text and graphical menu items.

- JProgressBar—A configurable bar that displays progress as a percentage of the bar's length.

- JRootPane—Uses a layered pane and a see-through plane to allow objects to be overlaid on the layered plane.

- JScrollBar—The Swing scrollbar implementation, typically used with objects of the JViewPort class.

- JScrollPane—The combination of a scrollbar and a viewport.

- JSeparator—Used to separate menu items.

- JSlider—Provides a slider GUI control that is analogous to the sliders found on audio equalizers.

- JSplitPane—A panel that is used to separate exactly two components.

- JTabbedPane—A panel that organizes components into tabs. The user clicks on the tabs to view the component groups.

- JTable—A very flexible table component that displays both text and graphic cells.

- JTableHeader—Column header for JTable objects.

- JTextComponent—Superclass of the Swing text fields.

- JToolBar—A draggable, floating toolbar container.

- JToolTip—A pop-up component that displays useful information about other components.

- JTree—A component that displays hierarchical data in a tree-like (outline) fashion.

- JViewport—A panel for holding information that is scrolled by a scrollbar.

12

INTRODUCING
SWING

FIGURE 12.2.

*Swing component
hierarchy.*

```
JComponent
   •  AbstractButton
         •   JButton
         •   JMenuItem
               •   JCheckBoxMenuItem
               •   JMenu
               •   JRadioButtonMenuItem
         •   JToggleButton
               •   JCheckBox
               •   JRadioButton
   •  JComboBox
   •  JInternalFrame
   •  JLabel
         •   DefaultTableCellRenderer(java.awt.swing.table)
   •J LayeredPane
         •   JDesktopPane
   •  JList
   •  JMenuBar
   •  JOptionPane
   •  JPanel
         •   ColorChooserPanel
   •  JPopupMenu
   •  JProgressBar
   •  JRootPane
   •  JScrollBar
   •  JScrollPane
   •  JSeparator
   •  JSlider
   •  JSplitPane
   •  JTabbedPane
   •  JTable
   •  JTableHeader(java.awt.swingn.table)
   •  JTextComponent(java.awt.swing.text)
               •   JEditorPane
                     •  JTextPane
               •   JTextArea
               •   JTextField
                     •  JPasswordField
   •  JToolBar
   •  JToolTip
   •  JTree
   •  JViewport
```

You'll see visual examples of many of these components later in this chapter and in the following chapter.

Swing Package Overview

Swing is a large API consisting of 9 packages and numerous classes and interfaces. Most of the Swing components are contained in the com.sun.java.swing package, which also provides classes and interfaces that support and manage the GUI components. The com.sun.java.swing.border package provides a number of interesting borders that can be used with Swing components. These borders help to tailor the look and feel of component sets.

The com.sun.java.swing.event package defines the events and event listeners used by Swing components. It is a good idea to look over the list of events and event listeners to get a feel for the types of user interactions supported by Swing.

The com.sun.java.swing.table package provides classes and interfaces that support the feature rich and flexible JTable object. You use these classes and interfaces to tailor a table's display features.

The com.sun.java.swing.text packages provides several classes and interfaces that support text components. These classes and interfaces control the caret, highlighting, formatting, and other aspects of text that is entered and edited within text components.

The com.sun.java.swing.text.html package contains the single HTMLEditorKit class. This class supports the implementation of a simple but powerful HTML editor. The com.sun.java.swing.text.rtf package is similar to the com.sun.java.swing.text.html package. It contains the single RTFEditorKit class, which provides the capability to edit Rich Text Format (RTF) text.

The com.sun.java.swing.tree package provides classes and interfaces that support the use of the JTree component.

The com.sun.java.swing.undo package provides support for undo and redo operations.

The com.sun.java.swing.plaf provides support for Swing's pluggable look-and-feel features.

Developing a Swing-Based GUI

Now that we've covered the components and packages that compose the Swing API, you'll develop a sample program that shows off some of Swing's features. You'll run the program first, to get an idea of what it does, and then you'll examine the Swing code used in its implementation.

Listing 12.1 shows the source code of the SwingStart program. Compile this program and run it. It displays the GUI shown in Figure 12.3. You'll notice four tabs labeled Buttons, Bars, Lists, and Table. You'll also notice two graphical buttons. Move your mouse over any of the tabs. After a second or two, an information tip is displayed, as shown in Figure 12.4. Move your mouse over each tab to see the tip associated with that tab.

FIGURE 12.3.

The initial display of the SwingStart *program.*

FIGURE 12.4.

Tips are displayed when you move your mouse over a tab.

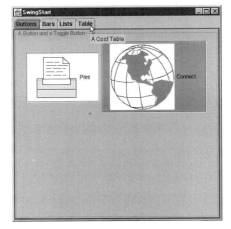

The Buttons tab shows two buttons. The button on the left is a standard button, but it is enhanced with a printer image. Wouldn't a button like this be more informative to a program user than a simple text button? The button on the right provides an extra capability—the button retains its state. When you click the button, it sticks in the in position. When you click it again, the button moves back out.

Click on the Bars tab. A slider and a progress bar are displayed, as shown in Figure 12.5. Use your mouse to move the slider, and the progress bar is updated to reflect the new slider position. Sliders and progress bars provide users with a fine level of control over a program parameter and display progress toward the completion of a task.

FIGURE 12.5.

The Bars tab shows examples of Swing's slider and progress bar controls.

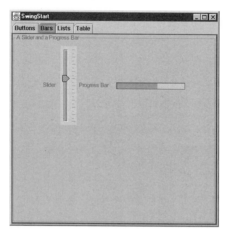

FIGURE 12.6.

A Swing list can contain icons.

Click on the Lists tab. The icon list, shown in Figure 12.6, is displayed. Click on any of the images to select it from the list. As you can see, Swing provides excellent integration of images into GUI controls.

FIGURE 12.7.

Swing makes it easy to create advanced tables.

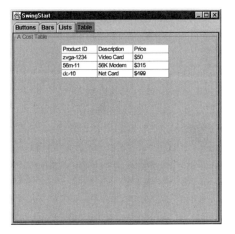

Click on the Table tab. The cost table, shown in Figure 12.7, is displayed. Swing tables not only provide the capability to display tabular information, but they can also be used to create tables that can be edited by users.

The GUI controls shown in the SwingStart program are just a small sample of the GUI capabilities of Swing. However, they are enough to introduce you to Swing programming, as discussed in the next section.

LISTING 12.1. THE SwingStart PROGRAM.

```java
import java.awt.*;
import java.awt.event.*;
import com.sun.java.swing.*;
import com.sun.java.swing.event.*;
import com.sun.java.swing.border.*;

public class SwingStart extends Frame {
  public static int WIDTH = 450;
  public static int HEIGHT = 450;
  public static String TITLE = "SwingStart";

  // Swing components
  JTabbedPane tabbedPane = new JTabbedPane();
  JPanel buttonPanel = new JPanel();
```

continues

LISTING 12.1. CONTINUED

```java
JPanel barPanel = new JPanel();
JPanel listPanel = new JPanel();
JPanel tablePanel = new JPanel();
JPanel[] panels = {buttonPanel,barPanel,listPanel,tablePanel};
Icon worldIcon = new ImageIcon("world.gif");
Icon printerIcon = new ImageIcon("printer.gif");
Icon leaf1Icon = new ImageIcon("leaf1.gif");
Icon leaf2Icon = new ImageIcon("leaf2.gif");
Icon leaf3Icon = new ImageIcon("leaf3.gif");
Icon[] leaves = {leaf1Icon, leaf2Icon, leaf3Icon};
JButton printerButton = new JButton("Print",printerIcon);
JToggleButton worldButton = new JToggleButton("Connect",worldIcon,true);
JList leafList = new JList(leaves);
JSlider slider = new JSlider(JSlider.VERTICAL, 0, 100, 60);
JProgressBar progressBar = new JProgressBar();
String[] columns = {"Product ID","Description","Price"};
Object[][] cells = {columns,{"zvga-1234","Video Card","$50"},
 {"56m-11","56K Modem","$315"},
 {"dc-10","Net Card","$499"}};
JTable table = new JTable(cells,columns);
{
 super(TITLE);
 addWindowListener(new WindowHandler());
 buildGUI();
 setSize(WIDTH,HEIGHT);
 setBackground(Color.darkGray);
 show();
}

void buildGUI() {
 // Set up tabbed pane
 String[] tabs = {"Buttons","Bars","Lists","Table"};
 String[] tabTips = {"A Button and a Toggle Button",
  "A Slider and a Progress Bar",
  "An Icon List",
  "A Cost Table"};
 for(int i=0;i<tabs.length;++i) {
 panels[i].setBackground(Color.lightGray);
 panels[i].setBorder(new TitledBorder(tabTips[i]));
 tabbedPane.addTab(tabs[i],null,panels[i],tabTips[i]);
 }
 addComponentsToTabs();
 add("Center",tabbedPane);
}

void addComponentsToTabs() {
 setupButtonPanel();
```

```
  setupBarPanel();
  setupListPanel();
  setupTablePanel();
}

void setupButtonPanel() {
 printerButton.setBackground(Color.white);
 worldButton.setBackground(Color.white);
 buttonPanel.add(printerButton);
 buttonPanel.add(worldButton);
 }

void setupBarPanel() {
 slider.setMajorTickSpacing(10);
 slider.setMinorTickSpacing(5);
 slider.setPaintTicks(true);
 slider.addChangeListener(new SliderHandler());
 progressBar.setOrientation(JProgressBar.HORIZONTAL);
 progressBar.setMinimum(0);
 progressBar.setMaximum(100);
 progressBar.setValue(60);
 progressBar.setBorderPainted(true);
 barPanel.add(new JLabel("Slider"));
 barPanel.add(slider);
 barPanel.add(new JLabel("Progress Bar"));
 barPanel.add(progressBar);
}

void setupListPanel() {
 leafList.setFixedCellHeight(123);
 listPanel.add(leafList);
 }

void setupTablePanel() {
 tablePanel.add(table);
 }

public static void main(String[] args) {
   SwingStart app = new SwingStart();
 }

public class WindowHandler extends WindowAdapter {
 public void windowClosing(WindowEvent e) {
  System.exit(0);
 }
}
public class SliderHandler implements ChangeListener {
 public void stateChanged(ChangeEvent e) {
```

continues

12

INTRODUCING
SWING

LISTING 12.1. CONTINUED

```
  progressBar.setValue(slider.getValue());
 }
 }
}
```

How SwingStart Works

The first thing that you should notice about SwingStart is that it imports the
com.sun.java.swing (Swing components), com.sun.java.swing.event (Swing event
handling), and com.sun.java.swing.border (custom borders) packages. The
SwingStart program extends the Frame class of java.awt. Swing provides its own window classes that extend java.awt. You'll learn about these classes in the following chapter. SwingStart uses the Frame class to show how Swing and AWT components can be
used interchangeably.

The SwingStart class begins by declaring a few constants used to define the window
size and title. After that, it declares and initializes a number of variables used to implement Swing components. These variables are used as follows:

- tabbedPane—References a JTabbedPane object that provides the four tabs of the
  SwingStart GUI.

- buttonPanel, barPanel, listPanel, and tablePanel—Reference JPanel objects
  that serve as containers for the objects added to the Buttons, Bars, Lists, and Table
  tabs.

- panels—An array of JPanel objects used to access each of the preceding four
  panels.

- worldIcon, printerIcon, leaf1Icon, leaf2Icon, and leaf3Icon—Reference
  objects of the ImageIcon class that are used in the Buttons and Lists tabs.

- leaves—An ImageIcon array consisting of the preceding three leaf icons. These
  objects are used in the Lists tab.

- printerButton—References the JButton object used in the Buttons tab. The button is created with the Print label and the ImageIcon object referenced by
  printerIcon.

- worldButton—References the JToggleButton object used in the Buttons tab. The
  button is created with the Connect label and the ImageIcon object referenced by
  worldIcon. Objects of the JToggleButton class are buttons that implement an
  on/off state. The button state is identified by whether or not the button is pushed in.

- leafList—References a JList object that is constructed from an ImageIcon array.

The JList class provides the capability to construct lists from arbitrary GUI objects.

- slider—References the JSlider object used in the Bars tab. The object is a vertical slider with a range of 0 to 100 and a starting value of 60.
- progressBar—References the JProgressBar object used in the Bars tab.
- columns—An array of column headings used to construct a table.
- cells—The contents of the table's cells.
- table—References the JTable object used in the Table tab. The table is constructed from its column headings and cell values.

The SwingStart constructor invokes the superclass constructor to set the window's title, adds a window event handler, and invokes the buildGUI() method to build the program's graphical user interface. The setSize() method is used to set the window's size, and the setBackground() method sets the window's background color to dark gray. Finally, the show() method is invoked to cause the window to be displayed.

The buildGUI() method sets up the tabbed pane that controls the program's display. It creates an array of tab labels and tips associated with those labels. It then uses a for statement to set the background color and border of each panel. The border used is a TitleBorder object. This border constructs an etched box around the panel's contents and displays a title in the upper-left corner of the pane. Refer to Figures 12.3 through 12.7 for examples of how the border is displayed. Each of the panels is then added to a tab via the addTab() method, which takes the names of the tabs, an icon, the objects to be added to each tab, and the tab tips as parameters. The addComponentsToTabs() method is invoked to add components to the panels of each tab. The tabbed pane is then added to the center of SwingStart's frame.

The addComponentsToTabs()method simply invokes other methods to set up the Buttons, Bars, Lists, and Table panes.

The setupButtonPanel() method adds the printer and world buttons to the Buttons tab. It sets the background color of the buttons to white and then adds the buttons to the pane. No event handling is provided for the buttons.

The setupBarPanel() method sets parameters for the slider and progress bar, adds an event handler for the slider, and then adds the slider and progress bar to the Bars tab. The setMajorTickSpacing() and setMinorTickSpacing() methods are used to add tick marks to the slider. The setPaintTicks() method is invoked to cause the ticks to be displayed. The addChangeListener() method sets up an event handler for the slider.

The `setOrientation()`, `setMinimum()`, `setMaximum()`, and `setValue()` methods set up the progress bar's orientation, range, and initial value. The `setBorderPainted()` method controls the display of the progress bar's border. The slider, progress bar, and two labels are added to the Bars tab via the `JPanel` object referenced by `barPanel`.

The `setupListPanel()` method sets the cell height of the icon list to 123 pixels. (I arrived at this value through trial and error. It seemed to be the most pleasing height for the icons.) The list (referenced by the `leafList` variable) is then added to the tab.

The `setupTablePanel()` method sets up the `JTable` object's parameters and then adds the table to the Table tab. It sets the intercell spacing to a 20 pixel border. The `sizeColumnsToFit()` method causes table columns to be automatically resized to fit in the space allocated to the table.

The `main()` method simply creates a `SwingStart` object. The `WindowHandler` inner class handles the window closing event by exiting the JVM.

The `SliderHandler` class implements the `ChangeListener` interface of `com.sun.java.swing.event`. The `stateChanged()` method handles changes to the slider position by getting the value of the slider and setting the value of the progress bar to the slider value.

Summary

In this chapter, you were introduced to the GUI controls of Swing. You learned what Swing is, where it comes from, and its relationship to the AWT and the JFC as a whole. You learned about the Swing component hierarchy and about the Swing packages. You then developed an example Swing-based GUI. In the next chapter, you'll encounter more examples that will expand upon your Swing programming skills.

Working with Swing Components

In the previous chapter, you were introduced to Swing and learned about some of the Swing components. This chapter takes the introduction to the next level. You'll learn about Swing windows, menus, toolbars, tables, trees, and other GUI components. You'll learn how Swing events are handled and how the JApplet class supports the development of applets that use Swing components. You'll also learn how to convert your existing applications and applets to Swing. When you finish this chapter, you'll be able to begin writing your own Swing-based applets and applications.

Swing GUI Building

Chapter 6, "GUI Building," covered GUI building using the component and container classes of the AWT. Swing GUI building is very similar to AWT GUI building, except that you have many more component classes with which to work. For the most part, everything you learned in Chapter 6 carries over to Swing. However, Swing provides a number of enhancements you'll need to know about in order to maximize Swing's potential. The following subsections describe the classes used for Swing GUI building and point out the enhancements provided by Swing.

Windows

Just as AWT provides a Window class hierarchy, so does Swing. Swing's window classes are extensions of the AWT Window class hierarchy. The JWindow class extends the AWT Window class. The JFrame class extends the AWT Frame class and the JDialog class extends the AWT Dialog class.

The JWindow, JFrame, and JDialog classes differ from their AWT counterparts in that they use a separate content pane for adding and laying out GUI components. This content pane is a Container object that is accessed via the getContentPane() method. The content pane is part of a JRootPane object that contains other panes used for overlaying components and intercepting mouse and keyboard events. You'll learn how to use the content pane to build a Swing GUI in the examples of this chapter.

Menus

Swing menus, like Swing windows, are analogous to their AWT counterparts. The JMenuBar, JMenu, JMenuItem, JCheckBoxMenuItem, and JRadioButtonMenuItem classes are used in the same manner as the AWT MenuBar, Menu, MenuItem, and CheckboxMenuItem classes but with one very important difference. The Swing menu classes are all subclasses of the JComponent class, and therefore, of the Component class. This means that Swing menus, unlike their AWT counterparts, are first-class components and can be used with any `Container` classes. The `JPopupMenu` class is analogous to the AWT `PopupMenu` class. Another nice feature provided by Swing menus is the capability to use icon images in menus. An image can be added to a menu item via its constructor.

SwingWin

The `SwingWin` program, shown in Listing 13.1, demonstrates the use of Swing's menus. The program's opening display is shown in Figure 13.1. Select the New menu item from the File menu, as shown in Figure 13.2. The menu item's label is displayed in the text field, as shown in Figure 13.3. Try experimenting with the menu items of the File and Edit menus.

FIGURE 13.1.

The SwingWin *opening window.*

FIGURE 13.2.

Selecting the New menu item from the File menu.

FIGURE 13.3.

The name of the menu item is displayed in the text field.

The Special menu is shown in Figure 13.4. Note that it contains two checkboxes and two menu items. The second checkbox is already checked. Check the first checkbox and then pull down the menu to see its effect. As you can see in Figure 13.5, multiple checkboxes may be checked.

FIGURE 13.4.

The Special menu.

FIGURE 13.5.

Multiple check-boxes can be checked.

Check the first radio button and then pull down the Special menu to verify that it has been checked. Now check the second radio button. Only one radio button can be checked at a time. Figure 13.6 shows that the checking of the second radio button causes the first radio button to become unchecked.

FIGURE 13.6.

Only a single radio button may be checked.

LISTING 13.1. THE SwingWin PROGRAM.

```java
import java.awt.*;
import java.awt.event.*;
import com.sun.java.swing.*;
import com.sun.java.swing.event.*;

public class SwingWin extends JFrame {
  public static int WIDTH = 300;
  public static int HEIGHT = 300;
  public static String TITLE = "SwingWin";

  Container frameContainer;
  // Swing components
  JTextField textField = new JTextField(50);
  JMenuBar menuBar = new JMenuBar();
  JMenu fileMenu = new JMenu("File");
  JMenuItem fileNew = new JMenuItem("New");
  JMenuItem fileOpen = new JMenuItem("Open");
  JMenuItem fileSave = new JMenuItem("Save");
  JMenuItem fileExit = new JMenuItem("Exit");
  JMenu editMenu = new JMenu("Edit");
  JMenuItem editCut = new JMenuItem("Cut");
  JMenuItem editCopy = new JMenuItem("Copy");
  JMenuItem editPaste = new JMenuItem("Paste");
  JMenu specialMenu = new JMenu("Special");
  JCheckBoxMenuItem specialCheck1 = new JCheckBoxMenuItem("Check 1");
  JCheckBoxMenuItem specialCheck2 = new JCheckBoxMenuItem("Check 2",true);
  JSeparator separator = new JSeparator();
  JRadioButtonMenuItem specialRadio1 = new JRadioButtonMenuItem("Radio 1");
  JRadioButtonMenuItem specialRadio2 = new JRadioButtonMenuItem("Radio 2");
  ButtonGroup buttonGroup = new ButtonGroup();

  public SwingWin() {
    super(TITLE);
    buildGUI();
    setupEventHandlers();
    setSize(WIDTH,HEIGHT);
    show();
  }

  void buildGUI() {
    setupMenuBar();
    layoutComponents();
  }

  void setupMenuBar() {
    fileMenu.add(fileNew);
    fileMenu.add(fileOpen);
    fileMenu.add(fileSave);
```

continues

13

WORKING WITH
SWING
COMPONENTS

LISTING 13.1. CONTINUED

```java
      fileMenu.add(fileExit);
      editMenu.add(editCut);
      editMenu.add(editCopy);
      editMenu.add(editPaste);
      specialMenu.add(specialCheck1);
      specialMenu.add(specialCheck2);
      specialMenu.add(separator);
      buttonGroup.add(specialRadio1);
      buttonGroup.add(specialRadio2);
      specialMenu.add(specialRadio1);
      specialMenu.add(specialRadio2);
      menuBar.add(fileMenu);
      menuBar.add(editMenu);
      menuBar.add(specialMenu);
      setJMenuBar(menuBar);
    }

    public void layoutComponents() {
      frameContainer = getContentPane();
      frameContainer.setLayout(null);
      textField.setBounds(100,100,100,20);
      frameContainer.add(textField);
    }

    void setupEventHandlers() {
      addWindowListener(new WindowHandler());
      fileNew.addActionListener(new MenuItemHandler());
      fileOpen.addActionListener(new MenuItemHandler());
      fileSave.addActionListener(new MenuItemHandler());
      fileExit.addActionListener(new MenuItemHandler());
      editCut.addActionListener(new MenuItemHandler());
      editCopy.addActionListener(new MenuItemHandler());
      editPaste.addActionListener(new MenuItemHandler());
      specialCheck1.addItemListener(new ItemHandler());
      specialCheck2.addItemListener(new ItemHandler());
      specialRadio1.addItemListener(new ItemHandler());
      specialRadio2.addItemListener(new ItemHandler());
    }

    public static void main(String[] args) {
      SwingWin app = new SwingWin();
    }

    public class WindowHandler extends WindowAdapter {
      public void windowClosing(WindowEvent e) {
        System.exit(0);
      }
    }

    public class MenuItemHandler implements ActionListener {
      public void actionPerformed(ActionEvent e) {
```

Borders

The com.sun.java.swing.border package provides the Border interface, which defines the methods that need to be implemented by all border classes. The AbstractBorder class implements the Border interface and is the superclass of the Swing border classes. Its subclasses include:

- BevelBorder   A border that is beveled and raised or lowered
- CompoundBorder   A border consisting of multiple other borders
- EmptyBorder   An empty border used to provide margins
- EtchedBorder   A border that is etched with highlight and shadow colors
- LineBorder   A border that draws a line around a component
- MatteBorder   A border that is comprised of an image or color
- SoftBevelBorder   A beveled border with softened corners
- TitledBorder   A boxed border with a title

The use of these classes is covered in the next example.

SwingBorder

The SwingBorder program, shown in Listing 13.2, illustrates the use of Swing's pre-defined borders. The opening window of SwingBorder is shown in Figure 13.7. Select Bevel from the Border menu and the window's border changes to a beveled border as shown in Figure 13.8. Note that the beveling can be changed from a lowered bevel to a raised bevel.

13

WORKING WITH
SWING
COMPONENTS

FIGURE **13.7.**

The SwingBorder
opening display.

Select Compound from the Border menu and a compound blue and red border is displayed, as shown in Figure 13.9. The compound border consists of two line borders, one of each color. Figure 13.10 shows an the empty border that is displayed when you select Empty from the Border menu. An empty border is used to provide vertical and horizontal margins, without displaying anything in those margins.

Figure 13.8.

A beveled border.

Figure 13.9.

A compound border.

Figure 13.10.

An empty border.

Selecting Etched from the Border menu results in the Etched border shown in Figure 13.11. Figure 13.12 shows the lined border that results from selecting Line from the border menu.

Probably the most interesting border is the matte border, shown in Figure 13.13. This border results from selecting matte from the Border menu. The border was created using a phone icon.

Figure 13.14 shows the raised soft beveled border that results from selecting Soft Bevel from the Border menu. Figure 13.15 provides an example of a titled border.

FIGURE 13.11.
An etched border.

FIGURE 13.12.
A lined border.

FIGURE 13.13.
A matte border.

FIGURE 13.14.
A soft beveled border.

13

WORKING WITH
SWING
COMPONENTS

FIGURE 13.15.

A titled border.

LISTING 13.2. THE SwingBorder PROGRAM.

```
import java.awt.*;
import java.awt.event.*;
import com.sun.java.swing.*;
import com.sun.java.swing.event.*;
import com.sun.java.swing.border.*;

public class SwingBorder extends JFrame {
 public static int WIDTH = 300;
 public static int HEIGHT = 300;
 public static String TITLE = "SwingBorder";

 Container frameContainer;
 // Swing components
 JPanel panel = new JPanel();
 JMenuBar menuBar = new JMenuBar();
 JMenu fileMenu = new JMenu("File");
 JMenuItem fileExit = new JMenuItem("Exit");
 JMenu borderMenu = new JMenu("Border");
 String[] borderTypes = {"Bevel","Compound","Empty","Etched",
  "Line","Matte","SoftBevel","Titled"};
 JRadioButtonMenuItem[] borders =
  new JRadioButtonMenuItem[borderTypes.length];
 AbstractBorder[] border = {new BevelBorder(BevelBorder.LOWERED),
  new CompoundBorder(new LineBorder(Color.blue,10),
   new LineBorder(Color.red,5)), new EmptyBorder(10,10,10,10),
  new EtchedBorder(), new LineBorder(Color.blue,10),
  new MatteBorder(new ImageIcon("phone.gif")),
  new SoftBevelBorder(BevelBorder.RAISED),
  new TitledBorder("TitledBorder")};
 ButtonGroup buttonGroup = .new ButtonGroup();

 public SwingBorder() {
  super(TITLE);
  buildGUI();
```

```
    setupEventHandlers();
    setSize(WIDTH,HEIGHT);
    show();
  }

  void buildGUI() {
   setupMenuBar();
   layoutComponents();
  }

  void setupMenuBar() {
   fileMenu.add(fileExit);
   for(int i=0;i<borderTypes.length;++i) {
    borders[i] = new JRadioButtonMenuItem(borderTypes[i]);
    buttonGroup.add(borders[i]);
    borderMenu.add(borders[i]);
   }
   menuBar.add(fileMenu);
   menuBar.add(borderMenu);
   setJMenuBar(menuBar);
  }

  public void layoutComponents() {
   frameContainer = getContentPane();
   frameContainer.setLayout(new BorderLayout());
   frameContainer.add("Center",panel);
  }

  void setupEventHandlers() {
   addWindowListener(new WindowHandler());
   fileExit.addActionListener(new MenuItemHandler());
   for(int i=0;i<borders.length;++i)
    borders[i].addItemListener(new ItemHandler());
  }

  public static void main(String[] args) {
    SwingBorder app = new SwingBorder();
  }

  public class WindowHandler extends WindowAdapter {
   public void windowClosing(WindowEvent e) {
    System.exit(0);
   }
  }

  public class MenuItemHandler implements ActionListener {
   public void actionPerformed(ActionEvent e) {
    String cmd = e.getActionCommand();
```

continues

LISTING 13.2. CONTINUED

```
    if(cmd.equals("Exit")) System.exit(0);
  }
}

public class ItemHandler implements ItemListener {
  public void itemStateChanged(ItemEvent e) {
   JRadioButtonMenuItem button = (JRadioButtonMenuItem) e.getItem();
   String label = button.getText();
   for(int i=0;i<borderTypes.length;++i) {
    if(label.equals(borderTypes[i])) {
     panel.setBorder(border[i]);
     repaint();
    }
   }
  }
 }
}
```

SwingBorder begins by declaring the constants and variables used to implement the borders. It uses an object of the JPanel class to display the border. This object is assigned to the panel variable. The borderTypes array is used to create the menu items of the Border menu. These menu items are implemented as objects of the JRadioButtonMenuItem class. An array of AbstractBorder objects is created to provide examples of each border type. These borders are implemented by the following objects:

- A BevelBorder object with a lowered bevel
- A CompoundBorder object consisting of a blue 10-pixel-wide LineBorder object and a red 5-pixel-wide LineBorder object
- An EmptyBorder object with 10-pixel margins
- An EtchedBorder object
- A blue 10-pixel-wide LineBorder object
- A MatteBorder object that displays the image contained in the phone.gif file on the border
- A SoftBevelBorder object that has a raised bevel
- A TitledBorder object with the TitledBorder title

The setupMenuBar() method creates each of the JRadioButtonMenuItem objects from the borderTypes array, adds the buttons to their button group, and then adds them to the Border menu. The setupEventHandlers() method sets up the event handlers for the window and menu items. The Border menu items are assigned objects of the ItemHandler class.

The itemStateChanged() method of the ItemHandler class retrieves the label of the JRadioButtonMenuItem that is selected. The border of the JPanel object referenced by panel is set to the selected border object and the repaint() method is invoked to bring the border into effect.

Tool Tips

The JToolTip class provides the capability to add popup text boxes that are displayed when the mouse is held over a component. Those components that support tool tips allow tool tips to be specified in their constructors. The setToolTipText() method of the JComponent class can also be used to specify a component's tool tip.

Toolbars

The JToolBar class provides the capability to use moveable and dockable toolbars with Swing. Objects of this class are containers for other Swing or AWT components. Typical JToolBar objects contain JButton objects that are constructed with image icons. The addSeparator() method is used to add a separator to a toolbar.

SwingBar

The SwingBar program, shown in Listing 13.3, illustrates Swing's toolbar and tool tip capabilities. The program's opening display is shown in Figure 13.16. A toolbar is positioned at the top of the window, underneath the menu bar. Position your mouse over the first button and the New tool tip is displayed, as shown in Figure 13.17. The toolbar is moveable. Drag it by the left side to another position within the SwingBar window as shown in Figure 13.18.

13

WORKING WITH SWING COMPONENTS

FIGURE 13.16.

The SwingBar opening window.

FIGURE **13.17.**

Tool tips are assigned to the toolbar's buttons.

FIGURE **13.18.**

The toolbar can be moved around the SwingBar *window.*

LISTING 13.3. THE SwingBar PROGRAM.

```java
import java.awt.*;
import java.awt.event.*;
import com.sun.java.swing.*;
import com.sun.java.swing.event.*;

public class SwingBar extends JFrame {
 public static int WIDTH = 400;
 public static int HEIGHT = 400;
 public static String TITLE = "SwingBar";

 Container frameContainer;
 // Swing components
 JToolBar toolBar = new JToolBar();
 String[] iconFiles = {"new.gif","open.gif","save.gif","cut.gif",
  "copy.gif","paste.gif"};
```

```
String[] buttonLabels = {"New","Open","Save","Cut","Copy","Paste"};
ImageIcon[] icons = new ImageIcon[iconFiles.length];
JButton[] buttons = new JButton[buttonLabels.length];
JMenuBar menuBar = new JMenuBar();
JMenu fileMenu = new JMenu("File");
JMenuItem fileExit = new JMenuItem("Exit");

public SwingBar() {
 super(TITLE);
 buildGUI();
 setupEventHandlers();
 setSize(WIDTH,HEIGHT);
 show();
}

void buildGUI() {
 setupMenuBar();
 layoutComponents();
}

void setupMenuBar() {
 fileMenu.add(fileExit);
 menuBar.add(fileMenu);
 setJMenuBar(menuBar);
}

public void layoutComponents() {
 frameContainer = getContentPane();
 frameContainer.setLayout(new BorderLayout());
 for(int i=0;i<buttonLabels.length;++i) {
  icons[i] = new ImageIcon(iconFiles[i]);
  buttons[i] = new JButton(icons[i]);
  buttons[i].setToolTipText(buttonLabels[i]);
  if(i==3) toolBar.addSeparator();
  toolBar.add(buttons[i]);
 }
 frameContainer.add("North",toolBar);
}

void setupEventHandlers() {
 addWindowListener(new WindowHandler());
 fileExit.addActionListener(new MenuItemHandler());
}

public static void main(String[] args) {
  SwingBar app = new SwingBar();
}

public class WindowHandler extends WindowAdapter {
 public void windowClosing(WindowEvent e) {
```

continues

LISTING 13.3. CONTINUED

```
    System.exit(0);
  }
}

public class MenuItemHandler implements ActionListener {
  public void actionPerformed(ActionEvent e) {
    String cmd = e.getActionCommand();
    if(cmd.equals("Exit")) System.exit(0);
  }
 }
}
```

The `SwingBar` program creates a `JToolBar` object and assigns it to the `toolBar` variable. The `iconFiles` array identifies the filenames of the toolbar's button icons. The `buttonLabels` array identifies the tool tips of the toolbar's buttons. The `icons` array is used to hold the images of the toolbar's buttons. The `buttons` array contains the actual buttons.

The `layoutComponents()` method creates the image icons from their image files, creates the buttons from their icons, and sets the tool tips of each button. A separator is added between the third and fourth buttons. The buttons are then added to the `JToolBar` object.

Labels and Buttons

The `JLabel` and `JButton` classes provide Swing analogs to the AWT `Label` and `Button` classes. The Swing implementation provides the advantage of being able to use icons along with text. The `JLabel()` and `JButton()` constructors allow an icon to be specified. In addition, both classes support the `setIcon()` method for setting an icon after the object has been constructed.

Text Components

The `JTextComponent`, `JTextField`, and `JTextArea` classes are the Swing analogs of the AWT `TextComponent`, `TextField`, and `TextArea` classes. In addition, Swing provides the `TextPane` class for working with text documents that can be marked up with different text styles.

Lists and Combo Boxes

The `JComboBox` and `JList` classes provide the capability to present the user with a list of text or graphic selections. The `JComboBox` class implements a drop-down list, similar to a

Motif option list. The JList class is a single or multiple selection list with a multi-element view. JList objects are typically added to a JScrollPane object so the list can be scrolled. You'll see examples of JComboBox and JList objects in the Calendar example of Listing 13.4.

Sliders and Progress Bars

You were introduced to sliders and progress bars in Chapter 12, "Introducing Swing." The JSlider and JProgressBar classes do not have AWT analogs. Both classes support horizontal and vertical orientations. The JProgressBar class is typically used to display the progress of a task, such as the loading of an image. The JSlider class is used to adjust or monitor the value of a variable within its allowed interval.

Scrollbars

The JScrollPane greatly simplifies the use of scrollbars. The getViewport() method returns a JViewport object to which components may be added. In most cases, you simply need to add components to the JViewport object and they are automatically scrolled. You'll see an example of this in the Calendar program of Listing 13.4.

Tables

The JTable class is another Swing component that does not have an AWT analog. JTable provides a very flexible capability for creating and displaying tables. It allows tables to be constructed from arrays, vectors of objects, or from objects that implement the TableModel interface.

The JTableModel interface defines methods for objects that specify a table's contents. The AbstractTableModel class provides a default implementation of the JTableModel interface. This class is typically extended to provide a custom table model implementation. You'll see an example of using the AbstractTableModel class in the Calendar program of Listing 13.4.

The JTable class provides the capability to edit tables. The setCellEditor() method allows an object of the TableCellEditor interface to be identified as a table's cell editor.

Calendar

The Calendar program, shown in Listing 13.4, illustrates the use of Swing tables. The program's opening display is shown in Figure 13.19. It consists of a combo box, list, and a table. When you select a year from the combo box, the calendar displayed by the table is updated. Select 1999 from the combo box and the calendar is updated, as shown in Figure 13.20. The selection of a month from the list also results in the calendar table being updated. Select December from the list to view the calendar for the end of this millennium, as shown in Figure 13.21.

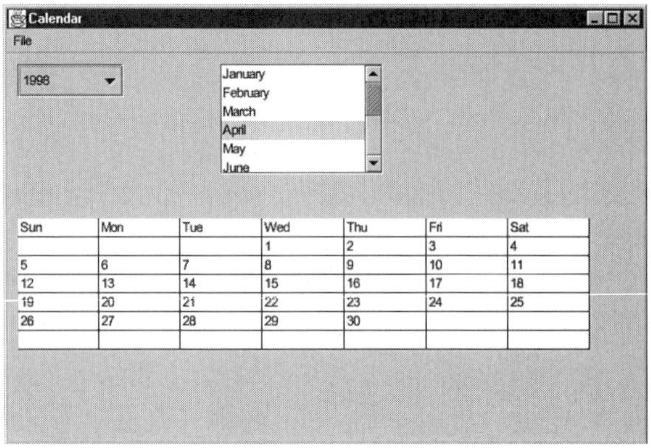

FIGURE 13.19.

The Calendar *opening display.*

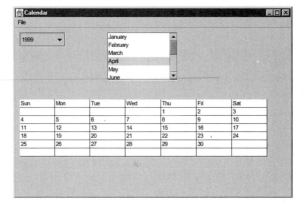

FIGURE 13.20.

Selecting a year from the combo box results in a new calendar.

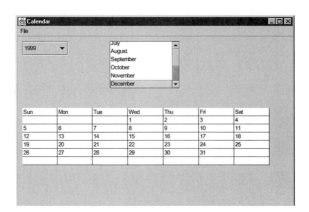

FIGURE 13.21.

Selecting a month from the list also results in a new calendar.

LISTING 13.4. THE Calendar PROGRAM.

```java
import java.awt.*;
import java.awt.event.*;
import com.sun.java.swing.*;
import com.sun.java.swing.event.*;
import com.sun.java.swing.table.*;
import java.util.Date;

public class Calendar extends JFrame {
 public static int WIDTH = 600;
 public static int HEIGHT = 400;
 public static String TITLE = "Calendar";

 Container frameContainer;
 // Swing components
 String[] years = {"1998","1999","2000","2001",
  "2002","2003","2004","2005"};
 JComboBox comboBox = new JComboBox(years);
 String[] months = {"January","February","March","April","May",
  "June","July","August","September","October","November",
  "December"};
 JList list = new JList(months);
 JScrollPane scrollPane = new JScrollPane(list);
 CalendarModel model = new CalendarModel();
 JTable table = new JTable(model);

 JMenuBar menuBar = new JMenuBar();
 JMenu fileMenu = new JMenu("File");
 JMenuItem fileExit = new JMenuItem("Exit");

 public Calendar() {
  super(TITLE);
  buildGUI();
  setupEventHandlers();
  setSize(WIDTH,HEIGHT);
  show();
 }

 void buildGUI() {
  setupMenuBar();
  layoutComponents();
 }

 void setupMenuBar() {
  fileMenu.add(fileExit);
  menuBar.add(fileMenu);
```

continues

13

WORKING WITH
SWING
COMPONENTS

LISTING 13.4. CONTINUED

```java
    setJMenuBar(menuBar);
  }

  public void layoutComponents() {
   frameContainer = getContentPane();
   frameContainer.setLayout(null);
   comboBox.setBounds(10,10,100,30);
   comboBox.setSelectedIndex(0);
   comboBox.addItemListener(new ComboHandler());
   scrollPane.setBounds(200,10,150,100);
   list.setSelectedIndex(3);
   list.addListSelectionListener(new ListHandler());
   table.setBounds(10,150,550,200);
   model.setMonth(comboBox.getSelectedIndex()+1998,
    list.getSelectedIndex());
   frameContainer.add(comboBox);
   frameContainer.add(scrollPane);
   table.setGridColor(Color.black);
   table.setShowGrid(true);
   frameContainer.add(table);
  }

  void setupEventHandlers() {
   addWindowListener(new WindowHandler());
   fileExit.addActionListener(new MenuItemHandler());
  }

  public static void main(String[] args) {
    Calendar app = new Calendar();
  }

  class CalendarModel extends AbstractTableModel {
   String[] days = {"Sun","Mon","Tue","Wed","Thu","Fri","Sat"};
   int[] numDays = {31,28,31,30,31,30,31,31,30,31,30,31};
   String[][] calendar = new String[7][7];
   public CalendarModel() {
    for(int i=0;i<days.length;++i)
     calendar[0][i]=days[i];
    for(int i=1;i<7;++i)
     for(int j=0;j<7;++j)
      calendar[i][j]=" ";
   }
   public int getRowCount() {
    return 7;
   }
   public int getColumnCount() {
    return 7;
   }
```

```
public Object getValueAt(int row, int column) {
 return calendar[row][column];
}
public void setValueAt(Object value,int row, int column) {
 calendar[row][column] = (String) value;
}
public void setMonth(int year,int month) {
 for(int i=1;i<7;++i)
  for(int j=0;j<7;++j)
   calendar[i][j]=" ";
 java.util.GregorianCalendar cal =
  new java.util.GregorianCalendar();
 cal.set(year,month,1);
 int offset = cal.get(java.util.GregorianCalendar.DAY_OF_WEEK)-1;
 offset += 7;
 int num = daysInMonth(year,month);
 for(int i=0;i<num;++i) {
  calendar[offset/7][offset%7]=Integer.toString(i+1);
  ++offset;
 }
}
public boolean isLeapYear(int year) {
 if(year % 4 ==0) return true;
 return false;
}
public int daysInMonth(int year,int month) {
 int days = numDays[month];
 if(month==1 && isLeapYear(year)) ++days;
 return days;
}
}

public class WindowHandler extends WindowAdapter {
 public void windowClosing(WindowEvent e) {
  System.exit(0);
 }
}

public class ComboHandler implements ItemListener {
 public void itemStateChanged(ItemEvent e) {
  model.setMonth(comboBox.getSelectedIndex()+1998,
   list.getSelectedIndex());
   table.repaint();
 }
}

public class ListHandler implements ListSelectionListener {
 public void valueChanged(ListSelectionEvent e) {
  model.setMonth(comboBox.getSelectedIndex()+1998,
```

13

WORKING WITH
SWING
COMPONENTS

continues

LISTING 13.4. CONTINUED

```
      list.getSelectedIndex());
      table.repaint();
  }
}

public class MenuItemHandler implements ActionListener {
  public void actionPerformed(ActionEvent e) {
    String cmd = e.getActionCommand();
    if(cmd.equals("Exit")) System.exit(0);
  }
 }
}
```

The Calendar program uses the years and months arrays to identify the years and months supported by the calendar. A JComboBox object is created from the years array and a JList object is created from the months array. The JList object is used to create a ScrollPane object that supports list scrolling. The CalendarModel class is an inner class that is used to implement the table's model. An object of this class is created and assigned to the model variable. A JTable object is created from the CalendarModel object and assigned to the table variable.

The layoutComponents() method sets the layout of the frame's container to a null layout. It then sets the bounds, selected index, and event handlers for the combo box and list. The table's bounds are set and then the table's model is updated based on the year selected in the combo box and month selected in the list. This is accomplished using the setMonth() method of the CalendarModel class.

The CalendarModel class is used as the table's model. It extends the AbstractTableModel class. It declares the days array for use in the table's column headings and the numDays array to keep track of the number of days in each month. The calendar array is set to a seven-row by seven-column array. It is used to keep track of the table's contents. The CalendarModel() constructor sets the column headings and then blanks the table's contents.

The getRowCount(), getColumnCount(), getValueAt(), and setValueAt() methods override those of the AbstractTableModel class.

The setMonth() method updates the calendar array with the contents of the calendar for the specified year and month. It blanks out the array's contents and creates a GregorianCalendar object for the first day of the month. It then uses the get() method to determine the day of the week associated with the first day of the month. The daysInMonth() method returns the number of days in the specified month. Using this information, setMonth() is able to fill in the array's contents.

The isLeapYear() method is used to identify leap years and the daysInMonth() method returns the number of days in a month adjusted for leap years.

Trees

One of the most interesting new classes provided by Swing is the JTree class. This class implements a tree structure that can be used to display hierarchical data. The TreeNode interface defines methods that are to be implemented by the nodes of a JTree object. The DefaultMutableTreeNode class provides a default implementation of the TreeNode interface. Trees are created by creating objects of the TreeNode interface and then adding them together (via the add() method). When all of the TreeNode objects have been added together, the resulting TreeNode object is passed to the JTree constructor.

The default rendering of a JTree object uses a folder icon to identify tree nodes that have child nodes and a file icon to identify tree leaves. The setCellRenderer() method of the JTree class is used to identify an alternative tree rendering. The setCellRenderer() method takes an object of the TreeCellRenderer interface as a parameter. The following example shows how to use a custom tree rendering object.

SwingTree

The SwingTree program, shown in Listing 13.5, illustrates the use of Swing trees. Its opening window is shown in Figure 13.22. A JTree object is used to display the teams of the National Basketball association, arranged by conference and division. Click the circles before the conferences and divisions to expand the tree, as shown in Figure 13.23. Note that scrollbars appear when you expand the tree to the bottom of its display area. Click any team and the team's win/loss record is displayed in the text field at the bottom of the window as shown in Figure 13.24.

FIGURE 13.22.

The SwingTree *initial display.*

FIGURE 13.23.

*Expand the tree
and scrollbars are
displayed.*

FIGURE 13.24.

*Click a team and
the team's record
is displayed.*

LISTING 13.5. THE SwingTree PROGRAM.

```
import java.awt.*;
import java.awt.event.*;
import com.sun.java.swing.*;
import com.sun.java.swing.event.*;
import com.sun.java.swing.tree.*;

public class SwingTree extends JFrame {
 public static int WIDTH = 400;
 public static int HEIGHT = 400;
 public static String TITLE = "SwingTree";

 Container frameContainer;
 // Swing components
 JTextField textField = new JTextField();
 JScrollPane scrollPane = new JScrollPane();
 JTree tree;
 Renderer renderer = new Renderer();
```

```
DefaultMutableTreeNode nba =
 new DefaultMutableTreeNode("National Basketball Association");
DefaultMutableTreeNode western =
 new DefaultMutableTreeNode("Western Conference");
DefaultMutableTreeNode pacific =
 new DefaultMutableTreeNode("Pacific Division Teams");
DefaultMutableTreeNode lalakers =
 new DefaultMutableTreeNode("Los Angeles (Lakers)");
DefaultMutableTreeNode seattle =
 new DefaultMutableTreeNode("Seattle");
DefaultMutableTreeNode phoenix =
 new DefaultMutableTreeNode("Phoenix");
DefaultMutableTreeNode portland =
 new DefaultMutableTreeNode("Portland");
DefaultMutableTreeNode sacramento =
 new DefaultMutableTreeNode("Sacramento");
DefaultMutableTreeNode goldengate =
 new DefaultMutableTreeNode("San Francisco");
DefaultMutableTreeNode laclippers =
 new DefaultMutableTreeNode("Los Angeles (Clippers)");
DefaultMutableTreeNode midwest =
 new DefaultMutableTreeNode("Midwest Division Teams");
DefaultMutableTreeNode utah =
 new DefaultMutableTreeNode("Utah");
DefaultMutableTreeNode sanantonio =
 new DefaultMutableTreeNode("San Antonio");
DefaultMutableTreeNode houston =
 new DefaultMutableTreeNode("Houston");
DefaultMutableTreeNode minnesota =
 new DefaultMutableTreeNode("Minnesota");
DefaultMutableTreeNode vancouver =
 new DefaultMutableTreeNode("Vancouver");
DefaultMutableTreeNode dallas =
 new DefaultMutableTreeNode("Dallas");
DefaultMutableTreeNode denver =
 new DefaultMutableTreeNode("Denver");
DefaultMutableTreeNode eastern =
 new DefaultMutableTreeNode("Eastern Conference");
DefaultMutableTreeNode atlantic =
 new DefaultMutableTreeNode("Atlantic Division Teams");
DefaultMutableTreeNode miami =
 new DefaultMutableTreeNode("Miami");
DefaultMutableTreeNode ny =
 new DefaultMutableTreeNode("New York");
DefaultMutableTreeNode nj =
 new DefaultMutableTreeNode("New Jersey");
DefaultMutableTreeNode washington =
 new DefaultMutableTreeNode("Washington");
DefaultMutableTreeNode orlando =
 new DefaultMutableTreeNode("Orlando");
```

13

WORKING WITH
SWING
COMPONENTS

continues

LISTING 13.5. CONTINUED

```java
DefaultMutableTreeNode boston =
 new DefaultMutableTreeNode("Boston");
DefaultMutableTreeNode philadelphia =
 new DefaultMutableTreeNode("Philadelphia");
DefaultMutableTreeNode central =
 new DefaultMutableTreeNode("Central Division Teams");
DefaultMutableTreeNode chicago =
 new DefaultMutableTreeNode("Chicago");
DefaultMutableTreeNode indiana =
 new DefaultMutableTreeNode("Indiana");
DefaultMutableTreeNode charlotte =
 new DefaultMutableTreeNode("Charlotte");
DefaultMutableTreeNode atlanta =
 new DefaultMutableTreeNode("Atlanta");
DefaultMutableTreeNode cleveland =
 new DefaultMutableTreeNode("Cleveland");
DefaultMutableTreeNode detroit =
 new DefaultMutableTreeNode("Detroit");
DefaultMutableTreeNode milwaukee =
 new DefaultMutableTreeNode("Milwaukee");
DefaultMutableTreeNode toronto =
 new DefaultMutableTreeNode("Toronto");
JMenuBar menuBar = new JMenuBar();
JMenu fileMenu = new JMenu("File");
JMenuItem fileExit = new JMenuItem("Exit");

public SwingTree() {
 super(TITLE);
 buildGUI();
 setupEventHandlers();
 setSize(WIDTH,HEIGHT);
 show();
}

void buildGUI() {
 setupMenuBar();
 setupTree();
 layoutComponents();
}

void setupMenuBar() {
 fileMenu.add(fileExit);
 menuBar.add(fileMenu);
 setJMenuBar(menuBar);
}

void setupTree() {
 nba.add(western);
```

```
        nba.add(eastern);
        western.add(pacific);
        western.add(midwest);
        eastern.add(atlantic);
        eastern.add(central);
        pacific.add(lalakers);
        pacific.add(laclippers);
        pacific.add(goldengate);
        pacific.add(seattle);
        pacific.add(phoenix);
        pacific.add(portland);
        pacific.add(sacramento);
        midwest.add(utah);
        midwest.add(sanantonio);
        midwest.add(houston);
        midwest.add(minnesota);
        midwest.add(vancouver);
        midwest.add(dallas);
        midwest.add(denver);
        atlantic.add(miami);
        atlantic.add(ny);
        atlantic.add(nj);
        atlantic.add(washington);
        atlantic.add(orlando);
        atlantic.add(boston);
        atlantic.add(philadelphia);
        central.add(chicago);
        central.add(indiana);
        central.add(charlotte);
        central.add(atlanta);
        central.add(cleveland);
        central.add(detroit);
        central.add(milwaukee);
        central.add(toronto);
        tree = new JTree(nba);
    }

    public void layoutComponents() {
     frameContainer = getContentPane();
     frameContainer.setLayout(new BorderLayout());
     tree.setCellRenderer(renderer);
     tree.addTreeSelectionListener(new TreeHandler());
     scrollPane.getViewport().add(tree);
     frameContainer.add("Center",scrollPane);
     frameContainer.add("South",textField);
    }

    void setupEventHandlers() {
     addWindowListener(new WindowHandler());
```

continues

13

WORKING WITH
SWING
COMPONENTS

LISTING 13.5. CONTINUED

```java
      fileExit.addActionListener(new MenuItemHandler());
  }

  public static void main(String[] args) {
    SwingTree app = new SwingTree();
  }

  public class WindowHandler extends WindowAdapter {
   public void windowClosing(WindowEvent e) {
    System.exit(0);
   }
  }

  public class MenuItemHandler implements ActionListener {
   public void actionPerformed(ActionEvent e) {
    String cmd = e.getActionCommand();
    if(cmd.equals("Exit")) System.exit(0);
   }
  }

  public class TreeHandler implements TreeSelectionListener {
   public void valueChanged(TreeSelectionEvent e) {
    TreePath path = e.getPath();
    String text = path.getPathComponent(
     path.getPathCount()-1).toString();
    if(path.getPathCount()>3) {
     text += ": ";
     text += Integer.toString((int)(Math.random()*50))+" Wins ";
     text += Integer.toString((int)(Math.random()*50))+" Losses";
    }
    textField.setText(text);
   }
  }

 class Renderer extends JLabel implements TreeCellRenderer {
  public Component  getTreeCellRendererComponent(JTree tree,
    Object value, boolean selected, boolean expanded,
    boolean leaf, int row, boolean hasFocus) {
    setText(value.toString()+"                ");
    return this;
  }
 }
}
```

The SwingTree program uses a TextField object to display team selections, a
ScrollPane object to support scrolling for the tree, a JTree object to implement the tree,
and a Renderer object to control the way the tree is rendered. The Renderer class is
declared as an inner class.

The nodes and leaves of the tree are implemented as `DefaultMutableTreeNode` objects. These objects are created with the names of NBA teams and organizational groupings. The `setupTree()` method connects the `DefaultMutableTreeNode` objects into the nodes of the tree. A new `JTree` object is created at the end of `setupTree()` method. This object is created from the tree's root node and assigned to the `tree` variable.

The `layoutComponents()` method lays out the frame's container using a `BorderLayout` object. The `setCellRenderer()` method sets the rendering object of the tree to the `Renderer` object referenced by the `renderer` variable. An object of the `TreeHandler` class is used to handle the selection of elements of the tree. The tree is then added to the view port of a scroll pane.

The `valueChanged()` method of the `TreeHandler` class handles the selection of elements of the tree by using the `getPathComponent()` method to get the path selected by the user and the `getPathCount()` method to identify the length of this path. The last element of the path is set as the text of the text field. If the element is a team (in other words, at the fourth level of the tree), random win/loss statistics are displayed along with the team's name.

Swing Event Handling

Swing events are handled using the event delegation model introduced by JDK 1.1. The event inheritance model of JDK 1.0 cannot be used with Swing. The `com.sun.java.swing.event` package defines a number of event listening interfaces and event classes for use with Swing components. In addition, many Swing components also use AWT events. The Swing events defined in the `com.sun.java.swing.event` package are the following:

- `AncestorEvent`   Generated when an ancestors of a `JComponent` is added, removed, or moved
- `ChangeEvent`   Generated when an object's state is changed
- `DragEvent`   Generated as the result of the dragging of an object
- `ListDataEvent`   Generated as the result of changes to list data
- `ListSelectionEvent`   Generated as the result of a change in a list selection
- `MenuEvent`   Generated as the result of the posting, selection, or canceling of a menu
- `TableColumnModelEvent`   Generated as the result of a change in a table column model
- `TableModelEvent`   Generated as the result of a change in a table model
- `TreeExpansionEvent`   Generated as the result of a change in a tree's expansion

- TreeModelEvent   Generated as the result of a change in a tree model
- TreeSelectionEvent   Generated as the result of a change in a tree selection

The com.sun.java.swing.event package defines event listener interfaces for the above events. The next chapter covers the Model View Controller (MVC) used by Swing components.

Swing Applets

The JApplet class is the Swing analog of the Applet class. JApplet is similar to JFrame in that it supports a separate content pane. This container is accessed via the getContentPane() method. If you ever wished you could use menus in an applet, you'll love the JApplet class. It provides the capability to use a menu bar with an applet via the setJMenuBar method. The menu bar must be an object of the JMenuBar class.

CalendarApplet

The CalendarApplet applet, shown in Listing 13.6, is an applet conversion of the Calendar application of Listing 13.4. CalendarApplet illustrates the menu feature of the JApplet class. The calendar.htm file of Listing 13.7 is used to display CalendarApplet using the appletviewer.

Figure 13.25 shows the opening display of CalendarApplet. Note the addition of the Year and Month menus at the top of the applet display area. The inability to include menus in applets was a shortcoming of the Applet class. This shortcoming is removed by JApplet. Select the year 2002 from the Year pull-down menu. The calendar is updated to display a calendar for April 2002, as shown in Figure 13.26. Note that the year displayed by the combo box is also updated.

FIGURE 13.25.

The CalendarApplet *initial display.*

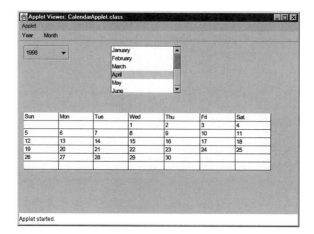

FIGURE 13.26.

Selecting a menu item from the Year menu causes the calendar and combo box to be updated.

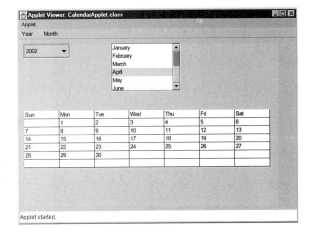

Select March from the Month menu. The calendar is updated to display March 2002, as shown in Figure 13.27. Also note that the list identifies the month of March as being selected.

FIGURE 13.27.

Selecting a menu item from the Month menu causes the calendar and list to be updated.

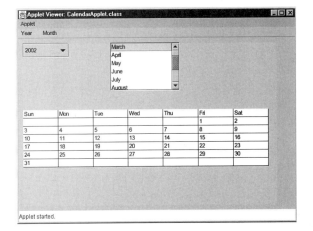

LISTING 13.6. THE CalendarApplet APPLET.

```
import java.awt.*;
import java.awt.event.*;
import com.sun.java.swing.*;
import com.sun.java.swing.event.*;
import com.sun.java.swing.table.*;
```

continues

13

WORKING WITH
SWING
COMPONENTS

LISTING 13.6. CONTINUED

```java
import java.util.Date;

public class CalendarApplet extends JApplet {
 public static int WIDTH = 600;
 public static int HEIGHT = 400;

 Container frameContainer;
 // Swing components
 String[] years = {"1998","1999","2000","2001",
  "2002","2003","2004","2005"};
 JComboBox comboBox = new JComboBox(years);
 String[] months = {"January","February","March","April","May",
  "June","July","August","September","October","November",
  "December"};
 JList list = new JList(months);
 JScrollPane scrollPane = new JScrollPane(list);
 CalendarModel model = new CalendarModel();
 JTable table = new JTable(model);

 JMenuBar menuBar = new JMenuBar();
 JMenu yearMenu = new JMenu("Year");
 JMenu monthMenu = new JMenu("Month");
 JMenuItem[] yearMenuItems = new JMenuItem[years.length];
 JMenuItem[] monthMenuItems = new JMenuItem[months.length];

 public CalendarApplet() {
  buildGUI();
  setupEventHandlers();
  setSize(WIDTH,HEIGHT);
 }

 void buildGUI() {
  setupMenuBar();
  layoutComponents();
 }

 void setupMenuBar() {
  for(int i=0;i<years.length;++i) {
   yearMenuItems[i] = new JMenuItem(years[i]);
   yearMenu.add(yearMenuItems[i]);
  }
  for(int i=0;i<months.length;++i) {
   monthMenuItems[i] = new JMenuItem(months[i]);
   monthMenu.add(monthMenuItems[i]);
  }
  menuBar.add(yearMenu);
  menuBar.add(monthMenu);
```

```
   setJMenuBar(menuBar);
 }
 public void layoutComponents() {
  frameContainer = getContentPane();
  frameContainer.setLayout(null);
  comboBox.setBounds(10,10,100,30);
  comboBox.setSelectedIndex(0);
  comboBox.addItemListener(new ComboHandler());
  scrollPane.setBounds(200,10,150,100);
  list.setSelectedIndex(3);
  list.addListSelectionListener(new ListHandler());
  table.setBounds(10,150,550,200);
  model.setMonth(comboBox.getSelectedIndex()+1998,
   list.getSelectedIndex());
  frameContainer.add(comboBox);
  frameContainer.add(scrollPane);
  table.setGridColor(Color.black);
  table.setShowGrid(true);
  frameContainer.add(table);
 }

 void setupEventHandlers() {
  for(int i=0;i<yearMenuItems.length;++i)
   yearMenuItems[i].addActionListener(new YearMenuItemHandler());
  for(int i=0;i<monthMenuItems.length;++i)
   monthMenuItems[i].addActionListener(new MonthMenuItemHandler());
 }

 class CalendarModel extends AbstractTableModel {
  String[] days = {"Sun","Mon","Tue","Wed","Thu","Fri","Sat"};
  int[] numDays = {31,28,31,30,31,30,31,31,30,31,30,31};
  String[][] calendar = new String[7][7];
  public CalendarModel() {
   for(int i=0;i<days.length;++i)
    calendar[0][i]=days[i];
   for(int i=1;i<7;++i)
    for(int j=0;j<7;++j)
     calendar[i][j]=" ";
  }
  public int getRowCount() {
   return 7;
  }
  public int getColumnCount() {
   return 7;
  }
  public Object getValueAt(int row, int column) {
   return calendar[row][column];
  }
```

13

WORKING WITH
SWING
COMPONENTS

continues

LISTING 13.6. CONTINUED

```java
public void setValueAt(Object value,int row, int column) {
  calendar[row][column] = (String) value;
}
public void setMonth(int year,int month) {
  for(int i=1;i<7;++i)
   for(int j=0;j<7;++j)
    calendar[i][j]=" ";
  java.util.GregorianCalendar cal =
   new java.util.GregorianCalendar();
  cal.set(year,month,1);
  int offset = cal.get(java.util.GregorianCalendar.DAY_OF_WEEK)-1;
  offset += 7;
  int num = daysInMonth(year,month);
  for(int i=0;i<num;++i) {
   calendar[offset/7][offset%7]=Integer.toString(i+1);
   ++offset;
  }
}
public boolean isLeapYear(int year) {
  if(year % 4 ==0) return true;
  return false;
}
public int daysInMonth(int year,int month) {
  int days = numDays[month];
  if(month==1 && isLeapYear(year)) ++days;
  return days;
}
}

public class ComboHandler implements ItemListener {
 public void itemStateChanged(ItemEvent e) {
  model.setMonth(comboBox.getSelectedIndex()+1998,
   list.getSelectedIndex());
   table.repaint();
 }
}

public class ListHandler implements ListSelectionListener {
 public void valueChanged(ListSelectionEvent e) {
  model.setMonth(comboBox.getSelectedIndex()+1998,
   list.getSelectedIndex());
   table.repaint();
 }
}

public class YearMenuItemHandler implements ActionListener {
 public void actionPerformed(ActionEvent e) {
```

```
    String cmd = e.getActionCommand();
    int year = (new Integer(cmd)).intValue() - 1998;
    comboBox.setSelectedIndex(year);
    model.setMonth(comboBox.getSelectedIndex()+1998,
     list.getSelectedIndex());
     table.repaint();
  }
}

public class MonthMenuItemHandler implements ActionListener {
 public void actionPerformed(ActionEvent e) {
   String cmd = e.getActionCommand();
   int month = 0;
   for(int i=0;i<months.length;++i) {
    if(cmd.equals(months[i])) {
     month = i;
     break;
    }
   }
   list.setSelectedIndex(month);
   model.setMonth(comboBox.getSelectedIndex()+1998,
    list.getSelectedIndex());
    table.repaint();
  }
 }
}
```

The `CalendarApplet` class is based on the `Calendar` class of Listing 13.4. Instead of extending `JFrame`, `CalendarApplet` extends `JApplet`. The only other significant difference between `CalendarApplet` and `Calendar` is the use of the Year and Month menus. These menus are set up in the `setupMenuBar()` and `setupEventHandlers()` methods. Note that separate classes are used to handle the Year and Month menu items.

The `actionPerformed()` method of the `YearMenuItemHandler` class determines the year that was selected and sets the corresponding index in the combo box. The table's model is updated based upon the indexes of the combo box and list. The `repaint()` method is invoked to cause the table to be redisplayed.

The `actionPerformed()` method of the `MonthMenuItemHandler` class is similar to that of the `YearMenuItemHandler` class. The month that was selected is determined and the corresponding index in the list is set. The table's model is then updated and the `repaint()` method is invoked.

LISTING 13.7. THE calendar.htm FILE.

```
<HTML>
<HEAD>
<TITLE>Calendar Applet</TITLE>
</HEAD>
<BODY>
<APPLET CODE="CalendarApplet.class" HEIGHT=400 WIDTH=600>
</APPLET>
</BODY>
</HTML>
```

Converting to Swing

Because Swing provides GUI components that are analogous to AWT components, it is easy to convert applications and applets to Swing. Applications are converted to Swing by replacing the Frame class with the JFrame class and using getContentPane() to access the frame's container. GUI components that were added to the Frame are added to the frame container. Applets are converted in a similar manner with the JApplet class replacing the Applet class. Most AWT GUI components can be converted to Swing by simply preceding the AWT class name with the letter 'J'.

Once you convert your AWT components to Swing components you may want to substitute new Swing components, such as sliders, trees, and tables to reduce the complexity of your user interface. You may also want to use icons with buttons, labels, and other components to make the interface more attractive and usable. Finally, you should experiment with borders and other Swing features that contribute to your application's or applet's look and feel.

Summary

In this chapter you learned about Swing windows, menus, toolbars, tables, trees, and other GUI components. You learned about Swing events and how the JApplet class supports the development of applets that use Swing components. You also learned how to convert your existing applications and applets to Swing. In the next chapter, Chapter 14, "Changing the Look and Feel of Your Swing Components" you'll learn about Swing's pluggable look and feel capabilities.

CHAPTER 14

Changing the Look and Feel of Your Swing Components

Swing is a powerful enhancement to the AWT because it provides a rich set of platform independent GUI components. Platform independence ensures that Swing components are supported in the same manner across all Java ports. Platform independence also enables the look-and-feel (L&F) of Swing components to be easily tailored. This feature, referred to as Pluggable Look and Feel (PL&F), lets you create applets and applications that use a look and feel that is independent of the windowing platform in which the applets and applications are executed. For example, you can create applications that use a Macintosh look and feel when they are executed on a Windows platform, and you can create applets that use a Motif look and feel no matter what browsers or windowing systems are used to run them.

This chapter covers PL&F. It explains what look and feel is and how the model-view-controller (MVC) architecture is used to achieve PL&F. It introduces you to the Swing classes and interfaces that implement PL&F and shows you how to change an applet or application's look and feel. It also shows you how to develop your own look and feel. When you finish this chapter, you'll be able to use PL&F to enhance the style and consistency of the applets and applications you develop.

Look and Feel Explained

The look and feel of a program consists of the way the program presents itself to the user (its look) and the way the user interacts with it (its feel). Most programs display their output to the user's console and receive input from a keyboard and pointer device (mouse or equivalent). However, look and feel is subtler than raw input and output.

Many operating systems, such as Microsoft Windows, Macintosh OS, and UNIX, support windowing systems, which allow windows to be opened, closed, moved, and sized based on keyboard and mouse operations. They also support GUI components, such as labels, buttons, text fields, and menus. However, look and feel is subtler still.

Look and feel is determined by how a window or other GUI component is displayed and how it responds to user input. The GUI components of Microsoft Windows share a display style and operational behavior that set them apart from the equivalent components of the Macintosh. We can look at a screen capture and determine whether it came from Microsoft Windows or Macintosh based on its look. We can interact with a GUI and identify it as Motif based upon its feel. We notice slight differences in the controls used with windows, the way menus are displayed, and the way buttons behave when clicked that enable us to make these decisions. These differences are what constitute look and feel.

The Model-View-Controller Architecture

Swing provides the capability to change the look and feel of an applet or application. This capability stems from the fact that Swing components (unlike AWT components) are not tied to the GUI components of the native windowing system. This capability allows you to create applets or applications that will use a specific look and feel (such as Motif) no matter whether the applet or application executes on a Macintosh, a UNIX system, or a PC. Figure 14.1 provides an example of a Java program that uses the Motif look and feel but executes under Windows 95. Figure 14.2 shows the very same program but with a Windows look and feel. The capability to easily change look and feel, referred to as pluggable look and feel (PL&F), also allows custom look and feel to be developed. For example, Swing defines the Metal look and feel as the standard look and feel for Java applets and applications that use Swing components. The Metal look and feel is named for the shiny sharp characteristics of its GUI components. Figure 14.3 provides an example of the Metal look and feel.

FIGURE 14.1.

The Motif look and feel.

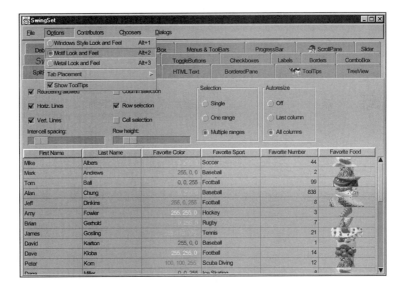

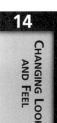

14

CHANGING LOOK AND FEEL

FIGURE 14.2.
The Windows look and feel.

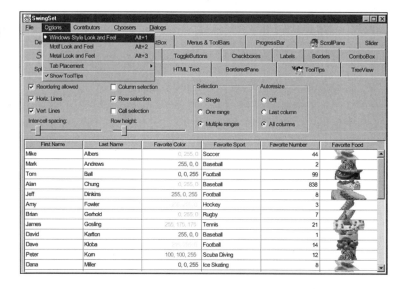

FIGURE 14.3.
The Metal look and feel.

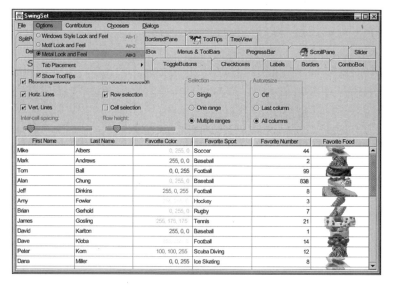

PL&F is implemented in terms of the model-view-controller (MVC) architecture. MVC is a software architecture that separates the state of an object (the model), the way the object is displayed to the user (the view), and the way that the object's state is updated (the controller). By separating these three perspectives, it is possible to define GUI components that are equivalent in terms of information state (model), but are displayed (view) and respond to the user (controller) in different ways. For example, a button's state may be defined in terms of a text label, an icon graphic, and whether the button is being clicked. The button's view can allow the button's label and icon to be displayed in a great variety of ways: square button, round button, etched button, label-only, text-only, different colors, and so on. The button's controller can cause the clicking of the button to be clicked in different ways: single-click, double-click, right-click, left-click, and so on.

By separating the model from its view and controller, Swing allows logically equivalent buttons to be implemented but rendered with different look and feels. MVC provides other advantages. For example, you can define a single GUI component with multiple simultaneous views. As another example, you can define a component that provides a separate controller for disabled users.

Combining the View and the Controller

In implementing PL&F, Swing allows GUI components to be tailored in terms of their model and L&F. L&F is a function of view and controller. The L&F of a component is implemented in terms of a *delegate*, which is the object that is used to display the component and interact with the user. The delegate encapsulates view and controller as a single object. This eliminates the need for all views to support all controllers, allowing L&F to exhibit richer, more varied behavior.

Each Swing component (subclass of JComponent) is defined in terms of a unique model and delegate. For example, the models of JButton components must implement the ButtonModel interface. However, this interface may be implemented in different ways by different classes. The model of a component is accessed via the getModel() and setModel() methods. Similarly, the delegates of JButton components must implement the ButtonUI interface. This interface can be implemented in different ways by different classes, thereby making PL&F possible for the JButton class. The delegate of a component is accessed via the getUI() and setUI() methods.

Changing Look and Feel

Delegates provide the basis for changing look and feel. In order to change the look and feel of a component, all you need to do is change the component's delegate. You change the component's delegate via the setUI() method. Consider the following example:

```
JButton button = new JButton("My Button");
button.setUI(new MotifButtonUI());
```

The button's delegate is changed to an object of the MotifButtonUI object.

The question naturally arises, "What delegates are available for a particular component?" The answer to this question lies in the PL&F packages that come with JDK 1.2 and the PL&F packages that you install. We'll cover the development and installation of custom PL&F packages later in this chapter in the section, "Look and Feel Programming."

The PL&F packages that come with JDK 1.2 are as follows:

- `com.sun.java.swing.plaf.basic`   The Basic look and feel
- `com.sun.java.swing.plaf.mac`   The Macintosh look and feel
- `com.sun.java.swing.plaf.motif`   The Motif look and feel
- `com.sun.java.swing.plaf.windows`   The Windows look and feel
- `com.sun.java.swing.plaf.organic`   The Organic look and feel
- `com.sun.java.swing.plaf.metal`   The Metal look and feel

The Macintosh, Motif, and Windows looks and feels are modeled after the looks and feels of popular windowing systems. The Basic, Organic, and Metal looks and feels are Java-specific. Each look and feel package provides classes that implement the delegate interfaces of Swing components. For example, the `com.sun.java.swing.plaf.motif` package provides the `MotifButtonUI` class and the `com.sun.java.swing.plaf.metal` package provides the `MetalButtonUI` class.

Delegate classes allow you to change the look and feel of a single component or a group of components (one component at a time). But what if you want to change the look and feel for all of your components? The `UIManager` class of `com.sun.java.swing` provides the solution. The `static setLookAndFeel()` method of `UIManager` lets you set the look and feel of all of the components used by an applet or application. For example, the following statement sets the look and feel to the Motif look and feel.

```
try {
 UIManager.setLookAndFeel("com.sun.java.swing.plaf.Motif");
}catch(Exception ex){
 System.out.println(ex);
}
```

There are two versions of `setLookAndFeel()`. One version takes the name of a look and feel package as a parameter. The other version takes the name of an object of the `LookAndFeel` class as a parameter. The first version throws the `LookAndFeelException` and the second version throws the `ClassNotFound` exception. After setting the look and feel, your GUI components must update their delegates to the new look and feel. The easiest way to do this is to invoke the `static updateComponentTreeUI()` method of the `SwingUtilities` class. This method asks each component that is contained in the component (or its subcomponents) passed as a parameter to update its delegate. For example, if `this` refers to a `JFrame` or `JApplet` object, all components contained in the application or applet will update their delegate to the new look and feel.

```
SwingUtilities.updateComponentTreeUI(this);
```

The next section provides an example application that changes its look and feel under user control.

The `SwingLF` Application

The `SwingLF` application, shown in Listing 14.1, shows how look and feel can be dynamically changed during program execution. When you run the program, it uses the default Metal look and feel, as shown in Figure 14.4. Play around with the menus and GUI controls to familiarize yourself with the Metal L&F. When you are finished, click the Motif button, and the program changes its look and feel to the Motif L&F, as shown in Figure 14.5. If you are not already familiar with Motif, you may want to take the time to familiarize yourself at this time. Finally, click the Windows button, and the program changes its look and feel to the Windows look and feel, as shown in Figure 14.6. Which L&F do you prefer? I find the Metal L&F to be very appealing. Compared to Metal, the Windows L&F appears pretty boring.

FIGURE 14.4.

The Metal L&F is the program's default L&F.

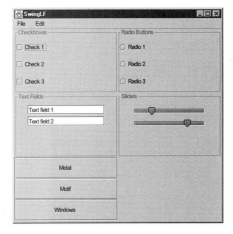

FIGURE 14.5.

The Motif L&F as displayed by SwingLF.

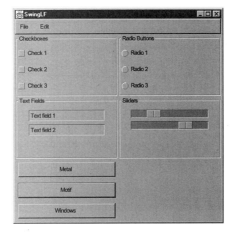

14

CHANGING LOOK
AND FEEL

FIGURE 14.6.

SwingLF *also displays the Windows L&F.*

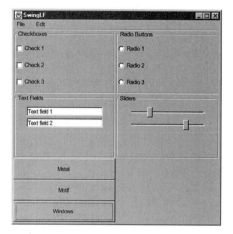

LISTING 14.1. THE SwingLF APPLICATION.

```
import java.awt.*;
import java.awt.event.*;
import javax.swing.*;
import javax.swing.event.*;
import javax.swing.border.*;
import com.sun.java.awt.swing.plaf.motif.*;
import javax.swing.plaf.metal.*;
import com.sun.java.awt.swing.plaf.windows.*;

public class SwingLF extends JFrame {
 public static int WIDTH = 450;
 public static int HEIGHT = 450;
 public static String TITLE = "SwingLF";

 Container frameContainer;
 // Swing components
 JPanel[] panels = new JPanel[6];
 JCheckBox checkbox1 = new JCheckBox("Check 1");
 JCheckBox checkbox2 = new JCheckBox("Check 2");
 JCheckBox checkbox3 = new JCheckBox("Check 3");
 ButtonGroup buttonGroup = new ButtonGroup();
 JRadioButton radioButton1 = new JRadioButton("Radio 1");
 JRadioButton radioButton2 = new JRadioButton("Radio 2");
 JRadioButton radioButton3 = new JRadioButton("Radio 3");
 JTextField textField1 = new JTextField("Text field 1",15);
 JTextField textField2 = new JTextField("Text field 2",15);
 JSlider slider1 = new JSlider(0,0,100,25);
 JSlider slider2 = new JSlider(0,0,100,75);
 JButton metalButton = new JButton("Metal");
```

```
JButton motifButton = new JButton("Motif");
JButton windowsButton = new JButton("Windows");
JMenuBar menuBar = new JMenuBar();
JMenu fileMenu = new JMenu("File");
JMenuItem fileNew = new JMenuItem("New");
JMenuItem fileOpen = new JMenuItem("Open");
JMenuItem fileSave = new JMenuItem("Save");
JMenuItem fileExit = new JMenuItem("Exit");
JMenu editMenu = new JMenu("Edit");
JMenuItem editCut = new JMenuItem("Cut");
JMenuItem editCopy = new JMenuItem("Copy");
JMenuItem editPaste = new JMenuItem("Paste");

//Look and Feel Classes
MetalLookAndFeel metalLF = new MetalLookAndFeel();
MotifLookAndFeel motifLF = new MotifLookAndFeel();
WindowsLookAndFeel windowsLF = new WindowsLookAndFeel();

public SwingLF() {
 super(TITLE);
 buildGUI();
 setupEventHandlers();
 setSize(WIDTH,HEIGHT);
 show();
}

void buildGUI() {
 setupMenuBar();
 layoutComponents();
}

void setupMenuBar() {
 fileMenu.add(fileNew);
 fileMenu.add(fileOpen);
 fileMenu.add(fileSave);
 fileMenu.add(fileExit);
 editMenu.add(editCut);
 editMenu.add(editCopy);
 editMenu.add(editPaste);
 menuBar.add(fileMenu);
 menuBar.add(editMenu);
 setJMenuBar(menuBar);
}

public void layoutComponents() {
 for(int i=0;i<panels.length;++i)
  panels[i] = new JPanel();
 panels[0].setBorder(new TitledBorder("Checkboxes"));
 panels[0].setLayout(new GridLayout(3,1));
```

14

continues

LISTING 14.1. CONTINUED

```
  panels[0].add(checkbox1);
  panels[0].add(checkbox2);
  panels[0].add(checkbox3);
  panels[1].setBorder(new TitledBorder("Radio Buttons"));
  panels[1].setLayout(new GridLayout(3,1));
  panels[1].add(radioButton1);
  panels[1].add(radioButton2);
  panels[1].add(radioButton3);
  panels[2].setBorder(new TitledBorder("Text Fields"));
  panels[2].add(textField1);
  panels[2].add(textField2);
  panels[3].setBorder(new TitledBorder("Sliders"));
  panels[3].add(slider1);
  panels[3].add(slider2);
  panels[4].setLayout(new GridLayout(3,1));
  panels[4].add(metalButton);
  panels[4].add(motifButton);
  panels[4].add(windowsButton);
  frameContainer = getContentPane();
  frameContainer.setLayout(new GridLayout(3,2));
  for(int i=0;i<panels.length;++i) frameContainer.add(panels[i]);
}

void setupEventHandlers() {
  addWindowListener(new WindowHandler());
  fileExit.addActionListener(new MenuItemHandler());
  metalButton.addActionListener(new ButtonHandler());
  motifButton.addActionListener(new ButtonHandler());
  windowsButton.addActionListener(new ButtonHandler());
}

public static void main(String[] args) {
  SwingLF app = new SwingLF();
}

public class WindowHandler extends WindowAdapter {
 public void windowClosing(WindowEvent e) {
  System.exit(0);
 }
}

public class MenuItemHandler implements ActionListener {
 public void actionPerformed(ActionEvent e) {
  System.exit(0);
 }
}
```

```
public class ButtonHandler implements ActionListener {
 public void actionPerformed(ActionEvent e) {
  String cmd = e.getActionCommand();
  if(cmd.equals("Motif")) {
   try {
    UIManager.setLookAndFeel(motifLF);
    SwingUtilities.updateComponentTreeUI(SwingLF.this);
   }catch(Exception ex){
    System.out.println(ex);
   }
  }else if(cmd.equals("Metal")) {
   try {
    UIManager.setLookAndFeel(metalLF);
    SwingUtilities.updateComponentTreeUI(SwingLF.this);
   }catch(Exception ex){
    System.out.println(ex);
   }
  }else if(cmd.equals("Windows")) {
   try {
    UIManager.setLookAndFeel(windowsLF);
    SwingUtilities.updateComponentTreeUI(SwingLF.this);
   }catch(Exception ex){
    System.out.println(ex);
   }
  }
 }
}

}
```

SwingLF begins by importing the packages that are used to implement the various L&Fs. It then declares the class constants and the Swing components to be displayed in the application window. You should be familiar with these components from Chapter 12, "Introducing Swing," and Chapter 13, "Working with Swing Components." Three look and feel variables are declared and used to refer to objects of the MetalLookAndFeel, MotifLookAndFeel, and WindowsLookAndFeel classes.

The SwingLF constructor sets its title, invokes buildGUI() to build the application's GUI and setupEventHandlers() to set up event handling, and then sizes and displays the window.

The buildGUI() method simply invokes setupMenuBar() and layoutComponents(). The setupMenuBar() method sets up the application's menu bar and the layoutComponents() method adds and arranges the previously declared Swing components to the application's GUI.

14

CHANGING LOOK
AND FEEL

The `setupEventHandlers()`method sets up the event handling for the window's closing, the Exit menu item, and the three buttons. Only the `ButtonHandler` is of interest. The clicking of a button is handled by invoking `getActionCommand()` to get the label of the button that was clicked. The program's look and feel is then changed based on the button. The `static setLookAndFeel()` method of `UIManager` is used to change the look and feel. The `static updateComponentTreeUI()` method of `SwingUtilities` is used to notify the program's GUI controls to update their L&F to the new delegates.

Changing the Model

Changing the delegate of a component results in a change in the component's look and feel. You can also change a component's model. However, this is rarely done because the state of a label, button, text field and other GUI components tends to be the same from platform-to-platform and across various look and feels. However, there are times when you may want to add state information to a component's model. As a hypothetical example, suppose you want to develop an animated button. In this case, you may want to store the button's animation frames as part of its model. Any new implementation of a component's model must implement the interface associated with that model. For example, the hypothetical `AnimatedButton` model would need to implement the `ButtonModel` interface. You could then change a button's model to `AnimatedButton` using the `setModel()` method, as follows:

```
JButton myCoolButton = new JButton("Cool Button");
myCoolButton.setModel(new AnimatedButton("frames.zip"));
```

The model of `myCoolButton` is set to an object of the `AnimatedButton` class. This object is created using the `frames.zip` file as an argument. This file would contain the frames of the animation sequence.

Look and Feel Programming

Now that you know what look and feel is, how it is implemented in terms of the MVC architecture, and how to use different looks and feels, you're probably wondering how you would go about developing your own look and feel. The answer is to create delegate classes for the components of your look and feel. The easiest way to do this is to extend an existing look and feel, such as the Basic L&F. You can then change selected GUI components and leave the others as they are. You would need to override some methods of the `BasicLookAndFeel` class and use the `initClassDefaults()` method to map component classes to your look and feel delegates.

Listing 14.2 shows the `RedLookAndFeel` class, which extends the `BasicLookAndFeel` class. This class overrides most of the methods inherited from `BasicLookAndFeel`.

- `getName()`   Returns the name of the L&F
- `getDescription()`   Returns a description of the L&F
- `getID()`   Returns an identifier for the L&F
- `isNativeLookAndFeel()`   Identifies the L&F as non-native
- `isSupportedLookAndFeel()`   Identifies the L&F as supported
- `initClassDefaults()`   Identifies that the `RedButtonUI` class is to be used where objects of the `ButtonUI` are required

The `initClassDefaults()` method is used to modify the default mapping between delegate interfaces and the L&F classes that implement those interfaces. The only change to the delegate mapping is the `RedButtonUI` class used to implement the look and feel for buttons. Whenever an object of the `ButtonUI` is required, an object of the `RedButtonUI` is used.

LISTING 14.2. THE `RedLookAndFeel` CLASS.

```
import java.awt.*;
import java.awt.event.*;
import javax.swing.*;
import javax.swing.event.*;
import javax.swing.plaf.*;
import javax.swing.plaf.basic.*;

public class RedLookAndFeel extends BasicLookAndFeel {
 public RedLookAndFeel() {
  super();
 }
 public String getName() {
  return "Red Look and Feel";
 }
 public String getDescription() {
  return "The Red Look and Feel";
 }
 public String getID() {
  return "RedLookAndFeel";
 }
 public boolean isNativeLookAndFeel() {
  return false;
 }
 public boolean isSupportedLookAndFeel() {
  return true;
```

14

CHANGING LOOK
AND FEEL

continues

LISTING 14.2. CONTINUED

```
}
protected void initClassDefaults(UIDefaults table) {
 super.initClassDefaults(table);
 table.put("ButtonUI", "RedButtonUI");
 }
}
```

The `RedButtonUI` Class

The `RedButtonUI` class (Listing 14.3) implements the button delegate for the `RedLookAndFeel`. All other delegates are inherited from `BasicLookAndFeel`. The `RedButtonUI` class extends the `BasicButtonUI` class of `com.sun.java.swing.plaf.basic`.

The `static createUI()` method is overridden to return an object of the `RedButtonUI` class.

The `paintFocus()` method is overridden to paint a red square around the perimeter of the button. The thickness of the red square is 5% of the button's height and 10% of the button's width.

LISTING 14.3. THE `RedButtonUI` CLASS.

```
import java.awt.*;
import java.awt.event.*;
import javax.swing.*;
import javax.swing.event.*;
import javax.swing.plaf.*;
import javax.swing.plaf.basic.*;

public class RedButtonUI extends BasicButtonUI {
 public RedButtonUI() {
  super();
 }
 public static ComponentUI createUI(JComponent c) {
  return new RedButtonUI();
 }
 public void paintFocus(Graphics g, Dimension size) {
  Color color = g.getColor();
  g.setColor(Color.red);
  int hpercentage = 5;
  int wpercentage = 10;
  int w = size.width;
  int h = size.height;
  int sw = w/wpercentage;
  int sh = h/hpercentage;
  g.fillRect(0,0,w,sh);
```

```
    g.fillRect(0,0,sw,h);
    g.fillRect(w-sw,0,sw,h);
    g.fillRect(0,h-sh,w,sh);
    g.setColor(color);
  }
}
```

Testing the Look and Feel

The `MyLF` program, shown in Listing 14.4, extends the `SwingLF` program of Listing 14.1 to use the `RedLookAndFeel`. When you run the program, it displays the opening window shown in Figure 14.7. Note the additional Red button. Click the Red button to use the Red look and feel. The Red look and feel uses the basic look and feel, except that it displays a red square around a button when it has the input focus, as shown in Figure 14.8.

FIGURE 14.7.

The opening display of the `MyLF` *program.*

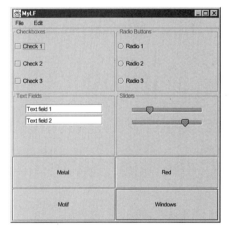

FIGURE 14.8.

Switching to the `RedLookAndFeel`.

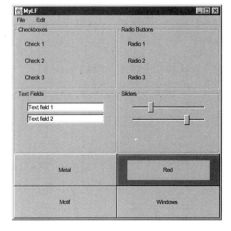

Press the Tab key to move the input focus to the Windows button.

Only a few changes are required to upgrade SwingLF to MyLF. The Red button is created, assigned an event handler, and displayed. The actionPerformed() method of ButtonHandler is updated to process the handling of the Red button and change the look and feel to the RedLookAndFeel class.

LISTING 14.4. THE MyLF PROGRAM.

```
import java.awt.*;
import java.awt.event.*;
import javax.swing.*;
import javax.swing.event.*;
import javax.swing.border.*;
import com.sun.java.awt.swing.plaf.motif.*;
import javax.swing.plaf.metal.*;
import com.sun.java.awt.swing.plaf.windows.*;

public class MyLF extends JFrame {
 public static int WIDTH = 450;
 public static int HEIGHT = 450;
 public static String TITLE = "MyLF";

 Container frameContainer;
 // Swing components
 JPanel[] panels = new JPanel[6];
 JCheckBox checkbox1 = new JCheckBox("Check 1");
 JCheckBox checkbox2 = new JCheckBox("Check 2");
 JCheckBox checkbox3 = new JCheckBox("Check 3");
 ButtonGroup buttonGroup = new ButtonGroup();
 JRadioButton radioButton1 = new JRadioButton("Radio 1");
 JRadioButton radioButton2 = new JRadioButton("Radio 2");
 JRadioButton radioButton3 = new JRadioButton("Radio 3");
 JTextField textField1 = new JTextField("Text field 1",15);
 JTextField textField2 = new JTextField("Text field 2",15);
 JSlider slider1 = new JSlider(0,0,100,25);
 JSlider slider2 = new JSlider(0,0,100,75);
 JButton metalButton = new JButton("Metal");
 JButton motifButton = new JButton("Motif");
 JButton windowsButton = new JButton("Windows");
 JButton redButton = new JButton("Red");
 JMenuBar menuBar = new JMenuBar();
 JMenu fileMenu = new JMenu("File");
 JMenuItem fileNew = new JMenuItem("New");
 JMenuItem fileOpen = new JMenuItem("Open");
 JMenuItem fileSave = new JMenuItem("Save");
 JMenuItem fileExit = new JMenuItem("Exit");
 JMenu editMenu = new JMenu("Edit");
 JMenuItem editCut = new JMenuItem("Cut");
```

```
JMenuItem editCopy = new JMenuItem("Copy");
JMenuItem editPaste = new JMenuItem("Paste");

//Look and Feel Classes
MetalLookAndFeel metalLF = new MetalLookAndFeel();
MotifLookAndFeel motifLF = new MotifLookAndFeel();
WindowsLookAndFeel windowsLF = new WindowsLookAndFeel();
RedLookAndFeel redLF = new RedLookAndFeel();

public MyLF() {
 super(TITLE);
 buildGUI();
 setupEventHandlers();
 setSize(WIDTH,HEIGHT);
 show();
}

void buildGUI() {
 setupMenuBar();
 layoutComponents();
}

void setupMenuBar() {
 fileMenu.add(fileNew);
 fileMenu.add(fileOpen);
 fileMenu.add(fileSave);
 fileMenu.add(fileExit);
 editMenu.add(editCut);
 editMenu.add(editCopy);
 editMenu.add(editPaste);
 menuBar.add(fileMenu);
 menuBar.add(editMenu);
 setJMenuBar(menuBar);
}

public void layoutComponents() {
 for(int i=0;i<panels.length;++i)
  panels[i] = new JPanel();
 panels[0].setBorder(new TitledBorder("Checkboxes"));
 panels[0].setLayout(new GridLayout(3,1));
 panels[0].add(checkbox1);
 panels[0].add(checkbox2);
 panels[0].add(checkbox3);
 panels[1].setBorder(new TitledBorder("Radio Buttons"));
 panels[1].setLayout(new GridLayout(3,1));
 panels[1].add(radioButton1);
 panels[1].add(radioButton2);
 panels[1].add(radioButton3);
 panels[2].setBorder(new TitledBorder("Text Fields"));
 panels[2].add(textField1);
```

14

CHANGING LOOK
AND FEEL

continues

LISTING 14.4. CONTINUED

```java
    panels[2].add(textField2);
    panels[3].setBorder(new TitledBorder("Sliders"));
    panels[3].add(slider1);
    panels[3].add(slider2);
    panels[4].setLayout(new GridLayout(2,1));
    panels[4].add(metalButton);
    panels[4].add(motifButton);
    panels[5].setLayout(new GridLayout(2,1));
    panels[5].add(redButton);
    panels[5].add(windowsButton);
    frameContainer = getContentPane();
    frameContainer.setLayout(new GridLayout(3,2));
    for(int i=0;i<panels.length;++i) frameContainer.add(panels[i]);
  }

  void setupEventHandlers() {
    addWindowListener(new WindowHandler());
    fileExit.addActionListener(new MenuItemHandler());
    metalButton.addActionListener(new ButtonHandler());
    motifButton.addActionListener(new ButtonHandler());
    windowsButton.addActionListener(new ButtonHandler());
    redButton.addActionListener(new ButtonHandler());
  }

  public static void main(String[] args) {
    MyLF app = new MyLF();
  }

  public class WindowHandler extends WindowAdapter {
   public void windowClosing(WindowEvent e) {
    System.exit(0);
   }
  }

  public class MenuItemHandler implements ActionListener {
   public void actionPerformed(ActionEvent e) {
    System.exit(0);
   }
  }

  public class ButtonHandler implements ActionListener {
   public void actionPerformed(ActionEvent e) {
    String cmd = e.getActionCommand();
    if(cmd.equals("Motif")) {
     try {
      UIManager.setLookAndFeel(motifLF);
      SwingUtilities.updateComponentTreeUI(MyLF.this);
     }catch(Exception ex){
      System.out.println(ex);
```

```
        }
      }else if(cmd.equals("Metal")) {
        try {
         UIManager.setLookAndFeel(metalLF);
         SwingUtilities.updateComponentTreeUI(MyLF.this);
        }catch(Exception ex){
         System.out.println(ex);
        }
      }else if(cmd.equals("Windows")) {
        try {
         UIManager.setLookAndFeel(windowsLF);
         SwingUtilities.updateComponentTreeUI(MyLF.this);
        }catch(Exception ex){
         System.out.println(ex);
        }
      }else{
        try {
         UIManager.setLookAndFeel(redLF);
         SwingUtilities.updateComponentTreeUI(MyLF.this);
        }catch(Exception ex){
         System.out.println(ex);
        }
      }
    }
  }
 }

}
```

Summary

This chapter covers Swing's PL&F capabilities. It explains what look and feel is and how
the model-view-controller (MVC) architecture is used to achieve PL&F. It introduces
you to the Swing classes and interfaces that implement PL&F and shows you how to
change an applet and application's look and feel. It also shows you how to develop your
own look and feel. In the next chapter, you'll learn how to perform clipboard cut and
paste operations using Java.

14

CHANGING LOOK
AND FEEL

Enhancing Your Applets and Applications

PART V

IN THIS PART

Using the Clipboard

IN THIS CHAPTER

Copying and pasting data to and from the clipboard is a fundamental capability that is expected by users of all windowing systems. The JDK provides the basis for full support of clipboard operations through the `Clipboard` class and other classes and interfaces of the `java.awt.transfer` package. This chapter introduces you to the classes of `java.awt.transfer`. You'll learn how to copy Java objects to the clipboard and paste them into other windows or programs. When you finish this chapter, you'll be able to implement clipboard support in your Java applications.

Clipboard Basics

The `java.awt.datatransfer` class was created to support platform-independent clipboard operations. It consists of three interfaces (`ClipboardOwner`, `FlavorMap`, and `Transferable`) and four classes (`Clipboard`, `DataFlavor`, `SystemFlavorMap`, and `StringSelection`). Each of these classes and interfaces is covered in the following sections.

The `Clipboard` Class

The `Clipboard` class, as you would expect, is the core class for implementing clipboard operations. It provides access to the system clipboard as well as to Java-internal clipboard objects. The system clipboard can be used to copy and paste data between Java and non-Java programs. The `Clipboard` object is returned by the `getSystemClipboard()` method of the `Toolkit` class. Other Java-internal `Clipboard` objects can be created using the `Clipboard()` constructor, which takes a `String` object (the name of the clipboard) as an argument.

The `Clipboard` class has two field variables: `owner` and `contents`. The `owner` variable refers to an object that implements the `ClipboardOwner` interface and identifies the process that owns the clipboard. The `contents` variable refers to an object that is placed on the clipboard. This object implements the `Transferable` interface.

The three clipboard access methods, `getName()`, `getContents()`, and `setContents()`, are used to identify a `Clipboard` object, get the contents of the clipboard, and put new data on the clipboard.

The `getContents()` method takes a single argument—the object requesting the clipboard's contents. It returns an object that implements the `Transferable` interface. This object is used to access the clipboard's contents.

The `setContents()` method takes two arguments: an object that implements the `Transferable` interface and an object that implements the `Clipboard` owner interface. The first object contains the data that is to be placed on the clipboard. The second object identifies the object that has placed the data on the clipboard.

The `Transferable` Interface

Objects that implement the `Transferable` interface are copied to and from `Clipboard` objects via the `setContents()` and `getContents()` method of the `Clipboard` class. The `Transferable` interface has three methods that allow the clipboard data to be read:

- `getTransferDataFlavors()`—Returns an array of `DataFlavor` objects that describe the type of data that is on the clipboard and the various format options in which the data can be accessed.

- `isDataFlavorSupported()`—Returns a `boolean` value indicating whether a particular `DataFlavor` object is supported. The `DataFlavor` object of interest is passed as an argument to this method.

- `getTransferData()`—Returns an object that identifies the actual data to be retrieved from the clipboard. The object returned depends on the `DataFlavor` object that is passed as an argument. This object must be cast to a class that is appropriate for the `DataFlavor` object.

The key to reading data from the clipboard is to read the data using the most appropriate data flavor (for example, PostScript, HTML, plain text, and so on). At present, choosing the correct flavor is easy because the `java.awt.datatransfer` package only provides useful support for simple text transfers. However, the classes and interfaces of `java.awt.datatransfer` provide a foundation from which more complex data flavors can be created.

The `DataFlavor` Class

The `DataFlavor` class encapsulates data types used to pass data to and from the clipboard. A `DataFlavor` object consists of the following information:

- A human-readable name
- A MIME type
- The Java class of the object to be returned (referred to as its *representation* class)

The naming scheme of the `DataFlavor` class bridges the gap between humans, MIME types, and Java. It provides a sound foundation from which complex clipboard operations can be supported.

> **NOTE**
>
> MIME types are covered in Chapter 11, "Using the Utility and Math Packages," and Chapter 33, "Content and Protocol Handlers."

The `DataFlavor` class provides several constructors that allow a `DataFlavor` object to be created for a particular Java class or for a specified MIME type. In the first case, a `Class` object (representing the class of the data to be sent to the keyboard) and a `String` that provides a human-readable name for the data are provided as arguments to the constructor. The MIME type associated with the `DataFlavor` object defaults to application/x-java-serialized-object.

In the second case, the MIME type and human-readable name are provided as arguments to the constructor, and the Java class name of the object defaults to either `InputStream` or `null`.

Several access methods of `DataFlavor` are used to get and set the human-readable name, MIME type, and Java class associated with `DataFlavor` objects:

- The `getHumanPresentableName()` and `setHumanPresentableName()` methods provide access to the human-readable name of a `DataFlavor` object.

- The `getMimeType()`, `normalizeMimeType()`, `normalizeMimeTypeParameter()`, and the two versions of the `isMimeTypeEqual()` method provide access to the MIME type of a `DataFlavor` object.

- The `getRepresentationClass()` method returns the Java class that is associated with a `DataFlavor` object.

- The `equals()` method is used to compare `DataFlavor` objects.

The `DataFlavor` class defines two constants, `plainTextFlavor` and `stringFlavor`, that are used to identify specific data flavors. The `plainTextFlavor` constant identifies data that is of the text/plain MIME type and that is associated with an `InputStream` class or with no class (`null`). The `stringFlavor` constant identifies an object of the `java.lang.String` class that has the application/x-java-serialized-object MIME type.

The `FlavorMap` Interface and `SystemFlavorMap` Class

The `FlavorMap` interface maps native type strings to their associated MIME types and data flavors. It consists of two methods, `getFlavorsForNatives()` and `getNativesForFlavors()`. The `SystemFlavorMap` class provides an implementation of the FlavorMap interface that also provides support for working with MIME types.

The `ReadClipApp` Program

The `ReadClipApp` program in Listing 15.1 shows how the `Clipboard` class, `Transferable` interface, and `DataFlavor` class are used to obtain information about data that is contained on the clipboard. Figure 15.1 shows the program's opening display.

Copy some text to the clipboard using a text editor such as Notepad. When you switch to
ReadClipApp and select Clipboard from the Read menu, ReadClipApp displays information about the flavor of the data contained on the clipboard, as shown in Figure 15.2. Try
copying nontext objects to the clipboard, such as an image that you create using the
Paint program. When you try to read information about these objects, the ReadClipApp
program displays the information shown in Figure 15.3. The reason the program does not
see the image data is because the DataFlavor class for the image data is not available.

FIGURE 15.1.

*The opening win-
dow of the
ReadClipApp pro-
gram.*

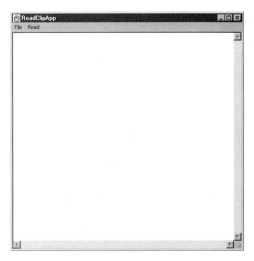

FIGURE 15.2.

*Displaying infor-
mation about the
clipboard's con-
tents.*

15

**USING THE
CLIPBOARD**

FIGURE 15.3.

How unknown data flavors are handled.

LISTING 15.1. THE SOURCE CODE OF THE ReadClipApp PROGRAM.

```java
import java.awt.*;
import java.awt.event.*;
import java.awt.datatransfer.*;

public class ReadClipApp extends Frame {
 TextArea textArea = new TextArea();
 Toolkit toolkit;
 int screenWidth = 500;
 int screenHeight = 500;
 public static void main(String args[]){
  ReadClipApp app = new ReadClipApp();
 }
 public ReadClipApp() {
  super("ReadClipApp");
  setup();
  setSize(screenWidth,screenHeight);
  addWindowListener(new WindowEventHandler());
  show();
 }
 void setup() {
  setupMenuBar();
  toolkit=getToolkit();
  add("Center",textArea);
 }
 void setupMenuBar() {
  MenuBar menuBar = new MenuBar();
  Menu fileMenu = new Menu("File");
  Menu readMenu = new Menu("Read");
  MenuItem fileExit = new MenuItem("Exit");
```

```
  MenuItem readClipboard = new MenuItem("Clipboard");
  fileExit.addActionListener(new MenuItemHandler());
  readClipboard.addActionListener(new MenuItemHandler());
  fileMenu.add(fileExit);
  readMenu.add(readClipboard);
  menuBar.add(fileMenu);
  menuBar.add(readMenu);
  setMenuBar(menuBar);
}
class MenuItemHandler implements ActionListener {
 public void actionPerformed(ActionEvent ev){
  String s=ev.getActionCommand();
  if(s=="Exit"){
   System.exit(0);
  }else if(s=="Clipboard"){
   // Use the Toolkit object to obtain access to the system clipboard
   Clipboard clip=toolkit.getSystemClipboard();
   String text="Object Name: ";
   // Get the name of the clipboard
   text+=clip.getName();
   text+="\n\nData Flavors:";
   // Get the clipboard contents
   Transferable contents=clip.getContents(ReadClipApp.this);
   if(contents==null) text+="\n\nThe clipboard is empty.";
   else{
    // Get the data flavors associated with the clipboard contents
    DataFlavor flavors[]=contents.getTransferDataFlavors();
    for(int i=0;i<flavors.length;++i){
     // Get the name, MIME type, and class associated with each flavor
     text+="\n\n Name: "+flavors[i].getHumanPresentableName();
     text+="\n MIME Type: "+flavors[i].getMimeType();
     text+="\n Class: ";
     Class cl = flavors[i].getRepresentationClass();
     if(cl==null) text+="null";
     else text+=cl.getName();
    }
   }
   textArea.setText(text);
  }
 }
}
class WindowEventHandler extends WindowAdapter {
 public void windowClosing(WindowEvent e){
  System.exit(0);
 }
}
}
```

The code that implements clipboard operations is contained in the actionPerfomed()
method of the MenuItemHandler class. When the Clipboard menu item is selected, the

getSystemClipboard() method of the Toolkit class is invoked to gain access to the system clipboard. This object is assigned to the clip variable. The getName() method of the Clipboard class is used to get the name of the Clipboard object that is returned.

A Transferable object representing the contents of the clipboard is returned by invoking the getContents() method of the Clipboard class. This object is assigned to the contents variable.

If a null value is returned by getContents(), the clipboard is identified as empty. Otherwise, the getTransferDataFlavors() method of the Transferable interface is invoked to obtain an array of data flavors corresponding to the clipboard data. The getHumanPresentableName(), getMimeType(), and getRepresentationClass() methods are used to obtain information about each of the supported DataFlavor objects. This information is then displayed to the user.

Clipboard Ownership

The ClipboardOwner interface of java.awt.datatransfer is used to provide a callback method, lostOwnership(), that notifies the current clipboard owner that it has lost ownership of the clipboard. The ClipboardOwner object can then take whatever action is necessary as the result of lost ownership. In most cases, no action is required at all.

The StringSelection Class

The StringSelection class implements both the Transferable and ClipboardOwner interfaces to support the transfer of String objects to and from the clipboard. This is a useful class that simplifies the copying and pasting of text.

The StringSelection class has a single constructor that takes a String object as an argument. This object is the data that is to be transferred via the clipboard. StringSelection implements the getTransferData(), getTransferDataFlavors(), and isDataFlavorSupported() methods of the Transferable interface and the lostOwnership() method of the ClipboardOwner interface. These methods provide all that is needed to copy and paste String objects, as you'll learn in the next section.

Copying and Pasting Text

The ClipTextApp program of Listing 15.2 shows how text can be copied to or pasted from the clipboard. Figure 15.4 shows the ClipTextApp opening window. Copy some text to the clipboard using a text editor and then switch back to the ClipTextApp program. Select Paste from the Edit menu. The text that you copied to the clipboard is pasted to the ClipTextApp window, as shown in Figure 15.5.

You have seen how `ClipTextApp` supports pasting from the system clipboard. It is also designed to copy the text `Hello from Java!` to the system clipboard. Select Copy from the Edit menu to copy text from `ClipTextApp` to the clipboard. Then select Paste to see which text was copied, as shown in Figure 15.6. `ClipTextApp` copied the text `Hello from Java!` to the clipboard. You can verify this by pasting the clipboard's contents using another program, such as Notepad, as shown in Figure 15.7.

FIGURE 15.4.

The opening window of the `ClipTextApp` *program.*

FIGURE 15.5.

Pasting text to the `ClipTextApp` *window.*

FIGURE 15.6.

The result of copying and pasting.

FIGURE 15.7.

The text copied by ClipTextApp *can be retrieved by other programs.*

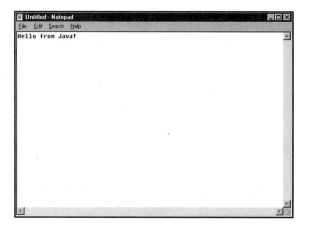

LISTING 15.2. THE SOURCE CODE OF THE ClipTextApp PROGRAM.

```
import java.awt.*;
import java.awt.event.*;
import java.awt.*;
import java.awt.datatransfer.*;
import java.util.*;
import java.io.*;

public class ClipTextApp extends Frame {
 Font defaultFont = new Font("default",Font.PLAIN,12);
 int screenWidth = 400;
 int screenHeight = 400;
 Toolkit toolkit;
 int baseline;
 int lineSize;
 FontMetrics fm;
 Canvas canvas = new MyCanvas();
```

```
Vector text = new Vector();
int topLine;
public static void main(String args[]){
 ClipTextApp app = new ClipTextApp();
}
public ClipTextApp() {
 super("ClipTextApp");
 setup();
 setSize(screenWidth,screenHeight);
 addWindowListener(new WindowEventHandler());
 show();
}
void setup() {
 setupMenuBar();
 setupFontData();
 text.addElement("");
 add("Center",canvas);
}
void setupMenuBar() {
 MenuBar menuBar = new MenuBar();
 Menu fileMenu = new Menu("File");
 Menu editMenu = new Menu("Edit");
 MenuItem fileExit = new MenuItem("Exit");
 MenuItem editCopy = new MenuItem("Copy");
 MenuItem editPaste = new MenuItem("Paste");
 fileExit.addActionListener(new MenuItemHandler());
 editCopy.addActionListener(new MenuItemHandler());
 editPaste.addActionListener(new MenuItemHandler());
 fileMenu.add(fileExit);
 editMenu.add(editCopy);
 editMenu.add(editPaste);
 menuBar.add(fileMenu);
 menuBar.add(editMenu);
 setMenuBar(menuBar);
}
void setupFontData() {
 setFont(defaultFont);
 toolkit = getToolkit();
 fm = toolkit.getFontMetrics(defaultFont);
 baseline = fm.getLeading()+fm.getAscent();
 lineSize = fm.getHeight();
}
public void paint(Graphics g) {
 canvas.repaint();
}
void copyToClipboard() {
 // Copy the string, "Hello from Java!" to the clipboard
 String toClipboard="Hello from Java!";
 StringSelection ss = new StringSelection(toClipboard);
```

continues

15

Listing 15.2. CONTINUED

```
  Clipboard clip=toolkit.getSystemClipboard();
  clip.setContents(ss,ss);
}
void pasteFromClipboard() {
  // Get the system clipboard using the toolkit
  Clipboard clip=toolkit.getSystemClipboard();
  // Get the clipboard contents
  Transferable contents=clip.getContents(ClipTextApp.this);
  text.removeAllElements();
  if(contents==null) text.addElement("The clipboard is empty.");
  else{
    // If the contents support the string data flavor then retrieve and
➥parse the data contained
    // on the clipboard
    if(contents.isDataFlavorSupported(DataFlavor.stringFlavor)){
     try{
      String data = (String) contents.getTransferData(
       DataFlavor.stringFlavor);
      if(data==null) text.addElement("null");
      else{
       StringTokenizer st = new StringTokenizer(data,"\n");
       while(st.hasMoreElements()) text.addElement(st.nextToken());
      }
     } catch(IOException ex){
      text.addElement("IOException");
     } catch(UnsupportedFlavorException ex){
      text.addElement("UnsupportedFlavorException");
     }
    }else text.addElement("Wrong flavor.");
  }
  repaint();
}
class MenuItemHandler implements ActionListener {
 public void actionPerformed(ActionEvent ev){
  String s=ev.getActionCommand();
  if(s=="Exit"){
   System.exit(0);
  }else if(s=="Copy") copyToClipboard();
  else if(s=="Paste") pasteFromClipboard();
 }
}
class WindowEventHandler extends WindowAdapter {
 public void windowClosing(WindowEvent e){
  System.exit(0);
 }
}
class MyCanvas extends Canvas {
 public void paint(Graphics g) {
  topLine = 0;
```

```
    int numLines = text.size();
    screenHeight = getSize().height;
    int y = baseline*2;
    int x = y;
    for(int i = topLine;(i < numLines) && (y < screenHeight +
➡lineSize);++i) {
      g.drawString((String) text.elementAt(i),x,y);
      y += lineSize;
    }
  }
 }
}
```

The copying of text to the clipboard is implemented by the copyToClipboard() method
of ClipTextApp. This method creates a StringSelection object with the text Hello
from Java!. It invokes the getSystemClipboard() method of the Toolkit class to
access the system clipboard and the setContents() method of the Clipboard class to
set the StringSelection object as the clipboard's contents.

The pasting of text from the clipboard is performed by the pasteFromClipboard()
method. This method invokes getSystemClipboard() to access the system clipboard and
getContents() to retrieve the clipboard contents as a Transferable object. If the
Transferable object is null, a Clipboard empty. message is displayed to the user.
Otherwise, the isDataFlavorSupported() method of the Transferable interface is used
to determine whether an object that is compatible with the StringSelection class is
contained on the clipboard. If not, a Wrong flavor. message is displayed to the user.

If the data on the clipboard can be accessed as a StringSelection object, the data is
retrieved using the getTransferData() method of the Transferable interface and
assigned to the data variable. A StringTokenizer object is constructed to parse the data
into separate lines and assign them to the Vector object referenced by the text variable.
The contents of text are then displayed to the screen via the paint() method of the
MyCanvas class.

Summary

In this chapter you were introduced to the classes of java.awt.transfer. You learned
how to copy data to and from the clipboard using the Clipboard API. In the next chapter,
you'll learn how to use the new drag-and-drop capabilities of JDK 1.2.

Working with Drag and Drop

Drag and drop is a capability that allows users to perform operations on objects by dragging files' GUI components to the GUI components of objects that represent the operations. Most windowing systems provide desktops that display icons representing programs, files, printers, and storage devices. You drag a file's icon to a program icon to have the file opened by the program, to a printer icon to send the file to the printer, or to a storage device to have the file copied to that device.

Drag-and-drop capabilities are introduced to the Core API with JDK 1.2. These capabilities allow you to use drag and drop within Java applications, between Java applications, and between Java applications and native applications. This chapter shows you how to use drag and drop in your Java programs. It covers the basic mechanics of drag and drop, describes the Drag and Drop API, and provides examples of Java programs that implement drag and drop. When you finish this chapter, you'll be able to use drag and drop in your Java applications.

Drag and drop consists of the following three levels of abstraction:

- The actual files, programs, devices, and other objects upon which operations are performed

- GUI components that represent the files, programs, and devices

- The drag-and-drop gesture, which associates the GUI component of the source object being dragged with the GUI component of the target upon which the source is dropped

Drag and drop is implemented using special objects, referred to as the *drag source* and *drop target* (see Figure 16.1). A GUI component that receives drops is associated with a drop target object that is activated and waits for drop events. The GUI creates the drag source at the beginning of the drag gesture. The drag source monitors the progress of the drag operation by handling events from the GUI. When the drag-and-drop operation is completed (the user drops the source component on the target component), the drop target coordinates with the drag source to transfer information from the source component to the target component. If the source and target components are associated with other objects (such as files or devices), these components effect data transfers between these other objects.

The Drag and Drop API

The Drag and Drop API consists of the `java.awt.dnd` package. However, it is implemented using other packages, most notably the `java.awt.datatransfer` package. The `java.awt.dnd` package consists of 4 interfaces and 15 classes. These interfaces and classes are summarized as follows:

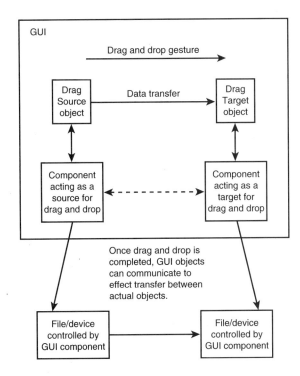

FIGURE 16.1.
How drag and drop works.

- `DnDConstants`—Defines constants used in drag-and-drop operations.
- `DragSource`—Provides field variables and methods that are used to originate a drag-and-drop operation.
- `DragSourceContext`—Implements the `DragSourceListener` interface and provides methods for managing the initiation of a drag-and-drop operation.
- `DropTarget`—A class that is associated with a component that acts as a target for drag-and-drop operations. The `DropTargetAutoScroller` inner class implements auto scrolling.
- `DropTargetContext`—The class of an object that is created as the result of a drag to a component that is associated with a `DropTarget`. `DragTargetContext` provides methods for providing feedback and completing the drag operation.
- `DropTargetContext.TransferableProxy`—An inner class of `DropTargetContext` that supports data transfer to the target.
- `Autoscroll`—An interface that defines methods that support the dropping of objects in a scrollable GUI area that is not currently visible.
- `DragSourceEvent`—Superclass of all drag-and-drop events that are provided to the drag source.

- `DragSourceDragEvent`— Provides feedback to the drag source about the drag state of a drag-and-drop operation.

- `DragSourceDropEvent`—Provides feedback to the drag source about the drop state of a drag-and-drop operation.

- `DragGestureEvent`—An event that is generated as the result of a platform dependent drag-and-drop action initiating gesture.

- `DragGestureListener`—Defines methods for handling the `DragGestureEven` event.

- `DragGestureRecognizer`—An abstract class for handling platform dependent drag-and-drop operations.

- `MouseDragGestureRecognizer`—Extends `DragGestureRecognizer` to support mouse-based gestures.

- `DragSourceListener`—An interface that defines methods for source objects to handle state changes associated with drag-and-drop events.

- `DropTargetEvent`—Superclass of all drag-and-drop events that are provided to the drag target.

- `DropTargetDragEvent`—Provides feedback to the drag target about the drag state of a drag-and-drop operation.

- `DropTargetDropEvent`—Provides feedback to the drag target about the drop state of a drag-and-drop operation.

- `DropTargetListener`—An interface that defines methods for target objects to handle state changes associated with drag-and-drop events.

Drag and drop is implemented by setting up `DragSource` and `DropTarget` objects for those GUI components that you want to use as a source or destination of drag-and-drop operations. You can implement only sources, only targets, or both sources and targets, depending on the requirements of your application. A `DragSource` object is associated with a GUI component from which you want to have data transferred, and a `DropTarget` component is associated with a GUI component that is to receive transferred data. Once these components are set up, the bulk of the drag-and-drop processing consists of handling events associated with the sources and targets.

A `DragSource` object is associated with a GUI component by specifying the component as an argument to the object's `start()` method. A `DropTarget` object is associated with a GUI component by passing the component as an argument to the object's constructor. Information is transferred from the source component to the target component via an object of the `Transferable` interface. You declare a class that implements this interface to effect the data transfer. The example in the following section illustrates the use of the `DragSource`, `DropTarget`, and `Transferable` objects.

Using Drag and Drop in Your Programs

Now that you've been introduced to the Drag and Drop API, we'll create an example application that implements both the source and target aspects of drag and drop. Listing 16.1 presents the DragNDrop application. This program displays the opening window, shown in Figure 16.2. Its GUI uses two text boxes to implement drag and drop. Type some text in the upper text box and then drag the text to the lower text box, as shown in Figure 16.3. Note how the cursor changes shape during the drag-and-drop operation. The program also displays text to the console window that identifies the drag-and-drop events that are handled.

FIGURE 16.2.

The DragNDrop application opening window.

FIGURE 16.3.

Dragging text from one text area to another.

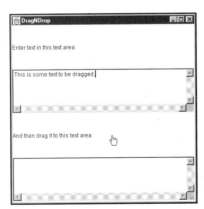

The `DragNDrop` application illustrates both source and target event-handling in support of drag and drop. The program declares the needed GUI components and then declares variables that are used to implement drag and drop. The `source` variable is assigned an object of the `DragSource` class, and the `target` variable is assigned an object of the `DropTarget` class. The `DropTarget()` constructor takes the following four arguments:

- The component that the target is associated with
- The type of drag-and-drop operation supported
- An event handler for target-related events
- A Boolean value indicating whether or not the target accepts drops

The `transferable` variable is assigned an object of the `TextTransfer` class, which is an inner class that implements the `Transferable` interface of `java.awt.datatransfer`.

The `sourceHandler` variable is assigned a `DragSourceHandler` object that is used to handle source-related events.

The `setup()` method sets the `DropTarget` object referenced by `target` to actively receive drops via the `setActive()` method. A `DragGestureRecognizer` is created with respect to the first `TextArea` object so that drag opertations can be detected and processed. The rest of the program (with the exception of `TextTransfer`) consists of event handlers.

The `DragSourceHandler` class implements the `DragSourceListener` interface to handle source-related events. The `dropActionChanged()`, `dragEnter()`, and `dragDropEnd()` methods just display notices about the occurrence of events. The `dragOver()` method doesn't display anything because it may be invoked many times during a drag-and-drop operation.

The `DropTargetHandler` class implements the `DropTargetListener` interface to handle target-related events. The `dragEnter()` method handles the event that occurs when a drag operation enters the component (the second `TextArea` object) associated with the `DropTarget`. This method checks if the data flavors of the object being dragged to the target support any of the standard text data flavors. If so, the drag is accepted. Otherwise, it is rejected. The `dragOver()`, `dragExit()`, and `dropAction()` methods are placeholders used to implement the `DropTargetListener` interface.

The `drop()` method implements the actual data transfer. It accepts the drop action and gets a `Transferable` object that contains the data being transferred. It retrieves the data flavors associated with the `Transferable` object and checks to see whether these flavors coincide with the target's flavors. If a match occurs, the associated `TextArea` object is updated with the transferred data. The successful completion of the drop is signaled by the `dropComplete()` method of the `DropTargetContext` class.

The TextTransfer class implements the Transferable interface and is used to transfer information from the DragSource object. The getTransferDataFlavors() method returns the flavors supported by the source. The isDataFlavorSupported() method reports information on a single data flavor. The getTransferData() method returns the data to be transferred.

The DragHandler class implements DragGestureListener to start the drag operation when a drag operation is initiated in the first text area. It handles this event by invoking the event's startDrag() method. This method takes the following arguments:

- The cursor to be used for dragging.
- An object that implements the Transferable interface that is used to accomplish the actual transfer.
- An event handler for source-related events.

The WindowEventHandler class handles the closing of the application window.

LISTING 16.1. THE DragNDrop APPLICATION.

```
import java.awt.*;
import java.awt.event.*;
import java.awt.dnd.*;
import java.awt.datatransfer.*;
import java.io.*;

public class DragNDrop extends Frame {
 int screenWidth = 400;
 int screenHeight = 400;
 Panel panel = new Panel();
 Label topLabel = new Label("Enter text in this text area:");
 Label bottomLabel = new Label("And then drag it to this text area:");
 TextArea textArea1 = new TextArea();
 TextArea textArea2 = new TextArea();

 //Drag and drop variables
 DragSource source = new DragSource();
 DropTarget target = new DropTarget(textArea2,
  DnDConstants.ACTION_COPY,new DropTargetHandler(),true);
 TextTransfer transferable = new TextTransfer();
 DragSourceHandler sourceHandler = new DragSourceHandler();

 public static void main(String[] args) {
  DragNDrop app = new DragNDrop();
 }
 public DragNDrop() {
  super("DragNDrop");
  setup();
  setSize(screenWidth,screenHeight);
```

continues

LISTING 16.1. CONTINUED

```
  addWindowListener(new WindowEventHandler());
  show();
 }
 void setup() {
  target.setActive(true);
  panel.setLayout(new GridLayout(4,1));
  panel.add(topLabel);
  panel.add(textArea1);
  Toolkit toolkit=Toolkit.getDefaultToolkit();
  try{
   toolkit.createDragGestureRecognizer(Class.forName(
    "java.awt.dnd.MouseDragGestureRecognizer"),source,textArea1,
    DnDConstants.ACTION COPY,new DragHandler());
  }catch(ClassNotFoundException ex){
   System.out.println("Recognizer class not found.");
   System.exit(o);
   }
  panel.add(bottomLabel);
  panel.add(textArea2);
  add("Center",panel);
 }
 class DragSourceHandler implements DragSourceListener {
  public void dropActionChanged(DragSourceDragEvent ev) {
   System.out.println("Source: Drop action changed");
  }
  public void dragEnter(DragSourceDragEvent ev) {
   System.out.println("Source: Drag enter");
  }
  public void dragOver(DragSourceDragEvent ev) {
  }
  public void dragExit(DragSourceEvent ev) {
   System.out.println("Source: Drag exit");
 }
  public void dragDropEnd(DragSourceDropEvent ev) {
   System.out.println("Source: Drag drop end");
  }
 }
 class DropTargetHandler implements DropTargetListener {
  public void dragEnter(DropTargetDragEvent ev) {
   System.out.println ("Target: Drag enter");
   DataFlavor df[] = ev.getCurrentDataFlavors();
   for (int i = 0; i < df.length; i++) {
    if (df[i].equals (DataFlavor.plainTextFlavor) ||
      df[i].equals (DataFlavor.stringFlavor)) {
     ev.acceptDrag(DnDConstants.ACTION_COPY);
     return;
    }
   }
```

```
    ev.rejectDrag();
   }
   public void dragOver(DropTargetDragEvent ev) {
   }
   public void dragExit(DropTargetEvent ev) {
    System.out.println ("Target: Drag exit");
   }
   public void dropActionChanged(DropTargetDragEvent ev) {
    System.out.println("Target: Drop action changed");
   }
   public void drop(DropTargetDropEvent ev) {
    System.out.println ("Target: Dropped");
    ev.acceptDrop (DnDConstants.ACTION_COPY);
    Transferable transfer = ev.getTransferable();
    DataFlavor df[] = ev.getCurrentDataFlavors();
    String input = "";
    try {
     for (int i=0;i<df.length;i++) {
      if (df[i].equals(DataFlavor.stringFlavor) ||
       df[i].equals(DataFlavor.plainTextFlavor)) {
       input = (String) transfer.getTransferData(df[i]);
      }
     }
     textArea2.setText(input);
    }catch (Exception e) {
     System.out.println(e.toString());
    }
    try {
     target.getDropTargetContext().dropComplete(true);
    }catch (Exception e) {
    }
   }
  }
  class TextTransfer implements Transferable {
   public DataFlavor[] getTransferDataFlavors() {
    DataFlavor[] flavors = new DataFlavor[1];
    flavors[0] = DataFlavor.plainTextFlavor;
    return flavors;
   }
   public boolean isDataFlavorSupported(DataFlavor flavor) {
    return (flavor.equals(DataFlavor.plainTextFlavor));
   }
   public Object getTransferData(DataFlavor flavor)
     throws UnsupportedFlavorException, IOException {
    return textArea1.getText();
   }
  }
  class DragHandler implements DragGestureListener {
   public void dragGestureRecognized(DragGestureEvent e) {
```

continues

LISTING 16.1. CONTINUED

```
      e.startDrag (new Cursor(Cursor.HAND CURSOR),
        transferable,sourceHandler);
    }
  }
  class WindowEventHandler extends WindowAdapter {
    public void windowClosing(WindowEvent e){
      System.exit(0);
    }
  }
}
```

Summary

This chapter showed you how to use the drag-and-drop capabilities of JDK 1.2. It covered the basic mechanics of drag and drop, described the Drag and Drop API, and provided examples of Java programs that implement drag and drop. In the next chapter you'll learn how to use the sophisticated input/output capabilities of the `java.io` package.

Input/Output Streams

CHAPTER 17

In this chapter you'll learn to use Java streams to perform sophisticated input and output using standard I/O, memory buffers, and files. You'll explore the input and output stream class hierarchy and learn to use stream filters to simplify I/O processing. You'll also learn how to perform random-access I/O and how to use the StreamTokenizer class to construct input parsers. When you finish this chapter, you'll be able to add sophisticated I/O processing to your Java programs.

Streams

Java input and output is based on the use of *streams*, or sequences of bytes that travel from a source to a destination over a communication path. If your program is writing to a stream, it is the stream's *source*. If it is reading from a stream, it is the stream's *destination*. The communication path is dependent on the type of I/O being performed. It can consist of memory-to-memory transfers, a file system, a network, and other forms of I/O.

Streams are not complicated. They are powerful because they abstract away the details of the communication path from input and output operations. This allows all I/O to be performed using a common set of methods. These methods can be tailored and extended to provide higher-level custom I/O capabilities.

Java defines two major classes of byte streams: InputStream and OutputStream. These streams are subclassed to provide a variety of I/O capabilities. Java 1.1 introduced the Reader and Writer classes to provide the foundation for 16-bit Unicode character-oriented I/O. These classes support internationalization of Java I/O. The Reader and Writer classes, such as InputStream and OutputStream, are subclassed to support additional capabilities. Unicode is covered in Chapter 19, "Internationalization."

The java.io Class Hierarchy

Figure 17.1 identifies the java.io class hierarchy. As described in the previous section, the InputStream, OutputStream, Reader, and Writer classes are the major components of this hierarchy. Other high-level classes include the File, FileDescriptor, RandomAccessFile, ObjectStreamClass, and StreamTokenizer classes.

The InputStream and OutputStream classes have complementary subclasses. For example, both have subclasses for performing I/O via memory buffers, files, and pipes. The InputStream subclasses perform the input and the OutputStream classes perform the output.

FIGURE 17.1.

The classes of the java.io *hierarchy.*

```
InputStream
        FilterInputStream
                BufferedInputStream
                DataInputStream
                LineNumberInputStream
                PushbackInputStream
        ByteArrayInputStream
        FileInputStream
        ObjectInputStream
                ObjectInputStream GetField(nested)
        PipedInputStream
        SequenceInputStream
        StringBufferInputStream
OutputStream
        FilterOutputStream
                BufferedOutputStream
                DataOutputStream
                PrintStream
        ByteArrayOutputStream
        FileOutputStream
        ObjectOutputStream
                ObjectOutputStream PutField(nested)
        PipedOutputStream
Reader
        BufferedReader
                LineNumberReader
        CharArrayReader
        FilterReader
                PushbackReader
        InputStreamReader
                FileReader
        PipedReader
        StringReader
Writer
        BufferedWriter
        CharArrayWriter
        FilterWriter
        OutputStreamWriter
                FileWriter
        PipedWriter
        PrintWriter
        StringWriter
File
RandomAccessFile
FileDescriptor
FilePermission
ObjectStreamClass
ObjectStreamField
SerializablePermission
StreamTokenizer
```

17

INPUT/OUTPUT STREAMS

The InputStream class has seven direct subclasses. The ByteArrayInputStream class is used to convert an array into an input stream. The StreamBufferInputStream class uses a StreamBuffer as an input stream. The FileInputStream class allows files to be used as input streams. The ObjectInputStream class is used to read primitive types and objects that have been previously written to a stream. The PipedInputStream class allows a pipe to be constructed between two threads and supports input through the pipe. The SequenceInputStream class allows two or more streams to be concatenated into a single stream. The FilterInputStream class is an abstract class from which other input-filtering classes are constructed.

> **NOTE**
>
> The process of preparing objects for stream input and output is referred to as *serialization*. In order for an object to be serialized, it must implement the java.io.Serializable interface.

Filters are objects that read from one stream and write to another, usually altering the data in some way as they pass it from one stream to another. Filters can be used to buffer data, read and write objects, keep track of line numbers, and perform other operations on the data they move. Filters can be combined, with one filter using the output of another as its input. You can create custom filters by combining existing filters.

FilterInputStream has four filtering subclasses. The BufferedInputStream class maintains a buffer of the input data that it receives. This eliminates the need to read from the stream's source every time an input byte is needed. The DataInputStream class implements the DataInput interface, a set of methods that allow objects and primitive data types to be read from a stream. The LineNumberInputStream is used to keep track of input line numbers. The PushbackInputStream provides the capability to push data back onto the stream that it is read from so that it can be read again.

> **NOTE**
>
> Other Java API packages, such as java.util, contain classes and interfaces that extend those of java.io. In particular, the java.util package defines input and output stream classes that can be used to support file and stream compression.

The OutputStream class hierarchy consists of five direct subclasses. The ByteArrayOutputStream, FileOutputStream, ObjectOutputStream, and PipedOutputStream classes are the output complements to the ByteArrayInputStream, FileInputStream, ObjectInputStream, and PipedInputStream classes. The FilterOutputStream class provides subclasses that complement the FilterInputStream classes.

The `BufferedOutputStream` class is the output analog to the `BufferedInputStream` class. It buffers output so that output bytes can be written to devices in larger groups. The `DataOutputStream` class implements the `DataOutput` interface. This interface complements the `DataInput` interface. It provides methods that write objects and primitive data types to streams so that they can be read by the `DataInput` interface methods. The `PrintStream` class provides the familiar `print()` and `println()` methods used in most of the sample programs that you've developed so far in this book. It provides a number of overloaded methods that simplify data output.

> **NOTE**
>
> The `PrintStream` class is not necessarily used to print to a printer. Chapter 18, "Printing," covers printing to a printer.

The `Reader` class is similar to the `InputStream` class in that it is the root of an input class hierarchy. `Reader` supports 16-bit Unicode character input, while `InputStream` supports 8-bit byte input. The `Reader` class has six direct subclasses:

- The `BufferedReader` class supports buffered character input. Its `LineNumberReader` subclass supports buffered input and keeps track of line numbers.
- The `CharArrayReader` class provides the capability to read a character input stream from a character buffer.
- The `FilterReader` class is an abstract class that provides the basis for filtering character input streams. Its `PushbackReader` subclass provides a filter that allows characters to be pushed back onto the input stream.
- The `InputStreamReader` class is used to convert byte input streams to character input streams. Its `FileReader` subclass is used to read character files.
- The `PipedReader` class is used to read characters from a pipe.
- The `StringReader` class is used to read characters from a `String`.

The `Writer` class is the output analog of the `Reader` class. It supports 16-bit Unicode character output. It has seven direct subclasses:

- The `BufferedWriter` class supports buffered character output.
- The `CharArrayWriter` class supports output to a character array.
- The `FilterWriter` class is an abstract class that supports character output filtering.

- The `OutputStreamWriter` class allows a character stream to be converted to a byte stream. Its `FileWriter` subclass is used to perform character output to files.
- The `PipedWriter` class supports character output to pipes.
- The `PrintWriter` class supports platform-independent character printing.
- The `StringWriter` class supports character output to `String` objects.

The `File` class is used to access the files and directories of the local file system. The `FileDescriptor` class is an encapsulation of the information used by the host system to track files that are being accessed. The `RandomAccessFile` class provides the capabilities needed to directly access data contained in a file. The `ObjectStreamClass` class is used to describe classes whose objects can be written (serialized) to a stream. The `StreamTokenizer` class is used to create parsers that operate on stream data.

New classes introduced with JDK 1.2 include the `ObjectInputStream.GetField`, `ObjectOutputStream.PutField`, and `ObjectStreamField` classes, which support object stream I/O. The `FilePermission` and `SerializablePermission` classes support I/O access controls (refer to Chapter 3, "The Extended Java Security Model").

> **NOTE**
>
> Other packages, such as `java.util.zip`, provide classes that extend the `java.io` class hierarchy shown in Figure 17.1.

The `java.io` Interfaces

The `java.io` package declares 10 interfaces. The `DataInput` and `DataOutput` interfaces provide methods that support machine-independent I/O. The `ObjectInput` and `ObjectOutput` interfaces extend `DataInput` and `DataOutput` to work with objects. The `ObjectInputValidation` interface supports the validation of objects that are read from a stream. The `ObjectStreamConstants` interface defines constants that are used to work with object streams. The `Serializable`, `Externalizable`, `Replaceable`, and `Resolvable` interfaces support the serialized writing of objects to streams. The `FileFilter` and `FilenameFilter` interfaces are used to select filenames from a list.

The `InputStream` Class

The `InputStream` class is an abstract class that lays the foundation for the Java `Input` class hierarchy. As such, it provides methods that are inherited by all `InputStream` classes.

The read() Method

The read() method is the most important method of the InputStream class hierarchy. It reads a byte of data from an input stream and blocks if no data is available. When a method *blocks*, it causes the thread in which it is executing to wait until data becomes available. This is not a problem in multithreaded programs. The read() method takes on several overloaded forms. It can read a single byte or an array of bytes, depending upon what form is used. It returns the number of bytes read, or -1 if an end of file is encountered with no bytes read.

The read() method is overridden and overloaded by subclasses to provide custom read capabilities.

The available() Method

The available()method returns the number of bytes that are available to be read without blocking. It is used to peek into the input stream to see how much data is available. However, depending on the input stream, it might not be accurate or useful. Some input streams on some operating systems may always report 0 available bytes. In general, it is not a good idea to blindly rely on this method to perform input processing.

The close() Method

The close() method closes an input stream and releases resources associated with the stream. It is always a good idea to close a stream to ensure that the stream processing is correctly terminated.

Markable Streams

Java supports *markable streams*. These are streams that provide the capability to mark a position in the stream and then later reset the stream so that it can be reread from the marked position. If a stream can be marked, it must contain some memory associated with it to keep track of the data between the mark and the current position of the stream. When this buffering capability is exceeded, the mark becomes invalidated.

The markSupported() method returns a boolean value that identifies whether a stream supports mark and reset capabilities. The mark() method marks a position in the stream. It takes an integer parameter that identifies the number of bytes that can be read before the mark becomes invalid. This is used to set the buffering capacity of the stream. The reset()method simply repositions the stream to its last marked position.

The `skip()` Method

The `skip()` method skips over a specified number of input bytes. It takes a `long` value as a parameter. You can use the `skip()` method to move to a specific position within an input stream.

The `OutputStream` Class

The `OutputStream` class is an abstract class that lays the foundation for the output stream hierarchy. It provides a set of methods that are the output analog to the `InputStream` methods.

The `write()` Method

The `write()` method allows bytes to be written to the output stream. It provides three overloaded forms to write a single byte, an array of bytes, or a segment of an array. The `write()` method, like the `read()` method, may block when it tries to write to a stream. The blocking causes the thread executing the `write()` method to wait until the write operation has been completed.

> **NOTE**
>
> The `OutputStream` class defines three overloaded forms for the `write()` method. These forms allow you to write an integer, an array of bytes, or a subarray of bytes to an `OutputStream` object. You will often see several overloaded forms for methods that perform the same operation using different types of data.

The `flush()` Method

The `flush()` method causes any buffered data to be immediately written to the output stream. Some subclasses of `OutputStream` support buffering and override this method to clean out their buffers and write all buffered data to the output stream. They must override the `OutputStream` `flush()` method because, by default, it does not perform any operations and is used as a placeholder.

The `close()` Method

It is generally more important to `close()` output streams than input streams, so that any data written to the stream is stored before the stream is deallocated and lost. The `close()` method of `OutputStream` is used in the same manner as that of `InputStream`.

Byte Array I/O

Java supports byte array input and output via the `ByteArrayInputStream` and `ByteArrayOutputStream` classes. These classes use memory buffers as the source and destination of the input and output streams. These streams do not have to be used together. They are covered in the same section here because they provide similar and complementary methods. The `StringBufferInputStream` class is similar to the `ByteArrayInput` class and is also covered in this section.

The `CharArrayReader`, `CharArrayWriter`, `StringReader`, and `StringWriter` classes support character-based I/O in a similar manner to the `ByteArrayInputStream`, `ByteArrayOutputStream`, and `StringBufferInputStream` classes. They are covered later in this chapter.

The `ByteArrayInputStream` Class

The `ByteArrayInputStream` class creates an input stream from a memory buffer. The buffer is an array of bytes. It provides two constructors that use a byte array argument to create the input stream. The class does not support any new methods, but overrides the `read()`, `skip()`, `available()`, and `reset()` methods of `InputStream`.

The `read()` and `skip()` methods are implemented as specified for `InputStream`. The `available()` method is reliable and can be used to check on the number of available bytes in the buffer. The `reset()` method resets the stream to the marked position.

The `ByteArrayOutputStream` Class

The `ByteArrayOutputStream` class is a little more sophisticated than its input complement. It creates an output stream on a byte array, but provides additional capabilities to allow the output array to grow to accommodate new data that is written to it. It also provides the `toByteArray()` and `toString()` methods for converting the stream to a byte array or `String` object.

`ByteArrayOutputStream` provides two constructors. One takes an integer argument that is used to set the output byte array to an initial size. The other constructor does not take an argument and sets the output buffer to a default size.

`ByteArrayOutputStream` provides some additional methods not declared for `OutputStream`. The `reset()` method resets the output buffer to allow writing to restart at the beginning of the buffer. The `size()` method returns the current number of bytes that have been written to the buffer. The `writeTo()` method is new. It takes an object of class `OutputStream` as an argument and writes the contents of the output buffer to the specified output stream. The `write()` methods override those of `OutputStream` to support array output.

The `ByteArrayIOApp` Program

Having learned about both sides of the byte array I/O classes, you now have a base from which to create a sample program. The source code of the `ByteArrayIOApp` program is provided in Listing 17.1.

LISTING 17.1. THE SOURCE CODE OF THE `ByteArrayIOApp` PROGRAM.

```
import java.lang.System;
import java.io.ByteArrayInputStream;
import java.io.ByteArrayOutputStream;
import java.io.IOException;

public class ByteArrayIOApp {
 public static void main(String args[]) throws IOException {
  // Create ByteArrayOutputStream object
  ByteArrayOutputStream outStream = new ByteArrayOutputStream();
  String s = "This is a test.";
  // Write output to stream
  for(int i=0;i<s.length();++i)
   outStream.write(s.charAt(i));
  System.out.println("outstream: "+outStream);
  System.out.println("size: "+outStream.size());
  ByteArrayInputStream inStream;
  inStream = new ByteArrayInputStream(outStream.toByteArray());
  // Determine how many input bytes are available
  int inBytes = inStream.available();
  System.out.println("inStream has "+inBytes+" available bytes");
  byte inBuf[] = new byte[inBytes];
  // Read input into a byte array
  int bytesRead = inStream.read(inBuf,0,inBytes);
  System.out.println(bytesRead+" bytes were read");
  System.out.println("They are: "+new String(inBuf));
 }
}
```

The program creates a `ByteArrayOutputStream` object, `outStream`, and an array, `s`, that contains the text `"This is a test."` to be written to the stream. Each `s` character is written, one at a time, to `outStream`. The contents of `outstream` are then printed, along with the number of bytes written.

A `ByteArrayInputStream` object, `inStream`, is created by invoking the `toByteArray()` method of `outStream` to create a byte array that is used as an argument to the

`ByteArrayInputStream` constructor. The `available()` method is used to determine the number of available input bytes stored in the buffer. This number is stored as `inBytes` and is used to allocate a byte array to store the data that is read. The `read()` method is invoked for `inStream` to read `inBytes` worth of data. The actual number of bytes read is stored in `bytesRead`. This number is displayed, followed on the next line by the bytes that were read from `inStream`, as follows:

```
outstream: This is a test.
size: 15
inStream has 15 available bytes
15 bytes were read
They are: This is a test.
```

The `StringBufferInputStream` Class

`StringBufferInputStream` is similar to `ByteArrayInputStream` except that it uses a `StringBuffer` to store input data. The input stream is constructed using a `String` argument. Its methods are identical to those provided by `ByteArrayInputStream`. The `StringBufferInputStream` was deprecated in Java 1.1. This means that it has been superceded. The `StringReader` class is now the preferred class for `String`-based input.

File I/O

Java supports stream-based file input and output through the `File`, `FileDescriptor`, `FileInputStream`, and `FileOutputStream` classes. It supports direct or random access I/O using the `File`, `FileDescriptor`, and `RandomAccessFile` classes. Random access I/O is covered later in this chapter. The `FileReader` and `FileWriter` classes support Unicode-based file I/O. These classes are also covered later in this chapter.

The `File` class provides access to file and directory objects and supports a number of operations on files and directories. The `FileDescriptor` class encapsulates the information used by the host system to track files that are being accessed. The `FileInputStream` and `FileOutputStream` classes provide the capability to read and write to file streams.

The `File` Class

The `File` class is used to access file and directory objects. It uses the file-naming conventions of the host operating system. The `File` class encapsulates these conventions using the `File` class constants.

`File` provides constructors for creating files and directories. These constructors take absolute and relative file paths and file and directory names.

The File class provides numerous access methods that can be used to perform all common file and directory operations. It is important for you to review the API page for this class because file I/O and file and directory operations are common to most programs.

File methods allow files to be created, deleted, and renamed. They provide access to a file's path/name and determine whether a File object is a file or directory. These methods also check read and write access permissions.

Directory methods allow directories to be created, deleted, renamed, and listed. Directory methods also allow directory trees to be traversed by providing access to the parent and sibling directories.

The FileDescriptor Class

The FileDescriptor class provides access to the file descriptors maintained by operating systems when files and directories are being accessed. This class is *opaque* in that it does not provide visibility into the specific information maintained by the operating system. It provides only one method, the valid() method, which is used to determine whether a file descriptor object is currently valid.

The FileInputStream Class

The FileInputStream class allows input to be read from a file in the form of a stream. Objects of class FileInputStream are created using a filename string or a File or FileDescriptor object as an argument. FileInputStream overrides the methods of the InputStream class and provides two new methods, finalize() and getFD(). The finalize() method is used to close a stream when it is processed by the Java garbage collector. The getFD() method is used to obtain access to the FileDescriptor associated with the input stream.

The FileOutputStream Class

The FileOutputStream class allows output to be written to a file stream. Objects of class FileOutputStream are created in the same way as those of class FileInputStream, using a filename string, File object, or FileDescriptor object as an argument. FileOutputStream overrides the methods of the OutputStream class and supports the finalize() and getFD() methods described for the FileInputStream class.

The FileIOApp Program

The program in Listing 17.2 illustrates the use of the FileInputStream, FileOutputStream, and File classes. It writes a string to an output file and then reads the file to verify that the output was written correctly. The file used for the I/O is then deleted.

LISTING 17.2. THE SOURCE CODE OF THE `FileIOApp` PROGRAM.

```java
import java.lang.System;
import java.io.FileInputStream;
import java.io.FileOutputStream;
import java.io.File;
import java.io.IOException;

public class FileIOApp {
 public static void main(String args[]) throws IOException {
  // Create output file test.txt
  FileOutputStream outStream = new FileOutputStream("test.txt");
  String s = "This is a test.";
  for(int i=0;i<s.length();++i)
   outStream.write(s.charAt(i));
  outStream.close();
  // Open test.txt for input
  FileInputStream inStream = new FileInputStream("test.txt");
  int inBytes = inStream.available();
  System.out.println("inStream has "+inBytes+" available bytes");
  byte inBuf[] = new byte[inBytes];
  int bytesRead = inStream.read(inBuf,0,inBytes);
  System.out.println(bytesRead+" bytes were read");
  System.out.println("They are: "+new String(inBuf));
  inStream.close();
  File f = new File("test.txt");
  f.delete();
 }
}
```

The `FileOutputStream` constructor creates an output stream on the file `test.txt`. The file is automatically created in the current working directory. It then writes the string `"This is a test."` to the output file stream. Note the similarity between this program and the previous one. The power of streams is that the same methods can be used no matter what type of stream is being used.

The output stream is closed to make sure that all the data is written to the file. The file is then reopened as an input file by creating an object of class `FileInputStream`. The same methods used in the `ByteArrayIOApp` program are used to determine the number of available bytes in the file and read these bytes into a byte array. The number of bytes read is displayed along with the characters corresponding to those bytes.

The input stream is closed and then a `File` object is created to provide access to the file. The `File` object is used to delete the file using the `delete()` method. The program's output follows:

```
inStream has 15 available bytes
15 bytes were read
They are: This is a test.
```

The `SequenceInputStream` Class

The `SequenceInputStream` class is used to combine two or more input streams into a single input stream. The input streams are concatenated, which allows the individual streams to be treated as a single, logical stream. The `SequenceInputStream` class does not introduce any new access methods. Its power is derived from the two constructors that it provides. One constructor takes two `InputStream` objects as arguments. The other takes an `Enumeration` of `InputStream` objects. The `Enumeration` interface is described in Chapter 10, "Writing Console Applications." It provides methods for dealing with a sequence of related objects.

The `SequenceIOApp` Program

The program in Listing 17.3 reads the two Java source files, `ByteArrayIOApp.java` and `FileIOApp.java`, as a single file courtesy of the `SequenceInputStream` class.

LISTING 17.3. THE SOURCE CODE OF THE `SequenceIOApp` PROGRAM.

```java
import java.lang.System;
import java.io.FileInputStream;
import java.io.SequenceInputStream;
import java.io.IOException;

public class SequenceIOApp {
 public static void main(String args[]) throws IOException {
  SequenceInputStream inStream;
  FileInputStream f1 = new FileInputStream("ByteArrayIOApp.java");
  FileInputStream f2 = new FileInputStream("FileIOApp.java");
  // Concatentate two files into a single input stream
  inStream = new SequenceInputStream(f1,f2);
  boolean eof = false;
  int byteCount = 0;
  while (!eof) {
   int c = inStream.read();
   if(c == -1) eof = true;
   else{
    System.out.print((char) c);
    ++byteCount;
```

```
      }
    }
    System.out.println(byteCount+" bytes were read");
    inStream.close();
    f1.close();
    f2.close();
  }
}
```

The program creates two objects of class `FileInputStream` for the files
`ByteArrayIOApp.java` and `FileIOApp.java`. The `SequenceInputClass` constructor is
used to construct a single input stream from the two `FileInputStream` objects. The program then uses a `while` loop to read all bytes in the combined file and display them to
the console window. The loop stops when the end of the combined file is encountered.
This is signaled when the `read()` method returns `-1`. The streams are closed after the
combined files have been read. The program's output is as follows:

```
import java.lang.System;
import java.io.ByteArrayInputStream;
import java.io.ByteArrayOutputStream;
import java.io.IOException;

public class ByteArrayIOApp {
 public static void main(String args[]) throws IOException {
  ByteArrayOutputStream outStream = new ByteArrayOutputStream();
  String s = "This is a test.";
  for(int i=0;i<s.length();++i)
   outStream.write(s.charAt(i));
  System.out.println("outstream: "+outStream);
  System.out.println("size: "+outStream.size());
  ByteArrayInputStream inStream;
  inStream = new ByteArrayInputStream(outStream.toByteArray());
  int inBytes = inStream.available();
  System.out.println("inStream has "+inBytes+" available bytes");
  byte inBuf[] = new byte[inBytes];
  int bytesRead = inStream.read(inBuf,0,inBytes);
  System.out.println(bytesRead+" bytes were read");
  System.out.println("They are: "+new String(inBuf));
 }
}

import java.lang.System;
import java.io.FileInputStream;
import java.io.FileOutputStream;
import java.io.File;
import java.io.IOException;

public class FileIOApp {
```

```
public static void main(String args[]) throws IOException {
 FileOutputStream outStream = new FileOutputStream("test.txt");
 String s = "This is a test.";
 for(int i=0;i<s.length();++i)
  outStream.write(s.charAt(i));
 outStream.close();
 FileInputStream inStream = new FileInputStream("test.txt");
 int inBytes = inStream.available();
 System.out.println("inStream has "+inBytes+" available bytes");
 byte inBuf[] = new byte[inBytes];
 int bytesRead = inStream.read(inBuf,0,inBytes);
 System.out.println(bytesRead+" bytes were read");
 System.out.println("They are: "+new String(inBuf));
 inStream.close();
 File f = new File("test.txt");
 f.delete();
 }
}
1763 bytes were read
```

The `SequenceIOApp` program displays the combined contents of the two source files, followed by a line identifying the number of bytes that were read.

Filtered I/O

The filtered input and output stream classes provide the capability to filter I/O in a number of useful ways. I/O filters are used to adapt streams to specific program needs. These filters sit between an input stream and an output stream and perform special processing on the bytes they transfer from input to output. You can combine filters to perform a sequence of filtering operations where one filter acts on the output of another, as shown in Figure 17.2.

FIGURE 17.2.
Combining filters.

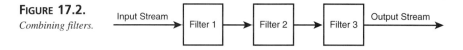

The `FilterInputStream` Class

The `FilterInputStream` class is an abstract class that is the parent of all filtered input stream classes. The `FilterInputStream` class provides the basic capability to create one stream from another. It allows one stream to be read and provided as output as another stream. This is accomplished through the use of the `in` variable, which is used to maintain a separate object of class `InputStream`. The design of the `FilterInputStream` class allows multiple chained filters to be created using several layers of nesting. Each subsequent class accesses the output of the previous class through the `in` variable. Because the `in` variable is an object of class `InputStream`, arbitrary `InputStream` objects can be filtered.

The `FilterOutputStream` Class

The `FilterOutputStream` class is the complement to the `FilterInputStream` class. It is an abstract class that is the parent of all filtered output stream classes. It is similar to the `FilterInputStream` class in that it maintains an object of class `OutputStream` as an `out` variable. Data written to an object of `FilterOutputStream` can be modified as needed to perform filtering operations and then forwarded to the `out` `OutputStream` object. Because `out` is declared to be of class `OutputStream`, arbitrary output streams can be filtered. Multiple `FilterOutputStream` objects can be combined in a manner that is analogous to `FilterInputStream` objects. The input of subsequent `FilterOutputStream` objects is linked to the output of preceding objects.

Buffered I/O

Buffered input and output is used to temporarily cache data that is read from or written to a stream. This allows programs to read and write small amounts of data without adversely affecting system performance. When buffered input is performed, a large number of bytes are read at a single time and stored in an input buffer. When a program reads from the input stream, the input bytes are read from the input buffer. Several reads may be performed before the buffer needs to be refilled. Input buffering is used to speed up overall stream input processing.

Output buffering is performed in a similar manner to input buffering. When a program writes to a stream, the output data is stored in an output buffer until the buffer becomes full or the output stream is flushed. Only then is the buffered output actually forwarded to the output stream's destination.

Java implements buffered I/O as filters. The filters maintain and operate the buffer that sits between the program and the source or destination of a buffered stream.

The `BufferedInputStream` Class

The `BufferedInputStream` class supports input buffering by automatically creating and maintaining a buffer for a designated input stream. This allows programs to read data from the stream one byte at a time without degrading system performance. Because the `BufferedInputStream` class is a filter, it can be applied to arbitrary objects of class `InputStream` and combined with other input filters.

The BufferedInputStream class uses several variables to implement input buffering. These variables are described in the Java API page for this class. However, because these variables are declared as protected, they cannot be directly accessed by your program.

BufferedInputStream defines two constructors. One allows the size of an input buffer to be specified and the other does not. Both constructors take an object of class InputStream as an argument. It is usually better to let BufferedInputStream select the best size for the input buffer than to specify one yourself, unless you have specific knowledge that one buffer size is better than another.

BufferedInputStream overrides the access methods provided by InputStream and does not introduce any new methods of its own.

The BufferedOutputStream Class

The BufferedOutputStream class performs output buffering in a manner that is analogous to BufferedInputStream. It allows the size of the output buffer to be specified in a constructor as well as providing for a default buffer size. It overrides the methods of the OutputStream class and does not introduce any new methods of its own.

The BufferedIOApp Program

The BufferedIOApp program (see Listing 17.4) builds on the SequenceIOApp example that was previously presented. It performs buffering on the SequenceInputStream object used to combine the input from two separate files. It also performs buffering on program output so that characters do not need to be displayed to the console window a single character at a time.

LISTING 17.4. THE SOURCE CODE OF THE BufferedIOApp PROGRAM.

```
import java.lang.System;
import java.io.BufferedInputStream;
import java.io.BufferedOutputStream;
import java.io.FileInputStream;
import java.io.SequenceInputStream;
import java.io.IOException;

public class BufferedIOApp {
 public static void main(String args[]) throws IOException {
   SequenceInputStream f3;
   FileInputStream f1 = new FileInputStream("ByteArrayIOApp.java");
   FileInputStream f2 = new FileInputStream("FileIOApp.java");
   f3 = new SequenceInputStream(f1,f2);
   // Create the buffered input and output streams
   BufferedInputStream inStream = new BufferedInputStream(f3);
   BufferedOutputStream outStream = new BufferedOutputStream(System.out);
```

```
  inStream.skip(500);
  boolean eof = false;
  int byteCount = 0;
  while (!eof) {
   int c = inStream.read();
   if(c == -1) eof = true;
   else{
    outStream.write((char) c);
    ++byteCount;
   }
  }
  String bytesRead = String.valueOf(byteCount);
  bytesRead+=" bytes were read\n";
  outStream.write(bytesRead.getBytes(),0,bytesRead.length());
  inStream.close();
  outStream.close();
  f1.close();
  f2.close();
 }
}
```

The program begins by creating two objects of FileInputStream and combining them into a single input stream using the SequenceInputStream constructor. It then uses this stream to create an object of BufferedInputStream using the default buffer size.

A BufferedOutputStream object is created using the System.out output stream and a default buffer size. The skip() method is used to skip over 500 bytes of the input stream. This is done for two reasons: to illustrate the use of the skip() method and to cut down on the size of the program output. The rest of the input is read and printed, as in the previous example.

The program output is similar to that of the preceding example. You should execute BufferedIOApp from the \ch17 directory. The skip() method was used to skip over 500 bytes of input. These bytes are also absent from the program's output, which is as follows:

```
rrayInputStream inStream;
  inStream = new ByteArrayInputStream(outStream.toByteArray());
  int inBytes = inStream.available();
  System.out.println("inStream has "+inBytes+" available bytes");
  byte inBuf[] = new byte[inBytes];
  int bytesRead = inStream.read(inBuf,0,inBytes);
  System.out.println(bytesRead+" bytes were read");
  System.out.println("They are: "+new String(inBuf));
 }
}

import java.lang.System;
```

```
import java.io.FileInputStream;
import java.io.FileOutputStream;
import java.io.File;
import java.io.IOException;

public class FileIOApp {
 public static void main(String args[]) throws IOException {
  FileOutputStream outStream = new FileOutputStream("test.txt");
  String s = "This is a test.";
  for(int i=0;i<s.length();++i)
   outStream.write(s.charAt(i));
  outStream.close();
  FileInputStream inStream = new FileInputStream("test.txt");
  int inBytes = inStream.available();
  System.out.println("inStream has "+inBytes+" available bytes");
  byte inBuf[] = new byte[inBytes];
  int bytesRead = inStream.read(inBuf,0,inBytes);
  System.out.println(bytesRead+" bytes were read");
  System.out.println("They are: "+new String(inBuf));
  inStream.close();
  File f = new File("test.txt");
  f.delete();
 }
}
1263 bytes were read
```

PushbackInputStream

PushbackInputStream is a filter that lets you push a byte that was previously read back onto the input stream so that it can be reread. This type of filter is commonly used with parsers. When a character indicating a new input token is read, it is pushed back onto the input stream until the current input token is processed. It is then reread when processing of the next input token is initiated. PushbackInputStream allows only a single byte to be pushed back. This is generally enough for most applications.

The pushback character is stored in a variable named pushBack.

The unread() method is the only new method introduced by this class. It is used to push a specified character back onto the input stream.

The PushbackIOApp Program

The PushbackIOApp program illustrates the use of the PushbackInputStream class (see Listing 17.5). It adds a pushback filter to the ByteArrayIOApp program shown earlier in this chapter.

LISTING 17.5. THE SOURCE CODE OF THE PushbackIOApp PROGRAM.

```java
import java.lang.System;
import java.io.PushbackInputStream;
import java.io.ByteArrayInputStream;
import java.io.ByteArrayOutputStream;
import java.io.IOException;

public class PushbackIOApp {
 public static void main(String args[]) throws IOException {
  ByteArrayOutputStream outStream = new ByteArrayOutputStream();
  String s = "This is a test.";
  for(int i=0;i<s.length();++i)
   outStream.write(s.charAt(i));
  System.out.println("outstream: "+outStream);
  System.out.println("size: "+outStream.size());
  ByteArrayInputStream inByteArray;
  inByteArray = new ByteArrayInputStream(outStream.toByteArray());
  PushbackInputStream inStream;
  inStream = new PushbackInputStream(inByteArray);
  char ch = (char) inStream.read();
  System.out.println("First character of inStream is "+ch);
  // Push 't' back onto stream
  inStream.unread((int) 't');
  int inBytes = inStream.available();
  System.out.println("inStream has "+inBytes+" available bytes");
  byte inBuf[] = new byte[inBytes];
  for(int i=0;i<inBytes;++i) inBuf[i]=(byte) inStream.read();
  System.out.println("They are: "+new String(inBuf));
 }
}
```

PushbackIOApp creates a stream to be used for byte array input using the code of the ByteArrayIOApp program. It applies a pushback filter to this stream by using the PushbackInputStream filter to create an object of class PushbackInputStream. It reads the first character of the input stream and displays it. It then pushes back a t onto the input stream. Note that any character could have been pushed back upon the input stream. The new input stream is then read and displayed.

The program output shows how the pushback filter was used to change the first character of the input stream from an uppercase T to a lowercase t. The program output consists of the following:

```
outstream: This is a test.
size: 15
First character of inStream is T
inStream has 15 available bytes
They are: this is a test.
```

The `LineNumberInputStream` Class

The `LineNumberInputStream` class provides a handy capability for keeping track of input line numbers. It is also a subclass of `FilterInputStream`. This class provides two new methods to support line number processing. The `setLineNumber()` method is used to set the current line number to a particular value. The `getLineNumber()` method is used to obtain the value of the current line number.

Up until Java 1.1, the `LineNumberInputStream` class was the preferred class for tracking input line numbers. In Java 1.1, significant support was added for internationalization. As a result, the `LineNumberInputStream` class has been deprecated. The `LineNumberReader` class (covered later in this chapter) is now the preferred class for tracking input line numbers.

Data I/O

The `DataInputStream` and `DataOutputStream` classes implement the `DataInput` and `DataOutput` interfaces. These interfaces identify methods that allow primitive data types to be read from and written to a stream. By implementing these interfaces, the `DataInputStream` and `DataOutputStream` classes provide the basis for implementing portable input and output streams.

The `DataInputStream` Class

The `DataInputStream` class provides the capability to read arbitrary objects and primitive types from an input stream. It implements the methods of the `DataInput` interface. These methods provide a full range of input capabilities:

- `readBoolean()`—Reads a `boolean` value.
- `readByte()`—Reads a byte as an 8-bit signed value.
- `readChar()`—Reads a Unicode character.
- `readDouble()`—Reads a `double` value.
- `readFloat()`—Reads a `float` value.
- `readFully()`—Reads an array of bytes.
- `readInt()`—Reads an `int` value.
- `readLine()`—Reads a line of text (deprecated).
- `readLong()`—Reads a `long` value.
- `readShort()`—Reads a `short` value.
- `readUnsignedByte()`—Reads a byte as an 8-bit unsigned value.

- `readUnsignedShort()`—Reads an unsigned 16-bit value.
- `readUTF()`—Reads a string that is in the UTF-8 format.
- `skipBytes()`—Skips over a specified number of input bytes.

Note that most, but not all, of these methods raise the `EOFException` when an end of file is encountered. The `readLine()` method returns a `null` value to signify a read past the end of a file. This method was deprecated in Java 1.1. The `readLine()` method of the `BufferedReader` class should be used instead. `BufferedReader` provides better support for internationalization. Its `readLine()` method corrects errors that exist in the `readLine()` method of `DataInputStream`.

The `DataOutputStream` Class

The `DataOutputStream` class provides an output complement to `DataInputStream`. It allows arbitrary objects and primitive data types to be written to an output stream. It also keeps track of the number of bytes written to the output stream. It is an output filter and can be combined with any output-filtering streams.

The `DataIOApp` Program

The program in Listing 17.6 shows how `DataInputStream` and `DataOutputStream` can be used to easily read and write a variety of values using streams.

LISTING 17.6. THE SOURCE CODE OF THE `DataIOApp` PROGRAM.

```
import java.lang.System;
import java.io.DataInputStream;
import java.io.DataOutputStream;
import java.io.FileInputStream;
import java.io.FileOutputStream;
import java.io.File;
import java.io.IOException;

public class DataIOApp {
 public static void main(String args[]) throws IOException {
  File file = new File("test.txt");
  FileOutputStream outFile = new FileOutputStream(file);
  DataOutputStream outStream = new DataOutputStream(outFile);
  // Write various data types to the output stream
  outStream.writeBoolean(true);
  outStream.writeInt(123456);
  outStream.writeChar('j');
  outStream.writeDouble(1234.56);
  System.out.println(outStream.size()+" bytes were written");
  outStream.close();
```

continues

LISTING 17.6. CONTINUED

```
    outFile.close();
    FileInputStream inFile = new FileInputStream(file);
    DataInputStream inStream = new DataInputStream(inFile);
    System.out.println(inStream.readBoolean());
    System.out.println(inStream.readInt());
    System.out.println(inStream.readChar());
    System.out.println(inStream.readDouble());
    inStream.close();
    inFile.close();
    file.delete();
  }
}
```

The program creates an object of class `File` that is used to access the `test.txt` file. This object is used to create an instance of class `FileOutputStream` that is assigned to the `outFile` variable. An object of class `DataOutputStream` is then constructed as a filter for the `FileOutputStream` object.

The `writeBoolean()`, `writeChar()`, `writeInt()`, and `writeDouble()` methods of `DataOutputStream` are used to write examples of primitive data types to the filtered output stream. The number of bytes written to the output stream is determined by the `size()` method and displayed to the console window. The output streams are then closed.

The `File` object, created at the beginning of the program, is then used to create an object of class `FileInputStream`. The output stream is then filtered by creating an object of `DataInputStream`.

The primitive data types that were written to the output file in the beginning of the program are now read from the filtered input stream and displayed to the console window.

The program's output shows that the data values were successfully written and read using the data I/O filters:

```
15 bytes were written
true
123456
j
1234.56
```

The `PrintStream` Class

The `PrintStream` class should be no stranger to you. The `System.out` object that you have been using for most of the sample programs is an instance of the `PrintStream` class. It is used to write output to the Java console window.

PrintStream's power lies in the fact that it provides two methods, print() and print-ln(), that are overloaded to print any primitive data type or object. Objects are printed by first converting them to strings using their toString() method, inherited from the Object class. To provide custom printing for any class, all you have to do is override the toString() method for that class.

PrintStream provides the capability to automatically flush all output bytes in the stream when a new line character is written to the stream. This feature can be enabled or disabled when the stream is created.

Because PrintStream is a filter, it takes an instance of OutputStream as an argument to its constructor. A second constructor adds the capability to use the autoflushing feature.

PrintStream introduces only one new method besides the extensively overloaded print() and println() methods. The checkError() method is used to flush stream output and determine whether an error occurred on the output stream. This capability is useful for printing output to devices, such as printers, where error status is needed to notify the user of any changes to the device state.

Piped I/O

Piped I/O provides the capability for threads to communicate via streams. A thread sends data to another thread by creating an object of PipedOutputStream that it connects to an object of PipedInputStream. The output data written by one thread is read by another thread using the PipedInputStream object.

The process of connecting piped input and output threads is symmetric. An object of class PipedInputThread can also be connected to an existing object of class PipedOutputThread.

Java automatically performs synchronization with respect to piped input and output streams. The thread that reads from an input pipe does not have to worry about any conflicts with tasks that are being written to the corresponding output stream thread.

Both PipedInputStream and PipedOutputStream override the standard I/O methods of InputStream and OutputStream. The only new method provided by these classes is the connect() method. Both classes provide the capability to connect a piped stream when it is constructed by passing the argument of the piped stream to which it is to be connected as an argument to the constructor.

The PipedIOApp Program

The PipedIOApp program creates two threads of execution, named Producer and Consumer, that communicate using connected objects of classes PipedOutputStream and PipedInputStream. Producer sends the message "This is a test." to Consumer one character at a time, and Consumer reads the message in the same manner. Producer displays its name and any characters that it writes to the console window. Consumer reads the message and displays its name and the characters it reads to the console window. The source code for the PipedIOApp program is shown in Listing 17.7.

LISTING 17.7. THE SOURCE CODE OF THE PipedIOApp PROGRAM.

```
import java.lang.Thread;
import java.lang.System;
import java.lang.InterruptedException;
import java.lang.Runnable;
import java.io.PipedInputStream;
import java.io.PipedOutputStream;
import java.io.IOException;

class PipedIOApp {
 public static void main(String args[]) {
  Thread thread1 = new Thread(new PipeOutput("Producer"));
  Thread thread2 = new Thread(new PipeInput("Consumer"));
  thread1.start();
  thread2.start();
  boolean thread1IsAlive = true;
  boolean thread2IsAlive = true;
  do {
   if(thread1IsAlive && !thread1.isAlive()){
    thread1IsAlive = false;
    System.out.println("Thread 1 is dead.");
   }
   if(thread2IsAlive && !thread2.isAlive()){
    thread2IsAlive = false;
    System.out.println("Thread 2 is dead.");
   }
  }while(thread1IsAlive || thread2IsAlive);
 }
}
class PipeIO {
 static PipedOutputStream outputPipe = new PipedOutputStream();
 static PipedInputStream inputPipe = new PipedInputStream();
 static {
  try {
   // Connect input and output pipes
   outputPipe.connect(inputPipe);
```

```
     }catch (IOException ex) {
      System.out.println("IOException in static initializer");
     }
    }
   String name;
   public PipeIO(String id) {
    name = id;
   }
  }
  class PipeOutput extends PipeIO implements Runnable {
   public PipeOutput(String id) {
    super(id);
   }
   public void run() {
    String s = "This is a test.";
    try {
     for(int i=0;i<s.length();++i){
      outputPipe.write(s.charAt(i));
      System.out.println(name+" wrote "+s.charAt(i));
     }
     outputPipe.write('!');
    } catch(IOException ex) {
     System.out.println("IOException in PipeOutput");
    }
   }
  }
  class PipeInput extends PipeIO implements Runnable {
   public PipeInput(String id) {
    super(id);
   }
   public void run() {
    boolean eof = false;
    try {
     while (!eof) {
      int inChar = inputPipe.read();
      if(inChar != -1) {
       char ch = (char) inChar;
       if(ch=='!'){
        eof=true;
        break;
       }else System.out.println(name+" read "+ch);
      }
     }
    } catch(IOException ex) {
     System.out.println("IOException in PipeOutput");
    }
   }
  }
```

This program is somewhat longer than the other examples in this chapter due to the overhead needed to set up the threading. The `main()` method creates the two `Producer` and `Consumer` threads as objects of classes `PipeOutput` and `PipeInput`. These classes are subclasses of `PipeIO` that implement the `Runnable` interface. The `main()` method starts both threads and then loops, checking for their death.

The `PipeIO` class is the superclass of the `PipeOutput` and `PipeInput` classes. It contains the `static` variables, `outputPipe` and `inputPipe`, that are used for interthread communication. These variables are assigned objects of classes `PipedOutputStream` and `PipeInputStream`. The `static` initializer is used to connect `outputPipe` with `inputPipe` using the `connect()` method. The `PipeIO` constructor provides the capability to maintain the name of its instances. This is used by the `PipeInput` and `PipeOutput` classes to store thread names.

The `PipeOutput` class extends `PipeIO` and implements the `Runnable` interface, making it eligible to be executed as a separate thread. The required `run()` method performs all thread processing. It loops to write the test message one character at a time to the `outputPipe`. It also displays its name and the characters that it writes to the console window. The `!` character is used to signal the end of the message transmission. Notice that `IOException` is handled within the thread rather than being identified in the `throws` clause of the `run()` method. In order for `run()` to properly implement the `Runnable` interface, it cannot throw any exceptions.

The `PipeInput` class also extends `PipeIO` and implements the `Runnable` interface. It simply loops and reads a character at a time from `inputPipe`, displaying its name and the characters that it reads to the console window. It also handles `IOException` in order to avoid having to identify the exception in its `throws` clause.

The output of `PipeIOApp` shows the time sequencing of the thread input and output taking place using the connected pipe I/O streams. The output generated by running the program on your computer will probably differ because of differences in your computer's execution speed and I/O performance. The output generated when I ran the program is as follows:

```
Producer wrote T
Producer wrote h
Producer wrote i
Producer wrote s
Producer wrote
Consumer read T
Consumer read h
Consumer read i
Producer wrote i
```

```
Producer wrote s
Producer wrote
Consumer read s
Consumer read
Producer wrote a
Producer wrote
Producer wrote t
Consumer read i
Consumer read s
Consumer read
Producer wrote e
Producer wrote s
Consumer read a
Consumer read
Consumer read t
Producer wrote t
Producer wrote .
Thread 1 is dead.
Consumer read e
Consumer read s
Consumer read t
Consumer read .
Thread 2 is dead.
```

Object I/O

The `ObjectOutputStream` and `ObjectInputStream` classes allow objects and values of primitive types to be written to and read from streams. These classes implement the `ObjectOutput` and `ObjectInput` interfaces. Of the methods specified by `ObjectOutput`, the `writeObject()` method is the most interesting; it writes objects that implement the `Serializable` interface to a stream. The `ObjectInput` interface provides the `readObject()` method to read the objects written to a stream by the `writeObject()` method.

The `Serializable` interfaces are used to identify objects that can be written to a stream. It does not define any constants or methods, but it does place some constraints on which classes are serializable. Chapter 40, "Using Object Serialization and JavaSpaces," covers the `Serializable` interface and object I/O in detail.

The `ObjectIOApp` Program

The `ObjectIOApp` program, shown in Listing 17.8, shows how the `ObjectOutputStream` and `ObjectInputStream` classes can be used to write and read objects from streams.

LISTING 17.8. THE SOURCE CODE OF THE `ObjectIOApp` PROGRAM.

```java
import java.io.ObjectInputStream;
import java.io.ObjectOutputStream;
import java.io.Serializable;
import java.io.FileInputStream;
import java.io.FileOutputStream;
import java.io.File;
import java.io.IOException;
import java.util.Date;

public class ObjectIOApp {
 public static void main(String args[]) throws IOException,
   ClassNotFoundException {
  File file = new File("test.txt");
  FileOutputStream outFile = new FileOutputStream(file);
  ObjectOutputStream outStream = new ObjectOutputStream(outFile);
  TestClass1 t1 = new TestClass1(true,9,'A',0.0001,"java");
  TestClass2 t2 = new TestClass2();
  String t3 = "This is a test.";
  Date t4 = new Date();
  // Write objects to stream
  outStream.writeObject(t1);
  outStream.writeObject(t2);
  outStream.writeObject(t3);
  outStream.writeObject(t4);
  outStream.close();
  outFile.close();
  FileInputStream inFile = new FileInputStream(file);
  ObjectInputStream inStream = new ObjectInputStream(inFile);
  // Read objects from stream and display them
  System.out.println(inStream.readObject());
  System.out.println(inStream.readObject());
  System.out.println(inStream.readObject());
  System.out.println(inStream.readObject());
  inStream.close();
  inFile.close();
  file.delete();
 }
}

class TestClass1 implements Serializable {
 boolean b;
 int i;
 char c;
 double d;
 String s;
 TestClass1(boolean b,int i,char c,double d,String s){
  this.b = b;
  this.i = i;
  this.c = c;
```

```
    this.d = d;
    this.s = s;
  }
  public String toString(){
    String r = String.valueOf(b)+" ";
    r += String.valueOf(i)+" ";
    r += String.valueOf(c)+" ";
    r += String.valueOf(d)+" ";
    r += String.valueOf(s);
    return r;
  }
}

class TestClass2 implements Serializable {
  int i;
  TestClass1 tc1;
  TestClass1 tc2;
  TestClass2(){
    i=0;
    tc1 = new TestClass1(true,2,'j',1.234,"Java");
    tc2 = new TestClass1(false,7,'J',2.468,"JAVA");
  }
  public String toString(){
    String r = String.valueOf(i)+" ";
    r += tc1.toString()+" ";
    r += tc2.toString();
    return r;
  }
}
```

17

INPUT/OUTPUT
STREAMS

ObjectIOApp is similar in design to the DataIOApp program in Listing 17.6. It creates a File object to support I/O to the test.txt file. The File object is used to create an object of class FileOutputStream. This object is then used to create an object of class ObjectOutputStream, which is assigned to the outStream variable.

Four objects are created and assigned to the t1 through t4 variables. An object of class TestClass1 is assigned to the t1 variable, and an object of class TestClass2 is assigned to the t2 variable. The TestClass1 and TestClass2 classes are declared at the end of Listing 17.8. A String object is assigned to t3, and a Date object is assigned to t4.

The objects referenced by the t1 through t4 variables are written to outStream using the writeObject() method. The stream and file are then closed. The test.txt file is reopened as a FileInputStream object, which is then converted to an ObjectInputStream object and assigned to the inStream variable. Four objects are read from inStream, using the readObject() method, and then written to standard output. The program's output is as follows:

```
true 9 A 1.0E-4 java
0 true 2 j 1.234 Java false 7 J 2.468 JAVA
This is a test.
Thu Jan 15 17:43:16 PST 1998
```

Note that you'll receive a different date value from this one. `TestClass1` and `TestClass2` are dummy test classes that are used to make the example work. Their `toString()` methods are automatically invoked by the `println()` method to convert objects to string values for printing.

The Reader and Writer Classes

The `Reader` and `Writer` classes are abstract classes at the top of a class hierarchy that support the reading and writing of Unicode character streams. These classes were introduced with Java 1.1.

The Reader Class

The `Reader` class supports the standard `read()`, `reset()`, `skip()`, `mark()`, `markSupported()`, and `close()` methods. In addition to these, the `ready()` method returns a `boolean` value that indicates whether the next read operation will succeed without blocking.

The direct subclasses of the `Reader` class are `BufferedReader`, `CharArrayReader`, `FilterReader`, `InputStreamReader`, `PipedReader`, and `StringReader`.

The Writer Class

The `Writer` class is the output complement to the `Reader` class. It declares the `write()`, `flush()`, and `close()` methods. Its direct subclasses are `BufferedWriter`, `CharArrayWriter`, `FilterWriter`, `OutputStreamWriter`, `PipedWriter`, `StringWriter`, and `PrintWriter`. Each of these subclasses, except `PrintWriter`, is an output complement to a `Reader` subclass.

Character Array and String I/O

The `CharArrayReader` and `CharArrayWriter` classes are similar to the `ByteArrayInputStream` and `ByteArrayOutputStream` classes in that they support I/O from memory buffers. The difference between these classes is that `CharArrayReader` and `CharArrayWriter` support 16-bit character I/O, and `ByteArrayInputStream` and `ByteArrayOutputStream` support 8-bit byte array I/O.

The `CharArrayReader` class does not add any new methods to those provided by `Reader`. The `CharArrayWriter` class adds the following methods to those provided by `Writer`:

- `reset()`—Resets the buffer so that it can be read.
- `size()`—Returns the current size of the buffer.
- `toCharArray()`—Returns a character array copy of the output buffer.
- `toString()`—Copies and converts the output buffer to a `String` object.
- `writeTo()`—Writes the buffer to another output stream (`Writer` object).

These methods are similar to those provided by the `ByteArrayOutputStream` class.

The `StringReader` class provides the capability to read character input from a string. Like `CharArrayReader`, it does not add any additional methods to those provided by `Reader`. The `StringWriter` class is used to write character output to a `StringBuffer` object. It adds the `getBuffer()` and `toString()` methods. The `getBuffer()` method returns the `StringBuffer` object corresponding to the output buffer. The `toString()` method returns a `String` copy of the output buffer.

The `CharArrayIOApp` and `StringIOApp` Programs

The `CharArrayIOApp` program (see Listing 17.9) is based on the `ByteArrayIOApp` program (see Listing 17.1) introduced at the beginning of this chapter. It writes the string `"This is a test."` one character at a time to a `CharArrayWriter` object. It then converts the output buffer to a `CharArrayReader` object. Each character of the input buffer is read and appended to a `StringBuffer` object. The `StringBuffer` object is then converted to a `String` object. The number of characters read and the `String` object are then displayed. The program output follows:

```
outstream: This is a test.
size: 15
15 characters were read
They are: This is a test.
```

The `StringIOApp` program (see Listing 17.10) is similar to `CharArrayIOApp`. It writes output to a `StringBuffer` instead of a character array. It produces the same output as `CharArrayIOApp`.

LISTING 17.9. THE SOURCE CODE OF THE `CharArrayIOApp` PROGRAM.

```
import java.lang.System;
import java.io.CharArrayReader;
import java.io.CharArrayWriter;
```

continues

LISTING 17.9. CONTINUED

```java
import java.io.IOException;

public class CharArrayIOApp {
 public static void main(String args[]) throws IOException {
  CharArrayWriter outStream = new CharArrayWriter();
  String s = "This is a test.";
  for(int i=0;i<s.length();++i)
   outStream.write(s.charAt(i));
  System.out.println("outstream: "+outStream);
  System.out.println("size: "+outStream.size());
  CharArrayReader inStream;
  inStream = new CharArrayReader(outStream.toCharArray());
  int ch=0;
  StringBuffer sb = new StringBuffer("");
  while((ch = inStream.read()) != -1)
   sb.append((char) ch);
  s = sb.toString();
  System.out.println(s.length()+" characters were read");
  System.out.println("They are: "+s);
 }
}
```

LISTING 17.10. THE SOURCE CODE OF THE `StringIOApp` PROGRAM.

```java
import java.lang.System;
import java.io.StringReader;
import java.io.StringWriter;
import java.io.IOException;

public class StringIOApp {
 public static void main(String args[]) throws IOException {
  StringWriter outStream = new StringWriter();
  String s = "This is a test.";
  for(int i=0;i<s.length();++i)
   outStream.write(s.charAt(i));
  System.out.println("outstream: "+outStream);
  System.out.println("size: "+outStream.toString().length());
  StringReader inStream;
  inStream = new StringReader(outStream.toString());
  int ch=0;
  StringBuffer sb = new StringBuffer("");
  while((ch = inStream.read()) != -1)
   sb.append((char) ch);
  s = sb.toString();
  System.out.println(s.length()+" characters were read");
  System.out.println("They are: "+s);
 }
}
```

The `InputStreamReader` and `OutputStreamWriter` Classes

The `InputStreamReader` and `OutputStreamWriter` classes are used to convert between byte streams and character streams. The `InputStreamReader` class converts an object of an `InputStream` subclass into a character-oriented stream. The `OutputStreamWriter` class converts a character output stream to a byte output stream.

The `InputStreamReader` Class

The `InputStreamReader()` constructor takes an `InputStream` object as a parameter and creates an `InputStreamReader` object. This provides a bridge between byte-oriented input streams and character-oriented input streams. A second `InputStreamReader` constructor also takes a `String` parameter that identifies the character encoding to be used in byte-to-character conversion. The `getEncoding()` method may be used to retrieve the encoding that is in effect. The `ready()` method is used to determine whether a character can be read without blocking.

The `InputConversionApp` Program

The `InputConversionApp` program, shown in Listing 17.11, converts the standard input stream (`System.in`) from a byte stream to a character stream. The input characters are echoed to standard output. It also prints out the encoding that is in effect on your system. The following is an example of the output generated when the program is run on my computer:

```
Encoding: 8859_1
>This is a test.
This is a test.
>
```

The `8859_1` encoding is the International Standard Organization (ISO) Latin-1 character encoding. Chapter 19, "Internationalization," identifies other encodings.

LISTING 17.11. THE SOURCE CODE OF THE `InputConversionApp` PROGRAM.

```
import java.lang.System;
import java.io.InputStreamReader;
import java.io.BufferedReader;
import java.io.IOException;

public class InputConversionApp {
```

continues

LISTING 17.11. CONTINUED

```
public static void main(String args[]) throws IOException {
  InputStreamReader in = new InputStreamReader(System.in);
  BufferedReader inStream = new BufferedReader(in);
  // Get the encoding that is in use
  System.out.println("Encoding: "+in.getEncoding());
  String inputLine;
  do {
   System.out.print(">");
   System.out.flush();
   inputLine=inStream.readLine();
   System.out.println(inputLine);
  } while (inputLine.length() != 0);
 }
}
```

The `OutputStreamWriter` Class

The `OutputStreamWriter` class allows a character stream to be converted to a byte
stream. Its constructor takes the name of an object of an `OutputStream` subclass as a
parameter. The characters written to an `OutputStreamWriter` object are translated and
written to the `OutputStream` object specified in the `OutputStreamWriter` object's constructor. The translation is performed according to the encoding specified in the `System`
property `file.encoding`. A different encoding scheme may be specified by supplying
the name of the encoding scheme in the `OutputStreamWriter` constructor. The
`getEncoding()` method may be used to retrieve the current character encoding that is in
effect.

The `FileReader` and `FileWriter` Classes

The `FileReader` and `FileWriter` classes are subclasses of `InputStreamReader` and
`OutputStreamWriter` that are used to perform character-based file I/O. These classes do
not provide any additional access methods. However, their constructors provide the capability to create input and output character streams using `String` objects that represent
filenames, `File` objects, and `FileDescriptor` objects.

The `CharFileIOApp` Program

Listing 17.12 demonstrates the use of the `FileReader` and `FileWriter` classes. It converts the `FileIOApp` program that was introduced earlier in the chapter (see Listing 17.2)
to character-oriented I/O and produces the following output:

15 characters were read
They are: This is a test.

The main difference between `CharFileIOApp` and `FileIOApp` is that `FileReader` and `FileWriter` classes are used instead of the `FileInputStream` and `FileOutputStream` classes. The other difference is the use of a `StringBuffer` object (instead of a byte array) to capture the characters read from the input file stream.

LISTING 17.12. THE SOURCE CODE OF THE `CharFileIOApp` PROGRAM.

```java
import java.lang.System;
import java.io.FileReader;
import java.io.FileWriter;
import java.io.File;
import java.io.IOException;

public class CharFileIOApp {
 public static void main(String args[]) throws IOException {
  FileWriter outStream = new FileWriter("test.txt");
  String s = "This is a test.";
  for(int i=0;i<s.length();++i)
   outStream.write(s.charAt(i));
  outStream.close();
  FileReader inStream = new FileReader("test.txt");
  StringBuffer sb = new StringBuffer("");
  int ch=0;
  while((ch = inStream.read()) != -1)
   sb.append((char) ch);
  s = sb.toString();
  System.out.println(s.length()+" characters were read");
  System.out.println("They are: "+s);
  inStream.close();
  File f = new File("test.txt");
  f.delete();
 }
}
```

Buffered Character I/O

Buffered character I/O is supported by the `BufferedReader` and `BufferedWriter` classes. These classes are character-based analogs to the `BufferedInputStream` and `BufferedOutputStream` classes. In Java 1.1, the `readLine()` method of the `BuffereddReader` class replaced the `readLine()` method of the `DataInputStream` class for reading lines of text from the console, a file, or other character-oriented input streams.

The `BufferedWriter` class provides the capability to write buffered data to character-based output streams. It adds the `newLine()` method to the methods that it inherits (and overrides) from the `Writer` class. The `newLine()` method allows new line characters to be written in a system-independent manner. It is preferable to simply writing an `\n` character to the output stream. The `line.separator` system property defines the system-specific new line character.

The `LineNumberReader` Class

The `LineNumberReader` class is a subclass of the `BufferedReader` class that is used to associate line numbers with each line of text that is read from a stream. Lines are terminated by a new line character (`\n`), a carriage return (`\r`), or a carriage return-new line combination (`\r\n`).

In addition to the methods that it inherits from `BufferedReader`, the `LineNumberReader` class declares the `getLineNumber()` and `setLineNumber()` methods. The `getLineNumber()` method returns the current line number. The `setLineNumber()` method sets the current line number to an integer value.

The `LineNumberIOApp` Program

The `LineNumberIOApp` program (see Listing 17.13) illustrates the use of the `LineNumberReader` class. It creates a `FileReader` on the `LineNumberIOApp.java` source file and then uses the `FileReader` object to create a `LineNumberReader` object. The character file is read, one line at a time, and its contents are displayed using line numbers obtained via the `getLineNumber()` method. The output of this program follows:

```
1.  import java.lang.System;
2.  import java.io.LineNumberReader;
3.  import java.io.FileReader;
4.  import java.io.BufferedWriter;
5.  import java.io.IOException;
6.
7.  public class LineNumberIOApp {
8.   public static void main(String args[]) throws IOException {
9.    FileReader inFile = new FileReader("LineNumberIOApp.java");
10.   LineNumberReader inLines = new LineNumberReader(inFile);
11.   String inputLine;
12.   while ((inputLine=inLines.readLine()) != null) {
13.    System.out.println(inLines.getLineNumber()+". "+inputLine);
14.   }
15.  }
16. }
```

LISTING 17.13. THE SOURCE CODE OF THE LineNumberIOApp PROGRAM.

```java
import java.lang.System;
import java.io.LineNumberReader;
import java.io.FileReader;
import java.io.BufferedWriter;
import java.io.IOException;

public class LineNumberIOApp {
 public static void main(String args[]) throws IOException {
  FileReader inFile = new FileReader("LineNumberIOApp.java");
  LineNumberReader inLines = new LineNumberReader(inFile);
  String inputLine;
  while ((inputLine=inLines.readLine()) != null) {
   // Get and print the line number
   System.out.println(inLines.getLineNumber()+". "+inputLine);
  }
 }
}
```

17

INPUT/OUTPUT
STREAMS

Filtered Character I/O

The FilterReader and FilterWriter classes are character-oriented analogs of the FilterInputStream and FilterOutputStream classes. The FilterReader class uses the in variable for input filtering and FilterWriter class uses the out variable for output filtering. Consult the section "Filtered I/O" earlier in this chapter for a description of I/O filtering.

The PushbackReader Class

The PushbackReader class is a subclass of FilterReader that provides the capability to push a character that was previously read back onto the input stream so that it can be read again. It is the character-oriented analog of the PushbackInputStream class that you studied earlier in the chapter.

The PipedReader and PipedWriter Classes

The PipedReader and PipedWriter classes support character-oriented piped I/O in the same way that PipedInputStream and PipedOutputStream support byte-oriented piped I/O. Consult the section "Piped I/O" earlier in this chapter for a description of piped input and output.

The `PrintWriter` Class

The `PrintWriter` class is the character-oriented replacement for the `PrintStream` class. The `PrintWriter` class improves `PrintStream` by using a platform-dependent line separator to print lines instead of the new line (\n) character. The `System line.separator` property identifies the system unique line separator. `PrintWriter` also provides better support for Unicode characters than `PrintStream`. The `checkError()` method is used to flush printed output and test for an error condition. The `setError()` method is used to set an error condition. `PrintWriter` provides support for printing primitive data types, character arrays, strings, and general objects. Objects are converted to a string (via the inherited or overridden `toString()` method) before being printed.

The `RandomAccessFile` Class

The `RandomAccessFile` class provides the capability to perform I/O directly to specific locations within a file. The name *random access* comes from the fact that data can be read from or written to random locations within a file rather than as a continuous stream of information. Random access is supported through the `seek()` method, which allows the pointer corresponding to the current file position to be set to arbitrary locations within the file.

`RandomAccessFile` implements both the `DataInput` and `DataOuput` interfaces. This provides the capability to perform I/O using primitive data types.

`RandomAccessFile` also supports basic file read/write permissions, allowing files to be accessed in read-only or read-write modes. A mode stream argument is passed to the `RandomAccessFile` constructor as r or rw, indicating read-only and read-write file access. The read-only access attribute may be used to prevent a file from being inadvertently modified.

`RandomAccessFile` introduces several new methods besides those inherited from `Object` and implemented from `DataInput` and `DataOutput`. These methods include `seek()`, `getFilePointer()`, and `length()`. The `seek()` method sets the file pointer to a particular location within the file. The `getFilePointer()` method returns the current location of the file pointer. The `length()` method returns the length of the file in bytes.

The `RandomIOApp` Program

The `RandomIOApp` program provides a simple demonstration of the capabilities of random-access I/O. It writes a `boolean`, `int`, `char`, and `double` value to a file and then uses the `seek()` method to seek to offset location 1 within the file. This is the position after the first byte in the file. It then reads the `int`, `char`, and `double` values from the file and displays them to the console window. Next, it moves the file pointer to the beginning of the file and reads the `boolean` value that was first written to the file. This value is also written to the console window. The source code of the `RandomIOApp` program is shown in Listing 17.14.

LISTING 17.14. THE SOURCE CODE OF THE `RandomIOApp` PROGRAM.

```java
import java.lang.System;
import java.io.RandomAccessFile;
import java.io.IOException;

public class RandomIOApp {
 public static void main(String args[]) throws IOException {
  RandomAccessFile file = new RandomAccessFile("test.txt","rw");
  file.writeBoolean(true);
  file.writeInt(123456);
  file.writeChar('j');
  file.writeDouble(1234.56);
  // Use seek() to move to a specific file location
  file.seek(1);
  System.out.println(filc.readInt());
  System.out.println(file.readChar());
  System.out.println(file.readDouble());
  file.seek(0);
  System.out.println(file.readBoolean());
  file.close();
 }
}
```

Although the processing performed by `RandomIOApp` is quite simple, it illustrates how random I/O allows you to move the file pointer to various locations within a file to directly access values and objects contained within the file.

The program's output is as follows:

```
123456
j
1234.56
true
```

The StreamTokenizer Class

The `StreamTokenizer` class is used by parsers to convert an input character stream into a stream of lexical tokens. It uses special methods to identify parser parameters, such as ordinary, whitespace, quote, and comment characters. These methods also enable and disable number and end-of-line parsing.

Seven variables are defined for the `StreamTokenizer` class, four of which are constant class variables. The `TT_EOF`, `TT_EOL`, `TT_NUMBER`, and `TT_WORD` constants are used to identify the type of input token encountered when parsing the input stream. The `ttype` variable is set either to one of these constants or to a single character based on the kind of token that is read from the input stream. The `TT_` constants are used to indicate a number, word, end of line, or end of file. When a word token is read, the actual word is stored in the `sval` variable and `ttype` is set to `TT_WORD`. When a number token is read, its value is stored in the `nval` variable and `ttype` is set to `TT_NUMBER`. When other special characters, such as @ or *, are read from the input stream, they are assigned directly to the `ttype` variable.

The `StreamTokenizer` constructor takes a `Reader` object as an argument and generates a `StreamTokenizer` object. The `StreamTokenizer` access methods can be divided into two groups: parser parameter-definition methods and stream-processing methods.

The parser parameter-definition methods are used to control the operation of the parser. The `commentChar()`, `slashSlashComments()`, and `slashStarComments()` methods are used to define comments. Comments are ignored by the parser. The `whitespaceChars()`, `wordChars()`, `quoteChar()`, `ordinaryChar()`, and `ordinaryChars()` methods are used to set the parser's token-generation parameters. The `parseNumbers()` and `eolIsSignificant()` methods toggle number and end-of-line parsing. The `lowerCaseMode()` method controls whether input words are converted to lowercase, and the `resetSyntax()` method is used to reset the syntax table, causing all characters to be treated as special characters.

The stream-processing methods are used to read tokens from the input stream, push tokens back out onto the input stream, and return the current line number associated with the input stream. The `nextToken()` method is used to get the next token from the input stream. The `pushBack()` method pushes the current token back out onto the input stream. The `lineno()` method returns the current line number associated with the input stream.

The `toString()` method of class `Object` is overwritten to allow printing of the current token.

The `StreamTokenApp` Program

The `StreamTokenApp` program demonstrates the ease with which `StreamTokenizer` can be used to create a parser. This program reads input from the standard input stream, parses input tokens, and displays the token type and value to the console window (see Listing 17.15).

LISTING 17.15. THE SOURCE CODE OF THE StreamTokenApp PROGRAM.

```
import java.lang.System;
import java.io.StreamTokenizer;
import java.io.InputStreamReader;
import java.io.BufferedReader;
import java.io.IOException;

public class StreamTokenApp {
 public static void main(String args[]) throws IOException {
  BufferedReader inData =
   new BufferedReader(new InputStreamReader(System.in));
  StreamTokenizer inStream = new StreamTokenizer(inData);
  inStream.commentChar('#');
  boolean eof = false;
  do {
   int token=inStream.nextToken();
   // Parse according to input token
   switch(token){
   case inStream.TT_EOF:
    System.out.println("EOF encountered.");
    eof = true;
    break;
   case inStream.TT_EOL:
    System.out.println("EOL encountered.");
    break;
   case inStream.TT_WORD:
    System.out.println("Word: "+inStream.sval);
    break;
   case inStream.TT_NUMBER:
    System.out.println("Number: "+inStream.nval);
    break;
   default:
    System.out.println((char) token+" encountered.");
    if(token=='!') eof=true;
   }
  } while(!eof);
 }
}
```

The program creates a new object of class BufferedReader using System.in as an argument. It then converts the BufferedReader object into a StreamTokenizer object and
assigns it to the inStream variable. It then sets the comment-line character to #.

Having set up the parser, StreamTokenApp reads tokens from inStream until the end of
file is encountered. It uses a switch statement to identify the type and value of each
token read.

The following is an example of the output produced by `StreamTokenizer`. Try running it with different input lines. An exclamation point (!) is used to terminate the program's execution:

```
This is a test.
Word: This
Word: is
Word: a
Word: test.
123 456
Number: 123.0
Number: 456.0
12.34 56.78
Number: 12.34
Number: 56.78
@ $ % ^
@ encountered.
$ encountered.
% encountered.
^ encountered.
#This is a comment
This is #a comment
Word: This
Word: is
!
! encountered.
```

Summary

In this chapter you learned how to work with Java input and output streams to perform input and output using standard I/O, memory buffers, and files. You explored the input and output stream class hierarchy and learned how to use stream filters to simplify I/O processing. You learned how the `Reader` and `Writer` classes support character-oriented I/O. You also learned how to perform random-access I/O and how to use the `StreamTokenizer` class to construct an input parser. In Chapter 18 you will learn how to print from your applications and applets.

Printing

IN THIS CHAPTER

One of the most useful capabilities that can be added to a Java program is printing information that is created with the program. Printing support was added in version 1.1 of the JDK but was both primitive and inconsistent. JDK 1.2 adds new printing support that corrects the deficiencies of JDK 1.1.

This chapter shows you how to print from your window programs. It identifies the AWT classes and methods used for printing, covers several programming examples that explain how to print text and graphics, and shows how to work with print jobs. When you finish this chapter, you'll be able to include printing capabilities in your applications and applets.

JDK 1.1 Printing Classes and Methods

The printing support provided with JDK 1.1 uses the `PrintJob` class of `java.awt`. This is an abstract class used to encapsulate print requests. An object of the `PrintJob` class is returned by the `getPrintJob()` method of the `Toolkit` class. This method initiates a platform-dependent print request using platform-specific dialog boxes. It has three parameters: a `Frame` object that identifies the application window from which the print request is generated, a `String` object that provides a title for the print job, and a `Properties` object that allows job-specific print properties to be specified and retrieved.

> **NOTE**
>
> In the Java vernacular, you *draw* on a `Graphics` object to display information to the screen or printer.

The `PrintJob` class provides the following six methods:

- `getGraphics()`—Returns a `Graphics` object that is drawn on to accomplish the printing. The `Graphics` object is sent to the printer when its `disposed()` method is invoked.
- `getPageDimension()`—Returns a `Dimension` object that identifies the width and height in pixels of the page to be printed.
- `getPageResolution()`—Identifies the page resolution in pixels per inch.

- `lastPageFirst()`—Returns a `boolean` value indicating whether the pages of a print job are printed in reverse order.
- `end()`—Completes the print job.
- `finalize()`—Invoked by the garbage collector when the `PrintJob` is no longer in use.

The `getGraphics()` method is key to printing—it provides a `Graphics` object that is used for drawing text and graphics. This `Graphics` object implements the `PrintGraphics` interface, which can be used to distinguish between a `Graphics` object that is used for printing and one that is used for screen display. The `PrintGraphics` interface consists of a single method, `getPrintJob()`, which returns the `PrintJob` associated with the `Graphics` object.

After drawing has been completed for a `Graphics` object, the object's `dispose()` method is invoked, which causes it to be printed. The `end()` method is invoked to end a print job.

The `getPageResolution()` and `getPageDimension()` methods are used to determine how a page is to be laid out. The `getPageResolution()` method returns the number of pixels per inch supported by a printer. The page dimensions returned by `getPageDimension()` are not the actual pixel dimensions of the page to be printed. Rather, the dimensions are a mapping (often unsuccessful) of screen coordinates to the graphics context used for printing. Because the dimensions returned by this method are inaccurate (as you'll see in the next section), it should not be used for page layout.

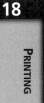

Working with Print Jobs

The `PrintJob` class is easy to use. To create a `PrintJob` object, invoke the `getPrintJob()` method of the `Toolkit` class. You can then invoke the methods of the `PrintJob` class to retrieve printer information, obtain a `PrintGraphics` object, or complete a print job. The `PrintTestApp` program, shown in Listing 18.1, shows how to work with `PrintJob` objects to obtain printer-related information. When you run this program, the opening window, shown in Figure 18.1, is displayed. Select Print from the File menu and a Print dialog box, similar to the one shown in Figure 18.2, is displayed. Click the OK button and the Print dialog box closes. The program window is updated to display the following information, as shown in Figure 18.3:

- The name of the print job
- Any `Properties` object returned by the `getPrintJob()` request
- The dimensions of the page in pixels

- The printer's resolution in pixels per inch
- Whether the printer prints the last page first

Depending on your printer and printer driver, the program may cause a blank page to be ejected.

LISTING 18.1. THE SOURCE CODE OF THE `PrintTestApp` PROGRAM.

```java
import java.awt.*;
import java.awt.event.*;
import java.util.Properties;
import ju.ch09.*;

public class PrintTestApp extends Frame {
 Object menuItems[][] = {{"File","Print","-","Exit"}};
 MenuItemHandler mih = new MenuItemHandler();
 MyMenuBar menuBar = new MyMenuBar(menuItems,mih,mih);
 TextArea textArea = new TextArea();
 Toolkit toolkit;
 int screenWidth = 300;
 int screenHeight = 300;
 public static void main(String args[]){
  PrintTestApp app = new PrintTestApp();
 }
 public PrintTestApp() {
  super("PrintTestApp");
  setup();
  setSize(screenWidth,screenHeight);
  addWindowListener(new WindowEventHandler());
  show();
 }
 void setup() {
  setMenuBar(menuBar);
  toolkit=getToolkit();
  add("Center",textArea);
 }
 class MenuItemHandler implements ActionListener, ItemListener {
  public void actionPerformed(ActionEvent ev){
   String s=ev.getActionCommand();
   String name="Test print job";
   Properties properties=new Properties();
   if(s=="Exit"){
    System.exit(0);
   }else if(s=="Print"){
    PrintJob pj=toolkit.getPrintJob(PrintTestApp.this,
     name,properties);
    if(pj==null) textArea.setText("A null PrintJob was returned.");
    else{
     String output="Name: "+name+"\nProperties: "+properties.toString();
```

```
        Dimension pageDim=pj.getPageDimension();
        int resolution=pj.getPageResolution();
        boolean lastPageFirst=pj.lastPageFirst();
        output+="\nPage dimension (in pixels):";
        output+="\n height: "+String.valueOf(pageDim.height);
        output+="\n width: "+String.valueOf(pageDim.width);
        output+="\nResolution (pixels/inch): "+String.valueOf(resolution);
        output+="\nLast Page First: "+String.valueOf(lastPageFirst);
        textArea.setText(output);
        Graphics g = pj.getGraphics();
        g.dispose();
        pj.end();
      }
    }
  }
  public void itemStateChanged(ItemEvent e){
  }
}
class WindowEventHandler extends WindowAdapter {
  public void windowClosing(WindowEvent e){
    System.exit(0);
  }
}
}
```

FIGURE **18.1.**

The opening window of the PrintTestApp *program.*

FIGURE **18.2.**

A Windows 95 Print dialog box.

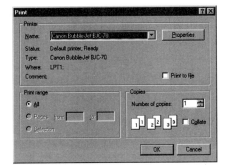

Figure 18.3 shows the parameters that are displayed for my Canon BJC-70 printer.

FIGURE 18.3.

The printer information for a Canon BJC-70 printer.

The `setup()` method of the `PrintTestApp` class creates a `Toolkit` object and assigns it to the `toolkit` variable. It also creates a `TextArea` object to display results to the user. The `MenuItemHandler` class handles the selection of the Print menu item by invoking the `Toolkit` class's `getPrintJob()` method to return a `PrintJob` object for printing. This object is assigned to the `pj` variable. The `pj` variable is checked to make sure that the print job is not `null`. In this case, the `getPageDimension()`, `getPageResolution()`, and `lastPageFirst()` methods are invoked to retrieve information about the printer. This information is displayed to the screen, along with the `Properties` object returned by the `getPrintJob()` method. The `getGraphics()` method of the `PrintJob` class is invoked to retrieve a `Graphics` object for printing. This object is immediately disposed by invoking its `dispose()` method. The `end()` method of the `PrintJob` class is then invoked to complete the processing of the print job.

The values of the page dimensions reported for the Canon BJC-70 printer were 792 pixels by 612 pixels. The values returned for other printers will differ. These dimensions are not the physical dimensions of a printed page, as you'll see in the next section. The printer resolutions in pixels per inch returned by `getPageResolution()` is 72. My printer is configured for 360 pixels per inch. However, 792 by 612 at 72 pixels per inch represents an 11 by 8.5 inch page.

Page Layout Controls

Java programs are required to perform their own page layout and pagination. The `getPageDimension()` and `getPageResolution()` methods provide the mechanism to do this. Unfortunately, these methods do not always return correct results. The methods return logical page dimensions that are used to provide compatibility with the screen display.

The `PrintDimApp` program, shown in Listing 18.2, illustrates the use of the `getPageDimension()` method in laying out pages for printing. The `PrintDimApp` opening screen is shown in Figure 18.4. When you select Print from the File menu, it prints a rectangle around the border of a page. On my Canon BJC-70 printer, it prints the rectangle with 10 percent margins around the page. You can use this program to determine how well the page dimensions returned by `getPageDimension()` work with your printer.

FIGURE 18.4.

*The opening
window of the*
`PrintDimApp`
program.

LISTING 18.2. THE SOURCE CODE OF THE `PrintDimApp` PROGRAM.

```java
import java.awt.*;
import java.awt.event.*;
import java.util.Properties;
import ju.ch09.*;

public class PrintDimApp extends Frame {
 Object menuItems[][] = {{"File","Print","-","Exit"}};
 MenuItemHandler mih = new MenuItemHandler();
 MyMenuBar menuBar = new MyMenuBar(menuItems,mih,mih);
 Toolkit toolkit;
 int screenWidth = 200;
 int screenHeight = 200;
 public static void main(String args[]){
  PrintDimApp app = new PrintDimApp();
 }
 public PrintDimApp() {
  super("PrintDimApp");
  setup();
  setSize(screenWidth,screenHeight);
  addWindowListener(new WindowEventHandler());
  show();
 }
 void setup() {
  setMenuBar(menuBar);
  toolkit=getToolkit();
 }
 void printDimensions(Graphics g,Dimension size){
  int width=size.width;
  int height=size.height;
```

continues

LISTING 18.2. CONTINUED

```
    int x1=(int) (width*0.1);
    int x2=(int) (width*0.9);
    int y1=(int) (height*0.1);
    int y2=(int) (height*0.9);
    g.drawRect(x1,y1,x2-x1,y2-y1);
    g.dispose();
  }
  class MenuItemHandler implements ActionListener, ItemListener {
    public void actionPerformed(ActionEvent ev){
      String s=ev.getActionCommand();
      String name="Test print job";
      Properties properties=new Properties();
      if(s=="Exit"){
        System.exit(0);
      }else if(s=="Print"){
        PrintJob pj=toolkit.getPrintJob(PrintDimApp.this,
         name,properties);
        if(pj!=null){
        printDimensions(pj.getGraphics(),pj.getPageDimension());
        pj.end();
        }
      }
    }
    public void itemStateChanged(ItemEvent e){
    }
  }
  class WindowEventHandler extends WindowAdapter {
    public void windowClosing(WindowEvent e){
      System.exit(0);
    }
  }
}
```

The overall structure of `PrintDimApp` is similar to `PrintTestApp`. The major difference between the two programs is the way that the Print menu item is handled.

The `PrintDimApp` program creates a `PrintJob` object using the `getPrintJob()` method of the `Toolkit` class. It invokes the `printDimensions()` method, passing it a `Graphics` object and `Dimension` object retrieved via the `getGraphics()` and `getPageDimension()` methods of `PrintJob`.

The `printDimensions()` method uses the `Dimension` object to draw a rectangle on the `Graphics` object. This rectangle is drawn with margins that are 10% of the page width and page height. The `dispose()` method is invoked to initiate printing of the `Graphics` object.

Printing Text and Graphics

The `PrintJob` class provides an easy-to-use interface for printing. Text and graphics are drawn to the printer in the same way they are drawn to the screen—you just display them to a different `Graphics` object. In fact, you can copy everything that is displayed to the screen to the printer by using a common drawing method for both. The `PrintSampleApp` program, shown in Listing 18.3, demonstrates how this can be accomplished.

When you run `PrintSampleApp`, it displays the opening window, shown in Figure 18.5. If you select Print from the File menu, the contents of the window can be sent to your printer. The `PrintSampleApp` program shows how graphics (rectangles, circles, and lines) and text are printed.

Figure 18.5.

The opening window of the `PrintSampleApp` *program.*

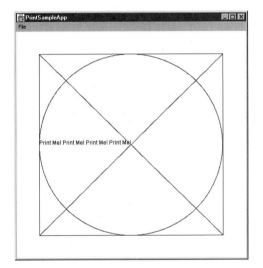

Listing 18.3. The source code for the `PrintSampleApp` program.

```java
import java.awt.*;
import java.awt.event.*;
import java.util.Properties;
import ju.ch09.*;

public class PrintSampleApp extends Frame {
  Object menuItems[][] = {{"File","Print","-","Exit"}};
  MenuItemHandler mih = new MenuItemHandler();
  MyMenuBar menuBar = new MyMenuBar(menuItems,mih,mih);
  MyCanvas canvas = new MyCanvas();
  Toolkit toolkit;
```

continues

LISTING 18.3. CONTINUED

```
int screenWidth = 500;
int screenHeight = 500;
public static void main(String args[]){
 PrintSampleApp app = new PrintSampleApp();
}
public PrintSampleApp() {
 super("PrintSampleApp");
 setup();
 setSize(screenWidth,screenHeight);
 addWindowListener(new WindowEventHandler());
 show();
}
void setup() {
 setMenuBar(menuBar);
 toolkit=getToolkit();
 add("Center",canvas);
}
class MenuItemHandler implements ActionListener, ItemListener {
 public void actionPerformed(ActionEvent ev){
   String s=ev.getActionCommand();
   String name="Test print job";
   Properties properties=new Properties();
   if(s=="Exit"){
    System.exit(0);
   }else if(s=="Print"){
    PrintJob pj=toolkit.getPrintJob(PrintSampleApp.this,
     name,properties);
    if(pj!=null){
     canvas.printAll(pj.getGraphics());
     pj.end();
    }
   }
 }
 public void itemStateChanged(ItemEvent e){
 }
}
class WindowEventHandler extends WindowAdapter {
 public void windowClosing(WindowEvent e){
   System.exit(0);
 }
}
}
class MyCanvas extends Canvas {
 public void paint(Graphics g){
  Dimension size=getSize();
  int width=size.width;
  int height=size.height;
  int x1=(int) (width*0.1);
  int x2=(int) (width*0.9);
  int y1=(int) (height*0.1);
```

```
  int y2=(int) (height*0.9);
  g.drawRect(x1,y1,x2-x1,y2-y1);
  g.drawOval(x1,y1,x2-x1,y2-y1);
  g.drawLine(x1,y1,x2,y2);
  g.drawLine(x2,y1,x1,y2);
  String text = "Print Me! ";
  text+=text;
  text+=text;
  g.drawString(text,x1,(int)((y1+y2)/2));
  g.dispose();
 }
}
```

The `PrintSampleApp` program creates an object of the `MyCanvas` class and adds it to the center of the application window. The `paint()` method of the `MyCanvas` class draws a rectangle, oval, two lines, and the text `Print Me! Print Me! Print Me!` on a graphics object. When the screen is initially painted and then repainted, the `Graphics` object is displayed to the application window. When the Print menu item is selected from the File menu, the `printAll()` method of the `Component` class is invoked for the `MyCanvas` object displayed in the application window. The `printAll()` method is passed the `Graphics` object of a `PrintJob` as an argument. The `printAll()` method prints a `Component` object (and all subcomponents) to a `Graphics` object. This causes the contents of the screen to be copied to the printer.

The `java.awt.print` Package

The `java.awt.print` package is a new AWT package that was added with JDK 1.2, replacing the print capabilities of JDK 1.1. The package consists of the following three interfaces and four classes:

- `Paper`—Specifies the physical characteristics of the paper used for printing. Provides methods for getting and setting the paper size and the drawing area.

- `PageFormat`—Specifies the size and orientation of a page to be printed. Provides methods for setting the `Paper` object to be used and the page orientation. Also provides methods for switching the drawing space between portrait and landscape mode and for retrieving the characteristics of the drawing area.

- `Pageable`—An interface specifying methods used for objects that represent a set of pages to be printed. These methods retrieve the number of pages to be printed and a specific page from within the page list.

- `PrinterJob`—Initiates, manages, and controls a printing request. Provides methods for printing `Pageable` objects and specifying print properties.

18

PRINTING

- Book—Maintains a list of pages to be printed. Provides methods for adding and managing pages. This class implements the Pageable interface.

- Printable—An interface that defines the print() method for printing a page on a Graphics object.

- PrinterGraphics—An interface that privides access to PrinterJob objects that are currently printing.

These classes provide the capability to create and process multiple page printouts using the current system printer. The GraphicsEnvironment class of java.awt provides the getPrinterJob() method, which can be used to create a PrinterJob object. The getLocalGraphicsEnvironment() method is used to produce an instance of the GraphicsEnvironment class.

Once you create a PrinterJob object, you invoke its print() method, passing it an object that implements the Pageable interface. The Book class implements this interface and is the type of object that you will most likely be printing.

Objects of the Book class are created using the Book() constructor and pages are added to the book via the append() method. This method takes an argument of the PageFormat class and an argument that implements the Printable interface. The PageFormat argument merely specifies the page format (letter, landscape, and so on). In most cases, you will be using a default page format. The object that implements the Printable interface is the heart of the printing application. You must create objects of a class that implements Printable to determine how text and graphics are drawn to each page.

The Printable interface specifies one method—the print() method. This method is invoked with an object of the Graphics class. You implement this method by drawing to the Graphics object. The PrintBookApp program, described in the next section, shows how this is accomplished.

The PrintBookApp Program

The PrintBookApp program, shown in Listing 18.4, shows how to use the classes and interfaces of the java.awt.print package. When you run the program, it displays the opening window, shown in Figure 18.6. Select Print from the file menu and the program prints three pages on your printer. The first page displays the text The JDK 1.2 Printing API really works! in the center of the page and a horizontal line at the bottom of the page. The second page displays an oval that is surrounded by a rectangle. The third page displays the text Last Page! in landscape mode. These three pages illustrate the printing versatility provided by the java.awt.print package.

FIGURE 18.6.

The opening window of the `PrintBookApp` *program.*

The `actionPerformed()` method of the `MenuItemHandler` class handles the selection of the Print menu item. It creates a `PrinterJob` object and assigns it to the `pj` variable. This variable is then passed to the `createBook()` method, which returns the `Book` object to be printed. The `setPageable()` method of the `PrinterJob` class is used to set the `Book` object to be printed. The `Book` object is printed using the `print()` method.

The `createBook()` method creates the three-page book that is printed. This method begins by creating a new `Book` object, followed by `PageFormat` objects representing the default page format (letter) and the landscape page format. A `PagePrinter` (described below) array is created to specify the `Printable` object for each page of the book.

The size of the printable area of each page is calculated in points. (A *point* is 1/72 of an inch.) The `getImageableWidth()` and `getImageableHeight` methods return the page's dimensions. These dimensions are assigned to `pageWidth` and `pageHeight`. The default font is then set to 18-point bold Helvetica.

The first page of the book is created as a `PagePrinter` object. The `addPrintElement()` method is used to specify what is to be printed to the page. The argument to `addPrintElement()` is an object of the `PrintElement` class (described later). The first print element consists of the text `The JDK 1.2 Printing API really works!`, which is printed using the value of `font` at x-position 100 (picas) and y-position `pageHeight/2` picas. The second print element consists of a line that is drawn from (0,`pageHeight`) to (`pageWidth`,`pageHeight`).

The second page draws a rectangle from (100,100) to (`pageWidth-100`,`pageHeight-100`) and an oval from (120,120) to (`pageWidth-120`,`pageHeight-120`).

The third page draws the text `Last Page!` at (`pageHeight/2`,`pageWidth/2`). However, these coordinates are switched when the page is printed in landscape mode.

18

PRINTING

The three pages are appended to the book, with the first two pages using the default format and the last page using a landscape format.

The PagePrinter class implements the Printable interface and supports the printing of each page of the book. It manages a Vector of PrintElement elements. This Vector is assigned to the pageContents variable. The print() method prints a page's contents to a Graphics object. This method is invoked by the underlying printing system, and the Graphics object is mapped to the printable portion of a page.

The print() method creates an Enumeration of the keys of the pageContents vector. It then loops through these keys, extracts each key's value, and invokes the print() method of PrintElement object.

The PrintElement class encapsulates the objects that are printed to a page. It supports text, lines, rectangles, and ovals. The type variable is set to text or graphics. The text variable is set to any text that is to be printed. The font variable specifies the text's font. The shape variable is used to identify the type of geometric shape to be displayed. The x, y, width, and height variables are used to specify the position and size of an object that is printed.

Two constructors are provided—one for creating text elements and the other for creating graphics elements. The print() method uses methods of the Graphics class to print text, lines, rectangles, and ovals.

LISTING 18.4. THE PrintBookApp PROGRAM.

```
import java.awt.*;
import java.awt.event.*;
import java.awt.print.*;
import java.awt.geom.*;
import java.utll.*;
import ju.cho9.*;

public class PrintBookApp extends Frame {
  Object menuItems [] [] = {{"File","Print","-","Exit"}};
  MenuItemHandler mih = new MenuItemHandler ();
  MyMenuBar menuBar = new MyMenuBar (menuItems,mih,mih);
  int screenWidth = 400;
  int screenHeight = 400;

  public static void main(String args [] ) {
   PrintBookApp app = new PrintBookApp ();
  }
  public PrintBookApp() {
   super("PrintBookApp")'
```

```
    setMenuBar(menuBar)'
    setSize(screenWidth,screenHeight);
    addWindowListener (new WindowEventHandler());
    show();
}
Book createBook(PrinterJob pj)  {
  Book book = neew Book();
  //Default page format
  PageFormat defaultFormat = new PageFormat ()'
  defaultFormat = pj.defaultPage (defaultFormat);
  //Landscape page format
  PageFormat landscapeFormat = new PageFormat ();
  landscapeFormat.setOrientation(PageFormat.LANDSCAPE);
  //Contents of each page
  PagePrinter [] page = new PagePrinter [3];
  //Determine page size in points (1/72 of an inch)
  int pageWidth = (int) defaultFormat.getImageableWidth ();
  int pageHeight = (int) defaultFormat.getImageableHeight ();
  Font font = new Font ("Helvetica", Font.BOLD,18);
  //Page 0
  page [0] = new PagePrinter();
  page[0].addPrintElement(
   new PrintElement("The JDK 1.2 Printing API really works!",font,
   100,pageHeight/2));
  page[0].addPrintElement (new PrintElement("line",
   0,pageHeight,pageWidth,pageHeight));
  //Page 1
  page[1] = new PagePrinter();
  page[1].addPrintElement (new
   PrintElement("rectangle",100,100,pageWidth-200,pageHeight-200));
  page[1].addPrintElement(new
  PrintElement("oval",120,120,pageWidth-240,pageHeight-240));
  //Page 2
  page[2] = new PagePrinter();
  page[2].addPrintElement (new
   PrintElement("Last Page!",font,pageheight/2,pageWidth/2));
  //Add pages to book
  book.append(page[0],defaultFormat);
  book append(page[1],defaultFormat);
  book append(page[2],landscapeFormat);
  return book;
}
class MenuItemHandler implements ActionListener, ItemListener {
  public void actionPerformed(ActionEvent ev) {
   String s=ev.getActionCommand();
   if(s=="Exit"){
    System.exit(0);
```

18

PRINTING

continues

LISTING 18.4. CONTINUED

```
   }else if(s=="Print"{
    PrinterJob pj=PrinterJob.getPrinterJob();
    Book book = createBook(pj);
    try{
     pj.setPageable(book);
     pj.print();
    }catch (Exception ex) {
     System.out.println(ex.toString());
    }
   }
  }
  public void itemStateChanged(ItemEvent e){
  }
 }
 class WindowEventHandler extends WindowAdapter {
  public voidd windowClosing(WindowEvent e){
   System.exit(0);
  }
 }
}

class PagePrinter implements Printable {
 Vector pageContents;
 public PagePrinter() {
  pageContents = new Vector();
 }
 public int print(Graphics g,PageFormat pageFormat, int pageIndex) {
  Enumeration printElements = pageContents.elements();
  while(printElements.hasMoreElements()) {
   PrintElement pe = (PrintElement) printElements.nextElement();
   pe.print(g);
  }
  return Printable.PAGE_EXISTS;
 }
 public void addPrintElement(PrintElement pe) {
  pageContents.addElement(pe);
 }
}

class PrntElement {
 static final int TEXT = 1;
 static final int GRAPHICS = 2;
 int type;
 String text;
 Font font;
 String shape;
 int x,y,width,height;
 public PrintElement(String text,Font font,int x, int y) {
  type = TEXT;
```

```
    this.text = text;
    this.font = font;
    this.x =x;
    this.y = y;
  }
  public PrintElement(String shape,int x,int y,int width,int height) {
    type = GRAPHICS;
    this.shape = shape.toUpperCase();
    this.x = x;
    this.y = y;
    this.width = width;
    this height = height;
  }
  public void print(Graphics g) {
   Font oldFont = g.getFont();
   if(type == TEXT) {
    g.setFont(font);
    g.drawString(text,x,y);
   }else if(type == GRAPHICS) {
    if(shape.equals("LINE")) {
     g.drawLine(x,y,width,height);
    }else if(shape.equals("OVAL")) {
     g.drawOval(x,y,width,height)'
    }else if(shape.equals(RECTANGLE")) {
     g.drawRect(x,y,width,height);
    }
   }
   g.setFont(oldFont);
  }
}
```

18

PRINTING

> **NOTE**
>
> The classes of the Java 2D API are covered in Chapter 20, "Working with 2D and 3D Graphics."

Summary

This chapter showed you how to include printing capabilities in your window programs, and covered the classes and methods used to support printing. You created examples that showed you how to print text and graphics and work with print jobs. Chapter 19, "Internationalization," shows how to develop Java programs that provide multilanguage capabilities.

Internationalization

CHAPTER 19

Being the de facto programming language of the Web, Java is an international programming language. It is being used in every country connected to the Web, and it is increasingly being called upon to develop applications and applets for use in the native languages of these countries. Fortunately, the developers of Java anticipated its international appeal and designed it accordingly. The decision to provide comprehensive support of the Unicode character set was a major step toward Java's internationalization. (Unicode is covered in the section "Using Unicode" later in this chapter.)

In addition to Unicode support, the JDK provides classes and interfaces that simplify the process of incorporating locale-specific resources (such as text strings, dates, and currencies) within Java programs. These classes and interfaces allow locale-specific resources to be separately maintained and easily converted.

This chapter covers Java's internationalization support. You'll be introduced to the Unicode character set, and you'll learn how to use the `Locale` and `ResourceBundle` classes to maintain locale-specific information. You'll also learn how the `java.text` package facilitates conversion of numbers, dates, and other units. When you finish this chapter, you'll be able to develop Java programs that adjust their output to the language and customs of the locale in which they execute.

What Is Internationalization?

In an age when individuals around the world are globally connected via the Internet, programs are often required to be tailorable to the language and customs of the locales in which they execute. Programs that provide these capabilities are referred to as *global* programs.

Global programs can be difficult to develop, but they don't have to be. If you write a program that mixes language-dependent text strings throughout its code and displays all its output using the customs of a single country, you will have a terrible time converting it to the language and customs of another locale. If and when you do complete the conversion, you will have to maintain multiple versions of the same program—one for each locale. When you take this kind of approach, developing global programs is complex, difficult, and time-consuming.

On the other hand, if you carefully isolate locale-specific resources, such as text strings, currencies, and dates, and maintain these resources separately from locale-independent code, global programs can be developed with a minimum of additional effort. Tailoring of such programs for use in specific locales can often be reduced to providing foreign-language equivalents of native-language text strings and specifying the use of alternative format sets.

Internationalization is the process of designing and developing global programs in such a way that locale-specific information is separately and efficiently maintained. Internationalization allows global programs to be more easily localized.

The JDK supports internationalization by using a multilanguage character set (Unicode 2.0), the `Locale`, `ResourceBundle` and other classes of `java.util`, the format conversion classes of `java.text`, and the Unicode character-stream support of `java.io`. This chapter focuses on `java.text` but also discusses how the internationalization-related classes and interfaces of other packages are used to develop global Java applications and applets.

Using Unicode

Unlike most other programming languages, Java provides comprehensive support for the Unicode 2.0 character set. Unicode is a 16-bit character set, meaning that it is capable of representing 65,536 characters. This is a large character set and can be used to represent the characters used by many of the world's popular languages. The 128 characters of the popular ASCII character set are the first 128 characters of Unicode.

> **NOTE**
>
> *ASCII* stands for *American Standard Code for Information Interchange*.

> **NOTE**
>
> More information about the Unicode character set can be found at `http://www.unicode.org`.

Unicode characters are written in Java using *Unicode escape character sequences*. These sequences are of the form \u*xxxx*, where the four x's are replaced with hexadecimal digits. Each of the four hexadecimal digits represents four bits of a 16-bit Unicode character.

To display Unicode characters other than ASCII, you need a Unicode font. In the absence of such a font, Java displays Unicode characters using the \u*xxxx* notation. The Bitstream Cyberbit font is an example of a font that supports Unicode. It can be downloaded from the Bitstream Web site at `http://www.bitstream.com/cyberbit/ftpcyber.htm`.

Managing Locales and Resources

The Locale class is defined in the java.util packages. This class provides internationalization support by describing geographic, political, or cultural regions. Locale objects are created by supplying the language and country arguments to the Locale() constructor or by using any of the predefined Locale constants. The access methods of Locale support the setting and retrieving of language, country, and variant-related values. The LocaleApp program, shown in Listing 19.1, illustrates the use of the Locale class in describing a locale in terms of a country and a language. Its output is as follows:

```
java LocaleApp
CURRENT LOCALE:
Country: United States
Language: English

OTHER LOCALES:
Country: ROC
Language: Chinese

Country: Korea
Language: Korean

Country: Italy
Language: Italian

Country: Canada
Language: English

Country: Canada
Language: French
```

LISTING 19.1. THE LocaleApp PROGRAM.

```
import java.util.*;

class LocaleApp {
 public static void main(String args[]) {
  Locale currentLocale = Locale.getDefault();
  Locale locales[]={Locale.TAIWAN,Locale.KOREA,
   Locale.ITALY,Locale.CANADA,Locale.CANADA_FRENCH};
  System.out.println("CURRENT LOCALE:");
  describeLocale(currentLocale);
  System.out.println("OTHER LOCALES:");
  for(int i=0;i<locales.length;++i)
   describeLocale(locales[i]);
 }
 static void describeLocale(Locale l){
  System.out.println("Country: "+l.getDisplayCountry());
```

```
    System.out.println("Language: "+l.getDisplayLanguage());
    System.out.println();
  }
}
```

The `LocaleApp` program invokes the `getDefault()` method of the `Locale` class to retrieve the current locale that is in effect. It then creates an array of sample `Locale` objects using the `Locale` constants to Taiwan, Korea, Italy, Canada, and French Canada. The `describeLocale()` method is then used to display the country and language associated with each `Locale` object.

> **NOTE**
>
> If you run the `LocaleApp` program with a default `Locale` other than the United States, the results will vary slightly.

The `ResourceBundle` Classes

The `ResourceBundle` class of `java.util` also supports internationalization. It is used to store locale-specific resources and tailor a program's appearance to the particular locale in which it is being run. The `ResourceBundle` class is extended by the `ListResourceBundle` and `PropertyResourceBundle` classes. The `ListResourceBundle` class organizes resources in terms of an array of object pairs, where the first object is a `String` key and the second object is the key's value. The `PropertyResourceBundle` class organizes locale-specific resources using a property file.

The `ResourceBundleApp` program in Listing 19.2 shows how resource bundles can be used to tailor a program's output. It is invoked with a two-character ISO-3166 country code and displays the names of five animals in English or Spanish, depending on the country code that was used.

> **NOTE**
>
> Lists of ISO-3166 country codes and ISO-639 language codes can be found at http://www.ics.uci.edu/pub/ietf/http/related/.

19

INTERNATIONALI-
ZATION

The following examples of program output show how the program tailors the information it displays using the methods of the `Locale`, `ResourceBundle`, and `ListResourceBundle` classes:

```
java ResourceBundleApp CA
cow
horse
cat
elephant
dog

java ResourceBundleApp US
cow
horse
cat
elephant
dog

java ResourceBundleApp GB
cow
horse
cat
elephant
dog

java ResourceBundleApp ES
vaca
caballo
gato
elefante
perro

java ResourceBundleApp MX
vaca
caballo
gato
elefante
perro
```

NOTE

The `TextBundle` and `TextBundle_es` classes, introduced later in this section, must be compiled before you run `ResourceBundleApp`.

LISTING 19.2. THE ResourceBundleApp PROGRAM.

```
import java.util.*;

class ResourceBundleApp {
 public static void main(String args[]) {
  if(args.length!=1){
   System.out.println("Usage: java ResourceBundleApp country_code");
   System.exit(0);
  }
  Locale mexico = new Locale("es","MX");
  Locale spain = new Locale("es","ES");
  Locale locales[] = {mexico,spain,Locale.US,Locale.CANADA,Locale.UK};
  Locale newLocale=null;
  for(int i=0;i<locales.length;++i){
   if(args[0].equals(locales[i].getCountry())){
    newLocale=locales[i];
    break;
   }
  }
  if(newLocale==null){
   System.out.println("Country not found.");
   System.exit(0);
  }
  ResourceBundle
resources=ResourceBundle.getBundle("TextBundle",newLocale);
  Enumeration enum=resources.getKeys();
  while(enum.hasMoreElements()){
   String key=(String) enum.nextElement();
   System.out.println(resources.getString(key));
  }
 }
}
```

The ResourceBundleApp program creates Locale objects for Mexico and Spain and creates a list of supported locales, including Mexico, Spain, the United States, Canada, and Great Britain. It checks the two-character country code that is passed to the program as a command-line argument with the list of supported locales. The newLocale variable is assigned the Locale object whose country code matches the one passed via the command line. The getCountry() method of the Locale class returns the two-character country code of a Locale object.

The getBundle()method of the ResourceBundle class is invoked to retrieve the ResourceBundle object associated with the Locale object stored in newLocale. Two resource bundle classes are available: the default (English) resource bundle, shown in Listing 19.3, and the Spanish language resource bundle, shown in Listing 19.4. The getBundle() method looks for classes of the following form until it finds one that matches: *ll* is the two-character (lowercase) language code of the locale, and *CC* is the two-character (uppercase) country code of the locale. The following are examples of these file name formats:

- TextBundle_*ll_CC*
- TextBundle_*ll*
- TextBundle

For example, if you pass the GB country code (Great Britain) to ResourceBundleApp, getBundle() will look for resource bundle classes TextBundle_en_GB and TextBundle_en before settling on TextBundle.

> **NOTE**
>
> The language code for English is en. The language code for Spanish is es. The country codes for Mexico, Spain, United States, Canada, and United Kingdom are MX, ES, US, CA, and GB.

The getKeys() method of the ResourceBundle class returns an enumeration of the keys used to access locale-specific resources. The getString() method of ResourceBundle returns a String representation of the resource object associated with the key.

LISTING 19.3. THE TextBundle CLASS.

```
import java.util.*;

public class TextBundle extends ListResourceBundle {
 public Object[][] getContents() {
  return contents;
 }
 static final Object[][] contents = {
  {"dog","dog"},
  {"cat","cat"},
  {"horse","horse"},
  {"cow","cow"},
  {"elephant","elephant"}
 };
}
```

The TextBundle class is a subclass of ListResourceBundle, which is a subclass of ResourceBundle. The getContents() method of ListResourceBundle is overridden to return an array of keys and their associated language-specific resources. The getContents() method is used to generate the information returned by the getKeys() and getString() methods used in ResourceBundleApp.

The contents array is an array of two-element arrays: the first element is the key, and the second element is its value.

The TextBundle_es class is a Spanish language version of the TextBundle class. It provides a Spanish translation of the words "dog," "cat," "horse," "cow," and "elephant."

LISTING 19.4. THE TextBundle_es CLASS.

```
import java.util.*;

public class TextBundle_es extends ListResourceBundle {
 public Object[][] getContents() {
  return contents;
 }
 static final Object[][] contents = {
  {"dog","perro"},
  {"cat","gato"},
  {"horse","caballo"},
  {"cow","vaca"},
  {"elephant","elefante"}
 };
}
```

Performing Locale-Specific Format Conversions

The classes of java.text are used to provide locale-specific format conversions for use with numbers, dates, and other objects. Format is an abstract class that is extended by other classes to support parsing and format conversion. It declares the format() method to convert objects to strings and the parseObject() method to convert strings to objects. These methods are overridden by its subclasses.

The DateFormat Class

DateFormat is an abstract class used to format and parse date and time values using locale-specific customs. It supports four formatting styles defined by the FULL, LONG, MEDIUM, and SHORT constants. These styles determine the length of the formatted output. DateFormat defines other constants for identifying specific date and time fields. The getInstance(), getDateInstance(), getTimeInstance(), and getDateTimeInstance() methods return instances of DateFormat that are specific to a locale. Other methods are provided for working with objects of the Calendar, TimeZone, and other date-related classes covered in Chapter 11, "Using the Utility and Math Packages."

The `SimpleDateFormat` Class

The `SimpleDateFormat` class extends the `DateFormat` class to provide a default implementation of date formatting and parsing capabilities. It allows date and time formatting patterns to be used to customize formatting and parsing. The `SimpleDateFormat` class makes use of special date and time pattern symbols that are discussed in the class's API description.

The `DateFormatApp` program, shown in Listing 19.5, illustrates the use of the date-formatting capabilities of the `SimpleDateFormat` class. When you run the program, it produces the following type-formatted output. The date and time displayed are the current date and time of the locale in which the program is run:

```
java DateFormatApp
The year is 1998 AD.
The month is July.
It is 09 o'clock PM, Pacific Standard Time.
```

> **NOTE**
>
> If `DateFormatApp` displays an incorrect time zone value, check your `user.timezone` system property to make sure that it is set correctly.

Although the output may not be that impressive, the formatting capabilities provided by `SimpleDateFormat` are efficient and easy to use. The pattern string places single quotes around text that is not a date/time formatting pattern. The formatting patterns used in the pattern string are as follows:

- `yyyy`—Year
- `GG`—Era
- `MMMMMMMMM`—Month
- `hh`—Hour
- `a`—AM/PM designator
- `zzzz`—Time zone

The pattern is supplied as an argument to the `SimpleDateFormat` constructor to create a format pattern-specific object. The current date is passed to the `format()` method of this object to create a `String` object that is formatted using the current date and the format pattern.

LISTING 19.5. THE `DateFormatApp` PROGRAM.

```
import java.text.*;
import java.util.*;

class DateFormatApp {
 public static void main(String args[]) {
  String pattern="'The year is '";
  pattern +="yyyy GG";
  pattern +="'.\nThe month is '";
  pattern+="MMMMMMMMM";
  pattern+="'.\nIt is '";
  pattern+="hh";
  pattern+="' o''clock '";
  pattern+="a, zzzz";
  pattern+="'.'";
  SimpleDateFormat format = new SimpleDateFormat(pattern);
  String formattedDate = format.format(new Date());
  System.out.println(formattedDate);
 }
}
```

The `DateFormatSymbols` Class

The `DateFormatSymbols` class is used to provide access to locale-specific date symbols, such as the names of days, months, and other date and time units. `DateFormatSymbols` objects are created using the `getDateFormatSymbols` method of the `SimpleDateFormat` class or via the `DateFormatSymbols()` constructor. Several `get` methods allow locale-specific formatting strings to be retrieved.

The `NumberFormat` Class

The `NumberFormat` class is an abstract class that supports the locale-specific formatting and parsing of numbers. The `INTEGER_FIELD` and `FRACTION_FIELD` constants are used to identify fields within decimal numbers. The `format()` and `parse()` methods support number formatting and parsing. Other methods are provided to access the number of digits to the left and right of the decimal point, to work with locales, and to access other number-formatting attributes.

The `NumberFormatApp` program, shown in Listing 19.6, illustrates the use of the `NumberFormat` class in supporting locale-specific currency formatting. It prints out a value of 1,000,000 currency units using the locale-specific currency value, as shown in the following:

```
java NumberFormatApp
$1,000,000.00
```

19

**INTERNATIONALI-
ZATION**

LISTING 19.6. THE NumberFormatApp PROGRAM.

```
import java.text.*;
import java.util.*;

class NumberFormatApp {
 public static void main(String args[]) {
  NumberFormat format = NumberFormat.getCurrencyInstance(
   Locale.getDefault());
  String formattedCurrency = format.format(1000000);
  System.out.println(formattedCurrency);
 }
}
```

The DecimalFormat Class

The DecimalFormat class extends the NumberFormat class to support the formatting of decimal numbers using locale-specific customs. The class supports the specification and use of custom formatting patterns. The format() and parse() methods are used to perform formatting and parsing. A number of get and set methods are provided to access specific formatting parameters. The DecimalFormat class makes use of special number formatting pattern symbols that are discussed in the class's API description.

The DecimalFormatSymbols Class

The DecimalFormatSymbols class provides access to the locale-specific symbols used in formatting numbers. These symbols include decimal separators, grouping separators, and others used by objects of the DecimalFormat class. Instances of DecimalFormatSymbols are created using the getDecimalFormatSymbols() method of the DecimalFormat class and the DecimalFormatSymbols() constructors. Several methods are provided to set and retrieve formatting information, such as the decimal separator character, grouping separators, the minus sign, the infinity symbol, the not-a-number symbol, and the percentage sign.

The ChoiceFormat Class

The ChoiceFormat class extends the NumberFormat class to identify strings that serve as labels for numbers within specific intervals. The ChoiceFormat constructor takes an array of double values used to specify numeric intervals and an array of String objects that identify the labels associated with those intervals. The double values are referred to as *limits*. The methods of the ChoiceFormat class support the formatting and parsing of strings based on the limits and their labels.

The `ChoiceFormatApp` program in Listing 19.7 illustrates the use of the `ChoiceFormat` class. It uses a random number generator to predict the likelihood of rain. Its output varies every time you run it. Sample output follows:

```
java ChoiceFormatApp
The likelihood of rain today is very low (0.05002163005399529).

java ChoiceFormatApp
The likelihood of rain today is high (0.954441890602895).

java ChoiceFormatApp
The likelihood of rain today is moderate (0.3000466839384621).
```

The `ChoiceFormatApp` program defines four limits: 0.0, 0.1, 0.3, and 0.7. It defines four labels that correspond to intervals defined by these limits:

- `very low`—From 0.0 up to, but not including, 0.1.

- `low`—From 0.1 up to, but not including, 0.3.

- `moderate`—From 0.3 up to, but not including, 0.7.

- `high`—From 0.7, on up.

An object of the `ChoiceFormat` class is created using the `limits` and `labels` arrays. A random number between 0 and 1 is fed into the `format()` method of the `ChoiceFormat` object to select the label associated with the interval in which the random number generator falls.

LISTING 19.7. THE `ChoiceFormatApp` PROGRAM.

```java
import java.text.*;
import java.util.*;

class ChoiceFormatApp {
 public static void main(String args[]) {
  double limits[] = {0.0,0.1,0.3,0.7};
  String labels[] = {"very low","low","moderate","high"};
  ChoiceFormat format = new ChoiceFormat(limits,labels);
  String prediction = "The likelihood of rain today is ";
  double r = Math.random();
  prediction += format.format(r)+" ("+r+").";
  System.out.println(prediction);
 }
}
```

19

INTERNATIONALI-
ZATION

The MessageFormat Class

The MessageFormat class extends the Format class to format objects as messages that are inserted into a String object. The MessageFormat constructor takes a String argument that specifies a message-formatting pattern. This pattern contains formatting elements where time, date, number, and choice objects may be inserted. Consult the API documentation of the MessageFormat class for a description of the syntax used to create formatting patterns. The format() method is used to insert objects into a message formatting pattern. The parse() method is used to parse the objects contained in a string according to a message-formatting pattern.

The MessageFormatApp program, shown in Listing 19.8, provides a simple introduction to the use of the MessageFormat class. It generates output in the following form:

```
java MessageFormatApp
The time is 4:16:05 PM and your lucky number is 620.
```

MessageFormatApp creates a format pattern with time and number fields and uses this pattern to construct a MessageFormat object. It creates an array of two objects: the current time (as a Date object) and a random Integer object. It then invokes the format() method of the MessageFormat object to produce the formatted output that is displayed to the console window.

LISTING 19.8. THE MessageFormatApp CLASS.

```java
import java.text.*;
import java.util.*;

class MessageFormatApp {
 public static void main(String args[]) {
  String pattern = "The time is {0,time} and ";
  pattern += "your lucky number is {1,number}.";
  MessageFormat format = new MessageFormat(pattern);
  Object objects[] = {new Date(),
   new Integer((int)(Math.random()*1000))};
  String formattedOutput=format.format(objects);
  System.out.println(formattedOutput);
 }
}
```

The FieldPosition and ParsePosition Classes

The FieldPosition class is used to identify fields in formatted output. It keeps track of the field's position within the formatted output. The FieldPosition() constructor takes an integer value that is used to identify the field. Its methods are used to retrieve the indices of the beginning and end of the field and the field's identifier.

The `ParsePosition` class is similar to the `FieldPosition` class. While `FieldPosition` is used for formatting, `ParsePosition` is used for parsing. Its constructor takes an integer that identifies its index within the string being parsed. The `getIndex()` and `setIndex()` methods are used to change this index.

Collation

Different languages have different alphabets and unique ways of sorting text strings written in those languages. *Collation*, as it applies to `java.text`, is the process of sorting or arranging text strings according to locale-specific customs. The `java.text` package supports collation through the `Collator`, `RuleBasedCollator`, `CollationKey`, and `CollationElementIterator` classes.

The `Collator` class is an abstract class that is used to compare `String` objects using locale-specific customs. It is subclassed to provide implement-specific collation algorithms. The `getInstance()` method is used to retrieve a locale-specific `Collation` instance. Some languages recognize different *strengths* in determining whether letters are identical or different; this is common to languages that support accented characters. The `setStrength()` of `Collator` may be used to set different collation strength levels. The `compare()` method compares two strings and returns an `int` value indicating the results of the comparison. The other methods of `Collator` support the decomposition of composite characters (for example, accented characters) and the creation of `CollationKey` objects.

The `CollationKey` class provides a compact representation of a `String` object according to the collation rules of a `Collator` object. `CollationKey` objects are optimized to support fast `String` comparisons and are preferred over the `compare()` method of the `Collator` class for extensive comparisons, such as those found in sorting algorithms. `CollationKey` objects are generated using the `getCollationKey()` method of the `Collator` class. The `compareTo()` and `equals()` methods of `CollationKey` are used to perform comparisons. The `toByteArray()` method can be used to convert a `CollationKey` object to a `byte` array. The `getSourceString()` method returns the String object from which a `CollationKey` object was generated.

The `RuleBasedCollator` class extends `Collator` to provide a concrete collator implementation. It allows you to define your own collation rules. However, in most cases, you'll want to use the predefined rules that are specific to your locale. The `getRules()` method may be used to retrieve the collation rules that are in effect for a

RuleBasedCollator object. The getCollationKey() method overrides that of the
Collator class. The getCollationElementIterator() method returns a
CollationElementIterator object for the collator. Iterator classes are covered in the
next section.

The CollateApp program, shown in Listing 19.9, shows how the RulesBasedCollator
and CollationKey classes can be used to sort a file. The CollateApp program takes a
filename as a command-line argument and produces a sorted version of the file's contents
as its output. The following output shows how the file CollateApp.java is sorted. Note
how the default collation rules treat blanks that appear at the beginning of a string:

```
java CollateApp CollateApp.java

}
 }
 }
  }
  }
  }
   }
    }
   }catch(Exception ex){
   boolean changes=true;
    BufferedReader in = new BufferedReader(new FileReader(args[0]));
    changes=false;
      changes=true;
class CollateApp {
  CollationKey keys[]=new CollationKey[keyVector.size()];
      CollationKey temp=keys[i];
    Collator.getInstance(defaultLocale);
   for(int i=0;i<keys.length;++i)
   for(int i=0;i<keys.length;++i)
    for(int i=0;i<keys.length-1;++i){
   if(args.length!=1){
     if(compare>0){
import java.io.*;
import java.text.*;
import java.util.*;
   in.close();
    int compare=keys[i].compareTo(keys[i+1]);
   keys[i]=(CollationKey) keyVector.elementAt(i);
     keys[i]=keys[i+1];
     keys[i+1]=temp;
   keys=sort(keys);
     keyVector.addElement(collator.getCollationKey(line));
    Locale defaultLocale = Locale.getDefault();
  public static void main(String args[]) {
   return keys;
   RuleBasedCollator collator = (RuleBasedCollator)
```

```
static CollationKey[] sort(CollationKey keys[]){
  String line;
  System.exit(0);
  System.exit(0);
  System.out.println("Usage: java CollateApp file");
  System.out.println(ex);
  System.out.println(keys[i].getSourceString());
  try {
  Vector keyVector = new Vector();
   while((line=in.readLine())!=null)
  while(changes){
```

LISTING 19.9. THE CollateApp PROGRAM.

```
import java.text.*;
import java.util.*;
import java.io.*;

class CollateApp {
 public static void main(String args[]) {
  if(args.length!=1){
   System.out.println("Usage: java CollateApp file");
   System.exit(0);
  }
  Locale defaultLocale = Locale.getDefault();
  RuleBasedCollator collator = (RuleBasedCollator)
   Collator.getInstance(defaultLocale);
  Vector keyVector = new Vector();
  try {
   BufferedReader in = new BufferedReader(new FileReader(args[0]));
   String line;
   while((line=in.readLine())!=null)
    keyVector.addElement(collator.getCollationKey(line));
   in.close();
  }catch(Exception ex){
   System.out.println(ex);
   System.exit(0);
  }
  CollationKey keys[]=new CollationKey[keyVector.size()];
  for(int i=0;i<keys.length;++i)
   keys[i]=(CollationKey) keyVector.elementAt(i);
  keys=sort(keys);
  for(int i=0;i<keys.length;++i)
   System.out.println(keys[i].getSourceString());
 }
 static CollationKey[] sort(CollationKey keys[]){
  boolean changes=true;
  while(changes){
```

19

INTERNATIONALI-
ZATION

continues

LISTING 19.9. CONTINUED

```
  changes=false;
  for(int i=0;i<keys.length-1;++i){
   int compare=keys[i].compareTo(keys[i+1]);
   if(compare>0){
    changes=true;
    CollationKey temp=keys[i];
    keys[i]=keys[i+1];
    keys[i+1]=temp;
   }
  }
 }
 return keys;
 }
}
```

The `CollateApp` program creates a `RulesBasedCollator` object using the `getInstance()` method of the `Collator` class. It selects the collator corresponding to the default locale. It reads in each line of the file, creates a `CollationKey` object corresponding to the input line, and stores the line in a `Vector` object. It then converts the vector to an array to simplify the sorting process. The `sort()` method is invoked to sort the `CollationKey` array. The `String` objects corresponding to the sorted `CollationKey` objects are retrieved via the `getSourceString()` method. These `String` objects are then printed.

The `sort()` method sorts the `CollationKey` array using the `CollationKey compareTo()` method. This method returns a positive integer if the `CollationKey` object being compared is greater than the one it is being compared to. It returns 0 if they are equal and a negative integer if the `CollationKey` object being compared is less than the one it is being compared to.

The Iterator Classes and Interfaces of `java.text`

The `CharacterIterator` interface defines methods that are implemented by classes that provide the capability to step through (iterate) a sequence of characters. These methods allow you to set your position within the text, move to other positions, and return the character at a specific position. The `StringCharacterIterator` class implements `CharacterIterator` to support string iteration and parsing.

The `BreakIterator` class is used to find text boundaries. It provides useful static methods for locale-specific parsing of character sequences by word, line, or sentence.

The CollationElementIterator class supports string iteration and returns information used to collate strings using locale-specific customs.

Summary

In this chapter you were introduced to Java's internationalization support. You learned about the Unicode character set and learned how to use the Locale and ResourceBundle classes to maintain locale-specific information. You also learned how the classes of the java.text package facilitate the conversion of numbers, dates, and other units. In the next chapter you'll be introduced to the new multimedia capabilities provided by JDK 1.2.

Multimedia Programming

PART

VI

Working with 2D and 3D Graphics

CHAPTER 20

Slick graphics can change an average program into an outstanding one. That's because
most of us are visually oriented. We prefer pictures over text descriptions, maps over
directions, and colorful graphs over equations. We also prefer programs that use graphics
to simplify the information they present. In Chapter 7, "Working with the Canvas," you
learned how to use the basic graphics capabilities of the AWT, which were present in
JDK 1.1. JDK 1.2 extends the JDK 1.1 graphics capabilities with the Java 2D API, which
provides comprehensive support for drawing, image processing, and text rendering.
Concurrent with JDK 1.2, but separate from it, JavaSoft also released the Java 3D API.
This API provides support for three-dimensional graphics used in advanced modeling
and virtual reality applications.

In this chapter, you'll explore the Java 2D and Java 3D APIs. You'll learn how the Java
2D API can be used to enhance line drawing, painting, and text rendering operations.
You'll then use the Java 3D API to display and manipulate three-dimensional objects.
When you finish this chapter, you'll be able to use these advanced graphics capabilities
in your programs.

The Java 2D API

The Java 2D API is a very large part of the JDK 1.2 AWT. It consists of the following six
packages, plus numerous classes and interfaces from the `java.awt` package:

- `java.awt.color`
- `java.awt.font`
- `java.awt.geom`
- `java.awt.image`
- `com.sun.java.image.codec.jpeg`
- `java.awt.image.renderable`

Because the 2D API is so large, it is impractical to learn this API by going directly to its
classes and interfaces. Instead, it is easier first to learn the capabilities that it provides,
and then which classes and interfaces are important in providing these capabilities.

The 2D API provides the following general capabilities:

- Graphics drawing—Complete line drawing support, including the capability to
  draw general 2D objects using a variety of line and fill patterns. General graphics
  transformations (such as rotation, scaling, and translation) are supported.

- Image processing and display—Advanced image creation, filtering, compositing,
  and display.

- Advanced text rendering and font support—Font faces are composed of glyphs that are displayed using normal drawing methods. Text can be filled, rotated, scaled, and so on. System-independent fonts can be developed.

- Device-independent graphics—Graphics operations take place in a device-independent user space. User space is then mapped to device-dependent coordinate systems and capabilities.

- Device-dependent graphics translation and display—Uniform rendering automatically performs the necessary conversions between user space and the device space of the target device.

- Advanced color definition—Support for a variety of color models and conversion between models.

By learning to use these capabilities, you can greatly improve the quality of the graphics in your applets and applications.

Moving from `Graphics` to `Graphics2D`

In Chapter 7, you learned how to draw line art and display text and images using the `Graphics` class. The Java 2D API extends the `Graphics` class with the `Graphics2D` class, which is the heart of the 2D API. It lets you do everything that you could with the AWT 1.1 `Graphics` class, plus a whole lot more.

You obtain a reference to a `Graphics2D` object in the same manner as a `Graphics` object. In most cases, you'll simply cast a `Graphics` object to a `Graphics2D` object. The following code shows how this is accomplished using the `paint()` method of the `Component` class:

```
public void paint(Graphics g) {
 Graphics2D g2d = (Graphics2D) g;
 /* Now I can use the methods of Graphics and Graphics2D
    with g2d. */
}
```

The `Graphics2D` class uses two coordinate spaces for drawing graphics, text, and images. The *user coordinate space* is a device-independent logical coordinate space. The origin (0,0) is in the upper-left corner. Horizontal (x) coordinates increase toward the right of the drawing area, and vertical (y) coordinates increase toward the bottom of the drawing area.

Each target rendering device (such as a monitor screen or a printer) has its own separate *device space.* The dimensions, orientation, and display capabilities of the display space vary with each device. The Java 2D rendering system automatically and transparently converts between user space and device space.

The available display devices are described by the GraphicsEnvironment class. The static getLocalGraphicsEnvironment() method returns a GraphicsEnvironment object for the local system. The getAllFonts() method returns a list of all available Font objects. The getScreenDevices() and getPrinterJob() methods provide access to screen and printer devices.

The GraphicsDevice class is used to describe graphics devices, such as screens or printers. Each of these devices may have one or more configurations. For example, a screen may be capable of both 640×480 and 800×600 resolution. The GraphicsConfiguration class is used to describe the configuration of a GraphicsDevice object. The getConfigurations() method of the GraphicsDevice class is used to obtain access to these configurations.

Drawing Graphics

The Shape interface defines the methods supported by all geometrical shapes. This interface is implemented by the following classes of the java.awt.geom and java.awt packages:

- GeneralPath—Defines a general geometric shape.
- Line2D—Defines a line that can be drawn using the 2D API. It is extended by Line2D.Float and Line2D.Double.
- Rectangle—A java.awt class that defines a rectangle.
- RectangularShape—Defines a shape that can be enclosed in a rectangle. It is extended by Arc2D, Ellipse2D, Rectangle2D, and RoundRectangle2D.
- Polygon—A java.awt class that defines a general polygon.
- CubicCurve2D—Defines a segment of a cubic parametric curve. It is extended by CubicCurve2D.Float and CubicCurve2D.Double.
- QuadCurve2D—Defines a segment of a quadratic curve. It is extended by QuadCurve2D.Float and QuadCurve2D.Double.
- Area—Used to specify an arbitrarily shaped area consisting of other shape objects.

These classes are extended by other, more specific shape classes in the java.awt.geom and java.awt packages. Subclasses with the .Float and .Double extensions are used to specify shapes using floating-point coordinates.

The Java 2D API also implements fonts in terms of the Shape interface. Individual characters or character combinations (*ligatures*) are represented as a combination of *glyphs*. Glyphs represent individual shapes that are used to display text using a particular font face. The GlyphSet, GlyphMetrics, and GlyphJustificationInfo classes are used to work with glyphs. However, in most cases you won't use these classes. Instead, you'll simply draw text on the screen using a particular font. The important point to remember is that your text is actually drawn as a set of shapes. This means that you can change the pen and fill style used to draw your text. (Refer to "Pen and Fill Styles" later in this chapter.) You can also rotate, translate, and manipulate text using the same methods that you use for other geometrical objects.

The basic drawing method of the Graphics2D class is draw(). You can use it to draw any object that implements the Shape interface. Graphics2D also supports drawImage() and drawString() methods that are tailored to image and text drawing. Finally, because Graphics2D is a subclass of Graphics, it supports all of the standard Graphics drawing methods.

Listing 20.1 illustrates the basics of line and text drawing using Java 2D. When you run this program, it displays the five geometric objects shown in Figure 20.1. These objects are a diagonal line, a rectangle, a circle, a tetragon, and a rounded rectangle.

FIGURE 20.1.

The Draw2D program displays a variety of geometric figures.

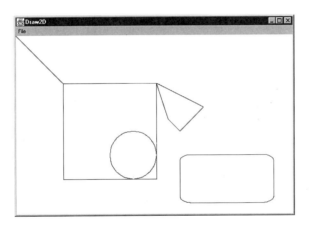

The shapes array contains the five objects shown in Figure 20.1. The elements of this array are created by the createShapes() method. These shapes consist of the following objects from the java.awt.geom package:

- A Line2D.Double object from (0,0) to (100,100).

- A Rectangle2D.Double object with the upper-left corner at (100,100) and a width and height of 200.

- An Ellipse2D.Double object with a bounding box beginning at (200,200) and width and height of 100.

20

WORKING WITH 2D AND 3D GRAPHICS

- A GeneralPath object composed of four line segments.

- A RoundRectangle2D.Double object with the upper-left corner at (350,250), a width of 200, and a height of 100.

The paint() method of the MyCanvas class displays the five objects. It casts its Graphics parameter to a Graphics2D object and then invokes the draw() method of Graphics2D for each of the objects in the shapes array.

LISTING 20.1. THE Draw2D PROGRAM.

```
import java.awt.*;
import java.awt.event.*;
import java.awt.geom.*;
import ju.ch09.MyMenu;
import ju.ch09.MyMenuBar;

public class Draw2D extends Frame {
 static final int numShapes = 5;
 Shape shapes[] = new Shape[numShapes];
 static final int width = 600;
 static final int height = 400;
 MyMenuBar menuBar;
 EventHandler eh = new EventHandler();
 public static void main(String args[]){
  Draw2D app = new Draw2D();
 }
 public Draw2D() {
  super("Draw2D");
  setupMenuBar();
  add("Center",new MyCanvas());
  createShapes();
  setSize(width,height);
  addWindowListener(eh);
  show();
 }
 void createShapes() {
  for(int i=0;i<shapes.length;++i) shapes[i] = null;
  shapes[0] = new Line2D.Double(0.0,0.0,100.0,100.0);
  shapes[1] = new Rectangle2D.Double(100.0,100.0,200.0,200.0);
  shapes[2] = new Ellipse2D.Double(200.0,200.0,100.0,100.0);
  GeneralPath path =
   new GeneralPath(new Line2D.Double(300.0,100.0,400.0,150.0));
  path.append(new Line2D.Double(400.0,150.0,350.0,200.0),true);
  path.append(new Line2D.Double(350.0,200.0,325.0,175.0),true);
  path.append(new Line2D.Double(325.0,175.0,300.0,100.0),true);
  shapes[3] = path;
  shapes[4] = new
RoundRectangle2D.Double(350.0,250.0,200.0,100.0,50.0,25.0);
 }
```

```
void setupMenuBar(){
 Object menuItems[][] = {{"File","Exit"}};
 menuBar = new MyMenuBar(menuItems,eh,eh);
 setMenuBar(menuBar);
}
class MyCanvas extends Canvas {
 public void paint(Graphics graphics) {
  Graphics2D g = (Graphics2D) graphics;
  for(int i=0;i<shapes.length;++i) {
   if(shapes[i]!=null) g.draw(shapes[i]);
  }
 }
}
class EventHandler extends WindowAdapter implements ActionListener,
  ItemListener {
 public void actionPerformed(ActionEvent e){
  String selection=e.getActionCommand();
  if("Exit".equals(selection)){
   System.exit(0);
  }
 }
 public void itemStateChanged(ItemEvent e){
 }
 public void windowClosing(WindowEvent e){
  System.exit(0);
 }
}
}
```

Antialiasing

When graphics and text are drawn to a particular device, they may appear to be somewhat jagged, depending on the device resolution. This effect, known as *aliasing*, occurs because the position of the pixels used to render the drawing differs from their ideal mathematical location. The jagged effect of aliasing can be reduced using a technique known as *antialiasing*, which sets the values of surrounding pixels to smooth out jagged contours. Antialiasing requires a fair amount of computational power and may slow down performance. To use antialiasing, use the setRenderingHints() method of Graphics2D to set the ANTIALIASING hint to ANTIALIAS_ON. You can also set the RENDERING hint to RENDER_QUALITY to improve the overall quality in which graphics and text are rendered. For example, the following code sets both the ANTIALIASING and RENDERING hints:

```
Graphics2D g = (Graphics2D) getGraphics();
g.setRenderingHints(Graphics2D.ANTIALIASING,Graphics2D.ANTIALIAS_ON);
g.setRenderingHints(Graphics2D.RENDERING,Graphics2D.RENDER_QUALITY);
```

20

WORKING WITH
2D AND 3D
GRAPHICS

You can check the state of ANTIALIASING and RENDERING using the getRenderingHints() method of Graphics2D.

Pen and Fill Styles

One of the advantages of the Java 2D API is its support for pen and fill styles. Pen styles can be used to change the type of line used to draw a Shape object. For example, you can change the thickness and pattern of a line so that it is displayed as a thin dotted line. The pen style of an object is specified by an object of a class that implements the Stroke interface. The BasicStroke class provides an implementation of this interface. It allows strokes to be defined based on the following:

- Stroke width
- End and join styles
- Dash pattern and phase

Fill patterns are defined by objects that implement the Paint interface. Three types of fill patterns are defined:

- Solid color fill
- Gradient fill
- Pattern fill

The Color class provides a default implementation of Paint for providing a solid color fill pattern. The GradientPaint class defines a fill pattern as a gradient between two colors. The TexturePaint class implements Paint to define a fill pattern, using a simple image fragment that is repeated uniformly throughout the interior of the object being filled.

Listing 20.2 illustrates the basics of pen and fill styles. Figure 20.2 shows the output generated by this program. Note that it draws the same objects as the Draw2D program in Listing 20.1. It just uses different pen and fill styles.

The PenFill program is essentially the same as Draw2D. The only notable differences are in the paint() method of MyCanvas. The dashPattern array is used to create a dash pattern consisting of a ten-unit dash, followed by a ten-unit space, five-unit dash, and five-unit space. The setStroke() method of Graphics2D is used to define the overall pen style. The CAP_ROUND and JOIN_MITER constants are used to specify the ends and joins of line segments.

The setPaint() method is used to set the background color of the rectangle to blue. The fill() method is used to perform the actual filling of the rectangle.

FIGURE 20.2.

The PenFill *program adds pen and fill styles to* Draw2D.

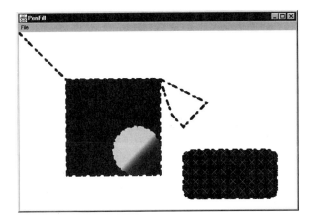

The setPaint() method is also used to set the fill color of the circle to a color gradient between red and green. The color gradient is specified as an object of the GradientPaint class.

The texture variable is assigned a new object of the TexturePaint class. The arguments to the TexturePaint constructor consist of a BufferedImage object containing the fill pattern, a Rectangle2D.Double object identifying the fill area, and the type of interpolation algorithm to be used in filling objects within the area.

The createBufferedImage() method returns a BufferedImage object containing the fill pattern. This fill pattern consists of a 20×20 image that uses a red-blue-green (RGB) color model. The pattern consists of two perpendicular diagonal lines that form an "X" pattern.

LISTING 20.2. THE PenFill PROGRAM.

```
import java.awt.*;
import java.awt.event.*;
import java.awt.geom.*;
import java.awt.image.*;
import ju.ch09.MyMenu;
import ju.ch09.MyMenuBar;

public class PenFill extends Frame {
  static final int numShapes = 5;
  Shape shapes[] = new Shape[numShapes];
  static final int width = 600;
  static final int height = 400;
  MyMenuBar menuBar;
```

continues

20

WORKING WITH
2D AND 3D
GRAPHICS

LISTING 20.2. CONTINUED

```
EventHandler eh = new EventHandler();
public static void main(String args[]){
 PenFill app = new PenFill();
}
public PenFill() {
 super("PenFill");
 setupMenuBar();
 add("Center",new MyCanvas());
 createShapes();
 setSize(width,height);
 addWindowListener(eh);
 show();
}
void createShapes() {
 for(int i=0;i<shapes.length;++i) shapes[i] = null;
 shapes[0] = new Line2D.Double(0.0,0.0,100.0,100.0);
 shapes[1] = new Rectangle2D.Double(100.0,100.0,200.0,200.0);
 shapes[2] = new Ellipse2D.Double(200.0,200.0,100.0,100.0);
 GeneralPath path =
  new GeneralPath(new Line2D.Double(300.0,100.0,400.0,150.0));
 path.append(new Line2D.Double(400.0,150.0,350.0,200.0),true);
 path.append(new Line2D.Double(350.0,200.0,325.0,175.0),true);
 path.append(new Line2D.Double(325.0,175.0,300.0,100.0),true);
 shapes[3] = path;
 shapes[4] = new
RoundRectangle2D.Double(350.0,250,200.0,100.0,50.0,25.0);
 }
 void setupMenuBar(){
  Object menuItems[][] = {{"File","Exit"}};
  menuBar = new MyMenuBar(menuItems,eh,eh);
  setMenuBar(menuBar);
}
class MyCanvas extends Canvas {
 public void paint(Graphics graphics) {
  Graphics2D g = (Graphics2D) graphics;
  float[] dashPattern = {10.0f,10.0f,5.0f,5.0f};
  g.setStroke(new BasicStroke(5,
   BasicStroke.CAP_ROUND,
   BasicStroke.JOIN_MITER,
   10.0f,
   dashPattern,
   0.0f));
  g.draw(shapes[0]);
  g.setPaint(Color.blue);
  g.draw(shapes[1]);
  g.fill(shapes[1]);
  g.setPaint(new GradientPaint(350.0f,200.0f,Color.red,
   325.0f,175.0f,Color.green));
```

```
      g.draw(shapes[2]);
      g.fill(shapes[2]);
      g.setColor(Color.black);
      g.draw(shapes[3]);
      TexturePaint texture = new TexturePaint(
       createBufferedImage(),
       new Rectangle2D.Double(350.0,250,200.0,100.0);
       g.setPaint(texture);
      g.draw(shapes[4]);
      g.fill(shapes[4]);
    }
    BufferedImage createBufferedImage() {
     BufferedImage image =
      new BufferedImage(20,20,BufferedImage.TYPE_INT_RGB);
     Graphics2D g = image.createGraphics();
     g.draw(new Line2D.Double(0.0,0.0,10.0,10.0));
     g.draw(new Line2D.Double(0.0,10.0,10.0,0.0));
     return image;
    }
   }
   class EventHandler extends WindowAdapter implements ActionListener,
     ItemListener {
    public void actionPerformed(ActionEvent e){
     String selection=e.getActionCommand();
     if("Exit".equals(selection)){
       System.exit(0);
     }
    }
    public void itemStateChanged(ItemEvent e){
    }
    public void windowClosing(WindowEvent e){
     System.exit(0);
    }
   }
 }
```

Clipping

In some cases, you may not want to display an entire Shape or Image object. The 2D API allows you to define a *clipping path*, which is a subset of the graphic or image to be displayed. Only the portions of a Shape or Image object that lies within the clipping path are displayed.

The setClip() method of the Graphics class (inherited by Graphics2D) is used to set the current clipping path. The setClip() method takes a Shape object as an argument, and any shape may be used for clipping.

Listing 20.3 illustrates how clipping is implemented. Figure 20.3 shows the output generated by this program. Note that it draws the same objects as the `PenFill` program in Listing 20.2. It just clips the objects to a 300×250 rectangle. The only significant difference between `Clipper` and `PenFill` is the inclusion of the following statement in the `paint()` method of `MyCanvas`:

```
g.setClip(new Rectangle2D.Double(75.0,75.0,300.0,250.0));
```

This statement invokes the `setClip()` method of `Graphics` to set the clipping area to a `Rectangle2D.Double` object, consisting of a 300×250 rectangle located at (75,75). All objects subsequently drawn to the `Graphics2D` object are clipped if they extend beyond this rectangle.

FIGURE 20.3.

The `Clipper` *program adds clipping to* `PenFill`.

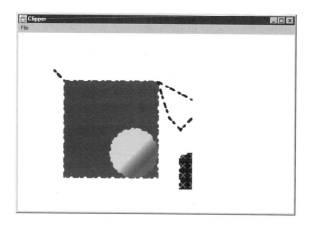

LISTING 20.3. THE `Clipper` PROGRAM.

```
import java.awt.*;
import java.awt.event.*;
import java.awt.geom.*;
import java.awt.image.*;
import ju.ch09.MyMenu;
import ju.ch09.MyMenuBar;

public class Clipper extends Frame {
  static final int numShapes = 5;
  Shape shapes[] = new Shape[numShapes];
  static final int width = 600;
  static final int height = 400;
  MyMenuBar menuBar;
```

```
EventHandler eh = new EventHandler();
public static void main(String args[]){
 Clipper app = new Clipper();
}
public Clipper() {
 super("Clipper");
 setupMenuBar();
 add("Center",new MyCanvas());
 createShapes();
 setSize(width,height);
 addWindowListener(eh);
 show();
}
void createShapes() {
 for(int i=0;i<shapes.length;++i) shapes[i] = null;
 shapes[0] = new Line2D.Double(0.0,0.0,100.0,100.0);
 shapes[1] = new Rectangle2D.Double(100.0,100.0,200.0,200.0);
 shapes[2] = new Ellipse2D.Double(200.0,200.0,100.0,100.0);
 GeneralPath path =
  new GeneralPath(new Line2D.Double(300.0,100.0,400.0,150.0));
 path.append(new Line2D.Double(400.0,150.0,350.0,200.0),true);
 path.append(new Line2D.Double(350.0,200.0,325.0,175.0),true);
 path.append(new Line2D.Double(325.0,175.0,300.0,100.0),true);
 shapes[3] = path;
 shapes[4] = new
RoundRectangle2D.Double(350.0,250,200.0,100.0,50.0,25.0);
}
void setupMenuBar(){
 Object menuItems[][] = {{"File","Exit"}};
 menuBar = new MyMenuBar(menuItems,eh,eh);
 setMenuBar(menuBar);
}
class MyCanvas extends Canvas {
 public void paint(Graphics graphics) {
  Graphics2D g = (Graphics2D) graphics;
  g.setClip(new Rectangle2D.Double(75.0,75.0,300.0,250.0));
  float[] dashPattern = {10.0f,10.0f,5.0f,5.0f};
  g.setStroke(new BasicStroke(5,
   BasicStroke.CAP_ROUND,
   BasicStroke.JOIN_MITER,
   10.0f,
   dashPattern,
   0.0f));
  g.draw(shapes[0]);
  g.setPaint(Color.blue);
  g.draw(shapes[1]);
  g.fill(shapes[1]);
```

continues

20

WORKING WITH
2D AND 3D
GRAPHICS

LISTING 20.3. CONTINUED

```
    g.setPaint(new GradientPaint(350.0f,200.0f,Color.red,
     325.0f,175.0f,Color.green));
    g.draw(shapes[2]);
    g.fill(shapes[2]);
    g.setColor(Color.black);
    g.draw(shapes[3]);
    TexturePaint texture = new TexturePaint(
     createBufferedImage(),
     new Rectangle2D.Double(350.0,250,200.0,100.0);
     g.setPaint(texture);
    g.draw(shapes[4]);
    g.fill(shapes[4]);
   }
  BufferedImage createBufferedImage() {
   BufferedImage image =
    new BufferedImage(20,20,BufferedImage.TYPE_INT_RGB);
   Graphics2D g = image.createGraphics();
   g.draw(new Line2D.Double(0.0,0.0,10.0,10.0));
   g.draw(new Line2D.Double(0.0,10.0,10.0,0.0));
   return image;
  }
 }
class EventHandler extends WindowAdapter implements ActionListener,
  ItemListener {
 public void actionPerformed(ActionEvent e){
  String selection=e.getActionCommand();
  if("Exit".equals(selection)){
   System.exit(0);
  }
 }
 public void itemStateChanged(ItemEvent e){
 }
 public void windowClosing(WindowEvent e){
  System.exit(0);
 }
 }
}
```

Using Text and Fonts

As mentioned earlier in this chapter in the "Drawing Graphics" section, Java font faces are comprised of glyphs, which are drawn in the same manner as other Shape objects. This means that text can be drawn using different pen and fill styles, and it can also be clipped and rotated. You'll learn how to rotate graphics and text in the "Using Transforms" section later in this chapter.

The Font class provides several methods for accessing information about how glyphs are drawn. The getGlyphOutline() method returns a Shape object that describes a glyph code. The getGlyphSet() returns a GlyphSet object that describes a text string. The GlyphSet object provides access to the glyph codes (int values) that define individual glyphs. The getGlyphMetrics() and getGlyphJustificationInfo() methods return metric and justification information about a glyph code.

The Java 2D API also provides extensive support for text formatting and layout. The TextAttribute class is used to specify the style attributes of text.

The TextLayout class is used to format and layout stylized text. The TextLayout class takes care of nearly all of your text processing needs and provides the following capabilities:

- Breaking, wrapping, and rendering text
- Support of bidirectional text (required to display text in some foreign languages)
- Working with multiple baselines
- Access to text metrics (ascent, descent, and so on)
- Font substitution
- Justification support
- Caret and cursor positioning and movement
- Highlighting
- Hit testing (Determining a text offset from the caret position)

TextLayout objects are constructed using String objects and displayed using the draw() method. TextLayout also provides numerous methods for obtaining information about the text that it processes.

Listing 20.4 shows how the TextLayout class is used to create text using multiple fonts. The StyledText program displays three lines of text, as shown in Figure 20.4.

The paint() method of MyCanvas invokes the createStyledStrings() method to create an array of TextLayout objects. The yOffset variable specifies the vertical position where the next string should be displayed. A for statement iterates through the TextLayout array and draws each string at a horizontal position of 100 and a vertical position of 100 plus the value of yOffset. The getAscent(), getDescent(), and getLeading() methods of TextLayout are used to calculate the new value of yOffset.

FIGURE 20.4.

The StyledText *program uses the* TextLayout *class to create and display text using multiple fonts.*

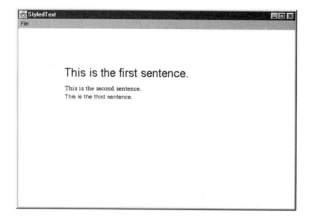

The createStyledStrings() method creates a three-element array of TextLayout, which it uses as a return value. Three fonts are used to provide variety to the text contained in these three strings.

LISTING 20.4. THE StyledText PROGRAM.

```
import java.awt.*;
import java.awt.event.*;
import java.awt.font.*;
import ju.ch09.MyMenu;
import ju.ch09.MyMenuBar;

public class StyledText extends Frame {
 static final int width = 600;
 static final int height = 400;
 MyMenuBar menuBar;
 FontRenderContext frc;EventHandler eh = new EventHandler();
 public static void main(String args[]){
  StyledText app = new StyledText();
 }
 public StyledText() {
  super("StyledText");
  setupMenuBar();
  add("Center",new MyCanvas());
  setSize(width,height);
  addWindowListener(eh);
  show();
 }
 void setupMenuBar(){
  Object menuItems[][] = {{"File","Exit"}};
  menuBar = new MyMenuBar(menuItems,eh,eh);
  setMenuBar(menuBar);
 }
```

```
class MyCanvas extends Canvas {
 public void paint(Graphics graphics) {
  Graphics2D g = (Graphics2D) graphics;frc=g.getFontRenderContext();
  TextLayout[] s = createStyledStrings();
  int yOffset = 0;
  for(int i=0;i<s.length;++i) {
   s[i].draw(g,100,100+yOffset);
   yOffset += s[i].getAscent()+s[i].getDescent()+s[i].getLeading();
  }
 }
}
TextLayout[] createStyledStrings() {
 TextLayout[] s = new TextLayout[3];
 Font f1 = new Font("Helvetica",Font.BOLD,24);
 Font f2 = new Font("TimesRoman",Font.ITALIC,14);
 Font f3 = new Font("Helvetica",Font.PLAIN,12);
 s[0] = new TextLayout("This is the first sentence.",f1,frc);
 s[1] = new TextLayout("This is the second sentence.",f2,frc);
 s[2] = new TextLayout("This is the third sentence.",f3.frc);
 return s;
}
class EventHandler extends WindowAdapter implements ActionListener,
  ItemListener {
 public void actionPerformed(ActionEvent e){
  String selection=e.getActionCommand();
  if("Exit".equals(selection)){
   System.exit(0);
  }
 }
 public void itemStateChanged(ItemEvent e){
 }
 public void windowClosing(WindowEvent e){
  System.exit(0);
 }
 }
}
```

Displaying Images

In addition to its extensive support for drawing graphics and text, the Java 2D API provides additional capabilities for image processing. Images are two-dimensional arrays of pixels. These arrays are often referred to as *raster images* or *rasters*. The color of each pixel is specified by a value that is either a color value or an index to a table of color values. In the first case, the image is said to use a *direct* color model. In the second case, the image uses an *indexed* color model. The Java 2D API supports both types of color models via the DirectColorModel and IndexedColorModel classes, which contain several subclasses that provide support for a variety of specific color models.

The Java 2D API also provides support for image compositing. *Compositing* is the process of rendering an image, graphic, or text based on the colors of objects that have already been rendered. For example, consider displaying a yellow sun on a blue sky. The yellow image can simply replace the pixels of the blue image, or it can blend in with the blue image. Compositing defines this blending process. The Composite interface defines methods that are implemented by classes that support compositing. Composite objects are used by Graphics2D objects when they draw graphics or text, or display images.

The AlphaComposite class provides a default implementation of the Composite interface. AlphaComposite supports the blending of new pixel data with existing pixel data using alpha color values in the new and existing pixel data. The alpha color values identify the transparency of a color using a scale of 0.0 to 1.0. If a value of 1.0 is used, the new pixel data completely replaces existing pixel data. If a value of 0.0 is used, any existing pixel data is used instead of new pixel data. If a number between 0.0 and 1.0 is used, the new and existing pixel data are used in proportion to this value. For example, a value of 0.6 causes the color of the new pixel data to contribute 60% of the value of the composite color and the existing pixel data to contribute 40% of the value. In addition to the alpha values of the new and existing pixel data, a separate alpha scale factor may also be specified. This scale factor ranges from 0.0 to 1.0 and is multiplied by the alpha values of the new and existing colors. In addition to this scale factor, the AlphaComposite class provides additional compositing rules. These rules are implemented as class constants and may be used to specify a particular compositing approach.

Listing 20.5 illustrates how the AlphaComposite class is used to implement compositing. The output of the Composite program is shown in Figure 20.5. It consists of a purple rectangle and a red rectangle. The red rectangle is displayed over the purple rectangle. Compositing is used to blend the colors of the two images together at their point of intersection. The Composite program uses a transparency value of 0.5 by default. You can change this value by supplying a new transparency value between 0.0 and 1.0 as a command-line argument.

The Composite program uses the alpha field variable to store the transparency value that is used to composite the two images. This value is modified if a command-line argument is supplied.

The paint() method of the MyCanvas class creates an AlphaComposite object using the static getInstance() method of the AlphaComposite class. This object uses a source-over-compositing approach and the alpha value specified by the alpha field variable. The setComposite() method of Graphics2D is used to specify the use of the AlphaComposite object.

FIGURE 20.5.

The Composite *program shows how images can be blended together using the* AlphaComposite *class.*

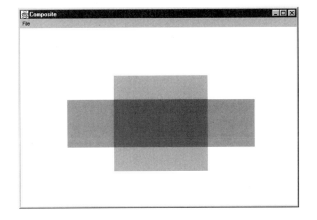

Having set up compositing, the images contained in the image0.gif and image1.gif files are displayed using the drawImage() method of the Graphics class. The first image is the purple rectangle, and the second image is the red rectangle.

LISTING 20.5. THE Composite PROGRAM.

```
import java.awt.*;
import java.awt.event.*;
import java.awt.image.*;
import ju.ch09.MyMenu;
import ju.ch09.MyMenuBar;

public class Composite extends Frame {
 static float alpha = 0.5f;
 static final int width = 600;
 static final int height = 400;
 MyMenuBar menuBar;
 EventHandler eh = new EventHandler();
 public static void main(String args[]){
  if(args.length>0) alpha = (new Float(args[0])).floatValue();
  Composite app = new Composite();
 }
 public Composite() {
  super("Composite");
  setupMenuBar();
  add("Center",new MyCanvas());
  setSize(width,height);
  addWindowListener(eh);
  show();
 }
```

continues

LISTING 20.5. CONTINUED

```java
void setupMenuBar(){
 Object menuItems[][] = {{"File","Exit"}};
 menuBar = new MyMenuBar(menuItems,eh,eh);
 setMenuBar(menuBar);
}
class MyCanvas extends Canvas {
 public void paint(Graphics graphics) {
  Graphics2D g = (Graphics2D) graphics;
  AlphaComposite composite =
   AlphaComposite.getInstance(AlphaComposite.SRC_OVER,alpha);
  g.setComposite(composite);
  Toolkit toolkit = Toolkit.getDefaultToolkit();
  Image image0 = toolkit.getImage("image0.gif");
  Image image1 = toolkit.getImage("image1.gif");
  g.drawImage(image0,200,100,this);
  g.drawImage(image1,100,150,this);
 }
}
class EventHandler extends WindowAdapter implements ActionListener,
  ItemListener {
 public void actionPerformed(ActionEvent e){
  String selection=e.getActionCommand();
  if("Exit".equals(selection)){
   System.exit(0);
  }
 }
 public void itemStateChanged(ItemEvent e){
 }
 public void windowClosing(WindowEvent e){
  System.exit(0);
 }
}
}
```

Using Transforms

One of the unique features of the Java 2D API is that it provides a uniform coordinate
transformation model. This model includes the `AffineTransformation` class, which supports linear transformations between sets of 2D coordinates. A *linear transformation*
calculates new coordinates by multiplying existing coordinates by a scaling factor and
then adding an offset value. The `AffineTransform` class can be used to translate (move),
scale, rotate, flip, and shear graphics, text, and images.

`AffineTransformation` objects are created by specifying a transformation matrix as an argument to the `AffineTransformation()` constructor. This matrix is defined as follows:

$$\begin{bmatrix} m00 & m01 & m02 \\ m10 & m11 & m12 \\ 0 & 0 & 1 \end{bmatrix}$$

The matrix is used to transform a point (x,y) to a new point (x',y') by first extending (x,y) to (x,y,1) and then multiplying the matrix by this point:

$$\begin{bmatrix} m00 & m01 & m02 & x = m00*x + m01*y + m02 \\ m10 & m11 & m12 & y = m10*x + m11*y + m12 \\ 0 & 0 & 1 & 1 = \qquad 1 \end{bmatrix}$$

(x',y') is then set to (m00*x + m01*y + m02,m10*x + m11*y + m12).

The `AffineTransformation` class provides a set of `static` convenience methods that can be used instead of specifying a transformation matrix. These methods are as follows:

- `getTranslateInstance()`—Creates an `AffineTransformation` object that is an (x,y) translation.
- `getRotateInstance()`—Creates an `AffineTransformation` object that is a rotation about a point using a specified angle.
- `getScaleInstance()`—Creates an `AffineTransformation` object that is an xy-scaling.
- `getShearInstance()`—Creates an `AffineTransformation` object that represents a *shearing*. Shearing is a transformation that scales coordinates of one axis (x or y) using coordinates of the other axis.

An `AffineTransformation` object is used by invoking the `transform()` method of the `Graphics2D` class. Multiple transforms can be used by repeatedly invoking `transform()`. The last transformation specified is the first transformation that is used. Once a transformation has been specified, it is used with all graphics, text, and images that are drawn to the `Graphics2D` object.

Listing 20.6 shows how the `AffineTransformation` class is used to transform graphics, text, and images. Figure 20.6 shows the output of the `Transform` program. It rotates the display of a line, a red rectangular image, and text by $\pi/16$ radians.

FIGURE 20.6.

The Transform *program shows how graphics, images, and text can be rotated using the* AffineTransformation *class.*

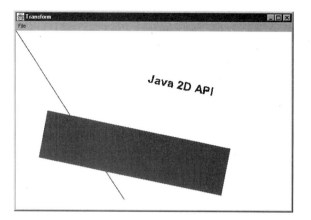

The paint() method of MyCanvas creates an AffineTransform object using the static getRotateInstance() method of the AffineTransform class. The rotation is specified as π/16 radians, which is about 11 degrees. The setTransform() method of Graphics2D is used to put the transform into effect. The following objects are then drawn to the Graphics2D object:

- A line from (0,0) to (300,300)
- The text "Java 2D API"
- The red rectangular image contained in image1.gif

These objects are rotated by π/16 radians when they are rendered.

LISTING 20.6. THE Transform PROGRAM.

```
import java.awt.*;
import java.awt.event.*;
import java.awt.font.*;
import java.awt.geom.*;
import java.awt.image.*;
import ju.ch09.MyMenu;
import ju.ch09.MyMenuBar;

public class Transform extends Frame {
  static final int width = 600;
  static final int height = 400;
  MyMenuBar menuBar;
  EventHandler eh = new EventHandler();
  public static void main(String args[]){
```

```
   Transform app = new Transform();
  }
 public Transform() {
  super("Transform");
  setupMenuBar();
  add("Center",new MyCanvas());
  setSize(width,height);
  addWindowListener(eh);
  show();
 }
 void setupMenuBar(){
  Object menuItems[][] = {{"File","Exit"}};
  menuBar = new MyMenuBar(menuItems,eh,eh);
  setMenuBar(menuBar);
 }
 class MyCanvas extends Canvas {
  public void paint(Graphics graphics) {
   Graphics2D g = (Graphics2D) graphics;
   AffineTransform transform =
    AffineTransform.getRotateInstance(Math.PI/16.0d);
   g.setTransform(transform);
   Line2D.Double shape =
    new Line2D.Double(0.0,0.0,300.0,300.0);
   g.draw(shape);
   g.getFont(new Font("Helvetica",Font.BOLD,24));
   String text = ("Java 2D API");
   g.drawString(text,300,50);
   Toolkit toolkit = Toolkit.getDefaultToolkit();
   Image image = toolkit.getImage("image1.gif");
   g.drawImage(image,100,150,this);
  }
 }
 class EventHandler extends WindowAdapter implements ActionListener,
   ItemListener {
  public void actionPerformed(ActionEvent e){
   String selection=e.getActionCommand();
   if("Exit".equals(selection)){
    System.exit(0);
   }
  }
  public void itemStateChanged(ItemEvent e){
  }
  public void windowClosing(WindowEvent e){
   System.exit(0);
  }
 }
}
```

> **NOTE**
>
> The rotate(), scale(), shear(), and translate() methods of the Graphics2D class can be used in lieu of working with AffineTransformation objects.

> **NOTE**
>
> An affine transformation always translates straight lines into straight lines and parallel lines into parallel lines.

The Java 3D API

The Java 3D API is a separate standard extension API that is used to create three-dimensional graphics, applets, and applications. It can be downloaded from JavaSoft's Web site at http://java.sun.com:80/products/java-media/3D/index.html. It consists of a self-installing executable file. After installing this file, follow the directions in the Readme.txt file for setting up your CLASSPATH. The Java 3D API is supported on Windows, UNIX, Macintosh, and JavaOS platforms. It uses the graphics APIs provided by these operating systems, such as OpenGL, Direct3D, and QuickDraw3D.

The 3D API consists of the two packages, javax.media.j3d and javax.vecmath, and supporting classes and interfaces from the com.sun.j3d.utils package. The javax.media.j3d package provides the basic classes and interfaces that implement the Java 3D API. The javax.vecmath class provides support for vector-based mathematics. The com.sun.j3d.utils package is not documented as part of the Java 3D API, but it contains classes and interfaces that simplify the building of 3D applications and applets.

The `javax.media.j3d` Package

The javax.media.j3d package consists of three interfaces and over 100 classes that support basic 3D operations. The features provided by these classes and interfaces include the following:

- A scene-graph-based programming model—Java 3D applications are compatible with popular approaches to modeling 3D worlds.
- 3D object representation—3D points, rectangles, triangles, text, and other objects are supported.

- 3D transformations—A number of 3D geometric transforms are provided.

- Multiple view support—3D worlds can be viewed from a variety of perspectives. These perspectives can be dynamically changed.

- Dynamic behavior and timing—Java 3D worlds support moving worlds, sophisticated event models, and dynamic sensor objects.

- Lighting—Comprehensive lighting support, including fog, is provided.

- High-performance 3D rendering—The rendering implementation supports many advanced features and may use native 3D rendering support.

- Compatibility support—Java 3D provides hooks for supporting current 3D file formats, including Virtual Reality Markup Language (VRML) 1.0 and VRML 2.0.

- Sound support—Indigenous support for 3D spatial sound is provided.

The classes and interfaces that support these operations were designed using the best features of the OpenGL, QuickDraw3D, Direct3D, and XGL graphics libraries.

The `javax.vecmath` Package

The `javax.vecmath` package consists of a number of classes that implement 3D objects.

The `Tuple3b` class represents a point in 3 space. It is extended by `Color3b`, which implements a 3-byte vector that is used for colors. The `Tuple3f` and `Tuple3d` classes provide floating-point and double-precision 3-space points. The `Tuple4b` class represents a point in 4 space. The `Tuple4f` and `Tuple4d` classes provide floating-point and double-precision representations. The `Color3f`, `Color4b`, and `Color4f` classes are used to represent three- and four-dimensional color values.

The `Point2f`, `Point3f`, `Point3d`, `Point4f`, and `Point4d` classes represent points in 2, 3, and 4 space.

The `Vector2f`, `Vector3f`, `Vector4f`, `Vector3d`, and `Vector4d` classes provide floating-point and double-precision vectors in 2, 3, and 4 space. The `GVector` class provides a general vector implementation.

The `Matrix3f`, `Matrix3d`, `Matrix4f`, and `Matrix4d` classes represent three- and four-dimensional matrices. The `GMatrix` class provides a general matrix implementation.

The `TexCoord2f` and `TexCoord3f` classes represent coordinates in 2 and 3 space.

The `Quat4f` and `Quat4d` classes represent four-dimensional quaternion values.

The `AxisAngle4d` and `AxisAngle4f` classes represent an angle about a vector. `AxisAngle4d` uses double values, and `AxisAngle4f` uses floating-point values.

Using 3D Graphics in Your Programs

A complete treatment of 3D programming with the Java 3D API could fill an entire book by itself. Rather than wading through all the classes of the Java 3D API, I'll shown you a simple 3D application and describe the classes and interfaces that make it work. You can then use this program as a basis for developing your own Java 3D applications and applets.

Listing 20.7 contains the source code of the Draw3D program. This program draws a 3D colored cube in the center of the application window and rotates the cube about the y-axis, as shown in Figure 20.7. In Java 3D, the default coordinate system is a right-handed system, with +y being up, +x horizontal to the right, and +z being outward toward the viewer.

FIGURE 20.7.

The Draw3D *program displays a moving 3D cube.*

The Draw3D program defines a Canvas3D object and assigns it to the canvas3D field variable. The Draw3D() constructor adds the Canvas3D object to the center of the application window. The Canvas3D class provides a canvas for 3D rendering. It is analogous to the Canvas class of java.awt.

The setup3DGraphics() method is invoked by the Draw3D constructor to set up the 3D scene to be rendered. This method creates a SimpleUniverse object. The SimpleUniverse class (from the com.sun.j3d.utils.universe package) simplifies the creation of a virtual 3D world. The getViewingPlatform() method is invoked to retrieve a ViewPlatform object for the universe. The setNominalViewingTransform() method sets up a simple default view of the universe. The Java 3D API provides the capability to view a 3D world from a variety of perspectives. The addBranchGraph() method adds a BranchGraph object to the universe. A BranchGraph is used to define a 3D scene.

The createSceneGraph() method creates the BranchGraph object that specifies the 3D scene to be displayed. It creates a BranchGraph object to be used as a return value and adds a TransformGroup object to it. The TransformGroup is used to define a 3D transformation on objects in the scene. In this case, it is used to rotate a colored cube. The setCapability() method is used to allow the TransformGroup object to be updated during program execution.

The ColorCube class of the com.sun.j3d.utils.geometry package provides a quick and easy way to create a colored 3D cube. This is an undocumented part of the Java 3D API. Without this class, we would have to construct and color our own 3D object. The relative size of the ColorCube object is set to 0.25, and the object is added to the TransformGroup.

A RotationInterpolator object is created to rotate the cube. It is constructed using a default Alpha object and the TransformGroup object. The Alpha object defines a default timing to be used in the rotation. A BoundingSphere object is constructed to define the bounds of the rotation. This object is centered at the origin and has a radius of 100. The setSchedulingBounds() method is used to associate the BoundingSphere object with the RotationInterpolator object. The RotationInterpolator object is then added to the TransformGroup object.

Note that no paint() method is needed to render the 3D scene. The Java 3D rendering engine automatically paints the Canvas3D object.

LISTING 20.7. THE Draw3D PROGRAM.

```
import java.awt.*;
import java.awt.event.*;
import javax.media.j3d.*;
import javax.vecmath.*;
import com.sun.j3d.utils.geometry.ColorCube;
import com.sun.j3d.utils.universe.*;
import ju.ch09.MyMenu;
import ju.ch09.MyMenuBar;

public class Draw3D extends Frame {
 Canvas3D canvas3D = new Canvas3D(null);
 static final int width = 600;
 static final int height = 400;
 MyMenuBar menuBar;
 EventHandler eh = new EventHandler();
 public static void main(String args[]){
  Draw3D app = new Draw3D();
 }
```

continues

LISTING 20.7. CONTINUED

```
public Draw3D() {
 super("Draw3D");
 setupMenuBar();
 add("Center",canvas3D);
 setSize(width,height);
 setup3DGraphics();
 addWindowListener(eh);
 show();
}
void setup3DGraphics() {
 // Create a simple universe that is used for the 3D world.
 SimpleUniverse universe = new SimpleUniverse(canvas3D);
 // Get the ViewPlatform for this universe and set its view.
 universe.getViewingPlatform().setNominalViewingTransform();
 // Create a scene and add it to the universe.
 universe.addBranchGraph(createSceneGraph());
}
BranchGroup createSceneGraph() {
 // Create the return object
 BranchGroup branchGroup = new BranchGroup();
 // Create a transform group for creating a 3D transformation.
 TransformGroup transGroup = new TransformGroup();
 // Allow the transform group to be updated during execution.
 transGroup.setCapability(TransformGroup.ALLOW_TRANSFORM_WRITE);
 // Add the transform group to the branch group
 branchGroup.addChild(transGroup);
 // Add a color cube to the transform group
 transGroup.addChild(new ColorCube(0.25));
 // Create a 3D transformation object.
 RotationInterpolator ri = new RotationInterpolator(
  new Alpha(), transGroup);
 BoundingSphere bounds =
  new BoundingSphere(new Point3d(0.0,0.0,0.0), 100.0);
 ri.setSchedulingBounds(bounds);
 transGroup.addChild(ri);
 return branchGroup;
}
void setupMenuBar(){
 Object menuItems[][] = {{"File","Exit"}};
 menuBar = new MyMenuBar(menuItems,eh,eh);
 setMenuBar(menuBar);
}
class EventHandler extends WindowAdapter implements ActionListener,
  ItemListener {
 public void actionPerformed(ActionEvent e){
  String selection=e.getActionCommand();
  if("Exit".equals(selection)){
   System.exit(0);
  }
```

```
   }
   public void itemStateChanged(ItemEvent e){
   }
   public void windowClosing(WindowEvent e){
    System.exit(0);
   }
  }
}
```

Summary

In this chapter, you explored the Java 2D and Java 3D APIs. You learned how the Java 2D API can be used to enhance line drawing, painting, and text rendering, and you created applications that demonstrated these capabilities. You also learned about the Java 3D API and used it to display and manipulate three-dimensional objects. In the next chapter, you'll learn how to add multimedia capabilities to your applets and applications.

CHAPTER 21

Using Audio and Video

One of the most interesting features that you can add to an applet or application is the capability to play multimedia files, such as audio or video. Recognizing the need for a multimedia API, JavaSoft developed the Java Media Framework (JMF), which consists of an API for playing and receiving multimedia files in a variety of audio and video formats. The JMF includes API packages, media stream/file players, codecs, and the Java Sound Engine.

In this chapter, you'll learn how to use the capabilities provided by the JMF to incorporate audio and video support into your applications and applets. You'll learn the basics of audio and video file formats, learn how to use the JMF player, and investigate the JMF API. You'll also learn about JMF's support for the Real-Time Transport Protocol (RTP). When you finish this chapter, you'll be able to add multimedia features to your applications and applets.

Audio and Video Basics

There are a number audio and video file formats that are used to store sounds and moving images. Each of these formats represents a compromise between fidelity, range, file size, and performance. For example, there is a limited range of frequencies that can be detected by the human ear. Within this range, the fidelity of an audio file is determined by the rate at which the sound is sampled (samples/second), the amount of information per sample (8, 16, or 32 bits), and the number of sound channels (mono or stereo). The greater the sample rate and sample size, the greater the file size. File size can be offset by the use of compression, but at higher compression rates there may be detectable impacts on system performance. Specialized *codecs* (compressors/decompressors) may be used to improve performance.

Video format tradeoffs are similar to audio tradeoffs. However, the size of most video files dwarfs that of audio files. Video fidelity is a function of the size of a video frame (in pixels), the number of colors per pixel, and the number of frames per second. Compression is extremely important in video because video files are so large. Specialized codecs are required for use in nearly all video formats.

Examples of common audio formats are as follows:

- WAVE—The Microsoft Windows audio file format.
- AIFF—The Audio Interchange File Format, typically used with Macintosh and Silicon Graphics computers.
- AU—The Sun audio file format.

- RMF—The Rich Music Format, an audio file format created by Headspace, Inc. for online playback through the Beatnik Plug-in.
- MIDI (type 1 and type 2)—The Musical Instrument Digital Interface, a digital format for musical instruments.

The use of these audio formats is organized along political lines. The most common audio format used with Microsoft Windows-based systems is Microsoft's Wave format (.WAV). The most common format used with Solaris is the Sun Audio Format (.AU). Historically, new audio file formats were introduced for use with different computer hardware and software platforms. The RMF format is intended to be a platform-independent format. The MIDI format is not based on sound sampling but is a digital format for identifying the instruments, rhythms, and notes used in a musical composition. In this respect, it is more like digital sheet music or an audio animation.

Examples of common video formats are as follows:

- MPEG—A sequence of video formats developed by the Moving Picture Experts Group.
- MOV—The Apple QuickTime video format.
- VIV—A streaming video format developed by Vivo Software, Inc.
- AVI—The Microsoft Video for Windows file format.
- ActiveMovie—Microsoft's streaming video format.

Of these video formats, MPEG produces the highest-quality video using the smallest file size. This is a result of the superior compression techniques it uses. The QuickTime and AVI formats were developed for use with the Macintosh and PC. The QuickTime format is more popular, and QuickTime players are available for a number of operating system platforms. The Vivo and ActiveMovie formats support *streaming video*, or video that is downloaded a little at a time from an Internet stream instead of as an entire file. The Vivo format is an excellent format for use with Web applications. ActiveMovie is Microsoft's venture into this area.

NOTE

Apple Computer provides an implementation of QuickTime that is independent of the JMF. It is referred to as QuickTime for Java and is available from Apple's Web site at http://www.apple.com/quicktime/.

The Java Media Framework

The Java Media Framework is an API for using audio and video within Java applications and applets. This API supports the playing of a wide variety of media types. It also provides examples of media-playing applications and applets. The JMF is available from JavaSoft's Web site at `http://www.javasoft.com/products/java-media/jmf/index.html`. It is packaged as a self-extracting, self-installing file. To install the JMF on Windows 95, 98, or NT, your system should include the following:

- ActiveMovie
- Direct X 2.0 (or greater)

Both ActiveMovie and Direct X 2.0 are available from Microsoft at `http://www.microsoft.com/directx/resources/devdl.htm`.

The media types supported by JMF 1.0 include the following:

- QuickTime (`.mov`)
- Video for Windows (`.avi`)
- Vivo (`.viv`)
- Sun Audio (`.au`)
- Audio Interchange File Format (`.aiff`)
- Wave (`.wav`)
- Musical Instrument Digital Interface (`.midi`)
- Rich Music Format (`.rmf`)
- Groupe Speciale Mobile (`.gsm`)
- MPEG-1 (`.mpg`)
- MPEG Audio (`.mp2`)
- Real-Time Transport Protocol (`.rtp`)

The JMF Player

The best way to get a feel for the capabilities provided by JMF is to use the JMF Player. If you installed the JMF under Windows, a JMF program group should have been created for you. Double-click the JMF Player icon to launch the JMF Player. Figure 21.1 shows its initial display.

FIGURE 21.1.
The JMF Player.

Select Open File from the File menu to launch an Open file dialog box. Navigate to the
samples\media subdirectory of the directory in which you installed the JMF. You should
find some example media files in this directory. Open Sample1.mov to play a QuickTime
movie. Figure 21.2 shows a snapshot of the movie that is displayed.

FIGURE 21.2.
*Playing a
QuickTime movie
with the JMF
Player.*

When you are finished playing the movie, click the pause icon in the lower-left corner of
the application window. Then open the Sample2.mpg movie from the same directory.
Figure 21.3 provides a snapshot of how this movie is displayed.

FIGURE 21.3.
*Playing an MPEG
movie with the
JMF Player.*

You can also try some of the audio samples that are included with the JMF. I was
impressed by the clarity of the sound that was played on my notebook computer.

The JMF API

Having had a taste of the capabilities provided by JMF, I'll bet you can't wait to start
using it in your applets and applications. We'll cover the JMF API first and then illustrate
the use of this API with an application and an applet.

The JMF API consists of the `javax.media` and the `javax.media.protocol` packages. These packages are standard extension APIs. The `javax.media` package is fairly large, consisting of 13 interfaces and 27 classes. Twenty-six of these classes and interfaces define events and event listeners. Event handling is a big part of media playing. However, we'll cover the other classes and interfaces before we introduce the JMF events and event handlers.

The `Player` interface is the most important element of the `javax.media` package. Classes that implement this interface are used to play actual multimedia objects. The `Player` interface extends the `MediaHandler`, `Controller`, and `Duration` interfaces. The `realize()` method (inherited from `Controller`) is used to construct the media-specific portions of a `Player` object. The `start()` method signals that the media should be played as soon as possible. Other methods are provided for accessing the visual component and controllers associated with the `Player` object.

The `Controller` interface extends the `Clock` interface to manage the state of a media object. Classes that implement this interface manage the following media states:

- Unrealized—The initial state of a `Controller`.
- Realizing—The `Controller` gathers all resources required to operate.
- Realized—The `Controller` has completed its realization.
- Prefetching—The `Controller` is filling its buffers with media content.
- Prefetched—The prefetch has been completed.
- Started—The `Controller` is rendering the prefetched media.

A `Controller` defines methods and generates events that support the management of these states. The `Player` interface is a subinterface of `Controller` that supports the playing of media.

The `Control` interface defines methods for exerting control over a media object. The `getControlComponent()` method returns a GUI component used to control a media object. The `CachingControl` interface extends the `Control` interface to define methods used to control the loading of media files/data. The `GainControl` interface defines methods for getting and setting audio signal gain.

The `MediaHandler` interface is implemented by classes that manage media that is retrieved from a `DataSource` object (defined in `javax.media.protocol`). This interface is extended by the `Player` and `MediaProxy` interfaces. The `MediaProxy` interface is implemented by classes that transform data from one `DataSource` object to another `DataSource` object.

The Manager class provides access to system-dependent media resources via static methods. The createPlayer() method is used to create a Player object that is capable of playing a media object referenced by a MediaLocator, URL, or DataSource object. Other methods allow DataSource and TimeBase objects to be created.

The MediaLocator class describes the location of media to be played. MediaLocator objects are constructed by passing a URL object, or a string that represents a URL, to the MediaLocator constructor. The MediaLocator class provides methods for accessing the media's location. The PackageManager class maintains a store of package prefix names used to locate protocol-handling and other media-related classes.

The Time class encapsulates time as used by media players. It provides time constants and methods for accessing time down to the nanosecond level. The TimeBase interface defines methods for a constant, uninterruptable source of time. The Clock interface defines methods for managing time with respect to the playing of media. The Duration interface defines the getDuration() method for obtaining information about the duration of a media object.

The `javax.media` Event Hierarchy

As previously mentioned, event handling is a big part of media playing. The javax.media package defines a variety of events to provide feedback to media handling software. The MediaEvent interface is implemented by all JMF events. These event handling classes form the class hierarchy.

ControllerEvent—Base interface for all Controller events.

TransitionEvent—Generated when a Controller changes to a new state.

StartEvent—Generated when a Controller enters the Start state.

RealizeCompleteEvent—Generated when a Controller changes from the Realizing to the Realized state.

PrefetchCompleteEvent—Generated when a Controller moves from the Prefetching to the Prefetched state.

StopEvent—Generated when a Controller enters the Stop state.

DataStarvedEvent—Generated when a Controller has lost data or stopped receiving data.

DeallocateEvent—Generated when the resources of a Controller have been deallocated and need to be reallocated to continue media operations.

EndOfMediaEvent—Generated when a Controller has reached the end of its media and is stopping.

RestartingEvent—Generated when a Controller changes from the Started state to the Prefetching state.

StopByRequestEvent—Generated when a Controller is stopped as a result of its stop() method being invoked.

StopAtTimeEvent—Generated when a Controller reaches its stop time.

StopTimeChangeEvent—Generated by a Controller when its stop time is updated.

ControllerClosedEvent—Generated when a Controller is no longer operational.

ControllerErrorEvent —Generated when an error occurs that causes a Controller to stop functioning.

ConnectionErrorEvent—Generated when an error occurs within a DataSource object.

ResourceUnavailableEvent—Generated when a Controller is unable to access a required resource.

InternalErrorEvent—Generated as the result of an internal error in a Controller.

CachingControlEvent—Generated by a CachingControl object when the caching state changes.

MediaTimeSetEvent—Generated when the media of a Controller has had its time updated.

RateChangeEvent—Generated when the rate of a Controller changes.

DurationUpdateEvent—Generated when the duration of a Controller changes.

GainChangeEvent—Generated by a GainControl object when its state changes.

The ControllerListener interface is used to handle events generated by Controller objects. These events consist of ControllerEvent and all of its subclasses. The GainChangeListener interface is used to handle the GainChangeEvent, which is generated by GainControl objects.

The `javax.media.protocol` Package

The javax.media.protocol package has nine interfaces and six classes that are used to transfer data from its source to a media player. These classes and interfaces are as follows:

- DataSource—An abstract class that encapsulates a media protocol handler. It implements the Controls and Duration interfaces, and provides methods for connecting to a media object and controlling the transfer of data from the object.

- PullDataSource—A subclass of DataSource whose data is "pulled" by a media player.

- URLDataSource—A subclass of PullDataSource whose data is retrieved from a URL.

- PushDataSource—A subclass of DataSource whose data is "pushed" to a media player.

- Positionable—An interface that is implemented by a DataSource that allows the media position within a stream to be changed.

- PullSourceStream—An interface that defines a stream that reads data from a DataSource.

- PushSourceStream—An interface that defines a stream used by a DataSource to push data to a media player.

- Seekable—An interface that is implemented by SourceStream objects that support repositioning within the stream.

- SourceStream—Defines methods that are implemented by a media data stream.

- SourceTransferHandler—Interface implemented to support handling of PushSourceStream objects.

- RateConfiguration—An interface for accessing streams that operate at a specific rate.

- RateConfigureable—An interface that is implemented by a DataSource that supports multiple rate configurations.

- RateRange—A class that maintains information about the range of rates at which data can be transferred from a DataSource.

- ContentDescriptor—A class that is used to describe the type of content contained in a DataSource.

- Controls—An interface that defines methods for obtaining objects that control other objects.

In many cases, you won't have to effect the actual transfer of data from a source to a Player. As you'll see in the MediaApplication application in Listing 21.1, Player implementations transfer data as part of their prefetch processing.

> **NOTE**
>
> Future versions of JMF will support media capture and media conferencing.

Adding Audio and Video Clips to Your Programs

Now that you've been introduced to the classes and interfaces of the JMF API, we'll put together an example of an application and applet that uses these classes and interfaces to play audio and video media. The `MediaApplication` program in the following section presents a simplified version of the JMF Player. This application can play all of the media that the JMF Player can play, but its GUI features have been minimized so that the application source code can fit in and be described within a single chapter. After presenting the `MediaApplication` program, the next section shows how to include media playing capabilities in an applet.

The `MediaApplication` Program

The `MediaApplication` program in Listing 21.1 covers all of the basics of media playing using the JMF. Make sure that you have the JMF installed before running the program. Its initial display is shown in Figure 21.4. The program isn't as pretty as the JMF Player, but at 20% of its size, it is much easier to understand. The `MediaApplication` program is capable of playing all of the media types that the JMF Player plays.

Select Open from the File menu and open the `Sample1.mov` file that is contained in the `samples\media` subdirectory of the JMF directory. Note that the program informs you that it is loading the media player and the media (see Figure 21.5).

When the appropriate media player and the selected media have been loaded, the program plays the media in the center of the application window. Note that a media control slider is displayed at the bottom of the application window, as shown in Figure 21.6.

Select Open from the File menu to play other media files, such as the MPEG movie or audio files that are provided with the JMF. Note that the old GUI components are removed and new ones are added when switching between media files.

FIGURE 21.4.

The MediaApplication *opening display.*

FIGURE 21.5.

The user is notified that the media is loading.

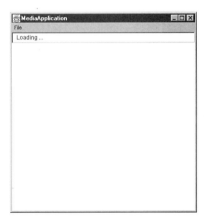

FIGURE 21.6.

The MediaApplication *displays a QuickTime movie.*

LISTING 21.1. THE MediaApplication SOURCE CODE.

```java
import java.awt.*;
import java.awt.event.*;
import ju.ch09.*;
import javax.media.*;

public class MediaApplication extends Frame
  implements ControllerListener {
// Declare media-related variables
Player player = null;
Player newPlayer = null;
Component visualComponent = null;
Component controllerComponent = null;

// Other variables
Object menuItems[][] = {{"File","Open","-","Exit"}};
MenuItemHandler mih = new MenuItemHandler();
MyMenuBar menuBar = new MyMenuBar(menuItems,mih,mih);
int screenWidth = 400;
int screenHeight = 400;
TextField text = new TextField();
String directory = ".";

public static void main(String args[]){
 MediaApplication app = new MediaApplication();
}
public MediaApplication() {
 super("MediaApplication");
 setMenuBar(menuBar);
 add("North",text);
 setSize(screenWidth,screenHeight);
 addWindowListener(new WindowEventHandler());
 show();
}
String getFileName() {
 // Display file dialog
 FileDialog dialog = new FileDialog(MediaApplication.this,
 "Open Media File", FileDialog.LOAD);
 dialog.setDirectory(directory);
 dialog.show();
 if(dialog.getFile()==null) return null;
 directory = dialog.getDirectory();
 String file = directory + dialog.getFile();
 return file;
}
Player createPlayer(String fileName) {
 Player newPlayer;
 try {
  MediaLocator locator = new MediaLocator("file:"+fileName);
  if(locator == null) return null;
  newPlayer = Manager.createPlayer(locator);
```

```
    }catch(Exception ex) {
      text.setText(ex.toString());
      return null;
    }
    return newPlayer;
  }
  void realizeComplete() {
    visualComponent = player.getVisualComponent();
    controllerComponent = player.getControlPanelComponent();
    if(visualComponent != null)
     add("Center",visualComponent);
    if(controllerComponent != null)
     add("South",controllerComponent);
    validate();
    player.prefetch();
  }
  void prefetchComplete() {
    text.setText("");
    if(player.getTargetState() != Controller.Started)
     player.start();
  }
  void controllerError() {
    player.close();
    if(visualComponent != null) remove(visualComponent);
    if(controllerComponent != null) remove(controllerComponent);
    validate();
    visualComponent = null;
    controllerComponent = null;
    player.removeControllerListener(this);
    player = null;
  }
  void controllerClosed() {
    if(visualComponent != null) remove(visualComponent);
    if(controllerComponent != null) remove(controllerComponent);
    player = null;
    System.gc();
    System.runFinalization();
    if(newPlayer!=null) {
     player = newPlayer;
     newPlayer = null;
     player.addControllerListener(this);
     text.setText("Loading ...");
     player.realize();
    }
    validate();
  }
  public synchronized void controllerUpdate(ControllerEvent e) {
   // Determine event type
   if(e instanceof RealizeCompleteEvent) realizeComplete();
   else if(e instanceof PrefetchCompleteEvent) prefetchComplete();
```

continues

LISTING **21.1.** CONTINUED

```
  else if(e instanceof ControllerErrorEvent) controllerError();
  else if(e instanceof ControllerClosedEvent) controllerClosed();
 }
 class MenuItemHandler implements ActionListener, ItemListener {
  public void actionPerformed(ActionEvent ev){
   String s=ev.getActionCommand();
   if(s.equals("Exit")){
    System.exit(0);
   }else if(s=="Open"){
    // Get the name of the media file
    String fileName = getFileName();
    if(fileName == null) return;
    // Create player for file
    newPlayer = createPlayer(fileName);
    // Stop old player
    boolean closingPlayer = false;
    if(player!=null){
     closingPlayer = true;
     player.close();
    }
    if(newPlayer == null) return;
    if(!closingPlayer) {
     player = newPlayer;
     player.addControllerListener(MediaApplication.this);
     text.setText("Loading ...");
     player.realize();
    }
   }
  }
  public void itemStateChanged(ItemEvent e){
  }
 }
 class WindowEventHandler extends WindowAdapter {
  public void windowClosing(WindowEvent e){
   // Stop the player
   if(player!=null) {
    player.close();
    while(player!=null) {
     // wait a half second
     try{
      Thread.currentThread().sleep(500);
     }catch(Exception ex) {
     }
    }
   }
   System.exit(0);
  }
 }
}
```

How the `MediaApplication` Works

The `MediaApplication` class implements the `ControllerListener` interface so that it can handle `Controller`-related events involved in the loading and playing of media. The `player` and `newPlayer` variables are used to manage the current `Player` object and any new `Player` object that is created. The `visualComponent` and `controllerComponent` variables reference the visual component displayed by a `Player` object and the component that is used to control the `Player`.

The user plays a new media file by opening it using the Open menu item in the File menu. To understand how this works, we'll start with the `actionPerformed()` method of the `MenuItemHandler` class and trace the thread of execution.

When the Open menu item is selected, the `actionPerformed()` method invokes the `getFileName()` method to retrieve the name of the file to be opened. The `getFileName()` method displays a File Open dialog box to the user. If the user selects a file, `actionPerformed()` passes the file name to the `createPlayer()` method. The `createPlayer()` method creates a `Player` object by first creating a `MediaLocator` object that identifies the selected media file's location, and then invoking the `createPlayer()` method of the `Manager` class to create a `Player` object that is suitable for the media. The new `Player` object is then returned to `actionPerformed()`.

The `actionPerformed()` method checks to see if there is currently a media file being played. If so, it invokes the `close()` method of the current `Player` object. The starting of the new player is then put off until the current player generates the `ControllerClosedEvent`.

If there is no current player, `actionPerformed()` adds the `MediaApplication` instance as a listener for `Controller`-related events and then invokes the `realize()` method of the new `Player` object. The `TextField` is also updated with a loading message.

At this point, a new media file has been opened. If there was no previous file being played, the new `Player` is in the Realizing state. Otherwise, the old `Player` is about to be changed into the Stop state. The rest of the media playing involves handling of `ControllerEvent` events.

The `controllerUpdate()` method implements the `ControllerListener` interface and provides a central point for handling all `Controller`-related events. Remember that all `Player` objects are also `Controller` objects. The `controllerUpdate()` method checks the event to see which subclass of `ControllerEvent` it is an instance of. It then invokes one of the following four methods, depending on the type of event:

- `realizeComplete()`—This method handles the `RealizeCompleteEvent`, which is the first event generated by a new player after its `realize()` method has been invoked. The `realizeComplete()` method gets the media's visual component (for video files) and adds it to the center of the application window. It also gets the media's controller component (the slider) and adds that to the bottom of the application window. The `validate()` method of the `Container` class is invoked so that the application's frame is laid out with the new components. The `prefetch()` method of the `Player` class is invoked to begin prefetching media data into available buffers.

- `prefetchComplete()`—This method handles the `PrefetchCompleteEvent`, which occurs after media data has been prefetched into the `Player` object's buffers. The `prefetchComplete()` method removes the loading message in the `TextField` and invokes the `Player` object's `start()` method to start playing the media file.

- `controllerError()`—This method handles the `ControllerErrorEvent`, which is generated as the result of any errors encountered by the `Player`. It closes the `Player` and removes its visual and controller components. It then removes the `MediaAppplication` instance as an event listener for the `Player`.

- `controllerClosed()`—This method handles the `ControllerClosedEvent`, which occurs after the current `Player` object has been closed. The `controllerClosed()` method removes the `Player`'s visual and controller components, sets the `Player` to `null`, and then garbage-collects the resources associated with the `Player`. If a new player has been selected, it sets up the `Player`'s `ControllerListener` and invokes the `Player`'s `realize()` method. The `TextField` is updated with the loading message.

As you can see from the `MediaApplication`'s description, very little code is required to set up a `Player`. Once a `Player` has been set up, the bulk of the processing involves handling the events that occur as the `Player` moves from state to state.

The `MediaApplet` Applet

The `MediaApplet`, shown in Listing 21.2, shows how media playing capabilities can be incorporated into an applet. The `MediaApplet` is a simplification of `MediaApplication` that plays a single QuickTime file. The HTML file shown in Listing 21.3 is used to run `MediaApplet`. Before running the applet, copy the `Sample1.mov` file from the `samples\media` directory of JMF to your `ju\ch21` directory. When you open `media.htm` with `appletviewer`, it displays the applet shown in Figure 21.7. `MediaApplet` can be easily tailored to play other media files.

FIGURE 21.7.

The MediaApplet *displays a QuickTime movie.*

Having covered MediaApplication, the source code of MediaApplet will be easy to understand. The MediaApplet class implements the ControllerListener interface and declares the player, visualComponent, and controllerComponent variables in the same manner as MediaApplication.

The init() method lays out the applet and creates the Player object. It creates a URL object for the Sample1.mov file and then passes this URL to the createPlayer() method of the Manager class. It then adds the MediaApplet instance as an event handler for ControllerEvent events and invokes the Player's realize() method.

The stop() method responds to the stopping of the applet by closing the current Player and waiting until it has been completely closed. It does this to keep the media from being played in the absence of a visible applet.

The realizeComplete(), prefetchComplete(), controllerError(), controllerClosed(), and controllerUpdate() methods handle Controller-related events in the same manner as MediaApplication.

LISTING 21.2. THE MediaApplet SOURCE CODE.

```
import java.applet.*;
import java.awt.*;
import java.awt.event.*;
import ju.ch09.*;
import javax.media.*;
import java.net.*;

public class MediaApplet extends Applet
```

continues

LISTING 21.2. CONTINUED

```java
 implements ControllerListener {
// Declare media-related variables
Player player = null;
Component visualComponent = null;
Component controllerComponent = null;

// Other variables
TextField text = new TextField();

public void init() {
 setLayout(new BorderLayout());
 add("North",text);
 // Create player
 try {
  URL url = new URL(getDocumentBase(),"Sample1.mov");
  player = Manager.createPlayer(url);
 } catch(Exception ex) {
  text.setText(ex.toString());
 }
 if(player != null) {
  player.addControllerListener(this);
  text.setText("Loading ...");
  player.realize();
 }else text.setText("Unable to play media.");
}
public void stop() {
 if(player!=null) player.close();
 while(player!=null) {
 // wait a half second
  try{
   Thread.currentThread().sleep(500);
  }catch(Exception ex) {
  }
 }
}
void realizeComplete() {
 visualComponent = player.getVisualComponent();
 controllerComponent = player.getControlPanelComponent();
 if(visualComponent != null)
  add("Center",visualComponent);
 if(controllerComponent != null)
  add("South",controllerComponent);
 validate();
 player.prefetch();
}
void prefetchComplete() {
 text.setText("");
 if(player.getTargetState() != Controller.Started)
  player.start();
```

```
}
void controllerError() {
 player.close();
 if(visualComponent != null) remove(visualComponent);
 if(controllerComponent != null) remove(controllerComponent);
 validate();
 visualComponent = null;
 controllerComponent = null;
 player.removeControllerListener(this);
 player = null;
}
void controllerClosed() {
 if(visualComponent != null) remove(visualComponent);
 if(controllerComponent != null) remove(controllerComponent);
 player = null;
 validate();
}
public synchronized void controllerUpdate(ControllerEvent e) {
 // Determine event type
 if(e instanceof RealizeCompleteEvent) realizeComplete();
 else if(e instanceof PrefetchCompleteEvent) prefetchComplete();
 else if(e instanceof ControllerErrorEvent) controllerError();
 else if(e instanceof ControllerClosedEvent) controllerClosed();
 }
}
```

LISTING 21.3. THE media.htm FILE.

```
<HTML>
<HEAD>
<TITLE>A Media-Playing Applet</TITLE>
</HEAD>
<BODY>
<APPLET CODE="MediaApplet.class" HEIGHT=400 WIDTH=400>
</APPLET>
</BODY>
</HTML>
```

The Real-Time Transport Protocol (RTP) Session Manager API

The JMF also provides support for the *Real-Time Transport Protocol (RTP)*. RTP is a protocol for transferring audio and video data in real-time from a media server to media players. It is a streaming protocol and does not guarantee error-free delivery of data. Typical media players drop late or error packets in order to keep up with new packets that are being received. RTP is designed to use the UDP transport protocol. It is supported by both Microsoft and Netscape and promises to be a popular protocol for streaming audio and video over the Internet. RTP is described in RFC 1889, which is available at `http://www.cis.ohio-state.edu/rfc/rfc1889`.

JMF supports RTP playback (client-side RTP) through the RTP Session Manager API. This API is contained in the `javax.medi.rtp` package. The RTP Session Manager API was not fully implemented at the time of this writing.

Summary

In this chapter, you learned how to use the capabilities provided by the JMF to incorporate audio and video support into your applications and applets. You covered the basics of audio and video file formats, learned how to use the JMF player, and investigated the JMF API. You also learned about JMF's support for RTP. In the next chapter, you'll learn how to create Java-based animations for use in applets and applications.

CHAPTER 22

Creating Animations

IN THIS CHAPTER

This chapter shows you how to include animation sequences in your window programs. It identifies the basic elements of implementing an animation and then describes approaches to improving the quality of an animation's display by selectively repainting parts of a window and using the MediaTracker class to support the loading of the images used in an animation. When you finish this chapter, you'll be able to include animation in your window programs.

Animation Basics

While including animation sequences in your Java programs may at first appear to be complicated, it is, in fact, rather easy once you learn the basics. Animations are nothing more than the rapid display of still images such that the pattern of image display causes the appearance of movement for the objects contained in the image. To create an animation, you need to produce the sequence of objects that are to be displayed and then write a Java program that will display that sequence at a particular display rate.

For many, the hardest part of developing an animation is producing the images that are to be displayed. This part requires drawing skills and is completely separate from Java programming. Don't fret if you are unable to easily draw these animation sequences. Chances are that you're better at it than most. The important point of this chapter is to learn how to display, in the form of an animation, the sequences that you do come up with.

Many animations display their image sequences in a looping fashion. A looping animation gives the appearance that it is much longer than it actually is and it can run indefinitely. Looping animations also require fewer image frames. If your animation displays 10 to 20 image frames per second and you want it to run for a minute, you will need 600 to 1,200 images. That's a lot of work for a one-minute animation. It is much easier to develop a small but varied looping animation and have it loop several times during the course of a minute.

The major parameter of an animation, besides the type and quality of the images it displays, is the number of image frames it displays per-second. This is typically a fixed number between 5 and 25. The more frames per-second that are displayed, the smoother the animation appears to be. For example, television is 30 frames per-second. The frames-per-second parameter translates into a frame delay parameter that is used to determine how long a program should wait before it displays the next image frame. This is typically measured in milliseconds. For example, frames-per-second rates of 5, 10, and 20 translate into frame delays of 200, 100, and 50 milliseconds.

A common approach to implementing an animation is to create a program thread that runs in an infinite loop and displays the frames of the animation sequence one-at-a-time, waiting frame-delay milliseconds between each frame's display.

A Simple Animation

In order to get a better understanding of the basics of the animation process, you can develop a simple, character-based animation. The source code of the SimpleAnimationApp program is shown in Listing 22.1.

LISTING 22.1. THE SOURCE CODE OF THE SimpleAnimationApp PROGRAM.

```java
import java.awt.*;
import java.awt.event.*;

public class SimpleAnimationApp extends Frame implements Runnable {
 Thread animation;
 // Set the frame delay
 int frameDelay = 100;
 // The objects to be displayed
 String frames[] = {"*","**","***","****","*****","****","***","**","*"};
 int numFrames = frames.length;
 int currentFrame = 0;
 long lastDisplay = 0;
 int screenWidth = 200;
 int screenHeight = 200;
 public static void main(String args[]) {
  SimpleAnimationApp app = new SimpleAnimationApp();
 }
 public SimpleAnimationApp() {
  super("Simple Animation");
  setup();
  setSize(screenWidth,screenHeight);
  addWindowListener(new WindowEventHandler());
  show();
  animation = new Thread(this);
  animation.start();
 }
 void setup() {
  setupMenuBar();
  setFont(new Font("default",Font.BOLD,18));
 }
 void setupMenuBar() {
  MenuBar menuBar = new MenuBar();
  Menu fileMenu = new Menu("File");
  MenuItem fileExit = new MenuItem("Exit");
```

continues

22

CREATING
ANIMATIONS

LISTING 22.1. CONTINUED

```java
    fileExit.addActionListener(new MenuItemHandler());
    fileMenu.add(fileExit);
    menuBar.add(fileMenu);
    setMenuBar(menuBar);
  }
  public void paint(Graphics g) {
   g.drawString(frames[currentFrame],60,60);
  }
  public void run() {
   // The animation loop
   do {
    long time = System.currentTimeMillis();
    if(time - lastDisplay > frameDelay) {
     repaint();
     try {
      Thread.sleep(frameDelay);
     }catch(InterruptedException ex){
     }
     ++currentFrame;
     currentFrame %= numFrames;
     lastDisplay = time;
    }
   } while (true);
  }
  class MenuItemHandler implements ActionListener, ItemListener {
   public void actionPerformed(ActionEvent ev){
    String s=ev.getActionCommand();
    if(s=="Exit"){
     System.exit(0);
    }
   }
   public void itemStateChanged(ItemEvent e){
   }
  }
  class WindowEventHandler extends WindowAdapter {
   public void windowClosing(WindowEvent e){
    System.exit(0);
   }
  }
}
```

Compile and run SimpleAnimationApp. Your program's display should look like the one shown in Figure 22.1.

FIGURE 22.1.

A simple animation.

A string of asterisks is modulated to give the appearance of movement.

While this short animation is by no means in line for any awards, it does illustrate all the basic elements of more complex and entertaining animations.

The SimpleAnimationApp class declares the animation Thread, the frameDelay variable, the array of frames[] used to implement the animation's display, the numFrames variable, the currentFrame variable, the time of the lastDisplay of a frame, and the standard menu bar and window size variables.

The setup of the SimpleAnimationApp program is fairly standard, with the exception of the creation of the animation thread at the end of the class constructor and the invocation of the animation thread's start() method.

The paint() method contains a single statement that is used to display a string of asterisks on the console window.

The run()method implements the animation loop. It checks the current system time and the time of the last image display to see if it is time to display a new frame. It uses the currentTimeMillis() method of the System class to read the current time in milliseconds. If it is time to display another frame, the run() method invokes the repaint() method to display the current frame and then tries to sleep for frameDelay milliseconds. It updates the currentFrame using modular arithmetic and changes the time of lastDisplay.

A Graphics Animation

Because the SimpleAnimationApp program provides all the basic elements required of an animation, we can easily modify the animation to support graphics. Figures 22.2 through 22.5 provide four stick figures I drew using the Windows Paint program. These crude figures can be used to create an animation of a stick figure that attempts to fly or exercise.

FIGURE 22.2.

stickman1.gif.

FIGURE 22.3.

stickman2.gif.

FIGURE 22.4.

stickman3.gif.

FIGURE 22.5.

stickman4.gif.

You may easily substitute your own figures for the ones used in this example.

The source code of the GraphicAnimationApp program is shown in Listing 22.2.

LISTING 22.2. THE SOURCE CODE OF THE GraphicAnimationApp PROGRAM.

```
import java.awt.*;
import java.awt.event.*;
```

```java
public class GraphicAnimationApp extends Frame implements Runnable {
 Thread animation;
 int frameDelay = 100;
 Image frames[];
 int numFrames;
 int currentFrame = 0;
 long lastDisplay = 0;
 int screenWidth = 400;
 int screenHeight = 400;
 public static void main(String args[]) {
  GraphicAnimationApp app = new GraphicAnimationApp();
 }
 public GraphicAnimationApp() {
  super("Graphic Animation");
  setup();
  setSize(screenWidth,screenHeight);
  addWindowListener(new WindowEventHandler());
  show();
  animation = new Thread(this);
  animation.start();
 }
 void setup() {
  setupMenuBar();
  setFont(new Font("default",Font.BOLD,18));
  Toolkit toolkit = getToolkit();
  frames = new Image[4];
  // Load the animation frames
  frames[0] = toolkit.getImage("stickman1.gif");
  frames[1] = toolkit.getImage("stickman2.gif");
  frames[2] = toolkit.getImage("stickman3.gif");
  frames[3] = toolkit.getImage("stickman4.gif");
  numFrames = frames.length;
 }
 void setupMenuBar() {
  MenuBar menuBar = new MenuBar();
  Menu fileMenu = new Menu("File");
  MenuItem fileExit = new MenuItem("Exit");
  fileExit.addActionListener(new MenuItemHandler());
  fileMenu.add(fileExit);
  menuBar.add(fileMenu);
  setMenuBar(menuBar);
 }
 public void paint(Graphics g) {
  g.drawImage(frames[currentFrame],125,80,this);
 }
 public void run() {
  // The animation loop
  do {
   long time = System.currentTimeMillis();
```

continues

LISTING 22.2. CONTINUED

```
   if(time - lastDisplay > frameDelay) {
    repaint();
    try {
     Thread.sleep(frameDelay);
    }catch(InterruptedException ex){
    }
    ++currentFrame;
    currentFrame %= numFrames;
    lastDisplay = time;
   }
  } while (true);
 }
 class MenuItemHandler implements ActionListener, ItemListener {
  public void actionPerformed(ActionEvent ev){
   String s=ev.getActionCommand();
   if(s=="Exit"){
    System.exit(0);
   }
  }
  public void itemStateChanged(ItemEvent e){
  }
 }
 class WindowEventHandler extends WindowAdapter {
  public void windowClosing(WindowEvent e){
   System.exit(0);
  }
 }
}
```

When you run GraphicAnimationApp, your display should look like the one shown in Figure 22.6.

FIGURE 22.6.

The Graphic-
AnimationApp *pro-
gram display.*

Unless you have a really fast computer and video card, your program display probably has some very noticeable flickering. Don't worry about that problem now. You'll learn about ways to improve the quality of an animation's display in the following section. For now, just focus on how you modified the SimpleAnimationApp program to support graphic-based animation.

The GraphicAnimationApp program is similar to the SimpleAnimationApp program. These are the differences between the two programs.

- In GraphicAnimationApp, the frames[] array was changed from an array of String objects to an array of Image objects.

- In GraphicAnimationApp, the setup() method was updated to create a Toolkit object and use it to load the stickman images.

These simple changes were all that was needed to convert the program from a simple text-based animation to a graphics-based animation.

Improving Animation Display Qualities

The GraphicAnimationApp program has some serious deficiencies in the way that it displays animation images. The first and probably the most noticeable problem is that it tries to start displaying the images before they are completely loaded. This is an easy problem to solve using the MediaTracker class.

The MediaTracker class provides the capability to manage the loading of image files. You use the addImage()method to add an image to the list of images being tracked. After adding an image to a MediaTracker object, you can check on the image or all images managed by the MediaTracker object using the access methods provided by the MediaTracker class.

The other major problem with the animation's display is that the entire screen is repainted with each new frame, which causes a significant amount of flickering. This image flickering can be mitigated by limiting the area of the window that is updated with each new image. The repaint() and update() methods of the component class provide this capability.

You are already familiar with limited screen repainting from using the repaint() method in Chapter 7, "Working with the Canvas." The update() method provides the capability to update a Graphics object without first clearing the current image. This allows successive images to be displayed as marginal increments to the currently displayed image.

Another option to improving an animation's display quality is to change the frame delay. By decreasing the number of frames-per-second being displayed, you are able to lower the rate at which flickering occurs. However, you do this at the expense of the overall quality of your animation, because higher frame display rates tend to smooth out any gaps between successive images.

An Updated Graphics Animation

The GraphicUpdateApp program shows how to use the MediaTracker class, together with limited repainting and frame-delay adjustments, to improve the quality of the GraphicAnimationApp program. Its source code is shown in Listing 22.3.

LISTING 22.3. THE SOURCE CODE OF THE GraphicUpdateApp PROGRAM.

```java
import java.awt.*;
import java.awt.event.*;

public class GraphicUpdateApp extends Frame implements Runnable {
 Thread animation;
 int frameDelay = 200;
 Image frames[];
 int numFrames;
 int currentFrame = 0;
 long lastDisplay = 0;
 boolean fullDisplay = false;
 MediaTracker tracker;
 int screenWidth = 400;
 int screenHeight = 400;
 public static void main(String args[]) {
  GraphicUpdateApp app = new GraphicUpdateApp();
 }
 public GraphicUpdateApp() {
  super("Updated Graphic Animation");
  setup();
  pack();
  setSize(screenWidth,screenHeight);
  addWindowListener(new WindowEventHandler());
  show();
  animation = new Thread(this);
  animation.start();
 }
 void setup() {
  setupMenuBar();
  setFont(new Font("default",Font.BOLD,18));
  Toolkit toolkit = getToolkit();
  frames = new Image[4];
  // Load animation frames
```

```
      frames[0] = toolkit.getImage("stickman1.gif");
      frames[1] = toolkit.getImage("stickman2.gif");
      frames[2] = toolkit.getImage("stickman3.gif");
      frames[3] = toolkit.getImage("stickman4.gif");
      numFrames = frames.length;
      tracker = new MediaTracker(this);
      // Use the MediaTracker object to manage the frames
      for(int i=0;i<numFrames;++i) tracker.addImage(frames[i],i);
    }
    void setupMenuBar() {
     MenuBar menuBar = new MenuBar();
     Menu fileMenu = new Menu("File");
     MenuItem fileExit = new MenuItem("Exit");
     fileExit.addActionListener(new MenuItemHandler());
     fileMenu.add(fileExit);
     menuBar.add(fileMenu);
     setMenuBar(menuBar);
    }
    public void paint(Graphics g) {
     if(allLoaded())
      g.drawImage(frames[currentFrame],125,80,this);
     else{
      String stars = "*";
      for(int i=0;i<currentFrame;++i) stars += "*";
      g.drawString(stars,60,60);
     }
    }
    boolean allLoaded() {
     for(int i=0;i<numFrames;++i) {
      if(tracker.statusID(i,true) != MediaTracker.COMPLETE) return false;
     }
     return true;
    }
    public void run() {
     // The animation loop
     do {
      long time = System.currentTimeMillis();
      if(time - lastDisplay > frameDelay) {
       if(allLoaded()) {
        if(fullDisplay) repaint (115,160,160,90);
        else{
         fullDisplay = true;
         repaint();
        }
       }else repaint();
       try {
        Thread.sleep(frameDelay);
       }catch(InterruptedException ex){
       }
```

continues

LISTING 22.3. CONTINUED

```
  ++currentFrame;
    currentFrame %= numFrames;
    lastDisplay = time;
    }
  } while (true);
}
class MenuItemHandler implements ActionListener, ItemListener {
  public void actionPerformed(ActionEvent ev){
   String s=ev.getActionCommand();
   if(s=="Exit"){
    System.exit(0);
   }
  }
  public void itemStateChanged(ItemEvent e){
  }
 }
 class WindowEventHandler extends WindowAdapter {
  public void windowClosing(WindowEvent e){
   System.exit(0);
  }
 }
}
```

When you run GraphicUpdateApp, it will display an animated string of asterisks while the image files are being loaded. After that, it will immediately display the image animation. This reduces the unsightly flickering caused when an image is displayed while it is being loaded.

Notice how GraphicUpdateApp implements the limited area repainting. You can run your mouse over the image display to determine the boundaries of the repaint area.

You should also notice that GraphicUpdateApp displays images at a slower rate. The frame-delay rate was increased from 100 microseconds to 200 microseconds, decreasing the frame display rate by a factor of 2.

The changes made to GraphicAnimationApp by GraphicUpdateApp consist of the declaration of the fullDisplay and tracker variables and modifications to the setup(), paint(), and run() methods. In addition, the allLoaded() method was created. The following summarizes the changes that were made.

- The fullDisplay variable is used to ensure that a full display of the stickman was accomplished before attempting a limited display using the repaint() method. The tracker variable is used to refer to a MediaTracker object.

- The setup() method is updated to create the MediaTracker object and to add the images being loaded with this object.

- The `paint()` method was updated to draw the images after they've been loaded and to draw asterisk strings before the images are loaded.

- The `allLoaded()` method uses the `statusID()` method of the `MediaTracker` class to determine whether all images have been completely loaded.

- The `run()` method has been modified to use the `allLoaded()` method and the `fullDisplay` variable to determine whether it should repaint the entire screen or only a limited portion of it.

The Animation API

Although it wasn't included in the JMF version 1.0, Sun intends to incorporate an Animation API in future versions of the JMF. The Animation API will provide a standard set of animation capabilities and will consist of two packages, referred to as Sprite and Scripting. The Sprite package will provide classes and methods for working with 2D images. The Scripting package will allow animations to be defined as scripted images. A scripting engine and animation player will be provided. The player will be capable of synchronizing animation effects with other JMF players. When it becomes available, the Animation API will provide a platform-independent solution for high-end business presentations, computer-aided training, games, and entertainment software.

Summary

This chapter showed how to include animation sequences in your window programs. It identified the basic elements of implementing an animation and described approaches to improving the quality of an animation's display. It showed you how to selectively repaint parts of a window and how to use the `MediaTracker` class to support the loading of the images used in an animation. Chapter 23, "Integrating Speech and Telephony Capabilities," completes Part VI, "Multimedia Programming," by discussing the Speech and Telephony APIs.

CHAPTER 23

Integrating Speech and Telephony Capabilities

In the previous chapters of Part 6, you learned a variety of approaches to making user interfaces more lively and attractive by incorporating multimedia features. Some of the most interesting new technologies in user interface design allow users and computers to talk to each other. Speech recognition enables users to translate speech into commands, data, and text, and simplifies the interface between the user and the computer. Speech synthesis enables the computer to provide output to the user via the spoken word. Although these technologies have been available for a few years, they haven't yet been integrated into mainstream software applications. The Java Speech API, which is being developed by Sun and several other companies, will bridge this gap and make speech capabilities standard features in Java applications.

One of the most common devices that we use to speak and listen is the telephone. Mobile devices, such as the Nokia 9000i, are being developed that integrate computer and telephone capabilities. The Java Telephony API is designed to incorporate telephony features into Java applications. This API will let you place and answer calls from within a Java application, provide touch-tone navigation, and manage multiple telephone connections. A number of advanced telephony capabilities are also being planned.

In this chapter, you'll preview the Speech and Telephony APIs and learn about the capabilities they will provide. You'll learn how Java Speech will be used to add speech recognition and synthesis to your programs, and how Java Telephony will be used to develop sophisticated telephony applications. When you finish this chapter, you'll understand what these two important APIs can bring to your Java programs.

The Java Speech API

The Java Speech API provides the capability to incorporate speech technology (both input and output) into Java applets and applications. When it becomes available, it will support speech-based program navigation, speech-to-text translation, and speech synthesis. The Java Speech API is being developed by Sun in collaboration with IBM, AT&T, Texas Instruments, Phillips, Apple, and other companies. At the time of this writing, the following specifications had been developed:

- Java Speech API Specification—Defines the packages used to implement basic Java Speech capabilities, speech recognition, and speech synthesis.

- Java Speech Programmer's Guide—Describes how to use the Java Speech API to develop speech-enabled applications.

- Java Speech Grammar Format (JSGF) Specification—Describes the JSGF and explains how it is used to create platform-independent speech recognition grammars. These grammars identify the words that a user speaks and their meaning in particular program contexts.

- Java Speech Markup Language (JSML) Specification—Describes the role of JSML and shows how it's used to mark up text documents for use with speech synthesizers.

These products are available at the Java Speech Web site, located at
`http://java.sun.com:80/products/java-media/speech/index.html`.

The Speech API consists of the following three packages:

- `javax.speech`—Provides classes and interfaces that support audio connectivity and manage the use of speech processing engines.

- `javax.speech.recognition`—Provides classes and interfaces that support speech recognition.

- `javax.speech.synthesis`—Provides classes and interfaces that support speech synthesis.

The `javax.speech` package consists of the following classes and interfaces:

- `Central`—Class that provides central access (via `static` methods) to all capabilities of the Speech API.

- `Engine`—Interface that is implemented by speech recognition and synthesis engines.

- `EngineAttributes`—Defines the attributes that are supported by an `Engine` object.

- `EngineCentral`—Provides the operating modes of a speech `Engine` in terms of `EngineModeDesc` objects.

- `EngineModeDesc`—Defines an `Engine` operating mode.

- `EngineList`—A collection of `EngineModeDesc` objects.

- `AudioManager`—Interface that defines methods for controlling audio input and output and managing audio events.

- `VocabManager`—Interface that defines methods for managing words that are used by a speech engine.

- `Word`—Encapsulates speakable words.

- SpeechEvent—The superclass of all speech events.
- AudioEvent—Subclass of SpeechEvent that is generated by speech Engine objects based on audio input and output processing.
- AudioListener—Defines methods for handling AudioEvent objects.
- AudioAdapter—Implementation of the AudioListener interface.
- EngineEvent—Reports changes in speech Engine status.
- EngineListener—Defines methods for handling EngineEvent objects.
- EngineAdapter—Implementation of the EngineListener interface.

The following sections cover the javax.speech.recognition and javax.speech.synthesis packages.

Speech Recognition

Speech recognition allows computers to listen to a user's speech and determine what the user has said. It can range from simple, discrete command recognition to continuous speech translation. Although speech recognition has made much progress over the last few years, most recognition systems still make frequent errors. These errors can be reduced by using better microphones, reducing background noise, and constraining the speech recognition task. Speech recognition constraints are implemented in terms of grammars that limit the variety in user input. The JSGF provides the capability to specify *rule grammars*, which are used for speech recognition systems that are command- and control-oriented. These systems only recognize speech as it pertains to program operation and do not support general dictation capabilities.

Even with the constraints posed by grammars, errors still occur and must be corrected. Almost all applications that employ speech recognition must provide error-correction facilities.

Speech recognition is supported by the javax.speech.recognition package, which consists of 15 interfaces and 19 classes. These classes and interfaces make up four major groups: Recognizer, Grammar, Rule, and Result.

The Recognizer interface extends the Engine interface to provide access to a speech recognition engine. RecognizerAttributes and RecognizerModeDesc are used to access the attributes and operational modes of the Recognizer. Recognizer objects generate RecognizerEvent objects as they change state during speech processing. The RecognizerInterface defines methods for handling these events. The

RecognizerAdapter class provides a default implementation of this interface. The AudioLevelEvent is generated as a result of a change in the audio level of a Recognizer. The RecognizerAudioListener interface defines methods for handling this event, and the RecognizerAudioAdapter class provides a default interface implementation.

The Grammar interface provides methods for handling the grammars used by a Recognizer. It is extended by RuleGrammar and DictationGrammar, which support rule grammars and dictation grammars. The GrammarSyntaxDetail class is used to identify errors in a grammar. The GrammarEvent class is used to signify the generation of Result object that matches a Grammar. The GrammarListener interface defines methods for handling this event, and the GrammarAdapter class provides a default implementation of this interface.

The Rule class encapsulates rules that are used with a RuleGrammar. It is extended by RuleAlternatives, RuleCount, RuleName, RuleParse, RuleSequence, RuleTag, and RuleToken, which specify different aspects of grammar rules.

The Result interface provides access to the recognition results generated by a Recognizer. The FinalResult interface is used for results that have been finalized (accepted or rejected). It is extended by FinalRuleResult and FinalDictationResult to provide additional information for RuleGrammar and DictationGrammar objects. The ResultToken interface provides access to a single word of a Result. The ResultEvent class is used to signal the status of results that are generated by a Recognizer. It is handled via the ResultListener interface and the default ResultAdapter class. The GrammarResultAdapter class is used to handle both ResultEvent and GrammarEvent objects.

The SpeakerManager interface is used to manage speaker profiles for a Recognizer.

Speech Synthesis

Speech synthesis is the opposite of speech recognition. It allows computers to generate spoken output to users. It can take the form of bulk text-to-speech translation, or of intricate speech-based responses that are integrated into an application's interface.

Speech synthesis systems must satisfy the two main requirements of understandability and naturalness. Understandability is improved by providing adequate pronunciation information to speech generators. This eliminates "guesses" on the part of the speech synthesizer. JSML is used to provide pronunciation information, as required. Naturalness is improved by using a non-mechanical voice and managing emphasis, intonation, phrasing, and pausing. JSML also provides markup capabilities that control these speech attributes.

When you're synthesizing speech, it is often desirable to select attributes of the voice that is generated. For example, you might want to choose between male and female voices or old and young voices. The Speech API provides control over these features. In addition, text that is to be synthesized can be marked up with event markers that cause events to be generated as they are processed. Event handlers can be designed to manipulate graphical interface components in synchronization with speech synthesis. For example, you can design a speaker's face that changes facial expressions as it "talks."

The flexibility of the synthesis component of the Speech API is provided by JSML. JSML, like HTML, is an SGML-based markup language. JSML allows text to be marked up using the following synthesis-related information:

- Paragraph and sentence boundaries
- Pronunciation of words and other text elements
- Pauses
- Emphasis
- Pitch
- Speaking rate
- Loudness

These capabilities may not have your computer reading poetry, but they will allow you to greatly enhance any speech that it generates. Listing 23.1 provides an example of a JSML file.

LISTING 23.1. AN EXAMPLE JSML FILE.

```
<?XML version="1.0" encoding="UCS-2"?>
<JSML>
<PARA><SENT>This is the <EMP>first</EMP> sentence of
the first paragraph.</SENT> <SENT>This is the second
sentence.</SENT><BREAK SIZE = "large"/><SENT>This is the
<EMP>last</EMP> sentence of this paragraph.</SENT></PARA>

<PARA><PROS RATE="+10%" VOL=".9"><SENT>This is the second
paragraph.</SENT></PARA>
</JSML>
```

The first line identifies the file as being XML version 1.0. The `<JSML>` and `</JSML>` tags surround the JSML markup. Within these tags are two paragraphs marked by the `<PARA>` and `</PARA>` tags. The first paragraph consists of three sentences marked by `<SENT>` and `</SENT>`. The second paragraph has a single sentence.

The word first is surrounded by <EMP> and </EMP>. This signifies that the word "first" should be emphasized. The <BREAK SIZE="large"/> tag specifies that a long pause should occur between the second and third sentences.

In the second paragraph, the <PROS RATE="+10%" VOL=".9"> tag is an example of a *prosody tag*. Prosody tags control the timing, intonation, and phrasing of speech. The RATE attribute specifies that the speech rate should be increased by 10%. The VOL attribute specifies that the volume of speech should be set at 90% of its maximum.

The example JSML file illustrates the use of JSML tags. However, the markup language is much richer than indicated by the example. For more information on JSML, download the JSML specification from the Java Speech Web site.

JSML is a subset of the eXtensible Markup Language (XML), which is a subset of the Standard Generalized Markup Language (SGML). JSML looks like HTML with different tags. (HTML is also a subset of SGML.) Figure 23.1 shows the relationship between JSML, XML, HTML, and SGML.

FIGURE 23.1.

The relationship between JSML and other markup languages.

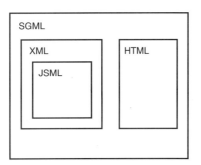

The Java Speech API supports speech generation via the javax.speech.synthesis package. This package provides the following five interfaces and six classes:

- Synthesizer—Extends Engine to implement a synthesizer engine.
- SynthesizerAttributes—Provides access to the control attributes of a Synthesizer.
- SynthesizerModeDesc—Used to specify an operational mode for a Synthesizer.
- SynthesizerEvent—Event generated by a Synthesizer as it changes state.
- SynthesizerListener—Defines methods for handling SynthesizerEvent objects.
- SynthesizerAdapter—An implementation of the SynthesizerListener interface.
- Speakable—An interface for providing JSML text to a Synthesizer.

- SpeakableEvent—Event generated by a Speakable object that identifies the state of JSML processing.
- SpeakableListener—Defines methods for handling SpeakableEvent objects.
- SpeakableAdapter—An implementation of the SpeakableListener interface.
- Voice—Allows the age and gender of a voice to be specified.

To use the synthesizer package, invoke the createSynthesizer() method of the Central class to create a Synthesizer object. Pass an argument of the SynthesizerModeDesc class to createSynthesizer() to specify the Synthesizer mode. Invoke the allocate() method of the Synthesizer (inherited from Engine) to start up the Synthesizer's engine. After that, use the speak() and speakPlainText() methods to put text in the Synthesizer's input queue.

The Java Telephony API

The Java Telephony API (JTAPI) is a set of APIs that provide telephony capabilities for Java applications. It supports basic telephony capabilities, such as call placement and call answering, and advanced capabilities, such as call centers and media streams. JTAPI provides both direct control over telephony resources and indirect access through networked resources. This means that you can create server applications that provide telephony resources over a network, and client applications that use these resources.

The JTAPI consists of the following 18 packages:

- javax.telephony—Provides the core classes and interfaces used by all telephony applications.
- javax.telephony.capabilities—Provides support for basic call and connection capabilities.
- javax.telephony.events—Defines the basic events used in all telephony applications.
- javax.telephony.callcenter—Provides support for developing call center applications.
- javax.telephony.callcenter.capabilities—Provides capabilities such as routing and automated call distribution used in call center applications.
- javax.telephony.callcenter.events—Defines the events used in call center applications.
- javax.telephony.callcontrol—Provides call control features, such as call hold, call transferring, and conferencing.

- `javax.telephony.callcontrol.capabilities`—Extends the interfaces of the basic `javax.telephony.capabilities` package to support call control applications.

- `javax.telephony.callcontrol.events`—Defines the events used in call control applications.

- `javax.telephony.media`—Supports media streams (touch tone and non-touch tone) used in telephony media-exchange applications.

- `javax.telephony.media.capabilities`—Defines the `MediaTerminalConnectionCapabilities` interface, which supports media streaming applications.

- `javax.telephony.media.events`—Defines the events used with media streams.

- `javax.telephony.phone`—Provides control over the physical features of telephone equipment.

- `javax.telephony.phone.capabilities`—Provides interfaces for controlling equipment components.

- `javax.telephony.phone.events`—Defines the events used with the `javax.telephone.phone` package.

- `javax.telephony.privatedata`—Provides classes for accessing telephone hardware switches.

- `javax.telephony.privatedata.capabilities`—Provides an interface that is used to access the capabilities provided by `javax.telephony.privatedata`.

- `javax.telephony.privatedata.events`—Defines the events used with the `javax.telephone.privatedata` package.

23

INTEGRATING
SPEECH AND
TELEPHONY

Although the number of packages provided with JTAPI may seem ominous, basic telephony applications are constructed using a few common elements of the `javax.telephony` package. The `Terminal` interface is used to provide access to a physical hardware device at the endpoint of a telephone connection. For example, telephone sets are accessed as `Terminal` objects. The `TerminalConnection` interface provides physical access to a telephone connection, while the `Connection` interface models a logical connection between a `Call` object and an `Address` object. An instance of the `Call` interface represents an actual telephone call. The `Address` interface is used with a telephone number, or in Internet telephony applications, an IP address combined with other endpoint information. The `Provider` interface is used to access a telephony/service provider software element.

The JTAPI home page, located at `http://java.sun.com/products/jtapi/index.html`, provides information about the current status of the JTAPI project.

Summary

In this chapter, you were introduced to the Speech and Telephony APIs and learned about their planned capabilities. You learned how Java Speech will be used to add speech recognition and synthesis to Java programs and how Java Telephony will be used to develop sophisticated telephony applications. This was the last chapter of Part VI. In Part VII, you'll learn how to develop component-based Java software using JavaBeans.

Creating JavaBeans

PART
VII

CHAPTER 24

The Software Component Assembly Model

In this book you develop almost all of your applications and applets from scratch because you're trying to learn Java. Once you become comfortable in Java programming and go out to develop real-world Java applications and applets, you won't be so eager to start from scratch. You'll want to use available off-the-shelf Java components whenever possible.

Java components are available in a number of forms. For example, you can go down to your local software superstore and purchase a set of Java API packages. You can then use these new APIs to create objects that are instances of the classes and interfaces of the new APIs. You're familiar with this process because you've been learning to do this with the API of JDK 1.2.

If you purchase a visual Java development tool, such as Symantec's Visual Café for Java, you'll be able to drag and drop GUI components onto the interface design of your applications and applets. Some of these GUI components may be new components that are not included with the JDK 1.2. Many of these components are made available as Java beans.

You don't need to purchase a visual design tool to get access to Java beans. Many beans are available for download via the Web. You can use these beans with freely available visual design tools, such as the JavaBeans Development Kit (BDK) from JavaSoft.

In this chapter, you'll be introduced to the JavaBeans software component model. You'll learn how the software component model works and how software components are used to simplify the development of complex software. You'll study the features of component-based software development and learn how JavaBeans supports these features. When you finish this chapter, you'll understand how JavaBeans are used in component-based software development.

> **NOTE**
>
> This chapter introduces the concepts of the software component model and summarizes how JavaBeans supports these concepts. Chapter 26, "Developing Beans," takes a detailed look at the JavaBeans API and shows how to develop simple beans.

Components and Containers

JavaBeans are Java software components that are designed for maximum reuse. They are often visible GUI components, but can also be invisible algorithmic components.

They support the software component model pioneered by Microsoft's Visual Basic and Borland's Delphi. This model focuses on the use of components and containers.

Components are specialized, self-contained software entities that can be replicated, customized, and inserted into applications and applets. Containers are simply components that contain other components. A container is used as a framework for visually organizing components. Visual development tools allow components to be dragged and dropped into a container, resized, and positioned.

You are familiar with the concept of components and containers from your study of the AWT. The components and containers of the JavaBeans component model are similar in many ways to the Component and Container classes of the AWT.

- Components come in a variety of different implementations and support a wide range of functions.

- Numerous individual components can be created and tailored for different applications.

- Components are contained within containers.

- Components can also be containers and contain other components.

- Interaction with components occurs through event handling and method invocation.

In other ways, the components and containers of JavaBeans extend beyond the Component and Container classes of the AWT.

- JavaBeans components and containers are not restricted to the AWT. Almost any kind of Java object can be implemented as a JavaBean.

- Components written in other programming languages can be reused in Java software development via special Java interface code. You'll learn how to use non-Java components, such as Component Object Model (COM) objects in Chapter 54, "Dirty Java."

- Components written in Java can be used in other component implementations, such as ActiveX, via special interfaces referred to as bridges. You'll also study bridges in Chapter 54, "Dirty Java."

The important point to remember about JavaBeans components and containers is that they support a hierarchical software development approach where simple components can be assembled within containers to produce more complex components. This capability allows software developers to make maximum reuse of existing software components when creating new software or improving existing software. Figure 24.1 summarizes the use of components and containers.

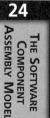

24

THE SOFTWARE
COMPONENT
ASSEMBLY MODEL

FIGURE 24.1.

Using components and containers.

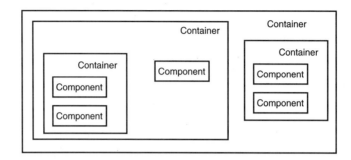

Introspection and Discovery

Component interfaces are well-defined and may be discovered during a component's execution. This feature, referred to as introspection, allows visual programming tools to drag and drop a component onto an application or applet design and dynamically determine what component interface methods and properties are available. Interface methods are public methods of a bean that are available for use by other components. Properties are attributes of a bean that are implemented by the bean class's field variables and accessed via *accessor* methods.

JavaBeans support introspection at multiple levels. At a low level, introspection can be accomplished using the reflection capabilities of the `java.lang.reflect` package. These capabilities allow Java objects to discover information about the public methods, fields, and constructors of loaded classes during program execution. Reflection allows introspection to be accomplished for all beans. All you have to do is declare a method or variable as `public` and it can be discovered using reflection.

An intermediate level introspection capability provided by JavaBeans utilizes design patterns. Design patterns are method naming conventions that are used by the introspection classes of `java.beans` to infer information about reflected methods based on their names. For example, design patterns can be used by visual design tools to identify a bean's event generation and processing capabilities by looking for methods that follow the naming conventions for event generation and event listening. Design tools can use design patterns to obtain a great deal of information about a bean in the absence of explicitly provided information.

Design patterns are a low overhead approach to supporting introspection in component development. All you have to do is adhere to the naming convention of design patterns and visual design tools will be able to make helpful inferences about how your components are used.

At the highest level, JavaBeans supports introspection through the use of classes and interfaces that provide explicit information about a bean's methods, properties, and events. By explicitly providing this information to visual design tools, you can add help information and extra levels of design documentation that will be automatically recognized and presented in the visual design environment.

Figure 24.2 illustrates the introspection and discovery capabilities of JavaBeans. These capabilities are important in that they allow software components to be developed in such a way that information about the components can be obtained automatically by visual design tools.

FIGURE 24.2.
Introspection and visual design.

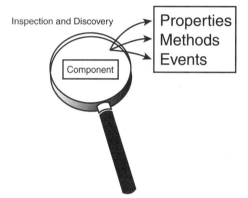

Interface Methods and Properties

Properties determine the appearance or behavior of a component. A component's properties can be modified during the visual design of an application. Most visual design tools provide property sheets to facilitate the setting of a component's properties. Property sheets identify all of the properties of a component and often provide help information related to specific properties. The properties and help information are discovered by visual design tools using introspection. Figure 24.3 provides an example of a property sheet.

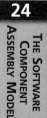

In JavaBeans, all properties are accessed through special interface methods, referred to as accessor methods. There are two types of accessor methods: *getter* methods and *setter* methods. Getter methods retrieve the values of properties, and setter methods set property values.

FIGURE 24.3.

Using property sheets to customize component properties.

Interface methods are methods that are used to modify the behavior or state of a component or to retrieve information about the state of a component. These methods are often used to support event handling. Most visual design tools provide the capability to connect events generated in one component with the interface methods of other components. For example, suppose a container contains two button components, labeled Start and Stop, and a ticker tape component, as shown in Figure 24.4. Also suppose that the buttons generate the button-clicked event when they are clicked and the ticker tape component provides the startTape() and stopTape() interface methods. Most visual design tools let you graphically connect the button-clicked events of the Start and Stop buttons with the startTape() and stopTape() methods. This allows you to implement your interface without having to write the code to connect your interface components.

FIGURE 24.4.

Interfaces methods can be connected to events.

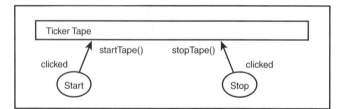

Persistence

The property sheets of visual design tools are used to tailor the properties of components for specific applications. The modified properties are stored in such a manner that they remain with the component from design to execution. The capability to store changes to a component's properties is known as persistence. Persistence allows components to be customized for later use. For example, during design, you can create two button beans— one with a blue background color and a yellow foreground color and another with a red background color and a white foreground color. The color modifications are stored along with instances of each bean object. When the beans are displayed during a program's execution, they are displayed using the modified colors.

JavaBeans supports persistence through object serialization. *Object serialization* is the capability to write a Java object to a stream in such a way that the definition and current state of the object are preserved. When a serialized object is read from a stream, the object is initialized and in exactly the same state it was in when it was written to the stream. Figure 24.5 summarizes how object serialization supports persistence. Chapter 40, "Using Object Serialization and JavaSpaces," covers object serialization.

FIGURE 24.5.

Persistence is implemented through object serialization.

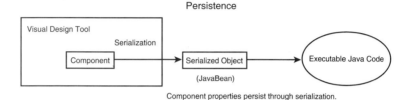

Persistence

Component properties persist through serialization.

Events

Visual development tools allow components to be dragged and dropped into a container, resized, and positioned. The visual nature of these tools greatly simplifies the development of user interfaces. However, component-based visual development tools go beyond simple screen layout. They also allow component event handling to be described in a visual manner.

You should be familiar with events, having worked with event handling code in most of the examples in this book. In general, events are generated in response to certain actions, such as the user clicking or moving the mouse or pressing a keyboard key. The event is handled by an event handler. Beans can handle events that occur local to them. For example, a button-based bean is required to handle the clicking of a button. Beans can also call upon other beans to complete the handling of an event. For example, a button bean can handle the button-clicked event by causing a text string to be displayed in a status-display bean. Visual development tools support the connection of event sources (for example, the button bean) with event listeners (for example, the status-display bean) using graphical design tools. In many cases, event handling can be performed without having to write event-handling code. You'll see a concrete example of this when you use the BDK in the next chapter. This code is automatically generated by the visual design tools. Figure 24.6 graphically depicts the relationship between event sources and event listeners.

FIGURE 24.6.
Event sources fire events that are handled by event listeners.

Visual Design

One of the ultimate benefits of using a component-based approach to software development is that you can use visual design tools to support your software development efforts. These tools greatly simplify the process of complex software development. They also allow you to develop higher-quality software, more quickly, and at a lower cost. Some of the features typically found in component-based visual design tools are as follows:

- Components and containers can be dragged onto a visual design worksheet.
- Components can be dragged into containers and assembled into more complex, higher-level components.
- Visual layout tools can be used to organize components within containers.
- Property sheets can be used to tailor component properties for different applications.
- Component interaction editors can be used to connect the events generated by one component with the interface methods of other components.
- Code can be automatically generated to implement visual interface designs.
- Traditional software development tools, such as source code editors, compilers, debuggers, and version control managers can be integrated within the visual design environment.

Figure 24.7 summarizes the various ways in which visual design tools simplify the process of component-based software development. If you've never used a visual design tool, you're in for a big surprise. Even the freely available BeanBox of the JavaBeans development kit provides a number of useful tools for facilitating the development of component-based software.

FIGURE 24.7.

Visual design tools greatly simplify the process of component-based software development.

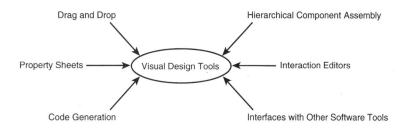

Summary

In this chapter you were introduced to component-based software development. You learned how the software component model works and how software components are used to simplify the development of complex software. You studied the features of component-based software development and learned how JavaBeans supports these features. In the next chapter you'll download, install, and familiarize yourself with the JavaBeans development kit (BDK) provided by JavaSoft.

24

THE SOFTWARE COMPONENT ASSEMBLY MODEL

The JavaBeans
Development Kit

CHAPTER 25

In the previous chapter you covered the basics of component-based software development. This background information will help you understand how the tools of the JavaBeans Development Kit (BDK) work. However, there is no substitute for hands-on experience. In this chapter you'll download and install the BDK and take a tour of what it has to offer. You'll learn how to use the BeanBox to develop and test your beans and investigate some of the example beans included with the BDK. When you finish this chapter, you'll know how to use the BDK to begin your own beans development.

Downloading and Installing the BDK

The BDK is freely available from the JavaBeans home page, which is located at `http://java.sun.com/beans/index.html`. This Web page also contains links to JavaBeans technical specifications and information on future plans for JavaBeans. Follow the links to the BDK 1.0 download page and download the version that is appropriate for your operating system. The rest of this section assumes that you are using Windows 95 or NT.

The Windows version of the BDK is available as a self-installing executable file. Just double-click the file's icon to start the installation program. Follow the installation instructions and install it in the default directory (`c:\bdk`).

Inside the BDK

The BDK provides several examples of JavaBeans, a tutorial, and supporting documentation. But most important, it provides a tool, referred to as the BeanBox, that can be used to display, customize, and test the beans that you'll develop. The BeanBox also serves as a primitive visual development tool. You'll use the BeanBox to see the important aspects of visual component-based software development as it applies to JavaBeans. Download and install the BDK before continuing on to the next section. Once you've installed the BDK, restart your system to make sure that all installation changes take effect.

> **NOTE**
>
> Through the rest of the chapter, it will be assumed that you've installed the BDK in its default location, the `c:\bdk` directory. If you install the BDK in a different directory, you'll have to map between `c:\bdk` and your installation directory.

Using the BeanBox

The BeanBox of the BDK is an example of a simple visual development tool for JavaBeans. It is located in the `c:\bdk\beanbox` directory. Change to this directory and start the BeanBox as follows:

`c:\bdk\beanbox>run`

The BeanBox application loads and displays three windows labeled ToolBox, BeanBox, and PropertySheet, as shown in Figures 25.1, 25.2, and 25.3.

The ToolBox window contains a list of available Java beans. These beans are components that can be used to build more complex beans, Java applications, or applets.

FIGURE 25.1.

The ToolBox window.

FIGURE 25.2.

The BeanBox window.

Figure 25.3.

The PropertySheet window.

Visual software development tools, such as the BeanBox, allow beans to be visually organized by placing them at the location where you want them to be displayed. Click the Juggler bean in the ToolBox window and then click in the BeanBox; the Juggler bean is placed in the BeanBox, as shown in Figure 25.4. The Juggler bean juggles when it is placed in the BeanBox.

Figure 25.4.

Adding a bean to the BeanBox.

Note that the PropertySheet is updated to display the properties of the Juggler bean (see Figure 25.5). You can customize the Juggler bean by changing its properties. Change the `animationRate` property to `500`, as shown in Figure 25.6. Note how the Juggler slows the rate at which it juggles the beans.

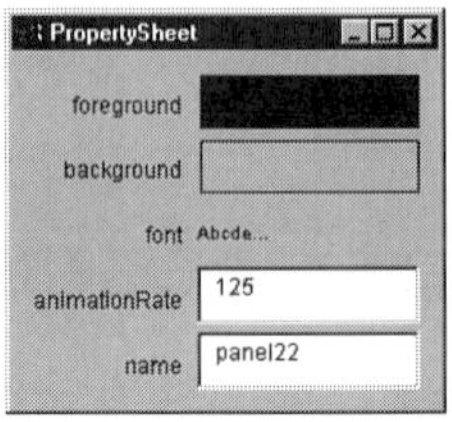

Figure 25.5.

The Juggler's PropertySheet.

FIGURE 25.6.

Changing the Juggler's `animationRate` *property.*

Now add a couple of buttons to the BeanBox. Select an OurButton bean in the ToolBox and then place it in the BeanBox, as shown in Figure 25.7. A button labeled Press is displayed. Use the button's property sheet to change its label to Start, as shown in Figure 25.8. Now create a second button labeled Stop, as shown in Figure 25.9.

FIGURE 25.7.

Adding a button to the BeanBox.

FIGURE 25.8.

*Editing the but-
ton's label.*

FIGURE 25.9.

*Adding a second
button to the
BeanBox.*

By now you can see where this application is going. You're going to use the Start and
Stop buttons to control the animation. To do this, you'll connect the Start button's
actionPerformed() event handler to the startJuggling() method of the Juggler bean
and the Stop button's actionPerformed() event handler to the stopJuggling() method
of the Juggler bean.

Click the Start button and then select Edit | Events | Action | ActionPerformed from the BeanBox menu bar, as shown in Figure 25.10. A red line is now shown emanating from the Start button. This line represents a logical connection from the Start button's `actionPerformed()` event handler. Click the Juggler bean to close the connection. When you do, the EventTargetDialog box, shown in Figure 25.11, is displayed. This dialog box lists the interface methods of the Juggler bean. Select startJuggling. By doing so, you connect the clicking of the Start button to the `startJuggling()` method via the `actionPerformed()` event handler of the Start button bean. The EventTargetDialog box notifies you that it is compiling an adapter class. The BeanBox creates a special class, referred to as an *adapter* class, to connect the clicking of the button with the `startJuggling()` method of the Juggler. It must compile this class and add it to the running BeanBox to support this connection.

FIGURE 25.10.

Selecting the
`actionPerformed()`
event handler.

FIGURE 25.11.

Connecting to the
`startJuggling()`
method.

Now that you know how to associate events with interface methods, connect the Stop button to the `stopJuggling()` method of the Juggler bean. Click the Stop button and select Edit | Events | action | actionPerformed from the BeanBox menu bar. Connect the red connector to the Juggler bean and select the `stopJuggling` method.

Now you can have some fun with the Juggler. Click the Stop button to stop the juggling and click the Start button to get it going again.

Understanding the Example Beans

You should be impressed by how easy it was to develop an interesting (or at least entertaining) application using the BeanBox and JavaBeans. In fact, you didn't have to write a single line of code to create the application. That's the power of component-based software development. Given a good stock of beans, you can quickly and easily assemble a large variety of useful applications.

In the example of the previous section, you learned how to use the OurButton and Juggler beans. The ToolBox that comes with the BeanBox lists 16 beans. I recommend that you play around with these beans to familiarize yourself with how they work. You studied the theory behind component-based software in the previous chapter. Now is the time to get some practical experience to back up your theoretical understanding. Try to see how the BeanBox and the example beans support the component-based model described in Chapter 24.

Just to whet your appetite, what follows is a short description of the beans that are in the ToolBox.

- BlueButton—A simple blue button with background, foreground, label, and font properties
- OrangeButton—A simple orange button with background, foreground, label, and font properties
- OurButton—A gray button with additional font properties
- ExplicitButton—A simple gray button with background, foreground, label, and font properties
- EventMonitor—A text area that is used to view events as they happen
- JellyBean—A jelly bean that is associated with a cost
- Juggler—A juggler animation
- TickTock—An interval timer
- Voter—A component that maintains a yes or no state
- ChangeReporter—A text field
- Molecule—A graphical field for displaying 3D pictures of molecules

- QuoteMonitor—A component that displays stock quotes received from a quote server
- JDBC SELECT—An SQL interface to a database
- SorterBean—An animation of a bubble sort
- BridgeTester—A bean used to test bean bridges (refer to Chapter 28, "Using Bridges")
- TransitionalBean—A button that changes colors

Now fire up the BeanBox and try out some of these beans. You'll learn how the `java.beans` packages support the implementation of the capabilities that you observe with the BeanBox.

Other Bean Development Tools

The BeanBox is a fairly basic visual design tool, yet it provides the important features of visual component-based software development. There are a number of very good visual design tools that support Java software development. If you're serious about developing your own beans, or using them to create applets or applications, it's recommended that you obtain one of these high-end tools. They'll save you plenty of time and effort in the long run. A list of available tools is available from JavaWorld at `http://www.javaworld.com/javaworld/tools/jw-tools-index.html`. Chapter 56, "Java Development Tools," describes the best of these tools. Table 25.1 provides a summary of popular tools that support bean development.

TABLE 25.1. BEAN DEVELOPMENT TOOLS.

Tool	Vendor	Retail Price	Description
Java Workshop 2.0	Sun Microsystems, Inc.	$110	Complete IDE that supports applet, application, and bean development
Java Studio	Sun Microsystems, Inc.	$69	Bean-oriented visual development tool
JavaPlan	Sun Microsystems, Inc.	$3,995/ seat	Enterprise-wide Java development tool; supports bean development

continues

TABLE 25.1. CONTINUED

Tool	Vendor	Retail Price	Description
Visual Café for Java 2.5	Symanted, Inc.	$99.95 to $499.95	Family of highly-rated visual development tools oriented around beans
Visual Age for Java	IBM	Free to $99.95	Bean-oriented visual development toolset
Visual J++	Microsoft, Inc.	$99.95	Microsoft's answer to Java software development
Jbuilder	Borland, Inc.	$99.95 to $2,495	Suit of bean-oriented Java development tools.
Super Mojo	Penumbra Software, Inc.	$39.95	Popular Java visual design tool.
JDesignerPro	BulletProof Corporation	$695	Application development environment and middleware
SuperCede Java Edition	SuperCede, Inc.	$29.95	A cost-effective Java visual design toolset
Jamba	Interleaf, Inc.	$149	Visual authoring environment aimed at minimizing the need for coding

Summary

In this chapter you downloaded and installed the BDK and took a tour of its contents. You learned how to use the BeanBox to develop and test beans and looked at some of the example beans included with the BDK. You also learned about some of the other bean development tools. In the next chapter you'll study the classes of the `java.beans` packages and learn how to use them to develop your own beans.

Developing Beans

CHAPTER 26

Now that you are familiar with the software component assembly model and the JavaBeans development kit, it's time to learn how to develop your own beans. In this chapter, you'll learn how beans work and take a tour of the `java.beans` packages. You'll also learn how to write bean code in Java. When you finish this chapter, you'll be able to create a few beans of your own.

How Do Beans Work?

Chapter 24, "The Software Component Assembly Model," presented the underlying concepts related to component-based software development. Chapter 25, "The JavaBeans Development Kit," showed how these concepts were embodied in an actual visual development tool. The point of the BeanBox tutorial in Chapter 25 was to give you some hands-on experience of how beans are used in software development. This section covers some of the underlying mechanisms that enable beans to be used in this manner. You may want to have your BeanBox up and running when you read through this section so that you can see how these mechanisms are implemented by it.

Graphic Representation and Visual Layout

One of the first things that you probably noticed when you started up the BeanBox was the ToolBox full of JavaBeans. Several of these beans had icons. JavaBeans have the capability to support a variety of icons for display by visual development tools.

Beans themselves can also be graphically displayed by visual development tools. When you placed the Juggler and OurButton beans in the BeanBox, they were displayed exactly how they appear in a final application. You can move them to their intended position and resize them to the desired dimensions.

Some beans are invisible in the sense that they do not have a graphical display. An example of an invisible bean could be a specialized algorithm, such as an image filter. Visual development tools usually create special graphical objects that allow the invisible beans to be manipulated in the same manner as visible beans during software development. Of course, the special graphical objects of the invisible beans are not displayed by the final application or applet.

Customizable and Persistent Properties

Properties are attributes of a bean that can be modified to change the appearance or behavior of a bean. They are accessed through special methods, referred to as *accessor* methods. Visual development tools allow properties to be changed through the use of *property sheets*, lists of properties that can be specified for a bean. Visual building tools, like the BeanBox, display a property sheet in response to a bean's selection. You used property sheets to change the `animationRate` property of the Juggler bean and the `label` property of the OurButton bean.

In addition to the simple property editing capabilities exhibited by the BeanBox example, individual beans can define custom property editors that allow properties to be edited using specialized dialog boxes. These custom property editors are implemented as special classes that are associated with the bean's class. The custom property editors are available to visual development tools, but because they are not part of the bean's class, they do not need to be compiled into applications or applets. This lets you provide extra *design* capabilities for a bean without having to develop bloated applications.

Suppose that you are using a bean that provides extensive customization support. You change the bean's background color to red and its foreground color to white, change a label associated with the bean, and alter a few other properties. You may wonder what happens to the property changes. How are the changes packaged along with the bean's class?

Beans store any property changes so that new property values come into effect and are displayed when the modified bean is used in an application. The capability to permanently store property changes is known as *persistence*. JavaBeans implement persistence by serializing bean objects that are instances of a bean class. *Serialization* is the process of writing the current state of an object to a stream. Because beans are serialized, they must implement the `java.io.Serializable` or `java.io.Externalizable` interfaces. Beans that implement `java.io.Serializable` are automatically saved. Beans that implement `java.io.Externalizable` are responsible for saving themselves.

> **NOTE**
>
> Chapter 40, "Using Object Serialization and JavaSpaces," covers object serialization in more detail.

When a bean object is saved through serialization, all of the values of the variables of the object are saved. In this way, any property changes are carried along with the object. The only exceptions to this are variables that are identified as `transient`. The values of `transient` variables are not serialized.

Bean Properties

Beans support a few different types of properties. In the BeanBox tutorial, you saw examples of *simple* properties. The `animationRate` property of the Juggler bean used a simple numeric value, and the `label` property of the OurButton bean used a text value.

An *indexed property* is a property that can take on an array of values. Indexed properties are used to keep track of a group of related values of the same type. For example, an indexed property could be used to maintain the values of a scrollable list.

A *bound* property is a property that alerts other objects when its value changes. For example, you could use a bound property to implement a temperature control dial. Whenever the user changes the control, notification of the change is propagated to objects that regulate temperature.

A *constrained* property differs from a bound property in that it notifies other objects of an *impending* change. Constrained properties give the notified objects the power to veto a property change. You could use a constrained property to implement a bean that fires a missile under two-person control. When one person initiates a missile launch, a notification is sent to a second user, who could either confirm or deny the launch.

Accessor Methods

All properties are accessed through accessor methods. There are two types of accessor methods: *getter* methods and *setter* methods. Getter methods retrieve the values of properties, and setter methods set property values. The names of getter methods begin with `get` and are followed by the name of the property to which they apply. The names of setter methods begin with `set` and are followed by the property name.

Methods Used with Simple Properties

If a bean has a property named `fooz` of type `foozType` that can be read and written, it should have the following accessor methods:

```
public foozType getFooz()
public void setFooz(foozType foozValue)
```

A property is read-only or write-only if one of the preceding accessor methods are missing.

> **NOTE**
>
> If a property is `boolean`, getter methods are written using `is` instead of `get`. For example, `isFooz()` would be used instead of `getFooz()` if `fooz` is a boolean property.

Methods Used with Indexed Properties

A bean that has an indexed property will have methods that support the reading and writing of individual array elements as well as the entire array. For example, if a bean has an indexed `widget` property in which each element of the array is of type `widgetType`, it will have the following accessor methods:

```
public widgetType getWidget(int index)
public widgetType[] getWidget()
public void setWidget(int index, widgetType widgetValue)
public void setWidget(widgetType[] widgetValues)
```

Methods Used with Bound Properties

Beans with bound properties have getter and setter methods, as previously identified, depending upon whether the property values are simple or indexed. Bound properties require certain objects to be notified when they change. The change notification is accomplished through the generation of a `PropertyChangeEvent`. Objects that want to be notified of a property change to a bound property must register as listeners. Accordingly, the bean that's implementing the bound property supplies methods of the form:

```
public void addPropertyChangeListener(PropertyChangeListener l)
public void removePropertyChangeListener(PropertyChangeListener l)
```

> **NOTE**
>
> The `PropertyChangeEvent` class and `PropertyChangeListener` interface are defined in `java.beans`.

The preceding listener registration methods do not identify specific bound properties. To register listeners for the `PropertyChangeEvent` of a specific property, the following methods must be provided:

```
public void addPropertyNameListener(PropertyChangeListener l)
public void removePropertyNameListener(PropertyChangeListener l)
```

In the preceding methods, `PropertyName` is replaced by the name of the bound property.

Objects that implement the `PropertyChangeListener` interface must implement the `propertyChange()` method. This method is invoked by the bean for all of its registered listeners to inform them of a property change.

Methods Used with Constrained Properties

The previously discussed methods used with simple and indexed properties also apply to constrained properties. In addition, the following event registration methods are provided:

```
public void addVetoableChangeListener(VetoableChangeListener l)
public void removeVetoableChangeListener(VetoableChangeListener l)
public void addPropertyNameListener(VetoableChangeListener l)
public void removePropertyNameListener(VetoableChangeListener l)
```

Objects that implement the `VetoableChangeListener` interface must implement the `vetoableChange()` method. This method is invoked by the bean for all of its registered listeners to inform them of a property change. Any object that does not approve of a property change can throw a `PropertyVetoException` within its `vetoableChange()` method to inform the bean whose constrained property was changed that the change was not approved.

Introspection

In order for beans to be used by visual development tools, the beans must be able to dynamically inform the tools of their interface methods and properties and also what kind of events they may generate or respond to. This capability is referred to as *introspection*. The `Introspector` class of `java.beans` provides a set of static methods for tools to obtain information about the properties, methods, and events of a bean.

The `Introspector` supports introspection in the following ways:

- Reflection and design patterns—The `java.lang.reflect` package provides the capability to identify the fields and methods of a class. The `Introspector` uses this capability to review the names of the methods of a bean's class. It identifies a bean's properties by looking at the method names for the getter and setter naming patterns, identified in previous sections of this chapter. It identifies a bean's event generation and processing capabilities by looking for methods that follow the naming conventions for event generation and event listening. The `Introspector` automatically applies reflection and design (naming) patterns to a bean class to obtain information for design tools in the absence of explicitly provided information.

- Explicit specification—Information about a bean may be optionally provided by a special bean information class that implements the `BeanInfo` interface. The `BeanInfo` interface provides methods for explicitly conveying information about a bean's methods, properties, and events. The `Introspector` recognizes `BeanInfo` classes by their name. The name of a `BeanInfo` class is the name of the bean class followed by `BeanInfo`. For example, if a bean was implemented via the `MyGizmo` class, the related `BeanInfo` class would be named `MyGizmoBeanInfo`.

Connecting Events to Interface Methods

Beans, being primarily GUI components, generate and respond to events. Visual development tools provide the capability to link events generated by one bean with event-handling methods implemented by other beans. For example, a button component may generate an event as the result of the user clicking on that button. A visual development tool would enable you to connect the handling of this event to the interface methods of other beans. The bean generating the event is referred to as the *event source*. The bean listening for (and handling) the event is referred to as the *event listener*.

Inside `java.beans`

Now that you have a feel for what beans are, how they are used, and some of the mechanisms they employ, let's take a look at the classes and interfaces of the `java.beans` packages. These classes and interfaces are organized into the categories of design support, introspection support, and change event-handling support.

Design Support

The classes in this category help visual development tools to use beans in a design environment.

The `Beans` class provides seven static methods that are used by application builders:

- `instantiate()`—Creates an instance of a bean from a serialized object.
- `isInstanceOf()`—Determines if a bean is of a specified class or interface.
- `getInstanceof()`—Returns an object that represents a particular view of a bean.
- `isDesignTime()`—Determines whether beans are running in an application builder environment.
- `setDesignTime()`—Identifies the fact that beans are running in an application builder environment.
- `isGuiAvailable()`—Determines whether a GUI is available for beans.
- `setGuiAvailable()`—Identifies the fact that a GUI is available for beans.

The `Visibility` interface is implemented by classes that support the capability to answer questions about the availability of a GUI for a bean. It provides the `avoidingGui()`, `dontUseGui()`, `needsGui()`, and `okToUseGui()` methods. The `VisibilityState` interface provides the `isOkToUseGui()` method.

The methods of the `PropertyEditor` interface are implemented by classes that support custom property editing. These methods support a range of property editors, from simple to complex. The `setValue()` method is used to identify the object that is to be edited. The `getValue()` method returns the edited value. The `isPaintable()` and `paintValue()` methods support the painting of property values on a `Graphics` object. The `getJavaInitializationString()` method returns a string of Java code that is used to initialize a property value. The `setAsText()` and `getAsText()` methods are used to set and retrieve a property value as a `String` object. The `getTags()` method returns an array of `String` objects that are acceptable values for a property. The `supportsCustomEditor()` method returns a `boolean` value indicating whether a custom editor is provided by a `PropertyEditor`. The `getCustomEditor()` method returns an object that is of a subclass of `Component` and is used as a custom editor for a bean's property. The `addPropertyChangeListener()` and `removePropertyChangeListener()` methods are used to register event handlers for the `PropertyChangeEvent` associated with a property.

The `PropertyEditorManager` class provides static methods that help application builders find property editors for specific properties. The `registerEditor()` method is used to register an editor class for a particular property class. The `getEditorSearchPath()` and `setEditorSearchPath()` methods support package name lists for finding property editors. The `findEditor()` method finds a property editor for a specified class. Unregistered property editors are identified by the name of the property followed by `Editor`.

The `PropertyEditorSupport` class is a utility class that implements the `PropertyEditor` interface. It is subclassed to simplify the development of property editors.

The methods of the `Customizer` interface are implemented by classes that provide a graphical interface for customizing a bean. These classes are required to be subclasses of `java.awt.Component` so that they can be displayed in a panel. The `addPropertyChangeListener()` method is used to enable an object that implements the `PropertyChangeListener` interface as an event handler for the `PropertyChangeEvent` of the object being customized. The `removePropertyChangeListener()` method is used to remove a `PropertyChangeListener`. The `setObject()` method is used to identify the object that is to be customized.

Introspection Support

The classes and interfaces in this category provide information to application builders about the interface methods, properties, and events of a bean.

The `Introspector` Class

The `Introspector` class provides static methods that are used by application builders to obtain information about a bean's class. The `Introspector` gathers this information using information explicitly provided by the bean designer whenever possible and uses reflection and design patterns when explicit information is not available. The `getBeanInfo()` method returns information about a class as a `BeanInfo` object. The `getBeanInfoSearchPath()` method returns a `String` array to be used as a search path for finding `BeanInfo` classes. The `setBeanInfoSearchPath()` method updates the list of package names used to find `BeanInfo` classes. The `decapitalize()` method is used to convert a `String` object to a standard variable name in terms of capitalization.

The `BeanInfo` Interface

The methods of the `BeanInfo` interface are implemented by classes that want to provide additional information about a bean. The `getBeanDescriptor()` method returns a `BeanDescriptor` object that provides information about a bean. The `getIcon()` method returns an `Image` object that is used as an icon to represent a bean. It uses the icon constants defined in `BeanInfo` to determine which type of icon should be returned. The `getEventSetDescriptors()` method returns an array of `EventSetDescriptor` objects that describe the events generated (fired) by a bean. The `getDefaultEventIndex()` method returns the index of the most commonly used event of a bean. The `getPropertyDescriptors()` method returns an array of `PropertyDescriptor` objects that support the editing of a bean's properties. The `getDefaultPropertyIndex()` method returns the most commonly updated property of a bean. The `getMethodDescriptors()` method returns an array of `MethodDescriptor` objects that describe a bean's externally accessible methods. The `getAdditionalBeanInfo()` method returns an array of objects that implement the `BeanInfo` interface.

The `SimpleBeanInfo` Class

The `SimpleBeanInfo` class provides a default implementation of the `BeanInfo` interface. It is subclassed to implement `BeanInfo` classes.

The `FeatureDescriptor` Class and Its Subclasses

The `FeatureDescriptor` class is the top-level class of a class hierarchy that is used by `BeanInfo` objects to report information to application builders. It provides methods that are used by its subclasses for information gathering and reporting.

The `BeanDescriptor` class provides global information about a bean, such as the bean's class and its `Customizer` class, if any. The `EventSetDescriptor` class provides information on the events generated by a bean. The `PropertyDescriptor` class provides information on a property's accessor methods and property editor. It is extended by the `IndexedPropertyDescriptor` class, which provides access to the type of the array implemented as an indexed property and information about the property's accessor methods.

The `MethodDescriptor` and `ParameterDescriptor` classes provide information about a bean's methods and parameters.

Change Event-Handling Support

The `PropertyChangeEvent` is generated by beans that implement bound and constrained properties as the result of a change in the values of these properties. The `PropertyChangeListener` interface is implemented by those classes that listen for the `PropertyChangeEvent`. It consists of a single method, `propertyChange()`, that is used to handle the event.

The `VetoableChangeListener` interface is implemented by classes that handle the `PropertyChangeEvent` and throw a `VetoableChangeEvent` in response to certain property changes. The `vetoableChange()` method is used to handle the `PropertyChangeEvent`.

The `PropertyChangeSupport` class is a utility class that can be subclassed by beans that implement bound properties. It provides a default implementation of the `addPropertyChangeListener()`, `removePropertyChangeListener()`, and `firePropertyChange()` methods.

The `VetoableChangeSupport` class, like the `PropertyChangeSupport` class, is a utility class that can be subclassed by beans that implement constrained properties. It provides a default implementation of the `addVetoableChangeListener()`, `removeVetoableChangeListener()`, and `fireVetoableChange()` methods.

Aggregation

The `Aggregate` interface has been added in JDK 1.2 as a means of aggregating several objects into a single bean. It is extended by the `Delegate` interface, which provides methods for accessing `Aggregate` objects. The `AggregateObject` class is an abstract class that implements the `Delegate` interface and provides a foundation for creating other aggregate classes. Note that aggregation has nothing to do with inheritance. It is just a way of combining multiple objects into a single bean.

The `java.beans.beancontext` Package

JDK 1.2 introduces the `java.beans.beancontext` package, which provides classes and interfaces for enabling beans to access their execution environment, referred to as their *bean context*. The `BeanContextChild` interface provides methods for getting and setting this context and for managing context-related event listeners. `BeanContextChild` is extended by the `BeanContext` interface, which provides methods by which beans can access resources and services that are available within their context. Objects that implement `BeanContext` function as containers for other beans. The `BeanContextMemberShipListener` interface provides an event listener interface for events that occur as the result of changes to the beans that are members of a bean context. The `DesignMode` interface of `java.beans` provides the capability for a `BeanContext` object to determine whether it is being executed in a design or execution mode.

In addition to the interfaces described in the previous paragraph, the `java.beans.beancontext` package provides the following six classes:

- `BeanContextEvent`—Events of this class are fired when the state of a bean context changes.
- `BeanContextMembershipEvent`—Extends `BeanContextEvent` to support changes in the membership of a bean context.
- `BeanContextAddedEvent`—Events of this class are fired when a bean is added to a bean context. This class extends `BeanContextMembershipEvent`.
- `BeanContextRemovedEvent`—Events of this class are fired when a bean is removed from a bean context. This class extends `BeanContextMembershipEvent`.
- `BeanContextSupport`—Provides an implementation of the `BeanContext` interface.
- `BeanContextSupport.BCSChildInfo`—Used to maintain information on the beans that are contained within a bean context.

The easiest way to implement a bean context is to extend the `BeanContextSupport` class. `BeanContextSupport` provides numerous methods for managing beans that are contained within a particular context.

Developing Beans

In this section, you'll learn how to create your own beans and use them in an applet. First, you'll create a simple gauge that can be used as a widget for applets and applications. Next, you'll create a bean that can be used to display text without the use of a `TextArea` or `TextField` object. After that, you'll learn how to use these beans in an applet that displays multiple-choice quiz questions.

A Gauge Bean

When you studied all of the classes and interfaces of `java.beans` in previous sections, you might have been left with the impression that beans are complicated and hard to develop. In fact, the opposite is true. You can easily convert existing classes to beans with minimal programming overhead.

Listing 26.1 contains the code for a bean that displays a simple gauge. The gauge is displayed as a 3D-style box that is filled somewhere between its minimum and maximum values. The color of the gauge's border and its fill color are both configurable. So are its dimensions and horizontal/vertical orientation.

LISTING 26.1. THE Gauge.java BEAN.

```java
import java.io.Serializable;
import java.beans.*;
import java.awt.*;
import java.awt.event.*;

public class Gauge extends Canvas implements Serializable {
  // Set constants and default values
  public static final int HORIZONTAL = 1;
  public static final int VERTICAL = 2;
  public static final int WIDTH = 100;
  public static final int HEIGHT = 20;
  public int orientation = HORIZONTAL;
  public int width = WIDTH;
  public int height = HEIGHT;
  public double minValue = 0.0;
  public double maxValue = 1.0;
  public double currentValue = 0.0;
  public Color gaugeColor = Color.lightGray;
  public Color valueColor = Color.blue;
  public Gauge() {
   super();
  }
  public Dimension getPreferredSize() {
   return new Dimension(width,height);
  }
  // Draw bean
  public synchronized void paint(Graphics g) {
   g.setColor(gaugeColor);
   g.fill3DRect(0,0,width-1,height-1,false);
   int border=3;
   int innerHeight=height-2*border;
   int innerWidth=width-2*border;
   double scale=(double)(currentValue-minValue)/
    (double)(maxValue-minValue);
   int gaugeValue;
   g.setColor(valueColor);
   if(orientation==HORIZONTAL){
    gaugeValue=(int)((double)innerWidth*scale);
    g.fillRect(border,border,gaugeValue,innerHeight);
   }else{
    gaugeValue=(int)((double)innerHeight*scale);
    g.fillRect(border,border+(innerHeight-
➥gaugeValue),innerWidth,gaugeValue);
```

```
    }
}
// Methods for accessing bean properties
public double getCurrentValue(){
 return currentValue;
}
public void setCurrentValue(double newCurrentValue){
 if(newCurrentValue>=minValue && newCurrentValue<=maxValue)
  currentValue=newCurrentValue;
}
public double getMinValue(){
 return minValue;
}
public void setMinValue(double newMinValue){
 if(newMinValue<=currentValue)
  minValue=newMinValue;
}
public double getMaxValue(){
 return maxValue;
}
public void setMaxValue(double newMaxValue){
 if(newMaxValue >= currentValue)
  maxValue=newMaxValue;
}
public int getWidth(){
 return width;
}
public void setWidth(int newWidth){
 if(newWidth > 0){
  width=newWidth;
  updateSize();
 }
}
public int getHeight(){
 return height;
}
public void setHeight(int newHeight){
 if(newHeight > 0){
  height=newHeight;
  updateSize();
 }
}
public Color getGaugeColor(){
 return gaugeColor;
}
public void setGaugeColor(Color newGaugeColor){
 gaugeColor=newGaugeColor;
}
public Color getValueColor(){
```

continues

LISTING 26.1. CONTINUED

```
  return valueColor;
}
public void setValueColor(Color newValueColor){
 valueColor=newValueColor;
}
public boolean isHorizontal(){
 if(orientation==HORIZONTAL) return true;
 else return false;
}
public void setHorizontal(boolean newOrientation){
 if(newOrientation){
  if(orientation==VERTICAL) switchDimensions();
 }else{
  if(orientation==HORIZONTAL) switchDimensions();
  orientation=VERTICAL;
 }
 updateSize();
}
void switchDimensions(){
 int temp=width;
 width=height;
 height=temp;
}
void updateSize(){
 setSize(width,height);
 Container container=getParent();
 if(container!=null){
  container.invalidate();
  container.doLayout();
 }
}
}
```

 To see how the bean works, copy the Gauge.jar file from your ch26 directory to the \bdk\jars directory and then start up the BeanBox using the following commands:

```
copy Gauge.jar \bdk\jars

cd \bdk\beanbox

run
```

The BeanBox opens and displays the ToolBox, BeanBox, and PropertySheet windows. You will notice a new bean at the bottom of the ToolBox. This is the Gauge bean from Listing 26.1. Note that it comes with its own icon, as shown in Figure 26.1.

FIGURE 26.1.

The Gauge bean now has an icon in the ToolBox.

Click the Gauge bean's ToolBox icon and then click in the BeanBox. The bean is displayed as a horizontal 3D box, as shown in Figure 26.2.

FIGURE 26.2.

Adding the Gauge bean to the BeanBox.

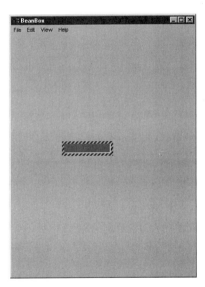

The bean's property sheet displays a number of properties that may be changed to alter the bean's appearance, as shown in Figure 26.3. The `foreground`, `background`, and `font` properties are the default properties of visible beans. These properties reflect the `getForeground()`, `setForeground()`, `getBackground()`, `setBackground()`, `getFont()`, and `setFont()` methods of the `Component` class.

FIGURE 26.3.

The Gauge bean's PropertySheet.

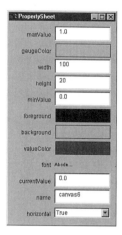

The rest of the properties shown in the style sheet were defined in Listing 26.1. The `minValue` and `maxValue` properties identify the minimum and maximum values associated with the gauge. The `currentValue` property identifies the current value of the gauge.

The `width` and `height` properties control the gauge's dimensions. The `horizontal` property takes on `boolean` values. When set to True, the gauge is displayed horizontally. When set to False, the gauge is displayed vertically. When the orientation of a gauge is switched, so are its width and height.

The `gaugeColor` and `valueColor` properties identify the color of the gauge's border and the color to be displayed to identify the gauge's current value.

To see how the gauge's properties work, make the following changes:

- Change the `currentValue` property to .7.
- Change the `horizontal` property to False.
- Change the `height` property to 200.
- Change the `gaugeColor` property to green.
- Change the `valueColor` property to orange.

Figure 26.4 shows the results of these changes on the bean's display.

FIGURE 26.4.

Changing the Gauge bean's properties.

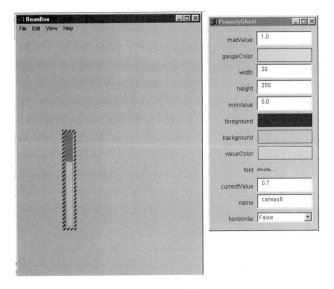

How the Gauge Bean Works

The first thing that you'll notice about the Gauge bean's source code is that it imports `java.io.Serializable`. All bean classes implement `Serializable` or `Externalizable`. These interfaces support bean persistence, allowing beans to be read from and written to permanent storage (for example, hard disk). When a bean implements `Serializable`, serialization of the bean's data is performed automatically by Java, meaning you don't have to figure out how to write objects to streams or read them back in. When a bean implements `Externalizable`, the bean is responsible for performing all the serialization overhead. `Serializable` is obviously the easiest to implement of the two interfaces. All you have to do is add `Serializable` to your class's `implements` clause and poof!—serialization is automatically supported. Chapter 40, "Using Object Serialization and JavaSpaces," covers object serialization.

Besides serialization, you won't notice anything bean-specific about the rest of the Gauge class. In fact, it looks just like any other custom AWT class. Gauge extends Canvas so that it can draw to a `Graphics` object. It defines a few constants for use in initializing its field variables. You should note that these field variables correspond to the Gauge bean's properties.

The `getPreferredSize()` method is an important method for visible beans to implement. It tells application builder tools how much room is needed to display a bean. All of your visible beans should implement `getPreferredSize()`.

The paint() method draws the bean on a Graphics object. Visible beans need to implement paint() in order to display themselves. The paint() method of Gauge works by drawing a 3D rectangle using the gaugeColor and then drawing an inner rectangle using the valueColor. The dimensions of the inner rectangle are calculated based on the value of currentValue and the orientation variables.

Gauge provides getter and setter methods for each of its properties. These methods adhere to the naming conventions used for bean properties. The Introspector class of java.beans automatically reports the properties corresponding to these methods to application builder tools, such as the BeanBox.

The switchDimensions() method is used to switch the values of width and height when the bean's orientation is switched.

The updateSize() method is invoked when the bean changes its size. It invokes setSize() to inform a layout manager of its new size. It invokes the invalidate() method of its container to invalidate the container's layout and doLayout() to cause the component to be redisplayed.

The GaugeBeanInfo Class

You may be wondering, "What about all of those other classes and interfaces of java.beans?" For simple beans, you don't really need them. However, we created a GaugeBeanInfo class so that the bean's icon can be displayed. The GaugeBeanInfo class is shown in Listing 26.2.

LISTING 26.2. THE GaugeBeanInfo CLASS.

```
import java.beans.*;
import java.awt.*;

public class GaugeBeanInfo extends SimpleBeanInfo {
 // Return icon to be used with bean
 public Image getIcon(int size) {
  switch(size){
  case ICON_COLOR_16x16:
   return loadImage("gauge16c.gif");
  case ICON_COLOR_32x32:
   return loadImage("gauge32c.gif");
  case ICON_MONO_16x16:
   return loadImage("gauge16m.gif");
  case ICON_MONO_32x32:
   return loadImage("gauge32c.gif");
  }
  return null;
 }
}
```

26

The `GaugeBeanInfo` class extends the `SimpleBeanInfo` class and implements one method—`getIcon()`. The `getIcon()` method is invoked by application builders to obtain an icon for a bean. It uses the constants defined in the `BeanInfo` interface to select a color or monochrome icon of size 16×16 or 32×32 bits.

The `Gauge.mf` Manifest File

The `Gauge.mf` manifest file is used to build the `Gauge.jar` file. It identifies the `Gauge.class` file as a bean. To create the `Gauge.jar` file, use the following command:

```
jar cfm Gauge.jar Gauge.mf Gauge*.class gauge*.gif
```

All the files that you need for this example are installed in your `ch26` directory. Remember to copy your beans' `.jar` files from the `ch26` directory to the `\bdk\jars` directory to have them loaded by the BeanBox. The contents of the `Gauge.mf` file are as follows:

```
Manifest-Version: 1.0

Name: Gauge.class
Java-Bean: True
```

A Text Canvas Bean

Did you ever wish that you could draw text on a canvas without having to fiddle around with fonts and font metrics? The bean that you'll develop next will make your wish come true. You can use it in place of the `TextArea` and `TextField` classes to display text in applets and window applications.

The name of this bean is `TCanv`, which is short for Text Canvas. The source code for the `TCanv` bean is shown in Listing 26.3. Let's start by learning how `TCanv` works. Copy the `TCanv.jar` file from the `ch26` directory to the `\bdk\jars` directory using the following command:

```
copy TCanv.jar \bdk\jars
```

When you open up your BeanBox, you will notice the `TCanv` bean at the bottom of your ToolBox, as shown in Figure 26.5.

Click on the `TCanv` icon and then in the BeanBox. The `TCanv` bean is displayed, as shown in Figure 26.6. Its property sheet is shown in Figure 26.7. The `background`, `foreground`, and `font` properties are the default properties of visible beans. The `leftMargin` and `topMargin` properties are used to insert space between the edges of the bean and the text it displays. The `border` property is used to display a border around the perimeter of the bean. The `width` and `height` properties control the bean's dimensions.

FIGURE 26.5.

The TCanv *bean is now in the ToolBox.*

FIGURE 26.6.

The TCanv *bean is in the BeanBox.*

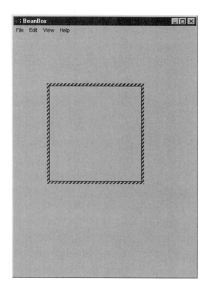

FIGURE 26.7.

The TCanv *bean's PropertySheet.*

The text property identifies the actual text that is displayed by the bean. Because some application builders, such as the BeanBox, do not let you enter a new line character in a text property, the vertical bar character (¦) is used to indicate a new line. At least one character should be contained on a line for the line to be displayed.

To distinguish it from the rest of the BeanBox and to show how its properties work, make the following changes:

- Change the text property to This¦is¦a¦test!.
- Change the leftMargin and topMargin properties to 20.
- Change the font property to a 14-point font. (Click on the font property to open the FontEditor dialog box.)
- Change the background property to yellow.

Figure 26.8 shows the effect of these changes on the bean.

FIGURE 26.8.

The result of changing the TCanv bean's properties.

LISTING 26.3. THE TCanv BEAN.

```
import java.io.*;
import java.util.*;
import java.beans.*;
import java.awt.*;
import java.awt.event.*;

public class TCanv extends Canvas implements Serializable {
  // Set constants and default values
```

continues

LISTING 26.3. CONTINUED

```
public static final int WIDTH = 200;
public static final int HEIGHT = 200;
public int width = WIDTH;
public int height = HEIGHT;
public int leftMargin = 5;
public int topMargin = 5;
public String text = "";
public boolean border = true;
public TCanv() {
 super();
}
public Dimension getPreferredSize() {
 return new Dimension(width,height);
}
// Draw bean
public synchronized void paint(Graphics g) {
 if(border) g.drawRect(0,0,width-1,height-1);
 Font font = g.getFont();
 FontMetrics fm = g.getFontMetrics(font);
 int lineHeight = fm.getHeight();
 int y=fm.getLeading()+fm.getAscent();
 StringTokenizer tokenizer = new StringTokenizer(text,"¦");
 String line;
 while(tokenizer.hasMoreTokens()){
  line=tokenizer.nextToken();
  if(border) g.drawString(line,leftMargin+1,topMargin+y+1);
  else g.drawString(line,leftMargin,topMargin+y);
  y+=lineHeight;
 }
}
// Methods for accessing bean properties
public String getText(){
 return text;
}
public void setText(String newTextValue){
 text=newTextValue;
}
public int getWidth(){
 return width;
}
public void setWidth(int newWidth){
 if(newWidth > 0){
  width=newWidth;
  updateSize();
 }
}
public int getHeight(){
 return height;
}
```

```
public void setHeight(int newHeight){
 if(newHeight > 0){
  height=newHeight;
  updateSize();
 }
}
public int getLeftMargin(){
 return leftMargin;
}
public void setLeftMargin(int newLeftMargin){
 if(newLeftMargin >= 0) leftMargin=newLeftMargin;
}
public int getTopMargin(){
 return topMargin;
}
public void setTopMargin(int newTopMargin){
 if(newTopMargin >= 0) topMargin=newTopMargin;
}
public boolean isBorder(){
 return border;
}
public void setBorder(boolean newBorder){
 border = newBorder;
}
void updateSize(){
 setSize(width,height);
 Container container=getParent();
 if(container!=null){
  container.invalidate();
  container.doLayout();
 }
}
}
```

Inside TCanv

The TCanv class, like the Gauge class, extends Canvas and implements Serializable.
It defines the field variables corresponding to its properties and implements
getPreferredSize() and paint(). It also implements a few getter and setter methods.
Starting to recognize a pattern?

The paint() method checks the border variable and draws a border around the bean, as
required. It then gets the value of the current font and the font's FontMetrics object. It
invokes the getHeight() method of the FontMetrics class to get the line height of the
current font in pixels. It then uses a StringTokenizer object to parse the String object
of the text variable based on the ¦ delimiter. Finally, the text is displayed one line at a
time. The hasMoreTokens() and nextToken() methods of StringTokenizer are used to

step through the parsed `text` string and to display them on the `Graphics` object of the bean's canvas.

Listing 26.4 shows the code for the `TCanvBeanInfo`. This class is similar to `GaugeBeanInfo` and is used to provide icons to application builders.

LISTING 26.4. THE `TCanvBeanInfo` CLASS.

```java
import java.beans.*;
import java.awt.*;

public class TCanvBeanInfo extends SimpleBeanInfo {
 // Return TCanv icon
 public Image getIcon(int size) {
  switch(size){
  case ICON_COLOR_16x16:
   return loadImage("tcanv16c.gif");
  case ICON_COLOR_32x32:
   return loadImage("tcanv32c.gif");
  case ICON_MONO_16x16:
   return loadImage("tcanv16m.gif");
  case ICON_MONO_32x32:
   return loadImage("tcanv32c.gif");
  }
  return null;
 }
}
```

The manifest file used to create `TCanv.jar` is as follows:

```
Manifest-Version: 1.0

Name: TCanv.class
Java-Bean: True
```

This file is used to identify the `TCanv` class as a bean. The following command is used to create the `TCanv.jar` file:

```
jar cvfm TCanv.jar TCanv.mf TCanv*.class tcanv*.gif
```

A Quiz Applet

Now that you have a couple of beans under your belt, let's use them in an applet. The `Quiz` applet, shown in Listing 26.5, uses both beans. It displays arithmetic multiple-choice quiz questions to the user. These questions are displayed in a `TCanv` bean. A second `TCanv` bean displays status information. A `Gauge` bean displays the user's quiz score in graphical form.

Figure 26.9 shows how the applet is initially displayed by `appletviewer`. The applet is displayed by opening the `quiz.htm` file contained in your `ch26` directory. The questions are randomized to reduce the likelihood of a question being asked twice. When you click on an answer, the `TCanv` beans are updated with new questions and status information. The `Gauge` bean updates the user's quiz score, as shown in Figure 26.10.

FIGURE 26.9.

The Quiz *applet as displayed by* `appletviewer`.

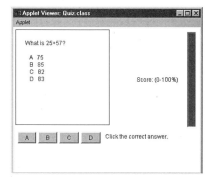

FIGURE 26.10.

Keeping track of the score using the Gauge *bean.*

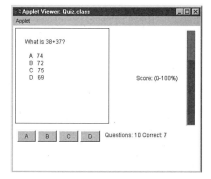

LISTING 26.5. THE Quiz APPLET.

```
import java.applet.*;
import java.awt.*;
import java.awt.event.*;

public class Quiz extends Applet {
 // Declare bean objects
 TCanv question = new TCanv();
 Gauge gauge = new Gauge();
 String labels[]={"  A   "," B   "," C   "," D   "};
 Button button[] = new Button[labels.length];
 TCanv status=new TCanv();
```

continues

LISTING 26.5. CONTINUED

```
int questions = 0;
int correctAnswers = 0;
int currentAnswer;

public void init() {
 Panel mainPanel = new Panel();
 Panel gaugePanel = new Panel();
 Panel bottomPanel = new Panel();
 Panel buttons = new Panel();
 // Set bean properties
 question.setLeftMargin(20);
 question.setTopMargin(20);
 gauge.setHorizontal(false);
 gauge.setMaxValue(100.0);
 gauge.setCurrentValue(100.0);
 gauge.setHeight(200);
 gauge.setWidth(20);
 status.setHeight(20);
 status.setWidth(200);
 status.setTopMargin(0);
 status.setBorder(false);
 mainPanel.setLayout(new BorderLayout());
 mainPanel.add("Center",question);
 gaugePanel.add(new Label("Score: (0-100%)"));
 gaugePanel.add(gauge);
 mainPanel.add("East",gaugePanel);
 bottomPanel.setLayout(new BorderLayout());
 for(int i=0;i<labels.length;++i){
  button[i] = new Button(labels[i]);
  button[i].addActionListener(new ButtonHandler());
  buttons.add(button[i]);
 }
 buttons.add(status);
 bottomPanel.add("Center",buttons);
 mainPanel.add("South",bottomPanel);
 add(mainPanel);
}

public void start(){
 displayQuestion();
}

void displayQuestion() {
 question.setText(nextQuestion());
 if(questions==0) status.setText("Click the correct answer.");
 else{
  String s="Questions: "+String.valueOf(questions);
```

```
   s+=" Correct: "+String.valueOf(correctAnswers);
   status.setText(s);
  }
}

String nextQuestion() {
 String q = "What is ";
 String operand[] = {"+","-","*"};
 int op1 = randomInt(100);
 int op2 = randomInt(100);
 int op = randomInt(3);
 String operator = operand[op];
 int ans=0;
 switch(op){
 case 0:
  ans=op1+op2;
  break;
 case 1:
  ans=op1-op2;
  break;
 case 2:
  ans=op1*op2;
  break;
 }
 currentAnswer=randomInt(labels.length);
 q+=String.valueOf(op1)+operator+String.valueOf(op2)+"?¦ ";
 for(int i=0;i<labels.length;++i){
  q+="¦"+labels[i];
  if(i==currentAnswer) q+=String.valueOf(ans);
  else{
   int delta = randomInt(10);
   if(delta==0) delta=1;
   int add = randomInt(2);
   if(add==1) q+=String.valueOf(ans+delta);
   else q+=String.valueOf(ans-delta);
  }
 }
 return q;
}

int randomInt(int max){
 int r = (int) (max*Math.random());
 r %= max;
 return r;
}

void answer(int i){
 ++questions;
 if(i==currentAnswer){
```

continues

LISTING 26.5. CONTINUED

```
    ++correctAnswers;
    displayQuestion();
  }else{
    status.setText("Try again!");
  }
  // Update bean properties
  double score = (double) correctAnswers/(double) questions;
  gauge.setCurrentValue(score*100.0);
  gauge.repaint();
  question.repaint();
  status.repaint();
  }

  class ButtonHandler implements ActionListener {
   public void actionPerformed(ActionEvent e){
    String s = e.getActionCommand();
    for(int i=0;i<labels.length;++i){
     if(labels[i].equals(s)){
       answer(i);
       break;
      }
     }
    }
   }
  }
}
```

Inside the `Quiz` Applet

The `Quiz` applet provides a very crude example of using beans in an applet. Normally, if you were using beans, you would slap together an applet using a visual programming tool. In this case, you could avoid having to do most of the applet programming.

The `Quiz` applet is valuable in that it shows you how beans can be used in the same manner as other GUI components. A second purpose of the applet is to make you appreciate the use of serialization. You'll learn about beans, serialization, and applets later in this chapter when you study a serialized clone of `Quiz`, named `Quiz2`.

The `Quiz` applet creates two `TCanv` beans and assigns them to the `question` and `status` variables. A `Gauge` bean is created and assigned to the `gauge` variable. The bean assigned to the `question` variable displays the text of a question. The bean assigned to the `status` variable displays the status information to the right of the answer buttons.

The applet's `init()` method lays out the applet and sets the properties of the beans. The left and top margins of the question bean are set to `20`. The `Gauge` bean is changed to vertical and its maximum value is set to `100`. Its current value is also set to `100`, giving the user a vote of confidence. The gauge's `width` and `height` dimensions are also modified. The dimensions of the `status` bean are adjusted. Its top margin is set to `0` and its `border` is turned off.

The applet's `start()` method simply invokes the `displayQuestion()` method to display a quiz question to the user. The `displayQuestion()` method invokes the question bean's `setText()` method to display the text of the question. The `setText()` method of the `status` bean is invoked to display status information to the user.

Questions are created by the `nextQuestion()` method. This method generates an arithmetic question based on the addition, subtraction, and multiplication of integers between `0` and `100`. It displays the answer along with three other incorrect answers. These answers are displayed in random order.

The `randomInt()` method generates a random integer from zero to one less than a specified maximum.

The `answer()` method supports the handling of the answer buttons by checking if the user answered correctly and then updating and displaying the `score` accordingly. The `repaint()` methods of the beans are invoked to cause the beans to update their respective displays.

The `ButtonHandler` class supports the handling of the events associated with clicking the answer buttons.

The `quiz.htm` file, shown in Listing 26.6, is used to display the `Quiz` applet.

LISTING 26.6. THE `quiz.htm` FILE.

```
<HTML>
<HEAD>
<TITLE>Quiz</TITLE>
</HEAD>
<BODY>
<APPLET CODE="Quiz.class" WIDTH=400 HEIGHT=300>
[Quiz applet]
</APPLET>
</BODY>
</HTML>
```

Using Serialization

While reading through the source code of the `Quiz` applet, you probably were wondering what benefit, if any, was derived from using beans. That's a legitimate concern. The answer is that in the absence of an application builder tool, beans are just a little easier to work with than other classes. The one feature of beans that is apparent, whether you are using them as part of an application builder or by hand, is their support for persistence.

The Quiz applet did not make use of persistence. Instead of customizing beans using the BeanBox, the Quiz applet included special code in the init() method to accomplish bean editing and customization. The Quiz2 applet, shown in Listing 26.7, which is a takeoff on the Quiz applet, does show how persistence is used. Listing 26.8 shows the quiz2.htm file used to display the applet. Go ahead and display quiz2.htm using the appletviewer. You should notice that the Quiz2 applet behaves in the same way as Quiz.

LISTING 26.7. THE Quiz2 APPLET.

```java
import java.applet.*;
import java.awt.*;
import java.awt.event.*;
import java.beans.*;

public class Quiz2 extends Applet {
 // Declare beans
 TCanv question, status;
 Gauge gauge;
 String labels[]={"   A   "," B   "," C   "," D   "};
 Button button[] = new Button[labels.length];
 int questions = 0;
 int correctAnswers = 0;
 int currentAnswer;

 public void init() {
  Panel mainPanel = new Panel();
  Panel gaugePanel = new Panel();
  Panel bottomPanel = new Panel();
  Panel buttons = new Panel();
  try{
   // Load serialized beans
   question = (TCanv) Beans.instantiate(null,"qcanv");
   gauge = (Gauge) Beans.instantiate(null,"vgauge");
   status = (TCanv) Beans.instantiate(null,"scanv");
  }catch(Exception ex){
  }
  mainPanel.setLayout(new BorderLayout());
  mainPanel.add("Center",question);
  gaugePanel.add(new Label("Score: (0-100%)"));
  gaugePanel.add(gauge);
  mainPanel.add("East",gaugePanel);
  bottomPanel.setLayout(new BorderLayout());
  for(int i=0;i<labels.length;++i){
   button[i] = new Button(labels[i]);
   button[i].addActionListener(new ButtonHandler());
```

```
  buttons.add(button[i]);
  }
 buttons.add(status);
 bottomPanel.add("Center",buttons);
 mainPanel.add("South",bottomPanel);
 add(mainPanel);
}

public void start(){
 displayQuestion();
}

void displayQuestion() {
 question.setText(nextQuestion());
 if(questions==0) status.setText("Click the correct answer.");
 else{
  String s="Questions: "+String.valueOf(questions);
  s+=" Correct: "+String.valueOf(correctAnswers);
  status.setText(s);
 }
}

String nextQuestion() {
 String q = "What is ";
 String operand[] = {"+","-","*"};
 int op1 = randomInt(100);
 int op2 = randomInt(100);
 int op = randomInt(3);
 String operator = operand[op];
 int ans=0;
 switch(op){
 case 0:
  ans=op1+op2;
  break;
 case 1:
  ans=op1-op2;
  break;
 case 2:
  ans=op1*op2;
  break;
 }
 currentAnswer=randomInt(labels.length);
 q+=String.valueOf(op1)+operator+String.valueOf(op2)+"? ";
 for(int i=0;i<labels.length;++i){
  q+=" "+labels[i];
  if(i==currentAnswer) q+=String.valueOf(ans);
  else{
   int delta = randomInt(10);
   if(delta==0) delta=1;
   int add = randomInt(2);
```

continues

LISTING 26.7. CONTINUED

```
    if(add==1) q+=String.valueOf(ans+delta);
    else q+=String.valueOf(ans-delta);
   }
  }
  return q;
 }

 int randomInt(int max){
  int r = (int) (max*Math.random());
  r %= max;
  return r;
 }

 void answer(int i){
  ++questions;
  if(i==currentAnswer){
   ++correctAnswers;
   displayQuestion();
  }else{
   status.setText("Try again!");
  }
  // Update bean properties
  double score = (double) correctAnswers/(double) questions;
  gauge.setCurrentValue(score*100.0);
  gauge.repaint();
  question.repaint();
  status.repaint();
 }

 class ButtonHandler implements ActionListener {
  public void actionPerformed(ActionEvent e){
   String s = e.getActionCommand();
   for(int i=0;i<labels.length;++i){
    if(labels[i].equals(s)){
     answer(i);
     break;
    }
   }
  }
 }
}
```

Quiz2 works in the same manner as Quiz. The only difference is in how the properties of
its beans are initialized. In Quiz, these properties are initialized through Java code in the
init() method. In Quiz2, the question, status, and gauge beans were customized in
the BeanBox and written to the qcanv.ser, scanv.ser, and vgauge.ser files. These files

not only contain class information but also the values of the bean's customized properties. The instantiate() method of the Beans class is used to read the beans from serialized storage in the .ser files.

LISTING 26.8. THE quiz2.htm FILE.

```
<HTML>
<HEAD>
<TITLE>Quiz</TITLE>
</HEAD>
<BODY>
<APPLET CODE="Quiz2.class" WIDTH=400 HEIGHT=300>
[Quiz applet]
</APPLET>
</BODY>
</HTML>
```

Creating the .ser Files

You probably want to know how the .ser files were created in the first place. I used the
BeanBox to customize each of the beans used by Quiz2 and saved them to .ser files
using the SerializeComponent command from the BeanBox File menu. (see Figure
26.11). I could have written a program to create the .ser file, but working with the
BeanBox is much easier.

FIGURE 26.11.
Using the
SerializeCompone
nt *command.*

Let's change the font used to display the text of the status bean. Run the BeanBox and
move a TCanv object into the box, as shown in Figure 26.12. Now edit the properties of
the TCanv object as follows:

- Set the height property to 20.
- Set the width property to 200.
- Set the topMargin property to 0.
- Set the border property to false.
- Change the font property to a 12-point italic Times Roman font.

When you have finished making these property changes, save the customized bean to a file using the SerializeComponent command under the File menu. Save the new file over the scanv.ser file that's in your ch26\ directory.

Now open quiz2.htm with appletviewer, as shown in Figure 26.12. Note how the sta-tus text is displayed in the new font you just selected.

FIGURE 26.12.

Displaying the changed proper-ties.

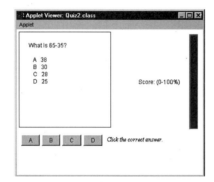

Summary

In this chapter, you learned how beans work and examined the classes and interfaces of the java.beans packages. You also learned how to write bean code in Java. In the next chapter, you'll look at some of the notable beans that have been developed by the industry.

Notable Beans

IN THIS CHAPTER

Since the debut of JavaBeans, thousands of beans have been developed. Hundreds of these beans are available as off-the-shelf Java components. You can find links to many of these beans from the JavaBeans Directory located at `http://www.javasoft.com/beans/directory/`. In this chapter you'll take a look at some of the beans that are being developed by the Java software development community. You'll look at the HotJava HTML Component bean, a product of JavaSoft. You'll work with the `RunningText` bean developed by Jayakrishnan Nair, a computer science student at the University of Victoria. You'll also look at some beans from IBM's WebRunner Toolkit. If you're not currently convinced of the power of JavaBeans, you will be after this chapter.

The HotJava HTML Component

One of the most powerful bean sets on the market is the HotJava HTML Component from JavaSoft. This product consists of several beans that can be used to add Web-browsing support to window applications. It parses and renders HTML files that are loaded from the Web and includes the following features:

- HTML 3.2 support
- HTTP 1.1 compatibility
- Frames and tables support
- The ability to use cookies
- Multimedia support
- JAR file support
- Implementation of the FTP, Gopher, SMTP, and SOCKS protocols

A trial version can be downloaded from `http://java.sun.com/products/hotjava/bean/index.html`. Go ahead and download it now so you can work along with the example in this section.

Installing the HotJava HTML Component

The HotJava HTML Component is easy to install. The Microsoft Windows version comes as a `.zip` file. UnZip the file to a temporary directory and copy the `HotJavaBean.jar` and `TextBean.jar` files to your `\bdk\jars` directory.

Running the HotJava HTML Component in the BeanBox

After installing `HotJavaBean.jar` and `TextBean.jar`, run your BeanBox. You will notice the following five beans have been added to the ToolBox:

- `TextBean`—A text field for entering the URL of a document to be browsed.
- `HotJavaDocumentStack`—A bean that keeps track of the URLs that have been browsed.
- `AuthenticatorBean`—An invisible bean that supports user authentication.
- `HotJavaBrowserBean`—An HTML-rendering bean.
- `HotJavaSystemState`—An invisible bean that maintains configuration information about the HotJava HTML Component.

We'll use three of these beans to visually design a browser in the BeanBox. Our browser won't support user authentication or URL history tracking, so we won't need `AuthenticatorBean` or `HotJavaDocumentStack`. However, you may want to experiment with these beans on your own.

1. Select the `HotJavaSystemState` bean from the ToolBox and click in the lower-right corner of the BeanBox. Use the properties sheet to edit the `SystemPropertDefaults` properties to set up any proxy servers that you may be using.

2. Select the `TextBean` in the Toolbox and click in the upper-left corner of the BeanBox.

3. Select the `HotJavaBrowserBean` in the Toolbox and click in the middle of the BeanBox. An evaluation notice is displayed. Click OK after you've read it. Resize the bean and organize the BeanBox as shown in Figure 27.1.

After completing these steps, your BeanBox should appear similar to Figure 27.1.

Now connect the `HotJavaBrowserBean` and the `TextBean` so that we can begin browsing URLs. If you are not currently connected to the Internet, now would be a good time to get online.

1. Select the `HotJavaBrowserBean` in the BeanBox. The bean's border is highlighted.

2. Select the `Bind` property from the Edit menu. The `PropertyNameDialog` is displayed.

3. Select the `documentString` property and click OK.

4. Move your mouse to the `TextBean`. A red line appears behind your cursor.

27

NOTABLE BEANS

FIGURE 27.1.

Laying out the
BeanBox for the
HotJava HTML
Component.

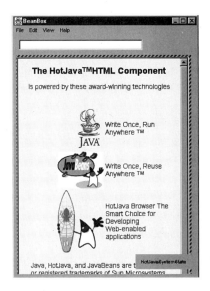

5. Click on the TextBean and the PropertyNameDialog appears.

6. Click on the text property and select OK. You've now connected the documentString property of the HotJavaBrowserBean to the text property of the TextBean. We'll make the connection in the other direction as well.

7. Select the TextBean.

8. Set the text property to www.javasoft.com.

9. Select Bind property from the Edit menu.

10. Select the text property in the PropertyNameDialog and click OK.

11. Move your mouse to the HotJavaBrowserBean and click OK. Note that the red line connects the TextBean to the HotJavaBrowserBean.

12. Select the documentString property in the PropertyNameDialog and click OK.

At this point, the HotJavaBrowserBean should try to establish an HTTP connection to www.javasoft.com, as shown in Figure 27.2.

With just a few drags and drops, you've created a full-blown browser within the BeanBox. Try using the TextBean to connect to other sites. For example, enter www.yahoo.com in the TextBean. The HotJavaBrowserBean should display the Yahoo! home page. Now click on any of the links on the Yahoo! home page. The TextBean is updated with the URL of the document you selected. When you are finished exploring the TextBean and HotJavaBrowserBean, exit the BeanBox.

FIGURE 27.2.
*Browsing the Web
with the HotJava
HTML
Component.*

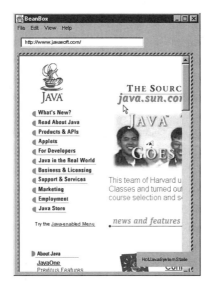

The `RunningText` Bean by Jayakrishnan Nair

You would expect a company like JavaSoft to come up with an impressive bean. However, you don't have to be a large company to build useful beans. Jayakrishnan Nair, a computer science student at the University of Victoria in Victoria, Canada, developed the `RunningText` bean that you'll study in this section. The `RunningText` bean provides a great example of animation and is perfect for Web page advertising. It allows you specify the text that you want to scroll, along with its foreground and background colors. Best of all, you can download the bean from Jayakrishnan's Web site at `http://csr.csc.uvic.ca/~jk/java.html`. Go ahead and download it so you can use it in the following example.

Installing the `RunningText` Bean

The `RunningText` bean, like most beans, is simple to install. It comes in a file named `RunningText.jar`. To install the bean, just copy `RunningText.jar` to the `\bdk\jars` directory to make it available to the BeanBox.

Running the `RunningText` Bean in the BeanBox

The `RunningText` bean is easy to use. Launch the BeanBox program and click on the `RunningText` bean in the ToolBox. Then click the center of the BeanBox. The `RunningText` bean should appear as shown in Figure 27.3.

FIGURE 27.3.

The initial display of the `RunningText` bean.

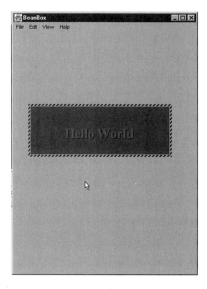

The `RunningText` bean is immediately up and running in your BeanBox. Look at the bean's property sheet. You'll see that it allows you to set the following properties:

- `fontSize`
- `width`
- `delay`
- `bgColor`
- `fgColor`
- `height`
- `text`
- `fontStyle`
- `shadowOn`
- `fontName`

Experiment with these properties to learn how you can tailor the bean's behavior.

1. Set the `text` property to `"JavaBeans"`.
2. Set the `bgColor` property to `yellow`.
3. Set the `fgColor` property to `blue`.
4. Set the `shadowOn` property to `false`.
5. Set the `fontSize` property to `32`.

You should notice that the bean's behavior is changed in the BeanBox instantly when you make these modifications.

The `RunningText` bean is a great way to add advertisements to Web pages. You may want to experiment further by adding the `RunningText` bean to an applet and displaying it in one of your Web pages. When you are finished with the `RunningText` bean, exit the BeanBox.

Beans by IBM

One of the most committed developers of beans is IBM. It has created dozens of handy beans and makes them available through its fine Java software development tools. In particular, the WebRunner Toolkit includes a number of beans that are great for building applets and window applications. Some of the beans available through the WebRunner Toolkit include the following:

- A collection of Network Beans that support the FTP, NNTP, SMTP, and POP3 protocols
- User interface beans including a `MultiColumnListbox` bean, a `ProgressBar` bean, and a `Charting` bean
- A `DatePicker` bean that provides full calendar support
- A `MaskedTextField` bean for controlling use input
- A set of `Gauge` beans that were designed by IBM's Human-Computer Interaction Strategy and Design Lab

Trial versions of these beans are available from `http://www.software.ibm.com/ad/webrunner/WRBeans.html`. Go ahead and download the `Gauge` beans. We'll use them in the following example.

Installing the `Gauge` Beans

The `Gauge` beans are contained in a file named `gauges1e.tgz`. The filename may vary for later versions of the `Gauge` beans. The file is a tarred, gzipped file. Use a program like WinZip to extract the files contained in `gauges1e.tgz` to a temporary directory.

You'll notice that IBM supplies copious documentation for these beans. The actual beans are extracted to the `\Jars` subdirectory. Copy `Gauges.jar` and `GaugeTest.jar` to the `\bdk\jars` directory to make the beans available to the BeanBox.

Running the Gauge Beans in the BeanBox

After installing the `.jar` files in the `\bdk\jars` directory, launch the BeanBox application. You should notice that the following beans have been added to the toolbox:

- `GaugeTest`—Increments/decrements a value through a specified range. Used to test the other beans.
- `Needle`—A semicircular needle gauge similar to an old-fashioned speedometer.
- `LightBulbIndicator`—A simulation of an actual light bulb.
- `TraceRecorder`—A data recorder/display device similar to those found in laboratory instruments.
- `BarIndicator`—A bar (horizontal or vertical) that displays a value similar to a thermometer.
- `RAGNeedle`—A speedometer-like gauge.
- `RollingCounter`—A counter that is similar to a car's odometer.
- `LEDCounter`—A counter that is similar to a calculator's display.
- `BlockIndicator`—Similar to the `BarIndicator`, but with hash marks.
- `Thermometer`—A thermometer simulation.
- `Oscilloscope`—An oscilloscope-like value display.

We'll start with the first four beans.

1. Place a `GaugeTest` bean in the upper-right corner of the BeanBox.
2. Place a `Needle` bean in the upper-left corner.
3. Place a `LightBulbIndicator` bean under the `Needle` bean.
4. Place a `TraceRecorder` bean under the `GaugeTest` bean.

At this point, your BeanBox should look like Figure 27.4.

Now connect the beans together. Bind the `value` property of the `GaugeText` bean to the `value` properties of the other three beans. Do this one bean at a time.

1. Select the `GaugeTest` bean.
2. Select the `Bind` property from the Edit menu.
3. Select the `value` property in the `PropertyNameDialog`.

FIGURE 27.4.

Laying out the first four Gauge *beans.*

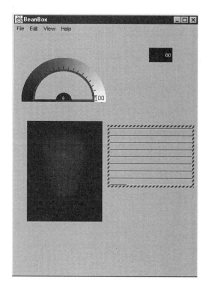

4. Click on the bean that you want to connect to.

5. Select the value property in the destination bean's PropertyNameDialog.

You'll notice that the value of the GaugeTest bean is reflected in the values of the other three beans, as shown in Figure 27.5.

FIGURE 27.5.

The GaugeTest *bean drives the* Needle, LightBulbIndicator, *and* TraceRecorder *beans.*

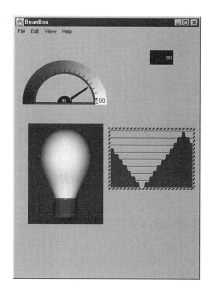

Now clear the BeanBox and examine some of the other Gauge beans.

1. Place the GaugeTest bean in the upper-right corner of the BeanBox, as before.
2. Place the BarIndicator bean to the left of the GaugeTest bean.
3. Set the background property of the BarIndicator to white so that you can see it against the background of the BeanBox.
4. Place the RAGNeedle bean underneath the BarIndicator bean.
5. Place the RollingCounter bean underneath the GaugeTest bean.
6. Place the LEDCounter bean underneath the RollingCounter bean.
7. Place the BlockIndicator bean underneath the RAGNeedle bean.
8. Set the background property of the BlockIndicator to white.
9. Place the Thermometer bean under the LEDCounter bean.
10. Place the Oscilloscope bean under the BlockIndicator bean.

Your BeanBox should now look similar to the one shown in Figure 27.6.

FIGURE 27.6.

Laying out the rest of the Gauge beans.

Now connect the value property of the GaugeTest bean to the value properties of the other beans. When you finish, the value of the GaugeTest bean will drive the value of the other beans, as shown in Figure 27.7.

FIGURE 27.7.

The gauges are all working in unison.

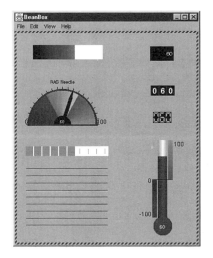

Summary

In this chapter you took a look at some of the beans that are being developed by the Java software development community. You learned how JavaSoft's HotJava HTML Component bean can be used to embed Web-browsing capabilities into any window application. You worked with the RunningText bean developed by Jayakrishnan Nair and learned how it can be used to add animated text to applets and applications. You also looked at some of the nifty Gauge beans from IBM's WebRunner Toolkit. In the next chapter, "Using InfoBus," you'll learn how Infobus is used to facilitate communication between beans.

Using InfoBus

CHAPTER 28

The goal of bean-based software development is to use beans to quickly and easily assemble applets and applications. To accomplish this, you need a suitable collection of beans and an approach to integrating them into your programs. The InfoBus, developed by Lotus Development Corporation and JavaSoft, provides a mechanism for bean integration. InfoBus supports a standard interface for communication between beans and allows information to be exchanged between beans in a structured way.

In this chapter, you'll be introduced to the InfoBus and learn how it works. You'll learn how InfoBus simplifies and standardizes bean communication, and about the classes and interfaces of the InfoBus API. You'll then develop an applet that uses InfoBus to exchange data between beans. When you finish this chapter, you'll be able to use InfoBus to simplify communication between the beans that you develop.

How InfoBus Works

Normally, all beans that are loaded from the same classloader are visible to each other. Beans can find each other by searching the container-component hierarchy or their bean context. They can then use reflection and design patterns to determine which services are provided by other beans. However, this approach is often cumbersome and prone to error. The software engineers at Lotus Development Corporation and JavaSoft recognized that a standard approach to data exchange between beans was needed and collaborated to simplify inter-bean communication. The InfoBus is the result of this effort.

The InfoBus is analogous to a PC system bus. Data producers and consumers connect to an InfoBus in the same way that PC cards connect to a PC's system bus. Data producers use the bus to send data items to data consumers. The InfoBus is asynchronous and symmetric. This means that the producer and consumer do not have to synchronize to exchange data, and any member of the bus can send data to any other member of the bus.

The InfoBus operates as follows:

> **NOTE**
>
> The unit of data exchanged on an InfoBus is referred to as a *data item*. A data item can be any object.

- Beans, components, and other objects join the InfoBus by implementing the `InfoBusMember` interface, obtaining an `InfoBus` instance, and using an appropriate method to join the instance.

- Data producers implement the `InfoBusDataProducer` interface, and data consumers implement the `InfoBusDataConsumer` interface. These interfaces define methods for handling events required for data exchange.

- Data producers signal that named data items are available on an `InfoBus` object by invoking the object's `fireItemAvailable()` method.

- Data consumers get named data items from an `InfoBus` object by invoking the `requestDataItem()` method of the `InfoBusItemAvailableEvent` event received via the `InfoBusDataConsumer` interface.

This list summarizes the typical usage of the InfoBus. However, the InfoBus is flexible and provides additional usage options, which you'll learn about in the next section. The advantage of InfoBus is that it eliminates the need for inference and discovery on the part of beans. Instead, it provides a standard, structured mechanism for named data items to be exchanged.

The InfoBus API

The InfoBus is a standard extension API consisting of the `javax.infobus` package, which defines 14 classes and 17 interfaces that support all aspects of InfoBus operation. The `InfoBus` class is the primary class of the package, supporting bus membership and communication between bus members. The `InfoBusMember` interface is the interface required of all bus members. The `InfoBusMemberSupport` class provides a default implementation of this interface.

28

USING INFOBUS

> **NOTE**
>
> The InfoBus API is a standard extension API. It can be downloaded from the JavaBeans home page at `http://www.javasoft.com/products/beans/`.

Data producers implement `InfoBusDataProducer`, and consumers implement `InfoBusDataConsumer`. The `InfoBusDataController` interface is implemented by members that control the operation of the InfoBus. By default, no bus controllers are required.

The `DataItem` interface is used to provide descriptive information about a data item. The data provided by a data item can be accessed through the following InfoBus access interfaces:

- `ImmediateAccess`—Used to access `String` or other objects.

- `ArrayAccess`—Used to access arrays.

- DbAccess—Used to provide access to a database.
- RowsetAccess—Used to access the rows of a database.
- ScrollableRowsetAccess—Used to access a set of database rows.

The DataItemView interface provides a two-dimensional database view. The RowsetValidate is used to validate the contents of a row of a database.

The DefaultPolicy class provides a default InfoBus security policy implementation. It implements the InfoBusPolicyHelper interface, which is required of InfoBus security policies.

The InfoBus supports two event hierarchies. The InfoBusEvent class is the base event class used with InfoBus communication. It is extended by InfoBusItemAvailableEvent, InfoBusItemRequestedEvent, and InfoBusItemRevokedEvent. The InfoBusEventListener interface is used to handle these events. The DataItemChangeEvent class is used to inform bus members about the availability and changes to a data item. It is extended by DataItemAddedEvent, DataItemDeletedEvent, DataItemRevokedEvent, DataItemValueChangedEvent, and RowsetCursorMovedEvent. The DataItemChangeListener interface handles these events.

The InfoBusPropertyMap interface is used with InfoBus 1.1 to support the DataItemChangeEvent. The DataItemChangeManager interface is used to manage multiple DataItemChangeListeners.

A Bean Communication Example

In this section, we'll use the InfoBus to enable communication between the following three beans:

- TimeGenerator—A bean that generates the time in the standard GMT time zone. The time is provided as a GregorianCalendar object and is placed on the InfoBus at one-second intervals. This data item is named "Time."
- TimeZoneList—A bean (subclass of List) that displays a list of time zone identifiers. When a time zone is selected by the user, a corresponding TimeZone object is put on the InfoBus. The data item is named "Zone."
- TimeDisplay—A bean that displays the time received from TimeGenerator and the time based on the TimeZone object received from TimeZoneList.

The TimeGenerator and TimeZoneList beans are data producers, and the TimeDisplay bean is a data consumer. All three beans are members of the Time Bus InfoBus.

The `TimeGenerator` Bean

Listing 28.1 shows the source code of the `TimeGenerator` bean. `TimeGenerator` extends the `InfoBusMemberSupport` class and implements `InfoBusDataProducer`, `Serializable`, and `Runnable`. The `Runnable` interface is required to run a `TimeGenerator` object as a separate thread.

Two constructors are provided. The first constructor has no parameters and passes a `null` value to the second constructor. The second constructor takes an `InfoBusMember` object as an argument and passes it to the superclass (`InfoBusMemberSupport`) constructor. This object is used to designate an alternative object to handle InfoBus-related events. A `null` value is used to let the `InfoBusMemberSupport` object handle these events.

The constructor invokes the `joinInfoBus()` method to join the Time Bus. The `getInfoBus()` and `addDataProducer()` methods add the object being constructed as a data producer on the InfoBus.

The `run()` method implements the `Runnable` interface by simply invoking `generateTime()`. The `generateTime()` method uses a `while` statement to loop forever and put Time data items in the InfoBus. The `fireItemAvailable()` method informs bus members that the Time data item is available. The thread then goes to sleep for a second to allow other threads to execute.

The `dateItemRequested()` method implements the `InfoBusDataProducer` interface. It creates a `GregorianCalendar` object for the GMT time zone and the current time. This object is then set into the `InfoBusItemRequestedEvent`, which is propagated back onto the data consumer.

28

USING INFOBUS

LISTING 28.1. THE `TimeGenerator` BEAN.

```
import java.util.*;
import java.io.*;
import javax.infobus.*;
import java.beans.*;

public class TimeGenerator extends InfoBusMemberSupport
  implements InfoBusDataProducer, Serializable, Runnable {

 public TimeGenerator() {
  this(null);
 }
 public TimeGenerator(InfoBusMember infoBusMember) {
  super(infoBusMember);
  try {
```

continues

LISTING 28.1. CONTINUED

```
    joinInfoBus("Time Bus");
    getInfoBus().addDataProducer(this);
  } catch (Exception e) {
    System.out.println(e.toString());
  }
}
public void run() {
 generateTime();
}
void generateTime() {
 while(true) {
   // Notify consumers
   getInfoBus().fireItemAvailable("Time",null,this);
   // Wait a second
   try{
    Thread.currentThread().sleep(1000);
   }catch(Exception ex) {
   }
 }
}
public void dataItemRequested(InfoBusItemRequestedEvent e) {
  // Get GMT time zone IDs
  String[] tzID = TimeZone.getAvailableIDs(0);
  SimpleTimeZone tz = new SimpleTimeZone(0,tzID[0]);
  GregorianCalendar calendar = new GregorianCalendar(tz);
  calendar.setTime(new Date());
  e.setDataItem(calendar);
}
public void propertyChange(PropertyChangeEvent e) {
}
}
```

The `TimeZoneList` Bean

The `TimeZoneList` bean, shown in Listing 28.2, extends the `List` class and implements
the `InfoBusMember`, `InfoBusDataProducer`, `ItemListener`, and `Serializable` interfaces. The `ItemListener` class is implemented so that `TimeZoneList` can handle its own
events.

An `InfoBusMemberSupport` field variable is used to simplify the implementation of the
`InfoBusMember` interface. The `TimeZoneList` methods pass on requests to the `ims` variable. The `tz` variable is used to reference the `TimeZone` object produced by objects of this
class. The `tzIDs` array consists of a list of time zone identifiers that are known to the
JDK.

The `TimeZoneList` constructor takes an argument that identifies the number of rows to
be made visible in the list's display. The object being constructed is added as a member

and data producer to the Time Bus. The time zone IDs are added to the list, and the addItemListener() method is invoked to allow the object being constructed to handle its own ItemEvents.

The itemStateChanged() method handles the selection of a list item. It constructs a TimeZone object based on the time zone ID selected by the user. The availability of this object is signaled by the fireItemAvailable() method. The data item is named Zone.

The setInfoBus(), getInfoBus(), addInfoBusVetoableListener(), removeVetoableListener(), addInfoBusPropertyListener(), and removeInfoBusPropertyListener() method implement the InfoBusMember interface and are redirected to the InfoBusMemberSupport object referenced by the ims variable.

The dataItemRequested() method implements the InfoBusDataProducer interface by setting the generated TimeZone object in the InfoBusItemRequestedEvent.

LISTING 28.2. THE TimeZoneList BEAN.

```
import java.awt.*;
import java.awt.event.*;
import java.util.*;
import java.io.*;
import javax.infobus.*;
import java.beans.*;

public class TimeZoneList extends java.awt.List
  implements InfoBusMember, InfoBusDataProducer,
    ItemListener, Serializable {
 InfoBusMemberSupport ims;
 TimeZone tz = TimeZone.getDefault();
 String[] tzIDs = TimeZone.getAvailableIDs();

 public TimeZoneList(int rows) {
  super(rows);
  ims = new InfoBusMemberSupport(null);
  try {
   ims.joinInfoBus("Time Bus");
   ims.getInfoBus().addDataProducer(this);
  }catch (Exception e) {
   System.out.println(e.toString());
  }
  for(int i=0;i<tzIDs.length;++i) add(tzIDs[i]);
  addItemListener(this);
 }
 public void itemStateChanged(ItemEvent e) {
  int index = ((Integer) e.getItem()).intValue();
  String tzID = tzIDs[index];
  tz = TimeZone.getTimeZone(tzID);
```

28

USING INFOBUS

continues

LISTING 28.2. CONTINUED

```
  getInfoBus().fireItemAvailable("Zone",null,this);
 }
 public void setInfoBus(InfoBus newInfoBus)
   throws PropertyVetoException {
  ims.setInfoBus(newInfoBus);
 }
 public InfoBus getInfoBus() {
  return ims.getInfoBus();
 }
 public void addInfoBusVetoableListener(VetoableChangeListener vcl) {
  ims.addInfoBusVetoableListener(vcl);
 }
 public void removeInfoBusVetoableListener(VetoableChangeListener vcl) {
  ims.removeInfoBusVetoableListener(vcl);
 }
 public void addInfoBusPropertyListener(PropertyChangeListener pcl) {
  ims.addInfoBusPropertyListener(pcl);
 }
 public void removeInfoBusPropertyListener(PropertyChangeListener pcl) {
  ims.removeInfoBusPropertyListener(pcl);
 }
 public void propertyChange(PropertyChangeEvent e) {
 }
 public void dataItemRequested(InfoBusItemRequestedEvent e) {
  e.setDataItem(tz);
 }
}
```

The TimeDisplay Bean

The TimeDisplay bean, shown in Listing 28.3, is an example of a data consumer. The TimeDisplay class extends Canvas and implements the InfoBusMember, InfoBusDataConsumer, and Serializable interfaces. The ims field variable is used in the same way as in TimeZoneList, to reference an InfoBusMemberSupport object that helps implement the InfoBusMember interface. The time1 and time2 variables reference String objects that are displayed on the canvas. The tz variable references the TimeZone object selected by the user. It is initially set to the current time zone.

The TimeDisplay constructor adds the object being constructed as a member and consumer to the Time Bus.

The getPreferredSize() and paint() methods are used to size and draw the component interface, which consists of two time displays. The first time display is based on the GregorianCalendar object received (via the InfoBus) from the TimeGenerator bean. The second time display is based on the TimeZone object received from the TimeZoneList bean.

The dataItemAvailable() method implements the InfoBusDataConsumer interface and allows the TimeDisplay object to receive data inputs from the other beans on the InfoBus. The InfoBusItemAvailableEvent passed as an argument to dataItemAvailable() contains the data item and information about the data item. The getDataItemName() method retrieves the data item's name. This name is used to determine whether the data item is from TimeGenerator or TimeZoneList.

If the data item is from TimeGenerator, the requestDataItem() method is used to return the GregorianCalendar object. This object is then used to update the time1 string. The time2 string is updated based on the current value of the tz variable. The repaint() method is invoked to cause the canvas to be repainted.

If the data item is from TimeZoneList, the requestDataItem() method is used to return the TimeZone object. This object is then used to update the tz variable.

The getTimeString() is used to retrieve the information to be displayed from a Calendar object.

LISTING 28.3. THE TimeDisplay BEAN.

```
import java.awt.*;
import java.util.*;
import java.io.*;
import javax.infobus.*;
import java.beans.*;

public class TimeDisplay extends Canvas
  implements InfoBusMember, InfoBusDataConsumer, Serializable {
  InfoBusMemberSupport ims;
  String time1 = "";
  String time2 = "";
  TimeZone tz = TimeZone.getDefault();

  public TimeDisplay() {
   ims = new InfoBusMemberSupport(null);
   try {
    ims.joinInfoBus("Time Bus");
    ims.getInfoBus().addDataConsumer(this);
   }catch (Exception e) {
    System.out.println(e.toString());
   }
  }
  public Dimension getPreferredSize() {
   return new Dimension(120,100);
  }
  public void paint(Graphics g) {
   g.drawString(time1,10,25);
```

28

USING INFOBUS

continues

LISTING 28.3. CONTINUED

```java
 g.drawString(time2,10,75);
}
public void setInfoBus(InfoBus newInfoBus)
  throws PropertyVetoException {
 ims.setInfoBus(newInfoBus);
}
public InfoBus getInfoBus() {
 return ims.getInfoBus();
}
public void addInfoBusVetoableListener(VetoableChangeListener vcl) {
 ims.addInfoBusVetoableListener(vcl);
}
public void removeInfoBusVetoableListener(VetoableChangeListener vcl) {
 ims.removeInfoBusVetoableListener(vcl);
}
public void addInfoBusPropertyListener(PropertyChangeListener pcl) {
 ims.addInfoBusPropertyListener(pcl);
}
public void removeInfoBusPropertyListener(PropertyChangeListener pcl) {
 ims.removeInfoBusPropertyListener(pcl);
}
public void propertyChange(PropertyChangeEvent e) {
}
public void dataItemAvailable(InfoBusItemAvailableEvent e) {
 String name = e.getDataItemName();
 if(name.equals("Time")) {
  GregorianCalendar calendar1 =
   (GregorianCalendar) e.requestDataItem(this,null);
  GregorianCalendar calendar2 = new GregorianCalendar(tz);
  time1 = getTimeString(calendar1);
  time2 = getTimeString(calendar2);
  repaint();
 }else if(name.equals("Zone")) {
  tz = (TimeZone) e.requestDataItem(this,null);
 }
}
String getTimeString(GregorianCalendar calendar) {
  String hour = String.valueOf(calendar.get(Calendar.HOUR_OF_DAY));
  if(hour.length()==1) hour = "0"+hour;
  String minute = String.valueOf(calendar.get(Calendar.MINUTE));
  if(minute.length()==1) minute = "0"+minute;
  String second = String.valueOf(calendar.get(Calendar.SECOND));
  if(second.length()==1) second = "0"+second;
  TimeZone timeZone = calendar.getTimeZone();
  return hour+":"+minute+":"+second+" "+timeZone.getID();
}
public void dataItemRevoked(InfoBusItemRevokedEvent e) {
}
}
```

The `TimeApplet` Class

Now that we have three InfoBus-enabled beans, let's combine them in an applet that will demonstrate their operation. The `TimeApplet` (Listing 28.4) shows how easy this is. This applet creates a new thread from the `TimeGenerator` bean and instances of the `TimeDisplay` and `TimeZoneList` beans. The applet's `init()` method adds the two visible beans as GUI components and then invokes the `TimeGenerator`'s `start()` method.

Listing 28.5 provides an HTML file that can be used to run the applet. When you run this file in `appletviewer`, the window shown in Figure 28.1, is displayed. Note that the time is displayed in GMT and in your local time zone. Select a new time zone from the list and the second time string displays time in the newly selected time zone, as shown in Figure 28.2.

FIGURE 28.1.

The `TimeApplet` initial display.

FIGURE 28.2.

The time is displayed using the newly selected time zone.

LISTING 28.4. THE TimeApplet CLASS.

```java
import java.applet.*;
import java.awt.*;
import java.awt.event.*;
import javax.infobus.*;

public class TimeApplet extends Applet {
 Thread generator = new Thread(new TimeGenerator());
 TimeDisplay display = new TimeDisplay();
 TimeZoneList tzl = new TimeZoneList(5);

 public void init() {
  add(tzl);
  add(display);
  generator.start();
 }
}
```

LISTING 28.5. THE time.htm FILE.

```html
<HTML>
<HEAD>
<TITLE>Using the InfoBus</TITLE>
</HEAD>
<BODY>
<APPLET CODE="TimeApplet.class" HEIGHT=300 WIDTH=300>
</APPLET>
</BODY>
</HTML>
```

Summary

In this chapter, you were introduced to the InfoBus. You learned how InfoBus simplifies and standardizes bean communication and about the classes and interfaces of the InfoBus API. You then developed an applet that uses InfoBus to exchange data between beans. In the next chapter, you'll study other facilities for integrating beans that were introduced with the Glasgow JavaBeans specification.

CHAPTER 29

Glasgow Developments

The capabilities of JDK 1.2 JavaBeans have been significantly enhanced since JDK 1.1. These enhancements are the result of an upgrade program, referred to as *Glasgow*. The Glasgow Specification (http://java.sun.com/beans/glasgow/) documents the objectives, rationale, requirements, and design of this upgrade. The JavaBeans improvements resulting from Glasgow can be grouped into the following three functional areas:

- The Extensible Runtime Containment and Services Protocol—A protocol that lets beans find out information about their container and the services that it provides.
- The JavaBeans Activation Framework (JAF)—A framework for mapping data to beans based on the data's types.
- The Drag and Drop Subsystem—The Drag and Drop API covered in Chapter 16.

Each of these three areas greatly enhances the capabilities of JavaBeans. The Extensible Runtime Containment and Services Protocol allows beans to be constructed in a hierarchical fashion, with bean containers providing direct services to their bean components. The JAF allows beans to be activated during execution time to process data of a variety of types. The Drag and Drop API allows JavaBeans to provide the same GUI capabilities as other component frameworks.

In this chapter, you'll focus on the first two Glasgow developments—Chapter 16, "Working with Drag and Drop," is dedicated to the third. You'll learn about the capabilities each area provides, and how to use them in the beans you develop. When you finish this chapter, you'll be familiar with the most recent developments in JavaBeans technology.

The Extensible Runtime Containment and Services Protocol

As described in Chapter 24, "The Software Component Assembly Model," the overall objective of component-based software development is to develop software components that can be used to assemble software on a component-by-component basis. In this model, existing components are used to assemble new components, which may be used to develop even more complex components. These components are then assembled into applets or applications via visual programming tools.

The JavaBeans implementation provided with JDK 1.1 allowed beans to be assembled into component hierarchies, with parent beans containing one or more child beans. However, the JDK 1.1 JavaBeans implementation did not provide any facilities for child beans to learn about their parent containers or the services they provide. As a result, child beans were not able to interact with their parents (or siblings) or make use of their (family) environment. For example, suppose that you want to use a multimedia bean as a container for part of an application, and you want to add custom bean controls to the multimedia bean. The bean controls have no way of obtaining information about their container or the multimedia services it provides.

The Extensible Runtime Containment and Services Protocol solves the lack of communication between child beans and their parent containers. This protocol adds the following capabilities to JDK 1.1 JavaBeans:

- Specifies the environment, or *context*, in which a bean executes.
- Allows services to be dynamically added to a bean's environment.
- Provides a mechanism for beans to interrogate their environment, discover which services are provided, and make use of those services.

These capabilities are provided through the `java.beans.beancontext` package, which is introduced in Chapter 26, "Developing Beans." This package provides classes and interfaces for enabling beans to access their execution environment, referred to as their *bean context*. The `BeanContextChild` and `BeanContext` interfaces implement this concept.

The `BeanContextChild` interface provides methods for getting and setting this context, and for managing context-related event listeners. All context-aware beans must implement this interface.

`BeanContextChild` is extended by the `BeanContext` interface, which provides methods by which beans can access resources and services that are available within their context. Objects that implement `BeanContext` function as containers for other beans (which implement `BeanChildContext`). When a child bean that implements `BeanChildContext` is added to a parent bean container that implements `BeanContext`, the parent invokes the `setBeanContext()` method of its child. When the child wants to access its environment (`BeanContext`), it invokes its `getBeanContext()` method.

A bean can access its environment through its `BeanContext`. A `BeanContext` may or may not expose its services to the beans that it contains. The `BeanContextServicesSupport` interface extends the `BeanContext` interface to provide child beans with access to the services of their `BeanContext`. A bean that provides services to its children must implement this interface. The `getCurrentServiceClasses()`, `hasServices()`, and `getService()` methods are invoked by the child beans to access these services. The `BeanContextServiceProvider` interface is implemented by objects that provide instances of a particular service. The `BeanContextContainer` interface is implemented by `BeanContext` objects that are associated with AWT containers.

29

GLASGOW DEVELOPMENTS

> **NOTE**
>
> Because a bean's `BeanContext` is subject to change, a bean's references to its `BeanContext` must be declared as `transient`.

The `BeanContextChildSupport` class provides a default implementation of the `BeanContextChild` interface.

The `BeanContextSupport` class extends `BeanContextChildSupport` to provide an implementation of the `BeanContext` interface. This class provides variables and methods for managing the beans that are contained in the context. It defines two inner classes: `BeanContextSupport.BCSChild` and `BeanContextSupport.BCSIterator`. These classes are used to maintain information on the beans that are contained within a bean context.

The `BeanContextServicesSupport` class extends `BeanContextSupport` and implements the `BeanContextServices` interface. It defines two inner classes: `BeanContextServicesSupport.BCSSChild` and `BeanContextServicesSupport.BCSSServiceProvider`. `BeanContextServicesSupport.BCSSChild` extends `BeanContextSupport.BCSChild`, and `BeanContextServicesSupport.BCSSServiceProvider` is used to access `BeanContextServiceProvider` objects.

BeanContext Event Handling

The Extensible Runtime Containment and Services Protocol allows a beans's `BeanContext` to change during a program's execution. It provides events and event handling interfaces to deal with changes in a bean's `BeanContext`. The `BeanContextEvent` class is the superclass of all `BeanContext`-related events. It is extended by `BeanContextMembershipEvent`, `BeanContextServiceAvailableEvent`, and `BeanContextServiceRevokedEvent`. The `BeanContextMembershipEvent` class defines events that occur as the result of changes in a bean's membership in a `BeanContext`. It is extended by `BeanContextAddedEvent` and `BeanContextRemovedEvent`. The `BeanContextServiceAvailableEvent` reports changes in the availability of services, and `BeanContextServiceRevokedEvent` reports the revocation of services.

The `BeanContextMemberShipListener` interface is used to handle the `BeanContextMembershipEvent` event. The `BeanContextServicesListener` interface is used to handle the `BeanContextServiceAvailableEvent` event. The `BeanContextServiceRevokedListener` interface is used to handle the `BeanContextServiceRevokedEvent` event.

A `BeanContext` Example

The `BeanContextApp` application, shown in Listing 29.1, illustrates the use of the `java.beans.beancontext` package. The program's output is nothing special (see Figure 29.1), but what's happening under the hood is quite interesting.

FIGURE 29.1.

The `BeanContextApp` *display.*

The text displayed in the text area is generated by a bean (an object of the `ChildBean` class) that is contained in another bean (an object of the `ParentBean` class). Listing 29.2 contains the source code of the `ChildBean` class, and Listing 29.3 contains the source code of the `ParentBean` class. The child bean obtains access to its `BeanContext` and queries the context about the services it provides. One of these services is the `TextArea` that is displayed in the program's frame window. The parent bean passes a reference to the `TextArea` object to the child, and the child uses it to display its output.

The `JAFApp` program is a simple component that displays a `TextArea` object. Its only processing of note is in the `setup()` method. After adding the `TextArea` object to the center of its frame, it creates a `ParentBean` object, passing a reference to the `TextArea` object in the `ParentBean` constructor. It then creates an object of the `ChildBean` class and adds it to the `ParentBean` object. Finally, it invokes the `useContext()` method of the `ChildBean` object.

The `ChildBean` class shows how to use a `BeanContext` to access services that are provided by a parent bean. The `ChildBean` class extends the `BeanContextChildSupport` class and implements the `BeanContextServiceRevokedListener` interface. It creates a `TextArea` object of its own, which it uses to pass parameters of the `Class` class to its parent.

29

GLASGOW
DEVELOPMENTS

The useContext() method invokes the getBeanContext() method to retrieve the bean's BeanContext and cast it into a BeanContextServices object. This object is used to determine whether the bean context provides a service of the TextArea class. The getService() method is used to obtain the object implementing this service (from the bean context). The TextArea object that is returned is then used to display the text message to the application window.

The serviceRevoked() method is a stub that is used to implement the BeanContextServiceRevokedListener interface. An object of this interface is required as an argument to the getService() method.

The ParentBean class provides the bean context of the ChildBean object. It extends the BeanContextServicesSupport class and implements the BeanContextServiceProvider interface. Its constructor receives and stores a TextArea object, and then adds a service related to this object.

Two getService() methods are provided. One overrides the method of the BeanContextServicesSupport class, and the other is used to implement the BeanContextServiceProvider interface. Both return the TextArea object.

The getCurrentServiceSelectors() and releaseService() methods are also used to implement the BeanContextServiceProvider interface.

LISTING 29.1. THE BeanContextApp PROGRAM.

```
import java.awt.*;
import java.awt.event.*;
import ju.ch09.*;

public class BeanContextApp extends Frame {
 Object menuItems[][] = {{"File","Exit"}};
 MenuItemHandler mih = new MenuItemHandler();
 MyMenuBar menuBar = new MyMenuBar(menuItems,mih,mih);
 int screenWidth = 400;
 int screenHeight = 400;
 TextArea textArea = new TextArea();

 public static void main(String args[]){
  BeanContextApp app = new BeanContextApp();
 }
 public BeanContextApp() {
  super("BeanContextApp");
  setMenuBar(menuBar);
  setup();
  setSize(screenWidth,screenHeight);
  addWindowListener(new WindowEventHandler());
  show();
```

```
    }
void setup() {
 add("Center",textArea);
 ParentBean parent = new ParentBean(textArea);
 ChildBean child = new ChildBean();
 parent.add(child);
 child.useContext();
}
class MenuItemHandler implements ActionListener, ItemListener {
 public void actionPerformed(ActionEvent ev){
  String s=ev.getActionCommand();
  if(s.equals("Exit")){
   System.exit(0);
  }
 }
 public void itemStateChanged(ItemEvent e){
 }
}
class WindowEventHandler extends WindowAdapter {
 public void windowClosing(WindowEvent e){
  System.exit(0);
 }
 }
}
```

LISTING 29.2. THE ChildBean BEAN.

```
import java.awt.*;
import java.beans.*;
import java.beans.beancontext.*;

public class ChildBean extends BeanContextChildSupport
  implements BeanContextServiceRevokedListener {

 TextArea textArea = new TextArea();

 public void useContext() {
  BeanContextServices beanContext =
   (BeanContextServices) getBeanContext();
  if(beanContext.hasService(textArea.getClass())) {
   try {
    textArea = (TextArea) beanContext.getService(this, this,
     textArea.getClass(), null, this);
   }catch(Exception ex){
    System.out.println(ex.toString());
   }
```

29

continues

LISTING 29.2. CONTINUED

```
   String msg = "The child was able to access the services of its
parent.";
   textArea.setText(msg);
  }
 }

 public void serviceRevoked(BeanContextServiceRevokedEvent ev) {
 }
}
```

LISTING 29.3. THE ParentBean BEAN.

```
import java.awt.*;
import java.beans.*;
import java.util.*;
import java.beans.beancontext.*;

public class ParentBean extends BeanContextServicesSupport
  implements BeanContextServiceProvider {

 TextArea textArea;

 public ParentBean(TextArea textArea) {
  this.textArea = textArea;
  addService(textArea.getClass(), this);
 }

 public Object getService(BeanContextChild child,
   Object requestor, Class serviceClass, Object serviceSelector,
   BeanContextServiceRevokedListener bcsrl)
   throws TooManyListenersException {
  return textArea;
 }

 public Object getService(BeanContextServices bcs,
   Object requestor, Class serviceClass, Object serviceSelector) {
  return textArea;
 }

 public Iterator getCurrentServiceSelectors(BeanContextServices bcs,
   Class serviceClass) {
  return null;
 }

 public void releaseService(BeanContextServices bcs,
   Object requestor, Object service) {
 }
}
```

The JavaBeans Activation Framework

In many applications, software is called upon to process data of arbitrary types. The application is required to determine the type of data that it is to process, determine which operations can be performed on the data, and instantiate software components for performing those operations. For example, consider a Web browser that displays data loaded from a URL. Some URLs reference HTML files, some reference image files, and others may reference files containing scripting data. The Web browser determines the type of data contained in the file using MIME type information provided by Web servers. It then selects external or internal components that display the file's data, launches instances of those components, and feeds the file data to those components for display.

The JavaBeans Activation Framework is used to support this type of data processing by associating beans with the types of data that they support. It provides the following capabilities:

- A mechanism for associating data types with different types of data.
- The capability to determine the operations supported by data of a particular type.
- A mapping of data operations to the beans that support those operations.
- The capability to instantiate beans to support specific data operations.

The JAF API is implemented by the `javax.activation` package, which is a standard API extension. This package consists of the following classes and interfaces:

- `DataHandler`—This class provides a standard interface to data of different types. It is the entry point to the JAF.
- `DataSource`—An interface that provides encapsulated access to data of different types. It reports the data's type and provides access to the data via input and output streams.
- `FileDataSource`—Extends `DataSource` to provide access to file data.
- `URLDataSource`—Extends `DataSource` to provide access to data that is accessible via a URL.
- `DataContentHandler`—Used by `DataHandler` to convert `DataSource` objects to the objects they represent, and to convert objects to byte streams of a particular MIME type.
- `DataContentHandlerFactory`—A factory for creating `DataContentHandler` objects for specific MIME types.

29

GLASGOW DEVELOPMENTS

- CommandMap—Provides access to the commands (operations) supported for a particular MIME type, and maps these commands to objects that support those commands.

- MailcapCommandMap—Extends CommandMap to support mailcap (RFC 1524) files.

- CommandObject—An interface implemented by JavaBeans to make them JAF-aware. It allows the beans to respond to commands and access the DataHandler associated with the data they are commanded to process.

- CommandInfo—Used by CommandMap to return the results of commands that have been made of JAF-aware beans.

- MimeType—Encapsulates a MIME type.

- FileTypeMap—Associated files with MIME types.

- MimetypesFileTypeMap—Extends FileTypeMap to identify a file's MIME type based on its extension.

- MimeTypeParameterList—Encapsulates the parameter list of a MIME type.

- ActivationDataFlavor—Extends java.awt.datatransfer.DataFlavor to provide better MIME type processing.

Before the JAF can be used, a CommandMap must be created that maps MIME types, and operations on those types, to bean classes. This is typically accomplished using the MailcapCommandMap class. External mailcap files can be used to set up the mapping, or it can be set up during program initialization. Once the CommandMap has been created, the JAF is ready for use.

The JAF is used by creating a DataSource for data that is to be processed. This data is typically stored in a file or referenced by a URL. A DataHandler is then constructed from the DataSource. The getContentType() method of DataHandler is used to retrieve the MIME type associated with the DataSource. This MIME type is used to retrieve a CommandInfo array from the CommandMap. The CommandInfo array presents the list of operations that are supported by the DataSource. A selected CommandInfo object is passed to the getBean() method of DataHandler to create an instance of a bean that supports a specific operation on a MIME type. The bean is added to the applet or application's GUI, and the bean's setCommandContext() method is invoked to cause the bean to perform the desired operation on the data contained in the DataSource.

JAF-compliant beans are required to implement the CommandObject interface. This interface consists of the single setCommandContext() method.

The JAFApp program in the next section illustrates the use of the interfaces and classes described in the previous paragraphs.

> **NOTE**
>
> Make sure that you download and install the JAF before going to the next section. It can be downloaded from JavaSoft's Web site at `http://java.sun.com/beans/glasgow/jaf.html`. To use the JAF, the `activation.jar` file must be placed in your CLASSPATH.

The JAFApp Program

The JAFApp program in Listing 29.4 shows how the JAF is used to read a file, determine its MIME type, and instantiate a bean to display the file's contents. The program's opening display is shown in Figure 29.2. It is a bare frame containing no GUI components. Use the Open menu item in the File menu to open the `test.txt` file that is provided in the ch29 directory. A bean is created to display the file's contents, as shown in Figure 29.3. Now open the `test.gif` file that is located in the same directory. The old bean is removed and a new bean is instantiated to display the GIF file, as shown in Figure 29.4.

> **NOTE**
>
> Make sure that the `ju.ch29` package is in your CLASSPATH before you run the JAFApp program.

FIGURE 29.2.

The JAFApp opening display.

FIGURE 29.3.

The TextDisplay *bean displays the text file.*

FIGURE 29.4.

The ImageDisplay *bean displays the GIF file.*

The JAFApp class declares a variable of the MailcapCommandMap class and assigns it to the mailcap variable. This variable is initialized in the setup() method. The bean variable is declared as an object that supports the CommandObject interface. This object is assigned to beans that are dynamically instantiated by the JAF.

The setup() method specifies that an object of the ju.ch29.TextDisplay class should be used to implement the view operation on data of the text/plain MIME type. It also specifies that an object of the ju.ch29.ImageDisplay class should be used to implement the view operation on data of the image/gif MIME type. This mapping is essential to specifying the behavior of the JAF.

The displayFile() method is invoked to display a file using the JAF. It creates a FileDataSource object from the name of the file to be displayed, and then creates a

DataHandler object from the FileDataSource object. The getContentType() method returns the MIME type of the data source. This MIME type is used to retrieve an array of CommandInfo objects that specify the commands that are supported on this MIME type. The array is searched for an object that implements the view command, and a bean implementing the CommandObject interface is created and instantiated via the getBean() method of the DataHandler interface. The CommandInfo object associated with the view command is passed as an argument to getBean().

The bean is cast to a Component and added to the program's GUI. The validate() method is then invoked to lay out the window. Finally, the bean is brought to life by invoking its setCommandContext() method, passing a reference to the DataHandler interface. This causes the bean to display the data source in its GUI component's display area.

The TextDisplay class, shown in Listing 29.5, extends TextArea and implements the CommandObject interface. This interface consists of the single setCommandContext() method. This method obtains an InputStream object from the DataHandler, reads the data contained in the stream, converts it to a String object, and displays it in its text area.

The ImageDisplay class (see Listing 29.6) is similar to TextDisplay. However, ImageDisplay extends a Canvas object instead of a TextArea object. Its setCommandContext() method reads the data from the InputStream object provided by the DataHandler and converts it to an Image object. The repaint() method is invoked to cause the Image object to be painted to the Graphics object associated with the Canvas.

LISTING 29.4. THE JAFApp PROGRAM.

```
import java.awt.*;
import java.awt.event.*;
import java.util.*;
import javax.activation.*;
import ju.ch09.*;
import ju.ch29.TextDisplay;
import ju.ch29.ImageDisplay;

public class JAFApp extends Frame {
  Object menuItems[][] = {{"File","Open","-","Exit"}};
  MenuItemHandler mih = new MenuItemHandler();
  MyMenuBar menuBar = new MyMenuBar(menuItems,mih,mih);
  int screenWidth = 400;
  int screenHeight = 400;
```

29

continues

LISTING 29.4. CONTINUED

```java
String directory = ".";
MailcapCommandMap mailcap = new MailcapCommandMap();
CommandObject bean = null;

public static void main(String args[]){
 JAFApp app = new JAFApp();
}
public JAFApp() {
 super("JAFApp");
 setMenuBar(menuBar);
 setup();
 setSize(screenWidth,screenHeight);
 addWindowListener(new WindowEventHandler());
 show();
}
void setup() {
 mailcap.addMailcap("text/plain; ; x-java-view=ju.ch29.TextDisplay");
 mailcap.addMailcap("image/gif; ; x-java-view=ju.ch29.ImageDisplay");
}
void displayFile(String fileName) {
 FileDataSource fds = new FileDataSource(fileName);
 DataHandler dh = new DataHandler(fds);
 String mimeType = dh.getContentType();
 try {
  CommandInfo[] commands = mailcap.getPreferredCommands(mimeType);
  for(int i=0;i<commands.length;++i) {
   if(commands[i].getCommandName().equals("view")) {
    if(bean!=null) remove((Component) bean);
    bean = (CommandObject) dh.getBean(commands[i]);
    add("Center",(Component) bean);
    validate();
    bean.setCommandContext("",dh);
   }
  }
 }catch(Exception ex){
  System.out.println(ex.toString());
 }
}
String getFileName() {
 // Display file dialog
 FileDialog dialog = new FileDialog(JAFApp.this,
 "Open File", FileDialog.LOAD);
 dialog.setDirectory(directory);
 dialog.show();
 if(dialog.getFile()==null) return null;
 directory = dialog.getDirectory();
```

```
    String file = directory + dialog.getFile();
    return file;
  }
  class MenuItemHandler implements ActionListener, ItemListener {
    public void actionPerformed(ActionEvent ev){
      String s=ev.getActionCommand();
      if(s.equals("Exit")){
        System.exit(0);
      }else if(s=="Open"){
        // Get the name of the file
        String fileName = getFileName();
        if(fileName == null) return;
        displayFile(fileName);
      }
    }
    public void itemStateChanged(ItemEvent e){
    }
  }
  class WindowEventHandler extends WindowAdapter {
    public void windowClosing(WindowEvent e){
      System.exit(0);
    }
  }
}
```

LISTING 29.5. THE `TextDisplay` BEAN.

```
package ju.ch29;

import java.awt.*;
import java.io.*;
import javax.activation.*;

public class TextDisplay extends TextArea
  implements Serializable, CommandObject {

  public void setCommandContext(String verb, DataHandler dh)
    throws IOException {
    if(dh!=null) {
      InputStream inStream = dh.getInputStream();
      byte[] bytes = new byte[inStream.available()];
      inStream.read(bytes);
      setText(new String(bytes));
    }
  }
}
```

LISTING 29.6. THE ImageDisplay BEAN.

```
package ju.ch29;

import java.awt.*;
import java.io.*;
import javax.activation.*;

public class ImageDisplay extends Canvas
  implements Serializable, CommandObject {
 public static final int WIDTH = 200;
 public static final int HEIGHT = 200;
 Image image = null;

 public ImageDisplay() {
  super();
 }
 public Dimension getPreferredSize() {
  return new Dimension(WIDTH,HEIGHT);
 }
 public Image getImage() {
  return image;
 }
 public void setImage(Image image) {
  this.image = image;
 }
 public synchronized void paint(Graphics g) {
  if(image!=null) g.drawImage(image,0,0,this);
 }
 public void setCommandContext(String verb, DataHandler dh)
   throws IOException {
  if(dh!=null) {
   InputStream inStream = dh.getInputStream();
   byte[] bytes = new byte[inStream.available()];
   inStream.read(bytes);
   image = Toolkit.getDefaultToolkit().createImage(bytes);
   repaint();
  }
 }
}
```

Summary

In this chapter, you learned about the Glasgow developments and how to use the capabilities they provide in the beans you develop. You learned about the Extensible Runtime Containment and Services Protocol and how it is used to create bean hierarchies. You also learned how the JAF is used to select beans based upon the MIME types they support. In the next chapter, you'll change course and learn about the network programming capabilities provided by JDK 1.2.

Network Programming

IN THIS PART

CHAPTER 30

Network Programming with the `java.net` Package

In this chapter you'll learn about Java's support of network programming. You'll learn the basics of client/server computing and TCP/IP socket programming, and then examine the classes of the java.net package and learn how to use them to develop client/server applications. This chapter provides an introduction to the java.net package. Other chapters in Part VIII, "Network Programming," explore the information presented here in greater detail.

The Internet Protocol Suite

The java.net package provides a set of classes that support network programming using the communication protocols employed by the Internet. These protocols are known as the *Internet protocol suite* and include the *Internet Protocol* (*IP*), the *Transport Control Protocol* (*TCP*), and the *User Datagram Protocol* (*UDP*) as well as other, less prominent supporting protocols. Although this section cannot provide a full description of the Internet protocols, it gives you the basic information that you need to get started with Java network programming. In order to take full advantage of this chapter, you will need an Internet connection.

What Is the Internet and How Does It Work?

Asking the question "What is the Internet?" may bring about a heated discussion in some circles. In this book, "the Internet" is defined as "the collection of all computers that can communicate, using the Internet protocol suite, with the computers and networks registered with the *Internet Network Information Center* (*InterNIC*)." This definition includes all computers to which you can directly send Internet Protocol packets (or indirectly, through a firewall).

Computers on the Internet communicate by exchanging packets of data, known as *Internet Protocol (IP)* packets. IP is the network protocol used to send information from one computer to another over the Internet. All computers on the Internet (by our definition in this book) communicate using IP, which moves information contained in IP packets. They are routed via special routing algorithms from a source computer that sends the packets to a destination computer that receives them. The routing algorithms figure out the best way to send the packets from source to destination.

In order for IP to send packets from a source computer to a destination computer, it must have some way of identifying these computers. All computers on the Internet are identified using one or more IP addresses. A computer may have more than one IP address if it has more than one interface to computers that are connected to the Internet.

IP addresses are 32-bit numbers. They may be written in decimal, hexadecimal, or other formats, but the most common format is dotted decimal notation. This format breaks the

32-bit address up into 4 bytes and writes each byte of the address as an unsigned decimal integer, separating them with dots. For example, one of my IP addresses is `0xCCD499C1`. Because `0xCC` = 204, `0xD4` = 212, `0x99` = 153, and `0xC1` = 193, my address in dotted decimal form is `204.212.153.193`.

IP addresses are not easy to remember, even using dotted decimal notation. The Internet has adopted a mechanism, the *Domain Name System* (*DNS*), whereby computer names can be associated with IP addresses. These computer names are referred to as *domain names*. The DNS has several rules that determine how domain names are constructed and how they relate to one another. For the purposes of this chapter, it is sufficient to know that domain names are computer names and that they are mapped to IP addresses.

The mapping of domain names to IP addresses is maintained by a system of *domain name servers*. These servers can look up the IP address corresponding to a domain name. They also provide the capability to look up the domain name associated with a particular IP address, if one exists.

As mentioned, IP enables communication between computers on the Internet by routing data from a source computer to a destination computer. However, computer-to-computer communication only solves half of the network communication problem. In order for an application program, such as a mail program, to communicate with another application, such as a mail server, there needs to be a way to send data to specific programs within a computer.

Ports, or addresses within a computer, are used to enable communication between programs. Port addresses are 16-bit addresses that are usually associated with a particular application protocol. An application server, such as a Web server or an FTP server, listens on a particular port for service requests, performs whatever service is requested of it, and returns information to the port used by the application program requesting the service.

Popular Internet application protocols are associated with *well-known ports*. The server programs that implement these protocols listen on these ports for service requests. The well-known ports for some common Internet application protocols are shown in Table 30.1.

TABLE 30.1. PORTS FOR COMMON INTERNET APPLICATION PROTOCOLS.

Port	Protocol
21	File transfer protocol
23	Telnet protocol

continues

30

NETWORK PROGRAMMING

TABLE 30.1. CONTINUED

Port	Protocol
25	Simple mail transfer protocol
80	Hypertext transfer protocol

The well-known ports are used to standardize the location of Internet services.

Connection-Oriented Versus Connectionless Communication

Transport protocols are used to deliver information from one port to another and thereby enable communication between application programs. They use either a connection-oriented or connectionless method of communication. TCP is a connection-oriented protocol, and UDP is a connectionless transport protocol.

The TCP connection-oriented protocol establishes a communication link between a source port/IP address and a destination port/IP address. The ports are bound together via this link until the connection is terminated and the link is broken. An example of a connection-oriented protocol is a telephone conversation. A telephone connection is established, communication takes place, and then the connection is terminated.

The reliability of the communication between the source and destination programs is ensured through error-detection and error-correction mechanisms that are implemented within TCP. TCP implements the connection as a stream of bytes from source to destination. This feature allows the use of the stream I/O classes provided by java.io.

The UDP connectionless protocol differs from the TCP connection-oriented protocol in that it does not establish a link for the duration of the connection. An example of a connectionless protocol is postal mail. To mail something, you just write down a destination address (and an optional return address) on the envelope of the item you're sending and drop it into a mailbox. When using UDP, an application program writes the destination port and IP address on a datagram and then sends the datagram to its destination. UDP is less reliable than TCP because there are no delivery-assurance or error-detection-and-correction mechanisms built into the protocol.

Application protocols such as FTP, SMTP, and HTTP use TCP to provide reliable, stream-based communication between client and server programs. Other protocols, such as the Time Protocol, use UDP because speed of delivery is more important than end-to-end reliability.

Multicast Addressing

Most TCP/IP communication is *unicast*—packets are sent from a source host to a destination host in a point-to-point fashion. Unicast communication is used by the majority of Internet services. However, there are some applications where it is desirable for a host to be able to simultaneously send IP packets to multiple destination hosts—for example, to transmit an audio or video stream. This form of communication is known as *multicast*. Multicast communication enables a host to transmit IP packets to multiple hosts, referred to as a *host group*, using a single destination IP address.

Host groups may be permanent or temporary. Permanent groups are assigned fixed IP addresses. Temporary groups are dynamically assigned IP address. Hosts may join or leave a host group in a dynamic fashion—even permanent groups. The existence of a host group is independent of its members. Multicast routers are used to send IP multicast packets to the members of host groups.

Client/Server Computing and the Internet

The Internet provides a variety of services that contribute to its appeal. These services include email, newsgroups, file transfer, remote login, and the Web. Internet services are organized according to a client/server architecture. Client programs, such as Web browsers and file transfer programs, create connections to servers, such as Web and FTP servers. The clients make requests of the server, and the server responds to the requests by providing the service requested by the client.

The Web provides a good example of client/server computing. Web browsers are the clients, and Web servers are the servers. Browsers request HTML files from Web servers on your behalf by establishing a connection with a Web server and submitting file requests to the server. The server receives the file requests, retrieves the files, and sends them to the browser over the established connection. The browser receives the files and displays them on your browser window.

Sockets and Client/Server Communication

Clients and servers establish *connections* and communicate via *sockets*. Connections are communication links that are created over the Internet using TCP. Some client/server applications are also built around the connectionless UDP. These applications also use sockets to communicate.

Sockets are the endpoints of Internet communication. Clients create client sockets and connect them to server sockets. Sockets are associated with a host address and a port address. The host address is the IP address of the host where the client or server program is located. The port address is the communication port used by the client or server program. Server programs use the well-known port number associated with their application protocol.

A client communicates with a server by establishing a connection to the socket of the server. The client and server then exchange data over the connection. Connection-oriented communication is more reliable than connectionless communication because the underlying TCP provides message-acknowledgment, error-detection, and error-recovery services.

When a connectionless protocol is used, the client and server communicate by sending datagrams to each other's sockets. The UDP is used for connectionless protocols. It does not support reliable communication like TCP.

Inside `java.net`

The `java.net` package provides several classes that support socket-based client/server communication.

The `InetAddress` class encapsulates Internet IP addresses and supports conversion between dotted decimal addresses and host names.

The `Socket`, `ServerSocket`, `DatagramSocket`, and `MulticastSocket` classes implement client and server sockets for connection-oriented and connectionless communication. The `DatagramPacket` class is used to construct UDP datagram packets. The `SocketImpl` and `DatagramSocketImpl` classes and the `SocketImplFactory` interface provide hooks for implementing custom sockets.

The `URL`, `URLConnection`, `HttpURLConnection`, and `URLEncoder` classes implement high-level browser-server Web connections. The `ContentHandler` and `URLStreamHandler` classes are `abstract` classes that have provided the basis for the implementation of Web content and stream handlers. They are supported by the `ContentHandlerFactory` and `URLStreamHandlerFactory` interfaces.

The `FileNameMap` interface is used to map filenames to MIME types. You'll learn about MIME types later in this chapter in the section "`ContentHandler`, `ContentHandlerFactory`, and `FileNameMap`."

The `InetAddress` Class

The `InetAddress` class encapsulates Internet addresses. It supports both numeric IP addresses and host names.

The `InetAddress` class has no public variables or constructors. It provides 10 access methods that support common operations on Internet addresses. Three of these methods are `static`.

The `getLocalHost()` method is a `static` method that returns an `InetAddress` object that represents the Internet address of the local host computer. The `static` `getByName()`-method returns an `InetAddress` object for a specified host. The `static` `getAllByName()` method returns an array of all Internet addresses associated with a particular host.

The `getAddress()` method gets the numeric IP address of the host identified by the `InetAddress` object, and the `getHostName()` method gets its domain name. The `getHostAddress()` method returns the numeric IP address of an `InetAddress` object as a dotted decimal string. The `isMulticastAddress()` method returns a `boolean` value that indicates whether an `InetAddress` object represents a multicast address.

The `equals()`, `hashCode()`, and `toString()` methods override those of the `Object` class.

The `NSLookupApp` program illustrates the use of the `InetAddress` class. It takes a host name as a parameter and identifies the primary IP address associated with that host (see Listing 30.1).

LISTING 30.1. THE SOURCE CODE OF THE NSLookupApp PROGRAM.

```
import java.net.InetAddress;
import java.net.UnknownHostException;
import java.lang.System;

public class NSLookupApp {
 public static void main(String args[]) {
  try {
   if(args.length!=1){
    System.out.println("Usage: java NSLookupApp hostName");
    return;
   }
   InetAddress host = InetAddress.getByName(args[0]);
   String hostName = host.getHostName();
   System.out.println("Host name: "+hostName);
   System.out.println("IP address: "+host.getHostAddress());
  }catch(UnknownHostException ex) {
```

continues

LISTING 30.1. CONTINUED

```
    System.out.println("Unknown host");
    return;
  }
 }
}
```

Compile `NSLookupApp` and run it as follows:

```
java NSLookupApp sun.com
Host name: sun.com
IP address: 192.9.9.100
```

This code example uses `NSLookupApp` to look up the primary IP address associated with the `sun.com` host. Try it with other Internet host names to look up their IP addresses.

`NSLookupApp` consists of a single `main()` method. A `try` statement surrounds most of the program's statements. It is used to catch the `UnknownHostException`, which is generated when an invalid host name is entered by the user or when a host name cannot be looked up from a DNS server.

`NSLookupApp` first checks the number of arguments supplied in the program invocation to make sure that a host name argument is provided by the user. It then uses the host name string of the first user argument with the `static getByName()` method of the `InetAddress` class to create an `InetAddress` object based on the user-supplied host name. This `InetAddress` object is assigned to the `host` variable. The `getHostName()` method gets the host's name from the `host` variable and assigns it to the `hostName` variable. The `getHostAddress()` method returns the four bytes of the host's IP address as a dotted decimal string. The host name and IP address then are printed.

The Socket Class

The `Socket` class implements client connection-based sockets. These sockets are used to develop applications that utilize services provided by connection-oriented server applications.

The `Socket` class provides eight constructors that create sockets and optionally connect them to a destination host and port. Two of these constructors were deprecated in JDK 1.1, but they still appear in JDK 1.2. The `DatagramSocket` constructor is the preferred constructor for creating UDP sockets.

The access methods of the `Socket` class are used to access the I/O streams and connection parameters associated with a connected socket. The `getInetAddress()` and `getPort()` methods get the IP address of the destination host and the destination host port number to which the socket is connected. The getLocalPort() method returns the source host local port number associated with the socket. The getLocalAddress() method returns the local IP address associated with the socket. The getInputStream() and getOutputStream() methods are used to access the input and output streams associated with a socket. The close() method is used to close a socket.

The getSoLinger() and setSoLinger() methods are used to get and set a socket's SO_LINGER option, which identifies how long a socket is to remain open after a close() method has been invoked and data remains to be sent over the socket.

The getSoTimeout() and setSoTimeout() methods are used to get and set a socket's SO_TIMEOUT option, which is used to identify how long a read operation on the socket is to be blocked before it times out and the blocking ends.

The getTcpNoDelay() and setTcpNoDelay() methods are used to get and set a socket's TCP_NODELAY option, which is used to specify whether Nagle's algorithm should be used to buffer data that is sent over a socket connection. When TCP_NODELAY is true, Nagle's algorithm is disabled.

The setSocketImplFactory() class method is used to switch from the default Java socket implementation to a custom socket implementation. The toString() method returns a string representation of the socket.

The PortTalkApp program is used to talk to a particular port on a given host on a line-by-line basis. It provides the options of sending a line to the specified port, receiving a line from the other host, or terminating the connection. Its source code is shown in Listing 30.2.

LISTING 30.2. THE SOURCE CODE OF THE PortTalkApp PROGRAM.

```java
import java.lang.System;
import java.net.Socket;
import java.net.InetAddress;
import java.net.UnknownHostException;
import java.io.*;

public class PortTalkApp {
 public static void main(String args[]){
  PortTalk portTalk = new PortTalk(args);
  portTalk.displayDestinationParameters();
  portTalk.displayLocalParameters();
  portTalk.chat();
  portTalk.shutdown();
 }
}
```

continues

30

NETWORK
PROGRAMMING

LISTING 30.2. CONTINUED

```java
class PortTalk {
 Socket connection;
 DataOutputStream outStream;
 BufferedReader inStream;
 public PortTalk(String args[]){
  if(args.length!=2) error("Usage: java PortTalkApp host port");
  String destination = args[0];
  int port = 0;
  try {
   port = Integer.valueOf(args[1]).intValue();
  }catch (NumberFormatException ex){
   error("Invalid port number");
  }
  try{
   connection = new Socket(destination,port);
  }catch (UnknownHostException ex){
   error("Unknown host");
  }
  catch (IOException ex){
   error("IO error creating socket");
  }
  try{
   inStream = new BufferedReader(
    new InputStreamReader(connection.getInputStream()));
   outStream = new DataOutputStream(connection.getOutputStream());
  }catch (IOException ex){
   error("IO error getting streams");
  }
  System.out.println("Connected to "+destination+" at port "+port+".");
 }
 public void displayDestinationParameters(){
  InetAddress destAddress = connection.getInetAddress();
  String name = destAddress.getHostName();
  byte ipAddress[] = destAddress.getAddress();
  int port = connection.getPort();
  displayParameters("Destination ",name,ipAddress,port);
 }
 public void displayLocalParameters(){
  InetAddress localAddress = null;
  try{
   localAddress = InetAddress.getLocalHost();
  }catch (UnknownHostException ex){
   error("Error getting local host information");
  }
  String name = localAddress.getHostName();
  byte ipAddress[] = localAddress.getAddress();
  int port = connection.getLocalPort();
  displayParameters("Local ",name,ipAddress,port);
 }
```

```
   public void displayParameters(String s,String name,
    ⮕byte ipAddress[],int port){
System.out.println(s+"host is "+name+".");
   System.out.print(s+"IP address is ");
   for(int i=0;i<ipAddress.length;++i)
    System.out.print((ipAddress[i]+256)%256+".");
   System.out.println();
   System.out.println(s+"port number is "+port+".");
   }
   public void chat(){
   BufferedReader keyboardInput = new BufferedReader(
    new InputStreamReader(System.in));
   boolean finished = false;
   do {
    try{
     System.out.print("Send, receive, or quit (S/R/Q): ");
     System.out.flush();
     String line = keyboardInput.readLine();
     if(line.length()>0){
      line=line.toUpperCase();
      switch (line.charAt(0)){
      case 'S':
       String sendLine = keyboardInput.readLine();
       outStream.writeBytes(sendLine);
       outStream.write(13);
       outStream.write(10);
       outStream.flush();
       break;
      case 'R':
       int inByte;
       System.out.print("***");
       while ((inByte = inStream.read()) != '\n')
       System.out.write(inByte);
       System.out.println();
       break;
      case 'Q':
       finished=true;
       break;
      default:
       break;
      }
     }
    }catch (IOException ex){
     error("Error reading from keyboard or socket");
    }
   } while(!finished);
   }
   public void shutdown(){
    try{
```

continues

LISTING 30.2. CONTINUED

```
  connection.close();
 }catch (IOException ex){
  error("IO error closing socket");
 }
}
public void error(String s){
 System.out.println(s);
 System.exit(1);
}
}
```

To see how `PortTalkApp` works, run it using the following command line:

```
java PortTalkApp jaworski.com 7
Connected to jaworski.com at port 7.
Destination host is jaworski.com.
Destination IP address is 204.212.153.193.
Destination port number is 7.
Local host is biscuit.jaworski.com.
Local IP address is 204.212.153.198.
Local port number is 1237.
Send, receive, or quit (S/R/Q):
```

`PortTalkApp` connects to my server at port 7. This is the port number for the `echo` server application. It is used to test Internet communication between hosts. It identifies my host's name, IP address, and destination port number. In this example, I am connecting from another computer on my local area network. Its name is `biscuit.jaworski.com` and it has the `204.212.153.198` IP address. When you run the program, your host name and IP address will be displayed. The local port number that I am connecting from is port 1237.

`PortTalkApp` asks you whether you want to send a line, receive a line, or quit the program. Whether you elect to send or receive is important. If you decide to receive a line and the host is not sending any data, your program will block while it waits to receive information from a socket-based stream.

Enter an `S` to send a line and then enter `This is a test!` on the following line, like this:

```
Send, receive, or quit (S/R/Q): s
This is a test!
Send, receive, or quit (S/R/Q):
```

`PortTalkApp` will send your line to port 7 on my host and then prompt you for your next command. Enter `R` to receive a line of text from my server:

```
Send, receive, or quit (S/R/Q): r
***This is a test!
Send, receive, or quit (S/R/Q):
```

PortTalkApp reads a line of text from the socket stream and displays it, prefixed with three asterisks. Now enter Q to close the connection and terminate the program. You can also use PortTalkApp to talk to other ports. For example, you can use it to talk to port 25 of hosts that support the Simple Mail Transport Protocol in order to send email to someone who is served by that host.

PortTalkApp consists of a simple main() function that creates an object of class PortTalk, passing it the user-supplied host and port arguments. It invokes the displayDestinationHostParameters() and displayLocalParameters() methods of the PortTalk class to provide the initial connection-status information. The chat() method is used to send and receive lines of text over an established connection. The shutdown() method terminates the connection.

The PortTalk class implements the bulk of the processing performed by the program. It declares three field variables. The connection variable keeps track of the socket used with the connection. The inStream and outStream variables maintain the input and output streams derived from the socket.

The PortTalk constructor checks the arguments supplied by the user to make sure that a host and port number were supplied, and converts the user-supplied port number to an integer. The error() method is used to display any errors to the console window. A new Socket object is created using the specified destination host name and port number and is assigned to the connection variable. The getInputStream() and getOutputStream() methods of the Socket class are used to attach input and output streams to the socket identified by the connection variable. These streams are then filtered as BufferedReader and DataOutputStream objects and assigned to the inStream and outStream variables. The constructor ends by displaying a connection status message to the console window.

The displayDestinationParameters() method uses the getInetAdress() method of the Socket class to get the InetAddress object associated with the destination host of the connection. It uses the getHostName() and getAddress() methods of the InetAddress class to obtain the name and IP address of the destination host. The getPort() method of the Socket class is used to get the destination port number. These parameters are displayed using the displayParameters() method.

The displayLocalParameters() method uses the getLocalHost(), getHostName(), and getAddress() methods of the InetAddress class to obtain the InetAddress object, name, and IP address of the local host. The getLocalPort() method of the Socket class

30

NETWORK PROGRAMMING

is used to get the local port number. These parameters are displayed using the displayParameters() method.

The displayParameters() method displays the host name, IP address, and port number of an end of a socket connection. The s string parameter is used to differentiate between a local host and a destination host.

The chat() method implements the heart of the PortTalkApp program. It displays the Send, receive, or quit (S/R/Q): prompt to the user and then reads an input line from the user's keyboard.

If the user enters S to send, another line is read from the user's keyboard. This line is then written to the output stream associated with the socket connection. A carriage return and a line-feed character are then written to the output stream to signal the end of the line. The carriage return-linefeed combination is the standard end-of-line identifier used with Internet application protocols.

If the user enters R to receive, three asterisks (***) are written to the console window to indicate input from the destination host. Then the input stream associated with the socket is read, a byte at a time, and displayed to the console window until a newline (\n) character is encountered.

If the user enters Q to quit, the do loop of the chat() method is terminated.

The shutdown() method closes the Socket object referenced by the connection variable.

The error() method prints an error message to the console window and then terminates the program using the exit() method of the System class.

The ServerSocket Class

The ServerSocket class implements a TCP server socket. It provides three constructors that specify the port to which the server socket is to listen for incoming connection requests, an optional maximum connection request queue length, and an optional Internet address. The Internet address argument allows *multihomed* hosts (that is, hosts with more than one Internet address) to limit connections to a specific interface.

The accept() method is used to cause the server socket to listen and wait until an incoming connection is established. It returns an object of class Socket once a connection is made. This Socket object is then used to carry out a service for a single client. The getInetAddress() method returns the address of the host to which the socket is connected. The getLocalPort() method returns the port on which the server socket listens for an incoming connection. The toString() method returns the socket's address and port number as a string in preparation for printing.

The getSoTimeout() and setSoTimeout() methods set the socket's SO_TIMEOUT parameter. The close() method closes the server socket.

The static setSocketFactory() method is used to change the default ServerSocket implementation to a custom implementation. The implAccept() method is used by subclasses of ServerSocket to override the accept() method.

The ReverServerApp program is a simple server that listens on port 1234 for incoming connections from client programs. When ReverServerApp connects to a client it reads one line of text at a time from the client, reverses the characters in the text line, and sends them back to the client. The source code of ReverServerApp is shown in Listing 30.3.

LISTING 30.3. THE SOURCE CODE OF THE ReverServerApp PROGRAM.

```
import java.lang.System;
import java.net.ServerSocket;
import java.net.Socket;
import java.io.*;

public class ReverServerApp {
 public static void main(String args[]){
  try{
   ServerSocket server = new ServerSocket(1234);
   int localPort = server.getLocalPort();
   System.out.println("Reverse Server is listening on port "+
   ➥localPort+".");
Socket client = server.accept();
   String destName = client.getInetAddress().getHostName();
   int destPort = client.getPort();
   System.out.println("Accepted connection to "+destName+" on port "+
   destPort+".");
   BufferedReader inStream = new BufferedReader(
   new InputStreamReader(client.getInputStream()));
   DataOutputStream outStream =
   ➥new DataOutputStream(client.getOutputStream());
boolean finished = false;
   do {
   String inLine = inStream.readLine();
   System.out.println("Received: "+inLine);
   if(inLine.equalsIgnoreCase("quit")) finished=true;
   String outLine=new ReverseString(inLine.trim()).getString();
   for(int i=0;i<outLine.length();++i)
    outStream.write((byte)outLine.charAt(i));
   outStream.write(13);
   outStream.write(10);
   outStream.flush();
```

continues

30

NETWORK
PROGRAMMING

LISTING 30.3. CONTINUED

```
    System.out.println("Sent: "+outLine);
  } while(!finished);
  inStream.close();
  outStream.close();
  client.close();
  server.close();
 }catch (IOException ex){
  System.out.println("IOException occurred.");
 }
 }
}
class ReverseString {
 String s;
 public ReverseString(String in){
  int len = in.length();
  char outChars[] = new char[len];
  for(int i=0;i<len;++i)
   outChars[len-1-i]=in.charAt(i);
  s = String.valueOf(outChars);
 }
 public String getString(){
  return s;
 }
}
```

To see how ReverServerApp works, you need to run it in a separate window and then use PortTalkApp to feed it lines of text. First, run ReverServerApp using the following command line:

```
java ReverServerApp
Reverse Server is listening on port 1234.
```

ReverServerApp notifies you that it is up and running. In a separate window, run PortTalkApp as follows, supplying your host name instead of athome.jaworski.com:

```
java PortTalkApp athome.jaworski.com 1234
Connected to athome.jaworski.com at port 1234.
Destination host is athome.jaworski.com.
Destination IP address is 204.212.153.194.
Destination port number is 1234.
Local host is athome.jaworski.com.
Local IP address is 204.212.153.194.
Local port number is 1302.
Send, receive, or quit (S/R/Q):
```

> **NOTE**
>
> You can use localhost or 127.0.0.1 as an IP address if you do not have a host name or cannot determine your IP address.

PortTalkApp displays all of the parameters of both endpoints of the connection. If you look in the window where ReverServerApp is running, you will see a message similar to the following:

```
Accepted connection to athome.jaworski.com on port 1302.
```

The port number reported by ReverServer is consistent with that reported by PortTalkApp. Now switch back to the PortTalkApp window and enter S to send a line of text, followed by the line of text This is a test!, as shown in the following output:

```
Send, receive, or quit (S/R/Q): s
This is a test!
```

The ReverServerApp window reports the following:

```
Received: This is a test!
Sent: !tset a si sihT
```

Enter an R in the PortTalkApp window, as shown in the following output:

```
Send, receive, or quit (S/R/Q): r
***!tset a si sihT
Send, receive, or quit (S/R/Q):
```

PortTalkApp displays the text that it received from ReverServerApp. Enter the S command followed by a quit text line:

```
Send, receive, or quit (S/R/Q): s
quit
```

The quit line is read by ReverServerApp, causing it to terminate the connection and exit. It displays the following:

```
Received: quit
Sent: tiuq
```

In the PortTalkApp window, type Q to terminate PortTalkApp, as shown in the following output:

```
Send, receive, or quit (S/R/Q): q
```

The ReverServerApp program is smaller in size than PortTalkApp. It consists of a single main() method. The ReverseString class is also declared.

30

NETWORK PROGRAMMING

The `main()`method begins by creating a `ServerSocket` object on port 1234. It then uses the `getLocalPort()` method to get the local port number associated with the socket. This is to verify that it is indeed using port 1234. It then displays the fact that it is up and running and displays the number of the port on which it is listening for connections.

The `accept()` method is used to accept an incoming client connection and return the `Socket` object associated with the connection. The `getHostName()` and `getPort()` methods are used to get the host name and port number associated with the client program. These parameters are displayed to the console window. Input and output streams are then associated with the socket.

The `main()` method enters a loop, where it reads a line of text from the input stream and then checks to see if it is the `quit` termination signal. The `ReverseString()`constructor and `getString()` method are used to reverse the line read from the input stream. The reversed line is then written to the output stream. If the `quit` line was received from the client, the loop is terminated and the input stream, output stream, client socket, and server socket are closed.

The `ReverseString` class provides a constructor that reverses a string and a `getString()` method for retrieving the reversed string.

The `DatagramSocket` Class

The `DatagramSocket` class implements client and server sockets using the UDP protocol. UDP is a connectionless protocol that allows application programs (both clients and servers) to exchange information using chunks of data known as *datagrams*.

`DatagramSocket` provides three constructors. The default constructor creates a datagram socket for use by client applications. No port number is specified. The second constructor allows a datagram socket to be created using a specified port. This constructor is typically used with server applications. The third constructor allows an Internet address to be specified in addition to the port. This is used to restrict service to a specific host interface.

The `send()` and `receive()` methods are used to send and receive datagrams using the socket. The datagrams are objects of class `DatagramPacket`. The `getLocalPort()` and `getLocalAddress()` methods return the local port and Internet address of the socket. The `close()` method closes this socket. The `getSoTimeout()` and `setSoTimeout()`methods get and set the socket's `SO_TIMEOUT` parameter.

The `DatagramPacket` Class

The `DatagramPacket` class encapsulates the actual datagrams that are sent and received using objects of class `DatagramSocket`. Two different constructors are provided: one for datagrams that are received from a datagram socket, and one for creating datagrams that are sent over a datagram socket. The arguments to the received datagram constructor are a byte array used as a buffer for the received data, and an integer that identifies the number of bytes received and stored in the buffer. The sending datagram constructor adds two additional parameters: the IP address and port where the datagram is to be sent.

Eight access methods are provided. The `getAddress()` and `getPort()` methods are used to read the destination IP address and port of the datagram. The `getLength()` and `getData()` methods are used to get the number of bytes of data contained in the datagram and to read the data into a byte array buffer. The `setAddress()`, `setPort()`, `setLength()`, and `setData()` methods allow the datagram's IP address, port, length, and data values to be set.

The `TimeServerApp` and `GetTimeApp` programs illustrate the use of client/server computing using datagrams. `TimeServerApp` listens on a UDP socket on port 2345 for incoming datagrams. When a datagram is received, it displays the data contained in the datagram to the console window and returns a datagram with the current date and time to the sending client program. It terminates its operation when it receives a datagram with the text `quit` as its data.

The `GetTimeApp` program sends five datagrams with the text `time` in each datagram to local port 2345. After sending each datagram, it waits for a return datagram from `TimeServerApp`. It displays the datagrams that it sends and receives to the console window. It then sends a `quit` datagram to `TimeServerApp` and terminates its operation.

The `TimeServerApp` program listing is shown in Listing 30.4. The code for `GetTimeApp` is in Listing 30.5.

LISTING 30.4. THE SOURCE CODE OF THE `TimeServerApp` PROGRAM.

```
import java.lang.System;
import java.net.DatagramSocket;
import java.net.DatagramPacket;
import java.net.InetAddress;
import java.io.IOException;
import java.util.Date;

public class TimeServerApp {
 public static void main(String args[]){
```

continues

30

NETWORK PROGRAMMING

LISTING 30.4. CONTINUED

```
try{
  DatagramSocket socket = new DatagramSocket(2345);
  String localAddress = InetAddress.getLocalHost().getHostName().trim();
  int localPort = socket.getLocalPort();
  System.out.print(localAddress+": ");
  System.out.println("Time Server is listening on port "+localPort+".");
  int bufferLength = 256;
  byte outBuffer[];
  byte inBuffer[] = new byte[bufferLength];
  DatagramPacket outDatagram;
  DatagramPacket inDatagram =
   new DatagramPacket(inBuffer,inBuffer.length);
boolean finished = false;
  do {
    socket.receive(inDatagram);
    InetAddress destAddress = inDatagram.getAddress();
    String destHost = destAddress.getHostName().trim();
    int destPort = inDatagram.getPort();
    System.out.println("\nReceived a datagram from "+destHost+" at port "+
     destPort+".");
    String data = new String(inDatagram.getData()).trim();
    System.out.println("It contained the data: "+data);
    if(data.equalsIgnoreCase("quit")) finished=true;
    String time = new Date().toString();
    outBuffer=time.getBytes();
    outDatagram =
    ➥new DatagramPacket(outBuffer,outBuffer.length,destAddress,
destPort);
    socket.send(outDatagram);
    System.out.println("Sent "+time+" to "+destHost+" at port "+
     ➥destPort+".");
} while(!finished);
  }catch (IOException ex){
   System.out.println("IOException occurred.");
  }
 }
}
```

LISTING 30.5. THE SOURCE CODE OF THE GetTimeApp PROGRAM.

```
import java.lang.System;
import java.net.DatagramSocket;
import java.net.DatagramPacket;
import java.net.InetAddress;
import java.io.IOException;

public class GetTimeApp {
 public static void main(String args[]){
```

```
  try{
    DatagramSocket socket = new DatagramSocket();
    InetAddress localAddress = InetAddress.getLocalHost();
    String localHost = localAddress.getHostName();
    int bufferLength = 256;
    byte outBuffer[];
    byte inBuffer[] = new byte[bufferLength];
    DatagramPacket outDatagram;
    DatagramPacket inDatagram =
     ➡new DatagramPacket(inBuffer,inBuffer.length);
for(int i=0;i<5;++i){
      outBuffer = new byte[bufferLength];
      outBuffer = "time".getBytes();
      outDatagram = new DatagramPacket(outBuffer,outBuffer.length,
       localAddress,2345);
      socket.send(outDatagram);
      System.out.println("\nSent time request to "+localHost+
      ➡" at port 2345.");
socket.receive(inDatagram);
      InetAddress destAddress = inDatagram.getAddress();
      String destHost = destAddress.getHostName().trim();
      int destPort = inDatagram.getPort();
      System.out.println("Received a datagram from "+destHost+" at port "+
       destPort+".");
      String data = new String(inDatagram.getData());
      data=data.trim();
      System.out.println("It contained the following data: "+data);
    }
    outBuffer = new byte[bufferLength];
    outBuffer = "quit".getBytes();
    outDatagram = new DatagramPacket(outBuffer,outBuffer.length,
     localAddress,2345);
    socket.send(outDatagram);
  }catch (IOException ex){
    System.out.println("IOException occurred.");
  }
 }
}
```

`TimeServerApp` and `GetTimeApp` should be run in separate windows. First, start
`TimeServerApp` using the following command line:

```
java TimeServerApp
biscuit.jaworski.com: Time Server is listening on port 2345.
```

`TimeServerApp` will respond by letting you know that it is up and running and listening
on port 2345.

Next, start `GetTimeApp` in a different window, as follows:

```
java GetTimeApp

Sent time request to biscuit.jaworski.com at port 2345.
Received a datagram from 204.212.153.198 at port 2345.
It contained the following data: Fri Dec 26 17:32:13 PST 1997

Sent time request to biscuit.jaworski.com at port 2345.
Received a datagram from 204.212.153.198 at port 2345.
It contained the following data: Fri Dec 26 17:32:14 PST 1997

Sent time request to biscuit.jaworski.com at port 2345.
Received a datagram from 204.212.153.198 at port 2345.
It contained the following data: Fri Dec 26 17:32:14 PST 1997

Sent time request to biscuit.jaworski.com at port 2345.
Received a datagram from 204.212.153.198 at port 2345.
It contained the following data: Fri Dec 26 17:32:14 PST 1997

Sent time request to biscuit.jaworski.com at port 2345.
Received a datagram from 204.212.153.198 at port 2345.
It contained the following data: Fri Dec 26 17:32:15 PST 1997
```

GetTimeApp reports the packets it sends to and receives from `TimeServerApp` and then terminates. `TimeServerApp` provides a similar display in its window, as shown in the following output:

```
Received a datagram from 204.212.153.198 at port 1325.
It contained the data: time
Sent Fri Dec 26 17:32:13 PST 1997 to 204.212.153.198 at port 1325.

Received a datagram from 204.212.153.198 at port 1325.
It contained the data: time
Sent Fri Dec 26 17:32:14 PST 1997 to 204.212.153.198 at port 1325.

Received a datagram from 204.212.153.198 at port 1325.
It contained the data: time
Sent Fri Dec 26 17:32:14 PST 1997 to 204.212.153.198 at port 1325.

Received a datagram from 204.212.153.198 at port 1325.
It contained the data: time
Sent Fri Dec 26 17:32:14 PST 1997 to 204.212.153.198 at port 1325.

Received a datagram from 204.212.153.198 at port 1325.
It contained the data: time
Sent Fri Dec 26 17:32:15 PST 1997 to 204.212.153.198 at port 1325.

Received a datagram from 204.212.153.198 at port 1325.
It contained the data: quit
Sent Fri Dec 26 17:32:15 PST 1997 to 204.212.153.198 at port 1325.
```

These two simple programs illustrate the basic mechanics of datagram-based client/ server applications. A UDP client sends a datagram to a UDP server at the server's port address. The UDP server listens on its port for a datagram, processes the datagram, and sends back information to the UDP client.

TimeServerApp

`TimeServerApp` begins by creating a `DatagramSocket` object on port 2345 and assigning it to the `socket` variable. It then obtains the host name and local port number using the `getHostName()` and `getLocalPort()` methods and displays this information to the console window.

`TimeServerApp` creates two byte buffers—`outBuffer` and `inBuffer`. `outBuffer` is an empty buffer that is used to send data in outgoing datagrams. `inBuffer` is initialized to a blank 256-byte buffer. `TimeServerApp` then declares two variables of the `DatagramPacket` class—a non-initialized `outDatagram` variable and an `inDatagram` variable that is initialized using the `inBuffer[]` array.

`TimeServerApp` executes a loop where it receives and processes datagrams received from client programs. It receives datagrams using the `receive()` method of the `DatagramSocket` class. It uses the `getAddress()` and `getPort()` methods of the `DatagramPacket` class to get the host address and port of the client program that sent the socket. It displays this information to the console window. It uses the `getData()` method of the `DatagramPacket` class to retrieve the data sent by the client program. It converts this data to a string and displays it on the console window. If the received data contains the `quit` string, it sets the finished flag to `true`. `TimeServerApp` processes the client time request by using the `Date()` constructor of the `java.util` package to construct a new `Date` object, converting the `Date` object to a `byte` array, and storing the data in `outBuffer`. It then creates a new `DatagramPacket` object, using `outBuffer`, with the destination address and port number of the sending client program. It sends the datagram to the client using the `send()` method of the `DatagramSocket` class. The console display is then updated with the data that was sent to the client program.

GetTimeApp

The `GetTimeApp` client program creates a `DatagramSocket` object and assigns it to the `socket` variable. It then creates a `DatagramPacket` objects in the same manner as the `TimeServerApp` program. `GetTimeApp` uses a `for` statement to loop five times, sending five datagrams to port 2345 of the local host. After each datagram is sent, it waits to receive a return datagram from `TimeServerApp`. It uses the `getAddress()`, `getPort()`, and `getData()` methods of the `DatagramPacket` class to report this information to the console window.

After sending and receiving five datagrams, `GetTimeApp` sends a datagram with the `quit` text to tell `TimeServerApp` that it should terminate its processing.

The `MulticastSocket` Class

The `MulticastSocket` class is used for developing clients and servers for IP multicasting. It provides the capability for hosts to join and leave multicast groups. All hosts in a multicast group receive UDP datagrams that are sent to the IP address of the group. Each host in the group listens on a common UDP port for the datagrams of the multicast application.

The `MulticastSocket` class has two constructors—a default parameterless constructor and a constructor that specifies the port number on which to listen for multicast datagrams. The `MulticastSocket` class has seven access methods:

- `joinGroup()`
- `leaveGroup()`
- `setInterface()`
- `getInterface()`
- `setTTL()`
- `getTTL()`
- `send()`

The `joinGroup()` and `leaveGroup()` methods are used to join and leave a multicast group at a specified Internet address. The `getInterface()` and `setInterface()` methods are used to get and set the IP address of the host interface that is used for multicasting. The `getTTL()` and `setTTL()` methods are used to get and set the *time-to-live* for multicast packets that are sent on the multicast socket. Time-to-live specifies the number of times that a packet is forwarded before it expires. The `send()` method is used to send a datagram to multicast IP address.

The `SocketImpl` and `DataSocketImpl` Classes and the `SocketImplFactory` Interface

The `SocketImpl` and `DataSocketImpl` classes are abstract classes that are used as a basis for defining custom socket implementations. The `SocketImplFactory` interface must be implemented by new socket implementations.

> **NOTE**
>
> The `setSocketImplFactory()` method of the `Socket` class can be used to set the system `SocketImplFactory`. Once it is set, it cannot be changed.

The `SocketImpl` class provides four variables that are used to define a socket: the destination IP address, the destination port, the local port, and a file descriptor used to create streams. The local IP address of the host need not be specified. The `DatagramSocketImpl` class uses only the local port and file descriptor because no connection with a destination IP address and port is required for UDP sockets.

Some of the access methods defined by `SocketImpl` are used to perform lower-level socket operations. These include listening for connections, accepting connections, binding a socket to a port, and implementing the actual connection. Other access methods are used to support stream-based I/O and to provide access to the IP address and port parameters of a socket. The `DatagramSocketImpl` class provides a similar set of methods that are oriented to the processing of UDP datagrams.

Web-Related Classes

In addition to providing the basic TCP- and UDP-based sockets used by almost all Internet client/server applications, the `java.net` package provides a useful set of classes that support higher-level, Web-specific applications. These classes are centered around the `URL` class, which encapsulates an object on the Web, typically a Web page, by its URL address.

URL stands for *uniform resource locator* and, as its name states, provides a uniform way to locate resources on the Web. Different types of URLs are used with different application protocols, the most common of which are the *Hypertext Transfer Protocol* (*HTTP*) and the *File Transfer Protocol* (*FTP*). URLs for these types of protocols are mainly used to identify the location of files, such as Web pages, supporting images, multimedia files, text files, and downloadable programs. HTTP URLs also refer to executable programs, such as CGI scripts, which perform Web-related services. *CGI scripts* are programs, usually written in a scripting language, that receive input and generate output in accordance with the *common gateway interface* (*CGI*) specification.

The URL Class

The URL class encapsulates Web objects by their URL address. It provides a set of constructors that allow URL objects to be easily constructed, and a set of access methods that allow high-level read and write operations to be performed using URLs.

Most URLs, but not all, consist of a protocol, host name, and the path and name of a file on the host. For example, the URL http://www.jaworski.com/jdg/index.htm refers to a Web page on my Web server. It specifies the HTTP protocol as the protocol used to access the Web page. It identifies my host name as www.jaworski.com, and it names the file as /jdg/index.htm, where /jdg/ is the directory path to the file (relative to my Web server's directory root) and index.htm is the file's name. In HTTP URLs, the path/filename is optional. For example, the URL http://www.jaworski.com/jdg/ is equivalent to the previous URL. My Web server uses the file name index.htm as the default name for a file. The path name can also be omitted. The URL http://www.jaworski.com would use the index.htm file in the Web server's root directory.

The four URL constructors allow URL objects to be created using a variety of URL parameters, such as protocol type, host name, port, and file path. These parameters may be supplied separately or in text form as part of an URL string. The URL class treats a file's path and name as a single entity to provide a more convenient way of working with URL components.

URLs can be constructed using their absolute address or using an address that is relative to another URL. Up until now we have been working with the complete or *absolute* address of an URL. A *relative address* is a path/filename or file offset that is specified relative to an absolute URL. For example, the absolute URL http://www.jaworski.com can be combined with the relative URL /jdg/index.htm to produce the URL to http://www.jaworski.com/jdg/index.htm.

The URL access methods provide a full set of URL processing capabilities. The getProtocol(), getHost(), getPort(), getFile(), and getRef() methods allow the individual address components of the URL to be determined. The getContent() and openStream() methods allow reading of the Web object pointed to by the URL. The toExternalForm() and toString()methods enable URLs to be converted into strings to support display and printing. The equals()method compares URLs, and the sameFile() method compares the Web objects pointed to by the URLs. The openConnection() method creates an object of class URLConnection to the Web object pointed to be the URL. This class is discussed in the "URLConnection and HttpURLConnection" section later in this chapter.

The GetURLApp program illustrates the power provided by the URL class. This small program implements a primitive Web browser. Just run the program with the name of an URL, and it makes a connection to the destination Web server and downloads the referenced document. The program's source code is shown in Listing 30.6.

LISTING 30.6. THE SOURCE CODE OF THE GetURLApp PROGRAM.

```
import java.lang.System;
import java.net.URL;
import java.net.MalformedURLException;
import java.io.*;

public class GetURLApp {
 public static void main(String args[]){
  try{
   if(args.length!=1) error("Usage: java GetURLApp URL");
   System.out.println("Fetching URL: "+args[0]);
   URL url = new URL(args[0]);
   BufferedReader inStream = new BufferedReader(
    new InputStreamReader(url.openStream()));
   String line;
   while ((line = inStream.readLine())!= null){
    System.out.println(line);
   }
   inStream.close();
  }catch (MalformedURLException ex){
   error("Bad URL");
  }catch (IOException ex){
   error("IOException occurred.");
  }
 }
 public static void error(String s){
  System.out.println(s);
  System.exit(1);
 }
}
```

After compiling the program, try running it with the URL http://www.jaworski.com/ java/GetURLApp.htm as follows. Make sure that you use the correct uppercase and lowercase characters:

java GetURLApp http://www.jaworski.com/java/GetURLApp.htm

The program will respond by displaying the following Web document from my Web server:

java GetURLApp http://www.jaworski.com/java/GetURLApp.htm
Fetching URL: http://www.jaworski.com/java/GetURLApp.htm

```
<!DOCTYPE HTML PUBLIC "-//SQ//DTD HTML 2.0 HoTMetaL + extensions//EN">
<HTML><HEAD><TITLE>GetURLApp Test Results</TITLE></HEAD>
<BODY><H1>GetURLApp Test Results</H1>
<P>Congratulations! You were able to successfully compile and run
➥GetURLApp.
</P>
</BODY></HTML>
```

Try running the program with other URLs to see how they are displayed.

GetURLApp consists of a short `main()` method and the `error()` method, used to display error messages to the console window.

The `main()` method checks the arguments supplied by the user to make sure that the correct number of arguments are present. It then displays a message to the console window identifying the URL that it is trying to fetch. It creates an URL object using the URL name supplied by the user and assigns it to the `url` variable. It then uses the `openStream()` method of the URL class to create an input stream from the URL. The input stream is filtered as a `BufferedReader` object and is assigned to the `inStream` variable. The `inStream` variable is used to read and display the input stream one line at a time.

URLConnection and HttpURLConnection

The URLConnnection class is an `abstract` class that encapsulates an active HTTP connection to a Web object represented by an URL. It provides a number of methods for getting information about the Web object and about the connection to the Web object, and for interacting with the Web object.

URLConnection defines several class variables that specify the connection state and associated parameters. It also supplies numerous methods that provide access to the HTTP-specific fields of the connection. This class is studied, in detail, in Chapter 31, "Client Programs." The next programming example covers a few aspects of its use.

The HttpURLConnection class is a subclass of URLConnection that provides direct access to the HTTP parameters involved in a client/server HTTP connection. HttpURLConnection is also covered in Chapter 31.

URLEncoder

The URLEncoder class is a simple class that provides a single `static` method, `encode()`, for converting text strings to a form that is suitable for use as part of an URL. This format is known as `x-www-form-urlencoded` and is typically used to encode form data that is sent to a CGI script.

The encode() method converts spaces to plus signs (+) and uses the percent character (%) as an escape code to encode special characters. The two characters that immediately follow a percent sign are interpreted as hexadecimal digits that are combined to produce an eight-bit value.

Listing 30.7 illustrates the use of the encode() method and the URLConnection class. The QueryURLApp program accesses the echo-query CGI program on my Web server, passing it the "/this/is/extra/path/information" query string and the "Query string with some special characters: @#$%?&+" query string. The query string is encoded using the encode() method of the URLEncoder class. The echo-query CGI program creates an HTML file that describes the parameters passed to it by my Web server and returns this file to the QueryURLApp program. This file shows how the query string was encoded by the encode() method.

LISTING 30.7. THE SOURCE CODE OF THE QueryURLApp PROGRAM.

```
import java.lang.System;
import java.net.URL;
import java.net.URLConnection;
import java.net.URLEncoder;
import java.net.MalformedURLException;
import java.net.UnknownServiceException;
import java.io.*;

public class QueryURLApp {
 public static void main(String args[]){
  try{
    String urlString = "http://www.jaworski.com/cgi-bin/echo-query";
    String extraPathInfo = "/this/is/extra/path/information";
    String queryString =
     URLEncoder.encode("Query string with some special characters:"+
     ➥" @#$%?&+");
URL url = new URL(urlString+extraPathInfo+"?"+queryString);
    URLConnection connection = url.openConnection();
    BufferedReader fromURL = new BufferedReader(
     new InputStreamReader(url.openStream()));
    String line;
    while ((line = fromURL.readLine())!= null){
     System.out.println(line);
    }
    fromURL.close();
  }catch (MalformedURLException ex){
   error("Bad URL");
  }catch (UnknownServiceException ex){
   error("UnknownServiceException occurred.");
  }catch (IOException ex){
```

continues

LISTING 30.7. CONTINUED

```
   error("IOException occurred.");
  }
 }
 public static void error(String s){
  System.out.println(s);
  System.exit(1);
 }
}
```

To run QueryURLApp, just type the following command line:

java QueryURLApp

QueryURLApp queries the echo-query program on my Web server and displays the HTML file generated by the echo-query program. Notice how the query string was encoded:

```
<HTML>
<HEAD>
<TITLE>Echo CGI Request</TITLE>
</HEAD>
<BODY>
<H1>CGI Request</H1>
<H2>Command Line Arguments</H2>
<P>Number of command line arguments: 7</P>
<P>Command line arguments: Query string with some special characters:
➥ @#\$%\?\&+
</P>
<H2>Environment Variables</H2>
<PRE>
AUTH_TYPE =
CONTENT_LENGTH =
CONTENT_TYPE =
GATEWAY_INTERFACE = CGI/1.1
HTTP_ACCEPT = text/html, image/gif, image/jpeg, *; q=.2, */*; q=.2
HTTP_USER_AGENT = Javainternal_build
PATH_INFO = /this/is/extra/path/information
PATH_TRANSLATED = /usr/local/etc/httpd/htdocs/this/is/extra/path/
➥ information
QUERY_STRING =
➥ Query+string+with+some+special+characters%3a+
➥ %40%23%24%25%3f%26%2b
REMOTE_ADDR = 204.212.153.194
REMOTE_HOST = athome.jaworski.com
REMOTE_IDENT =
REMOTE_USER =
REQUEST_METHOD = GET
SCRIPT_NAME = /cgi-bin/echo-query
SERVER_NAME = www.jaworski.com
SERVER_PORT = 80
```

```
SERVER_PROTOCOL = HTTP/1.0
SERVER_SOFTWARE = NCSA/1.4.2
</PRE>
<H2>Standard Input</H2>
</BODY>
</HTML>
```

QueryURLApp creates an URL by concatenating the URL for the echo-query program, the extra path information, and the encoded query string. It then uses the openConnection() method of the URL class to create an URLConnection object, which it assigns to the connection variable. The connection is then read and displayed in the same manner as the GetURLApp program.

ContentHandler, ContentHandlerFactory, and FileNameMap

The ContentHandler class is an abstract class that is used to develop specialized objects that can extract and process data associated with new MIME types.

MIME, or *multipurpose Internet mail extension,* is a general method by which the content of different types of Internet objects can be identified. MIME was originally developed to include different types of objects, such as sounds, images, and videos, in Internet email messages. It was also adopted and popularized by the Web and is used to identify multimedia and other types of Web objects so that appropriate external viewers or plug-in modules can be used to process and display these objects.

The ContentHandler class provides the basis for developing new viewers for processing MIME types that are not currently supported by Java. It consists of a single method, getContent(), that extracts an object of a particular MIME type from an URL connection.

The ContentHandlerFactory interface provides a standard method of associating a content handler with a MIME type. The FileNameMap interface provides the capability to associate a filename with a MIME type.

Chapter 33, "Content and Protocol Handlers," provides a detailed description of how content handlers are developed.

30

NETWORK
PROGRAMMING

The `URLStreamHandler` Class and the `URLStreamHandlerFactory` Interface

The `URLStreamHandler` class is an `abstract` class that is used to develop specialized objects that can communicate with Web resources using protocols that are currently not supported by Java. For example, suppose you develop a new protocol for a custom client/server application and you want that protocol to be accessible to Web browsers. You would develop an `URLStreamHandler` for that protocol. The `URLStreamHandlerFactory` interface is used to associate a stream handler with a particular protocol. Chapter 33 also covers protocol stream handlers.

Summary

In this chapter you learned about Java's support of network programming and about the basics of client/server computing and TCP/IP socket programming. You toured the classes of the `java.net` package and learned how to use them to develop client/server applications. You also learned about the URL-centric classes that support Web-based applications. The next chapter shows you how to apply what you've learned to develop Internet client software.

Client Programs

In this chapter you'll learn how to write client programs that support networked client/server applications. You'll learn about the typical client programs found on the Internet and how they are structured. You'll develop simple client programs that support remote login and fetch a list of Web pages. This chapter builds on the material presented in Chapter 30, "Network Programming with the `java.net` Package."

Types of Clients

Of the client/server applications that are found on the Internet, only a small group is typically used. These include email, the Web, FTP, Usenet newsgroups, and Telnet. Gopher and WAIS, both precursors of the Web, have declined in popularity, having been subsumed by the Web. Typical Internet client programs include email programs, Web browsers, FTP programs, news reader programs, and Telnet clients.

- *Email programs* provide an easy-to-use interface by which mail can be created, sent, retrieved, displayed, and managed. Popular Windows-based clients include Eudora and Outlook. UNIX systems provide a number of popular email clients including Pine, Elm, and mh.

- *Web browsers* provide a window on the World Wide Web and support the display of Web pages, including Java programs. The Netscape Navigator and Microsoft Internet Explorer browsers are the most popular browsers on the Web and are Java-capable. They are supported on UNIX, Windows, Macintosh, and other systems.

- *FTP programs* provide a convenient way to retrieve files from public Internet file servers and from private file directories. Although a number of user-friendly FTP client programs are available, the simple text-based FTP client is still the most popular and most widely supported. WS_FTP is a popular GUI-based FTP client for Windows platforms.

- *News reader* programs simplify the process of working with messages that are posted to Usenet newsgroups. A number of netnews client programs are available for Windows, Macintosh, UNIX, and other operating system platforms.

- *Telnet clients* are used to remotely log in to other systems. These systems are usually UNIX or other operating systems that are powerful enough to provide the underlying capabilities needed to implement multiuser support. Windows and Macintosh systems, because of their inherent limitations, do not support Telnet server applications.

Some client programs, such as Netscape Communicator, consist of an integrated suite of popular programs. For example, Netscape Communicator includes a Web browser, a mail client, and a news reader, among other clients.

Client Responsibilities

Client programs perform a service for their users by connecting with their server counterparts, forwarding service requests based on user inputs, and providing the service results back to the user.

In most cases, the client must initiate the connection. Typically, the server listens on a well-known port for a client connection. The client initiates the connection, which is accepted by the server. The client sends a service request to the server, based on user inputs. The server receives the service request, performs the service, and returns the results of the service to the client. The client receives the service results and displays them to the user.

A Simple Telnet Client

A Telnet client program provides users with the capability to log in to remote systems. It connects to a Telnet server (called a *Telnet daemon*) that listens on port 23 for an incoming connection. The Telnet client connects to the daemon, which usually runs a login program and, upon successful login, runs a shell program.

The Telnet client must be capable of simultaneously exchanging data with both the user and the remote system. The protocol used for communication between the client and the server is specified in RFC 854, the Telnet Protocol Specification. RFC 854 identifies three basic elements of the Telnet protocol: the network virtual terminal, negotiated options, and the symmetry between terminals and processes.

The Network Virtual Terminal

The *network virtual terminal* (NVT) is a simple device that forms the basis for establishing Telnet-based communication. All Telnet clients and servers are required to support the NVT as a minimum capability. It is an abstract device that consists of a printer and a keyboard. The user types characters on the keyboard that are forwarded to the server. The server returns data to the user and the NVT displays it on the printer. The NVT provides local character echoing and half-duplex operation, although remote echoing and full-duplex operation can be used as negotiated options. Lines are terminated using a standard carriage return/line feed combination.

The NVT also provides for control operations that support process interruption and the discarding of excessive output. These operations are signaled by using the *Interpret as Command (IAC)* code, as described in the next section.

The Interpret as Command Code

The IAC code is used to send a control code or to negotiate an option from a client or server to a program on the other end of a Telnet connection, as described in the next section. The IAC is a single byte consisting of the value 255 or hex 0xFF. The IAC may be followed by a single byte to send a control code, or by two or more bytes to negotiate an option. For example, the IAC followed by a byte with the decimal value of 243 is used to send a break command.

Because the IAC is used to indicate a command or option negotiated, a special byte sequence is needed to send the byte value 255 used for the IAC. This is accomplished by sending two IACs in succession.

Negotiated Options

Because all Telnet clients and servers are required to implement the NVT, they all have a common, but primitive, basis from which to begin operation. Additional options, such as full-duplex operation and character echoing, can be used based on the principle of negotiated options.

Options are *negotiated* when either the client or server program sends an IAC code to the other. The IAC code is followed by a WILL or DO code and an option code. The WILL code informs the program on the other side of the connection that it intends to use a particular option. The other program may respond with a DO or a DONT response consisting of the IAC, followed by the DO or DONT code, followed by the option.

A program can also request the program on the other side of the connection to implement an option. This is accomplished by sending the IAC code, the DO code, and the option code. The other program can respond with a WILL or WONT response. A WILL response is indicated by sending the IAC, followed by the WILL code, followed by the option code. A WONT response is sent in the same manner, with the WONT code being used instead of the WILL code.

Symmetry Between Terminals and Processes

As you've probably surmised from reading the previous sections, the communication between client and server is highly symmetrical. Either the client or server can initiate option negotiation. The use of symmetry between client and host simplifies the implementation of the Telnet protocol and allows client and host software to be developed from a common base. The TelnetApp program, presented in the next section, makes use of two I/O filters, `NVTInputStream` and `NVTOutputStream`, that implement some of the basic elements of the Telnet protocol. These streams do not support control characters or additional options. Option negotiation is handled by refusing any additional options other than those provided by the basic NVT.

The `TelnetApp` Program

The `TelnetApp` program implements a minimum set of features of the Telnet protocol in order to accomplish a remote login to a Telnet server. The purpose of the program is not to provide you with a Telnet client, but to show you the basics of how these clients work. More sophisticated and powerful Telnet client programs can be retrieved from the Internet. In addition, many operating systems supply Telnet client programs. The source code of the `TelnetApp` program is shown in Listing 31.1.

LISTING 31.1. THE SOURCE CODE FOR THE `TelnetApp` PROGRAM.

```
import java.lang.*;
import java.net.*;
import java.io.*;
import ju.ch31.NVTInputStream;
import ju.ch31.NVTOutputStream;
import ju.ch31.NVTPrinter;

public class TelnetApp {
 public static void main(String args[]){
  PortTalk portTalk = new PortTalk(args);
  portTalk.start();
 }
}

class PortTalk extends Thread {
 Socket connection;
 OutputStream outStream;
 NVTInputStream inStream;
 NVTPrinter printer;
 public PortTalk(String args[]){
  if(args.length!=2) error("Usage: java TelnetApp host port");
  String destination = args[0];
  int port = 0;
  try {
   port = Integer.valueOf(args[1]).intValue();
  }catch (NumberFormatException ex) { error("Invalid port number"); }
  try{
   connection = new Socket(destination,port);
  }catch (UnknownHostException ex) { error("Unknown host"); }
  catch (IOException ex) { error("IO error creating socket"); }
```

continues

LISTING 31.1. CONTINUED

```
  try{
   outStream = connection.getOutputStream();
   inStream = new NVTInputStream(connection.getInputStream(),outStream);
  }catch (IOException ex) { error("IO error getting streams"); }
  System.out.println("Connected to "+destination+" at port "+port+".");
 }
 public void run() {
  printer = new NVTPrinter(inStream);
  printer.start();
  yield();
  processUserInput();
  shutdown();
 }
 public void processUserInput() {
  try {
   String line;
   boolean finished = false;
   BufferedReader userInputStream = new BufferedReader(
    new InputStreamReader(System.in));
   do {
    line = userInputStream.readLine();
    if(line == null) finished = true;
    else{
     try {
      for(int i=0;i<line.length();++i)
       outStream.write(line.charAt(i));
      outStream.write('\n');
     } catch (IOException ex) {
     }
    }
   } while(!finished);
  } catch(IOException ex) {
   error("Error reading user input");
  }
 }
 public void shutdown(){
  try{
   connection.close();
  }catch (IOException ex) { error("IO error closing socket"); }
 }
 public void error(String s){
  System.out.println(s);
  System.exit(1);
 }
}
```

> **NOTE**
>
> The `TelnetApp` class uses the `NVTPrinter`, `NVTInputStream`, and `NVTOutputStream` classes that are supplied in the following sections. You must type in the `NVTPrinter.java`, `NVTInputStream.java`, and `NVTOutputStream.java` files before compiling `TelnetApp.java`. The Java compiler will automatically compile these files when `TelnetApp.java` is compiled. These files must be placed in the `ju\ch31` directory, since they are part of the `ju.ch31` package.

You use the `TelnetApp` program in the same way as any other Telnet program, but bear in mind that it is only a minimal Telnet client. Run the program by invoking it with the host name of a computer that supports Telnet and the well-known Telnet port number, port 23.

In the following example, I use the program to log in to my account at CTS. Note that the program operates in half-duplex mode, so characters are echoed locally. I substituted asterisks (*) for my password. Take caution when using this program because it will display your password characters in the same manner as any other text that you type. In addition, like other Telnet client programs, it sends unencrypted passwords to the system to which a Telnet connection is being made.

Notice that commands that I type were echoed by my `cts.com` host:

```
java TelnetApp cts.com 23
Connected to cts.com at port 23.


UNIX System V Release 3.2 (crash.cts.com) (ttyp2)

 login: jaworski
Password: ****

Last    successful login for jaworski: Sun Dec 28 22:51:04 PST 1997 on
ttyp6
Last unsuccessful login for jaworski: Mon Nov 17 02:57:41 PST 1997 on
ttyp5

                    Welcome to CTSNET!

            Enter 'help' for assistance and information.

TERM = (vt100)
 Terminal type is vt100
1% l
l
```

```
total 426
-rw-rw-r--  1 jaworski guest      4216 Dec 10 21:40 HIST_S90.TXT
drwx------  2 jaworski guest       272 Sep 08  1995 Mail
drwxr-xr-x  2 jaworski guest       208 Dec 07  1995 News
drwxr-xr-x  2 jaworski guest       224 Sep 08  1995 bin
-rw-------  1 jaworski guest     47682 Oct 06 17:30 cute.jpg
drwxr-xr-x  2 jaworski guest       384 Apr 04  1996 download
lrwxrwxrwx  1 root     root         15 Mar 15  1996 dropbox ->
/ftp/j/jaworski
drwxrwxr-x  2 jaworski guest       128 Dec 14 19:15 finished
drwx------  2 jaworski guest       160 Dec 08  1995 ga
drwxrwxr-x  2 jaworski guest       144 Dec 08 13:12 java_unleashed
drwx------  2 jaworski guest       288 Nov 11 01:30 mail
drwx------  2 jaworski guest       720 Nov 07 13:42 temp
-rw-------  1 jaworski guest        18 Oct 11 19:28 test
-rw-rw-r--  1 jaworski guest    150528 Nov 25 11:30 whmc.doc
drwxr-xr-x  3 jaworski guest       112 Dec 01  1995 writing
2% exit
exit
3% logout
```

Connection broken.

The `TelnetApp` program creates an object of class `PortTalk` to perform its processing. This class extends the `Thread` class in order to implement multithreading capabilities. Its constructor uses the parameters passed in the `TelnetApp` command-line invocation to set up the connection to the specified host and port.

The `run()` method creates an object of the `NVTPrinter` class to interface with the destination host and invokes the `processUserInput()` method to interface with the user. The `processUserInput()` method reads a line at a time from the user's console and sends it to the Telnet server.

The `NVTPrinter` Class

The `NVTPrinter` class performs most of the interesting processing because it interfaces with the server. It does this using the `NVTInputStream` class covered in the next section. `NVTPrinter` is also implemented as a subclass of `Thread`. Its source code is shown in Listing 31.2.

LISTING 31.2. THE SOURCE CODE FOR THE `NVTPrinter` CLASS.

```
package ju.ch31;

import java.io.*;

public class NVTPrinter extends Thread {
```

```
NVTInputStream inStream;
public NVTPrinter(NVTInputStream in) {
 super();
 inStream = in;
}
public void run() {
 boolean finished = false;
 try {
  do {
   int i = inStream.read();
   if(i == -1) finished = true;
   else{
    System.out.print((char) i);
    System.out.flush();
    yield();
   }
  } while(!finished);
  System.out.println("\nConnection broken.");
  System.exit(0);
 } catch (IOException ex) {
  System.out.println("NVTPrinter error");
  System.exit(1);
 }
}
}
```

The `NVTInputStream` Class

The `NVTInputStream` class implements the NVT input interface. Its source code is shown in Listing 31.3.

LISTING 31.3. THE SOURCE CODE FOR THE `NVTInputStream` CLASS.

```
package ju.ch31;

import java.io.*;

public class NVTInputStream extends FilterInputStream {
 byte IAC = (byte) 0xff;
 byte DO = (byte) 0xfd;
 byte WILL = (byte) 0xfb;
 byte CR = 13;
 byte LF = 10;
 int WONT = 252;
 int DONT = 254;
 int BUFFER_SIZE = 1024;
 OutputStream out;
```

continues

LISTING 31.3. CONTINUED

```java
byte lineBuffer[] = new byte[BUFFER_SIZE];
int numBytes = 0;
public NVTInputStream(InputStream inStream,OutputStream outStream) {
 super(inStream);
 out = outStream;
}
public int read() throws IOException {
 boolean recIAC;
 int i;
 do {
  recIAC = false;
  i = in.read();
  if(i == -1) return i;
  byte b = (byte) i;
  if(b == IAC) {
   recIAC = true;
   int cmd = in.read();
   if(cmd == -1) return cmd;
   byte b2 = (byte) cmd;
   if(b2 == IAC) return 255;
   else if(b2 == DO) {
    int opt = in.read();
    if(opt == -1) return opt;
    out.write(255);
    out.write(WONT);
    out.write(opt);
    out.flush();
   }else if(b2 == WILL) {
    int opt = in.read();
    if(opt == -1) return opt;
    out.write(255);
    out.write(DONT);
    out.write(opt);
    out.flush();
   }
  }
 } while(recIAC);
 return i;
}
public String readLine() throws IOException {
 numBytes = 0;
 boolean finished = false;
 do {
  int i = read();
  if(i == -1) return null;
  byte b = (byte) i;
  if(b == LF) {
   if(numBytes>0) {
    if(lineBuffer[numBytes-1] == 13)
```

```
      return new String(lineBuffer,0,numBytes-1);
    }
   }
   lineBuffer[numBytes] = b;
   ++numBytes;
  } while (!finished);
  return null;
 }
}
```

`NVTInputStream` uses the NVT conventions, covered earlier in this chapter, to filter the input stream associated with the connection. It implements the basic `read()` method and also a convenient `readLine()` method.

The `NVTOutputStream` Class

The `NVTOutputStream` class provides an output analog to the `NVTInputStream` class. It implements the basic `write()` method according to the NVT conventions. It also provides a `println()` method that uses the carriage return/line feed (CR-LF) end-of-line conventions. Its source code is shown in Listing 31.4.

LISTING 31.4. THE SOURCE CODE FOR THE `NVTOutputStream` CLASS.

```
package ju.ch31;

import java.io.*;

public class NVTOutputStream extends FilterOutputStream {
 int IAC = 255;
 byte CR = 13;
 byte LF = 10;
 public NVTOutputStream(OutputStream outStream) {
  super(outStream);
 }
 public void write(int i) throws IOException {
  if(i == IAC) super.write(i);
  super.write(i);
 }
 public void println(String s) {
  try {
   byte[] sBytes = s.getBytes();
   for(int i=0;i<sBytes.length;++i)
    super.write(sBytes[i]);
   super.write(CR);
   super.write(LF);
   super.flush();
```

continues

LISTING 31.4. CONTINUED

```
    } catch(IOException ex) {
    }
  }
}
```

The Web Fetcher Program

Web browsers are the most popular client programs found on the Internet. They allow users to download and display Web pages, usually one at time. The program shown in Listing 31.5 allows the user to specify a list of Web pages to be retrieved, and retrieves these Web pages and stores them on the local file system. This is an example of how custom Web clients can be implemented in Java.

LISTING 31.5. THE SOURCE CODE FOR THE `WebFetchApp` PROGRAM.

```
import java.util.Vector;
import java.io.*;
import java.net.*;

public class WebFetchApp {
 public static void main(String args[]){
  WebFetch fetch = new WebFetch();
  fetch.run();
 }
}

class WebFetch {
 String urlList = "url-list.txt";
 Vector URLs = new Vector();
 Vector fileNames = new Vector();
 public WebFetch() {
  super();
 }
 public void getURLList() {
  try {
   BufferedReader inStream = new BufferedReader(new FileReader(urlList));
   String inLine;
   while((inLine = inStream.readLine()) != null) {
    inLine = inLine.trim();
    if(!inLine.equals("")) {
     int tabPos = inLine.lastIndexOf('\t');
     String url = inLine.substring(0,tabPos).trim();
     String fileName = inLine.substring(tabPos+1).trim();
     URLs.addElement(url);
```

```
      fileNames.addElement(fileName);
    }
  }
 }catch(IOException ex){
  error("Error reading "+urlList);
 }
}
public void run() {
 getURLList();
 int numURLs = URLs.size();
 for(int i=0;i<numURLs;++i)
  fetchURL((String) URLs.elementAt(i),(String) fileNames.elementAt(i));
 System.out.println("Done.");
}
public void fetchURL(String urlName,String fileName) {
 try{
  URL url = new URL(urlName);
  System.out.println("Getting "+urlName+"...");
  File outFile = new File(fileName);
  PrintWriter outStream = new PrintWriter(new FileWriter(outFile));
  BufferedReader inStream = new BufferedReader(
   new InputStreamReader(url.openStream()));
  String line;
  while ((line = inStream.readLine())!= null) outStream.println(line);
  inStream.close();
  outStream.close();
 }catch (MalformedURLException ex){
  System.out.println("Bad URL");
 }catch (IOException ex){
  System.out.println("IOException occurred.");
 }
}
public void error(String s){
 System.out.println(s);
 System.exit(1);
}
}
```

To use the program, create a file named `url-list.txt` that contains the names of the URLs you want to retrieve and the names of the files in which you want them stored. The following `url-list.txt` file was used to retrieve some pretty famous Web pages. It is included on the CD-ROM that comes with this book, in the `\ju\ch31` directory:

```
http://www.yahoo.com        yahoo.htm
http://www.cnn.com          cnn.htm
http://home.netscape.com    netscape.htm
```

The output generated for the `WebFetchApp` program was as follows:

```
java WebFetchApp
Getting http://www.yahoo.com...
Getting http://www.cnn.com...
Getting http://home.netscape.com...
Done.
```

Note that only the HTML file associated with each Web site is retrieved. Supporting graphics files are not downloaded unless they are identified in `url-list.txt`.

Summary

In this chapter you have learned how to write client programs that implement the client end of Internet client/server applications. You have learned about the common client programs found on the Internet and how they are structured. You have developed a simple Telnet client and the Web fetcher program. In Chapter 32, "Server Programs," you'll learn how to write simple server applications.

Server Programs

CHAPTER 32

In this chapter you'll learn how to write server programs to support Internet client/server applications. You'll also learn about the server programs found on the Internet and how they are written. You'll develop a Web server that implements version 0.9 of the Hypertext Transfer Protocol. This chapter builds on the material presented in Chapters 30, "Network Programming with the `java.net` Package," and 31, "Client Programs." You might want to review these chapters before continuing with the material presented in this chapter.

Types of Servers

Chapter 30 introduced you to the types of client programs found on the Internet. For every client, there must be a server. Typical servers include email, Web, FTP, Telnet, Netnews, and DNS. Other, less-popular servers such as Echo, Ping, and Finger are also commonly supported.

Email servers move mail from client programs through the Internet to its destination hosts and store it until it is retrieved. The *Simple Message Transfer Protocol* (SMTP) is used to move mail. The *Post Office Protocol* (POP) is used to store mail and serve it to destination client programs.

Web servers implement the *Hypertext Transfer Protocol* (HTTP) in order to serve Web pages over the Internet. The most popular Web server is the Apache Web server. It is publicly available and may be freely downloaded. Commercial Web servers, such as those provided by Netscape and Microsoft, are only a small percentage of those that are in current operation.

FTP servers implement the File Transfer Protocol to make files available over the Internet. The most popular FTP server is a publicly available server developed by Washington University in St. Louis, Missouri.

The *domain name system* provides the backbone for Internet communication by translating domain names to their IP addresses. The most popular DNS software is the publicly available BIND software developed by the University of California at Berkeley.

Telnet servers are found in UNIX, VMS, and other multiuser operating systems. These servers allow remote login and implement the Telnet protocol covered in Chapter 30.

Server Responsibilities

A server program listens for incoming connections on the well-known port associated with its service protocol. When an incoming connection is initiated by a client, the server accepts the connection and typically spawns a separate thread to service that client. The client sends service requests over the connection. The server performs the service and then returns the results to the client.

A Multithreaded Server Framework

The operation of most servers involves listening for connections, accepting connections, processing requests received over the connections, and terminating connections after all requests have been processed. The handling of multiple connections is generally performed using multiple threads. As such, a general framework for multithreaded servers can be developed. Listing 32.1 provides such a framework for a generic server named GenericServer. Appendix A, "Java Language Summary," summarizes how multithreading is accomplished in Java.

The GenericServer class is the main class of the program. It defines serverPort as the number of the port that the server is to listen on. You would change 1234 to the well-known port of the service that the server is to implement. The main() method creates an instance of GenericServer and invokes the instance's run() method. The run() method creates a new ServerSocket and assigns the socket to the server variable. It then executes an infinite loop where it listens for an incoming connection and creates a Socket instance to service the connection. The Socket instance is assigned to the client variable. A new ServerThread object is created to process client requests and the start() method of this object is invoked to get the thread up and running.

The ServerThread class extends the Thread class. It declares the client field variable to keep track of the client socket. Its run() method creates objects of class ServiceInputStream and ServiceOutputStream to communicate with the client. These streams are buffered to enhance I/O performance. A while statement is used to repeatedly invoke the processRequest() method to process client requests. If processRequest() returns a value of false, the service is completed, the while loop ends, and the client socket is closed. The processRequest() method is a stub for implementing service-specific request processing.

The ServiceInputStream, ServiceOutputStream, and ServiceRequest classes are placeholders for implementing client I/O and request processing.

32

SERVER PROGRAMS

> **NOTE**
>
> `GenericServer` handles exceptions by exiting. In real server implementations this may not be the best response. To implement a real server based on `GenericServer`, you should substitute your own exception handling code.

LISTING 32.1. THE GenericServer CODE.

```java
import java.net.*;
import java.io.*;
import java.util.*;

public class GenericServer {
    // Replace 1234 with the well-known port used by the server.
    int serverPort = 1234;
    public static void main(String args[]){
        // Create a server object and run it
        GenericServer server = new GenericServer();
        server.run();
    }
    public GenericServer() {
        super();
    }
    public void run() {
        try {
            // Create a server socket on the specified port
            ServerSocket server = new ServerSocket(serverPort);
            do {
                // Loop to accept incoming connections
                Socket client = server.accept();
                // Create a new thread to handle each connection
                (new ServerThread(client)).start();
            } while(true);
        } catch(IOException ex) {
            System.exit(0);
        }
    }
}

class ServerThread extends Thread {
    Socket client;
    // Store a reference to the socket to which the client is connected
    public ServerThread(Socket client) {
        this.client = client;
    }
    // Thread's entry point
    public void run() {
        try {
```

```
            // Create streams for communicating with client
            ServiceOutputStream outStream = new ServiceOutputStream(
                new BufferedOutputStream(client.getOutputStream())));
            ServiceInputStream inStream =
             new ServiceInputStream(client.getInputStream());
            // Read client's request from input stream
            ServiceRequest request = inStream.getRequest();
            // Process client's request and send output back to client
            while (processRequest(outStream)) {};
        }catch(IOException ex) {
            System.exit(0);
        }
        try {
            client.close();
        }catch(IOException ex) {
            System.exit(0);
        }
    }
    // Stub for request processing
    public boolean processRequest(ServiceOutputStream outStream) {
        return false;
    }
}

// Input stream filter
class ServiceInputStream extends FilterInputStream {
    public ServiceInputStream(InputStream in) {
        super(in);
    }
    // Method for reading client requests from input stream
    public ServiceRequest getRequest() throws IOException {
        ServiceRequest request = new ServiceRequest();
        return request;
    }
}

// Output stream filter
class ServiceOutputStream extends FilterOutputStream {
    public ServiceOutputStream(OutputStream out) {
        super(out);
    }
}

// Class to implement client requests
class ServiceRequest {
}
```

Writing Your Own Web Server

Web servers implement the Hypertext Transfer Protocol (HTTP) in order to retrieve Web resources identified by URLs. HTTP is an application-level protocol that is designed to be quick and efficient. It is based on the request-response paradigm. Web browsers initiate connections with Web servers and submit service requests. The servers, upon receiving a request, locate the specified resource and perform the requested operation. Typical Web browser requests are to retrieve a designated file or send data to a CGI program. HTTP supports several request types, referred to as *methods*. These include the GET, HEAD, and POST methods.

The Web server developed in the following section only supports the GET request. It responds to GET requests by returning the requested resource to the browser. The server implements version 0.9 of HTTP. This is the earliest documented version of the protocol. HTTP 0.9 operates as follows:

- Clients (Web browsers) send single-line requests to the HTTP server of the form: GET *absoluteFilePath* where *absoluteFilePath* is an absolute path to a requested file relative to the server's root directory.
- Client requests are terminated by a carriage return and a line feed character.
- The HTTP server responds by sending the requested file to the client.

HTTP 0.9 is documented as part of Request For Comments (RFC) 1945 "Hypertext Transfer Protocol — HTTP/1.0."

The HTTP09Server Program

The HTTP09Server program illustrates the basic operation of a Web server. (See Listing 32.2.) It is a multithreaded Web server that implements the HTTP 0.9 protocol. Many Web servers are multithreaded, allowing them to simultaneously support multiple browser connections. HTTP09Server tailors the multithreaded server framework covered earlier in this chapter to the HTTP-specific processing. The server is configurable and supports logging of HTTP requests received from clients.

LISTING 32.2. THE SOURCE CODE FOR THE HTTP09Server PROGRAM.

```
import java.net.*;
import java.io.*;
import java.util.*;

public class HTTP09Server {
    // Version constants
```

```
static final String NAME = "HTTP09Server";
static final String VERSION = "1.0";
// Variables for accessing configuration and logging objects
ServerConfiguration config = new ServerConfiguration();
Logger logger = new Logger();

public static void main(String args[]){
    // Create a new server
    HTTP09Server server = new HTTP09Server();
    // Process command line arguments
    if(args.length>0) server.processCommandLine(args);
    // Run the server
    server.run();
}
public HTTP09Server() {
    super();
}
public void processCommandLine(String[] args) {
    for(int i=0;i<args.length;++i) {
        // Look for a configuration file
        if(args[i].equals("-CONFIG")) {
            if(i+1<args.length)
                config.processConfigurationFile(args[i+1]);
            else
            System.out.println("Configuration file argument is
            ➥missing.");
             break;
        }
    }
    String logFile = config.getLogFile();
    if(logFile!="") logger = new
    ➥Logger(logFile,config.echoToConsole());
}
public void displayVersionInfo(){
    System.out.println("HTTP09Server version "+VERSION);
}
public void run() {
    displayVersionInfo();
    // Configure server
    config.display();
    try {
        // Create server socket, listen for and process incoming
        // connections
        ServerSocket server = new
        ➥ServerSocket(config.getServerPort());
        int localPort = server.getLocalPort();
        logger.datedLog(NAME+" is listening on port "+localPort+".");
        do {
            Socket client = server.accept();
```

continues

32

SERVER
PROGRAMS

LISTING 32.2. CONTINUED

```
                // Create a new thread to handle the connection
                (new HTTP09ServerThread(client,config,logger)).start();
            } while(true);
        } catch(IOException ex) {
            logger.datedLog("Unable to listen on "+
            config.getServerPort()+".");
            System.exit(0);
        }
    }
}

class HTTP09ServerThread extends Thread {
    Socket client;
    ServerConfiguration config;
    Logger logger;
    public HTTP09ServerThread(Socket client,
            ServerConfiguration config, Logger logger) {
        this.client = client;
        this.config = config;
        this.logger = logger;
    }
    public void run() {
        try {
            // Send output to logging device
            describeConnection(client);
            // Set up I/O streams
            HTTPOutputStream outStream = new HTTPOutputStream(
                new BufferedOutputStream(client.getOutputStream()));
                HTTPInputStream inStream =
             new HTTPInputStream(client.getInputStream());
            // Get and process client requests
            HTTPRequest request = inStream.getRequest();
            request.log(logger);
            if(request.isGetRequest())
                processGetRequest(request,outStream);
            logger.datedLog("Request completed. Closing connection.");
        }catch(IOException ex) {
            logger.datedLog("IOException occured when processing
            ➥request.");
        }
        try {
            client.close();
        }catch(IOException ex) {
            logger.datedLog("IOException occured when closing socket.");
        }
    }
    void describeConnection(Socket client) {
        String destName = client.getInetAddress().getHostName();
        String destAddr = client.getInetAddress().getHostAddress();
```

```
            int destPort = client.getPort();
            logger.datedLog("Accepted connection to "+destName+" ("
                +destAddr+")"+" on port "+destPort+".");
        }
        void processGetRequest(HTTPRequest request,HTTPOutputStream outStream)
                throws IOException {
            // What file is the client requesting?
            String fileName = request.getFileName(config);
            File file = new File(fileName);
            if(file.exists()) {
                // Figure out the file's full path name
                String fullPath = file.getCanonicalPath();
                // Is the file in the server root directory (or
            ➥subdirectories)?
                if(inServerRoot(fullPath)) {
                    int len = (int) file.length();
                    // Send the file to the requesting client
                    sendFile(outStream,file);
                }else logger.datedLog("File is not in server root.");
             }else logger.datedLog("File "+file.getCanonicalPath()+
           " does not exist.");
        }
        public boolean inServerRoot(String fileName) {
            String serverRoot = config.getServerRoot();
            int fileLength = fileName.length();
            int rootLength = serverRoot.length();
            if(fileLength<rootLength) return false;
            if(serverRoot.equals(fileName.substring(0,rootLength))) return
            ➥true;
            return false;
        }
        void sendFile(HTTPOutputStream out,File file) {
            try {
                 DataInputStream in =
                 new DataInputStream(new FileInputStream(file));
                int len = (int) file.length();
                byte buffer[] = new byte[len];
                in.readFully(buffer);
                in.close();
                for(int i=0;i<len;++i) out.write(buffer[i]);
                out.flush();
                out.close();
                logger.datedLog("File sent: "+file.getCanonicalPath());
                logger.log("Number of bytes: "+len);
            }catch(Exception ex){
                logger.datedLog("Error retrieving "+file);
            }
        }
    }
```

32

SERVER
PROGRAMS

continues

LISTING 32.2. CONTINUED

```java
class HTTPInputStream extends FilterInputStream {
    public HTTPInputStream(InputStream in) {
        super(in);
    }
    public String readLine() throws IOException {
        StringBuffer result=new StringBuffer();
        boolean finished = false;
        boolean cr = false;
        do {
            int ch = -1;
            ch = read();
            if(ch==-1) return result.toString();
            result.append((char) ch);
            if(cr && ch==10){
                result.setLength(result.length()-2);
                return result.toString();
            }
            if(ch==13) cr = true;
            else cr=false;
        } while (!finished);
        return result.toString();
    }
    // Read and HTTP request from the input stream
    public HTTPRequest getRequest() throws IOException {
        HTTPRequest request = new HTTPRequest();
        String line;
        do {
            line = readLine();
            if(line.length()>0) request.addLine(line);
            else break;
        }while(true);
        return request;
    }
}

class HTTPOutputStream extends FilterOutputStream {
    public HTTPOutputStream(OutputStream out) {
        super(out);
    }
    public void println() throws IOException {
        write(13);
        write(10);
    }
    public void println(String s) throws IOException {
        for(int i=0;i<s.length();++i) write(s.charAt(i));
        println();
    }
}
```

```java
// Class for encapsulating an HTTP request
class HTTPRequest {
    Vector lines = new Vector();

    public HTTPRequest() {
    }
    public void addLine(String line) {
        lines.addElement(line);
    }
    boolean isGetRequest() {
        if(lines.size() > 0) {
            String firstLine = (String) lines.elementAt(0);
            if(firstLine.length() > 0)
                if(firstLine.substring(0,3).equalsIgnoreCase("GET"))
                    return true;
        }
        return false;
    }
    String getFileName(ServerConfiguration config) {
        if(lines.size()>0) {
            String firstLine = (String) lines.elementAt(0);
            String fileName = firstLine.substring(firstLine.indexOf("
            ➥")+1);
            int n = fileName.indexOf(" ");
            if(n!=-1) fileName = fileName.substring(0,n);
            try {
                if(fileName.charAt(0) == '/')
                fileName =  fileName.substring(1);
            } catch(StringIndexOutOfBoundsException ex) {}
            if(fileName.equals("")) fileName = config.getDefaultFile();
            if(fileName.charAt(fileName.length()-1)=='/')
                fileName+=config.getDefaultFile();
            return config.getServerRoot()+fileName;
        }else return "";
    }
    void log(Logger logger) {
        logger.datedLog("Received the following request:");
        for(int i=0;i<lines.size();++i)
            logger.log((String) lines.elementAt(i));
    }
}

// Class for configuring the server
class ServerConfiguration {
    static final char CONFIG_COMMENT_CHAR = '#';
    int serverPort = 80;
    String serverRoot = "";
    String defaultFile = "index.htm";
    String logFile = "";
```

continues

LISTING 32.2. CONTINUED

```
    boolean echoLogToConsole = true;
    public ServerConfiguration() {
    }
    public char getCommentChar() {
        return CONFIG_COMMENT_CHAR;
    }
    public int getServerPort() {
        return serverPort;
    }
    public String getServerRoot() {
        return serverRoot;
    }
    public String getDefaultFile() {
        return defaultFile;
    }
    public String getLogFile() {
        return logFile;
    }
    public boolean echoToConsole() {
        return echoLogToConsole;
    }
    public void display() {
        System.out.println("  serverPort: "+serverPort);
        System.out.println("  serverRoot: "+serverRoot);
        System.out.println("  defaultFile: "+defaultFile);
        System.out.println("  logFile: "+logFile);
        System.out.println("  echoLogToConsole: "+echoLogToConsole);
    }
    public void processConfigurationFile(String fname) {
        try {
            File file = new File(fname);
            if(file.exists()) {
                BufferedReader reader =
                new BufferedReader(new FileReader(file));
                String line;
                while((line=reader.readLine())!=null)
                    processConfigurationLine(line);
                reader.close();
            }
        }catch(Exception ex) {
            System.out.println("Unable to process configuration file.");
        }
    }
    public void processConfigurationLine(String line)
            throws NumberFormatException {
        line = removeLeadingWhiteSpace(line);
        if(line.length()==0) return;
        int n;
        int n1 = line.indexOf(' ');
```

```
            int n2 = line.indexOf('\t');
            if(n1 == -1) n = n2;
            else if(n2 == -1) n = n1;
            else if(n1 < n2) n = n1;
            else n = n2;
            if(n==-1 || n==line.length()-1) return;
            String param = line.substring(0,n);
            String value = line.substring(n+1);
            if(param.equals("serverPort"))
                serverPort = (new Integer(value)).intValue();
            else if(param.equals("serverRoot")){
                serverRoot = value;
                if(!serverRoot.equals("")){
                    char ch = serverRoot.charAt(serverRoot.length()-1);
                    if(ch!='/' && ch!='\\') serverRoot+="/";
                }
            }else if(param.equals("defaultFile"))
                defaultFile = value;
            else if(param.equals("logFile"))
                logFile = value;
            else if(param.equals("echoLogToConsole"))
                echoLogToConsole = (new Boolean(value)).booleanValue();
        }
        String removeLeadingWhiteSpace(String line) {
            boolean finished = false;
            do {
                if(line.length()==0) return "";
                char ch = line.charAt(0);
                if(ch==CONFIG_COMMENT_CHAR) return "";
                if(ch!=' ' && ch!='\t') return line;
                line=line.substring(1);
            } while (!finished);
            return "";
        }
    }

// Class for logging information about the server's operation
class Logger {
    public String logFile;
    public boolean echoLogToConsole = true;
    public BufferedWriter writer = null;
    public Logger() {
    }
    public Logger(String fname, boolean echo) {
        logFile = fname;
        echoLogToConsole = echo;
        try {
            writer = new BufferedWriter(new FileWriter(fname,true));
        }catch(IOException ex){}
```

continues

LISTING 32.2. CONTINUED

```
    }
    void logMsg(String msg) {
        if(writer!=null) {
            try {
                writer.write(msg);
                writer.newLine();
                writer.flush();
            }catch(IOException ex){}
        }
        if(echoLogToConsole) System.out.println(msg);
    }
    public synchronized void log(String msg) {
        logMsg("  "+msg);
    }
    public synchronized void datedLog(String msg) {
        logMsg((new Date()).toString()+" "+msg);
    }
}
```

When you run `HTTP09Server` it displays the following output.

```
HTTP09Server version 1.0
  serverPort: 80
  serverRoot:
  defaultFile: index.htm
  logFile:
  echoLogToConsole: true
Fri Jan 16 19:33:43 PST 1998 HTTP09Server is listening on port 80.
```

The output identifies the server port as port 80, the server root directory as blank (indicating the directory from which the server was run), the default filename as `index.htm`, no logging file, and logging being displayed to the console window. You'll learn how to configure these parameters in the section "Configuring `HTTP09Server`."

 I have supplied a default Web page, `index.htm`, that is retrieved by `HTTP09Server`. (See Listing 32.3.) I've also included the `test.htm` file shown in Listing 32.4. You can also retrieve other Web pages by placing them in a path off the server's root directory.

LISTING 32.3. THE CONTENTS OF THE `index.htm` FILE.

```
<HTML>
<HEAD>
<TITLE>Index</TITLE>
</HEAD>
<BODY>
```

```
<H1>This is index.htm</H1>
</BODY>
</HTML>
```

LISTING 32.4. THE CONTENTS OF THE test.htm FILE.

```
<HTML>
<HEAD>
<TITLE>Test</TITLE>
</HEAD>
<BODY>
<H1>This is test.htm</H1>
</BODY>
</HTML>
```

Because HTTP09Server is a server, you need to use a client program to interact with it. Launch your favorite Web browser and open the URL of your machine. For example, if your host name is my.host.name.com, open the URL http://my.host.name.com/. HTTP09Server responds by identifying the browser connection and sending the index.htm file. You can access other files by appending their names to the URL. For example, to access the test.htm file in the directory where you launched HTTP09Server, use the URL http://my.host.name.com/index.htm. You can also use localhost or 127.0.0.1 if you do not have a host name or know your IP address. Figure 32.1 shows how index.htm is displayed by Netscape Communicator 4.0. Figure 32.2 shows how test.htm is displayed.

When I request index.htm using my browser, the following output is displayed by HTTP09Server on the console window:

```
Fri Jan 16 19:47:17 PST 1998 Accepted connection to localhost (127.0.0.1)
on port 1759.
Fri Jan 16 19:47:17 PST 1998 Received the following request:
  GET / HTTP/1.0
  Connection: Keep-Alive
  User-Agent: Mozilla/4.04   (Win95; U)
  Host: localhost
  Accept: image/gif, image/x-xbitmap, image/jpeg, image/pjpeg, image/png,
*/*
  Accept-Language: en
  Accept-Charset: iso-8859-1,*,utf-8
Fri Jan 16 19:47:18 PST 1998 File sent: D:\jdk1.2beta2\ju\ch32\index.htm
  Number of bytes: 101
Fri Jan 16 19:47:18 PST 1998 Request completed. Closing connection.
```

32

SERVER PROGRAMS

You'll receive more or less output depending on the browser you use, its version, and how it is configured. The previous output identifies the date and time at which a connection was accepted, the request received from the browser, the file that was sent in response, and the time the connection was closed. You will see similar, but different, output when you request files from your installation of HTTP09Server.

When you access the URL http://my.host.name.com, HTTP09Server is instructed to return the default-no-name HTML file. It responds by sending index.htm to the Web browser.

> **NOTE**
>
> If you cannot find your host name, you can use localhost instead. For example, the URL http://localhost/ can be used instead of http://my.host.name.com/.

FIGURE 32.1.

Web browser displaying the default file (index.htm).

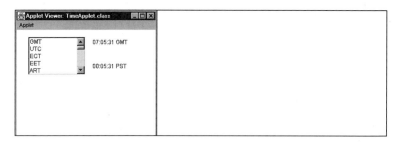

FIGURE 32.2.

Web browser displaying test.htm.

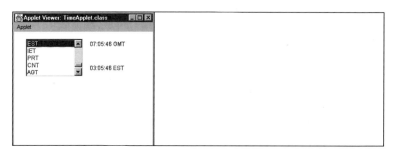

Experiment by creating your own HTML files and using your browser to access them using HTTP09Server. Use Ctrl+C to terminate the operation of HTTP09Server.

How `HTTP09Server` Works

`HTTP09Server` is implemented using the following seven classes:

- `HTTP09Server`—The main application class
- `HTTP09ServerThread`—Thread for servicing a client connection
- `HTTPInputStream`—Stream to read requests from the client
- `HTTPOutputStream`—Stream to send responses to the client
- `HTTPRequest`—The encapsulation of a client request
- `ServerConfiguration`—Provides the capability to configure the server
- `Logger`—Logs client requests

These classes are covered in the following subsections.

`HTTP09Server`

This class is similar in structure to `GenericServer`, but adds additional field variables and methods. The `config` variable is assigned an object of the `ServerConfiguration` class. This object encapsulates all configuration information needed by `HTTP09Server`. The `logger` variable is assigned a `Logger` object that is used to support request logging.

The `processCommandLine()` method checks to see if a configuration file was included as an argument to `HTTP09Server`. If so, it invokes the `processConfigurationFile()` method on the `ServerConfiguration` object referenced by `config`. A `Logger` object is created, initialized based on the server configuration, and assigned to the `logger` variable.

The `displayVersionInfo()` method displays version information about `HTTP09Server`.

The `run()` method displays version and configuration information, listens on the server port, and creates `HTTP09ServerThread` objects to service client requests.

`HTTP09ServerThread`

`HTTP09ServerThread` follows the structure of `ServerThread` and adds a few methods. The `describeConnection()` method uses the logger to display log information about the connection being handled. The `processGetRequest()` method determines the name of the file requested by the client, checks to see if the file exists and is accessible from the server root, and sends the file to the client. The `inServerRoot()` method checks a filename to see if it is accessible from the server root. The `sendFile()` method sends the file requested by the client.

HTTPInputStream and HTTPOutputStream

The HTTPInputStream and HTTPOutputStream classes are analogous to the ServiceInputStream and ServiceOutputStream classes of GenericServer. The readLine() method of HTTPInputStream reads a carriage return, linefeed terminated line. The getRequest() method reads multiline client requests. HTTPOutputStream provides the println() method to send response data to the client.

HTTPRequest

The HTTPRequest class is analogous to the ServiceRequest class of GenericServer. It stores requests using a Vector object. The isGetRequest() method verifies that a client request is an HTTP GET, as opposed to a PUT, POST, or other request. The getFileName() method extracts the file requested by the client from the request Vector object. The log() method is used to log a client request.

ServerConfiguration

The ServerConfiguration class provides the capability to configure HTTP09Server. It maintains the configuration information described in the section "Configuring HTTP09Server" later in this chapter. It provides several methods for accessing this configuration information. The processConfigurationFile() and processConfigurationLine() methods read and parse the configuration file.

Logger

The Logger class implements a logging capability. It displays logging information to a file, the console, or both. The logMsg() method writes data to the log devices. The log() and datedLog() methods are synchronized methods that use logMsg(). The datedLog() method prepends the current date and time to the log data.

Configuring HTTP09Server

You can configure the following parameters of HTTP09Server:

- The server port
- The server root directory
- The default file returned when none is specified
- The log filename
- Whether log information is displayed on the console window

Listing 32.5 presents a sample configuration file. Configuration parameters are placed on separate lines. Each line begins with the name of the parameter to be configured, followed by its value. The configuration parameter names are `serverPort`, `serverRoot`, `defaultFile`, `logFile`, and `echoToConsole`.

The pound character (#) indicates a comment in the configuration file when it is placed at the beginning of a line. Lines beginning with the comment character are ignored.

To use a configuration file with `HTTP09Server`, run `HTTP09Server` as follows:

`java HTTP09Server -CONFIG configurationFileName`

Substitute your configuration file for *configurationFileName*.

LISTING 32.5. EXAMPLE `HTTP09Server` CONFIGURATION FILE.

```
# Example HTTP09Server configuration file

# Set the server port to port 8080 instead of the default port 80.

serverPort 8080

# Set the server root to the D:\temp directory.

serverRoot D:\temp\

# Set the default file to default.htm.

defaultFile default.htm

# Set the log file to log.txt.

logFile log.txt

# Disable logging to the console window.

echoLogToConsole false
```

Summary

In this chapter you learned how to write programs that implement the server end of Internet client/server applications. You learned about the common server programs found on the Internet and how they are structured. You have developed a Web server that implements HTTP version 0.9. In Chapter 33, "Content and Protocol Handlers," you'll learn how to write content and protocol handlers that are used with Web client applications.

Content and Protocol Handlers

IN THIS CHAPTER

In this chapter you'll learn how to write Java content handlers and protocol handlers. Content handlers support the retrieval of objects by Web browsers. They use the Multipurpose Internet Mail Extensions (MIME) to identify the type of objects that are provided by Web servers. Protocol handlers enable browsers to work with protocols other than HTTP. Both content and protocol handlers allow you to expand the capabilities of your browser. In this chapter you'll develop examples of both types of handlers.

Using Content Handlers

If you have been extensively involved with using your Web browser, you probably have encountered a number of external viewers or plug-ins that are used to supplement the capabilities provided by your browser. These external viewers are used to display and process files that are not normally supported by browsers.

Java supports additional internal or external viewers through the content handler mechanism. Content handlers are used to retrieve objects via an URLConnection object.

Content handlers are implemented as subclasses of the ContentHandler class. A content handler is only required to implement a single method, the getContent() method, which overrides the method provided by the ContentHandler class. This method takes an URLConnection object as a parameter and returns an object of a specific MIME type. You'll learn about MIME types in the following section of this chapter.

The purpose of a content handler is to extract an object of a given MIME type from an URLConnection object's input stream. Content handlers are not directly instantiated or accessed. The getContent() methods of the URL and URLConnection classes cause content handlers to be created and invoked to perform their processing.

A content handler is associated with a specific MIME type through the use of the ContentHandlerFactory interface. A class that implements the ContentHandlerFactory interface must implement the createContentHandler() method. This method returns a ContentHandler object to be used for a specific MIME type. A ContentHandlerFactory object is installed using the static setContentHandlerFactory() method of the URLConnection class.

Multipurpose Internet Mail Extensions (MIME)

Content handlers are associated with specific MIME types. Many Internet programs, including email clients, Web browsers, and Web servers, use MIME to associate an object type with a file. These object types include text, multimedia files, and application-specific files. MIME types consist of a type and a subtype. Examples are text/html, text/plain, image/gif, and image/jpeg, where text and image are the types and html, text, gif, and jpeg are the subtypes. The URL classes provided by Java support the processing of each of these types. However, the number of MIME type/subtype combinations is large and growing. Content handlers are used to support MIME type processing.

Web servers map MIME types to the files they serve using the files' extensions. For example, files with the .htm and .html extensions are mapped to the text/html MIME type/subtype. Files with the .gif and .jpg extensions are mapped to image/gif and image/jpeg. The MIME type of a file is sent to Web browsers by Web servers when the servers send the designated files to the browsers in response to browser requests.

Developing Content Handlers

The first step in implementing a content handler is to define the class of the object to be extracted by the content handler. The content handler is then defined as a subclass of the ContentHandler class. The getContent() method of the content handler performs the extraction of objects of a specific MIME type from the input stream associated with an URLConnection object.

A content handler is associated with a specific MIME type through the use of a ContentHandlerFactory object. The createContentHandler() method of the ContentHandlerFactory interface is used to return a content handler for a specific MIME type.

Finally, the setContentHandlerFactory() method of the URLConnection class is used to set a ContentHandlerFactory as the default ContentHandlerFactory to be used with all MIME types.

A Content Handler Example

This section presents an example of implementing a simple content handler. A bogus MIME type, text/cg, is created to implement objects of the character grid type. A *character grid type* is a two-dimensional grid made up of a single character. An example follows:

```
0   0
 0 0
  0
 0 0
0   0
```

This example is a character grid object that is five characters wide and five characters high. It uses the O character to draw the grid. The grid is specified by a `boolean` array that identifies how the drawing character is to be displayed.

This particular character grid is represented using the following text string:

550100010101000100010101010001

The first character (5) represents the grid's height. The second character (also 5) represents the grid's width. The third character is the grid's drawing character. The remaining characters specify whether the draw character should be displayed at a particular grid position. A one (1) signifies that the draw character should be displayed and a zero (0) signifies that it should not be displayed. The array is arranged in row order beginning at the top of the grid.

The definition of the `CharGrid` class is shown in Listing 33.1.

LISTING 33.1. THE SOURCE CODE FOR THE `CharGrid` CLASS.

```
public class CharGrid {
 public int height;
 public int width;
 public char ch;
 public boolean values[][];
 public CharGrid(int h,int w,char c,boolean vals[][]) {
  height = h;
  width = w;
  ch = c;
  values = vals;
 }
}
```

The `GridContentHandler` Class

The `GridContentHandler` class is used to extract `CharGrid` objects from an `URLConnection`. Its source code is shown in Listing 33.2.

LISTING 33.2. THE SOURCE CODE FOR THE `GridContentHandler` CLASS.

```
import java.net.*;
import java.io.*;

public class GridContentHandler extends ContentHandler {
 public Object getContent(URLConnection urlc) throws IOException {
  DataInputStream in = new DataInputStream(urlc.getInputStream());
  int height = (int) in.readByte() - 48;
  int width = (int) in.readByte() - 48;
```

```
    char ch = (char) in.readByte();
    boolean values[][] = new boolean[height][width];
    for(int i=0;i<height;++i) {
     for(int j=0;j<width;++j) {
      byte b = in.readByte();
      if(b == 48) values[i][j] = false;
      else values[i][j] = true;
     }
    }
    in.close();
    return new CharGrid(height,width,ch,values);
  }
}
```

The `GridContentHandler` class extends the `ContentHandler` class and provides a single method. The `getContent()` method takes an `URLConnection` object as a parameter and returns an object of the `Object` class. It also throws the `IOException` exception.

The `getContent()` method creates an object of class `DataInputStream` and assigns it to the `in` variable. It uses the `getInputStream()` method of the `URLConnection` class to access the input stream associated with an URL connection.

The height, width, and draw character of the `CharGrid` object are read one byte at a time from the input stream. The `values` array is read and converted to a `boolean` representation. A `CharGrid` object is then created from the extracted values and returned.

The `GetGridApp` Program

The `GetGridApp` program illustrates the use of content handlers. It retrieves an object of the `CharGrid` type from my Web server. I use the NCSA HTTPD server on a Linux system. I've set up the server's MIME type file to recognize files with the `.cg` extension as text/cg.

The source code of the `GetGridApp` program is shown in Listing 33.3.

LISTING 33.3. THE SOURCE CODE FOR THE `GetGridApp` PROGRAM.

```
import java.net.*;
import java.io.*;

public class GetGridApp {
 public static void main(String args[]){
  try{
   GridFactory gridFactory = new GridFactory();
   URLConnection.setContentHandlerFactory(gridFactory);
```

continues

LISTING 33.3. CONTINUED

```java
      if(args.length!=1) error("Usage: java GetGridApp URL");
      System.out.println("Fetching URL: "+args[0]);
      URL url = new URL(args[0]);
      CharGrid cg = (CharGrid) url.getContent();
      System.out.println("height: "+cg.height);
      System.out.println("width: "+cg.width);
      System.out.println("char: "+cg.ch);
      for(int i=0;i<cg.height;++i) {
       for(int j=0;j<cg.width;++j) {
        if(cg.values[i][j]) System.out.print(cg.ch);
        else System.out.print(" ");
       }
       System.out.println();
      }
     }catch (MalformedURLException ex){
      error("Bad URL");
     }catch (IOException ex){
      error("IOException occurred.");
     }
    }
   public static void error(String s){
    System.out.println(s);
    System.exit(1);
   }
  }
  class GridFactory implements ContentHandlerFactory {
   public GridFactory() {
   }
   public ContentHandler createContentHandler(String mimeType) {
    if(mimeType.equals("text/cg")) {
     System.out.println("Requested mime type: "+mimeType);
     return new GridContentHandler();
    }
    return null;
   }
  }
```

Compile `CharGrid.java` and `GridContentHandler.java` before compiling
`GetGridApp.java`. When you invoke the `GetGridApp` program, provide it with the
`http://www.jaworski.com/java/chargrid.cg` URL as a parameter.

The `GetGridApp` program's output is as follows:

```
java GetGridApp http://www.jaworski.com/java/chargrid.cg
Fetching URL: http://www.jaworski.com/java/chargrid.cg
Requested mime type: text/cg
height: 5
width: 5
char: j
```

```
jjjjj
   j
   j
j j
 jj
```

This connects to my Web server, retrieves the `chargrid.cg` file, extracts the `CharGrid` object contained in the file, and displays it in the console window. The character grid object displays a grid of j characters.

The `main()` method creates an object of the `GridFactory` class, which implements the `ContentHandlerFactory` interface. It then sets the object as the default content handler. An `URL` object is created using the URL string passed as the program's parameter. The `getContent()` method of the `URL` class is then used to extract the `CharGrid` object from the URL. The `getContent()` method results in the `GridFactory` object assigned to the `gridFactory` variable being invoked to retrieve an appropriate content handler. An object of class `GridContentHandler` is returned and its `getContent()` method is invoked to extract the `CharGrid` object. This is performed behind the scenes as the result of invoking the `URL` class's `getContent()` method. The `CharGrid` object is then displayed.

The `GetGridApp` program defines the `GridFactory` class as a `ContentHandlerFactory`. It implements the `createContentHandler()` method and checks to see if the MIME type passed to it is text/cg. If it is not, the `null` value is returned to signal that the Java-supplied content handler should be used. If the MIME type is text/cg, the requested MIME type is displayed and a `GridContentHandler` object is returned.

TIP

Check your Web server's documentation if you want to learn how to set up your Web server to work with a new MIME type. Almost all Web servers provide the capability to define new MIME types. However, there is no common approach to doing this that works across all Web servers.

Using Protocol Handlers

Most popular Web browsers support protocols other than HTTP. These other protocols include FTP, gopher, email, and application-specific protocols. Support for these protocols is usually built into the browser, causing the browsers to become larger and slower to load.

Java supports additional protocols through the use of *protocol handlers*, also referred to as *stream handlers*. These protocol handlers are used to retrieve Web objects using application-specific protocols, which are specified in the URL referencing the object.

Protocol handlers are implemented as subclasses of the URLStreamHandler class. The URLStreamHandler class defines four access methods that can be overridden by its subclasses, but only the openConnection() method is required to be overridden.

The openConnection() method takes an URL with its assigned protocol as a parameter and returns an object of class URLConnection. The URLConnection object can then be used to create input and output streams and to access the resource addressed by the URL.

The parseURL() and setURL() methods are used to implement custom URL syntax parsing. The toExternalForm() method is used to convert an URL of the protocol type to a String object.

The purpose of a protocol handler is to implement a custom protocol needed to access Web objects identified by URLs that require the custom protocol. Protocol handlers, like content handlers, are not directly instantiated or accessed. The methods of the URLConnection object that is returned by a protocol handler are invoked to access the resource referenced by the protocol.

A protocol is identified beginning with the first character of the URL and continuing to the first colon (:) contained in the URL. For example, the protocol of the URL http://www.jaworski.com is http, and the protocol of the URL fortune:// jaworski.com is fortune.

A protocol handler is associated with a specific protocol through the use of the URLStreamHandlerFactory interface. A class that implements the URLStreamHandlerFactory interface must implement the createURLStreamHandler() method. This method returns an URLStreamHandler object to be used for a specific protocol. An URLStreamHandlerFactory object is installed using the static setURLStreamHandlerFactory() method of the URL class.

Developing Protocol Handlers

The first step in implementing a protocol handler is to define it as a subclass of the URLStreamHandler class. The openConnection() method of the protocol handler creates an URLConnection object that can be used to access an URL designating the specified protocol.

A protocol handler is associated with a specific protocol type through the use of an URLStreamHandlerFactory object. The createURLStreamHandler() method of the URLStreamHandlerFactory interface is used to return a protocol handler for a specific protocol type.

The setURLStreamHandlerFactory() method of the URL class is used to set an URLStreamHandlerFactory as the default URLStreamHandlerFactory to be used with all protocol types.

A Protocol Handler Example

This section presents an example of implementing a simple protocol handler. My Web server comes with a CGI program, named fortune, that returns a fortune cookie–type message when the program's URL is accessed. This section will define the fortune protocol to access the fortune program on my Web server. The fortune protocol is not a real Internet protocol; I contrived it to illustrate the use of protocol handlers. The URL for the fortune protocol consists of fortune:// followed by the host name. For example, fortune://jaworski.com accesses the fortune protocol on my Web server.

The definition of the URLFortuneHandler class is shown in Listing 33.4.

LISTING 33.4. THE SOURCE CODE FOR THE URLFortuneHandler CLASS.

```
import java.net.*;
import java.io.*;

public class URLFortuneHandler extends URLStreamHandler {
 public URLConnection openConnection(URL url) throws IOException {
  String host=url.getHost();
  URL newURL = new URL("http://"+host+"/cgi-bin/fortune");
  return newURL.openConnection();
 }
}
```

The URLFortuneHandler class extends the URLStreamHandler class and provides a single method. The openConnection() method takes an URL object as a parameter and returns an object of the URLConnection class. It also throws the IOException exception.

The openConnection() method uses the getHost() method of the URL class to extract the host name contained in the URL. It then uses a new HTTP URL by concatenating http:// with the host name and the location of the fortune CGI program, /cgi-bin/fortune. The openConnection() method of the URL class is used to return the URLConnection object associated with the new URL.

33

CONTENT AND
PROTOCOL
HANDLERS

The URLFortuneHandler class wraps the fortune CGI program using the fortune pro-tocol. This protocol is implemented through an HTTP connection to the CGI program.

The GetFortuneApp Program

The GetFortuneApp program illustrates the use of protocol handlers. It accesses the for-tune CGI program on my Web server using the fortune protocol. The source code of the GetFortuneApp program is shown in Listing 33.5. Be sure to compile URLFortuneHandler.java before compiling GetFortuneApp.java.

LISTING 33.5. THE SOURCE CODE FOR THE GetFortuneApp PROGRAM.

```java
import java.net.*;
import java.io.*;

public class GetFortuneApp {
 public static void main(String args[]){
  try{
   FortuneFactory fortuneFactory = new FortuneFactory();
   URL.setURLStreamHandlerFactory(fortuneFactory);
   if(args.length!=1) error("Usage: java GetFortuneApp FortuneURL");
   System.out.println("Fetching URL: "+args[0]);
   URL url = new URL(args[0]);
   BufferedReader inStream = new BufferedReader(
    new InputStreamReader(url.openStream()));
   String line = "";
   while((line = inStream.readLine()) != null)
    System.out.println(line);
  }catch (MalformedURLException ex){
   error("Bad URL");
  }catch (IOException ex){
   error("IOException occurred.");
  }
 }
 public static void error(String s){
  System.out.println(s);
  System.exit(1);
 }
}
class FortuneFactory implements URLStreamHandlerFactory {
 public FortuneFactory() {
 }
 public URLStreamHandler createURLStreamHandler(String protocol) {
  if(protocol.equals("fortune")){
   System.out.println("Requested protocol: "+protocol);
   return new URLFortuneHandler();
  }
  return null;
 }
}
```

When you invoke the `GetFortuneApp` program, provide it with the `fortune://jaworski.com` URL as a parameter. The `GetFortuneApp` program's output is as follows (you will get a different fortune each time you execute the program):

```
java GetFortuneApp fortune://jaworski.com
Fetching URL: fortune://jaworski.com
Requested protocol: fortune
                    JACK AND THE BEANSTACK
                      by Mark Isaak

        Long ago, in a finite state far away, there lived a JOVIAL
character named Jack.  Jack and his relations were poor.  Often their
hash table was bare.  One day Jack's parent said to him, "Our matrices
are sparse.  You must go to the market to exchange our RAM for some
BASICs."  She compiled a linked list of items to retrieve and passed it
to him.
        So Jack set out.  But as he was walking along a Hamilton path,
he met the traveling salesman.
        "Whither dost thy flow chart take thou?" prompted the salesman
in high-level language.
        "I'm going to the market to exchange this RAM for some chips
and Apples," commented Jack.
        "I have a much better algorithm.  You needn't join a queue
there; I will swap your RAM for these magic kernels now."
        Jack made the trade, then backtracked to his house.  But when
he told his busy-waiting parent of the deal, she became so angry she
started thrashing.
        "Don't you even have any artificial intelligence?  All these
kernels together hardly make up one byte," and she popped them out the
window ...
```

GetFortuneApp connects to my Web server, invokes the `fortune` CGI program, and then displays the program's results. The source code of the `fortune` CGI program is available at `http://www.jaworski.com/jdg/`.

The `main()` method creates an object of the `FortuneFactory` class that implements the `URLStreamHandlerFactory` interface. It then sets the object as the default protocol handler. An `URL` object is created using the URL string passed as the program's parameter. The `openStream()` method of the `URL` class is then used to open an input stream to extract the information generated by accessing the URL via the `fortune` protocol. The `openStream()` method results in the `FortuneFactory` object assigned to the `fortuneFactory` variable being invoked to retrieve an appropriate protocol handler. An object of class `URLFortuneHandler` is returned and its `openConnection()` method is invoked to extract the `URLConnection` object. This is performed behind the scenes as the result of invoking the `URL` class's `openStream()` method. The information returned from accessing the URL is then displayed.

33

CONTENT AND
PROTOCOL
HANDLERS

The GetFortuneApp program defines the FortuneFactory class as implementing the URLStreamHandlerFactory interface. It implements the createURLStreamHandler() method and checks to see if the protocol type passed to it is fortune. If it is not, the null value is returned to signal that the Java-supplied protocol handler should be used. If the protocol type is fortune, the requested protocol is displayed and an URLFortuneHandler object is returned.

Summary

In this chapter you learned how to write content handlers to support the retrieval of objects by Web browsers. You learned about the Multipurpose Internet Mail Extensions and how they are used to identify the type of objects that are provided by Web servers. You developed the GridContentHandler class and integrated it with the GetGridApp program.

You also learned how to write protocol handlers to access URLs via custom protocols. You developed the URLFortuneHandler and integrated it with the GetFortuneApp program. In the next chapter you will learn how to use the JavaMail API to develop electronic mail applications.

Using JavaMail

34

CHAPTER

Email is one of the most important functions provided by the Internet. Many of us send and receive email on a daily basis. The JavaMail API provides the capability to develop email clients and mail-enabled Java applications. In this chapter, you'll learn how mail systems work and how the JavaMail API is used to create email clients. You'll finish the chapter by developing a simple Internet mail client.

How Email Systems Work

Email systems consist of two major components: a mail client or *user agent (UA)*, and a mail server or *message transfer agent (MTA)*. User agents let users compose and send email and retrieve email from message transfer agents. Message transfer agents store and forward email for user agents and support the exchange of mail across a network or group of networks (see Figure 34.1).

FIGURE 34.1.

How email systems work.

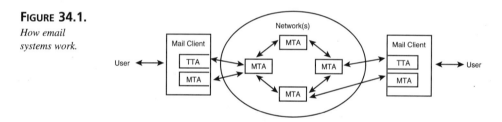

Examples of user agents are email programs, such as Eudora and Outlook. These programs also provide limited message transfer capabilities. Examples of message transfer agents are email server programs, such as Sendmail and Exchange. On the Internet, the Post Office Protocol 3 (POP3) is the most popular protocol for user agents to receive mail from message transfer agents. The Simple Message Transfer Protocol (SMTP) is the most popular protocol for user agents to send mail to message transfer agents, and for message transfer agents to exchange mail with each other. The POP3 protocol is described in Request for Comments (RFC) 1225, and the SMTP protocol is covered in RFC 821. Figure 34.2 shows how POP3 and SMTP are used on the Internet.

The Internet Message Access Protocol (IMAP4) protocol allows user agents to directly access mail folders that are stored on a mail server. IMAP4 leaves mail on the mail server, and POP3 downloads it to the user's computer. IMAP4 lets the user access his mail no matter what computer he is using. IMAP4 is described in RFC 2060.

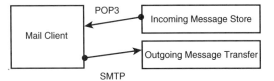

FIGURE 34.2.
How POP3 and
SMTP are used on
the Internet.

The JavaMail API

The JavaMail API supports the development of user agents. It can be used to create email client programs in Java, to mail-enable other programs (such as editors and browsers), or to implement special email features in embedded products, such as Web phones. The JavaMail API is not designed to support the development of mail servers, although it does provide the capability to interface with message transfer agents.

The JavaMail API consists of the following four packages:

- `javax.mail`—Provides the basic classes for implementing the user agent of a messaging system.
- `javax.mail.event`—Defines events, event listeners, and adapters for the events associated with mail clients.
- `javax.mail.internet`—Provides classes and interfaces for working with Internet mail headers (RFC 822) and MIME (RFC 2045) headers.
- `javax.mail.search`—Provides classes that can be used for performing searches of messages and message parts.

These packages are contained in the `mail.jar` file that is distributed with the JavaMail API. The `mail.jar` file also contains several other packages that, although they are not part of the JavaMail API, support the development of mail clients. These undocumented packages are as follows:

- `com.sun.mail.util`—Provides support for parsing, encoding, and decoding of messages.
- `com.sun.mail.smtp`—Provides support for the SMTP.
- `com.sun.mail.iap`—Provides protocol support classes.
- `com.sun.mail.imap`—Provides support for manipulating IMAP folders.
- `com.sun.mail.imap.protocol`—Provides support for the IMAP4.
- `com.sun.mail.handlers`—Provides RFC 822 and MIME mail-handling capabilities.

34

USING JAVAMAIL

Because these packages are not officially part of the JavaMail API, they may not be available in future versions.

Figure 34.3 shows how the JavaMail API supports the development of user agent software. The email client provides an application layer consisting of the application's GUI and application-specific logic. The application logic consists of mail functions, such as composition, addressing, and mail management. These functions use the classes and interfaces of the JavaMail API to implement general mail-processing capabilities. The JavaMail API classes and interfaces provide basic mail system objects, such as messages, addresses, headers, folders, and so on. The JavaMail API does not presume or provide the underlying messaging protocols, such as POP3, SMTP, or IMAP4. Instead, it provides a general framework for working with messaging systems. The undocumented Sun packages provide support for SMTP and IMAP4. It is expected that Sun or other vendors will provide support for protocols, such as POP3 or the Network News Transfer Protocol (NNTP).

FIGURE 34.3.

The JavaMail API layer.

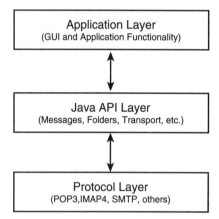

NOTE

JavaMail does not provide all the pieces needed to develop user agent software. It only provides classes for dealing with basic message system objects. You must add your own application logic and messaging protocols.

> **NOTE**
>
> The JavaMail API is not part of JDK 1.2. It must be downloaded separately from the JavaSoft Web site at `http://www.javasoft.com/products/javamail/`. The JavaMail API requires that the JavaBeans Activation Framework (JAF) be installed. The JAF may be downloaded from `http://java.sun.com/beans/glasgow/jaf.html`.

> **NOTE**
>
> The `mail.jar` (JavaMail) and `activation.jar` (JAF) files must be added to your `CLASSPATH` before you can use JavaMail. To do this, copy `mail.jar` and `activation.jar` to your `C:\jdk1.2\lib\ext` directory and set your `CLASSPATH` using the following:
>
> ```
> set
> CLASSPATH=%CLASSPATH%;C:\jdk1.2\lib\ext\mail.jar;C:\jdk1.2\lib\ext\
> activation.jar
> ```

The `javax.mail` Package

The `javax.mail` package provides the basic objects used by mail clients. It consists of 20 classes and three interfaces, as follows:

- `Address`—Encapsulates message addresses.
- `Authenticator`—Used to support authentication of network connections.
- `BodyPart`—Implements a single body part of a multipart message.
- `FetchProfile`—Used to specify a profile of the messages that the mail client is to fetch from a mail server.
- `FetchProfile.Item`—A specific item within a `FetchProfile`.
- `Flags`—A set of message flags.
- `Flags.Flag`—A specific message flag.
- `Folder`—A folder for storing messages.
- `Header`—An encapsulation of a message header.
- `Message`—Provides the basic object of an email system. All other classes are built around the `Message` class.

- `Message.RecipientType`—Used to specify the types of recipients of a message.
- `Multipart`—A container for the multiple body parts of a multipart message.
- `MultipartDataSource`—An interface that provides support for multipart messages.
- `Part`—An interface that implements a message part.
- `PasswordAuthentication`—Supports password-based authentication.
- `Provider`—A description of a protocol implementation.
- `Provider.Type`—Identifies the type of a protocol implementation.
- `Session`—Used to implement a mail session.
- `Store`—A message store that defines a protocol for storing and retrieving messages.
- `Transport`—A message transport used to exchange messages with a message transfer agent.
- `UIDFolder`—An interface that provides support for message folders that can be used offline. It supports unique IDs for messages in a folder.
- `UIDFolder.FetchProfileItem`—An extension of `FetchProfile` for use with `UIDFolder` objects.
- `URLName`—The name of a URL.

The most important classes in this list are `Message`, `Store`, `Folder`, `Session`, and `Transport`. The `Message` class provides the basic encapsulation of message objects. It implements the attributes of a message sender, message recipient, message subject, and message content. These attributes are implemented by the supporting classes of the `javax.mail` package. The `Message` class supports message types and multipart messages. Message types are integrated with the JavaBeans Activation Framework (JAF) described in Chapter 29, "Glasgow Developments."

The `Store` class supports the storing and retrieving of messages. A `Store` object is a collection of `Folder` objects, which are used to store and organize messages. The `Store` and `Folder` classes do not assume a particular implementation. Message storage can be implemented in a variety of ways, ranging from simple files to complex databases. Message storage can be accessed online (IMAP4) or offline (POP3) or a combination of both.

The `Transport` class is used to exchange messages with message transfer agents. It provides an abstract interface to a message transfer protocol, such as SMTP. It also provides connection management capabilities. In order to use the `Transport` class, you must start a mail transfer session with a message transfer agent. That's where the `Session` class comes in. It allows you to establish a session to a mail host using a specific transfer protocol. You'll learn how to use these classes in the mail client example later in this chapter.

The `javax.mail.event` Package

The `javax.mail.event` package defines events, event listeners, and adapters for handling mail system events. The following events are defined:

- `ConnectionEvent`—Implements events associated with mail connections.
- `FolderEvent`—Implements events related to access to message folders.
- `MailEvent`—The superclass of all other mail events.
- `MessageChangedEvent`—Signals changes to messages.
- `MessageCountEvent`—Generated as the result of changes in the number of messages in a folder.
- `StoreEvent`—Signals alerts and notices from the message store.
- `TransportEvent`—Implements events associated with message delivery.

The event listener interfaces used to implement event handlers for these events are as follows:

- `ConnectionListener`—Implemented by classes that handle connection events.
- `FolderListener`—Implemented by classes that handle folder events.
- `MessageChangedListener`—Implemented by classes that handle message changed events.
- `MessageCountListener`—Implemented by classes that handle message count events.
- `StoreListener`—Implemented by classes that handle store events.
- `TransportListener`—Implemented by classes that handle transport events.

The following adapter classes are defined as basic implementations of these event listener interfaces:

- `ConnectionAdapter`
- `FolderAdapter`
- `MessageCountAdapter`
- `TransportAdapter`

All JavaMail event handling uses the JDK 1.1 event delegation model.

The `javax.mail.internet` Package

The `javax.mail.internet` package provides classes and interfaces for working with Internet mail headers (RFC 822) and MIME headers. These classes and interfaces are as follows:

- `MimePart`—An interface that implements a MIME entity.
- `ContentType`—A MIME content type.
- `HeaderTokenizer`—Used to parse MIME and RFC 822 headers.
- `HeaderTokenizer.Token`—A parse token returned by `HeaderTokenizer`.
- `InternetAddress`—An RFC 822 Internet email address.
- `InternetHeaders`—Provides support for managing RFC 822 headers.
- `MimeBodyPart`—Implements the body of a MIME message.
- `MimeMessage`—Encapsulates a MIME message.
- `MimeMessage.RecipientType`—Identifies the type of recipient of a MIME message.
- `MimeMultipart`—Provides access to multipart data within a MIME message.
- `MimePartDataSource`—Implements a MIME data source for multipart messages.
- `MimeUtility`—Provides common functions for working with MIME messages.
- `NewsAddress`—Used to implement a RFC 1036 newsgroup address.
- `ParameterList`—Provides access to MIME parameters.

These classes provide the basic functionality needed to develop an email client that supports standard Internet mail formats.

The `javax.mail.search` Package

The `javax.mail.search` package provides classes that can be used for performing searches of messages and message parts. These classes are as follows:

- `AddressTerm`—Used to compare message addresses.
- `AndTerm`—Used to perform the logical and of search terms.
- `BodyTerm`—Supports searches on message bodies.
- `ComparisonTerm`—Implements a comparison operator.
- `DateTerm`—Supports date comparisons.
- `FlagTerm`—Used to compare message flags.

- FromTerm—Used to perform searches on from addresses.
- HeaderTerm—Supports comparisons of message headers.
- IntegerComparisonTerm—Used to compare integers.
- MessageIDTerm—Implements comparison of RFC 822 message IDs.
- MessageNumberTerm—Used to compare message numbers.
- NotTerm—Supports logical negation of search terms.
- OrTerm—Supports logical or of search terms.
- ReceivedDateTerm—Used to perform searches based on message receive date.
- RecipientTerm—Performs searches on message recipients.
- SearchTerm—The basic class used to implement searching.
- SentDateTerm—Used to perform searches based on date sent.
- SizeTerm—Supports comparisons based on message size.
- StringTerm—Supports string comparisons.
- SubjectTerm—Supports subject-based searches.

You can use these classes to add message-searching capabilities to email clients.

A Mail Client

Now that we've covered all the packages of the JavaMail API, let's work on an example so you can see which classes are important and how they are used to implement a mail client.

Listing 34.1 provides the source code for the MailClient application. This program implements a simple mail client that lets you send email to a specific address. The program is kept simple so that you can learn to use the basic classes used in implementing any mail application. Once you understand how MailClient works, feel free to experiment with it by adding other capabilities.

When you run MailClient, it displays the window shown in Figure 34.4. Fill in a destination email address, your source (return) email address, a subject, and then the message's content. When you are finished, click the Send Message button and the program sends the message to the specified destination. It informs you of its progress by displaying information in the status text area. Figure 34.5 shows the results of a message that I sent to myself. If you encounter any errors while running MailClient, make sure that you've entered a valid destination email address.

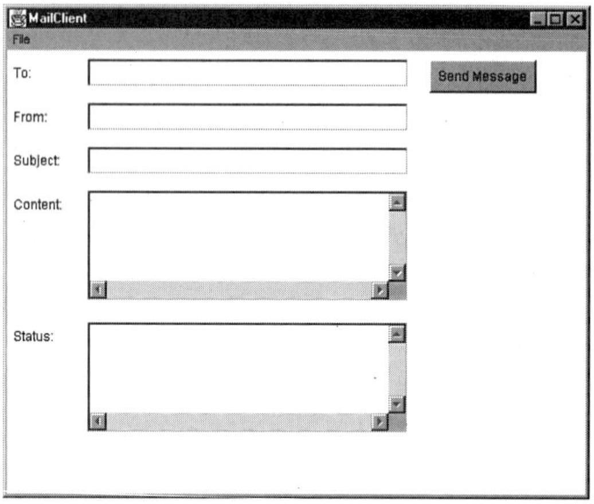

FIGURE 34.4.

The MailClient *opening display.*

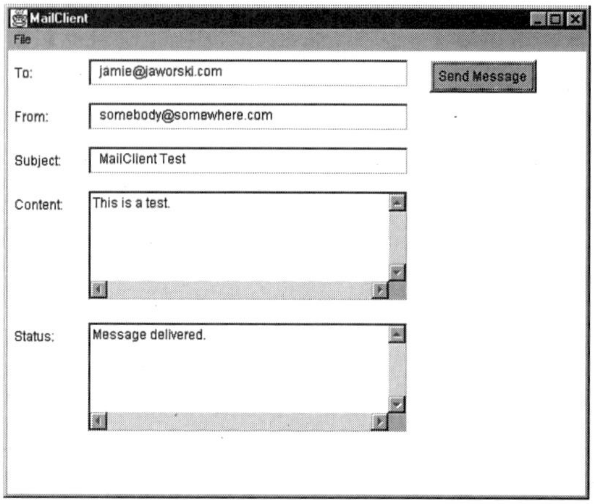

FIGURE 34.5.

Sending a message.

MailClient shows how to use the MimeMessage (a subclass of Message), InternetAddress, Session, and Transport classes. It also shows how to perform basic message event handling.

The program begins by setting the mailHost variable to jaworski.com. Feel free to change this variable to the name of your SMTP mail host. After the mail host is identified, the program's GUI components are created.

The program's main(), setup(), and setupMenuBar() methods are fairly routine. The layoutComponents() method is somewhat long, but all it does is lay out the GUI components and add them the application window. A blank label is added at the end of this method. This is done to overcome a bug in the AWT that sometimes fails to display the last component added to a Frame using a null layout.

The sendMessage() method is the heart of the program's message processing. It declares a Properties object that is used to create an SMTP session with my mail host. The mail.smtp.host property is set to the mail host, and the mail.from property is set to the contents of the Source text field. The getInstance() method of the Session class is used to set up a connection with my mail server.

An object of the MimeMessage class is created using the Session object as an argument. The destination addresses are set to the single address specified in the Destination text field. The messages from address, subject, and content are taken from the Source and Subject text fields and the Content text area. The message's MIME type is set to text/plain.

A Transport object is created using the getTransport() method of the Session object. This object is used to perform the actual message transfer. ConnectionHandler and TransportHandler objects are used to handle events associated with the connection itself and the transport of messages across the connection. The connect() method establishes a connection with my mail server, and the sendMessage() method sends the message to the specified address.

The ConnectionHandler class provides three methods that handle the opening, disconnecting, and closing of connections to the mail server. The TransportHandler class provides methods for handling events associated with message delivery. The event handlers display status messages in the Status text area.

The ButtonHandler, MenuItemHandler, and WindowEventHandler classes handle events associated with the program's GUI.

LISTING 34.1. THE MailClient APPLICATION.

```
import java.awt.*;
import java.awt.event.*;
import java.util.*;
import javax.mail.*;
import javax.mail.event.*;
import javax.mail.internet.*;

public class MailClient extends Frame {

 String mailHost = "jaworski.com";
 Label toLabel = new Label("To:");
 Label fromLabel = new Label("From:");
 Label subjectLabel = new Label("Subject:");
```

continues

34

USING JAVAMAIL

LISTING 34.1. CONTINUED

```java
Label contentLabel = new Label("Content:");
Label statusLabel = new Label("Status:");
TextField destination = new TextField();
TextField source = new TextField();
TextField subject = new TextField();
TextArea content = new TextArea();
Button send = new Button("Send Message");
TextArea status = new TextArea();

public static void main(String args[]){
 MailClient app = new MailClient();
}

public MailClient() {
 super("MailClient");
 setup();
 addWindowListener(new WindowEventHandler());
 setSize(550,450);
 show();
}

void setup() {
 setupMenuBar();
 layoutComponents();
 send.addActionListener(new ButtonHandler());
}

void setupMenuBar() {
 MenuBar menuBar = new MenuBar();
 Menu fileMenu = new Menu("File");
 MenuItem fileExit = new MenuItem("Exit");
 fileExit.addActionListener(new MenuItemHandler());
 fileMenu.add(fileExit);
 menuBar.add(fileMenu);
 setMenuBar(menuBar);
}

void layoutComponents() {
 int x = 10;
 int y = 50;
 // Set bounds
 toLabel.setBounds(x,y,50,25);
 destination.setBounds(x+70,y,300,25);
 fromLabel.setBounds(x,y+40,50,25);
 source.setBounds(x+70,y+40,300,25);
 subjectLabel.setBounds(x,y+80,50,25);
 subject.setBounds(x+70,y+80,300,25);
 contentLabel.setBounds(x,y+120,50,25);
 content.setBounds(x+70,y+120,300,100);
```

```
        statusLabel.setBounds(x,y+240,50,25);
        status.setBounds(x+70,y+240,300,100);
        send.setBounds(400,y,100,30);
        // Add components
        add(toLabel);
        add(destination);
        add(send);
        add(fromLabel);
        add(source);
        add(subjectLabel);
        add(subject);
        add(contentLabel);
        add(content);
        add(statusLabel);
        add(status);
        add(new Label(""));
       }

     void sendMessage() {
      Properties properties = new Properties();
      properties.put("mail.smtp.host",mailHost);
      properties.put("mail.from",source.getText());
      Session session = Session.getInstance(properties, null);
      try {
       Message message = new MimeMessage(session);
       InternetAddress[] address =
        {new InternetAddress(destination.getText())};
       message.setRecipients(Message.RecipientType.TO, address);
       message.setFrom(new InternetAddress(source.getText()));
       message.setSubject(subject.getText());
       message.setContent(content.getText(),"text/plain");
       Transport transport = session.getTransport(address[0]);
       transport.addConnectionListener(new ConnectionHandler());
       transport.addTransportListener(new TransportHandler());
       transport.connect();
       transport.sendMessage(message,address);
      }catch(Exception e){
       status.setText(e.toString());
      }
     }

     class ConnectionHandler extends ConnectionAdapter {
      public void opened(ConnectionEvent e) {
       status.setText("Connection opened.");
      }
      public void disconnected(ConnectionEvent e) {
       status.setText("Connection disconnected.");
      }
      public void closed(ConnectionEvent e) {
```

continues

34

LISTING 34.1. CONTINUED

```
   status.setText("Connection closed.");
  }
 }

 class TransportHandler extends TransportAdapter {
  public void messageDelivered(TransportEvent e) {
   status.setText("Message delivered.");
  }
  public void messageNotDelivered(TransportEvent e) {
   status.setText("Message NOT delivered.");
  }
  public void messagePartiallyDelivered(TransportEvent e) {
   status.setText("Message partially delivered.");
  }
 }

 class ButtonHandler implements ActionListener {
  public void actionPerformed(ActionEvent ev){
   String s=ev.getActionCommand();
   if(s.equals("Send Message")) sendMessage();
  }
 }

 class MenuItemHandler implements ActionListener {
  public void actionPerformed(ActionEvent ev){
   String s=ev.getActionCommand();
   if(s=="Exit"){
    System.exit(0);
   }
  }
 }

 class WindowEventHandler extends WindowAdapter {
  public void windowClosing(WindowEvent e){
   System.exit(0);
  }
 }
}
```

Summary

In this chapter, you learned how mail systems work and how the JavaMail API is used to create email clients. You used this knowledge to develop a simple Internet mail client. In the next chapter, you'll learn how to use the directory service capabilities provided by the Java Naming and Directory Interface.

CHAPTER 35

Naming and Directory Services

Naming and directory services provide critical user support in large enterprise networks. They allow users to access information about the network's services, applications, computers, shared devices, and users. Without naming and directory services, a user's knowledge of network capabilities is severely limited, often confined to whatever he can learn from user manuals and word of mouth.

As an enterprise software development platform, Java provides comprehensive support for naming and directory services. The *Java Naming and Directory Interface (JNDI)* is a standard extension API that allows naming and directory services to be integrated with Java applications and applets. JNDI is independent of any specific naming and directory services, such as X.500 or the NetWare Directory Service (NDS), and allows a wide variety of these services to be used in a common way.

In this chapter, you'll learn about directory services and how they simplify enterprise networking. You'll be introduced to JNDI and learn how it can be used to interface Java programs with these directory services. You'll also learn how to use specific directory service providers with JNDI. When you finish this chapter, you'll be able to develop directory service-enabled applications.

What Are Naming and Directory Services?

Naming services map names to network objects and are essential to network communication. Imagine using the phone without a phone book or a directory information service. Or worse, imagine using the Internet without the Domain Name Service (DNS). The phone book is an example of a naming service. It maps people's names and addresses to their phone numbers. DNS is another name service. It maps computer names to their IP addresses. You'll learn about other naming services later in this book. When you study Java remote method invocation (RMI) in Part IX, you'll learn about the naming service that RMI uses to map object names (URLs) to distributed objects. When you study CORBA in Chapter 41, "Java IDL and ORBs," you'll learn how the CORBA naming service maps object names to their implementation.

Naming services are said to *bind* an object name with the object being named. A *context* is a set of name-to-object bindings. This terminology is commonly used in the DNS, RMI, and CORBA naming services, but not in naming services such as the phone book. A naming service *lookup* results in the named object being retrieved based on its name. The process of using a name to look up a named object is *name resolution*.

Names may be atomic, compound, or composite. *Atomic* names are indivisible names that identify an object. For example, the name `index.htm` names a file on my Web server. *Compound* names are names that consist of one or more atomic names. For example, the relative path `/java/examples/index.htm` names a file on my Web server. *Composite* names are names that are composed of multiple naming services. For example, the URL `http://www.jaworski.com/java/examples/index.htm` consists of a protocol identifier (`http://`), a DNS name (`www.jaworski.com`), and a file system path (`/java/examples/index.htm`).

Directory services build upon and extend naming services. Directory services usually organize name spaces in a hierarchical fashion and include attributes that provide additional information about named objects. For example, consider the DOS and UNIX file systems. File and directory names are mapped to file and directory objects. These objects are organized in a hierarchical fashion, with subdirectories and files extending the directories in which they are contained. Size, date, and access attributes provide additional information about the files and directories of the file system.

Network directory services provide information about the enterprise network, computers, devices (such as printers), network services and applications, users, security information, and other objects. Examples of directory services include the International Standards Organization's X.500 directory service, the Novell NetWare Directory Service (NDS), and Sun's Network Information Service Plus (NIS+). NDS and NIS+ are both proprietary protocols.

Lightweight Directory Access Protocol

The *Lightweight Directory Access Protocol (LDAP)* is a popular protocol for accessing directory service. It was developed at the University of Michigan as a front-end for the X.500 directory service but has grown to replace X.500 servers with its own directory servers. Its principal advantages are that it is non-proprietary, runs over TCP/IP networks, and is a manageable subset of the X.500 international standard. LDAP version 3 is the current version and is described in RFC 2251.

LDAP's popularity stems from X.500's shortcomings. X.500 provides the basis for large directory services that are distributed over wide area networks; LDAP scales X.500 services to the needs of large enterprises. X.500 requires the use of the higher-level OSI protocol layers; LDAP works over TCP/IP. LDAP simplifies the management of X.500 directories and makes these directories globally accessible via the Internet.

35

NAMING AND
DIRECTORY
SERVICES

LDAP directories consist of individual *entries* that contain information about an object, such as a person. Each entry consists of a set of attributes. Each attribute consists of a type and a value. Figure 35.1 provides an example of an LDAP entry.

FIGURE 35.1.

An LDAP entry describes an object.

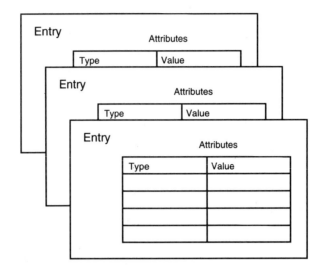

LDAP entries are organized in a hierarchical fashion. For example, an LDAP server could contain information about the Federal Government, one part of which is the Department of Defense (DOD). DOD directories can be organized into the Army, Navy, and Air Force, as shown in Figure 35.2. These directories are refined into smaller organizational units until all Federal Government employees are included in the directory name space.

FIGURE 35.2.

LDAP directories are organized in a hierarchical structure.

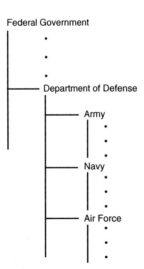

The JNDI API

The JNDI API consists of three packages: `javax.naming`, `javax.naming.directory`, and `javax.naming.spi`. The `javax.naming` package supports naming operations, and `javax.naming.directory` supports directory operations. The `javax.naming.spi` package provides support for service provider interfaces, such as LDAP, NDS, and NIS+. These packages are covered in the following subsections.

> **NOTE**
>
> The JNDI is a standard extension API. It can be downloaded from the JavaSoft Web site at `http://www.javasoft.com/jndi/index.html`.

The `javax.naming` Package

The `javax.naming` package provides five interfaces and 10 classes that support basic naming operations. These interfaces and classes are used as follows:

- `Context`—Specifies a naming context, which represents a set of name-to-object bindings. It provides methods for adding and deleting bindings and looking up objects.

- `InitialContext`—Provides a default implementation of the `Context` interface and acts as a starting point for name resolution.

- `Name`—Implemented by names (atomic, compound, or composite). It provides methods for name manipulation.

- `CompoundName`—Implements the `Name` interface and supports hierarchical names.

- `CompositeName`—Implements the `Name` interface and supports names that are composed of multiple name spaces.

- `NameParser`—Supports the parsing of `Name` objects.

- `NamingEnumeration`—Extends `Enumeration` to provide support for naming and directory information.

- `NameClassPair`—Represents the name and class of a bound object.

- `Binding`—Extends `NameClassPair` to implement a name-to-object mapping found in a `Context`.

- `Reference`—Provides address and class information about the object being referenced. This object is outside the naming and directory system.

35

NAMING AND
DIRECTORY
SERVICES

- `Referenceable`—Allows address information to be associated with objects that are outside the naming system. Objects that are referenced by a `Reference` object should implement this interface.

- `LinkRef`—Extends `Reference` to use a link name that is bound to an atomic name in a `Context`.

- `RefAddr`—Provides address information about an object.

- `StringRefAddr`—Extends `RefAddr` to support a `String` format.

- `BinaryRefAddr`—Extends `RefAddr` to support a binary format.

The `javax.naming` package provides the basic classes and interfaces for managing name spaces. These classes and interfaces are used in conjunction with those of the `javax.naming.directory` and `javax.naming.spi` packages.

The `javax.naming.directory` Package

The `javax.naming.directory` package consists of three interfaces and six classes that provide directory services to Java programs. These interfaces and classes are as follows:

- `DirContext`—Extends the `Context` interface to provide support for directory services.

- `InitialDirContext`—Extends `InitialContext` and implements the `DirContext` interface. Each directory consists of zero or more `Attribute` objects.

- `Attribute`—An interface that is implemented by an attribute associated with a named object.

- `BasicAttribute`—A default implementation of the `Attribute` interface.

- `Attributes`—A collection of `Attribute` objects.

- `BasicAttributes`—An implementation of the `Attributes` interface.

- `ModificationItem`—Used to perform operations on a set of attributes.

- `SearchControls`—Supports attribute-based searches.

- `SearchResult`—Returns a search result as a binding.

Since `DirContext` and `InitialDirContext` extend `Context` and `InitialContext`, from an API perspective, you can view a directory service as an extension of a naming service with additional support provided for `Attribute` objects.

The `javax.naming.spi` Package

The `javax.naming.spi` package provides the interface between the JNDI and provider-specific naming and directory service implementations, such as LDAP and NDS. This package consists of the following five interfaces and three classes:

- `NamingManager`—Provides `static` methods for creating `Context` objects.

- `DirectoryManager`—Extends `NamingManager` to provide `static` methods for creating `DirContext` objects.

- `Resolver`—Supports name resolution outside of a `Context`.

- `ResolveResult`—Provides the result of a name resolution.

- `InitialContextFactory`—Supports the creation of an initial context implementation.

- `InitialContextFactoryBuilder`—Allows for the specification of an `InitialContextFactory` at runtime.

- `ObjectFactory`—Used to create objects from `Reference` objects and to load those objects dynamically.

- `ObjectFactoryBuilder`—Allows for the specification of an `ObjectFactory` at runtime.

The next section will show you how to use JNDI with the specific service providers.

> **NOTE**
>
> A *service provider* is an implementation of a naming or directory service, such as LDAP or NDS, that is accessible via JNDI.

Incorporating Service Providers in Your Applications

JNDI can be viewed as an API for developing naming and directory service clients that work with multiple naming and directory services. These services are implemented by specific service providers, such as LDAP or NIS+. Figure 35.3 shows how the JNDI API fits into this architecture. A Java application uses the classes and interfaces of the JNDI API to access local naming and directory service capabilities, which are provided through a Naming Manager (see the `NamingManager` class of the `javax.naming.spi` package). The Naming Manager provides access to locally installed service provider implementations through the JNDI Service Provider Interface (refer to the `javax.naming.spi` package). These service provider implementations, such as LDAP and NDS, provide access to enterprise naming services.

35

NAMING AND DIRECTORY SERVICES

FIGURE 35.3.
*The JNDI archi-
tecture.*

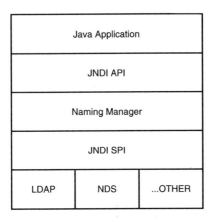

Figure 35.1 shows that using JNDI requires the use of specific service providers and naming/directory services. Service providers for LDAP, NIS+, NDS, and the File System Service Provider are available from the JNDI Web site at `http://www.javasoft.com/products/jndi/index.html`. With the exception of the File System Service Provider, using these service providers requires the availability of naming and directory servers. If you have access to an enterprise naming and directory server, you should download a service provider that is appropriate for your enterprise server. The File System Service Provider is a directory service that operates on your local file system.

To get you started with JNDI, JavaSoft includes in the JNDI 1.1 distribution a test service provider that operates out of a flat, local name space. We'll use this service provider to illustrate JNDI programming. However, you can easily substitute other service providers that are compatible with your enterprise network. Each service provider will provide its own unique installation instructions.

Before going on, download the JNDI 1.1 distribution from JavaSoft's Web site. It consists of a single `jndi11.zip` file that unzips into the following:

- `README.txt` file—Provides general information about the JNDI distribution.
- `lib` directory—Contains the `jndi.jar` file. You need to put `jndi.jar` in your `CLASSPATH` to use the JNDI API.
- `examples` directory—Contains examples of JNDI clients and the flat service provider. Put the `examples` directory in your `CLASSPATH`, and compile the files in the `examples\spi\flat` directory. These files implement the flat service provider. You can take a look at these files to see how this simple service provider is implemented.

Make sure that you compile the flat service provider before going to the next section. You can run the `TestFlat` program included in the `examples\spi\flat` directory to verify that the flat service provider is set up correctly. It will generate the following output:

```
original
b:binding_b
a:binding_a
c:binding_c
after changes
aa:binding_a
d:binding_d
c:new_binding
```

Using the Flat Service Provider

The flat service provider implements a simple flat (non-hierarchical) naming service. However, it illustrates the basics of using the JNDI API to access any naming service. The `JNDITest` program, shown in Listing 35.1, shows how to create a simple client to use the flat name service.

When you run `JNDITest` from a console window, it displays the following output:

```
Commands:
  add name objectString
  delete name
  change oldName newName
  lookup name
  names
  bindings
  exit
>
```

Use the `add` command to add a name-to-object binding to the name space. For example:

```
add Jamie jamie@jaworski.com
```

This binds the name `Jamie` to the email address `jamie@jaworski.com`. Use the `add` command to add this binding. Also add the following bindings:

```
add Z kenz@cts.com
add Tim timdel@ix.netcom.com
```

You can then enter the `bindings` command to obtain a list of the bindings that you entered:

```
> bindings
Jamie -> jamie@jaworski.com
Tim -> timdel@ix.netcom.com
Z -> kenz@cts.com
```

The `names` command simply lists all names in the name space. You can use it as follows:

```
> names
Jamie
Tim
Z
```

The `change` command can be used to rename a name to a new name. Change the name `Z` to `Ken` using the following command:

```
change Z Ken
```

You can verify the change with another `bindings` command:

```
> bindings
Ken -> kenz@cts.com
Jamie -> jamie@jaworski.com
Tim -> timdel@ix.netcom.com
```

The `lookup` command returns the object to which a name is bound. When you look up `Tim` it returns Tim's email address, as follows:

```
> lookup Tim
timdel@ix.netcom.com
```

The `delete` command deletes a name and its binding from the name space. Let's use it to delete `Tim`, as follows:

```
delete Tim
```

Then run a `bindings` command to verify the contents of the name space:

```
> bindings
Ken -> kenz@cts.com
Jamie -> jamie@jaworski.com
```

Play around with the program to become familiar with its operation. When you finish, enter `exit` to exit the program.

How `JNDITest` Works

The `JNDITest` program uses the `javax.naming` and `examples.spi.flat` packages in addition to `java.util` and `java.io`. These packages must be in your `CLASSPATH` for the program to compile and execute.

The `JNDITest` class declares the `environment` variable as a `Hashtable` to hold the `java.naming.factory.initial` property. This property identifies the naming factory used to create the service provider. Its value is set to `examples.spi.flat.FlatInitCtxFactory` in the `JNDITest()` constructor so that the flat service provider is configured for use. You may set this property to that of another installed service provider.

Other configuration parameters may also need to be supplied, as described in the service provider's documentation.

The `context` variable is used to reference a naming context. The `in` variable is used to access an input reader. The `command`, `parm1`, and `parm2` variables reference the command and parameters entered by the user.

After setting up the `java.naming.factory.initial` property, the `JNDITest()` constructor creates a new initial naming context. This context is created with respect to the flat service provider, using the `FlatInitCtxFactory` class.

The `run()` method displays the list of commands to the user and then loops forever, getting the next command and then processing it. An `exit` command causes the loop to terminate.

The `getCommand()` method prompts the user to enter a command and then reads the line entered by the user. It invokes the `parseCommand()` method to parse the line into its command and parameters. The `parseCommand()` method uses a `StringTokenizer` to parse the input line.

The `processCommand()` method is the heart of this example and shows how the methods of the `Context` interface are used to implement naming service operations. These methods are as follows:

- `bind()`—Binds a name with its object.
- `unbind()`—Deletes a bound name and its associated object.
- `rename()`—Changes a name to a new value.
- `lookup()`—Returns the object associated with a name.
- `listBindings()`—Returns a `NamingEnumeration` of the bindings that are available through a specified `Context`.

The `hasMore()` and `next()` methods are used to iterate through a `NamingEnumeration` and retrieve individual `Binding` objects. The `getName()` and `getObject()` methods of `Binding` return the name and object to which a name is bound.

LISTING 35.1. THE JNDITest APPLICATION.

```
import java.util.*;
import java.io.*;
import javax.naming.*;
import examples.spi.flat.*;
```

continues

35

NAMING AND
DIRECTORY
SERVICES

LISTING 35.1. CONTINUED

```java
public class JNDITest {
 Hashtable environment = new Hashtable();
 Context context;
 BufferedReader in = new BufferedReader(new
  InputStreamReader(System.in));
 String command;
 String parm1;
 String parm2;

 public static void main(String[] args) {
  JNDITest app = new JNDITest();
  app.run();
 }

 public JNDITest() {
  // Setup SPI
  environment.put("java.naming.factory.initial",
   "examples.spi.flat.FlatInitCtxFactory");
  try {
   context = new InitialContext(environment);
  } catch (NamingException e) {
    e.printStackTrace();
    System.exit(0);
  }
 }

 void run() {
  displayHelp();
  for(;;) {
   getCommand();
   if(command.equals("exit")) break;
   processCommand();
  }
 }

 void getCommand() {
  try {
   System.out.print("> ");
   System.out.flush();
   String newLine = in.readLine();
   if(newLine == null) command = "exit";
   else parseCommand(newLine);
  } catch(Exception e) {
   e.printStackTrace();
   System.exit(0);
  }
 }
```

```java
void parseCommand(String line) {
 StringTokenizer tokenizer = new StringTokenizer(line);
 if(tokenizer.hasMoreElements())
  command = ((String) tokenizer.nextElement()).toLowerCase();
 else command = "";
 if(tokenizer.hasMoreElements())
  parm1 = (String) tokenizer.nextElement();
 else parm1 = "";
 if(tokenizer.hasMoreElements())
  parm2 = (String) tokenizer.nextElement();
 else parm2 = "";
}

void processCommand() {
 try {
  if(command.equals("add")) {
   if(!parm1.equals("") && !parm2.equals("")) {
    context.bind(parm1,parm2);
   }else System.out.println("*** missing parameter");
  }else if(command.equals("delete")) {
   if(!parm1.equals("")) {
    context.unbind(parm1);
   }else System.out.println("*** missing parameter");
  }else if(command.equals("change")) {
   if(!parm1.equals("") && !parm2.equals("")) {
    context.rename(parm1,parm2);
   }else System.out.println("*** missing parameter");
  }else if(command.equals("lookup")) {
   if(!parm1.equals("")) {
    System.out.println(context.lookup(parm1));
   }else System.out.println("*** missing parameter");
  }else if(command.equals("names")) {
   NamingEnumeration bindings = context.listBindings("");
   if(bindings != null) {
    while(bindings.hasMore()) {
     Binding b = (Binding) bindings.next();
     System.out.println(b.getName());
    }
   }
  }else if(command.equals("bindings")) {
   NamingEnumeration bindings = context.listBindings("");
   if(bindings != null) {
    while(bindings.hasMore()) {
     Binding b = (Binding) bindings.next();
     System.out.println(b.getName()+" -> "+b.getObject());
    }
   }
  }else System.out.println("*** unrecognized command");
 }catch(Exception e) {
```

35

NAMING AND
DIRECTORY
SERVICES

continues

LISTING 35.1. CONTINUED

```
        e.printStackTrace();
        System.exit(0);
    }
}

void displayHelp() {
  System.out.println("Commands:");
  System.out.println("  add name objectString");
  System.out.println("  delete name");
  System.out.println("  change oldName newName");
  System.out.println("  lookup name");
  System.out.println("  names");
  System.out.println("  bindings");
  System.out.println("  exit");
  }
}
```

Summary

In this chapter, you learned about directory services and how they simplify enterprise networking. You were introduced to JNDI, and you learned how it can be used to interface Java programs with directory services. You also learned how to use specific directory service providers with JNDI. In the next chapter, you'll learn how the Java Management API supports the management of enterprise networks.

CHAPTER 36

Working with the Java Management API

With the growing reliance by companies and other organizations on their enterprise networks, the management of these networks and the systems and services they support have become critical. Network administrators use a wide array of system monitoring and management tools to ensure continuous reliable operation. These tools are designed to detect and respond to potential problems that could affect service continuity. However, with the heterogeneous nature of modern networks, these tools run on a variety of operating system platforms, do not operate well together, and sometimes conflict.

The Java Management API is being developed by JavaSoft to provide an integrated solution for system, network, and service management. Because of Java's platform-independent nature, it eliminates the need to use several nonintegrated, platform-specific system and network management tools to manage the diverse computing resources that are common to medium-to-large-sized enterprise networks.

In this chapter, you'll learn about the Java Management API (JMAPI). You'll be given an overview of the typical problems confronting system and network administrators. You'll then be introduced to JMAPI and learn how it can be used to provide a common integrated solution for system, network, and service management. You'll cover the Java management architecture and learn how it allows enterprise resources to be managed from a browser interface. You'll learn about the components of JMAPI and how they are used to support this architecture. When you finish this chapter, you'll have an understanding of how JMAPI works and insight into how you can use it to solve your organization's system, network, and service management problems.

Overview of System, Network, and Service Management

Imagine that you are responsible for the management of a medium-to-large-scale enterprise network. Your primary responsibilities are to keep the network up and running, keep its systems operational, make sure that its services are available, and keep its users happy. Your users demand the latest Internet and intranet services from the moment that they read about them on a Web page or in a magazine. Continuous, reliable operation is expected 24 hours a day, 7 days a week.

In a typical medium-to-large-scale enterprise network, you'll find thousands of users, some quite sophisticated and some not. These users will have workstations, PCs, Macintoshes, X terminals, and dumb terminals. They will use several flavors of UNIX, all versions of Windows and MacOS, Netware, DOS, and anything else that's available. Your networks will run TCP/IP, IPX, NetBEUI, AppleTalk, and other protocols. Your

enterprise will maintain legacy systems that run on DEC VAXes and IBM minicomputers and mainframes. You'll also interface with customers, vendors, and suppliers via the Internet, dedicated lines, and dial-up connections. You'll have one or more firewalls, several routers, a slew of network hubs, and all sorts of system, network, and service management tools.

The tools that you'll use to manage your network will run on a variety of platforms, mostly UNIX and Windows. These tools will be independent. They will not know about or interoperate with each other, and will sometimes conflict when run concurrently.

Some of these tools will be system-specific. They'll let you manage the legacy applications that you have running on DEC and IBM minicomputers and mainframes. They'll tell you that you need to change disk volumes, do a backup, or perform some application-specific maintenance.

Some tools will be protocol- and service-specific. You'll use them to manage specific protocols, such as TCP/IP, IPX, AppleTalk, and SNA. They'll tell you what your network traffic load is like, when you have interruptions in service, and what network components are malfunctioning. You'll also have a sniffer or two to tell you what these other tools can't. Service-specific tools will tell you what types of hits your Web and FTP servers are taking, what your email situation looks like, and how file and print servers are behaving.

Some tools try to be integrated network management solutions, at least from the vendor's viewpoint. You'll run HP OpenView, Microsoft's System Management Server, and possibly one or two other management tools. In the end, you'll need a chair that rolls easily in order to move between the computers that run each of your system management tools.

The JMAPI Solution

Is this scenario far-fetched? Not at all. If you are a system or network manager, you are probably working in an environment like this right now—the type of environment that JMAPI is being developed to deal with.

If Java's motto is "Write Once. Run Everywhere," then JMAPI's is "Why can't we all just work together?" The goal of JMAPI is to leverage Java's platform independence to provide a set of system management building blocks that can be used to integrate a diverse set of system and network management tools under a common look and feel.

> **NOTE**
>
> The Java Management home page is located at
> http://www.javasoft.com/products/JavaManagement/index.html.

The look and feel of JMAPI is provided by a Java-enabled browser. All management applications are run from a browser. Not only do you have a common, cross-platform user interface, but the organization of this interface is governed by the recommendations and standards of the JMAPI User Interface Style Guide. This guide describes a standard approach to developing browser-based interfaces for use with JMAPI.

Not only does JMAPI provide you with a standard browser-based interface, it also provides you with a common architecture for managing systems, networks, and services. This architecture, referred to as the Java management architecture, is shown in Figure 36.1.

Administrators use Java-enabled Web browsers to manage the systems, networks, and services of a network. The browsers interface with managed object servers that manage one or more appliances within their domain. An appliance is any system that is to be managed. It can be a network computer, PC, workstation, or any other type of computer or device that is capable of running the JVM.

Agents are objects that execute on appliances and communicate with managed object servers. Agent objects maintain information about the configuration and status of the appliances they manage, and they report this information to managed object servers. The agent objects provide methods that allow managed object servers to control and reconfigure their appliances. The agent software can be dynamically updated and is installed on appliances as Java classes that are loaded from Web servers.

Managed object servers are the link between the browser interface and the managed appliances of an enterprise. They consist of Java applications that provide the following capabilities:

- Appliance configuration and status reporting—Appliance configuration and status information that was retrieved from agent objects is available as managed objects that can be browsed by administrators.

- Control and configuration of appliances—The managed objects provide methods that can be used to control the appliances or modify their configuration data.

- SNMP agent interfaces—These interfaces are presented to administrators as browsable managed objects.

Working with the Java Management API

CHAPTER 36

777

36

JAVA
MANAGEMENT
API

FIGURE 36.1.

*The Java manage-
ment architecture.*

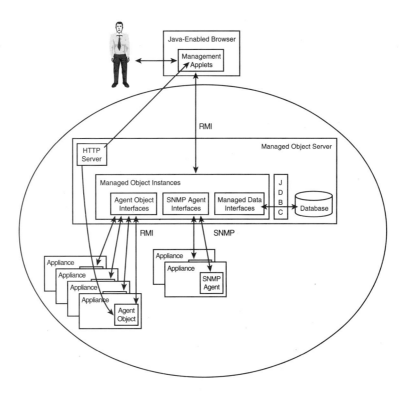

- Managed data interfaces—These data interfaces allow management information to be maintained by relational database servers.

- Database connectivity through JDBC—Managed object servers use JDBC to interface with relational database servers.

- A Web server—HTTP servers make management applets available to the browsers used by administrators. These applets provide GUI controls that are used to browse and display managed objects. The HTTP servers are also used to distribute agent objects throughout the domains of the managed object servers.

The Java Management API and architecture help system and network administrators solve the problem of managing multiple heterogeneous components. By leveraging Java's platform-independence and the classes and interfaces of JMAPI, agent software can be quickly developed and deployed to any appliance that is capable of running the JVM. New and updated software can be easily distributed via the Web server components of the managed object servers. These same Web servers provide the management applets that are used by administrators to monitor and control network resources as managed objects.

The managed object servers create managed object abstractions that allow resources to be managed without knowing the details of the object's implementation. This separation between management and implementation allows administrators to concentrate on the problem at hand. Resources can be monitored, reconfigured, and controlled independently of the protocols, vendor packages, or hardware and software platforms used to provide these resources.

By using a common browser interface, administrators are able to take advantage of consistent, intuitive GUI controls for managing all system and network resources. By providing access to all managed resources as managed objects, administrators can use the single browser interface for all management functions. Administrators no longer have to move from station to station to use the tools that are independently implemented at each one. In addition, the single browser interface can be accessed via any computer that supports a Java-enabled Web browser. When an administrator is paged in the middle of the night, he can securely access the managed object server by launching his browser from home, a hotel, a coffee shop, or anywhere.

The Components of JMAPI

JMAPI is distributed as a set of Java classes, interfaces, and associated documentation. It can be downloaded from the Java Management home page. It consists of the following components:

- Admin View Module—A set of classes and interfaces for developing the GUI components of management applets. It builds on the AWT and is oriented toward applications that run as applets within the context of a Web browser. It can also be used to develop standalone applications.

- Base Object Interfaces—Java interfaces that are used to create managed objects. These interfaces allow managed objects to be created quickly, easily, and consistently.

- Managed Container Interfaces—Java interfaces that allow managed objects to be collected and managed as a group.

- Managed Notification Interfaces—Used to support event delivery between the elements of the Java management architecture. These interfaces are also used to support event handling.

- Managed Data Interfaces—Used to maintain system management data via a relational database. These interfaces use JDBC to support database connectivity.

- Managed Protocol Interfaces—Support the secure communication of management information. These interfaces use the Security API and remote method invocation.

- SNMP Interfaces—Used to provide access to existing SNMP agents. These interfaces allow you to incorporate your existing network management agents into the Java management architecture.
- Applet Integration Interfaces—The Applet Integration Interfaces allow developers to integrate their applets within the Java management architecture. Support of applet, page, and link registration is provided.

The Java Management API User Interface Style Guide is also included. The style guide describes a standard approach to developing browser-based interfaces for use with JMAPI.

The JMAPI components previously listed are used to create all elements of the Java management architecture. The Admin View Module and Applet Integration Interfaces simplify the task of creating management applets that conform to the JMAPI User Interface Style Guide. The other interfaces are used to create managed objects and agent objects, to interface with existing SNMP agents, and to provide database connectivity.

Summary

In this chapter, you learned how JMAPI can be used to provide a common integrated solution to system, network, and service management. You learned about the Java management architecture and how it is deployed within an organization. You were introduced to the components of JMAPI and learned how they are used to support this architecture. You should now have an understanding of how JMAPI works and some insight into how it can be used to solve your organization's system, network, and service management problems.

Developing
Distrbuted
Applications

PART

IX

IN THIS PART

Distributed Application Architecture

CHAPTER 37

This chapter provides background information on Java's distributed programming capabilities. It discusses the various approaches to designing and implementing distributed applications and shows how Java's distributed object model compares to these approaches. It describes how Java's RMI capabilities are implemented using a three-tiered protocol set, and finishes with a discussion of the security issues involved with using RMI. When you finish this chapter, you'll have the background information you need to understand how RMI works and how it is used to develop distributed applications.

Distributed Application Design Approaches

A *distributed application* is an application whose processing is distributed across multiple networked computers. Distributed applications are able to concurrently serve multiple users and, depending on their design, make more optimal use of processing resources.

Distributed applications are typically implemented as client/server systems that are organized according to the user interface, information processing, and information storage layers, as shown in Figure 37.1.

The user interface layer is implemented by an application client. Email programs and

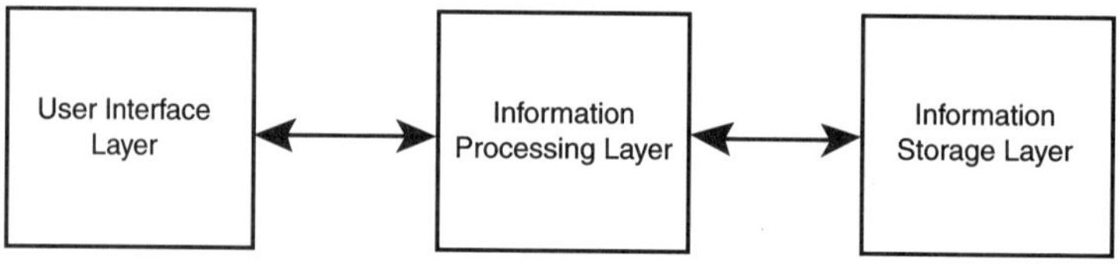

FIGURE 37.1.
The organization of distributed systems.

Web browsers are examples of the user-interface component of distributed applications.

The information processing layer is implemented by an application client, an application server, or an application support server. For example, a database application may utilize a database client to convert user selections into SQL statements, a database access server may be used to support communication between the client and a database server, and the database server may use reporting software to process the information requested by a client.

The information storage layer is implemented by database servers, Web servers, FTP servers, file servers, and any other servers whose purpose is to store and retrieve information.

Distributed Applications on the Internet

The popularity of the Internet and the Web has resulted in an almost fully networked world. Computers on opposite ends of the world are directly accessible to each other via the TCP/IP protocol suite. This worldwide connectivity has given rise to distributed applications that run within the Internet's client/server framework. These first-generation applications support client/server communication using application-specific protocols such as HTTP, FTP, and SQL*NET. Figure 37.2 illustrates a typical Internet application.

FIGURE 37.2.

A distributed Internet application.

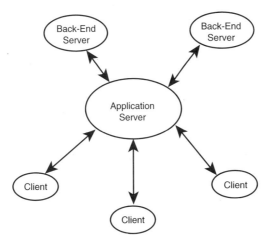

Typically, a client program is executed on multiple host computers. The client uses TCP to connect to a server that listens on a well-known port. The client makes one or more requests of the server. The server processes the client's requests, possibly using gateway programs or back-end servers, and forwards the response to the client.

> **NOTE**
>
> Chapter 30, "Network Programming with the `java.net` Package," describes the basics of TCP/IP client-server computing.

Applets on an Intranet

In an intranet environment, corporate information systems support services that are tailored to the organizational needs of the company. These services consist of applications that support business areas such as management, accounting, marketing, manufacturing, customer support, vendor interface, shipping and receiving, and so on. These intranet services can be implemented using client/server services, such as a company-internal Web. Java applets provide the capability to run the client interface layer and part of the information processing layer of business applications within the context of a Web browser. Figure 37.3 shows an approach to implementing corporate information services using the applet paradigm. Applets are represented by the small filled-in squares within browsers.

FIGURE 37.3.
Implementing intranet services using applets.

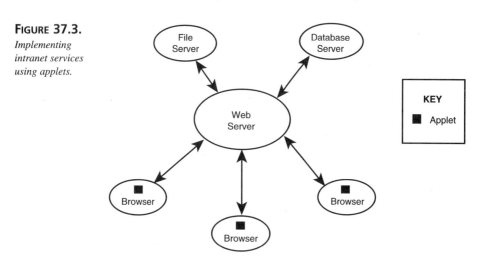

The approach shown in Figure 37.3 is essentially the Internet client/server approach shown in Figure 37.2 but applied to an intranet, using Java applets to program client information system interfaces. This approach is popular for developing distributed intranet applications, and can also be used with Internet applications. It allows business applications to be distributed among browsers, Web servers, and other back-end servers.

The Distributed Computing Environment

The *Distributed Computing Environment (DCE)* is another approach to building distributed applications. DCE was developed by the Open Software Foundation, now referred to as the Open Group. DCE integrates a variety of fundamental services and technologies to build distributed applications. Distributed systems are organized into *cells*, which are groups of processing resources, services, and users that support a common function and share a common set of DCE services. For example, cells can be organized according to company functions. In this case, you may have separate cells for your finance, manufacturing, and marketing departments.

The DCE services of a cell are used to implement distributed applications that serve the users of the cell and interface with the applications implemented by other cells. The services and technologies used within a DCE cell consist of the following:

- Directory Services—Store the names of resources that are available within the distributed environment. The Cell Directory Service (CDS) supports naming within a cell, and the Global Directory Service (GDS) supports naming across all cells within an enterprise. GDS implements the X.500 directory service standard.

- Distributed File Service (DFS)—An optional DCE service that provides a seamless file system that operates across all computers contained within a cell.

- Distributed Time Service (DTS)—Used to synchronize time across all computers within a cell.

- Security Service—Used to authenticate cell users and control access to the available resources within a cell.

- Remote Procedure Calls (RPCs)—Replace TCP sockets as the basic mechanism for client/server communication. RPCs are implemented as a layer that is built on top of the TCP/IP transport layer and transparently manages connection management and protocol-specific concerns.

- DCE Threads—Similar to Java threads. They are lightweight processes that simplify the design of client/server applications.

DCE is referred to as *middleware* because it is not a standalone product, but rather a bundle of services that are integrated into an operating system or operating environment. These services are used as an alternative approach to constructing distributed applications. They are used to build the same kinds of applications as the Web-based example covered in the previous section, but they go about it in a different manner.

> **NOTE**
>
> The DCE FAQ, located at http://www.camb.opengroup.org/dce/info/faq-mauney.html, provides a good introduction to the DCE services identified in this section.

The Distributed Component Object Model

The *Distributed Component Object Model*, or *DCOM*, is Microsoft's approach to developing distributed systems. DCOM is based on COM, which is the heart of Microsoft's object-oriented development strategy. Because DCOM is essentially a distributed system extension to COM, understanding COM is essential to understanding DCOM.

37

DISTRIBUTED
APPLICATION
ARCHITECTURE

Understanding COM

COM is an outgrowth of Microsoft's *Object Linking and Embedding* technology, or *OLE*. OLE was used in early versions of windows to support *compound documents*, or documents that are the product of multiple applications. COM was a solution to early problems in OLE, and like most great solutions, it solved a much more fundamental problem—how general objects should interact with and provide services to each other.

COM objects are instances of classes and are organized into interfaces. Interfaces are simply collections of methods. COM objects can only be accessed via their methods, and every COM object is implemented inside a server. A server may be implemented as a dynamic-link library, independent process, or an operating service. COM abstracts away the implementation details and presents a single uniform interface to all objects, no matter how each object is implemented.

The COM library is key to implementing this common interface between objects. It is present on any system that supports COM and provides a directory to all classes that are available on that system. The COM library maintains information about available classes in the system registry. When one COM object accesses another, it first invokes functions in the COM library. These functions can be used to create a COM object from its class or obtain a pointer to its interfaces. The COM runtime is a process that supports the COM library in implementing its functions. It is supported by the Service Control Manager. The invoking object uses interface pointers to invoke the methods of the object that it accesses through the COM library. The pointers used by COM objects can be used by objects written in any programming language.

The interface definition language used to define COM interfaces and methods is borrowed from DCE. COM also defines a binary interface standard. This standard helps to promote language-independence.

> **NOTE**
>
> COM differs from other object-oriented systems in its support of inheritance. COM classes do not inherit the implementation of methods from their superclasses. They only inherit the definition of those interfaces. This means that all methods must be reimplemented every time a subclass is declared. COM provides a workaround to this problem called *aggregation*. Using aggregation, a class may inherit an entire interface by copying the interface of its superclass. However, the inheriting class may not override individual methods in the inherited interface.

From COM to DCOM

DCOM is essentially COM distributed over multiple computers. DCOM allows COM objects executing on one computer to create COM objects on other computers and access their methods. The location of the remote object is transparent. Using DCOM, remote objects are accessed in exactly the same manner as local objects.

In order for an object on a local system to access the methods of an object on a remote system, the local system must have the remote object's class registered in its local registry. The local object, oblivious of the location of the object that it is accessing, creates the remote object and/or obtains a pointer to its methods by invoking the functions of its local COM library. The COM library processes the function calls using its local COM runtime. The COM runtime checks the system registry for the class of the object being accessed. If the registry indicates that the class is defined in the registry of a remote machine, the local COM runtime contacts the COM runtime on the remote machine and requests that it perform the creation of the remote object or invocation of its methods. The remote COM runtime carries out the request if the request is allowed by the system's security policy. This policy typically defaults to the Windows NT security policy, but may be tailored and made more restrictive for a particular application. Figure 37.4 summarizes DCOM's operation.

The COM runtime processes on separate machines communicate with each other using an RPC mechanism referred to as *Object RPC*, or *ORPC*. ORPC is based on Microsoft RPC (which is essentially DCE RPC. ORPC) may be configured to use a number of transport protocols, but works best with UDP. Refer to Chapter 30 for a description of UDP. Because most firewalls block UDP, it is necessary to use TCP with ORPC to build distributed applications that work over the Internet.

Although DCOM is a Microsoft product, it is an open standard and has been ported to other platforms, such as UNIX. Microsoft intends DCOM to be a cross-platform solution for distributed application development. So far it has received a high level of acceptance by Windows users but mediocre success in cross-platform applications.

One of the prominent features of DCOM is its application support. DCOM security integrates with and extends the Windows NT security model. It allows access control decisions to be made with a fine level of granularity. For example, it is possible to specify whether one object is allowed to create or invoke the methods of another. DCOM also provides strong and flexible communication security. A variety of encryption mechanisms may be used to protect information as it is transmitted from one COM object to another. Windows NT 5.0 extends these encryption capabilities to Kerberos-based authentication, encryption, and access control. Kerberos is a very strong security protection mechanism developed at the Massachusetts Institute of Technology. Information on Kerberos may be found at `http://www.ov.com/misc/krb-faq.html`.

FIGURE 37.4.

How DCOM works.

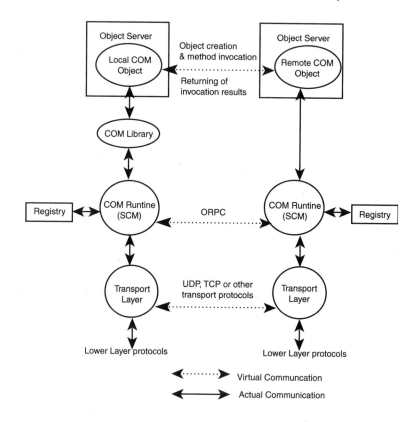

The Microsoft Java Software Development Kit includes a JVM and API that provides an interface to COM and DCOM. Chapter 54, "Dirty Java," shows how to use the capabilities provided by the Microsoft JVM and API.

The Common Object Request Broker Architecture (CORBA)

The *Common Object Request Broker Architecture (CORBA)* provides another approach to building distributed systems. CORBA, like DCOM but unlike DCE, is object-oriented. It allows objects on one computer to invoke the methods of objects on other computers. CORBA, unlike DCOM, is an open standards solution and is not tied to any particular operating system vendor. Because of this, CORBA is a great choice for building distributed object-oriented applications.

CORBA makes use of objects that are accessible via *Object Request Brokers (ORBs)*. ORBs are used to connect objects to one another across a network. An object on one computer (client object) invokes the methods of an object on another computer (server object) via an ORB.

The client's interface to the ORB is a stub that is written in the *Interface Definition Language (IDL)*. The stub is a local proxy for a remote object. The IDL provides a programming language-independent mechanism for describing the methods of an object.

The ORB's interface to the server is through an IDL skeleton. The skeleton provides the ORB with a language-independent mechanism for accessing the remote object.

Remote method invocation under CORBA takes place as follows: The client object invokes the methods of the IDL stub corresponding to a remote object. The IDL stub communicates the method invocations to the ORB. The ORB invokes the corresponding methods of the IDL skeleton. The IDL skeleton invokes the methods of the remote server object implementation. The server object returns the result of the method invocation via the IDL skeleton, which passes the result back to the ORB. The ORB passes the result back to the IDL stub, and the IDL stub returns the result back to the client object. Figure 37.5 summarizes this process.

37

DISTRIBUTED APPLICATION ARCHITECTURE

FIGURE 37.5.

How CORBA works.

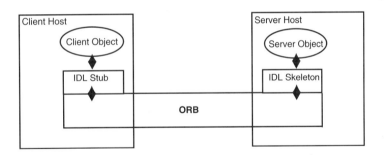

Figure 37.5 shows the ORB as being a single layer across the client and server hosts. This is the standard way in which the ORB is viewed. A number of possible ORB implementations are possible. For example, peer ORBs could be implemented on the client and server hosts or a central system ORB could be implemented on a local server. Other ORB implementations are also possible.

Now that you know how CORBA works, you may be wondering how it is used to develop distributed applications. The answer is that CORBA provides a flexible approach to distributed application development. It provides a finer level of granularity in the implementation of client/server systems. Instead of relying on monolithic clients and servers (as is the case of the browsers and servers of the Web), both clients and servers can be distributed over several hosts.

The advantages of CORBA over other distributed application integration approaches are significant:

- It provides a true object-oriented approach to developing distributed applications.

- It is language-independent. It can be used to connect objects that are developed in any programming language, as long as an IDL stub for the objects can be furnished.

- It is recognized as an international standard and is supported by nearly all major software vendors.

We'll cover CORBA more in Chapter 41, "JavaIDL and ORBs," where you'll learn how to use Java objects with CORBA.

Java Remote Method Invocation

Given the various approaches to distributed application development discussed in the previous sections, you may be wondering why Java just doesn't pick the best approach and go with it instead of using RMI. There are a number of reasons for this:

- TCP sockets—Java does support them, as you learned in Part VIII, "Network Programming." You can build traditional socket-based client/server applications using Java for an intranet and the Internet. Java applets and servlets can be used to distribute the application's information processing layer between the client and server. Even though Java supports TCP sockets, JavaSoft decided that a more fine-grained, low-overhead approach to distributed application development, such as that provided by CORBA, would be needed to develop advanced distributed applications using Java.

- DCE—Based on RPC, which is a procedure-oriented approach to developing distributed applications. RPC does not mesh well with distributed object-oriented applications. The remote method invocation approach supported by CORBA is much better suited to the Java object model.

- DCOM—Based on DCE's RPC, but provides object-oriented programming capabilities through COM objects, interfaces, and methods. In addition, DCOM provides extensive security services. Microsoft's Java development environment, Visual J++, provides the capability to access COM and DCOM objects from Java. However, this capability is more of a bridge to legacy technologies than a distributed extension of the Java object model.

- CORBA—Provides an excellent approach to building distributed object-oriented applications. And Java does support CORBA, as you'll learn in Chapter 41. However, CORBA is designed to support a language-independent object model.

Java RMI has all the benefits of CORBA, but is specifically tailored to the Java object model. This makes Java RMI far more efficient and easier to use than CORBA for pure Java applications.

Chapter 38, "Building Distributed Applications with the `java.rmi` Packages," provides an introduction to Java RMI and covers the RMI API. It also shows you how to develop a simple distributed application using RMI. In the next section, I'll describe the Java distributed object model and explain why it is a natural extension of the Java object model used within a single JVM.

The Java Distributed Object Model

The distributed object model used by Java allows objects that execute in one JVM to invoke the methods of objects that execute in other JVMs. These other JVMs may execute as a separate process on the same computer or on other remote computers. The object making the method invocation is referred to as the *client object*. The object whose methods are being invoked is referred to as the *server object*. The client object is also referred to as the *local object* and is said to execute locally. The server object is also referred to as the *remote object* and is said to execute remotely.

In the Java distributed object model, a client object never references a remote object directly. Instead, it references a remote interface that is implemented by the remote object. The use of remote interfaces allows server objects to differentiate between their local and remote interfaces. For example, an object could provide methods to objects that execute within the same JVM that are in addition to those that it provides via its remote interface. The use of remote interfaces also allows server objects to present different remote access modes. For example, a server object can provide both a remote administration interface and a remote user interface. Finally, the use of remote interfaces allows the server object's position within its class hierarchy to be abstracted away from the manner in which it is used. This allows client objects to be compiled using the remote interface alone, eliminating the need for server class files to be locally present during the compilation process.

The Three-Tiered Layering of the Java RMI

In addition to remote interfaces, the model makes use of stub and skeleton classes in much the same way as CORBA. *Stub classes* serve as local proxies for the remote objects. *Skeleton classes* act as remote proxies. Both stub and skeleton classes implement the remote interface of the server object. The client interface invokes the methods of the local stub object. The local stub communicates these method invocations to the remote skeleton, and the remote skeleton invokes the methods of the server object. The server object returns a value to the skeleton object. The skeleton object returns the value to the stub object, and the stub object returns the value to the client. Figure 37.6 summarizes the use of stubs and skeletons.

FIGURE 37.6.

The use of stubs and skeletons in the Java distributed object model.

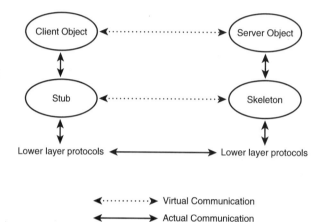

If you are a CORBA programmer, you'll notice the conspicuous absence of IDL and ORBs in Figure 37.6. (IDL and ORBs are required by CORBA because it is language-neutral). The stub and skeleton classes are automatically generated by the `rmic` compiler from the server object. (The `rmic` compiler is a standard JDK tool.) These classes are true Java classes and do not rely on an external IDL. No ORB is required because the Java RMI is a pure Java solution. The client object and stub communicate using normal Java method invocations, and so do the skeleton and the server object. The stub and the skeleton communicate via a remote reference layer.

The remote reference layer supports communication between the stub and the skeleton. If the stub communicates with more than one skeleton instance (not currently supported), the stub object communicates with the multiple skeletons in a multicast fashion. The RMI API currently only defines classes that support unicast communication between a stub and a single skeleton. The remote reference layer may also be used to activate server objects when they are invoked remotely.

The remote reference layer on the local host communicates with the remote reference layer on the remote host via the RMI transport layer. The transport layer sets up and manages connections between the address spaces of the local and remote hosts, keeps track of objects that can be accessed remotely, and determines when connections have timed out and become inoperable. The transport layer uses TCP sockets, by default, to communicate between the local and remote hosts. However, other transport layer protocols, such as SSL and UDP, may also be used.

Figure 37.7 illustrates the three-tier layering used to implement Java RMI. In this expanded view of the model, the client object invokes the methods of the local stub of the server object. The local stub uses the remote reference layer to communicate with the server skeleton. The remote reference layer uses the transport layer to set up a connection between the local and remote address spaces and to obtain a reference to the skeleton object.

FIGURE 37.7.

The three-tier layering of Java RMI.

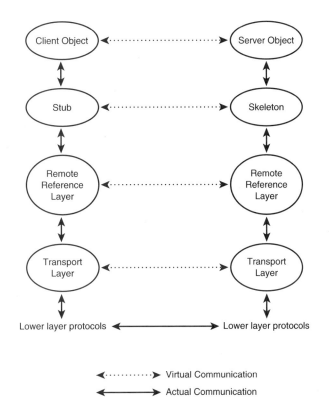

In order for a server object to be accessed remotely, it must register itself with the remote registry. It does this by associating its object instance with a name. The remote registry is a process that runs on the server host, and is created by running the `rmiregistry` program, another JDK tool.

The remote registry maintains a database of server objects and the names by which these objects can be referenced. When a client creates an instance of a server object's interface (that is, its local stub), the transport layer on the local host communicates with the transport layer on the remote host to determine if the referenced object exists and to find out type of interface the referenced object implements. The server-side transport layer uses the remote registry to access this information. A separate process, referred to as the Java RMI Activation System Daemon, supports the activation of remote objects. The Java RMI Activation System Daemon is run by executing the `rmid` program of the JDK on the remote system.

Passing Arguments and Returning Values

In order for a client object to pass an argument as part of a remote method invocation, the type of the argument must be *serializable*. A serializable type is a primitive or reference type that can be written to and read from a stream. In practice, all Java primitive types are serializable, and so are all classes and interfaces that implement or extend the `Serializable` interface. The `Serializable` interface is defined in the `java.io` package.

> **NOTE**
>
> Chapter 40, "Using Object Serialization and JavaSpaces," covers object serialization in more detail.

Object references are used within the JVM that contains the object. When a local object is passed as an argument to a remote method invocation, the local object is copied from the local JVM to the remote JVM. Only non-static and non-transient field variables are copied.

When a remote object is passed via a remote method invocation within the same JVM, the reference to the remote object is passed. This is because the remote JVM already contains the object being referenced.

When an object is returned by a server object as the result of a remote method invocation, the object is copied from the remote JVM to the local JVM.

Objects and Remote Method Invocation

The Java distributed object model is a natural extension of the Java object model used within a single JVM. It implements RMI in an easy-to-use fashion and places minimal requirements on objects in order for them to be accessed remotely. These requirements are as follows:

- The object's class must implement an interface that extends the Remote interface. This interface must define the methods that the object will allow to be remotely invoked. These methods must throw RemoteException.

- The object's class must extend the RemoteServer class. This is typically done by extending the UnicastRemoteObject subclass of RemoteServer.

- The stub and skeleton classes of the object's class must be created using the rmic compiler. The stub must be distributed to the client host.

- The remote object's class, interface, and skeleton class must be in the CLASSPATH of the remote host.

- The remote activation daemon and remote registry must be started.

- A remote object instance must be created and registered with the remote registry. The bind() and rebind() methods of the Naming class are used to register an object with its associated name. The remote object should install a security manager to enable loading of RMI classes.

Chapter 38 builds a simple distributed application that shows how each of these requirements are accomplished. Chapter 39, "Working with Remote Objects," provides more advanced examples of implementing remote objects.

Distributed Application Security

The Java distributed object model implements security through the use of class loaders and security managers in the same way that it does for applications and applets. The class loader trusts classes that are loaded from the local host. Classes are not allowed to be loaded from the network unless a security manager is in place that permits remote class loading.

An applet security manager is automatically put into place for applets as they are loaded. The security manager used in distributed Java applications is the RMISecurityManager class. An instance of this class should be set via the setSecurityManager() method of the System class at the beginning of the execution of a client or server object. Less restrictive security managers can be developed by subclassing RMISecurityManager and overriding its methods.

Transport Security

Because RMI uses TCP/IP for network communication, it is subject to the vulnerabilities of the TCP/IP protocol suite. JDK 1.2 enhancements to RMI provide the capability to create custom sockets on a per-object basis. Custom sockets can enable RMI to use Netscape's Secure Sockets Layer protocol to protect information as it is communicated

37

between local and remote objects. This is accomplished by creating a custom RMISocketFactory.

Authentication and Access Control

Authentication is the process of verifying the identity of an individual or an object that acts on the individual's behalf. *Access control* is the process of restricting access to resources or services based on an object or individual's identity. Authentication and access control work hand in hand. Without strong authentication, unscrupulous individuals may be able to masquerade as trusted individuals. Without access control, authentication has no teeth.

Authorization and access control are important in distributed applications. For example, you may want to limit the objects that are able to remotely invoke the methods of a particular server object to those objects that execute on a specific host or set of hosts, or that act on behalf of a particular individual.

The RMI API does not provide classes and interfaces that directly support authentication and access control. However, these capabilities may be built on top of the classes that are provided by the RMI API. For example, the `getClientHost()` method of the `RemoteServer` class can be used by a server object to determine the name of the host from which a remote method invocation is initiated. This may be used to limit RMI access to a specified list of hosts, but this approach is not foolproof. There are ways for malicious hosts to masquerade as trusted hosts. However, it may be used to provide a limited degree of protection. More advanced authentication and access control can be implemented through the use of digital certificates in the overall distributed application supported by RMI.

Firewalls may be used to protect distributed applications that run on an intranet. They are typically used to restrict access to the distributed application to those hosts that are on a corporate intranet or on a selected segment of an intranet. However, firewalls introduce problems of their own. If a firewall exists in the communication path between client and server objects, it can prevent remote method invocations from occurring. Fortunately, JavaSoft recognized this problem, and the `RMISocketFactory` class provides the capability for RMI to be used with a firewall. This class uses alternative approaches to client/server communication that can be used to circumvent the security restrictions imposed by many firewalls.

Summary

In this chapter you covered background information about approaches to designing and implementing digital applications, and learned how Java's distributed object model compares to these approaches. You delved into the details of Java's distributed object model, and learned how RMI is implemented using a three-layered protocol set. You then investigated the security issues involved with using RMI. In the next chapter, you'll cover RMI in more detail and use it to develop sample distributed applications.

Building Distributed Applications with the `java.rmi` Packages

The Remote Method Invocation (RMI) API adds the capability to develop fully distributed applications to Java's overwhelming list of credentials. This capability is provided by a set of intuitive and easy-to-use packages that make distributed application development a natural extension of single host programming. The RMI API is much simpler to use than other currently available distributed application programming frameworks, including Common Object Request Broker Architecture (CORBA) and Distributed Component Object Model (DCOM).

In this chapter, you'll learn why the RMI API provides a superior development approach for distributed programming in Java. You'll learn about the packages of the RMI API and then use them to develop a simple distributed application. When you finish this chapter, you'll be thoroughly introduced to the `java.rmi` packages.

RMI and Distributed Applications

Distributed applications are those that execute across multiple host systems. Objects executing on one host invoke methods of objects on other hosts to help them perform their processing. These methods execute on the remote hosts—hence the name *remote method invocation*. The remotely invoked objects perform computations and may return values that are used by the local objects. Figure 38.1 illustrates this concept.

FIGURE 38.1.

A distributed application.

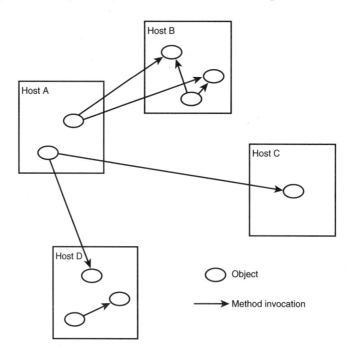

A number of approaches to implementing distributed systems have been developed. The Internet and the Web are examples of distributed systems that have been developed using the TCP/IP client/server approach. Clients and servers communicate via TCP and UDP sockets. While the Internet and the Web are remarkably successful, the use of sockets requires separate application-level protocols for client/server communication. The overhead associated with these protocols prohibits the fine-grain parallel operation that is possible through other approaches.

The Distributed Component Object Model (DCOM) makes use of remote procedure calls to allow objects executing on one system to invoke the methods of objects that run on other systems. DCOM provides an excellent framework for developing distributed object-based systems. However, its major shortcoming, from a Java perspective, is that it is oriented toward legacy Windows applications and does not provide a 100% pure Java solution. The use of DCOM with Java is covered in Chapter 54, "Dirty Java."

The Common Object Request Broker Architecture (CORBA) supports an object-oriented framework for developing distributed systems. CORBA's strong point is that it supports a language-independent model. However, this advantage is a disadvantage when it comes to Java because it forces Java applications to use an external, albeit neutral, object model. CORBA is covered in Chapter 41, "Java IDL and ORBs."

The Remote Method Invocation (RMI) API of Java is a Java-specific approach to developing distributed systems. RMI's major advantage is that it is fully integrated with the Java object model, highly intuitive, and easy to use. The main disadvantage of RMI is that its use is limited to Java. RMI, unlike CORBA, cannot be used with objects written in other programming languages. Consequently, RMI is optimal for pure Java enterprise applications. However, if you need to build distributed systems containing objects that are written in languages other than Java, CORBA is a better solution.

RMI Terminology

Before describing the RMI API, let's cover some of the terminology it uses.

RMI is built upon the fundamental notion of local and remote objects. This concept is relative. *Local objects* are objects that execute on a particular host. *Remote objects* are objects that execute on all other hosts. Objects on remote hosts are *exported* so that they can be invoked remotely. An object exports itself by registering with a *remote registry server*. The remote registry server helps objects on other hosts to remotely access its registered objects. It does this by maintaining a database of names and the objects that are associated with those names (see Figure 38.2).

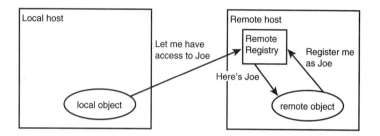

FIGURE 38.2.

Remote objects register themselves for remote access.

Objects that export themselves for remote access must implement the `Remote` interface. This interface identifies the object as capable of being accessed remotely. Any methods that are to be invoked remotely must throw the `RemoteException`. This exception is used to indicate errors that may occur during an RMI.

Java's RMI approach is organized into a client/server framework. A local object that invokes a remote object's method is referred to as a *client object*, or simply a *client*. A remote object whose methods are invoked by a local object is referred to as a *server object*, or a *server*.

Java's RMI approach makes use of stubs and skeletons. A *stub* is a local object that acts as a local proxy for the remote object. The stub provides the same methods as the remote object. Local objects invoke the methods of the stub as if they were methods of the remote object. The stub then communicates these method invocations to the remote object via a skeleton which is implemented on the remote host. The skeleton is a proxy for the remote object that is located on the same host as the remote object. The skeleton communicates with the local stub and propagates method invocations on the stub to the actual remote object. It then receives the value returned by the remote method invocation (if any) and passes this value back to the stub. The stub, in turn, sends the return value on to the local object that initiated the remote method invocation.

Stubs and skeletons communicate through a remote reference layer. This layer provides stubs with the capability to communicate with skeletons via a transport protocol. RMI currently uses TCP for information transport, although it is flexible enough to use other protocols. Figure 38.3 shows how stubs and skeletons are used in Java RMI.

The `java.rmi` Packages

The RMI API is implemented by the following five packages:

- `java.rmi`—Provides the `Remote` interface, a class for accessing remote names, the `MarshalledObject` class, and a security manager for RMI.

- `java.rmi.registry`—Provides classes and interfaces that are used by the remote registry.

FIGURE 38.3.

Java RMI uses stubs and skeletons to support client/server communication.

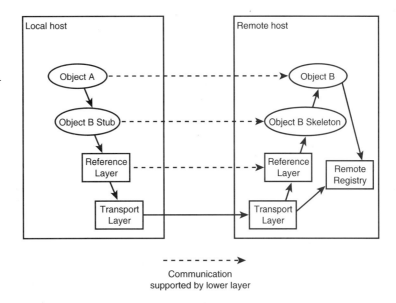

- `java.rmi.server`—Provides the classes and interfaces used to implement remote objects, stubs, and skeletons, and to support RMI communication. This package implements the bulk of the RMI API.

- `java.rmi.activation`—Supports persistent object references and remote object activation.

- `java.rmi.dgc`—Provides classes and interfaces that are used by the RMI distributed garbage collector.

The following sections describe each of these packages. Don't worry if it seems like there's a lot of material to learn. When you actually use RMI, you'll only use a fraction of the RMI API. When you read over the description of the RMI packages, try to get a feel for the classes and interfaces that are available to you.

The `java.rmi` Package

The `java.rmi` package declares the `Remote` interface, the `MarshalledObject`, `Naming` and `RMISecurityManager` classes, and a number of exceptions that are used with remote method invocation.

The `Remote` interface must be implemented by all remote objects. This interface has no methods. It is used for identification purposes.

38

BUILDING DISTRIBUTED APPLICATIONS

The MarshalledObject class was added in JDK 1.2. It is used to maintain a serialized byte stream of an object. Its get() method is used to retrieve a deserialized version of the object.

The Naming class provides static methods for accessing remote objects via RMI URLs. The bind() and rebind() methods bind a remote object name to a specific RMI URL. The unbind() method removes the binding between an object name and an RMI URL. The lookup() method returns the remote object specified by an RMI URL. The list() method returns the list of URLs that are currently known to the RMI registry.

The syntax for RMI URLs is as follows:

```
rmi://host:port/remoteObjectName
```

The *host* and TCP *port* are optional. If the *host* is omitted, the local host is assumed. The default TCP *port* is 1099. For example, the following URL names the MyObject remote object that is located on the host athome.jaworski.com and is accessible via TCP port 1234:

```
rmi://athome.jaworski.com:1234/MyObject
```

The RMISecurityManager class defines the default security policy used for remote object stubs. It only applies to applications. Applets use the AppletSecurityManager class even if they perform RMI. You can extend RMISecurityManager and override its methods to implement your own RMI security policies. Use the setSecurityManager() method of the System class to set an RMISecurityManager object as the current security manager to be used for RMI stubs.

The java.rmi package defines a number of exceptions. The RemoteException class is the parent of all exceptions that are generated during RMI. It must be thrown by all methods of a remote object that can be accessed remotely.

> **NOTE**
>
> A remote object is allowed to have local methods that can be invoked locally. These methods do not need to throw RemoteException.

The java.rmi.registry Package

The java.rmi.registry package provides the Registry and RegistryHandler interfaces and the LocateRegistry class. These interfaces and classes are used to register and access remote objects by name. Remote objects are registered when they are identified to a host's registry process. The registry process is created when the rmireg-istry program is executed.

The Registry interface defines the bind(), rebind(), unbind(), list(), and lookup() methods that are used by the Naming class to associate object names and RMI URLs. The registry interface also defines the REGISTRY_PORT constant that identifies the default TCP port used by the registry service.

The RegistryHandler interface provides methods for accessing objects that implement the Registry interface. The registryStub() method returns the local stub of a remote object that implements the Registry interface. The registryImpl() method constructs a Registry object and exports it via a specified TCP port.

The LocateRegistry class provides the static getRegistry() method for retrieving Registry objects on the local host or a remote host. It also provides the createRegistry() method to construct a Registry object and export it via a specified TCP port.

The java.rmi.server Package

The java.rmi.server package implements several interfaces and classes that support both client and server aspects of RMI.

The RemoteObject class implements the Remote interface and provides a remote implementation of the Object class. All classes that implement remote objects, both client and server, extend RemoteObject.

The RemoteServer class extends RemoteObject and is a common class that is subclassed by specific types of remote object implementations. It provides the static setLog() and getLog() methods for setting and retrieving an output stream used to log information about RMI accesses. It also provides the getClientHost() method that is used to retrieve the host name of the client performing the remote method invocation.

The UnicastRemoteObject class extends RemoteServer and provides the default remote object implementation. Classes that implement remote objects usually subclass UnicastRemoteObject. Objects of the UnicastRemoteObject class are accessed via TCP connections on port 1099, exist only for the duration of the process that creates them, and rely on a stream-based protocol for client/server communication.

The RemoteStub class extends RemoteObject and provides an abstract implementation of client side stubs. A *client stub* is a local representation of a remote object that implements all remote methods of the remote object. The static setRef() method is used to associate a client stub with its corresponding remote object.

The `RemoteCall` interface provides methods that are used by stubs and skeletons to implement remote method invocations.

The `RemoteRef` interface is used by `RemoteStub` objects to reference remote objects. It provides methods for comparing and invoking remote objects and for working with objects that implement the `RemoteCall` interface.

The `ServerRef` interface extends the `RemoteRef` interface and is implemented by remote objects to gain access to their associated `RemoteStub` objects.

The `Skeleton` interface is implemented by remote skeletons. It provides methods that are used by the skeleton to access the methods being requested of the remote object, and for working with method arguments and return values.

The `Unreferenced` interface is implemented by a remote object to enable it to determine when it is no longer referenced by a client.

The `RMIClassLoader` class supports the loading of remote classes. The location of a remote class is specified by either an URL or the `java.rmi.server.codebase` system property. The static `loadClass()` method loads a remote class, and the static `getSecurityContext()` returns the security context in which the class loader operates. The `LoaderHandler` interface defines methods that are used by `RMIClassClassLoader` to load classes.

The `Operation` class is used to store a reference to a method. The `getOperation()` method returns the name of the method. The `toString()` method returns a `String` representation of the method's signature.

The `ObjID` class is used to create objects that serve as unique identifiers for objects that are exported as remote by a particular host. It provides methods for reading the object ID from and writing it to a stream. The `UID` class is an abstract class for creating unique object identifiers.

The `LogStream` class extends the `PrintStream` class to support the logging of errors that occur during RMI processing.

The `RMISocketFactory` class is used to specify a socket implementation for transporting information between clients and servers involved in RMI. This class provides three alternative approaches to establishing RMI connections that can be used with firewalls. The static `setSocketFactory()` method can be used to specify a custom socket implementation. The `RMIClientSocketFactory` and `RMIServerSocketFactory` interfaces provide support for both client and server sockets. The `RMIFailureHandler` interface defines methods that handle the failure of a server socket creation. The `RMIFailureHandler` interface provides the `failure()` method for handling exceptions that occur in the underlying RMI socket implementation.

The `java.rmi.activation` Package

The `java.rmi.activation` package is a new RMI package that was added to JDK 1.2. It provides the capabilities to activate remote objects as needed and to use persistent object references.

> **NOTE**
>
> Examples of using the `java.rmi.activation` package are provided in the next chapter.

The `Activatable` class defines the basic methods implemented by activatable, persistent objects. It contains two constructors. One constructor is used to create and register (with the activation system) objects that can be accessed via specific TCP ports. The other constructor is used to activate an object based upon an `ActivationID` object and persistent data that has been stored for that object. The `export()` object methods are used to make an object available for use via a specific TCP port. The `getID()` method returns an object's `ActivationID` (used to uniquely identify the object). The `register()` and `unregister()` methods register (and unregister) an object with the runtime system. The `inactive()` method is used to tell the activation system that an object is inactive, or, if active, that it should be deactivated.

Objects of the `ActivationID` class are used to uniquely identify activatable objects and contain information about how objects are to be activated. An object's `ActivationID` is created when the object is registered with the activation system. The `activate()` method is used to activate the object referenced by an `ActivationID` object. The `equals()` and `hashCode()` methods are used to compare two `ActivationID` objects. Two `ActivationID` objects are equal if they reference the same object.

The `ActivationDesc` class encapsulates the information necessary to activate an object. It provides five methods that can be used to retrieve this information. The `getClassName()` method returns the described object's class name. The `getCodeSource()` method returns a `CodeSource` object that identifies the described object's location and other source information. The `getData()` method returns a `MarshalledObject` object that contains serialized information used to initialize the described object. The `getGroupID()` method returns the described object's `ActivationGroupID` object. The `getRestartMode()` method returns the restart mode associated with the activation descriptor.

38

BUILDING
DISTRIBUTED
APPLICATIONS

The `ActivationGroup` class is used to group activatable objects so that they execute in the same JVM. `ActivationGroup` objects are used to create instances of the activatable objects within their group. The `activeObject()` method is used to inform an `ActivationGroup` that an activatable object has been activated. The `createGroup()` method is used to specify the current `ActivationGroup` object for the current JVM instance. The `currentGroupID()` method returns the `ActivationGroupID` object of the current `ActivationGroup` object. The `getSystem()` method returns the current `ActivationSystem` object. The `inactiveObject()` method is invoked when an object in the group is deactivated (becomes inactive). This method deactivates the object if the object is still active. The `inactiveGroup()` method is used to report an inactive group to the group's `ActivationMonitor` object. The `newInstance()` method creates a new instance of an activatable object. The `setSystem()` method sets the `ActivationSystem` object for the current JVM.

The `ActivationGroupID` class uniquely identifies an `ActivationGroup` object and contains information about the object's activation system. The `getSystem()` method returns the `ActivationSystem` object that is used to activate the referenced `ActivationGroup` object. The `equals()` and `hashCode()` methods are used to compare `ActivationGroupID` objects in terms of their referenced `ActivationGroupID` objects.

The `ActivationGroupDesc` class encapsulates the information necessary to create an `ActivationGroup` object. The `getClassName()` method returns the described `ActivationGroup` object's class name. The `getCodeSource()` method returns the described `ActivationGroup` object's `CodeSource` object. The `getData()` method returns a `MarshalledObject` object that contains serialized data about the described `ActivationGroup` object. The `CommandEnvironment` inner class provides support for implementation-specific options.

The `ActivationSystem` interface is implemented by objects that register activatable objects and activatable object groups. The `SYSTEM_PORT` constant identifies the TCP port used by the activation system. The `registerGroup()`, `registerObject()`, `unregisterGroup()`, and `unregisterObject()` methods are used to register and unregister `Activatable` and `ActivationGroup` objects. The `activeGroup()` method is used to inform the activation system about an active `ActivationGroup` object.

The `Activator` interface is implemented by objects that activate objects that are registered with an `ActivationSystem` (object). The `activate()` method activates an object based upon its associated `ActivationID` object.

The `ActivationInstantiator` interface provides methods for classes that create instances of activatable objects. The `newInstance()` method creates new object instances based on their associated `ActivationID` and `ActivationDesc` objects.

The `ActivationMonitor` provides methods for maintaining information about active and inactive objects. The `activeObject()`, `inactiveObjet()`, and `inactiveGroup()` methods are used to collect this information.

The `java.rmi.dgc` Package

The `java.rmi.dgc` package contains classes and interfaces that are used by the distributed garbage collector. The `DGC` interface is implemented by the server side of the distributed garbage collector. It defines two methods: `dirty()` and `clean()`. The `dirty()` method indicates that a remote object is being referenced by a client. The `clean()` method is used to indicate that a remote reference has been completed.

The `Lease` class creates objects that are used to keep track of object references. The `VMID` class is used to create an ID that uniquely identifies a Java virtual machine on a particular host.

Implementing RMI

Now that you've been introduced to the RMI API and covered each of its packages, you're probably wondering how you go about implementing a remote method invocation. I'll summarize the process in this section and then explain it in detail in the next chapter. I'll organize the discussion according to the steps performed on the remote host (server) and local host (client).

Implementing the RMI Server on the Remote Host

Because a remote object must exist before it can be invoked, we'll first cover the steps involved in creating the remote object and registering it with the remote registry. In the following section, we'll look at what it takes for a local object to access a remote object and invoke its methods.

Create the Remote Interface

Remote objects are referenced via interfaces. In order to implement a remote object, you must first create an interface for that object. This interface must be `public` and must extend the `Remote` interface. Define the remote methods that you want to invoke within this interface. These methods must throw `RemoteException`.

Listing 38.1 provides an example of a remote interface. The `MyServer.java` file is defined in the `ju.ch38.server` package. This file is located in the `ju\ch38\server` directory. The reason that I put it in a named package is so it can be found relative to your CLASSPATH. Edit your CLASSPATH, if necessary, to make sure that the ju.ch38.serv-er package is accessible.

MyServer defines two methods: getDataNum() and getData(). The getDataNum() method returns an integer indicating the total number of data strings that are available on the server. The getData() method returns the *n*th data string.

Compile MyServer.java before going on to the next section.

LISTING 38.1. THE MyServer CLASS.

```
package ju.ch38.server;

import java.rmi.*;

public interface MyServer extends Remote {
  int getDataNum() throws RemoteException;
  String getData(int n) throws RemoteException;
}
```

Create a Class that Implements the Remote Interface

After creating the remote interface, you must create a class that implements the remote interface. This class typically extends the UnicastRemoteObject class. However, it could also extend other subclasses of the RemoteServer class.

The implementation class should have a constructor that creates and initializes the remote object. It should also implement all of the methods defined in the remote interface. It should have a main() method so that it can be executed as a remote class. The main() method should use the setSecurityManager() method of the System class to set an object to be used as the remote object's security manager. It should register a name by which it can be remotely referenced with the remote registry.

Listing 38.2 provides the implementation class for the MyServer interface. The MyServerImpl class is also in the ju.ch38.server package. You should change the hostName value to the name of the host where the remote object is to be located.

The data array contains five strings that are retrieved by the client object via the getDataNum() and getData() methods. The getDataNum() method returns the length of data, and the getData() method returns the *n*th element of the data array.

The main() method sets the security manager to an object of the RMISecurityManager class. It creates an instance of the MyServerImpl class and invokes the rebind() method of Naming to register the new object with remote registry. It registers the object with the name `MyServer` and then informs you that it has successfully completed the registration process.

Compile `MyServerImpl.java` before going on to the next section.

LISTING 38.2. THE `MyServerImpl` CLASS.

```
package ju.ch38.server;

import java.rmi.*;
import java.rmi.server.*;

public class MyServerImpl extends UnicastRemoteObject
 implements MyServer {
 static String hostName="athome.jaworski.com";
 static String data[] = {"Remote","Method","Invocation","Is","Great!"};
 public MyServerImpl() throws RemoteException {
  super();
 }
 public int getDataNum() throws RemoteException {
  return data.length;
 }
 public String getData(int n) throws RemoteException {
  return data[n%data.length];
 }
 public static void main(String args[]){
  System.setSecurityManager(new RMISecurityManager());
  try {
   MyServerImpl instance = new MyServerImpl();
   Naming.rebind("//"+hostName+"/MyServer", instance);
   System.out.println("I'm registered!");
  } catch (Exception ex) {
   System.out.println(ex);
  }
 }
}
```

38

BUILDING
DISTRIBUTED
APPLICATIONS

Create Stub and Skeleton Classes

Once you have created the class that implements the remote interface, use the `rmic` compiler to create the stub and skeleton classes:

`rmic ju.ch38.server.MyServerImpl`

Run the `rmic` compiler from the `ju\ch38\server` directory. The `rmic` compiler creates the files `MyServerImpl_Stub.class` and `MyServerImpl_Skel.class` in this directory.

> **NOTE**
>
> You must supply the fully qualified package name of the class that you compile with `rmic`.

Copy the Remote Interface and Stub File to the Client Host

You'll need the `MyServer.class` interface file to compile your client software, and you'll need `MyServer.class` and `MyServerImpl_Stub.class` to run your client. Before going any further, you should copy these files to an appropriate location on your client host. They must be in a path `ju\ch38\server` that is accessible via the client's `CLASSPATH`. I suggest putting them in `c:\jdk1.2\ju\ch38\server` and putting `c:\jdk1.2` in your `CLASSPATH`. If you run both the client and server on the same computer, the directory structure and files should already be in position.

> **NOTE**
>
> In the next chapter, I'll show you how to use applets and a Web server to automatically distribute client files.

Start Up the Remote Registry

Now you must start your remote registry server. This program listens on the default port 1099 for incoming requests to access named objects. The named objects must register themselves with the remote registry program in order to be made available to requesters. You start up the remote registry server as follows:

```
start rmiregistry
```

Under Windows 95, this command creates a new DOS window and runs the remote registry program as a background task.

Create and Register the Remote Object

You're almost done with the remote server. The last thing to do is to execute the `MyServerImpl` program to create an object of the `MyServerImpl` class that registers itself with the remote registry. You do this as follows:

```
java ju.ch38.server.MyServerImpl
I'm registered!
```

The program displays the `I'm registered!` string to let you know that it has successfully registered itself. Leave the server running (don't exit the server program by pressing Ctrl+C) while you start the client. If you run the client and server on the same computer, you'll need to open up a separate command line window for the client.

Implementing the RMI Client on the Local Host

Now that you have the remote server up and running, let's create a client program to remotely invoke the methods of the `MyServer` object and display the results it returns.

Listing 38.3 contains the `MyClient` program. You must change the `hostName` variable to the name of the remote server host where the remote object is registered. Compile this program and copy it to a `ju\ch38\client` directory that is accessible from the `CLASSPATH` of the client host. Once you have compiled it, you can run it as follows:

```
java ju.ch38.client.MyClient
Remote
Method
Invocation
Is
Great!
```

The `MyClient` program remotely invokes the methods of the server object and displays the data returned to the console window.

`MyClient` consists of a single `main()` method that invokes the `lookup()` method of the `Naming` class to retrieve a reference to the object named `MyServer` on the specified host. It casts this object to the `MyServer` interface. It then invokes the `getDataNum()` method of the remote object to retrieve the number of available data items, and the `getData()` method to retrieve each specific data item. The retrieved data items are displayed in the console window.

You can shut down the client and server by terminating the programs and closing their command line windows.

LISTING 38.3. The `MyClient` PROGRAM.

```
package ju.ch38.client;

import ju.ch38.server.*;
import java.rmi.*;

public class MyClient {
 static String hostName="athome.jaworski.com";
 public static void main(String args[]) {
```

continues

LISTING 38.3. CONTINUED

```
try {
 MyServer server = (MyServer) Naming.lookup("//"+hostName+"/MyServer");
 int n = server.getDataNum();
 for(int i=0;i<n;++i) {
  System.out.println(server.getData(i));
 }
} catch (Exception ex) {
 System.out.println(ex);
 }
 }
}
```

Summary

This chapter introduced you to distributed applications. You learned why the RMI API provides a superior development approach for distributed programming in Java. You learned about the packages of the RMI API and then used them to develop a simple distributed application. In the next chapter, you'll discover more details about implementing distributed applications using RMI.

CHAPTER 39

Working with Remote Objects

In Chapter 38, "Building Distributed Applications with the `java.rmi` Packages," you learned about the RMI API and how it is used to develop distributed applications. In this chapter, you'll develop a few distributed applications of your own to get some practical experience using RMI. You'll create an applet that uses RMI to connect to a server object, retrieve information, and display the information in a text area. You'll create a random number server and a client that accesses the server. You'll learn how to use class loaders and security managers to bootstrap the client from a remote host. You'll develop a program that contacts the remote registry of a host and obtains a list of the remote objects that it services. You'll also learn how to use RMI to develop remotely activatable objects that are persistent. When you finish this chapter, you'll have enough experience using RMI to build your own distributed applications.

Using Remote Objects

In Chapter 38, you learned how to use RMI to develop simple client and server objects. The server object contained a `main()` method that set a security manager. It also registered the server object with the remote registry. The client performed a remote lookup of the server object in order to gain access to a local stub. It then used the stub to access the server object. The approach used in this example is common to most distributed applications that use RMI.

In order to use the client object, you copied its class file, the stub's class file, and the class file of the remote interface to the client computer. Although this may not have seemed to be an inconvenience at the time, one of the features of Java is the capability to automatically distribute software to clients. In this section, you'll learn how to use applets as clients for distributed applications. In the following section, you'll learn how to bootstrap clients from a remote host.

The `InfoClient` Applet

Listing 39.1 presents an applet that is used as a local client to access a remote server. The server generates news flashes that the client displays in a text area. The `InfoClient.java` file is stored in the `ch39\info\client` directory and is implemented as part of the `ju.ch39.info.client` package. Note that it imports the `ju.ch39.info.server` package. This package contains the classes and interfaces of the remote server.

LISTING 39.1. THE `InfoClient` APPLET.

```
package ju.ch39.info.client;

import ju.ch39.info.server.*;
```

```
import java.applet.*;
import java.awt.*;
import java.awt.event.*;
import java.net.*;
import java.rmi.*;

public class InfoClient extends Applet {
 String text = "Click Update for an InfoServer update.";
 TextArea textArea = new TextArea(15,50);
 Button update = new Button("Update");
 InfoServer server;
 public void init() {
  setLayout(new BorderLayout());
  add("Center",textArea);
  update.addActionListener(new ButtonHandler());
  add("South",update);
  try {
   URL hostURL = getCodeBase();
   String host = hostURL.getHost();
   server = (InfoServer) Naming.lookup("//"+host+"/InfoServer");
   textArea.setText(text);
  } catch (Exception ex) {
   textArea.setText(ex.toString());
  }
 }
 class ButtonHandler implements ActionListener {
  public void actionPerformed(ActionEvent ev){
   String s=ev.getActionCommand();
   if("Update".equals(s)){
    try {
     String newText=server.getInfo();
     text=newText+"\n"+text;
     textArea.setText(text);
    } catch (Exception ex){
     textArea.setText(ex.toString());
    }
   }
  }
 }
}
```

You won't get to run the applet until a little later in this chapter. I have to show you how to compile, run, and install it first. However, I'll give you a preview of its operation so that you'll be able to more easily follow the discussion.

The InfoClient applet displays a text area and an Update button to the user, as shown in Figure 39.1. When you click the Update button, the applet invokes a method of an object that executes remotely on a Web server. The remote object returns a news update to the applet, and the applet displays this news update in the text area. See Figure 39.2.

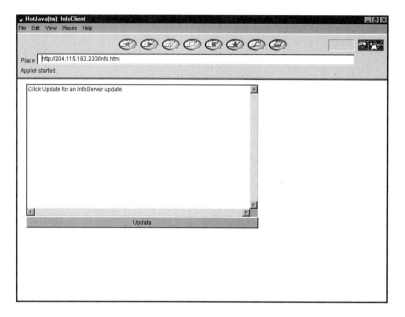

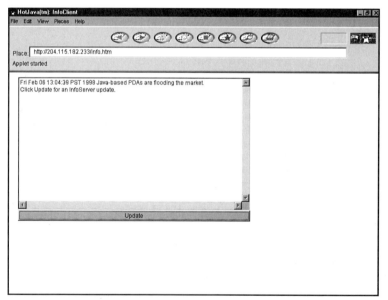

The processing performed by InfoClient consists of creating and laying out the applet's
GUI, establishing access to the remote server object, and processing the event associated
with the clicking of the Update button.

The server object implements the `InfoServer` interface. The server field variable is declared as the `InfoServer` type and is used to refer to the server object via a local stub. The `init()` method sets up the GUI and accesses the server object. The `getCodebase()` method retrieves the applet's URL, and the `getHost()` method retrieves the name of the host from which the applet was served. The `lookup()` method of the `Naming` class returns a local stub for the remote object named `InfoServer`. The `InfoServer` object executes on the Web server from which the applet was served. The local stub of the remote `InfoServer` object is referenced by the `server` variable.

The `ButtonHandler` class handles the clicking of the Update button by invoking the `getInfo()` method of the server object. This causes the server object to return a news flash in the form of a `String`. The returned `String` is then prepended to the text displayed in the text area.

Listing 39.2 contains the `info.htm` file that is used to display the applet. Note that it sets the `CODEBASE` attribute to the URL from which the applet's class file is retrieved. You must set this URL to the URL of your Web server. The actual applet is loaded from the following URL:

`http://your.host.com/codebase/ju/ch39/info/client/InfoClient.class`

You'll need to create a codebase directory on your Web server's root directory. You'll also store the compiled applet in the path `/codebase/ju/ch39/info/client/`. Refer to the section "Compiling and Installing the `InfoServer` Application" later in this chapter for information on how to compile both the client and server parts of the `InfoServer` application.

LISTING 39.2. THE `info.htm` FILE USED TO DISPLAY THE `InfoClient` APPLET.

```
<HTML>
<HEAD>
<TITLE>InfoClient</TITLE>
</HEAD>
<BODY>
<APPLET CODEBASE="http://204.115.182.233/codebase/"
CODE="ju.ch39.info.client.InfoClient.class"
WIDTH=500 HEIGHT=300>
[InfoClient Applet]
</APPLET>
</BODY>
</HTML>
```

39

WORKING WITH REMOTE OBJECTS

> **NOTE**
>
> Make sure that you substitute your server's host name or IP address for
> 204.115.182.233 in the InfoClient applet's CODEBASE attribute. You can use
> localhost if you are running both the client and server on the same computer.

The InfoServer Interface

Listing 39.3 contains the InfoServer interface that is implemented by the server object
and referenced by the InfoClient applet. It is contained in the ju.ch39.info.server
package and defines the getInfo() method.

LISTING 39.3. THE InfoServer INTERFACE.

```
package ju.ch39.info.server;

import java.rmi.*;

public interface InfoServer extends Remote {
  String getInfo() throws RemoteException;
}
```

The InfoServerImpl Class

Listing 39.4 shows the InfoServerImpl class that implements the InfoServer interface.
It declares and initializes the info array to a list of five news flashes. The getInfo()
method retrieves the current date/time as a Date object and then randomly selects one of
the elements of the info array. It converts the Date to a String, appends the info element, and returns the String to the invoking object.

The main() method sets the default security manager and creates an instance of the
InfoServerImpl object. It invokes the rebind() method of the Naming class to register
the new object with the remote registry under the name InfoServer. It then displays a
message to the console window notifying you that the server object was successfully registered.

LISTING 39.4. THE InfoServerImpl CLASS.

```
package ju.ch39.info.server;

import java.rmi.*;
```

```
import java.rmi.server.*;
import java.util.*;

public class InfoServerImpl extends UnicastRemoteObject
 implements InfoServer {
 String info[] = {"Gold is up to $500 per ounce.",
  "The Chargers beat the Raiders 41-0.",
  "The weather will be hot and sunny.",
  "Computer prices are coming down.",
  "Java-based PDAs are flooding the market."};
 public InfoServerImpl() throws RemoteException {
  super();
 }
 public String getInfo() throws RemoteException {
  String newInfo;
  Date date=new Date();
  int n = new Double(100.0*Math.random()).intValue();
  n %= info.length;
  newInfo=date.toString()+" "+info[n];
  return newInfo;
 }
 public static void main(String args[]){
  System.setSecurityManager(new RMISecurityManager());
  try {
   InfoServerImpl instance = new InfoServerImpl();
   Naming.rebind("///InfoServer", instance);
   System.out.println("InfoServer is registered.");
  } catch (Exception ex) {
   System.out.println(ex.toString());
  }
 }
}
```

Compiling and Installing the `InfoServer` Application

Now that you've learned about each of the four source files, let's compile and install them on the server.

The `InfoServer.java` and `InfoServerImpl.java` files are in your `ch39\info\server` directory. Compile them and then use the `rmic` compiler to create a stub and skeleton for the `InfoServerImpl` class:

```
rmic ju.ch39.info.server.InfoServerImpl
```

Next, switch over to the client directory and compile `InfoClient.java`.

39

WORKING WITH
REMOTE OBJECTS

Your class files are ready to go. All you need to do is to move them to your Web server. Create the following codebase\ju\ch39\info\client and codebase\ju\ch39\ info\server paths on your Web server's root directory. Move the InfoClient.class and InfoClient$ButtonHandler.class classes to the codebase\ju\ch39\info\client directory and the InfoServer.class, InfoServerImpl.class, InfoServerImpl_Stub.class, and InfoServerImpl_Skel.class classes to the codebase\ju\ch39\info\server directory. Also, copy the info.htm file to your Web server's root directory. Your class files should now be organized as follows:

- *WebRoot*—info.htm
- *WebRoot*\codebase\ju\ch39\info\client—InfoClient.class and InfoClient$ButtonHandler.class
- *WebRoot*\codebase\ju\ch39\info\server—InfoServer.class, InfoServerImpl.class, InfoServerImpl_Stub.class, and InfoServerImpl_Skel.class

Substitute your Web server's root directory for *WebRoot*.

In order to execute the InfoServerImpl class, you'll need to include the codebase directory in the CLASSPATH of the computer that's hosting your Web server. Do this before going on to the next section. If you are running Windows 95, you'll have to restart your system for the new CLASSPATH to go into effect.

Running the `InfoServer` Application

Hang on. We're almost there. Just a few more things to do and we can run the InfoServer application.

At this time, you should start your Web server if it isn't already up and running. I'm using Sun's Java Web Server as my Web server for this example. I configured it so that it listens for HTTP requests on port 80 instead of the default port 8080.

Start the remote registry program as follows:

```
start rmiregistry
```

On Windows 95 systems, the preceding command will create and open a blank DOS window. Just minimize the window and go on.

Now start up the server object as follows:

```
java ju.ch39.info.server.InfoServerImpl
InfoServer is registered.
```

The server object will inform you that it has successfully registered itself with the remote registry program. That completes the server setup.

To run the application, you will need a Web browser that supports at least JDK 1.1. I'll use HotJava 1.1. You can also use Internet Explorer 4.0, Netscape Communicator 4.0, or `appletviewer`. From the same host or a different host, launch your browser and open up the URL `http://your.server.com/info.htm`, where `your.server.com` is the host name or IP address of the Web server where you installed the HTML and class files and ran the server object. If you are running the client and server on the same host, you can use `localhost` for your host name. Figure 39.1 shows the initial browser window. Now click the Update button a few times to receive news flashes from the remote object (refer to Figure 39.2).

Working with Class Loaders and Security Managers

The previous example showed how easy it is to use applets as the clients of distributed applications. After creating and compiling the required classes and starting the remote object, you just load the appropriate classes on your Web server. Users download the client applet as part of a Web page. No client installation is required.

The applet-based approach that you learned in the previous section works great for many distributed applications. However, there may be times when you want to run the client as an application and not as an applet. In this section, I'll show you an approach to distributing application clients that is almost as easy to use as the applet approach. This approach makes use of class loaders and security managers, and provides a practical introduction to these topics.

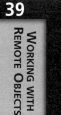

A Random Number Server

In many numerical applications such as simulations, applied genetic algorithms, and cryptography, it is important to have a good random number generator. All software-based random number generators are only pseudorandom and create repeating patterns after a time. Hardware-based random number generators, such as noisy diodes, have been developed that overcome the problems with software random number generators. Unfortunately, not everyone has immediate access to high-grade random number generators. That's where random number servers come in. You ask the server for a random number, and it gives you one.

The distributed application that you'll develop is a random number server. You'll be using the `Math.random()` function to generate random numbers. However, you can use this application as a basis for developing more advanced random number generators if you wish. The distributed application makes use of a random number client that is a window application program, as opposed to an applet. The client is maintained on a Web server, along with the random number server. A bootstrap program is developed that allows clients to remotely load the client. This bootstrap program is generic in nature and may be used with other distributed applications. The bootstrap program illustrates the use of class loaders and security managers within the context of distributed applications.

The `RandomServer` Interface

Listing 39.5 shows the `RandomServer` interface. This interface defines the `getRandom()` function that returns a double value between 0 and 1. Note that the interface is contained in the `ju.ch39.random.server` package.

LISTING 39.5. THE RandomServer INTERFACE.

```
package ju.ch39.random.server;

import java.rmi.*;

public interface RandomServer extends Remote {
  double getRandom() throws RemoteException;
}
```

The `RandomServerImpl` Class

The `RandomServerImpl` class, shown in Listing 39.6, implements the `RandomServer` interface. The `getRandom()` method just returns a random number generated by the standard `Math.random()` method. To implement a high-grade random number server, you would replace this method with one that obtains its data from an external random number source. You would probably use a native method to accomplish this (see Chapter 53, "Native Methods").

The `main()` method installs a default `RMISecurityManager` object as the security manager and registers an instance of the `RandomServerImpl` class with the remote registry. It then displays a message to the console window informing you of its success.

LISTING 39.6. THE RandomServerImpl CLASS.

```
package ju.ch39.random.server;

import java.rmi.*;
import java.rmi.server.*;

public class RandomServerImpl extends UnicastRemoteObject
 implements RandomServer {
 public RandomServerImpl() throws RemoteException {
  super();
 }
 public double getRandom() throws RemoteException {
  return Math.random();
 }
 public static void main(String args[]){
  System.setSecurityManager(new RMISecurityManager());
  try {
   RandomServerImpl instance = new RandomServerImpl();
   Naming.rebind("///RandomServer", instance);
   System.out.println("RandomServer is registered.");
  } catch (Exception ex) {
   System.out.println(ex.toString());
  }
 }
}
```

The `RandomClient` Class

The client application used with the random number server is shown in Listing 39.7. This application has an interesting twist. There's no `main()` method because the client's class file remains on the Web server and is loaded remotely (and executed) by a second bootstrap program. The bootstrap program is a generic program that can be used to remotely load distributed application clients. We'll cover the bootstrap program in the following section.

As a point of reference, Figure 39.3 shows the initial display of the `RandomClient` program. You click the New Random button and a new random number is displayed, as shown in Figure 39.4.

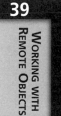

39

WORKING WITH
REMOTE OBJECTS

FIGURE 39.3.

*The initial display
of* RandomClient.

FIGURE 39.4.

*The random num-
ber returned by*
RandomServer.

Note that the host variable is assigned the IP address 204.115.182.233. You'll need to change this to your Web server's host name or IP address in order to run it with your Web server.

RandomClient implements the Runnable interface. This is so it can be executed as a sep-arate thread by the bootstrap program. It implements an empty run() method in order to satisfy the Runnable interface. The main processing performed by RandomClient is cre-ating the application window and handling the clicking of the New Random button.

During the creation of the application window, the connectToServer() method is invoked to obtain a reference to the RandomServer object. This reference is stored in the server variable.

The ButtonHandler class handles the clicking of the New Random button by invoking the getRandom() method of the RandomServer object and displaying the returned value as a text string.

LISTING 39.7. THE RandomClient CLASS.

```
package ju.ch39.random.client;

import ju.ch39.random.server.*;
import java.awt.*;
import java.awt.event.*;
import java.net.*;
import java.rmi.*;
import java.rmi.server.*;

public class RandomClient extends Frame implements Runnable {
 String host="204.115.182.233";
 TextField text = new TextField(50);
 Button newRandom = new Button("New Random");
 RandomServer server;
 int screenWidth = 500;
 int screenHeight = 100;
 public void run(){
```

```
    }
    public RandomClient() {
     super("RandomClient");
     setup();
     setSize(screenWidth,screenHeight);
     addWindowListener(new WindowEventHandler());
     show();
    }
    void setup() {
     setLayout(new FlowLayout(FlowLayout.LEFT));
     newRandom.addActionListener(new ButtonHandler());
     add(newRandom);
     add(text);
     connectToServer();
    }
    void connectToServer() {
     try {
      server = (RandomServer) Naming.lookup("//"+host+"/RandomServer");
     } catch (Exception ex) {
      text.setText(ex.toString());
     }
    }
    class ButtonHandler implements ActionListener {
     public void actionPerformed(ActionEvent ev){
      String s=ev.getActionCommand();
      if("New Random".equals(s)){
       try {
        double rand=server.getRandom();
        text.setText(new Double(rand).toString());
       } catch (Exception ex){
        text.setText(ex.toString());
       }
      }
     }
    }
    class WindowEventHandler extends WindowAdapter {
     public void windowClosing(WindowEvent e){
      System.exit(0);
     }
    }
}
```

The Bootstrap Class

We finally get to the Bootstrap class, shown in Listing 39.8. This class implements the most interesting processing of the RandomServer application. However, before I get into the details of this processing, let me summarize its operation. You run the Bootstrap program on the client and specify the URL and name of a client application (that is,

RandomClient). Bootstrap retrieves the client application from a remote Web server and executes it locally. The client application (running locally) uses RMI to invoke the methods of server objects (that is, RandomServer) executing on the Web server. The Bootstrap program solves the problem of maintaining and distributing client programs. The clients are maintained and stored on a central Web server. They can be upgraded and modified without having to be installed on users' computers. You only need to distribute the Bootstrap program, a small program that can be used to load and execute clients from any host.

The Bootstrap program is invoked with the -D option to set the java.rmi.server.codebase property to the URL where all classes should be loaded. The name of the class of the client program is also identified. The following is an example of the program's invocation:

```
java -Djava.rmi.server.codebase=http://host.com/codebase/ Bootstrap Client
```

The preceding command runs Bootstrap and sets the java.rmi.server.codebase property to http://host.com/codebase/. All classes are loaded from this URL. In particular, the Client class is loaded remotely and executed locally. Any classes that are loaded by Client are also loaded from the identified URL. If you can't picture how Bootstrap works, hang in there. When you actually run it, its function will be obvious.

Bootstrap is a simple console program. Its first few lines just display directions on how it is to be used. It is important to note that in the first line, it sets the security manager to an object of the BootstrapSecurityManager class. This class overrides RMISecurityManager and supports a more liberal policy for remotely loaded clients. BootstrapSecurityManager is covered in the next section.

The main processing performed by Bootstrap takes place within the try statement. It invokes the static loadClass() method of the RMIClassLoader class to load the class named as a command-line argument. This class is the name of the client application. The class is loaded from the URL specified by the java.rmi.server.codebase property.

The loaded class is assigned to the clientClass variable. An instance of the loaded class is then created and cast as a Runnable object. This creates a separate thread of execution. (That's why we implemented RandomClient as Runnable.) The run() method of the newly created thread is then invoked to cause the thread to be executed.

The three lines of code within the try statement accomplish quite a bit. They load a user-selected client application from a specified URL and execute it locally.

LISTING 39.8. THE Bootstrap CLASS.

```
import java.rmi.*;
import java.rmi.server.*;

public class Bootstrap {
 public static void main(String args[]) {
  System.setSecurityManager(new BootstrapSecurityManager());
  if(args.length!=1){
   System.out.print("Usage: java -Djava.rmi.server.codebase=URL ");
   System.out.println("Bootstrap clientName");
   System.out.println("\n  Notes:");
   System.out.print("    Use a URL of the form: ");
   System.out.println("http://host.com/codebase/");
   System.out.print("    Substitute the name of the client's ");
   System.out.println("class for clientName");
   System.out.println("\n  Example:");
   System.out.print("    java -Djava.rmi.server.codebase=");
   System.out.println("http://host.com/codebase/ Bootstrap Client");
   System.exit(0);
  }
  System.out.println("Loading "+args[0]+" ...");
  try {
   Class clientClass = RMIClassLoader.loadClass(args[0]);
   Runnable clientInstance = (Runnable) clientClass.newInstance();
   clientInstance.run();
  } catch (Exception ex) {
   System.out.println(ex.toString());
  }
 }
}
```

The `BootstrapSecurityManager` Class

The `BootstrapSecurityManager` class is needed for `Bootstrap` to run without any security exceptions. The default `RMISecurityManager` is somewhat restrictive in the capabilities it permits for remotely loaded applications. It is similar to the security manager used with applets in this regard. How do we overcome these restrictions? By extending `RMISecurityManager` and overriding the methods that perform certain security checks.

Listing 39.9 shows the methods of `RMISecurityManager` that are overridden by `BootstrapSecurityManager`. These methods check a variety of operations to determine whether they are permissible under the RMI security policy. The `RMISecurityManager` methods with a void return value raise a `SecurityException` when an operation that violates the RMI security policy is detected. By overriding them in

BootstrapSecurityManager, you prevent the SecurityException from occurring. The checkTopLevelWindow() method returns a boolean value indicating whether it is permissible for a remotely loaded class to open a top-level application window. By always returning a true value, you ensure that a top-level window can be created and opened by the remotely loaded client.

The methods that have been overridden by BootstrapSecurityManager are described in the RMISecurityManager class. You can override other methods in addition to these. The methods that were overridden were selected to allow clients, like RandomClient, to execute without a SecurityException.

LISTING 39.9. THE BootstrapSecurityManager CLASS.

```
import java.rmi.*;
import java.io.*;

public class BootstrapSecurityManager extends RMISecurityManager {
 public synchronized void checkAccess(Thread t){}
 public synchronized void checkAccess(ThreadGroup g){}
 public synchronized void checkExit(int status){}
 public synchronized void checkPropertiesAccess(){}
 public synchronized void checkAccept(String host,int port){}
 public synchronized void checkConnect(String host,int port){}
 public synchronized boolean checkTopLevelWindow(Object window){
  return true;
 }
 public synchronized void checkPackageAccess(String pkg){}
 public void checkAwtEventQueueAccess(){}
 public synchronized void checkRead(FileDescriptor fd){}
 public synchronized void checkRead(String file){}
}
```

Compiling and Installing the RandomServer Application

You compile and install the RandomServer application using the following steps:

1. Compile RandomServer.java, RandomServerImpl.java, and RandomClient.java.

2. Run rmic on RandomServerImpl to create RandomServerImpl_Stub.class and RandomServerImpl_Skel.class. Remember to run rmic using the full package name of RandomServerImpl (that is, rmic ju.ch39.random.server. RandomServerImpl).

3. Move RandomServer.class, RandomServerImpl.class, RandomServerImpl_Stub.class, and RandomServerImpl_Skel.class to the /codebase/ju/ch39/random/server directory off of your Web server's root.

4. Move RandomClient.class, RandomClient$WindowEventHandler.class, and RandomClient$ButtonHandler.class to the /codebase/ju/ch39/random/client directory off of your Web server's root.

5. Make sure that the codebase directory is in your CLASSPATH.

6. Compile BootstrapSecurityManager.java and Bootstrap.java.

7. Copy Bootstrap.class and BootstrapSecurityManager.class to the client computer.

This may seem like a lot of work, but you'll only have to do all but the last step once. You'll need to copy the Bootstrap classes to any clients that want to load a client application remotely.

Running the RandomServer Application

To run the RandomServer application, do the following:

1. Make sure that your Web server is running.

2. Start rmiregistry on your Web server host.

3. Run java ju.ch39.random.server.RandomServerImpl on your Web server host.

4. Run the Bootstrap program on the client.

The last step is performed as follows:

```
java -Djava.rmi.server.codebase=http://204.115.182.233/codebase/
↪Bootstrap ju.ch39.random.client.RandomClient
```

Substitute your Web server's host name or IP address for 204.115.182.233.

> **NOTE**
>
> If you intend to use the Bootstrap program, you may want to consider putting the long command line in a batch file.

When you run Bootstrap, it loads RandomClient from your Web server and executes it locally. Figure 39.3 shows its opening display. When you click the New Random button, RandomClient invokes the getRandom() method of the RandomServer object (executing on your Web server) and displays the value returned by getRandom().

39

WORKING WITH REMOTE OBJECTS

Locating Remote Objects

In a large network running a multitude of server objects, it is sometimes difficult to keep track of which objects are running on which hosts. In this section, we'll develop a client application named Browser that enables you to browse a host's registry to see which remote objects it supports.

Listing 39.10 shows the Browser program. You compile it using javac Browser.java and run it using java Browser. Before you run Browser, start rmiregistry and run RandomServerImpl and InfoServerImpl. This will put two object names in your remote registry.

The Browser application's opening window is shown in Figure 39.5. Enter the name of the host running the remote registry and click the Browse host button. The text area in the center of the program window displays the objects that are maintained in the local registry. (See Figure 39.6.) You can also use this program to browse the remote registries of other hosts.

FIGURE 39.5.

The Browser *opening display.*

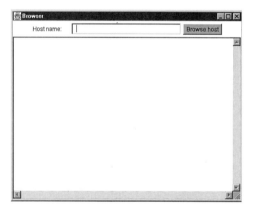

Browser's ButtonEventHandler uses the static getRegistry() method of the LocateRegistry class to return a Registry object for a specified host. The list() method of the Registry interface returns an array that contains the names of all objects that are currently registered in the registry. These objects are displayed to the text area in the middle of the Browser window.

FIGURE 39.6.

Browser *displays the remote objects maintained by the remote registry on the specified host.*

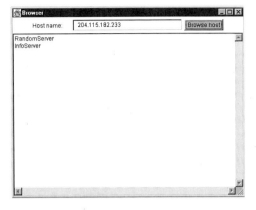

LISTING 39.10. THE Browser PROGRAM.

```
import java.awt.*;
import java.awt.event.*;
import java.rmi.registry.*;

public class Browser extends Frame {
 TextField host = new TextField(30);
 TextArea objectNames = new TextArea(15,50);
 Button browse = new Button("Browse host");
 int screenWidth = 500;
 int screenHeight = 400;
 public static void main(String args[]){
  Browser app = new Browser();
 }
 public Browser() {
  super("Browser");
  setup();
  setSize(screenWidth,screenHeight);
  addWindowListener(new WindowEventHandler());
  show();
 }
 void setup() {
  browse.addActionListener(new ButtonHandler());
  Panel panel = new Panel();
  panel.add(new Label("Host name: "));
  panel.add(host);
  panel.add(browse);
  add("North",panel);
  add("Center",objectNames);
 }
```

39

WORKING WITH
REMOTE OBJECTS

continues

LISTING 39.10. CONTINUED

```
class ButtonHandler implements ActionListener {
  public void actionPerformed(ActionEvent ev){
    String s=ev.getActionCommand();
    if("Browse host".equals(s)){
      try {
        Registry registry = LocateRegistry.getRegistry(host.getText());
        String objectList[] = registry.list();
        String objects="";
        for(int i=0;i<objectList.length;++i){
          objects+=objectList[i]+"\n";
        }
        objectNames.setText(objects);
      } catch (Exception ex){
        objectNames.setText(ex.toString());
      }
    }
  }
}
class WindowEventHandler extends WindowAdapter {
  public void windowClosing(WindowEvent e){
    System.exit(0);
  }
}
}
```

Automatic Object Activation

One of the new RMI features introduced in JDK 1.2 is the remote object activation framework. This framework allows you to activate remote objects remotely, deactivate the objects when they are not being used, and then reactivate the objects when needed. This capability is very important when you're developing large distributed systems consisting of many objects running on many computers. In these large distributed systems, it is impractical to have all objects running at the same time. Remote object activation allows you to build distributed systems that are more reliable and resource-efficient. Reliability is increased because remote object references are not transient references to object instances, but persistent references to objects that can be reactivated across multiple instances.

How Remote Activation Works

Remote activation is easy to understand and use, once you learn its terminology and work through an example. This section covers the terminology and introduces the concepts involved. The following section describes the mechanics of creating an activatable object. The section after that provides a remote activation example.

A remote object is *active* when it is instantiated within a Java Virtual Machine and exported for access via RMI. A remote object is *inactive* when it is not yet instantiated or exported. *Activation* is the process of transforming an inactive object into an active object. This involves instantiating the object within a JVM and restoring its state. An *activatable* object is an object that is capable of being activated.

RMI uses a form of remote activation that is referred to as *lazy activation*. Lazy activation does not mean that activation is slow or reticent. It means that a remote object is not activated until one of its methods has been invoked.

Lazy activation is implemented using a technique called *faulting remote references*. A remote reference to an object consists of the following two components:

A transient remote object reference.

A persistent object activation ID.

The transient remote object reference, or *live* reference, is a reference to an instance of a remote object. When a remote object is no longer active, the live reference is no longer valid. The persistent object activation ID is an object identifier that is valid whether the object is active or inactive. The activation ID provides a reference to the object's activator, which you'll learn about shortly.

When a client object invokes a method of an activatable remote object, the live reference is checked to determine whether it is valid. If it is not valid (that is, a faulting remote reference), the remote object's activation ID is used to activate the remote object and create a valid live reference. Activation of the remote object is performed using the *activation protocol*.

The activation protocol makes use of a special object, referred to as the *activator*. The activator is executed on a remote host as the result of running the `rmid` program that comes with JDK 1.2. The activator maintains a database of information that maps activatable objects to information that is needed to activate them, such as an object's class name and its code source (location). This information is referred to as an *activation descriptor*. The activator also maintains information on activation groups and instances of the JVM that are executing on the remote computer.

Each executing JVM is associated with an *activation group*. The activation group of a JVM is used to activate objects on that JVM. When the activator receives a faulting remote reference, it uses the object's activation ID (included in the reference) to look up the object's activation descriptor. The activation descriptor tells the activator what class to load, where to load it from (its code source), where to activate it (its activation group), and how to initialize the object. The activator checks for an executing JVM with the required activation group. If none is found, it creates one. The activator then requests the activation group to activate the object within the JVM. The activation group returns a valid live reference to the activated object, which is passed back to the client object making the method invocation.

> **NOTE**
>
> In order to use remote activation, you must first run the remote activation system daemon, rmid. You run it by typing start rmid in a console window.

Creating an Activatable Object

In order to create an activatable object, you must do three things:

1. Register an activation descriptor for a remote object.
2. Provide special constructors to be used for initial creation and activation.
3. Export the object for remote access.

You must register the activation descriptor with the activator so the activator will have the information it needs to activate the object. The object's activation group uses the special constructors to create and activate (or reactivate) the object.

There are two ways to accomplish steps 1 and 2—the easy way and the hard way. The easy way is to have your object's class extend `java.rmi.activation.Activatable`. When you do this, registration and export are taken care of when your object is constructed. You still need to provide the special constructors, but you can take advantage of the constructors provided by `Activatable`. The hard way requires you to use the static `register()` and `exportObject()` methods of `Activatable`. The hard way isn't very difficult; it just involves more work. The advantage of not extending `Activatable` is that your class can appear somewhere else in the class hierarchy.

The special constructors that you need to implement have the following signatures:

- *className*(CodeSource source, MarshalledObject data, int port)—This constructor is used initially to create the remote object, register it, and export it for access on a particular port. The first line of this type of constructor is usually a call to the superclass constructor (via super()) passing along these parameters. The CodeSource parameter identifies the location of the class's code. The MarshalledObject parameter is used to initialize the object. The int port parameter is used to identify the TCP port on which the object is accessed. Setting this parameter to 0 causes an anonymous port to be used.

- *className*(ActivationID id, MarshalledObject data)—This constructor is used to activate or reactivate an inactive object. The ActivationID parameter is used to identify the object's activation descriptor. The MarshalledObject parameter is used to initialize the object.

You'll see examples of both of these constructors in the following sections.

A Remote Activation Example

Now that you've covered the terminology and mechanics of remote activation, you'll create and use an example of a remotely activatable object. This example will consist of the following classes and interfaces:

- ActivationClient—This class implements the application's client software. The client displays activation state information and the value of a counter received from the remote server (see Listing 39.11).

- ActivationServer—This interface specifies the methods that are made available from the remote server (see Listing 39.12).

- ActivationServerImpl—This class implements the remote server (see Listing 39.13).

- ActivationServerImpl_Stub and ActivationServerImpl_Skel—These classes are the stub and skeleton classes used with ActivationServerImpl. These classes are generated by running rmic with ActivationServerImpl.

We'll examine the code of the client, server interface, and server before going on to the example.

The ActivationClient class

The ActivationClient class is located in its own package, ju.ch39.activation.client, and consists of a single main() method. It displays the string ActivationClient to let you know that it is up and running, and then creates a remote reference to an ActivationServer object by using the lookup() method of the Naming class. I've hardcoded the IP address of my remote server (204.212.153.194) as an argument to the lookup() method. Substitute your server's host name or IP address for 204.212.153.194.

The main() method loops three times and displays the values returned by the getCount() and getState() methods that are invoked on the ActivationServer object. The getCount() method retrieves the value of a counter. The getState() method retrieves the activation state of the remote server object.

After the first for loop, the deactivate() method is invoked to cause the server object to deactivate itself. Another for loop follows that displays the results of getCount() and getState() after the server has been deactivated.

LISTING 39.11. THE ActivationClient CLASS.

```
import ju.ch39.activation.server.*;
import java.rmi.*;

public class ActivationClient {
 public static void main(String args[]){
  System.out.println("ActivationClient");
  try {
   ActivationServer server = (ActivationServer)
    Naming.lookup("//204.212.153.194/ActivationServer");
   for(int i=0;i<3;++i) {
    System.out.print(server.getCount()+" ");
    System.out.println(server.getState());
   }
   server.deactivate();
   for(int i=0;i<3;++i) {
    System.out.print(server.getCount()+" ");
    System.out.println(server.getState());
   }
  } catch (Exception ex){
   System.out.println(ex);
  }
 }
}
```

The ActivationServer Interface

The ActivationServer interface declares the getCount(), getState(), and deactivate() methods used by ActivationClient and implemented by ActivationServerImpl. It is part of the ju.ch39.activation.server package.

LISTING 39.12. THE ActivationServer INTERFACE.

```
package ju.ch39.activation.server;

import java.rmi.*;

public interface ActivationServer extends Remote {
 int getCount() throws RemoteException;
 String getState() throws RemoteException;
 void deactivate() throws RemoteException;
}
```

The `ActivationServerImpl` Class

The `ActivationServerImpl` class implements the `ActivationServer` remote interface and extends the `Activatable` class. It defines the `activationState` variable to keep track of whether it has been initially created or has been reactivated. The `count` variable is used to implement a simple counter.

The `ActivationServerImpl` constructors illustrate the special constructors that are used with activatable objects. The first constructor is used for initially creating, registering, and exporting an object. It uses the superclass constructor to perform most of the processing. It then sets `activationState` to `object created` and binds itself to `ActivationServer`. The second constructor is used for activating and reactivating objects that have been created but have been deactivated. Like the first constructor, it uses the superclass constructor to perform most of the processing. It then sets `activationState` to `object reactivated` and binds itself to `ActivationServer`.

The `getCount()` and `getState()` methods return the value of `count` and `activationState`. The `deactivate()` method uses the `getID()` method to get its activation ID and passes the ID to the static `inactive()` method of the `Activatable` class. This causes the object to be deactivated. Once deactivated, an object must be reactivated in order to receive subsequent method invocations.

The `main()` method constructs a new `ActivationServerImpl` object and displays a message identifying that an `ActivationServer` object has been registered. I've put the required `.class` files on my Web server and used them as the code source. You should substitute your Web server's name within the code source's URL.

LISTING 39.13. THE `ActivationServerImpl` CLASS.

```
package ju.ch39.activation.server;

import java.rmi.*;
import java.rmi.server.*;
import java.rmi.activation.*;
import java.util.*;
import java.net.*;
import java.security.*;

// Extend Activatable instead of UnicastRemoteObject
public class ActivationServerImpl extends Activatable
 implements ActivationServer {
 String activationState = "undefined";
 int count = 0;
// Constructor used for creation
 public ActivationServerImpl(CodeSource source,
```

39

WORKING WITH
REMOTE OBJECTS

continues

LISTING 39.13. CONTINUED

```
 MarshalledObject data,int port)
 throws RemoteException, ActivationException {
super(source,data,port);
activationState="object created";
try {
 Naming.rebind("///ActivationServer", this);
}catch(Exception ex){
 System.out.println(ex);
}
}
// Constructor used for activation
public ActivationServerImpl(ActivationID id,
 MarshalledObject data)
 throws RemoteException {
super(id,0);
activationState="object reactivated";
try {
 Naming.rebind("///ActivationServer", this);
}catch(Exception ex){
 System.out.println(ex);
}
}
public int getCount() throws RemoteException {
 ++count;
 return count;
}
public String getState() throws RemoteException {
 String temp = activationState;
 activationState = "object active";
 return temp;
}
public void deactivate() throws RemoteException {
 try {
  Activatable.inactive(this.getID());
 }catch(ActivationException ex){
  System.out.println(ex);
 }
}
public static void main(String args[]){
 try {
  String className = "ju.ch39.activation.server.ActivationServerImpl";
  URL url = new URL("http://204.212.153.194/codebase/");
  CodeSource source = new CodeSource(url,null);
  new ActivationServerImpl(source,null,0);
  System.out.println("ActivationServer is registered.");
 } catch (Exception ex) {
  System.out.println(ex);
 }
}
}
```

Compiling, Installing, and Running Activation Server

To compile, install, and run the client and server objects, follow these steps:

1. Edit `ActivationClient.java` and `ActivationServerImpl.java`, substituting your host name or IP address for `204.212.153.194`.

2. Compile `ActivationServer.java` and then `ActivationServerImpl.java`.

3. Compile `ActivationClient.java`.

4. Copy the `ActivationClient.class` and `ActivationServerImpl_Stub.class` files to the client machine. Make sure that `ActivationServerImpl_Stub.class` is accessible from the `CLASSPATH` of the client machine.

5. Copy `ActivationServer.class`, `ActivationServerImpl.class`, and `ActivationServerImpl_Skel.class` to the `codebase\ju\ch39\activation\` server directory on your Web server's root directory. This should be the server machine.

6. Run `start rmiregistry` on the server machine.

7. Run `start rmid` on the server machine.

8. Run `java ju.ch39.activation.server.ActivationServerImpl` on the server machine.

9. Run `java ActivationClient` on the client machine.

When you run `java ju.ch39.activation.server.ActivationServerImpl` on the server machine, it displays the following message to let you know that it is up and running:

```
ActivationServer is registered.
```

When you run `java ActivationClient` on the client machine, it displays the following output:

```
ActivationClient
1 object created
2 object active
3 object active
1 object reactivated
2 object active
3 object active
```

You should follow the code in Listings 39.11 and 39.13 when examining this output. The first line indicates that `ActivationClient` is up and running. The second line indicates that the value of `count` is 1 and that `activationState` is `object created`. The next two lines indicate that `count` has been incremented and that the same object continues to be active. The fifth line occurs after `ActivationClient` invokes the `deactivate()` method

39

WORKING WITH
REMOTE OBJECTS

of `ActivationServer`. It indicates that the remote object became inactive and was later reactivated. Note that when the object was reactivated, the value of `count` was reset. The last two lines show `count` being incremented while the remote object continues to be active.

Summary

In this chapter, you developed a few distributed applications that gave you some practical experience using RMI. You created an applet that uses RMI to connect to a server object, retrieve information, and display the information in a text area. You created a random number server and a client that accesses the server. You learned how to use class loaders and security managers to bootstrap the client from a remote host. You developed a program that contacts the remote registry of a host and obtains a list of the remote objects that it services. You also learned how to use remote activation. In the next chapter, you'll learn about object serialization, an important topic for RMI and JavaBeans.

Using Object Serialization and JavaSpaces

CHAPTER **40**

Most meaningful Java applications provide a way to save the Java objects they create and to restore these objects at a later point in time. For example, in Chapter 26, "Developing Beans," you saw how the BeanBox lets you change the properties of a component and then save the component's state. The BeanBox also lets you restore the state of a saved component.

The capability for an object to exist beyond the execution of the program that created it is known as *persistence. Serialization* is the key to implementing persistence, providing the capability to write an object to a stream and to read the object back in at a later time.

Serialization allows you to store objects in files, communicate them across networks, and use them in distributed applications. In this chapter, you'll be introduced to object serialization. You'll learn how it works and how it is used in both distributed and non-distributed applications. You'll cover the `Serializable` and `Externalizable` interfaces and the security issues related to object serialization. When you finish this chapter, you'll be better able to use serialization in your programs.

Storing Objects to Streams

On the surface, the process of storing an object to a stream may seem trivial. But in fact, it is quite involved. When an object is written to a stream, information about its class must be stored along with the object. Without class information, there is no way to reconstruct an object that is read from a stream. In addition to class information, all objects that are referenced by that object must also be stored. If the referenced objects are not stored along with the object, the references of the stored object become meaningless.

The `Serializable` Interface

The JDK 1.2 provides the `Serializable` and `Externalizable` interfaces of the `java.io` package to support object serialization. The `Serializable` interface is easy to use. It contains no methods. You just declare your class as being `Serializable` and use the `ObjectOutputStream` filter to write objects to a stream. The `writeObject()` method of `ObjectOutputStream` automatically takes care of storing the correct information when objects of the class are written to a stream. Objects are read back in using the `readObject()` method of the `ObjectInputStream` class. The objects that are read back in are cast to their original types.

Listing 40.1 provides an example of using the `Serializable` interface. The `SerialApp` program creates an instance of `ObjectOutputStream` on the `temp` file and assigns it to the `outputStream` variable. It invokes the `getProperties()` method of the `System` class to obtain the current system properties. It invokes the `writeObject()` method of `ObjectOutputStream` to write the `Properties` object to the output stream. Note that the `Properties` class is `Serializable`. It then closes the output stream and creates an instance of `ObjectInputStream` on the `temp` file. It reads an object from the input stream using the `readObject()` method of the `ObjectInputStream` class. The object is cast into an object of the `Properties` class and assigned to the `newProp` variable. The `list()` method of the `Properties` class displays the object as follows:

```
-- listing properties --
java.specification.name=Java Platform API Specification
awt.toolkit=sun.awt.windows.WToolkit
java.version=1.2beta2
java.awt.graphicsenv=sun.awt.Win32GraphicsEnvironment
java.tmpdir=C:\WINDOWS\TEMP\
user.timezone=PST
java.specification.version=1.2beta2
user.home=D:\JDK1.2BETA2\BIN\..
java-vm.name=non-JIT
os.arch=x86
java.awt.fonts=C:\WINDOWS\Fonts
java.vendor.url=http://www.sun.com/
user.region=US
file.encoding.pkg=sun.io
java.home=D:\JDK1.2BETA2\BIN\..
java-vm.specification.vendor=Sun Microsystems Inc.
java-vm.specification.version=1.0
java.class.path=.;D:\JDK1.2BETA2\BIN\..\classes;D:\JD...
line.separator=

os.name=Windows 95
java.vendor=Sun Microsystems Inc.
java.library.path=D:\JDK1.2BETA2\BIN;.;C:\WINDOWS;C:\WI...
java-vm.version=1.2beta2
file.encoding=8859_1
java.specification.vendor=Sun Microsystems Inc.
user.name=jaworskij
user.language=en
java.vendor.url.bug=http://java.sun.com/cgi-bin/bugreport...
java.class.version=45.3
os.version=4.0
path.separator=;
java-vm.specification.name=Java Virtual Machine Specification
user.dir=D:\jdk1.2beta2\ju\ch36
file.separator=\
java-vm.vendor=Sun Microsystems Inc.
```

The properties that are displayed on your computer will differ depending on your operating system and how you have set up the JDK.

Java's object serialization capabilities make it easy to read and write objects from a file. Without these capabilities, you would be forced to read and write each primitive value of each property.

LISTING 40.1. THE SerialApp PROGRAM.

```
import java.io.*;
import java.util.*;

public class SerialApp {
 public static void main(String args[]) {
  try {
   ObjectOutputStream outputStream = new ObjectOutputStream(
    new FileOutputStream("temp"));
   Properties prop = System.getProperties();
   outputStream.writeObject(prop);
   outputStream.close();
   ObjectInputStream inputStream = new ObjectInputStream(
    new FileInputStream("temp"));
   Properties newProp = (Properties) inputStream.readObject();
   inputStream.close();
   newProp.list(System.out);
  } catch(Exception ex) {
   System.out.println(ex.toString());
  }
 }
}
```

Special Requirements for Using `Serializable`

Only objects that are `Serializable` can be stored to a stream using the `ObjectOuputStream` class. This includes all objects that are referenced by the object being written. If the object being written to a stream refers to an object that is not `Serializable`, the `NotSerializableException` is thrown.

When a serialized object is written to a stream, the class of the object, the class's signature, and the values of all non-transient and non-static field variables are written to the stream. If an object references other objects (except in `transient` or `static` fields), those objects are also written to the stream.

> **NOTE**
>
> TStatic and `transient` field variables are not saved when a `Serializable` object is written to a stream using the `writeObject()`. These field variables are ignored by `readObject()` when a `Serializable` object is read from a stream.

In order for a class to be `Serializable`, its parent class must either be `Serializable` or have a default constructor that does not take any arguments. The no-argument constructor is used to initialize an object's parent class when the object is read from a stream. If a parent class is not `Serializable`, it is the responsibility of the `Serializable` subclass to save and restore the state of its parent beyond the default initialization. A `Serializable` class can tailor the way that it is serialized by declaring `readObject()` and `writeObject()`methods of the following form:

```
private void writeObject(ObjectOutputStream stream) throws IOException {
}
private void readObject(ObjectInputStream stream) throws IOException,
ClassNotFoundException {
}
```

In general, because all primitive types and most classes are `Serializable`, you don't need to mess around with tailoring the way that your classes are serialized.

The serialver Tool

You can determine if a class is `Serializable` by looking up its API description or writing a program to see if its objects are instances of the `Serializable` interface. In some cases, the first alternative may not be possible—you may be using a class that is not documented. The second alternative is somewhat of an inconvenience. The `serialver` tool that is included with the JDK 1.2 provides a quick and easy way to determine if a class is `Serializable`. It also returns the `serialVersionUID` of the class. The `serialVersionUID` is used to uniquely identify the class of an object that is written to a stream. The `serialver` tool can be run from the command line by identifying the fully qualified name of a class as an argument. Examples of its use follow:

```
serialver java.lang.Object
Class java.lang.Object is not Serializable.

serialver java.lang.String
java.lang.String:    static final long serialVersionUID =
➥-6849794470754667710L;
```

You can also run `serialver` as a window application by invoking it with the `-show` option. For example, `serialver -show` creates the application window shown in Figure 40.1. You can then enter the name of the class you want to check and click the Show button. The program displays the results of the query, as shown in Figures 40.2 and 40.3.

FIGURE 40.1.

The window version of serialver.

FIGURE 40.2.

The serialver *program identifies the* serialVersionUID *of a class.*

FIGURE 40.3.

The serialver *program identifies a class as not being* Serializable.

The Externalizable Interface

The Serializable interface and the writeObject() and readObject() methods of ObjectOutputStream and ObjectInputStream provide the most convenient way to save objects to a stream and restore them at a later time. This convenience comes at the expense of relinquishing control of how the objects are stored in and read from streams.

The `Externalizable` interface extends the `Serializable` interface to provide you with additional control over how objects are written to and read from streams. Because the `Externalizable` interface extends the `Serializable` interface, you can use `Externalizable` objects with `ObjectOutputStream` and `ObjectInputStream` in the same manner that you could use `Serializable` objects. The only difference being that the class of an `Externalizable` object must implement the `writeExternal()` and `readExternal()` methods defined by the `Externalizable` interfaces. These methods are of the following form:

```
public void writeExternal(ObjectOutput out) throws IOException {
}

public void readExternal(ObjectInput in) throws IOException,
ClassNotFoundException {
}
```

The `writeExternal()` method is implemented by an `Externalizable` object to write itself to an output stream represented by an `ObjectOutput` interface. The `ObjectOutput` interface provides methods for writing objects to an output stream. The `ObjectOutput` interface extends the `DataOutput` interface, which provides methods for writing primitive types to an output stream.

The `readExternal()` method is the input analog of the `writeExternal()` method. It is implemented by an `Externalizable` object to read its values from an input stream represented by an `ObjectInput` interface. The `ObjectInput` interface provides methods for reading objects from an input stream. It extends the `DataInput` interface, which provides methods for reading primitive data types from an input stream. When an `Externalizable` object is read from an input stream, an instance of the object is created using its default no-argument constructor. The object's `readExternal()` method is then invoked.

The `Externalizable` interface gives you complete control over the way that objects are written to and read from streams. This control comes at the expense of having to implement your own methods for reading and writing the objects. The `Exteralizable` objects are responsible for storing and retrieving the state of their parent class, as well as any objects that they reference.

Listing 40.2 provides an example of using the `Externalizable` interface. The `main()` method of `ExternalApp` is similar to the `main()` method of `SerialApp`. The only difference is that you are writing and reading an object of `MyClass`.

The `MyClass` class implements the `Externalizable` interface. It declares three variables that are of the `GregorianCalendar` and `String` types. Its no-argument constructor creates a default `GregorianCalendar` object and two strings that are set to `uninitialized`. Its other constructor takes a `Date` parameter. It invokes the `setFieldValues()` method to set the `cal`, `timeVal`, and `dateVal` variables based on the value of the `Date` object that is passed as a parameter.

The `writeExternal()` method saves a `MyClass` object to a stream as a `Date` object. The `Date` object is created using the `getTime()` method of the `Calendar` class. The `readExternal()` method reads a `MyClass` object as a `Date` object and invokes the `setFieldValues()` method to initialize the fields of the `MyClass` object.

The `toString()` method returns a `String` value of a `MyClass` object. The `setFieldValues()` method initializes the field variables of a `MyClass` object based on the value of a `Date` parameter.

The `ExternalApp` program shows how the `Externalizable` interface is used to control the manner in which objects are serialized. The `writeExternal()` and `readExternal()` methods serialize `MyClass` objects as `Date` objects. This allows these objects to be stored in a more compact form.

The program displays the current date and time as shown:

```
java ExternalApp
1/15/1998 2:5:4
```

LISTING 40.2. THE `ExternalApp` PROGRAM.

```
import java.io.*;
import java.util.*;

public class ExternalApp {
 public static void main(String args[]) {
   try {
     ObjectOutputStream outputStream = new ObjectOutputStream(
       new FileOutputStream("temp"));
     MyClass obj = new MyClass(new Date());
     outputStream.writeObject(obj);
     outputStream.close();
     ObjectInputStream inputStream = new ObjectInputStream(
       new FileInputStream("temp"));
     MyClass newObj = (MyClass) inputStream.readObject();
     inputStream.close();
     System.out.println(newObj);
   } catch(Exception ex) {
     System.out.println(ex.toString());
   }
 }
}
```

```
class MyClass implements Externalizable {
 GregorianCalendar cal;
 String timeVal;
 String dateVal;
 public MyClass() {
  cal = new GregorianCalendar();
  timeVal="uninitialized";
  dateVal="uninitialized";
 }
 public MyClass(Date d){
  cal = new GregorianCalendar();
  setFieldValues(d);
 }
 public void writeExternal(ObjectOutput out) throws IOException {
  out.writeObject(cal.getTime());
 }
 public void readExternal(ObjectInput in) throws IOException,
  ClassNotFoundException {
  Date date = (Date) in.readObject();
  setFieldValues(date);
 }
 public String toString() {
  if(timeVal=="uninitialized") return timeVal;
  return dateVal+" "+timeVal;
 }
 void setFieldValues(Date d){
  cal.setTime(d);
  timeVal = String.valueOf(cal.get(cal.HOUR))+":";
  timeVal += String.valueOf(cal.get(cal.MINUTE))+":";
  timeVal += String.valueOf(cal.get(cal.SECOND));
  dateVal = String.valueOf(cal.get(cal.MONTH)+1)+"/";
  dateVal += String.valueOf(cal.get(cal.DATE))+"/";
  dateVal += String.valueOf(cal.get(cal.YEAR));
 }
}
```

Object Serialization and RMI

Object serialization is used extensively in remote method invocation. It is used to send the arguments of a method invocation from the client object to the remote object, and to send return values from the server object back to the client object. As a consequence, all arguments to a remote method invocation must be `Serializable`. Similarly, any values returned by a remote object must also be `Serializable`.

The serialization used by RMI is transparent to the client and server objects. It is performed by the stubs and skeletons, remote reference layer, and transport layer. This is a great convenience and a major benefit of RMI. Applications that use TCP sockets for client/server communication are responsible for serializing and deserializing objects via input and output streams. With RMI, you only need to ensure that your arguments and return values are `Serializable`, and RMI takes care of serialization and deserialization. Refer to Chapter 39, "Remote Method Invocation."

Security Considerations

Because object serialization is used as the primary mechanism to store and retrieve Java objects and to send them over a network, it is of considerable importance to the security of Java objects and programs. While a Java object is stored in a file or is being transmitted over a network, it is outside of the Java Virtual Machine and is vulnerable to deliberate or accidental modification. In addition, any sensitive data contained in the object can be read.

Whenever an object is read from a stream, the object cannot be trusted to be a faithful representation of the object that was written to the stream. The validity of an object must be determined when it is read. This can be accomplished by implementing the `readObject()` and `writeObject()` or `readExternal()` and `writeExternal()` methods. A digital signature of the object can be created, using the methods of the Security API, and stored with the object. The object's signature can be verified when the object is read from the stream.

When sensitive information contained in an object is written to a stream, that information is subject to disclosure. One solution to this problem is to encrypt objects when they are serialized. This can be readily accomplished using the Security API by creating output and input streams that act as filters for the `ObjectOutputStream` and `ObjectInputStream` classes. Refer to Chapter 3, "The Extended Java Security Model," and Chapter 8, "Applet Security," for information on using encryption with Java.

Another solution involves the judicious use of static and transient variables. Because static and transient variables are never serialized, the information contained in these variables is never exposed. The drawback to this approach is that the sensitive information is not persistent and expires at the termination of the program that created it. An even harsher solution would be to ensure that sensitive objects do not implement the `Serializable` or `Externalizable` interfaces.

JavaSpaces

JavaSoft is currently researching new approaches to building distributed systems. Part of this research is referred to as *JavaSpaces* and is aimed at providing more advanced mechanisms to supported distributed object persistence and data exchange. The JavaSpaces model is shown in Figure 40.4. In this model, JavaSpaces are objects that hold other objects called *entries*. Each entry is a typed group of objects that is stored in the JavaSpace. Entries can be written to, read from, and deleted from a JavaSpace. JavaSpaces can be searched to find entries using *templates*. Templates are entries whose fields are set to search patterns. A JavaSpace can also provide notification of events related to entries. JavaSpaces support secure transaction processing and eliminate the need for distributed coordination between objects that concurrently access a JavaSpace. Access controls are performed by identifying the objects that make requests of a particular JavaSpace and entry.

FIGURE 40.4.

The JavaSpaces model.

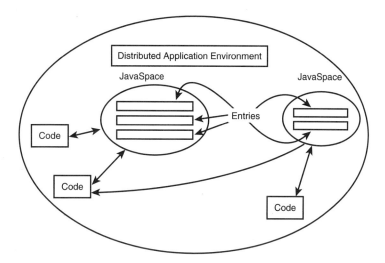

JavaSpaces are useful for building distributed applications because they allow distributed objects to be stored in a persistent manner and managed independently of the applications they support. They provide distributed access controls, enable distributed event processing, and support *flow of objects* application models. Flow of objects models implement work flows using objects that are read to and taken from JavaSpaces. JavaSpaces is not part of JDK 1.2 but may be integrated within future JDK releases.

Summary

In this chapter, you were introduced to object serialization. You learned how it works and how it is used in both distributed and non-distributed applications. You learned about the Serializable and Externalizable interfaces and about security issues related to object serialization. You also learned about the capabilities that will be provided by JavaSpaces. In the next chapter, you'll extend your distributed application programming capabilities by learning how Java fits into the Common Object Request Broker Architecture (CORBA).

40

USING OBJECT
SERIALIZATION
AND JAVASPACES

Java IDL and ORBs

CHAPTER 41

In Chapter 37, "Distributed Application Architecture," you learned about different approaches to developing distributed applications. One of these approaches was the Common Object Request Broker Architecture (CORBA). You learned about the similarities and differences between Java RMI and CORBA, and how RMI provides a pure Java implementation of the distributed object model used by CORBA. Although RMI is much easier to use to develop distributed applications in Java, it is limited to pure Java applications. CORBA, on the other hand, is language-neutral and allows you to interface Java objects with objects written in other programming languages.

In this chapter, you'll learn how to create CORBA objects using Java and how to connect Java objects to CORBA objects. You'll learn how Object Request Brokers (ORBs) are used to connect distributed objects, how the Interface Definition Language (IDL) is used to define object interfaces, and how the `idltojava` compiler is used to create Java stub and skeleton classes. You'll also learn about Java IDL and the `tnameserv` naming service tool. When you finish this chapter, you'll know how to integrate Java with CORBA.

The Object Management Group and CORBA

The Object Management Group (OMG), which can be reached at `http://www.omg.org`, is a consortium of companies and other organizations that was founded in 1989 to promote the development of component-based software through the establishment of object-oriented software standards and guidelines. The OMG has hundreds of member organizations.

Since its creation, the OMG has focused on standards for implementing distributed objects. CORBA is a result of this effort. It provides a standard architecture for developing distributed object-oriented systems. This architecture specifies how a client object written in one language can invoke the methods of a remote server object developed in a different language.

> **NOTE**
>
> An overview of CORBA is provided in Chapter 37, "Distributed Application Architecture."

CORBA uses stubs and skeletons in much the same way as Java RMI. A *stub* is a local proxy for a remote object. It presents the same interface as the server object, but runs on the same computer as the client. A *skeleton* is a remote interface to the server object's implementation. It runs on the same computer as the server object and provides an interface between the server object's implementation and other objects.

The stub and skeleton are connected via an ORB. The ORB forwards method invocations from the stub to the skeleton and uses a special object called an Object Adapter (OA), which runs on the same computers as the server object. The OA activates the server object, if required, and helps to manage its operation. You can think of the ORB as analogous to the remote reference and transport layers of Java RMI, and the OA as being like the remote registry. The OA is sometimes referred to as a *Basic Object Adapter (BOA)*.

Figure 41.1 provides an overview of how client and server objects communicate using CORBA. When a client object invokes the methods of a server object, it does so via the local stub of the server object. The stub presents two interfaces: its interface to the client object is in a form that is recognized by the client object's implementation, and its interface to the ORB is in a form that is common to the ORB.

FIGURE 41.1.

How client and server objects communicate using CORBA.

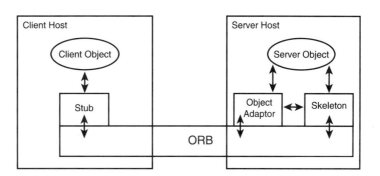

The local stub communicates with an ORB and provides it with the name of the object, the method being invoked, and any arguments to the method invocation. The ORB finds the referenced object in its network domain (often using a CORBA name service) and contacts the OA running on the same computer as the server object. The ORB passes the method invocation and argument information to the OA.

The OA will do a number of things based on the way that it manages objects on the server's computer. Its basic responsibility, however, is to activate the server object's implementation and then pass the method invocation and arguments to the server object's implementation via the skeleton. The server object processes the method invocation and returns any results to the skeleton, which forwards them to the ORB.

The skeleton, like the stub, presents two interfaces. Its interface to the OA and ORB is a standard interface that each expects. Its interface with the server object is in a form that is known to the server object. Later in this chapter, you'll learn how stubs and skeletons are specified in the Interface Definition Language and automatically generated.

When the skeleton returns a value to the ORB, the ORB forwards the return value to the stub and the stub returns the value to the client object.

ORBs

The ORB is the key to making CORBA work, the glue that holds together stubs, skeletons, naming services, and OAs. It is responsible for communicating with the stub, finding the server object, and communicating with the OA and skeleton. It provides a language-neutral interface to the stub and skeleton, and helps the stub and skeleton to abstract away the fact that the client and server objects are implemented on different computers and in different languages. To the client, there must be no difference between invoking the methods of a local object and a remote object. To the server, the fact that its methods are being invoked remotely is transparent. The transparency that the ORB, stub, and skeleton provide to the client and server objects is the greatest feature of CORBA.

In Figure 41.1, the ORB is shown as a single entity between the client and server. This is a logical representation of the ORB. The actual implementation may vary depending upon the ORB. It may be implemented as peer components that are installed on both the client and server's computers, or as an ORB server that resides on a separate computer. Other ORB implementations are also possible.

> **NOTE**
>
> The part of the ORB that provides the basic representation of objects and communication of requests is referred to as the *ORB core*.

Interoperability Between ORBs

There may be multiple ORB implementations from different vendors within the same network that are used in the same distributed application. A client may simultaneously use two different ORBs to access multiple objects, or one ORB to access an object that is serviced by another ORB. Because multiple ORBs may exist within the same application, it is necessary that the ORBs be able to communicate with each other.

The *General Inter-ORB Protocol (GIOP)* is the common interface that is used to support communication between ORBs. The GIOP specifies a syntax and a set of message formats for inter-ORB communication. Because ORBs may be implemented on networks that use a variety of transport protocols, such as TCP/IP, IPX, or SNA, the protocol used to transport information between ORBs is not specified in GIOP.

The *Internet Inter-ORB Protocol (IIOP)* is used to map the GIOP to the TCP/IP protocol suite. Different ORBs can communicate with each other across TCP/IP networks using GIOP and IIOP, as shown in Figure 41.2.

FIGURE 41.2.

Different ORBs communicate using GIOP and IIOP across TCP/IP networks.

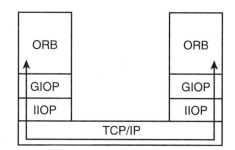

In addition to GIOP and IIOP, CORBA also provides *Environment-Specific Inter-ORB Protocols (ESIOPs)*, which are used to connect legacy applications to distributed applications that are CORBA-compliant. Legacy systems use ESIOPs to communicate with ORBs. ESIOPs, like the GIOP, need to be tailored to their networking environment. The *DCE Common Inter-ORB Protocol (DCE-CIOP)* is used with ESIOP to integrate DCE applications with CORBA applications.

The Interface Definition Language

Now that you have the big picture on CORBA, we'll cover one more important element of it before we look at Java IDL. Because one of CORBA's main goals is to provide a distributed object-oriented framework in which objects created in a variety of programming languages can interact, it needs a way to bridge the gap between multiple programming language interfaces and the ORB. IDL is the key to achieving this goal.

IDL provides a language-neutral way of describing the interfaces of objects. It describes an interface in the same manner that Java interfaces do. It defines the methods contained in an interface, their arguments, and their return values, but does not specify how the interfaces are implemented.

A server object's interface is specified in IDL, and the IDL specification is compiled to produce the stub and skeleton to be used for that object. For example, you could specify the interface of a server in IDL and then compile the IDL to create the C++ source code for the server's skeleton. You could also compile the same IDL to create a Java stub.

IDL compilers are available for C, C++, Smalltalk, Ada, and (of course) Java. These compilers translate IDL into stubs and skeletons in the source code of these languages.

You then use a language-specific compiler to compile the stubs and skeletons to binary code or byte code.

In order to develop an IDL compiler for a particular language, a language mapping must be developed that shows how the datatypes and method invocation semantics of IDL map to the language. The Java language mapping has been completed and is available at `http://splash.javasoft.com/products/jdk/idl/docs/idl-java.html`. An IDL-to-Java compiler, aptly named `idltojava`, is also available from the Java Developer Connection at `http://developer.javasoft.com`. You should download `idltojava` to perform the example in this chapter. Copy the `idltojava` program to a directory that is in your execution path.

Using Java IDL

The capability to use Java objects within CORBA is referred to as *Java IDL* and has been incorporated into JDK 1.2. Java IDL is based upon the following:

- The IDL-to-Java mapping—Takes each element of the IDL and maps it to Java language elements.
- The `idltojava` compiler—Produces stub and skeleton files from IDL definitions.
- A Java ORB that supports IIOP—Supports communication between stubs and skeletons and the transparent creation of OAs. It also supports communication with other ORBs.
- A transient object nameserver (`tnameserv`)—Provides the capability to obtain remote object references from a hierarchical object space.
- The `org.omg.CORBA` and `org.omg.CosNaming` families of API packages—Provides the Java API classes and interfaces needed to integrate Java objects with CORBA.

You don't need to understand the IDL-to-Java mapping to use Java with CORBA. However, downloading and reading the mapping will help you to learn IDL, which you'll need to do if you want to use CORBA. Luckily, it is an easy language to learn. The CORBA/IIOP 2.1 specification can be downloaded from `http://www.omg.org`. Section 3 provides an introduction to IDL.

Listing 41.1 provides a small sample IDL description. It defines the `MyServer` interface that is contained in the sample module. An IDL interface corresponds to a Java interface. An IDL module corresponds to a Java package. The `getServerData()` method takes the `string` input argument identified by the `dataID` variable and returns an IDL `string` value. (In our example, the `getServerData()` method will simply convert its `string` argument to uppercase.)

You can create Java stubs and skeletons for this interface using the following command:

```
idltojava MyServer.idl
```

This generates the following five Java files in the `example` subdirectory of your `ch41` directory:

- `MyServer.java`—Defines the `MyServer` interface resulting from the `MyServer.idl` IDL-to-Java mapping. (Refer to Listing 41.2.)
- `_MyServerImplBase.java`—The skeleton file for the `MyServer` interface. The `_MyServerImplBase` class is the superclass of the class used to implement the remote object server. (Refer to Listing 41.3.)
- `_MyServerStub.java`—The stub file for the `MyServer` interface. (Refer to Listing 41.4.)
- `MyServerHelper.java`—Defines `static` auxiliary methods that can be used by the client. (Refer to Listing 41.5.)
- `MyServerHolder.java`—Defines a class for holding an object of the `MyServer` interface. This class is used to support parameter passing between Java and CORBA. (Refer to Listing 41.6.)

Note how the `example` IDL module was translated into the `example` Java package, and the `MyServer` IDL interface was translated into the `MyServer` Java interface. Also note how the `getServerData()` method was created. You can look through the rest of the Java files that were generated. These files are used to implement the skeleton and stub of the `MyServer` interface.

> **NOTE**
>
> The example files are created in the `example` subdirectory of your `ch41` directory.

LISTING 41.1. AN IDL DESCRIPTION OF THE MyServer INTERFACE.

```
module example {
 interface MyServer {
  string getServerData(in string dataID);
 };
};
```

> **NOTE**
>
> The `idltojava` tool requires a C/C++ preprocessor to be installed on your system. If you have a C or C++ compiler on your system, `idltojava` should find it. You can suppress the use of the preprocessor by using the `-fno-cpp` option with `idltojava`. The preprocessor supports the IDL-to-Java translation process. If you are using Visual C++, you should adjust your PATH to include the path to `CL.EXE`. You can find `CL.EXE` using the Windows 95, 98, or NT Find command, which is accessible from the Start button.

LISTING 41.2. THE `MyServer.java` FILE GENERATED BY `idltojava`.

```
/*
 * File: ./EXAMPLE/MYSERVER.JAVA
 * From: MYSERVER.IDL
 * Date: Mon Feb 23 00:28:16 1998
 *   By: C:\JDK1~1.2BE\BIN\IDLTOJ~1.EXE Java IDL 1.2 Nov 10 1997 13:52:11
 */

package example;
public interface MyServer
    extends org.omg.CORBA.Object {
    String getServerData(String dataID)
;
}
```

LISTING 41.3. THE `_MyServerImplBase.java` FILE GENERATED BY `idltojava`.

```
/*
 * File: ./EXAMPLE/_MYSERVERIMPLBASE.JAVA
 * From: MYSERVER.IDL
 * Date: Mon Feb 23 00:28:16 1998
 *   By: C:\JDK1~1.2BE\BIN\IDLTOJ~1.EXE Java IDL 1.2 Nov 10 1997 13:52:11
 */

package example;
public abstract class _MyServerImplBase extends
org.omg.CORBA.DynamicImplementation implements example.MyServer {
    // Constructor
    public _MyServerImplBase() {
        super();
    }
    // Type strings for this class and its superclasses
    private static final String _type_ids[] = {
        "IDL:example/MyServer:1.0"
```

```
    };

    public String[] _ids() { return (String[]) _type_ids.clone(); }

    private static java.util.Dictionary _methods = new
    ➥java.util.Hashtable();
    static {
      _methods.put("getServerData", new java.lang.Integer(0));
     }
    // DSI Dispatch call
    public void invoke(org.omg.CORBA.ServerRequest r) {
        switch (((java.lang.Integer) _methods.get(r.op_name())).intValue()){
            case 0: // example.MyServer.getServerData
              {
              org.omg.CORBA.NVList _list = _orb().create_list(0);
              org.omg.CORBA.Any _dataID = _orb().create_any();
              _dataID.type(org.omg.CORBA.ORB.init().get_primitive_tc
              ➥(org.omg.CORBA.TCKind.tk_string));
              _list.add_value("dataID", _dataID, org.omg.CORBA.ARG_IN.
              ➥value);
              r.params(_list);
              String dataID;
              dataID = _dataID.extract_string();
              String ___result;
                        ___result = this.getServerData(dataID);
              org.omg.CORBA.Any __result = _orb().create_any();
              __result.insert_string(___result);
              r.result(__result);
              }
              break;
            default:
              throw new org.omg.CORBA.BAD_OPERATION(0,
              ➥org.omg.CORBA.CompletionStatus.COMPLETED_MAYBE);
        }
    }
  }
}
```

LISTING 41.4. THE `_MyServerStub.java` FILE GENERATED BY `idltojava`.

```
/*
 * File: ./EXAMPLE/_MYSERVERSTUB.JAVA
 * From: MYSERVER.IDL
 * Date: Mon Feb 23 00:28:16 1998
 *   By: C:\JDK1~1.2BE\BIN\IDLTOJ~1.EXE Java IDL 1.2 Nov 10 1997 13:52:11
 */

package example;
public class _MyServerStub
```

continues

LISTING 41.4. CONTINUED

```
    extends org.omg.CORBA.portable.ObjectImpl
        implements example.MyServer {

    public _MyServerStub(org.omg.CORBA.portable.Delegate d) {
        super();
        _set_delegate(d);
    }

    private static final String _type_ids[] = {
        "IDL:example/MyServer:1.0"
    };

    public String[] _ids() { return (String[]) _type_ids.clone(); }

    //     IDL operations
    //         Implementation of ::example::MyServer::getServerData
    public String getServerData(String dataID)
{
            org.omg.CORBA.Request r = _request("getServerData");
            r.set_return_type(org.omg.CORBA.ORB.init().get_primitive_tc
            ➥(org.omg.CORBA.TCKind.tk_string));
            org.omg.CORBA.Any _dataID = r.add_in_arg();
            _dataID.insert_string(dataID);
            r.invoke();
            String __result;
            __result = r.return_value().extract_string();
            return __result;
    }

};
```

LISTING 41.5. THE MyServerHelper.java FILE GENERATED BY idltojava.

```
/*
 * File: ./EXAMPLE/MYSERVERHELPER.JAVA
 * From: MYSERVER.IDL
 * Date: Mon Feb 23 00:28:16 1998
 *   By: C:\JDK1~1.2BE\BIN\IDLTOJ~1.EXE Java IDL 1.2 Nov 10 1997 13:52:11
 */

package example;
public class MyServerHelper {
    // It is useless to have instances of this class
    private MyServerHelper() { }

    public static void write(org.omg.CORBA.portable.OutputStream out,
    ➥example.MyServer that) {
```

```
            out.write_Object(that);
    }
    public static example.MyServer read(org.omg.CORBA.portable.InputStream
➥in) {
        return example.MyServerHelper.narrow(in.read_Object());
    }
    public static example.MyServer extract(org.omg.CORBA.Any a) {
      org.omg.CORBA.portable.InputStream in = a.create_input_stream();
      return read(in);
    }
    public static void insert(org.omg.CORBA.Any a, example.MyServer that) {
      org.omg.CORBA.portable.OutputStream out = a.create_output_stream();
      write(out, that);
      a.read_value(out.create_input_stream(), type());
    }
    private static org.omg.CORBA.TypeCode _tc;
    synchronized public static org.omg.CORBA.TypeCode type() {
            if (_tc == null)
                _tc = org.omg.CORBA.ORB.init().create_interface_tc(id(),
                ➥"MyServer");
        return _tc;
    }
    public static String id() {
        return "IDL:example/MyServer:1.0";
    }
    public static example.MyServer narrow(org.omg.CORBA.Object that)
        throws org.omg.CORBA.BAD_PARAM {
        if (that == null)
            return null;
        if (that instanceof example.MyServer)
            return (example.MyServer) that;
    if (!that._is_a(id())) {
        throw new org.omg.CORBA.BAD_PARAM();
    }
        org.omg.CORBA.portable.Delegate dup =
        ➥((org.omg.CORBA.portable.ObjectImpl)that)._get_delegate();
        example.MyServer result = new example._MyServerStub(dup);
        return result;
    }
}
```

LISTING 41.6. THE `MyServerHolder.java` FILE GENERATED BY `idltojava`.

```
/*
 * File: ./EXAMPLE/MYSERVERHOLDER.JAVA
 * From: MYSERVER.IDL
 * Date: Mon Feb 23 00:28:16 1998
 *   By: C:\JDK1~1.2BE\BIN\IDLTOJ~1.EXE Java IDL 1.2 Nov 10 1997 13:52:11
 */
```

continues

LISTING 41.6. CONTINUED

```
package example;
public final class MyServerHolder
      implements org.omg.CORBA.portable.Streamable{
    //    instance variable
    public example.MyServer value;
    //    constructors
    public MyServerHolder() {
    this(null);
    }
    public MyServerHolder(example.MyServer __arg) {
    value = __arg;
    }

    public void _write(org.omg.CORBA.portable.OutputStream out) {
        example.MyServerHelper.write(out, value);
    }

    public void _read(org.omg.CORBA.portable.InputStream in) {
        value = example.MyServerHelper.read(in);
    }

    public org.omg.CORBA.TypeCode _type() {
        return example.MyServerHelper.type();
    }
}
```

Developing Clients and Servers

Now that you've used idltojava to generate stub and skeleton files, you need to develop a client that remotely accesses the server and provide an implementation of the server interface.

Creating the Client

The client will simply pass the strings "java", "corba", "orb", and "idl" to the remote server and display the values returned by the server. Most of its processing will involve setting up the connection to the remote object, invoking the remote object, and processing the results of the method invocations. Listing 41.7 shows the source code for the MyClient program. (I could have named this program anything. There is no naming relationship between MyClient and MyServer. I point this out because there are conventions that should be followed when naming the server source code files.)

LISTING 41.7. THE `MyClient` PROGRAM.

```java
import org.omg.CORBA.*;      // Access the Java ORB
import org.omg.CosNaming.*;  // Acccess the CORBA name service
import example.*;  // Access the MyServer interface and stub

public class MyClient {
 public static void main(String[] args) {
  try {
   // Obtain a reference to the Java ORB and initialize it
   ORB orb = ORB.init(args,null);
   // Obtain a reference to the name service
   org.omg.CORBA.Object objRef =
    orb.resolve_initial_references("NameService");
   // Cast the reference to a NamingContext object
   NamingContext ncRef = NamingContextHelper.narrow(objRef);
   // Define the first (and only) component of MyServer's name
   NameComponent nc = new NameComponent("MyServer", "");
   // Create a path name for MyServer
   NameComponent path[] = {nc};
   // Use the naming service to obtain a reference to MyServer
   // and cast the reference to a MyServer object
   MyServer serverRef = MyServerHelper.narrow(ncRef.resolve(path));
   String[] data = {"java","corba","orb","idl"};
   for(int i=0;i<data.length;++i) {
    System.out.println("Sent: "+data[i]);
    // Invoke the getServerData() method of MyServer and
    // display the result returned
    System.out.println("Received: "+serverRef.getServerData(data[i]));
   }
  }catch(Exception ex){
   System.out.println(ex.toString());
  }
 }
};
```

The `MyClient` program is a simple console program that exercises the `MyServer` CORBA object. It illustrates the basics of developing a CORBA client in Java. The first items of interest are the `import` statements. The `org.omg.CORBA` package is imported by all Java CORBA clients and servers because it provides access to the `ORB` class. The `ORB` class is the Java implementation of a CORBA object request broker. The `org.omg.CosNaming` package is imported to access the CORBA naming service. The naming service is used to obtain a local reference to a named CORBA object—that is, an instance of `MyServer`. The `examples` package is the Java package corresponding to the `MyServer` IDL module. This package contains the classes and interfaces defined in Listings 41.2 through 41.6.

The processing within the main() method is wrapped in a try-catch statement to catch any exceptions that may occur in using the CORBA interface. The first thing that we do within the try statement is to obtain a reference to the ORB and then initialize it. The args command-line arguments are passed on to the ORB initialization. This simplifies the setup of the ORB on a particular port. You'll see how this works when we run MyClient.

The next thing we do in setting up the CORBA interface is to obtain a reference to the name service. The name service is used to locate a remote object by its name. The reference is returned as an object of class org.omg.CORBA.Object. This class is at the top of the CORBA class hierarchy and is a subclass of java.lang.Object. The narrow() method of the NamingContextHelper class is used to convert the reference from an object of the org.omg.CORBA.Object class to an object of the NamingContext class. The NamingContext class provides access to the naming service.

CORBA supports names that are made up of multiple name components. The MyServer object consists of only a single MyServer name component. A NameComponent object is created for MyServer. This component is converted into a path consisting of this single component. The path is implemented as a NameComponent array.

A reference to an instance of MyServer is obtained by invoking the resolve() method of the NamingContext object (that is, the name server). The reference returned by resolve() is cast into an object of the MyServer interface by invoking the static narrow() method of the MyServerHelper class. The MyServerHelper class was automatically generated by idltojava. This class provides methods for converting CORBA objects to and from the MyServer interface.

We now have a local reference to an instance of MyServer. The setup portion of MyClient is complete. The rest of the program uses the MyServer reference to carry out the program's processing. An array of strings is created to test the getServerData() method of MyServer. A for statement is used to invoke getServerData() with these strings and display the results that getServerData()returns.

Creating the Server

Java IDL supports a two-tiered server implementation. The first tier consists of a *servant* class that provides the actual implementation of the remote object interface. The second tier consists of a *server* class that creates *servant* instances. The servant class is named by appending Servant to the name of the object's IDL interface. The server class is named by appending Server to the interface name. Our interface is MyServer, so MyServerServant and MyServerServer are the names of the servant and server classes.

Listing 41.8 shows the source code of the `MyServerServant` class. This class extends the skeleton `_MyServerImplBase` and implements the `getServerData()` method. This method simply converts strings to uppercase.

LISTING 41.8. THE `MyServerServant` CLASS.

```
import org.omg.CORBA.*;
import org.omg.CosNaming.*;
import org.omg.CosNaming.NamingContextPackage.*;
import example.*;

public class MyServerServant extends _MyServerImplBase {
 public String getServerData(String in) {
  return in.toUpperCase();
 }
}
```

The `MyServerServer` class is shown in Listing 41.9. This class is responsible for instantiating the servant and registering it with the ORB and name service. You'll notice that the CORBA setup processing is very similar to that performed by `MyClient`. It begins by initializing the ORB and then creates an instance of `MyServerServant`. It then connects the servant to the ORB.

Next, the server registers the servant with the name service. It does this by obtaining a reference to the name service, creating a path name for `MyServer`, and binding the servant instance to the path name in the name service.

Finally, an object is created that puts the server thread in a wait state so that method invocations from the client (`MyClient`) can be received.

LISTING 41.9. THE `MyServerServer` CLASS.

```
import org.omg.CORBA.*;
import org.omg.CosNaming.*;
import org.omg.CosNaming.NamingContextPackage.*;
import example.*;

public class MyServerServer {
 public static void main(String[] args){
  try{
   // Access and initialize the ORB
   ORB orb = ORB.init(args, null);
   // Create a servant instance
   MyServerServant myServerRef = new MyServerServant();
   // Connect the servant to the ORB
```

continues

LISTING 41.9. CONTINUED

```
  orb.connect(myServerRef);
  // Obtain a reference to the name service
  org.omg.CORBA.Object objRef =
   orb.resolve_initial_references("NameService");
  // Cast the name service reference as a NamingContext object
  NamingContext ncRef = NamingContextHelper.narrow(objRef);
  // Create the name component for MyServer
  NameComponent nc = new NameComponent("MyServer", "");
  // Create the path name for MyServer
  NameComponent path[] = {nc};
  // Bind the path name with the servant in the name service
  // This registers the servant with the MyServer name
  ncRef.rebind(path, myServerRef);
  // Wait for and respond to remote method invocations
  java.lang.Object sync = new java.lang.Object();
  synchronized(sync){
   sync.wait();
  }
 }catch(Exception ex){
  System.out.println(ex.toString());
 }
 }
}
```

Compiling and Running the Client and Server

You've covered all the code needed to create client and server objects in Java that communicate using the Java ORB and naming service provided with the JDK. All you need to do is to compile the server and client and run them with the name service:

1. Change directories to the ch41\example directory and compile the stub, skeleton, interface, and support files by entering javac *.java.

2. Change directories to the ch41 directory and compile MyServerServant.java.

3. Compile MyServerServer.java.

4. Compile MyClient.java.

5. Start the name service by entering tnameserv.

6. Start the MyServerServer program by entering java MyServerServer in a separate console window.

7. Run MyClient in another console window (or on another host) using java MyClient.

NOTE

To run `tnameserv` and `MyServerServer` on another host, pass the `-ORBInitialHost` argument to `MyClient`. For example, if the servers run on server.com, you would invoke `MyClient` with `java MyClient -ORBInitialHost server.com`.

The `MyClient` program displays the following results:

```
Sent: java
Received: JAVA
Sent: corba
Received: CORBA
Sent: orb
Received: ORB
Sent: idl
Received: IDL
```

The name service, `MyServerServer`, and `MyClient` programs all communicate on TCP port 900 as a default. Use of this port requires root access on UNIX machines and Administrator privilege under Windows NT. If you'd like to use a different TCP port, pass the `-ORBInitialPort` option to each of the programs, as follows:

```
tnameserv -ORBInitialPort port
java MyServerServer -ORBInitialPort port
java MyClient -ORBInitialPort port
```

Substitute the desired TCP port number for `port`.

Summary

In this chapter, you learned the basics of how CORBA works and how Java objects can be integrated with CORBA. You learned how ORBs are used to connect distributed objects, how IDL is used to define object interfaces, and how Java IDL supports Java-CORBA integration. You also developed client and server objects in Java that communicated with each other using the Java ORB and naming service. In the next chapter, you'll learn about network computers and how Sun's JavaStation provides a pure Java solution to network computing.

Network
Computers

CHAPTER 42

Of all the available technologies for implementing a distributed intranet, network computers (NCs) have received the most attention. NCs have been brought to market by computer giants such as Sun, IBM, Oracle, and others. Even Microsoft and Intel are trying to jump on the NC bandwagon with their NetPC. As you might have guessed, Java is the programming language of choice for NC software.

In this chapter you'll be introduced to NCs and learn about their advantages and disadvantages. You'll learn about the NC-1 specification and review the NCs that are currently in the market. You'll then focus on the architecture and operation of one particular NC—Sun's JavaStation. You'll learn how the JavaStation works and how it supports both intranet and Internet applications. When you finish this chapter, you'll understand what NCs are all about and how they may be deployed within your organization.

What Are NCs?

An NC is designed to operate as an integral component of a network rather than as a desktop computer with network connectivity. This difference is subtle, yet significant.

In a desktop PC computer environment, each desktop computer is its own separate domain. Each PC boots locally, maintains its own local file storage, and locally installs most of its applications. These applications are typically compiled into the machine code language that is native to the computer's microprocessor.

The desktop computer's resources consist mainly of application files (word processing, graphics, spreadsheet, database, and so on) that are developed by the desktop user. These resources are "owned" by the user and may be shared over the network. The desktop uses the network for file and printer sharing, access to client/server intranet applications, and access to Internet/Web services.

The desktop user is responsible for maintaining his computer using the help provided by his PC support group. The user is also responsible for backing up his files. If his computer fails, his productivity comes to a halt until his files are recovered and made available on a desktop of a similar configuration.

Contrast the desktop computer environment with that of the NC. In an NC environment, the network is a single common shared resource in which all corporate information resides. NCs extend this resource to employees. Business applications are installed on the network and execute in a distributed fashion across NCs and network servers.

NCs are clients that provide access to the information and applications served by the network. They boot from distributed network servers, load their application programs from these servers, and access files that are stored on the servers. Network applications execute as Java programs on NCs, but their current state is maintained on NC servers. This enables a high level of fault tolerance. If an NC breaks down, you can toss it, plug in a new one, and bring up your network application right where you left off.

Maintenance of network applications and the backing up of user files is periodically performed by server administrators.

Advantages of NCs

The advantages of NCs are tremendous. First and foremost, deployment of NCs causes an important shift in the way computers are perceived and used within an organization. Instead of being the personal information repositories for individual users, NCs are the conduits by which corporate resources are accessed. This shift in perspective from the individual to the organization affects the way that information is created, stored, and disseminated. The end result is greater online collaboration, coordination, and communication. In a desktop environment, employees must leave their computers to attend meetings in order to collaborate, share information, reach consensus, and make decisions. In an NC environment, the enterprise network replaces unproductive meetings with dynamic, online information exchanges that solve critical problems in a timely manner.

NC applications are tailored to organizational and user needs. Instead of purchasing and installing mass market software applications that try to be all things to all people, network applications are developed around NC software products that are tailored to the needs of the enterprise as well as specific users.

The capability to tailor NC applications makes them easier to use. Instead of being locked into a windowed desktop metaphor, NC applications can be designed using whatever works best for the user. For example, the HotJava Views user environment eschews multiple overlapping windows for an easy-to-use pushbutton interface.

Network applications can also balance flexibility and ease of use with standardization. Users are free to tailor network applications to their needs, but they all use the same application. Gone are the problems associated with trying to disseminate files to users running PCs, Macs, and UNIX workstations that run incompatible versions of word processing, graphics, spreadsheet, and other desktop software. Once a new or upgraded network application is installed, it is immediately available throughout the enterprise. Because network applications are configured at the server, the days of scurrying around to each and every user's computer to install new software are gone for good.

Because software is installed centrally on network servers, the organization has more control over the software being run by users. This may mean that users will spend less time playing Free Cell and more time using work-related software.

In addition to the benefits described in the previous paragraphs, an NC is less than half the price of a PC and much cheaper to maintain. Because all software is installed and maintained on network servers, large organizations do not require the huge support staffs needed by those that deploy PCs.

The NC environment is based on the use of open standards. This means that proprietary bottlenecks are eliminated, lowering overall enterprise computing costs. This lower total cost of ownership is a primary consideration for organizations that deploy NCs.

Finally, NCs are based around the use of the Java Virtual Machine and Java Runtime Environment, greatly enhancing application security. In addition, network server security controls can be used to limit the access of individual users.

Disadvantages of NCs

While there are a number of advantages to using NCs, there are also some disadvantages. The most significant shortcoming is the current lack of software applications. This disadvantage is quickly diminishing, however. Major software houses, such as Star Division GmbH, are porting complete office suites to Java. Given the current interest in Java, it is expected that additional vendors will develop Java application software.

Another short-term disadvantage of NCs is that they are new. Some individuals do not like change, and the transition to network computing is a significant one. In any organization there will be individuals who whine, "I liked it better when we used Windows."

> **NOTE**
>
> While the adoption of the NC-1 standard has completed the standardization of NCs, no standard has been adopted (as of this writing) for the network servers that are used to provide services to NCs. Sun, IBM, and other companies are currently developing this network server standard.

A common problem for any organization that moves to a network computing environment is figuring out what to do with legacy hardware and systems. Until legacy applications are ported to the network computing environment, the most prudent solution is to let the legacy systems peacefully coexist. After porting, the system hardware can be converted to network computing resources. (Sun is working on a product, called JavaPC, that will convert low-end PCs into NCs.) PCs, UNIX, and Macintosh systems can be used to run NC applications by running Java client software on browsers or local JDK installations.

Some people fear a lack of control when they make the transition to network computing. Because network applications are configured on network servers, users no longer need to tinker with their systems to install, uninstall, and reinstall software. This is a blessing in disguise. By removing the capability to install and configure applications, you are freeing users to perform their jobs instead of playing with their computers. On the other hand, any sizable NC environment will require a suitable stable of wizards to maintain the network servers.

Because NC applications are distributed across the enterprise network, continuous and reliable network service is essential to business operation. Any significant network failure can bring an organization to its knees. The potential for network failure can be offset by the use of redundant servers, network topologies, and routing strategies that minimize failure impacts.

The NC Standard

Now that we've summarized the advantages and disadvantages of NCs, you're probably wondering exactly what an NC consists of. In order to standardize NCs, Sun, IBM, Oracle, Netscape, and Apple created the Network Computer-1 (NC-1) specification. This specification identifies the following minimum hardware and software capabilities:

- VGA monitor
- Keyboard
- Mouse
- Network interface card
- Sound card and speakers
- Java virtual machine
- Java runtime environment
- Java API class libraries
- TCP/IP networking support
- Web browser
- Email support
- Multimedia support

From the preceding list, you can see that NCs are reasonably well-stocked. What's missing from the list is hard or floppy disk support. Instead, the specification encourages the use of the BOOTP protocol to boot the NC from a network server.

> **NOTE**
>
> Most companies provide additional features besides those identified in NC-1.

NC Products

A number of vendors have released NC products that meet the NC-1 standard (or at least come close). These products are summarized in the following subsections. The Sun JavaStation is covered later in this chapter in the "JavaStation" section.

IBM Network Station Series 100, 300, and 1000

The IBM Network Station family of products (http://www.ibm.com) meet the NC-1 specification and run on PowerPC microprocessors. The Network Station 1000 is the most powerful product in this family. It comes with 32MB of RAM and is expandable to 64MB. All Network Stations provide extensive terminal emulation capabilities, including X Window, IBM 3270, and IBM 5250 terminal support. They also provide the capability to run Windows applications remotely.

Network Computing Devices Explora

The Network Computing Devices Explora NC (http://www.ncd.com) runs on a high-performance 64-bit R4700 processor. It offers a 1600×1200 pixel monitor and an array of advanced multimedia options. It also provides options for accessing UNIX, using X-Windows, and Windows applications, using the WinCenter Windows Application Server.

HDS @workstation

The HDS Network Systems @workstation (http://www.ncns.com) is an NC that is comprised of an X terminal with the JVM and Netscape Navigator. It runs on the Intel i960 processor using the HDS netOS operating system. It comes with 4MB RAM and is expandable to 128MB. A number of other expansion options are available, such as hard and floppy disk drives and PCMCIA slots. A wireless version of the workstation is also available.

NCI NC Software

Network Computer, Inc. (http://www.nc.com) is a wholly owned subsidiary of Oracle that provides the NC Desktop, NC Server, and NC Card products. NC Desktop is a software product that provides an HTML- and Java-enabled interface for NCs as well as

Web browsing, email, and other applications. The NC Server product provides the software needed to manage a network of NCs. The NC Card is used to authenticate NC users to the network.

JavaStation

The Sun JavaStation was the first computer to meet the NC-1 specification and is the premier NC on the market. It provides a 100MHz microSPARC II microprocessor and 8MB of RAM that is expandable to 64MB. It supports 10-BaseT or 100-BaseT Ethernet cards and a single RS-232C serial port. It adds 16-bit audio and a speaker.

The graphics card supports 8- or 16-bit color and screen resolutions up to 1024×768 pixels. Both 14- and 17-inch monitors are available with .28 millimeter dot pitch. It comes with a PS-2 keyboard and a two-button mouse.

The best feature of the JavaStation isn't its hardware, but that it runs JavaSoft's JavaOS operating system, which is designed from the ground up to support Java applications in a networked environment. The JavaOS is a fast, small-memory-footprint operating system for NCs, PDAs, and consumer electronic devices. The JavaOS optimizes the JavaStation for distributed Java applications.

> **NOTE**
>
> Chapter 52, "JavaOS," is dedicated to the JavaOS.

The JavaStation also comes with the HotJava browser and the HotJava Views user interface environment. These applications provide Web browsing, email, distributed calendar, and other capabilities to NC users.

Using Network Servers with JavaStation

What makes the JavaStation so special is that it is a true NC—it boots from a network server, loads applications from the server, and uses the server's file system. Furthermore, the JavaStation is stateless in the sense that it maintains all information about the current state of an application on the server.

The fact that JavaStation relies so heavily on the server is a distinct advantage. It enables all client administration to be performed on the server. Support personnel never have to visit a JavaStation. Users never have to install or configure software. This provides a significant cost savings in terms of reduced maintenance costs and millions of man-hours spent by users tinkering with their computers.

The stateless nature of the JavaStation provides other advantages. The user never has to worry about losing data. If his JavaStation fails, he can replace it with a new one, even in the middle of an application. He never has to back up his data because it resides on the server and periodic backup is performed by the server administrator.

NC/Network Server Interaction

JavaStations depend heavily on the network server for their operation. When a JavaStation powers up, it boots the JavaOS from the server using the boot protocol (BOOTP).

After initializing JavaOS, the NC responds to user inputs by loading the client part of network applications from the server and executing this software on the NC. The NC maintains state information on the server and stores application information using the file systems of the network server and other dedicated file servers. The NC makes use of services provided by Web, FTP, mail, and other servers, and uses Java remote method invocation and database capabilities to interact with enterprisewide applications and information repositories.

Netra j Server

The Netra j server is the server used by Sun to support NC applications that use the JavaStation. The Netra j server enables network booting of JavaStations using the BOOTP protocol. It also supports the centralized management of applications used by the JavaStations. The Netra j server provides connectivity to legacy systems and databases via the OpenConnect and OpenVista software packages.

Netra j runs the Solaris operating system on UltraSPARC computers. It comes with the Netscape Enterprise Server, JavaStation management and support software, Java software development tools, and Java applications written for the JavaStation. These tools make it easy to set up a JavaStation network. It only takes about an hour to install the Netra server and a JavaStation network.

Developing Java Software Applications for JavaStation

Software for the JavaStation and other NC-1–compliant NCs is written as Java applets and applications. Applets are the preferred solution because they can be executed from the HotJava browser or other Java-enabled browsers that run on the NC. The use of applets is encouraged because they can also run on non-NC hosts via a browser interface.

NC software can be written as Java application programs. The advantages of applications over applets are that they do not run in the context of a browser window and the security restrictions associated with applets are removed. The disadvantages of applications are that they are less portable and are more difficult to distribute to non-NC hosts.

In general, any Java applet or application that runs on a browser or via the JDK will run on an NC. The advantage of using NCs stems from the low cost of the NC hardware and the even lower costs of maintaining the network application software.

What kinds of applications are being targeted to NCs? Although it is technically possible to run any application written in Java, some applications are more suited to the NC environment. Sun recommends that NC networks be used to initially support a single mission-critical business function (such as customer support, manufacturing, or shipping) and provide general office productivity software (such as Corel Office for Java).

The reason for focusing on a single business function is to make the NC network and its applications more focused and easier to deploy. It's much easier to deploy an NC network to replace a legacy inventory management system than it is to replace all corporate information systems. By handling off a single function at a time, your support staff will be able to incorporate valuable lessons learned into subsequent NC deployments.

The most well-suited applications for NCs are those that require information dissemination and access to databases, and that are limited to a few process-oriented software applications. A good example in the medical field is patient reception and registration. A receptionist could use a JavaStation to enter patient information into a database and schedule a room, nurse, and doctor to treat the patient. NCs could be provided to nurses, doctors, pharmacists, and cashiers for updating the patient's record, entering diagnosis and treatment notes, prescribing/dispensing medication, and billing.

Applications that are ill-suited to NCs are those that require extensive processing and memory support, such as modeling and simulation, event prediction, and software development. However, even these applications could be supported by NC clients as long as the bulk of the computation is performed on application-specific servers.

42

NETWORK
COMPUTERS

JavaStation and the Intranet

The focus of the JavaStation is the intranet, and it works well in this environment. A typical intranet deployment of the JavaStation is shown in Figure 42.1. JavaStation *thin clients* are managed by Netra j servers that provide boot-up, application loading, and data storage capabilities. The JavaStations also make use of other network file, print, mail, and directory servers. The Netra j servers support connectivity to legacy applications hosted on mainframes and high-end workstations. They also provide bridges to legacy database applications. New network applications are developed using open standards and make use of Web, database, multimedia, VRML, and other technologies. These applications are implemented on Web-, database-, and application-specific servers and are accessed via Java-based client software that executes on the JavaStations. The simplicity of JavaStation software maintenance makes it possible to deploy new network applications throughout an enterprise within a single day.

FIGURE 42.1.

The integration of JavaStations within a company's intranet.

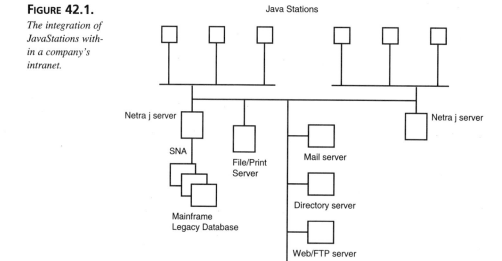

The JavaStation also supports Internet applications. The integrated HotJava browser and email capabilities, combined with telnet and FTP support, provide JavaStation users with the typical Internet client software used on PCs. The multimedia features of the JavaStation support the audio, video, and graphics capabilities expected by desktop PC users.

Summary

In this chapter you learned how NCs work and how they are deployed within an organization's intranet. You learned about a few of the popular NC products, but focused on Sun's JavaStation. This chapter completes Part IX, "Developing Distributed Applications." In Part X, "Database Programming," you'll learn how to connect Java applets and applications to databases.

Database Programming

PART

X

Database Fundamentals

IN THIS CHAPTER

Advanced Web applications often interface with database management systems. These database systems serve as repositories for large amounts of information that is collected and used by the application. For example, search sites maintain database information about the URLs that are searched. Online employee directories use databases to store contact information about employees. Web-based product catalogs maintain product descriptions and sales information in the form of a database.

In this chapter, you'll learn the fundamentals of database programming. You'll learn how relational databases work and how SQL is used to update and retrieve data from relational databases. You'll learn how databases are accessed and about the different types of drivers that can be used. When you finish this chapter, you'll have the background you need to begin Java database programming. Even if you are an experienced database programmer, you should still skim over this chapter. It contains useful introductory information on aspects of database programming with Java.

What Is a Database?

A *database* is a collection of data that is organized so that it may be easily searched and updated. The most important feature of a database is its organization, which supports both ease of use and efficient data retrieval. Consider an office that is organized with numbered file cabinets containing carefully labeled folders. Office information is stored by subject in specific folders that are kept in designated file cabinets. In such a system, every folder has its place and it is easy to find a particular folder.

Now consider a different environment where information is stored in folders, but the folders are haphazardly stored in boxes that are placed at seemingly random locations throughout an office building. How do you find a particular folder in such an environment? Where do you store a folder when you're finished with it?

The well-organized environment is analogous to a database. Information that is entered into a database is stored in specific locations within it. Because of the database's structure and organization (assuming the database is well designed), information can be easily retrieved. The database can be accessed remotely and is shared between many users.

The unorganized environment is analogous to a situation where information is stored in files on various user's computers. In such an environment, it is very hard to locate specific information. What file contains the information you need? Whose computer contains that file? Where is the computer located? Where is the file located in the user's file system?

A *database server* is a software program that manages databases, keeps them organized, and provides shared access to them. Database servers manage and organize databases at both a physical level and at a logical level. At a *physical level*, database servers store database information in specific locations within the particular files, directories, and disk volumes used by the server. The server keeps track of what information goes where so that you don't have to worry about it. The server is like a trusty office assistant—you can turn to and say, "Get me the file on…" and the assistant immediately retrieves the information you need and places it on your desk.

As previously mentioned, database servers also manage and organize information at a *logical level*. This logical level corresponds to the type of information that you store in a database. For example, you may have a database that stores the names, companies, email addresses, and phone numbers of your business contacts. The logical organization of the database could consist of a `Contacts` table with five columns: `LastName`, `FirstName`, `Company`, `Email`, and `Phone`. Specific contacts would be identified by rows of the table, as shown in Table 43.1.

TABLE 43.1. A BUSINESS CONTACT TABLE.

LastName	FirstName	Company	Email	Phone
Smith	Joe	XYZ, Corp.	joe@xyz.com	123-456-7890
Jones	Sally	UVW, Corp.	sally@uvw.com	234-567-8901
Woods	Al	RST, Corp.	al@rst.com	345-678-9012

Relational Databases

Although there are a number of different ways that databases can be logically organized, one particular organization, called the *relational model*, is the predominant method. The relational model was developed by E.F. Codd, a mathematician at IBM, during the late 1960s. Databases that adhere to the relational model are referred to as *relational databases*.

Relational databases are organized into tables that consist of rows and columns. As shown in Table 43.1, the columns of the table identify what type of information is contained in each row. The rows of the table contain specific records that have been entered in the database. The first row of Table 43.1 indicates that Joe Smith works for XYZ, Corp. and has email address joe@xyz.com and phone number 123-456-7890. (The table column headings are not counted as rows within the table.)

Organizing Tables

A relational database can have one table or 1,000 tables. The number of tables is only limited by the relational database server software and the amount of available physical storage. Some relational database servers, also referred to as *relational database management systems (RDBMs)*, organize tables into schemas. A *schema* is a way of partitioning the tables of a database. Each table in a database belongs to exactly one schema. In a similar fashion, schemas are organized into *catalogs*. Each schema belongs to exactly one catalog, as shown in Figure 43.1. The purpose of schemas and catalogs is to organize tables into related groups and control access to the information contained in a database according to these groups.

> **NOTE**
>
> Not all relational database management systems support schemas and catalogs.

Working with Keys

Access to information contained within tables is organized by keys. A *key* is a column or group of columns that uniquely identifies a row of a table. Keys are used to find a particular row within a table and to determine whether a new row is to be added to a table or to replace an existing row. Suppose that Table 43.1 was updated to include everybody in the world with an email address. What columns should we use as a key?

At first glance we may choose the LastName column. However, many people have the same last names. After further consideration, even if we chose the LastName, FirstName, and Company columns as our key, we would still run into problems with companies that had more than one Joe Smith working for them. The Email column would make a good key, though. If two people in the same company have the same name, they are still given unique email addresses, such as joe@xyz.com and joe.smith@xyz.com. (For the purpose of the example, we'll ignore the cases where people share the same email address or a person has more than one email address.)

Using Email as our key, we can easily manage our business contacts table. When we update the table, we can check to see if the Email column of the new row is already in the table. In this case, we can overwrite the existing row with new information. If the Email column of the new row is not in the table, we can add a new row to the table.

FIGURE 43.1.
*Tables are orga-
nized into
schemas and cata-
logs.*

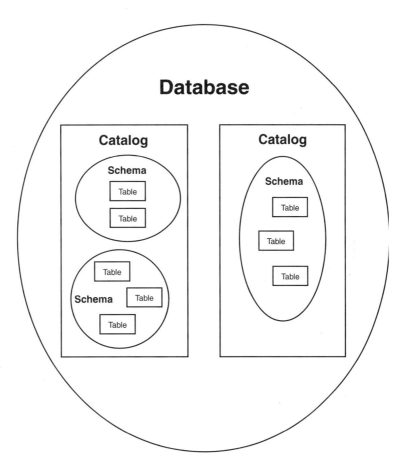

Normalizing Tables

When we design the tables of a database, how do we decide which information to put in which tables? Is it better to use one big table or lots of little tables?

The answer to these questions was provided by Codd in his paper on the relational data model. He described a process called *normalization*, which could be used to optimize the way that data is organized into tables. The purpose of normalization is to minimize the number of columns in database tables and promote data consistency. More tables with fewer columns are the result of normalization. Five levels of normalization are recognized. A database that is normalized to a particular level is said to be in *normal form* for that level (that is, first normal form through fifth normal form). The purpose of normalization is to remove redundant information from the database to simplify database updating and maintenance.

First normal form is the simplest and easiest to achieve. In it, duplicate columns of a table are eliminated. For example, consider Table 43.2, which keeps track of the taxes an individual paid in the years 1995 through 1997. The first column is the person's social security number and is the key for the table. The second through fourth columns represent the amount of tax the individual paid.

TABLE 43.2. INDIVIDUAL TAXES PAID TABLE.

SSN	Tax95	Tax96	Tax97
123-45-6789	10,000	11,000	11,500
234-56-7890	4,500	5,000	5,250

Because the second through fourth columns contain the same type of information, the table can be put into first normal form by organizing it as shown in Table 43.3.

TABLE 43.3. FIRST NORMAL FORM OF INDIVIDUAL TAXES PAID TABLE.

SSN	Year	Tax
123-45-6789	95	10,000
123-45-6789	96	11,000
123-45-6789	97	11,500
234-56-7890	95	4,500
234-56-7890	96	5,000
234-56-7890	97	5,250

Subsequent normal forms are more complicated and harder to achieve. In most cases, achieving high levels of normalization is neither necessary nor desired. For example, databases that are put in fifth normal form have a high degree of consistency because redundant database columns are eliminated. However, this consistency comes at the expense of requiring more tables. The additional number of tables increases the storage space required by the database as a whole, and also increases the time to perform a database search. In general, database design is a trade-off between data consistency, database size, and database performance.

Structured Query Language

The *Structured Query Language*, or *SQL* (pronounced "sequel"), is a language for interacting with relational databases. It was developed by IBM during the '70s and '80s and standardized in the late '80s. The SQL standard has been updated over the years, and several versions currently exist. In addition, several database vendors have added product-specific extensions and variations to the language. The JDBC requires JDBC-compliant drivers to support the American National Standards Institute (ANSI) SQL-92 Entry Level version of the standard that was adopted in 1992.

SQL has many uses. When SQL is used to create or design a database, it is a *data definition language*. When it's used to update the data contained in a database, it is a *data maintenance language*. When it's used to retrieve information from a database, it is a *data query language*. We'll cover each of these uses in the following subsections.

> **NOTE**
>
> The following sections present enough SQL to get you started in database programming. For a complete description of SQL, check out the SQL Standards home page (http://www.jcc.com/sql_stnd.html) for links to standards and books on SQL. More sophisticated versions of the described SQL statements may be available. Consult the ANSI SQL standard for a complete description of each statement.

Using SQL as a Data Definition Language

You can use SQL to define a database. For example, there are SQL statements for creating a database, creating tables and adding them to a database, updating the design of existing tables, and removing tables from a database. However, most database systems provide GUI tools for database definition, and these tools are far easier to work with than SQL for designing a database. For example, Microsoft Access 97 provides wizards that guide you through the entire process of creating a database and the tables that it contains. If you have access to a GUI-based database design tool, use it. It will save you time in creating your database and make it much easier to update. For those of you who do not have a GUI database design tool, I'll describe some of the basic SQL statements.

The CREATE DATABASE Statement

The CREATE DATABASE statement can be used to create a database:

CREATE DATABASE *databaseName*

Substitute the name of the table to be created for *databaseName*. For example, the following statement creates a database named MyDB:

CREATE DATABASE MyDB

> **NOTE**
>
> The CREATE DATABASE statement is not supported by all SQL implementations.

The CREATE TABLE Statement

The CREATE TABLE statement creates a table and adds it to the database:

```
CREATE TABLE tableName (columnDefinition, ... ,columnDefinition)
```

Each `columnDefinition` is of the form

```
columnName columnType
```

The `columnName` is unique to a particular column in the table. The `columnType` identifies the type of data that may be contained in the table. Common data types are

- `char(n)`—An *n* character text string
- `int`—An integer value
- `float`—A floating point value
- `bit`—A boolean (1 or 0) value
- `date`—A date value
- `time`—A time value

> **NOTE**
>
> The Types class of java.sql identifies the SQL data types supported by Java. The get methods of the ResultSet interface are used to convert SQL data types into Java data types. The set methods of the PreparedStatement interface are used to convert Java types into SQL data types. These classes are covered in more detail in the next chapter.

The following is an example of a CREATE TABLE statement:

```
CREATE TABLE Contacts (
 LastName char(30),
 FirstName char(20),
 Company char(50),
 Email char(40),
 Phone char(20)
)
```

The preceding statement creates a Contacts table with the following columns:

- LastName—A 30-character-wide text field
- FirstName—A 20-character-wide text field
- Company—A 50-character-wide text field
- Email—A 40-character-wide text field
- Phone—A 20-character-wide text field

The ALTER TABLE Statement

The ALTER TABLE statement adds a row to an existing table:

```
ALTER TABLE tableName ADD (columnDefinition ... columnDefinition)
```

The row values of the newly added columns are set to NULL. Columns are defined as described in the previous section.

The following is an example of the ALTER TABLE statement that adds a column named Fax to the Contacts table:

```
ALTER TABLE Contacts ADD (Fax char(20))
```

The DROP TABLE Statement

The DROP TABLE statement deletes a table from the database:

```
DROP TABLE tableName
```

The dropped table is permanently removed from the database. The following is an example of the DROP TABLE statement:

```
DROP TABLE Contacts
```

The preceding statement removes the Contacts table from the database.

Using SQL as a Data Maintenance Language

One of the primary uses of SQL is to update the data contained in a database. There are SQL statements for inserting new rows into a database, deleting rows from a database, and updating existing rows.

The INSERT Statement

The INSERT statement inserts a row into a table:

```
INSERT INTO tableName VALUES ('value1', ..., 'valuen')
```

In the preceding form of the INSERT statement, *value1* through *valuen* identify all column values of a row. Values should be surrounded by single quotes.

43

DATABASE FUNDAMENTALS

The following is an example of the preceding form of the INSERT statement:

```
INSERT INTO Contacts VALUES (
 'Zepernick',
 'Ken',
 'SAIZ, Inc.',
 'kenz@cts.com',
 '619-555-5555'
)
```

The preceding statement adds Ken Zepernick to the Contacts table. All columns of Ken's row are filled in.

An alternative form of the INSERT statement may be used to insert a partial row into a table. The following is an example of this alternative form of the INSERT statement:

```
INSERT INTO tableName (columnName1, ..., columnNamem) VALUES ('value1',
..., 'valuem')
```

The values of *columnName1* through *columnNamem* are set to *value1* through *valuem*. The value of the other columns of a row are set to NULL.

An example of this form of the INSERT statement follows:

```
INSERT INTO Contacts (LastName, Email) VALUES (
 'Deloach',
'timdel@ix.netcom.com'
)
```

The preceding statement adds a person with the last name of Deloach and the email address timdel@ix.netcom.com to the Contacts table. The person's FirstName, Company, and Phone fields are set to NULL.

The DELETE Statement

The DELETE statement deletes a row from a table:

```
DELETE FROM tableName [WHERE condition]
```

All rows of the table that meet the condition of the WHERE clause are deleted from the table. The WHERE clause is covered in a subsequent section of this chapter.

> **WARNING**
>
> If the WHERE clause is omitted, all rows of the table are deleted.

The following is an example of the DELETE statement:

```
DELETE FROM Contacts WHERE LastName = 'Zepernick'
```

The preceding statement deletes all contacts with the last name of Zepernick from the Contacts table.

The UPDATE Statement

The UPDATE statement is used to update an existing row of a table:

```
UPDATE tableName SET columnName1 = 'value1', ... ,columnNamen = 'valuen'
[WHERE condition]
```

All the rows of the table that satisfy the condition of the WHERE clause are updated by setting the value of the columns to the specified values. If the WHERE clause is omitted, all rows of the table are updated.

An example of the UPDATE statement follows:

```
UPDATE Contacts SET FirstName = 'Tim' WHERE LastName = 'Deloach'
```

The preceding statement changes the FirstName of all contacts with the LastName of Deloach to Tim.

Using SQL as a Data Query Language

The most important use of SQL for many users is for retrieving data contained in a database. The SELECT statement specifies a database query:

```
SELECT columnList1 FROM table1, ..., tablem [WHERE condition] [ORDER BY
columnList2]
```

In the preceding syntax description, columnList1 and columnList2 are comma-separated lists of column names from the tables table1 through tablem. The SELECT statement returns a result set consisting of the specified columns of the table1 through tablem, such that the rows of these tables meet the condition of the WHERE clause. If the WHERE clause is omitted, all rows are returned.

43

DATABASE
FUNDAMENTALS

> **NOTE**
>
> An asterisk (*) may replace columnList1 to indicate that all columns of the table(s) are to be returned.

The ORDER BY clause is used to order the result set by the columns of *columnSet2*. Each of the column names in the column list may be followed by the ASC or DESC keywords. If DESC is specified, the result set is ordered in descending order. Otherwise, the result set is ordered in ascending order.

An example of the SELECT statement follows:

```
SELECT * FROM Contacts
```

This statement returns all rows and columns of the Contact table.

The WHERE Clause

The WHERE clause is a boolean expression consisting of column names, column values, relational operators, and logical operators. For example, suppose you have columns Department, Salary, and Bonus. You could use the following WHERE clause to match all employees in the Engineering department that have a salary over 100,000 and a bonus less than 5,000:

```
WHERE Department = 'Engineering' AND Salary > '100000' AND Bonus < '5000'
```

Relational operators are =, !=, <, >, <=, and >=. Logical operators are AND, OR, and NOT.

> **NOTE**
>
> The ANSI SQL standard provides additional operators besides those listed in this section.

Remote Database Access

Most useful databases are accessed remotely. In this way, shared access to the database can be provided to multiple users at the same time. For example, you can have a single database server that is used by all employees in the accounting department.

In order to access databases remotely, users need a *database client*. A database client communicates to the database server on the user's behalf. It provides the user with the capability to update the database with new information or to retrieve information from the database. In this book, you'll learn to write Java applications and applets that serve as database clients. Your database clients talk to database servers using SQL statements. (See Figure 43.2.)

FIGURE 43.2.

A database client talks to a database server on the user's behalf.

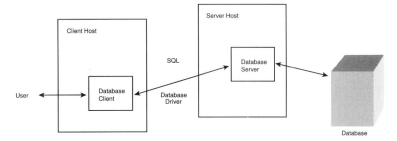

ODBC and JDBC Drivers

Database clients use database drivers to send SQL statements to database servers and to receive result sets and other responses from the servers. JDBC drivers are used by Java applications and applets to communicate with database servers. Officially, Sun says that JDBC is an acronym that does not stand for anything. However, it is associated with "Java database connectivity."

Microsoft's ODBC

Many database servers use vendor-specific protocols. This means that a database client has to learn a new language to talk to a different database server. However, Microsoft established a common standard for communicating with databases, called *Open Database Connectivity (ODBC)*. Until ODBC, most database clients were server-specific. ODBC drivers abstract away vendor-specific protocols, providing a common application programming interface to database clients. By writing your database clients to the ODBC API, you enable your programs to access more database servers. (See Figure 43.3.)

FIGURE 43.3.

A database client can talk to many database servers via ODBC drivers.

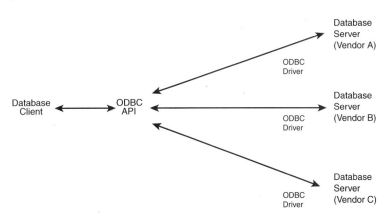

43

DATABASE FUNDAMENTALS

Enter JDBC

So where does JDBC fit into this picture? It's not a competitor to ODBC yet, but it soon will be. JDBC provides a common database-programming API for Java programs. However, JDBC drivers do not directly communicate with as many database products as ODBC drivers. Instead, many JDBC drivers communicate with databases using ODBC. In fact, one of the first JDBC drivers was the JDBC-ODBC bridge driver developed by JavaSoft and Intersolv.

Why did JavaSoft create JDBC? What was wrong with ODBC? There are a number of reasons why JDBC was needed, which boil down to the simple fact that JDBC is a better solution for Java applications and applets:

- ODBC is a C language API, not a Java API. Java is object-oriented and C is not. C uses pointers and other "dangerous" programming constructs that Java does not support. A Java version of ODBC would require a significant rewrite of the ODBC API.

- ODBC drivers must be installed on client machines. This means that applet access to databases would be constrained by the requirement to download and install a JDBC driver. A pure Java solution allows JDBC drivers to be automatically downloaded and installed along with the applet. This greatly simplifies database access for applet users.

JavaSoft created the Java-ODBC bridge driver as a temporary solution to database connectivity until suitable JDBC drivers were developed. The JDBC-ODBC bridge driver translates the JDBC API into the ODBC API and is used with an ODBC driver. The JDBC-ODBC bridge driver is not an elegant solution, but it allows Java developers to use existing ODBC drivers. (See Figure 43.4.)

FIGURE 43.4.

The JDBC-ODBC bridge lets Java database clients talk to databases via ODBC drivers.

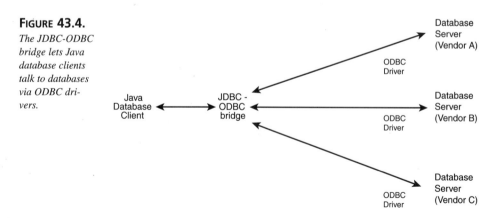

Since the release of the JDBC API, a number of JDBC drivers have been developed. These drivers provide varying levels of capability. As a service to Java developers, JavaSoft has classified JDBC drivers into the following four driver types:

- JDBC-ODBC bridge plus ODBC driver—This driver category refers to the original JDBC-ODBC bridge driver. The JDBC-ODBC bridge driver uses Microsoft's ODBC driver to communicate with database servers. It is implemented in both binary code and Java and must be preinstalled on a client computer before it can be used.

- Native-API partly Java driver—This driver category consists of drivers that talk to database servers in the server's native protocol. For example, an Oracle driver would speak SQLNet, while a DB2 driver would use an IBM database protocol. These drivers are implemented in a combination of binary code and Java, and they must be installed on client machines. (See Figure 43.5.)

FIGURE 43.5.

A Type 2 JDBC driver uses a vendor-specific protocol and must be installed on client machines.

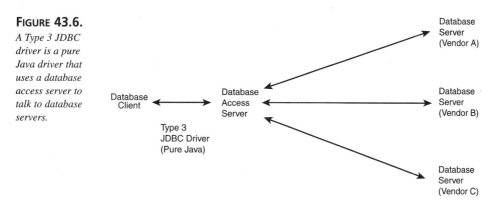

- JDBC-Net pure Java driver—This driver category consists of pure Java drivers that speak a standard network protocol (such as HTTP) to a database access server. The database access server then translates the network protocol into a vendor-specific database protocol (possibly using an ODBC driver). (See Figure 43.6.)

FIGURE 43.6.

A Type 3 JDBC driver is a pure Java driver that uses a database access server to talk to database servers.

43

DATABASE
FUNDAMENTALS

- Native-protocol pure Java driver—This driver category consists of a pure Java driver that speaks the vendor-specific database protocol of the database server that it is designed to interface with. (See Figure 43.7.)

FIGURE 43.7.

A Type 4 JDBC driver is a pure Java driver that uses a vendor-specific protocol to talk to database servers.

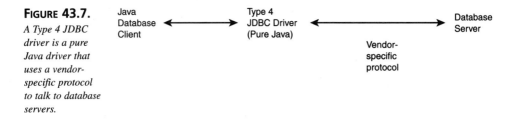

Of the four types of drivers, only Type 3 and Type 4 are pure Java drivers. This is important to support zero installation for applets, as you'll learn in Chapter 46, "Integrating Database Support into Web Applications." The Type 4 driver communicates with the database server using a vendor-specific protocol, such as SQLNet. The Type 3 driver makes use of a separate database access server. It communicates with the database access server using a standard network protocol, such as HTTP. The database access server communicates with database servers using vendor-specific protocols or ODBC drivers. The IDS JDBC driver that you'll use in Chapter 44, "Connecting to Databases with the java.sql Package," (and also in Chapters 45, "Using JDBC," and 46, "Integrating Database Support into Web Applications") is an example of a Type 3 driver.

Summary

In this chapter, you learned the basics of database programming. You learned how relational databases work and how SQL is used to update and retrieve data from relational databases. You also learned how databases are accessed and about the different types of drivers that can be used to access databases. In the following chapter, you'll learn how to use JDBC to connect to databases, execute SQL statements, and access the results of database queries.

Connecting to Databases with the `java.sql` Package

IN THIS CHAPTER

One of the most powerful and exciting elements in the Java API is the `java.sql` package. This package adds database programming capabilities to Java and is referred to as the *JDBC API*. The JDBC was originally developed as a separate package from the JDK 1.02 but is an integral part of the JDK as of JDK 1.1. JDK 1.2 supports JDBC 2.0.

> **NOTE**
>
> Many people think JDBC stands for Java Database Connectivity. However, according to JavaSoft, JDBC is not an acronym.

The JDBC is a powerful tool for Java development. By providing database connectivity to applications and applets, it enables these programs to tap into commercial, government, university, and other databases. This results in information-rich Java applications that can be used to replace and enhance current legacy information systems.

In this chapter, you'll learn the basics of the JDBC. You'll learn about the classes of the `java.sql` package and how to work with JDBC drivers. You'll also learn how to connect to databases, execute SQL statements, and work with result sets. This chapter provides a quick introduction to the `java.sql` package. Chapter 45, "Using JDBC," expands on the programming concepts introduced in this chapter.

Setting Up a Database Connection

In order to use JDBC, you'll need a database server and a database driver. Because most readers have access to Windows 95, I'll be using Microsoft Access as my database server. You can choose to use Access or some other server. After you learn how to connect to your database, the type of server that you're using won't matter—JDBC provides a server-independent approach to database access. That's one of JDBC's major benefits!

You'll also need a database driver, which provides the linkage between the JDBC and your database. The JDBC comes with a JDBC-ODBC bridge. This bridge allows you to access databases via Microsoft's Open Database Connectivity API. However, the JDBC-ODBC bridge is a temporary solution to database connectivity and has some significant drawbacks, such as requiring the bridge to be installed on your database users' computers.

I will use the JDBC driver of IDS Software (`http://www.idssoftware.com`). The IDS JDBC driver is a pure Java driver that supports *zero installation* for applets. This means that you can provide database access via applets without requiring software to be preinstalled on the computers of applet users.

> **NOTE**
>
> Consult the JDBC home page at `http://www.javasoft.com/products/jdbc/` for information on the JDBC drivers that will work with your database server.

While you may use the JDBC driver of your choice for the examples in this book, I recommend the IDS driver because of its ease of use, great documentation, and zero installation features. If you are interested in using the IDS JDBC driver, check the IDS Web page for the availability of an evaluation copy. If you intend to develop Java-based database applications, it will be well worth obtaining a licensed version of the IDS software.

> **NOTE**
>
> If you use the IDS JDBC driver with Microsoft Access, make sure you have installed version 3.5 or later of Microsoft's ODBC database drivers. These drivers are available at `ftp://ftp.microsoft.com/Softlib/MSLFILES/WX1350.EXE`.

> **TIP**
>
> You can check the version of your ODBC database drivers by opening the 32-bit ODBC Control Panel applet and clicking on the ODBC Drivers tab.

The `DriverManager` Class

The `DriverManager` class of `java.sql` is used to manage the JDBC drivers that are installed on your system. These drivers may be installed by setting the `jdbc.drivers` system property or by loading the driver class using the `forName()` method of the `Class` class. The `DriverApp` program, presented in the section "The `DriverApp` Program" later in this chapter, shows how to load a JDBC driver using the `forName()` method.

The `DriverManager` class does not provide a constructor, and all of its methods are static. The `getDrivers()` method returns an enumeration of all the JDBC drivers that are installed on your system. The `getConnection()` method is used to establish a connection to a database. This method is provided in the following three forms:

```
getConnection(String url)
getConnection(String url,String userID,String password)
getConnection(String url,Properties arguments)
```

44

THE JAVA.SQL
PACKAGE

The first form takes a `String` argument that specifies the URL of the database. You'll learn about database URLs shortly. The second form takes two additional strings: the user ID and password required to access a database. The third form takes an additional `Properties` argument that specifies a list of connection arguments, such as user ID, password, database name, and so on. Consult your JDBC driver documentation for more information on which method to use with those drivers.

The URLs used to establish database connections vary with the JDBC drivers that you use, but they are of the following form:

`jdbc:subprotocol:subname`

All JDBC database protocols begin with `jdbc:`. The subprotocol is used to identify either the connection mechanism or the JDBC driver. For example, the JDBC-ODBC bridge uses protocols of the form `jdbc:odbc:subname` and the IDS JDBC driver uses protocols of the form `jdbc:ids:subname`.

The subname of a database protocol identifies the database and provides other parameters that depend on the subprotocol and JDBC driver. For example, I use the following URL to establish a database connection to the Microsoft Access database named `DataSetName` on the host `cx122974-a.cv1.sdca.home.com` on protocol port 80:

```
jdbc:ids://cx122974-a.cv1.sdca.home.com:80/
conn?dbtype=odbc&dsn=DataSetName
```

The IDS Server can be configured to support Web service and database access via the same TCP protocol port (80).

> **NOTE**
>
> Consult your JDBC driver's documentation for information on the subprotocol and subname you should use to establish a database connection.

Although the `getDrivers()` and `getConnection()` methods are the most important methods of the `DriverManager` class, it provides other methods that support driver and general database management:

- `getDriver()`—Returns a driver that can support a connection via a specified URL.
- `registerDriver()`—Invoked by drivers to register themselves with `DriverManager`.
- `deregisterDriver()`—Invoked by drivers to deregister themselves with `DriverManager`.

- `getLoginTimeout()`—Returns the maximum time for drivers to wait while trying to log in to a database.

- `setLoginTimeout()`—Sets the maximum time for drivers to wait while trying to log in to a database.

- `getLogStream()`—Returns the stream that is to be used for logging and tracing.

- `setLogStream()`—Specifies a stream to be used for logging and tracing.

- `println()`—Prints data to the log stream.

The `Driver` Interface

The `Driver` interface is implemented by JDBC drivers. Writing a JDBC driver consists of creating a Java class that implements the `Driver` interface. Although you most likely won't have to worry about writing your own JDBC driver, there are a few useful methods in the `Driver` interface:

- `connect()`—An abstract method that is overridden by a driver to establish a database connection. This method is invoked for the driver by `DriverManager`.

- `acceptsURL()`—Returns a `boolean` value indicating whether a driver is capable of opening a database connection via a specified URL.

- `getPropertyInfo()`—Returns a `DriverPropertyInfo` array that provides information about how to use a driver to connect to a database.

- `getMajorVersion()`—Returns the driver's major version number.

- `getMinorVersion()`—Returns the driver's minor version number.

- `jdbcCompliant()`—Returns a `boolean` value indicating whether a driver is fully JDBC-compliant. It must pass the JDBC-compliance tests to return `true`.

The `DriverPropertyInfo` Class

An array of objects of the `DriverPropertyInfo` class is returned by the `getPropertyInfo()` method of the `Driver` class to provide information about a driver that can be used to establish a database connection. The `DriverPropertyInfo` class provides the following five field variables to describe a property of a driver:

- `name`—The property's name.

- `description`—A description of the property.

- `value`—The current value of the property.

- `choices`—A list of possible values.

- `required`—A variable that indicates whether the property is required.

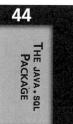

44

THE JAVA.SQL PACKAGE

The `DriverApp` Program

The `DriverApp` program, shown in Listing 44.1, illustrates the use of the `DriverManager` and `DriverPropertyInfo` classes and the `Driver` interface.

When I run the program, it provides the following output:

```
Available drivers:
  Driver: ids.sql.IDSDriver
  Major version: 2
  Minor version: 5
  JDBC compliant: true
  Properties:
    Name: dsn
      Description: Data Source Name or Database Name
      Value: null
      Required: true
    Name: user
      Description: User ID
      Value: null
      Required: false
    Name: password
      Description: Password
      Value: null
      Required: false
  Driver: sun.jdbc.odbc.JdbcOdbcDriver
  Major version: 1
  Minor version: 2001
JDBC compliant: true
```

If you use a different driver than the IDS driver, you'll have to replace the class name `ids.sql.IDSDriver` in the statement

```
Class.forName("ids.sql.IDSDriver");
```

with your JDBC driver's class name in order for the program to work properly. If you delete the preceding statement, the program only displays information about the Sun JDBC-ODBC driver.

The IDS Server runs on both Windows 95 and Windows NT.

> **NOTE**
>
> Make sure that you put the IDS classes (`C:\IDSServer\classes`) in your CLASSPATH. Otherwise, `DriverApp` won't be able to find your IDS driver (`ids.sql.IDSDriver`).

DriverApp provides useful information about your driver that you can use to set up a database connection. It loads the `ids.sql.IDSDriver` and the `sun.jdbc.odbc.JdbcOdbcDriver` classes by invoking the `forName()` method of the `Class` class. It then invokes the `getDrivers()` method of `DriverManager` to return an `Enumeration` of the loaded drivers. A `while` loop is used to iterate through the `Enumeration` object and display information about each driver.

The name of the driver is retrieved by invoking the `getClass()` method to retrieve the driver's class and the `getName()` method to retrieve the name of the class. The `getMajorVersion()`, `getMinorVersion()`, and `jdbcCompliant()` methods return additional information about each driver.

An array of `DriverPropertyInfo` objects is returned by the `getPropertyInfo()` method of the `Driver` class. The `name`, `description`, `value`, `choices`, and `required` fields of each object are displayed.

The sample program output shows that the `ids.sql.IDSDriver` driver is version 2.5, is JDBC-compliant, and takes the required `dsn` and optional `user` and `password` properties. However, the `sun.jdbc.odbc.JdbcOdbcDriver` driver revealed little information about itself.

LISTING 44.1. THE DriverApp PROGRAM.

```
import java.sql.*;
import java.util.*;

class DriverApp {
 public static void main(String args[]) {
  try{
   // Load the database drivers
   Class.forName("ids.sql.IDSDriver");
   Class.forName("sun.jdbc.odbc.JdbcOdbcDriver");
   // Obtain a list of the loaded drivers
   Enumeration drivers = DriverManager.getDrivers();
   System.out.println("Available drivers:");
   while(drivers.hasMoreElements()){
    Driver driver=(Driver)drivers.nextElement();
    // Display information about each driver
    System.out.println("  Driver: "+driver.getClass().getName());
    System.out.println("  Major version: "+driver.getMajorVersion());
    System.out.println("  Minor version: "+driver.getMinorVersion());
    System.out.println("  JDBC compliant: "+driver.jdbcCompliant());
    // Get driver properties
    DriverPropertyInfo props[] = driver.getPropertyInfo("",null);
    if(props!=null){
     // Display each property and its value
```

44

THE JAVA.SQL
PACKAGE

continues

LISTING 44.1. CONTINUED

```
    System.out.println("  Properties: ");
    for(int i=0;i<props.length;++i){
     System.out.println("    Name: "+props[i].name);
     System.out.println("      Description: "+props[i].description);
     System.out.println("      Value: "+props[i].value);
     if(props[i].choices!=null){
      System.out.println("        Choices: ");
      for(int j=0;j<props[i].choices.length;++j)
       System.out.println("          "+props[i].choices[j]);
     }
     System.out.println("        Required: "+props[i].required);
    }
   }
  }
 }catch(Exception ex){
  System.out.println(ex);
  System.exit(0);
 }
 }
}
```

Connecting to the Database

The getConnection() method of DriverManager is used to establish a connection to a database. In this section, you'll see how a database connection is established. But first let's cover two important interfaces related to database connections—Connection and DatabaseMetaData. You'll then use the ConnectApp program to connect to a database and return information about the database to which you are connected.

The Connection Interface

When a database connection is established using the getConnection() method of DriverManager, the getConnection() method returns an object that implements the Connection interface. This interface defines methods for interacting with the database via the established connection. It also defines several constants that describe the manner in which the database supports the committing of database transactions. Approaches to committing transactions are covered in Chapter 45. You don't need to understand these concepts to complete this chapter.

The methods of the Connection interface are used to manage a database connection, obtain information about a connection, roll back or commit database transactions, and prepare SQL statements for execution.

A number of methods are defined by the `Connection` interface. Consult the API documentation of the `Connection` interface for a complete description of these methods. Particular methods of interest include the following:

- `close()`—Closes a database connection.
- `getMetaData()`—Returns an object of the `DatabaseMetaData` interface that can be used to obtain detailed information about the structure and capabilities of a database.
- `createStatement()`—Creates an SQL `Statement` object.
- `prepareStatement()`—Creates an SQL `PreparedStatement` object using an SQL string. `PreparedStatement` objects are precompiled SQL statements that are more efficiently executed.
- `prepareCall()`—Creates an SQL `CallableStatement` object using an SQL string. `CallableStatement` objects are SQL-stored procedure call statements.

> **NOTE**
>
> *SQL* stands for *Structured Query Language*. It is a language for adding information to a database or retrieving information that is contained in a database. Chapter 43, "Database Fundamentals," covers SQL in more detail.

The `DatabaseMetaData` Interface

The `DatabaseMetaData` interface provides a vast amount of information about the database to which a connection is established. It defines several constants for describing database attributes and over 100 methods. You can use these methods to retrieve almost any type of information about a database's structure and capabilities. It is well worth the time to scan through the API documentation of `DatabaseMetaData` to see what kind of information is available through these methods.

> **NOTE**
>
> Databases differ in the extent to which they support the methods of `DatabaseMetaData`. For example, Microsoft Access 97 supports the simple methods used in the `ConnectApp` program in the following section, but tends to choke on more advanced metadata queries. In addition, a database may provide a particular capability, but that capability may not be supported by the driver you use to access the database.

44

THE JAVA.SQL
PACKAGE

The ConnectApp Program

The ConnectApp program, shown in Listing 44.2, establishes a connection to a database and returns information about that database. It illustrates the use of the Connection and DatabaseMetaData classes. The ConnectApp program connects to a sample database provided with the IDS JDBC driver. If you've downloaded and installed an evaluation copy of the IDS Server and JDBC driver, you'll be able to run ConnectApp as shown. Otherwise, if you feel comfortable doing so, you can tailor ConnectApp to your driver and database. Otherwise, just try to read through the program's output and correlate it with its description.

> **NOTE**
>
> If you are using the IDS Server and JDBC driver, don't forget to install the IDSExamples data set, as specified in the installation instructions contained in the IDS User Guide.

> **WARNING**
>
> If you use a different driver than the IDS driver, you'll have to adjust the parameters you use to establish a database connection. Check your driver's documentation for instructions on how to set up a database connection.

Be sure to start your IDS Server before running ConnectApp. When ConnectApp is run, it generates the following output:

```
Database: ACCESS version 3.5 Jet
User name: admin
```

The name of my database is reported as ACCESS with version number 3.5 Jet. It also identifies me as accessing the database as user admin.

The output produced by ConnectApp may be underwhelming, but don't be concerned— you'll be able to produce mountains of information once you learn how to use ResultSet objects. The important point is that we established a successful database connection and were able to access metadata about the database.

ConnectApp begins by loading the IDS driver using the forName() method of the Class class. It then creates a database URL for that driver and the IDSExamples data set that comes with the IDS Server and driver.

> **NOTE**
>
> The IDS Server is a database access server and a Web server. It is used to support the connection of the IDS JDBC driver with a variety of database servers. See Chapter 43 for more information about database access servers.

The URL of the database consists of the JDBC protocol identifier (`jdbc:`), followed by the IDS subprotocol identifier (`ids:`), followed by the subname. The subname consists of the host name and port of my database server (`cx122974-a.cv1.sdca.home.com:80`), the connection parameter identifier (`conn`), the database type (`dbtype=odbc`), and the data set name (`dsn='IDSExamples'`). Other characters of the URL are used as separators.

> **NOTE**
>
> Substitute your host name for `cx122974-a.cv1.sdca.home.com` in the database URL.

The `getConnection()` method of `DriverManager` establishes the connection and returns an object of the `Connection` interface. The `getMetaData()` method is invoked for this `Connection` object to obtain information about the database to which the connection is established.

The `getDatabaseProductName()`, `getDatabaseProductVersion()`, and `getUserName()` methods of the `DatabaseMetaData` interface are used to retrieve information about the database product and the user name associated with the connection.

LISTING 44.2. THE `ConnectApp` PROGRAM.

```
import java.sql.*;
import java.util.*;

class ConnectApp {
 public static void main(String args[]) {
  try{
   // Load the IDS driver
   Class.forName("ids.sql.IDSDriver");
   String url="jdbc:ids://cx122974-a.cv1.sdca.home.com:80/";
   url+="conn?dbtype=odbc&dsn='IDSExamples'";
   // Connect to the database
   Connection connection=DriverManager.getConnection(url);
```

44

THE JAVA.SQL
PACKAGE

continues

LISTING 44.2. CONTINUED

```
    // Get database meta data
    DatabaseMetaData meta=connection.getMetaData();
    // Display meta data information
    System.out.print("Database: "+meta.getDatabaseProductName());
    System.out.println(" version "+meta.getDatabaseProductVersion());
    System.out.println("User name: "+meta.getUserName());
    // Close the database
    connection.close();
  }catch(Exception ex){
   System.out.println(ex);
   System.exit(0);
  }
 }
}
```

Working with Result Sets

When a database query is executed, the results of the query are returned as a table of data organized according to rows and columns. The ResultSet interface is used to provide access to this tabular data. Query results are returned as ResultSet objects that provide access to the tabular data, one row at a time.

A ResultSet object maintains a pointer to a row within the tabular results. This pointer is referred to as a *cursor*. When a ResultSet object is returned from a query, the cursor initially points immediately before the first row of the table. The next() method of the ResultSet class is used to move the cursor to the next row of the table. The next() method returns a boolean value that is true if the next row is returned and false if the end of the table is reached. The next() method is used to successively step through the rows of the tabular results.

The ResultSet interface provides a number of get methods that allow the column entries for a row to be returned as a variety of primitive and reference types, ranging from simple integers to streams and arbitrary objects. The getMetaData() method returns a ResultSetMetaData object that contains information about a row.

The ResultSetMetaData Interface

The ResultSetMetaData interface provides constants and methods that are used to obtain information about ResultSet objects. The getColumnCount() method returns the number of columns in the tabular data accessed by a ResultSet. The getColumnName() method returns the names of each column in the database from which the data was retrieved. The getColumnType() method returns a column's SQL type. The Type class defines constants that are used to identify SQL types. Other methods of `ResultMetaData` are used to access additional column properties, such as the column's display width, number formats, and read/write status.

> **NOTE**
>
> The columns in a `ResultSet` are accessed beginning with index 1 instead of index 0.

The `ResultApp` Program

The `ResultApp` program, shown in Listing 44.3, illustrates the use of the `ResultSet` and `ResultMetaData` interfaces. It retrieves information from the `IDSExamples` database that comes with the IDS JDBC driver. This database defines three tables (`courses`, `departments`, and `employees`) that correspond to those of a typical university. The tables are filled with sample data. The `ResultApp` program executes an SQL statement that queries the database for the entire contents of the `courses` table. The program's results follow:

```
Course_ID | Department_ID | CourseNumber | CourseLevel | CourseName
35 | BIOL | 100 | Basic        | Physiology
37 | BIOL | 300 | Intermediate | Plant Biology
38 | BIOL | 600 | Advanced     | Microbiology
39 | BIOL | 310 | Intermediate | Neurobiology
40 | BIOL | 620 | Advanced     | Neurobiology
41 | CHEM | 100 | Basic        | General Chemistry
42 | CHEM | 300 | Intermediate | Analytical Chemistry
44 | ECON | 100 | Basic        | Financial Accounting
45 | ECON | 110 | Basic        | Business Law
51 | MATH | 100 | Basic        | Calculus I
52 | MATH | 300 | Intermediate | Calculus II
59 | MATH | 600 | Advanced     | Linear Algebra
60 | ECON | 220 | Intermediate | Microeconomics
61 | CHEM | 600 | Advanced     | Organic Chemistry
```

The first line displays the column names of the table. Subsequent lines display the data contained in the table.

> **NOTE**
>
> You'll learn how to execute SQL statements in the next section.

44

THE JAVA.SQL
PACKAGE

The ResultApp program begins by establishing a connection to the IDSExamples database in the same manner as the ConnectApp program. It invokes the createStatement() method of the Connection class to create a Statement object to be used to query the database. The SELECT * FROM customer SQL query statement is then executed using the executeQuery() method of the Statement class. This statement queries the database, and its results are returned as a ResultSet object. The ResultSet object is displayed using the displayResults() method.

The displayResults() method invokes the getMetaData() method of a ResultSet object to access a ResultSetMetaData object that describes the ResultSet object. The getColumnCount() method of the ResultSetMetaData object identifies the number of columns in the ResultSet object. The names of these columns are retrieved using the getColumnName() method of ResultSetMetaData.

A while loop steps through each row of the ResultSet object using the next() method. The getString() method of the ResultSet class is used to retrieve each row's column entry and display it to the console. Note that the columns are accessed beginning with index 1.

LISTING 44.3. THE ResultApp PROGRAM.

```java
import java.sql.*;
import java.util.*;

class ResultApp {
 public static void main(String args[]) {
  try{
   // Load the IDS driver
   Class.forName("ids.sql.IDSDriver");
   String url="jdbc:ids://cx122974-a.cv1.sdca.home.com:80/";
   url+="conn?dbtype=odbc&dsn='IDSExamples'";
   // Connect to the database
   Connection connection=DriverManager.getConnection(url);
   Statement statement = connection.createStatement();
   String sql="SELECT * FROM courses";
   // Execute the SQL statement and retrieve the result set
   ResultSet result = statement.executeQuery(sql);
   displayResults(result);
   // Close the database connection
   connection.close();
  }catch(Exception ex){
   System.out.println(ex);
   System.exit(0);
  }
 }
 static void displayResults(ResultSet r) throws SQLException {
  // Get result set meta data
```

```
    ResultSetMetaData rmeta = r.getMetaData();
    // Use meta data to determine the number of columns in each row
    // of the result set
    int numColumns=rmeta.getColumnCount();
    // Print out values of each column
    for(int i=1;i<=numColumns;++i) {
     if(i<numColumns)
       System.out.print(rmeta.getColumnName(i)+" ¦ ");
     else
       System.out.println(rmeta.getColumnName(i));
    }
    while(r.next()){
     for(int i=1;i<=numColumns;++i) {
      if(i<numColumns)
        System.out.print(r.getString(i)+" ¦ ");
      else
        System.out.println(r.getString(i).trim());
     }
    }
   }
}
```

Executing SQL Statements

SQL is the language used to interact with database servers. SQL statements can be used to add information to a database, update or delete existing database information, or retrieve information from a database. The purpose of the java.sql package is to let you execute SQL statements from Java. Chapter 43 provides an introduction to SQL. This section discusses the JDBC API interfaces that are used to execute SQL statements.

The `Statement` Interface

In the ResultApp program, you created an object of the Statement interface by invoking the createStatement() method of the Connection interface. You then invoked the executeQuery() method of the Statement interface, passing it the SELECT * FROM courses SQL statement as an argument. This resulted in the query being processed by the database and a ResultSet object being returned. This example illustrates the simplicity with which SQL statements are executed via the JDBC.

The Statement interface defines methods that are used to interact with databases via the execution of SQL statements. These methods also support the processing of query results returned via ResultSet objects and provide control over the mechanics of query processing. The execute(), executeQuery(), and executeUpdate() methods are the primary methods of interest in the Statement interface.

The executeQuery() method executes an SQL statement (such as the SELECT statement) that queries a database and returns a ResultSet object. The executeUpdate() method executes an SQL statement (such as an INSERT, UPDATE, or DELETE statement) that updates the database and returns the integer value of the row count associated with the SQL statement, or 0 if the statement did not return a result.

The execute() method executes an SQL statement that is written as a String object. It returns a boolean value indicating whether a ResultSet object was produced as the result of the statement's execution. The getResultSet() and getMoreResults() methods are used to retrieve the ResultSet object. If the statement's execution returns an update count, execute() returns false. The update count can be retrieved using the getUpdateCount() method.

The PreparedStatement Interface

The PreparedStatement interface extends the Statement interface to define methods that are used to work with precompiled SQL statements. The use of precompiled SQL statements provides a more efficient way of executing frequently used SQL statements.

PreparedStatement objects may be used with parameterized SQL statements. These parameterized SQL statements replace a constant SQL expression with a question mark (?). For example, the following parameterized statement retrieves an unspecified column from the courses table:

```
SELECT ? FROM courses
```

The preceding statement needs to be instantiated with the name of the column to be retrieved. The parameterized fields are said to be instantiated by IN parameter values.

> **NOTE**
>
> The implementation of SQL varies from database to database. However, the SQL presented in this book is commonly supported by all databases.

The PreparedStatement interface provides several set methods for setting the values of IN parameters. These methods are organized into the type of value to which a parameter is to be set.

PreparedStatement provides its own version of the execute(), executeQuery(), and executeUpdate() methods of the Statement interface. These methods do not specify the

SQL statement to be used in the query. Instead, the SQL statement is specified as an argument to the prepareStatement() method of the Connection interface that is used to create the PreparedStatement object.

The CallableStatement Interface

The CallableStatement interface extends the PreparedStatement interface to implement stored SQL procedures. CallableStatement objects are created via the prepareCall() method of the Connection class. A stored SQL procedure is passed as an argument to the prepareCall() method. It may be parameterized using question marks in the same manner as that discussed for the PreparedStatement interface. However, the CallableStatement interface allows some parameters to be OUT parameters, which are used to return values from the SQL procedure call. The registerOutParameter() method of the CallableStatement interface is used to identify the type of OUT parameter. In addition, several get methods are provided to retrieve the value returned by an OUT parameter.

The StatementApp Program

The StatementApp program, shown in Listing 44.4, allows you to execute an SQL statement that is passed as a command-line parameter. The program uses the IDS driver to link to the IDSExamples data set used in the previous examples of this chapter. You can use this program to brush up on your SQL. Execute the program with the "SELECT * FROM courses" SQL statement to obtain a listing of the contents of the courses table:

```
java StatementApp "SELECT * FROM courses"
SELECT * FROM courses
Course_ID ¦ Department_ID ¦ CourseNumber ¦ CourseLevel ¦ CourseName
35 ¦ BIOL ¦ 100 ¦ Basic        ¦ Physiology
37 ¦ BIOL ¦ 300 ¦ Intermediate ¦ Plant Biology
38 ¦ BIOL ¦ 600 ¦ Advanced     ¦ Microbiology
39 ¦ BIOL ¦ 310 ¦ Intermediate ¦ Neurobiology
40 ¦ BIOL ¦ 620 ¦ Advanced     ¦ Neurobiology
41 ¦ CHEM ¦ 100 ¦ Basic        ¦ General Chemistry
42 ¦ CHEM ¦ 300 ¦ Intermediate ¦ Analytical Chemistry
44 ¦ ECON ¦ 100 ¦ Basic        ¦ Financial Accounting
45 ¦ ECON ¦ 110 ¦ Basic        ¦ Business Law
51 ¦ MATH ¦ 100 ¦ Basic        ¦ Calculus I
52 ¦ MATH ¦ 300 ¦ Intermediate ¦ Calculus II
59 ¦ MATH ¦ 600 ¦ Advanced     ¦ Linear Algebra
60 ¦ ECON ¦ 220 ¦ Intermediate ¦ Microeconomics
61 ¦ CHEM ¦ 600 ¦ Advanced     ¦ Organic Chemistry
```

The economics classes don't belong with all of the math and science courses. Let's delete them by using the "DELETE FROM courses WHERE Department_ID = 'ECON'" SQL statement:

44

THE JAVA.SQL PACKAGE

```
java StatementApp "DELETE FROM courses WHERE Department_ID
➥= 'ECON'"
DELETE FROM courses WHERE Department_ID = 'ECON'
```

Use the "SELECT * FROM courses" statement to verify that the economics classes have been deleted:

```
java StatementApp "SELECT * FROM courses"
SELECT * FROM courses
Course_ID ¦ Department_ID ¦ CourseNumber ¦ CourseLevel ¦ CourseName
35 ¦ BIOL ¦ 100 ¦ Basic        ¦ Physiology
37 ¦ BIOL ¦ 300 ¦ Intermediate ¦ Plant Biology
38 ¦ BIOL ¦ 600 ¦ Advanced     ¦ Microbiology
39 ¦ BIOL ¦ 310 ¦ Intermediate ¦ Neurobiology
40 ¦ BIOL ¦ 620 ¦ Advanced     ¦ Neurobiology
41 ¦ CHEM ¦ 100 ¦ Basic        ¦ General Chemistry
42 ¦ CHEM ¦ 300 ¦ Intermediate ¦ Analytical Chemistry
51 ¦ MATH ¦ 100 ¦ Basic        ¦ Calculus I
52 ¦ MATH ¦ 300 ¦ Intermediate ¦ Calculus II
59 ¦ MATH ¦ 600 ¦ Advanced     ¦ Linear Algebra
61 ¦ CHEM ¦ 600 ¦ Advanced     ¦ Organic Chemistry
```

Which courses are missing from the list? These poor students are being deprived of a Java education. Enter the following INSERT SQL statements to round out their education:

```
java StatementApp "INSERT INTO courses VALUES ('34', 'JAVA',
➥ '999', 'Basic', 'Intro to Java')"
INSERT INTO courses VALUES ('34', 'JAVA', '999', 'Basic', 'Intro to Java')

java StatementApp "INSERT INTO courses VALUES ('43', 'JAVA',
➥ '999', 'Intermediate', 'AWT Programming')"
INSERT INTO courses VALUES ('43', 'JAVA', '999', 'Intermediate', 'AWT
Programmin
➥g')

java StatementApp "INSERT INTO courses VALUES ('62', 'JAVA'
➥, '999', 'Advanced', 'Database Programming')"
INSERT INTO courses VALUES ('62', 'JAVA', '999', 'Advanced', 'Database
Programmi
➥ng')
```

Use the "SELECT * FROM courses" statement to redisplay the courses table:

```
java StatementApp "SELECT * FROM courses"
SELECT * FROM courses
Course_ID ¦ Department_ID ¦ CourseNumber ¦ CourseLevel ¦ CourseName
35 ¦ BIOL ¦ 100 ¦ Basic        ¦ Physiology
37 ¦ BIOL ¦ 300 ¦ Intermediate ¦ Plant Biology
38 ¦ BIOL ¦ 600 ¦ Advanced     ¦ Microbiology
39 ¦ BIOL ¦ 310 ¦ Intermediate ¦ Neurobiology
40 ¦ BIOL ¦ 620 ¦ Advanced     ¦ Neurobiology
41 ¦ CHEM ¦ 100 ¦ Basic        ¦ General Chemistry
42 ¦ CHEM ¦ 300 ¦ Intermediate ¦ Analytical Chemistry
```

```
51 | MATH | 100 | Basic        | Calculus I
52 | MATH | 300 | Intermediate | Calculus II
59 | MATH | 600 | Advanced     | Linear Algebra
61 | CHEM | 600 | Advanced     | Organic Chemistry
34 | JAVA | 999 | Basic        | Intro to Java
43 | JAVA | 999 | Intermediate | AWT Programming
62 | JAVA | 999 | Advanced     | Database Programming
```

All the Java courses were appended to the end of the table. Let's sort the result set by the Course_ID column:

```
java StatementApp "SELECT * FROM courses ORDER BY Course_ID"
SELECT * FROM courses ORDER BY Course_ID
Course_ID | Department_ID | CourseNumber | CourseLevel | CourseName
34 | JAVA | 999 | Basic        | Intro to Java
35 | BIOL | 100 | Basic        | Physiology
37 | BIOL | 300 | Intermediate | Plant Biology
38 | BIOL | 600 | Advanced     | Microbiology
39 | BIOL | 310 | Intermediate | Neurobiology
40 | BIOL | 620 | Advanced     | Neurobiology
41 | CHEM | 100 | Basic        | General Chemistry
42 | CHEM | 300 | Intermediate | Analytical Chemistry
43 | JAVA | 999 | Intermediate | AWT Programming
51 | MATH | 100 | Basic        | Calculus I
52 | MATH | 300 | Intermediate | Calculus II
59 | MATH | 600 | Advanced     | Linear Algebra
61 | CHEM | 600 | Advanced     | Organic Chemistry
62 | JAVA | 999 | Advanced     | Database Programming
```

The Database Programming course could apply to any programming language. Let's use the UPDATE statement to change it to Advanced JDBC.

```
java StatementApp "UPDATE courses SET CourseName = 'Advanced
➥JDBC' WHERE Department_ID = 'JAVA' AND CourseLevel = 'Advanced'"
UPDATE courses SET CourseName = 'Advanced JDBC' WHERE Department_ID =
'JAVA' AND
➥ CourseLevel = 'Advanced'
```

Once again, we'll display the courses table, sorted by the Course_ID column:

```
java StatementApp "SELECT * FROM courses ORDER BY Course_ID"
SELECT * FROM courses ORDER BY Course_ID
Course_ID | Department_ID | CourseNumber | CourseLevel | CourseName
34 | JAVA | 999 | Basic        | Intro to Java
35 | BIOL | 100 | Basic        | Physiology
37 | BIOL | 300 | Intermediate | Plant Biology
38 | BIOL | 600 | Advanced     | Microbiology
39 | BIOL | 310 | Intermediate | Neurobiology
40 | BIOL | 620 | Advanced     | Neurobiology
41 | CHEM | 100 | Basic        | General Chemistry
42 | CHEM | 300 | Intermediate | Analytical Chemistry
```

44

THE JAVA.SQL
PACKAGE

```
43 ¦ JAVA ¦ 999 ¦ Intermediate ¦ AWT Programming
51 ¦ MATH ¦ 100 ¦ Basic        ¦ Calculus I
52 ¦ MATH ¦ 300 ¦ Intermediate ¦ Calculus II
59 ¦ MATH ¦ 600 ¦ Advanced     ¦ Linear Algebra
61 ¦ CHEM ¦ 600 ¦ Advanced     ¦ Organic Chemistry
62 ¦ JAVA ¦ 999 ¦ Advanced     ¦ Advanced JDBC
```

The StatementApp program provides a lot of capability in a few lines of code. That's because it allows you to enter SQL statements directly to the database. It begins in the same way as ResultApp by loading the ids.sql.IDSDriver, connecting to the IDSExamples data set, and creating a Statement object. It then passes the program's command-line argument to the execute() method of the Statement interface. If the execute() method returns a true value, it invokes the getResultSet() method of the Statement interface to retrieve the ResultSet object of a query operation. It then invokes the displayResults() method to display the ResultSet.

LISTING 44.4. THE StatementApp PROGRAM.

```java
import java.sql.*;
import java.util.*;

class StatementApp {
 public static void main(String args[]) {
  if(args.length!=1){
   System.out.println("Usage: java StatementApp sql");
   System.exit(0);
  }
  try{
   // Load IDS driver
   Class.forName("ids.sql.IDSDriver");
   String url="jdbc:ids://cx122974-a.cv1.sdca.home.com:80/";
   url+="conn?dbtype=odbc&dsn='IDSExamples'";
   // Connect to database
   Connection connection=DriverManager.getConnection(url);
   Statement statement = connection.createStatement();
   String sql=args[0];
   System.out.println(sql);
   // Execute SQL statement
   boolean hasResults = statement.execute(sql);
   if(hasResults){
    // Retrieve result set
    ResultSet result = statement.getResultSet();
    if(result!=null) displayResults(result);
   }
   // Close database connection
   connection.close();
  }catch(Exception ex){
   System.out.println(ex);
```

```
     System.exit(0);
   }
 }
 static void displayResults(ResultSet r) throws SQLException {
  // Get meta data about result set
  ResultSetMetaData rmeta = r.getMetaData();
  // Use meta data to determine the number of columns
  // in the result set
  int numColumns=rmeta.getColumnCount();
  // Display values of each column
  for(int i=1;i<=numColumns;++i) {
   if(i<numColumns)
    System.out.print(rmeta.getColumnName(i)+" ¦ ");
   else
    System.out.println(rmeta.getColumnName(i));
  }
  while(r.next()){
   for(int i=1;i<=numColumns;++i) {
    if(i<numColumns)
     System.out.print(r.getString(i)+" ¦ ");
    else
     System.out.println(r.getString(i).trim());
   }
  }
 }
}
```

The `Date`, `Time`, and `Timestamp` Classes

The `java.sql` package provides the `Date`, `Time`, and `Timestamp` classes as extensions to `java.util.Date`. They may be used as objects within database transactions. The `Date` class represents ANSI SQL `DATE` values in the `YYYY-MM-DD` format. The `Time` class represents ANSI SQL `TIME` values in the `HH:MM:SS` format. The `Timestamp` class represents ANSI SQL `TIMESTAMP` (`DATE` and `TIME`) values.

Summary

In this chapter, you were introduced to the JDBC. You learned about the classes of the `java.sql` package and learned how to work with JDBC drivers, connect to databases, execute SQL statements, and work with result sets. This chapter provided a quick introduction to the `java.sql` package. The next chapter, "Using JDBC," expands upon this chapter and provides further examples of the information you've learned.

44

THE JAVA.SQL PACKAGE

Using JDBC

CHAPTER

45

Chapter 44, "Connecting to Databases Using the `java.sql` Package," provided an introduction to database programming using JDBC. This chapter continues your introduction to database programming by showing you how to work with vendor-specific JDBC drivers and database servers. You'll get more hands-on experience using SQL, and you'll learn how to work with the results of SQL queries. You'll also learn about transaction processing and database security. When you finish this chapter, you'll be able to write more advanced Java database applications.

Using Alternate JDBC Drivers and Databases

In Chapter 43, you learned about the four different types of JDBC drivers:

- JDBC-ODBC bridge plus ODBC driver
- Native-API partly Java driver
- JDBC-Net pure Java driver
- Native-protocol pure Java driver

In this section, you'll work with three of the four driver types. You'll learn how to access a Microsoft Access 97 database using the JDBC-ODBC bridge driver and the IDS JDBC driver. You'll also learn how to access an mSQL database using a Type 4 JDBC driver. When you finish this section, you'll have enough experience working with database drivers to figure out how to use other vendor-specific JDBC drivers.

Setting Up ODBC Drivers to Work with Microsoft Access Databases

 I've provided a small Microsoft Access 97 database named `action.mdb` in the `ch45` directory. In order to use this database, you'll have to set it up as an ODBC data source. You do this using the 32-bit ODBC applet found in the Control Panel.

> **NOTE**
>
> If you have Microsoft Access 97 and want to use it to run the examples of this chapter, install it before setting up the `action.mdb` database.

After you open the applet, click the System DSN tab and then the Add button to add a new data source. Enter `Actions` as the name for the data source in the Data Source

Name field. Click the Select button to set the path to the database to the location of the ch45 directory. (See Figure 45.1.)

> **NOTE**
>
> A System DSN is accessible to more than one user, while a User DSN is limited to a single user. It is important to set up your database as a System DSN, rather than a User DSN, to make it accessible to other users.

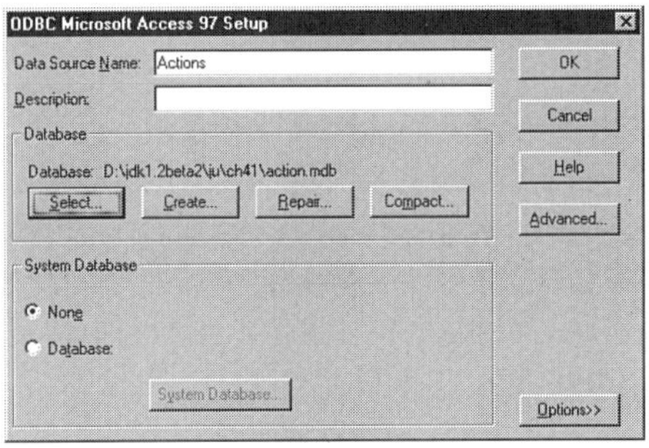

FIGURE 45.1.

Setting up the Actions *data source.*

If you do not have Microsoft Access 97, you'll still be able to follow the example. In a later section of this chapter, "Setting Up the mSQL Server," I'll show you how to download and install the mSQL database server.

Setting Up the IDS Server and IDS JDBC Driver

As mentioned in Chapter 44, I highly recommend using the IDS JDBC driver provided by IDS Software. It is a Type 3 JDBC driver that works with the IDS Server—a database access server that connects the IDS JDBC driver with your database. You can download an evaluation copy of the IDS Server and JDBC driver from the IDS Software Web site at http://www.idssoftware.com. The IDS software is distributed as a self-extracting executable file. Open this file and follow the installation instructions.

After installing the IDS software, read through the User's Guide. In particular, Section 1 describes how to set up the IDS Server, and Section 4 describes how to set up the IDS JDBC driver. Don't worry. You probably won't have to make many changes to configure the server and driver for your particular needs. I installed the software in the default C:\IDSServer directory on the same machine as Microsoft Access. Be sure to include the IDS JDBC driver in your CLASSPATH. I added C:\IDSServer\classes to my CLASSPATH.

45

USING JDBC

> **NOTE**
>
> If your organization is intent on pursuing Java database programming, you should seriously consider obtaining a production version of the IDS Server and JDBC driver. They are an excellent solution to providing database connectivity to Java applications and applets.

Setting Up the mSQL Server

Whether you have Microsoft Access or not, it will be worth your time to download and install the mSQL database server. If you don't have Microsoft Access 97, you can use mSQL to work some of the examples in this book. If you do have Microsoft Access 97, using mSQL will broaden your base of experience. You can obtain a copy of the Windows version of mSQL from

`ftp://bond.edu.au/pub/Minerva/msql/Contrib/Win-mSQL/`.

The Windows version of mSQL is a zipped file that you must unzip before installing mSQL. After unzipping the file, read the `Readme` and `Readme.w32` files for installation instructions. The mSQL server is easy to install and use if you follow these instructions. The `mSQL.htm` file located in the `\DOC` directory of the unzipped files provides you with all the information you need to run mSQL.

Make sure that you read the license that comes with mSQL. It is distributed as shareware and must be registered as specified in the license.

Setting Up the mSQL JDBC Driver

In order to connect to an mSQL server from Java, you need an appropriate JDBC driver. Luckily, an mSQL JDBC driver was developed by George Reese. You can download the latest version from `http://www.imaginary.com/Java/`.

The driver is distributed as a tarred, gzipped file. You can extract the contents of this file using an unarchiving tool such as WinZip. After extracting the file, add the `imaginary.zip` file to your CLASSPATH.

Setting Up the `ActMSQL` Database

 An mSQL database is provided in the `ch45\ActmSQL` directory. To use this database with mSQL, move the entire `ActmSQL` directory under `c:\msql\msqldb`. The `c:\msql\msqldb` directory is where mSQL keeps its database files. The `c:\msql\msqldb\ActmSQL` directory is the directory used for the `ActmSQL` database.

Using the `AccessApp` Program

Now that you've gone to all the trouble of installing and configuring the IDS Server, the IDS JDBC driver, the mSQL server, and the mSQL JDBC driver, you can reap the fruits of your labor. The `AccessApp` program, shown in Listing 45.1, allows you to use a variety of JDBC drivers to access the Microsoft Access 97 database (`action.mdb`) and the mSQL database (`ActmSQL`).

LISTING 45.1. THE `AccessApp` PROGRAM.

```java
import java.awt.*;
import java.awt.event.*;
import java.sql.*;

public class AccessApp extends Frame {
 TextField driver = new TextField(60);
 TextField url = new TextField(60);
 TextField sql = new TextField(60);
 Button doIt = new Button("Do it!");
 TextArea resultArea = new TextArea(10,60);
 public static void main(String args[]){
  AccessApp app = new AccessApp();
 }
 public AccessApp() {
  super("AccessApp");
  setup();
  pack();
  addWindowListener(new WindowEventHandler());
  show();
 }
 void setup() {
  setupMenuBar();
  setLayout(new GridLayout(2,1));
  Panel topPanel = new Panel();
  topPanel.setLayout(new GridLayout(4,1));
  Panel panels[]=new Panel[4];
  for(int i=0;i<panels.length;++i){
   panels[i]=new Panel();
   panels[i].setLayout(new FlowLayout(FlowLayout.LEFT));
  }
  panels[0].add(new Label("Driver:"));
  panels[0].add(driver);
  panels[1].add(new Label("URL: "));
  panels[1].add(url);
  panels[2].add(new Label("SQL: "));
  panels[2].add(sql);
  doIt.addActionListener(new ButtonHandler());
```

continues

LISTING 45.1. CONTINUED

```java
    panels[3].add(doIt);
    for(int i=0;i<panels.length;++i)
     topPanel.add(panels[i]);
    add(topPanel);
    add(resultArea);
  }
  void setupMenuBar() {
   MenuBar menuBar = new MenuBar();
   Menu fileMenu = new Menu("File");
   MenuItem fileExit = new MenuItem("Exit");
   fileExit.addActionListener(new MenuItemHandler());
   fileMenu.add(fileExit);
   menuBar.add(fileMenu);
   setMenuBar(menuBar);
  }
  void accessDB() {
   try{
    // Load JDBC driver
    Class.forName(driver.getText());
    // Connect to database
    Connection connection=DriverManager.getConnection(url.getText());
    Statement statement = connection.createStatement();
    // Execute SQL
    boolean hasResults = statement.execute(sql.getText());
    if(hasResults){
     // Get results of query
     ResultSet result = statement.getResultSet();
     if(result!=null) displayResults(result);
    }else resultArea.setText("");
    // Close database connection
    connection.close();
   }catch(Exception ex){
    resultArea.setText(ex.toString());
   }
  }
  void displayResults(ResultSet r) throws SQLException {
   ResultSetMetaData rmeta = r.getMetaData();
   // Use meta data to obtain the number of columns
   int numColumns=rmeta.getColumnCount();
   String text="";
   for(int i=1;i<=numColumns;++i) {
    if(i<numColumns)
     text+=rmeta.getColumnName(i)+" ¦ ";
    else
     text+=rmeta.getColumnName(i);
   }
   text+="\n";
   while(r.next()){
    for(int i=1;i<=numColumns;++i) {
```

```
  if(i<numColumns)
    text+=r.getString(i)+" ¦ ";
  else
    text+=r.getString(i).trim();
   }
  text+="\n";
 }
 resultArea.setText(text);
}
class ButtonHandler implements ActionListener {
 public void actionPerformed(ActionEvent ev){
  String s=ev.getActionCommand();
  if(s=="Do it!") accessDB();
 }
}
class MenuItemHandler implements ActionListener {
 public void actionPerformed(ActionEvent ev){
  String s=ev.getActionCommand();
  if(s=="Exit"){
   System.exit(0);
  }
 }
}
class WindowEventHandler extends WindowAdapter {
 public void windowClosing(WindowEvent e){
  System.exit(0);
 }
 }
}
```

Before you run the AccessApp program, start the IDS Server by selecting it from the Start menu. Also, open an MS-DOS window and change the directory to C:\msql. Start up the mSQL server by running the msqld.bat file.

When you run AccessApp, it displays the window shown in Figure 45.2. The Driver text field allows you to enter the name of a JDBC driver. The URL field allows you to enter the URL of a database to be accessed by the driver. The SQL field allows you to enter an SQL command to update the database or retrieve information from it. You can use this program to access the Access 97 database and the mSQL database using the JDBC-ODBC bridge, IDS JDBC driver, and mSQL JDBC driver.

Let's start with the JDBC-ODBC bridge. This driver comes with the JDK 1.2.

1. Enter sun.jdbc.odbc.JdbcOdbcDriver into the Driver field to load the JDBC-ODBC bridge driver.

2. Enter jdbc:odbc:Actions in the URL field to tell the driver to access the Actions data set that you set up earlier in this chapter.

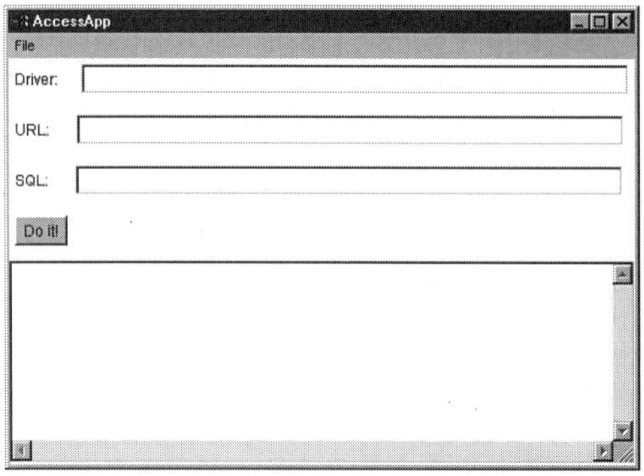

FIGURE 45.2.

Opening window for AccessApp.

3. Now enter SELECT * FROM ActionItem in the SQL field to dump the contents of the ActionItem table.

4. Click the Do it! button to execute the SQL statement.

The program displays the contents of the ActionItem table, as shown in Figure 45.3.

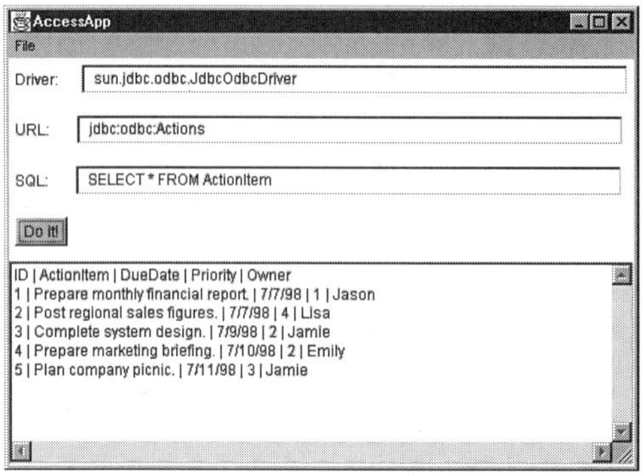

FIGURE 45.3.

Using the JDBC-ODBC bridge driver.

Now let's execute the same command using the IDS JDBC driver. The IDS driver will access the same Actions data set, but it will access it through the IDS Server.

1. Enter ids.sql.IDSDriver in the Driver field to load the IDS driver.

2. Enter jdbc:ids://your.host.com:port/conn?dbtype=odbc&dsn='Actions' in the URL field. Substitute the name of the host where you installed the IDS Server for *your.host.com* and your IDS Server's port number for *port*. (The default port is 12.)

3. Now click the Do it! button.

Figure 45.4 shows the results of the query.

FIGURE 45.4.

Using the IDS JDBC driver.

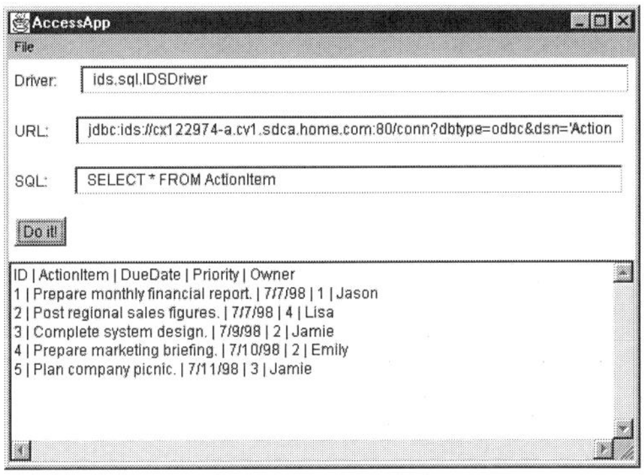

What, no change? Don't worry—the results should stay the same. You just executed the same command using a different driver. Try executing some other SQL commands. It really works!

So far, we've accessed the `Actions` data set using the JDBC-ODBC bridge driver and the IDS JDBC driver. Now we'll access the `ActmSQL` database using the mSQL database server and the mSQL JDBC driver.

1. Enter `com.imaginary.sql.msql.MsqlDriver` in the Driver field.
2. Enter `jdbc:msql://your.host.com:port/ActmSQL` in the URL field. Substitute the name of the host where you installed the mSQL server for *your.host.com* and your server's port number for *port*. (The default port is 1112.)
3. Enter `SELECT * from Action` in the SQL field.
4. Click the Do it! button.

Voilà! You have done it again, as shown in Figure 45.5.

FIGURE 45.5.

Using the mSQL JDBC bridge driver.

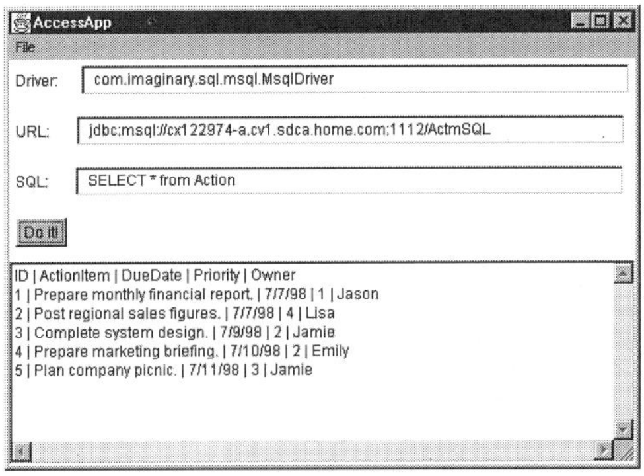

45

USING JDBC

How `AccessApp` Works

`AccessApp` begins by creating and laying out the three text fields, the Do it! button, and the text area. The `ButtonHandler` class handles the clicking of the Do it! button by invoking the `accessDB()` method.

The `accessDB()` method invokes the `forName()` method of the `Class` class to load the JDBC driver identified by the `driver` variable. It then invokes the `getConnection()` method of the `DriverManager` class to establish a connection to the database at the specified URL. The `createStatement()` method of the `Connection` class is invoked to create a `Statement` object. The `execute()` method of this object is invoked to execute the SQL statement entered in the text field referenced by the `sql` variable.

If the `execute()` method returns a `true` value, indicating that it has produced a `ResultSet` object, the `getResultSet()` method is invoked to retrieve this object. The `displayResults()` method is then invoked to display the returned results in the text area.

If no results were returned by the `execute()` method, the text area is emptied. The `close()` method of the `Connection` interface is invoked to close the database connection.

The `displayResults()` method takes a `ResultSet` object as an argument. It invokes the `getMetaData()` method of the `ResultSet` class to retrieve a `ResultSetMetaData` object that describes the `ResultSet` object. It invokes the `getColumnCount()` method to determine the number of columns in the result set. Then the `displayResults` method retrieves each column name using the `getColumnName()` method of the `ResultSetMetaData` class. It builds a column header using these names. Each column is separated using a vertical bar (¦).

After building the column header, `displayResults()` executes a `while` loop that reads each row of the `ResultSet` object. It uses the `next()` method to move between rows of the result set. It reads the column values of the row using the `getString()` method of the `ResultSet` class. The rows of the result set are formatted in the same manner as the column header. The columns of each row are separated by vertical bars. The resulting text string is then displayed in the `TextArea` object referenced by the `resultArea` variable.

Interacting with the Database

Now that you have broadened your knowledge of how to use JDBC drivers to connect to databases, you are on your way to becoming a JDBC programmer. Once you connect to a database, the bulk of your programming involves executing SQL statements and displaying the results of those statements. Chapter 43 introduced you to SQL and Chapter

44 showed you how to use SQL with Java. This chapter provides you with more examples of using SQL.

The `AccessApp` program provides you with a good opportunity to practice the SQL that you learned in Chapter 43. You'll be executing SQL statements directly. If you were writing a Java program to act as an SQL client, you would write a GUI front end to the SQL. The GUI front end would shield your users from having to learn SQL.

Open `AccessApp` and enter the name of a JDBC driver in the Driver field and the URL of the `Actions` data set in the URL field, as shown in Figure 45.6. I'll be using the JDBC-ODBC driver this time. You can use the IDS driver or any other driver that works with ODBC.

FIGURE 45.6.

Specifying the JDBC driver and database URL.

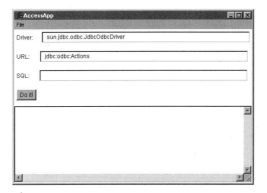

Enter the following SQL statement in the SQL field, as shown in Figure 45.7. Click Do it! to execute this statement:

```
CREATE TABLE Test (Col1 char(20), Col2 int, Col3 float)
```

This statement creates a new table named `Test` in the `Actions` data set (Microsoft Access 97 `action.mdb` database). The table has columns named `Col1`, `Col2`, and `Col3`. `Col1` is a 20-character-wide text column. `Col2` stores integer values, and `Col3` stores floating point values.

Enter the following SQL statement and click the Do it! button (see Figure 45.8.):

```
INSERT INTO Test VALUES ('Java', 1, 10.0)
```

This statement inserts a new row into the database with the value of `Col1` set to `'Java'`, `Col2` set to 1, and `Col3` set to `10.0`.

45

USING JDBC

FIGURE 45.7.

Using the CREATE
TABLE *statement to*
create the Test
table.

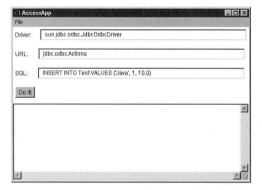

FIGURE 45.8.

Using the INSERT
statement to add
new rows to the
Test *table.*

Enter the following two rows in the same manner:

```
INSERT INTO Test VALUES ('JDBC', 10, 1.0)
```

```
INSERT INTO Test VALUES ('ODBC', 100, 0.1)
```

Now let's see what our database looks like. Enter the following and click the Do it! button:

```
SELECT * FROM Test
```

The text area displays the contents of the Test table, as shown in Figure 45.9.

Enter the following statement to delete all rows where the value of Col2 is 100 (see Figure 45.10.):

```
DELETE FROM Test WHERE Col2 = 100
```

Click the Do it! button to execute the DELETE statement.

FIGURE 45.9.

Checking the results of the INSERT *statements.*

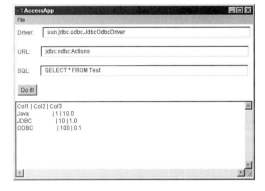

FIGURE 45.10.

Using the DELETE *statement to delete the last row.*

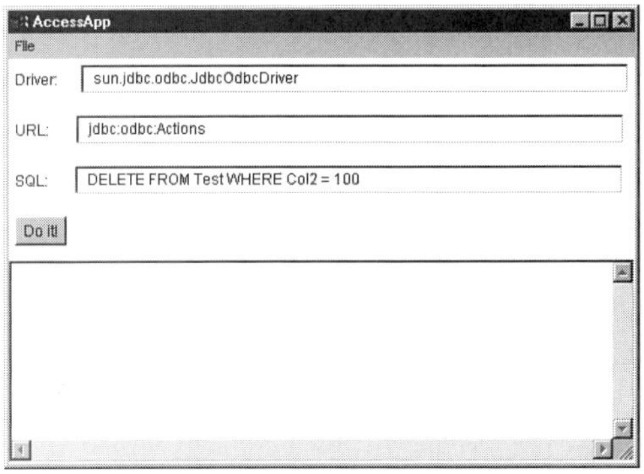

Let's replace the deleted row using the following INSERT statement:

```
INSERT INTO Test VALUES ('SQL', 50, 2.5)
```

Now execute the UPDATE statement, shown in Figure 45.11:

```
UPDATE Test SET Col2 = 99 WHERE Col3 < 10.0
```

FIGURE 45.11.

Using the UPDATE *statement to change selected rows.*

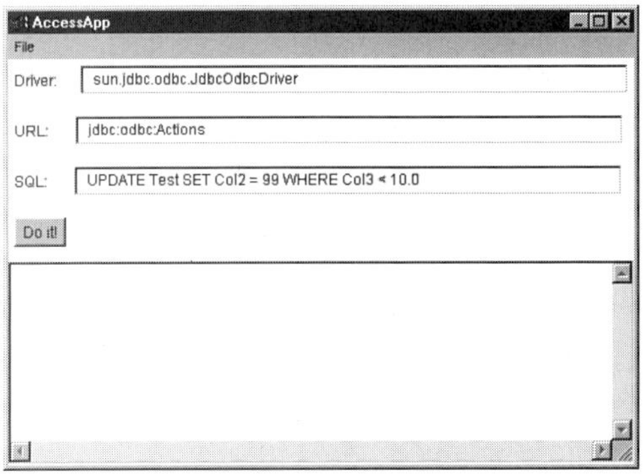

45

USING JDBC

Are you curious to see what the `Test` table looks like? Execute the following statement to dump all rows of `Test`:

```
SELECT * FROM Test
```

Figure 45.12 shows the results of the query.

FIGURE 45.12.

Checking the updated Test *table.*

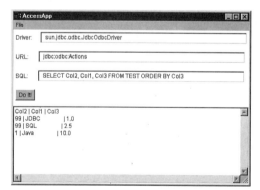

Execute the following `SELECT` statement to rearrange the first and second columns and sort by the third column:

```
SELECT Col2, Col1, Col3 FROM TEST ORDER BY Col3
```

Figure 45.13 shows the modified output.

FIGURE 45.13.

Sorting the results of a query.

Working with Result Sets

As you saw in the previous section, working with SQL is pretty easy. There are only a handful of important SQL statements. Once you learn their syntax, you can accomplish quite a bit.

Connecting to databases and executing SQL statements enables you to add information to the databases and retrieve information in the form of ResultSet objects. You can think of ResultSet objects as custom tables that are generated by the database as the result of processing a SELECT statement. The SELECT statement identifies the columns to be selected and the way results should be ordered.

Accessing the data contained in a ResultSet object is pretty straightforward. However, like laying out a GUI, it can be somewhat tedious. A ResultSet object can be thought of as a window on the custom table returned as the result of processing a SELECT statement. This window lets you view only one row of the table at a time. You can move the window forward to the next row (using the next() method), but you can never move it back. This means that you have to store the information of interest in a particular row before moving onto the next row. The get methods of the ResultSet interface allow you to retrieve the information contained in a particular column of the current row. These methods convert the column data from its SQL type to a Java type. In most cases, you will use the getString() method to retrieve information as a Java String object. However, there are methods that work with all primitive types and objects. The getAsciiStream(), getUnicodeStream(), and getBinaryStream() methods that are used to retrieve large column values are Java streams. You can use the read() methods of the particular stream class to access the contents of the stream in manageable amounts.

The ResultSet interface does not provide any methods to find out how many columns are in a particular row. Instead, it provides the getMetaData() method to return a ResultSetMetaData object.

A ResultSetMetaData object provides quite a bit of information about its corresponding ResultSet object. There are several methods that return information about the columns of the ResultSet object and the table from which the columns originated, as well as other helpful information. Although you probably won't use all of these methods, you will find yourself using some of them, such as the getColumnCount() and getColumnName() methods, in almost all of your Java database applications.

Transaction Processing

So far, whenever we've executed an SQL statement, the statement has automatically updated the contents of the database. This approach to database updating works fine for some database applications but not as well for others.

Consider the case where several database tables need to be updated to input a new customer order into a database that supports an online ordering application. For example, a Customers table may need to be updated with information about the new customer, an

Orders table may need to be updated with information about the order, and a ProductAvailability table may need to be updated to mark a product as sold. What happens if a database connection is broken before all three tables are updated? The database is left in a corrupted state.

Transaction processing was invented as a solution to this database update problem. A *transaction* consists of a group of related database operations. The SQL statements that make up a transaction update the database at the same time. Even though the statements are executed in sequence, they do not permanently update the database until they are *committed*. If an error occurs during the processing of a transaction, the SQL statements that make up the transaction can be *rolled back*.

The setAutoCommit(), commit(), and rollback() methods of the Connection interface are used to implement transaction processing. The setAutoCommit() method turns off automatic committing of SQL statements. When setAutoCommit() is turned off, SQL statements are organized into a single transaction until a commit() or rollback() method is invoked. The commit() method completes a transaction by committing all SQL statements that were executed since the last commit or rollback. The rollback() method reverses a transaction that is in progress by erasing the effects of all SQL statements that were executed since the last commit or rollback.

Transaction Isolation

Transaction processing helps eliminate many problems associated with multiple database updates. However, it creates some problems of its own. Consider the case where two separate transactions occur simultaneously. An SQL statement of the first transaction changes a row in a table, and an SQL statement of the second transaction performs a query that reads the changed row. If the first transaction has not yet been committed, what row value should be reported in the query?

Transaction isolation levels are used to specify how potential conflicts between transactions should be resolved. Higher levels of transaction isolation prevent conflicts from occurring between concurrent transactions. However, this isolation comes at the expense of reduced database performance. At the highest level of transaction isolation, transactions must occur in a serial fashion, eliminating concurrent database transactions completely.

The Connection interface defines constants that can be used to specify transaction isolation levels. The getTransactionIsolation() and setTransactionIsolation() methods of the Connection interface are used to access transaction isolation levels. The supportsTransactionIsolation() method of the DatabaseMetaData interface can be used to determine what levels of transaction isolation are supported by a particular database.

The `CommitApp` Program

The `CommitApp` program, shown in Listing 45.2, illustrates the use of transaction processing. I use the IDS JDBC driver in `CommitApp`. You can use a different driver, but you'll have to change the first couple lines of the `setupDB()` method to reflect your driver and database URL. If you decide to stick with the IDS driver, make sure that you start the IDS Server before running `CommitApp`.

LISTING 45.2. THE `CommitApp` PROGRAM.

```
import java.awt.*;
import java.awt.event.*;
import java.sql.*;

public class CommitApp extends Frame {
 TextField sql = new TextField(60);
 Button commit = new Button("Commit");
 Button execute = new Button("Execute");
 TextArea resultArea = new TextArea(10,60);
 Connection connection;
 public static void main(String args[]){
  CommitApp app = new CommitApp();
 }
 public CommitApp() {
  super("CommitApp");
  setup();
  setupDB();
  pack();
  addWindowListener(new WindowEventHandler());
  show();
 }
 void setup() {
  setupMenuBar();
  setLayout(new GridLayout(2,1));
  Panel topPanel = new Panel();
  topPanel.setLayout(new GridLayout(2,1));
  Panel panels[]=new Panel[2];
  for(int i=0;i<panels.length;++i){
   panels[i]=new Panel();
   panels[i].setLayout(new FlowLayout(FlowLayout.LEFT));
  }
  panels[0].add(new Label("SQL: "));
  panels[0].add(sql);
  commit.addActionListener(new ButtonHandler());
  execute.addActionListener(new ButtonHandler());
  panels[1].add(commit);
  panels[1].add(execute);
```

continues

LISTING 45.2. CONTINUED

```
  for(int i=0;i<panels.length;++i)
   topPanel.add(panels[i]);
  add(topPanel);
  add(resultArea);
 }
 void setupMenuBar() {
  MenuBar menuBar = new MenuBar();
  Menu fileMenu = new Menu("File");
  MenuItem fileExit = new MenuItem("Exit");
  fileExit.addActionListener(new MenuItemHandler());
  fileMenu.add(fileExit);
  menuBar.add(fileMenu);
  setMenuBar(menuBar);
 }
 void setupDB() {
  try{
   // Load IDS driver
   Class.forName("ids.sql.IDSDriver");
   String url = "jdbc:ids:// cx122974-a.cv1.sdca.home.com:80/";
   url+="conn?dbtype=odbc&dsn='Actions'";
   // Connect to database
   connection=DriverManager.getConnection(url);
   // Get meta data about database
   DatabaseMetaData meta=connection.getMetaData();
   // Determine if database supports transaction processing
   if(meta.supportsTransactions())
    // Turn off automatic committing of transactions
    connection.setAutoCommit(false);
   else{
    String err="Your database server/driver does not support
   ➡transactions.";
    System.out.println(err);
    System.exit(0);
   }
  }catch(Exception ex){
   resultArea.setText(ex.toString());
  }
 }
 void commitTransactions() {
  try{
   // Commit current transaction
   connection.commit();
  }catch(Exception ex){
   resultArea.setText(ex.toString());
  }
 }
 void executeTransaction() {
  try{
   Statement statement = connection.createStatement();
```

```
   // Execute SQL statement
   boolean hasResults = statement.execute(sql.getText());
   if(hasResults){
    // Retrieve and display results
    ResultSet result = statement.getResultSet();
    if(result!=null) displayResults(result);
   }else resultArea.setText("");
  }catch(Exception ex){
   resultArea.setText(ex.toString());
  }
 }
 void displayResults(ResultSet r) throws SQLException {
  ResultSetMetaData rmeta = r.getMetaData();
  int numColumns=rmeta.getColumnCount();
  String text="";
  for(int i=1;i<=numColumns;++i) {
   if(i<numColumns)
    text+=rmeta.getColumnName(i)+" ¦ ";
   else
    text+=rmeta.getColumnName(i);
  }
  text+="\n";
  while(r.next()){
   for(int i=1;i<=numColumns;++i) {
    if(i<numColumns)
     text+=r.getString(i)+" ¦ ";
    else
     text+=r.getString(i).trim();
   }
   text+="\n";
  }
  resultArea.setText(text);
 }
 void closeConnection(){
  try {
   connection.close();
  }catch(Exception ex){
  }
 }
 class ButtonHandler implements ActionListener {
  public void actionPerformed(ActionEvent ev){
   String s=ev.getActionCommand();
   if(s=="Commit") commitTransactions();
   else if(s=="Execute") executeTransaction();
  }
 }
 class MenuItemHandler implements ActionListener {
  public void actionPerformed(ActionEvent ev){
   String s=ev.getActionCommand();
```

continues

LISTING 45.2. CONTINUED

```
   if(s=="Exit"){
    closeConnection();
    System.exit(0);
   }
  }
 }
 class WindowEventHandler extends WindowAdapter {
  public void windowClosing(WindowEvent e){
   closeConnection();
   System.exit(0);
  }
 }
}
```

Open `CommitApp` and list the current content of the `ActionItem` table using the `SELECT *
FROM ActionItem` SQL statement. See Figure 45.14. (Click the Execute button to execute an SQL statement.)

FIGURE 45.14.

*Displaying the
original*
`ActionItem` *table.*

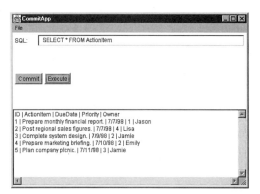

Now insert a new row into the `ActionItem` table by executing the following SQL statement, as shown in Figure 45.15 (make sure that you *don't* click the Commit button):

```
INSERT INTO ActionItem VALUES('6', 'Close out quarter.', '7/15/98', 1,
'Jason')
```

When you redisplay the `ActionItem` table, the newly added row is shown, as in Figure 45.16.

Exit the `CommitApp` program, restart IDS server, and then open `CommitApp` a second time. When you redisplay the `ActionItem` table this time, the newly added row is not displayed. (See Figure 45.17.) That's because you terminated the database connection before committing the new row.

FIGURE 45.15.

Inserting a new row into the ActionItem *table.*

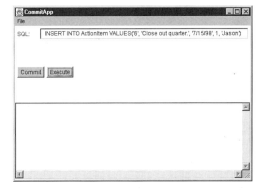

FIGURE 45.16.

Displaying the updated table.

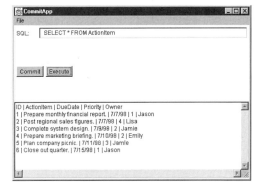

FIGURE 45.17.

The transaction was not committed.

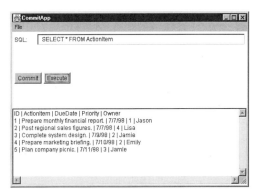

Reinsert the row by executing the following statement again:

```
INSERT INTO ActionItem VALUES('6', 'Close out quarter.', '7/15/98', 1,
'Jason')
```

45

Now click the Commit button to commit the transaction. Exit CommitApp and then open it a third time. When you list the ActionItem table, the newly inserted row is displayed because you committed the new transaction before exiting the CommitApp program.

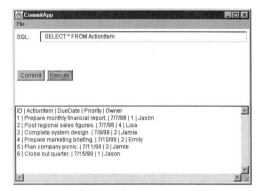

How CommitApp Works

CommitApp is similar to AccessApp in that it allows you to enter SQL commands directly into a database. It differs in that it uses the IDS JDBC driver (and IDS Server) and works with the action.mdb Microsoft Access 97 database that you used earlier in the chapter.

The setupDB() method is invoked during the program's initialization. It establishes a connection with the Actions data set via the IDS JDBC driver and IDS server. The getMetaData() method is invoked to retrieve the DatabaseMetaData object that describes the database to which the connection was established. The supportsTransactions() method is invoked to determine whether the database supports transaction processing. If the database does support transaction processing, the setAutoCommit() method is invoked to turn off the automatic committing of database transactions. Note that the database connection is left open.

When a user clicks the Commit or Execute button, the ButtonHandler object associated with the button checks to see what button was clicked and invokes the commitTransactions() or executeTransactions() methods.

The commitTransactions() method invokes the commit() method of the Connection interface to close the database connection.

The executeTransactions() method invokes the execute() method of the Statement class to execute the SQL statement entered by the user. If the SQL statement returns a ResultSet object, it invokes getResultSet() to retrieve the ResultSet object and displayResults() to display it.

The `displayResults()` method is the same method used in the `AccessApp` program.

Note that the `MenuItemHandler` and `WindowEventHandler` classes invoke the `closeConnection()` method to terminate the database connection before exiting the program.

Database Security

Until now, we haven't addressed the issue of database security, which is a serious concern for most organizations. Because databases may contain sensitive information about a company's operation, it is often imperative that such information be restricted to those who are trusted to handle it in a secure manner.

The integrity of database information is also paramount. Unauthorized changes to critical database information could have an adverse impact on a company's capability to carry out business operations.

Finally, data availability is important. Users must be able to get access to database information when they need it. This access often needs to be provided 24 hours a day, seven days a week.

How does the JDBC support database security? The answer is not very comforting. The JDBC currently relies on the database server to provide security protection. You probably noticed that we didn't even need to use a password to access the databases used as examples for this chapter. That's because we were working with personal database products (Microsoft Access and mSQL). Enterprisewide database servers, such as Microsoft SQL Server, do require a user ID and password in order to establish a database connection. However, even password protection is not very secure. If passwords are not encrypted between client and server, they can be easily intercepted and compromised.

Fortunately, vendors have developed solutions to Java database security. The folks at IDS Software have incorporated *Secure Socket Layer (SSL)* version 3 into their IDS server product line. This feature is referred to as *Secure JDBC* and provides encrypted communication between the database driver and server. The Secure JDBC solution is very flexible, uses the industry standard SSL, and provides a high level of security. Chapter 5 of the IDS Server User's Manual explains the security features provided by Secure JDBC.

> **NOTE**
>
> The SSL protocol is an industry standard developed by Netscape Communications, Inc.

Summary

In this chapter you learned how to work with vendor-specific JDBC drivers and database servers. You used type 1 and 3 drivers with Microsoft Access, and a type 4 driver with mSQL. You then gained some more hands-on experience working with SQL and the results of SQL queries. You also learned about transaction processing and database security. In the next chapter, you'll learn how to access databases with applets.

CHAPTER 46

Integrating Database Support into Web Applications

The Web is a global medium from which you can find information on any topic. Because of the Web's capability to distribute information to a worldwide audience, different approaches to integrating databases with the Web have been explored. Early Web pioneers relied on the Common Gateway Interface (CGI) as a way to marry Web and database technologies. The complexities, inefficiencies, and security problems associated with CGI programs resulted in second-generation approaches to database integration. Major Web software vendors, such as Netscape, have devised solutions to connecting databases to Web applications, such as LiveWire Pro.

In this chapter, you'll learn how to use the JDBC to connect applets with online databases. You'll learn what kind of JDBC drivers to use to support zero installation database connectivity. You'll develop an applet that inserts form data directly into an online database. You'll create a general SQL statement processing applet for searching online databases and for testing other database-enabled applets. You'll then explore approaches to integrating multimedia and databases and develop a multimedia photo album. When you finish this chapter, you'll find the JDBC to be a superior conduit for connecting the Web to online databases.

Using `java.sql` with Applets

Although applets can communicate with databases using any type of JDBC driver, the elegance or crudeness of the solution depends on which type of driver you use. The following is a list of the available drivers:

- JDBC-ODBC bridge plus ODBC driver—This is the crudest possible solution. Applets access your database using a combination of the JDBC-ODBC bridge and an ODBC driver. This requires both drivers to be installed on the user's computer— a very cumbersome solution for both Internet and intranet users.

- Native-API partly Java driver—This solution is also cumbersome. Applets use a hybrid Java-native API driver that also must be installed on the client machine. Its only benefit is that its installation is easier than installing both the JDBC-ODBC bridge *and* an ODBC driver.

- JDBC-Net pure Java driver—This is an ideal solution for both intranets and the Internet. Applets use pure Java drivers that are served from Web servers along with the applets. The Java drivers are automatically installed on the user's machine in a transparent manner. The pure Java drivers communicate with a database access server using a protocol such as HTTP or Secure HTTP that can be proxied by a firewall. The database access server translates database requests into a vendor-specific protocol. The IDS JDBC driver and IDS server fit into this category.

- Native-protocol pure Java driver—This solution is also useful because it uses a pure Java driver. However, instead of communicating with a database server using a proxiable protocol, the JDBC driver uses a database vendor-specific protocol. This approach is efficient for intranet applications but suffers from the drawback that the vendor's protocol may not be supported by a firewall. Lack of firewall support may rule out some potential Internet applications for security reasons.

> **NOTE**
>
> Chapter 45 introduces and describes each of the preceding JDBC driver types.

As you can tell by now, I am sold on the JDBC-Net pure Java driver—that's why I use the IDS driver. The first two approaches are just too cumbersome for Web applications. Users should not have to install database drivers on their machines to use an applet.

Security and standardization are important considerations for Internet use. When I am not writing books, I am involved in Internet security, sometimes in the area of Internet firewalls. Because of the significant lack of firewall proxies for vendor-specific database protocols, any database-enhanced Web application should consider the availability of a standard protocol for database access (like HTTP and SHTTP). The JDBC-Net pure Java driver solution allows you to use a standard protocol. This is important so that both your firewall *and* the user's firewall can support applet-to-database communication.

> **NOTE**
>
> *Proxies* are programs that support secure use of a protocol through a firewall. In order for a firewall to support a protocol in a secure manner, it needs a proxy for that protocol.

The third and fourth types of drivers support zero installation applets. Because the JDBC drivers are written entirely in Java, they are downloaded from the Web server along with the applet. In order to support zero installation, the drivers must be placed on the Web server in the same directory as the applet. In this chapter, I'll be placing the applets in the \ch46 directory off of my Web server root. You should also create a \ch46 directory off of your Web server's root if you intend to run the examples in this chapter. Copy the C:\IDSServer\classes\ids directory and all of its subdirectories to your Web server so that it is accessible as /ch46/ids. By doing so, you're making the IDS JDBC driver accessible to applets so that zero installation can be accomplished. If you are not using the IDS driver, you will need to consult your driver's documentation to determine how to make that driver available for installation by applet users.

Trusted vs. Untrusted Applets

Another important consideration when you're setting up a database-enabled Web application using applets is the location of your database server and database access server. Untrusted applets can only communicate with the host from which they are served. This means that they can talk back only to the Web server from which they are loaded. The purpose of this restriction is to prevent applets from obtaining sensitive information (such as that entered into a form) and disclosing that information to other hosts on the Internet.

If you are using type 1, 2, or 4 JDBC drivers, you have to put your database server on the same host as your Web server. This can lead to a performance problem for a busy Web site that supports a high level of database accesses. Your alternative is to require users to trust your applets to talk to other Internet hosts in a secure manner. This is an imposition on the user for two reasons: 1) Technically, there is no reason why they should have to reconfigure their browser to run your applet, other than your inability to come up with a workable solution, and 2) Any trust that the user extends creates a potential security risk.

If you use a type 3 driver, you can place the database access server on the same host as your Web server (enabling the use of untrusted applets) and the actual database server on a separate machine. This can greatly reduce any potential performance problems with running the database server and the Web server on the same host. Several of the database access servers are integrated with a Web server and share the HTTP protocol port. This supports greater combined performance of the Web server and database access server. In addition, a separate database access server allows you to use multiple database servers that are located on independent hosts. Overall, type 3 drivers provide the most flexible and easy-to-use solution.

Form Handling and Database Access

Now that we've explored the virtues of different JDBC driver types as they relate to applets, we'll develop an applet that displays a survey form to a user and updates a database with the data entered by the user.

Integrating Database Support into Web Applications

Chapter 46

955

46

INTEGRATING
DATABASE
SUPPORT

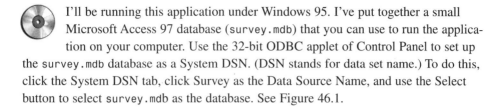 I'll be running this application under Windows 95. I've put together a small Microsoft Access 97 database (`survey.mdb`) that you can use to run the application on your computer. Use the 32-bit ODBC applet of Control Panel to set up the `survey.mdb` database as a System DSN. (DSN stands for data set name.) To do this, click the System DSN tab, click Survey as the Data Source Name, and use the Select button to select `survey.mdb` as the database. See Figure 46.1.

FIGURE 46.1.

Setting up the Survey DSN.

I've installed the System DSN on a host named `cx122974-a.cv1.sdca.home.com`. I've also installed an evaluation copy of the IDS server (database access server) on this machine. The IDS server doubles as a Web server. Feel free to use your own Web server. However, if you use a type 3 JDBC driver and a database access server, you'll have a lot fewer installation hassles.

The `Survey` applet is shown in Listing 46.1. To run it, you'll have to tailor the first few lines of the `updateDatabase()` method for your JDBC driver and host name:

```
void updateDatabase(){
  try{
    Class.forName("ids.sql.IDSDriver");
    String url="jdbc:ids://cx122974-a.cv1.sdca.home.com:80/";
    url+="conn?dbtype=odbc&dsn='Survey'";
    Connection connection=DriverManager.getConnection(url);
```

As a minimum, you'll have to change `cx122974-a.cv1.sdca.home.com` to your database server's (or database access server's) host name. If you use a driver other than the IDS driver, you'll need to consult your driver's documentation for information on how to do this.

When you're finished with these changes, compile `Survey.java` and then copy the `survey.htm` (see Listing 46.2), `Survey.class`, and `Survey$ButtonHandler.class` files to the `/ch46` directory off of your Web server's root.

Now you're ready for action. Use your browser to access the applet, as shown in Figure 46.2.

TIP

You can get a copy of the HotJava browser from `http://java.sun.com/products/hotjava/`.

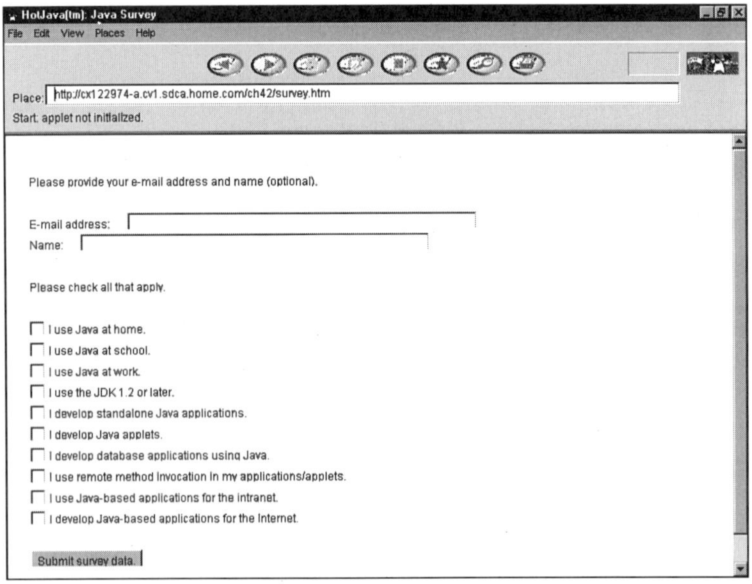

FIGURE 46.2.

The Survey *applet opening display.*

Use your Web server's host name instead of `cx122974-a.cv1.sdca.home.com` to access the applet. You can run your browser from the same host or a different host. If you've used a type 3 or 4 driver and copied the driver to the `/ch46` directory, you'll be able to easily access the applet from any host. Otherwise, you'll have to install your JDBC drivers on the host from which you run your browser.

Fill out the Survey form as you want and click the Submit survey data button. Your survey results are added to your database. The applet then displays a Thank you! message, as shown in Figure 46.3.

To verify that the survey information was added to the database, start up Microsoft Access 97, open the `survey.mdb` database, and view the contents of the `RawData` table.

The alternative is to wait until we create a general-purpose database search applet in the next section.

FIGURE 46.3.

The applet completes the survey by thanking the user.

LISTING 46.1. THE Survey APPLET.

```
import java.applet.*;
import java.awt.*;
import java.awt.event.*;
import java.sql.*;

public class Survey extends Applet {
 Label blankLine = new Label(" ");
 TextField email = new TextField(50);
 TextField name = new TextField(50);
 Checkbox home = new Checkbox("I use Java at home.");
 Checkbox school = new Checkbox("I use Java at school.");
 Checkbox work = new Checkbox("I use Java at work.");
 Checkbox jdk12 = new Checkbox("I use the JDK 1.2 or later.");
 Checkbox standalone = new Checkbox("I develop standalone Java
➥applications.");
 Checkbox applets = new Checkbox("I develop Java applets.");
 Checkbox database = new Checkbox("I develop database applications using
➥Java.");
 Checkbox rmi = new Checkbox("I use remote method invocation in my
➥applications/applets.");
```

continues

LISTING 46.1. CONTINUED

```java
Checkbox intranet = new Checkbox("I use Java-based applications for the
➥intranet.");
Checkbox internet = new Checkbox("I develop Java-based applications for
➥the Internet.");
Button submitButton = new Button("Submit survey data.");
public void init() {
 setLayout(new GridLayout(21,1));
 Panel panels[]=new Panel[21];
 for(int i=0;i<panels.length;++i){
  panels[i]=new Panel();
  panels[i].setLayout(new FlowLayout(FlowLayout.LEFT));
 }
 submitButton.addActionListener(new ButtonHandler());
 panels[0].add(blankLine);
 panels[1].add(new Label("Please provide your e-mail address and name
➥(optional)."));
 panels[2].add(blankLine);
 panels[3].add(new Label("E-mail address:"));
 panels[3].add(email);
 panels[4].add(new Label("Name:"));
 panels[4].add(name);
 panels[5].add(blankLine);
 panels[6].add(new Label("Please check all that apply."));
 panels[7].add(blankLine);
 panels[8].add(home);
 panels[9].add(school);
 panels[10].add(work);
 panels[11].add(jdk12);
 panels[12].add(standalone);
 panels[13].add(applets);
 panels[14].add(database);
 panels[15].add(rmi);
 panels[16].add(intranet);
 panels[17].add(internet);
 panels[18].add(blankLine);
 panels[19].add(submitButton);
 panels[20].add(blankLine);
 for(int i=0;i<panels.length;++i) add(panels[i]);
}
void updateDatabase(){
 try{
  // Load IDS driver
  Class.forName("ids.sql.IDSDriver");
  String url="jdbc:ids://cx122974-a.cv1.sdca.home.com:80/";
  url+="conn?dbtype=odbc&dsn='Survey'";
  // Connect to database
  Connection connection=DriverManager.getConnection(url);
  Statement statement = connection.createStatement();
  String sql="INSERT INTO RawData VALUES ('"+email.getText()+"'";
```

```
    sql+=",'"+name.getText()+"'";
    sql+=toDigit(home);
    sql+=toDigit(school);
    sql+=toDigit(work);
    sql+=toDigit(jdk12);
    sql+=toDigit(standalone);
    sql+=toDigit(applets);
    sql+=toDigit(database);
    sql+=toDigit(rmi);
    sql+=toDigit(intranet);
    sql+=toDigit(internet);
    sql+=")";
    // Execute SQL
    statement.executeUpdate(sql);
    // Close database connection
    connection.close();
    displayPanel("Thank you!");
   }catch(Exception ex){
    displayPanel(ex.toString());
   }
  }
  String toDigit(Checkbox ch){
   boolean state = ch.getState();
   if(state) return ",'1'";
   else return ",'0'";
  }
  void displayPanel(String s){
   removeAll();
   setLayout(new BorderLayout());
   Font currentFont = getFont();
   setFont(new Font(currentFont.getName(),Font.ITALIC+Font.BOLD,18));
   add("Center",new Label(s,Label.CENTER));
   invalidate();
   doLayout();
  }
  class ButtonHandler implements ActionListener {
   public void actionPerformed(ActionEvent e){
    String s = e.getActionCommand();
    if("Submit survey data.".equals(s)){
     updateDatabase();
    }
   }
  }
}
```

LISTING 46.2. THE `survey.htm` FILE.

```
<HTML>
<HEAD>
<TITLE>Java Survey</TITLE>
</HEAD>
<BODY>
<APPLET CODE="Survey.class" WIDTH=550 HEIGHT=475>
[Survey applet]
</APPLET>
</BODY>
</HTML>
```

How the Survey Applet Works

Most of the code of the Survey applet is used to present the survey form to the user. This involves the creation and layout of the text fields and checkbox buttons that you saw in Figure 46.2.

The clicking of the Submit survey data button is handled by the ButtonHandler class. The updateDatabase() method is invoked to update the database with the information collected in the form.

The updateDatabase() method loads the JDBC driver and establishes a connection to the database specified in the database URL. It executes the "INSERT INTO RawData VALUE (...)" SQL statement with the values of the form fields inserted into the statement at the appropriate column positions. The toDigit() method is invoked to convert the values of the checkbox fields into strings of 1 or 0 so that they are in the correct format for Microsoft Access.

> **TIP**
>
> You can open the survey.mbd database with Microsoft Access 97 to see how the RawData table is structured.

Performing Database Searches

The Survey applet shows how form data can be collected and stored in a database. You typically would not let a user search a database that collected data from users via forms (mainly because of privacy considerations). In this case, you would use your database management system's reporting features to view the stored form data.

However, there are some cases where you'll want to provide users with the capability to search your databases. The SQL applet shown in Listing 46.3 provides the general capability to search (and update) selected databases. Although you most likely won't want to provide your users with this much flexibility, you can use the processing performed by this applet and tailor it to your specific search and update needs.

Because the SQL applet is a general-purpose applet, you'll only need to tailor the first couple of lines of processQuery() to work with your JDBC driver:

```
void processQuery(){
  try{
    Class.forName("ids.sql.IDSDriver");
    String url="jdbc:ids://"+hostPort.getText()+"/";
    url+="conn?dbtype=odbc&dsn='"+dsn.getText()+"'";
    Connection connection=DriverManager.getConnection(url);
```

Compile SQL.java and then copy SQL.class, SQL$ButtonHandler.class, and sql.htm (see Listing 46.4) to the /ch46 directory of your Web server.

Open sql.htm with your browser, as shown in Figure 46.4.

FIGURE 46.4.

The SQL applet can query or update a variety of databases.

The SQL applet provides a great deal of flexibility for accessing different databases. You can use it to maintain your databases and test other database-enabled applets. It allows you to specify the host name and port of the database access server, the data set name, and an SQL statement. Click the Submit query button to send an SQL statement to the database server for execution. If the SQL statement returns a result, the results of the query are displayed in the text area.

Let's use the SQL applet to view the contents of the Survey data set. First, enter your database access server's host name and port number. Then enter the data set that you want to access. Finally, enter the SQL statement that you want to execute and click the Submit query button. The results of the query are displayed in the text area. Figure 46.5 shows a query that displays the contents of the RawData table of the Survey data set.

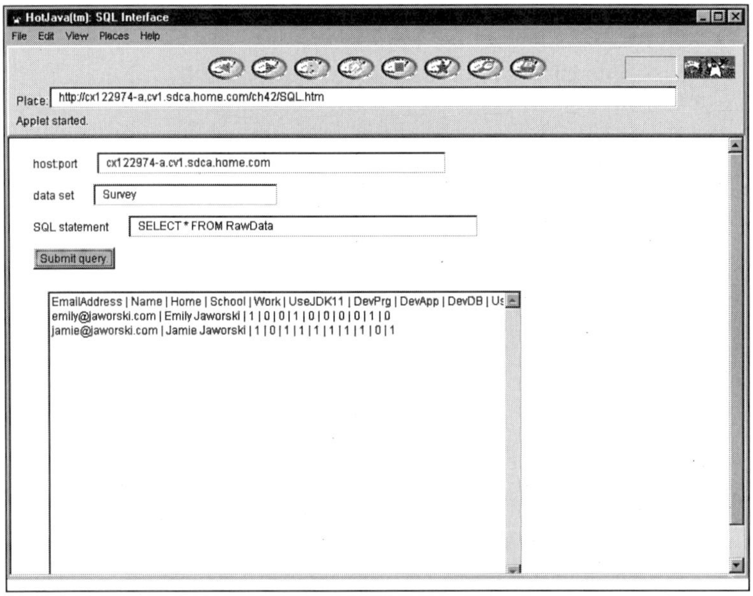

FIGURE 46.5.

Using the SQL applet to view the Survey database.

LISTING 46.3. THE SQL APPLET.

```
import java.applet.*;
import java.awt.*;
import java.awt.event.*;
import java.sql.*;

public class SQL extends Applet {
  Label blankLine = new Label(" ");
  TextField hostPort = new TextField(50);
  TextField dsn = new TextField(25);
  TextField sqlStatement = new TextField(50);
  TextArea results = new TextArea(20,70);
  Button submitButton = new Button("Submit query.");
  public void init() {
    Panel topPanel = new Panel();
    Panel bottomPanel = new Panel();
```

```java
  Panel topPanels[] = new Panel[4];
  for(int i=0;i<topPanels.length;++i){
   topPanels[i]=new Panel();
   topPanels[i].setLayout(new FlowLayout(FlowLayout.LEFT));
  }
  topPanel.setLayout(new GridLayout(4,1));
  topPanels[0].add(new Label("host:port "));
  topPanels[0].add(hostPort);
  topPanels[1].add(new Label("data set "));
  topPanels[1].add(dsn);
  topPanels[2].add(new Label("SQL statement "));
  topPanels[2].add(sqlStatement);
  submitButton.addActionListener(new ButtonHandler());
  topPanels[3].add(submitButton);
  for(int i=0;i<topPanels.length;++i)
   topPanel.add(topPanels[i]);
  bottomPanel.add(results);
  setLayout(new BorderLayout());
  add("North",topPanel);
  add("South",bottomPanel);
 }
 void processQuery(){
  try{
   // Load IDS driver
   Class.forName("ids.sql.IDSDriver");
   String url="jdbc:ids://"+hostPort.getText()+"/";
   url+="conn?dbtype=odbc&dsn='"+dsn.getText()+"'";
   // Connect to database
   Connection connection=DriverManager.getConnection(url);
   Statement statement = connection.createStatement();
   String sql=sqlStatement.getText();
   // Execute SQL and retrieve results
   boolean hasResults = statement.execute(sql);
   if(hasResults){
    // Retrieve result set
    ResultSet result = statement.getResultSet();
    if(result!=null) displayResults(result);
   }else results.setText("");
   // Close database connection
   connection.close();
  }catch(Exception ex){
   results.setText(ex.toString());
  }
 }
 void displayResults(ResultSet r) throws SQLException {
  // Get meta data from result set
  ResultSetMetaData rmeta = r.getMetaData();
  // Use the meta data to obtain information about the columns
  // of the result set
```

continues

LISTING 46.3. CONTINUED

```
   int numColumns=rmeta.getColumnCount();
   String text="";
   for(int i=1;i<=numColumns;++i) {
    if(i<numColumns)
     text+=rmeta.getColumnName(i)+" ¦ ";
    else
     text+=rmeta.getColumnName(i);
   }
   text+="\n";
   while(r.next()){
    for(int i=1;i<=numColumns;++i) {
     if(i<numColumns)
      text+=r.getString(i)+" ¦ ";
     else
      text+=r.getString(i).trim();
    }
    text+="\n";
   }
   results.setText(text);
  }
  class ButtonHandler implements ActionListener {
   public void actionPerformed(ActionEvent e){
    String s = e.getActionCommand();
    if("Submit query.".equals(s)){
     processQuery();
    }
   }
  }
 }
}
```

LISTING 46.4. THE sql.htm FILE.

```
<HTML>
<HEAD>
<TITLE>SQL Interface</TITLE>
</HEAD>
<BODY>
<APPLET CODE="SQL.class" WIDTH=550 HEIGHT=475>
[SQL applet]
</APPLET>
</BODY>
</HTML>
```

How the SQL Applet Works

The main bulk of the SQL applet involves creating and laying out the form fields. The ButtonHandler class handles the clicking of the Submit query button by invoking the

`processQuery()` method. The `processQuery()` method loads the JDBC driver and connects to the database access server specified in the `hostPort` text field and the data set specified in the `dsn` text field. The `execute()` method of the `Statement` class is invoked to execute the SQL statement specified in the `sql` text field.

If the `execute()` method returns a value of `true`, the `getResultSet()` method is invoked to retrieve a `ResultSet` object and the `displayResults()` method is invoked to display the `ResultSet` object in the text area.

The `displayResults()` method displays the column names separated by the vertical bar character (¦). It then displays each row of the result table, also separating columns using the vertical bar.

Accessing Multimedia Databases

So far the database results that we've been displaying have consisted of boring text. Most databases allow you to store images, audio files, and other multimedia. The JDBC provides the capability to read arbitrary objects from the columns of a `ResultSet` object. However, in many cases, it is inconvenient to do so. To work with multimedia objects from a database, you must put the objects in the database in the first place. Your database server has to retrieve the objects and forward them to your applet. Then your applet has to convert the object to a format that is suitable to display.

Although each of these steps is technically feasible, there is an easier way. Instead of putting all of your multimedia files in your database, just put their names or URLs in the database. Move the actual multimedia files to your Web server. This will speed up your database access and let you use the applet methods for loading multimedia files.

The `Multimedia` applet in Listing 46.5 shows how easy it is to combine applets, databases, and multimedia. I've provided a `multimed.mdb` database with the descriptions of image and audio files and a `\ch46\multimedia` directory containing multimedia files. These multimedia files include circus photographs and audio files that comment on the photographs. The photographs were taken by a Kodak DC-20 digital camera and converted to JPEG format. The audio files were recorded by the Windows 95 sound recorder and converted to Sun audio (`.au`) format. Copy the `\ch46\multimedia` directory to your Web server so that it is `\ch46\multimedia` under your server's root. Use the Windows 95 Control Panel's 32-bit `ODBC` applet to set up the `multimed.mdb` file as a system data set, as shown in Figure 46.6.

FIGURE 46.6.

Setting up the system data set for the Multimedia database.

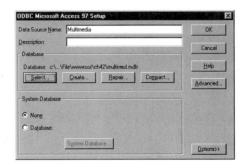

In order to run the `Multimedia` applet, you need to tailor `Multimedia.java` to your host name and JDBC driver. First, modify the `init()` method to change `cx122974-a.cv1.sdca.home.com` to your host name:

```
public void init() {
  try{
   baseURL = new
    URL("http://cx122974-a.cv1.sdca.home.com/ch46/multimedia/");
  }catch(Exception ex){
  }
```

Second, change the first few lines of `getQueryResults()` to use your JDBC driver and substitute your host name for `cx122974-a.cv1.sdca.home.com`:

```
String[][] getQueryResults(String sql){
  try{
   Class.forName("ids.sql.IDSDriver");
   String url="jdbc:ids://cx122974-a.cv1.sdca.home.com:80/";
   url+="conn?dbtype=odbc&dsn='Multimedia'";
   Connection connection=DriverManager.getConnection(url);
```

Finally, compile `Multimedia.java` and copy the `Multimedia.class`, `Multimedia$ChoiceHandler.class`, `Multimedia$MyCanvas.class`, and `multimedia.htm` (see Listing 46.6) files to your Web server.

Open `multimedia.htm` with your browser, as shown in Figure 46.7. Be sure to substitute your Web server's host name for `cx122974-a.cv1.sdca.home.com`.

Select an item from the choice list. A photograph is displayed, as shown in Figure 46.8, and an audio file is played. You can browse through the circus photos for amusement.

This applet is very simple, and it was designed that way. However, it is a good example of how applets, databases, and multimedia files can be combined into an easy-to-use (and easy-to-develop) Web application.

FIGURE 46.7.

The Multimedia *applet's opening screen.*

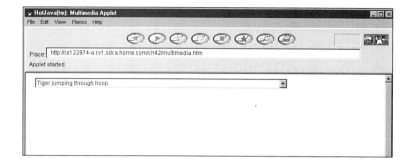

FIGURE 46.8.

Combining applets, databases, and multimedia.

LISTING 46.5. THE Multimedia APPLET.

```
import java.applet.*;
import java.awt.*;
import java.awt.event.*;
import java.sql.*;
import java.util.*;
import java.net.*;

public class Multimedia extends Applet {
 Choice choice = new Choice();
 MyCanvas canvas = new MyCanvas();
 Image photo = null;
```

continues

LISTING 46.5. CONTINUED

```java
AudioClip audio = null;
String imageName="";
String audioName="";
URL baseURL;
public void init() {
 try{
  baseURL = new
   URL("http://cx122974-a.cv1.sdca.home.com/ch46/multimedia/");
 }catch(Exception ex){
 }
 String choices[]=getChoices();
 if(choices!=null){
  try{
   for(int i=0;i<choices.length;++i)
    choice.add(choices[i]);
  }catch(Exception ex){
   choice.add(ex.toString());
  }
 }
 setLayout(new BorderLayout());
 choice.addItemListener(new ChoiceHandler());
 add("North",choice);
 add("Center",canvas);
}
String[] getChoices(){
 String results[][] =
  getQueryResults("SELECT Description FROM Photographs");
 if(results == null){
  String err[]= {"No choices returned from database."};
  return err;
 }
 String column[] = new String[results.length];
 for(int i=0;i<results.length;++i)
  column[i]=results[i][0];
 return column;
}
String[][] getQueryResults(String sql){
 try{
  // Load IDS driver
  Class.forName("ids.sql.IDSDriver");
  String url="jdbc:ids://cx122974-a.cv1.sdca.home.com:80/";
  url+="conn?dbtype=odbc&dsn='Multimedia'";
  // Connect to database
  Connection connection=DriverManager.getConnection(url);
  Statement statement = connection.createStatement();
  // Execute SQL and obtain result set
  ResultSet results = statement.executeQuery(sql);
  // Obtain meta data about result set
  ResultSetMetaData rmeta = results.getMetaData();
```

```java
   // Use meta data to get info about columns
   int numColumns=rmeta.getColumnCount();
   Vector v = new Vector();
   while(results.next()){
    String row[] = new String[numColumns];
    for(int i=0;i<numColumns;++i)
     // Retrieve results
     row[i]=results.getString(i+1);
    v.addElement(row);
   }
   int numRows=v.size();
   String resultTable[][] = new String[numRows][];
   for(int i=0;i<numRows;++i)
    resultTable[i]=(String[]) v.elementAt(i);
   // Close database connection
   connection.close();
   return resultTable;
  }catch(Exception ex){
   return null;
  }
 }
void loadMedia(String s){
 String sql = "SELECT Image, Audio FROM Photographs";
 sql += " WHERE Description = '"+s+"'";
 String results[][] = getQueryResults(sql);
 if(results!=null){
  imageName = results[0][0];
  audioName = results[0][1];
  if(imageName != "TBD") photo=getImage(baseURL,imageName);
  if(audioName != "TBD") audio=getAudioClip(baseURL,audioName);
 }
 canvas.repaint();
}
class ChoiceHandler implements ItemListener {
 public void itemStateChanged(ItemEvent e){
  String s = choice.getSelectedItem();
  imageName="";
  audioName="";
  photo=null;
  if(audio!=null){
   audio.stop();
   audio=null;
  }
  loadMedia(s);
 }
}
class MyCanvas extends Canvas {
 public void paint(Graphics g){
  if(photo!=null) g.drawImage(photo,20,20,this);
```

continues

LISTING 46.5. CONTINUED

```
    else g.drawString(imageName,10,20);
    if(audio!=null) audio.play();
    else g.drawString(audioName,10,40);
  }
 }
}
```

LISTING 46.6. THE `multimedia.htm` FILE.

```
<HTML>
<HEAD>
<TITLE>Multimedia Applet</TITLE>
</HEAD>
<BODY>
<APPLET CODE="Multimedia.class" WIDTH=540 HEIGHT=450>
[Multimedia applet]
</APPLET>
</BODY>
</HTML>
```

How the `Multimedia` Applet Works

The `Multimedia` applet displays a `Choice` object referenced by the `choice` variable and a `MyCanvas` object referenced by the canvas variable. The values of the `Choice` object are retrieved from the `Photographs` table of the `Multimedia` data set. The `photo` and `audio` variables are used to reference the `Image` object that is displayed on the `MyCanvas` object and the `AudioClip` object that is played. The `baseURL` variable is used to identify the URL of the directory where the image and audio files are located.

The `init()` method initializes the `baseURL` variable. (Be sure to substitute your server's URL.) It then invokes the `getChoices()` method to retrieve the list of photograph descriptions from the `Multimedia` data set. It then adds this list of descriptions to the `Choice` object referenced by the `choice` variable. The `Choice` object and `MyCanvas` objects are then laid out for display.

The `getChoices()` method invokes the `getQueryResults()` method with the `"SELECT Description FROM Photographs"` SQL statement. It then converts the results (if not null) from a two-dimensional `String` array to a one-dimensional `String` array. The `String` array is then returned to the caller.

The `getQueryResults()` method executes an SQL statement and returns the tabular results as a two-dimensional array. It begins by loading the JDBC driver and connecting to the `Multimedia` data set. It executes the SQL query and converts the result set to a

Vector object containing a one-dimensional array for each row of the result set. A vector is used because there is no way to determine the size of the result set without stepping through it. The Vector object is then converted to a two-dimensional String array.

The ChoiceHandler class handles the ItemEvent associated with selecting an item from the choice list. It resets the values of the imageName, audioName, photo, and audio variables and then invokes loadMedia() with the value of the selected choice.

The loadMedia() method invokes getQueryResults() with the "SELECT Image, Audio FROM Photographs WHERE Description = 'description'" SQL statement where the selected choice (as identified by the s variable) is substituted for *description*. This statement returns the values of the Image and Audio columns for the row with the Description column set to *description*. The imageName and audioName variables are updated based on the results returned. If the imageName is not "TBD", the getImage() method of the Applet class is used to load the image from the Web server and assign it to the photo variable. If the audioName is not "TBD", the getAudioClip() method of the Applet class is used to load the audio file from the Web server and assign it to the audio variable. Using getImage() and getAudioClip() is much easier than retrieving an image or audio file from the database. The repaint() method of the MyCanvas class is invoked to cause the image to be displayed and the audio file to be played.

The paint() method of the MyCanvas class checks to see if the photo variable references a valid image. If it does, the image then is drawn on the canvas. Otherwise, the image name is displayed. Similarly, the audio file is played if it is valid. Otherwise, its name is displayed.

JavaBlend and the Future of Java Database Programming

Having completed four chapters on Java database programming, you should be confident in your ability to develop your own Java database applications and applets. As you know by now, database programming is an involved process and requires expertise in working with database drivers, SQL, and the classes and interfaces of the java.sql package. The folks at JavaSoft realize the complex work that is involved in database programming, even with a language as easy to use as Java. They are in the process of developing a new product, JavaBlend, that will greatly simplify the process of building database applications using JDBC. JavaBlend will automatically map Java objects to information that is stored in databases. All operations on those objects will result in automatic querying and updating of the corresponding information stored in the databases. Once a Java object-to-database mapping is constructed, JavaBlend will free Java programmers from having to deal with the execution of SQL statements and the processing of result sets. JavaBlend will automatically generate, execute, and process the SQL statements corresponding to the methods that are invoked on Java objects. This will allow JDBC and SQL programming to be abstracted out of database application development. JavaBlend is not included in JDK 1.2.

Summary

In this chapter, you learned how to use the JDBC to connect applets with online databases. You learned what kind of JDBC drivers you should use to support zero installation database connectivity. You developed an applet that inserts form data directly into an online database. You then created a general SQL statement processing applet for searching databases and for testing other database-enabled applets. You also developed a multimedia photo album that explored approaches to integrating multimedia and databases. Finally, you learned about the future capabilities to be provided by JavaBlend.

This chapter concludes Part X, "Database Programming." In Part XI, "Server-Side Java," you'll learn how to develop server-side programs that implement CGI applications.

Server-Side Java

PART
XI

IN THIS PART

Sun's Java Web Server

In Chapter 32, "Server Programs," you learned how to write server programs in Java. You saw how easy it is to listen for incoming connections, read requests from the connection's input stream, process the requests, and write responses to the connection's output stream. JavaSoft also realizes that it has a winner in Java when it comes to server development and server-side programming, and has developed the JavaServer Toolkit and Service API. The JavaServer Toolkit is a server framework from which other servers can be developed. One of the servers developed from this framework is the Java Web Server, formerly named Jeeves. Jeeves doesn't stand for anything—it's the name of a butler (and hence a SERVant).

One of the key features (among many) of the JavaServer Toolkit is its support for Java server-side programming in the form of servlets. Servlets are the server-side analog to applets. JavaSoft has developed a Servlet API for servlet programming. This API is a standard extension to JDK 1.2.

In this chapter, you'll install Java Web Server and learn how it works. You'll learn about servlets, cover the basics of the Servlet API, and develop a few servlets of your own. When you finish this chapter, you'll be able to use Java Web Server and servlets to build advanced Web sites.

What Are the JavaServer Toolkit and Java Web Server?

The JavaServer Toolkit is a framework for building Internet and intranet servers. It implements the functions that are common to many servers:

- It listens on a port (or ports) for connection requests.
- It accepts connection requests.
- It creates threads to handle the requests.
- It hands the connections to the threads for processing.
- It manages the threads and connections.

Besides providing these basic server functions, the Java Server Toolkit makes it easier to integrate the following advanced capabilities into the servers you develop:

- Web-based remote administration
- Authentication and access controls
- Secure Sockets Layer (SSL)
- Servlets support
- HTTP 1.0 support
- Dynamic Web page generation

The JavaServer Toolkit provides a framework for developing Java-based server software. This framework was used to develop Java Web Server. Java Web Server is a top-of-the-line, fully HTTP 1.1-compliant Web server that provides a number of attractive features:

- Java servlets can be used to replace CGI programs written in other languages.

- Web pages can be dynamically compiled based on server code that is embedded in HTML files.

- User connections with the Web server can be tracked and managed as interactive sessions.

- Secure Sockets Layer and X.509 digital certificates can be used to provide privacy, integrity, and authentication services.

- Templates for the presentation of HTML content are separately managed by the server.

Of these features, this chapter will focus on the development of Java servlets. Information on other Java Web Server capabilities is covered in the server documentation.

How Does Java Web Server Work?

Because Java Web Server is built using the Java Server framework, it follows its basic execution paradigm. An acceptor listens for incoming connection requests on the TCP ports managed by the server. It hands off accepted connections to connection handlers. The connection handlers receive HTTP requests from Web server clients and load and invoke servlets to process the HTTP requests. Figure 47.1 provides an overview of Java Web Server's operation.

FIGURE 47.1.
How Java Web Server works.

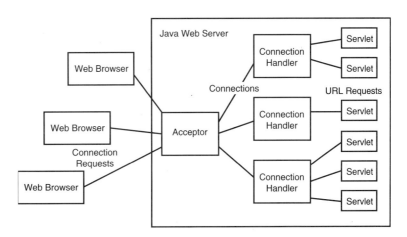

What's unique about the Java Server Toolkit, in general, and Java Web Server, in particular, is the use of servlets. *Servlets* are server extensions that are written in Java and are associated with particular URLs. When a request for the URL of a servlet is received from a Web browser, Java Web Server invokes the servlet to process the request. Java Web Server provides the servlet with all the information it needs to process the request. It also provides a mechanism for the servlet to send response information back to the Web browser. The Servlet API (covered later in this chapter in the section "The Servlet API") is used to develop servlets. Servlets can be preloaded by Java Web Server or loaded on-the-fly as they are needed.

Installing Java Web Server

In order to run the examples in this chapter, you'll need to download and install Java Web Server. It is available from JavaSoft at `http://jserv.javasoft.com/products/java-server/webserver/index.html`. Java Web Server for Windows 95 and NT is distributed as a self-extracting executable file. Run the file and follow the installation instructions to install Java Web Server on your system.

Running Java Web Server

Java Web Server comes with extensive documentation that describes its features and shows how they work. I'm not going to duplicate the documentation here, but I will give you enough information to get you up and running and to show you how to develop and use servlets.

To start Java Web Server, open a DOS window, change to Java Web Server's `bin` directory, and run `httpd`, as follows:

```
C:\JavaWebServer1.0.3\bin>httpd
```

> **NOTE**
>
> If you installed Java Web Server as a service under Windows NT, it is automatically started when you reboot your machine.

Java Web Server provides Web service on port 8080 as a default. This lets you use Java Web Server without having to stop your current Web server (if any). I've temporarily installed Java Web Server on a host named `athome.jaworski.com`. Figure 47.2 shows the server's default Web page, located at `http://athome.jaworski.com:8080/`.

FIGURE 47.2.

The Java Web Server default Web page.

The default Web page provides a link for you to administer your server. Follow this link to the server administration applet, shown in Figure 47.3. Note that server administration takes place on port 9090, as a default.

FIGURE 47.3.

The Java Web Server administration applet.

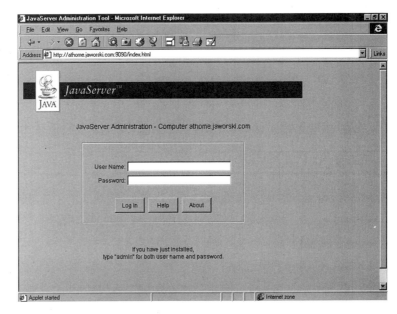

You can log in to this applet to administer your server. I won't cover server administration in any more detail than you'll need to install a servlet. The Java Web Server documentation explains all aspects of server administration.

To stop Java Web Server, just press Ctrl+C from within the DOS window in which it was started. On Windows NT, use the Services applet in the Control Panel to stop the Java Server service.

Using Servlets

Before I show you how to develop servlets, I'm going to whet your appetite by taking you on a tour of the servlets that come with Java Web Server.

Open your Web server to the default Web page (`http://your.host.name.com:8080`). Next, click on the link to Administer the Web Server. Here you'll find two Health Check servlets, as shown in Figure 47.4.

FIGURE 47.4.

Links to Health Check Servlets.

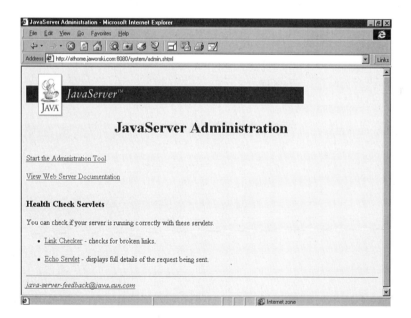

Click on the link to the Link Checker servlet. This servlet provides a handy tool to check for broken links in your Web documents, as shown in Figure 47.5.

Go back to the previous page and click on the link to the Echo Servlet. This servlet echoes the Common Gateway Interface (CGI) parameters that are passed to it, as shown in Figure 47.6. You can use this servlet to debug your URLs.

FIGURE 47.5.

The Link Checker Servlet.

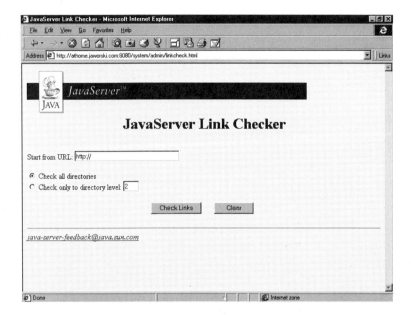

FIGURE 47.6.

The Echo Servlet.

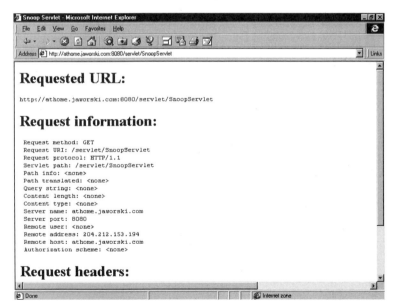

Now use your browser to open the following URL:

```
http://your.host.com:8080/servlet/ProtectedServlet
```

Substitute your host name for your.host.name. The Protectedservlet illustrates the use of the access control features of Java Web Server. It prompts you with the login dialog, shown in Figure 47.7. If you fail to log in correctly three times, it displays the notice shown in Figure 47.8. If you do log in correctly (User name=jeeves and Password=jeeves), it displays the Web page shown in Figure 47.9.

FIGURE 47.7.

The authorization dialog box.

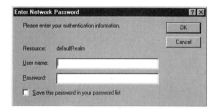

FIGURE 47.8.

Wrong password!

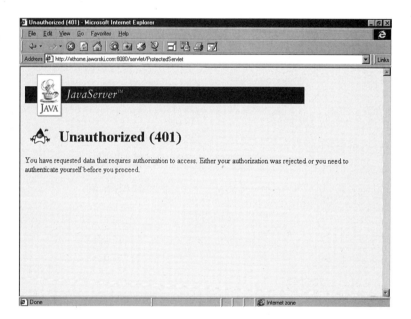

FIGURE 47.9.

The protected Web page.

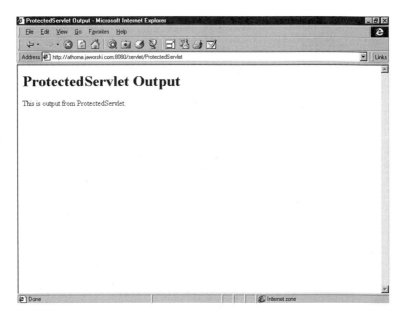

Writing Servlets

Now that you have a taste for servlets, I'll show you how they work and help you to develop a couple of your own.

Servlets are the server-side analog of applets. They are written to the Servlet API (covered in the next section) and are installed on a Web server. Besides Java Web Server, a number of Web servers support servlets and the Servlet API. The following list identifies some of these Web servers. A complete list can be obtained from `http://jserv.javasoft.com/products/java-server/servlets/environments.html`.

- Apache 1.1.3
- Netscape FastTrack 2.0, Enterprise 2.0, Enterprise 3.0
- Microsoft IIS 2.0, IIS 3.0
- Weblogic Tengah
- Lotus Domino Go Webserver
- IBM Internet Connection Server

Servlets are located in the `servlets` directory of the Web server and can be invoked via the following URL:

`http://your.host.com:port/servlet/ServletName.class[?arguments]`

The name of your Web server host (and port number) are substituted for `your.host.com:port`, and the class name of your servlet is substituted for `ServletName.class`. The optional *arguments* are a standard URL-encoded query string.

Java Web Server can also be configured to associate servlets with other URLs or to be invoked as the result of processing a particular type of URL. Consult the Java Web Server documentation for information on how to do this. Most likely, the servlets that you'll develop will be similar to CGI programs in the services they provide. The advantages of servlets over CGI programs are that there is minimal server overhead in invoking them, they are provided with direct access to server resources, and they are written in Java.

The Servlet API

The Servlet API is a Standard Extension API, meaning that it is not a part of the core Java Platform. See Chapter 51, "Java Platforms and Extensions," for a description of the Java Platform, the Core API, and the Standard Extension API. The Servlet API packages include the `javax.servlet` package and the `javax.servlet.http` package.

The `javax.servlet` Package

The `javax.servlet` package defines the following six interfaces and three classes:

- `javax.servlet` interfaces
  - `Servlet`—The `Servlet` interface must be implemented by all servlets. The `init()` and `destroy()` methods are invoked by the server to start and stop a servlet. The `getServletConfig()` and `getServletInfo()` methods are overridden to return information about a servlet. The `service()` method is invoked by the server so that a servlet can perform its service. It has two parameters—one of the `ServletRequest` interface and one of the `ServletResponse` interface.
  - `ServletRequest`—The `ServletRequest` interface encapsulates a client request for service. It defines a number of methods for obtaining information about the server, requester, and request. The `getInputStream()` method returns an object of the `ServletInputStream` class that may be used to read request information sent by the client.

- ServletResponse—The ServletResponse interface is used by a servlet to respond to a request by sending information back to the requester. The getOutputStream() method returns an object of the ServletOutputStream class that is used to send response information to the client. The getWriter() method returns a PrintWriter object that is used for client communication. The setContentType() method sets the MIME type of the response information. The setContentLength() method specifies the length of the response in bytes. The getCharacterEncoding() method returns the MIME type associated with the response.

- ServletConfig—The ServletConfig interface is used by the server to pass configuration information to a servlet. Its methods are used by the servlet to retrieve this information.

- ServletContext—The ServletContext interface defines the environment in which an applet is executed. It provides methods that are used by applets to access environment information.

- SingleThreadModel—The SingleThreadModel interface is used to identify servlets that must be thread-safe. If a servlet implements this interface, the Web server will not concurrently execute the service() method of more than one instance of the servlet.

- javax.servlet classes

- GenericServlet—The GenericServlet class is a convenience class that implements the Servlet interface. You can subclass this class to define your own servlets.

- ServletInputStream—The ServletInputStream class is used to access request information supplied by a Web client. An object of this class is returned by the getInputStream() method of the ServletRequest interface.

- ServletOutputStream—The ServletOutputStream class is used to send response information to a Web client. An object of this class is returned by the getOutputStream() method of the ServletResponse interface.

The `javax.servlet.http` Package

The javax.servlet.http package is used to define HTTP-specific servlets. It defines the following interfaces and classes.

- javax.servlet.http interfaces

  - HttpServletRequest—The HttpServletRequest interface extends the ServletRequest interface and adds methods for accessing the details of an HTTP request.

- HttpServletResponse—The HttpServletResponse interface extends the ServletResponse interface and adds constants and methods for returning HTTP-specific responses.

- HttpSession—This interface is implemented by servlets to enable them to support browser-server sessions that span multiple HTTP request-response pairs. Since HTTP is a stateless protocol, session state is maintained externally using client-side cookies or URL rewriting. This interface provides methods for reading and writing state values and managing sessions.

- HttpSessionBindingListener—This event listening interface is implemented by classes whose objects are associated with HTTP sessions. The valueBound() method is used to notify an object that it is bound to an HTTP session, and the valueUnbound() method is used to notify an object that it is unbound from an HTTP session.

- HttpSessionContext—This interface is used to represent a collection of HttpSession objects that are associated with session IDs. The getIds() method returns a list of session IDs. The getSession() method returns the HttpSession object associated with a particular session ID. Session IDs are implemented as String objects.

- javax.servlet.http classes

  - Cookie—This class represents an HTTP cookie. Cookies are used to maintain session state over multiple HTTP requests. They are named data values that are created on the Web server and stored on individual browser clients. The Cookie class provides the method for getting and setting cookie values and attributes.

  - HttpServlet—The HttpServlet class extends the GenericServlet class to use the HttpServletRequest and HttpServletResponse interfaces.

  - HttpSessionBindingEvent—This class implements the event that is generated when an object is bound to or unbound from an HTTP session.

  - HttpUtils—The HttpUtils class provides the parseQueryString() method for parsing a query string contained in an HTTP request.

The TimeServlet Class

The TimeServlet class, shown in Listing 47.1, is a simple servlet that will ease you into servlet programming. Compile the servlet and move the TimeServlet.class file to Java Web Server's servlets directory. Don't worry about the deprecation warning. I'll explain it in the next section.

LISTING 47.1. THE `TimeServlet` CLASS.

```java
import javax.servlet.*;
import java.util.*;
import java.io.*;

public class TimeServlet extends GenericServlet  {
 public String getServletInfo() {
  return "Time Servlet";
 }
 public void service(ServletRequest request, ServletResponse response)
  throws ServletException, IOException {
  String date=new Date().toString();
  PrintStream outputStream = new PrintStream(response.getOutputStream());
  outputStream.println(date);
 }
}
```

Next, you must install the servlet on Java Web Server. To do this, open the URL `http://your.server.com:9090/`. Your server's administration applet is loaded and displays the login, shown in Figure 47.10. Log in as `admin` with the `admin` password.

FIGURE 47.10.

The server admin-istration applet.

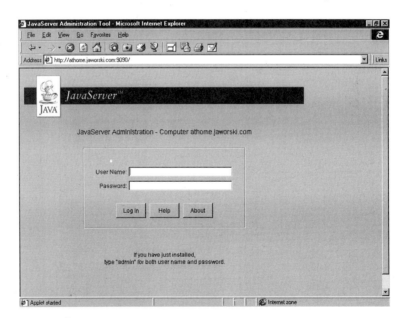

After you log in, the administration main screen is displayed, as shown in Figure 47.11. Highlight the Web service and click on the Manage button to configure the Web service.

FIGURE **47.11.**

The server admin-
istration main
screen.

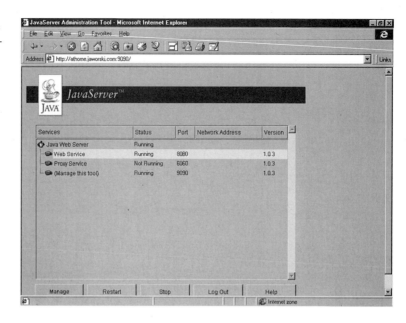

The Web service administration screen is displayed, as shown in Figure 47.12. Click the Servlets button to add the `TimeServlet`.

FIGURE **47.12.**

The Web service
administration
applet.

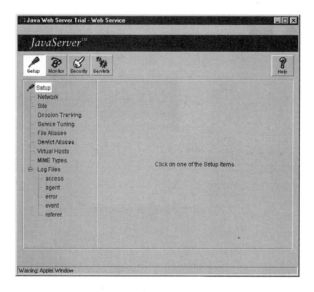

The Servlets configuration screen is displayed, as shown in Figure 47.13. Click on Add in the selection list on the left of the screen to add a servlet to the list of servlets known to Java Web Server.

FIGURE 47.13.

The Servlet administration applet.

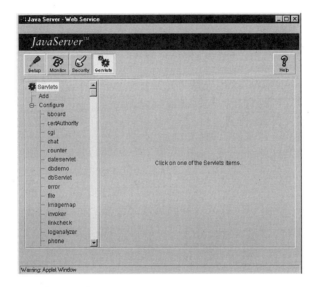

An Add a New Servlet dialog appears, as shown in Figure 47.14. Enter `TimeServlet` for the servlet's name and `TimeServlet.class` for the servlet's class. Then click the Add button to add the servlet.

FIGURE 47.14.

The Add a New Servlet dialog.

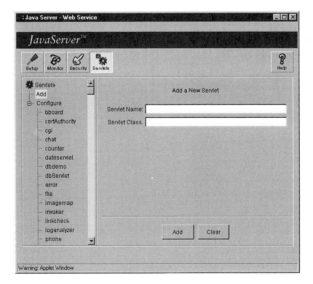

The screen is updated to display information about the servlet. Click the Load at Startup radio button to cause the servlet to be loaded automatically when the server starts. Then click the Save button to save the change. (See Figure 47.15.)

FIGURE 47.15.

Completing the servlet's configuration.

You're finished configuring the servlet. Click the Load button to load the servlet, close the applet window, and then click the Log Out button to log out of the administration applet.

Now you're ready to use the `TimeServlet` servlet. Open the URL `http://your.server.com:8080/servlet/TimeServlet.class` to access the servlet. It displays the output shown in Figure 47.16.

If that seems like a lot of work just to get the time, hang in there. The next servlet will be more interesting and informative.

How `TimeServlet` Works

In order to use servlets, you must import the `javax.servlet` package, as shown in Listing 47.1. The `TimeServlet` class extends the `GenericServlet` class and overrides the `getServletInfo()` and `service()` methods. The `getServletInfo()` method returns a string that provides information about the servlet. The `service()` method implements the actual servlet request handling and response handling. It is invoked by the Web server when the URL of the servlet is requested. The server passes the `ServletRequest` and `ServletResponse` arguments to the servlet.

FIGURE 47.16.

The TimeServlet*'s output display.*

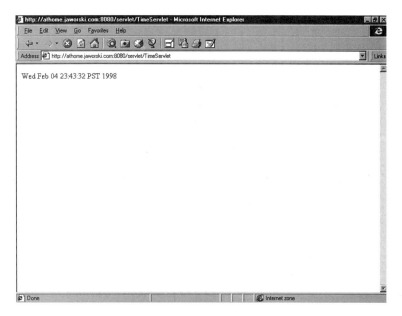

The TimeServlet is pretty simple and does not need any particular information contained in the ServletRequest object to perform its processing. It creates a new Date object, converts it to a String, and stores it using the date variable. It uses the getOutputStream() method of the ServletResponse class to create a ServletOutputStream object for sending response information back to the browser client. The ServletOutputStream object is filtered as a PrintStream.

> **NOTE**
>
> When you compile TimeServlet, you get a deprecation warning because you used PrintStream instead of its PrintWriter replacement.

Finally, you write the date string to the output stream to send it to the browser client.

The EchoRequest Servlet

The EchoRequest servlet, shown in Listing 47.2, shows how ServletRequest parameters are processed. Compile EchoRequest.java and copy the EchoRequest.class file to the servlets directory used by Java Web Server. Again, don't worry about the deprecation warning. Configure EchoRequest using the administration applet, as discussed for TimeServlet. Set its name to EchoRequest and its class name to EchoRequest.class. (See Figure 47.17.)

LISTING 47.2. THE EchoRequest SERVLET.

```java
import javax.servlet.*;
import java.util.*;
import java.io.*;

public class EchoRequest extends GenericServlet  {
 public String getServletInfo() {
  return "Echo Request Servlet";
 }
 public void service(ServletRequest request, ServletResponse response)
  throws ServletException, IOException {
  response.setContentType("text/plain");
  PrintStream outputStream = new PrintStream(response.getOutputStream());
  outputStream.print("Server: "+request.getServerName()+":");
  outputStream.println(request.getServerPort());
  outputStream.print("Client: "+request.getRemoteHost()+" ");
  outputStream.println(request.getRemoteAddr());
  outputStream.println("Protocol: "+request.getProtocol());
  Enumeration params = request.getParameterNames();
  if(params != null) {
   while(params.hasMoreElements()){
     String param = (String) params.nextElement();
     String value = request.getParameter(param);
     outputStream.println(param+" = "+value);
   }
  }
 }
}
```

FIGURE 47.17.

Configuring the
EchoRequest
servlet.

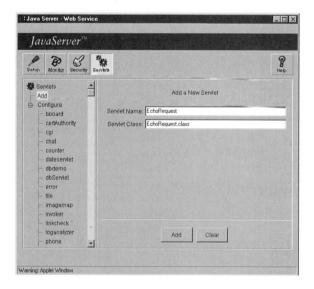

Open the URL `http://your.server.com/servlet/EchoRequest.class`. It displays the IP address and port number of the Java Web Server Web server, and the host name and address of the computer on which your browser resides. It also displays the version of the HTTP protocol being used. (See Figure 47.18.)

FIGURE 47.18.

Using the EchoRequest servlet.

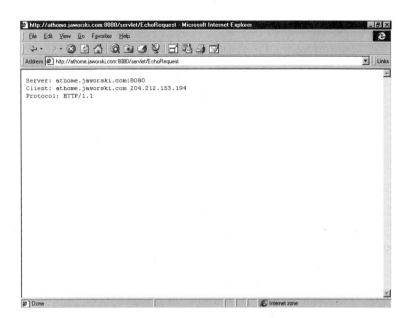

Now open the same URL with the `?n1=v1&n2=v2&n3=v3` query string appended. `EchoRequest` displays the name value pairs in the query string, as shown in Figure 47.19.

You can also use `EchoRequest` with forms. Copy the `formtest.htm` file, shown in Listing 47.3, to the `public_html` directory of your Web server. Open it with the URL `http://your.server.com:8080/formtest.htm`. The form shown in Figure 47.20 is displayed.

LISTING 47.3. THE `formtest.htm` FILE.

```
<HTML>
<HEAD>
<TITLE>Using a form with EchoRequest</TITLE>
</HEAD>
<BODY>
<FORM ACTION="servlet/EchoRequest.class">
Enter text: <INPUT NAME="textField" TYPE="TEXT" SIZE="30"><P>
```

continues

LISTING 47.3. CONTINUED

```
Check this out: <INPUT NAME="checkbox" TYPE="CHECKBOX"><P>
Select me: <SELECT NAME="mySelection">
<OPTION>Number one
<OPTION>Number two
<OPTION>Number three
</SELECT><P>
<INPUT NAME="Submit" TYPE="SUBMIT">
</FORM>
</BODY>
</HTML>
```

FIGURE 47.19.

Using the
EchoRequest
servlet with a
query string.

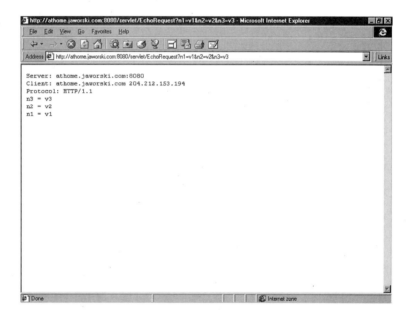

Enter a value for the text field, check or uncheck the text box, and make a selection from the selection list. Then click the Submit button. The EchoRequest servlet is invoked to process the form. It displays the output shown in Figure 47.21. Note that it correctly identifies the form values that you submitted.

FIGURE 47.20.

Using the
`EchoRequest`
servlet with an
HTML form.

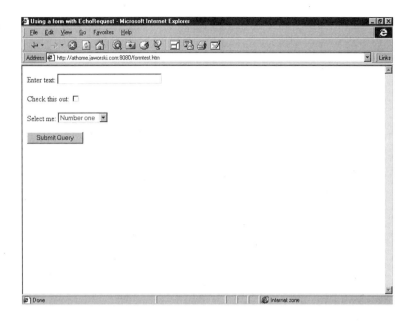

FIGURE 47.21.

`EchoRequest` *displays the data you entered in the form.*

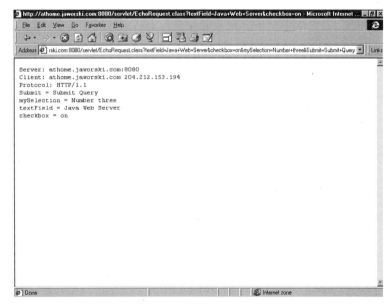

How `EchoRequest` Works

As you would expect, the overall structure of `EchoRequest` is the same as `TimeServlet`. Both servlets extend `GenericServlet` and override the `getServletInfo()` and `service()` methods.

The `service()` method of `EchoRequest` begins by setting the content type of the response to the `text/plain` MIME type. We set the MIME type because we'll be generating more than one line of output and we don't want the browser client to mistake it for HTML.

Next, `service()` creates an output stream in the same manner as `TimeServlet`, using the `getOutputStream()` method of the `ServletResponse` interface. It then prints information about the server, client, and protocol that it obtains using the `getServerName()`, `getServerPort()`, `getRemoteHost()`, `getRemoteAddr()`, and `getProtocol()` methods of the `ServletRequest` interface.

The `service()` method invokes the `getParameterNames()` method of the `ServletRequest` interface to retrieve an enumeration of the parameter names that are passed in the query string of the HTTP request. It displays each parameter name along with its value. The parameter values are retrieved via the `getParameter()` method of the `ServletRequest` interface.

Summary

In this chapter, you installed Java Server and learned how it works. You learned about servlets and about the basics of the Servlet API. You then developed the `TimeServlet` and the `EchoRequest` servlet and learned how servlets can be used to process form data. In the next chapter, you'll learn more about the Servlet API and how to use servlets with other Web servers.

Programming Other Servers

In the previous chapter, you learned how to use the Servlet API to write servlets that run on the Java Web server. The Servlet API is supported by a wide range of Web servers, including the popular Apache Web server, the Netscape Enterprise and FastTrack servers, and the Microsoft Internet Information Server. Support for these servers is provided with the Java Server Development Kit (JSDK), which is available from JavaSoft's Web site.

In this chapter, you'll take a look at server-side programming using Java. You'll learn about the Common Gateway Interface (CGI) and learn why the CGI is not conducive to server-side Java programming. You'll explore some of the server-side Java workarounds developed by Netscape and Microsoft for use with their servers. You'll then learn how to install the JSDK to support servlet programming on popular servers other than Java Web server. Finally, you'll be introduced to the servletrunner tool of JDK 1.2 and learn how to use it to run and test your servlets. When you finish this chapter, you'll have a better understanding of the Java server-side programming options that are available to you.

Java and the Common Gateway Interface

The Common Gateway Interface was adopted early on as a standard for interfacing external programs to Web servers. The CGI allows these external programs, referred to as *CGI programs* or *CGI scripts*, to be written in such a way that they are not dependent on the particular Web server being used. The CGI specification describes a standard interface for a Web server to send browser requests to the CGI program and for the CGI program to return response data to the browser, via the Web server. These interfaces are summarized as follows.

> **NOTE**
>
> A variation of the CGI, known as WinCGI, has been popularized by some early Windows-based Web servers.

Web Server to CGI Program Communication

Web servers communicate with CGI programs using environment variables, command-line arguments, and the standard input stream. These three communication methods are used as follows:

- Environment variables—These are the most common way that a Web server passes information to a CGI program. Environment variables are variables that are defined outside of a program but in the program's execution context, or environment. The CGI defines a number of environment variables for communicating with a CGI program. These variables are described in Table 48.1. The capability of a program to read environment variables is important for CGI programming, and, unfortunately, the Java API does not support this capability well.

- Command-line arguments—Certain types of browser requests, such as HTTP ISINDEX queries, cause the Web server to pass information to CGI programs using the command-line arguments of the CGI program. For example, in the following Java program invocation, v1, v2, and v3 would be command-line arguments:

```
java ProgramName v1 v2 v3
```

A Java program reads the command-line variables via the args parameter of its main() function.

- Standard input—Browser requests that are submitted using the POST method are sent to the CGI program via its standard input stream. This allows the CGI program to read the data using its standard I/O capabilities. Java programs use the methods of the java.io package to read data via an input stream.

CGI Program to Web Server Communication

Although there are three ways that information is provided to a CGI program, there is only one way that the CGI program returns information to the Web server (and on to the browser). CGI program output is simply written to the standard output stream. Java programs use the methods of the java.io package to write data to an output stream.

There are some additions to the CGI, such as the use of non-parsed header programs, but these additions are not significant for Java programming.

TABLE 48.1. ENVIRONMENT VARIABLES USED WITH THE CGI.

Variable	Description
AUTH_TYPE	The authentication scheme used with the request
CONTENT_LENGTH	The length of standard input in bytes
CONTENT_TYPE	The MIME type of the standard input
GATEWAY_INTERFACE	The version of the CGI in use by the server
PATH_INFO	Extra path information added to the URL of the CGI program
PATH_TRANSLATED	The full path name of the CGI program
QUERY_STRING	The query string appended to the request URL
REMOTE_ADDR	The IP address of the requestor

continues

48

TABLE 48.1. CONTINUED

Variable	*Description*
REMOTE_HOST	The host name of the requestor
REMOTE_IDENT	The verified host name of the requestor
REMOTE_USER	The name of the user making the request
REQUEST_METHOD	The HTTP method used to make the request
SCRIPT_NAME	The name of the CGI program
SERVER_NAME	The host name of the server
SERVER_PORT	The TCP port used by the Web server
SERVER_PROTOCOL	The protocol used to submit the request
SERVER_SOFTWARE	The name and version of the Web server software

Most CGI programs are written in scripting languages. Perl and UNIX shell languages are the most popular scripting languages. CGI programs can also be written in compiled languages, such as C and C++. Some Windows-based CGI programs are written in Visual Basic, Delphi, and other Windows-specific programming languages.

Java is not a good programming language for writing CGI programs, for two reasons: It doesn't support environment variables well, and the loading of the Java interpreter adds quite a bit of overhead to CGI processing.

Java's inability to read environment variables is an API problem. The pre-JDK 1.0 API was used to support the getenv() method of the System class for obtaining access to environment variables. However, this method has been deprecated and is no longer supported. Instead, the preferred solution is to use the getProperties() and getProperty() methods of the System class to access environmental properties of the Java program. When the Java interpreter is loaded and executed by a Web server, the server sets the CGI-standard environment variables in the interpreter's environment. However, the Java interpreter does not pass these variables on to the Java program as properties. This fundamental flaw makes Java incompatible with the CGI.

Even if Java programs could read the environment variables of the Java interpreter, the overhead of loading the Java interpreter for every Java CGI program is prohibitive. This is not a showstopper as far as Java CGI programming is concerned, but it is a serious limiting factor.

Because Java is a popular programming language and many people want to develop server-side programs in Java, there have been a number of approaches to making Java suited for server-side programming. The Servlet API is an optimal approach to server-side Java programming and will eventually become the standard. The following sections cover some of the other approaches to server-side Java programming. Then, we'll show how to use the JSDK to implement the Servlet API on popular Web servers.

> **NOTE**
>
> Additional information on the Common Gateway Interface can be obtained at the URL `http://hoohoo.ncsa.uiuc.edu/cgi/interface.html`.

Server-Side Java Programming with Netscape Servers

Netscape and Microsoft, being major Web server vendors, have created their own solutions to Java Web server programming. However, neither of these solutions is as elegant as the Servlet API. We'll discuss Netscape's approach in this section and Microsoft's in the next.

> **NOTE**
>
> Netscape's Enterprise and FastTrack servers and Microsoft's Internet Information Server provide separate support for the Servlet API, in addition to the standard Java support identified in this section and next.

Netscape solved the processing overhead problem of loading the Java interpreter with each CGI request by building the Java interpreter inside its FastTrack and Enterprise Web servers. The Java interpreter is loaded and started with the Web server and remains in memory throughout the server's operation. Server-side Java programs (referred to as *server-side applets* by Netscape) are placed in a special `applets` directory and installed with the Web server. The server is also configured to map specific URLs to the server-side applets.

> **NOTE**
>
> Netscape servers support servlets in a separate `servlets` directory. Servlets support the Servlet API. Server-side applets are Netscape's equivalent to servlets.

When a browser requests the URL of an applet, the server invokes the applet and passes the request information to the applet via special classes defined in the `netscape.server.applet` package. These classes are as follows:

- `ServerApplet`—The top-level class implemented by server applets. It is similar to the `Servlet` interface of Jeeves's Servlet API. It provides methods for accessing browser request information and for obtaining an output stream to be used to return information to the browser.

- `HttpApplet`—Extends `ServerApplet` to support HTTP-specific requests. `ServerApplet` can also be extended for other types of requests, such as `Gopher` and `FTP`. Your server applets are written by subclassing `HttpApplet` and overriding its `run()` method.

- `Server`—Contains methods that provide information about the Web server.

- `URIUtil`—Contains methods used to process the URL requested by the browser.

Developing server applets using the `netscape.server.applet` package is a snap. You simply subclass `HttpApplet` with your applet and override its `run()` method to implement the applet's processing. Use the various methods of `HttpApplet` to access request information, and the `getOutputStream()` method of `HttpApplet` to obtain a stream that you can use to send response information back to the browser. The `netscape.server.applet` package is the next best thing to the Servlet API for server-side Java programming.

Netscape is gradually phasing out its server-side applet support in favor of the standard Servlet API of JDK 1.2. The `netscape.server.applet` package has been deprecated as of Enterprise Server 3.5.1.

Server-Side Java Programming with Microsoft Servers

Microsoft's Internet Information Server (IIS) provides the capability to develop server-side programs in Java. This capability is buried inside of its Active Server Pages (ASP) scripting environment, however.

ASP is an environment for developing dynamic Web applications, primarily using VBScript and JScript (Microsoft's clone of JavaScript). ASP was developed as a substitute for the CGI and supports the embedding of scripts within HTML files. The Web server executes these scripts when browsers request the HTML files. The results of the scripts' execution are embedded in the files before they are sent to the browsers.

Scripts may use objects to access request information provided by Web browsers and to send response information back to the browsers. The five primary objects supported by ASP are as follows:

- Request—Encapsulates a browser request.
- Response—Provides the capability to send response information back to the browser.
- Server—Provides access to the server environment.
- Application—Provides the capability to communicate with other users of the same Web application.
- Session—Stores information about the current browser session.

The preceding objects are referred to as *built-in objects*. You use the properties and methods of these objects in scripts in much the same way you would use a Java object's variables and methods.

ActiveX server components are server-side components (think of them as server-side JavaBeans) that can be used by scripts. These components can be used to provide interfaces with databases, legacy applications, or just about anything that you would use a CGI program for. You can create server-side components using a variety of languages, one of which is Java.

To build an ActiveX server component using Java, you use the object interfaces that are provided in the asp package. These interfaces are as follows:

- IScriptingContext—Used to access the five built-in ASP objects.
- IRequest—Used to access the Request object.
- IResponse—Used to access the Response object.
- IServer—Used to access the Server object.
- IApplicationObject—Used to access the Application object.
- ISessionObject—Used to access the Session object.
- IReadCookie—Allows cookies to be read.
- IWriteCookie—Supports writing of cookies.
- IRequestDictionary—Used to access client certificates.
- IStringList—Used to access the individual values of a browser request.

The ASP approach to Web applications wasn't exactly developed with Java in mind. You can develop ActiveX server components in Java, but you're probably better off using the ASP scripting languages. If you have the urge to develop server-side programs in Java on IIS, by all means use the Servlet API and the Java Servlet Development Kit.

The Java Servlet Development Kit

Given the diverging approaches taken by Netscape and Microsoft to support server-side Java programming, JavaSoft developed the Servlet API to provide a standard approach to supporting server-side Java. In addition, JavaSoft developed the JSDK as a means of ensuring that "Write Once, Run Everywhere" holds true for the Web server as well as the Web browser. The JSDK provides the `servletrunner` tool for supporting the development and testing of servlets as well as code that enables servlets to run on Apache, Netscape, and Microsoft Web servers. The following subsections discuss how to install the JSDK to run servlets on these Web servers.

Installing the JSDK with the Apache Web Server

The Apache freeware Web server is the world's most popular Web server. More Apache Web servers are deployed on the Web than Netscape and Microsoft Web servers combined. The Apache server is available in both source and binary distributions from the Apache Web site at `http://www.apache.org`. Although Apache was designed to take advantage of features of the Linux and UNIX operating systems, it is also available for Windows 98, 95, and NT platforms. However, the JSDK only supports Linux and UNIX implementations of Apache.

In order to use the Servlet API with the Apache Web server, you must download a source code distribution, version 1.1.3 or later. The JSDK provides the Apache servlet module, `mod_servlet.c`, which you must compile into the Apache server. You do this by copying `mod_servlet.c` to the `src` directory of the Apache distribution, editing the Apache `Configuration` file to include the following line, and compiling the Web server.

```
Module servlet_module    mod_servlet.o
```

After compiling Apache, you'll also need to edit the `srm.conf` file used to configure the server and add the following lines:

```
<Location /servlet>
 SetHandler servlet-handler
 </Location>
```

These lines configure the server to use the servlet module with client requests of the `servlet` directory. Additional configuration commands may be added to the `srm.conf` file to tailor the execution of the servlet module. These commands are covered in the servlet module's installation instructions.

This installation approach takes advantage of Apache's support for custom modules. The Java-Apache Project (`http://java.apache.org/`) is developing an external servlet engine for supporting the Servlet API that can be used with all Apache implementations. The overall goals of the project are to promote, plan, and develop server-side Java software for the Apache Web server.

Installing the JSDK with Netscape Servers

Next to Java Web Server, the Netscape family of Web server products provides the most platform-independent Web server solution. Netscape servers run on all major operating system platforms, from low-end Windows platforms to high-end UNIX servers. The JSDK provides support for the Servlet API on both Enterprise and FastTrack servers (versions 2.0 and higher). This support consists of class files that must be unzipped in the `plugins\java\local-classes` directory of the server's home directory.

Once the class files are put in place, you must configure your server to run Java. This is accomplished via the server administration interface. After turning Java on, you also need to edit your server's `obj.conf` file to map URLs containing `/servlet` to the directory where your servlets are stored. Then add the following lines to the bottom of this file:

```
<Object name="servlet">
Service fn="java-run" class="sun/servlet/netscape/NSRunner"
vpath="/servlet" initfile="<nshome>/https-<hostname>/config/
servlets.properties"
</Object>
```

Make sure to apply these changes and restart your server so that the changes take effect.

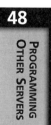

48

PROGRAMMING
OTHER SERVERS

> **NOTE**
>
> Version 2.x and 3.0 Netscape servers use a JVM that supports JDK 1.02 but not higher JDK versions. This means that your servlets are limited in the classes that they may use.

Installing the JSDK with Microsoft Servers

Installation of the JSDK for versions 2.0 through 4.0 of Microsoft Internet Information Server is a breeze. Simply run the `jsdk-iis.exe` program that is distributed with the JSDK. This program copies the necessary files into your Web server's directory structure and makes changes, as required, to your system registry. After running the installation, make sure that you reboot your server so that all changes go into effect.

Using the Servlet API

After installing the JSDK support for your Web server, you can take advantage of the "Write Once, Run Anywhere" feature of the Servlet API. This means that you can develop and test your servlets on one Web server (for example, Java Web Server) and then run them on a different production Web server (such as Apache). This greatly enhances the portability and reusability of your servlets. The standardization provided by the Servlet API will allow the development of a market for platform-independent server-side programs. It is reasonable to expect that servlets and server-side Java beans will be available as commercial products in the same manner as applet-side classes and beans.

Using `servletrunner`

One of the most useful tools for developing and testing server-side programs is the `servletrunner` tool that is included with the JSDK 1.2. This tool provides a configurable, multithreaded environment that can be used to test multiple concurrent servlets. The `servletrunner` is configured to run a list of named servlets with a predefined set of initialization arguments. Configuration of `servletrunner` is accomplished using a properties file. The `servlet.properties` file is the default file used by `servletrunner`, but other files may be substituted using the `-s` command-line option.

The properties file consists of property statements of the form *propertyName* = *propertyValue*, where each statement is on a single logical line. A single logical line may be extended over multiple physical lines by using a backslash (\) as a line continuation character.

Property names are used to name a servlet and identify its initialization arguments. Properties of the form

```
servlet.name.code
```

are used to assign a name to a servlet. For example, the following statement gives the name `time` to the `TimeServlet` of Chapter 47, "Sun's Java Web Server":

```
servlet.time.code=TimeServlet
```

In some cases, you may want to specify initialization parameters for a servlet. Consider the `MessageServlet` of Listing 48.1. It uses an initialization argument to determine which message it should display. This initialization argument is named `message`, and its value is read by the `getInitParameter()` method. The properties file for this servlet is as follows:

```
servlet.message.code=MessageServlet
servlet.message.initArgs=\
 message=This is the message of the day.
```

These statements are provided in the `message.properties` file on the book's CD. The first statement names `MessageServlet` as message. The second statement (continued over two lines) specifies the value of the message argument as `This is the message of the day`.

> **NOTE**
>
> Make sure that the `servlet.jar` file is in your CLASSPATH before compiling any of the servlet examples.

Compile `MessageServlet.java` in the `ch48` directory. Make sure that you copy the `message.properties` file from the CD. Then run `servletrunner` from the `ch48` directory using the following command:

```
servletrunner -s message.properties
```

The above command runs `servletrunner` using the `message.properties` file. The default TCP port of `servletrunner` is 8080. You can view the results of the servlet with your Web browser at `http://your.host.com:8080/servlet/message`. Figure 48.1 shows the result when I run it on my computer, `athome.jaworski.com`, and view it with my Web browser. Make sure that your TCP/IP software is up and running before starting `servletrunner`.

FIGURE 48.1.
Viewing the results of the `MessageServlet`.

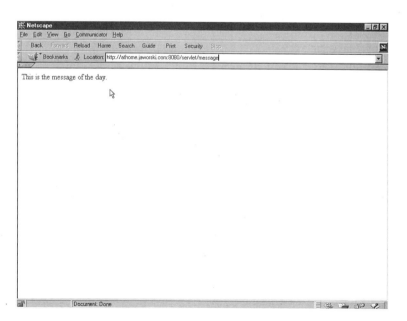

48

PROGRAMMING
OTHER SERVERS

LISTING 48.1. THE MessageServlet SOURCE CODE.

```
import javax.servlet.*;
import java.util.*;
import java.io.*;

public class MessageServlet extends GenericServlet  {
 public String getServletInfo() {
  return "Message Servlet";
 }
 public void service(ServletRequest request, ServletResponse response)
  throws ServletException, IOException {
  PrintStream outputStream = new PrintStream(response.getOutputStream());
  outputStream.println(getInitParameter("message"));
 }
}
```

Using `servletrunner` to Test HTML Form Handling

You can use `servletrunner` to debug the servlets that you use to handle HTML forms.
Listing 48.2 presents the `FormTestServlet`, which is a scaled-down version of the
`EchoRequest` servlet of Chapter 47. Compile `FormTestServlet.java` in the `ch48` directory and copy `formtest.properties` from the CD. The `formtest.properties` file contains the single property statement:

`servlet.formtest.code=FormTestServlet`

This statement simply names the `FormTestServlet` as `formtest`. Listing 48.3 provides
an HTML form that submits the results of the form to the `FormTestServlet`. You must
edit the `ACTION` attribute of the `FORM` tag to replace `athome.jaworski.com` with your host
name.

Run `servletrunner` from within the `ch48` directory using the following command:

`servletrunner -s formtest.properties`

Open `formtest.htm` with your Web browser, edit the form's data, and click the Submit
button. Figure 48.2 shows the results of submitting the form.

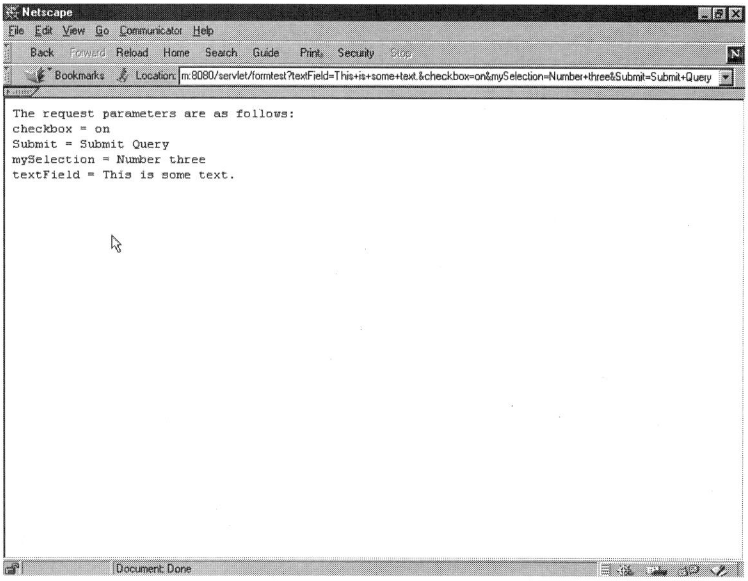

FIGURE 48.2.

The results generated by the FormTestServlet.

LISTING 48.2. THE FormTestServlet SOURCE CODE.

```java
import javax.servlet.*;
import java.util.*;
import java.io.*;

public class FormTestServlet extends GenericServlet  {
 public String getServletInfo() {
  return "Form Test Servlet";
 }
 public void service(ServletRequest request, ServletResponse response)
  throws ServletException, IOException {
  response.setContentType("text/plain");
  PrintStream outputStream = new PrintStream(response.getOutputStream());
  outputStream.println("The request parameters are as follows:");
  Enumeration params = request.getParameterNames();
  if(params != null) {
   while(params.hasMoreElements()){
    String param = (String) params.nextElement();
    String[] values = request.getParameterValues(param);
    outputStream.print(param+" = ");
    for(int i=0;i<values.length;++i)
     outputStream.print(values[i]+" ");
    outputStream.println("");
   }
  }
 }
}
```

LISTING 48.3. THE formtest.htm FILE.

```
<HTML>
<HEAD>
<TITLE>Testing a form with FormTestServlet</TITLE>
</HEAD>
<BODY>
<FORM ACTION="http://athome.jaworski.com:8080/servlet/formtest">
Enter text: <INPUT NAME="textField" TYPE="TEXT" SIZE="30"><P>
Check this out: <INPUT NAME="checkbox" TYPE="CHECKBOX"><P>
Select me: <SELECT NAME="mySelection">
<OPTION>Number one
<OPTION>Number two
<OPTION>Number three
</SELECT><P>
<INPUT NAME="Submit" TYPE="SUBMIT">
</FORM>
</BODY>
</HTML>
```

The servletrunner Command-Line Options

The servletrunner program supports a number of command-line options:

- -p *port*—Identifies the port number to listen on.
- -b *backlog*—Identifies the size of the listen backlog queue.
- -m *max*—Specifies the maximum number of connection handlers.
- -t *timeout*—Specifies the connection timeout in milliseconds.
- -d *dir*—Identifies the directory in which servlets are to be found.
- -r *root*—Identifies the document root directory.
- -s *filename*—Names the servlet property file name to be used.
- -v—Specifies that servletrunner should generate verbose output.

Experiment with these options (especially the -p option) to tailor servletrunner's execution to your needs.

Summary

In this chapter, you took a look at server-side programming using Java. You learned about the Common Gateway Interface (CGI) and learned why the CGI is not conducive to server-side Java programming. You also explored some of the server-side Java workarounds developed by Netscape and Microsoft for use on their servers. You then learned how to install the JSDK with Apache, Netscape, and Microsoft Web servers. Finally, you were introduced to the servletrunner tool and learned how to use it to run and test your servlets. In the next chapter, you'll learn how Java is used with push technologies, such as Marimba's Castanet.

Pushing Java

CHAPTER 49

One of the new and interesting technologies developed using Java is the Castanet product for automating the distribution of Web applications and software. Castanet, developed by Marimba, Inc., consists of a client/server publishing system that automatically updates users' computers with Web applications and software that are made available over specific distribution channels. Castanet's paradigm for Web publishing has since been adopted by both Netscape and Microsoft. The Netcaster component of Netscape Communicator incorporates Castanet technology, as well as more general channel capabilities. Microsoft and Marimba collaborated on the Channel Definition Format used by Internet Explorer 4.0.

In this chapter, you'll be introduced to Castanet and learn how the Castanet Transmitter and Tuner are used to publish applets and other executable content. You'll also learn about the channel publishing support provided by Netcaster and Active Channels. When you finish this chapter, you'll be able to use channels to publish your own Java applets.

Castanet

Castanet is a new paradigm for distributing Web applications and software that was developed by Marimba, Inc. (`http://www.marimba.com`), a company that was started by four of the original members of the Java team. Marimba provides three main products that are used to implement Castanet:

- Castanet Tuner—A freely distributed client for accessing Castanet channels. It is similar to a TV or radio tuner, allowing users to select channels over which specific Web applications are distributed. Castanet Tuner receives applications that are published on a channel and stores them on users' computers. It also provides a GUI front-end for managing and executing these applications.

- Castanet Transmitter—The server component of Castanet. It is used to publish Web applications over specific channels that are received, installed, and executed by the Castanet Tuner client.

- Bongo—A visual development environment that is used to create applications, called *presentations*, that are published using Castanet. Bongo greatly speeds up the process of application development. However, it is not needed to develop Castanet applications, which can be developed just using HTML and Java.

All three of these Marimba products were developed in Java. They are available for Windows 95, Windows NT, and Solaris platforms. Ports of these products are also available for Linux and other operating system platforms.

> **NOTE**
>
> Version 2.1 of Castanet only supports the Java Development Kit 1.1.5. Applications written using the newer JDK 1.2 API do not work with this version of Castanet.
>
> Castanet also provides repeater and proxy products. Repeaters are used to add supplementary transmission capabilities. Proxies are used to support transmission through a firewall.

How Castanet Works

Castanet uses the analogy of radio and television broadcasting. Web applications are published using Castanet Publish, a component of Castanet Transmitter. These applications may consist of simple HTML files, Java applets, presentations developed using Bongo, or Java applications. The applications are published to a Castanet Transmitter and are associated with a named channel. The Castanet Transmitter is analogous to a Web server. A channel is analogous to a Web site. For example, Marimba provides a transmitter on the host `trans.marimba.com`. This transmitter provides access to a number of channels, ranging from Castanet documentation to a couple of interesting games.

The Castanet Tuner is a client that is run by users in order to access Castanet channels. The tuner allows users to subscribe to a particular Castanet Transmitter and channel. When a user subscribes to a channel, the tuner contacts the transmitter responsible for that channel and downloads all of the files published on that channel to a directory on the user's computer. It then allows the user to execute these applications locally. The tuner also periodically checks back with the transmitter to see if the application files have been updated, and if so, downloads any changes to the user's computer. In this way, the user is ensured of having the latest information that is published on a channel available locally on his computer.

Figure 49.1 summarizes how Castanet works. A content developer creates HTML files, Java applets and applications, and Bongo presentations that he wants to publish. He organizes these files into three channels: A, B, and C. For example, A could be news and weather, B could be art and literature, and C could be games. He uses Castanet Publisher to publish these files to a transmitter. Different users subscribe to these channels using their tuner clients. The tuners download the files for the subscribed channels and store them on the users' hard drives. The users execute the application files locally using the tuner. The tuner also periodically checks back with the transmitter and updates the locally stored application files after they have been updated and republished by the content developer.

What's So Good About Castanet?

As you can see from Figure 49.1, Castanet uses a much different approach than most other Internet client/server systems, in which the interaction between a client and server is limited to a single transaction or a single group of transactions. For example, when a Web browser fetches a Web page from a Web server, the interaction between the browser and the server is complete. The user may never go back to that Web page again. In Castanet, once you subscribe to a channel, your tuner periodically checks back with the transmitter to make sure that you have the latest content published on the channel. If new information is published on the channel, the tuner automatically downloads it to the user's hard drive. This is a great benefit to the user, allowing him to keep abreast of the latest information of interest without having to continually check back with the server. The tuner does all the legwork for him.

Another advantage of the Castanet approach is that the tuner maintains the information that is published on a channel locally on the user's hard disk. This means that the user does not have to be connected to the Internet to access this information. For example, suppose you were using a notebook computer. You could dial in to your Internet service provider and use your tuner to subscribe to a channel. Your tuner would download the channel's content and store it on your hard drive. You could then take your notebook computer on a plane and access the channel's content while you were flying away to a distant location. When you arrived at your destination, you could call into your ISP and get an update of any new content that was added to the channel.

Castanet is especially helpful to users who have low-bandwidth Internet connections. Because the tuner works in the background to update your channels, it can be checking on your favorite channels while you are running other applications or doing other things. You can leave your computer running overnight and when you wake up the next day, it will be automatically updated with the latest channel content.

As mentioned earlier, Castanet channels support HTML, Java applets and applications, and Bongo presentations. Bongo presentations are a scripted hybrid of applets and applications. Think of them as Java applets or applications that are implemented using scripts rather than byte code.

When HTML files are published over a channel, the tuner executes them by invoking your default browser. You must configure your browser to use Castanet as a local proxy for accessing the Web. Castanet works with both Netscape Navigator and Microsoft Internet Explorer, as well as other popular browsers. The main advantage of Castanet when used for HTML publishing is that it maintains the HTML files on your system. When you need to access them, they're there. You don't have to worry about accessing the Internet or whether the destination Web server is down.

When Java applets are published over a channel, the tuner executes the applet in much the same way as the `appletviewer` tool of the JDK. The tuner provides the applet with all of the capabilities that it would have if it were executed via a browser. For example, an applet can retrieve and display images and play audio files. Castanet is an advantage for applet developers and users because it maintains the applet and the files used by the applet on users' computers, so the applet developer can use more bandwidth-consuming audio, image, and video files. When users access the applet, they don't have to wait for the multimedia files to be downloaded. They're waiting for them on their hard disks. Most applets can be used with Castanet without modification.

When Java applications are published over a channel, the tuner executes the application locally on your machine. However, the tuner implements a security manager that prevents the application from causing any damage to your system. The security manager confines all application disk I/O to a specific directory on your hard disk, prevents applications from making network connections to any host other than the transmitter, and keeps applications from executing local programs or dynamic link libraries. Castanet facilitates the installation and execution of Java applications, while limiting the exposure of users to accidental or deliberate damage.

The Castanet Tuner

The Castanet Tuner is freely available for download from Marimba's Web site. It is supported on Windows 95, Windows NT, Macintosh, and Solaris platforms. It has also been
ported to Linux and other operating systems. The Linux version is available from the
Java Linux Web site at `http://www.blackdown.org/java-linux/Products.html`. The
Windows 95 version of Castanet Tuner is distributed as a self-extracting executable file
that installs quickly and easily on your system. Go ahead and download and install
Castanet Tuner. When you have finished, select Castanet Tuner from the Start menu to
run it.

Figure 49.2 shows how the tuner appears when you execute it. It provides four tabs that
are used to access various parts of the application. The Marimba tab displays the
Marimba logo and copyright information.

NOTE

When you first run the tuner, it will connect to Marimba's transmitter and
update itself with the latest version of the tuner software. This may take a few
minutes.

FIGURE 49.2.

*The Castanet
Tuner.*

The Channels tab lists the channels that you are currently subscribed to and allows you to execute these channels by double-clicking on them (see Figure 49.3).

FIGURE 49.3.

The Channels tab lists the channels that you've subscribed.

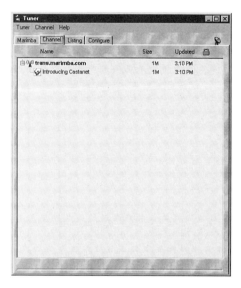

The Listing tab allows you to list all of the channels that are available from a particular transmitter, as shown in Figure 49.4. Just enter the host name of the transmitter and click on the List button. You can subscribe to a channel by double-clicking on it.

FIGURE 49.4.

The Listings tab lists the channels of a transmitter.

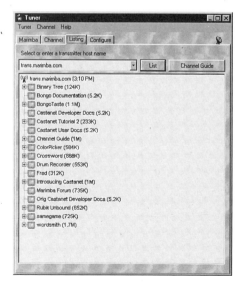

49

PUSHING JAVA

The Configure tab, shown in Figure 49.5, allows you to configure your tuner. It contains the Updates, User, Network, and Options subtabs. The Updates subtab lets you control how frequently the tuner contacts transmitters. The User subtab allows you to enter name and address information. The Network subtab is used to configure a firewall proxy. The Options subtab is used to configure your network connection.

FIGURE 49.5.

The Configure tab lets you configure your tuner.

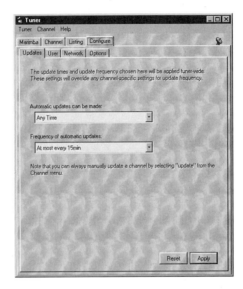

Subscribing to a Channel

We'll subscribe to a transmitter and channel to show you how it works. Click on the Listing tab, enter `trans.marimba.com` in the pull-down text field, and click on the List button. A listing of the Marimba channels is displayed, as shown in Figure 49.4. Double-click on the SameGame channel to subscribe to it. The SameGame application is downloaded and then executed, as shown in Figure 49.6. You can play the game by clicking twice on groups of two or more squares of the same color. The objective is to remove all of the squares.

When you are finished with the SameGame channel, close it and return to the Listing tab. Enter `gday.bloke.com:81` and click the List button. The channels for the `gday.bloke.com` transmitter are listed. Double-click on the WhatsNew channel to subscribe to it. This channel provides a great starting place to learn about other channels.

FIGURE 49.6.

The SameGame channel.

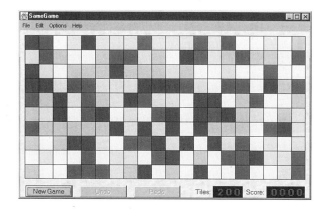

> **WARNING**
>
> When using Castanet tuner to access transmitter channels, remember that it stores all channel content locally on your hard disk. If you are not vigilant about your channel usage, you'll find yourself running out of hard disk storage space.

The Castanet Transmitter

The Castanet Transmitter is a product of Marimba, Inc. It is not freeware or shareware. However, Marimba makes evaluation copies available for download from its Web site. Castanet Transmitter also comes in Windows 95, Windows NT, and Solaris versions. The Windows 95 version is distributed as a self-extracting executable installation program.

> **NOTE**
>
> To run the examples later in this chapter, you'll need to download and install Castanet Transmitter.

Castanet Transmitter allows you to create your own channels for distributing executable content and HTML files over the Internet. It consists of two products: the transmitter itself and Castanet Publisher. The transmitter is self-installing and provides excellent help support. Castanet Publisher is covered in the next section.

Castanet Publisher

You use Castanet Publisher to publish your executable content to a transmitter. Castanet Publisher doesn't provide any Web content development capabilities. You develop your Java and HTML files using your normal development tools. All Castanet Publisher does is move your files from your development directory to a directory on the transmitter and configure your transmitter to make the files available over a particular channel.

Castanet comes with a few demo channels. These channels are contained in the `C:\Program Files\Marimba\Castanet Publisher\developers\channels` directory. I'll show you how to publish one so that you'll learn how Castanet Publisher works. If you do not have your transmitter running, now is a good time to start it. I use the `C:\Channels` directory as my transmitter channels directory.

> **WARNING**
>
> You cannot circumvent Castanet Publisher by copying files directly to your transmitter. Castanet Publisher must copy your files so that it can properly configure them on a channel.

Open Castanet Publisher from the Start menu. It displays the window shown in Figure 49.7.

FIGURE 49.7.

The Castanet Publisher opening window.

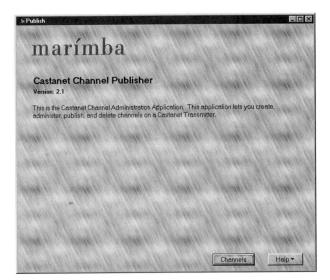

Click on the Channels button to go to the Channels Under Development window, shown in Figure 49.8.

FIGURE 49.8.

The Channels Under Development window.

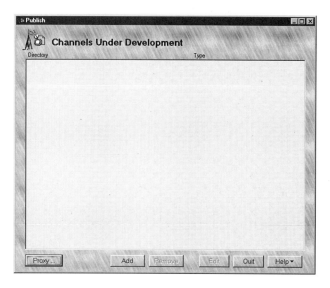

Click the Add button to go to the Directory Finder dialog box, shown in Figure 49.9.

FIGURE 49.9.

The Directory Finder dialog box.

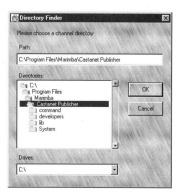

49

PUSHING JAVA

Enter `C:\Program Files\Marimba\Castanet Publisher\developers\channels\Crossword` and click the Add button. The channel is added to the Channels under Development window, as shown in Figure 49.10.

Now click the Edit button. The nine-tabbed window, shown in Figure 49.11, is displayed. You can use these tabs to configure your channel before publishing it. These tabs are described in the following paragraphs:

FIGURE **49.10.**

*The channel is
added to the
Channels Under
Development win-
dow.*

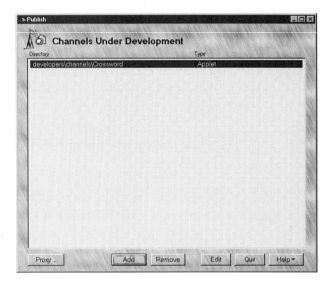

- The Transmitter tab is used to identify the host name and port of the transmitter. Use `localhost` if you are publishing to a transmitter on the same host as Castanet Publisher. You can enter a password for your transmitter or the channel you are publishing. You can also specify file types that are excluded from being published. Never exclude `*.txt` files, because they are used by the transmitter to store channel configuration information.

- The General tab allows you to name your channel and to identify the type of channel that you are publishing. Four different types of channels can be published: HTML, Java Applet, Java Application, and Bongo Presentation. When you select one of these types, configuration fields for that type are displayed.

- The Update tab lets you specify the frequency with which tuners should check back with the transmitter for channel updates. The Inactive parameters refer to when your channel application is not executing. The Active parameters refer to when your channel application is executing. The Data Available Action field tells the tuner what to do with new channel updates.

- The Icons tab allows you to specify icons to be used with your channel.

- The Contacts tab allows you to specify information that channel users can use to contact you.

- The Description tab allows you to specify descriptive information about your channel.

- The Parameters tab is used to specify applet parameters.

- The Repeaters tab is used to specify the use of Castanet Repeaters. Castanet Repeaters are similar to mirrored FTP sites.

- The Security tab is used to implement security controls for your channel.

FIGURE 49.11.

The channel configuration tabs.

Now that you've taken a brief tour through Castanet Publisher, click the Publisher button to publish the Crossword channel.

Click the Done button twice and then the Quit button to exit Castanet Publisher.

FIGURE 49.12.

Publishing the Crossword channel.

49

PUSHING JAVA

Running the Crossword Application

Now that you've published the Crossword channel to your transmitter, you can use your tuner to execute it. Open your tuner and turn to the Listing tab. Enter the host name of your transmitter and click the List button. The Crossword channel is displayed under your transmitter, as shown in Figure 49.13. Double-click on the Crossword channel to execute it.

FIGURE 49.13.

Listing the Crossword channel on your transmitter.

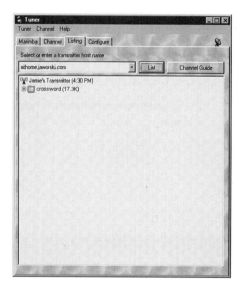

Figure 49.14 shows the Crossword channel. It displays a crossword puzzle that you can complete.

FIGURE 49.14.

Executing the Crossword channel.

Creating an Applet and Publishing It with Castanet

Although we haven't covered all of Castanet's features or capabilities, you now know enough to develop an applet and publish it using Castanet. Listing 49.1 shows the `Gallery` applet, which is contained in the `ch49\publish` directory.

After you compile the `Gallery` applet, the `ch49\publish` directory contains the following files:

- `Gallery.java`
- `Gallery.class`
- `Gallery$ButtonHandler.class`
- `MyCanvas.class`
- `image.jpg`
- `audio.au`

The `image.jpg` file contains a photographic image. The `audio.au` file contains an audio description of the photo.

Now use Castanet Publisher to distribute the applet and its supporting files via a channel. When you open Castanet Publisher, click the Channels button to go to the Channels Under Development window. Then click the Add button. Type `c:\jdk1.2\ju\ch49\pub-lish` in the Path field (as shown in Figure 49.15), and then click the OK button.

FIGURE 49.15.

Specifying the channel's source directory.

Now click on the Edit button in the Channels Under Development window. The channel configuration window is displayed. Click on the General tab. Set the Name field to `Daily Photo Gallery`. Set the Type field to `Applet`. Set the Code field to `Gallery`. Set the Width field to `500` and the Height field to `450` (see Figure 49.16).

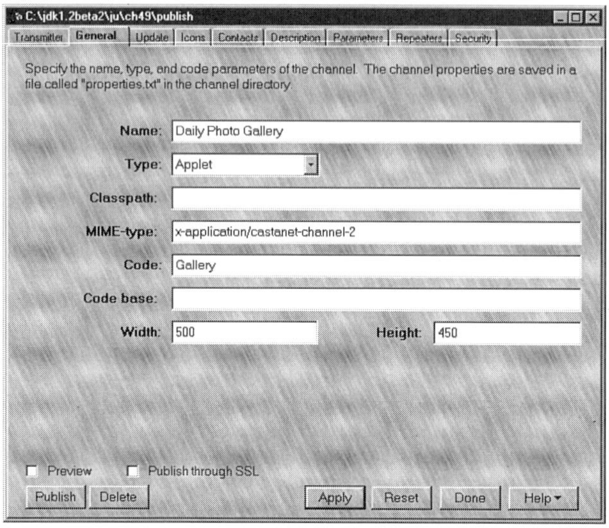

FIGURE 49.16.

Specifying the channel's name and type.

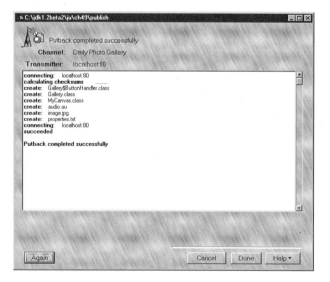

Click on the Update tab and then set the Update Frequency for an Inactive application to Daily. Then click the Publisher button. The Gallery channel is published to your transmitter. Castanet Publisher displays a confirmation, as shown in Figure 49.17. Go ahead and exit Castanet Publisher.

FIGURE 49.17.

Confirming the channel's publication.

Start your tuner and click on the Listing tab. Enter the host name of your transmitter and click the List button. The name of the new channel is displayed, as shown in Figure 49.18.

FIGURE 49.18.

Listing the new channel under your transmitter.

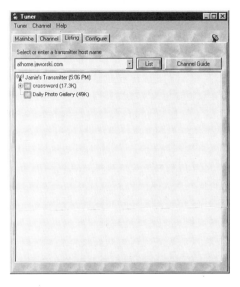

Double-click on the Daily Photo Gallery channel and the Gallery applet is executed, as shown in Figure 49.19. You can click the Audio Description button to find out information about the photograph that is displayed. Close the applet and the tuner.

FIGURE 49.19.

The Daily Photo Gallery channel.

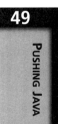

49

PUSHING JAVA

Updating the Information Displayed by the Applet

The previous example shows how easy it is to publish an applet using Castanet. In this section, I'll show you how easy it is to update the information displayed by the applet. In your ch49 directory are files named image2.jpg and audio2.au. These files contain a new image and audio description. Copy these files over the image.jpg and audio.au files contained in the publish subdirectory.

You've just updated the Daily Photo Gallery's source directory. Now let's publish the new information to the transmitter. Open Castanet Publisher and click the Channels button. Select the channel and click the Edit button. Now click the Publisher button to republish the channel. That's all you need to do to update your channel. You can exit from Castanet Publish.

Because your channel specified a daily update frequency, all channel tuners will check back with your transmitter in about a day to get the updated channel information. Let's check out the new information that you published. Open your tuner and click on the Channels tab. Now double-click on the Daily Photo Gallery channel. The same photo that was displayed in Figure 49.19 is displayed. That's because your tuner didn't check in with your transmitter yet.

Close the Daily Photo Gallery channel, but keep it selected in the Channels tab of your tuner. Select Update from the Channel pull-down menu to force your tuner to check back with the transmitter. Now double-click on the Daily Photo Gallery channel again. This time it displays the photo shown in Figure 49.20.

FIGURE 49.20.

The Daily Photo Gallery channel.

How the `Gallery` Applet Works

Up to this point, we've been focusing on how Castanet works. In this section we'll describe how the `Gallery` applet works. It creates two field variables named `image` and `audio` to refer to the image that is displayed and its associated audio description. The `init()` method invokes the `getCodeBase()` method of the `Applet` class to retrieve the URL associated with the applet's code base. This URL is used to read the image and audio files that are located in the same directory as the applet. Even though the applet, image file, and audio file are executed by a tuner from the user's hard disk, we can still use `getCodeBase()` to refer to their location. The `getImage()` and `getAudioClip()` methods retrieve the image and audio files. The rest of `init()` consists of applet layout.

The `stop()` method simply stops the playing of the audio file.

The `actionPerformed()` method of the `ButtonHandler` class handles the clicking of the button by playing the audio file.

The `MyCanvas` class is used to display the image in the middle of the applet window. The `paint()` method calculates the difference between the canvas size and the image size and adjusts the image to the center of the canvas.

LISTING 49.1. THE `Gallery` APPLET.

```
import java.applet.*;
import java.awt.*;
import java.awt.event.*;
import java.net.*;

public class Gallery extends Applet {
 AudioClip audio;
 Image image;
 public void init() {
  try {
   URL base = getCodeBase();
   image = getImage(base,"image.jpg");
   audio = getAudioClip(base,"audio.au");
   setLayout(new BorderLayout());
   add("Center",new MyCanvas(image));
   Button button = new Button("Audio Description");
   button.addActionListener(new ButtonHandler());
   add("South",button);
  }catch (Exception ex) {
  }
 }
 public void stop() {
```

49

PUSHING JAVA

continues

LISTING 49.1. CONTINUED

```java
    audio.stop();
  }
  class ButtonHandler implements ActionListener {
   public void actionPerformed(ActionEvent event) {
    audio.play();
   }
  }
 }
class MyCanvas extends Canvas {
 Image image;
 public MyCanvas(Image image) {
  this.image = image;
 }
 public void paint(Graphics g) {
  Dimension canvasSize = getSize();
  int imageHeight = image.getHeight(this);
  int imageWidth = image.getWidth(this);
  int x = (canvasSize.width - imageWidth)/2;
  int y = (canvasSize.height - imageHeight)/2;
  if(x<0) x=0;
  if(y<0) y=0;
  g.drawImage(image,x,y,this);
 }
}
```

Other Castanet Publishing Capabilities

So far, you have seen how easy it is to publish applets with Castanet. However, Castanet provides many more capabilities than we've covered here. Some of these capabilities are as follows:

- Java applications can be published using Castanet. Marimba provides special classes that can be used to implement applications as channels.

- Java applications can be updated while they are executing to take advantage of information that is dynamically published.

- Java applications can maintain information locally on the user's hard disk.

- Java applications can send information back to transmitters that can be used to keep track of user preferences.

- Bongo presentations can be published using Castanet and are easy to develop using Bongo's visual development environment and Java-based scripting language.

The use of these capabilities in channels is a book in itself. For more information, I suggest that you subscribe to the Castanet Developer Docs channel that is published by trans.marimba.com.

Netcaster

The Castanet approach to delivering Web content was adopted by Netscape in Netscape Communicator 4.0. The Netcaster component of Communicator 4.0 supports the push delivery of Web content and includes support for Java and JavaScript. Netcaster provides direct support for Castanet channels. However, Netcaster does not support Microsoft's Channel Definition Format (CDF).

Netcaster, like Castanet, is channel-oriented. The user subscribes to certain channels that are delivered to the user as a background or foreground operation. Netcaster implements push in the same way as Castanet by having the client download data from the server and store it on the user's local computer. Netcaster supports the notion of a "Webtop" as a channel that is anchored to the user's desktop. The Webtop channels are similar to the Active Channels supported by Microsoft's Internet Explorer 4.0.

Netcaster supports offline browsing, which is implemented by downloading Web sites to the user's hard disk. The user browses local files instead of going out to the Web.

Netcaster Versus Castanet

One of the major advantages of Netcaster is that it works with the existing HTML, Java, and JavaScript infrastructure of the Web. No special transmitter or server-side publishing is required. Existing Web sites do not need to be reconfigured to work with Netcaster. All the user needs to do is identify the URL of a Web site, the number of levels of links to download, and an update period. Netcaster takes care of the rest.

Castanet support is embedded in Netcaster. Netcaster can be used to access Castanet channels by simply identifying the URL of the Castanet transmitter. Castanet URLs begin with `castanet://` and are followed by the name of the host, port, and channel to be accessed. Netcaster provides the best of both worlds—support of Castanet channels and general HTTP, Java, and JavaScript support.

Developing Channels

There are no special requirements for developing Netcaster channels. For basic channel support, all you have to do is publish your HTML files, scripts, and Java `.class` files to your Web site. If you want to publish Castanet channels for use with Netcaster, you can use the Castanet publishing tools covered earlier in this chapter. Castanet channels require the use of a Castanet transmitter.

49

PUSHING JAVA

Active Channels

Active Channels are Microsoft's answer to pushing Web content. They are based on the Channel Definition Format (CDF), which is a channel specification developed by Microsoft and Marimba. The CDF has been submitted to the World Wide Web Consortium for international standardization. Active Channels are incorporated into Internet Explorer 4.0.

Active Channels are similar to Castanet channels in that channel content is loaded in the background, at regular intervals, by the user's client program. Internet Explorer 4.0 is the Active Channel client. Active Channels are also similar to the Netcaster Webtop in that Active Channels can be integrated within the Windows 95, 98, and NT desktop. Since Active Channels are targeted toward Windows platforms, Active Channels provide tighter desktop integration. This is a major feature of Windows 98.

Active Channel content consists of anything that you could publish to a Web site: HTML files, scripts, Java applets, and ActiveX controls. Active Channels are implemented in the same manner as Netcaster channels. However, special testing of Active Channels is required because ActiveX controls and some Java applets may not work correctly in the channel's offline mode. This generally occurs when the control or applet needs access to network resources.

The Channel Definition Format

Unlike Netcaster channels, Active Channels require the use of a separate CDF file. The CDF file is used to specify the channel content, its structure, and information about the scheduling of channel updates. CDF files are syntactically similar to HTML files in that they use HTML-like tags. CDF files also specify the URLs of the channel files, the structure of the channel pages, and scheduling options.

CDF is an application of the eXtensible Markup Language (XML). Its syntax is covered in the Channel Definition Format specification, which is available at `http://www.microsoft.com/standards/cdf-f.htm`. A CDF file begins with a line that identifies the XML version being used:

```
<?XML Version="1.0"?>
```

This is then followed by a CHANNEL tag that identifies the channel's main page:

```
<CHANNEL HREF="url">
```

In the preceding statement, *url* is replaced by the URL of the channel's main HTML page.

ABSTRACT and TITLE tags can be used to specify an abstract and title for the channel:

```
<ABSTRACT>This is a summary of what my channel is all about.</ABSTRACT>
<TITLE>This is my channel's title</TITLE>
```

The LOGO tag may be used to specify a logo for a channel:

```
<LOGO HREF="url" STYLE="iconType" />
```

The *url* identifies the location of the channel's logo (a GIF file). The *iconType* identifies the type of icon. Three icon types are supported: icon, image, or image-wide. These icons are placed on the Channel Bar and Active Desktop.

A series of ITEM tags follow the LOGO tags. The ITEM tags are used to specify the *subpages* (other pages) of a channel. ITEM tags are used as follows:

```
<ITEM HREF="url">
<ABSTRACT>Abstract of subpage.</ABSTRACT>
<TITLE>Title of subpage</TITLE>
</ITEM>
```

The *url* refers to the URL of the subpage. The ABSTRACT and TITLE tags are used to provide additional information about the subpage.

The closing CHANNEL tag follows the last ITEM tag and marks the end of the CDF file.

```
</CHANNEL>
```

Creating Active Channels

Listing 49.2 provides an example CDF file. This file identifies the URL of the main page as http://www.jaworski.com/ju/ch49/hello.htm. Listing 49.3 displays the contents of the hello.htm file. An abstract and title are provided for the main page. However, I skipped the logos. The channel contains a single subpage—the HelloChannel applet. Listing 49.4 shows the source code for HelloChannel. This applet just displays the text Hello Channel! to the applet display area.

I've put the hello.htm and HelloChannel.class files on my Web server. To view the channel with Internet Explorer 4.0, simply open the example.cdf file. Figure 49.21 shows how the channel is displayed by Internet Explorer.

As you can see, Active Channels are easy to create. Basically, you create a Web site as you normally would and then specify the channel's contents using a CDF file. Active Channels are equal in capability to basic Netcaster channels, but they are far less sophisticated than Castanet channels. Active Channels have a significant disadvantage in that they require the creation of a separate CDF file.

FIGURE 49.21.

Displaying the example Active Channel.

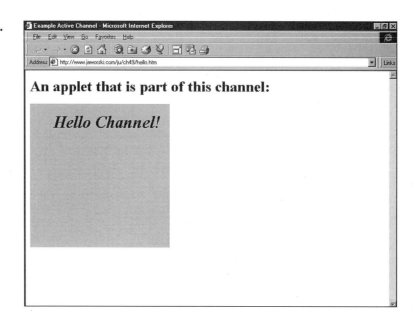

LISTING 49.2. AN EXAMPLE CDF FILE (EXAMPLE.CDF).

```
<?XML Version="1.0"?>

<CHANNEL HREF="http://www.jaworski.com/ju/ch49/hello.htm">
<ABSTRACT>This is a example Active Channel.</ABSTRACT>
<TITLE>Example Active Channel</TITLE>
<ITEM HREF="http://www.jaworski.com/ju/ch49/HelloChannel.class">
<ABSTRACT>HelloChannel applet.</ABSTRACT>
<TITLE>HelloChannel</TITLE>
</ITEM>
</CHANNEL>
```

LISTING 49.3. AN HTML FILE USED IN AN ACTIVE CHANNEL (HELLO.HTM).

```
<HTML>
<HEAD>
<TITLE>Example Active Channel</TITLE>
</HEAD>
<BODY>
<H1>An applet that is part of this channel:</H1>
<APPLET CODE="HelloChannel.class" HEIGHT=300 WIDTH=300>
</APPLET>
</BODY>
</HTML>
```

LISTING 49.4. THE `HelloChannel` APPLET.

```java
import java.applet.*;
import java.awt.*;
public class HelloChannel extends Applet {
 public void paint(Graphics g) {
  g.setFont(new Font("TimesRoman",Font.BOLD+Font.ITALIC,36));
  g.drawString("Hello Channel!",50,50);
 }
}
```

Summary

In this chapter, you were introduced to Castanet and learned how the Castanet Transmitter and Tuner are used to publish applets and other executable content. You also learned about the channel publishing support provided by Netcaster and Active Channels. In the next chapter, you'll learn about the electronic commerce capabilities supported by the Java Commerce and JavaCard APIs.

49

PUSHING JAVA

Java Commerce and JavaCard

CHAPTER 50

Not only is the Web changing the way that we share information, it is also changing the way that we do business. Since the earliest days of the Web, businesses arrived in droves to advertise their wares and set up electronic storefronts. With the omnipresence of business activity throughout the Web, approaches to implementing electronic commerce were eagerly sought. JavaSoft answers the call for a practical approach to electronic commerce with its Java Electronic Commerce Framework (JECF).

In this chapter, you'll be introduced to the JECF and learn about its key components. You'll learn about the JECF architecture and how it supports a multiplicity of electronic commerce protocols. You'll learn about the Commerce API and the services it provides. You'll also learn about the Java Commerce Toolkit and Java Wallet. Finally, you'll learn how the Java Card API is being developed to bring smart cards to electronic commerce. When you finish this chapter, you'll be familiar with the various ways in which Java is being used to support electronic commerce applications.

Java Electronic Commerce Framework

The JECF is a framework for developing products and applications that are used in electronic commerce. This framework was developed by JavaSoft to leverage Java's platform-independence to create secure and reliable software components for carrying out financial transactions.

> **NOTE**
>
> The Java Commerce home page is located at `http://www.javasoft.com/products/commerce/`.

The JECF consists of an architecture and a set of APIs for implementing electronic commerce solutions. Its architecture consists of the following four layers:

- The Java Environment Layer—This layer provides the foundation for the other layers. It consists of the Java Virtual Machine and other elements of the Java Runtime Environment. It may be implemented in the context of a browser, as part of the normal JDK distribution, or in hardware such as a Java microprocessor.
- The Java Commerce Package Layer—This layer consists of those classes and interfaces that provide the foundation for developing electronic commerce applications. These classes consist of the Java Commerce API and supporting APIs, such as the

Security API, JDBC, the AWT, and others. The Java Commerce Package Layer is built on top of the Java Environment Layer and supports the other layers of the JECF architecture.

- The Cassette Layer—The Cassette Layer consists of cassettes that implement specific electronic commerce transaction protocols. Cassettes store sensitive and valuable information related to electronic financial transactions, such as account numbers, digital certificates, and payment information. They make extensive use of the encryption capabilities supported by the Java API. Unique cassettes are developed for different payment protocols, such as Secure Electronic Transaction (SET), electronic money, and online banking. The Cassette Layer is built on top of the Java Commerce Package and Java Environment Layers.

> **NOTE**
>
> Java Commerce cassettes are *logical* objects, not *physical* objects.

- The Merchant Applet Layer—The Merchant Applet Layer consists of Java applets that are designed to provide an interface to financial transactions. Examples are shopping applets, banking applets, and financial investment applets. The Merchant Applet Layer is built on top of the other three layers of the JECF architecture.

Figure 50.1 provides an overview of the JECF architecture. The Java Environment and Java Commerce Layers provide the foundation for implementing electronic commerce. These layers consist of the classes and interfaces from which cassettes are built.

FIGURE 50.1.
The JECF architecture.

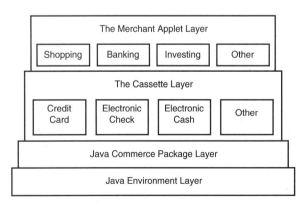

50

JAVA COMMERCE AND JAVACARD

The JECF provides a flexible framework for the development of electronic commerce applications. Instead of limiting itself to a particular payment protocol, the JECF allows standard and custom payment protocols to be implemented in terms of cassettes.

Cassettes are used as the building blocks for developing electronic commerce services. Some, but not all, of these services may be presented to consumers, businesses, and other organizations in the form of Java applets. Other cassettes may be embedded in stand-alone applications. Applets will provide attractive, easy-to-use interfaces to their customers and will use cassettes to carry out commerce transactions. For example, a shopping applet may use a number of alternative cassettes to support credit card payments, electronic checks, or electronic cash.

The Java Commerce API

The Java Commerce API provides the classes and interfaces for building commerce applications within the JECF. These APIs are implemented within the Java Commerce Package Layer of the JECF architecture and support a number of capabilities, including the following:

- The downloading, installation, operation, and management of cassettes
- The secure storage of sensitive and valuable information such as account numbers, transaction details, and encryption keys
- A database interface
- Special GUI controls

At the time this chapter was written, the Java Commerce API was in the Alpha 0.8 release and consisted of the following packages:

- `com.sun.commerce.example.post`—Provides two classes that are used to post credit card information and drive cassette installation.
- `com.sun.commerce.gencc`—Provides classes and an interface for the handling of credit cards.
- `javax.commerce.base`—Provides base classes and interfaces that are used by other packages of the Commerce API.
- `javax.commerce.cassette`—Provides classes and interfaces for the installation and operation of cassettes.
- `javax.commerce.database`—Provides classes and interfaces that support database access.
- `javax.commerce.gui`—Provides a number of classes that implement custom GUI controls.

- `java.commerce.smartcards`—Provides classes that support smartcards.
- `java.commerce.log`—Provides classes that support the logging of financial transactions.
- `javax.commerce.util`—Provides classes that encapsulate money.

These packages make use of other packages of the Java Commerce Package Layer, such as those of the Security API.

The Java Commerce Toolkit

The Java Commerce Toolkit is a set of tools for developing electronic commerce applications using the Java Commerce API. You can use it to quickly get a commerce application off the ground. It includes the Java Wallet, sample Java cassettes, and a sample shopping cart applet.

The cassettes implement common electronic commerce protocols. The shopping cart applet is used by customers to hold items to be purchased while browsing through an electronic store. The Java Wallet is covered in the next section.

Java Wallet

The Java Wallet provides GUI controls that are used to carry out financial transactions. These GUI controls are designed to provide a graphical representation of a traditional wallet. Figure 50.2 provides a screen capture of the Java Wallet interface.

FIGURE 50.2.

The Java Wallet.

The purpose of the Java Wallet is to make users comfortable using electronic commerce applications. The Java Wallet interfaces with cassettes that carry out electronic commerce protocols. It's extensible and can support a number of different cassettes. It was also designed with financial institutions in mind. It provides institutions with the capability to tailor the wallet to display institution-specific information, such as logos and address information, in a manner similar to credit cards, such as Master Card and Visa.

The Java Wallet is not tied to any particular implementation. It is written in pure Java and will run on all platforms that support the Commerce API.

The Java Card API

The Java Card API is designed for creating specialized applications that run on smart cards. A *smart card* is the size, shape, and appearance of a normal credit card. The difference is that it has a small programmable computer embedded within it that contains memory and is capable of storing a limited amount of information. The availability and use of smart cards are expected to grow tremendously in the next few years.

The Java Card API was developed to program smart cards. It is a specialized API, in that it runs on a limited version of the JVM that is designed for the tight constraints of a smart card.

The Java Card API is compliant with ISO 7816-4. This means that it will run on any standard smart card. The Java Card API can be used to program smart cards for a variety of applications, such as identification and authentication, storage of medical information, and, of course, electronic commerce. The Java Card API is intended to provide a smart card implementation of the Java Wallet.

The Java Card API consists of a single `java.iso7816` package that is based on the ISO 7816-4 standard (`http://www.iso.ch`). This package provides very low-level methods for controlling smart card operation.

Summary

In this chapter, you were introduced to the JECF and learned about its key components. You learned about the JECF architecture and how it uses cassettes to support a range of electronic commerce protocols. You learned about the Commerce API and about the services it provides. You also learned about the Java Commerce Toolkit and Java Wallet. Finally, you learned about how the Java Card API is being used to implement electronic commerce with smart cards. In the next chapter, you'll learn about the variety of execution platforms that support Java.

EmbeddedJava, and JavaCard, are subsets of the Core API. Figure 51.1 shows the relationship between the Java Platform, Personal Java, Embedded Java, and Java Card.

Figure 51.1.

The Java application environments.

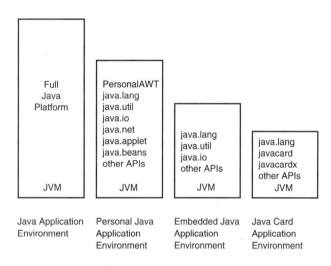

Full Java Platform

PersonalAWT
java.lang
java.util
java.io
java.net
java.applet
java.beans
other APIs

java.lang
java.util
java.io
other APIs

java.lang
javacard
javacardx
other APIs

JVM   JVM   JVM   JVM

Java Application Environment

Personal Java Application Environment

Embedded Java Application Environment

Java Card Application Environment

Core API

Because the Core API must be supported by all Java Platforms, it is the API to which most Java applications will be written. The Core API is quite extensive. It includes all of the packages of the JDK 1.2, plus other packages that will be added to the next JDK 1.3 release. These packages include the following:

- Java 3D API—Provides a 3D library that supports VRML.

- Java Animation API—Supports 2D animation.

- Java Media Framework (JMF)—Provides a common API for multimedia players, multimedia capture, and multimedia conferencing.

- Java Commerce API—Part of this will be Core, and the rest will be Standard Extension. This provides the capability to perform electronic financial transactions. The part of the Java API to be included in the Core is referred to as *Java Wallet* and supports the client-side functions of electronic commerce.

Other APIs that are part of the Standard Extension will be added to the Core after they are widely supported.

Standard Extensions

The Standard Extension API includes all packages that are not part of the Core API. It's not supported on all Java platforms, but it contains the most exciting new API developments. The following Standard Extension API packages are being developed:

- Java Naming and Directory Interface (JNDI)—Provides access to common naming and directory services, such as the Lightweight Directory Access Protocol or LDAP.

- Java Server and Servlet APIs—The Server API facilitates the development of Internet servers, such as Web servers. The Servlet API supports the development of server-side applications.

- Java Commerce API—The Standard Extension part of the Commerce API includes classes and interfaces for implementing the server-side components of electronic financial transactions.

- Java Collaboration API—Supports the development and sharing of multiuser applications over a network.

- Java Telephony API—Provides access to telephonic communication and supports call control.

- Java Speech API—Supports speech recognition and synthesis.

- Java Management API—Supports network and system management functions.

JavaSoft is continually adding to its list of new APIs that are being developed. If the preceding list does not quench your thirst for Java, check the Java API Overview and Schedule Web page (`http://www.javasoft.com/products/api-overview/index.html`) for new developments.

Personal Java

Personal Java has been defined as a subset of the Java Platform for use in consumer electronic devices and mobile computing devices. Examples of Personal Java applications include handheld PCs, set-top Internet boxes, Web phones, and game controllers. Personal Java is designed to be upward-compatible with the Java Platform but still capable of executing in memory-constrained devices. Personal Java includes the JVM, PersonalAWT (a fine-tuned implementation of the Abstract Window Toolkit), and most of the applet, JavaBeans, I/O, networking, language, and utility packages. Optional APIs may be added to tailor Personal Java to specific application environments. Personal Java is capable of running on systems with 2MB of ROM and 1MB of RAM.

Embedded Java

Embedded Java is a subset of the Java Platform that is intended for high-volume embedded devices, such as mobile phones, pagers, printers, copiers, fax machines, medical instruments, and factory automation systems. Embedded Java is upward-compatible with Personal Java. It supports a text-only user interface and a selectable subset of the Java Platform. The Embedded Java API is still under development. Embedded Java is intended to be capable of running on systems with .5MB of ROM and .5MB of RAM.

Java Card

Java Card is a Java API for embedding Java in devices such as smart cards. It allows applications to be written once in Java and run on all smart cards for which the Java Card API has been ported. It also allows multiple applications to run on a single card. The Java Card API is currently in version 2.0. The Java Card API consists of parts of the `java.lang` package, plus the `javacard.framework`, `javacardx.crypto`, `javacardx.cryptEnc`, and `javacardx.framework` packages. These packages provide low-level control of smart card devices and provide security encryption and authentication services. Java Card is designed for hardware environments that have at least 16KB of ROM, 8KB of EEPROM, and 256 bytes of RAM.

Java Runtime Environment

The Java Runtime Environment, or JRE, is the implementation of the Java Platform and consists of the JVM, Core APIs, and supporting files. It is the JDK without the JDK tools, associated documentation, and source code. Although the JRE has been ported to many operating system platforms, Sun only distributes the JRE for Win32 (Windows NT, Windows 95, and Windows 98) and Solaris (Sparc and Intel versions). The JRE has been tailored to support languages other than English. It is also distributed with Java-enabled products, such as Netscape Communicator, Microsoft Internet Explorer, and Marimba Castanet Tuner.

Java Performance Enhancements

The Win32 Performance Pack is also distributed by Sun as an extension of the JRE. It includes a *Just-In-Time compiler (JIT)* that increases the speed of Java applications by a factor of 10. The JIT compiler compiles Java bytecodes into native x86 machine code so that they can execute directly on Intel x86 and Pentium-class processors.

Navigator Classes

Netscape has added its own extensions to the Java Platform for use within the Netscape Navigator. These extensions are referred to as *Internet Foundation Classes (IFC)*. The IFC is an API for developing Web applications that execute within the context of the Netscape browser. The API includes additional graphical user interface (GUI) controls besides those included with the AWT, a multifont text object for developing word processor-like applications, drag-and-drop support, animation support, and other capabilities. The IFC can be downloaded from Netscape at

`http://developer.netscape.com/library/ifc/index.html`.

Netscape intended that the *Java Foundation Classes (JFC)* would eventually include and replace the IFC. However, this is not the case as of JDK 1.2. Eventually, the JFC will incorporate the IFC into the Java API and develop a common set of GUI interface controls implemented as JavaBeans.

Internet Explorer Classes

Not to be left out, Microsoft has developed its own Java API extensions, referred to as the *Application Foundation Classes (AFC)*. The AFC consists of a set of class libraries that implement GUI controls, multimedia capabilities, and support for Microsoft extract cabinet (CAB) files. CAB files are compressed archive files similar to ZIP files. The AFC consists of the following packages:

- `com.ms.ui`—Classes that provide user interface controls.
- `com.ms.fx`—Classes for multimedia effects.
- `com.ms.util.cab`—Classes for working with CAB files.

The AFC is written entirely in Java and is built on top of the AWT. It is intended to run on all Java platforms. The AFCs are available at

`http://www.microsoft.com/java/afc/`.

Other Class Libraries

A number of vendors offer their class libraries as freeware, shareware, and commercial products. The Gamelan Web site has an excellent directory of these libraries at

`http://www.developer.com/directories/pages/dir.java.html`.

ObjectSpace, Inc. has made their Generic Collection Library for Java (JGL) free for commercial use by Java Developers from its Web Site (`http://www.objectspace.com`).

The JGL contains 11 collection objects (such as lists) used to organize other objects, and 40 algorithms (such as sorting) used to manipulate groups of objects. The JGL is licensed and provided by most major Java tool vendors.

Native Methods

All of the Java API extensions that we've mentioned so far have been pure Java extensions. Although it is technically possible to extend Java using native methods, this approach is not recommended because you lose the platform-independent capability of Java.

There are some special circumstances in which native methods may be an appropriate solution for Java software development. For example, when interfacing Java to legacy systems, it may be necessary to create a Java wrapper around the API of the legacy system that you're attempting to salvage. In this case, you would use native methods to provide the interface with your legacy code. Other reasons to use native methods are based on the absence of appropriate features within the Java API. For example, you may need to access the native NetBEUI or IPX protocols of your operating system. Native methods can be used to wrap a Java interface on these protocols. Chapter 53, "Native Methods," shows how to extend the Java Platform using native methods.

Summary

In this chapter, you learned about the Java Platform and examined each of its parts, as well as the Personal Java, Embedded Java, and Java Card application environments. You looked at the most popular extensions to the Java Platform, including Netscape's Internet Foundation Classes, Microsoft's Application Foundation Classes, and ObjectSpace's JGL. In the next chapter, you'll learn about one of the most promising platforms for Java deployment—JavaOS.

JavaOS

CHAPTER 52

One of the most exciting new products released by JavaSoft is the JavaOS version 1.0. JavaOS promises to be the operating system of choice for network computers (NCs), Personal Digital Assistants (PDAs), and commercial electronics devices. This chapter looks at JavaOS, describes its architecture, and examines its features.

Why JavaOS?

With Java supported on Windows, Macintosh, Linux, and UNIX platforms, why would JavaSoft create JavaOS? Rather than porting an existing operating system to new hardware and running Java on top of that operating system, the engineers at JavaSoft and Sun decided to create JavaOS as a small, memory-efficient, fast, and highly portable operating system (OS) that provides direct support for the Java runtime environment, windowing system, networking capabilities, and other features of the Java API. The goal of JavaOS is to make Java available on low-powered and low-memory devices, such as NCs and PDAs.

JavaOS 1.0 is currently available for the Intel X86, Sun SPARC, and StrongARM hardware platforms. Of course, JavaOS will also run on the JavaChip family of processors (picoJava, microJava, and UltraJava). These processors are targeted to a range of products including consumer electronics devices (Web phones and PDAs), network computers, and network servers.

JavaOS Features

Besides providing native Java support, JavaOS has a number of features that make it an ideal operating system for intranet applications. Its small memory footprint and efficient use of processing resources make it an ideal OS for running thin-client applications on network computers. Four megabytes of RAM are sufficient to run JavaOS, HotJava, and other common applications. JavaOS is being ported to low-end x86 machines, extending their lives as network computers. It can be burnt into ROM, allowing it to run on PDAs, hand-held PCs, and consumer electronics devices.

The integrated networking support of JavaOS provides the TCP/IP communication capabilities required in an intranet environment. Its remote boot and network login capabilities enable Java applications and support files to be installed on and managed from a central server. This allows system administrators to automatically upgrade client software across the enterprise and to back up client data at periodic intervals. The central management of JavaOS clients enables zero client administration and facilitates enterprise-wide software distribution and management.

The JavaOS windowing system supports the HotJava and HotJava Views user environments, providing users with a full graphical user interface and the capability to browse Web pages, run Java applets, and exchange email. With JavaOS, users are able to log into a network, from any location, and instantly access their personal workspaces.

Finally, because Java supports the complete Java API, any pure Java application will run on JavaOS. This means that new Java applications, such as the Star Office suite, will run on JavaOS as-is. It also means that even small Java platforms, such as PDAs, will be able to take advantage of the mulithreading, memory management, graphics, and networking capabilities of the Java API.

The JavaOS Architecture

JavaOS is organized into platform-dependent and platform-independent code. The platform-dependent code is referred to as the *kernel* and consists of the *microkernel* and *Java Virtual Machine (JVM)*. The microkernel provides memory management, interrupt and trap handling, multithreading, DMA, and other low-level operating system functions. The JVM interprets and executes Java byte codes. The purpose of the kernel is to abstract hardware-specific details and provide a platform-neutral interface for the rest of JavaOS.

The platform-independent code of JavaOS is referred to as the Java *runtime*. The runtime is written in Java, enabling it to be easily ported and upgraded. It consists of device drivers, networking support, a graphics system, a windowing system, and other elements of the Java API. The device drivers support communication with a display monitor, keyboard, mouse, and network interface card. The networking support classes implement the TCP/IP protocol suite using the network device driver. The graphics and windowing systems provide and implement the *Abstract Windowing Toolkit (AWT)*. Other layers support stream I/O and the remaining elements of the Java API.

Figure 52.1 provides an overview of the JavaOS architecture. JavaOS is a layered operating system that may be tailored for a particular application environment. The layers are functionally independent and may be added or omitted to support the needs of the operating environment. For example, a network computer would utilize all layers of JavaOS and add the HotJava browser and HotJava Views application environments. A consumer electronics device, on the other hand, may only require a limited number of JavaOS layers to run custom application software.

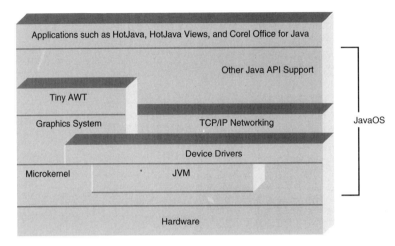

FIGURE 52.1.

*The JavaOS archi-
tecture.*

The JavaOS Kernel

Because the JavaOS runtime provides many operating system elements, such as device drivers, file I/O, and windowing and networking support, the JavaOS kernel needs only to provide an interface with the underlying hardware and implement the JVM. This enables the kernel to be small, fast, and portable. The following sections cover the functions performed by the kernel.

System Booting

Since JavaOS is intended for a number of different hardware platforms, it must be capable of booting from a variety of sources including disks, ROM, and network devices. The kernel booting software need not provide all booting capabilities on all hardware platforms, but may be individually tailored for a specific hardware implementation.

Memory Management

Different microprocessors provide varying levels of memory management features to allow memory to be allocated and made available to executing programs. Some microprocessors convert real memory addresses into virtual addresses in order to simplify memory access. Others implement memory access controls that prevent conflicts between programs and enhance system security and integrity. The objective of the memory management function of the JavaOS kernel is to remove these hardware details from the concern of the runtime software by providing a common interface for the allocation and deallocation of memory resources. It uses the underlying hardware memory management capabilities to translate physical memory addresses into virtual addresses and manage the allocation of virtual memory units. The kernel memory management software does not require physical-to-virtual address translation hardware. Instead, it utilizes whatever capabilities are provided by the hardware platform and makes up for any shortcomings using software translation.

JavaOS operates in a single virtual address space that it shares with the runtime and application programs. This address space is never seen outside of the JVM, because the Java memory model does not provide access to memory pointers.

Interrupt and Exception Handling

External devices, such as keyboards, mice, disks, and I/O cards, communicate with an operating system by generating interrupts that are handled and processed by the operating system. Software interrupts, referred to as *traps*, are used in a similar manner by application programs to request services of the OS. Exceptions consist of traps and other OS calls that are used to signal the occurrence of an error or anomalous condition. The interrupt, trap, and exception processing components of the JavaOS kernel utilize the underlying hardware's interrupt vectoring capabilities to assign interrupts, traps, and exceptions to the appropriate handling routines and device drivers.

Timer Management

The system clock and timer devices generate periodic interrupts to the operating system that are used to keep track of the current time, perform thread scheduling, control the operation of device drivers, and provide API timer support. The JavaOS timer management software utilizes the platform-dependent clock and timer hardware to provide these functions.

Direct Memory Access Control

Direct memory access (DMA) is used by high-speed devices, such as disks, to quickly move information in and out of RAM. The DMA support software of the kernel uses the hardware DMA capabilities to communicate with system devices that use DMA. This software provides a hardware-independent DMA interface to device drivers.

Multithreading Support

The multithreading support function of the kernel manages the memory used by executable threads, saves the current context of a thread, schedules the next thread to be executed, and performs context-switching. The multithreading support function interfaces with the memory management, timer management, and other kernel functions in order to implement multithreading capabilities.

File System Access

Low-level kernel file system support is required in environments, such as a network boot environment, where the kernel must interface with foreign file systems prior to the loading of the device drivers of the runtime system.

Native Code Interface

The kernel may provide the capability to interface with native machine code when that code is required to implement OS functions. An example would be an interface to native code that would drive an advanced video card.

Debugging Support

Certain types of software debugging require the capability to step between machine or byte code instructions under hardware control. Many microprocessors support a special debugging mode of execution. The kernel debugging support software utilizes native debugging facilities to accommodate application-level debugging requirements.

The JVM

The previously discussed kernel components focus on the utilization of the underlying hardware capabilities to support the needs of the JavaOS runtime. The JVM takes `.class` files in the Java byte code format and executes them using the machine code instructions of the underlying microprocessor. In order to do this, the JVM must synchronize and control the operation of the rest of the kernel functions. It utilizes the memory management function to control the allocation of memory resources in the form of Java objects, the interrupt handling, DMA, and timer management functions to support Java device drivers, the multithreading and timer management functions to support Java threads, and so on. The JVM is the nucleus of the Java kernel. The other kernel functions provide support to the JavaOS runtime under the direction and control of the JVM.

JavaOS Runtime Components

The JavaOS runtime consists of operating system-specific functions that are written in Java. The JavaOS kernel provides a platform-independent JVM interface by removing hardware-specific characteristics from consideration. The runtime provides the platform-independent resources of the Java API to application programs. The components of the Java runtime are covered in the following sections.

Device Drivers

Device drivers are used to enable communication between the operating system and external devices such as display monitors, keyboards, mice, and network interface cards. The availability of device drivers is a critical factor in determining the success or failure of an operating system. How many times have you heard, "I couldn't get Windows NT to work with my sound card," or "The Macintosh doesn't have a driver for that scanner"? The popularity of an operating system and the availability of device drivers are so closely related that it's hard to determine which one causes the other. Operating systems are popular because they support a variety of devices. Device drivers were written for popular operating systems long before they were written for not-so-popular operating systems.

In JavaOS, all device drivers are written in Java (with two minor exceptions, as discussed in the following note). This has advantages and disadvantages. The primary advantage is that device drivers are highly portable. Once a device driver is written for JavaOS, it is highly likely that the device driver will run across all JavaOS hardware implementations.

52

JAVAOS

> **NOTE**
>
> Device drivers require the capability to directly address specific physical memory addresses and to handle device interrupts. The software to implement these capabilities is implemented in C language code and made available via the Memory and Interrupt classes. The Memory class provides direct access to memory addresses. The Interrupt class supports interrupt handling. These classes can only be accessed by registered device drivers.

The disadvantage of using only Java device drivers is that no existing device drivers will work with JavaOS. All device drivers have to be written from scratch. Fortunately, JavaOS is so popular that many device drivers are being written by hardware vendors and third-party software developers.

TCP/IP Networking

One of the strongest features of JavaOS is its support for TCP/IP networking. In fact, JavaOS provides more comprehensive TCP/IP networking support than Windows NT. JavaOS supports the basic IP, TCP, and UDP protocols you learned about in Part VIII, "Network Programming." It also supports the Internet Control Message Protocol used by the Ping command and network management functions, the Dynamic Host Configuration Protocol (DHCP) used to dynamically assign IP addresses, the Reverse Address Resolution Protocol (RARP) used to determine a host's address, the Domain Name

Service (DNS) for hostname-to-IP address translation, and the Network Information Service (NIS) to support network login. It also supports the Network File System (NFS) protocol to share files across a network and the Simple Network Management Protocol (SNMP) to manage network clients and servers. Such extensive networking support alone is reason enough to dump your old desktop OS and install JavaOS.

Graphics System

The graphics system of the JavaOS runtime consists of the basic graphics functions required to manage a display monitor and provide the foundation for an AWT implementation. These functions provide the capability to draw and fill geometric objects, render fonts, and control and display cursors. For performance reasons, some of these functions require direct access to physical memory locations and are implemented as native C language methods.

Windowing System

The windowing system of the JavaOS runtime is none other than the AWT. A special Tiny AWT library is used to implement GUI components. The Tiny AWT does not rely on platform-dependent peer classes of the GUI components.

Other API Classes

The Java runtime provides full support for all classes and interfaces of the Java API. This includes stream input and output, applets, math functions, and all of the other goodies found in the core Java API classes.

HotJava and HotJava Views

Although HotJava and HotJava Views are not part of JavaOS, they are a welcome addition to any Java system and provide the graphical desktop environment for running user applications. HotJava is a full-featured Web browser, written entirely in Java. It supports HTML 3.2, FTP downloading, email, and, of course, the execution of Java applets. HotJava Views is a user interface environment referred to by JavaSoft as a *webtop*. It provides pushbutton access to email, calendaring, Web browsing, and other networked applications. HotJava Views was developed to provide a user interface for network computer users.

Summary

In this chapter, you examined the software architecture of JavaOS and looked at its main features. You also learned about the HotJava browser and the HotJava Views user environment. In the next chapter, you'll learn how to interface Java code with code written in other languages.

Native Methods

CHAPTER 53

The power of Java is its portability. Once you write a pure Java applet or program, it can run on any hardware and operating system that supports the Java platform. That's fine for applications that are written entirely in Java, but what happens if you need to access some non-Java code from your Java program? Java will let you do this, but it comes at the expense of portability. Once you use non-Java code in an application or applet, it can only run on those platforms to which the non-Java code is also ported.

The Java Native Interface (JNI) is the link between your Java application and native code. It allows you to invoke native methods from an application or applet, pass arguments to these methods, and use the results returned by the methods. In this chapter you'll learn how to write a Java application that invokes a native method to perform a specialized calculation. You'll use the javah header generation tool to generate a C header file for the native method and implement the native method in the C programming language. You'll also learn important information about the conversion of Java types to and from C types. When you finish this chapter, you'll be able to use native methods in your Java applications.

The Java Native Interface

Java's motto is "Write Once, Run Anywhere." In order to accomplish this, Java is designed to provide all that you would need to write a platform-independent program. However, there may be a time when you need to access a platform-dependent function or method. These platform-dependent functions or methods are written in a non-Java language (typically C or C++) and are referred to as *native methods*. Reasons for using native methods include interfacing with a legacy application and accessing capabilities that aren't present (yet) in the Java API.

The Java Native Interface (JNI) provides the capability to access native methods through shared dynamic link libraries, referred to as *DLLs* on Windows systems. The JNI allows Java programs to invoke the native method, pass arguments to it, and receive the results returned by it. The JNI also provides programmers with the capability to include the JVM in non-Java applications.

Accessing Native Methods

In order to access a native method from a Java program, you create a class for the native method and invoke the native method using the normal Java method invocation syntax. Native methods are created using the following steps:

1. Create a Java class for the native method and include code to load the native method's shared library.

2. Use `javah` to create C language header files for the native method.

3. Implement the native method as a C function.

4. Compile and link the C code to create the shared library.

We'll cover each of these steps in an extended example that uses a native method to calculate Fibonacci numbers.

Listing 53.1 contains the `NativeApp` program that is used to calculate and display Fibonacci numbers. The Fibonacci numbers are an important sequence of numbers in mathematics. They were developed by Leonardo of Pisa, who was also called Fibonacci, meaning "son of good fortune" in Italian. The first Fibonacci number is 0 and the second Fibonacci number is 1. Subsequent Fibonacci numbers are the sum of the previous two Fibonacci numbers. For example, the first 10 Fibonacci numbers are 0, 1, 1, 2, 3, 5, 8, 13, 21, and 34.

> **NOTE**
>
> For more information on Fibonacci numbers, check out the Web page at
> `http://www.ee.surrey.ac.uk/Personal/R.Knott/Fibonacci/fib.html`.

Anyway, back to the `NativeApp` program. It takes an integer command-line parameter and assigns it to the variable n. It then creates a new instance of the `Native` class and invokes the instance's `fibonacci()` method, passing it the value of n. The result returned by the method is assigned to the `answer` variable and then displayed to the console window.

> **NOTE**
>
> The names `NativeApp` and `Native` are my own. These names are not required to use native methods.

The `NativeApp` program looks pretty simple (see Listing 53.1). You are probably wondering where the native methods are declared and used. The `fibonacci()` method is a native method that is declared in the `Native` class. To find out how this is done, you must move along to the next section.

LISTING 53.1. THE NativeApp PROGRAM.

```
class NativeApp {
 public static void main(String[] args) {
  if(args.length!=1) {
   System.out.println("Usage: java NativeApp n");
   System.exit(0);
  }
  int n=new Integer(args[0]).intValue();
  int answer = new Native().fibonacci(n);
  System.out.println(answer);
 }
}
```

Creating a Class for Native Methods

In order to simplify the use of native methods, it is always a good idea to put them in their own class. The Native class is the class used to declare the fibonacci() method, as shown in Listing 53.2. Note that the fibonacci() method is declared just like Java methods, except that it is preceded by the native keyword and its body is replaced by a semicolon (;). In addition, the loadLibrary() method of the System class is invoked to load the shared library specified by native. In Windows 95 and Windows NT, this causes the native.dll dynamic link library to be loaded. The loadLibary() method is invoked as part of a static initializer of the Native class. A static initializer is used so that the library is loaded only once, when the Native class itself is loaded.

Go ahead and compile Native.java and NativeApp.java before proceeding to the next section.

LISTING 53.2. THE Native CLASS.

```
class Native {
 public native int fibonacci(int n);
 static {
  System.loadLibrary("native");
 }
}
```

Using javah

The javah tool is part of the JDK. It is used to create C language header files that specify the interface between C language native methods and Java. It provides a number of options, which you can read about by invoking the -help option:

```
javah -help
Usage: JAVAH.EXE [-v] [-options] classes...

where options include:
    -help       print out this message
    -o          specify the output file name
    -d          specify the output directory
    -jni        create a JNI-style header file
    -td         specify the temporary directory
    -stubs      create a stubs file
    -trace      adding tracing information to stubs file
    -v          verbose operation
    -classpath <directories separated by colons>
    -version    print out the build version
```

In practice, the only option that you'll ever need is -jni, which creates a JNI-style header file instead of the old-style header files used with the JDK 1.02.

Create a header for the Native class as follows:

```
javah -jni Native
```

This creates the Native.h file, shown in Listing 53.3. It is a C language header file. Heed the warning of the first line of the file.

```
/* DO NOT EDIT THIS FILE - it is machine generated */
```

The second line of the file includes the jni.h file that defines the types used in Native.h. The jni.h file contains a number of type and function definitions. If you are a C programmer, you may want to scan this file to see what's in it. The jni.h file is located in the \jdk1.2\include directory. It is accessed using the following:

```
#include <jni.h>
```

After that, several conditional compilation directives and a comment are included:

```
#ifndef _Included_Native
#define _Included_Native
#ifdef __cplusplus
extern "C" {
#endif
/*
 * Class:     Native
 * Method:    fibonacci
```

53

NATIVE METHODS

```
* Signature: (I)I
*/
```

The lines beginning with # are of no consequence and are included in all header files generated by `javah`. They are used to determine whether `Native.h` was previously included in the current compilation.

The comment identifies the `Native` class, the `fibonacci()` method, and the method's signature.

The heart of the `Native.h` file is the declaration of the `Java_Native_fibonacci()` method. This is the method that you'll need to implement. It specifies that it has three parameters of the types `JNIEnv *`, `jobject` and `jint`. The `JNIEnv *` and `jobject` parameters are passed to all native methods and usually can be ignored. The `JNIEnv *` parameter is a pointer to the environment in which the method is invoked. The `jobject` parameter is a reference to the object or class in which the method is defined (for example, `Native`). The `jint` parameter corresponds to the `int` parameter of the `fibonacci()` method, shown in Listing 53.2. You'll use this parameter to calculate a Fibonacci number.

The return value of the `Java_Native_fibonacci()` method looks pretty complicated, but it's not:

```
JNIEXPORT jint JNICALL Java_Native_fibonacci
  (JNIEnv *, jobject, jint);
```

`JNIEXPORT` and `JNICALL` surround the actual `jint` return value. This `jint` return value is the type of value that you'll actually return from the native method. `JNIEXPORT` and `JNICALL` are used to define the function-calling sequence and are defined in the `jni_md.h` file, which is located in the `\jdk1.2\include\win32` directory on Windows 95 and NT implementations.

The remainder of the file ends the conditional compilation directives (see Listing 53.3).

LISTING 53.3. THE `Native.h` FILE.

```
/* DO NOT EDIT THIS FILE - it is machine generated */
#include <jni.h>
/* Header for class Native */

#ifndef _Included_Native
#define _Included_Native
#ifdef __cplusplus
extern "C" {
```

```
#endif
/*
 * Class:     Native
 * Method:    fibonacci
 * Signature: (I)I
 */
JNIEXPORT jint JNICALL Java_Native_fibonacci
  (JNIEnv *, jobject, jint);

#ifdef __cplusplus
}
#endif
#endif
```

Implementing Native Methods

The Native.h header file tells you what the C implementation of the fibonacci()
method must look like. In order to implement this method, you must create a C language
file with the implementation of Java_Native_fibonacci(), as shown in Listing 53.4.

The file begins with the following two include statements:

```
#include <jni.h>
#include "Native.h"
```

The first line includes the jni.h header file that was mentioned earlier. The second line
includes the Native.h header file that you generated in the previous section.

Following the include statements is the C language fibo() function, which calculates
the *n*th Fibonacci number:

```
int fibo(int n){
 if(n<=1) return 0;
 if(n==2) return 1;
 return fibo(n-1)+fibo(n-2);
}
```

And finally, we include an implementation for Java_Native_fibonacci():

```
JNIEXPORT jint JNICALL
Java_Native_fibonacci(JNIEnv *env, jobject obj, jint n) {
 return fibo(n);
}
```

This method is defined in the same manner as in the Native.h header file. All it does is
retrieve the n parameter, pass it to fibo(), and return the result. The complete code of
the NativeImp.c file is shown in Listing 53.4.

53

NATIVE METHODS

LISTING 53.4. THE `NativeImp.c` FILE.

```c
#include <jni.h>
#include "Native.h"

int fibo(int n){
 if(n<=1) return 0;
 if(n==2) return 1;
 return fibo(n-1)+fibo(n-2);
}

JNIEXPORT jint JNICALL
Java_Native_fibonacci(JNIEnv *env, jobject obj, jint n) {
 return fibo(n);
}
```

Creating a Shared Library

At this point, all of our coding is done. All we need to do is compile `NativeImp.c` in such a way that it produces a shared library (that is, a DLL on Windows systems). I use an old version 2.0 of the Microsoft C++ compiler. After Java came out as an alpha version on Windows NT in 1995, I stopped using C++. This is how I compile `NativeImp.c` using the Microsoft C++ compiler:

```
cl -Ic:\jdk1.2\include -Ic:\jdk1.2\include\win32 -Ic:\msvc20\include -LD
➥NativeImp.c c:\msvc20\lib\*.lib -Fenative.dll
```

The same command line works with subsequent versions of Microsoft C++. If you use a different compiler, you'll have to check with its documentation to see how to build a DLL. Note that I included the `c:\jdk1.2\include` and `c:\jdk1.2\include\win32` directories. These directories are where the `jni.h` and `jni_md.h` files are located.

Your compiler should produce the `native.dll` file, which is the shared library loaded to implement the native method. This file is contained in the `ch53` directory.

Putting It All Together

Now that you've gone through the trouble of implementing the `fibonacci()` native method, you can enjoy your reward. Use the program to generate as many Fibonacci numbers as you desire. For example, you can generate the 13th Fibonacci number as follows:

```
java NativeApp 13
144
```

You could have easily implemented `fibonacci()` in Java, but the point of the example was to show you how to create and invoke a native method, pass an argument to the method, and receive the value returned by the method.

Converting Between Java Types and C Types

The one thing that we haven't talked about yet is the use of the `jint` type. The JNI defines a list of C language types that correspond to Java types. These types are defined in `jni.h`. The primitive Java `boolean`, `byte`, `char`, `short`, `int`, `long`, `float`, and `double` types are represented by the C `jboolean`, `jbyte`, `jchar`, `jshort`, `jint`, `jlong`, `jfloat`, and `jdouble` types. See a pattern here?

Java objects are represented by the `jobject` type, arrays by the `jarray` type, and `String` objects by the `jstring` type. In addition, the `jni.h` file defines other C types for other kinds of Java objects.

The Java `void` type is implemented by the C `void` type. (They must have run out of Js.)

The Java primitive types are converted to C types in a natural fashion and can be used without problems. However, nonprimitive types, including the `String` type, are not converted to C types in a natural, easy-to-use manner. For example, Java `String` objects are 16-bit Unicode strings, whereas C strings are 8-bit ASCII strings. The `jni.h` file defines a number of conversion functions that can be used to access the converted types. These conversion functions are provided as a convenience. You can use DLLs that are compiled without `jni.h`.

Summary

In this chapter you learned how to write a Java application that invokes a native method to calculate a Fibonacci number. You used the `javah` header generation tool to generate a C header file for the native method, and implemented the native method in the C programming language. You also learned important information about the conversion of Java types to and from C types. In the next chapter you'll learn how to write Java programs that take advantage of Microsoft's Java extensions.

Dirty Java

CHAPTER 54

Java's promise to provide a platform-independent programming language has resulted in its rapid growth in popularity. This popularity has led to some opposition, principally by industry-giant Microsoft. Although Microsoft was one of Java's original licensees, it has done little to advance Java's platform-independent appeal, instead opting to tie Java to its Windows platform. This has resulted in a significant impact on the Java programmer.

In this chapter, you'll learn about Microsoft's impact on Java and about the capabilities of the Visual J++ development environment. You'll also learn how Java can be integrated with legacy Component Object Model (COM) technology and how the Java plug-in can be used to provide full JDK support across browser platforms. When you finish this chapter, you'll have a thorough introduction to the pitfalls and advantages of Microsoft-style Java.

Microsoft and Java

One of the biggest controversies in the Java world in the last year has been Microsoft's subversion of the Java API. Microsoft's failure to implement the full JDK 1.1 with their Internet Explorer 4.0 browser has landed them a lawsuit from Sun Microsystems. From its initial release in 1995, Java has been perceived as a threat to Microsoft's hegemony in the PC operating system world. An omnipresent, platform-independent Java could result in the Windows platform being relegated to a one-among-many carrier of the Java run-time system, and Microsoft's leverage in the PC operating system and application software market could be significantly eroded. Microsoft fought back against Java with their typical tactics—using their dominance in the PC operating system world to build a better but non-standard product. Their Visual J++ 1.0 and 1.1 development tools provide excellent access to Windows-specific resources. However, using these capabilities eliminates Java's "Write Once, Run Anywhere" features.

Sun fought back with its 100% pure Java campaign. Visual J++ amassed a large market share among Java development tools nevertheless, but its popularity among serious Java developers was eclipsed by pure Java tools, such as Symantec's Visual Café and Sun's Java Studio. In addition, many hardcore Java programmers have forsaken the niceties of these visual programming tools and still use the JDK tool set.

On another front, Microsoft's battle with Netscape in the browser wars had a significant impact of JDK 1.1 software development. Both Netscape and Microsoft were significantly behind schedule in implementing JDK 1.1 support in their version 4.0 browsers. Netscape provided incremental JDK 1.1 support that eventually encompassed the entire JDK 1.1 API. Microsoft provided support for a majority of the JDK 1.1 API. However, having wrested browser dominance away from Netscape, Microsoft simply declared their browser to be JDK 1.1-compliant without providing full JDK 1.1 support. This eventually led to Sun filing a lawsuit over Microsoft's failure to live up to the terms of using the Java-compatible logo. At the time of this writing, the court had ruled that Microsoft could not use the Java-compatible logo with Internet Explorer 4.0.

The impact of Microsoft's actions on Java applet developers was that they could not use all of the JDK 1.1 features in their applets and still be compatible with Navigator, HotJava, and Internet Explorer. This stifled JDK 1.1 applet development.

One of the JDK 1.1 APIs conspicuously left out of Internet Explorer 4.0 is the Remote Method Invocation (RMI) API. RMI's popularity has eclipsed industry interest in Microsoft's solution to distributed object programming—the Distributed Component Object Model (DCOM). DCOM is the combination of two legacy technologies—the Component Object Model (COM) and the Distributed Computing Environment (DCE). An RMI-capable Internet Explorer could obviate the need for a flailing ActiveX (COM spinoff) and DCOM. Microsoft's tradeoff between providing complete JDK 1.1 support and eliminating ActiveX/DCOM competition has resulted in a significant inconvenience to the Java programmer.

> **NOTE**
>
> Chapter 37, "Distributed Application Architecture," provides an introduction to COM and DCOM.

The Microsoft JVM

The Microsoft JVM is a reimplementation of the JavaSoft JVM that provides additional Windows-specific features. These features allow Java code to access native Win32 code, such as ActiveX components, dynamic-link libraries (DLLs), and COM interfaces. The J/Direct feature allows Java code to access DLLs without going through the Java Native Interface (JNI). The advantage of J/Direct is that it is more efficient and easier to use. Its disadvantage is that it reduces the portability of Java code between operating system platforms.

The Microsoft JVM also supports ActiveX/JavaBeans integration. This support allows ActiveX components to be accessed as JavaBeans and vice versa. This interoperability between JavaBeans and ActiveX makes a large number of ActiveX components available to Java programmers. It also allows beans to be used within the COM environment. These advantages are offset by the fact that using ActiveX confines applications to

Microsoft Windows platforms, a high price to pay for a Java programmer. The capability to access JavaBeans from a COM environment is certainly a boon for Windows programmers.

The Microsoft JVM also supports the Raw Native Interface (RNI), which provides highly efficient access to native code from Java. The RNI is not compatible with JavaSoft's JNI. The RNI requires native code to conform to Java constraints, such as naming conventions, data representation, and garbage collection. Use of RNI requires the native code programmer to be familiar with low-level Java programming details. RNI can provide very high code performance at the expense of complexity and lack of portability.

COM is Microsoft's legacy to object-oriented programming. Although COM lacks some object-oriented programming features, such as true inheritance, it is widely used throughout the Windows world. Support for COM is one of the primary features of the Microsoft JVM. This support allows Java code to access COM objects as Java classes.

Visual J++

Visual J++ is Microsoft's development environment for Java. Visual J++ 1.0 corresponds to the JDK 1.02 and quickly became popular for its low cost, full development environment, and fast compiler. Microsoft also included the Microsoft JVM with Visual J++, providing support for ActiveX and COM. Of course, the objective for this support was to skew Java's use toward the Microsoft Windows family of operating systems and the Internet Explorer browser. Visual J++ 1.0 provides a number of features that makes it more attractive than the tools of JDK 1.02.

- Visual J++, unlike the JDK, is a *visual* tool. Visual programming tools are much easier for beginners to learn and work with than non-visual tools.

- Visual J++ provides an integrated development environment, including a syntax-aware source code editor, a fast compiler, and a graphical debugger.

- Visual J++ provides access to Windows ActiveX and COM technologies.

- Visual J++ is similar to Visual Basic and Visual C++ and is easy for Windows programmers to learn.

In addition, Microsoft priced Visual J++ very low. This made it very competitive with high-end visual Java programming tools, such as Symantec's Visual Café and JavaSoft's Java Studio.

Visual J++ 1.1 was released in the same timeframe as the JDK 1.1. However, Visual J++ 1.1 provided little support for the JDK 1.1 API. Instead, it introduced the Application

Foundation Classes (AFC), a Microsoft API that supports GUI development and graphics effects.

Visual J++ 1.1 also includes the following features:

- Database Wizard—Allows Java code to circumvent the JDBC and use ODBC databases directly.
- ActiveX Wizard—Simplifies the development of ActiveX components.
- IDE Enhancements—Supports Visual Basic scripting and other features.
- Compiler—Even faster than before.
- CAB tool—An attempt to replace JAR files with Microsoft's file archive and compression technology.

Visual J++ 6.0 is Microsoft's latest version, released at the same time as the JDK 1.2. (Microsoft must have been so impressed with the new version that it skipped versions 2 through 5!) Visual J++ 6.0 adds a number of features that lock it tighter with Windows programming and ignore Java's platform-independent programming capabilities. These features include the Windows Foundation Classes (WFC), which is another attempt to substitute a Microsoft API for a JavaSoft API. The WFC promotes even greater dependence on Win32, Microsoft's version of Dynamic HTML (DHTML), and Internet Explorer. WFC takes advantage of J/Direct technology in providing Win32 integration. This support includes access to the Windows clipboard, Windows threads, Windows registry, Windows messaging, OLE, ActiveX, DHTML, and other Windows-specific capabilities.

Other features included with Visual J++ 6.0 include the following:

- IDE Enhancements—Both visual design enhancements and overall performance improvements.
- Database Support Enhancements—This support includes ActiveX Data Objects (ADO) 2.0 and an interface to OLE DB, both of which are Windows technologies.
- Packaging—The capability to deploy applications as .CAB, .EXE, .DLL, and other non-Java file formats.
- Enhanced COM support—Even more support for legacy COM objects.

For more information on Visual J++, check out the Microsoft Visual J++ Web site at http://www.microsoft.com/visualj/prodinfo/.

Microsoft APIs

Microsoft's Java APIs include the AFC and the new WFC. In this section, we'll take a look at the packages comprising these APIs.

The AFC consists of five packages that provide support for graphics, GUI components, event handling, Win32 access, and .CAB files. These packages consist of the following:

- com.ms.fx—Provides basic graphics support, such as curves, text, colors, and textures.
- com.ms.ui—Provides GUI controls that are similar to those found in the Java Foundations Classes (JFC).
- com.ms.ui.event—Provides support for the JDK 1.1 event delegation model.
- com.ms.ui.resource—Provides support for Win32 resource files.
- com.ms.util.cab—Provides support for the Microsoft .CAB file format.

The WFC consists of 10 packages that provide support for native Windows capabilities. These packages consist of the following:

- wfc.app—Provides access to Windows-specific capabilities, such as the Windows clipboard, the Windows registry, and Windows threads.
- wfc.ax—Provides ActiveX support.
- wfc.core—Provides core WFC classes and interfaces.
- wfc.data.ui—Provides support for data-bound controls.
- wfc.html—Provides DHTML support.
- wfc.io—Provides Microsoft's version of I/O stream support.
- wfc.ole32—Provides Windows OLE support.
- wfc.ui—Provides various GUI components.
- wfc.util—Provides utility classes and interfaces.
- wfc.win32—Provides access to the Win32 API.

At the time of this writing, the WFC were only in preview release 1. Additional capabilities may be present in the final WFC release.

Using Java and COM Objects

The unifying principle behind Microsoft's JVM, Visual J++, and class libraries is the capability to integrate Java with COM objects. COM has been the hub of Microsoft's object-oriented software development strategy since Windows 3.1. It has undergone a few marketing name changes (OLE, OLE2, COM, and the recent ActiveX), but the technology centers around Microsoft's Component Object Model. As such, COM is very important to Microsoft's product strategy: operating systems, application software, and enterprise server software.

The existence of Java objects, separate from COM, poses a direct threat to COM's future. That's why it is so important for Microsoft to bring Java into its COM strategy. By integrating Java with COM, Microsoft can keep Java from becoming a wholly separate and competing object technology.

This strategy is flawed because COM is a legacy object technology and Java represents the future of object and component development. Rolling Java into COM is a step backwards in the evolution of object-oriented programming. However, the capability to integrate Java objects with COM objects is important to support Java migration while leveraging prior investments in COM technology.

Accessing COM Objects from Java Objects

Visual J++ 6.0 provides the `jactivex` command line tool, which enables COM objects to be accessed by Java objects. The `jactivex` tool generates Java source files that correspond to a COM object's type library. A *type library* provides a standardized description of a COM object's interfaces. The Java source files generated by `jactivex` provide the required Java-to-COM connectivity by wrapping the interface methods of COM objects. Java applications can then invoke the methods of the Java classes generated by `jactivex`, and these methods in turn provide a pass-through to the interface methods of COM objects.

> **NOTE**
>
> COM objects must be registered with the Windows Registry before they can be accessed.

54

DIRTY JAVA

Accessing Java Objects from COM

The capability to access Java objects from COM is also important to any COM-to-Java migration strategy. The migration of legacy COM-based applications to Java can be initiated by selectively reimplementing and replacing COM objects with Java objects. To accomplish this, newly developed Java objects must present an identical interface to existing COM objects.

COM programming, like Windows programming in general, is full of arcane terminology and programming requirements. Fortunately, the Microsoft JVM and Visual J++ tools shield the Java programmer from the complexities of the COM world. For example, Java programmers don't have to worry about implementing the COM IUnknown interface, initializing COM objects, or retrieving interface pointers. Writing COM objects in Java is actually easier than writing them in C++.

COM interfaces are described using the COM Interface Definition Language (IDL). The IDL description of a COM interface is compiled into a COM type library using the Microsoft IDL (MIDL) compiler or the jactivex tool. The type library is then imported into your Java code. The jactivex tool generates an appropriate Java interface for the type library description. You then implement your COM object by implementing each of its interfaces (imported from the object's type library). To make the COM object available for use, you must register it with the Windows registry by using the javareg command line tool. The javareg tool is included with all versions of Visual J++.

Using Java with DCOM

Distributed COM, or DCOM, was introduced with Windows NT 4.0 and Windows 95. DCOM allows COM objects to be accessed remotely over a network. It's the integration of COM with the DCE remote procedure call (RPC) protocols and can be thought of as COM objects connected via Microsoft's implementation of DCE. Version 2.0 of the javareg tool (included with Visual J++ 6.0) allows Java classes to be registered as remote objects that can be accessed via DCOM.

The JavaBeans Bridge for ActiveX

In order to promote the widespread use of JavaBeans, JavaSoft developed the JavaBeans Bridge for ActiveX. This bridge allows Windows users to use beans in legacy Windows applications, such as Microsoft Office or Visual Basic. The bridge wraps beans in an ActiveX container that makes the beans appear as native COM objects to Windows programs. The purpose of the bridge is to give bean developers backward-compatibility with Windows. This means that you can write beans that take advantage of the latest Java advances and be sure that they will interoperate with legacy software. As such, the bridge allows a smooth transition path from Windows, COM, and ActiveX to Web-enabled, platform-independent Java applications.

The bridge consists of a utility that creates OLE type library information and Win32 registry information for a bean. This information is needed so that COM objects can correctly access and use beans. The bridge also allows bean events to be used by COM objects, thus allowing full interaction between the bean and its COM container.

The bridge also allows beans to function as COM servers. This allows other COM objects to invoke bean methods and use beans as building blocks in larger COM applications.

The JavaBeans Bridge for ActiveX is available from the JavaSoft Web site at `http://java.sun.com:80/beans/software/bridge/`.

Migrating from ActiveX to JavaBeans

While COM and ActiveX have played an important role in the development of components for Windows platforms, many software development organizations want to develop future components for the platform-independent Java runtime environment. In order to support this migration from ActiveX to Java, IBM, Taligent, and JavaSoft developed the JavaBeans Migration Assistant for ActiveX. This tool simplifies the process of porting ActiveX components to JavaBeans by using available ActiveX information to create equivalent JavaBeans interfaces. The tool identifies interface methods and their parameters and maps Windows types to their equivalent Java types. It also generates Java stubs for ActiveX components that are being migrated. Migration from ActiveX to JavaBeans is accomplished by implementing these interfaces in Java.

The JavaBeans Migration Assistant for ActiveX is available from IBM's Web site at `http://www3.software.ibm.com/segdown?segment=AD&family=JV`.

Working with the Java Plug-In

The failure of Microsoft and Netscape to provide complete JDK 1.1 support with their version 4.0 browsers put a dent in the development and deployment of JDK 1.1 applets. In order to prevent future versions of the JDK from being undermined, JavaSoft developed the Java Plug-In, formally named Activator. The Java Plug-In lets Web publishers specify the use of JavaSoft's Java Runtime Environment (JRE) in Internet Explorer (version 3.02 or later) and Netscape Navigator (version 3.0 or later). The JavaSoft JVM is used instead of the browser's default JVM. This assures applet developers that the applets they develop can use the latest version of the JDK and that they will be supported on the two most popular browsers. The JDK 1.2 Java Plug-In support is included with Win 32 JDK. An installation option allows the Plug-In to be used with Navigator and Internet Explorer. Java Plug-In is also available from JavaSoft's Web site at `http://www.java.sun.com/products/plugin/index.html`.

Web publishers are required to make changes to their HTML pages to specify the use of the Java Plug-In. When Internet Explorer or Navigator browsers process the modified HTML, they load the plug-in, which loads and uses the JavaSoft JVM with any applets

54

DIRTY JAVA

contained in the HTML pages. JavaSoft provides an HTML converter that simplifies the integration of Java Plug-In with existing HTML pages.

When an Internet Explorer browser initially loads a Web page that specifies the use of the plug-in, it automatically downloads and installs the plug-in. This causes the latest JRE to be installed also. The initial installation can be time-consuming, depending on the user's computing power and network bandwidth. However, after the initial installation, the plug-in does not pose any additional performance impact. Navigator supports the same type of installation, although it is somewhat less automated.

Summary

In this chapter, you learned about Microsoft's impact on Java and about the capabilities of the Visual J++ development environment. You also learned how Java can be integrated with COM technology, and how the Java plug-in can be used to provide full JDK support across browser platforms. In the next chapter, you'll learn how the Java Command Language (Jacl) adds a scripting capability to Java.

Java Command Language

IN THIS CHAPTER

Java is a remarkable programming language, but it isn't the only programming language to be developed at Sun. The Tool Command Language, or Tcl, is another extraordinary programming language that was developed (by John Ousterhout) at Sun. Tcl is an embedded scripting language that was originally created to support the rapid development of applications that run under the X Window System. However, Tcl's power, flexibility, and ease of use have caused it to be ported to almost all popular operating systems. Tcl is associated with the GUI toolkit named Tk, which provides a rich set of components for developing GUIs.

> **NOTE**
>
> Tcl is pronounced "tickle."

Because Java is a general-purpose, platform-independent programming language and Tcl is a cross-platform scripting language, the software engineers at Sun launched a research project to determine how the languages could be used together. The result of this effort is the Java Command Language (Jacl). Jacl is a 100% Java implementation of Tcl that allows Tcl scripts to take full advantage of the Java API. Jacl allows Tcl to be used as the scripting language for Java.

In this chapter, you'll be introduced to Jacl and learn how it provides programmers with the best features of both Java and Tcl. You'll use Tcl to quickly script an AWT-based Java application. You'll also learn how another product of the Java-Tcl research team, Tcl Blend, can be used to convert legacy C applications to Java. When you finish this chapter, you'll be able to use Tcl to script Java applications.

What's Jacl?

Jacl is the result of a very successful research effort to combine the best features of Java and Tcl. In a nutshell, Jacl is a 100% pure Java implementation of Tcl that give Tcl scripts full access to the Java API. Jacl enables Tcl to be used as the scripting language for Java applications. It lets you very quickly and easily generate GUI-based Java programs with just a few lines of Tcl code.

The power of Jacl lies in its capability to expose the Java API to Tcl. It does this through a software component referred to as the *Java Package*, which provides an interface between Java and Tcl. This interface provides Tcl scripts with the following capabilities:

- Scripts can create instances of Java classes.
- Scripts can invoke the methods of Java objects and classes. (Both static and non-static methods.)
- Scripts can access the public fields of Java objects.
- Scripts can determine the class of an object and its position within the overall Java class hierarchy.
- Scripts can load classes from a class path.
- Scripts can define new classes from byte streams.

Jacl also exploits the Reflection API to provide Tcl scripts with the capability to access the methods, properties, and events of JavaBeans. It allows Tcl scripts to create JavaBeans, invoke their methods, and get and set their properties. It also provides exceptional support of bean event handling. Bean events are exposed to Tcl, and these events may be handled in Tcl by binding Tcl code to the events.

Note

Don't worry if you are unfamiliar with Tcl. The next section provides an introductory Tcl primer.

One benefit of Jacl-to-Tcl programmers is that Jacl provides a platform-independent implementation of Tcl. This means that anywhere that Java will run, Tcl will also run. Another advantage is the feature-rich Java API. The capabilities of the Java API are reason alone for a Tcl programmer to switch from a C-based Tcl environment to Jacl.

Jacl is available for download from Sun's Web site at `http://sunscript.sun.com/java/`. It is packaged as a self-extracting installation file. You should download and install Jacl before going to the next section. Also, make sure that you put the `\Jacl1.0` directory in your PATH.

Note

Jacl supports Tcl version 8.0. You do not need to install Tcl to run Jacl.

A Tcl Primer

This section teaches you how Tcl works and shows you how to write simple Tcl scripts. Having made it through 54 chapters of this book, you are on your way to becoming an accomplished programmer and should be able to pick up Tcl's syntax rather easily. The next section shows how to use Jacl to access the Java API from within Tcl scripts.

The syntax of Tcl, like Java, is based on C. It is organized into a set of commands that are executed by a Tcl interpreter. Tcl supports a single datatype—the `string` datatype. Everything in Tcl, including commands, is implemented using strings. The Tcl interpreter can be viewed as a very flexible and efficient string processor.

Command Syntax

Tcl commands are line-oriented, separated by the new line character or by semicolons. Commands consist of one or more fields, separated by spaces or tabs, where the first field is the name of the command. All fields after the first field are the arguments to the command. For example, the following command sets the value of the variable x to 5:

```
set x 5
```

Including Spaces as Part of a Field

Double quotes are used to include a space as part of a field. The following command sets the value of x to `This is a test`:

```
set x "This is a test"
```

Curly braces ({ and }) may also be used to delimit a field.

Command Substitution

Brackets ([and]) are used to delimit commands that are embedded in a field. Embedded commands are executed and their values are returned as part of the field in which they occur. Bracketed commands may span multiple lines. For example, the following commands set the value of x to 12:

```
set y 12
set x [set y]
```

In this command, the value returned by the command set y is 12.

Variable Substitution

The dollar sign ($) is used to substitute the value of a variable for the variable itself. For example, if the value of the variable y is 12, the following statement sets the value of x to 12:

```
set x $y
```

Arrays

Tcl arrays associate values with array elements. Array indices are not ordered as Java arrays and may consist of non-integer string values. Paired opening and closing parentheses are used to identify array indices. If a variable name is followed by an opening parenthesis, all characters up to the closing parenthesis are used to determine the array index. For example, if y(5) is 10, the following command assigns 10 to x:

```
set x y(5)
```

Escape Characters

Backslashes are used as escape characters in a similar manner as Java. For example, \n represents a new line character.

Comments

Tcl comments begin with the pound character (#) and extend to the end of the line on which they occur.

Expressions

Some Tcl commands treat their arguments as expressions. The operators used in Tcl expressions are based on C and are very similar to Java operators.

Lists

Tcl also supports list processing. Tcl lists are strings in which the individual list elements are separated by spaces, tabs, or new line characters. List elements are also delimited by curly braces. For example, the following list consists of the three elements a, {b c}, and {c {d e}}:

```
a {b c} {c {d e}}
```

The last element of the list is itself a list consisting of c and {d e}.

Variable Declaration

Tcl variables do not need to be declared.

Built-In Commands

Tcl supports a rich set of built-in commands. The following subsections cover some of the most important commands.

set

The set command is used to assign a value to a variable. It has the following syntax:

```
set variableName expression
```

The value of *variableName* is set to the result of *expression*. The set command can also be used to return a value when enclosed within brackets. The expression [set *variableName*] returns the value of *variableName*.

if

The Tcl if command is similar to that of other languages. It has the following form:

```
if { expression1 } {
 commands1
} elseif { expression2 }
 commands2
} else {
 commands3
}
```

Multiple elseif clauses may be used. The elseif and else clauses are optional and may be omitted. Note that the expressions are enclosed in curly braces instead of the parentheses used with Java.

for

The for command is similar to the Java statement. Its syntax follows:

```
for {start} {test} {update} {body}
```

The *start* is typically a set command that assigns a value to a loop iterator variable. The *test* is a condition that is evaluated to determine whether the loop should continue. The *update* updates the iterator between loop iterations. The *body* consists of commands that are the body of the for loop.

The following Tcl for command iterates i from 0 to 10 and executes commands:

```
for {set i 0} {$i < 10} {incr i} { commands }
```

break

The break command may be used to break out of a for command. It is used in the same way it is in Java. For example, the break command causes the following for loop to be exited when i is 5:

```
for {set i 0} {$i < 10} {incr i} {
 if {i == 5} break
}
```

Other Commands

Tcl supports many other commands, such as while, case, continue, and others. Consult an introductory Tcl book for more information on these commands. *Tcl and the Tk Toolkit* by John Ousterhout is the definitive reference on Tcl.

Built-In Variables

Tcl also supports several built-in variables that provide access to the environment and error codes.

Accessing Java from Tcl Scripts

Jacl makes it easy to access Java objects from Tcl scripts. The best way to learn how to do this is through an example. Listing 55.1 shows an example program named Demo.tcl. We'll run this program and then examine how it works. Make sure that you have Jacl installed and the \Jacl1.0 directory in your PATH.

> **TIP**
>
> The C:\Jacl\jacl.bat file assumes you have JDK 1.1. You must modify this file so that it contains the correct CLASSPATH for your JDK installation.

Open a console window and switch to the \ju\ch55 directory. Launch Jacl and enter the following command at the Jacl prompt:

```
%source Demo.tcl
```

The Java window shown in Figure 55.1 is displayed. This window contains a text field, a label, and a button. Click on the button and the text field is updated, as shown in Figure 55.2. When you are finished, close the window and exit Jacl by entering exit at the Jacl prompt.

FIGURE 55.1.

The Demo.tcl
opening window.

FIGURE 55.2.

*The text field is
updated when the
button is clicked.*

LISTING 55.1. THE Demo.tcl SCRIPT.

```
set frame [java::new java.awt.Frame]
set panel [java::new java.awt.Panel]
$frame setLayout [java::new java.awt.BorderLayout]
$frame setTitle "Jacl Demo"
set label [java::new java.awt.Label]
$label setText "Click to update the text field:"
set button [java::new java.awt.Button]
$button setLabel "Update text"
$panel {add java.awt.Component} $label
$panel {add java.awt.Component} $button
$frame {add java.lang.String java.awt.Component} "Center" $panel
set text [java::new java.awt.TextField]
$text setText "An AWT TextField"
$frame {add java.lang.String java.awt.Component} "North" $text
$frame setSize 400 400
```

```
$frame show
$frame toFront
java::bind $frame windowClosing "set done yes"
set newText {"THE TEXT HAS BEEN UPDATED!!!"}
java::bind $button actionPerformed "$text setText $newText"
vwait done
$frame dispose
```

The first line of the script sets the value of [java::new java.awt.Frame] to the frame variable. The java::new command creates a new Java object. In this case, it is a Frame object. The end result is that a Frame object is created and assigned to the frame variable.

The next line creates a Panel object and assigns it to the panel variable.

The third line invokes the setLayout() method of the Frame object, passing it a new object of the BorderLayout class. Whenever a Java object is the first field in a command, the second field identifies the method being invoked and the remaining fields identify the arguments for the method invocation.

The next line invokes the setTitle() method of the Frame object with the "Jacl Demo" argument.

The fifth and sixth lines of the script create a Label object and assign it to the label variable. The label's text is set to "Click to update the text field:".

The next two lines create a Button object that is labeled Update text.

The ninth line of the script adds the Label object to the Panel object. The add() method of the container class has more than one version, so the specific version must be identified by placing the method name and its argument types in a list (surrounded by braces).

The tenth line adds the Button object to the Panel object.

The eleventh line adds the Panel object to the center of the Frame object. Note that the add() method with two arguments (String and Component) is used.

The next two lines create a TextField object and initialize its text to An AWT TextField.

In lines 14-17, the text field is added to the frame, the frame's size is set to 400 by 400, the frame is shown, and it is set to the front window.

The next line shows how Java events are handled by Tcl. The java::bind command is used to bind a Java event with a Tcl command. The first argument to java::bind is the Java object whose events are being handled. The second argument is the event name, and the third argument is the Tcl command that is executed to handle the event. This command sets the done variable to yes.

The following line sets the value of newText to the list containing the string "THE TEXT HAS BEEN UPDATED!!!". The text is put in a list so that it appears as a single argument to a method.

The actionPerformed event of the button is handled by this command:

```
$text setText $newText
```

This command updates the text of the TextField object referenced by the text variable.

The vwait command causes the script to wait while events are handled. The vwait command waits until the done variable is set by an event handler and the event handler has completed its processing. This variable is set by the handling of the windowClosing event. The Frame object is disposed after the vwait command finishes its processing.

Jacl Versus Tcl

Because Jacl supports the integration of both Java and Tcl, it is natural to ask which part of an application should be written in Java and which part should be written in Tcl. The developers of Jacl envisioned a development approach in which Java would be used to develop reusable components, such as JavaBeans. As such, Java is referred to as a *component developer*. Tcl, on the other hand, is referred to as an *application assembler*. Tcl scripts are the "glue" used to integrate Java components into applications.

This symbiosis between Java and Tcl can be compared to the complimentary relationship between Microsoft's Visual C++ and Visual Basic. Visual C++ is used to develop Component Object Model (COM) components, and Visual Basic is used to assemble COM components into final applications. In the same way, Java is used to create JavaBeans, and Tcl is used to integrate the beans into Jacl applications.

Jacl can also be used in another context that has a Microsoft analogy. The individual programs of Microsoft Office, such as Word and Excel, support Visual Basic as an application scripting language. Visual Basic can be used to extend the capabilities of the Office application programs. It is envisioned that Tcl will be used in the same manner to extend Jacl-enabled Java applications. Imagine a Java-based office suite that uses Tcl to create extensions to the individual office programs.

Tcl Blend

Tcl Blend is another product of the Java-Tcl research team. It's an extension to the C-based Tcl environment that allows the C-based Tcl interpreter to interact with the JVM, and vice versa. Tcl Blend is the middle ground between the standard Tcl environment and Jacl. It supports Tcl, C, and Java, and provides a bridge between the C and Java-based Tcl environments so that legacy code, written in C, can be incrementally ported to Java.

Tcl Blend uses the same Java Package software component as Jacl. This means that Tcl scripts have the same visibility into the Java API as they do in Jacl. For this reason, Tcl Blend is a great way for Tcl programmers to move over to Java without sacrificing their investment in C code. Tcl programmers can write Tcl scripts that use both the Java API and C-based Tcl extensions. As the C-based Tcl extensions are replaced by the Java API, the Tcl applications can be ported to the 100-percent Java environment of Jacl.

Tcl Blend is available from the Sun Web site at `http://sunscript.sun.com/java/`.

> **NOTE**
>
> Tcl Blend requires Tcl version 8.0.

Summary

In this chapter, you were introduced to Jacl and learned how it provides programmers with the best features of both Java and Tcl. You used Tcl to script an AWT-based Java application. You were then introduced to Tcl Blend and learned how it can be used to convert legacy C applications to Java. In the next chapter, you'll learn about the visual design tools that are available to support Java software development.

Java Development Tools

CHAPTER 56

The purpose of this book is to teach you to program in Java. Because of this, I have avoided visual development tools and instead have concentrated on programming examples that are built from scratch. By taking this learning approach, you'll be better prepared to understand the code that is generated by visual development tools.

There is certainly a place for Java development tools. These tools help you develop Java applications and applets more quickly and effectively. They make you a better-organized programmer and help you to build a more maintainable, higher-quality product.

In this chapter you'll examine some of the popular Java development tools and learn how they can be used to simplify the process of developing Java applications and applets.

Visual Development Tools

Visual development tools simplify the software development process, letting you create the graphical user interface (GUI) of applets and applications by dragging and dropping user-interface components to their desired locations. These tools provide hooks for event handling associated with GUI components, typically letting you create and maintain event-handling code by clicking on the GUI components.

Visual development tools commonly provide a class browser for viewing and traversing the application class hierarchy. They also include a source code editor that highlights Java syntax elements using special colors. Most tools support automatic code generation and a just-in-time compiler.

Second-generation Java development tools provide JavaBeans support, team programming capabilities, JDBC drivers for popular database products, CORBA compatibility, and tools that simplify connectivity with legacy applications.

Java Workshop

Java Workshop 2.0 from Sun Microsystems (`http://www.sun.com/software/Developer-products/java/`) is an integrated development environment (IDE) for Java applets, applications, and beans. It provides a graphical user interface and uses Sun's Visual Java GUI builder for developing applets and standalone applications. It includes a compiler, editor, profiler, debugger, and several wizards and online tutorials.

Java Workshop 2.0 runs on Solaris (Sparc and Intel versions), HP-UX, UnixWare, Windows NT, and Windows 95. Java Workshop 2.0 retails for $110.

Java Development Tools

CHAPTER 56

1097

56

JAVA
DEVELOPMENT
TOOLS

> **NOTE**
>
> All prices are in U.S. dollars. Prices may vary from the time of this writing.

Java Studio

Java Studio from Sun Microsystems (`http://www.sun.com/studio/`) is a visual software development environment that maximizes the use of prebuilt JavaBeans components and minimizes the need for coding. Java Studio provides an extensive set of JavaBeans and a set of tools for integrating beans into applets and applications. Java Studio provides beans that support multimedia, GUI development, database access, data flow, and mathematical computation.

Java Studio is built in Java and runs on all Java platforms that support the core API. It costs $69.

JavaPlan

JavaPlan from Lighthouse Design, Limited (recently purchased by Sun Microsystems) is an enterprisewide visual development tool for Java applets and applications (`http://www.lighthouse.com/Product.html`). JavaPlan consists of an integrated set of tools that are aimed at the development of reusable Java components, such as JavaBeans.

JavaPlan supports graphical modeling of applications via an electronic *whiteboard*, a tool that enables multiuser collaboration over a network. It provides a reverse-engineering capability for analyzing compiled bytecode files, and supports the porting of C and C++ legacy applications. JavaPlan also provides extensive documentation-generation capabilities.

JavaPlan runs on Solaris and Windows NT 4.0. It can be purchased for $3,995 per single user license.

Visual Café for Java

Visual Café for Java version 2.5 from Symantec (`http://cafe.symantec.com/`) provides a top-of-the-line, integrated visual development environment for Java applets and applications. It supports drag-and-drop visual application development and comes with an extensive prebuilt component library.

Visual Café for Java supports a sophisticated automated code-generation capability that lets users interact with and edit the generated code. It comes in three development editions: Web, Professional, and Database. The Web Development Edition includes the

Visual Café for Java IDE, the Visual Page HTML authoring tool, and a copy of Netscape Communicator 4.0. The Professional Development Edition includes the Web Development Edition and adds a native code compiler, an advanced debugger, additional JavaBeans support, and other features. The Database Development Edition includes the Professional Development Edition and adds a dbANYWHERE Workgroup Server, a Sybase SQL Anywhere Database, and a Netscape Fast Track Server.

Visual Café for Java 2.5 runs on Windows NT, Windows 98, and Windows 95. Prices range from $99.95 to $499.95, depending on the edition purchased.

VisualAge for Java

VisualAge for Java (http://www.software.ibm.com/ad/vajava/) is IBM's solution for Java software development. It uses the same technology as other VisualAge products, and is an enterprisewide Java software development environment that focuses on the development of Java applications that connect to existing server data, transactions, and applications. It also makes extensive use of JavaBeans components, via the VisualAge WebRunner Toolkit and tools that provide the capability to convert ActiveX components into JavaBeans.

VisualAge for Java includes a source code editor, debugger, class browser, and extensive class library. These tools are provided in a team programming environment. The Enterprise Access Builder tool facilitates the connection of Java code with legacy applications and data.

VisualAge for Java comes in three versions: Entry, Professional, and Enterprise. The Entry version is scaled down from the Professional version and may be downloaded for free. The Professional version is the Enterprise version without the Enterprise Access Builder and team software development features.

VisualAge for Java runs on Windows NT, Windows 98, Windows 95, and OS/2. The Entry version is a free download. The Professional version costs $99. The price of the Enterprise version has not been determined at the time of this writing.

Visual J++

Visual J++ (http://www.microsoft.com/visualj/) is Microsoft's answer to Java development. It includes wizards for applet development, a class browser, an advanced color syntax highlighted source code editor, a visual debugger, and a just-in-time compiler. Besides providing all of the traditional integrated visual development capabilities, Visual J++ Professional includes database support for a plethora of popular database products. Visual J++ also supports Microsoft's COM, DCOM, and ActiveX technologies.

Visual J++ runs on Windows NT, Windows 98, and Windows 95 and retails for $99.95.

JBuilder Client/Server Suite

JBuilder Client/Server Suite Inprise, formerly by Borland (http://www.borland.com/jbuilder/), is a component-oriented visual development environment for developing enterprisewide Java applications. It provides connectivity to SQL databases, supporting both JDBC and ODBC. It supports team programming and provides distributed object support through CORBA connectivity. JBuilder Client/Server retails for $2,495.

JBuilder also comes in Standard ($99.95) and Professional ($799) versions. The Standard version is for entry-level programmers. The Professional version is the same as the Client/Server version, minus some CORBA and database support.

JBuilder runs on Windows NT, Windows 98, and Windows 95.

Super Mojo

Super Mojo by Penumbra Software, Inc. (http://www.penumbrasoftware.com/) uses a component-oriented approach to developing Java software. It consists of a GUI Designer, Visual Scripter, and a Coder. The Designer provides drag-and-drop development of an applet or application's GUI. The Visual Scripter is used to add functionality to an application's visual design. The Coder organizes objects in a way that facilitates code development. An integrated class and method browser lets users view code that is automatically generated.

Super Mojo is written in Java and runs on all platforms that support the Java core API. Super Mojo is priced at $39.95.

JDesignerPro

JDesignerPro version 2.3 by the BulletProof Corporation (http://www.bulletproof.com) consists of an application development environment and application middleware. The application development environment provides traditional visual development tools. The middleware consists of the JAGGServer, which provides JDBC/ODBC database connectivity. BulletProof plans to enhance the JAGGServer to handle IIOP and CORBA connectivity.

JDesignerPro is written in Java and runs on Windows NT, Windows 98, Windows 95, and UNIX platforms. It retails for $695.

SuperCede Java Edition

SuperCede Java Edition 2.0 by SuperCede, Inc. (`http://www.supercede.com`) is an IDE that includes a compiler, debugger, editor, and drag-and-drop visual design tools. It provides database connectivity, C++ and ActiveX development support, and native compilation capabilities.

SuperCede 2.0 runs on Windows NT 4.0, Windows 98, and Windows 95. It costs $29.95.

Jamba

Jamba 2.0 from Interleaf, Inc. (`http://www.jamba.com`) is a visual authoring environment that supports the development of Java applets and applications with little or no programming. It provides wizards that simplify program development, advanced animation tools, drag-and-drop support, and an extensive collection of predefined objects.

Jamba 2.0 runs on Windows NT, Windows 98, and Windows 95. It is available for $149.

Summary

In this chapter you've examined some of the popular Java development tools and learned how they can be used to simplify the process of Java application and applet development.

Congratulations! You've completed the last chapter of this book. Appendixes A through C provide a summary of the Java language, environment variables, and JDK development tools. Appendix D shows how to use the JDK's tools to automatically generate Java software documentation and help files. Appendix E covers the Java Extensions Framework. Appendix F provides a JDK 1.2 API description.

APPENDIX A

Java Language Summary

This appendix summarizes the syntax of the Java language and serves as a quick reference guide to look up specific points of language usage.

Java Packages

Java programs are organized into *packages* that contain the source code declarations of Java classes and interfaces. Packages are identified by the package statement. It is the first statement in a source code file:

```
package packageName;
```

If a package statement is omitted, the classes and interfaces declared within the package are put into the default no-name package. The package name and the CLASSPATH are used to find a class. Only one class or interface may be declared as public for a given source code file (compilation unit). For example, you can define classes X and Y and interface Z within a compilation unit, but only one of these three can be declared public. The name of the compilation unit must be the name of the public class or interface followed by the .java extension.

The import Statement

The import statement is used to reference classes and interfaces that are declared in other packages. There are three forms of the import statement:

```
import packageName.className;
import packageName.interfaceName;
import packageName.*;
```

The first and second forms allow the identified classes and interfaces to be referenced without specifying the name of their package. The third form allows all classes and interfaces in the specified package to be referenced without specifying the name of their package.

Comments

Java provides three styles of comments:

```
/* This is a
   multiline comment. */

// This is a single line comment.

/** This is a
   multiline javadoc comment */
```

The first comment style supports traditional C-language comments. All text appearing between /* and */ is treated as a comment. Comments of this style can span multiple lines.

The second comment style supports single-line C++ comments. All text following the // until the end of the line is treated as a comment.

The third comment style is used by the javadoc documentation-generation tool. All text between the /** and */ is treated as a javadoc comment. javadoc comments may span multiple lines. The use of javadoc comments is covered in Appendix D, "Generating Documentation and Help Files."

Comments cannot be nested and cannot appear within string and character literals.

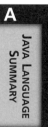

Identifiers

Identifiers are used to name Java language entities. They begin with a letter, underscore character (_), or dollar sign ($). Subsequent characters consist of these characters and digits. Identifiers are case sensitive and cannot be the same as a reserved word. Avoid using the dollar sign character; it is used for compiler-generated identifiers.

Reserved Words

The following words are reserved by the Java language, and cannot be used as identifiers:

abstract	default	if	private	throw
boolean	do	implements	protected	throws
break	double	import	public	transient
byte	else	instanceof	return	try
case	extends	int	short	void
catch	final	interface	static	volatile
char	finally	long	super	while
class	float	native	switch	
const	for	new	synchronized	
continue	goto	package	this	

Primitive Data Types and Literal Values

Java defines eight primitive types. Variables that are declared as a primitive type are not objects. They are only placeholders to store primitive values. The eight primitive types are byte, short, int, long, float, double, char, and boolean.

The byte, short, int, and long types represent 8-, 16-, 32-, and 64-bit integer values. The literal values of these types are written using positive or negative decimal, hexadecimal, or octal integers. Hexadecimal values are preceded by 0x or 0X and use the letters a through f (upper- or lowercase) to represent the digits 10 through 15. Octal numbers are preceded by 0. Long decimal values have an l or L appended to the end of the number.

The float and double types represent 32- and 64-bit IEEE 754 floating-point numbers. float numbers have the f or F suffix. double numbers have d or D. If no suffix is provided, the default double type is assumed. Floating-point numbers may be written in any of the following four forms:

```
digits . optionalDigits optionalExponentPart suffix
. digits optionalExponentPart suffix
digits exponentPart suffix
NaN
```

The suffix is optional. It consists of f, F, d, or D, as described previously.

The exponent part is optional in the first two forms but required in the third form. It consists of an e or E followed by a signed integer. It is used to identify the exponent of 10 of the number written in scientific notation. For example, 1000000.0 could be represented as 1.0E6.

The special value NaN is used to represent the value "not a number," which occurs as the result of undefined mathematical operations such as division by zero.

The char type represents 16-bit Unicode characters. Unicode is a 16-bit superset of the ASCII character set that provides many foreign-language characters. A single character is specified by putting the character within single quotes ('). There are three exceptions: single quote ('), double quote ("), and backslash (\). The backslash character (\) is used as an escape code to represent special character values. The character escape codes are shown in Table A.1.

TABLE A.1. CHARACTER ESCAPE CODES.

Escape Code	Character
\b	Backspace
\t	Tab
\n	Linefeed
\f	Form feed
\r	Carriage return
\"	Double quote
\'	Single quote
\\	Backslash

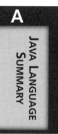

The backslash can also be followed by an 8-bit octal value, or by a u or U followed by a four-digit hexadecimal value. The four-digit value is used to specify the value of Unicode characters.

The boolean type represents the logical values true and false.

String literals are also provided by Java, although strings are not primitive values. Strings consist of characters enclosed by double quotes ("). The character escape codes may be used within strings.

The literal value null is used to identify the fact that an object is not assigned to a value. It may be used with any variable that is not of a primitive data type.

Class literals were introduced with Java 1.1. A class literal is formed by appending .class to the name of a primitive or reference type. It evaluates to an object of type Class, which is the Class object for the identified type. The expression void.class evaluates to void. You can use class literals to directly refer to the class of a variable. For example, suppose Test is a class that you've declared. The following statement displays the name of the Test class:

```
System.out.println(Test.class);
```

Classes and Objects

Objects are the basic elements of Java programs. They are executable entities that contain data and provide methods for manipulating that data. Every object is an instance of a class. Classes are the templates from which objects are created. They define the type of data that an object contains and the methods for manipulating that data. Objects are created (or instantiated) via constructors. An object is instantiated by assigning specific values to the field variables defined by the class.

Class Declarations

Class declarations allow new classes to be defined for use in Java programs. Classes are declared as follows:

`classModifiers class className extendsClause implementsClause classBody`

The class modifiers, extends clause, and `implements` clause are optional.

The class modifiers are `abstract`, `public`, and `final`. An `abstract` class provides an abstract class declaration that cannot be instantiated. In general, `abstract` classes are used as building blocks for the declaration of subclasses. A class that is declared as `public` can be referenced outside its package. If a class is not declared as `public`, it can be referenced only within its package. A `final` class cannot be subclassed. A class cannot be declared as both `final` and `abstract`.

The `extends` clause is used to identify the immediate superclass of a class and thereby position the class within the overall class hierarchy. It is written as follows:

`extends immediateSuperclass`

The `implements` clause identifies the interfaces that are implemented by a class. It is written as follows:

`implements interfaceNames`

The interface names consist of one or more interface names separated by commas.

The class body declares the members of a class. It is written as follows:

`{ memberDeclarations }`

The member declarations consists of zero or more of the following declarations:

- Field variables
- Constructors and methods
- Static and object initializers
- Inner classes

Object initializers and inner classes were introduced with Java 1.1. Object initializers are used to initialize a non-static field variable as part of a class's declaration. Inner classes are classes that are declared within the body of another class. Inner classes may also be declared local to a statement block. They are used to declare classes for use within a limited local scope.

Java also allows inner classes to be declared anonymously within an expression. These classes are referred to as *anonymous classes*.

Variable Declarations

Variables are used to refer to objects and primitive data types. They are declared as follows:

```
variableModifiers type extendedVariableName variableInitialization ;
```

The variable modifiers and variable initialization are optional. A variable's `type` may be a primitive data type, class type, or interface type. The extended variable name is a variable name followed by zero or more bracket sets (`[]`) indicating that the variable is an array.

The variable initialization consists of an equal sign (`=`) followed by an expression yielding a value of the variable's type. If the variable being declared is an array, it can be assigned to an array initializer. Array initializers are written as follows:

```
{elementInitializers}
```

The element initializers are expressions that yield values that are consistent with the element type of the array.

There are seven variable modifiers: `public`, `protected`, `private`, `static`, `final`, `transient`, and `volatile`.

The `public`, `protected`, and `private` modifiers are used to designate the specific manner in which a variable can be accessed. Variables that are declared as `public` can be accessed anywhere that the class in which they are declared can be accessed. Variables that are declared as `protected` can be accessed within the package in which they are declared and in subclasses of the class in which they are declared. Variables that are declared as `private` are only accessible in the class in which they are defined and not in any of its subclasses. If a variable isn't declared as `public`, `protected`, or `private`, it can be accessed only within the package in which it is declared.

A variable that is declared as `static` is associated with its class and is shared by objects that are instances of its class. A `static` variable is also known as a *class variable*.

A variable that is declared as `final` is a constant and cannot be modified. `final` variables must be initialized before they are used. Java 1.1 allows the initialization of a `final` variable to be separated from its declaration.

A variable that is declared as `transient` is not saved as part of an object when the object is serialized. The `transient` keyword identifies a variable that does not maintain a persistent state.

A variable that is declared as volatile refers to objects and primitive values that can be modified asynchronously by separate threads of execution. They are treated in a special manner by the compiler to control the manner in which they can be updated.

Constructor Declarations

Constructors are methods that are used to initialize newly created objects of a class. They are declared as follows:

```
constructorModifiers constructorName(ParameterList) throwsClause
constructorBody
```

The constructor modifiers are public, protected, and private. They control access to the constructor and are used in the same manner as they are for variables.

The constructor name is the same as the class name in which it is declared. It is followed by a parameter list, consisting of an opening parenthesis, followed by zero or more parameter declarations, followed by a closing parenthesis. The parameter declarations are separated by commas. Parameter declarations are written as follows:

```
type parameterName
```

Each parameter declaration consists of a type followed by a parameter name. A parameter name may be followed by sets of matched brackets ([]) to indicate that it is an array.

The throws clause identifies all uncaught exceptions that are thrown within the constructor. It is written as follows:

```
throws uncaughtExceptions
```

The exceptions are separated by commas.

The body of a constructor specifies the manner in which an object of the constructor's class is to be initialized. It is written as follows:

```
{constructorCallStatement blockBody}
```

The constructor call statement and block body are optional, but the opening and closing braces must be supplied.

The constructor call statement allows another constructor of the class or its superclass to be invoked before the constructor's block body. It is written using one of the two following forms:

```
this(argumentList);
```

```
super(argumentList);
```

The first form results in a constructor for the current class being invoked with the specified arguments. The second form results in the constructor of the class's superclass being invoked. The argument list consists of expressions that evaluate to the allowed values of a particular constructor.

If no constructor call statement is specified, a default `super()` constructor is invoked before the constructor block body.

Method Declarations

Methods are used to perform operations on the data contained in an object. They are written as follows:

```
methodModifiers returnType methodName(ParameterList) throwsClause
methodBody
```

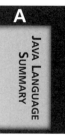

The parameters and `throws` clause are declared in the same method as in constructor declarations.

The method body differs from the constructor body in that it does not allow a constructor call statement.

The method modifiers include the `public`, `protected`, and `private` modifiers defined for constructors, as well as the `final`, `static`, `abstract`, `native`, and `synchronized` modifiers.

The `final` modifier identifies a method that cannot be overridden.

The `static` modifier identifies a class method. Class methods are only allowed to access `static` class variables. `static` methods are `final`.

An `abstract` method is used to identify a method that cannot be invoked and must be overridden by any non-abstract subclasses of the class in which it is declared. An `abstract` method does not have a method body. Instead, it has a semicolon (`;`).

A `native` method is a method written in a language other than Java. It is like an `abstract` method in that its body is replaced by a semicolon.

A `synchronized` method is a method that must acquire a lock on an object or on a class before it can be executed.

Static and Object Initializers

A *static initializer* is a block of code that is used to initialize the `static` variables of a class. It is written as follows:

```
static block
```

Static initializers can only access `static` class variables. They are executed in the order in which they appear in a class declaration.

Object initializers do not have the `static` keyword. They are used to initialize non-static variables of a class and are executed immediately after a class's superclass constructor is invoked.

Interfaces

An *interface* specifies a collection of `abstract` methods that must be overridden by classes that implement the interface. Interfaces are declared as follows:

interfaceModifiers `interface` *interfaceName extendsClause interfaceBody*

The interface modifiers are `public` and `abstract`. `public` interfaces can be accessed in other packages. All interfaces are `abstract`. The `abstract` modifier is superfluous.

The optional `extends` clause is used to identify any interfaces that are extended by an interface. It is written as follows:

`extends` *interfaceNames*

The interface names are separated by commas. An interface inherits all the methods of all interfaces that it extends.

The interface body is enclosed within braces and consists of zero or more variable (constant) and abstract method declarations. Variables declared within an interface are `public`, `static`, and `final`. Methods are `public` and `abstract`. These variable and method modifiers need not be specified.

Blocks

Blocks consist of sequences of local variable declarations and statements. They are written as follows:

`{ blockBody }`

The block body is a sequence of local variable or class declarations or statements. A block can also consist of a single statement without the enclosing braces.

Local Variable Declarations

Local variables are declared in the same manner that field variables are declared, except that local variables do not include modifiers. They are accessible within the block in

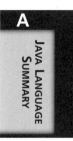

which they are declared. The this and super variables are predefined. They refer to the current object for which a method is invoked and the superclass of the current object being invoked.

Statements

The programming statements supported by Java are described in the following subsections.

Empty Statement

The *empty statement* performs no processing. It consists of a single semicolon.

Block Statement

A *block statement* consists of a sequence of statements and declarations that are treated as a single statement block. The statements are enclosed within braces ({ and }).

Method Invocation

A *method invocation* invokes a method for an object or class. Method invocations may be used within an expression or as a separate statement. Method invocation statements take the following forms:

```
objectName.methodName(argumentList);
className.methodName(argumentList);
```

The *argumentList* consists of a comma-separated list of zero or more expressions that are consistent with the method's parameters.

Allocation Statements

When an object is *allocated*, it is typically assigned to a variable. However, it is not required to be assigned when it is allocated. An allocation statement is of the following form:

```
new constructor(argumentList);
```

The new operator is used to allocate an object of the class specified by the *constructor*. The *constructor* is then invoked to initialize the object using the arguments specified in the *argumentList*.

Assignment Statements

The *assignment statement* assigns an object or value to a variable. Its general form is

```
variableName = expression;
```

where the expression yields a value that is consistent with the variable's type.

Other assignment operators may be used in addition to the = operator. See the section titled "Operators" later in this appendix.

The `if` Statement

The `if` statement is used to select among alternative paths of execution. It is written in the following two forms:

```
if ( booleanExpression ) statement
if ( booleanExpression ) statement1 else statement2
```

In the first form, `statement` is executed only if the `booleanExpression` is `true`. In the second form, `statement1` is executed if the `booleanExpression` is `true` and `statement2` is executed if the `booleanExpression` is `false`.

Statement Labels

A statement can be *labeled* by prefixing an identifier to the statement as follows:

```
label: statement
```

The label can be a name or integer.

The `switch` Statement

The `switch` statement is similar to the `if` statement in that it enables a selection from alternative paths of execution. It is written as follows:

```
switch (expression) caseBlock
```

The expression must evaluate to a `byte`, `char`, `short`, or `int` value. Control is transferred to the next statement in the block that is labeled with a value that matches the expression.

The case block contains a sequence of case-labeled statements. These statements are written as follows:

```
case value: statement
```

An optional default-value statement may also appear in the case block. It is written as follows:

```
default: statement
```

If no value matches the expression and a default-value statement is provided, control is transferred to this statement. If there is no default-value statement, the next statement following the `switch` statement is executed.

The `break` Statement

The `break` statement is used to transfer control to a labeled statement or out-of-statement block. It takes the following forms:

```
break;
```

```
break label;
```

The first form transfers control to the first statement following the current statement block. The second form transfers control to the statement with the identified label.

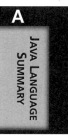

The `for` Statement

The `for` statement is used to iteratively execute a statement. It takes the following form:

```
for (initializationStatement ; booleanExpression ; incrementStatement)
    iteratedStatement
```

The initialization statement is executed at the beginning of the `for` statement, and then the `boolean` expression is tested. If the expression is `true`, the iterated statement is executed. The increment statement is executed after the iterated statement and then the `boolean` expression is retested. The iterated statement-increment-statement loop continues until the `boolean` expression evaluates to `false`. The increment statement does not end with a semicolon.

The `while` Statement

The `while` statement is used to execute a statement while a `boolean` expression is `true`. It is written as follows:

```
while (booleanExpression) iteratedStatement
```

The `boolean` expression is evaluated; if it is `true`, the iterated statement is executed. It continues to execute until the `boolean` expression is `false`.

The do Statement

The do statement, like the while statement, is used to execute a statement until a boolean expression becomes false. The only difference is that the expression is tested after the statement is executed. The do statement is written as follows:

```
do iteratedStatement while (booleanExpression);
```

The continue Statement

The continue statement is used to continue execution of a loop (for, do, or while) without completing execution of the iterated statement. The continue statement may take an optional label. It is written as follows:

```
continue label;
```

If a label is supplied, the loop continues at the labeled loop.

The synchronized Statement

The synchronized statement is used to execute a statement after acquiring a lock on an object. It is written as follows:

```
synchronized ( expression ) statement
```

The expression yields the object for which the lock must be acquired.

The try Statement

The try statement executes a block of statements while setting up exception handlers. If an exception occurs, the appropriate handler, if any, is executed to handle the exception. A finally clause may also be specified to perform absolutely required processing.

The try statement is written as follows:

```
try block catchClauses finallyClause
```

At least one catch clause or a finally clause must be provided.

The format of the catch clause is as follows:

```
catch (exceptionDeclaration) block
```

If an exception is thrown within the block executed by the try statement and it can be assigned to the type of exception declared in the catch clause, the block of the catch clause is executed.

The `finally` clause, if it is provided, is always executed regardless of whether an exception is generated.

The `return` Statement

The `return` statement is used to return an object or value as the result of a method's invocation. It is written as follows:

```
return expression;
```

The value of the expression must match the return value identified in the method's declaration.

Operators

Java defines arithmetic, relational, logical, bit-manipulation, caste, class, selection, and assignment operators. Table A.2 summarizes these operators.

TABLE A.2. JAVA OPERATORS.

Operator Type	Operator	Description	Example
Arithmetic	+	Addition	a + b
	-	Subtraction	a - b
	*	Multiplication	a * b
	/	Division	a / b
	%	Modulus	a % b
Relational	>	Greater than	a > b
	<	Less than	a < b
	>=	Greater than or equal	a >= b
	<=	Less than or equal	a <= b
	!=	Not equal	a != b
	==	Equal	a == b
Logical	!	Not	!a
	&&	AND	a && b
	¦¦	OR	a ¦¦ b

continues

TABLE A.2. CONTINUED

Operator Type	Operator	Description	Example
Bit-manipulation	~	Complement	~a
	&	AND	a & b
	¦	OR	a ¦ b
	^	Exclusive or	a ^ b
	<<	Left-shift	a << b
	>>	Right-shift	a >> B
	>>>	Zero-filled right-shift	a >>> b
Assignment	=	Assignment	a = b
	++	Increment and assign	a++
	--	Decrement and assign	a--
	+=	Add and assign	a += b
	-=	Subtract and assign	a -= b
	*=	Multiply and assign	a *= b
	/=	Divide and assign	a /= b
	%=	Take modulus and assign	a %= b
	¦=	OR and assign	a ¦= b
	&=	AND and assign	a &= b
	^=	XOR and assign	a ^= b
	<<=	Left-shift and assign	a <<= b
	>>=	Right-shift and assign	a >>= b
	>>>=	Zero-filled left-shift and assign	a >>>= b
Caste	(type)	Convert to type	(char) b
Instance	instanceof	Is instance of class?	a instanceof b
Allocation	new	Create a new object of a class	new A()
Selection	? :	If...Then selection	a ? b : c

Multithreading

Java's multithreading support is provided through the Thread class of the java.lang package. Objects of the Thread class have their own separate flow of control.

Java provides two approaches to creating threads. In the first approach, you create a subclass of class Thread and override the run() method to provide an entry point into the thread's execution. When you create an instance of your Thread subclass, you invoke its start() method to cause the thread to execute as an independent sequence of instructions. The start() method is inherited from the Thread class. It initializes the Thread object using your operating system's multithreading capabilities and invokes the run() method.

Subclassing the Thread class is a simple and direct approach to multithreading. However, there are times when you may want your thread to be an object of a class that is outside of the Thread class hierarchy. This is often the case when you develop components for multithreaded applets. Java's other approach to creating threads does not limit your threads to the Thread class hierarchy. In this approach, your class implements the Runnable interface of java.lang. The Runnable interface consists of a single method, the run() method, which must be overridden by your class. The run() method provides an entry point into your thread's execution. In order to run an object of your class as an independent thread, you pass it as an argument to a constructor of class Thread.

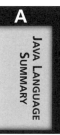

A

JAVA LANGUAGE
SUMMARY

JDK 1.2 Changes to Multithreading

The stop(), suspend(), and resume() methods of the Thread class have been deprecated in JDK 1.2, which means that they'll be phased out of future versions of Java. These methods have been deprecated because of inherent problems that cannot easily be remedied. Chapter 1, "What's New in JDK 1.2," summarizes these problems.

Java Environment Variables

This appendix describes important environment variables used with the tools of JDK 1.2 and discusses how to set up these variables during JDK 1.2 installation. This appendix is specific to Windows-based operating systems (Windows 95, Windows 98, and Windows NT). For information about the environment variables used by other ports of JDK 1.2, consult the documentation that comes with that port.

Adding the JDK Tools to Your PATH

The JDK 1.2 installation software installs the JDK files in the C:\jdk1.2 directory by default. The JDK 1.2 tools (compiler, debugger, and so on) are installed in the C:\jdk1.2\bin directory by default. To run these tools without having to type in their full path name, add C:\jdk1.2\bin to your PATH variable. The easiest way to do this is to add the following line to your AUTOEXEC.BAT file:

```
PATH=[other_paths;]C:\jdk1.2\bin;
```

The *other_paths* is a semicolon-separated list of any other paths that you want to add to your PATH. Windows NT users may also use the System option in the Control Panel to set the PATH variable. If you are using Windows 95, you can also use the following line (in your AUTOEXEC.BAT file) to set your PATH:

```
PATH=%PATH%;C:\jdk1.2\bin;
```

%PATH% is used to prepend your existing path to C:\jdk1.2\bin.

> **NOTE**
>
> If you install the JDK in a directory other than C:\jdk1.2, you'll have to adjust your PATH accordingly.

Setting Your CLASSPATH

The CLASSPATH environment variable identifies the location of compiled Java classes. The CLASSPATH is set on Windows 95 and Windows 98 systems by including the following line in the AUTOEXEC.BAT file:

```
SET CLASSPATH=pathlist
```

The *pathlist* is a semicolon-separated list of paths where compiled Java classes are to be found. On Windows NT, the CLASSPATH is set using the System option in the Control Panel.

By default, the JDK tools append the following path list to the CLASSPATH variable:

```
.;C:\jdk1.2\src.jar
```

This tells the tools to look in the current directory (.), and the JAR file `C:\jdk1.2\src.jar` for compiled Java classes.

If you installed the JDK in a directory other than `C:\jdk1.2`, the JDK tools will adjust the appended paths to the directory where the JDK was installed.

Many of the extension APIs, such as JavaMail, are distributed as .jar files. To add a .jar file to your CLASSPATH, add the file's full path name. For example, I copied `mail.jar` to my `C:\jdk1.2\lib` directory and added `mail.jar` to my CLASSPATH using the following:

```
set CLASSPATH=%CLASSPATH%;C:\jdk1.2\lib\mail.jar
```

The statement appends the `mail.jar` file to my current CLASSPATH.

Using JDK_HOME and JRE_HOME

The environment variables JDK_HOME and JRE_HOME are environment variables that are used by the HotJava browser. As of version 1.1, HotJava comes with its own copy of the Java runtime environment. If you want HotJava to use another installation of the JDK or JRE, set JDK_HOME or JRE_HOME, as appropriate. For example, adding the following line to your AUTOEXEC.BAT file tells HotJava to use the JDK installed in `C:\jdk1.2`:

```
SET JDK_HOME=C:\jdk1.2
```

If both JDK_HOME and JRE_HOME are set, JDK_HOME is used.

The JDK 1.2 Toolset

APPENDIX C

This appendix describes the tools that are provided with JDK 1.2 and summarizes their usage options.

Development Tools

Because the purpose of the JDK is Java software development, most of the JDK tools are development tools. These tools include the Java compiler, bytecode interpreter, debugger, disassembler, documentation generator, and applet viewer. The C-language header file and stub generator tool are also provided.

javac

The `javac` compiler is used to compile Java source code files (ending with `.java`) into bytecode files (ending with `.class`). It is invoked as follows:

```
javac [options] SourceFileNames
```

The source file names are a space-separated list of source code files ending with `.java`. The options are used to control the compiler's operation. They are as follows:

- `-classpath path`—Specifies an alternative `classpath`.
- `-d directory`—Specifies the destination directory for the compiled `.class` files.
- `-depend`—Causes the source files upon which the files being compiled depend to be recompiled.
- `-deprecation`—Causes explanations of deprecation warnings to be displayed.
- `-encoding encoding`—Specifies the encoding of the source file.
- `-g`—Causes debugging information to be generated.
- `-g:nodebug`—Suppresses the generation of line number and local variable debugging information.
- `-nowarn`—Suppresses the display of warnings.
- `-O`—Optimizes compiled code for performance.
- `-O:interclass`—Further optimizes generated code as a single code unit.
- `-Joption`—Passes *option* on to the interpreter that runs the compiler.
- `-verbose`—Causes the compiler to display information about the source files being compiled and the `.class` files being loaded.

java

The Java interpreter, `java`, is used to execute Java bytecode (`.class`) files. It is invoked in the following ways:

```
java [options] className [arguments]
java [options] -jar jarFile [arguments]
```

In the first form, the class name is the name of the class whose `main()` method is to be executed. The arguments are the program's arguments and are separated by spaces.

In the second form, `java` executes a program contained in the JAR file. The class to be executed must be specified by the `Main-Class` manifest header.

The options to the Java interpreter are as follows:

- `-classpath` *path*—Specifies an alternative `classpath`.
- `-Dname=value`—Sets the named property to the specified value.
- `-help`—Displays help information.
- `-usepolicy`—Allows a security policy to be specified.
- `-v` or `-verbose`—Displays information about the classes being loaded.
- `-verbosegc`—Causes the garbage collector to display status messages.
- `-verbosejni`—Displays information about the use of local methods.
- `-version`—Displays information about the current interpreter version.
- `-X`—Prints help information on non-standard options.

In addition to these options, a number of non-standard options are also used with `java`. These options are defined in the JDK 1.2 tool documentation.

A special version of `java`, `javaw`, creates a separate console window for output.

In most cases, unless you are doing advanced debugging, you will not need any of the specialized versions of java.

jdb

The Java debugger, `jdb`, is used to debug Java programs. It is invoked as follows:

`jdb [options] [className]`

The `jdb` options are as follows:

- `-help`—Displays help information.
- `-host` *hostName*—Specifies the name of the host machine with which the debugger is to be used.
- `-password` *password*—Specifies the password to be used to attach the debugger to an interpreter executing on a remote system.
- `-version`—Displays version information about the debugger.

The -host and -password parameters are used to attach the debugger to an interpreter that is currently executing. In addition to the preceding debugger options, a number of options can be forwarded to the process being debugged. These options are covered in the JDK 1.2 documentation.

javap

The Java disassembler, javap, is used to recover Java source code from bytecode files. The disassembler is invoked as follows:

```
javap [options] className
```

The following options are supported by javap:

- -b—Used for backward-compatibility with javap of JDK 1.1.
- -c—Causes disassembled code to be displayed.
- -classpath path—Specifies an alternative classpath.
- -J flag—Passes flag to the runtime system.
- -l—Causes line and local variable tables to be displayed.
- -package—Displays information about package, protected, and public classes and members.
- -private—Displays information about all classes and members.
- -protected—Displays information about protected and public classes and members.
- -public—Displays information about public classes and members.
- -s—Controls the display of type signatures.
- -verbose—Displays information about the stack, local variables, and method arguments.
- -version—Displays version information.

If no options are specified, javap prints the public fields and methods of the class it is disassembling.

javadoc

The Java documentation generator, javadoc, is used to produce the fine Web pages used to document Java packages. The javadoc tool is invoked as follows:

```
javadoc [options] targets
```

The targets are a space-separated list of package names or Java source files for which documentation is to be generated. The `javadoc` options are as follows:

- `-classpath` *path*—Specifies an alternative `classpath`.
- `-doclet` *className*—Specifies the doclet to be used in the documentation generation.
- `-encoding` *name*—Specifies the source file encoding scheme.
- `-J` *flag*—Passes *flag* to the runtime system.
- `-package`—Displays documentation for `package`, `protected`, and `public` classes and members.
- `-private`—Displays documentation on all classes and members.
- `-protected`—Displays documentation for `protected` and `public` classes and members.
- `-public`—Displays documentation for `public` classes and members.
- `-sourcepath` *path*—Specifies the path to be used for source files.

Appendix D, "Generating Documentation and Help Files," covers the use of `javadoc`.

appletviewer

The `appletviewer` is used to view and test applets. It is invoked as follows:

```
appletviewer [options] url
```

The URL is the URL of the HTML file containing the applet to be viewed. It can also be the name of a file in the local file system. The options are as follows:

- `-debug`—Starts `appletviewer` in the debugger.
- `-J` *flag*—Passes *flag* to the runtime system.
- `-encoding` *coding*—Specifies the encoding of the HTML file at the specified URL.

In addition to these options, `appletviewer` allows the following properties to be set:

- HTTP proxy server—The name/IP address of a proxy server to be used. You set this option if your connection to the Internet is mediated by a proxy server.
- HTTP proxy port—The TCP port used by the proxy server.
- Network access—Specifies the access that applets may make to other hosts on the Internet.
- Class access—Specifies whether or not the applet should be restricted to the sandbox.
- Allow unsigned applets—Specifies whether unsigned applets should be allowed.

C

THE JDK 1.2
TOOLSET

These properties are set by selecting Properties from the Applet pulldown menu. Refer to Figure C.1.

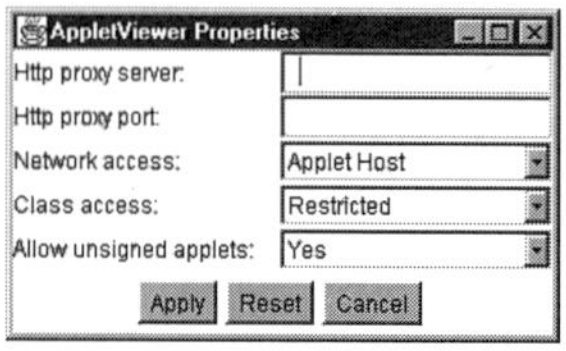

FIGURE C.1.

Setting the properties of the `appletviewer`.

javah

The Java header file and stub generator, `javah`, creates C header files and code stubs for writing native methods. It is invoked as follows:

```
javah [options] className
```

The class name is the name of the class for which the header and stub files are to be generated. The options used with `javah` are as follows:

- `-o` *outputFile*—Causes all output to be written to the specified output file.
- `-d` *directory*—Specifies the directory in which header and stub files are to be saved.
- `-td` *directory*—Specifies the directory to be used for temporary files.
- `-stubs`—Causes stub files to be generated.
- `-v`—Displays information about the status of the files that are generated.
- `-help`—Displays help information.
- `-trace`—Causes trace information to be generated in the stub file.
- `-version`—Displays version information.
- `-jni`—Causes Java native interface function prototypes to be generated.
- `-classpath` *path*—Specifies an alternative `classpath`.

A special version of `javah`, `javah_g`, is non-optimized and more suitable for use in debugging.

Chapter 53, "Native Methods," illustrates the use of the `javah` tool.

Conversion Tools

The JDK provides a tool, `native2ascii`, for converting non-Unicode files to Unicode files. This tool converts non-Unicode Latin-1 text files to Unicode Latin-1 files. It is invoked as follows:

```
native2ascii [options] [inputFile [outputFile]]
```

The input file is the name of the file to be converted, and the output file is the file to which the converted output is to be written. If the output file is not specified, results are written to the standard output stream. If the input file is not specified, input is taken from the standard input stream. The native2ascii tool supports two options: -reverse and -encoding. The -reverse option is used to reverse the conversion process. Instead of converting from non-Unicode to Unicode, conversion takes place in the other direction. The -encoding option is used to specify the encoding name that is used in the conversion. The JDK 1.2 documentation for native2ascii specifies a number of encoding constants that encompass many of the common international character sets.

Archive Tools

The JDK provides the jar tool to archive a number of files into a single .jar file. The jar tool is covered in Chapter 8, "Applet Security." The jar tool is invoked as follows:

```
jar [options] [manifestFile] destinationFile inputFiles
```

The manifest file is used to store information about the archive. If a manifest file is not supplied, jar will automatically create one named META-INF/MANIFEST.INF.

The destination file is the .jar file that is to contain the archive. The input files are a space-separated list of the files that are to be added to the archive. Wildcard characters may be used to specify these files. If one of the input file names is the name of a directory, the directory is processed recursively, adding all of the files and subdirectories contained in the directory to the archive.

The options used with jar are as follows:

- c—Creates a new archive file.
- t—Lists the contents of the archive file.
- x files—Extracts the specified files from the archive. If files is omitted, all files are extracted.
- f—Used to identify the jar file name. If f is not specified, the standard output is used.
- v—Causes verbose output to be displayed to the standard error stream.
- m—Used to specify that a user-specified manifest file should be used.
- 0—Suppresses ZIP compression.
- M—Suppresses the creation of a manifest file.
- u—Used to update an existing .jar file.
- -C—Used to change directories during execution of the jar command.

The @ character is used to specify the name of a file containing an additional jar argument. The contents of the file are inserted into the command line (one argument per input file line) at the point where the @ character occurs.

Security Tools

JDK 1.2 provides three tools that are used to implement the Java security policy: policytool, keytool, and jarsigner. These tools are covered in the following subsections.

policytool

The policytool is a GUI-based tool that provides a convenient way to edit the security policy of a local JDK installation. This tool is invoked as follows:

policytool

The policytool displays the opening window shown in Figure C.2. Select Open from the File menu and then select the policy file that you want to edit. The default policy is jdk1.2\lib\security\java.policy. Use the Add Policy Entry, Edit Policy Entry, and Remove Policy Entry buttons to edit the policy, and select Save from the File menu to save the updated policy.

FIGURE C.2.

The policytool opening display.

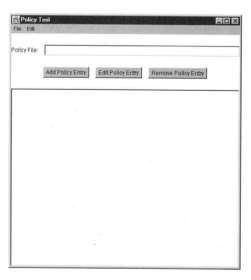

keytool

The keytool is used to manage a local database of keys and certificates. It is invoked as follows:

```
keytool [commands]
```

Entering keytool -help provides a list of the keytool commands and their options. These commands and options are described in the JDK 1.2 documentation of the keytool. Chapter 8 covers the use of the keytool.

jarsigner

The jarsigner tool is used to sign a jar file and to verify the signature of a signed jar file. It is invoked as follows:

```
jarsigner [options] jarFile alias
```

The jarFile argument identifies the name of the jar file to be signed or verified. The alias argument is the alias of the keystore entry containing the private key used to generate the signature. The keystore is a database of keys and certificates maintained by the keytool.

The options used with jarsigner are as follows:

- -keystore *file*—Specifies the file to be used as a keystore.
- -storepass *password*—Specifies the password to be used to access the keystore.
- -keypass *password*—Specifies the password to be used to access the private key of the keystore entry.
- -sigfile *file*—Specifies the file name (without extensions) to be used for the generation of .sf and .dsa files.
- -signedjar *file*—Specifies the name of the signed jar file.
- -verify—Causes the jar file's signature to be verified, as opposed to signed.
- -ids—Causes information about the identities of the signers to be displayed.
- -verbose—Causes status information about the signing or verification to be displayed.

Chapter 8 covers the use of the jarsigner tool.

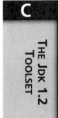

Remote Method Invocation Tools

JDK 1.2 provides four remote method invocation (RMI) tools to enable the development and execution of distributed applications. These tools are covered in the following sub-sections and in Chapter 38, "Building Distributed Applications with the `java.rmi` Packages," and Chapter 39, "Remote Method Invocation."

rmic

The RMI compiler, `rmic`, is used to generate the skeleton and stub files for an object that is to be accessed using RMI. It is invoked as follows:

```
rmic [options] classNames
```

The class names are the fully qualified class names of the classes for which stubs and skeletons are to be generated. The `rmic` options are as follows:

- `-classpath path`—Specifies an alternative `classpath`.
- `-d directory`—Specifies the directory to which stub and skeleton files are to be written.
- `-depend`—Causes the compiler to recompile classes upon which the target classes depend.
- `-g`—Causes debugging tables to be generated.
- `-keepgenerated`—Writes the source `.java` files to the same directory as the stub and skeleton files.
- `-nowarn`—Suppresses the display of warning messages.
- `-O`—Optimizes compiled code for performance.
- `-show`—Causes a GUI version of `rmic` to be launched.
- `-verbose`—Causes status information to be displayed concerning the compilation and loading of classes.

The GUI version of `rmic`, generated using the `-show` option, is shown in Figure C.3.

FIGURE C.3.

The GUI-based `rmic` *tool.*

rmiregistry

The rmiregistry tool is used to start a remote object registry, which makes remote objects available to distributed applications. It is invoked as follows:

```
start rmiregistry [port]
```

The port is the TCP port used by the remote object registry. If the port is not specified, the default port of 1099 is used.

rmid

The RMI activation system daemon is a server process that supports the activation and registration of objects on a remote system. The rmid tool starts the RMI activation system daemon. It is used as follows:

```
rmid [-port port] [-log dir]
```

The port option specifies the TCP port to be used by the daemon. The default port is 1098. The -log option is used to specify the directory that the daemon uses for its database. The default directory is the log subdirectory of the directory in which rmid is invoked.

serialver

The serialver tool is used to calculate the serialVersionUID of a class. The serialVersionUID is a unique object identifier used in distributed applications. The serialver tool is invoked as follows:

```
serialver [-show] [className]
```

The -show option is used to launch the GUI implementation of serialver. Refer to Figure C.4.

FIGURE C.4.

The GUI-based serialver *tool.*

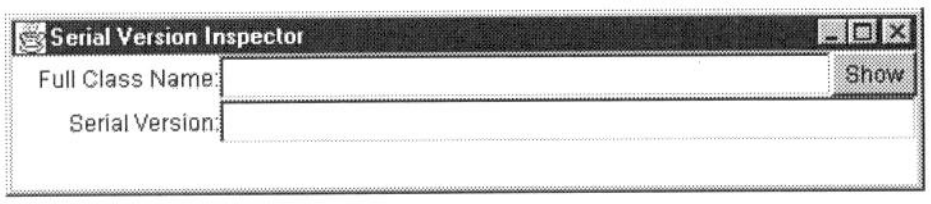

Serial Version Inspector

Full Class Name:
Serial Version:

Show

Java IDL Tools

The tnameserv tool is used to start the Java IDL nameserver on a specified port. The Java IDL nameserver provides a simple implementation of the CORBA Common Object Services (COS) Naming Service. It is invoked as follows:

```
tnameserv [-ORBInitialPort port]
```

The optional port specifies the TCP port to be used with the naming service. The default port is 900. Chapter 41, "Java IDL and ORBs," covers the use of tnameserv.

Servlet Tools

The servletrunner is used to run and test servlets. Although servletrunner is no longer part of the JDK 1.2, it is summarized here for your convenience. The servletrunner tool is invoked using the following:

```
servletrunner [options]
```

The servletrunner options are used to control the operation of servletrunner. These options are as follows:

- -p *port*—The TCP port used by servletrunner.
- -b *backlog*—The maximum size of the backlogged listening queue.
- -m *max*—The maximum number of connection handlers.
- -t *timeout*—The number of milliseconds before a connection times out.
- -d *dir*—The directory where servlets are located.
- -r *root*—The document root directory.
- -s *filename*—The property file name to be used with servlets.
- -v—Specifies that verbose output should be displayed.
- -help—Causes help information to be displayed.

Chapter 48, "Programming Other Servers," covers the use of servletrunner.

Generating Documentation and Help Files

One of the main goals of object-oriented software development is that objects can be reused, and Java is an excellent language for developing reusable objects. The extensive API provided by the JDK is testimony to this fact. One of the most important factors in making software usable and reusable is good documentation. This is another area where Java excels. The API packages of the JDK are examples of great software documentation. This documentation is automatically generated by the javadoc tool of the JDK.

In this chapter you'll learn how to use javadoc to automate the documentation for your software. You'll cover the basic documentation tags that are used with javadoc. You'll then learn how doclets are used to alter the output of javadoc. Finally, you'll explore JavaHelp, a new documentation technology being developed at JavaSoft. When you finish this chapter, you'll be able to quickly and easily document your software using javadoc.

How javadoc Works

javadoc examines your source code and generates HTML files that provide a fully integrated set of documentation for your Java software. The HTML files generated by javadoc document the classes, interfaces, variables, methods, and exceptions that you declare and use in your programs. These files describe your software at the package and class level. The linking capabilities of HTML are used to provide extensive cross-referencing between related software components. These links allow you to quickly access all of the documentation that is relevant to a particular topic.

javadoc differs from other documentation generators in that it goes beyond simple comment-scanning, actually parsing your source code to generate documentation that describes the structure and behavior of your programs. It makes judicious use of HTML links to generate documentation that allows you to easily traverse the structure of your software.

The javadoc program recognizes special types of comments that you insert into your source code. When it parses your source code, it combines these comments with the structural information it generates. Your comments then are integrated into your software's HTML description. The special comments recognized by javadoc consist of doc comments, javadoc tags, and HTML tags.

Doc comments are based on the traditional C /* and */ comment delimiters. They are distinguished from ordinary C comments in that they begin with /** instead of /*. However, doc comments still end with */.They are used to identify comments that are to be automatically added to the HTML documentation produced by javadoc.

The javadoc tags are special tags that are embedded in doc comments. These tags allow you to include reference information in your software. For example, you can include a javadoc comment that says See also: class X. Some references result in links being automatically inserted into your software's documentation.

javadoc also allows you to insert HTML tags directly into your source code. However, javadoc recommends that you limit your HTML to small, simple, and correctly formatted HTML elements so as not to conflict with the HTML that it generates. Your HTML tags are combined with those produced by javadoc to create an integrated set of HTML pages.

Using javadoc

The best way to understand how javadoc works is by using it and then exploring the documentation that it produces. javadoc is so simple to use that it only requires a single command line to generate integrated software documentation for multiple software packages.

To use javadoc, create a separate appxd directory under your ju path. This directory will be used to store the HTML files that javadoc produces. You could store these files in the same directory in which you store your Java API documentation, but it's not a good idea to clutter up your API directory with other documentation.

NOTE

javadoc is a real memory hog, requiring at least 32MB of RAM. To make more memory available to javadoc, close any other open applications.

To run javadoc, launch a DOS shell, switch to the ju\appxd directory, and enter the following DOS command line:

```
javadoc -J-mx20m ju.ch09
```

The -J-mx20m option is passed to the java interpreter. It tells java to allow the heap to grow to a maximum of 20MB. javadoc generates the following output:

```
Loading source files for ju.ch09
Constructing Javadoc information.
Generating tree.html
Generating index.html
Generating deprecatedlist.html
Generating frame.html
Generating packages.html
```

D

GENERATING
DOCUMENTATION
AND HELP FILES

```
Generating packages-frame.html
Generating package-ju.ch09.html
Generating package-tree-ju.ch09.html
Generating package-frame-ju.ch09.html
Generating ju.ch09.MessageDialog.html
Generating ju.ch09.MyMenu.html
Generating ju.ch09.MyMenuBar.html
```

As the result of that single command line, javadoc generates a complete set of HTML documentation for the menu software you produced in Chapter 9, "Creating Window Applications." This documentation will have the same look and feel as the Java API documentation.

When javadoc has finished producing the documentation, use your browser to view it. (I'll be using Internet Explorer 4.0.)

Launch your browser and use its local file open feature to open the file packages.html, located in the appxd directory. Your browser will display a Sun-style Package Summary page, as shown in Figure D.1.

FIGURE D.1.

The Package Summary page.

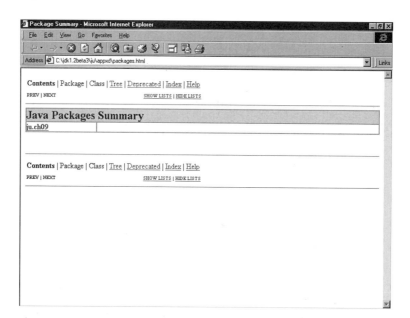

With your browser open to the Package Summary, click on the Tree link. A Web page showing all the classes in the ju.ch09 package is presented to you. The page shows how your classes fit within the rest of the Java class hierarchy. It also identifies the interfaces that are implemented by your classes. The information presented in the class hierarchy page is extremely useful in understanding the structure of Java programs. See Figure D.2.

While you have the Class Hierarchy page loaded, click on the Index link. Another great Web page is displayed that contains an alphabetized index of all the fields (variables) and methods declared in the ju.ch09 package. Click around this page to see some of the items that you've used in your programs. When you have finished, click on the Contents link to go back to the Package Summary (see Figure D.3).

From the Package Summary, click on the ju.ch09 link. This will bring you into the Class Summary for the ju.ch09 package. This page documents the classes that are declared in this package (see Figure D.4).

From here, click on the MyMenu link. The class's description is displayed. Notice how it identifies the branch of the class hierarchy leading to the MyMenu class. A list consisting of a single constructor appears under the class hierarchy diagram. Click on the link to find a more detailed description of the constructor (see Figure D.5).

Under the constructor list is a list of the single method that is declared for the MyMenu class. Following that is a list of methods inherited from other classes. Then a detailed description of the MyMenu() constructor and getItem() method are provided.

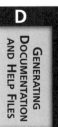

FIGURE D.3.

The Index page.

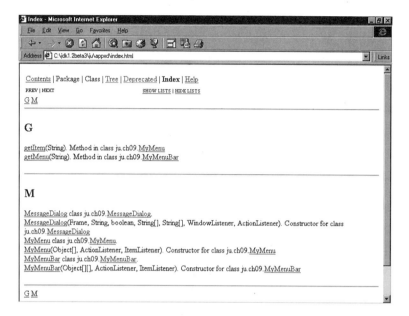

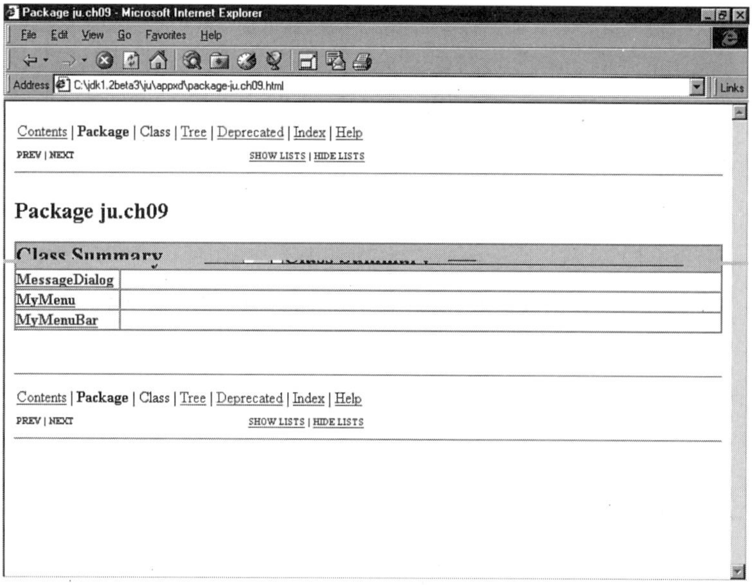

FIGURE D.4.

The ju.ch09 Class Summary page.

FIGURE D.5.

The MyMenu *class page.*

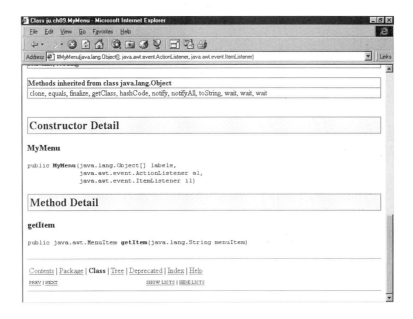

You should now have a pretty good idea of the kind of documentation that can be produced using javadoc. The most remarkable fact about the documentation produced in this section is that you did not have to write a single comment in your source code. It was generated automatically and is far more effective than any traditional program comments. However, if this level of documentation is not enough to satisfy your requirements, you can insert additional comments into your source code that will be integrated with the documentation produced by javadoc.

Placing Doc Comments

Doc comments, as discussed in the beginning of this chapter, are normal Java comments that begin with an extra asterisk. They are easy to insert into your Java programs, and they add implementation-specific information to your documentation. To show how they are used, I've added doc comments to the MyMenu.java source code. These comments can be easily identified in the new program listing for MyMenu (see Listing D.1). If you want to duplicate what I have done, you have to copy and paste the doc comments into the MyMenu.java file and then regenerate its documentation using javadoc.

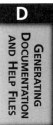

LISTING D.1. THE NEW MyMenu.java.

```java
package ju.ch09;

import java.awt.*;
import java.awt.event.*;

/**
 * The MyMenu class is used to facilitate
 * the creation of menus.
 */
public class MyMenu extends Menu {
 /**
  * A MyMenu object is constructed from an
  * array of labels, an ActionListener,
  * and an ItemListener.
  */
 public MyMenu(Object labels[],ActionListener al,ItemListener il) {
  super((String)labels[0]);
  String menuName = (String) labels[0];
  char firstMenuChar = menuName.charAt(0);
  if(firstMenuChar == '~' || firstMenuChar =='!'){
   setLabel(menuName.substring(1));
   if(firstMenuChar == '~') setEnabled(false);
  }
  for(int i=1;i<labels.length;++i) {
   if(labels[i] instanceof String){
    if("-".equals(labels[i])) addSeparator();
    else{
     String label = (String)labels[i];
     char firstChar = label.charAt(0);
     switch(firstChar){
     case '+':
      CheckboxMenuItem checkboxItem = new
CheckboxMenuItem(label.substring(1));
      checkboxItem.setState(true);
      add(checkboxItem);
      checkboxItem.addItemListener(il);
      break;
     case '#':
      checkboxItem = new CheckboxMenuItem(label.substring(1));
      checkboxItem.setState(true);
      checkboxItem.setEnabled(false);
      add(checkboxItem);
      checkboxItem.addItemListener(il);
      break;
     case '-':
      checkboxItem = new CheckboxMenuItem(label.substring(1));
      checkboxItem.setState(false);
      add(checkboxItem);
      checkboxItem.addItemListener(il);
```

```
        break;
      case '=':
        checkboxItem = new CheckboxMenuItem(label.substring(1));
        checkboxItem.setState(false);
        checkboxItem.setEnabled(false);
        add(checkboxItem);
        checkboxItem.addItemListener(il);
        break;
      case '~':
        MenuItem menuItem = new MenuItem(label.substring(1));
        menuItem.setEnabled(false);
        add(menuItem);
        menuItem.addActionListener(al);
        break;
      case '!':
        menuItem = new MenuItem(label.substring(1));
        add(menuItem);
        menuItem.addActionListener(al);
        break;
      default:
        menuItem = new MenuItem(label);
        add(menuItem);
        menuItem.addActionListener(al);
      }
    }
   }else{
    add(new MyMenu((Object[])labels[i],al,il));
   }
  }
 }
 /**
  * The getItem() method returns the MenuItem
  * object identified by a String.
  */
 public MenuItem getItem(String menuItem) {
  int numItems = getItemCount();
  for(int i=0;i<numItems;++i)
   if(menuItem.equals(getItem(i).getLabel())) return getItem(i);
  return null;
 }
}
```

You can see how these doc comments were integrated into the appropriate class, variable, and constructor descriptions by looking for them in my browser's display (see Figure D.6).

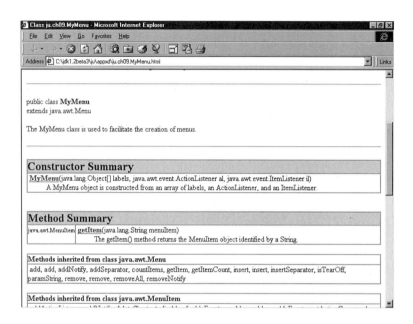

FIGURE D.6.

Doc comments as displayed by a browser.

Using `javadoc` Tags

`javadoc` tags are special tags that are inserted into doc comments. They are used to identify specific references in your code. Special `javadoc` tags are provided for documenting classes, variables, and methods.

`javadoc` tags consist of an at sign (@) followed by a tag type and then a specific comment reference. Their syntax is as follows:

```
@tagType commentReference
```

Java classes and interfaces are allowed to use the `see`, `version`, `author`, `since`, and `deprecated` tag types. Variables can only use the `see`, `since`, and `deprecated` tag types. Methods are allowed to use the `see`, `param`, `return`, `exception`, `since`, and `deprecated` tag types.

The `see` tag type has the following syntax:

```
@see HTMLlink
@see className
@see fullClassName
@see fullClassName#methodName
```

The `see` tag is used to reference other classes and methods that are related to the class, interface, variable, or method being documented.

The version and author tag types are used like this:

```
@version versionID
@author authorNames
```

The `version` tag is used to associate a software version identifier with a class or interface. The `author` tag is used to identify the author of the class or interface.

The `param`, `return`, and `exception` tags are used as follows:

```
@param parameterName description
@return description
@exception fullClassName description
```

The `param` tag is used to document a method parameter. The `return` tag is used to describe the value returned by a method. The `exception` tag is used to document the exceptions that are thrown by a method.

The `deprecated` tag is a new tag introduced with the JDK 1.1. It is used to mark old API classes, interfaces, variables, and methods as superseded and about to be phased out. It is used as follows:

```
@deprecated comment
```

The optional comment is used to provide instructions on how to replace the superseded API element. For a good example of the `deprecated` tag, check out the JDK 1.2 API's description of the `readLine()` method of the `java.io.DataInputStream` class. If you used the JDK 1.0, you probably used `readLine()` to read console input. This method has been replaced by the `readLine()` method of the `java.io.BufferedReader` class.

The `since` tag is used to identify the JDK version in which a language feature was added. It is used as follows:

```
@since version
```

In order to demonstrate the use of these tags, I have modified the `ju.ch09.MyMenuBar.java` file to include `param` tags (see Listing D.2).

LISTING D.2. THE NEW MyMenuBar.

```
package ju.ch09;

import java.awt.*;
import java.awt.event.*;

public class MyMenuBar extends MenuBar {
/**
```

D

**GENERATING
DOCUMENTATION
AND HELP FILES**

continues

```
 * @param labels[] Menu labels
 * @param al ActionListener for menu selections
 * @param il ItemListener for menu checkboxes
 */
public MyMenuBar(Object labels[][],ActionListener al,
  ItemListener il) {
 super();
 for(int i=0;i<labels.length;++i)
  add(new MyMenu(labels[i],al,il));
}
/**
 * @param menuName Name of menu item
 */
public MyMenu getMenu(String menuName) {
 int numMenus = getMenuCount();
 for(int i=0;i<numMenus;++i)
  if(menuName.equals(getMenu(i).getLabel())) return((MyMenu)getMenu(i));
 return null;
}
}
```

Figure D.7 shows how the javadoc tags are integrated by javadoc and displayed by my browser.

FIGURE D.7.

The browser's display of the javadoc tags.

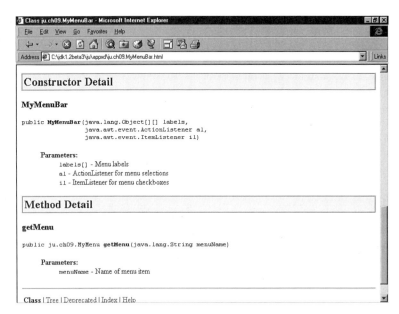

Embedding Standard HTML

If the doc comments and `javadoc` tags still aren't enough to meet your documentation requirements, you can always insert your own HTML markup into a doc comment. However, using HTML is a little bit dangerous because your HTML tags might conflict with the HTML tags inserted by `javadoc`. If you're going to use HTML in your documentation, try to keep it as simple as possible.

I've modified the source code in `MessageDialog.java` to include HTML address tags so that I can put my email address in the doc comment. See Listing D.3.

LISTING D.3. THE NEW `MessageDialog`.

```
package ju.ch09;

import java.awt.*;
import java.awt.event.*;

/**
 * Send your bug reports to:
 * <ADDRESS>jamie@jaworski.com</ADDRESS>
 */
public class MessageDialog extends Dialog {
 public MessageDialog(Frame parent,String title,boolean modal,String
text[],
  String buttons[], WindowListener wh, ActionListener bh) {
  super(parent,title,modal);
  int textLines = text.length;
  int numButtons = buttons.length;
  Panel textPanel = new Panel();
  Panel buttonPanel = new Panel();
  textPanel.setLayout(new GridLayout(textLines,1));
  for(int i=0;i<textLines;++i) textPanel.add(new Label(text[i]));
  for(int i=0;i<numButtons;++i){
   Button b = new Button(buttons[i]);
   b.addActionListener(bh);
   buttonPanel.add(b);
  }
  add("North",textPanel);
  add("South",buttonPanel);
  setBackground(Color.lightGray);
  setForeground(Color.black);
  pack();
  addWindowListener(wh);
 }
}
```

D

GENERATING
DOCUMENTATION
AND HELP FILES

Figure D.8 shows how the HTML tags are integrated by `javadoc` and displayed by my browser.

Figure D.8

How a browser displays javadoc *tags.*

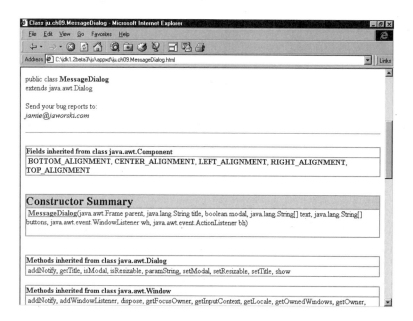

Doclets

javadoc generates its documentation using *doclets*, which are Java programs that specify the content and format of the output of javadoc. In this appendix, you've been using javadoc's default doclet. However, you can create your own doclets to customize javadoc's output. Doclets can also be used to perform analyses of Java source and compiled code.

Doclets are written using the Doclet API, which consists of the sun.tools.javadoc package. This package is included with the classes.zip file that is located in the lib directory of the JDK 1.2 files. The sun.tools.javadoc package contains 1 interface and 16 classes. Figure D.9 shows the class hierarchy and describes the classes and interfaces.

Doclets are executed by the javadoc tool and are different from both applets and applications. The execution entry point for a doclet is a start() method of the following form:

```
public static boolean start(Root root) {
    .
    .
    .
}
```

FIGURE D.9.

The
sun.tools.javadoc
package.

```
Doc - Superclass of all other Doc classes.
    Root - Holds the information generated by running javadoc.
    PackageDoc - Provides information about a Java package.
    ProgramElementDoc - Base class for providing information about Java package elements.
        ClassDoc - Provides information about Java classes.
        MemberDoc - Base class for providing information about class members.
            FieldDoc - Provides information about a class's fields.
            ExecutableMemberDoc - Provides information about a class's constructors and methods.
                ConstructorDoc - Provides information about class constructors.
                MethodDoc - Provides information about a class's methods.
Tag - Provides access to documentation tags.
    SeeTag - Provides access to information contained in a See tag.
    ParamTag - Provides access to information contained in a Param tag.
    ThrowsTag - Provides access to information contained in a Throws tag.
Doclet - Provides an entry point for generating doclet information. Also provides information about a doclet's options.
Type - Defines methods for obtaining information about Java types: classes, interfaces, and primitive types.
Parameter - Provides information about a parameter's name and type.
```

The Root object provides the doclet with methods for gaining access to the information generated by javadoc.

Listing D.4 provides an example doclet that displays all packages, interfaces, classes, and class/interface members that have been processed by javadoc. Compile the doclet using javac, and then run it using the following command:

```
javadoc -J-mx20m -doclet MyDoclet ju.ch09
```

The -doclet option tells javadoc to use the MyDoclet class for generating its output. This output is as follows:

```
Loading source files for ju.ch09
Constructing Javadoc information.
Package: ju.ch09
 Class: MyMenu
  Constructor: MyMenu
  Method: getItem
 Class: MessageDialog
  Constructor: MessageDialog
 Class: MyMenuBar
  Constructor: MyMenuBar
  Method: getMenu
```

The MyDoclet class contains three static methods: start(), displayClasses(), and displayMembers(). The start() method is the doclet's entry point. It is passed an object of the Root class, which contains the information gathered by javadoc. The packages array is used to access the PackageDoc objects for each of the packages that were processed. These objects are returned by the specifiedPackages() method of Root. The indent string is used to format the doclet's output. A for statement is used to iterate through packages, and to display the package name and its interfaces and classes. The interfaces() and ordinaryClasses() methods of the PackageDoc class provide access to information about the interfaces and classes of a package.

The displayClasses() method is used to display information about a class or interface. It takes the following arguments:

- outputType—A String that is either "Interface:" or "Class: ".
- indent—A String that is used to format displayed output.
- classes—An array of ClassDoc objects that are to be displayed.

The method iterates through the classes array and displays the name of the interface or class. It then uses the fields(), constructors(), and methods() methods of ClassDoc to retrieve the members of the interface or class. The displayMembers() method is invoked to display these members.

The displayMembers() method uses the outputType and indent arguments in the same manner as displayClasses(). Its other argument is an array of MemberDoc objects. It iterates through this array and displays the type and name of each member.

LISTING D.4. THE MyDoclet CLASS.

```
import sun.tools.javadoc.*;

public class MyDoclet {
 public static boolean start(Root root) {
  PackageDoc[] packages = root.specifiedPackages();
  String indent="";
  for (int i = 0; i < packages.length; ++i) {
   System.out.println(indent+"Package: "+packages[i].name());
   ClassDoc[] interfaces = packages[i].interfaces();
   displayClasses("Interface: ",indent+" ",interfaces);
   ClassDoc[] classes = packages[i].ordinaryClasses();
   displayClasses("Class: ",indent+" ",classes);
  }
  return true;
 }
 public static void displayClasses(String outputType,
   String indent,ClassDoc[] classes) {
  for(int i=0;i<classes.length;++i) {
   System.out.println(indent+outputType+classes[i].name());
   FieldDoc[] fields = classes[i].fields();
   displayMembers("Field: ",indent+" ",fields);
   ConstructorDoc[] constructors = classes[i].constructors();
   displayMembers("Constructor: ",indent+" ",constructors);
   MethodDoc[] methods = classes[i].methods();
   displayMembers("Method: ",indent+" ",methods);
  }
 }
 public static void displayMembers(String outputType,
   String indent, MemberDoc[] members) {
  for(int i=0;i<members.length;++i) {
   System.out.println(indent+outputType+members[i].name());
  }
 }
}
```

JavaHelp

In addition to the excellent documentation capabilities provided by `javadoc`, JavaSoft is in the process of developing a separate JavaHelp API that will allow software developers to incorporate online help for applets, applications, JavaBeans, and other Java software. The JavaHelp API will support the development of Help applications that run in the context of other software components or that run separately. These Help applications will contain sophisticated methods for searching and navigating through help information.

At the time of this writing, the JavaHelp specification was still in development. This specification calls for a Help Viewer that displays help information using HTML 3.2. The Help Viewer also supports Java applets. The JavaHelp specification also identifies Help Navigators that provide tables of contents, indices, and full-text search capabilities. The JavaHelp files will be distributed as compressed archives in the Java Archive (JAR) file format. JavaHelp will also support the merging of help information about multiple components and the dynamic online update of help information.

For more information about JavaHelp, check out its Web page at `http://java.sun.com/ products/javahelp/index.html`.

The Java
Extensions
Framework

The Java Extensions Framework allows the Core API to be extended with user-developed packages. This capability is useful in a number of scenarios. For example, if your organization maintains an intranet that uses Java applets and applications, it may be useful to install organization-specific packages (especially those that use native code) as standard extensions. In this way, these packages are available to all users and needed classes and interfaces are treated as extensions to the Core API.

In another scenario, consider a set of consumer-oriented, Web-based applets. Suppose these applets all use a set of common packages. You can create a downloaded extension that is referenced in the applets' JAR files. This frees you from having to package the common classes in each applet's JAR file.

JDK 1.2 supports two types of extension: *installed extensions* and *downloaded extensions*. As you might have guessed, installed extensions are installed in the local classpath, and downloaded extensions are downloaded from URLs. Both installed and downloaded extensions are packaged as JAR files.

Installed Extensions

Installed extensions consist of JAR files that are placed in a particular location within the local file system. These JAR files are installed in the /lib/ext subdirectory of the JAVA_HOME directory. Refer to Appendix B, "Java Environment Variables," for a definition of the JAVA_HOME environment variable. On Windows-based systems, native code is installed in the /bin subdirectory of the JAVA_HOME directory. When the Java virtual machine looks for a class, it first searches its list of system classes. After that, it searches the /lib/ext directory. If the class is still not found, it searches through the downloaded extension classes, and finally, throughout other directories in the CLASSPATH.

Installed extensions are particularly useful when a number of packages that use native code must be distributed throughout an organization.

Downloaded Extensions

Downloaded extensions consist of JAR files that are referenced in the JAR files of applets and applications. The extension's JAR file is referenced in the manifest of the applet's JAR file. This reference occurs in the Class-Path header field. For example, consider the following header field:

```
Class-Path: MyExtensions.jar YourExtensions.jar TheirExtensions.jar
```

This references three extension JAR files. The URLs of these files are relative to the applet's URL. Consult Chapter 8, "Applet Security," for information on how to specify the header fields in the manifest of a JAR file. Extension files are subject to the Java security policy. If extensions are referenced by applets, it is a good idea to sign the extensions.

> **NOTE**
>
> Installed extensions may contain native code, but downloaded extensions may not.

JDK 1.2 API
Description

This appendix describes the packages of the JDK 1.2 API in terms of their interfaces, classes, exceptions, and errors. Also, hierarchical relationships between package elements are identified. This appendix is based on the API defined for JDK 1.2 release candidate 2 (RC2).

java.applet	java.rmi.server
java.awt	java.security
java.awt.color	java.security.acl
java.awt.datatransfer	java.security.cert
java.awt.dnd	java.security.interfaces
java.awt.event	java.security.spec
java.awt.font	java.sql
java.awt.geom	java.text
java.awt.im	java.util
java.awt.image	java.util.jar
java.awt.image.renderable	java.util.zip
java.awt.print	javax.accessibility
javax.swing	javax.swing
javax.swing	javax.swing.border
javax.swing	javax.swing.colorchooser
javax.swing	javax.swing.event
javax.swing	javax.swing.filechooser
javax.swing	javax.swing.plaf
javax.swing	javax.swing.plaf.basic
javax.swing	javax.swing.plaf.metal
javax.swing	javax.swing.plaf.multi
java.beans	javax.swing.table
java.beans.beancontext	javax.swing.text
java.io	javax.swing.text.html
java.lang	javax.swing.tree
java.lang.ref	javax.swing.undo
java.lang.reflect	org.omg.CORBA
java.math	org.omg.CORBA.DynAnyPackage
java.net	org.omg.CORBA.ORBPackage
java.rmi	org.omg.CORBA.portable
java.rmi.activation	org.omg.CORBA.TypeCodePackage
java.rmi.dgc	org.omg.CosNaming
java.rmi.registry	org.omg.CosNaming.NamingContextPackage

Package `java.applet`

The `java.applet` package is one of the smallest packages in the Core API. It consists of one class and three interfaces that provide the basic functionality needed to implement applets.

Interfaces

AppletContext

The `AppletContext` interface defines methods that allow an applet to access the context in which it is being run.

AppletStub

The `AppletStub` interface supports communication between an applet and its browser environment, and is used to develop custom applet viewers.

AudioClip

The `AudioClip` interface provides methods that support the playing of audio clips.

Classes

Applet

The `Applet` class is the superclass of all applets. It provides methods to display images, play audio files, respond to events, and obtain information about an applet's execution environment. The `Applet` class is a subclass of `java.awt.panel`.

Exceptions and Errors

None.

Package `java.awt`

The `java.awt` package implements the core classes and interfaces of the Abstract Windowing Toolkit (AWT). It is a large package, containing 64 classes and 14 interfaces. These classes and interfaces provide the standard AWT GUI controls, as well as drawing, printing, and other capabilities. The `java.awt` package is covered in Chapter 5, "JDK 1.2 Applet Writing Basics."

Interfaces

ActiveEvent

The ActiveEvent interface defines methods that are implemented by event classes that are self-dispatching.

Adjustable

The Adjustable interface is implemented by classes, such as sliders and scrollbars, that allow a value to be selected from a range of values.

Composite

The Composite interface defines methods that are implemented by classes that allow drawing to be composed with an underlying graphics area.

CompositeContext

The CompositeContext interface defines methods for classes that provide a context for compositing drawing operations.

ItemSelectable

The ItemSelectable interface is implemented by classes whose objects, such as choices or lists, may contain selectable items.

LayoutManager

The LayoutManager interface is implemented by classes that can lay out Container objects.

LayoutManager2

The LayoutManager2 interface extends the LayoutManager interface to provide support for layout constraints.

MenuContainer

The MenuContainer interface defines methods for classes that may contain Menu objects.

Paint

The Paint interface extends the Transparency interface, providing support for defining color patterns for use in graphics operations.

PaintContext

The PaintContext interface provides methods that define the context for paint operations.

PrintGraphics

The `PrintGraphics` interface defines a graphics context for printing a single page.

Shape

The `Shape` interface defines methods that are implemented by classes that encapsulate geometric shapes.

Stroke

The `Stroke` interface provides methods that are implemented by classes that define pen strokes.

Transparency

The `Transparency` interface defines methods for classes that support transparency-related graphics operations.

Classes

AlphaComposite

The `AlphaComposite` class is a subclass of `Object` that implements alpha compositing rules for combining source and destination image pixels. It implements the `Composite` interface.

AWTEvent

The `AWTEvent` class is a subclass of `java.util.EventObject` that serves as the base class for all AWT-related events.

AWTEventMulticaster

The `AWTEventMulticaster` class is a subclass of `Object` that provides thread-safe multicast event dispatching capabilities. It implements the following interfaces of the `java.awt.event` package: `ActionListener`, `AdjustmentListener`, `ComponentListener`, `ContainerListener`, `FocusListener`, `InputMethodListener`, `ItemListener`, `KeyListener`, `MouseListener`, `MouseMotionListener`, `TextListener`, and `WindowListener`.

AWTPermission

The `AWTPermission` class is a subclass of `java.security.BasicPermission` that implements security permissions for a variety of AWT-related operations.

BasicStroke

The BasicStroke class is a subclass of Object that provides a set of properties for a basic implementation of the Stroke interface.

BorderLayout

The BorderLayout class is a subclass of Object that is used to lay out the components of a container along the container's border. It implements the LayoutManager2 and java.lang.Serializable interfaces.

Button

The Button class is a subclass of Component that encapsulates a GUI text-labeled push-button.

Canvas

The Canvas class is a subclass of Component that provides a rectangular drawing area.

CardLayout

The CardLayout class is a subclass of Object that provides the capability to lay out a Container object in a card-like fashion. It implements the LayoutManager2 and java.io.Serializable interfaces.

Checkbox

The Checkbox class is a subclass of Container that provides the capability to display and work with checkbox and radio button GUI controls. It implements the ItemSelectable interface.

CheckboxGroup

The CheckboxGroup class is a subclass of Object that is used to group Checkbox objects together as a set of radio buttons. It implements the java.io.Serializable interface.

CheckboxMenuItem

The CheckboxMenuItem class is a subclass of MenuItem that is used to create a menu item that may be in an on or off state. It implements the ItemSelectable interface.

Choice

The Choice class is a subclass of Component that provides a pop-up menu of choices. It implements the ItemSelectable interface.

Color

The Color class is a subclass of Object that is used to define colors within a particular color space. It implements the Paint and java.io.Serializable interfaces.

Component

The Component class is a subclass of Object that provides the base class for the development of GUI components. It implements the MenuContainer, java.awt.imaga.ImageObserver, and java.io.Serializable interfaces.

ComponentOrientation

The ComponentOrientation class is a subclass of Object that implements the Serializable interface. It is used to specify the language-specific orientation of text.

Container

The Container class is a subclass of Component that acts as a container for other GUI components.

Cursor

The Cursor class is a subclass of Object that encapsulates a changeable cursor associated with a pointing device. It implements the java.io.Serializable interface.

Dialog

The Dialog class is a subclass of Window that provides a base class for the development of dialog boxes.

Dimension

The Dimension class is a subclass of java.awt.geom.Dimension2D that provides the capability to specify the height and width of an object. It implements the java.io.Serializable interface.

Event

The Event class is a subclass of Object that provides the base class for implementing events in the JDK 1.0 event model. It implements the java.io.Serializable interface.

EventQueue

The EventQueue class is a subclass of Object that implements the system event queue.

FileDialog

The FileDialog class is a subclass of Dialog that encapsulates a file system dialog box.

FlowLayout

The FlowLayout class is a subclass of Object that is used to lay out Container objects in a left-to-right and top-to-bottom fashion. It implements the LayoutManager and java.io.Serializable interfaces.

Font

The Font class is a subclass of Object that encapsulates text fonts. It implements the java.io.Serializable interface.

FontMetrics

The FontMetrics class is a subclass of Object that provides information about the properties of a font. It implements the java.io.Serializable interface.

Frame

The Frame class is a subclass of Window that provides a top-level application window. It implements the MenuContainer interface.

GradientPaint

The GradientPaint class is a subclass of Object that provides the capability to fill a drawing area with a linear gradient color fill. It implements the Paint interface.

Graphics

The Graphics class is a subclass of Object that is the base class for the development of graphics drawing contexts.

Graphics2D

The Graphics2D class is a subclass of Graphics that serves as the basic graphics context for the Java 2D API.

GraphicsConfigTemplate

The GraphicsConfigTemplate class is a subclass of Object that is used as a template for the creation of GraphicsConfiguration objects. It implements the java.io.Serializable interface.

GraphicsConfiguration

The GraphicsConfiguration class is a subclass of Object that specifies the physical characteristics of a graphics display device.

GraphicsDevice

The GraphicsDevice class is a subclass of Object that describes the graphics display devices available to the system.

GraphicsEnvironment

The GraphicsEnvironment class is a subclass of Object that describes the entire graphics environment available to the system, including all of the accessible GraphicsDevice objects.

GridBagConstraints

The GridBagConstraints class is a subclass of Object that is used to specify how containers are to be laid out using GridBagLayout objects. It implements the java.lang.Cloneable and java.io.Serializable interfaces.

GridBagLayout

The GridBagLayout class is a subclass of Object that is used to lay out a container according to the properties of a GridBagConstraints object. It implements the LayoutManager2 and java.io.Serializable interfaces.

GridLayout

The GridLayout class is a subclass of Object that is used to lay out a container in a grid-like fashion. It implements the LayoutManager and java.io.Serializable interfaces.

Image

The Image class is a subclass of Object that encapsulates a displayable image.

Insets

The Insets class is a subclass of Object that specifies the border of a GUI component. It implements the java.lang.Cloneable and java.io.Serializable interfaces.

Label

The Label class is a subclass of Component that implements a GUI text label.

List

The List class is a subclass of Component that encapsulates a scrollable list GUI control. It implements the ItemSelectable interface.

MediaTracker

The MediaTracker class is a subclass of Object that is used to track the loading status of multimedia objects. It implements the java.io.Serializable interface.

F

JDK 1.2 API
DESCRIPTION

Menu

The Menu class is a subclass of MenuItem that encapsulates a pull-down menu. It implements the MenuContainer interface.

MenuBar

The MenuBar class is a subclass of MenuComponent that provides the capability to attach a menu bar to a Frame object. It implements the MenuContainer interface.

MenuComponent

The MenuComponent class is a subclass of Object that is the base class for all other AWT menu-related classes. It implements the java.io.Serializable interface.

MenuItem

The MenuItem class is a subclass of MenuComponent that implements a menu item value that is selectable from a Menu object.

MenuShortcut

The MenuShortcut class is a subclass of Object that provides the capability to associate a keyboard accelerator with a MenuItem object. It implements the java.io.Serializable interface.

Panel

The Panel class is a subclass of Container that provides a rectangular container for other GUI components.

Point

The Point class is a subclass of java.awt.geom.Point2D that encapsulates a point in the xy-plane. It implements the java.io.Serializable interface.

Polygon

The Polygon class is a subclass of Object that is used to describe a mathematical polygon. It implements the Shape and java.io.Serializable interfaces.

PopupMenu

The PopupMenu class is a subclass of Menu that provides a menu that can be popped up at a specific location within a component.

PrintJob

The `PrintJob` class is a subclass of `Object` that is used to implement a system-specific printing request.

Rectangle

The `Rectangle` class is a subclass of `java.awt.geom.Rectangle2D` that encapsulates a mathematical rectangle. It implements the `Shape` and `java.io.Serializable` interfaces.

RenderingHints

The `RenderingHints` class is a subclass of `Object` that implements the `Map` and `Cloneable` interfaces. It is used to provide information for rendering objects for display.

RenderingHints.Key

The `RenderingHints.Key` class is an inner class of `RenderingHints` that provides a base class for specifying keys used in the rendering process.

Scrollbar

The `Scrollbar` class is a subclass of `Component` that provides a GUI scrollbar component. It implements the `Adjustable` interface.

ScrollPane

The `ScrollPane` class is a subclass of `Container` that provides a combination of a panel and vertical and horizontal scrollbars.

SystemColor

The `SystemColor` class is a subclass of `Color` that is used to specify the color scheme used with GUI components. It implements the `java.io.Serializable` interface.

TextArea

The `TextArea` class is a subclass of `TextComponent` that provides a GUI text area control.

TextComponent

The `TextComponent` class is a subclass of `Component` that is the base class for `TextField` and `TextArea`.

TextField

The `TextField` class is a subclass of `TextComponent` that implements a GUI text input field.

TexturePaint

The TexturePaint class is a subclass of Object that provides the capability to fill a geometrical shape with a texture image. It implements the Paint interface.

Toolkit

The Toolkit class is a subclass of Object that provides access to implementation-specific AWT resources.

Window

The Window class is a subclass of Container that provides a basic window object.

Exceptions and Errors

AWTError

The AWTError class is a subclass of java.lang.Error that is thrown when a fundamental error occurs in the AWT operation.

AWTException

The AWTException class is a subclass of java.lang.Exception that signals the occurrence of an AWT-specific exception.

IllegalComponentStateException

The IllegalComponentStateException class is a subclass of java.lang.IllegalStateException that identifies that an AWT component is in the wrong state for a particular operation.

Package java.awt.color

The java.awt.color package is part of the Java 2D API. It provides five classes that support the capability to work with different color models. The java.awt.color package is covered in Chapter 20, "Working with 2D and 3D Graphics."

Interfaces

None.

Classes

ColorSpace

The `ColorSpace` class is an abstract subclass of `Object` that specifies the color space used with other objects. It provides constants that define popular color spaces and methods for converting colors between color spaces.

ICC_ColorSpace

The `ICC_ColorSpace` class is a subclass of `ColorSpace` that provides a non-abstract implementation of the `ColorSpace` methods. It represents color spaces in accordance with the ICC Profile Format Specification, Version 3.4, August 15, 1997, from the International Color Consortium. For more information, refer to `http://www.color.org`.

ICC_Profile

The `ICC_Profile` class is a subclass of `Object` that provides a representation of color profile data for color spaces based on the ICC Profile Format Specification. Color profiles represent transformations from the color space of a device, such as a monitor, to a profile connection space, as defined by the ICC Profile Format Specification.

ICC_ProfileGray

The `ICC_ProfileGray` class is a subclass of `ICC_Profile` that supports color conversion to monochrome color spaces.

ICC_ProfileRGB

The `ICC_ProfileRGB` class is a subclass of `ICC_Profile` that supports color conversion between RGB and CIEXYZ color spaces.

Exceptions and Errors

CMMException

The `CMMException` class is a subclass of `java.lang.RuntimeException` that defines an exception that is thrown when the color model manager returns an error.

ProfileDataException

The `ProfileDataException` class is a subclass of `java.lang.RuntimeException` that defines an exception that is thrown when an error occurs in accessing or processing an `ICC_Profile` object.

Package `java.awt.datatransfer`

The `java.awt.datatransfer` package provides four classes and three interfaces that support clipboard operations. It is covered in Chapter 15, "Using the Clipboard."

Interfaces

ClipboardOwner

The `ClipboardOwner` interface defines the `lostOwnership()` method, which is invoked to notify an object that it has lost ownership of a clipboard. This interface is implemented by classes that copy data to a clipboard.

FlavorMap

The `FlavorMap` interface maps MIME types to Java data flavors.

Transferable

The `Transferable` interface defines methods that support the transfer of data via the clipboard or other mechanisms. It is implemented by classes that support clipboard-related data transfers.

Classes

Clipboard

The `Clipboard` class is a subclass of `Object` that provides access to system- and user-defined clipboards. It provides methods for getting and setting the contents of a clipboard and retrieving the name of a clipboard.

DataFlavor

The `DataFlavor` class is a subclass of `Object` that defines the types of data available for a transfer operation (such as those that take place via a clipboard). Flavors are implemented as MIME types. The `DataFlavor` class provides methods for reading and writing objects to be transferred and for accessing MIME type information. It implements the `java.io.Serializable` and `java.lang.Cloneable` interfaces.

StringSelection

The `StringSelection` class is a subclass of `Object` that supports the transfer of `String` objects as plain text. It provides methods for working with string-related data flavors. It implements the `Transferable` and `ClipboardOwner` interfaces.

SystemFlavorMap

The `SystemFlavorMap` class extends the `Object` class and provides a default implementation of the `FlavorMap` interface.

Exceptions and Errors

UnsupportedFlavorException

The `UnsupportedFlavorException` class is a subclass of `java.lang.Exception` that is used to signal that transferable data is not supported in a particular flavor.

Package `java.awt.dnd`

The `java.awt.dnd` package supports the new JDK 1.2 drag-and-drop capability. It contains 12 classes and four interfaces and is covered in Chapter 16, "Working with Drag and Drop."

Interfaces

Autoscroll

The `Autoscroll` interface provides methods that support automatic scrolling through GUI components in support of drag-and-drop operations.

DragGestureListener

The `DragGestureListener` interface extends the `EventListener` interface to allow for the handling of the `DragGestureEvent` event.

DragSourceListener

The `DragSourceListener` interface extends the `java.util.EventListener` interface to define methods that are implemented by objects that originate drag-and-drop operations. These methods track the state of drag-and-drop operations and enable feedback to be provided to the user.

DropTargetListener

The `DropTargetListener` interface extends the `java.util.EventListener` interface to define methods that are implemented by objects that are the target of drag-and-drop operations.

Classes

DnDConstants

The DnDConstants class is a subclass of Object that defines constants that are used in drag-and-drop operations.

DragGestureEvent

The DragGestureEvent class extends the EventObject class to define an event to signal that a user has gestured that a drag-and-drop operation should be initiated.

DragGestureRecognizer

The DragGestureRecognizer class extends Object to provide an abstract class for the development of platform-dependent event listeners for drag-and-drop operations.

DragSource

The DragSource class is a subclass of Object that implements the source originator of a drag-and-drop operation. It defines several java.awt.Cursor objects that define the cursor state during drag-and-drop. Its startDrag() method is used to initiate drag-and-drop.

DragSourceContext

The DragSourceContext class is a subclass of Object that is used to manage the source-side of drag-and-drop operations. It manages events associated with the drag source and implements the DragSourceListener interface.

DragSourceDragEvent

The DragSourceDragEvent class is a subclass of DragSourceEvent. It implements the event that is handled by a DragSourceListener during the dragging stage of a drag-and-drop operation.

DragSourceDropEvent

The DragSourceDropEvent class is a subclass of DragSourceEvent. It implements the event that is handled by a DragSourceListener during the dropping stage of a drag-and-drop operation.

DragSourceEvent

The DragSourceEvent class is a subclass of java.util.EventObject that is used as the base class for DragSourceDragEvent and DragSourceDropEvent.

DropTarget

The DropTarget class is a subclass of Object that is used to implement the target of a drag-and-drop operation. Objects of DropTarget are associated with components that function as drop targets. These objects are typically GUI components. DropTarget implements the DropTargetListener and java.io.Serializable interfaces.

DropTarget.DropTargetAutoScroller

The DropTarget.DropTargetAutoScroller class is an inner class of DropTarget that supports scrolling operations.

DropTargetContext

The DropTargetContext class is a subclass of Object that is used to implement the context of a drop operation. Objects of this class are dynamically created when an object is dragged over a potential drop target. This class is used by the drop target to provide feedback to the user and to initiate the data transfer associated with the drag-and-drop operation.

DropTargetDragEvent

The DropTargetDragEvent class is a subclass of DropTargetEvent that informs DropTargetListener objects of the dragging state of a drag-and-drop operation.

DropTargetDropEvent

The DropTargetDropEvent class is a subclass of DropTargetEvent that informs DropTargetListener objects of the dropping state of a drag-and-drop operation.

DropTargetEvent

The DropTargetEvent class is a subclass of java.util.EventObject that serves as the base class for DropTargetDragEvent and DropTargetDropEvent.

MouseDragGestureRecognizer

The MouseDragGestureRecognizer class extends DragGestureRecognizer and implements the MouseListener and MouseMotionListener interfaces. This class provides support for mouse-based drag-and-drop listeners.

Exceptions and Errors

InvalidDnDOperationException

The InvalidDnDOperationException class is a subclass of java.lang.IllegalStateException that signals that a drag-and-drop operation cannot be carried out.

Package `java.awt.event`

The `java.awt.event` package provides the foundation for JDK 1.1-style event processing. It contains 20 classes and 13 interfaces, and is covered in Chapter 6, "GUI Building."

Interfaces

ActionListener

The `ActionListener` interface extends the `java.util.EventListener` interface and defines methods that are implemented by classes that handle `ActionEvent` events.

AdjustmentListener

The `AdjustmentListener` interface extends the `java.util.EventListener` interface and defines methods that are implemented by classes that handle `AdjustmentEvent` events.

AWTEventListener

The `AWTEventListener` interface extends the `java.util.EventListener` interface and defines methods that are implemented by classes that handle the `AWTEvent`.

ComponentListener

The `ComponentListener` interface extends the `java.util.EventListener` interface and defines methods that are implemented by classes that handle `ComponentEvent` events.

ContainerListener

The `ContainerListener` interface extends the `java.util.EventListener` interface and defines methods that are implemented by classes that handle `ContainerEvent` events.

FocusListener

The `FocusListener` interface extends the `java.util.EventListener` interface and defines methods that are implemented by classes that handle `FocusEvent` events.

InputMethodListener

The `InputMethodListener` interface extends the `java.util.EventListener` interface and defines methods that are implemented by classes that handle `InputMethodEvent` events.

ItemListener

The `ItemListener` interface extends the `java.util.EventListener` interface and defines methods that are implemented by classes that handle `Item` events.

KeyListener

The KeyListener interface extends the java.util.EventListener interface and defines methods that are implemented by classes that handle KeyEvent events.

MouseListener

The MouseListener interface extends the java.util.EventListener interface and defines methods that are implemented by classes that handle MouseEvent events.

MouseMotionListener

The MouseMotionListener interface extends the java.util.EventListener interface and defines methods that are implemented by classes that handle MouseEvent events.

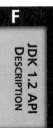

TextListener

The TextListener interface extends the java.util.EventListener interface and defines methods that are implemented by classes that handle TextEvent events.

WindowListener

The WindowListener interface extends the java.util.EventListener interface and defines methods that are implemented by classes that handle WindowEvent events.

Classes

ActionEvent

The ActionEvent class is a subclass of java.awt.AWTEvent that implements an event generated by user interface actions, such as clicking on a button or selecting a menu item.

AdjustmentEvent

The AdjustmentEvent class is a subclass of java.awt.AWTEvent that implements an event generated by scrolling actions.

ComponentAdapter

The ComponentAdapter class is a subclass of Object that provides a basic implementation of the ComponentListener interface.

ComponentEvent

The ComponentEvent class is a subclass of java.awt.AWTEvent that implements an event generated by changes to the position, focus, or sizing of a window component, or by a keyboard input or other mouse action.

ContainerAdapter

The ContainerAdapter class is a subclass of Object that provides a basic implementation of the ContainerListener interface.

ContainerEvent

The ContainerEvent class is a subclass of java.awt.ComponentEvent that implements an event generated by adding and removing components from a container.

FocusAdapter

The FocusAdapter class is a subclass of Object that provides a basic implementation of the FocusListener interface.

FocusEvent

The FocusEvent class is a subclass of ComponentEvent that implements an event generated by a change in the status of a component's input focus.

InputEvent

The InputEvent class is a subclass of ComponentEvent that is the base class for defining events generated by user keyboard and mouse actions.

InputMethodEvent

The InputMethodEvent class is a subclass of java.awt.AWTEvent that implements an event generated by changes to the text being entered via an input method.

InvocationEvent

The InvocationEvent class extends the java.awt.AWTEvent class and implements the java.awt.ActiveEvent interface. It signals the invocation of a Runnable object.

ItemEvent

The ItemEvent class is a subclass of AWTEvent that implements an event generated by a component state change, such as selecting an item from a list.

KeyAdapter

The KeyAdapter class is a subclass of Object that provides a basic implementation of the KeyListener interface.

KeyEvent

The KeyEvent class is a subclass of InputEvent that implements an event generated by user keyboard actions.

MouseAdapter

The `MouseAdapter` class is a subclass of `Object` that provides a basic implementation of the `MouseListener` interface.

MouseEvent

The `MouseEvent` class is a subclass of `InputEvent` that implements an event generated by low-level mouse actions.

MouseMotionAdapter

The `MouseMotionAdapter` class is a subclass of `Object` that provides a basic implementation of the `MouseMotionListener` interface.

PaintEvent

The `PaintEvent` class is a subclass of `ComponentEvent` that implements an event generated by the painting/repainting of a window.

TextEvent

The `TextEvent` class is a subclass of `java.awt.AWTEvent` that implements an event generated by text-related events, such as changing the value of a text field.

WindowAdapter

The `WindowAdapter` class is a subclass of `Object` that provides a basic implementation of the `WindowListener` interface.

WindowEvent

The `WindowEvent` class is a subclass of `ComponentEvent` that implements an event generated by events such as the opening, closing, and minimizing of a window.

Exceptions and Errors

None.

Package `java.awt.font`

The `java.awt.font` package is new to JDK 1.2. It provides 13 classes and two interfaces that support advanced font capabilities. The `java.awt.font` package is covered in Chapter 20.

Interfaces

MultipleMaster

The MultipleMaster interface defines methods that are implemented by classes that support Type 1 Multiple Master fonts.

OpenType

The OpenType interface defines methods that are implemented by classes that support Open Type and Truc Type fonts.

Classes

FontRendererContext

The FontRendererContext class extends the Object class to provide a container for the information needed to correctly measure text.

GlyphJustificationInfo

The GlyphJustificationInfo class is a subclass of Object that provides information about the justification of a glyph.

GlyphMetrics

The GlyphMetrics class is a subclass of Object that defines the properties of a single glyph.

GlyphVector

The GlyphVector class is a subclass of Object that represents text as a sequence of integer glyph codes. It implements the java.lang.Cloneable interface.

GraphicAttribute

The GraphicAttribute class is a subclass of Object that is used to identify a graphic that is embedded in text.

ImageGraphicAttribute

The ImageGraphicAttribute class is a subclass of GraphicAttribute that is used to identify an image that is embedded in text.

LineBreakMeasurer

The LineBreakMeasurer class is a subclass of Object that organizes lines of text according to a wrapping width.

LineMetrics

The LineMetrics class extends the Object class to provide access to line-oriented text metrics.

ShapeGraphicAttribute

The ShapeGraphicAttribute class is a subclass of GraphicAttribute that is used to identify a Shape object that is embedded in text.

TextAttribute

The TextAttribute class is a subclass of java.text.AttributedCharacterIterator.Attribute that maintains a set of attributes for rendering text.

TextHitInfo

The TextHitInfo class is a subclass of Object that is used to specify a position within text.

TextLayout

The TextLayout class is a subclass of Object that provides support for laying out styled text. It implements the java.lang.Cloneable interface.

TextLayout.CaretPolicy

The TextLayout.CaretPolicy class is an inner class of TextLayout that specifies how the caret should be used with a TextLayout object. It is a subclass of Object.

TextLine.TextLineMetrics

The TextLine.TextLineMetrics class extends Object to provide basic metrics for working with text.

TransformAttribute

The TransformAttribute class extends Object and implements the Serializable interface. It allows transforms to be used as attributes.

Exceptions and Errors

None.

Package `java.awt.geom`

The `java.awt.geom` package is a new JDK 1.2 package that is part of the Java 2D API. It provides 30 classes and one interface that support standard geometrical objects and transformations. The `java.awt.geom` package is covered in Chapter 20.

Interfaces

PathIterator

The `PathIterator` interface provides constants and methods for iterating over the points in a path.

Classes

AffineTransform

The `AffineTransform` class is a subclass of `Object` that provides the capability to compute two-dimensional affine transformations. It implements the `java.lang.Cloneable` interface.

Arc2D

The `Arc2D` class is a subclass of `RectangularShape` that defines an arc within a bounding rectangle.

Arc2D.Double

The `Arc2D.Double` class is an inner class of `Arc2D` that specifies the arc in `double` precision.

Arc2D.Float

The `Arc2D.Float` class is an inner class of `Arc2D` that specifies the arc in `float` precision.

Area

The `Area` class is a subclass of `Object` that encapsulates an arbitrary 2D area. It implements the `java.awt.Shape` and `java.lang.Cloneable` interfaces.

CubicCurve2D

The `CubicCurve2D` class is a subclass of `Object` that encapsulates a cubic curve.

CubicCurve2D.Double

The CubicCurve2D.Double class is an inner class of CubicCurve2D that specifies the curve in double precision.

CubicCurve2D.Float

The CubicCurve2D.Float class is an inner class of CubicCurve2D that specifies the curve in float precision.

Dimension2D

The Dimension2D class is a subclass of Object that encapsulates width and height dimensions. It implements the java.lang.Cloneable interface.

Ellipse2D

The Ellipse2D class is a subclass of RectangularShape that represents an ellipse.

Ellipse2D.Double

The Ellipse2D.Double class is an inner class of Ellipse2D that specifies the ellipse in double precision.

Ellipse2D.Float

The Ellipse2D.Float class is an inner class of Ellipse2D that specifies the ellipse in float precision.

FlatteningPathIterator

The FlatteningPathIterator class is a subclass of Object that is used to flatten a path. It implements the PathIterator interface.

GeneralPath

The GeneralPath class is a subclass of Object that represents a general 2D path. It implements the java.awt.Shape and java.lang.Cloneable interfaces.

Line2D

The Line2D class is a subclass of Object that encapsulates a 2D line. It implements the java.awt.Shape and java.lang.Cloneable interfaces.

Line2D.Double

The Line2D.Double class is an inner class of Line2D that specifies the line in double precision.

Line2D.Float

The Line2D.Float class is an inner class of Line2D that specifies the line in float precision.

Point2D

The Point2D class is a subclass of Object that represents a 2D point. It implements the java.lang.Cloneable interface.

Point2D.Double

The Point2D.Double class is an inner class of Point2D that specifies the point in double precision.

Point2D.Float

The Point2D.Float class is an inner class of Point2D that specifies the point in float precision.

QuadCurve2D

The QuadCurve2D class is a subclass of Object that encapsulates a 2D quadratic curve. It implements the java.awt.Shape and java.lang.Cloneable interfaces.

QuadCurve2D.Double

The QuadCurve2D.Double class is an inner class of QuadCurve2D that specifies the curve using a double value.

QuadCurve2D.Float

The QuadCurve2D.Float class is an inner class of QuadCurve2D that specifies the curve using a float value.

Rectangle2D

The Rectangle2D class is a subclass of RectangularShape that encapsulates a 2D rectangle.

Rectangle2D.Double

The Rectangle2D.Double class is an inner class of Rectangle2D that specifies the rectangle using double values.

Rectangle2D.Float

The Rectangle2D.Float class is an inner class of Rectangle2D that specifies the rectangle using float values.

RectangularShape

The RectangularShape class is a subclass of Object that is the base class for other rectangular shapes. It implements the java.awt.Shape and java.lang.Cloneable interfaces.

RoundRectangle2D

The RoundRectangle2D class is a subclass of RectangularShape that defines a rectangle with rounded corners.

RoundRectangle2D.Double

The RoundRectangle2D.Double class is an inner class of RoundRectangle2D that specifies the rectangle using double values.

RoundRectangle2D.Float

The RoundRectangle2D.Float class is an inner class of RoundRectangle2D that specifies the rectangle using float values.

Exceptions and Errors

IllegalPathStateException

The IllegalPathStateException class is a subclass of java.lang.RuntimeException that signals an attempt to perform an operation on a path when it is in the incorrect state for that operation.

NoninvertibleTransformException

The NoninvertibleTransformException class is a subclass of java.lang.Exception indicating that an operation requiring an invertible transform was performed using a noninvertible transform.

Package java.awt.im

The java.awt.im package is a new package that supports the Input Method API. It contains two classes and one interface. The Input Method API is covered in Chapter 19, "Internationalization."

Interfaces

InputMethodRequests

The InputMethodRequests interface defines methods that must be implemented by an input handling class in order to function within the Input Method API. These methods are used to obtain information about the text being entered by the user.

Classes

InputContext

The InputContext class is a subclass of Object that is used to implement the connection between text editing components and input methods. It does this by generating events that are handled by the text editing components and input methods.

InputMethodHighlight

The InputMethodHighlight class is a subclass of Object that supports the highlighting and conversion of text that is input via an input method.

Exceptions and Errors

None.

Package java.awt.image

The java.awt.image package is a Java 2D API package that supports image processing. It provides 40 classes and 10 interfaces that support common image filters. The java.awt.image package is covered in Chapter 20.

Interfaces

BufferedImageOp

The BufferedImageOp interface defines methods for classes that perform operations on BufferedImage objects.

ImageConsumer

The ImageConsumer interface defines methods for classes that receive image data from ImageProducer objects.

ImageObserver

The ImageObserver interface defines methods for classes that observe the loading/construction of Image objects.

ImageProducer

The ImageProducer interface defines methods for classes that produce image data for use by ImageConsumer objects.

RasterOp

The RasterOp interface is implemented by classes that support operations on Raster objects.

RenderedImage

The RenderedImage interface is implemented by classes that produce image data in the form of Raster objects.

TileObserver

The TileObserver interface defines methods for handling events generated by changes to tiles of an image.

WritableRenderedImage

The WritableRenderedImage interface defines methods for classes that implement images that can be overwritten.

Classes

AffineTransformOp

The AffineTransformOp class is a subclass of Object that performs a 2D affine transform between two images. It implements the BufferedImageOp and RasterOp interfaces.

AreaAveragingScaleFilter

The AreaAveragingScaleFilter class is a subclass of ReplicateScaleFilter that supports image resizing using an area-averaging algorithm.

BandCombineOp

The BandCombineOp class is a subclass of Object that performs operations that combine bands in a Raster object. It implements the RasterOp interface.

BandedSampleModel

The BandedSampleModel class is a subclass of SampleModel that provides advanced band control.

BufferedImage

The BufferedImage class is a subclass of Image that provides access to buffered image data. It implements the WritableRenderedImage interface.

BufferedImageFilter

The `BufferedImageFilter` class is a subclass of `ImageFilter` that supports `BufferedImage` objects. It implements the `RasterImageConsumer` and `java.lang.Cloneable` interfaces.

ByteLookupTable

The `ByteLookupTable` class is a subclass of `LookupTable` that supports byte data.

ColorConvertOp

The `ColorConvertOp` class is a subclass of `Object` that supports pixel-by-pixel color conversions. It implements the `BufferedImageOp` and `RasterOp` interfaces.

ColorModel

The `ColorModel` class is a subclass of `Object` that provides the base class for the development of a variety of color models. It implements the `Transparency` interface.

ComponentColorModel

The `ComponentColorModel` class is a subclass of `ColorModel` that provides support for a variety of color spaces.

ComponentSampleModel

The `ComponentSampleModel` class is a subclass of `SampleModel` that supports the separate storage of color component data.

ConvolveOp

The `ConvolveOp` class is a subclass of `Object` that supports convolution operations on image data. It implements the `BufferedImageOp` and `RasterOp` interfaces.

CropImageFilter

The `CropImageFilter` class is a subclass of `ImageFilter` that supports image cropping.

DataBuffer

The `DataBuffer` class is a subclass of `Object` that supports the buffering of image data.

DataBufferByte

The `DataBufferByte` class is a subclass of `DataBuffer` that supports byte-oriented image buffering.

DataBufferInt

The DataBufferInt class is a subclass of DataBuffer that supports int-oriented image buffering.

DataBufferShort

The DataBufferShort class is a subclass of DataBuffer that supports short-oriented image buffering.

DataBufferUShort

The DataBufferUShort class is a subclass of DataBuffer that supports unsigned short-oriented image buffering.

DirectColorModel

The DirectColorModel class is a subclass of PackedColorModel that supports direct RGB pixel colors.

FilteredImageSource

The FilteredImageSource class is a subclass of Object that combines an ImageProducer with an ImageFilter. It implements the ImageProducer interface.

ImageFilter

The ImageFilter class is a subclass of Object that supports general image filtering operations. It implements the ImageConsumer and java.lang.Cloneable interfaces.

IndexColorModel

The IndexColorModel class is a subclass of ColorModel that represents pixels as indices into a color map.

Kernel

The Kernel class is a subclass of Object that defines matrices for filtering operations.

LookupOp

The LookupOp class is a subclass of Object that supports image lookup operations. It implements the BufferedImageOp and RasterOp interfaces.

LookupTable

The LookupTable class is a subclass of Object that defines a lookup table for use in imaging operations.

MemoryImageSource

The MemoryImageSource class is a subclass of Object that provides image data from a memory source. It implements the ImageProducer interface.

MultiPixelPackedSampleModel

The MultiPixelPackedSampleModel class is a subclass of SampleModel that supports the processing of multiple one-sample pixels.

PackedColorModel

The PackedColorModel class is a subclass of ColorModel that represents color values directly within pixel data.

PixelGrabber

The PixelGrabber class is a subclass of Object that is used to retrieve a subset of the pixels of an image. It implements the ImageConsumer interface.

PixelInterleavedSampleModel

The PixelInterleavedSampleModel class extends ComponentSampleModel to provide the capability to store interleaved pixel image data.

RGBImageFilter

The RGBImageFilter class is a subclass of ImageFilter that supports the filtering of RGB color values.

Raster

The Raster class is a subclass of Object that implements a rectangular array of pixels.

ReplicateScaleFilter

The ReplicateScaleFilter class is a subclass of ImageFilter that implements a simple scaling algorithm.

RescaleOp

The RescaleOp class is a subclass of Object that supports image-rescaling operations. It implements the BufferedImageOp and RasterOp interfaces.

SampleModel

The SampleModel class is a subclass of Object that provides a base class for developing approaches to sampling image data.

ShortLookupTable

The ShortLookupTable class is a subclass of LookupTable that supports short-valued data.

SinglePixelPackedSampleModel

The SinglePixelPackedSampleModel class is a subclass of SampleModel that packs single-pixel samples in a single data element.

WritableRaster

The WritableRaster class is a subclass of Raster that provides support for image updating.

Exceptions and Errors

ImagingOpException

The ImagingOpException class is a subclass of java.lang.RuntimeException that indicates errors encountered during filtering operations.

RasterFormatException

The RasterFormatException class is a subclass of java.lang.RuntimeException that indicates format errors in Raster objects.

Package java.awt.image.renderable

The java.awt.image.renderable package provides four classes and three interfaces that support image rendering. It is covered in Chapter 20.

Interfaces

ContextualRenderedImageFactory

The ContextualRenderedImageFactory interface extends the RenderedImageFactory interface to provide methods that support rendering-independent operations. It is implemented by subclasses of RenderableImageOp.

RenderableImage

The RenderableImage interface provides a common set of methods for rendering-independent images. These methods support image operations that are independent of any specific image rendering.

RenderedImageFactory

The RenderedImageFactory interface defines the create() method for use by classes that provide different image renderings, depending on a particular set of rendering parameters.

Classes

ParameterBlock

The ParameterBlock class is a subclass of Object that provides a common set of parameters for use with RenderableImageOp objects. It implements the java.lang.Cloneable and java.io.Serializable interfaces.

RenderContext

The RenderContext class is a subclass of Object that specifies contextual information for rendering a RenderableImage object. This contextual information includes the area of interest, transforms, and rendering hints. It implements the java.lang.Cloneable interface.

RenderableImageOp

The RenderableImageOp class is a subclass of Object that supports context-specific image rendering. It implements the RenderableImage interface.

RenderableImageProducer

The RenderableImageProducer class is a subclass of Object that supports the asynchronous production of a RenderableImage object. It implements the java.awt.image.ImageProducer and java.lang.Runnable interfaces.

Exceptions and Errors

None.

Package java.awt.print

The java.awt.print package is a Java 2D API package that supports the printing of text and graphics. It contains eight classes and three interfaces. This package is covered in Chapter 18, "Printing."

Interfaces

PrinterGraphics

The PrinterGraphics interface provides access to a PrinterJob object.

Pageable

The Pageable interface specifies methods used for objects that represent a set of pages to be printed. These methods retrieve the number of pages to be printed and a specific page from within the page list.

Printable

The Printable interface defines the print() method for printing a page on a Graphics object.

Classes

Book

The Book class is a subclass of Object that maintains a list of pages to be printed. It provides methods for adding and managing pages. It implements the Pageable interface.

PageFormat

The PageFormat class is a subclass of Object that specifies the size and orientation of a page to be printed. It provides methods for setting the Paper object to be used and the page orientation. It also provides methods for switching the drawing space between portrait and landscape mode and for retrieving the characteristics of the drawing area. It implements the java.lang.Cloneable interface.

Paper

The Paper class is a subclass of Object that specifies the physical characteristics of the paper used for printing. It provides methods for getting and setting the paper size and the drawing area.

PrinterJob

The PrinterJob class is a subclass of Object that initiates, manages, and controls a printing request. Provides methods for printing Pageable objects and specifying print properties.

Exceptions and Errors

PrinterAbortException

The PrinterAbortException class is a subclass of PrinterException that indicates a print job has been aborted.

PrinterException

The PrinterException class extends java.lang.Exception to provide a base class for printing-related exceptions.

PrinterIOException

The `PrinterIOException` class extends `PrinterException` to indicate a printing I/O error.

Package `java.beans`

The `java.beans` package contains 15 classes and eight interfaces that provide the basic JavaBeans functionality. The `java.beans` package is covered in Part 7, "Creating JavaBeans."

Interfaces

AppletInitializer

The `AppletInitializer` interface provides support for initializing beans that are also applets.

BeanInfo

The `BeanInfo` interface is used to provide explicit information about a bean.

Customizer

The `Customizer` interface provides methods for customizing a bean's GUI.

DesignMode

The `DesignMode` interface is used to signal that a bean is in design (as opposed to execution) mode.

PropertyChangeListener

The `PropertyChangeListener` interface defines methods for handling events that result from changes to bound bean properties. It extends `java.util.EventListener`.

PropertyEditor

The `PropertyEditor` interface provides support for changing the properties of a bean.

VetoableChangeListener

The `VetoableChangeListener` interface extends `java.util.EventListener` to provide support for handing constrained property change events.

Visibility

The `Visibility` interface is used to signal whether a bean needs a GUI to perform its processing.

Classes

BeanDescriptor

The BeanDescriptor class is a subclass of FeatureDescriptor that provides global information about a bean.

Beans

The Beans class is a subclass of Object that provides general-purpose bean support.

EventSetDescriptor

The EventSetDescriptor class is a subclass of FeatureDescriptor that describes the events supported by a bean.

FeatureDescriptor

The FeatureDescriptor class is a subclass of Object that serves as a base class for explicit bean descriptions.

IndexedPropertyDescriptor

The IndexedPropertyDescriptor class is a subclass of PropertyDescriptor that supports indexed property descriptions.

Introspector

The Introspector class is a subclass of Object that provides static methods for obtaining information about a bean.

MethodDescriptor

The MethodDescriptor class is a subclass of FeatureDescriptor that provides information about a bean's methods.

ParameterDescriptor

The ParameterDescriptor class is a subclass of FeatureDescriptor that describes the parameters supported by a bean method.

PropertyChangeEvent

The PropertyChangeEvent class is a subclass of java.util.EventObject that signals a change in a bean's properties.

PropertyChangeSupport

The PropertyChangeSupport class is a subclass of Object that provides support for PropertyChangeEvent handling. It implements the java.io.Serializable interface.

PropertyDescriptor

The `PropertyDescriptor` class is a subclass of `FeatureDescriptor` that describes a bean property.

PropertyEditorManager

The `PropertyEditorManager` class is a subclass of `Object` that is used to access bean property editors.

PropertyEditorSupport

The `PropertyEditorSupport` class is a subclass of `Object` that provides a basic implementation of the `PropertyEditor` interface.

SimpleBeanInfo

The `SimpleBeanInfo` class is a subclass of `Object` that provides a basic implementation of the `BeanInfo` interface.

VetoableChangeSupport

The `VetoableChangeSupport` class is a subclass of `Object` that provides support for property change event handling. It implements the `java.io.Serializable` interface.

Exceptions and Errors

IntrospectionException

The `IntrospectionException` class is a subclass of `java.lang.Exception` that indicates that an exception occurred during introspection.

PropertyVetoException

The `PropertyVetoException` class is a subclass of `java.lang.Exception` that indicates an invalid property change.

Package `java.beans.beancontext`

The `java.beans.beancontext` package provides 13 classes and eight interfaces that implement an execution context for beans. The `java.beans.beancontext` package is covered in Chapter 29, "Glasgow Developments."

Interfaces

BeanContext

The BeanContext interface is implemented by classes that act as containers for other beans. It extends the BeanContextChild, java.util.Collection, java.beans.DesignMode, and java.beans.Visibility interfaces.

BeanContextChild

The BeanContextChild interface defines methods that allow classes to access their execution environment.

BeanContextChildComponentProxy

The BeanContextChildComponentProxy interface provides access to the AWT component associated with a BeanContextChildren object.

BeanContextContainerProxy

The BeanContextContainerProxy interface provides access to the AWT container associated with a BeanContext object.

BeanContextMembershipListener

The BeanContextMembershipListener interface defines methods for handling events associated with changes in membership in a bean context. It extends the java.util.EventListener interface.

BeanContextProxy

The BeanContextProxy interface is implemented by beans that use the context of other beans.

BeanContextServiceProvider

The BeanContextServiceProvider interface defines methods that are used to provide services to a bean context.

BeanContextServiceProviderBeanInfo

The BeanContextServiceProviderBeanInfo interface extends the BeanInfo interface to provide explicit information about the services of an interface.

BeanContextServiceRevokedListener

The BeanContextServiceRevokedListener interface supports the handling of events associated with revocation of a service to a bean context. It extends the java.util.EventListener interface.

BeanContextServices

The BeanContextServices interface defines methods that allow a BeanContext object to make services available to its contained BeanContextChild objects. It extends the BeanContext and BeanContextServicesListener interfaces.

BeanContextServicesListener

The BeanContextServicesListener interface defines methods for handling events associated with a service becoming available to a bean context. It extends the BeanContextServiceRevokedListener interface.

Classes

BeanContextChildSupport

The BeanContextChildSupport class is a subclass of Object that provides a basic implementation of the BeanContextChild interface. It also implements the BeanContextServicesListener and java.io.Serializable interfaces.

BeanContextEvent

The BeanContextEvent class is a subclass of java.util.EventObject that serves as the base class for bean context-related events.

BeanContextMembershipEvent

The BeanContextMembershipEvent class is a subclass of BeanContextEvent that is used to signal a change in the set of beans that is contained in a bean context.

BeanContextServiceAvailableEvent

The BeanContextServiceAvailableEvent class is a subclass of BeanContextEvent that indicates that a service has been made available to a bean context.

BeanContextServiceRevokedEvent

The BeanContextServiceRevokedEvent class is a subclass of BeanContextEvent that indicates that a service is no longer available to a bean context.

BeanContextServicesSupport

The BeanContextServicesSupport class is a subclass of BeanContextSupport that provides a basic implementation of the BeanContextServices interface.

BeanContextServicesSupport.BCSSChild

The BeanContextServicesSupport.BCSSChild class is an inner class of BeanContextServicesSupport that is inherited from BeanContextSupport. It is a subclass of BeanContextSupport.BCSChild.

BeanContextSupport

The BeanContextSupport class is a subclass of BeanContextChildSupport that provides a basic implementation of the BeanContext interface. It also implements the java.beans.PropertyChangeListener, java.beans.VetoableChangeListener, and java.io.Serializable interfaces.

BeanContextSupport.BCSIterator

The BeanContextSupport.BCSIterator class is an inner class of BeanContextSupport that is used as an iterator within its parent. It is a subclass of Object that implements the java.util.Iterator interface.

Exceptions and Errors

None.

Package `java.io`

The java.io package provides 49 classes and 11 interfaces that implement stream-based input and output. Chapter 17, "Input/Output Streams," shows how to use java.io to perform a wide variety of input and output.

Interfaces

DataInput

The DataInput interface provides methods for reading primitive types from a byte stream.

DataOutput

The DataOutput interface provides methods for writing primitive types to a byte stream.

Externalizable

The Externalizable interface extends the Serializable interface to provide methods for writing objects to a stream and for reading them back from a stream.

FileFilter

The FileFilter interface provides the capability to filter path names.

FilenameFilter

The FilenameFilter interface provides the capability to filter file names during file name selection.

ObjectInput

The `ObjectInput` interface extends the `DataInput` interface to support the reading of objects from input streams.

ObjectInputValidation

The `ObjectInputValidation` interface supports the validation of objects within a graph.

ObjectOutput

The `ObjectOutput` interface extends the `DataOutput` interface to support the writing of objects to output streams.

ObjectStreamConstants

The `ObjectStreamConstants` interface provides constants that are used to perform object-based input and output.

Serializable

The `Serializable` interface identifies an object as being capable of being written to and read from a stream.

Classes

BufferedInputStream

The `BufferedInputStream` class is a subclass of `FilterInputStream` that supports input buffering.

BufferedOutputStream

The `BufferedOutputStream` class is a subclass of `FilterOutputStream` that supports output buffering.

BufferedReader

The `BufferedReader` class is a subclass of `Reader` that supports input buffering.

BufferedWriter

The `BufferedWriter` class is a subclass of `Writer` that supports output buffering.

ByteArrayInputStream

The `ByteArrayInputStream` class is a subclass of `InputStream` that supports input from a byte array.

ByteArrayOutputStream

The ByteArrayOutputStream class is a subclass of OutputStream that supports output to a byte array.

CharArrayReader

The CharArrayReader class is a subclass of Reader that supports input from a character array.

CharArrayWriter

The CharArrayWriter class is a subclass of Writer that supports output to a character array.

DataInputStream

The DataInputStream class is a subclass of FilterInputStream that allows primitive types to be read from an input stream. It implements the DataInput interface.

DataOutputStream

The DataOutputStream class is a subclass of FilterOutputStream that allows primitive types to be written to an output stream. It implements the DataOutput interface.

File

The File class is a subclass of Object that encapsulates a disk file. It implements the Serializabe and java.lang.Comparable interfaces.

FileDescriptor

The FileDescriptor class is a subclass of Object that encapsulates a file descriptor.

FileInputStream

The FileInputStream class is a subclass of InputStream that supports file-based input.

FileOutputStream

The FileOutputStream class is a subclass of OutputStream that supports file-based output.

FilePermission

The FilePermission class is a subclass of java.security.Permission that is used to control access to files. It implements the Serializable interface.

FileReader

The FileReader class is a subclass of InputStreamReader that supports file-based input.

FileWriter

The FileWriter class is a subclass of OutputStreamWriter that supports file-based output.

FilterInputStream

The FilterInputStream class is a subclass of InputStream that is used to filter data that is being read from a stream.

FilterOutputStream

The FilterOutputStream class is a subclass of OutputStream that is used to filter data that is being written to a stream.

FilterReader

The FilterReader class is a subclass of Reader that allows filtering of data that is being read.

FilterWriter

The FilterWriter class is a subclass of Writer that allows filtering of data that is being written.

InputStream

The InputStream class is a subclass of Object that provides the base class for all stream-based input.

InputStreamReader

The InputStreamReader class is a subclass of Reader that is used to read a stream using a Reader object.

LineNumberInputStream

The LineNumberInputStream class is a subclass of FilterInputStream that supports line number identification.

LineNumberReader

The LineNumberReader class is a subclass of BufferedReader that supports line number identification.

ObjectInputStream

The ObjectInputStream class is a subclass of InputStream that supports the reading of objects from streams. It implements the ObjectInput and ObjectStreamConstants interfaces.

ObjectInputStream.GetField

The ObjectInputStream.GetField class is an inner class of ObjectInputStream that provides support for the reading of individual object fields. It is a subclass of Object.

ObjectOutputStream

The ObjectOutputStream class is a subclass of OutputStream that supports the writing of objects to streams. It implements the ObjectOutput and ObjectStreamConstants interfaces.

ObjectOutputStream.PutField

The ObjectOutputStream.PutField class is an inner class of ObjectOutputStream that allows individual object fields to be accessed. It is a subclass of Object.

ObjectStreamClass

The ObjectStreamClass class is a subclass of Object that describes a serialized class. It implements the Serializable interface.

ObjectStreamField

The ObjectStreamField class is a subclass of Object that describes a field of a serialized class. It implements the java.lang.Comparable interface.

OutputStream

The OutputStream class is a subclass of Object that provides the basis for stream-based output.

OutputStreamWriter

The OutputStreamWriter class is a subclass of Writer that allows output streams to be accessed as Writer objects.

PipedInputStream

The PipedInputStream class is a subclass of InputStream that supports communication between threads.

F

JDK 1.2 API
DESCRIPTION

PipedOutputStream

The PipedOutputStream class is a subclass of OutputStream that supports communication between threads.

PipedReader

The PipedReader class is a subclass of Reader that supports communication between threads.

PipedWriter

The PipedWriter class is a subclass of Writer that supports communication between threads.

PrintStream

The PrintStream class is a subclass of FilterOutputStream that supports printing to the standard output stream.

PrintWriter

The PrintWriter class is a subclass of Writer that supports printing to the standard output stream.

PushbackInputStream

The PushbackInputStream class is a subclass of FilterInputStream that allows data that is read in to be pushed back onto the input stream.

PushbackReader

The PushbackReader class is a subclass of FilterReader that allows data that is read in to be pushed back onto the input source.

RandomAccessFile

The RandomAccessFile class is a subclass of Object that supports random file input and output. It implements the DataInput and DataOutput interfaces.

Reader

The Reader class is a subclass of Object that provides the basis for Unicode character input.

SequenceInputStream

The SequenceInputStream class is a subclass of InputStream that supports the concatenation of two or more input streams.

SerializablePermission

The SerializablePermission class is a subclass of java.security.BasicPermission that controls access to object serialization.

StreamTokenizer

The StreamTokenizer class is a subclass of Object that supports input stream parsing.

StringBufferInputStream

The StringBufferInputStream class is a subclass of InputStream that supports input from String objects.

StringReader

The StringReader class is a subclass of Reader that supports input from String objects.

StringWriter

The StringWriter class is a subclass of Writer that supports output to String objects.

Writer

The Writer class is a subclass of Object that provides the basis for Unicode character-based output.

Exceptions and Errors

CharConversionException

The CharConversionException class is a subclass of IOException that signals that an error occurred during character conversion.

EOFException

The EOFException class is a subclass of IOException that signals that the end of a file has been encountered.

FileNotFoundException

The FileNotFoundException class is a subclass of IOException that signals that a file cannot be located.

IOException

The IOException class is a subclass of java.lang.Exception that serves as the base class for defining I/O-based exceptions.

InterruptedIOException

The InterruptedIOException class is a subclass of IOException signals that an I/O operation has been interrupted.

InvalidClassException

The InvalidClassException class is a subclass of ObjectStreamException that signals that an invalid class was encountered during object serialization.

InvalidObjectException

The InvalidObjectException class is a subclass of ObjectStreamException that signals that an invalid object was encountered during object serialization.

NotActiveException

The NotActiveException class is a subclass of ObjectStreamException that signals that serialization is not active.

NotSerializableException

The NotSerializableException class is a subclass of ObjectStreamException that signals that an object is not serializable.

ObjectStreamException

The ObjectStreamException class is a subclass of IOException that serves as a base class for defining exceptions that occur during object I/O.

OptionalDataException

The OptionalDataException class is a subclass of ObjectStreamException that signals that additional data was encountered when reading an object from an input stream.

StreamCorruptedException

The StreamCorruptedException class is a subclass of ObjectStreamException that an object stream contains errors.

SyncFailedException

The SyncFailedException class is a subclass of IOException that synchronization of I/O could not take place.

UTFDataFormatException

The UTFDataFormatException class is a subclass of IOException that an invalid UTF-8 string was read.

UnsupportedEncodingException

The UnsupportedEncodingException class is a subclass of IOException that identifies the use of unsupported data encoding.

WriteAbortedException

The WriteAbortedException class is a subclass of ObjectStreamException indicating that the writing of an object was aborted.

Package `java.lang`

The java.lang package provides 28 classes and four interfaces that implement fundamental Java objects. Because of its importance, the java.lang package is included with all Java platforms, ranging from EmbeddedJava to the full-blown JDK. The java.lang package is covered in Chapter 10, "Writing Console Applications."

Interfaces

Cloneable

The Cloneable interface identifies a class as being cloneable by the clone() method of the Object class.

Comparable

The Comparable interface provides the compareTo() method for ordering the objects of a class.

Runnable

The Runnable interface identifies a class as being runnable as a separate thread.

Classes

Boolean

The Boolean class is a subclass of Object that wraps the primitive boolean type as a class. It implements the java.io.Serializable interface.

Byte

The Byte class is a subclass of Number that encapsulates a byte value. It implements the Comparable interface.

Character

The Character class is a subclass of Object that encapsulates a two-byte Unicode character value. It implements the Comparable and java.io.Serializable interfaces.

Character.Subset

The Character.Subset class is an inner class of Character that defines Unicode constants. It is a subclass of Object.

Character.UnicodeBlock

The Character.UnicodeBlock class extends Character.Subset to provide Unicode support.

Class

The Class class is a subclass of Object that is used to refer to classes as objects. It implements the java.io.Serializable interface.

ClassLoader

The ClassLoader class is a subclass of Object that is the base class for implementing custom class loaders for use with the runtime system.

Compiler

The Compiler class is a subclass of Object that is used to implement Just-In-Time (JIT) compilation.

Double

The Double class is a subclass of Number that encapsulates the double primitive type. It implements the Comparable interface.

Float

The Float class is a subclass of Number that encapsulates the float primitive type. It implements the Comparable interface.

InheritableThreadLocal

The InheritableThreadLocal class extends ThreadLocal to provide support for inheritance of thread values.

Integer

The Integer class is a subclass of Number that encapsulates the int primitive type. It implements the Comparable interface.

Long

The Math class is a subclass of Number that encapsulates the long primitive type. It implements the Comparable interface.

Math

The Math class is a subclass of Object that provides access to mathematical constants and functions.

Number

The Number class is a subclass of Object that is used as the base class for the wrapping of primitive numerical types. It implements the java.io.Serializable interface.

Object

The Object class is the highest class in the Java class hierarchy. It provides methods that are inherited by all Java classes.

Package

The Package class is a subclass of Object that is used to provide version information about a Java package.

Process

The Process class is a subclass of Object that is used to control external processes that are executed from within the Java runtime environment.

Runtime

The Runtime class is a subclass of Object that provides access to the Java runtime environment.

RuntimePermission

The RuntimePermission class is a subclass of java.security.BasicPermission that is used to control access to the runtime environment.

SecurityManager

The SecurityManager class is a subclass of Object that is used to implement a Java security policy.

Short

The Short class is a subclass of Number that encapsulates a short integer value. It implements the Comparable interface.

F

JDK 1.2 API
DESCRIPTION

String

The String class is a subclass of Object that encapsulates a growable Unicode text string. It implements the Comparable and java.io.Serializable interfaces.

StringBuffer

The StringBuffer class is a subclass of Object that provides a buffer for the implementation of String objects. It implements the java.io.Serializable interface.

System

The System class is a subclass of Object that provides access to operating system-specific resources.

Thread

The Thread class is a subclass of Object that provides the capability to create objects that run as separate threads. It implements the Runnable interface.

ThreadGroup

The ThreadGroup class is a subclass of Object that represents a collection of Thread objects.

ThreadLocal

The ThreadLocal class is a subclass of Object that provides variables that are local to a specific thread instance.

Throwable

The Throwable class is a subclass of Object that is the base class for all Java errors and exceptions. It implements the java.io.Serializable interface.

Void

The ArithmeticException class is a subclass of Object that represents the class of the void primitive type.

Exceptions and Errors

AbstractMethodError

The AbstractMethodError class is a subclass of IncompatibleClassChangeError that indicates an attempt to invoke an abstract method.

ArithmeticException

The ArithmeticException class is a subclass of RuntimeException that is used to signal an arithmetic error, such as divide by zero.

ArrayIndexOutOfBoundsException

The ArrayIndexOutOfBoundsException class is a subclass of IndexOutOfBoundsException that indicates that an array index has exceeded its legal range.

ArrayStoreException

The ArrayStoreException class is a subclass of RuntimeException that indicates an attempt to store the wrong type of object in an array.

ClassCastException

The ClassCastException class is a subclass of RuntimeException that indicates an attempt to perform an illegal object cast.

ClassCircularityError

The ClassCircularityError class is a subclass of LinkageError that indicates a circularity in a class definition.

ClassFormatError

The ClassFormatError class is a subclass of LinkageError that indicates an error in the format of a class's bytecode file.

ClassNotFoundException

The ClassNotFoundException class is a subclass of Exception that signals that the class loader is unable to locate a particular class.

CloneNotSupportedException

The CloneNotSupportedException class is a subclass of Exception that signals an attempt to clone an object that does not implement the Cloneable interface.

Error

The Error class is a subclass of Throwable that is the base class of all Java error classes.

Exception

The Exception class is a subclass of Throwable that is the base class of all Java exception classes.

ExceptionInInitializerError

The ExceptionInInitializerError class is a subclass of LinkageError that indicates the occurrence of an unexpected exception.

IllegalAccessError

The IllegalAccessError class is a subclass of IncompatibleClassChangeError that indicates an attempt to access a field or method that violates the access modifier assigned to the field or method.

IllegalAccessException

The IllegalAccessException class is a subclass of Exception that signals an illegal attempt to load a class.

IllegalArgumentException

The IllegalArgumentException class is a subclass of RuntimeException that indicates an illegal attempt to pass an argument.

IllegalMonitorStateException

The IllegalMonitorStateException class is a subclass of RuntimeException that signals an attempt to use a monitor without owning it.

IllegalStateException

The IllegalStateException class is a subclass of RuntimeException that signals that a method invocation occurred while the runtime environment was not in an appropriate state for the method invocation.

IllegalThreadStateException

The IllegalThreadStateException class is a subclass of IllegalArgumentException that signals that a thread is not in an appropriate state for a requested operation.

IncompatibleClassChangeError

The IncompatibleClassChangeError class is a subclass of LinkageError that indicates an incompatible change to a class definition has occurred.

IndexOutOfBoundsException

The IndexOutOfBoundsException class is a subclass of RuntimeException that indicates an index has exceeded its range.

InstantiationError

The `InstantiationError` class is a subclass of `IncompatibleClassChangeError` indicating that an attempt to instantiate an abstract class or interface has occurred.

InstantiationException

The `InstantiationException` class is a subclass of `Exception` that indicates an attempt to instantiate an abstract class or interface.

InternalError

The `InternalError` class is a subclass of `VirtualMachineError` that indicates an unexpected internal error has occurred in the virtual machine.

InterruptedException

The `InterruptedException` class is a subclass of `Exception` that is thrown when a thread is interrupted.

LinkageError

The `LinkageError` class is a subclass of `Error` that indicates a class has changed in such a way that dependencies on that class are no longer valid.

NegativeArraySizeException

The `NegativeArraySizeException` class is a subclass of `RuntimeException` that is thrown as the result of attempting to allocate an array of negative size.

NoClassDefFoundError

The `NoClassDefFoundError` class is a subclass of `LinkageError` that indicates that a class definition cannot be found.

NoSuchFieldError

The `NoSuchFieldError` class is a subclass of `IncompatibleClassChangeError` that indicates an attempt to access a field that no longer exists.

NoSuchFieldException

The `NoSuchFieldException` class is a subclass of `Exception` that indicates that a referenced field name does not exist.

NoSuchMethodError

The `NoSuchMethodError` class is a subclass of `IncompatibleClassChangeError` that indicates an attempt to access a method that no longer exists.

NoSuchMethodException

The `NoSuchMethodException` class is a subclass of `Exception` indicating that a referenced method name does not exist.

NullPointerException

The `NullPointerException` class is a subclass of `RuntimeException` that is thrown by the use of a `null` reference.

NumberFormatException

The `NumberFormatException` class is a subclass of `IllegalArgumentException` that is thrown when an attempt is made to convert a `String` object to a number and the object does not have a valid numeric representation.

OutOfMemoryError

The `OutOfMemoryError` class is a subclass of `VirtualMachineError` that indicates that the JVM is out of memory and no memory could be made available.

RuntimeException

The `RuntimeException` class is a subclass of `Exception` that serves as the base class for defining exceptions that occur at runtime during normal JVM operation.

SecurityException

The `SecurityException` class is a subclass of `RuntimeException` that is thrown by a security policy violation.

StackOverflowError

The `StackOverflowError` class is a subclass of `VirtualMachineError` that indicates that a stack overflow has occurred.

StringIndexOutOfBoundsException

The `StringIndexOutOfBoundsException` class is a subclass of `IndexOutOfBoundsException` that indicates an attempt to access an element of a `String` object that is outside the string's bounds.

ThreadDeath

The `ThreadDeath` class is a subclass of `Error` that is thrown after a thread is stopped.

UnknownError

The `UnknownError` class is a subclass of `VirtualMachineError` that indicates that an unknown error occurred in the JVM.

UnsatisfiedLinkError

The `UnsatisfiedLinkError` class is a subclass of `LinkageError` that signals an attempt to access a nonexistent native method.

UnsupportedClassVersionError

The `UnsupportedClassVersionError` class extends `ClassFormatError` to identify situations where the JVM does not support the version of Java used by a class file.

UnsupportedOperationException

The `UnsupportedOperationException` class is a subclass of `RuntimeException` that is thrown by an object to indicate that it does not support a particular method.

VerifyError

The `VerifyError` class is a subclass of `LinkageError` that is thrown when the verifier encounters an inconsistency in a class file that it is verifying.

VirtualMachineError

The `VirtualMachineError` class is a subclass of `Error` that indicates that the virtual machine is incapable of further processing.

Package `java.lang.ref`

The `java.lang.ref` package provides six classes that implement the new JDK 1.2 reference object capability. Reference objects are objects that are used to refer to other objects. They are similar to C and C++ pointers. The `java.lang.ref` package is covered in Chapter 10.

Interfaces

None.

Classes

PhantomReference

The `PhantomReference` class is a subclass of `Reference`. When the referent of a registered `PhantomReference` object is no longer strongly, guardedly, or weakly reachable, the `PhantomReference` object is cleared and added to the `ReferenceQueue` to which it is registered.

Reference

The Reference class is a subclass of Object that implements a reference to another object.

ReferenceQueue

The ReferenceQueue class is a subclass of Object that is used to collect Reference objects whose reachability has changed.

SoftReference

The SoftReference class is a subclass of Reference. An instance of this class is automatically cleared when memory is low and its referent is reachable only via soft references.

WeakReference

The WeakReference class is a subclass of Reference. When the referent of a registered WeakReference object is no longer strongly or guardedly reachable, the WeakReference object is cleared and added to the ReferenceQueue to which it is registered. The referent is then subject to finalization.

Exceptions and Errors

None.

Package `java.lang.reflect`

The java.lang.reflect package contains seven classes and one interface that provide the capability to implement runtime discovery of information about an object's class. The java.lang.reflect package is covered in Chapter 10.

Interfaces

Member

The Member interface is used to provide information that is reflected about a Field, Constructor, or Method.

Classes

AccessibleObject

The AccessibleObject class is a subclass of Object that is the superclass of the Constructor, Field, and Method classes. It was added to the class hierarchy in JDK 1.2 to provide the capability to specify whether an object suppresses reflection access control checks.

Array

The Array class is a subclass of Object that is used to obtain information about, create, and manipulate arrays.

Constructor

The Constructor class is a subclass of AccessibleObject that is used to obtain information about class constructors. It implements the Member interface.

Field

The Field class is a subclass of AccessibleObject that is used to obtain information about and access the field variables of a class. It implements the Member interface.

Method

The Method class is a subclass of Object that is used to obtain information about and access the methods of a class. It implements the Member interface.

Modifier

The Modifier class is a subclass of Object that is used to decode integers that represent the modifiers of classes, interfaces, field variables, constructors, and methods.

ReflectPermission

The ReflectPermission class is a subclass of java.security.BasicPermission that is used to specify whether the default language access checks should be suppressed for reflected objects.

Exceptions and Errors

InvocationTargetException

The InvocationTargetException class is a subclass of java.lang.Exception that wraps an exception thrown by an invoked method or constructor.

Package java.math

The java.math package provides two classes, BigDecimal and BigInteger, that provide the capability to perform arbitrary-precision arithmetic. This package is covered in Chapter 11, "Using the Utility and Math Packages."

Interfaces

None.

Classes

BigDecimal

The `BigDecimal` class is a subclass of `java.lang.Number` that provides the capability to perform arbitrary-precision decimal arithmetic. It implements the `java.lang.Comparable` interface.

BigInteger

The `BigInteger` class is a subclass of `java.lang.Number` that provides the capability to perform arbitrary-length integer arithmetic. It implements the `java.lang.Comparable` interface.

Exceptions and Errors

None.

Package `java.net`

The `java.net` package provides 20 classes and four interfaces for TCP/IP network programming. Six new classes are introduced with JDK 1.2. The `java.net` package is covered in Part 8, "Network Programming."

Interfaces

ContentHandlerFactory

The `ContentHandlerFactory` interface is implemented by classes that create `ContentHandler` objects.

FileNameMap

The `FileNameMap` interface is implemented by classes that map file names to MIME types.

SocketImplFactory

The `SocketImplFactory` interface is implemented by classes that create `SocketImpl` objects.

SocketOptions

The `SocketOptions` interface defines constants that can be used to tailor a socket configuration.

URLStreamHandlerFactory

The URLStreamHandlerFactory interface is implemented by classes that create URLStreamHandler objects.

Classes

Authenticator

The Authenticator class is a subclass of Object that is used to authenticate a network connection.

ContentHandler

The ContentHandler class is a subclass of Object that is used to handle downloaded content based on its MIME type.

DatagramPacket

The DatagramPacket class is a subclass of Object that is used to implement UDP socket communication.

DatagramSocket

The DatagramSocket class is a subclass of Object that is used for UDP communication.

DatagramSocketImpl

The DatagramSocketImpl class is a subclass of Object that is a base class for implementing connectionless socket-based communication.

HttpURLConnection

The HttpURLConnection class is a subclass of URLConnection that supports the Hypertext Transfer Protocol (HTTP).

InetAddress

The InetAddress class is a subclass of Object that encapsulates an IP address.

JarURLConnection

The JarURLConnection class is a subclass of URLConnection that is used to access a JAR file via a network connection.

MulticastSocket

The MulticastSocket class is a subclass of DatagramSocket that supports multicast communication.

NetPermission

The NetPermission class is a subclass of java.security.BasicPermission that supports network security policy implementation.

PasswordAuthentication

The PasswordAuthentication class is a subclass of Object that supports network authentication by password.

ServerSocket

The ServerSocket class is a subclass of Object that is used to implement the server side of client-server applications.

Socket

The Socket class is a subclass of Object that provides an encapsulation of the client side of TCP and UDP sockets.

SocketImpl

The SocketImpl class is a subclass of Object that is used to create custom socket implementations.

SocketPermission

The SocketPermission class is a subclass of java.security.Permission that is used to define socket-level access controls. It implements the java.io.Serializable interface.

URL

The URL class is a subclass of Object that encapsulates a Universal Resource Locator. It implements the java.lang.Comparable and java.io.Serializable interfaces.

URLClassLoader

The URLClassLoader class is a subclass of java.security.SecureClassLoader that is used to load classes from a location specified by a URL.

URLConnection

The URLConnection class is a subclass of Object that is used as a base class for implementing TCP connections to a URL-referenced resource.

URLDecoder

The URLDecoder class extends Object to support x-www-form-urlencoded decoding.

URLEncoder

The URLEncoder class is a subclass of Object that supports x-www-form-urlencoded encoding.

URLStreamHandler

The URLStreamHandler class is a subclass of Object that is used to support the development of stream-based protocol handlers.

Exceptions and Errors

Exceptions

BindException

The BindException class is a subclass of SocketException that indicates that an error occurred during socket binding.

ConnectException

The ConnectException class is a subclass of SocketException that indicates that an error occurred during socket connection.

MalformedURLException

The MalformedURLException class is a subclass of java.io.IOException that identifies the use of an incorrectly formed URL.

NoRouteToHostException

The NoRouteToHostException class is a subclass of SocketException that indicates that the network was not able to establish a route to a remote host.

ProtocolException

The ProtocolException class is a subclass of java.io.IOException indicating that an error occurred in the protocol stack.

SocketException

The SocketException class is a subclass of java.io.IOException that indicates that an error occurred in the underlying socket implementation.

UnknownHostException

The UnknownHostException class is a subclass of java.io.IOException that is thrown by a reference to a host whose IP address could not be resolved.

UnknownServiceException

The UnknownServiceException class is a subclass of java.io.IOException that is thrown by an attempt to use a network service that is unknown to the requestor.

Package java.rmi

The java.rmi package provides three classes and one interface that support basic remote method invocation (RMI) capabilities. It is covered in Chapter 38, "Building Distributed Applications with the java.rmi Packages," and Chapter 39, "Remote Method Invocation."

Interfaces

Remote

The Remote interface is used to identify an object as being remotely accessible. It does not define any constants or methods.

Classes

MarshalledObject

The MarshalledObject class is a subclass of Object that supports object persistence for remote object activation by representing method arguments and return values as serialized byte streams. It implements the java.io.Serializable interface.

Naming

The Naming class is a subclass of Object that provides static methods for accessing remote objects via RMI URLs. It is used to bind object names to the remote objects they represent.

RMISecurityManager

The RMISecurityManager class is a subclass of java.lang.SecurityManager that defines the default security policy used with remote objects. This class can be extended to implement custom RMI security policies.

Exceptions and Errors

AccessException

The AccessException class is a subclass of RemoteException that is used to signal an access violation.

AlreadyBoundException

The AlreadyBoundException class is a subclass of java.lang.Exception that is used to signal that a name has already been bound.

ConnectException

The ConnectException class is a subclass of RemoteException that signals that a connection was refused by the remote host.

ConnectIOException

The ConnectIOException class is a subclass of RemoteException that signals that an I/O error occurred during connection establishment.

MarshalException

The MarshalException class is a subclass of RemoteException that identifies that an error in object marshalling occurred.

NoSuchObjectException

The NoSuchObjectException class is a subclass of RemoteException that identifies an attempt to invoke a method on an object that is no longer available.

NotBoundException

The NotBoundException class is a subclass of java.lang.Exception that identifies an attempt to look up a name that has not been bound.

RMISecurityException

The RMISecurityException class is a subclass of java.lang.SecurityException that identifies that a security exception has occurred during RMI.

RemoteException

The RemoteException class is a subclass of java.io.IOException that serves as a base class for RMI-related exceptions.

ServerError

The ServerError class is a subclass of RemoteException that identifies that an error occurred on a remote server as the result of processing a method invocation.

ServerException

The ServerException class is a subclass of RemoteException that identifies that an exception occurred on a remote server as the result of processing a method invocation.

ServerRuntimeException

The ServerRuntimeException class is a subclass of RemoteException that identifies that a runtime exception occurred on a remote server as the result of processing a method invocation.

StubNotFoundException

The StubNotFoundException class is a subclass of RemoteException that identifies that the stub of a requested remote object has not been exported.

UnexpectedException

The UnexpectedException class is a subclass of RemoteException that identifies that an exception occurred during a remote method invocation that was not specified in the method's signature.

UnknownHostException

The UnknownHostException class is a subclass of RemoteException that identifies an attempt to access the registry of an unknown host.

UnmarshalException

The UnmarshalException class is a subclass of RemoteException that identifies that an error occurred in the unmarshalling of a marshalled object.

Package java.rmi.activation

The java.rmi.activation package supports persistent object references and remote object activation. It contains six classes and four interfaces. Chapter 39 shows how to work with these classes and interfaces.

Interfaces

ActivationInstantiator

The ActivationInstantiator interface is implemented by classes that create remotely activatable objects. It extends the Remote interface.

ActivationMonitor

The ActivationMonitor interface is implemented by classes that monitor the activation status of an ActivationGroup object. The ActivationGroup object notifies its ActivationMonitor when objects in the group change their activation status or when the group as a whole becomes inactive. ActivationMonitor extends the Remote interface.

ActivationSystem

The `ActivationSystem` interface is implemented by classes that support the registration of activatable objects and `ActivationGroup` objects. It extends the `Remote` interface.

Activator

The `Activator` interface is implemented by a class that activates classes whose objects are remotely activatable. The system `Activator` object is invoked by a faulting remote reference. It then initiates the activation of the object needed to complete the remote reference. It extends the `Remote` interface.

Classes

Activatable

The `Activatable` class is a subclass of `RemoteServer` that is the base class for developing remotely activatable classes. It is extended by classes that require remote activation or object persistence.

ActivationDesc

The `ActivationDesc` class is a subclass of `Object` that encapsulates the information needed to activate a remotely activatable object. This information includes the object's class name, activation group, code location, and initialization data. The `ActivationDesc` class implements the `java.io.Serializable` interface.

ActivationGroup

The `ActivationGroup` class is a subclass of `UnicastRemoteObject` that is used to manage a group of activatable objects. It implements the `ActivationInstantiator` interface.

ActivationGroupDesc

The `ActivationGroupDesc` class is a subclass of `Object` that encapsulates the information needed to activate an `ActivationGroup` object. This information includes the object's class name, code location, and initialization data. The `ActivationGroupDesc` class implements the `java.io.Serializable` interface.

ActivationGroupDesc.CommandEnvironment

The `ActivationGroupDesc.CommandEnvironment` class is an inner class of `ActivationGroupDesc` that supports the implementation of startup options for `ActivationGroup` objects.

ActivationGroupID

The `ActivationGroupID` class is a subclass of `Object` that uniquely identifies an `ActivationGroup` object as well as its `ActivationSystem` object. It implements the `java.io.Serializable` interface.

ActivationID

The `ActivationID` class is a subclass of `Object` that uniquely identifies a remotely activatable object as well as its `Activator` object. It implements the `java.io.Serializable` interface.

Exceptions and Errors

ActivateFailedException

The `ActivateFailedException` class is a subclass of `java.rmi.RemoteException` that identifies the failure to activate a remotely activatable object.

ActivationException

The `ActivationException` class is a subclass of `java.lang.Exception` that is the superclass of `UnknownGroupException` and `UnknownObjectException`.

UnknownGroupException

The `UnknownGroupException` class is a subclass of `ActivationException` that is generated by an attempt to activate an object from an unknown `ActivationGroup` object.

UnknownObjectException

The `UnknownObjectException` class is a subclass of `ActivationException` that is generated by an attempt to activate an object that is unknown to an `Activator` object.

Package `java.rmi.dgc`

The `java.rmi.dgc` package supports distributed garbage collection. It contains two classes and one interface and is covered in Chapter 38.

Interfaces

DGC

The `DGC` interface is implemented by the server side of the distributed garbage collector. It defines the `clean()` and `dirty()` methods for keeping track of which objects should be garbage-collected.

Classes

Lease

The Lease class is a subclass of Object that creates objects that are used to keep track of object references. It implements the java.io.Serializable interface.

VMID

The VMID class is a subclass of Object that implements an ID that uniquely identifies a Java virtual machine on a particular host. It implements the java.io.Serializable interface.

Exceptions and Errors

None.

Package `java.rmi.registry`

The java.rmi.registry package supports distributed registry operations. It contains one class and two interfaces. It is covered in Chapter 38.

Interfaces

Registry

The Registry interface provides methods for associating names with remotely accessible objects. It is implemented by classes that provide the RMI registry. It extends the Remote interface.

RegistryHandler

The RegistryHandler interface provides methods for accessing a Registry implementation. These methods have been deprecated in JDK 1.2.

Classes

LocateRegistry

The LocateRegistry class is a subclass of Object that provides methods for accessing the RMI registry on a particular host.

Exceptions and Errors

None.

Package `java.rmi.server`

The `java.rmi.server` package provides the low-level classes and interfaces that implement RMI. It contains 10 classes and 9 interfaces. It is covered in Chapter 38.

Interfaces

LoaderHandler

The `LoaderHandler` interface provides methods for working with RMI class loaders.

RMIFailureHandler

The `RMIFailureHandler` interface defines methods for handling RMI failure events.

RMIClientSocketFactory

The `RMIClientSocketFactory` interface provides access to client sockets for RMI calls.

RMIServerSocketFactory

The `RMIServerSocketFactory` interface provides access to server sockets for RMI calls.

RemoteCall

The `RemoteCall` interface defines methods for supporting a remote method invocation.

RemoteRef

The `RemoteRef` interface extends the `java.io.Externalizable` interface and provides methods for implementing a reference to a remote object.

ServerRef

The `ServerRef` interface extends the `RemoteRef` interface to provide a server-side reference to a remote object.

Skeleton

The `Skeleton` interface provides methods that are implemented by server-side skeletons.

Unreferenced

The `Unreferenced` interface provides methods that are implemented by a remote object to determine when the object is no longer remotely referenced.

Classes

LogStream

The LogStream class is a subclass of java.io.PrintStream that supports the logging of RMI errors.

ObjID

The ObjID class is a subclass of Object that uniquely identifies a remote object. It implements the java.io.Serializable interface.

Operation

The Operation class is a subclass of Object that encapsulates a remote method.

RMIClassLoader

The RMIClassLoader class is a subclass of Object that supports class loading during RMI.

RMISocketFactory

The RMISocketFactory class is a subclass of Object that is used to load custom RMI socket implementations.

RemoteObject

The RemoteObject class is a subclass of Object that is the base class for developing remote objects. It implements the Remote and java.io.Serializable interfaces.

RemoteServer

The RemoteServer class is a subclass of RemoteObject that is the base class for implementing an RMI server.

RemoteStub

The RemoteStub class is a subclass of RemoteObject that is the base class of all RMI stubs.

UID

The UID class is a subclass of Object that uniquely identifies an object on a particular host. It implements the java.io.Serializable interface.

UnicastRemoteObject

The UnicastRemoteObject class is a subclass of RemoteServer that provides a default RMI server implementation.

Exceptions and Errors

ExportException

The ExportException class is a subclass of java.rmi.RemoteException indicating that an error occurred during object export.

ServerCloneException

The ServerCloneException class is a subclass of java.rmi.RemoteException that indicates an attempt to clone a non-cloneable remote object.

ServerNotActiveException

The ServerNotActiveException class is a subclass of java.lang.Exception that indicates that the remote server is not currently active.

SkeletonMismatchException

The SkeletonMismatchException class is a subclass of java.rmi.RemoteException indicating that the skeleton of a remote object is inappropriate for the object being referenced.

SkeletonNotFoundException

The SkeletonNotFoundException class is a subclass of java.rmi.RemoteException that signals that the skeleton of a remote object cannot be located.

SocketSecurityException

The SocketSecurityException class is a subclass of ExportException that signals a socket operation that violates the current security policy.

Package java.security

The java.security package provides 39 classes and 8 interfaces that provide the foundation for the Security API. Refer to Chapter 3 and Chapter 8.

Interfaces

Certificate

The Certificate interface is a deprecated interface that provides support for digital certificates.

Guard

The Guard interface defines methods for objects that protect other objects.

Key

The Key interface extends the java.io.Serializable interface to encapsulate a cryptographic key.

Principal

The Principal interface provides methods for a subject that may have an identity.

PrivateKey

The PrivateKey interface extends the Key interface to provide support for a private key.

PrivilegedAction

The PrivilegedAction interface is used to perform privileged actions that do not throw checked exceptions.

PrivilegedExceptionAction

The PrivilegedExceptionAction interface is used to perform privileged actions that do throw checked exceptions.

PublicKey

The PublicKey interface extends the Key interface to provide support for a public key.

Classes

AccessControlContext

The AccessControlContext class is a subclass of Object that is used to make access control decisions.

AccessController

The AccessController class is a subclass of Object that implements security access controls.

AlgorithmParameterGenerator

The AlgorithmParameterGenerator class is a subclass of Object that generates parameters for use with cryptographic algorithms.

AlgorithmParameterGeneratorSpi

The AlgorithmParameterGeneratorSpi class is a subclass of Object that defines a service provider interface for an AlgorithmParameterGenerator class.

AlgorithmParameters

The AlgorithmParameters class is a subclass of Object that encapsulates parameters used with cryptographic algorithms.

AlgorithmParametersSpi

The AlgorithmParametersSpi class is a subclass of Object that provides a service provider interface for an AlgorithmParameters class.

AllPermission

The AllPermission class is a subclass of Permission that implies all other permissions.

BasicPermission

The BasicPermission class is a subclass of Permission that provides a base class for implementing permissions that use the same naming approach. It implements the java.io.Serializable interface.

CodeSource

The CodeSource class is a subclass of Object that identifies the location from which code is loaded. It implements the java.io.Serializable interface.

DigestInputStream

The DigestInputStream class is a subclass of java.io.FilterInputStream that is used to read a message digest.

DigestOutputStream

The DigestOutputStream class is a subclass of java.io.FilterOutputStream that is used to write a message digest.

GuardedObject

The GuardedObject class is a subclass of Object that is used to protect other objects. It implements the java.io.Serializable interface.

Identity

The Identity class is a subclass of Object that implements an identity used for making access control decisions. It implements the Principal and java.io.Serializable interfaces.

IdentityScope

The IdentityScope class is a subclass of Identity that defines the scope of an identity.

KeyFactory

The KeyFactory class is a subclass of Object that is used to create Key objects.

KeyFactorySpi

The KeyFactorySpi class is a subclass of Object that provides a service provider interface to a KeyFactory class.

KeyPair

The KeyPair class is a subclass of Object that encapsulates a public-private key pair.

KeyPairGenerator

The KeyPairGenerator class is a subclass of KeyPairGeneratorSpi that is used to create key pairs.

KeyPairGeneratorSpi

The KeyPairGeneratorSpi class is a subclass of Object that provides a service provider interface to a KeyPairGenerator object.

KeyStore

The KeyStore class is a subclass of Object that supports the management of cryptographic keys.

KeyStoreSpi

The KeyStoreSpi class extends Object to provide a service provider interface for the KeyStore class.

MessageDigest

The MessageDigest class is a subclass of MessageDigestSpi that implements a message digest.

MessageDigestSpi

The MessageDigestSpi class is a subclass of Object that provides a service provider interface to a MessageDigest class.

Permission

The Permission class is a subclass of Object that defines a permission to a protected resource. It implements the Guard and java.io.Serializable interfaces.

PermissionCollection

The `PermissionCollection` class is a subclass of `Object` that implements a collection of `Permission` objects. It implements the `java.io.Serializable` interface.

Permissions

The `Permissions` class is a subclass of `PermissionCollection` that supports a mixed collection of `Permission` objects. It implements the `java.io.Serializable` interface.

Policy

The `Policy` class is a subclass of `Object` that implements a Java security policy.

ProtectionDomain

The `ProtectionDomain` class is a subclass of `Object` that identifies a set of classes with the same permissions.

Provider

The `Provider` class is a subclass of `java.util.Properties` that implements a service provider.

SecureClassLoader

The `SecureClassLoader` class is a subclass of `java.lang.ClassLoader` that supports secure class loading.

SecureRandom

The `SecureRandom` class is a subclass of `java.util.Random` that provides secure random-number-generation capabilities.

SecureRandomSpi

The `SecureRandomSpi` class extends `Object` and implements `Serializable` to provide a service provider interface for the `SecureRandom` class.

Security

The `Security` class is a subclass of `Object` that provides common access to security-related objects.

SecurityPermission

The `SecurityPermission` class is a subclass of `BasicPermission` that defines security-related permissions.

Signature

The Signature class is a subclass of SignatureSpi that provides digital signature support.

SignatureSpi

The SignatureSpi class is a subclass of Object that provides a service provider interface to a Signature class.

SignedObject

The SignedObject class is a subclass of Object that represents an object that has been signed. It implements the java.io.Serializable interface.

Signer

The Signer class is a subclass of Identity that is capable of signing a signature-related object.

UnresolvedPermission

The UnresolvedPermission class is a subclass of Permission that does not have an accessible permission class. It implements the java.io.Serializable interface.

Exceptions and Errors

AccessControlException

The AccessControlException class is a subclass of SecurityException that indicates a violation of security access controls.

DigestException

The DigestException class is a subclass of GeneralSecurityException that is thrown by errors in message digest calculation.

GeneralSecurityException

The GeneralSecurityException class is a subclass of java.lang.Exception that is used as the base class for defining the security-related exceptions.

InvalidAlgorithmParameterException

The InvalidAlgorithmParameterException class is a subclass of GeneralSecurityException that indicates that an invalid parameter was supplied to a cryptographic algorithm.

InvalidKeyException

The `InvalidKeyException` class is a subclass of `KeyException` that indicates that an invalid key was supplied to a cryptographic algorithm.

InvalidParameterException

The `InvalidParameterException` class is a subclass of `IllegalArgumentException` indicating that an invalid parameter was supplied to a cryptographic algorithm.

KeyException

The `KeyException` class is a subclass of `GeneralSecurityException` that identifies an exception related to a cryptographic key.

KeyManagementException

The `KeyManagementException` class is a subclass of `KeyException` that identifies an exception in the management of keys.

KeyStoreException

The `KeyStoreException` class is a subclass of `GeneralSecurityException` that identifies an exception in the storage of keys.

NoSuchAlgorithmException

The `NoSuchAlgorithmException` class is a subclass of `GeneralSecurityException` indicating that a requested algorithm does not exist.

NoSuchProviderException

The `NoSuchProviderException` class is a subclass of `GeneralSecurityException` indicating that a requested service provider does not exist.

PrivilegedActionException

The `PrivilegedActionException` class extends `Exception` to indicate that the performance of a privileged action resulted in a checked exception.

ProviderException

The `ProviderException` class is a subclass of `java.lang.RuntimeException` that is generated by a service provider.

SignatureException

The `SignatureException` class is a subclass of `GeneralSecurityException` that identifies an exception occurring during signature calculation.

UnrecoverableKeyException

The UnrecoverableKeyException class is a subclass of GeneralSecurityException that signals that a key cannot be recovered from a key store.

Package java.security.acl

The java.security.acl package provides five interfaces that provide the basic elements for implementing security access controls. This package is covered in Chapter 8.

Interfaces

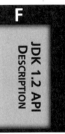

Acl

The Acl interface extends the Owner interface to define methods for classes that implement access control lists. An Acl object consists of zero or more AclEntry objects.

AclEntry

The AclEntry interface defines methods for an entry in an access control list. It identifies a set of permissions for a principal. It extends the java.lang.Cloneable interface.

Group

The Group interface extends the java.security.Principal interface to provide methods for working with a group of Principal objects. A Group object may also contain other Group objects.

Owner

The Owner interface defines methods for working with the owners of an access control list.

Permission

The Permission interface defines methods for implementing permissions to access-protected resources.

Classes

None.

Exceptions and Errors

AclNotFoundException

The AclNotFoundException class is a subclass of java.lang.Exception that signals a reference to a nonexistent access control list.

LastOwnerException

The LastOwnerException class is a subclass of java.lang.Exception that signals an attempt to delete the last owner of an access control list.

NotOwnerException

The NotOwnerException class is a subclass of java.lang.Exception that signals an attempt to modify an access control list by an object that is not its owner.

Package java.security.cert

The java.security.cert package provides four classes and one interface that implement digital certificates. It is covered in Chapter 8.

Interfaces

X509Extension

The X509Extension interface provides methods that encapsulate extensions defined for X.509 v3 certificates and v2 certificate revocation lists.

Classes

Certificate

The Certificate class is a subclass of Object that provides an abstract base class for implementing identity certificates.

CertificateFactory

The CertificateFactory class extends Object to provide a factory for creating certificates and certificate revocation lists.

CertificateFactorySpi

The CertificateFactorySpi class extends Object to provide a security provider interface for the CertificateFactory class.

CRL

The CRL class extends Object to provide an abstract implementation of a certificate revocation list.

X509CRLEntry

The X509CRLEntry class extends Object and implements the X509Extension interface to provide an abstract class for a revoked certificate in a CRL.

X509CRL

The X509CRL class is a subclass of Object that implements an X.509 certificate revocation list. It implements the X509Extension interface.

X509Certificate

The X509Certificate class is a subclass of Certificate that provides an abstract base class for implementing X.509 digital certificates.

Exceptions and Errors

CRLException

The CRLException class is a subclass of java.security.GeneralSecurityException that identifies an exception occurring in the processing of a certificate revocation list.

CertificateEncodingException

The CertificateEncodingException class is a subclass of CertificateException that identifies that an exception occurred during the encoding of a certificate.

CertificateException

The CertificateException class is a subclass of java.security.GeneralSecurityException that acts as a base class for other certificate-related exceptions.

CertificateExpiredException

The CertificateExpiredException class is a subclass of CertificateException that identifies that an expired certificate has been encountered.

CertificateNotYetValidException

The CertificateNotYetValidException class is a subclass of CertificateException that identifies that a certificate has been processed before its valid date range.

CertificateParsingException

The CertificateParsingException class is a subclass of CertificateException that indicates that an error occurred in the parsing of a certificate.

Package java.security.interfaces

The java.security.interfaces package provides five interfaces that support implementation of the NIST digital signature algorithm. It is covered in Chapter 8.

Interfaces

DSAKey

The DSAKey interface defines the getParams() method for accessing a Digital Signature Algorithm (DSA) public or private key.

DSAKeyPairGenerator

The DSAKeyPairGenerator interface is implemented by objects that can generate DSA key pairs.

DSAParams

The DSAParams interface defines methods for accessing a set of DSA key parameters.

DSAPrivateKey

The DSAPrivateKey interface extends the DSAKey and java.security.PrivateKey interfaces to provide access to a DSA private key.

DSAPublicKey

The DSAPublicKey interface extends the DSAKey and java.security.PublicKey interfaces to provide access to a DSA public key.

RSAPrivateCrtKey

The RSAPrivateCrtKey interface extends RSAPrivateKey with support for the Chinese Remainder Theorem.

RSAPrivateKey

The RSAPrivateKey interface extends PrivateKey to provide support for RSA private keys.

RSAPublicKey

The RSAPublicKey interface extends PublicKey to provide support for RSA public keys.

Classes

None.

Exceptions and Errors

None.

Package `java.security.spec`

The `java.security.spec` package provides six classes and two interfaces that provide specifications for cryptographic keys. It is covered in Chapter 8.

Interfaces

AlgorithmParameterSpec

The `AlgorithmParameterSpec` interface provides no constants or methods. It is used to identify an object that provides cryptographic algorithm parameters.

KeySpec

The `KeySpec` interface provides no constants or methods. It is used to identify an object that is a key for a cryptographic algorithm.

Classes

DSAParameterSpec

The `DSAParameterSpec` class is a subclass of `Object` that provides parameters for a Digital Signature Algorithm (DSA) implementation. It implements the `AlgorithmParameterSpec` and `java.security.interfaces.DSAParams` interfaces.

DSAPrivateKeySpec

The `DSAPrivateKeySpec` class is a subclass of `Object` that implements a private DSA key. It implements the `KeySpec` interface.

DSAPublicKeySpec

The `DSAPublicKeySpec` class is a subclass of `Object` that implements a public DSA key. It implements the `KeySpec` interface.

EncodedKeySpec

The `EncodedKeySpec` class is a subclass of `Object` that implements an encoded public or private key. It implements the `KeySpec` interface.

PKCS8EncodedKeySpec

The `PKCS8EncodedKeySpec` class is a subclass of `EncodedKeySpec` that represents the PKCS #8 standard encoding of a private key.

RSAPrivateCrtKeySpec

The `RSAPrivateCrtKeySpec` class extends `RSAPrivateKeySpec` to specify an RSA private key using Chinese Remainder Theorem values.

RSAPrivateKeySpec

The RSAPrivateKeySpec class extends Object and implements KeySpec to provide support for RSA private keys.

RSAPublicKeySpec

The RSAPublicKeySpec class extends Object and implements KeySpec to provide support for RSA public keys.

X509EncodedKeySpec

The X509EncodedKeySpec class is a subclass of EncodedKeySpec that represents the X.509 standard encoding of a public or private key.

Exceptions and Errors

InvalidKeySpecException

The InvalidKeySpecException class is a subclass of java.security.GeneralSecurityException that identifies an invalid key specification.

InvalidParameterSpecException

The InvalidParameterSpecException class is a subclass of java.security.GeneralSecurityException that identifies an invalid parameter specification.

Package java.sql

The java.sql package provides six classes and 16 interfaces that provide Java database connectivity. This package is covered in Part 10, "Database Programming."

Interfaces

Array

The Array interface provides a reference to an array that is stored by the database server.

Blob

The Blob interface provides a reference to a binary large object that is stored by the database server.

CallableStatement

The CallableStatement interface extends the PreparedStatement interface to provide support for stored procedures.

Clob

The Clob interface provides a reference to a character large object that is stored by the database server.

Connection

The Connection interface encapsulates a database connection.

DatabaseMetaData

The DatabaseMetaData interface provides access to information about the database itself.

Driver

The Driver interface encapsulates a database driver.

PreparedStatement

The PreparedStatement interface provides access to precompiled, stored SQL statements.

Ref

The Ref interface provides a reference to a stored SQL value.

ResultSet

The ResultSet interface encapsulates the results of a database query.

ResultSetMetaData

The ResultSetMetaData interface provides information about a ResultSet object.

SQLData

The SQLData interface provides support for mapping SQL and Java data types.

SQLInput

The SQLInput interface represents an input stream of a SQL UDT instance.

SQLOutput

The SQLOutput interface represents a SQL UDT output stream.

Statement

The Statement interface provides support for executing SQL statements.

Struct

The Struct interface encapsulates a SQL structured type.

StructLocator

The StructLocator interface provides a reference to a stored SQL structured type.

Classes

Date

The Date class is a subclass of java.util.Date that supports SQL date objects.

DriverManager

The DriverManager class is a subclass of Object that is used to manage database drivers.

DriverPropertyInfo

The DriverPropertyInfo class is a subclass of Object that provides information about a database driver.

Time

The Time class is a subclass of java.util.Time that supports SQL time objects.

Timestamp

The Timestamp class is a subclass of Object that encapsulates a SQL time stamp.

Types

The Types class is a subclass of Object that defines constants for use with SQL types.

Exceptions and Errors

BatchUpdateException

The BatchUpdateException class is a subclass of SQLException that signals the occurrence of errors during batch update operations.

DataTruncation

The DataTruncation class is a subclass of SQLWarning that indicates that a date value has been truncated.

SQLException

The SQLException class is a subclass of java.lang.Exception that serves as a base class for database exceptions.

SQLWarning

The SQLWarning class is a subclass of SQLException that signals warnings about database operations.

Package java.text

The java.text package provides 17 classes and four interfaces that support internationalization. The java.text package is covered in Chapter 19.

Interfaces

AttributedCharacterIterator

The AttributedCharacterIterator interface extends the CharacterIterator interface to provide support for iterating through text that is associated with style, internationalization, or other attributes.

CharacterIterator

The CharacterIterator interface provides internationalization support for bidirectional text iteration.

Classes

Annotation

The Annotation class is a subclass of Object that is used to work with text attribute values.

AttributedCharacterIterator.Attribute

The AttributedCharacterIterator.Attribute class extends Object and implements Serializable to define attribute keys that are used to identify text attributes.

AttributedString

The AttributedString class is a subclass of Object that encapsulates text and related attribute information.

BreakIterator

The BreakIterator class is a subclass of Object that provides support for identifying text-break boundaries. It implements the java.lang.Cloneable and java.io.Serializable interfaces.

ChoiceFormat

The `ChoiceFormat` class is a subclass of `NumberFormat` that allows number formatting to be associated with a range of numbers.

CollationElementIterator

The `CollationElementIterator` class is a subclass of `Object` that is used to iterate through international text strings.

CollationKey

The `CollationKey` class is a subclass of `Object` that is used to compare two `Collator` objects. It implements the `java.lang.Comparable` interface.

Collator

The `Collator` class is a subclass of `Object` that supports locale-specific string comparisons. It implements the `java.lang.Comparable`, `java.lang.Cloneable`, and `java.io.Serializable` interfaces.

DateFormat

The `DateFormat` class is a subclass of `Format` that provides international date formatting support.

DateFormatSymbols

The `DateFormatSymbols` class is a subclass of `Object` that provides support for locale-specific date formatting information. It implements the `java.lang.Cloneable` and `java.io.Serializable` interfaces.

DecimalFormat

The `DecimalFormat` class is a subclass of `Object` that provides international decimal point formatting support.

DecimalFormatSymbols

The `DecimalFormatSymbols` class is a subclass of `Object` that provides locale-specific decimal formatting information. It implements the `java.lang.Cloneable` and `java.io.Serializable` interfaces.

FieldPosition

The `FieldPosition` class is a subclass of `Object` that is used to identify fields in formatted output.

Format

The Format class is a subclass of Object that is the base class for international formatting support. It implements the java.lang.Cloneable and java.io.Serializable interfaces.

MessageFormat

The MessageFormat class is a subclass of Format that supports international message concatenation.

NumberFormat

The NumberFormat class is a subclass of Format that provides international number formatting support.

ParsePosition

The ParsePosition class is a subclass of Object that is used to keep track of the current parsing position.

RuleBasedCollator

The RuleBasedCollator class is a subclass of Collator that supports rule-based sorting.

SimpleDateFormat

The SimpleDateFormat class is a subclass of DateFormat that supports basic international date formatting.

StringCharacterIterator

The StringCharacterIterator class is a subclass of Object that provides a basic implementation of the CharacterIterator interface. It also implements the java.io.Serializable interface.

Exceptions and Errors

ParseException

The ParseException class is a subclass of java.lang.Exception that signals a parsing error.

Package `java.util`

The java.util package, like java.lang and java.io, is fundamental to any Java platform. It provides 34 classes and 13 interfaces that cover a wide variety of common programming needs. Most of the new classes and interfaces support the Collections API. The java.util package is covered in Chapter 11.

Interfaces

Collection

The Collection interface defines methods for working with arbitrary collections of objects.

Comparator

The Comparator interface defines methods for implementing a comparison function.

Enumeration

The Enumeration interface defines methods for working with an ordered collection of objects.

EventListener

The EventListener interface provides the basic interface to support Java event handling.

Iterator

The Iterator interface defines methods for iterating through an ordered collection.

List

The List interface extends the Collection interface to an ordered list of objects.

ListIterator

The ListIterator interface extends the Iterator interface to support iteration through a List object.

Map

The Map interface provides methods for mapping between two object sets.

Map.Entry

The Map.Entry interface defines methods for a single mapping element.

Observer

The Observer interface defines methods for observing the occurrence of an event, action, or processing.

Set

The Set interface extends the Collection interface to implement a collection in which each element occurs only once.

SortedMap

The SortedMap interface extends the Map interface to identify an ordering between the map elements.

SortedSet

The SortedSet interface extends the Set interface to order the collection of set elements.

Classes

AbstractCollection

The AbstractCollection class is a subclass of Object that provides an abstract implementation of the Collection interface.

AbstractList

The AbstractList class is a subclass of AbstractCollection that provides an abstract implementation of the List interface.

AbstractMap

The AbstractMap class is a subclass of Object that provides an abstract implementation of the Map interface.

AbstractSequentialList

The AbstractSequentialList class is a subclass of AbstractList that provides a sequential access data store.

AbstractSet

The AbstractSet class is a subclass of AbstractCollection that provides an abstract implementation of the Set interface.

ArrayList

The ArrayList class is a subclass of AbstractList that is implemented in terms of an array. It implements the List, java.lang.Cloneable, and java.io.Serializable interfaces.

Arrays

The Arrays class is a subclass of Object that provides support for array manipulation.

BitSet

The BitSet class is a subclass of Object that provides a growable vector of bits. It implements the java.lang.Cloneable and java.io.Serializable interfaces.

Calendar

The Calendar class is a subclass of Object that provides basic support for date, time, and calendar functions. It implements the java.lang.Cloneable and java.io.Serializable interfaces.

Collections

The Collections class is a subclass of Object that provides static methods for working with collections of objects.

Date

The Date class is a subclass of Object that provides basic date/time support. It implements the java.lang.Comparable, java.lang.Cloneable, and java.io.Serializable interfaces.

Dictionary

The Dictionary class is a subclass of Object that maps names to values.

EventObject

The EventObject class is a subclass of Object that provides the basic class from which most Java events are derived. It implements the java.io.Serializable interface.

GregorianCalendar

The GregorianCalendar class is a subclass of Calendar that implements a Gregorian calendar.

HashMap

The HashMap class is a subclass of AbstractMap that provides an implementation of the Map interface using a hash table. It implements the Map, java.lang.Cloneable, and java.io.Serializable interfaces.

HashSet

The HashSet class is a subclass of AbstractSet that implements the Set interface using a hash table. It implements the Set, java.lang.Cloneable, and java.io.Serializable interfaces.

Hashtable

The Hashtable class is a subclass of Dictionary that maps keys to their values. It implements the Map, java.lang.Cloneable, and java.io.Serializable interfaces.

LinkedList

The LinkedList class is a subclass of AbstractSequentialList that encapsulates a linked list data structure. It implements the List, java.lang.Cloneable, and java.io.Serializable interfaces.

ListResourceBundle

The ListResourceBundle class is a subclass of ResourceBundle that provides internationalization in the form of a list.

Locale

The Locale class is a subclass of Object that encapsulates a local region for internationalization purposes. It implements the java.lang.Cloneable and java.io.Serializable interfaces.

Observable

The Observable class is a subclass of Object that represents observable data in the model-view paradigm.

Properties

The Properties class is a subclass of Hashtable that represents a set of properties and property values.

PropertyPermission

The PropertyPermission class is a subclass of java.security.BasicPermission that implements access controls on system properties.

PropertyResourceBundle

The PropertyResourceBundle class is a subclass of ResourceBundle that manages internationalization resources using properties.

Random

The Random class is a subclass of Object that provides random-number generation capabilities. It implements the java.io.Serializable interface.

ResourceBundle

The ResourceBundle class is a subclass of Object that is used to manage internationalization resources.

SimpleTimeZone

The `SimpleTimeZone` class is a subclass of `TimeZone` that provides basic time zone information.

Stack

The `Stack` class is a subclass of `Vector` that implements a stack data structure.

StringTokenizer

The `StringTokenizer` class is a subclass of `Object` that supports the parsing of strings. It implements the `Enumeration` interface.

TimeZone

The `TimeZone` class is a subclass of `Object` that encapsulates the notion of a time zone. It implements the `java.lang.Cloneable` and `java.io.Serializable` interfaces.

TreeMap

The `TreeMap` class is a subclass of `AbstractMap` that provides a tree-based implementation of the `Map` interface. It implements the `SortedMap`, `java.lang.Cloneable`, and `java.io.Serializable` interfaces.

TreeSet

The `TreeSet` class is a subclass of `AbstractSet` that provides a tree-based implementation of the `Set` interface. It implements the `SortedSet`, `java.lang.Cloneable`, and `java.io.Serializable` interfaces.

Vector

The `Vector` class is a subclass of `AbstractList` that provides a growable array of objects. It implements the `List`, `java.lang.Cloneable`, and `java.io.Serializable` interfaces.

WeakHashMap

The `WeakHashMap` class extends `AbstractMap` and implements the `Map` interface to provide a hashtable-based `Map` implementation with weak keys.

Exceptions and Errors

ConcurrentModificationException

The `ConcurrentModificationException` class is a subclass of `java.lang.RuntimeException` that identifies invalid concurrent accesses to collections objects.

EmptyStackException

The EmptyStackException class is a subclass of java.lang.RuntimeException that signals an attempt to pop an object from an empty stack.

MissingResourceException

The MissingResourceException class is a subclass of java.lang.RuntimeException that signals an access to a missing resource.

NoSuchElementException

The NoSuchElementException class is a subclass of java.lang.RuntimeException that indicates an Enumeration contains no more elements.

TooManyListenersException

The TooManyListenersException class is a subclass of java.lang.Exception indicating that too many event listeners are associated with an event.

Package java.util.jar

The java.util.jar package provides seven classes for working with JAR files. It is covered in Chapter 11. Chapter 8 shows how to use the jar tool to create JAR files.

Interfaces

None.

Classes

Attributes

The Attributes class is a subclass of Object that maps Manifest attribute names to string values. It implements the java.util.Map and java.lang.Cloneable interfaces.

Attributes.Name

The Attributes.Name class is an inner class of Attributes that represents a specific attribute name of the Attributes map. It is a subclass of Object.

JarEntry

The JarEntry class is a subclass of java.util.zip.ZipEntry that represents an entry in a JAR file. It provides methods for reading the attributes and identities of JAR file entries.

JarFile

The `JarFile` class is a subclass of `java.util.zip.ZipFile` that is used to read JAR files. It supports reading of the manifest as well as individual JAR file entries.

JarInputStream

The `JarInputStream` class is a subclass of `java.util.zip.ZipInputStream` that is used to read a JAR file from an input stream.

JarOutputStream

The `JarOutputStream` class is a subclass of `java.util.zip.ZipOutputStream` that is used to write the contents of a JAR file to an output stream.

Manifest

The `Manifest` class is a subclass of `Object` that implements a JAR file manifest. It provides methods for accessing manifest names and their attributes. It implements the `java.lang.Cloneable` interface.

Exceptions and Errors

JarException

The `JarException` class is a subclass of `java.util.zip.ZipException` that is used to report errors that occur in the reading or writing of a JAR file.

Package `java.util.zip`

The `java.util.zip` package provides 14 classes and one interface for working with compressed files. It is covered in Chapter 11.

Interfaces

Checksum

The `Checksum` interface provides a common set of methods for classes that compute a checksum.

Classes

Adler32

The `Adler32` class is a subclass of `Object` that computes an Adler-32 checksum on an input stream. It implements the Checksum interface.

CRC32

The CRC32 class is a subclass of Object that computes an CRC-32 checksum on an input stream. It implements the Checksum interface.

CheckedInputStream

The CheckedInputStream class is a subclass of java.io.FilterInputStream that computes a checksum of the data being read.

CheckedOutputStream

The CheckedOutputStream class is a subclass of java.io.FilterOutputStream that computes a checksum of the data being written.

Deflater

The Deflater class is a subclass of Object that supports compression using the ZLIB compression library.

DeflaterOutputStream

The DeflaterOutputStream class is a subclass of java.io.FilterOutputStream that compresses stream output using the deflate format of the ZLIB compression library.

GZIPInputStream

The GZIPInputStream class is a subclass of InflatorInputStream that supports the reading of GZIP-compressed data.

GZIPOutputStream

The GZIPOutputStream class is a subclass of DeflatorOutputStream that supports the writing of GZIP-compressed data.

Inflater

The Inflater class is a subclass of Object that supports decompression using the ZLIB compression library.

InflaterInputStream

The InflaterInputStream class is a subclass of java.io.FilterIntputStream that decompresses stream input using the inflate format of the ZLIB compression library.

ZipEntry

The ZipEntry class is a subclass of Object that encapsulates a ZIP file entry. It implements the java.lang.Cloneable interface.

ZipFile

The ZipFile class is a subclass of Object that supports the reading of ZipEntry objects from ZIP files.

ZipInputStream

The ZipInputStream class is a subclass of InflaterInputStream that is used for reading streams that are in the compressed or uncompressed ZIP format.

ZipOutputStream

The ZipOutputStream class is a subclass of DeflaterOutputStream that is used to write compressed and uncompressed ZIP file entries to an output stream.

Exceptions and Errors

DataFormatException

The DataFormatException class is a subclass of java.lang.Exception that is used to identify the occurrence of a data format error during compression or decompression.

ZipException

The ZipException class is a subclass of java.io.IOException that signals an error in the reading or writing of a ZIP file or stream.

Package javax.accessibility

The javax. accessibility package provides seven classes and seven interfaces that support the use of assistive technologies for disabled users. It is covered in Chapter 9, "Creating Window Applications."

Interfaces

Accessible

The Accessible interface is implemented by all components that support accessibility. It defines the single getAccessibleContext() method to return an object that implements the AccessibleContext interface.

AccessibleAction

The AccessibleAction interface defines methods that can be used to determine which actions are supported by a component. It also provides methods for acccessing these actions.

AccessibleComponent

The AccessibleComponent interface defines methods for controlling the behavior and display of GUI components that support assistive technologies.

AccessibleHypertext

The AccessibleHypertext interface is implemented by GUI components that display hypertext. It supports assistive technologies for hypertext display.

AccessibleSelection

The AccessibleSelection interface provides support for determining which subcomponents of a GUI component have been selected, and for controlling the selection status of those components.

AccessibleText

The AccessibleText interface provides constants and methods for use with GUI components that display text. It allows assistive technologies to control the content, attributes, and layout of displayed text.

AccessibleValue

The AccessibleValue interface is implemented by GUI components that support the selection of a numerical value from a range of values, such as a scrollbar. This interface provides methods for getting and setting the numerical value and for determining the range of values.

Classes

AccessibleBundle

The AccessibleBundle class is a subclass of Object that provides access to resource bundles and supports string conversions.

AccessibleContext

The AccessibleContext class is a core accessibility API class and provides access to other assistive technology objects. It defines the information that is used by all accessible objects and is subclassed by objects that implement assistive technologies. It is a subclass of Object.

AccessibleHyperlink

The AccessibleHyperlink extends Object to provide accessibility support for a hyperlink or set of hyperlinks.

AccessibleResourceBundle

The `AccessibleResourceBundle` class is a subclass of `java.util.ListResourceBundle` that implements a resource bundle for assistive technology applications. It provides localized accessibility properties for a particular locale.

AccessibleRole

The `AccessibleRole` class is a subclass of `AccessibleBundle` that provides constants that describe the role of an accessibility GUI component, such as `LIST`, `MENU`, and `CHECK_BOX`.

AccessibleState

The `AccessibleState` class is a subclass of `AccessibleBundle` that describes the state of an accessibility object. `AccessibleState` objects are contained in `AccessibleStateSet` objects. The `AccessibleState` class provides constants that define common object states, such as `BUSY`, `CHECKED`, and `ENABLED`.

AccessibleStateSet

The `AccessibleStateSet` class is a subclass of `Object` that implements a collection of `AccessibleState` objects. `AccessibleStateSet` objects are used to define the overall state of an accessibility object.

Exceptions and Errors

None.

Package `javax.swing`

The `javax.swing` package is the core Swing package. It contains 90 classes and 22 interfaces that provide the foundation for the Swing API. This package is introduced in Chapter 12, "Introducing Swing."

Interfaces

Action

The `Action` interface extends the `java.awt.ActionListener` interface defines methods for defining, enabling, and disabling a unit of program operation.

BoundedRangeModel

The `BoundedRangeModel` interface defines a data model used for range-bounded components, such as sliders and progress bars.

ButtonModel

The ButtonModel interface extends the java.awt.ItemSelectable interface to provide methods that define the state of a button.

CellEditor

The CellEditor interface defines methods that are used to edit the cell values of GUI components, such as tables.

ComboBoxEditor

The ComboBoxEditor interface defines methods for editing combo boxes.

ComboBoxModel

The ComboBoxModel interface extends the ListModel interface and defines methods for supporting the data model of a combo box.

DesktopManager

The DesktopManager interface provides methods that are implemented by classes that support a Java-based desktop.

Icon

The Icon interface defines methods that are implemented by classes that provide desktop and application icons.

JComboBox.KeySelectionManager

The JComboBox.KeySelectionManager interface defines a key for selecting items from a combo box.

ListCellRenderer

The ListCellRenderer interface defines methods for painting the cells in a JList object.

ListModel

The ListModel interface defines methods that support the data model for a list.

ListSelectionModel

The ListSelectionModel interface defines methods for selecting elements from a list.

MenuElement

The MenuElement interface defines methods that are implemented by items that are placed in a menu.

MutableComboBoxModel

The MutableComboBoxModel interface extends the ComboBoxModel interface to provide update support.

Renderer

The Renderer interface defines methods for obtaining access to and setting the value of GUI components.

RootPaneContainer

The RootPaneContainer interface defines methods that are implemented by top-level window components.

ScrollPaneConstants

The ScrollPaneConstants interface defines constants that are used by scrollable pane classes.

Scrollable

The Scrollable interface defines methods that are implemented by scrollable container classes.

SingleSelectionModel

The SingleSelectionModel interface defines methods for selecting a single item from a list of items.

SwingConstants

The SwingConstants interface defines constants for laying out GUI components.

UIDefaults.ActiveValue

The UIDefaults.ActiveValue interface supports an active (preset) approach to defining user interface default values.

UIDefaults.LazyValue

The UIDefaults.LazyValue interface supports a lazy (as-needed) approach to defining user interface default values.

WindowConstants

The WindowConstants interface defines constants that are used in window operations.

Classes

AbstractAction

The AbstractAction class is a subclass of Object that provides a default implementation of the Action interface. It also implements the java.lang.Cloneable and java.io.Serializable interfaces.

AbstractButton

The AbstractButton class is a subclass of JComponent that serves as a base class for developing other JFC buttons. It implements the SwingConstants and java.awt.ItemSelectable interfaces.

AbstractListModel

The AbstractListModel class is a subclass of Object that provides an abstract data model for list-related classes. It implements the ListModel and java.io.Serializable interfaces.

BorderFactory

The BorderFactory class is a subclass of Object that provides support for creating Border objects.

Box

The Box class is a subclass of java.awt.Container that lays out components in a BoxLayout. It implements the java.awt.accessibility.Accessible interface.

Box.Filler

The Box.Filler class is an inner class of Box that supports the layout of Box objects. It is a subclass of java.awt.Component.

BoxLayout

The BoxLayout class is a subclass of Object that supports the layout of containers in a box-like, top-to-bottom, left-to-right fashion. It implements the java.awt.LayoutManager2 and java.io.Serializable interfaces.

ButtonGroup

The ButtonGroup class is a subclass of Object that supports the development of radio button-like button groups in which only one button in the group can be selected at a time. It implements the java.io.Serializable interface.

CellRendererPane

The CellRendererPane class is a subclass of java.awt.Container that supports the organization of cell-oriented components, such as lists and tables. It implements the java.awt.accessibility.Accessible interface.

DebugGraphics

The DebugGraphics class is a subclass of java.awt.Graphics that provides debugging support.

DefaultBoundedRangeModel

The DefaultBoundedRangeModel class is a subclass of Object that provides a default implementation of the BoundedRangeModel interface. It also implements the java.io.Serializable interface.

DefaultButtonModel

The DefaultButtonModel class is a subclass of Object that provides a default implementation of the ButtonModel interface. It also implements the java.io.Serializable interface.

DefaultCellEditor

The DefaultCellEditor class is a subclass of Object that provides a default implementation of the javax.swing.table.TableCellEditor and javax.swing.tree.TreeCellEditor interfaces. It also implements the java.io.Serializable interface.

DefaultComboBoxModel

The DefaultComboBoxModel class is a subclass of AbstractListModel and implements the MutableComboBoxModel and java.io.Serializable interfaces. It provides a default model for combo boxes.

DefaultDesktopManager

The DefaultDesktopManager class is a subclass of Object that provides a default implementation of the DesktopManager interface.

DefaultFocusManager

The DefaultFocusManager class is a subclass of FocusManager that provides support for accessing the components governed by the focus manager.

DefaultListCellRenderer

The DefaultListCellRenderer class extends JLabel and implements the ListCellRenderer and Serializable interfaces to provide a default rendering for a list cell.

DefaultListCellRenderer.UIResource

The DefaultListCellRenderer.UIResource class is an inner class of DefaultListCellRenderer that implements the UIResource interface.

DefaultListModel

The DefaultListModel class is a subclass of AbstractListModel that provides support for managing the addition and deletion of list elements.

DefaultListSelectionModel

The DefaultListSelectionModel class is a subclass of Object that provides a default implementation of the ListSelectionModel interface. It also implements the java.lang.Cloneable and java.io.Serializable interfaces.

DefaultSingleSelectionModel

The DefaultSingleSelectionModel class is a subclass of Object that provides a default implementation of the SingleSelectionModel interface. It also implements the java.io.Serializable interface.

FocusManager

The FocusManager class is a subclass of Object that is used to manage the current input focus.

GrayFilter

The GrayFilter class is a subclass of java.awt.image.RGBImageFilter that provides a grayscale rendering of an image.

ImageIcon

The ImageIcon class is a subclass of Object that provides a default implementation of the Icon interface. It also implements the java.io.Serializable interface.

JApplet

The JApplet class is a subclass of java.applet.Applet that provides Swing support. It implements the java.awt.accessibility.Accessible and RootPaneContainer interfaces.

JButton

The JButton class is a subclass of AbstractButton that provides a Swing pushbutton. It implements the java.awt.accessibility.Accessible interface.

JCheckBox

The JCheckBox class is a subclass of JToggleButton that provides a Swing checkbox. It implements the java.awt.accessibility.Accessible interface.

JCheckBoxMenuItem

The JCheckBoxMenuItem class is a subclass of JMenuItem that implements a checkbox that can be used as a menu item. It implements the SwingConstants and java.awt.accessibility.Accessible interfaces.

JColorChooser

The JColorChooser class extends JComponent and implements the Accessible interface. It provides the capability for users to select a color from a color selection panel.

JComboBox

The JComboBox class is a subclass of JComponent that provides a combo box GUI component. It implements the java.awt.ItemSelectable, java.awt.event.ActionListener, javax.swing.event.ListDataListener, and java.awt.accessibility.Accessible interfaces.

JComponent

The JComponent class is a subclass of java.awt.Container that is the base class for all Swing components. It implements the java.io.Serializable interface.

JDesktopPane

The JDesktopPane class is a subclass of JLayeredPane that supports the implementation of a desktop manager. It implements the java.awt.accessibility.Accessible interface.

JDialog

The JDialog class is a subclass of java.awt.Dialog that provides a Swing dialog box. It implements the RootPaneContainer, WindowConstants, and java.awt.accessibility.Accessible interface.

JEditorPane

The JEditorPane class is a subclass of JTextComponent that supports text editing.

JFileChooser

The JFileChooser class extends JComponent and implements the Accessible interface. It allows a user to select a file from a file chooser panel.

JFrame

The JFrame class is a subclass of java.awt.Frame that adds Swing support. It implements the RootPaneContainer, WindowConstants, and java.awt.accessibility.Accessible interfaces.

JInternalFrame

The JInternalFrame class is a subclass of JComponent that provides a frame that can be used within a JDesktopPane object. It implements the RootPaneContainer, WindowConstants, java.awt.accessibility.Accessible, java.awt.event.ComponentListener, java.awt.event.MouseListener, and java.awt.event.MouseMotionListener interfaces.

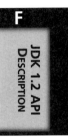

JInternalFrame.JDesktopIcon

The JInternalFrame.JDesktopIcon class is an inner class of JInternalFrame that provides an icon for use with the JInternalFrame object. It is a subclass of JComponent and implements the java.awt.accessibility.Accessible interface.

JLabel

The JLabel class is a subclass of JComponent that provides a Swing label (text or image). It implements the SwingConstants and java.awt.accessibility.Accessible interfaces.

JLayeredPane

The JLayeredPane class is a subclass of JComponent that provides a multi-layered pane. It implements the java.awt.accessibility.Accessible interface.

JList

The JList class is a subclass of JComponent that provides a basic list component. It implements the Scrollable and java.awt.accessibility.Accessible interfaces.

JMenu

The JMenu class is a subclass of JMenuItem that provides a Swing menu. It implements the MenuElement and java.awt.accessibility.Accessible interfaces.

JMenuBar

The `JMenuBar` class is a subclass of `JComponent` that provides a Swing menu bar. It implements the `MenuElement` and `java.awt.accessibility.Accessible` interfaces.

JMenuItem

The `JMenuItem` class is a subclass of `AbstractButton` that provides a Swing menu item. It implements the `MenuElement` and `java.awt.accessibility.Accessible` interfaces.

JOptionPane

The `JOptionPane` class is a subclass of `JComponent` that provides support for option dialog boxes.

JPanel

The `JPanel` class is a subclass of `JComponent` that provides a generic Swing panel. It implements the `java.awt.accessibility.Accessible` interface.

JPasswordField

The `JPasswordField` class is a subclass of `JTextField` that provides the capability to enter a password without it being displayed.

JPopupMenu

The `JPopupMenu` class is a subclass of `JComponent` that provides a popup menu capability. It implements the `java.awt.accessibility.Accessible` and `MenuElement` interfaces.

JPopupMenu.Separator

The `JPopupMenu.Separator` class is an inner class of `JPopupMenu` that provides accessibility support. It implements a menu separator.

JProgressBar

The `JProgressBar` class is a subclass of `JComponent` that provides a vertical or horizontal progress bar. It implements the `SwingConstants` and `java.awt.accessibility.Accessible` interfaces.

JRadioButton

The `JRadioButton` class is a subclass of `JToggleButton` that provides a basic radio button. It implements the `java.awt.accessibility.Accessible` interface.

JRadioButtonMenuItem

The `JRadioButtonMenuItem` class is a subclass of `JComponent` that provides the root pane for window container operations. It implements the `java.awt.accessibility.Accessible` interface.

JScrollBar

The `JScrollBar` class is a subclass of `JComponent` that provides a basic scrollbar. It implements the `java.awt.Adjustible` and `java.awt.accessibility.Accessible` interfaces.

JScrollPane

The `JScrollPane` class is a subclass of `JComponent` that provides a scrollable panel. It implements the `ScrollPaneConstants` and `java.awt.accessibility.Accessible` interfaces.

JSeparator

The `JSeparator` class is a subclass of `JComponent` that provides a menu separator. It implements the `java.awt.accessibility.Accessible` interface.

JSlider

The `JSlider` class is a subclass of `JComponent` that provides a slider control. It implements the `SwingConstants` and `java.awt.accessibility.Accessible` interfaces.

JSplitPane

The `JSplitPane` class is a subclass of `JComponent` that is used to split exactly two components. It implements the `java.awt.accessibility.Accessible` interface.

JTabbedPane

The `JTabbedPane` class is a subclass of `JComponent` that provides a tabbed multi-layer pane. It implements the `SwingConstants`, `java.io.Serializable`, and `java.awt.accessibility.Accessible` interfaces.

JTable

The `JTable` class is a subclass of `JComponent` that provides a basic table implementation. It implements the `Scrollable`, `java.awt.accessibility.Accessible`, `javax.swing.event.TableModelListener`, `javax.swing.event.TableColumnModelListener`, `javax.swing.event.ListSelectionListener`, and `javax.swing.event.CellEditorListener` interfaces.

JTextArea

The JTextArea class is a subclass of JTextComponent that provides a Swing text area component.

JTextField

The JTextField class is a subclass of JTextComponent that provides a Swing text field. It implements the SwingConstants interface.

JTextPane

The JTextPane class is a subclass of JEditorPane that supports styled text.

JToggleButton

The JToggleButton class is a subclass of AbstractButton that supports a two-state button. It implements the java.awt.accessibility.Accessible interface.

JToggleButton.ToggleButtonModel

The JToggleButton.ToggleButtonModel class is an inner class of JToggleButton that supports button configuration. It is a subclass of DefaultButtonModel.

JToolBar

The JToolBar class is a subclass of JComponent that provides a basic tool bar. It implements the java.awt.accessibility.Accessible interface.

JToolBar.Separator

The JToolBar.Separator class is an inner class of JToolBar that acts as a toolbar separator. It is a subclass of java.awt.Component.

JToolTip

The JToolTip class is a subclass of JComponent that provides a popup tool tip. It implements the java.awt.accessibility.Accessible interface.

JTree

The JTree class is a subclass of JComponent that provides a basic tree component. It implements the Scrollable and java.awt.accessibility.Accessible interfaces.

JTree.DynamicUtilTreeNode

The JTree.DynamicUtilTreeNode class is an inner class of JTree that supports dynamic tree node management. It is a subclass of DefaultMutableTreeNode.

JTree.EmptySelectionModel

The JTree.EmptySelectionModel class is an inner class of JTree that supports tree selection. It is a subclass of DefaultTreeSelectionModel.

JViewport

The JViewport class is a subclass of JComponent that acts as a porthole for viewing displayed information. It implements the java.awt.accessibility.Accessible interface.

JWindow

The JWindow class is a subclass of java.awt.Window that provides Swing support. It implements the RootPaneContainer and java.awt.accessibility.Accessible interfaces.

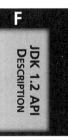

KeyStroke

The KeyStroke class is a subclass of Object that implements a user-typed keystroke. It implements the java.io.Serializable interface.

LookAndFeel

The LookAndFeel class is a subclass of Object that supports pluggable look and feel.

MenuSelectionManager

The MenuSelectionManager class is a subclass of Object that supports the management of menu selections.

OverlayLayout

The OverlayLayout class is a subclass of Object that supports overlay-type container layout. It implements the java.awt.LayoutManager2 and java.io.Serializable interfaces.

ProgressMonitor

The ProgressMonitor class is a subclass of Object that supports the monitoring of an operation in progress.

ProgressMonitorInputStream

The ProgressMonitorInputStream class is a subclass of java.io.FilterInputStream that supports the monitoring of data that is read from an input stream.

RepaintManager

The RepaintManager class is a subclass of Object that supports the repainting of JComponent objects.

ScrollPaneLayout

The ScrollPaneLayout class is a subclass of Object that is used to lay out a JScrollPane object. It implements the ScrollPaneConstants, java.awt.LayoutManager, and java.io.Serializable interfaces.

ScrollPaneLayout.UIResource

The ScrollPaneLayout.UIResource class is an inner class of ScrollPaneLayout that provides access to a UIResource.

SizeRequirements

The SizeRequirements class is a subclass of Object that provides information used by layout managers. It implements the java.io.Serializable interface.

SwingUtilities

The SwingUtilities class is a subclass of Object that provides general static methods that are used by Swing components. It implements the SwingConstants interface.

Timer

The Timer class is a subclass of Object that provides a timer/event generator. It implements the java.io.Serializable interface.

ToolTipManager

The ToolTipManager class is a subclass of java.awt.event.MouseAdapter that is used to provide tool tip support. It implements the java.awt.event.MouseMotionListener interface.

UIDefaults

The UIDefaults class is a subclass of java.util.Hashtable that supports the storage of user interface parameter information.

UIManager

The UIManager class is a subclass of Object that supports look and feel management. It implements the java.io.Serializable interface.

UIManager.LookAndFeelInfo

The UIManager.LookAndFeelInfo class is an inner class of UIManager that supports the storage of look and feel information. It is a subclass of Object.

ViewportLayout

The ViewportLayout class is a subclass of Object that supports the layout of JViewport objects. It implements the java.awt.LayoutManager and java.io.Serializable interfaces.

Exceptions and Errors

UnsupportedLookAndFeelException

The UnsupportedLookAndFeelException class is a subclass of java.lang.Exception that signals that an unsupported look and feel has been selected.

Package javax.swing.border

The javax.swing.border package provides nine classes and one interface that implement borders and border styles. It is covered in Chapter 13, "Working with Swing Components."

Interfaces

Border

The Border interface provides methods for rendering a border around a Swing component.

Classes

AbstractBorder

The AbstractBorder class is a subclass of Object that provides an abstract base class used to implement other javax.swing.border classes. It implements the Border and java.io.Serializable interfaces.

BevelBorder

The BevelBorder class is a subclass of AbstractBorder that implements a two-line bevel border.

CompoundBorder

The CompoundBorder class is a subclass of AbstractBorder that combines two Border objects into a single border.

EmptyBorder

The EmptyBorder class is a subclass of AbstractBorder that implements an empty, spaceless border. It implements the java.io.Serializable interface.

EtchedBorder

The EtchedBorder class is a subclass of AbstractBorder that implements an etched border. The border can be etched either in or out.

LineBorder

The LineBorder class is a subclass of AbstractBorder that draws a line border around an object. The line thickness and color of the border may be specified.

MatteBorder

The MatteBorder class is a subclass of EmptyBorder that implements a matte-like border. The border can consist of a specified color or a javax.swing.Icon object.

SoftBevelBorder

The SoftBevelBorder class is a subclass of BevelBorder that implements a bevel border with softened (rounded) corners. The beveling may be raised or lowered.

TitledBorder

The TitledBorder class is a subclass of AbstractBorder that specifies a text tile at a specified position on the border.

Exceptions and Errors

None.

Package javax.swing.colorchooser

The javax.swing.colorchooser package provides three classes and one interface that support color selection. It is covered in Chapters 12 through 14.

Interfaces

ColorSelectionModel

The ColorSelectionModel interface defines methods that support the selection of colors.

Classes

AbstractColorChooserPanel

The `AbstractColorChooserPanel` class extends `JPanel` to provide an abstract class for the implementation of color choosers.

ColorChooserComponentFactory

The `ColorChooserComponentFactory` class extends `Object` to provide a factory for the generation of components used in color choosers.

DefaultColorSelectionModel

The `DefaultColorSelectionModel` class extends `Object` and implements the `ColorSelectionModel` and `Serializable` interfaces. It provides a base class for the implementation of color selection models.

Exceptions and Errors

None.

Package `javax.swing.event`

The `javax.swing.event` package provides 23 classes and 23 interfaces that implement Swing events and event listeners. It is covered in Chapters 12 and 13.

Interfaces

AncestorListener

The `AncestorListener` interface extends the `java.util.EventListener` interface to support handling of the `AncestorEvent`.

CaretListener

The `CaretListener` interface extends the `java.util.EventListener` interface to support handling of the `CaretEvent`.

CellEditorListener

The `CellEditorListener` interface extends the `java.util.EventListener` interface to support table cell editing by the handling of the `ChangeEvent`.

ChangeListener

The `ChangeListener` interface extends the `java.util.EventListener` interface to support general handling of the `ChangeEvent`.

DocumentEvent

The DocumentEvent interface provides methods for handling document change notifications.

DocumentEvent.ElementChange

The DocumentEvent.ElementChange interface provides methods for handling changes made to a document element.

DocumentListener

The DocumentListener interface extends the java.util.EventListener interface to support handling of the DocumentEvent.

HyperlinkListener

The HyperlinkListener interface extends the java.util.EventListener interface to support handling of the HyperlinkEvent.

InternalFrameListener

The InternalFrameListener interface extends the java.util.EventListener interface to support handling of the InternalFrameEvent.

ListDataListener

The Listener interface extends the java.util.EventListener interface to support handling of the ListDataEvent.

ListSelectionListener

The ListSelectionListener interface extends the java.util.EventListener interface to support handling of the ListSelectionEvent.

MenuDragMouseListener

The MenuDragMouseListener interface extends EventListener to provide support for the MenuDragMouseEvent.

MenuKeyListener

The MenuKeyListener interface extends EventListener to provide support for the MenuKeyEvent.

MenuListener

The MenuListener interface extends the java.util.EventListener interface to support handling of the MenuEvent.

MouseInputListener

The MouseInputListener interface extends MouseListener and MouseMotionListener to support a combined mouse event handler.

PopupMenuListener

The PopupMenuListener interface extends the java.util.EventListener interface to support handling of the PopupMenuEvent.

TableColumnModelListener

The TableColumnModelListener interface extends the java.util.EventListener interface to support handling of the TableColumnModelEvent.

TableModelListener

The TableModelListener interface extends the java.util.EventListener interface to support handling of the TableModelEvent.

TreeExpansionListener

The TreeExpansionListener interface extends the java.util.EventListener interface to support handling of the TreeExpansionEvent.

TreeModelListener

The TreeModelListener interface extends the java.util.EventListener interface to support handling of the TreeModelEvent.

TreeSelectionListener

The TreeSelectionListener interface extends the java.util.EventListener interface to support handling of the TreeSelectionEvent.

TreeWillExpandListener

The TreeWillExpandListener interface extends the java.util.EventListener interface to support handling of the TreeExpansionEvent.

UndoableEditListener

The UndoableEditListener interface extends the java.util.EventListener interface to support handling of the UndoableEditEvent.

Classes

AncestorEvent

The AncestorEvent class is a subclass of java.AWT.AWTEvent that indicates changes in a component's ancestor.

CaretEvent

The CaretEvent class is a subclass of java.util.EventObject that indicates a change in the text caret.

ChangeEvent

The ChangeEvent class is a subclass of java.util.EventObject that indicates a change in the state of a component.

DocumentEvent.EventType

The DocumentEvent.EventType class is a subclass of Object that is used to enumerate the types of document events.

EventListenerList

The EventListenerList class is a subclass of Object that provides a list of EventListener objects. It implements the java.io.Serializable interface.

HyperlinkEvent

The HyperlinkEvent class is a subclass of java.util.EventObject that indicates an action with respect to a hypertext link.

HyperlinkEvent.EventType

The HyperlinkEvent.EventType class is an inner class of HyperlinkEvent that enumerates the types of hyperlink events.

InternalFrameAdapter

The InternalFrameAdapter class is a subclass of Object that provides a default implementation of the InternalFrameListener interface.

InternalFrameEvent

The InternalFrameEvent class is a subclass of java.awt.AWTEvent that provides events related to javax.swing.JInternalFrame objects.

ListDataEvent

The ListDataEvent class is a subclass of java.util.EventObject that identifies changes in list-type components.

ListSelectionEvent

The ListSelectionEvent class is a subclass of java.util.EventObject that identifies changes in the current list selection.

MenuDragMouseEvent

The MenuDragMouseEvent class extends MouseEvent to provide support for menu-related drag-and-drop operations.

MenuEvent

The MenuEvent class is a subclass of java.util.EventObject that is used to signal menu-related events.

MenuKeyEvent

The MenuKeyEvent class is a subclass of KeyEvent that supports menu-related key actions.

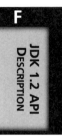

MouseInputAdapter

The MouseInputAdapter class is a subclass of Object that provides a default implementation of the MouseInputListener interface.

PopupMenuEvent

The PopupMenuEvent class is a subclass of java.util.EventObject that is used to signal popup menu-related events.

SwingPropertyChangeSupport

The SwingPropertyChangeSupport class extends java.beans.PropertyChangeSupport to provide Swing support.

TableColumnModelEvent

The TableColumnModelEvent class is a subclass of java.util.EventObject that is used to identify changes in a table column model.

TableModelEvent

The TableModelEvent class is a subclass of java.util.EventObject that is used to identify changes in a table model.

TreeExpansionEvent

The TreeExpansionEvent class is a subclass of java.util.EventObject that indicates that a tree has been expanded.

TreeModelEvent

The TreeModelEvent class is a subclass of java.util.EventObject that is used to signal a change in a tree model.

TreeSelectionEvent

The TreeSelectionEvent class is a subclass of java.util.EventObject that is used to signal a change in the current tree selection. It implements the java.lang.Cloneable interface.

UndoableEditEvent

The UndoableEditEvent class is a subclass of java.util.EventObject indicating that an operation that can be undone has been performed.

Exceptions and Errors

None.

Package javax.swing.filechooser

The javax.swing.filechooser package provides three classes and no interfaces that support basic file system operations. It is covered in Chapters 12 through 14.

Interfaces

None.

Classes

FileFilter

The FileFilter class extends Object to provide an abstract class for file filtering operations.

FileSystemView

The FileSystemView class extends Object to provide a default file system view.

FileView

The FileView class extends Object to provide a default information about a file.

Exceptions and Errors

None.

Package `javax.swing.plaf`

The `javax.swing.` `plaf` package provides 42 classes and one interface that support pluggable look-and-feel. It is covered in Chapters 12 through 14.

Interfaces

UIResource

The `UIResource` interface is used to identify an object as supporting pluggable look-and-feel.

Classes

BorderUIResource

The `BorderUIResource` class extends `Object` and implements the `Border`, `UIResource`, and `Serializable` interfaces to define a `UIResource` for `Border` objects.

BorderUIResource.BevelBorderUIResource

The `BorderUIResource.BevelBorderUIResource` class extends `BevelBorder` and implements `UIResource` to support pluggable look-and-feel.

BorderUIResource.CompoundBorderUIResource

The `BorderUIResource.CompoundBorderUIResource` class extends `CompoundBorder` and implements `UIResource` to support pluggable look-and-feel.

BorderUIResource.EmptyBorderUIResource

The `BorderUIResource.EmptyBorderUIResource` class extends `EmptyBorder` and implements `UIResource` to support pluggable look-and-feel.

BorderUIResource.EtchedBorderUIResource

The `BorderUIResource.EtchedBorderUIResource` class extends `EtchedBorder` and implements `UIResource` to support pluggable look-and-feel.

BorderUIResource.LineBorderUIResource

The `BorderUIResource.LineBorderUIResource` class extends `LineBorder` and implements `UIResource` to support pluggable look-and-feel.

BorderUIResource.MatteBorderUIResource

The `BorderUIResource.MatteBorderUIResource` class extends `MatteBorder` and implements `UIResource` to support pluggable look-and-feel.

BorderUIResource.TitledBorderUIResource

The `BorderUIResource.TitledBorderUIResource` class extends `TitledBorder` and implements `UIResource` to support pluggable look-and-feel.

ButtonUI

The `ButtonUI` class extends `ComponentUI` to support pluggable look-and-feel for `JButtonUI` objects.

ColorChooserUI

The `ColorChooserUI` class extends `ComponentUI` to support pluggable look-and-feel for `JColorChooser` objects.

ColorUIResource

The `ColorUIResource` class extends `Color` and implements `UIResource` to support pluggable look-and-feel for `Color` objects.

ComboBoxUI

The `ComboBoxUI` class extends `ComponentUI` to support pluggable look-and-feel for `JComboBoxUI` objects.

ComponentUI

The `ComponentUI` class extends `Object` to support pluggable look-and-feel for Swing component objects.

DesktopIconUI

The `DesktopIconUI` class extends `ComponentUI` to support pluggable look-and-feel for `JDesktopIcon` objects.

DesktopPaneUI

The `DesktopPaneUI` class extends `ComponentUI` to support pluggable look-and-feel for `JDesktopPane` objects.

DimensionUIResource

The `DimensionUIResource` class extends `Dimension` and implements `UIResource` to support pluggable look-and-feel for `Dimension` objects.

FileChooserUI

The `FileChooserUI` class extends `ComponentUI` to support pluggable look-and-feel for `JFileChooser` objects.

FontUIResource

The FontUIResource class extends Font and implements UIResource to support pluggable look-and-feel for Font objects.

IconUIResource

The IconUIResource class extends Object and implements UIResource, Icon and Serializable to support pluggable look-and-feel for Icon objects.

InsetsUIResource

The InsetsUIResource class extends Insets and implements UIResource to support pluggable look-and-feel for Insets objects.

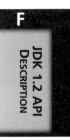

InternalFrameUI

The InternalFrameUI class extends ComponentUI to support pluggable look-and-feel for JInternalFrame objects.

LabelUI

The LabelUI class extends ComponentUI to support pluggable look-and-feel for JLabel objects.

ListUI

The ListUI class extends ComponentUI to support pluggable look-and-feel for JList objects.

MenuBarUI

The MenuBarUI class extends ComponentUI to support pluggable look-and-feel for JMenuBar objects.

MenuItemUI

The MenuItemUI class extends ButtonUI to support pluggable look-and-feel for JMenuItem objects

OptionPaneUI

The OptionPaneUI class extends ComponentUI to support pluggable look-and-feel for JOptionPane objects.

PanelUI

The PanelUI class extends ComponentUI to support pluggable look-and-feel for JPanel objects.

PopupMenuUI

The `PopupMenuUI` class extends `ComponentUI` to support pluggable look-and-feel for `JPopupMenu` objects.

ProgressBarUI

The `ProgressBarUI` class extends `ComponentUI` to support pluggable look-and-feel for `JProgressBar` objects.

ScrollBarUI

The `ScrollBarUI` class extends `ComponentUI` to support pluggable look-and-feel for `JScrollBar` objects.

ScrollPaneUI

The `ScrollPaneUI` class extends `ComponentUI` to support pluggable look-and-feel for `JScrollPane` objects.

SeparatorUI

The `SeparatorUI` class extends `ComponentUI` to support pluggable look-and-feel for `JSeparator` objects.

SliderUI

The `SliderUI` class extends `ComponentUI` to support pluggable look-and-feel for `JSlider` objects.

SplitPaneUI

The `SplitPaneUI` class extends `ComponentUI` to support pluggable look-and-feel for `JSplitPane` objects.

TabbedPaneUI

The `TabbedPaneUI` class extends `ComponentUI` to support pluggable look-and-feel for `JTabbedPane` objects.

TableHeaderUI

The `TableHeaderUI` class extends `ComponentUI` to support pluggable look-and-feel for `JTableHeader` objects.

TableUI

The `TableUI` class extends `ComponentUI` to support pluggable look-and-feel for `JTable` objects.

TextUI

The TextUI class extends ComponentUI to support pluggable look-and-feel for JText objects.

ToolBarUI

The ToolBarUI class extends ComponentUI to support pluggable look-and-feel for JToolBar objects.

ToolTipUI

The ToolTipUI class extends ComponentUI to support pluggable look-and-feel for JToolTip objects.

TreeUI

The TreeUI class extends ComponentUI to support pluggable look-and-feel for JTree objects.

ViewportUI

The ViewportUI class extends ComponentUI to support pluggable look-and-feel for JViewport objects.

Exceptions and Errors

None.

Package `javax.swing.plaf.basic`

The javax.swing.plaf.basic package provides 65 classes and one interface that support the basic look-and-feel. It is covered in Chapters 12 through 14.

Interfaces

ComboPopup

The ComboPopup interface defines methods required to implement a BasicComboBoxUI.

Classes

BasicArrowButton

The BasicArrowButton class extends JButton and implements the SwingConstants interface to support an arrow button with the basic look-and-feel.

BasicBorders

The BasicBorders class extends Object to provide a border factory for the basic look-and-feel.

BasicBorders.ButtonBorder

The BasicBorders.ButtonBorder class extends AbstractBorder and implements UIResource to provide a button border with the basic look-and-feel.

BasicBorders.FieldBorder

The BasicBorders.FieldBorder class extends AbstractBorder and implements UIResource to provide a field border with the basic look-and-feel.

BasicBorders.MarginBorder

The BasicBorders.MarginBorder class extends AbstractBorder and implements UIResource to provide a margin border with the basic look-and-feel.

BasicBorders.MenuBarBorder

The BasicBorders.MenuBarBorder class extends AbstractBorder and implements UIResource to provide a menu bar border with the basic look-and-feel.

BasicBorders.RadioButtonBorder

The BasicBorders.RadioButtonBorder class extends BasicBorders.ButtonBorder to provide a border with the basic look-and-feel.

BasicBorders.SplitPaneBorder

The BasicBorders.SplitPaneBorder class extends Object and implements the Border and UIResource interfaces to provide a split pane border with the basic look-and-feel.

BasicBorders.ToggleButtonBorder

The BasicBorders.ToggleButtonBorder class extends BasicBorders.ButtonBorder to provide a border with the basic look-and-feel.

BasicButtonListener

The BasicButtonListener class extends Object and implements the MouseListener, MouseMotionListener, FocusListener, ChangeListener, and PropertyChangeListener interfaces to handle button-related events for the basic look-and-feel.

BasicButtonUI

The BasicButtonUI class extends ButtonUI to support the basic look-and-feel.

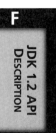

BasicCheckBoxMenuItemUI

The BasicCheckBoxMenuItemUI class extends BasicMenuItemUI to support the basic look-and-feel for checkbox menu items.

BasicCheckBoxUI

The BasicCheckBoxUI class extends BasicRadioButtonUI to support the basic look-and-feel for checkboxes.

BasicColorChooserUI

The BasicColorChooserUI class extends ColorChooserUI to support the basic look-and-feel.

BasicComboBoxEditor

The BasicComboBoxEditor class extends Object and implements the ComboBoxEditor and FocusListener interfaces to provide a default editor for editable combo boxes.

BasicComboBoxEditor.UIResource

The BasicComboBoxEditor.UIResource class extends BasicComboBoxEditor and implements UIResource to provide a UIResource for the BasicComboBoxEditor class.

BasicComboBoxRenderer

The BasicComboBoxRenderer class extends JLabel and implements the ListCellRenderer and Serializable interfaces to support the rendering of combo boxes with the basic look-and-feel.

BasicComboBoxRenderer.UIResource

The BasicComboBoxRenderer.UIResource class extends BasicComboBoxRenderer and implements UIResource to provide a UIResource for the BasicComboBoxRenderer class.

BasicComboBoxUI

The BasicComboBoxUI class extends ComboBoxUI to support the basic look-and-feel.

BasicComboPopup

The BasicComboPopup class extends JPopupMenu and implements ComboPopup to provide a combo popup component for the basic look-and-feel.

BasicDesktopIconUI

The BasicDesktopIconUI class extends DesktopIconUI to support the basic look-and-feel.

BasicDesktopPaneUI

The BasicDesktopPaneUI class extends DesktopPaneUI to support the basic look-and-feel.

BasicDirectoryModel

The BasicDirectoryModel class extends AbstractListModel and implements the PropertyChangeListener interface to implement a file list with the basic look-and-feel.

BasicEditorPaneUI

The BasicEditorPaneUI class extends BasicTextUI to support the basic look-and-feel.

BasicFileChooserUI

The BasicFileChooserUI class extends FileChooserUI to support the basic look-and-feel.

BasicGraphicsUtils

The BasicGraphicsUtils class extends Object to provide graphic utilities used with the basic look-and-feel.

BasicIconFactory

The BasicIconFactory class extends Object and implements Serializable to provide a factory for the creation of icons with the basic look-and-feel.

BasicInternalFrameTitlePane

The BasicInternalFrameTitlePane class extends JComponent to provide a basic look-and-feel implementation of a title bar.

BasicInternalFrameUI

The BasicInternalFrameUI class extends InternalFrameUI to support the basic look-and-feel.

BasicLabelUI

The BasicLabelUI class extends LabelUI and implements the PropertyChangeListener interface to support the basic look-and-feel.

BasicListUI

The BasicListUI class extends ListUI to support the basic look-and-feel.

BasicLookAndFeel

The BasicLookAndFeel class extends Object and implements Serializable to provide the basic look-and-feel specification.

BasicMenuBarUI

The BasicMenuBarUI class extends MenuBarUI to support the basic look-and-feel.

BasicMenuItemUI

The BasicMenuItemUI class extends MenuItemUI to support the basic look-and-feel.

BasicMenuUI

The BasicMenuUI class extends BasicMenuItemUI to support the basic look-and-feel for menus.

BasicOptionPaneUI

The BasicOptionPaneUI class extends OptionPaneUI to support the basic look-and-feel.

BasicOptionPaneUI.ButtonAreaLayout

The BasicOptionPaneUI.ButtonAreaLayout class extends Object and implements LayoutManager to support the layout of option panes with the basic look-and-feel.

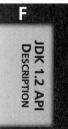

BasicPanelUI

The BasicPanelUI class extends PanelUI to support the basic look-and-feel.

BasicPasswordFieldUI

The BasicPasswordFieldUI class extends BasicTextFieldUI to support the basic look-and-feel for password fields.

BasicPopupMenuSeparatorUI

The BasicPopupMenuSeparatorUI class extends BasicSeparatorUI to support the basic look-and-feel for menu separators.

BasicPopupMenuUI

The BasicPopupMenuUI class extends PopupMenuUI to support the basic look-and-feel.

BasicProgressBarUI

The BasicProgressBarUI class extends ProgressBarUI to support the basic look-and-feel.

BasicRadioButtonMenuItemUI

The BasicRadioButtonMenuItemUI class extends BasicMenuItemUI to support the basic look-and-feel for radio button menu items.

BasicRadioButtonUI

The `BasicRadioButtonUI` class extends `BasicToggleButtonUI` to support the basic look-and-feel for radio buttons.

BasicScrollBarUI

The `BasicScrollBarUI` class extends `ScrollBarUI` and implements the `LayoutManager` and `SwingConstants` interfaces to support the basic look-and-feel.

BasicScrollPaneUI

The `BasicScrollPaneUI` class extends `ScrollPaneUI` and implements the `ScrollPaneConstants` interface to support the basic look-and-feel.

BasicSeparatorUI

The `BasicSeparatorUI` class extends `SeparatorUI` to support the basic look-and-feel.

BasicSliderUI

The `BasicSliderUI` class extends `SliderUI` to support the basic look-and-feel.

BasicSplitPaneDivider

The `BasicSplitPaneDivider` class extends `Container` and implements `PropertyChangeListener` to provide a divider used by `BasicSplitPaneUI`.

BasicSplitPaneUI

The `BasicSplitPaneUI` class extends `SplitPaneUI` to support the basic look-and-feel.

BasicTabbedPaneUI

The `BasicTabbedPaneUI` class extends `TabbedPaneUI` and implements the `SwingConstants` interface to support the basic look-and-feel.

BasicTableHeaderUI

The `BasicTableHeaderUI` class extends `TableHeaderUI` to support the basic look-and-feel.

BasicTableUI

The `BasicTableUI` class extends `TableUI` to support the basic look-and-feel.

BasicTextAreaUI

The `BasicTextAreaUI` class extends `BasicTextUI` to support the basic look-and-feel.

BasicTextPaneUI

The `BasicTextPaneUI` class extends `BasicEditorPaneUI` to support the basic look-and-feel.

BasicTextUI

The BasicTextUI class extends TextUI and implements the ViewFactory interface to support the basic look-and-feel.

BasicTextUI.BasicCaret

The BasicTextUI.BasicCaret class extends DefaultCaret and implements UIResource to provide a text caret with the basic look-and-feel.

BasicTextUI.BasicHighlighter

The BasicTextUI.BasicHighlighter class extends DefaultHighlighter and implements UIResource to provide a text highlighter with the basic look-and-feel.

BasicToggleButtonUI

The BasicToggleButtonUI class extends BasicButtonUI to support the basic look-and-feel.

BasicToolBarSeparatorUI

The BasicToolBarSeparatorUI class extends BasicSeparatorUI to support the basic look-and-feel.

BasicToolBarUI

The BasicToolBarUI class extends ToolBarUI and implements SwingConstants to support the basic look-and-feel.

BasicToolTipUI

The BasicToolTipUI class extends ToolTipUI to support the basic look-and-feel.

BasicTreeUI

The BasicTreeUI class extends TreeUI to support the basic look-and-feel.

BasicViewportUI

The BasicViewportUI class extends ViewportUI to support the basic look-and-feel.

DefaultMenuLayout

The DefaultMenuLayout class extends BoxLayout and implements UIResource to provide a menu layout manager with the basic look-and-feel.

Exceptions and Errors

None.

Package `javax.swing.plaf.metal`

The `javax.swing.plaf.metal` package provides 47 classes and no interfaces that support the metal look-and-feel. It is covered in Chapters 12 through 14.

Interfaces

None.

Classes

DefaultMetalTheme

The `DefaultMetalTheme` class extends the `Object` class to provide a default implementation of the Metal look and feel.

MetalBorders

The `MetalBorders` class extends the `Object` class to provide a border with the Metal look and feel.

MetalBorders.ButtonBorder

The `MetalBorders.ButtonBorder` class extends the `AbstractBorder` class and implements the `UIResource` interface to create a border class with the Metal look and feel.

MetalBorders.Flush3DBorder

The `MetalBorders.Flush3DBorder` class extends the `AbstractBorder` class and implements the `UIResource` interface to create a border class with the Metal look and feel.

MetalBorders.InternalFrameBorder

The `MetalBorders.InternalFrameBorder` class extends the `AbstractBorder` class and implements the `UIResource` interface to create a border class with the Metal look and feel.

MetalBorders.MenuBarBorder

The `MetalBorders.MenuBarBorder` class extends the `AbstractBorder` class and implements the `UIResource` interface to create a border class with the Metal look and feel.

MetalBorders.MenuItemBorder

The `MetalBorders.MenuItemBorder` class extends the `AbstractBorder` class and implements the `UIResource` interface to create a border class with the Metal look and feel.

MetalBorders.PopupMenuBorder

The MetalBorders.PopupMenuBorder class extends the AbstractBorder class and implements the UIResource interface to create a border class with the Metal look and feel.

MetalBorders.RolloverButtonBorder

The MetalBorders.RolloverButtonBorder class extends the AbstractBorder class and implements the UIResource interface to create a border class with the Metal look and feel.

MetalBorders.ScrollPaneBorder

The MetalBorders.ScrollPaneBorder class extends the AbstractBorder class and implements the UIResource interface to create a border class with the Metal look and feel.

MetalBorders.TextFieldBorder

The MetalBorders.TextFieldBorder class extends the AbstractBorder class and implements the UIResource interface to create a border class with the Metal look and feel.

MetalBorders.ToolBarBorder

The MetalBorders.ToolBarBorder class extends the AbstractBorder class and implements the UIResource interface to create a border class with the Metal look and feel.

MetalButtonUI

The MetalButtonUI class extends the BasicButtonUI class with the Metal look and feel.

MetalCheckBoxIcon

The MetalCheckBoxIcon class extends the Object class and implements the Icon, UIResource, and Serializable interfaces to create a checkbox icon with the Metal look and feel.

MetalCheckBoxUI

The MetalCheckBoxUI class extends the MetalRadioButtonUI class to create a metal checcbox.

MetalComboBoxButton

The MetalComboBoxButton class extends the JButton class with the Metal look and feel.

MetalComboBoxEditor

The MetalComboBoxEditor class extends the BasicComboBoxEditor class with the Metal look and feel.

MetalComboBoxEditor.UIResource

The MetalComboBoxEditor.UIResource class is an inner class of the MetalComboBoxEditor class that implements the UIResource interface to provide a UIResource for the MetalComboBoxEditor class.

MetalComboBoxIcon

The MetalComboBoxIcon class extends the Object class and implements the Icon and Serializable interfaces to create a combo box icon with the Metal look and feel.

MetalComboBoxUI

The MetalComboBoxUI class extends the BasicComboBoxUI class with the Metal look and feel.

MetalDesktopIconUI

The MetalDesktopIconUI class extends the BasicDesktopIconUI class with the Metal look and feel.

MetalFileChooserUI

The MetalFileChooserUI class extends the BasicFileChooserUI class with the Metal look and feel.

MetalIconFactory

The MetalIconFactory class extends the Object class and implements the Serializable interface to create an icon factory with the Metal look and feel.

MetalIconFactory.FileIcon16

The MetalIconFactory.FileIcon16 class extends the Object class and implements the Icon and Serializable interfaces to provide a file icon with the Metal look and feel.

MetalIconFactory.FolderIcon16

The MetalIconFactory.FolderIcon16 class extends the Object class and implements the Icon and Serializable interfaces to provide a folder icon with the Metal look and feel.

MetalIconFactory.TreeControlIcon

The `MetalIconFactory.TreeControlIcon` class extends the `Object` class and implements the `Icon` and `Serializable` interfaces to provide a tree control icon with the Metal look and feel.

MetalIconFactory.TreeFolderIcon

The `MetalIconFactory.TreeFolderIcon` class extends the `MetalIconFactory.FolderIcon16` class to create a tree folder icon with the Metal look and feel.

MetalIconFactory.TreeLeafIcon

The `MetalIconFactory.TreeLeafIcon` class extends the `MetalIconFactory.FileIcon16` class to create a tree file icon with the Metal look and feel.

MetalInternalFrameUI

The `MetalInternalFrameUI` class extends the `BasicInternalFrameUI` class with the Metal look and feel.

MetalLabelUI

The `MetalLabelUI` class extends the `BasicLabelUI` class with the Metal look and feel.

MetalLookAndFeel

The `MetalLookAndFeel` class extends the `BasicLookAndFeel` class with the Metal look and feel.

MetalPopupMenuSeparatorUI

The `MetalPopupMenuSeparatorUI` class extends the `MenuSeparatorUI` class to create a popup menu separator with the Metal look and feel.

MetalProgressBarUI

The `MetalProgressBarUI` class extends the `BasicProgressBarUI` class with the Metal look and feel.

MetalRadioButtonUI

The `MetalRadioButtonUI` class extends the `BasicRadioButtonUI` class with the Metal look and feel.

MetalScrollBarUI

The `MetalScrollBarUI` class extends the `BasicScrollBarUI` class with the Metal look and feel.

MetalScrollButton

The MetalScrollButton class extends the BasicArrowButton class with the Metal look and feel.

MetalScrollPaneUI

The MetalScrollPaneUI class extends the BasicScrollPaneUI class with the Metal look and feel.

MetalSeparatorUI

The MetalSeparatorUI class extends the BasicSeparatorUI class with the Metal look and feel.

MetalSliderUI

The MetalSliderUI class extends the BasicSliderUI class with the Metal look and feel.

MetalSplitPaneUI

The MetalSplitPaneUI class extends the BasicSplitPaneUI class with the Metal look and feel.

MetalTabbedPaneUI

The MetalTabbedPaneUI class extends the BasicTabbedPaneUI class with the Metal look and feel.

MetalTextFieldUI

The MetalTextFieldUI class extends the BasicTextFieldUI class with the Metal look and feel.

MetalTheme

The MetalTheme class extends the Object class to provide a general description of the Metal look and feel.

MetalToggleButtonUI

The MetalToggleButtonUI class extends the BasicToggleButtonUI class with the Metal look and feel.

MetalToolBarUI

The MetalToolBarUI class extends the BasicToolBarUI class with the Metal look and feel.

MetalToolTipUI

The MetalToolTipUI class extends the BasicToolTipUI class with the Metal look and feel.

MetalTreeUI

The MetalTreeUI class extends the BasicTreeUI class with the Metal look and feel.

Exceptions and Errors

None.

Package `javax.swing.plaf.multi`

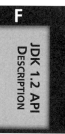

The javax.swing.plaf.multi package provides 29 classes and no interfaces that supports the multiplexing look-and-feel. It is covered in Chapters 12 through 14.

Interfaces

None.

Classes

MultiButtonUI

The MultiButtonUI class extends the ButtonUI class with the multiplexing look and feel.

MultiColorChooserUI

The MultiColorChooserUI class extends the ColorChooserUI class with the multiplexing look and feel.

MultiComboBoxUI

The MultiComboBoxUI class extends the ComboBoxUI class with the multiplexing look and feel.

MultiDesktopIconUI

The MultiDesktopIconUI class extends the DesktopIconUI class with the multiplexing look and feel.

MultiDesktopPaneUI

The MultiDesktopPaneUI class extends the DesktopPaneUI class with the multiplexing look and feel.

MultiFileChooserUI

The `MultiFileChooserUI` class extends the `FileChooserUI` class with the multiplexing look and feel.

MultiInternalFrameUI

The `MultiInternalFrameUI` class extends the `InternalFrameUI` class with the multiplexing look and feel.

MultiLabelUI

The `MultiLabelUI` class extends the `LabelUI` class with the multiplexing look and feel.

MultiListUI

The `MultiListUI` class extends the `ListUI` class with the multiplexing look and feel.

MultiLookAndFeel

The `MultiLookAndFeel` class extends the `LookAndFeel` class with the multiplexing look and feel.

MultiMenuBarUI

The `MultiMenuBarUI` class extends the `MenuBarUI` class with the multiplexing look and feel.

MultiMenuItemUI

The `MultiMenuItemUI` class extends the `MenuItemUI` class with the multiplexing look and feel.

MultiOptionPaneUI

The `MultiOptionPaneUI` class extends the `OptionPaneUI` class with the multiplexing look and feel.

MultiPanelUI

The `MultiPanelUI` class extends the `PanelUI` class with the multiplexing look and feel.

MultiPopupMenuUI

The `MultiPopupMenuUI` class extends the `PopupMenuUI` class with the multiplexing look and feel.

MultiProgressBarUI

The `MultiProgressBarUI` class extends the `ProgressBarUI` class with the multiplexing look and feel.

MultiScrollBarUI

The MultiScrollBarUI class extends the ScrollBarUI class with the multiplexing look and feel.

MultiScrollPaneUI

The MultiScrollPaneUI class extends the ScrollPaneUI class with the multiplexing look and feel.

MultiSeparatorUI

The MultiSeparatorUI class extends the SeparatorUI class with the multiplexing look and feel.

MultiSliderUI

The MultiSliderUI class extends the SliderUI class with the multiplexing look and feel.

MultiSplitPaneUI

The MultiSplitPaneUI class extends the SplitPaneUI class with the multiplexing look and feel.

MultiTabbedPaneUI

The MultiTabbedPaneUI class extends the TabbedPaneUI class with the multiplexing look and feel.

MultiTableHeaderUI

The MultiTableHeaderUI class extends the TableHeaderUI class with the multiplexing look and feel.

MultiTableUI

The MultiTableUI class extends the TableUI class with the multiplexing look and feel.

MultiTextUI

The MultiTextUI class extends the TextUI class with the multiplexing look and feel.

MultiToolBarUI

The MultiToolBarUI class extends the ToolBarUI class with the multiplexing look and feel.

MultiToolTipUI

The MultiToolTipUI class extends the ToolTipUI class with the multiplexing look and feel.

MultiTreeUI

The MultiTreeUI class extends the TreeUI class with the multiplexing look and feel.

MultiViewportUI

The MultiViewportUI class extends the ViewportUI class with the multiplexing look and feel.

Exceptions and Errors

None.

Package javax.swing.table

The javax.swing.table package provides seven classes and four interfaces that implement the Swing table component. It is covered in Chapter 13.

Interfaces

TableCellEditor

The TableCellEditor interface extends the javax.swing.CellEditor interface to provide support for the text editing of table cells.

TableCellRenderer

The TableCellRenderer interface defines methods for rendering the cells of JTable objects.

TableColumnModel

The TableColumnModel interface defines methods for manipulating the rows of a table.

TableModel

The TableModel interface defines methods that are implemented by a data model that provides data for a JTable object.

Classes

AbstractTableModel

The AbstractTableModel class is a subclass of Object that provides an abstract implementation of the TableModel interface. It also implements the java.io.Serializable interface.

DefaultTableCellRenderer

The DefaultTableCellRenderer class is a subclass of javax.swing.JLabel that is used to render the individual cells of a table. It implements the TableCellRenderer and java.io.Serializable interfaces.

DefaultTableCellRenderer.UIResource

The DefaultTableCellRenderer.UIResource class is an inner class of DefaultTableCellRenderer that provides support for cell rendering.

DefaultTableColumnModel

The DefaultTableColumnModel class is a subclass of Object that provides a default implementation to the TableColumnModel interface. It also implements the java.beans.PropertyChangeListener, javax.swing.event.ListSelectionListener, and java.io.Serializable interfaces.

DefaultTableModel

The DefaultTableModel class is a subclass of AbstractTableModel that organizes its data using java.util.Vector objects. It implements the java.io.Serializable interface.

JTableHeader

The JTableHeader class is a subclass of javax.swing.JComponent that encapsulates the column header of a JTable object. It implements the TableColumnModelListener and java.awt.accessibility.Accessible interfaces.

TableColumn

The TableColumn class is a subclass of Object that defines the properties of a column in a JTable object. It implements the java.io.Serializable interface.

Exceptions and Errors

None.

Package `javax.swing.text`

The javax.swing.text package provides 63 classes and 21 interfaces that implement text-processing components. It is covered in Chapter 12.

Interfaces

AbstractDocument.AttributeContext

The AbstractDocument.AttributeContext interface supports attribute compression.

AbstractDocument.Content

The AbstractDocument.Content interface describes a sequence of editable content.

AttributeSet

The AttributeSet interface defines a read-only set of text attributes.

AttributeSet.CharacterAttribute

The AttributeSet.CharacterAttribute interface defines an attribute type signature.

AttributeSet.ColorAttribute

The AttributeSet.ColorAttribute interface defines a color type signature.

AttributeSet.FontAttribute

The AttributeSet.FontAttribute interface defines a font type signature.

AttributeSet.ParagraphAttribute

The AttributeSet.ParagraphAttribute interface defines a paragraph type signature.

Caret

The Caret interface defines a document insertion point caret.

Document

The Document interface defines a container for editable text.

Element

The Element interface defines a structural piece of a Document object.

Highlighter

The Highlighter interface provides support for highlighted text.

Highlighter.Highlight

The Highlighter.Highlight interface defines the location of highlighted text.

Highlighter.HighlightPainter

The Highlighter.HighlightPainter interface defines the manner in which highlighted text is to be painted.

Keymap

The Keymap interface binds keystrokes to actions.

MutableAttributeSet

The MutableAttributeSet interface extends the AttributeSet interface to provide methods for updating the set of attributes.

Position

The Position interface defines a location within a Document object.

Style

The Style interface defines text, paragraph, and other document-related styles.

StyledDocument

The StyledDocument interface extends the Document interface to provide style support.

TabExpander

The TabExpander interface provides support for tab settings.

TabableView

The TabableView interface provides support for viewing expanded tabs within a document.

ViewFactory

The ViewFactory interface provides support for creating different views of a document.

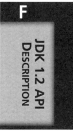

Classes

AbstractDocument

The AbstractDocument class is a subclass of Object that provides a basic implementation of the Document interface. It also implements the java.io.Serializable interface.

AbstractDocument.ElementEdit

The AbstractDocument.ElementEdit class is an inner class of AbstractDocument that provides undo/redo support. It is a subclass of javax.swing.undo.AbstractUndoableEdit.

AbstractWriter

The `AbstractWriter` class is an subclass of `Object` that supports the display of text.

BoxView

The `BoxView` class is a subclass of `CompositeView` that provides a box-like organization of document content.

ComponentView

The `ComponentView` class is a subclass of `View` that provides a view of a single document component.

CompositeView

The `CompositeView` class is a subclass of `View` that provides a view of multiple document components.

DefaultCaret

The `DefaultCaret` class is a subclass of `Object` that provides a default implementation of the `Caret` interface. It also implements the `java.awt.event.FocusListener`, `java.awt.event.MouseListener`, `java.awt.event.MouseMotionListener`, and `java.io.Serializable` interfaces.

DefaultEditorKit

The `DefaultEditorKit` class is a subclass of `EditorKit` that provides a basic text editing capability.

DefaultEditorKit.BeepAction

The `DefaultEditorKit.BeepAction` class is an inner class of `DefaultEditorKit` that creates a beep sound. It is a subclass of `Object`.

DefaultEditorKit.CopyAction

The `DefaultEditorKit.CopyAction` class is an inner class of `DefaultEditorKit` that copies data to the clipboard. It is a subclass of `Object`.

DefaultEditorKit.CutAction

The `DefaultEditorKit.CutAction` class is an inner class of `DefaultEditorKit` that cuts data to the clipboard. It is a subclass of `Object`.

DefaultEditorKit.DefaultKeyTypedAction

The `DefaultEditorKit.DefaultKeyTypedAction` class is an inner class of `DefaultEditorKit` that handles key presses. It is a subclass of `Object`.

DefaultEditorKit.InsertBreakAction

The DefaultEditorKit.InsertBreakAction class is an inner class of
DefaultEditorKit that inserts a line break into a document. It is a subclass of Object.

DefaultEditorKit.InsertContentAction

The DefaultEditorKit.InsertContentAction class is an inner class of
DefaultEditorKit that inserts content into a document. It is a subclass of Object.

DefaultEditorKit.InsertTabAction

The DefaultEditorKit.InsertTabAction class is an inner class of DefaultEditorKit
that inserts a tab into a document. It is a subclass of Object.

DefaultEditorKit.PasteAction

The DefaultEditorKit.PasteAction class is an inner class of DefaultEditorKit that
pastes content into a document from the clipboard. It is a subclass of Object.

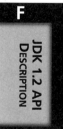

DefaultHighlighter

The DefaultHighlighter class is a subclass of Object that provides a default implementation of the Highlighter interface.

DefaultHighlighter.DefaultHighlightPainter

The DefaultHighlighter.DefaultHighlightPainter class is an inner class of
DefaultHighlighter that implements the Highlighter.HighlightPainter interface. It
is a subclass of Object.

DefaultStyledDocument

The DefaultStyledDocument class is a subclass of AbstractDocument and implements
the StyledDocument interface.

DefaultStyledDocument.AttributeUndoableEdit

The DefaultStyledDocument.AttributeUndoableEdit class is an inner class of
DefaultStyledDocument that supports undoable edit operations.

DefaultStyledDocument.ElementSpec

The DefaultStyledDocument.ElementSpec class is an inner class of
DefaultStyledDocument that supports the building of document elements. It is a subclass of Object.

DefaultTextUI

The DefaultTextUI class is a subclass of javax.swing.plaf.TextUI that provides a default implementation of the ViewFactory interface. It also implements the java.io.Serializable interface.

EditorKit

The EditorKit class is a subclass of Object that provides a base class for developing a text editor. It implements the java.lang.Cloneable and java.io.Serializable interfaces.

ElementIterator

The ElementIterator class extends Object and implements the Cloneable interface. It is used to iterate through the elements of a document.

FieldView

The FieldView class is a subclass of PlainView that supports a single-line editing view.

GapContent

The GapContent class extends Object and implements the AbstractDocument.Content and Serializable interfaces to provide an encapsulation of a gap buffer.

IconView

The IconView class is a subclass of View that provides support for viewing an icon.

JTextComponent

The JTextComponent class is a subclass of javax.swing.JComponent that provides the base class for Swing text components. It implements the javax.swing.Scrollable and java.awt.accessibility.Accessible interfaces.

JTextComponent.KeyBinding

The JTextComponent.KeyBinding class is an inner class of JTextComponent that provides key binding support. It is a subclass of Object.

LabelView

The LabelView class is a subclass of View that implements the TabableView interface.

LabelView2D

The LabelView2D class extends View to provide the capability to render a 2D label.

LayeredHighlighter

The LayeredHighlighter class is a subclass of object that implements the Highlighter interface.

LayeredHighlighter.LayerPainter

The LayeredHighlighter.LayerPainter class is an inner class of LayeredHighlighter that supports layered highlight rendering.

ParagraphView

The ParagraphView class is a subclass of BoxView that provides the capability to display styled paragraphs. It implements the TabExpander interface.

PasswordView

The PasswordView class is a subclass of FieldView that provides password-hiding support.

PlainDocument

The PlainDocument class is a subclass of AbstractDocument that supports one text font and color.

PlainView

The PlainView class is a subclass of View that supports the display of one font and one color. It implements the TabExpander interface.

Position.Bias

The Position.Bias class extends Object to provide the capability to specify a bias in a character position.

Segment

The Segment class is a subclass of Object that represents a text fragment.

SimpleAttributeSet

The SimpleAttributeSet class is a subclass of Object that provides a default implementation of the MutableAttributeSet interface. It also implements the java.io.Serializable interface.

StringContent

The StringContent class is a subclass of Object that provides a default implementation of the AbstractDocument.Content interface. It also implements the java.io.Serializable interface.

F

JDK 1.2 API
DESCRIPTION

StyleConstants

The StyleConstants class is a subclass of Object that provides constants and methods for implementing text, paragraph, and document styles.

StyleConstants.CharacterConstants

The StyleConstants.CharacterConstants class is an inner class of StyleConstants that supports character styles. It is a subclass of Object and implements the AttributeSet.CharacterAttribute interface.

StyleConstants.ColorConstants

The StyleConstants.ColorConstants class is an inner class of StyleConstants that supports text colors. It is a subclass of Object and implements the AttributeSet.ColorAttribute and AttributeSet.CharacterAttribute interfaces.

StyleConstants.FontConstants

The StyleConstants.FontConstants class is an inner class of StyleConstants that supports fonts. It is a subclass of Object and implements the AttributeSet.FontAttribute and AttributeSet.CharacterAttribute interfaces.

StyleConstants.ParagraphConstants

The StyleConstants.ParagraphConstants class is an inner class of StyleConstants that supports paragraph styles. It is a subclass of Object and implements the AttributeSet.ParagraphAttribute interface.

StyleContext

The StyleContext class is a subclass of Object that provides style constants and resources. It implements the java.io.Serializable and AbstractDocument.AttributeContext interfaces.

StyledEditorKit

The StyledEditorKit class is a subclass of DefaultEditorKit that provides a text editor that supports text styles.

StyledEditorKit.AlignmentAction

The StyledEditorKit.AlignmentAction class is an inner class of StyledEditorKit that supports paragraph alignment. It is a subclass of StyledEditorKit.StyledTextAction.

StyledEditorKit.BoldAction

The StyledEditorKit.BoldAction class is an inner class of StyledEditorKit that supports text bolding. It is a subclass of StyledEditorKit.StyledTextAction.

StyledEditorKit.FontFamilyAction

The StyledEditorKit.FontFamilyAction class is an inner class of StyledEditorKit that supports the use of fonts. It is a subclass of StyledEditorKit.StyledTextAction.

StyledEditorKit.FontSizeAction

The StyledEditorKit.FontSizeAction class is an inner class of StyledEditorKit that supports the control of text font size. It is a subclass of StyledEditorKit.StyledTextAction.

StyledEditorKit.ForegroundAction

The StyledEditorKit.ForegroundAction class is an inner class of StyledEditorKit that supports the setting of text foreground color. It is a subclass of StyledEditorKit.StyledTextAction.

StyledEditorKit.ItalicAction

The StyledEditorKit.ItalicAction class is an inner class of StyledEditorKit that supports the use of italics. It is a subclass of StyledEditorKit.StyledTextAction.

StyledEditorKit.StyledTextAction

The StyledEditorKit.StyledTextAction class is an inner class of StyledEditorKit that supports text operations. It is a subclass of TextAction.

StyledEditorKit.UnderlineAction

The StyledEditorKit.UnderlineAction class is an inner class of StyledEditorKit that supports underlining. It is a subclass of StyledEditorKit.StyledTextAction.

TabSet

The TabSet class is a subclass of Object that defines a set of tab stops. It implements the java.io.Serializable interface.

TabStop

The TabStop class is a subclass of Object that encapsulates a single tab stop. It implements the java.io.Serializable interface.

TableView

The TableView class is a subclass of BoxView that provides table support.

TextAction

The TextAction class is a subclass of AbstractAction that is used to define key mappings for text operations.

Utilities

The `Utilities` class is a subclass of `Object` that provides utility methods for text operations.

View

The `View` class is a subclass of `Object` that defines a view of part of a document.

WrappedPlainView

The `WrappedPlainView` class is a subclass of `BoxView` that supports wrapped plain text. It implements the `TabExpander` interface.

Exceptions and Errors

BadLocationException

The `BadLocationException` class is a subclass of `java.lang.Exception` that identifies errors in `Document` objects.

ChangedCharSetException

The `ChangedCharSetException` class extends `java.io.IOException` to signal a change from one character set to another.

Package `javax.swing.text.html`

The `javax.swing.text.html` package consists of 28 classes that provide basic HTML editing capabilities. This package is covered in Chapter 12.

Interfaces

None.

Classes

BlockView

The `BlockView` class extends `BoxView` to provide the capability to display and HTML block with CSS attributes.

CSS

The `CSS` class extends `Object` to define an enumeration of CSS attributes.

CSS.Attribute

The CSS.Attribute class extends Object to define keys for CSS-related attribute sets.

FormView

The FormView class extends ComponentView and implements the ActionListener interface to provide a view implementation for HTML form elements.

HTML

The HTML class extends Object to define constants used in HTML documents.

HTML.Attribute

The HTML.Attribute class extends Object to provide an enumeration of HTML attributes.

HTML.Tag

The HTML.Tag class extends Object to provide an enumeration of HTML tags.

HTML.UnknownTag

The HTML.UnknownTag class extends Object and implements the Serializable interface to identify an unknown HTML tag.

HTMLDocument

The HTMLDocument class extends DefaultStyledDocument to encapsulate an HTML document.

HTMLDocument.Iterator

The HTMLDocument.Iterator class extends Object to provide the capability to iterate over HTML tags.

HTMLEditorKit

The HTMLEditorKit class is a subclass of javax.swing.text.StyledEditorKit that provides a basic HTML editing capability.

HTMLEditorKit.HTMLFactory

The HTMLEditorKit.HTMLFactory class extends Object and implements the ViewFactory interface to provide the capability to build HTML views.

HTMLEditorKit.HTMLTextAction

The HTMLEditorKit.HTMLTextAction class extends StyledEditorKit.StyledTextAction to provide basic support for HTML text editing.

HTMLEditorKit.InsertHTMLTextAction

The HTMLEditorKit.InsertHTMLTextAction class extends Object to

HTMLEditorKit.LinkController

The HTMLEditorKit.LinkController class is an inner class of HTMLWriter that provides basic mouse event-handling support. It is a subclass of java.awt.event.MouseAdapter.

HTMLEditorKit.Parser

The HTMLEditorKit.Parser class extends HTMLEditorKit.HTMLTextAction to provide the capability to insert HTML into an existing document.

HTMLEditorKit.ParserCallback

The HTMLEditorKit.ParserCallback class extends Object to support HTML parsing.

HTMLFrameHyperlinkEvent

The HTMLFrameHyperlinkEvent class extends HyperlinkEvent to signal that an HTML link is activated.

HTMLWriter

The HTMLWriter class extends AbstractWriter to provide a basic Writer object for HTML documents.

InlineView

The InlineView class extends LabelView to display inline HTML elements with CSS attributes.

ListView

The ListView class extends BlockView to provide the capability to display an HTML list.

MinimalHTMLWriter

The MinimalHTMLWriter class extends AbstractWriter to provide an HTML Writer that displays HTML that is not produced by the HTML editor kit API.

ObjectView

The ObjectView class extends ComponentView to support the <OBJECT> tag.

Option

The Option class extends Object to provide support for the <OPTION> tag.

ParagraphView

The ParagraphView class extends javax.swing.text.ParagraphView to display an HTML paragraph with CSS attributes.

StyleSheet

The StyleSheet class extends StyleContext to provide CSS support.

StyleSheet.BoxPainter

The StyleSheet.BoxPainter class extends Object and implements the Serializable interface to support CSS box-like formatting.

StyleSheet.ListPainter

The StyleSheet.ListPainter class extends Object and implements the Serializable interface to support CSS list-like formatting.

Exceptions and Errors

None.

Package javax.swing.tree

The javax.swing.tree package provides ten classes and seven interfaces that provide the capability to work with javax.swing.JTree components. The JTree component is a GUI component that displays a set of hierarchical data as an outline. The javax.swing.tree package is covered in Chapter 13.

Interfaces

MutableTreeNode

The MutableTreeNode interface extends the TreeNode interface to provide methods for modifying the properties of a TreeNode object.

RowMapper

The RowMapper interface is used to identify the row corresponding to a TreeNode object.

TreeCellEditor

The TreeCellEditor interface extends the javax.swing.CellEditor interface to support the editing of tree elements.

TreeCellRenderer

The TreeCellRenderer interface is used to render the nodes of a tree.

TreeModel

The TreeModel interface is used to model the data used to build a tree.

TreeNode

The TreeNode interface defines methods for classes that implement the nodes of a tree.

TreeSelectionModel

The TreeSelectionModel interface defines constants and methods for working with the current selection state of the nodes of a tree.

Classes

AbstractLayoutCache

The AbstractLayoutCache class extends Object and implements the RowMapper interface to support layout development.

AbstractLayoutCache.NodeDimensions

The AbstractLayoutCache.NodeDimensions class is an inner class of AbstractLayoutCache that provides support for size and positioning in support of layout development.

DefaultMutableTreeNode

The DefaultMutableTreeNode class is a subclass of Object that provides a default, modifiable tree node. It implements the MutableTreeNode, java.lang.Cloneable, and java.io.Serializable interfaces.

DefaultTreeCellEditor

The DefaultTreeCellEditor class extends Object and implements the ActionListener, TreeCellEditor, and TreeSelectionListener interfaces. It provides a basic capability to edit tree cells.

DefaultTreeCellRenderer

The DefaultTreeCellRenderer class extends JLabel and implements the TreeCellRenderer interface to provide the capability to render a tree cell.

DefaultTreeModel

The DefaultTreeModel class is a subclass of Object that provides a default TreeModel implementation. It also implements the java.io.Serializable interface.

DefaultTreeSelectionModel

The DefaultTreeSelectionModel class is a subclass of Object that provides a default TreeSelectionModel implementation. It also implements the java.lang.Cloneable and java.io.Serializable interfaces.

FixedHeightLayoutCache

The FixedHeightLayoutCache class extends AbstractLayoutCache to support fixed height layout.

TreePath

The TreePath class is a subclass of Object that identifies a path to a node of a tree. It implements the java.io.Serializable interface.

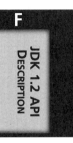

VariableHeightLayoutCache

The VariableHeightLayoutCache class extends AbstractLayoutCache to support variable height layout.

Exceptions and Errors

ExpandVetoException

The ExpandVetoException class extends java.lang.Exception to provide the capability to veto the expanding or collapsing of a tree.

Package javax.swing.undo

The javax.swing.undo package provides five classes and two interfaces that support the implementation of undo and redo capabilities. It is covered in Chapter 13.

Interfaces

StateEditable

The StateEditable interface is implemented by classes whose state can be undone or redone by the StateEdit class.

UndoableEdit

The UndoableEdit interface is implemented by classes that support the undoing or redoing of edit operations.

Classes

AbstractUndoableEdit

The `AbstractUndoableEdit` class is a subclass of `Object` that provides an abstract implementation of the `UndoableEdit` interface.

CompoundEdit

The `CompoundEdit` class is a subclass of `AbstractUndoableEdit` that provides the capability to implement compound undo/redo operations.

StateEdit

The `StateEdit` class is a subclass of `AbstractUndoableEdit` that supports undo/redo operations on objects that change state.

UndoManager

The `UndoManager` class is a subclass of `CompoundEdit` that provides for thread-safe undo/redo operations. It implements the `javax.swing.event.UndoableEditListener` interface.

UndoableEditSupport

The `UndoableEditSupport` class is a subclass of `Object` that supports the management of undoable editing operations.

Exceptions and Errors

CannotRedoException

The `CannotRedoException` class is a subclass of `RuntimeException` that indicates a redo operation cannot be performed.

CannotUndoException

The `CannotUndoException` class is a subclass of `RuntimeException` that indicates an undo operation cannot be performed.

Package `org.omg.CORBA`

The `org.omg.CORBA` package consists of 40 classes and 29 interfaces that implement the foundation for supporting Java-CORBA integration.

Interfaces

ARG_IN

The ARG_IN interface identifies a method input argument.

ARG_INOUT

The ARG_INOUT interface identifies an argument that may be used as both an input and an output in a method invocation.

ARG_OUT

The ARG_OUT interface identifies a method output argument.

BAD_POLICY

The BAD_POLICY interface is used to indicate a bad policy.

BAD_POLICY_TYPE

The BAD_POLICY_TYPE interface is used to indicate a bad policy type.

BAD_POLICY_VALUE

The BAD_POLICY_VALUE interface is used to indicate a bad policy value.

CTX_RESTRICT_SCOPE

The CTX_RESTRICT_SCOPE interface is used as a flag to restrict the search scope of the get_values() method.

Current

The Current interface extends the Object interface to provide the capability to access information associated with a particular thread of execution.

DomainManager

The Current interface extends the Object interface to provide the capability to manage the policy associated with a particular domain.

DynAny

The Current interface extends the Object interface to support the dynamic traversal of CORBA Any values.

DynArray

The Current interface extends the Object and DynAny interfaces to support arrays.

DynEnum

The Current interface extends the Object and DynAny interfaces to support IDL enum types.

DynFixed

The Current interface extends the Object and DynAny interfaces to support IDL fixed types.

DynSequence

The Current interface extends the Object and DynAny interfaces to support IDL sequence types.

DynStruct

The Current interface extends the Object and DynAny interfaces to support IDL structs.

DynUnion

The Current interface extends the Object and DynAny interfaces to support IDL union types.

DynValue

The Current interface extends the Object and DynAny interfaces to support name value pairs.

IDLType

The IDLType interface encapsulates an IDL IDLType. It extends the Object and IRObject interfaces.

IRObject

The IRObject interface encapsulates an interface repository object. It extends the Object interface.

Object

The Object interface represents a CORBA object reference.

Policy

The Policy interface extends the Object interface to provide a basic mechanism for policy implementation.

PRIVATE_MEMBER

The PRIVATE_MEMBER interface extends the Object interface to support the implementation of private members.

PUBLIC_MEMBER

The PUBLIC_MEMBER interface extends the Object interface to support the implementation of public members.

UNSUPPORTED_POLICY

The UNSUPPORTED_POLICY interface extends the Object interface to support the specification of unsupported policy.

UNSUPPORTED_POLICY_VALUE

The UNSUPPORTED_POLICY_VALUE interface extends the Object interface to support the specification of unsupported policy.

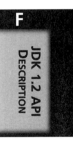

VM_ABSTRACT

The VM_ABSTRACT interface extends the Object interface to support the specification of an abstract virtual machine.

VM_CUSTOM

The VM_CUSTOM interface extends the Object interface to support the specification of a custom virtual machine.

VM_NONE

The VM_NONE interface extends the Object interface to support the specification of an non-existent virtual machine.

VM_TRUNCATABLE

The VM_TRUNCATABLE interface extends the Object interface to support the specification of a truncatable virtual machine.

Classes

Any

The Any class is a subclass of Object that acts as a container for data of any primitive IDL type.

AnyHolder

The `AnyHolder` class is a subclass of `Object` that acts as a holder for `Any` objects used as `INOUT` and `OUT` method parameters.

BooleanHolder

The `BooleanHolder` class is a subclass of `Object` that is used to hold `boolean` values for use as `INOUT` and `OUT` arguments.

ByteHolder

The `ByteHolder` class is a subclass of `Object` that is used to hold `byte` values for use as `INOUT` and `OUT` arguments.

CharHolder

The `CharHolder` class is a subclass of `Object` that is used to hold `char` values for use as `INOUT` and `OUT` arguments.

CompletionStatus

The `CompletionStatus` class is a subclass of `Object` that identifies the completion status of a method that throws a `SystemException`.

Context

The `Context` class is a subclass of `Object` that provides information about the context in which a method invocation request takes place.

ContextList

The `ContextList` class is a subclass of `Object` that specifies properties associated with a `Context` object.

DefinitionKind

The `DefinitionKind` class is a subclass of `Object` that is used to hold Boolean types for use as `INOUT` and `OUT` arguments.

DoubleHolder

The `DoubleHolder` class is a subclass of `Object` that is used to hold `double` values for use as `INOUT` and `OUT` arguments.

DynamicImplementation

The `DynamicImplementation` class is a subclass of `org.omg.CORBA.portable.ObjectImpl` that provides support for the dynamic servant interface.

Environment

The Environment class is a subclass of Object that is used to make exceptions available to the client that requested a method invocation.

ExceptionList

The ExceptionList class is a subclass of Object that lists the exceptions that can be thrown by a method.

FixedHolder

The FixedHolder class is a subclass of Object that is used to hold fixed IDL type values for use as INOUT and OUT arguments.

FloatHolder

The FloatHolder class is a subclass of Object that is used to hold float values for use as INOUT and OUT arguments.

IntHolder

The IntHolder class is a subclass of Object that is used to hold int values for use as INOUT and OUT arguments.

LongHolder

The LongHolder class is a subclass of Object that is used to hold long values for use as INOUT and OUT arguments.

NVList

The NVList class is a subclass of Object that provides a list of NamedValue objects.

NamedValue

The NamedValue class is a subclass of Object that is used to describe method arguments and return values.

NameValuePair

The NameValuePair class extends Object to hold names and values of IDL structs in the DynStruct API.

ORB

The ORB class is a subclass of Object that serves as the CORBA object request broker.

ObjectHolder

The ObjectHolder class is a subclass of Object that is used to hold object references for use as INOUT and OUT arguments.

Principal

The Principal class is a subclass of Object that identifies a client making a remote method invocation request.

PrincipalHolder

The PrincipalHolder class is a subclass of Object that is used to hold Principal objects for use as INOUT and OUT arguments.

Request

The Request class is a subclass of Object that encapsulates a client request to invoke a remote method.

ServerRequest

The ServerRequest class is a subclass of Object that encapsulates a dynamic skeleton interface request.

ServiceDetail

The ServiceDetail class extends Object that implements the IDLEntity interface. It is used to provide service information.

ServiceDetailHelper

The ServiceDetailHelper class extends Object to provide helper support for service detail information.

ServiceInformation

The ServiceInformation class extends Object to provide information to a service information IDL struct.

ServiceInformationHelper

The ServiceInformationHelper class extends Object to provide helper support for the service information IDL struct.

ServiceInformationHolder

The ServiceInformationHolder class extends Object to provide holder support for the service information IDL struct.

SetOverrideType

The SetOverrideType class extends Object and implements the IDLEntity interface to provide support for the override type.

ShortHolder

The ShortHolder class is a subclass of Object that is used to hold short values for use as INOUT and OUT arguments.

StringHolder

The StringHolder class is a subclass of Object that is used to hold String objects for use as INOUT and OUT arguments.

StructMember

The StructMember class is a subclass of Object that describes a member of a CORBA data structure.

TCKind

The TCKind class is a subclass of Object that encapsulates the IDL TCKind object.

TypeCode

The TypeCode class is a subclass of Object that is used to identify a primitive IDL value type.

TypeCodeHolder

The TypeCodeHolder class is a subclass of Object that is used to hold TypeCode objects for use as INOUT and OUT arguments.

UnionMember

The UnionMember class is a subclass of Object that provides support for IDL union constructs.

ValueMember

The ValueMember class extends Object and implements the IDLEntity interface to provide an interface repository description of the value object.

Exceptions and Errors

BAD_CONTEXT

The BAD_CONTEXT class is a subclass of SystemException that supports the CORBA BAD_CONTEXT exception.

BAD_INV_ORDER

The BAD_INV_ORDER class is a subclass of SystemException that supports the CORBA BAD_INV_ORDER exception.

BAD_OPERATION

The BAD_OPERATION class is a subclass of SystemException that supports the CORBA BAD_OPERATION exception.

BAD_PARAM

The BAD_PARAM class is a subclass of SystemException that supports the CORBA BAD_PARAM exception.

BAD_TYPECODE

The BAD_TYPECODE class is a subclass of SystemException that supports the CORBA BAD_TYPECODE exception.

Bounds

The Bounds class is a subclass of UserException that provides support for the user-defined bounds exception.

COMM_FAILURE

The COMM_FAILURE class is a subclass of SystemException that supports the CORBA COMM_FAILURE exception.

DATA_CONVERSION

The DATA_CONVERSION class is a subclass of SystemException that supports the CORBA DATA_CONVERSION exception.

FREE_MEM

The FREE_MEM class is a subclass of SystemException that supports the CORBA FREE_MEM exception.

IMP_LIMIT

The IMP_LIMIT class is a subclass of SystemException that supports the CORBA IMP_LIMIT exception.

INITIALIZE

The INITIALIZE class is a subclass of SystemException that supports the CORBA INITIALIZE exception.

INTERNAL

The INTERNAL class is a subclass of SystemException that supports the CORBA INTERNAL exception.

INTF_REPOS

The INTF_REPOS class is a subclass of SystemException that supports the CORBA INTF_REPOS exception.

INVALID_TRANSACTION

The INVALID_TRANSACTION class is a subclass of SystemException that supports the CORBA INVALID_TRANSACTION exception.

INV_FLAG

The INV_FLAG class is a subclass of SystemException that supports the CORBA INV_FLAG exception.

INV_IDENT

The INV_IDENT class is a subclass of SystemException that supports the CORBA INV_IDENT exception.

INV_OBJREF

The INV_OBJREF class is a subclass of SystemException that supports the CORBA INV_OBJREF exception.

INV_POLICY

The INV_POLICY class is a subclass of SystemException that supports the CORBA INV_POLICY exception.

MARSHAL

The MARSHAL class is a subclass of SystemException that supports the CORBA MARSHAL exception.

NO_IMPLEMENT

The NO_IMPLEMENT class is a subclass of SystemException that supports the CORBA NO_IMPLEMENT exception.

NO_MEMORY

The NO_MEMORY class is a subclass of SystemException that supports the CORBA NO_MEMORY exception.

NO_PERMISSION

The NO_PERMISSION class is a subclass of SystemException that supports the CORBA NO_PERMISSION exception.

NO_RESOURCES

The NO_RESOURCES class is a subclass of SystemException that supports the CORBA NO_RESOURCES exception.

NO_RESPONSE

The NO_RESPONSE class is a subclass of SystemException that supports the CORBA NO_RESPONSE exception.

OBJECT_NOT_EXIST

The OBJECT_NOT_EXIST class is a subclass of SystemException that supports the CORBA OBJECT_NOT_EXIST exception.

OBJ_ADAPTER

The OBJ_ADAPTER class is a subclass of SystemException that supports the CORBA OBJ_ADAPTER exception.

PERSIST_STORE

The PERSIST_STORE class is a subclass of SystemException that supports the CORBA PERSIST_STORE exception.

PolicyError

The PolicyError class extends UserException to provide support for identifying policy-related errors.

SystemException

The SystemException class is a subclass of java.lang.RuntimeException that serves as the base class for implementing CORBA exceptions.

TRANSACTION_REQUIRED

The TRANSACTION_REQUIRED class is a subclass of SystemException that supports the CORBA TRANSACTION_REQUIRED exception.

TRANSACTION_ROLLEDBACK

The TRANSACTION_ROLLEDBACK class is a subclass of SystemException that supports the CORBA TRANSACTION_ROLLEDBACK exception.

TRANSIENT

The TRANSIENT class is a subclass of SystemException that supports the CORBA TRANSIENT exception.

UNKNOWN

The UNKNOWN class is a subclass of SystemException that supports the CORBA UNKNOWN exception.

UnknownUserException

The UnknownUserException class is a subclass of UserException that identifies an unknown user exception returned by the remote server.

UserException

The UserException class is a subclass of java.lang.Exception that supports the implementation of IDL-defined user exceptions.

WrongTransaction

The WrongTransaction class is a subclass of UserException that identifies a requested transaction as being from an incorrect transaction scope.

Package org.omg.CORBA.DynAnyPackage

The org.omg.CORBA.DynAnyPackage package defines four exceptions, which are used to support the DynAny interface.

Interfaces

None.

Classes

None.

Exceptions and Errors

Invalid

The Invalid class extends UserException to indicate that a bad DynAny or Any is passed as a parameter.

InvalidSeq

The InvalidSeq class extends UserException to indicate an invalid array sequence.

InvalidValue

The InvalidValue class extends UserException to a bad DynAny value was encountered.

TypeMismatch

The TypeMismatch class extends UserException to indicate that the type of an object does not match the type being accessed.

Package org.omg.CORBA.ORBPackage

The org.omg.CORBA.ORBPackage package defines the InconsistentTypeCode and InvalidName exceptions.

Interfaces

None.

Classes

None.

Exceptions and Errors

InconsistentTypeCode

The InconsistentTypeCode class is a subclass of org.omg.CORBA.UserException that indicates an attempt to create a dynamic any with a type code that does not match the particular subclass of DynAny.

InvalidName

The InvalidName class is a subclass of org.omg.CORBA.UserException that indicates that the ORB was passed a name for which there is no initial reference.

Package org.omg.CORBA.TypeCodePackage

The org.omg.CORBA.TypeCodePackage package defines the BadKind and Bounds exceptions, which are used to signal exceptions related to type usage and constraints.

Interfaces

None.

Classes

None.

Exceptions and Errors

BadKind

The BadKind class is a subclass of org.omg.CORBA.UserException that indicates that an inappropriate operation was attempted on an org.omg.CORBA.TypeCode object.

Bounds

The Bounds class is a subclass of org.omg.CORBA.UserException that indicates that an out-of-bounds exception occurred as the result of an operation on an org.omg.CORBA.TypeCode object.

Package org.omg.CORBA.portable

The org.omg.CORBA.portable package consists of five classes and four interfaces that are used to support vendor-specific CORBA implementations.

Interfaces

IDLEntity

The IDLEntity interface extends the Serializable interface to indicate that an implementing class is a Java value type from IDL that has a corresponding helper class.

InvokeHandler

The InvokeHandler interface provides the capability to invoke a ResponseHandler object.

ResponseHandler

The ResponseHandler interface provides the capability to respond to a method invocation.

Streamable

The Streamable interface provides methods for marshalling and unmarshalling holders to and from streams.

Classes

Delegate

The Delegate class is a subclass of Object that specifies a portable API for ORB-vendor-specific implementation of the org.omg.CORBA.Object methods.

InputStream

The InputStream class is a subclass of Object that provides methods for reading IDL types from streams.

ObjectImpl

The ObjectImpl class is a subclass of Object that provides a default implementation of the org.omg.CORBA.Object interface.

OutputStream

The OutputStream class is a subclass of Object that provides methods for writing IDL types to streams.

ServantObject

The ServantObject class extends Object to encapsulate a CORBA servant.

Exceptions and Errors

ApplicationException

The ApplicationException class extends java.lang.Exception to indicate that an exception occurred in the current application.

RemarshalException

The RemarshalException class extends java.lang.Exception to indicate that an exception occurred while remarshalling a method invocation.

Package org.omg.CosNaming

The org.omg.CosNaming package consists of 20 classes and two interfaces that implement a tree-structured naming service.

Interfaces

BindingIterator

The BindingIterator interface extends the org.omg.CORBA.Object interface and provides the capability to iterate through a list of name-object bindings.

NamingContext

The `NamingContext` interface extends the `org.omg.CORBA.Object` interface and provides access to the naming service.

Classes

Binding

The `Binding` class is a subclass of `Object` that associates a name with an object.

BindingHelper

The `BindingHelper` class is a subclass of `Object` that provides static methods for manipulating bindings.

BindingHolder

The `BindingHolder` class is a subclass of `Object` that holds the value of a `Binding` object.

BindingIteratorHelper

The `BindingIteratorHelper` class is a subclass of `Object` that provides static methods for manipulating binding iterators.

BindingIteratorHolder

The `BindingIteratorHolder` class is a subclass of `Object` that holds the value of a binding iterator.

BindingListHelper

The `BindingListHelper` class is a subclass of `Object` that provides static methods for manipulating binding lists.

BindingListHolder

The `BindingListHolder` class is a subclass of `Object` that holds the value of a binding list.

BindingType

The `BindingType` class is a subclass of `Object` that identifies the type of a `Binding` object.

BindingTypeHelper

The `BindingTypeHelper` class is a subclass of `Object` that provides static methods for manipulating binding types.

BindingTypeHolder

The `BindingTypeHolder` class is a subclass of `Object` that holds the value of a binding type.

IstringHelper

The `IstringHelper` class is a subclass of `Object` that provides static methods for manipulating strings.

NameComponent

The `NameComponent` class is a subclass of `Object` that is used to build hierarchical names.

NameComponentHelper

The `NameComponentHelper` class is a subclass of `Object` that provides static methods for manipulating name components.

NameComponentHolder

The `NameComponentHolder` class is a subclass of `Object` that holds the value of a name component. It implements the `org.omg.CORBA.portable.Streamable` interface.

NameHelper

The `NameHelper` class is a subclass of `Object` that provides static methods for manipulating names.

NameHolder

The `NameHolder` class is a subclass of `Object` that holds the value of a name. It implements the `org.omg.CORBA.portable.Streamable` interface.

NamingContextHelper

The `NamingContextHelper` class is a subclass of `Object` that provides static methods for manipulating name contexts.

NamingContextHolder

The `NamingContextHolder` class is a subclass of `Object` that holds the value of a naming context. It implements the `org.omg.CORBA.portable.Streamable` interface.

_BindingIteratorImplBase

The `_BindingIteratorImplBase` class is a subclass of `org.omg.CORBA.DynamicImplementation` that supports the implementation of binding iterators. It implements the `BindingIterator` interface.

_BindingIteratorStub

The BindingIteratorStub class is a subclass of org.omg.CORBA.portable.ObjectImpl that supports the implementation of a binding iterator stub.

_NamingContextImplBase

The _NamingContextImplBase class is a subclass of org.omg.CORBA.DynamicImplementation that supports the implementation of naming contexts. It implements the NamingContext interface.

_NamingContextStub

The NamingContextStub class is a subclass of org.omg.CORBA.portable.ObjectImpl that supports the implementation of a naming context stub.

Exceptions and Errors

None.

Package org.omg.CosNaming.NamingContextPackage

The org.omg.CosNaming.NamingContextPackage package consists of 13 classes that implement aspects of the naming service's name context. The name context implements nodes within the tree-structured naming scheme.

Interfaces

None.

Classes

AlreadyBoundHelper

The AlreadyBoundHelper class is a subclass of Object that provides support for the AlreadyBound exception.

AlreadyBoundHolder

The AlreadyBoundHolder class is a subclass of Object that provides support for the AlreadyBound exception. It implements the org.omg.CORBA.portable.Streamable interface.

CannotProceedHelper

The CannotProceedHelper class is a subclass of Object that provides support for the CannotProceed exception.

CannotProceedHolder

The CannotProceedHolder class is a subclass of Object that provides support for the CannotProceed exception. It implements the org.omg.CORBA.portable.Streamable interface.

InvalidNameHelper

The InvalidNameHelper class is a subclass of Object that provides support for the InvalidName exception.

InvalidNameHolder

The InvalidNameHolder class is a subclass of Object that provides support for the InvalidName exception. It implements the org.omg.CORBA.portable.Streamable interface.

NotEmptyHelper

The NotEmptyHelper class is a subclass of Object that provides support for the NotEmpty exception.

NotEmptyHolder

The NotEmptyHolder class is a subclass of Object that provides support for the NotEmpty exception. It implements the org.omg.CORBA.portable.Streamable interface.

NotFoundHelper

The NotFoundHelper class is a subclass of Object that provides support for the NotFound exception.

NotFoundHolder

The NotFoundHolder class is a subclass of Object that provides support for the NotFound exception.

NotFoundReason

The NotFoundReason class is a subclass of Object that provides support for the NotFound exception.

NotFoundReasonHelper

The NotFoundReasonHelper class is a subclass of Object that provides support for the NotFoundReason object.

NotFoundReasonHolder

The NotFoundReasonHolder class is a subclass of Object that provides storage for a NotFoundReason object. It implements the org.omg.CORBA.portable.Streamable interface.

Exceptions and Errors

AlreadyBound

The AlreadyBound class is a subclass of org.omg.CORBA.UserException that identifies a name as being already bound with an object.

CannotProceed

The CannotProceed class is a subclass of org.omg.CORBA.UserException that signals that the CORBA implementation has come to a standstill.

InvalidName

The InvalidName class is a subclass of org.omg.CORBA.UserException that indicates that an invalid name has been used.

NotEmpty

The NotEmpty class is a subclass of org.omg.CORBA.UserException that signals a nonempty reference was encountered when one was not expected.

NotFound

The NotFound class is a subclass of org.omg.CORBA.UserException that signals that a referenced name cannot be found.

INDEX

H

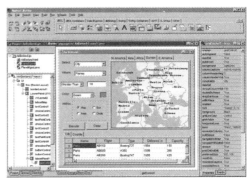

What's on the CD-ROM

This book's CD-ROM is a hybrid that works on Windows 95 and 98, Macintosh, and UNIX operating systems. The CD-ROM includes all the code from the book, sample applets, and additional Java utilities and tools.

The best way to view the contents of this CD-ROM is with a Web browser.

Example Code from the Book

All the code listings in the book can be found on the CD-ROM; the listings are organized by chapter number.

Software

This CD-ROM contains the following software to help you in programming Java.

JBuilder™ 2 Publisher's Edition

JBuilder™ 2 Tutorials

Tek-Tools, Inc.'s Kawa

Netscape Communicator 4.04

Microsoft's Internet Explorer 4.01

Adobe System, Inc.'s Acrobat Reader 3.01

EarthLink Network's TotalAccess 2.0

Read This Before Opening Software